Elinor Glyn,
Volume ONE

In this book:

Man and Maid

Three Weeks

Beyond The Rocks, A Love Story

His Hour

Red Hair

The Reason Why

The Damsel and the Sage,

A Woman's Whimsies

The letter of her mother to Elizabeth

Elinor Glyn (1864 – 1943), born Elinor Sutherland, was a British novelist and scriptwriter who specialised in risqué romantic fiction which was considered scandalous for its time. She popularized the concept of It. She had tremendous influence on early 20th century popular culture, and perhaps on the careers of notable Hollywood stars such as Rudolph Valentino, Gloria Swanson, and Clara Bow. Everyone who has read "The Visits of Elizabeth," in which a girl of seventeen describes her adventures to her mother in a series of entertaining and clever letters, has instinctively asked the question: "What sort of woman was Elizabeth's Mother?"

Perhaps an answer that will satisfy all will be found in the following "Letters of her Mother to Elizabeth."

In this book:

Man and Maid....................................Pag. 3
Three Weeks....................................Pag. 81
Beyond The Rocks.............................Pag. 131
His Hour...Pag. 192
Red Hair..Pag. 244
The Reason Why................................Pag. 293
The Damsel and the Sage......................Pag. 339
The letter of her mother to Elizabeth..........Pag. 398

Man and Maid

I

February, 1918.

I am sick of my life—The war has robbed it of all that a young man can find of joy.

I look at my mutilated face before I replace the black patch over the left eye, and I realize that, with my crooked shoulder, and the leg gone from the right knee downwards, that no woman can feel emotion for me again in this world.

So be it—I must be a philosopher.

Mercifully I have no near relations—Mercifully I am still very rich, mercifully I can buy love when I require it, which under the circumstances, is not often.

Why do people write journals? Because human nature is filled with egotism. There is nothing so interesting to oneself as oneself; and journals cannot yawn in one's face, no matter how lengthy the expression of one's feelings may be!

A clean white page is a sympathetic thing, waiting there to receive one's impressions!

Suzette supped with me, here in my *appartement* last night—When she had gone I felt a beast. I had found her attractive on Wednesday, and after an excellent lunch, and two Benedictines, I was able to persuade myself that her tenderness and passion were real, and not the result of some thousands of francs,—And then when she left I saw my face in the glass without the patch over the socket, and a profound depression fell upon me.

Is it because I am such a mixture that I am this rotten creature?—An American grandmother, a French mother, and an English father. Paris—Eton—Cannes—Continuous traveling. Some years of living and enjoying a rich orphan's life.—The war—fighting—a zest hitherto undreamed of—unconsciousness—agony—and then?—well now Paris again for special treatment.

Why do I write this down? For posterity to take up the threads correctly?—Why?

From some architectural sense in me which must make a beginning, even of a journal, for my eyes alone, start upon a solid basis?

I know not—and care not.

Three charming creatures are coming to have tea with me to-day. They had heard of my loneliness and my savageness from Maurice—They burn to give me their sympathy—and have tea with plenty of sugar in it—and chocolate cake.

I used to wonder in my salad days what the brains of women were made of—when they have brains!—The cleverest of them are generally devoid of a logical sense, and they seldom understand the relative value of things, but they make the charm of life, for one reason or another.

When I have seen these three I will dissect them. A divorcée—a war widow of two years—and the third with a husband fighting.

All, Maurice assures me, ready for anything, and highly attractive. It will do me a great deal of good, he protests. We shall see.

Night. They came, with Maurice and Alwood Chester, of the American Red Cross. They gave little shrill screams of admiration for the room.

"*Quel endroit delicieux!*—What *boiserie*! English?—Yes, of course, English *dix-septième*, one could see—What silver!—and cleaned—And everything of a *chic*!—And the hermit so *séduisant* with his air *maussade*!—*Hein.*"

"Yes, the war is much too long—One has given of one's time in the first year—but now, really, fatigue has overcome one!—and surely after the spring offensive peace *must* come soon—and one must live!"

They smoked continuously and devoured the chocolate cake, then they had liqueurs.

They were so well dressed! and so lissome. They wore elastic corsets, or none at all. They were well painted; cheeks of the new tint, rather apricot coloured—and magenta lips. They had arranged themselves when they had finished munching, bringing out their gold looking-glasses and their lip grease and their powder—and the divorcee continued to endeavour to enthrall my senses with her voluptuous half closing of the eyes, while she reddened her full mouth.

They spoke of the theatre, and the last *bons mots* about their *chères amies*—the last liasons—the last passions—They spoke of Gabrielle—her husband was killed last week—'So foolish of him, since one of Alice's 'friends' among the Ministers could easily have got him a soft job, and one must always help one's friends! Alice adored Gabrielle.—But he has left her well provided for—Gabrielle will look well in her crepe—and there it is, war is war—*Que voulez vous?*

"After all, will it be as agreeable if peace does come this summer?—One will be able to dance openly—that will be nice—but for the rest? It may be things will be more difficult—and there may be complications. One has been very well during the war—very well, indeed—*N'est ce pas ma cherie—n'est ce pas?*"

Thus they talked.

The widow's lover is married, Maurice tells me, and has been able to keep his wife safely down at their place in Landes, but if peace should come he must be *en famille*, and the wife can very well be disagreeable about the affair.

The divorcée's three lovers will be in Paris at the same time. The married one's husband returned for good—"Yes, certainly, peace will have its drawbacks—The war knows its compensations—But considerable ones!"

When they had departed, promising to return very soon—to dinner this time, and see all the "exquisite *appartement*," Burton came into the room to take away the tea things. His face was a mask as he swept up the cigarette ash, which had fallen upon the William and Mary English lac table, which holds the big lamp, then he carefully carried away the silver ash trays filled with the ends, and returned with them cleaned. Then he coughed slightly.

"Shall I open the window, Sir Nicholas?"

"It is a beastly cold evening."

He put an extra log on the fire and threw the second casement wide.

"You'll enjoy your dinner better now, Sir," he said, and left me shivering.

I wish I were a musician, I could play to myself. I have still my two hands, though perhaps my left shoulder hurts too much to play often. My one eye aches when I read for too long, and the stump below the knee is too tender still to fit the false leg on to, and I cannot, because of my shoulder, use my crutch overmuch, so walking is out of the question. These trifles are perhaps, the cause of my ennui with life.

I suppose such women as those who came to-day fulfill some purpose in the scheme of things. One can dine openly with them at the most exclusive restaurant, and not mind meeting one's relations. They are rather more expensive than the others—pearl necklaces—sables—essence for their motor cars—these are their prices.—They are so decorative, too, and before the war were such excellent tango partners. These three are all of the best families, and their relations stick to them in the background, so they are not altogether *déclassé*. Maurice says they are the most agreeable women in Paris, and get the last news out of the Generals. They are seen everywhere, and Coralie, the married one, wears a Red Cross uniform sometimes at tea—if she happens to remember to go into a hospital for ten minutes to hold some poor fellow's hand.

Yes, I suppose they have their uses—there are a horde of them, anyway.

To-morrow Maurice is bringing another specimen to divert me—American this time—over here for "war work." Maurice says one of the cleverest adventuresses he has ever met; and I am still irresistible, he assures me, so I must be careful—(for am I not disgustingly rich!)

Burton is sixty years old—He is my earliest recollection. Burton knows the world.

Friday—The American adventuress delighted me. She was so shrewd. Her eyes are cunning and evil—her flesh is round and firm, she is not extremely painted, and her dresses are quite six inches below her knees.

She has two English peers in tow, and any casual Americans of note whom she can secure who will give her facilities in life. She, also, is posing for a 'lady' and 'a virtuous woman,' and an ardent war worker.

All these parasites are the product of the war, though probably they always existed, but the war has been their glorious chance. There is a new verb in America, Maurice says—"To war work"—It means to get to Paris, and have a splendid time.

Their *toupé* is surprising! To hear this one talk one would think she ruled all the politics of the allies, and directed each General.

Are men fools?—Yes, imbeciles—they cannot see the wiles of woman. Perhaps I could not when I was a human male whom they could love!

Love?—did I say love?

Is there such a thing?—or is it only a sex excitement for the moment!—That at all events is the sum of what these creatures know.

Do they ever think?—I mean beyond planning some fresh adventure for themselves, or how to secure some fresh benefit.

I cannot now understand how a man ever marries one of them, gives his name and his honour into such precarious keeping. Once I suppose I should have been as easy a prey as the rest. But not *now*—I have too much time to think, I fear. I seem to find some ulterior motive in whatever people say or do.

To-day another American lunched with me, a bright girl, an heiress of the breezy, jolly kind, a good sort before the war, whom I danced with often. She told me quite naturally that she had a German prisoner's thigh bone being polished into an umbrella handle—She had assisted at the amputation—and the man had afterwards died—"A really cute souvenir," she assured me it was going to be!

Are we all mad—?

No wonder the finest and best "go West."—Will they come again, souls of a new race, when all these putrid beings have become extinguished by time? I hope so to God....

These French women enjoy their crepe veils—and their high-heeled shoes, and their short black skirts, even a cousin is near enough for the trappings of woe.—Can any of us feel woe now?—I think not....

Maurice has his uses—Were I a man once more I should despise Maurice—He is so good a creature, such a devoted hanger on of the very rich—and faithful too. Does he not pander to my every fancy, and procure me whatever I momentarily desire?

How much better if I had been killed outright! I loathe myself and all the world.

Once—before the war—the doing up of this flat caused me raptures. To get it quite English—in Paris! Every *antiquaire* in London had exploited me to his heart's content. I paid for it through the nose, but each bit is a gem. I am not quite sure now what I meant to do with it when finished, occupy it when I did come to Paris—lend it to friends?—I don't remember—Now it seems a sepulchre where I can retire my maimed body to and wait for the end.

Nina once proposed to stay with me here, no one should know, Nina?—would she come now?—How dare they make this noise at the door—what is it?—Nina!

Sunday—it was actually Nina herself—"Poor darling Nicholas," she said. "The kindest fate sent me across—I 'wangled' a passport—really serious war work, and here I am for a fortnight, even in war time one *must* get a few clothes—"

I could see I was a great shock to her, my attraction for her had gone—I was just "poor darling Nicholas," and she began to be motherly—Nina motherly!—She would have been furious at the very idea once. Nina is thirty-nine years old, her boy has just gone into the flying corps, she is so glad the war will soon be over.

She loves her boy.

She gave me news of the world, our old world of idle uselessness, which is now one of solid work.

"Why have you completely cut yourself off from everything and everybody, ever since you first went out to fight?—Very silly of you."

"When I was a *man* and could fight, I liked fighting, and never wanted to see any of you again. You all seemed rotters to me, so I spent my leaves in the country or here. Now you seem glorious beings, and I the rotter. I am no use at all—"

Nina came close to me and touched my hand—

"Poor darling Nicholas," she said again.

Something hurt awfully, as I realized that to touch me now caused her no thrill. No woman will ever thrill again when I am near.

Nina does know all about clothes! She is the best-dressed Englishwoman I have ever seen. She has worked awfully well for the war, too, I hear, she deserves her fortnight in Paris.

"What are you going to do, Nina?" I asked her.

She was going out to theatres every night, and going to dine with lots of delicious 'red tabs' whose work was over here, whom she had not seen for a long time.

"I'm just going to frivol, Nicholas, I am tired of work."

Nothing could exceed her kindness—a mother's kindness.

I tried to take an interest in everything she said, only it seemed such aeons away. As though I were talking in a dream.

She would go plodding on at her war job when she got back again, of course, but she, like everyone else, is war weary.

"And when peace comes—it will soon come now probably—what then?"

"I believe I shall marry again."

I jumped—I had never contemplated the possibility of Nina marrying, she has always been a widowed institution, with her nice little house in Queen Street, and that wonderful cook.

"What on earth for?"

"I want the companionship and devotion of one man."

"Anyone in view?"

"Yes—one or two—they say there is a shortage of men, I have never known so many men in my life."

Then presently, when she had finished her tea, she said—

"You are absolutely out of gear, Nicholas—Your voice is rasping, your remarks are bitter, and you must be awfully unhappy, poor boy."

I told her that I was—there was no use in lying.

"Everything is finished," I said, and she bent down and kissed me as she said good-bye—a mother's kiss.

And now I am alone, and what shall I do all the evening? or all the other evenings—? I will send for Suzette to dine.

Night—Suzette—was amusing—. I told her at once I did not require her to be affectionate.

"You can have an evening's rest from blandishments, Suzette."

"*Merci!*"—and then she stretched herself, kicked up her little feet, in their short-vamped, podgy little shoes, with four-inch heels, and lit a cigarette.

"Life is hard, *Mon ami*"—she told me—"And now that the English are here, it is difficult to keep from falling in love."

For a minute I thought she was going to insinuate that I had aroused her reflection—I warmed—but no—She had taken me seriously when I told her I required no blandishments.

That ugly little twinge came to me again.

"You like the English?"

"Yes."

"Why?"

"They are very *bons garçons*, they are clean, and they are fine men, they have sentiment, too—Yes, it is difficult not to feel," she sighed.

"What do you do when you fall in love then, Suzette?"

"*Mon ami*, I immediately go for a fortnight to the sea—one is lost if one falls in love *dans le metier*—The man tramples then—tramples and slips off—For everything good one must never feel."

"But you have a kind heart Suzette—you feel for me?"

"*Hein?*"—and she showed all her little white pointed teeth—"Thou?—Thou art very rich, *mon chou*. Women will always feel for thee!"

It went in like a knife it was so true—.

"I was a very fine Englishman once," I said.

"It is possible, thou art still, sitting, and showing the right profile—and full of *chic*—and then rich, rich!"
"You could not forget that I am rich, Suzette?"
"If I did I might love you—*Jamais!*"
"And does the sea help to prevent an attack?"—
"Absence—and I go to a poor place I knew when I was young, and I wash and cook, and make myself remember what *la vie dure*was—and would be again if one loved—Bah! that does it. I come back cured—and ready only to please such as thou, Nicholas!—rich, rich!"

And she laughed again her rippling gay laugh—
We had a pleasant evening, she told me the history of her life—or some of it—They were ever the same from Lucien's Myrtale.

When all of me is aching—Shall I too, find solace if I go to the sea?
Who knows?

II

I have been through torture this week—The new man wrenches my shoulder each day, it will become straight eventually, he says. They have tried to fit the false leg also, so those two things are going on, but the socket is not yet well enough for anything to be done to my left eye—so that has defeated them. It will be months before any real improvement takes place.

There are hundreds of others who are more maimed than I—in greater pain—more disgusting—does it give them any comfort to tell the truth to a journal?—or are they strong enough to keep it all locked up in their hearts?—I used to care to read, all books bore me now—I cannot take interest in any single thing, and above all, I loathe myself—My soul is angry.

Nina came again, to luncheon this time. It was pouring with rain, an odious day. She told me of her love affairs—as a sister might—Nina a sister!

She can't make up her mind whether to take Jim Bruce or Rochester Moreland, they are both Brigadiers now, Jim is a year younger than she is.

"Rochester is really more my mate, Nicholas," she said, "but then there are moments when I am with him when I am not sure if he would not bore me eventually, and he has too much character for me to suppress—Jim fascinates me, but I only hold him because he is not sure of me—If I marry him he will be, and then I shall have to watch my looks, and remember to play the game all the time, and it won't be restful—above all, I want rest and security."

"You are not really in love with either, Nina?"

"Love?" and she smoothed out the fringe on her silk jersey with her war-hardened hand—the hand I once loved to kiss—every blue vein on it!—"I often, wonder what really is love, Nicholas—I thought I loved you before the war—but, of course, I could not have—because I don't feel anything now—and if I had really loved you, I suppose it would not have made any difference."

Then she realized what she had said and got up and came closer to me.

"That was cruel of me, I did not mean to be—I love you awfully as a sister—always."

"Sister Nina!—well, let us get back to love—perhaps the war has killed it—or it has developed everything, perhaps it now permits a sensitive, delicious woman like you to love two men."

"You see, we have become so complicated"—she puffed smoke rings at me—"One man does not seem to fulfill the needs of every mood—Rochester would not understand some things that Jim would, and *vice versa*—I do not feel any glamour about either, but it is rest and certainty, as I told you, Nicholas, I am so tired of working and going home to Queen Street alone."

"Shall you toss up?"

"No—Rochester is coming up from the front to-morrow just for the night, I am going to dine with him at Larue's—alone, I shall sample him all the time—I sampled Jim when he was last in London a fortnight ago—"

"You will tell me about it when you have decided, won't you, Nina. You see I have become a brother, and am interested in the psychological aspects of things."

"Of course I will"—then she went on meditatively, her rather plaintive voice low.

"I think all our true feeling is used up, Nicholas—our souls—if we have souls—are blunted by the war agony. Only our senses still feel. When Jim looks at me with his attractive blue eyes, and I see the D.S.O. and the M.C., and his white nice teeth—and how his hair is brushed, and how well his uniform fits, I have a jolly all-overish sensation—and I don't much listen to what he is saying—he says lots of love—and I think I would really like him all the time. Then, when he has gone I think of other things, and I feel he would not understand a word about them, and because he isn't there I don't feel the delicious all-overish sensation, so I rather decide to marry Rochester—there would be such risk—because when you are married to a man, it is possible to get much fonder of him. Jim is a year younger than I am—It would be a strain, perhaps in a year or two—especially if I got fond."

"You had better take the richer," I told her—"Money stands by one, it is an attraction which even the effects of war never varies or lessens," and I could hear that there was bitterness in my voice.

"You are quite right," Nina said, taking no notice of it—"but I don't want money—I have enough for every possible need, and my boy has his own. I want something kind and affectionate to live with."

"You want a master—and a slave."

"Yes."

"Nina, when you loved me—what did you want?"

"Just you, Nicholas—just you."
"Well, I am here now, but an eye and a leg gone, and a crooked shoulder, changes me;—so it is true love—even the emotion of the soul, depends upon material things—"
Nina thought for a while.
"Perhaps not the emotion of the soul—if we have souls?—but what we know of love now certainly does. I suppose there are people who can love with the soul, I am not one of them."
"Well, you are honest, Nina."
She had her coffee and liqueur, she was graceful and composed and refined, either Jim or Rochester will have a very nice wife.
Burton coughed when she had left.
"Out with it, Burton!"
"Mrs. Ardilawn is a kind lady, Sir Nicholas."
"Charming."
"I believe you'd be better with some lady to look after you, Sir—."
"To hell with you. Telephone for Mr. Maurice—I don't want any woman—we can play piquet."
This is how my day ended—.
Maurice and piquet—then the widow and the divorcée for dinner—and now alone again! The sickening rot of it all.

Sunday—Nina came for tea—she feels that I am a great comfort to her in this moment of her life, so full of indecision—It seems that Jim has turned up too, at the Ritz, where Rochester still is, and that his physical charm has upset all her calculations again.
"I am really very worried Nicholas," she said, "and you, who are a dear family friend"—I am a family friend now!—"ought to be able to help me."
"What the devil do you want me to do, Nina?—outset them both, and ask you to marry me?"
"My dearest Nicholas!" it seemed to her that I had suggested that she should marry father Xmas! "How funny you are!"
Once it was the height of her desire—Nina is eight years older than I am—I can see now her burning eyes one night on the river in the June of , when she insinuated, not all playfully, that it would be good to wed.
"I think you had better take Jim my dear, after all. You are evidently becoming in love with him and you have proved to me that the physical charm matters most,—or if you are afraid of that, you had better do as another little friend of mine does when she is attracted—she takes a fortnight at the sea!"
"The sea would be awful in this weather! I should send for both in desperation!" and she laughed and began to take an interest in the furnishings of my flat. She looked over it, and Burton pointed out all its merits to her (My crutch hurts my shoulder so much to-day I did not want to move out of my chair). I could hear Burton's remarks, but they fell upon unheeding ears—Nina is not cut out for a nurse, my poor Burton, if you only knew—!
When she returned to my sitting room tea was in, and she poured it out for me, and then she remarked.
"We have grown so awfully selfish, haven't we, Nicholas, but we aren't such hypocrites as we were before the war. People still have lovers, but they don't turn up their eyes so much at other people having them, as they used. There is more tolerance—the only thing you cannot do is to act publicly so that your men friends cannot defend you—'You must not throw your bonnet over the windmills'—otherwise you can do as you please—."
"You had not thought of taking either Jim or Rochester for a lover to make certain which you prefer?"
Nina looked unspeakably shocked—.
"What a dreadful idea Nicholas!—I am thinking of both *seriously*, not only to pass the time of day remember."
"That is all lovers are for, then Nina?—I used to think—."
"Never mind what you thought, there is no reason to insult me."
"Nothing was farther from my desire."
Nina's face cleared, as it had darkened ominously.
"What will you do if, having married Rochester, you find yourself bored—Will you send for Jim again?"
"Certainly not, that would be disaster. I shan't plunge until I feel pretty certain I am going to find the water just deep enough, and not too deep—and if I do make a mistake, well I shall have to stick to it."
"By Jove what a philosopher," and I laughed—She poured out a second cup of tea, and then she looked steadily at me, as though studying a new phase of me.
"You are not a bit worse off than Tom Green, Nicholas, and he has not got your money, and Tom is as jolly as anything, and everybody loves him, though he is a hopeless cripple, and can't even look decent, as you will be able to in a year or two. There is no use in having this sentiment about war heroes that would make one put up with their tempers, and their cynicism! Everybody is in the same boat, women and men, we chance being maimed by bombs, and we are losing our looks with rough work—for goodness sake stop being so soured—."
I laughed outright—it was all so true.

Friday—Maurice brings people to play bridge every afternoon now. Nina has gone back to England—having decided to take Jim!
It came about in this way—She flew in to tell me the last evening before she left for Havre. She was breathless running up the stairs, as something had gone wrong with the lift.
"Jim and I are engaged!"
"A thousand congratulations."
"Rochester had a dinner for me on Wednesday night. All the jolliest people in Paris—some of those dear French who have been so nice to us all along, and some of the War Council and the Ryvens, and so on—and, do

you know, Nicholas—I *heard* Rochester telling Madame de Clerté the same story about his *bon mot* when a shell broke at Avicourt—as I had already heard him tell Admiral Short, and Daisy Ryven!—that decided me—. There was an element of self-glorification in that modest story—and a man who would tell it *three times*, is not for me! In ten years I should grow into being the listener victim—I could not face it! So I said good-bye to him in the corridor, before up to my room—and I telephoned to Jim, who was in his room on the Cambon side, and he came round in the morning!"

"Was Rochester upset?"

"Rather! but a man of his age—he is forty-two, who can tell a self-story three times is going to get cured soon, so I did not worry."

"And what did Jim say?"

"He was enchanted, he said he knew it would end like that—give a man of forty-two rope enough and he'll be certain to hang himself, he said, and, Oh! Nicholas—Jim is a darling, he is getting quite masterful—I adore him!"

"Senses winning, Nina! Women only like physical masters."

She grew radiant. Never has she seemed so desirable. "I don't care a fig Nicholas! If it is senses, well, then, I know it is the best thing in the World, and a woman of my age can't have everything. I adore Jim! We are going to be married the first moment he can get leave again—and I shall 'wangle' him into being a 'red tab'—he has fought enough."

"And if meanwhile he should get maimed like me—what then, Nina?"

She actually paled.

"Don't be so horrid Nicholas—Jim—Oh! I can't bear it!" and being a strict Protestant, she crossed herself—to avert bad luck!

"We won't think of anything but joy and happiness, Nina, but it is quite plain to me you had better have a fortnight at the sea!"

She had forgotten the allusion, and turned puzzled brown eyes upon me.

"You know—to balance yourself when you feel you are falling in love"—I reminded her.

"Oh! It is all stuff and nonsense! I know now I adore Jim—good-bye Nicholas"—and she hugged me—as a sister—a mother—and a family friend—and was off down the stairs again.

Burton had brought me in a mild gin and seltzer, and it was on the tray, near, so I drank it, and said to myself, "Here is to the Senses—jolly good things"—and then I telephoned to Suzette to come and dine.

There is a mole on the left cheek of Suzette, high up near her eye, there are three black hairs in it—I had never seen them until this morning—*c'est fini—je ne puis plus*!

Of course we have all got moles with three black hairs in them—and the awful moment is when suddenly they are seen—That is the tragedy of life—disillusion.

I cannot help being horribly introspective, Maurice would agree to whatever I said, so there is no use in talking to him—I rush to this journal, it cannot look at me with fond watery eyes of reproach and disapproval—as Burton would if I let myself go to him.

May th—The times have been too anxious to write, it is over two months since I opened this book. But it cannot be, it cannot be that we shall be beaten—Oh! God—why am I not a man again to fight! The raids are continuous—All the fluffies and nearly everyone left Paris in the ticklish March and April times, but now their fears are lulled a little and many have returned, and they rush to cinemas and theatres, to kill time, and jump into the rare taxis to go and see the places where the raid bombs burst, or Bertha shells, and watch the houses burning and the crushed bodies of the victims being dragged out. They sicken me, this rotten crew—But this is not all France—great, dear, brave France—It is only one section of useless society. To-day the Duchesse de Courville-Hautevine came to call upon me—mounted all the stairs without even a wheeze—(the lift gave out again this morning!)—What a personality!—How I respect her! She has worked magnificently since the war began, her hospital is a wonder, her only son was killed fighting gloriously at Verdun.

"You look as melancholy as a sick cat," she told me.

She likes to speak her English—"Of what good *Jeune homme*! We are not done yet—I have cut some of my relatives who ran away from Paris—Imbeciles! Bertha is our diversion now, and the raids at night—jolly loud things!"—and she chuckled, detaching her scissors which had got caught in the purple woolen jersey she wore over her Red Cross uniform. She is quite indifferent to coquetry, this grande dame of the *ancien regime*!

"My *blessés* rejoice in them—*Que voulez vous?*—War is war—and there is no use in looking blue—Cheer up, young man!"

Then we talked of other things. She is witty and downright, and her every thought and action is kindly. I love la Duchesse—My mother was her dearest friend.

When she had stayed twenty minutes—she came over close to my chair.

"I knew you would be bitter at not being in the fight, my son," she said, patting me with her once beautiful hand, now red and hardened with work, "So I snatched the moments to come to see you. On your one leg you'll defend if the moment should come,—but it won't! And you—you wounded ones, spared—can keep the courage up. *Tiens!* you can at least pray, you have the time—I have not—*Mais le Bon Dieu* understands—."

And with that she left me, stopping to arrange her tightly curled fringe (she sticks to all old styles) at the lac mirror by the door. I felt better after she had gone—yes, it is that—God—why can't I fight!

III

Is some nerve being touched by the new treatment? I seem alternately to be numb and perfectly indifferent to how the war is going, and then madly interested. But I am too sensitive to leave my flat for any meals—I drive whenever one of the "fluffies" (this is what Maurice calls the widow, the divorcée and other rejoicers of men's war hearts) can take me in her motor—No one else has a motor—There is no petrol for ordinary people.

"It reminds one of Louis XV's supposed reply to his daughters"—I said to Maurice yesterday. "When they asked him to make them a good road to the Château of their dear *Gouvernante*, the Duchesse de la Bove—He assured them he could not, his mistresses cost him too much! So they paid for it themselves, hence the '*Chemin des Dames*.'"

"What reminds you of what—?" Maurice asked, looking horribly puzzled.

"The fluffies being able to get the petrol—."

"But I don't see, the connection?"

"It was involved—the mistresses got the money which should have made the road in those days, and now—."

Maurice was annoyed with himself; he could not yet see, and no wonder, for it *was* involved!—but I am angry that the widow and the divorcée both have motors and I none!

"Poor Odette—she hates taxis! Why should she not have a motor?—You are *grinchant, mon cher*!—since she takes you out, too!"

"Believe me, Maurice, I am grateful, I shall repay all their kindnesses—they have all indicated how I can best do so—but I like to keep them waiting, it makes them more keen."

Maurice laughed again nervously.

"It is divine to be so rich, Nicholas"!

All sorts of people come to talk to me and have tea (I have a small hoard of sugar sent from a friend in Spain). Amongst them an ancient guardsman in some inspection berth here—He, like Burton, knows the world.

He tests women by whether or no they take presents from him, he tells me. They profess intense love which he returns, and then comes the moment (he, like me, is disgustingly rich). He offers them a present, some accept at once, those he no longer considers; others hesitate, and say it is too much, they only want his affection—He presses them, they yield—they too, are wiped off the list—and now he has no one to care for, since he has not been able to find one who refuses his gifts. It would be certainly my case also—were I to try.

"Women"—he said to me last night—"are the only pleasure in life—men and hunting bring content and happiness, work brings satisfaction, but women and their ways are the only *pleasure*."

"Even when you know it is all for some personal gain?"

"Even so, once you have realized that, it does not matter, you take the joy from another point of view, you have to eliminate vanity out of the affair, your personal vanity is hurt, my dear boy, when you feel it is your possessions, not yourself, they crave, but if you analyse that, it does not take away from the pleasure their beauty gives you—the tangible things are there just as if they loved you—I am now altogether indifferent as to their feelings for me, as long as their table manners are good, and they make a semblance of adoring me. If one had to depend upon their real disinterested love for their kindness to one, then it would be a different matter, and very distressing, but since they can always be caught by a bauble—you and I are fortunately placed, Nicholas."

We laughed our vile laughs together.—It is true—I hate to hear my own laugh. I agree with Chesterfield, who said that no gentleman should make that noise!

As I said before, all sorts of people come to see me, but I seem to be stripping them of externals all the time. What is the good in them? What is the truth in them? Strip me—if I were not rich what would anyone bother with me for? Is anyone worth while underneath?

One or other of the fluffies come almost daily to play bridge with me, and any fellow who is on leave, and the neutrals who have no anxieties, what a crew! It amuses me to "strip" them. The married one, Coralie, has absolutely nothing to charm with if one removes the ambience of success, the entourage of beautiful things, the manicurist and the complexion specialist, the Reboux hats, and the Chanel clothes. She would be a plain little creature, with not too fine ankles,—but that self-confidence which material possessions bring, casts a spell over people.—Coralie *is* attractive. Odette, the widow, is beautiful. She has the brain of a turkey, but she, too, is exquisitely dressed and surrounded with everything to enhance her loveliness, and the serenity of success has given her magnetism. She announces platitudes as discoveries, she sparkles, and is so ravishing that one finds her trash wit. She thinks she is witty, and you begin to believe it!

Odette can be best stripped, people could like her just for her looks. Alice, the divorcée, appeals to one.—She is gentle and feminine and clinging—she is the cruelest and most merciless of the three, Maurice tells me, and the most difficult to analyse: But most of one's friends would find it hard to stand the test of denuding them of their worldly possessions and outside allurements, it is not only the fluffies, who would come out of not much value!

Oh! the long, long days—and the ugly nights!

One does not sleep very well now, the noise of "Bertha" from six A.M. and the raids at night!—but I believe I grow to like the raids—and last night we had a marvelous experience. I had been persuaded by Maurice to have quite a large dinner party. Madame de Clerté, who is really an amusing personality, courageous and agreeable, and Daisy Ryven, and the fluffies, and four or five men. We were sitting smoking afterwards, listening to de Volé playing, he is a great musician. People's fears are lulled, they have returned to Paris. Numbers of men are being killed,—"The English in heaps—but what will you!" the fluffies said, "they had no business to make that break with the Fifth Army! Oh! No! and, after all, the country is too dull—and we have all our hidden store of petrol. If we must fly at the last moment, why on earth not go to the theatre and try to pass the time!"

de Volé was playing "Madame Butterfly"—when the sirens went for a raid—and almost immediately the guns began—and bombs crashed. One very seldom sees any fear on people's faces now, they are accustomed to the noise. Without asking any of us, de Volé commenced Chopin's Funeral March. It was a very wonderful moment, the explosions and the guns mingling with the splendid chords. We sat breathless—a spell seemed to be upon us all—We listened feverishly. de Volé's face was transfigured. What did he see in the dim light?—He played and played. And the whole tragedy of war—and the futility of earthly interests—the glory, the splendour and the agony seemed to be brought home to us. From this, as the noise without became less loud, he glided into Schubert, and so at last ceased when the "all clear" commenced to rend the air. No one had spoken a word, and then Daisy Ryven laughed—a queer little awed laugh. She was the only Englishwoman there.

"We are keyed up," she said.

And when they had all gone I opened my window wide and breathed in the black dark night. Oh! God—what a rotter I am.

Friday—Maurice has a new suggestion—he says I should write a book—he *knows* I am becoming insupportable, and he thinks if he flatters me enough I'll swallow the bait, and so be kept quiet and not try him so much.—A novel?—A study of the causes of altruism? What?—I feel—yes, I feel a spark of interest. If it could take me out of myself—I shall consult the Duchesse—I will tell Burton to telephone and find out if I can see her this afternoon. She sometimes takes half an hour off between four and five to attend to her family.

Yes—Burton says she will see me and will send me one of her Red Cross cars to fetch me, then I can keep my leg up.

I rather incline to a treatise upon altruism and the philosophical subjects. I fear if I wrote a novel it would be saturated by my ugly spirit, and I should hate people to read it. I must get that part of me off in my journal, but a book about—Altruism?

I must have a stenographer of course, a short-hand typist, if I do begin this thing. There are some English ones here no doubt. I do not wish to write in French—Maurice must find me a suitable one.—I won't have anything young and attractive. In my idiotic state she might get the better of me! The idea of some steady employment quite bucks me up.

I felt rather jarred when I arrived at the Hotel Courville—the paving across the river is bad; but I found my way to the Duchesse's own sitting room on the first floor—the only room apparently left not a ward—and somehow the smell of carbolic had not penetrated here. It was too hot, and only a little window was open.

How wonderfully beautiful these eighteenth century rooms are! What grace and charm in the panelling—what dignity in the proportions! This one, like all rooms of women of the Duchesse's age, is too full—crammed almost, with gems of art, and then among them, here and there, a shocking black satin stuffed and buttoned armchair, with a bit of woolwork down its centre, and some fringe! And her writing table!—the famous one given by Louis XV to the ancestress, who refused his favours—A mass of letters and papers, and reports, a bottle of creosote and a feather! A servant in black, verging upon ninety, brought in the tea, and said Madame la Duchesse would be there immediately—and she came.

Her twinkling eyes kindly as ever "Good day Nicholas," she said and kissed me on both cheeks, "Thou art thy mother's child—*Va!*—And I thank thee for the fifty thousand francs for my *blessés*—I say no more—*Va!*—."

Her scissors got caught in her pocket, not the purple jersey this time, and she played with them for a minute.

"Thou art come for something—out with it!"

"Shall I write a book?, that's it. Maurice thinks it might divert me—What do you think?"

"One must consider," and she began pouring out the tea, "paper is scarce—I doubt, my son, if what you would inscribe upon it would justify the waste—but still—as a *soulagement*—an asperine so to speak—perhaps—yes. On what subject?"

"That is what I want your advice about, a novel?—or a study upon Altruism, or—or—something like that?"

She chuckled and handed me my tea, thin tea and a tiny slice of black bread, and a scrape of butter. There is no cheating of the regulations here, but the Sevres cup gave me satisfaction.

"You have brought me your bread coupon, I hope?" she interrupted with,—"if you eat without it one of my household has less!"

I produced it.

"Two days old will do here," then she became all interest in my project again and chuckled anew.

"Not a novel my son, at your age and with your temperament, it would arouse emotions in you if you created them in your characters, you are better without them.—No!—Something serious; Altruism as well as another, by all means!"

"I expected you to say that, you are always so practical and kind, then we will choose a research subject to keep me busy."

"Why not the history of Blankshire, your old county where the Thormondes have sat since the conquest—*hein*?"

This delighted me, but I saw the impossibility. "I cannot get at the necessary reference books, and it is impossible to receive anything from England."

She realized this before I spoke.

"No—philosophy it must be—or your pet hobby, the furniture of your William and Mary!"

This seemed the best of all, and I decided in a moment. This shall be my subject. I really know something of William and Mary furniture! So we settled it. Then she became reflective.

"The news is *très grave* to-day, my son," she whispered softly, "the fearful ones predict that the Boche will be within range in a few days.—Why not leave Paris?"

"Are you going, Duchesse?"

"I,—*Mon Dieu!*—Of course not!—I must stay to get my *Blessés* out—if the worst should come—but I never believe it.—Let the cowards flee—. Some of my relatives have gone again. Those I speak to will have become a minority when peace arrives, it would seem!"—then she frowned angrily. "Many are so splendid—devoted, untiring, but there are some—!—*Mon Dieu!* the girls play tennis at the *tix aux pigeons*!—and the Germans are sixty-five kilometers from Paris!"

I did not speak, and then, as though I had said something disparaging and she must defend them—"But you must not judge them hardly—No!—it is not possible with our National temperament that young girls of the world can nurse men—No—No—and our ministry of War won't employ women—what can they do—ask yourself, what can they do?—but wait and pray! Other nations must not judge us—our men know what they want of us—yes, yes—"

"Of course they do."

"My niece Madelaine—a lighthead—dragged me to the Ritz to lunch last week, before the wild rush cleared them off again—*Mon Dieu!* what a sight there in that restaurant!—Olivier and the waiters are the only things of dignity left! The women dressed to the eyes as Red Cross nurses. Some Americans, and, yes, French—nursing the well English officers I must believe—no nearer wounded than that!—floating veils, painted lips—high heels—Heavens! it filled me with rage—I who know the devoted and good of both nations who are not seen, and you English—. But there it is easy for you with your temperament to be good and really work—France is full of sensible kind Americans and English—but those in Paris—they make me sick! Quarter of an hour twice a day—to have the right to a passport to come—and to wear a uniform—Pah! Sick, sick!—"

I thought of the fluffies!—they too played at something the first year of the war, but now have given up even the pretence of that.

The Duchesse was still angry.

"My nephew Charles, le Prince de Vimont, eats chicken and cutlets on the meatless days, he told me with pride, his *maître d'hôtel*—he of the one eye—like thou, Nicholas, is able to procure plenty on the day before from friends in the trade, and with ice—*Mon Dieu!*—and I pay twenty-eight francs apiece for the best poulets for my *blessés* for extra rations!—and ice!—impossible to procure—. Oh! I would punish them all, choke them with their own meat—it is they who should be "food for the guns" as you English say,—they, these few disgrace our brave France, and make the other nations laugh at us."

I tried to assure her that no one laughed, and that we all understood and worshipped the spirit of France, that it was only the few, and that we were not deceived, but I could not calm her.

"It makes me weep" at last she said and I could not comfort her.

"Heloise de Tavantaine—my Cousin's Jew daughter-in-law—paid four thousand francs for a new evening dress, which did not cover a tenth of her fat body—Four thousand francs would have given my *blessés*—Ah!—well—I rage, I rage."

Then she checked herself—.

"But why do I say this to thee Nicholas?—because I am sore—it is ever thus—we are all human, and must cry to someone."

So after all there is some meaning in my journal.

"*One must cry to someone!*"

Burton is delighted that I shall write a book!—He wrote at once to my aunt Emmeline to tell her that I was better. I have her letter with congratulations in it to-day. Burton does the correspondence with my few relations, all war working hard in England. I am becoming quite excited, I long to begin, but there is no use until Maurice finds me a stenographer. He has heard of two. One a Miss Jenkins, aged forty—sounds good, but she can only give three hours a day—and I must have one at my beck and call—There is a second one, a Miss Sharp—but she is only twenty-three—plain though, Maurice says, and wears horn spectacles—that should not attract me! She makes bandages all the evening, but is obliged to work for her living so could come for the day. She is not out of a job, because she is very expert, but she does not like her present one. I would have to pay her very highly Maurice says—I don't mind that, I want the best.—I had better see Miss Sharp, and judge if I can stand her. She may have a personality I could not work with. Maurice must bring her to-morrow.

The news to-night is worse.—The banks have sent away all their securities.—But I shall not leave—one might as well die in a bombardment as any other way. The English Consul has to know all the names of the English residents in case of evacuation. But I will not go.

Bertha is making a most fiendish noise, there were two raids last night,—and she began at six this morning—one gets little sleep. I have a one horse Victoria now, driven by Methusala; I picked Maurice up at the Ritz this evening at nine o'clock—there was not a human soul to be seen in the *Rue de la Paix*, or the *Place Vendôme*, or the *Rue Castiglione*—a city of the dead—And the early June sky full of peace and soft light.

What does it all mean?

IV

Maurice brought Miss Sharp to-day to interview me. I do not like her much, but the exhibition she gave me of her speed and accuracy in short-hand satisfied me and made me see that I should be a fool to look further. So I have engaged her. She is a small creature, palish with rather good bright brown hair—She wears horn rimmed spectacles with yellow glasses in them so I can't see her eyes at all. I judge people by their eyes. Her hands look as if she had done rather a lot of hard work—they are so very thin. Her clothes are neat but shabby—that is not the last look like French women have—but as if they had been turned to "make do"—I suppose she is very poor. Her manner is icily quiet. She only speaks when she is spoken to. She is quite uninteresting.

It is better for me to have a nonentity—then I can talk aloud my thoughts without restriction. I am to give her double what she is getting now— francs a month—war price.

Some colour came into her cheeks when I offered that and she hesitated,

I said "Don't you think it is enough?"

She answered so queerly.

"I think it is too much, and I was wondering if I would be able to accept it. I want to."

"Then do."

"Very well—I will of course do my very best to earn it"—and with that she bowed and left me.

Anyhow she won't make a noise.

Nina writes since she has married Jim—which she did just before the offensive in March—she has been too happy—or too anxious, to remember her friends—even dear old ones—but now fortunately Jim is wounded in the ankle bone which will keep him at home for two months so she has a little leisure.

"You can't think, Nicholas, what a different aspect the whole war took on when I knew Jim was in the front line—I adore him—and up to now I have managed to keep him adoring me—but I can see I'll have to be careful if he is going to be with me long at a time."

So it would seem that Nina had not obtained the rest and security she hoped for.

I hope my writing a book will rest me. I have arranged all my first chapter in my head—and to-morrow I begin.

June th—Miss Sharp came punctually at ten—she had a black and white cotton frock on—There is nothing of her—she is so slight—(a mass of bones probably in evening dress—but thank goodness I shall not see her in evening dress,) she goes at six—She is to have her lunch here—Burton has arranged it. An hour off for lunch which she can have on a tray in the small salon, which I have had arranged for her work room.—Of course it won't take her an hour to eat—but Burton says she must have that time, it is always done. It is a great nuisance for perhaps when : comes I shall just be in the middle of an inspiration and I suppose off she'll fly like the housemaids used when the servants' hall bell went at home. But I can't say anything.

I was full of ideas and the beginning of my first chapter spouted out, and when Miss Sharp had read it over to me I found she had not made any mistake. That is a mercy.

She went away and typed it, and then had her lunch—and I had mine, but Maurice dropped in and mine took longer than hers—it was half past two when I rang my hand bell for her (it is a jolly little silver one I bought once in Cairo) She answered it promptly—the script in her hand.

"I have had half an hour with nothing to do," she said—"Can you not give me some other work which I can turn to, if this should happen again?"

"You can read a book—there are lots in the book case" I told her—"Or I might leave you some letters to answer."

"Thank you, that would be best"—(She is conscientious evidently).

We began again.

She sits at a table with her notebook, and while I pause she is absolutely still—that is good. I feel she won't count more than a table or chair. I am quite pleased with my work. It is awfully hot to-day and there is some tension in the air—as though somethingwas going to happen. The news is the same—perhaps slightly better.—I am going to have a small dinner to-night. The widow and Maurice and Madame de Clerté—just four and we are going to the play. It is such a business for me to go I seldom turn out.—Maurice is having a little supper in his rooms at the Ritz for us. It is my birthday—I am thirty-one years old.

Friday—What an evening that th of June! The theatre was hot and the cramped position worried me so—and the lights made my eye ache—Madame de Clerté and I left before the end and ambled back to the Ritz in my one horse Victoria and went and sat in Maurice's room. We talked of the situation, and the effect of the Americans coming in, bucking everyone up—we were rather cheerful. Then the sirens began—and the guns followed just as Maurice and Odette got back—They seemed unusually loud—and we could hear the bits of shrapnel falling on the terrace beneath us, Odette was frightened and suggested going into the cellar—but as Maurice's rooms are only on the second floor, we did not want to take the trouble.

Fear has a peculiar effect upon some people—Odette's complexion turned grey and she could hardly keep her voice steady. I wondered how soon she would let restraint slip from her and fly out of the room to the cellar. Madame de Clerté was quite unmoved.

Then the dramatic happened—Bang!—the whole house shook and the glass of the window crashed in fragments—and Maurice turned out the one light—and lifted a corner of the thick curtain to peep out.

"I believe they got the *Colome Vendôme*" he said awed—and as he spoke another bomb fell on the Ministaire beside us—and some of the splinters shot into space and buried themselves in our wall.

We were all blown across the room—and Madame de Clerté and I fell in a heap together by the door, which gave way outwards—Odette's shrieks made us think that she was hurt, but she was not, and subsided into a gibbering prayer—Maurice helped Madame de Clerté to rise and I turned on the torch I keep in my pocket, for a minute. I was not conscious of any pain. We sat in the dark and listened to the commotion beneath us for some time, and the crashing bombs but never one so near again.—Maurice's voice soothing Odette was the only sound in our room.

Then Madame de Clerté laughed softly and lit a cigarette.

"A near thing that, Nicholas!" she said—"Let us go down now and see who is killed, and where the explosion actually occurred—The sight is quite interesting you know you can believe me."

"When Bertha hit the —— two days ago, we rushed for taxis to go down to see the place—Coralie—has petrol for her motor since two weeks you know"—and she smiled wickedly—"Monsieur le Ministre must show his gratitude somehow mustn't he?—Coralie is such a dear—Yes—?—So some of us packed in with her—we were quite a large party—and when we got there they were trying to extinguish the fire, and bringing out the bodies—You ought to come with us sometime when we go on these trips—anything for a change."

These women would not have looked on at the sufferings of a mouse before the war—.

The sight in the hall when we did arrive there after the "all clear" went—was remarkable—the great glass doors of the salon blown in and all the windows broken—and the *Place Vendôme* a mass of debris—not a pane whole there I should think.

But nobody seems very much upset—these things are all in the days work—.

I wonder if in years to come we shall remember the queer recklessness which has developed in almost everyones mentality, or shall we forget about the war and go on just as we were before—Who knows?

I said to Miss Sharp this morning—

"What do you do in the evenings when you leave here"?

I had forgotten for a moment that Maurice had told me that she makes bandages. She looked at me and her manner froze—I can't think why I *felt* she thought I had no right to question her—I say "looked at me"—but I am never quite sure what her eyes are doing, because she never takes off her yellow glasses—Those appear to be gazing at me at all events.

"I make bandages."

"Aren't you dead tired after working all day with me?"

"I have not thought about it—the bandages are badly needed."

Her pencil was in her hand, and the block ready—she evidently did not mean to go on conversing with me. This attitude of continuous diligence on her part has begun to irritate me. She never fidgets—just works all the time.

I'll ask Burton what he thinks of her at luncheon to-day—As I said before, Burton knows the world.

"What do you think of my typist, Burton?"

He was putting a dish of make-believe before me—it is a meatless day—my one-legged cook is an artist but he thinks me a fool because I won't let him cheat—our want of legs makes us friendly though.

"And with a brother in the trade I could get Monsieur chickens and what he would wish!" he expostulates each week.

"A-hem"—Burton croaked.

I repeated the question.

"The young lady works very regular."

"Yes—That is just it—a kind of a machine."

"She earns her money Sir Nicholas."

"Of course she does—I know all that—But what do you think of her?"

"Beg pardon Sir Nicholas—I don't understand?"

I felt irritated.

"Of course you do—What kind of a creature I mean—?"

"The young lady don't chatter Sir—She don't behave like bits of girls."

"You approve of her then Burton?"

"She's been here a fortnight only, Sir Nicholas, you can't tell in the time"—and that is all I could get out of him—but I felt the verdict when he did give it would be favourable.

Insignificant little Miss Sharp—!

What shall I do with my day—? that is the question—my rotten useless idle day?—I have no more inspiration for my book—besides Miss Sharp has to type the long chapter I gave her yesterday. I wonder if she knows anything about William and Mary furniture really?—she never launches a remark.

Her hands are very red these last days—does making bandages redden the hands?

I wonder what colour her eyes are—one can't tell with that blurred yellow glass—.

Suzette came in just as I wrote that; she seldom turns up in the afternoon. She caught sight of Miss Sharp typing through the open door.

"*Tiens!*" she spit at me—"Since when?"

"I am writing a book, Suzette."

"I must see her face," and without waiting for permission, Suzette flounced into the small salon.

I could hear her shrill little voice asking Miss Sharp to be so good as to give her an envelope—She must write an address! I watched her—Miss Sharp handed her one, and went on with her work.

Suzette returned, closing the door, without temper, behind her.

"Wouff!" she announced to me—"No anxiety there—an *Anglaise*—not appetizing—not a *fausse maigre* like us, as thin as a hairpin! Nothing for thou Nicholas—and *Mon Dieu!*—she does the family washing by her hands—I know! mine look like that when I have taken one of my fortnights at the sea!"

"You think it is washing?—I was wondering—."

"Does she take off her glasses ever, Nicholas?"

"No perhaps she has weak light eyes. One never can tell!"

Suzette was not yet quite at ease about it all—. I was almost driven to ask Miss Sharp to remove her glasses to reassure her.

Women are jealous even of one-legged half blind men! I would like to ask my cook if he has the same trouble—but—Oh! I wish anything mattered!

Suzette showed affection for me after this—and even passion! I would be quite good-looking she said—when I should be finished. Glass eyes were so well made now—"and as for legs!—truly my little cabbage, they are as nimble as a goat's!"
Of course I felt comforted when she had gone.

The hot days pass—Miss Sharp has not asked for a holiday, she plods along, we do a great deal of work—and she writes all my letters. And there are days when I know I am going to be busy with my friends, when I tell her she need not come—there was a whole week at the end of July. Her manner never alters, but when Burton attempted to pay her she refused to take the cheque.
"I did not earn that" she said.
I was angry with Burton because he did not insist.
"It was just, Sir Nicholas."
"No, it was not, Burton—If she did not work here, she was out of pocket not working anywhere else. You will please add the wretched sum to this week's salary."
Burton nodded stubbornly, so I spoke to Miss Sharp myself.
"It was my business as to whether I worked or did not work for a week—therefore you are owed payment in any case—that is logic——."
A queer red came into her transparent skin, her mouth shut firmly—I knew that I had convinced her, and that yet for some reason she hated having to take the money.
She did not even answer, just bowed with that strange aloofness that is not insolent. Her manner is never like a person of the lower classes, trying to show she thinks she is an equal. It has exactly the right note—perfectly respectful as one who is employed, but with the serene unselfconsciousness that only breeding gives. Shades of manner are very interesting to watch. Somehow I *know*that Miss Sharp, in her washed cotton, with her red little hands, is a lady.
I have not seen my dear Duchesse lately—she has been down to one of her country places—where she sends her convalescents, but she is returning soon. She gives me pleasure—.

August th—The interest in the book has flagged lately—I could not think of a thing, so I proposed to Miss Sharp to have a holiday. She accepted the fortnight without enthusiasm. Now she is back and we have begun again—Still I have no *flair*—Why do I stick to it?—Just because I have said to the Duchesse that I *will* finish it?——I have an uneasy feeling that I do not want to probe my real reason—I would like to lie even to this Journal. Lots of fellows have been upon the five days' leave lately, things are going better—they jolly one, and I like to see them, but after they go I feel more of a rotten beast than ever. The only times I forget are when Maurice brings the fluffies to dine with me—when they rush up to Paris from Deauville. We drink champagne—(they love to know how much it costs) and I feel gay as a boy—and then in the night I have once or twice reached out for my revolver. They have all gone back to Deauville now.
Perhaps it is Miss Sharp who irritates me with her eternal diligence—What is her life—who are her family? I would like to know but I will not ask—I sit and think and think what to write about in my book. I have almost come to the end of grinding out facts about Walnut and ball fringe—and she sits taking it all down in short-hand, never raising her head, day after day—.
Her hair is pretty—that silky sort of nut brown with an incipient wave in it—her head is set on most gracefully, I must admit, and the complexion is very pale and transparent—But what a firm mouth!—Not cold though—only firm. I have never seen her smile. The hands are well shaped really—awfully well shaped, if one watches them—How long would it take to get them white again I wonder? She has got good feet, too, thin like the hands—. How worn her clothes look—does she never have a new dress—?
Yes Burton, I will see Madame de Clerté—.

Solonge de Clerté is a philosopher—she has her own aims—but I do not know them.
"Writing a book, Nicholas?" There was the devil of a twinkle in her eye—"There is a poor boy wounded in the leg who would make a perfect secretary if you are not satisfied."
I grew irritated—.
"I am quite satisfied"—we heard the noise of the typing machine from beyond—these modern doors allow nothing to be unknown.
"Young, is she?" Madame de Clerté asked turning her glance in that direction.
"I don't know and don't care—she types well"—.
"*Hein?*"
She saw that I was becoming enraged.—My dinners are good and the war is not yet over—.
"We shall all be terribly interested—yes—when we read the result—."
"Probably"—.
Then she told me of complications occurring about Coralie's husband.
"Of an insanity to attempt the three at once" she sighed—.
And now I can turn to my journal again—Good God—the last pages have all been about Miss Sharp—ridiculous, exasperating Miss Sharp! did I write ridiculous?—No—it is I who am ridiculous—I shall go for a drive—!

God! what is the meaning of it all—!

I have been in hell——I came in from my drive very quietly, it was early, a quarter to six, Miss Sharp goes at six—It was a horribly chilly evening and Burton had lit a bright wood fire—and I suppose its crackling prevented my hearing the sounds which were coming from the next room for a minute. I sat down in my chair—.

What was that?—the *roucoulements* of a dove?—No, a woman's voice cooing foolish love words in French and English—and a child's treble gurgling fondness back to her. It seemed as if my heart stopped beating—as if every nerve in my spine quivered—a tremendous emotion of I know not what convulsed me.—I lay and listened and suddenly I felt my cheek wet with tears—then some shame, some anger shook me, and I started to my feet, and hobbled to the door which was ajar—I opened it wide—there was Miss Sharp with the *concierge's* daughter's baby on her lap fondling it—the creature may be six months old. Her horn spectacles lay on the table. She looked up at me, the slightest flash of timidity showing—but her eyes—Oh! God! the eyes of the Madonna—heavenly blue, tender as an angel's—soft as a doe's—. I could have cried aloud with some pain in the soul—and so that brute part of me spoke—.

"How dare you make this noise"?—I said rudely—"do you not know that I have given orders for complete quiet"—.

She rose, holding the child with the greatest dignity—The picture she made could be in the Sistine Chapel.

"I beg your pardon" she said in a voice which was not quite steady—"I did not know you had returned, and Madame Bizot asked me to hold little Augustine while she went to the next floor—it shall not occur again!"

I longed to stay and gaze at them both—I would have liked to have touched the baby's queer little fat fingers—I would have liked—Oh—I know not what—And all the time Miss Sharp held the child protectively, as though something evil would come from me and harm it.—Then she turned and carried it out of the room—and I went back into my sitting-room and flung myself down in my chair—.

What had I done—Beast—brute—What had I done?

And will she never come back again?—and will life be emptier than ever—?

I could kill myself—.

It shall not be only Suzette but six others for supper to-night—.

Five a.m.—The dawn is here and it is not the rare sound of an August pigeon that I am listening to, but the tender cooing of a woman and a child—God, how can I get it out of my ears.

V

This morning I feel as if I could hardly bear it until Miss Sharp arrives—I dressed early, ready to begin a new chapter although I have not an idea in my head, and, as the time grows nearer, it is difficult for me to remain still here in my chair.

Have I been too impossible?—Will she not turn up?—and if she does not, what steps can I take to find her?—Maurice is at Deauville with the rest, and I do not know Miss Sharp's home address—nor if she has a telephone—probably not. My heart beats—I have every feeling of excitement as stupid as a woman! I analyse it all now, how mental emotion reacts on the physical—even the empty socket of my eye aches—I could hardly control my voice when Burton began a conversation about my orders for the day just now.

"You would not be wishin' for the company of your Aunt Emmeline, Sir Nicholas"?—he asked me—.

"Of course not, Burton, you old fool—"

"You seem so much more restless, sir—lately—"

"I am restless—please leave me alone."

He coughed and retired.

Now I am listening again—it wants two minutes to the hour—she is never late.

One, two, three, four, five, six, seven, eight, nine, ten—. It feels as if the blood would burst the veins—I cannot write.

She came after all, only ten minutes beyond her usual time, but they seemed an eternity when I heard the ring and Burton's slow step. I could have bounded from my chair to open the door myself.—It was a telegram! How this always happens when one is expecting anyone with desperate anxiety—A telegram from Suzette.

"I shall return to-night, *Mon Chou.*"

Her cabbage!—*Bah!* I never want to see her again—.

Miss Sharp must have entered when the door was opened for the telegram, for I had begun to feel pretty low again when I heard her knock at the door of the sitting-room.

She came in and up to my chair as usual—but she did not say her accustomary cold good morning. I looked up—the horn spectacles were over her eyes again, and the rest of her face was very pale—while there was something haughty in the carriage of her small head, it seemed to me. Her eternal pad and pencil were in her little thin, red hands.

"Good morning"—I said tentatively, she made a slight inclination as much as to say—"I recognize you have spoken," then she waited for me to continue.

I felt an egregious ass, I knew I was nervous as a bird, I could not think of anything to say—I, Nicholas Thormonde, accustomed to any old thing! nervous of a little secretary!

"Er—would you read me aloud the last chapter we finished"—I barked at last lamely.

She turned to fetch the script from the other room—.

I must apologize to her, I knew.

She came back and sat down stiffly, prepared to begin.

"I am sorry I was such an uncouth brute yesterday," I said—"It was good of you to come back—. Will you forgive me?"

She bowed again. I almost hated her at that moment, she was making me feel so much—A foolish arrogance rose in me—

"We had better get to work I suppose," I went on pettishly.

She began to read—how soft her voice is, and how perfectly cultivated.—Her family must be very refined gentlefolk—ordinary English typists have not that indescribable distinction of tone.

What voices mean to one!—The delight of that exquisite sound of refinement in the pronunciation. Miss Sharp never misplaces an inflection or slurs a word, she never uses slang, and yet there is nothing pedantic in her selection of language—it is just as if her habitual associates were all of the same class as herself, and that she never heard coarse speech.—Who can she be—?

The music of her reading calmed me—how I wish we could be friends—!

"How old is Madame Bizot's grandchild?" I asked abruptly, interrupting.

"Six months," answered Miss Sharp without looking up.

"You like children?"

"Yes—."

"Perhaps you have brothers and sisters?"

"Yes—."

I knew that I was looking at her hungrily—and that she was purposely keeping her lids lowered—.

"How many?"

"Two—."

The tone said, "I consider your questions impertinent—."

I went on—

"Brothers?"

"One brother."

"And a sister?"

"Yes."

"How old?"

"Eleven and thirteen."

"That is quite a gap between your ages then?"

She did not think it necessary to reply to this—there was the faintest impatience in the way she moved the manuscript.

I was so afraid to annoy her further in case she should give me notice to go, that I let her have her way, and returned to work.

But I was conscious of her presence—thrillingly conscious of her presence all the morning. I never once was able to take the work naturally, it was will alone which made me grind out the words.

There was no sign of nervousness in Miss Sharp's manner—I simply did not exist for her—I was a bore, a selfish useless bore of an employer, who was paying her twice as much as anyone else would, and she must in return give the most perfect service. As a man I had no meaning. As a wounded human being she had no pity for me—but I did not want her pity—what did I want?—I cannot write it—I cannot face it—. Am I to have a new torment in my life?—Desiring the unattainable?—Eating my heart out; not that woman can never really love me again, but that, well or ill, the consideration of *one* woman is beyond my reach—.

Miss Sharp is not influenced because I am or am not a cripple—If I were as I was when I first put on my grenadier's uniform, I should still not exist for her probably—she can see the worthless creature that I am—Need I always be so?—I wish to God I knew.

Night.

She worked with her usual diligence the entire day almost, not taking the least notice of me, until at five o'clock when my tea came I rang for her—Perhaps it was the irritation reacting upon my sensitive wrenched nerves, but I felt pretty rotten, my hands were damp—another beastly unattractive thing, which as a rule does not happen to me—I asked her to pour out the tea.

"If you will be so kind," I said—"I have let Burton go out"—Mercifully this was true—she came in as a person would who knew you had a right to command—you could not have said if she minded or no.

When she was near me I felt happier for some reason.

She asked me how I took my tea—and I told her—.

"Are you not going to have some with me?" I pleaded.

"Mine is already on my table in the next room—thank you"—and she rose.

In desperation I blurted out—.

"Please—do not go!—I don't know why, but I feel most awfully rotten to-day."

She sat down again and poured out her cup.

"If you are suffering shall I read to you?" she said—"It might send you to sleep—" and somehow I fancied that while her firm mouth never softened, perhaps the eyes behind the horn spectacles might not be so stony. And yet with it all something in me resented her pity, if she felt any. Physical suffering produces some weaknesses which respond to sympathy, and the spirit rages at the knowledge that one has given way. I never felt so mad in all my year of hell that I cannot be a man and fight—as I did at that moment.

A French friend of mine said—In English books people were always having tea—handing cups of tea! Tea, tea—every chapter and every scene—tea! There is a great deal of truth in it—tea seems to bring the characters together—at tea time people talk, it is the excuse to call at that hour of leisure. We are too active as a nation to meet at any other time in the day, except for sport—So tea is our link and we shall go down through the ages as tea fiends—because our novelists who portray life accurately, chronicle that most of the thrilling scenes of our lives pass among tea cups!—I ventured to say all this to Miss Sharp by way of drawing her into conversation.

"What could one describe as the French doing most often?"—I asked her—.

She thought a moment.

"They do not make excuses for anything they do, they have not to have a pretext for action as we have—They are much less hypocritical and self-conscious."

I wanted to make her talk—.

"Why are we such hypocrites?"

"Because we have set up an impossible standard for ourselves, and hate to show each other that we cannot act up to it."

"Yes, we conceal every feeling—We show indifference when we feel interest—We pretend we have come on business when we have come simply to see someone we are attracted by—."

She let the conversation drop. This provoked me, as her last remark showed how far from stupid she is.

That nervous feeling overcame me again—Confound the woman!

"Please read," I said at last in desperation, and I closed my one eye.

She picked up a book—it happened to be a volume of de Musset—and she read at random—her French is as perfect as her English—The last thing I remember was "*Mimi Pinson*"—and when I awoke it was past six o'clock and she had gone home.

I wonder how many of us, since the war, know the desolation of waking—alone and in pain—and helpless—Of course there must be hundreds. If I am a rotter and a coward about suffering, at all events it does not come out in words—and perhaps it is because I am such a mixture that I am able to write it in this journal—If I were purely English I should not be able to let myself go even here—.

Suzette came to dinner—I thought how vulgar she looked—and that if her hands were white they were podgy and the nails short. The three black hairs irritated my cheek when she kissed me—I was brutal and moved my head in irritation—.

"*Tiens?! Mon Ami!*"—she said and pouted.

"Amuse me!" I commanded—.

"So! it is not love then, Nicholas, thou desirest—Bear!"

"Not in the least—I shall never want love again probably. Divert me!—tell me—tell me of your scheming little mouse's brain, and your kind little heart—How is it '*dans le metier*'?"

Suzette settled herself on the sofa, curled up among the pillows like a plump little tabby cat. She lit a cigarette—.

"Very middling," she whiffed—"Cases of love where all my good counsel remains untaken—a madness for drugs—very foolish—A drug—yes to try—but to continue!—*Mon Dieu!* they will no longer make fortunes '*dans le metier*'—"

"When you have made your fortune, Suzette, what will you do with it?"

"I shall buy that farm for my mother—I shall put Georgine into a convent for the nobility, and arrange a large dot for her—and for me?—I shall gamble in a controlled way at Monte Carlo—."

"You won't marry then, Suzette?"

"Marry!" she laughed a shrill laugh—"For why, Nicholas?—A tie-up to one man, *hein*?—to what good?—and yet who can say—to be an honored wife is the one experience I do not know yet!"—she laughed again—.

"And who is Georgine—you have not spoken of her before, Suzette?"

She reddened a little under her new terra cotta rouge.

"No?—Oh! Georgine is my little first mistake—but I have her beautifully brought up, Nicholas—with the Holy Mother at St. Brieux. I am then her Aunt—so to speak—the wife of a small shop keeper in Paris, you must know—She adores me—and I give all I can to *St. Georges-des-Près*—. Georgine will be a lady and marry the Mayor's son—one day—."

Something touched me infinitely. This queer little *demi-mondaine* mother—her thoughts set on her child's purity, and the conventional marriage for her—in the future. Her plebeian, insolent little round face so kindly in repose.

I respect Suzette far more than my friends of the world—.

When she left—it was perhaps in bad taste, but I gave her a quite heavy four figure cheque.

"For the education of Georgine—Suzette."

She flung her arms round my neck and kissed me frankly on both cheeks, and tears were brimming over in her merry black eyes.

"Thou hast after all a heart, and art after all a gentleman, Nicholas— *Va!*—"—and she ran from the room.

VI

For two days after I last wrote, I tried not to see Miss Sharp—I gave short moments to my book—and she answered a number of business letters. She knows most of my affairs now,—Burton transmits all the bills and papers to her.—I can hear them talking through the thin door. The excitement of that time I was so rude seems to have used up my vitality, an utter weariness is upon me, I have hardly stirred from my chair.

The ancient guardsman, George Harcourt, came to lunch yesterday. He was as cynically whimsical as ever—He has a new love—an Italian—and until now she has refused all his offers of presents, so he is taking a tremendous interest in her—.

"In what an incredible way the minds of women work, Nicholas!" he said—"They have frequently a very definite aim underneath, but they 'grasshopper'—."

I looked puzzled I suppose—.

"To 'grasshopper' is a new verb!" he announced—"Daisy Ryven coined it.—It means just as you alight upon a subject and begin tackling it, you spring to another one—These lovely American war workers 'grasshopper' continuously.—It is impossible to keep pace with them."

I laughed.

"Yet they seem to have quite a definite aim—to get pleasure out of life."

"To 'grasshopper' does not prevent pleasure to the grasshopper.—It is only fatiguing to the listener. You can have no continued sensible conversation with any of these women—they force you to enjoy only their skins—"

"Can the Contessa talk?"

"She has the languour of the South—She does not jump from one subject to another, she is frankly only interested in love."

"Honestly, George—do you believe there is such a thing as real love?"

"We have discussed this before, Nicholas—You know my views—but I am hoping Violetta will change them. She has just begun to ask daily if I love her"—

"Why do women always do that—even one's little friends continually murmur the question?"

"It is the working of their subconscious minds——Damn good cigars these, my dear boy—pre-war eh?——Yes it is to justify their surrender—They want to be assured *in words* that you adore them—because you see the actions of love really prove nothing of love itself. A stranger who has happened to appeal to the senses can call them forth quite as successfully as the lady of one's heart!"

"It is logical of women then to ask that eternal question?"

"Quite—I make a point of answering them always without irritation."

——I wonder—if Miss Sharp loved anyone would she?——but I am determined not to speculate further about her—.

When Colonel Harcourt had gone—I deliberately rang my bell—and when she came into the room I found I was not sure what I had rung for—It is the most exasperating fact that Miss Sharp keeps me in a continual state of nervous consciousness.

Her manner was indifferently expectant, if one can use such a paradoxical description—.

"I—I—wondered if you played the piano?—"I blurted out.

She looked surprised—if one can ever say she looks anything, with the expression of her eyes completely hidden. She answered as usual with one word—.

"Yes."

"I suppose you would not play to me?—er—it might give me an inspiration for the last chapter—"

She went and opened the lid of the instrument.

"What sort of music do you like?" she asked.

"Play whatever you think I would appreciate."

She began a Fox trot, she played it with unaccountable spirit and taste, so that the sound did not jar me—but the inference hurt a little. I said nothing, however. Then she played "Smiles," and the sweet commonplace air said all sorts of things to me—Desire to live again, and dance, and enjoy foolish pleasures—How could this little iceberg of a girl put so much devilment into the way she touched the keys? If it had not been for the interest this problem caused me, the longing the sounds aroused in me to be human again, would have driven me mad.

No one who can play dance music with that lilt can be as cold as a stone—.

From this she suddenly turned to Debussy—she played a most difficult thing of his—I can't remember its name—then she stopped.

"Do you like Debussy?" I asked.

"No, not always."

"Then why did you play it?"

"I supposed you would."

"If you had said in plain words, 'I think you are a rotter who wants first dance music, then an unrestful modern decadent, brilliantly clever set of disharmonies,' you could not have expressed your opinion of me more plainly."

She remained silent—I could have boxed her ears.

I leaned back in my chair, perhaps I gave a short harsh sigh—if a sigh can be harsh—I was conscious that I had made some explosive sound.

She turned back to the piano again and began "Waterlily" and then ""—and the same strange quivering came over me that I experienced when I heard the cooing of the child.—My nerves must be in an awful rotten state—Then a longing to start up and break something shook me, break the windows, smash the lamp—yell aloud—I started to my one leg—and the frightful pain of my sudden movement did me good and steadied me.

Miss Sharp had left the piano and came over to me—.

"I am afraid you did not like that," she said—"I am so sorry"—her voice was not so cold as usual.

"Yes I did—" I answered—"forgive me for being an awful ass—I—I—love music tremendously, you see—"

She stood still for a moment—I was balancing myself by the table, my crutch had fallen. Then she put out her hand.

"Can I help you to sit down again?"—she suggested.

And I let her—I wanted to feel her touch—I have never even shaken hands with her before. But when I felt her guiding me to the chair, the maddest desire to seize her came over me—to seize her in my arms to tear off those glasses, to kiss those beautiful blue eyes they hid—to hold her fragile scrap of a body tight against my breast, to tell her that I loved her—and wanted to hold her there, mine and no one else's in all the world——My God! what am I writing—I must crush this nonsense—I must be sane—. But—what an emotion! The strongest I have ever felt about a woman in my life—.

When I was settled in the chair again—things seemed to become blank for a minute and then I heard Miss Sharp's voice with a tone—could it be of anxiety? in it? saying "Drink this brandy, please." She must have gone to the dining-room and fetched the decanter and glass from the case, and poured it out while I was not noticing events.

I took it.

Again I said—"I am awfully sorry I am such an ass."

"If you are all right now—I ought to go back to my work," she remarked—.

I nodded—and she went softly from the room. When I was alone, I used every bit of my will to calm myself—I analysed the situation. Miss Sharp loathes me—I cannot hold her by any means if she decides to go—. The only way I can keep her near me is by continuing to be the cool employer—And to do this I must see her as little as possible—because the profound disturbance she is able to cause in me, reacts upon my raw nerves—and with all the desire in the world to behave like a decent, indifferent man, the physical weakness won't let me do so, and I am so bound to make a consummate fool of myself.

When I was in the trenches and the shells were coming, and it was beastly wet and verminy and uncomfortable, I never felt this feeble, horrible quivering—I know just what funk is—I felt it the day I did the thing they gave me the V.C. for. This is not exactly funk—I wish I knew what it was and could crush it out of myself—.

Oh! if I could only fight again!—that was the best sensation in life—the zest—the zest!—What is it which prompts us to do decent actions? I cannot remember that I felt any exaltation specially—it just seemed part of the day's work—but how one slept! How one enjoyed any old thing—!

Would it be better to end it all and go out quite? But where should I go?—the *me* would not be dead.—I am beginning to believe in reincarnation. Such queer things happened among the fellows—I suppose I'd be born again as ugly of soul as I am now—I must send for some books upon the subject and read it up—perhaps that might give me serenity.

The Duchesse returned yesterday. I shall go and see her this afternoon I think,—perhaps she could suggest some definite useful work I could do—It is so abominably difficult, not being able to get about. What did she say?—She said I could pray—I remember—she had not time, she said—but the *Bon Dieu* understood—I wonder if He understands me—? or am I too utterly rotten for Him to bother about?

The Duchesse was so pleased to see me—she kissed me on both cheeks—.

"Nicholas! thou art better!" she said—"As I told you—the war is going to end well—!"

"And how is the book?" she asked presently—"It should be finished—I am told that your work is intermittent—."

My mind jumped to Maurice as the connecting link—the Duchesse of course must have seen him—but I myself have seen very little of Maurice lately—how did he know my work was intermittent—?

"Maurice told you?" I said.

"Maurice?"—her once lovely eyes opened wide—she has a habit of screwing them up sometimes when she takes off her glasses.—"Do you suppose I have been on a *partie de plaisir*, my son—that I should have encountered Maurice—!"

I dared not ask who was her informant—.

"Yes, I work for several days in succession, and then I have no ideas. It is a pretty poor performance anyway—and is not likely to find a publisher."

"You are content with your Secretary?"

This was said with an air of complete indifference. There was no meaning in it of the kind Madame de Clerté would have instilled into the tone.

"Yes—she is wonderfully diligent—it is impossible to dislodge her for a moment from her work. She thinks me a poor creature I expect."

The Duchesse's eyes, half closed now, were watching me keenly—.

"Why should she think that, Nicholas—you can't after all fight."

"No——but—."

"Get well, my boy—and these silly introspective fancies will leave you—Self analysis all the time for those who sit still—they imagine that they matter to the *Bon Dieu* as much as a *Corps d'Armée*—!"

"You are right, Duchesse, that is why I said Miss Sharp—my typist—probably thinks me a poor creature—she gets at my thoughts when I dictate."

"You must master your thoughts——"

And then with a total change of subject she remarked.

"Thou art not in love, Nicholas?"

I felt a hot flush rise to my face—What an idiotic thing to do—more silly than a girl—Again how I resent physical weakness reacting on my nerves.

"In love!"—I laughed a little angrily—"With whom could I possibly be in love, *chère amie*?! You would not suggest that Odette or Coralie or Alice could cause such an emotion!"

"Oh! for them perhaps no—they are for the senses of men—they are the exotic flowers of this forcing time—they have their uses—although I myself abhor them as types—but—is there no one else?"

"Solonge de Clerté?—Daisy Ryven?—both with husbands—."

"Not as if that prevented things" the Duchesse announced reflectively—"Well, well—Some of my *blessés* show just your symptoms, Nicholas, and I discover almost immediately it is because they are in love—with the brain—with the imagination you must understand—that is the only dangerous kind—. When it is with a pretty face alone—a good dose and a new book helps greatly."

"There would be no use in my being in love, Duchesse—"

"It would depend upon the woman—you want sympathy and a guiding hand— *Va!*—"
Sympathy and a guiding hand!
"I liked ruling and leading when I was a man—"
"——We all have our ups and downs—I like my own bed—but last night an extra batch of *blessés* came in—and I had to give it up to one whose back was a mass of festers—he would have lain on the floor else—. What will you—*hein?*—We have to learn to accommodate ourselves to conditions, my son."
Suddenly the picture of this noble woman's courage came to me vividly, her unvarying resourcefulness—her common sense—her sympathy with humanity—her cheerfulness—I never heard her complain or repine, even when fate took her only son at Verdun—Such as these are the glory of France—and Coralie and Odette and Alice seemed to melt into nothingness—.
"The war will be finished this autumn—" she told me presently—"and then our difficult time will begin—. Quarrels for all the world—Not good fighting—But you will live to see a Renaissance, Nicholas—and so prepare for it."
"What can I do, dear friend—If you knew how much I want to do something!"
"Your first duty is to get well.—Have yourself patched together—finished so to speak, and then marry and found a family to take the place of all who have perished. It was good taste when I was young not to have too many—but now!—France wants children—and England too. There is a duty for you, Nicholas!"
I kissed her hand—.
"If I could find a woman like you!" I cried—"indeed then I would worship her—."
"So—so—! There are hundreds such as I—when I was young I lived as youth lives—You must not be too critical, Nicholas."
She was called away then, back to one of the wards, and I hobbled down the beautiful staircases by myself—the lift was not working. The descent was painful and I felt hot and tired when I reached the ground floor, it was quite dusk then, and the one light had not yet been lit. A slight wisp of a figure passed along the end of the corridor. I could not see plainly, but I could have sworn it was Miss Sharp—I called her name—but no one answered me so I went on out,—the servant, aged ninety, now joining me, he assisted me into my one horse Victoria beyond the concierge's lodge.
Miss Sharp and the Duchesse!—? Why if this is so have I never been told about it?—The very moment Maurice returns I must get him to investigate all about the girl—In the meantime I think I shall go to Versailles—. I cannot stand Paris any longer—and the *masseur* can come out there, it is not an impossible distance away.

VII

RESERVOIRES, VERSAILLES.
September th.
How I love Versailles—the jolliest old hole on earth—(I wonder why one uses slang like this, I had written those words as an exact reflection of my thoughts—and nothing could be more inexact as a description of Versailles! It is as far from being "jolly" as a place can be—nor is it a "hole!") It is the greatest monument which the vanity of one man ever erected, and like all other superlatives it holds and interests. If the *Grand Monarque* squandered millions to build it, France has reaped billions from the pockets of strangers who have come to look at it. And so everything that is well done brings its good. Each statue is a personal friend of mine—and since I was a boy I have been in love with the delicious nymph with the shell at the bottom of the horse-shoe descent before you come to the *tapis vert* on the right hand side. She has two dimples in her back—I like to touch them—.
Why did I not come here sooner? I am at peace with the world—Burton wheels me up onto the terrace every evening to watch the sunset from the top of the great steps. All the masterpieces are covered with pent houses of concrete faced with straw, but the lesser gods and goddesses must take their chance.
And sitting here with peaceful families near me—old gentlemen—soldiers on leave—a pretty war widow with a great white dog—children with spades—all watching the glorious sky, seated in groups on the little iron park chairs, a sense of stupefaction comes over me—for a hundred or two kilometres away men are killing one another—women are searching for some trace of their homes—the ground is teeming with corpses—the air is fœtid with the smell of death! And yet we enjoy the opal sunset at Versailles and smile at the quaint appearance of the camouflaged bronzes!
Thus custom deadens all painful recollections and so are we able to live.
I wonder what Louis XIV would say if he could return and be among us? He, with all his faults being a well bred person, would probably adapt himself to circumstances, as the Duchesse does.
Suzette suggested that she should come and stay the week end out here—She wants change of air she says. I have consented.—Miss Sharp does not bring her eternal block and pencil until Tuesday—when Suzette will have left.
Now that I am peaceful and have forgotten my perturbations, Suzette will jolly me up—I have used the right term there!—Suzette does jolly one—! I feel I could write out here, but not about William and Mary furniture—! I could write a cynical story of the Duc de Richelieu's loves.—Armande, the present duc, tells me that he has a dispatch box filled with the love letters his ancestor received—their preservation owed to a faithful valet who kept them all separated in bundles tied with different ribbons—and every lock of hair and souvenir attached to each.—There is an idea!—I wonder if Burton has ever thought of keeping mine? He would not have had a heavy job in these last years—!
I read all the mornings, seated in the sun—I read Plato—I want to furbish up my Greek—For no reason on earth except that it is difficult, and perhaps if I start doing difficult things I may get more will.

Suzette arrived in an entirely new set of garments—the "*geste*" had altered, she said, one had to have a different look, and she was sure the autumn fashions would be even more pronounced.

"As you can readily understand, my friend, one cannot be *démodé, dans le metier*,—especially in war time!—"

Naturally I agreed with her—.

"The only unfortunate part is that it obliged me to break into the sum for Georgine's education."

"That is at least reparable"—I answered, and reached for my cheque-book—Suzette is such a good little sort—and clothes give her pleasure—and fancy being able to give *real pleasure* for a few thousand francs—pleasure, not comfort, or charity, or any respectable thing, but just *pleasure*! The only worry about this cheque was that Suzette was a little too affectionate after it!—I would nearly always rather only talk to her—now.

She accompanied my bath chair on to the terrace. Her ridiculous little outline and high heels contradicting all ideas of balance, and yet presenting an indescribable elegance. She prattled gaily—then when no one was looking she slipped her hand into mine.

"*Mon cher! Mon petit chou!*" she said.

We had the gayest dinner in my sitting-room—.

"The war was certainly nearing its close—Toinette, the friend of one of the Generals, assured her—people were thoroughly bored, and it was an excellent thing to finish it—."

"But even when peace comes, never again the restaurants open all night to dance, Nicholas!—there is a sadness, my friend!"

That was one of the really bad aspects of wars—the way they upset people's habits—, she told me. Even "*dans le metier*" things became of an uncertainty! '—One was never sure if the *amant* would not be killed—and it might be difficult to replace him advantageously!'

"It is perhaps fortunate for you that I am wounded and an institution, Suzette!"

"Thou—Nicholas!—Just as if I did not understand—I represent nothing but an agreeable passing of some moments to thee—Thou art not an *Amant*!—Not even a little pretense of loving me thou showest!"—

"But you said you never allowed yourself to care—perhaps I have the same idea—"

She shook with laughter.

"An artist at love thou, Nicholas—but no lover!"

"It is a nice distinction—would you like me better if I were a lover?"

"We have before spoken of this, *Mon ami*—If you were a lover—that is, if you loved—you would be dangerous even with your one leg and your one eye—a woman could be foolish for you. There is that air of *Grand seigneur*—that air of—mocking—of—*Mon Dieu!* Something which I can't find my word for—Thou art *rudement chic cheri*!"

I wished then that I had made the cheque larger—because there was something in her merry black eyes which told me she meant what she said—at the moment. I must be grateful to my money though after all—I could not be "*rudement chic*" or a "*Grand seigneur*" without it—Thus we get back to material things again!

——I wonder if material things could affect Miss Sharp?—One side of her certainly—or she could not have played that dance music——What can she think about all day?—certainly not my affairs, attending to them must be purely mechanical—. I know she is not stupid. She plays beautifully—she thinks—she has an air, and knowledge of the world. If I were not so afraid of losing her I would act toward her quite differently—I would chance annoying her by making her talk—but that fear holds me back.

George Harcourt says that between men and women, no matter what the relation may be, one or the other holds the reins and is the real arbiter of things, and that if you find yourself not in the happy position of master, there are many occasions when a man must look ridiculous.—I feel ridiculous when I think about Miss Sharp. I am "demand" and she is "supply"—I am wanting every moment of her time, and to know all her thoughts—and she is entirely uninterested in me, and grants nothing.

Suzette left last evening in the best of moods—I made the cheque larger—and now I am awaiting Miss Sharp in my sitting-room—I love this hotel—it has an air of indifference about it which is soothing, and the food is excellent.

Miss Sharp arrived about eleven to-day. Her cheeks were quite pink when she came in, and I could see she was warm with walking.—I wish I had remembered to send to the station to meet her.

"Do you think we shall be able to work here?" I asked her—"we have only the *résumé* chapter to do, and then the book will be finished."

"Why not here as well as any other place?"

"Does not environment matter to you?"

"I suppose it would if I were creating it, it does not matter now."

"Do you ever write—I mean write on your own?"

"Sometimes."

"What sort of things?"

She hesitated for a moment and then said as though she regretted having to speak the truth.—

"I write a journal."

I could not prevent myself from replying too eagerly—.

"Oh! I should like to see it!—er—I write one too!"—

She was silent. I felt nervous again—.

"Do you put down your impressions of people—and things?"

"I suppose so—."
"Why does one write a journal?—" I wanted to hear what she would answer.
"One writes journals if one is lonely."
"Yes, that is true. Then you are lonely?"
Again she conveyed to me the impression that I had shown bad taste in asking a personal question—and I felt this to be unjust, because in justice, she would have been forced to admit that her words were a challenge.
"You explain to me why one writes journals, and then when I presume upon the inference you snub me—You are not fair, Miss Sharp—"
"It would be better to stick to business," was all she answered—"will you dictate, please?"
I was utterly exasperated—.
"No, I won't!—If you only admit by inference that you are lonely, I say it right out—I am abominably lonely this morning and I want to talk to you.—Did I see you at the Duchesse de Courville-Hautevine's on Wednesday last?"
"Possibly."
I literally had not the pluck to ask her what she was doing there. However, she went on—.
"There are still many wounded who require bandages—."
That was it! of course—she was bringing bandages!
"She is a splendid woman, the Duchesse, she was a friend of my mother's—" I said.
Miss Sharp looked down suddenly—she had her head turned towards the window.
"There are many splendid women in France—but you don't see them—the poor are too wonderful, they lose their nearest and dearest and never complain, they only say it is '*la Guerre*!'."
"Have you any near relations fighting?"—
"Yes"—
It was too stupid having to drag information out of her like this—I gave it up—and then I was haunted by the desire to know what relations they were?—If she has a father he must be at least fifty—and he must be in the English Army—why then does she seem so poor?—It can't be a brother—her's is only thirteen—would a cousin count as a near relation?—or—can she have a *fiancé*—?!
The sudden idea of this caused me a nasty twinge—But no, her third finger has no ring on it.—I grew calmer again—.
"I feel you have a hundred thousand interesting things to say if you would only talk!" I blurted out at last.
"I am not here to talk, Sir Nicholas—I am here to do your typing."
"Does that make a complete barrier?—Won't you be friends with me?"
Burton came into the room at that moment—and while he was there she slipped off to her typing without answering me. Burton has arranged a place for her in his room, which is next to mine, so that I shall not be disturbed by the noise of her machine clicking.
"Miss Sharp must lunch with me"—I said.
Burton coughed as he answered.
"Very good, Sir Nicholas."
That meant that he did not approve of this arrangement—why?—Really these old servants are unsupportable.
The antediluvian waiters come in to lay the table presently, and I ordered peaches and grapes and some very special chablis—I felt exultant at my having manoeuvred that Miss Sharp should eat with me!
She came in when all was ready with her usual serene calm—and took her place at right angles to me.
Her hands are not nearly so red to-day, and their movements when she began to eat pleased me—her wrists are tiny, and everything she does is dainty.
She did not peck her food like a bird, as very slight people sometimes do—and she was entirely at ease—it was I who was nervous—.
"Won't you take off your glasses," I suggested—but she declined—.
"Of what use—I can see with them on."
This disconcerted me.
The waiter poured out the chablis carefully. She took it casually without a remark, but for an instant a cynical expression grew round her mouth—What was she thinking of?—it is impossible to tell, not seeing her eyes—but some cynical thought was certainly connected with the wine—By the direction of her head she may have been reading the label on the bottle—Does she know how much it cost and disapprove of that in war time—or what?
We talked of French politics next,—that is, she answered everything I said with intelligence, and then let the subject drop immediately—Nothing could be more exasperating because I knew it was deliberate and not that she is stupid, or could not keep up the most profound conversation. She seemed to know the war situation very well—Then I began about French literature—and at the end of the meal had dragged out enough replies to my questions to know that she is an exquisitely cultivated person—Oh! what a companion she would make if only I could break down this wretched barrier of her reserve!
She ate a peach—and I do hope she liked it—but she refused a cigarette when I offered her one—.
"I don't smoke."
"Oh, I am so sorry I did not know—" and I put out mine.
"You need not do that—I don't mind other people smoking, so long as I need not do it myself."
I re-lit another one—.
"Do you know—I believe I shall have my new eye put in before Christmas!" I told her just before she rose from the table—and for the first time I have known her, the faintest smile came round her mouth—a kindly smile—.
—"I am so very glad," she said.

And all over me there crept a thrill of pleasure.

After lunch I suggested the *parc*, and that I should dictate in some lovely cool spot. She made no objection, and immediately put on her hat—a plain dark blue straw. She walked a little behind my bath chair as we turned out of the Reservoires courtyard and began ascending the avenue in the *parc*, so that I could not converse with her. By the time we had reached the *parterre* I called to her—

"Miss Sharp"—

She advanced and kept beside me—.

"Does not this place interest you awfully?" I hazarded.

"Yes."

"Do you know it well?"

"Yes."

"What does it say to you?"

"It is ever a reminder of what to avoid."

"What to avoid! but it is perfectly beautiful. Why should you want to avoid beauty?!"

"I do not—it is what this was meant to stand for and what human beings failed in allowing it to do—that is the lesson."

I was frightfully interested.

"Tell me what you mean?"

"The architects were great, the king's thought was great—but only in one way—and everyone—the whole class—forgot the real meaning of *noblesse oblige*, and abused their power—and so the revolution swept them away—They put false value upon everything—false values upon birth and breeding—and no value upon their consequent obligations, or upon character—."

"You believe in acknowledging your obligations I know"—

"Yes—I hope so—Think in that palace the immense importance which was given to etiquette and forms and ceremonies—and to a quite ridiculous false sense of honour—they could ruin their poor tradesmen and—yet—."

"Yes"—I interrupted—"it was odd, wasn't it?—a gentleman was still a gentleman, never paying his tailor's bills—but ceased to be one if he cheated at cards—."

Miss Sharp suddenly dropped her dark blue parasol and bent to pick it up again—and as she did she changed the conversation by remarking that there were an unusual quantity of aeroplanes buzzing from Buc.

This was unlike her—I cannot think why she did so. I wanted to steer her back to the subject of Versailles and its meaning—.

Burton puffed a little as we went up the rather steep slope by the *Aile du Nord*, and Miss Sharp put her hand on the bar and helped him to push the chair.

"Is it not hateful for me being such a burden"—I could not help saying—.

"It leaves you more time to think—."

"Well! that is no blessing—that is the agony—thinking."

"It should not be—to have time to think must be wonderful"—and she sighed unconsciously.

Over me came a kind of rush of tenderness—I wanted to be strong again, and protect her and make her life easy, and give her time and love and everything in the world she could wish for—But I dared not say anything, and she hung back again a little, and once more it made the conversation difficult—and when we reached a sheltered spot by the "*point du jour*" I felt there was a sort of armour around her, and that it would be wiser to go straight to work and not talk further to-day.

She went directly from the *parc* to catch her train at five o'clock—and I was wheeled back to the hotel.

And now I have the evening alone before me—but the day is distinctly a step onward in the friendship line.

VIII

I spent a memorable day with Miss Sharp in the *parc* yesterday. I do not even remember what I did in the intermediate time—it seems of so little importance—but this Thursday will always stand out as a landmark of our acquaintance.

We drove in a fiacre to the Little Trianon after she arrived, with Burton on the box to help me out, and then I walked with my crutch to a delicious spot I know, rather near the grotto, and yet with a view of the house—I was determined I would entice her to talk as much as I could, and began very cautiously so as not to provoke her to suggest work.

"Have you ever read that wonderful story called 'An Adventure'—The two old ladies seeing Marie Antoinette and some other ghosts here?"

"No."

So I told her about it, and how they had accounted for it.

"I expect it was true," she said.

"You believe in ghosts then?"

"Some ghosts."

"I wish I did—then I should know that there is a beyond—."

I felt she was looking surprised.

"But of course there is a beyond—we have all been there many times during our evolution, after each life."

"That is what I want to know about—that theory of reincarnation," I responded eagerly—"can you tell me?"

"I could get you a book about it—."

"I would much rather hear it personally explained—the merest outline,—please tell me, it might help me not to be such a rotter—."

She looked away toward the giant trees, her mouth had a slightly sad expression, I could have torn those glasses off her blue eyes!

"We came up through the animal group soul—and finally were re-born individualized, into man—and from then onward the life on this earth is but a school for us to learn experience in, to prepare us eventually for higher spheres. When we advance far enough we need not be re-born again—."

"Yes—as a theory—I follow that—."

She went on—

"Everything is *cause* and *effect*—We draw the result of every action we commit, good or bad—and sometimes it is not until the next re-birth we pay for the bad ones, or receive the result of the good ones—."

"Is that why then that I am a cripple and life seems a beastly affair—?"

"Of course—You drew that upon yourself by some actions in your last life—. Also it may be to teach you some lesson in the improvement of the soul—."

"I don't seem to have learned anything—I believe I am rebellious all the time—."

"Probably."

"Miss Sharp—you could really help me if you would. Please explain to me—I will be a diligent pupil."

"Perhaps you were in a position of great power the last time, and were lavish and kind to people in a way—or you would not be so rich now—but you caused suffering and relied upon yourself, not on anything divine—you must have caused much suffering, perhaps mentally even, and so you had to be re-born and be wounded—to teach you the lesson of it all;—that is called your Karma. Our Karma is what we bring on with us from life to life in the way of obligations which we must discharge—so you see it rests with each one of us not to lay up more debts to pay in the future."

Her refined voice was level, as though she were controlling herself, not to allow any personal feeling to enter her discourse—her gloved hands were perfectly still in her lap—She was in profile to me so that I could see that her very long eyelashes seemed to be rather pressed against the glasses—I have not before been so close to her in a bright light.—Why does she wear those damned spectacles? I was thinking, when she said—

"You find it hard to be confined to your chair and not to be able to fight, don't you?—Well when you could fight it was not always the pleasure of going over the top? You had to have times in the trenches too, hadn't you—when you just had to bear it?"

"Of course—?"

"Well—you are in the trenches now, don't you see—and it is according to how your soul learns the lesson of them, as to whether in this life you will ever be allowed to go over the top again—or even to have peace."

"What is the lesson?"

"I am not God—I cannot tell you—but we would all know what our lesson to learn is, if we were not too vain to face the truth into ourselves."

"The aim being?"—

"Why of course to improve character and learn strength."

"What qualities do you most admire in a person, Miss Sharp?"

"Self control and strength."

"You have no sympathy with weaklings?"

"None whatever—bad strong people are better than weak good ones."

I knew this was true. This fragile creature suggests infinite repose and strength—what could she have done in a former life to bring her back in such unkind surroundings, that she must spend her days in drudgery, so that she has never even leisure to think?—I longed to ask her, but did not dare.

"Shall we not begin work now," she suggested—and I demonstrated my first lesson in self control by agreeing, and we did not talk again until luncheon time.

"If you don't mind we shall go to the little café by the *lac*," I said—"and then afterwards we can find another place and work again—Burton will have had my wheeled chair brought down there, so we can choose a decent spot in one of the *bosquets*."

She nodded slightly—Now that it was not to help my moral regeneration she did not intend to talk any more, it seemed!

As we got into the fiacre I slipped in the slightest degree, and caught on to her arm—It was bare to the elbow in the little cheap cotton frock, and as I touched the fine, fine skin, that maddening feeling came over me again to clasp her in my arms.—I pulled myself together, and she got in beside me. She has a darling tiny curl which comes behind her ear, slipped down probably because her hair is so unfashionably dressed—None of Suzette's "*geste*," nor even the subtle perfect taste of the fluffies.—It is just torn back and rolled into a tight twist. But now that I see her out of doors and in perspective I realize that she has a lovely small figure, and that everything is in the right place. I had told Burton to order the nicest lunch he could think of in that simple place, and our table under one of the umbrellas was waiting for us when we arrived.

There were only four other people there besides ourselves, and a few came in afterwards.

I had forgotten my bread tickets, so Miss Sharp gave me one of hers. She had relapsed into absolute silence. The only words she had uttered as we came down that avenue from The Trianon to the *lac* were when I exclaimed at the beauty of it—I judged by her mouth that she was admiring it too—and she said softly—

"For me, Versailles is the loveliest spot on earth!"

My mind flew then to the thought of what it would be to buy a really nice house here and spend the summers—with her—for my own—. I found myself clutching at my crutch—.

I tried to make conversation at lunch. There is nothing in the world so difficult as to keep this up when you are nervous with interest, and the other person is determined not to say a sentence which is unnecessary. A chill crept over me.

Burton turned up in time to pay the bill and put me into my chair.
"I don't think you look well enough to stay out the afternoon, Sir Nicholas"—he said—"Better go straight back to the hotel and rest—."
Miss Sharp joined in.
"I was going to say that"—she said.
I felt like a cross, disappointed child—I knew they were both right though; I was feeling pretty tired and had not an idea in my head. But if I did that, there would be a chance to see her lost—and all the long hours to face alone—.
"I am quite all right and I want to work," I said fretfully—and we started off.
We went up through the lovely *allées* past *Enceledus*—and on to the *Quinconce du Nord*, Miss Sharp walking a little behind my chair.
Here Burton bent over me—.
"It would be good for you to be taking a nap, Sir Nicholas—Indeed it would."
It seemed as if Miss Sharp was abetting him, for she came to my side—.
"If you can get quite comfortable—I would read to you, and you might sleep," she said—.
"We've no book"—I retorted—peeved, and yet pleased at the idea.
"I have one here which, will do"—and she took a little volume from her bag.—"I have wanted it for a long time, and I bought it at the *Foire* as I came from the station to-day—it cost a franc!"
It was a worn eighteenth century copy of François Villon—.
"Yes, that will be nice," I agreed—and leaned back while Burton settled my cushion, and then retired to a distance. Twelve years on and off of Paris has not taught him French—at least not the French of François Villon!
Miss Sharp took a little *parc* chair and I was able to watch her as she read—I did not even hear the words—because, as she was looking down I had not to guard myself, but could let my eye devour her small oval face. All my nerves were thrilling again and there was no peace—how I longed—ached—to take her into my arms!
She looked up once after an hour, to see if I were asleep, I suppose.—She must have observed passionate emotion in my eye—she looked down at the book instantly, but a soft pink flush came into her cheeks—which have a mother of pearl transparency usually. This caused me deep pleasure—I had been able to make her feel something at any rate! but then I was frightened—perhaps she would suggest going if she found the situation uncomfortable. Her voice had a fresh tone in it as she went on, and finally it faltered, and she stopped.
"If it is not putting you to sleep" she remarked—"perhaps you would not object if I walked on and typed what I took down this morning—It seems a pity to waste this time."
I knew that if I did not let her have her way there might be difficulties, so I agreed—and said that I would go back to the hotel and rest upon the sofa in the salon—So the procession started, and as we took the *allée*, to bring us to the Reservoirs on the level—I suddenly caught sight of Coralie and her last favoured one!—both of whom are supposed to be at Deauville with the rest!
Coralie was exquisitely dressed, Duquesnois in uniform.
I realized that she had seen us, and that she could not avoid coming up to talk, although that had not been her intention—When one is supposed to be at Deauville with one's family, and is in reality at Versailles with one's lover—one does not seek to recognize one's friends!
She came forward with *empressement* when she found the meeting was inevitable—.
"Nicholas!" she cooed "—what happiness!"—
Then she eyed Miss Sharp mischievously, making a movement as though she expected me to introduce them—.
But Miss Sharp defeated this by immediately walking on—.
"*Tiens!*" said Coralie—.
"That is Miss Sharp—my secretary—What are you doing—here Coralie?"
"Perhaps the same as you, *cher ami*—" and she rippled with laughter—"Versailles is so tranquil a place!"
I could have slapped her—fortunately Miss Sharp was out of earshot—.
Jean Duquesnois now joined in—he was back from the front for two days—things were going better—peace would certainly be declared before Christmas—.
Coralie meanwhile was looking after Miss Sharp with an expression upon her clever face which only a Frenchwoman is able to put there—It said as plainly as words, "So this is the reason Nicholas!—Well you have chosen something very every-day and inexpensive this time!—Men are certainly crazy in their tastes!"
I pretended not to notice, and so she spoke.
"Why if you can come here cannot you come to Deauville, Nicholas?—there must be some irresistible attraction stronger than to be with your friends!"
"Yes—he is an excellent Swedish masseur who is glued to Paris.—Also I like solitude sometimes—."
"Solitude!" and Coralie glanced at Miss Sharp's rapidly disappearing figure—. "*Hein?*"
I would not permit myself to grow angry.
"The book is nearly finished—you can tell the rest—."
"That old book! You were much more entertaining before you commenced it, Nicholas! Perhaps the idea has come to me why!"
I would not be drawn—I threw the war into the enemy's country.
"You are staying at the Reservoirs?"
I saw that she was—and that now the thought of my being there disconcerted her—.
"But no!" she lied sweetly—"I am merely out here for the day to see Louise, who has a son in the hospital—."
It was my turn to say—
"*Tiens?*"

And then we both laughed—and I let them go on—.

But when I got into my salon—I heard no typing—only there was a note from Miss Sharp to say that some slight thing had gone wrong with the machine, so she had taken the work to finish it at home—.

I cursed Coralie and all the fluffies in the world, and then in pain laid down upon my bed.

IX

Saturday Morning:

Yesterday I was so restless I could not settle to anything. I read pages and pages of Plato and was conscious that the words were going over in my head without conveying the slightest meaning, and that the other part of my mind was absorbed with thoughts of Miss Sharp—. If I only dared to be natural with her we surely could be friends, but I am always obsessed with the fear that she will leave me if I transgress in the slightest beyond the line she has marked between us—. I see that she is determined to remain only the secretary, and I realize that it is her breeding which makes her act as she does—. If she were familiar or friendly with me, she would feel it was not correct to come to my flat alone—She only comes at all because the money is so necessary to her—and having to come, she protects her dignity by wearing this ice mask.—I know that she was affronted by Coralie's look on Thursday, and that is why she went home pretending the typing machine was out of order—Now if any more of these *contretemps* happen she will probably give me warning. Burton instinctively sensed this, and that is why he disapproved of my asking her to lunch—If she had been an ordinary typist Burton would not have objected in the least,—as I said before, Burton knows the world!

Now what is to be done next?—I would like to go and confide in the Duchesse, and tell her that I believe I have fallen in love with my secretary, who won't look at me, and ask her advice—but that I fear with all her broad-minded charity, her class prejudice is too strong to make her really sympathetic. Her French mind of the *Ancien Régime* could not contemplate a Thormonde—son of Anne de Mont-Anbin—falling in love with an insignificant Miss Sharp who brings bandages to the Courville hospital!

These thoughts tormented me so all yesterday that I was quite feverish by the evening—and Burton wore an air of thorough disapproval. A rain shower came on too, and I could not go up on the terrace for the sunset.

I would like to have taken asperines and gone to sleep, when night came—but I resisted the temptation, telling myself that to-morrow she would come again.

I am dawdling over this last chapter on purpose—and I have re-read the former ones and decided to rewrite one or two, but at best I cannot spread this out over more than six weeks, I fear, and then what excuse can I have for keeping her? I feel that she would not stay just to answer a few letters a day, and do the accounts and pay the bills with Burton. I feel more desperately miserable than I have felt since last year—And I suppose that according to her theory, I have to learn a lesson. It seems if I search, as she said one must do without vanity, that the lesson is to conquer emotion, and be serene when everything which I desire is out of reach.

Saturday Night:

To-day has been one of utter disaster and it began fairly well. Miss Sharp turned up at eleven as I shut my journal. I had sent to the station to meet her this time—She brought all the work she had taken away with her on Thursday, quite in order—and her face wore the usual mask. I wonder if I had not ever seen her without her glasses if I should have realized now that she is very pretty—I can see her prettiness even with them on—her nose is so exquisitely fine, and the mouth a Cupid's bow really—if one can imagine a Cupid's bow very firm. I am sure if she were dressed as Odette, or Alice, or Coralie, she would be lovely. This morning when she first came I began thinking of this and of how I should like to give her better things than any of the fluffies have ever had—how I would like her to have some sapphire bangles for those little wrists and a great string of pearls round that little throat—my mother's pearls—and perhaps big pearls in those shell ears—And how I would like to take her hair down and brush it out, and let it curl as it wanted to—and then bury my face in it—those stiff twists must take heaps of hair to make.—But why am I writing all this when the reality is further off than ever, and indeed has become an impossibility I fear.

We worked in the sitting-room—it was a cloudy day—and presently, after I had been dreaming on in this way, I asked her to read over the earlier chapters of the book.—She did—.

"Now what do you think of the thing as a whole?" I asked her.

She was silent for a moment as though trying not to have to answer directly, then that weird constitutional honesty seemed to force out the words.

"It perhaps tells what that furniture is."

"You feel it is awful rot?"

"No—."

"What then?"

"It depends if you mean to publish it?"

I leaned back and laughed—bitterly! the realization that she understood so completely that it was only a "*soulagement*"—an "asperine" for me, so to speak as the Duchesse said—cut in like a knife. I had the exasperated feeling that I was just being pandered to, humored by everyone, because I was wounded. I was an object of pity, and even my paid typist—but I can't write about it.

Miss Sharp started from her chair, her fine nostrils were quivering, and her mouth had an expression I could not place.

"Indeed, it is not bad," she said—"You misunderstand me—."

I knew now that she was angry with herself for having hurt me—and that I could have made capital out of this, but something in me would not let me do that.

"Oh—it is all right—" I replied, but perhaps my voice may have been flat and discouraged—for she went on so kindly.

"You know a great deal about the subject of course—but I feel the chapters want condensing—May I tell you just where?"

I felt that the thing did not interest me any more, one way or another, it was just a ridiculous non-essential—. I saw it all in a new perspective—but I was glad she seemed kindly—though for a moment even that appeared of less importance. Something seemed to have numbed me. What, what could be the good of anything?—the meaning of anything?—I unconsciously put my head back against the cushion of my chair in weariness—I felt the soft silk and shut my eye for a moment.

When Miss Sharp spoke again, her voice was full of sympathy—and was it remorse—?

"I would like to help you to take interest in it—again—won't you let me?" she pleaded.

I was grateful that she did not say she was sorry she had hurt me—that I could not have stood—.

I opened my eye now and looked at her, she was bending nearer to me, but I felt nothing particular, only a desire to go to sleep and have done with it all. It was as if the fabric of my make-believe had been rent asunder.

"It is very good of you," I answered politely—"Yes—say what you think."

Her tact is immense—she plunged straight into the subject without further imputation of sympathy,—her voice, full of inflections of interest and friendliness, her constrained self-control laid aside for the time. She spoke so intelligently, showing trained critical faculties—and at last my numbness began gradually to melt, and I could not help some return of sensation. There may have been soothing syrup in the fact that she must have been interested in the work, or she could not have dissected it chapter by chapter, point by point, as she was doing.

She grew animated as we discussed things, and once unconsciously took off her glasses—It was like the sun coming out after days of storm clouds—her beautiful, beautiful blue eyes!—My "heart gave a bound"—(I believe that is the way to express what I mean!)—I felt a strange emotion of excitement and pleasure—I had not time to control my admiration, I expect,—for she took fright and instantly replaced them, a bright flush in her cheeks—and went on talking in a more reserved way—Alas!—

Of course then I realized that she does not wear the glasses for any reason of softening light or of defective sight, but simply to hide those blue stars and make herself unattractive—.

How mysterious it all is!—

I wish I had been able to conceal the fact that I had noticed that the glasses were off—Another day I would certainly have taken advantage of this moment and would have tried to make her confess the reason of her wearing them; but some odd quality in me prevented me from reaping any advantage from this situation, so I let the chance pass.—Perhaps she was grateful to me, for she warmed up a little again.

I began to feel that I might write the fool of a book right over from the beginning—and suggested to her that we should take it in detail.

She acquiesced—.

Then it suddenly struck me that she had not only spoken of style in writing, of method in book making—but had shown an actual knowledge of the subject of the furniture itself.—How could little Miss Sharp, a poverty stricken typist, be familiar with William and Mary furniture? She has obviously not "seen better days," and only taken up a stenographic business lately, because such proficiency as she shows, not only in this work but in account keeping and all the duties of a secretary, must have required a steady professional training.

Could she have studied in Museums?

But the war has been on for four years and I had gathered that she has been in Paris all that time—Even if she had left England in , she could only have been eighteen or nineteen then, and girls of that age do not generally take an interest in furniture. This thought kept bothering me—and I was silent for some moments. I was weighing things up.

Her voice interrupted my thoughts.

"The Braxted chair has the first of the knotted fringes known"—it was saying.

I had spoken of the Braxted chair—but had not recorded this fact—.

How the devil could she have known about it?

"Where did you find that?"

"I knew someone who had seen it—" she answered in the same voice, but her cheeks grew pinker—.

"You have never seen it yourself?"

"No—I have never been in England—."

"——Never been in England?"

I was stupefied.

She went on hurriedly—I was going to write feverishly,—so quickly did she rush into questions of method in arranging the chapters, her armour was on again—she had become cautious, and was probably annoyed with herself for ever having allowed herself to slip off her guard.

I knew that I could disconcert her, and probably obtain some interesting admissions from her—and have a thrilling fencing match, but some instinct warned me not to do so—I might win out for the time being, but if she has a secret which she does not wish me to discover, she will take care not again to put herself in a situation where this can happen. I have the apprehension always hanging, like Damocles' sword, over my head, of her relinquishing her post. Besides, why should I trouble her for my own satisfaction?—However, I registered a vow then that I would find out all I could from Maurice.

The inference of everything she says, does and unconsciously infers, is that she is a cultivated lady, accustomed to talking with people of our world—people who know England and its great houses well enough to have made her familiar with the knowledge of where certain pieces of famous furniture are.—The very phrasing of her sentences is the phrasing of our Shibboleth, and not the phrasing of the professional classes.

And yet—she is meanly dressed—does housework—and for years must have been trained in professional business methods. It is profoundly interesting.

I have never even questioned Maurice as to how he heard of her.

Well, I write all this down calmly, the record of the morning, to let myself look back on it, and to where the new intimacy might have led us, but for the sickening end to the day.

Burton did not question her lunching with me this time—he had given the order as a matter of course—He is very fine in his distinctions, and understood that to make any change after she once had eaten with me would be invidious.

By the time the waiters came in to lay the table, that sense of hurt, and then of numbness, had worn off—I was quite interested again in the work, and intensely intrigued about the possible history of the Sharp family!

I was using cunning, too, and displaying casual indifference, so watchfulness was allowed to rest a little with the strange girl.

"I believe if you will give me your help I shall be able to make quite a decent book of it after all,—but does it not seem absurd to trouble about such thing's as furniture with the world in ruins and Empires tottering!"—I remarked while the ark-relic handed the omelette—.

"All that is only temporary—presently people will be glad to take up civilized interests again."

"You never had any doubt as to how the war would end?"

"Never."

"Why?"

"Because I believe in the gallantry of France, and the tenacity of England, and the—youth of America."

"And what of Germany?"

"The vulgarity."

This was quite a new reason for Germany's certain downfall—! It delighted me—.

"But vulgarity does not mean weakness!"

"Yes it does—Vulgar people have imperfect sensibilities, and cannot judge of the psychology of others, they appraise everything by their own standard—and so cannot calculate correctly possible contingencies—that shows weakness."

"How wise you are—and how you think!"

She was silent.

"All the fighting nations will be filled with vulgarians even when we do win, though with most of the decent people killed—" I ventured to say—.

"Oh! no—Lots of their souls are not vulgar, only their environment has caused their outward self-expression to seem so. Once you get below the pompous *bourgeoisie* in France, for instance, the more delightful you find the spirit, and I expect it is the same in England. It is the pretentious aspiring would-bes who are vulgar—and Germany seems filled with them,"

"You know it well?"

"Yes, pretty well."

"If it is not a frightfully impertinent question—how old are you really, Miss Sharp—?" I felt that she could not be only twenty-three after this conversation.

She smiled—the second smile I have seen—.

"On the twentieth of October I shall be twenty-four."

"Where on earth did you learn all your philosophy of life in the time!"

"It is life which teaches us everything—if we are not half asleep—especially if it is difficult—."

"And the stupid people are like me—not liking to learn any lessons and kicking against the pricks—.",

"Yes—."

"I would try to learn anything you would teach me though, Miss Sharp."

"Why?"

"Because I have confidence in you"—I did not add—because I loved her voice and respected her character and——.

"Thank you"—she said.

"Will you teach me?"

"What?"

"How not to be a rotter—."

"A man knows that himself—."

"How to learn serenity then?"

"That would be difficult."

"Am I so impossible?"

"I cannot say—but."

"But—what?"

"One would have to begin from the beginning—."

"Well?"

"And I have not time—."

I looked at her as she said this—there was in the tone a faint echo of regret, so I wanted to see the expression of her mouth—It told me nothing.

I could not get anything further out of her, because the waiters came in and out after this rather frequently, changing the courses—and so I did not have any success.

After lunch I suggested as it had cleared up that we should go at least as far as the parterre, and sit under the shadow of the terrace—the flower beds are full of beans now—their ancient glories departed. Miss Sharp followed my bath chair,—and with extreme diligence kept me to the re-arranging of the first chapter. For an hour I watched her darling small face whenever I could. A sense of peace was upon me. We were certainly on the first rung of the ladder of friendship—and presently—presently—If only I could keep from annoying her in any way!

When we had finished our task she rose—.

"If you don't mind, as it is Saturday I have promised Burton"—and she looked at him, seated on a chair beyond earshot enjoying the sun—"to do up the accounts and prepare the cheques for you to sign—. So I will go in now and begin."

I wanted to say "Damn the accounts"—but I let her go—I must play the tortoise in this game, not the hare. She smiled faintly—the third smile—as she made me a little bow, and walked off.

After a few paces she came back again.

"May I ask Burton for the bread ticket I lent you on Thursday," she said—"No one can afford to be generous with them now, can they!"

I was delighted at this. I would have been delighted at anything which kept her with me an extra minute.

I watched her as she disappeared down towards the Reservoirs with longing eyes, then I must have dozed for a while, because it was a quarter to five when I got back to my sitting-room.

And when I was safely in my chair there was a knock on the door, and in she came—with a cheque-book in her hand. Before I opened it or even took it up I knew something had happened which had changed her again.

Her manner had its old icy respect as of a person employed, all the friendliness which had been growing in the last two or three days had completely departed. I could not imagine why—.

She put the cheque-book open, and handed me a pen to sign with, and then I signed the dozen that she had filled in, and tore them off as I did so. She was silent, and when I had finished she took them, saying casually that she would bring the corrected chapter typed again on Tuesday, and was now going to catch her train—and before I could reply, she had gone into the other room—.

A frightful sense of depression fell upon me—What could it possibly be—?

Idly I picked up the cheque-book—and absently fingered the leaves—then my eye caught a counterfoil where I had chanced to open it. It was not in Miss Sharp's handwriting, although this was the house cheque-book which Burton usually keeps, but in my own and there was written, just casually as I scribble in my private account.—"For Suzette francs" and the date of last Saturday—and on turning the page there was the further one of "For Suzette francs" and the date of Monday!!

The irony of fate!—I had picked this cheque-book up inadvertently I suppose on these two days instead of my own.

X

It is quite useless for me to comment upon the utterly annoying circumstance of that mixup of cheque-books—Such things are fate—and fate I am beginning to believe is nothing but a reflex of our own actions. If Suzette had not been my little friend, I should not have given her eight thousand francs—but as she has been—and I did—I must stand by the consequences.

After all—a man?—Well—what is the use of writing about it. I am so utterly mad and resentful that I have no words.

It is Sunday morning, and this afternoon I shall hire the one motor which can be obtained here, at a fabulous price, and go into Paris. There are some books I want to get out of my bookcase—and somehow I have lost interest here. But this morning I shall go and sit in the parish church and hear Mass.—I feel so completely wretched, the music may comfort me and give me courage to forget all about Miss Sharp. And in any case there is a soothing atmosphere in a Roman Catholic church, which is agreeable. I love the French people! They are a continual tonic, if one takes them rightly. So filled with common sense, simply using sentiment as an ornament, and a relaxation; and never allowing it to interfere with the practical necessities of life. Ignorant people say they are hysterical, and over passionate—They are nothing of the kind—They believe in material things, and in the "*beau geste*." Where they require a religion, they accept a comforting one; and meanwhile they enjoy whatever comes in their way and get through disagreeables philosophically. *Vive la France!*

I am waiting for the motor now—and trying to be resigned.—Mass did me good—I sat in a corner and kept my crutch by me. The Church itself told me stories, I tried to see it in Louis XV's time—I dare say it looked much the same, only dirtier—And life was made up with etiquette and forms and ceremonies, more exasperating than anything now. But they were ahead of us in manners, and a sense of beauty.

A little child came and sat beside me for about ten minutes, and looked at me and my crutch sympathetically.

"*Blessé de la guerre*," I heard her whisper to her mother—"*Comme Jean*."

The organ was not bad—and before I came out I felt calmer.

After all it is absurd of Miss Sharp to be disgusted about Suzette—She must know, at nearly twenty-four, and living in France, that there are Suzettes—and I am sure she is not narrow-minded in any way—What can have made her so censorious? If she took a personal interest in me it would be different, but entirely indifferent as she is, how can it matter to her?—As I write this, that hot sense of anger and rebellion arises in me—I'll have to keep saying to myself that I am in the trenches again and must not complain.

I'll make Burton find out if Coralie is really staying here, and get her to dine with me to-night—Coralie always pretended to have a *béguin* for me—even when most engaged elsewhere.

Monday:

Sunday was a memorable day—.

I went through the *Bois de Marne* on that bad road because the trees were so lovely—and then through the *parc de St. Cloud.* Even in war time this wonderful people can enjoy the open air life!—

I think of Henriette d' Angleterre looking from the terrace of her Château over the tree tops—The poor Château! not a stone of which is standing to-day—Did she feel sentimental with her friend the Comte de Guiche—as I would like to feel now?—If I had someone to be sentimental with. Alas! There was an ominous hot stillness in the air, and the sky beyond the Eiffel tower had a heavy, lurid tone in it.

When we got across the river into the *Bois de Boulogne* it seemed as if all Paris was enjoying a holiday. I told the chauffeur to go down a side *allée* and to go slowly, and presently I made him draw up at the side of the road. It was so hot, and I wanted to rest for a little, the motion was jarring my leg.

I think I must have been half asleep, when my attention was caught by three figures coming up another by-path obliquely—the tallest of them was undoubtedly Miss Sharp—but Miss Sharp as I had never seen her before!—

And a boy of thirteen, and a girl of eleven were at either side of her, the boy clinging on to her arm, he was lame and seemed to be a dreadfully delicate, rickety person. The little girl was very small and sickly looking too—but Miss Sharp—my secretary!—appeared blooming and young and lovely in her inexpensive foulard frock—No glasses hid her blue eyes. Her hair was not torn back and screwed into a knot, but might have been dressed by Alice's maid—and her hat, the simplest thing possible, was most becoming, with the proper modish "look."—

Refinement and perfect taste proclaimed themselves from every inch of her, even if everything had only cost a small sum.

So that dowdy get-up is for my benefit, and is not habitual to her!—Or is it, that she has only one costume and keeps it for Sundays and days of *fête*?—

In spite of my determination to put all thought of her from me—a wild emotion arose—a passionate longing to spring from the car and join her—to talk to her, and tell her how lovely I thought she was looking.

They came nearer and nearer—I could see that her face was rippling with smiles at something the little brother had said—Its expression was gentle and sympathetic and it was obvious that fond affection held all three.

The children might have been drawn by Du Maurier in Punch long ago, to express a family who were overbred. Race run to seed expressed itself in every line of them. The boy wore an Eton jacket and collar and a tall hat—and it looked quite strange in this place.

As they got close to me I could hear him cough in the hollow way which tells its own story—.

I cowered down behind the hood of the motor, and they passed without seeing me—or perhaps Miss Sharp did see me but was determined not to look—. I felt utterly alone and deserted by all the world—and the same nervous trembling came over me which once before made me suffer so, and again I was conscious that my cheek was wet with a tear.

The humiliation of it! the disgrace of such feebleness!—

When they had gone by, I started forward again to watch them—I could hear the little girl cry, "Oh! look Alathea!" as she pointed to the sky, and then all three began to quicken their pace down another *allée*, in the direction of Auteuil, and were soon out of sight.

Then, still quivering with emotion, I too glanced heavenward—Ye Gods! what a storm was coming on—!

Where were they going? there into the deep wood?—it was a good mile or two from the Auteuil gate—They would be soaked to the skin when the rain did commence to fall—and there was a thunder storm beginning also—were they quite safe?

All these thoughts tormented me, and I gave the chauffeur orders to take a road I thought might cut across the path they had followed, and when we reached the spot, I made him wait.

The livid lightning rent the sky and the thunder roared like guns, and the few people in sight rushed, panic-stricken, in a hopeless search for shelter—far greater fear on their faces than they show at German bombs.

My chauffeur complained audibly, as he got down to shut the car—Did Monsieur wish to be struck by lightning? he demanded, very enraged.

Still I waited—but no Sharp family appeared—and at last I knew I had missed them somehow—a very easy thing in that path-bisected wood. So I told him he could drive like hell to my *appartement* in the *Place des Etats Unis*—and off we rushed in the now torrential rain—It was one of the worst thunder storms I have ever seen in my life.

I was horribly worried as to what could have happened to that little party, for that *alleé* where I had seen them, was in the very middle of the *Bois*, and far from any gate or shelter. They must have got soaking wet if nothing worse had happened to them. And how could I hear anything about them?—What should I do? Was the Duchesse in Paris?—Could I find the address possibly from her? But would she be likely to know it? just because Miss Sharp—"Alathea"—(what a lovely Greek name!) brought bandages to the hospital?

However, this was worth trying, and I could hardly wait to get out of the motor, and get to the telephone. The *concierge* came out with an umbrella in great concern and took me up in the lift herself—and there was Burton waiting for me, he had come in by train to take me back safely later on.

How I cursed my folly in not having asked Miss Sharp herself for her address! Could Burton possibly know it?—How silly of me not to have thought of that before!

"Burton, I saw Miss Sharp and her family in the *Bois*—do you know their address by chance?—I want to ring up and find out if they got home all right."

Burton could see my anxiety—and actually hurried in his reply!

"They live in Auteuil, Sir Nicholas, but I can't exactly say where—the young lady never seems very particular to give me the address. She said I should not be needing it, and that they were likely to move."

"Get on to the Duchesse de Courville-Hautevine as quickly as you can—."

Burton did so at once, but it seemed a long time.

—No, Madame la Duchesse was down at Hautevine taking some fresh convalescents, and would not return until the middle of the week—if then!

I nearly swore aloud—.

"Are they talking from the *concierge's* lodge or the hotel?—Burton ask at both if they know the address of a Miss Sharp who brings bandages to the hospital!"

Of course by this time the connection had been cut off, and it took quite ten minutes to get on again, and by that time I could have yelled aloud with the feverish fret of it all, and the pain!

No one knew anything of a "Mees Shearp."

"Mees Shearp—*Mais non*!"

Many ladies brought bandages, *hein*?!

I mastered myself as well as I could and got into my chair—.

And in a few moments Burton brought me a brandy and soda, and put it into my hand.

"It won't be cleared up enough to go back to Versailles before dinner, Sir Nicholas," he said—and coughed—"I was just thinking maybe—you'd be liking some friends to come in and dine—Pierre can get something in from the restaurant, if you'd feel inclined."

The cough meant that Burton knows I am dreadfully upset, and that under the circumstances anything to distract me is the lesser of two evils—!

"Ask whom you please," I answered and drank the brandy and soda down.

Presently, after half an hour, Burton came back to me, beaming—I had been sitting in my chair too exhausted even to feel pain meanwhile—.

He had telephoned everywhere, and no one was in town, but at last, at the Ritz, where the *concierge* knows all my friends, he had been informed that Mrs. Bruce (Nina) had arrived the night before, alone—he had got connected up at her *appartement*, and she would be "round at eight o'clock, very pleased to dine!'

Nina!—A pleasant thrill ran through me—Nina, and without Jim—!

The wood fire was burning brightly, and the curtains were drawn when Nina, fresh as a rose, came in—.

"Nicholas!" she cried delightedly—and held out both hands.

"Nina!—this is a pleasure, you old dear!—now let me look at you and see what marriage has done—."

Nina drew back and laughed!

"Everything, Nicholas!" she said—.

A feeling of envy came over me—Jim's ankle is stiff for life—it seems hard that an eye can make such a difference!—Nina is in love with Jim, but no woman can be in love with me.

Her face is much softer, she is more attractive altogether.

"You look splendid, Nina," I told her—"I want to hear all about it."

"So you shall when we have finished dinner," and she handed me my crutch as I got up from my chair.

Pierre had secured some quite respectable food, and during dinner and afterwards when we were cosily smoking our cigarettes in the sitting-room, Nina gave me all the news of our friends at home.—Every single one of them was still working, she said.

"It is marvelous how they have stuck it," I responded—.

"Oh no, not at all," Nina answered. "We as a nation are people of habit—the war is a habit to us now—heaps of us work from a sense of duty and patriotism, others because they are afraid what would be said of them if they did not—others because they are thankful to have some steady job to get off their superfluous energy on—So it ends by everyone being roped in—and you can't think, Nicholas, how divine it is to get home after long hours of drudgery, to find the person you love waiting for you, and to know you are going to have all the rest of the time together, until next day!"

"No, I can't imagine the bliss of that, Nina—."

She looked at me suddenly—.

"Well, why don't you marry then, dear boy?"

"I would, if I thought I could secure bliss—but you forget, it would be from pity and not love that a woman would be kind to me."

"I am—not quite sure of that, Nicholas"—and she looked at me searchingly—"You are changed since last time—you are not so bitter and sardonic—and you, always have that—oh! you know what Elinor Glyn writes of in her books—that "it."—Some kind of attraction that has no name—but I am sure has a lot to do with love—."

"So you think I have got 'it,' Nina?"

"Yes, your clothes fit so well—and you say rather whimsical things—Yes, decidedly, Nicholas, now that you are not so bitter—I am sure—."

"What a pity you did not find that out before you took Jim, Nina!"

"Oh! Jim! that is different—You have much more brain than Jim, and would not have been nearly so easy to live with!"

"Is it going well, Nina?"

"Yes—perfectly—that is why I came to Paris alone—I knew it would be good for him—besides I wanted a rest, Nicholas."

"I thought you had married for a rest!"

"Well, if a man 'in love' is what you really want,—and not his just 'loving' you—you have to use your wits; it can't be a rest, not if he has made you care too.—When I was just tossing up between Jim and Rochester, then I had not to bother about how I behaved to them. You see I was the, as yet, unattained desired thing—but having accepted one of them, he has time to think of things, not having to fight to get me, and so I have to keep him thinking of things which have still speculation in them—don't you see?"

"You have to keep the hunting instinct alive, in fact."

"Yes—"
"You don't think it would be possible to find someone who was just one's mate so that no game of any sort would be necessary?"
She thought hard for a moment.
"That, of course, would be heaven—" then she sighed—"I am afraid it is no use in hoping for that, Nicholas!"
"Someone who would understand so well that silence was eloquent—someone who would read books with one, and think thoughts with one. Someone who would lie in one's arms and respond to caresses—and not be counting the dollars—or—doing her knitting—. Someone who was tender and kind and true—Oh! Nina!"
I suppose my voice had taken on a tone of emotion—I was thinking of Miss Sharp—Alathea—that shall be her name always for me now—.
"Nicholas!" Nina exclaimed—"My dear boy, of course you are in love!"
"And if so?"
Instantly I became of more value to Nina—she realized that she had lost me, and that some other woman drew me and not herself—and although Nina is the best sort in the world and more or less really in love with Jim, I knew that a new note could grow in our friendship if I wished to encourage it—Nina's fighting instinct had been aroused to try to get me back!
"Who with?" she demanded laconically.
"With a dream—."
"Nonsense! you are much too cynical—Is it anyone I know?"
"I should not think so—she has not materialised yet."
"This is frightfully interesting, my dear old boy!"
"So you think I'll have a chance then?"
"Certainly when you are all finished."
"My new eye is to be in before Christmas, and my new leg after the new year, and my shoulder gets straighter every day!"
Nina laughed—.
"Real love would be—I suppose—if you could make her adore you before you looked any handsomer!"
And this sentence of Nina's rang in my ears long after she had gone, and often in the night. I could not sleep, I felt something had happened and that fate might be going to take Miss Sharp—Alathea—from me—.

And then before morning in fretful dreams I seemed to be obsessed by the cooing of love words between a woman and a child—.

XI

Monday was a perfectly impossible day—I spent all the morning before I returned to Versailles in writing to Maurice, telling him he must find out all about Miss Sharp—Alathea—I felt if I told him her Christian name it would be a clue—and yet even to assist in that, which was, at the moment, my heart's desire, I could not overcome my personal dislike to pronounce it to Maurice!—it seemed as something sacred to me alone—which makes me reflect upon how egotistical we all are—and how we would all rather fail in attaining what is our greatest wish than not to be able to express our own personality—!
Nina had suggested before she left that I should stay in Paris and come to the theatre with her—.
"We could have some delicious old times, Nicholas, now that you are so much better."
Once this would have thrilled me—only last Spring! but now the contrariness in me made me say that it was absolutely necessary that I returned immediately to Versailles. I believe I should have answered like that even if there had been no Miss Sharp,—Alathea—in the case, just because I now knew Nina really wanted me to stay—every man is like that, more or less, if only women knew!—The whole sex relation is one of fence—until the object has been secured—and then emotion dies out altogether, or is revived in one or the other, but very seldom in both. Love—real love—is beyond all this I suppose, and does not depend upon whether or no the other person excites one's desire for conquest. Love must be wonderful—I believe Alathea—(I have actually written it naturally this time!—) could love. I never used to think I could, at the best of moments I have analysed my emotions, and stood aside as it were, and measured just how much things were meaning to me.
But when I think of that scrap of a girl, with her elusive ways, her pride, her refinement, even her little red hands—! I have a longing—a passionate longing to hold her always near me—to know that she is mine—that for the rest of time I should be with her, learning from her high thoughts, comforted by her strength of character—believing in her—respecting her—Yes, that is it—*respecting her*. How few women one meets with attractions that one really respects.—One respects many elderly ones, of course, and abstract splendid creatures, but bringing it down to concrete facts, how few are the women who have drawn one's admiration or excited one's desire, who at the same time one reverenced!—Love must mean reverence—that is it.
And what is reverence—?
The soul's acknowledgment of the purity of another—and purity in this sense means truth and honor, and lofty aims—not the denial of all passion, or the practice of asceticism.
I utterly reverence Alathea, and yet I am sure with that mouth—if she loved me she would be anything but cold. How on God's earth can I make her love me—?
I went back to Versailles after luncheon, having had to see the specialist about my eye, he thinks the socket is so marvelously healed lately, that I could have the glass one in now much sooner than Christmas. I wonder if some self confidence will return when I can feel people are not revolted when looking at me?—That again is super-

sensitiveness. Of course no one is revolted—they feel pity—and that is perhaps worse. When I get my leg too, shall I have the nerve to make love to Alathea and use all the arts which used to be so successful in the old days?

I believe if I were back in —I should still be as nervous as a cat when with her—Is this one of the symptoms of love again?

George Harcourt has many maxims upon the subject of love—One is that a Frenchman thinks most of the methods of love—An Englishman more of the sensations of love—and an Austrian of the emotions of love—. I wonder if this is true? He also says that a woman does not really appreciate a man who reverences her sex in the abstract, and is chivalrous about all women,—she rather thinks him a simpleton—. What she does appreciate is a man who holds cynical views about the female sex in general, and shows reverence and chivalry towards herself in particular!

This I feel is probably the truth—!

I did not expect to hear anything of Alathea on the Monday, she was not due until Tuesday at eleven o'clock, but when I came in from my sunset on the terrace, I found two telegrams, all the first one said was—

"Extremely sorry will be unable to come to-morrow, brother seriously ill.

A. Sharp—."

And no address!

So I could not send sympathy, or even offer any help—I could have sworn aloud! The storm had wrecked its vengeance on someone, then, and the poor little chap had probably taken cold.

If I could only be of some use to them—Perhaps getting the best Doctor is out of their reach. I was full of turmoil while I tore open the other blue paper—this was from Suzette—.

"I come this evening at eight."

It was nearly seven o'clock now, so I could not put her off—and I am not sure that I wanted to—Suzette is a human being and kindly, and her heart is warm.

When Burton was dressing me I told him of Miss Sharp's telegram.

"The poor young lady!" he said—.

Burton always speaks of her as the "young lady"—he never makes a mistake about class.

Suzette for him is "Mam'zell"—and he speaks of her as a mother might about her boy's noisy, tiresome rackety school friends—necessary evils to be put up with for the boy's sake—The fluffies he announces always by their full titles—"Madame la Comtesse"—etc., etc., with a face of stone. Nina and the one or two other Englishwomen he is politely respectful to, but to Miss Sharp he is absolutely reverential—she might be a Queen!

"I expect the poor little fellow got wet through yesterday," I hazarded—.

"He's that delicate," Burton remarked.

So Burton knows something more about the family than I do after all—!

"How did you know he was delicate, Burton, or even that Miss Sharp had a brother?"

"I don't exactly know, Sir Nicholas—it's come out from one time to another—the young lady don't talk."

"How did you guess, then?"

"I've seen her anxious when I've brought in her tray—sometimes, and once I ventured to say to her—'I beg pardon Miss, but can I do anything for you,' and she took off her glasses sudden like—and thanked me, and said it was her little brother she was worrying about—and you may believe me or not as you like, Sir Nicholas, but her eyes were full of tears."

I wonder if Burton guessed the deep emotion he was causing me—My little darling! with her beautiful blue eyes full of tears, and I impotent to comfort or help her—!

"Yes—yes?" I said—.

"She told me then that he'd been delicate since birth, and she feared the winter in Paris for him—I do believe Sir, it's that she works so hard for, to get him away south."

"Burton—what the devil can we do about it?"

"I don't very well know, Sir Nicholas—Many's the time I've badly wanted to offer her the peaches and grapes and other things, to take back to him—but of course I know my place better than to insult a lady—tisn't like as if she were of another class you see Sir—she'd have grabbed 'em then, but bein' as she is, she'd have been bound to refuse them, and it might have tempted her for him and made things awkward."

Burton not only knows the world but has tact—!

He went on, now once started.

"I saw her outside a wine shop once when I got off the tram at Auteuil—She was looking at the bottles of port—and I made so as to pass, and her not see me, but she turned and said friendly like—'Burton, do you suppose this shop would keep really good port—?' I said as how I would go in and see, and she came with me—They had some fairly decent—though too young, Sir Nicholas, and it was thirty-five francs the bottle—I saw she had not an idea it would be as much as that—her face fell—Do you know, Sir, I could see she hadn't that much with her,—it was the day before she's paid you see—her colour came and went—then she said—'I wonder Burton if you could oblige me with paying the ten extra francs until to-morrow—I must have the best!'—You may believe me, Sir Nicholas, I got out my purse quick enough—and then she thanked me so sweet like—'The Doctor has ordered it for my mother, Burton,' she said—'and of course she couldn't drink any but the best!'"

"Who on earth can she be, Burton? It does worry me—can't you possibly find out? I would so like to help them."

"I feel that, Sir—but here's the way I figure it—When gentry lives in foreign towns and don't seem anxious for you to know their address it don't seem right like to pry into it."

"Burton, you dear old brick!—well supposing we don't try to pry, but just try how we can possibly help her—You could certainly be sympathetic about the brother since she has spoken to you—and surely something can be done—? I saw her at the Duchesse's you know—do you suppose she knows her—?"

"I do, Sir Nicholas—I never meant to speak of it, but one day Her Grace came to see you and you were out and she caught sight of Miss Sharp through the half open door—and she jumped like a cat, Her Grace did, 'Halthee'—she cried out—or some name like that,—and Miss Sharp started up and went down the stairs with her—She seemed to be kind of explaining, and I am not sure that Her Grace was too pleased—."

(Burton thinks all Duchesses should be called "Grace" whether they are French or English.)

"Then we should certainly be able to find out from the Duchesse—."

"Well, I would not be so sure of that Sir Nicholas—You see the Duchesse is a very kind lady, but she is a lady of the world, and she may have her reasons."

"Then what do you suggest, Burton?"

"Why, I hardly know—perhaps to wait and see, Sir Nicholas."

"Masterly inactivity!"

"It might be that I could do a bit of finding out if I felt sure no harm could come of it."

I was not quite certain what Burton meant by this—What possible harm could come of it?

"Find out all you can and let me know—."

Suzette opened the door and came in just as I finished dressing—Burton left the room.—She was pouting.

"So the book is not completed, Nicholas?—and the English Mees comes three times a week—*hein*?"

"Yes—does that upset you?"

"I should say!"

"May I not have a secretary?—You will be objecting to my Aunt coming to stay with me, or my dining with my friends—next!"

I was angry—.

"No—*mon ami*—not that—they are not for me—those—but a secretary—a 'Mees'—*tiens*?—for why do you want us two?"

"You *two*! good Lord! Do you think, Suzette—*Mon Dieu!*"—I now became very angry. "My secretary is here to type my book—. Let us understand one another quite—You have overstepped the mark this time, Suzette, and there must be an end. Name whatever sum you want me to settle on you and then I don't ever wish to see you again."

She burst into frantic weeping. She had meant nothing—she was jealous—she loved me—even going to the sea could do nothing for her! I was her *adoré*—her sun, moon and stars—of what matter a leg or an eye—! I was her life—her *Amant*!!

"Nonsense, Suzette!—you have told me often it was only because I was very rich—now be sensible—these things have to have an end some day. I shall be going back to England soon, so just let me make you comfortable and happy and let us part friends—."

She still stormed and raged—'There was someone else—it was the "Mees"—I had been different ever since she had come to the flat—She, Suzette, would be revenged—she would kill her—!'

Then I flew into a rage, and dominated her, and when I had her thoroughly frightened I appealed to the best in her—and when she was sobbing quietly Burton came in to say that dinner was ready—his face was eloquent!

"Don't let the waiters see you like that," I said.

Suzette rushed to the glass and looked at herself, and then began opening her gold chain bag to get out her powder and lip grease—I went on into the salon and left her—.

What an irony everything is—! When I was yearning for tenderness and love—, even Suzette's, I was unable to touch her, and now because I am quite indifferent, both she and Nina, in their separate ways, have begun to find me attractive. So there is nothing in it really, it is only as to whether or no you arouse the hunting instinct!

Suzette wore an air of deep pathos during our repast—. She had put some blue round her eyes to heighten the effect of the red of the real tears, and she appeared very pretty and gentle—It had not the slightest effect upon me—I found myself looking on like a third person. The mole with its three black hairs seemed to be the only salient point about her.

Poor little Suzette!—How glad I felt that I had never even pretended a scrap of love for her!

That astonishing sense of the fitness of things which so many of these women possess, showed itself as the evening wore on—. Finding the situation hopeless, Suzette accepted it, curbed the real emotion in herself and played the game—She tried to amuse me—and then we discussed plans for her future. A villa at Monte Carlo she decided at last—A *bijou* of a place! which she knew of—. And when we parted at about eleven o'clock everything was arranged satisfactorily. Then she said good-bye to me—She would go back to Paris by the last train—.

"Good-bye, Suzette!"—and I bent down and kissed her forehead—"You have been the jolliest little pal possible—and remember that I have appreciated it,—and you will always have a real friend in me!"

She burst into tears once more—real tears—.

"*Je t'aime bien!*" she whispered—"I shall go to Deauville—*Va!*"

We wrung hands, and she went to the door, but there she turned, and some of her old fire came back to her—.

"Pah! these English Meeses! thin, stiff, *ennuyeuse*!—thou wilt yet regret thy Suzette, Nicholas!" and with this she left me.

So that episode in my life is ended—and I shall never repeat the experiment.

But are not women the most amazing creatures!

You adore them and give them abject devotion and they treat you as dirt—nothing can be so cruel as the tenderest hearted woman is to a male slave—! Another woman appears upon the scene—then the first one begins to treat you with some respect. You grow masterful—love is aroused in her. You become indifferent—and very often it is she who then turns into the slave!—The worst of it is that when you really care you are incapable of playing a game successfully. The woman's subconscious mind *knows* that it is merely pretense—and so she remains a tyrant.—It is only when she herself has ceased to put forth sufficient attraction to keep you and you are growing numb that you can win out and find your self-respect again.

There was a moment when I was very angry with Suzette and almost shaking her, when I saw in her eyes the first look of real passionate affection—!

Are there any women in the world who could be mates?—who would be able to love one, and hold one at the same time—satisfying one's mind and one's spirit and one's body—?—Could Alathea—?—I do not know.

I had got this far in my speculations when a note was brought to me by a smart French maid—it was now past eleven at night—.

It was from Coralie—.

"I am here, *cher Ami*—I am rather in a difficulty—Can I come to your sitting-room?"

I scribbled "of course"—and in a moment she came—seductive and distressful. Duquesnois had been recalled to the front suddenly—her husband would be back on the morrow—. Might she stay and have some St. Galmier water with me—could we ring the bell and order it, so that the waiter might see her there?—because if the husband asked anything—he could be sure it was only the much wounded Englishman, and he would not mind—!!

I was sympathetic!—the St. Galmier came.

Coralie did not seem in a hurry to drink it, she sat by the fire and talked, and looked at me with her rather small expressive eyes—and suddenly I realized that it was not to save any situation that even a complacent and much-tried war-husband might object to, but just to talk to me alone—!!

She put forth every charm she possessed for half an hour—I led her on—watching each move with interest and playing right cards in return. Coralie is very well born and never could be vulgar or blatant, so it was all entertaining for me. This is the first time she has had the chance of being quite alone. We fenced—I showed enough *empressement* not to discourage her too soon—and then I allowed myself to be natural, which was being completely indifferent—and it worked its usual charm!

Coralie grew restless—she got up from the sofa she stood by the fire—she came at last quite close up to my chair—.

"What is there about you, Nicholas," she cooed, "which makes one forget that you are wounded—. When I saw you even in the *parc*—with that *demoiselle* I felt—that—"—She looked down with a sigh—.

"How hard upon Duquesnois, Coralie! a good-looking, whole man!"

"I have tired of him, *Mon ami*—he loves me too much—the affair has become tame—."

"And I am wild, is that it?"

"A savage—yes—One feels that you would break one's bones if you were angry—and would mock most of the time,—but if you loved. *Mon Dieu!*—it would be worth while!"

"You have had immense experience of love Coralie, haven't you?"

She shrugged her shoulders—.

"I am not sure that it has been love—."

"Neither am I."

"They say that you have given millions to the little *demi-mondaine* Suzette la Blonde——and that you are crazy about her, Nicholas—Did I see her on the stairs just now?"—

I frowned—. She saw in a moment it was not the right line—. "For that! it is nothing, Nicholas—they are very attractive, those ladies—one understands—but—your book and your secretary?—*hein?*—"

I lit a cigarette with supreme calm, and did not answer, so that she was obliged to go on—.

"Her face is pretty in spite of those glasses, Nicholas—and one saw that she walked well as she went on."

"May not a secretary have a decent appearance then?"

"When they have they do not remain secretaries long."

"You had better ask Miss Sharp if she means to stay when next you chance upon her then—I don't exchange much conversation with her myself."

There is no exact English word which would describe Coralie's face—She was longing to believe me—but felt she could not—quite—! She knew it was foolish to bait me, and yet the female in her was too strong for any common sense to win—Her personality had to express herself just as strongly about her jealousy of my secretary, as mine had to express itself about not telling Maurice, Alathea's name,—in both cases we cut off our noses to spite our faces. I was aware of my folly, I do not know if Coralie was aware of hers. Her exasperation so increased in a few moments that she could not control herself—and she spoke right out—.

"When we have all been so kind to you, Nicholas, it is too bad for you to waste your time upon that—!"

I became stern, then, as I had earlier become with Suzette, and made Coralie understand that I would have no interference from anyone. I frightened her—and presently she left me more attracted than she has ever been—. As I said before, women are amazing creatures.

XII

On Wednesday morning I received a reply from Maurice at Deauville—he hastened to answer he said—He had heard of Miss Sharp through a man in the American Red Cross, where Miss Sharp had been employed. He knew nothing more about her, he had seen her once when he was interviewing her, and Miss whatever the other woman's name was, he had forgotten now—and he had thought her suitable and plain and capable, that is all.

I had tried to word my letter not to give the impression of peculiar interest, but no doubt Coralie, who had returned to the band on Monday, had given him her view of the case, for he added that these people were often designing although they looked simple—and in my loneliness he felt sure I would be happier and better at the sea with my friends—!

I would have been angry, only there was something humorous in the way everyone seems to think I am incapable of managing my own affairs!—What is it they all want of me—? Not that I should be happy in my own way, but that I should contribute to their happiness—they want to participate in what my money is able to procure—and they do not want interference from outside. Every one of my friends—and relations—would be hostile if I were to announce that I was in love with Miss Sharp, and wanted to marry her—Even though it was proved to them that she was pretty—a perfect lady—intelligent—virtuous—clever! She is not of their set and might, and probably would, be a stumbling block in their path when they wished to make use of me!—so she would be taboo! None of them would put it in that way of course, their opposition would be (and they might even think they were sincere) because they were thinking of *my* happiness!

Burton is the only person whose sympathy I could count upon!

How about the Duchesse?—that is the deepest mystery of all—I must find out from Burton what was the date about when she came to my *appartement* and found Alathea. Was it before that time when she asked me if I were in love—and I saw that dear little figure in the passage?—Could she have been thinking of her—?

By Thursday when there was no further news I began to feel so restless that I determined to go back to Paris the following week. It was all very well to be out in the *parc* at Versailles with a mind at ease, but it feels too far away when I am so troubled.

I sent Burton in on Friday to Auteuil—.

"Just walk about near the wine shop, Burton, and try to find out by every clue your not unintelligent old pate can invent, where Miss Sharp lives, and what is happening? Then go to the Hotel de Courville and chat with the concierge—or whatever you think best—I simply can't stand hearing nothing!"

Burton pulled in his lips.

"Very good, Sir Nicholas."

I tried to correct my book in the afternoon. I really am trying to do the things I feel she thinks would improve my character—But I am one gnawing ache for news—Underneath is the fear that some complication may occur which will prevent her returning to me. I find myself listening to every footstep in the passage in case it might be a telegram, so of course quite a number of messages and things were bound to come from utterly uninteresting sources, to fill me with hope and then disappoint me—It is always like that. I really was wild on Friday afternoon, and if George Harcourt had not turned up—he is at the Trianon Palace now with the Supreme War Council—I don't know what I should have done with myself. Lots of those fellows would come and dine with me if I wanted them—some are even old pals—but I am out of tune with my kind.

George was very amusing.

"My dear boy," he said, "Violetta is upsetting all my calculations—she has refused everything I have offered her—But I fear she is beginning to show me too much devotion!"

This seemed a great calamity to him.

"It is terribly dangerous that, Nicholas!—because you know, my dear boy, when a woman shows absolute devotion, a man is irresistibly impelled to offer her a back seat—it is when she appeals to his senses, shows him caprice, and remains an insecure possession, that he will offer her the place his mother held of highest honour."

"George, you impossible cynic!"

"Not at all—I am merely a student of human instincts and characteristics—Half a cynic is a poor creature—A complete one has almost reached the mercy and tolerance of Christ."

This was quite a new view of the subject—!

He went on—.

"You see, when men philosophize about women, they are generally unjust, taking the subject from the standpoint that whatever frailties they have, the male is at all events exempt from them. Now that is nonsense—Neither sex is exempt—and neither sex as a rule will contemplate or admit its failings.—For instance, the sense of abstract truth in the noblest woman never prevents her lying *for* her lover or her child, yet she thinks herself quite honest—In the noblest man the sense is so strong that it enables him to make only the one exception, that of invariably lying *to* the woman!"

I laughed—he puffed one of my pre-war cigars—.

"Women have no natural sense of truth—they only rise to it through sublime effort,"—

"And men?"

"It is ingrained in them, they only sink from it to cover their natural instincts of infidelity."

His voice was contemplative now—.

"How we lie to the little darlings, Nicholas! How we tell them we have no time to write—when of course we have always time if we really want to—we never are at a loss for the moments before the creatures are a secure possession!"

"The whole thing gets back to the hunting instinct, my dear George—I can't see that one can be blamed for it—."

"I am not blaming, I am merely analysing. Have you remarked that when a man feels perfectly secure about the woman he will give his hours of duty to his country, his hours of leisure to his friends who flatter him, and the crumbs snatched from either to the poor lady of his heart! But if she excites his senses, and remains problematic, he will skimp his duty, neglect his friends, and snatch even hours from sleep to spend them in her company!"

"You don't think then that there is something higher and beyond all this in love, George?—something which you and I have never come across perhaps?"

"If one met a woman who was all man in mind, all woman in body, and all child in soul—it is possible—but where are these phoenixes to be discovered, my son?—It is wiser not to dissatisfy oneself by thinking of them—but just go on accepting that which is always accorded to the very rich!—By the way, I saw Suzette la Blonde dining last night with old Solly Jesse—*Monsieur le Comte Jessé!*—She had a new string of pearls on and was stroking his fat hand, while her lips curled with love—I thought—??"

I lay back in my chair and laughed and laughed—And I had imagined that Suzette really felt for me, and would grieve for at least a week or two—but I am replaced in four days—!

I do not think I even felt bitter—all those things seem so far away now.

When George had gone, I said to myself—"All man in mind"—yes I am sure she is—"All woman in body"—Certainly that—"All child in soul"—I want to know about her soul—if we have souls, as Nina says—by the way, I will send a messenger into the Ritz with a note to ask Nina to spend the day with me to-morrow. We have got accustomed to the impossible difficulty of telephoning to Paris, and waiting hours for telegrams—a messenger is the quickest in the end.

How the war drags on—! Will it really finish this year after all—people are very depressed these last days—I do not write of any of this in my journal—others will chronicle every shade—When I let myself think of it I grow too wild. I become feverish with longing to be up and with the old regiment—When I read of their deeds—then I grow rebellious.

Monday:

No news—yet—It is unbearable—Burton returned from Auteuil with no clue whatsoever—except that the *concierge* at the Hotel de Courville had never heard of the name of Sharp! That proves to me that "Sharp" is not Alathea's name at all. He was a newcomer—and there were so many young ladies who came and went to see Madame la Duchesse that he could not identify anyone in particular by description.

Nina turned up early on Saturday in time for lunch—She was looking ravishing in entirely new clothes—like Suzette, she has found that the "*geste*" is altering—Germans may be attacking Paris—Friends and relations may be dying in heaps, but women must have new clothes and fashion must have her say as to their shapes—And what a mercy it is so! If there was nothing to relieve war and seriousness—all the nations would be raving lunatics by now.

"Jim will be crazy about you, Nina, when he sees you in that hat!"

"Yes, won't he! I put it on to make you crazy now!"

"Of course I always am!"

"No, Nicholas—you were once—but you are altered, some quite new influence has come into your life—you don't say half such horrid things."

We lunched in the restaurant. Some of the Supreme War Council were about at the different tables, and we exchanged a few words—Nina preferred it to my sitting-room.

"Englishmen do look attractive in uniform, Nicholas, don't they," she said—. "I wonder if I had seen Jim in ordinary things if I would have been so drawn to him?"

"Who knows? Do you remember how sensible you were about him and Rochester!—it is splendid that it has turned out so well."

" ... Where is happiness, Nicholas?" and her eyes became dreamy,—"I have a well balanced nature, and am grateful for what has been given me in Jim, but I can't pretend that I have found perfect content—because some part of me is always hungry—. I believe really that you were the only person who could have fulfilled all I wanted in a man!"

"Nina, you had not the least feeling for me when you first saw me after I was wounded, do you remember you felt like a sister—a mother—and a family friend!"

"Yes, was not that odd!—because of course the things which used to attract me in you and which could again now, were there all the time."

"At that moment you were so occupied with 'Jim's blue eyes,' and his 'white nice teeth,' and 'how his hair was brushed,' and 'how well his uniform fitted'—to say nothing of his D.S.O. and his M.C. that you could not appreciate anything else."

"You have a V.C., your teeth are divine, and you too have blue eyes, Nicholas—."

"Eye—please,—the singular or plural in this case makes all the difference, but I shall have my new one in fairly soon now and then illusion will help me!"

Nina sighed—.

"Illusion! I am just not going to think of what perhaps might have happened if I had not been surrounded with illusion, last February—."

"Well, you can always have the satisfaction of knowing that as your interest in Jim diminishes, so his will increase—George Harcourt and I thrashed it all out the other day—and you yourself admitted it, when we dined. To keep the hunting instinct alive is the thing—You will have the fondest lover when you go back to Queen Street, Nina!"

"I—suppose so—. But would it not be wonderful if one had not to play any game, but could just love and be so satisfied with each other that there would not be any fear—."

Nina's eyes were sad—Did she remember my words at our last meeting?

"Yes that would be heaven!"

"Is that what you are dreaming about, Nicholas?"

"Perhaps."

"What a fortunate woman she will be!—And of yourself, what shall you give her?"
"I shall give her passion—and tenderness, and protection, and devotion—she shall share the thoughts of my mind and the aspirations of my soul—."
"Nicholas!—you talking in this romantic way—she must be a miracle!"
"No—she is just a little girl."
"And it is she who has made you think about souls?"
"I expect so—."
"Well, I must not think of them, or of anything but what a good time we shall all have when the war is over, and what nice things I've bought in Paris—and of how good-looking Jim is—Let us talk of something else!"
So we spoke of every-day matters—and then we went into the *parc*—and Nina stayed by my bath chair and amused me. But she does not know anything about Versailles or its history—and she cannot make psychological deductions—and all the time I was understanding with one part of me that her hat was awfully becoming, and everything about her perfect; and with another part I was seeing that her brain is limited—and that if I had married her I should have been bored to death!
And when the evening came and she left me, after our long day, I felt a sense of relief—Oh! there can be no one in the world like my Alathea—with her little red hands, and cheap cotton garments! I realize now that life used to be made up of the physical—and that something,—perhaps suffering, has taught me that the mental and the spiritual matter more.
Even if she does come back—how am I to break through the wall of ice which she has surrounded herself with since the Suzette cheque business?—I can't explain—she won't even know that I have parted with her.
Of course she has heard the fluffies often in the next room when they have come to play bridge in the afternoon. Perhaps she may even have heard the idiotic things they talk about—yes—of course she must have an awful impression of me—.
The contrast of her life and theirs—and mine! I shall go on with my Plato—it bores me—it is difficult, and I am tired—but *I will*!.

XIII

Suspense is the hardest thing to bear—what a ridiculous truism! It has been said a thousand times before and will be said a thousand times again!—because it has come to everyone at some moment, and so its pain is universally understood. To have attained serenity would mean that one was strong enough not to allow suspense to cause one a moment's doubt or distress. I am far from serenity, I fear—for I am filled with unrest—I try to tell myself that Alathea Sharp does not matter in my life at all—that this is the end—that I am not to be influenced by her movements or her thoughts, or her comings and goings—I try not to think of her even as "Alathea"—And then when I have succeeded in some measure in all this, a hideous feeling of sinking comes over me—that physical sensation of a lead weight below the heart. What on earth is the good of living an ugly maimed life?
It was ten times easier to carry on under the most disgusting and fearsome circumstances when I was fighting, than it is now when everything is done for my comfort, and I have all that money can buy.
What money cannot buy is of the only real consequence though. I must read Henley again, and try to feel the thrill of pride I used to feel when I was a boy at the line "I am the master of my fate, I am the captain of my soul."
——What if she does not come back, and I do not hear any more of her?
Stop! Nicholas Thormonde, this is contemptible weakness!

This evening it was wonderful on the terrace, the sun set in a blaze of crimson and purple and gold, every window in the *Galerie des Glasses* seemed to be on fire—strange ghosts of by-gone courtiers appeared to be flitting past the mirrors.
What do they think of the turmoil they have left behind them, I wonder? Each generation torn by the same anguish which the worries of love bring?—And what is love for?—Just to surround the re-creative instinct with glamour and render it æsthetic?
Did cave men love?—They were exempt from pain of the mind at all events. Civilization has augmented the mental anguishes, and pleasures of love, and when civilization is in excess it certainly distorts and perverts the whole passion.
But what is love anyway? the thing itself I mean. It is a want, and an ache and a craving—I know what I want. I want firstly Alathea for my own, with everything which that term implies of possession. Then I want to share her thoughts, and I want to feel all the great aspirations of her soul—I want her companionship—I want her sympathy—I want her understanding.
When I was in love with Nina—and five or six others—I never thought of any of these things—I just wanted their bodies: Therefore it is only when the spiritual enters into the damned thing, I suppose, that one could call it love. By that reasoning I have loved only Alathea in all my life. But I am stumped with this thought—If she had one eye and no leg below the knee—should I be in love with her? and feel all these exalted emotions about her? I cannot honestly be certain how I would answer that question yet, so this shows that the physical plays the chief rôle even in a love that seems spiritual.
Matho—in Flaubert's Salammbô was beaten to a jelly but his eyes still flamed with love for his princess—But when she saw him as this revolting mass, did her love flame for him? Or was she exalted only by the incense to her vanity—and a pity for his sufferings? Heloise and Abelard were pretty wonderful in their love, but his love became transmuted much sooner than hers, because all physical emotions were gone from him. Plato's idea that man gravitates towards beauty for some subconscious soul desire to re-create himself through perfection, and so attain immortality, is probably the truth. And that is why we shrink from mutilated bodies—. Until I can be quite

sure that I should love Alathea just the same were she disfigured as I am—I cannot in justice expect her to return my passion—.

Nina became re-attracted (if I can coin that word)—because I was out of reach. The predatory instinct in woman had received a rebuff, and demanded renewed advance.—She still keeps a picture in some part of her mental vision of what I was too, therefore, I am not so revolting to her—but Alathea has not this advantage, and has seen me only wounded.

I have done nothing to earn her respect—She has apprehended my useless life in these last months—She has heard the chattering of my companions, whom I have been free to choose—the obvious deduction being that these are what I desire—And finally, she knows that I have had a mistress.—In heaven's name *why* should she be anything but what she is in her manner to me!—Of course she despises me. So that the only thing I could possibly allure her by would be that intangible something which Nina and Suzette and even Coralie—have inferred that I possess—"It"!!—. And how would that translate itself to a mind like Alathea's?—It might mean nothing to her—It probably would not. The only times I have ever seen any feeling at all in her for me were when she thought she had destroyed a wounded man's interest in a harmless hobby—and felt remorse—And the freezing reserve which showed when she handed me the cheque-book—and the perturbation and contempt when I was rude about the child.—At other times she has shown a blank indifference—or a momentary consciousness that there was admiration in my eye for her.

Now what do I get out of the iciness over Suzette's cheque?

Two possibilities—.

One—that she is more prudish than one of her literary cultivation, and worldly knowledge is likely to be, so that she strongly disapproves of a man having a "*petite amie*"—or—

Two—that she has sensed that I love her and was affronted at the discovery that at the same time I had a—friend?—

The second possibility gives me hope, and so I fear to entertain a belief in it—but taken coldly it seems the most likely.—Now if she had *not* been affronted at this stage, would she have gone on believing I loved her, and so eventually have shown some reciprocity?

It is just possible—.

And as it is, will that same instinct which is in the subconscious mind of all women—and men too for the matter of that—which makes them want to fight to retain or retake what was theirs, influence her now unconsciously to feel some, even contemptuous, interest in me? This also is possible—.

If only fate brings her to me again—. That is where one is done—when absence cuts threads.

To-morrow it will be Monday—a whole week since I received her telegram.

I shall go up to Paris in the morning if I hear nothing and go myself to the Hotel de Courville to try and obtain a trace of her—if that is impossible I will write to the Duchesse.—

Reservoirs—Night:

As I wrote the last words—a note was brought to me by Burton—someone had left at the Hotel.

"Dear Sir Nicholas—(it ran)

I am very sorry I have been unable to come out to
do my work—but my brother died last Tuesday, and
I have been extremely occupied—I will be at Versailles
at eleven on Thursday as usual.

Yours truly,

A. Sharp."

Her firm writing, more like a man's than a woman's looked a little shaky at the end—Was she crying perhaps when she wrote the letter—the poor little girl—What will the death mean to her eventually? Will the necessity to work be lessened?

But even the gravity of the news did not prevent a feeling of joy and relief in me—I would see her again—Only four days to wait!

But what a strange note!—not any exhibition of feeling! she would not share even that natural emotion of grief with me. Her work is business, and a well bred person ought not to mix anything personal into it.—How will she be—? Colder than ever? or will it have softened her—.

She will probably be more unbending to Burton than to me.

The weather has changed suddenly, the wind is sighing, and I know that the summer is over—I shall have the sitting-room fire lighted and everything as comfortable as I can when she does turn up, and I shall have to stay here until then since I cannot communicate with her in any way. This ridiculous obscurity as to her address must be cleared away. I must try to ask her casually, so as not to offend her.

A week has passed—.

Alathea came on Thursday—I was sickeningly nervous on Thursday morning. I resented it extremely. As yet the only advance I have made is that I can control most of the outward demonstrations of my perturbations, but not the sensations themselves. I was sitting in my chair quite still when the door opened, and in she came—Just the scrap of a creature in dead black. Although there was no crepe, one could see that the garments were French trappings of woe, that is, she had a veil hanging from her simple small hat. I felt that she had had to buy these things for the funeral, and probably could not afford a second set of more dowdy ones for her working clothes, so that there was that indescribable air of elegance about her appearance which had shown in the *Bois* that Sunday. The black was supremely becoming to her transparent white skin, and seemed to set off the bright bronze brown of her hair—the rebellious little curls had slipped out beside her ears, but the yellow horn spectacles were as uncompromising as ever—I could not see whether her eyes were sad or no—her mouth was firm as usual.

"I want to tell you of my sympathy," I said immediately—"I was so sorry not to know your address that I might have expressed it to you before—I would have wished to send you some flowers."

"Thank you," was all she answered—but her voice trembled a little.

"It was so stupid of me not to have asked you for your address before—you must have thought it was so careless and unsympathetic."

"Oh! no"—.

"Won't you give it to me now that I may know in the future?"

"We are going to move—It would be useless—it is not decided where we go yet."

I knew I dared not insist.

"Is there some place where I could be certain of a message reaching you then? because I would have asked you to come to the flat to-day and not out here if I could have found you."

She was silent for a moment. I could see she was in a corner—I felt an awful brute but I had said it all quite naturally as any employer would who was quite unaware that there could be any reluctance to give the information, and I felt it was better to continue in this strain not to render her suspicious.

After a second or two she gave the number of a stationer's shop in the Avenue Mosart—.

"I pass there every day," she said.

I thanked her—.

"I hope you did not hurry back to your work—I can't bear to think that perhaps you would have wished to remain at home now."

"No, it does not matter"—There was an infinite weariness in her tone—A hopeless flatness I had never heard before, it moved me so that I blurted out—.

"Oh! I have felt so anxious, and so sorry—I saw you in the *Bois* two Sundays ago in the thunder storm, and I tried to get near the path I thought you would cross to offer you the carriage to return in, but I missed you—Perhaps your little brother caught cold then?"

There was a sob in her voice—.

"Yes—will you—would you mind if we just did not speak of anything but began work."

"Forgive me—I only want you to know that I'm so awfully sorry—and Oh, if there was anything in the world I could do for you—would you not let me?"

"I appreciate your wish—it is kind of you—but there is nothing—You were going to begin the last chapter over again—Here is the old one—I will take off my hat while you look at it," and she handed it to me.

Of course I could not say anything more—I had had a big bunch of violets put on the table where she types, in Burton's room adjoining—they were the first forced ones which could be got in Paris—and I had slipped a card by them with just "my sympathy" on it.

When she came back into the room hatless, her cheeks were bright pink below the glasses—and all she said was "Thank you" and then I saw a little streak of wet trickle from under the horn rims. I have never had such a temptation in my life—to stretch out myarms and cry "Darling one, let me comfort you, here clasped close to me!"—I longed to touch her—to express somehow that I felt profoundly for her grief.—

"Miss Sharp—" I did burst out—"I am not saying anything because I know you don't want me to—but it is not because I do not feel—I'm—I'm—awfully sorry—May not I perhaps send some roses to—your home—or, perhaps there is someone there who would like them—flowers are such jolly things!"—Then I felt the awfully ill chosen word "jolly" was—but I could not alter it.

I believe that *gaucherie* on my part helped though a little, her fine senses understood it was because I was so nervously anxious to offer comfort—a much kinder note came into her voice—.

"I'll take the violets with me if you will let me," she said—"Please don't trouble about anything more—and do let us begin work."

So we started upon the Chapter.

Her hands were not so red I noticed. I am becoming sensitive to what is called "atmosphere" I suppose, for I felt all the currents in the room were disturbed—that ambience of serenity did not surround Alathea and keep me unconsciously in awe of her as it always has before—I was aware that my natural emotions were running riot and that my one eye was gazing at her with love in it, and that my imagination was conjuring up scenes of delight with her as a companion. Her want of complete control allowed the waves to reach her, I expect—for I knew that she was using all her will to keep her attention upon the work, and that she was nearly as disturbed as I was myself—.

But how was she disturbed?—was she just nervous from events—or was I causing her any personal trouble? The moment I felt that perhaps I was, a feeling of assurance and triumph came over me—! Then I used every bit of the cunning I possess—I tried to say subtle things—I made her talk about the ridiculous book, and the utterly unimportant furniture—I made her express her opinion about styles, and got out of her that a simple Queen Anne was what she herself preferred.—I *knew* that she was giving way and talking with less stiffness because she was weak with sorrow, and probably had not had much sleep—I *knew* that it was not because she had forgotten about the Suzette cheque or really was more friendly. I *knew* that I was taking an unfair advantage of her—but I continued—Men are really brutes after all!—and gloried in my power every time the slightest indication showed that I possessed it! I lost some of my diffidence—If I could only have stood upon two feet and seen with two eyes—I know that even the morning would have ended by my taking her in my arms, cost what might; but as I was glued to my chair she was enabled always at this stage to stay out of reach—and fenced gallantly with me by silence and stiff answers—but by luncheon time there was a distinct gain on my side—I had made her feel something, I no longer was a nonentity who did not count—.

Her skin is so transparent that the colour fluctuates with every emotion. I love to watch it. What a mercy that I had very strong sight!—for my one eye sees quite clearly.

At luncheon we talked of the time of the Fronde—Alathea is so wonderfully well read. I make dashes into all sorts of subjects, and find she knows more of them than I do myself—What a mind she must have to have acquired all this in her short twenty-three years.

"You are not thinking of leaving Paris, I hope when you move," I said as we drank coffee. "I am going to begin another book directly this one is finished."

"It is not yet decided," she answered abruptly.

"I could not write without you."

Silence.

"I would love to think that you took an interest in teaching me how to be an author—."

The faintest shrug of the shoulders—.

"You don't take any interest?"

"No."

"Are not you very unkind?"—

"No—If you have anything to complain of in my work I will listen attentively and try and alter it."

"You will never allow the slightest friendship?"

"No."

"Why?"

"Why should I?"

"I must be grateful even that you ask a question, I suppose—Well, I don't know quite myself why you should—You think I am a rotter—You despise my character—you think my life is wasted and that—er—I have undesirable friends."

Silence.

"Miss Sharp! you drive me crazy never answering—I can't think why you like to be so provoking!" I was stung to exasperation.

"Sir Nicholas," and she put down her cup with displeasure—"If you will not keep to the subject of work—I am sorry but I cannot stay as your secretary."

Terror seized me—.

"I shall have to if you insist upon it—I suppose—but I am longing to be friends with you—and I can't think why you should resent it so—We are both English, we are both—unhappy—we are both lonely—."

Silence!—

"Somehow I don't feel it is altogether because I am a revolting object to look at that you are so unkind—you must have seen lots like me since the war—."

"I am not unkind—I think you are—May I go to my work now?"

We rose from the table—And for a second she was so near to me the pent up desire of weeks mastered me and the tantalization of the morning overcame me so that a frantic temptation seized me—I *could not* resist it—I put out one arm while I steadied myself with the other by the back of a chair, and I drew her tiny body towards me, and pressed my lips to her Cupid's bow of a mouth—And Oh God the pleasure of it—right or wrong!

She went dead white when I released her, she trembled, and in her turn held on to the back of the chair—.

"How dare you!" she panted—"How dare you!—I will go this minute—You are not a gentleman."

The reaction came to me—.

"That is it, I suppose—" I said hoarsely—"I am not a gentleman underneath—the civilization is mere veneer—and the *man* breaks through it—I have nothing to say—I was mad, that is all. You will have to weigh up as to whether it is worth your while to stay with me or not. I cannot judge of that. I can only assure you that I will try not to err again—perhaps some day you will know how you have been making me suffer lately—I shall go to my room now, and you can let me have your decision in an hour or so—."

I could not move because my crutch had fallen to the floor out of my reach—She stood in indecision for a moment and then she bent and picked it up and gave it to me. She was still as white as a ghost. As I got to the door I turned and said—.

"I apologize for having lost my self-control—I am ashamed of that—and do not ask you to forgive me—Your staying or not is a business arrangement. I give you my word I will try never to be so weak again."

She was gazing at me—For once I had taken the wind out of her sails—.

Then I bowed and hobbled on into my bedroom, shutting the door after me.

Here my courage deserted me. I got to the bed with difficulty and threw myself down upon it and lay there, too filled with emotion to stir. The thought tormenting me always. Have I burnt my boats—or is this only the beginning of a new stage?

Time will tell.

XIV

I lay and wondered and wondered what were Alathea's emotions after I left her. Should I ever know? When the hour was up I went back into the sitting-room. I had struggled against the awful depression which was overcoming me. I suppose every man has committed some action he is sorry and ashamed of, forced thereto by some emotion, either of anger or desire, which has been too strong for his will to control—. This is the way murders must often have been committed, and other crimes—I had not the slightest intention of behaving like a cad—or of doing anything which I knew would probably part us forever.—If my insult had been deliberate or planned, I would have held her longer, and knowing I was going to lose her by my action, I would have profited by it. As I lay on my bed in great pain from the wrench in getting there alone—I tried to analyse things. The nervous excitement in which she always plunges me must have come to the culminating point. The only thing I was glad about was that I had not attempted to ask forgiveness, or to palliate my conduct. If I had done so she would undoubtedly have walked straight out of the hotel—but having just had the sense to leave her to think for a while—perhaps—?

Well—I was sitting in my chair—feeling some kind of numb anguish—which I suppose those going to be hanged experience, when Burton brought in my tea—and I heard no sound of clicking next door—I asked him as naturally as I could if Miss Sharp had gone—.

"Yes, Sir Nicholas," he answered, and the shock, even though it was expected, was so great that for a second I closed my eye.

She had left a note, he further added,—putting the envelope down on the table beside the tray—.

I made myself light a cigarette and not open it, and I made myself say casually—

"I am afraid she feels her brother's death dreadfully, Burton!"

"The poor young lady, Sir Nicholas!—She must have kept up brave like all the time this morning, and then after lunch when I come in—while you were resting, Sir—it got too much for her, I expect, sittin' alone—for she was sobbin' like to break her heart—as I opened the door. She looked that forlorn and huddled up—give you my word, Sir Nicholas—I was near blubberin' myself."

"I am so awfully sorry—What did you do, Burton?"

"I said, '—Let me bring you a nice cup of tea, Miss.'—It is always best to bring ladies tea when they are upset, Sir Nicholas, as you may know—She thanked me sweet like, as she always does—and I made so bold as to say how sorry I was, and I did hope she had not had any extra trouble to deal with over it; and how I'd be so glad to advance her her next week's salary if it would be any convenience to her—knowing funerals and doctors is expensive—Out of my own money of course I gave her to understand—because I knew she'd be bound to refuse yours, Sir Nicholas.

"—At that her tears burst out afresh—She had no glasses on, and she looked no more than sixteen years old, give you my word Sir—She thanked me like as if it was something real kind I'd thought of—I felt sort of ashamed I could not do more—

"Then she seemed to be having a struggle with herself—just as if she'd rather die than take anything from anybody—and yet knew she had to—She turned them, blue eyes on me streamin' with tears, and I had to turn away, Sir Nicholas—I had really.—

"'Burton,' she says—. 'Have you ever felt that you wanted to be dead and done with it all—that you couldn't fight any more?'

—"'I can't say as I have, Miss,' I answered her—'but I know my master feels that way often—' Perhaps she felt kinder, sorry for you too, Sir Nicholas, because as I said that, she gave a sort of extra sharp sob and buried her face in her hands—.

"I slipped out of the room then and brought the tea as quick as I could you may believe me Sir—and by that time she had pulled herself together—'It is stupid to have any proud feelings—if you have to work Burton' she said—'I will be—grateful for the loan of your money—and I am happy to have such a friend' ... and she put out her little bit of a hand—She did, Sir Nicholas—and I never felt so proud in my life—She's just a real lady to her finger tips. She is, Sir—I shook it as gentle as I could, and then was obliged to blow my nose, I felt that blubberish—I left the room at once, and when I come back for the tray, and to bring the money she had her hat on, and the note written for you Sir—I took the violets and began putting them in the box for her to take—but she stopped me—.

"'Violets fade so soon—I will not take them, thanks,' she said—'I have to do some shopping before I go home and I could not carry them.' But I knew it was not that.—She did not want to take them—perhaps she felt she'd given up enough of her pride to take my money—for one day—So I said nothing,—but that I did hope she would be feeling better by the time she came to the *appartement* on Saturday. She did not speak, she just nodded her head and smiled kind like at me and went."

I could not answer Burton—I too just nodded my head—and the dear old boy left me alone—My very heart seemed bursting with pain and remorse—When he had gone—I seized the letter and opened it.

"To Sir Nicholas Thormonde, Bart, V.C.," (it began, and then)

"Dear Sir:

Circumstances force me to work—so I shall have to remain in your service—if you require me. I am unfortunately quite defenceless, so I appeal to whatever chivalry there is in you not to make it so impossible that I must again give in my resignation.

Yours faithfully,

A. Sharp."

I fell back in my chair in an agony of emotion—My darling! My queen!—whose very footprints I worship—to have had to write such a letter—to me!

The unspeakable brute beast I felt! All my cynical calculations about women fell from me—I saw myself as I had been all day—utterly selfish—not really feeling for her grief, only making capital out of it for my own benefit—. At that moment, and for the rest of the day and night, I suffered every shade of self reproach and abasement a man can feel. And next day I had to stay in bed because I had done some stupid thing to my leg in lying down without help.

When I knew I could not get into Paris by Saturday when Alathea was to come to the flat—I sent Burton in with a note to the shop in the Avenue Mosart.

"Dear Miss Sharp—(I wrote)

"I am deeply grateful for your magnanimity. I am utterly ashamed of my weakness—and you will not have called upon my chivalry in vain, I promise you.—I have to stay in bed, so I cannot be at the flat, and if you receive this in time I shall be obliged if you will come out here again on Saturday.

Yours very truly,

Nicholas Thormonde."

Then I never slept all night with thoughts of longing and wondering if she would get it soon enough to come.

Over and over in my vision I saw the picture of her sitting there in Burton's room sobbing—My action was the last straw—My shameful action!—Burton showed the good taste and the sympathy and understanding for her which I should have done—. And to think that she is troubled about money, so that she had to take a loan from my dear old servitor—far greater gentleman than I am—. And that I cannot be the least use to her—and may not help her in any way! I can go on no longer in this anguish—as soon as I feel that peace is in the smallest measure restored between us—I will ask her to marry me, just so that I can give her everything. I shall tell her that I expect nothing from her—only the right to help her family and give her prosperity and peace—.

Sunday:

I was still in bed on Saturday morning at eleven—the Doctor came out to see me very early and insisted that I be kept quite still until Monday—So Burton had my bed table brought, and all my papers and things—There had come a number of letters to answer, and he had asked me if Miss Sharp could not do them as soon as she arrived.

"Burton, perhaps she'll feel not quite at ease with me alone in here like this. Could you not make some excuse to be tidying drawers and stay while I am dictating," I said.

"Very good, Sir Nicholas."

When he replies with those words I know that he is agreeing—with reservations—.

"Out with what you are thinking, Burton."

"Well, Sir Nicholas"—and he coughed—"Miss Sharp—is that understandin' sh'd know in a minute your things wasn't likely to be in a mess, and that you'd got me there on purpose—It might make her awkward like—."

"You may be right, we will see how things turn out."

Presently I heard Alathea in the sitting-room and Burton went in to see her.

"Sir Nicholas is very poorly to-day, Miss"—I heard him say—"The Doctor won't let him out of bed—I wonder if you'd be so kind as to take down his letters—they are too much for him himself not being able to sit up—and I have not the time."

"Of course I will, Burton," her soft voice answered.

"I've put the table and everything ready—and I thank you kindly—" Burton went on—"I am glad to see you looking better, Miss."

I listened intently—It seemed as if I could hear her taking off her hat—and then she came into the room to me—but by that time my heart was beating so that I could not speak loud.

I said "good morning" in some half voice, and she answered the same—then she came forward to the table. Her dear little face was very pale and there was something pathetic in the droop of her lips—her hands, I noticed, were again not so red—.

"All the letters are there"—and I pointed to the pile—"It will be so good of you if you will do them now."

She took each one up and handed it to me without speaking and I dictated the answer.—I had had one from Suzette that morning thanking me for the villa—but I was clearly under the impression that I had put it with the one from Maurice and one from Daisy Ryven at the other side of the bed, so I had no anxiety about it—Then suddenly I saw Alathea's cheeks flame crimson and her mouth shut with a snap—and I realized that the irony of fate had fallen upon me again, and that she had picked up Suzette's lavender tinted, highly scented missive. She handed it to me without a word—.

The letter ended:

"*Adieu Nicholas! tu es,*
Toujours Mon Adoré
Ta Suzette."

but the way it was folded only showed "*Toujours Mon Adoré—Ta Suzette*"—and this much Alathea had certainly seen—.

I felt as if there was some evil imp laughing in the room—There was nothing to be said or done. I could not curse aloud—so I simply took the letter, put it with Daisy Ryven's—and indicated that I was waiting for the next one to be handed to me—So Alathea continued her work.—But could anything be more maddening—more damnably provoking!—and inopportune—Why must the shadow of Suzette fall upon me all the time?—

This of course will make any renewal of even the coldest friendliness impossible, between my little girl and me—. I cannot ask her to marry me now, and perhaps not for a long time, if ever the chance comes to me again, in any case. Her attitude, carriage of head, and expression of mouth, showed contempt, as she finished the short-hand notes. And then she rose and went into the other room to type, closing the door after her.

And I lay there shivering with rage and chagrin,

I saw no more of Alathea that morning—She had her lunch in the sitting-room alone, and Burton brought the dishes in to me, and after luncheon he insisted that I should sleep for an hour until half-past two o'clock. He had some accounts for Miss Sharp to do, he said.

I was so exhausted that when I did fall asleep I slept until nearly four—and awoke with a start and an agony of apprehension that she might have gone—but no—Burton said she was still there when I rang for him—and I asked her to come in again—.

We went over one of the earlier chapters in the book and I made some alterations in it; she never showed the slightest interest, nor did she speak—; she merely took down what I told her to—.

"Do you think that will do now?" I asked when it was complete.

"Yes."

Tea came in then for us both.—She poured it out, still without uttering a word—she remembered my taste of no sugar or milk, and put the cup near me so that I could reach it. She handed me the plate of those nasty make-believe biscuits, which is all we can get now—then she drank her own tea.

The atmosphere had grown so tense it was supremely uncomfortable. I felt that I must break the ice.

"How I wish there was a piano here," I remarked *à propos* of nothing—and of course she greeted this, with her usual silence.

"I am feeling so rotten if I could hear some music it would make me better."

She made the faintest movement with her head, to show me I suppose that she was listening respectfully, but saw no occasion to reply.

I felt so unspeakably wretched and helpless and useless lying there, I had not the pluck to go on trying to talk, so I closed my eye and lay still, and then I heard Alathea rise and softly go towards the door—.

"I will type this at home—and return it to the flat on Tuesday if that will be all right," she said—and: I answered:

"Thank you" and turned my face to the wall—And after a little, when she had gone, Burton came in and gave me the medicine the Doctor had told him to give me, he said—but I have a strong suspicion it was simply asperine, for then I fell into a dreamy sleep and forgot my aching body and my troubled mind.

And now I am much better in health again—and am back in Paris and to-night Maurice, up from Deauville at last, is coming to dine with me.

But what is the good of it all?

XV

I was awfully glad to see old Maurice again—he was looking brown and less dilettante—though his socks and tie and eyes matched as well as ever! He congratulated me on the improvement in health in myself too, and then he gave me all the news—.

Odette has been "painting the lily," and used some new skin tightener which has disfigured her for the moment, and she has retired to the family place near Bordeaux to weep until her complexion is restored again—.

"Very unfortunate for her," Maurice said—"because she had nearly secured a roving English peer who had enjoyed 'cushy' jobs during the war, and had been recruiting from the fatigues of red-taping at Deauville—and now, with this whisper of a spoiled skin, he had transferred his attentions to Coralie—and there was trouble among the graces!"—Alice's plaintiveness had actually caught a very rich neutral who was forwarding philanthropic schemes for great ladies—and she hoped soon to wed.

Coralie seemed in the most secure and happy case, since she is already established, and can enjoy herself without anxiety.—Maurice hinted that but for her *béguin* for me, she could land the English peer, and divorce poor René—her docile war husband—and become an English Countess!

"Thou hast upset everything, Nicholas. Duquesnois is desolated—Coralie changed directly she saw you here—he says—and then to divert herself and forget you, took Lord Brockelbank from Odette!"

"*Vieux coquin! Va!*" and Maurice patted me on the back—.

They were enchanted with my presents to them lately, he added, and were all longing to return to Paris soon and thank me.

The war was simply growing into a nuisance and the quicker it was over the better for everyone.(!)

Then he beat about the bush for a little longer and at last began to grow nearer the vital subject!—

He had seen some of my Mont Aubin relations—fortunately for me, they have been far from Paris in this last year—and they had anxiously asked him if I thought of marrying?—What in fact *was* I doing with myself now that my wounds were healing?

I laughed—.

"I am so glad my mother was an only child and they are none of them near enough to have the right to bore me—they had better continue their good works at Biarritz—I am told my cousin Marguerite's convalescent home is a marvel! I have sent her frequent donations."

Then Maurice plunged in—.

"You are not—becoming entangled in any way with your secretary, are you *Mon ami*?" he asked.

I had decided beforehand that I would not get angry at anything he said—so I was ready for this.

"No, Maurice—" and I poured out a second glass of port for him—Burton had left us alone by now—. "Miss Sharp does not know that I exist—she is simply here to do her work, and is the best secretary any man could want—I knew Coralie would infect you with some silly idea."

Maurice sipped his port.—"Coralie said that in spite of the girl's glasses there was some air of distinction about her—as she walked on—and that she *knew* and *felt* you were interested."

I remained undisturbed.

"I am, immensely interested—I want to know who she really is. She is a lady—even a lady of our world.—I mean she knows about things in England—where she has never been—that she could not possibly know unless her family had spoken of them always. She has that unconscious air of familiarity and ease with subjects which would surprise you. Can't you find anything out for me, old boy, as to who she is?"

"I will certainly try—Sharp?—it is not a name of the great world—no—?"

"Of course that is not her real name—"

"Why not ask her yourself, *Mon brave*!"

"I'd like to find a man with pluck enough to ask her anything she did not wish him to!"

"That little girl!—but she appeared meek and plain, and respectable, Nicholas—You intrigue me!"

"Well, put your wits to work Maurice, and promise me you will not talk to the others about anything. I shall be very angry if you do."

He gave me every assurance he would be silent as the grave—and then he changed the topic to that of Suzette—He was sorry I had given her her congé, because I would find it hard to replace her—Those so honest and really not too rapacious, were very difficult to find—Since he had heard that Suzette was no longer my little friend, he had been looking out for me, but as yet had seen nothing suitable!!

"You need not trouble, Maurice," I told him, "I am absolutely finished with that part of my life—I loathe the whole idea of it now—."

Maurice inspected me with grave concern—.

"My dear chap—this appears serious—You are not *in love* with your secretary are you?—or is it possible that you are bluffing, and that she has replaced Suzette, and you wish tranquility about the subject?"

I felt a hot flush mounting to my forehead—The very thought of my adored little girl in the category of Suzette!—I could have struck my old friend—but I had just sense enough to reason things. Maurice was only speaking as any of the Paris world would speak. A secretary, whom a man was obviously interested in, was certainly not out of the running for the post of "*Maitresse-en-titre!*"

He meant no personal disrespect to Alathea. For him women were either of the world or they were not!—True, there was an intermediate class "*Les braves gens*"—*Bourgeoises*—servants, typists, etc., etc.—But one could only be interested in one of these for one reason. That is how things appeared to Maurice. I knew his views; perhaps I had shared them in some measure in my unregenerate days.

"Look here Maurice—I want you to understand—that Miss Sharp is a lady in every way—I have already told you this but you don't seem to have grasped it—and that she has my greatest respect—and it makes me sick to think of anyone talking of her as you have just done. Although I know you did not mean anything low, you old owl!—She treats me as though I were a tiresome, elderly employer—whom she must give obedience to, but is not obliged to converse with. She would not permit the slightest friendship or familiarity from any man she worked for."

"Your interest is then serious, Nicholas?"

Maurice was absolutely aghast!

"My *respect* is serious—my curiosity is hot—and I want information."——

Maurice tried to feel relieved—.

"Supposing financial disaster fell upon your family, old boy—would you consider your sister less of a lady because she had to earn bread for you all by being a typist!"

"Of course not—but it would be very dreadful!—Marie!—Oh! I could not think of it!"

"Then try to get the idea into your thick head that Miss Sharp is Marie—and behave accordingly—That is how I look at her."

Maurice promised that he would, and our talk turned to the Duchesse—he had seen her at a cross country station as he came up, and she would be back in Paris the following week—This thought gave me comfort. Everyone would be back by the fifteenth of October he assured me, and then we could all amuse ourselves again—.

"You will be quite well enough to dine out, Nicholas—Or if not you must move to the Ritz with me, so that you at least have entertainment on the spot, *Mon cher*!"

We spoke then of the book—Furniture was a really refined and interesting subject for me to be delving into. Maurice longed to read the proofs, he averred.

When he had left me, I lay back in my chair and asked myself what had happened to me?—that Maurice and all that lot seemed such miles and miles away from me—as miles and miles as they would have seemed in their triviality, when we used to discuss important questions in "Pop" at Eton.

How I must have sunk in the years which followed those dear old days, ever even to have found divertisement among the people like Maurice and the fluffies. Surely even a one-eyed and one-legged man ought to be able to do something for his country politically, it suddenly seemed to me—and what a glorious picture to gaze at!—If I could some day go into Parliament, and have Alathea beside me, to give me inspiration and help me to the best in myself. How her poise would tell in English political society! How her brain and her power of exercising her critical faculties! Apart from the fact that I love every inch of her wisp of a body—What an asset that mind would be to any man!—And I dreamed and dreamed in the firelight—things all filled with sentiment and exaltation, which of course no fellow could ever say aloud, or let anyone know of—A journal is certainly an immense comfort, and I do not believe I could have gone through this hideous year of my life without it.

How I would love to have Alathea for my wife—and have children—It can't be possible that I have written that! I loathe children in the abstract—they bore me to death—Even Solonge de Clerté's two entertaining angels—but to have a son—with Alathea's eyes——God! how the thought makes me feel!—How I would like to sit and talk with her of how we should bring him up—I reached out my hand and picked up a volume of Charles Lamb and read "Dream Children"—and as I finished I felt that idiotic choky sensation which I have only begun to know since something in me has been awakened by Alathea—or since my nerves have been on the rack—I don't remember ever feeling much touched, or weak, or silly, before the war—.

And now what have I to face—?
A will, stronger, or as strong as my own—A prejudice of the deepest which I cannot explain away—A knowledge that I have no power to retain the thing I love—No guerdon to hold out to her mentally or physically—Nothing but the material thing of money—which because of her great unselfishness and desire to benefit her loved ones, she might be forced to consider. My only possibility of obtaining her at all is to buy her with money. And when once bought,—when I had her here in my house,—would I have the strength to resist the temptation to take advantage of the situation?—Could I go on day after day never touching her,—never having any joys?—until the greatness of my love somehow melted her dislike and contempt of me—?
I wish to God I knew.
She will never marry me unless I give my word of honour that the thing will only be an empty ceremony—of that I feel sure even if circumstances aid me to force her into doing this much. And then one has to keep one's word of honour. And might not that be a greater hell than I am now in of suffering?
Perhaps I had better go to the sea—like Suzette—and try to break the whole chain and forget her—.
I rang the bell for Burton then, and told him of my new plan, as he put me to bed. We would go off to St. Malo,—for a week, and I gave orders that he should make the necessary arrangements to get permits. To travel anywhere now is no end of a difficulty.
I wrote to Alathea without weakening—I asked her to collect the Mss. and make notes of what she thought still should be altered—during my absence—I wrote as stiffly, and in as business like a manner as possible—and finally I went to sleep, and slept better than I have done for some time.

St. Malo:
How quaint these places are! I am at this deserted corner by the sea—where the hotel is comfortable, and hardly touched by the war—I am not happy—the air is doing me good, that is all—I have brought books—I am not trying to write—I just read and endeavor to sleep—and the hours pass. I tell myself continually that I am no more interested in Alathea—that I am going to get well, and go back to England—that I have emerged, and am a man with a free will once more—and I am a great deal better—.
After all, how absurd to be thinking of a woman, from morning to night!
When I get my new leg, and everything is all healed, up in a year or two, shall I be able to ride again?—Of course I shall, no doubt, and even play a little tennis?—I can shoot anyway—if we will be allowed to preserve partridges and pheasants when the war is over in England.
Yes, of course life is a gorgeous thing—I like the fierce wind to blow in my face—and yesterday, much to Burton's displeasure, I went out sailing—.
How could I be such a fool, he inferred—as to chance a wrench putting me back some months again—But one has to chance things occasionally. I never enjoyed a sail more because of this very knowledge.

A week has passed since we came to this end of the earth—and again I have grown restless—perhaps it is because Burton came in just now with a letter in his hand—. I recognized immediately Alathea's writing.
"I made so bold as to leave the young lady our address before we left, Sir Nicholas, in case she wanted to communicate with us, and she writes now to say, would I be good enough to ask you if you took with you Chapter Seven, because she cannot find it anywhere."
Then he went on with evident constraint to tell me that the rest of the letter said that while she was working on Friday a "Mademoiselle la Blonde" called, and insisted upon passing Pierre who answered the door—and coming in to her—("It was Mam'zelle of course, Sir Nicholas!" Burton snapped!) And that she had demanded my address—but Miss Sharp had not felt she was justified in giving it to her—but had said letters would be forwarded—.
"I hope to goodness that the baggage made no scene with the young lady, Sir Nicholas," Burton growled—"Of course she don't say in the letter—but it's more than likely—I would not have her insulted for the world."
"Nor I either," I retorted angrily—"Suzette ought to know better now that I have given her everything she wanted—Will you let her understand please that this must not occur again—."
"I'll see that the lawyer does it, Sir—that is the only way to deal with them persons—though Mam'zelle was the best of her sort. Seems to me Sir Nicholas, they are more bother than they are worth. I said it always, even when I was younger—They leave their trail of trouble where ever they go."
How I agreed with him!
So here was a fresh barrier arisen between Alathea and myself!—a fresh barrier which I cannot explain away. The only comfort I get out of the whole thing is that imperative necessity must have been driving my little darling—or she would not put up with any of these things for a moment, and would have given her *demission* at the same time as she wrote.
If money is so necessary to her—perhaps after all I could get her consent to marry me—The very thought made my pulses bound again—and all my calm flew to the winds! All the sage reasoning which was beginning to have an effect upon me evaporated!—I knew that once more I was as utterly under the spell of her attraction, as the moment when my passionate lips touched her soft reluctant ones—Ah! that thought! that memory—One I have never let myself indulge in—but now, all resistance broken on every side,—I spent the rest of the day dreaming about the joy of that kiss—until by night time I was as mad as a hatter, and more full of cruel unrest than ever—.
I hate this place—I hate the sea—It is all of no use—I shall go back to Paris.

XVI

The first thing I learned when I reached the *appartement* was that the Duchesse had returned, and wished to see me. This was good news—and without even telephoning to Maurice, I got into my one horse Victoria and repaired to the Hotel de Courville—.

The Duchesse was sitting in her boudoir upstairs when I got in.—She had a quaint expression upon her face. I was not certain that her greeting was as cordial as usual—Has gossip reached her ears also?

I sat down near her and she took my crutch from me tenderly, her instinct for "*blessés*" never failing her.

I thought I would begin at once before she could say anything which might make questioning her impossible.

"I have been longing to see you, Duchesse, to ask you if you could help me to find out who my secretary, Miss Sharp, is?—because I saw her here in the passage one day, and I thought you might possibly be able to identify her—."

"*Tiens?*"

"Her christian name is 'Alathea'—I heard her little sister call her that once when I saw them and they did not see me, in the *Bois*—She is a lady—and I feel Sharp is not her name at all."

The Duchesse put on her eyeglasses—.

"She has not shown a sign that she wishes you to know her history?"

"No—"

"Then, my son, do you think it is very good taste to endeavor to discover it?"

"Perhaps not—" I was nettled—I hated that the Duchesse should be displeased with me, then I went on—"I fear that she is very poor and I know that her little brother died just lately, and I would give anything in the world to help them in some way."

"Sometimes one helps more by showing discretion."

"You won't assist me then, Duchesse? I *feel* that you know Miss Sharp."

She frowned—.

"Nicholas—if I did not love you really, I should be angry.—Am I the character to betray friends—presuming that I have friends—for a young man's curiosity?"

"Indeed it is not curiosity—it is because I want to help—."

"Camouflage!"

I felt angry now.

"You assume that your secretary is a *demoiselle du monde*"—she went on—"if you have reached that far—you should know that there is some honor, some *tenue* left in old families,—and so you should treat her with consideration, and respect her incognito.—All this is not like you, my son!"

The Duchesse had dropped the "thee and thou"—it hurt me.

"I want to treat her with every respect—" I reiterated.

"Then believe me it is unnecessary for you to know her name—I am not altogether pleased with you, Nicholas."

"Dear Duchesse! that grieves me—I wish I could explain—I have only wanted to be kind—and I don't even know her address and could not send flowers when her brother died."

"They did not want flowers, perhaps—Take my advice—of the best I can give—Pay your secretary her wages—as high ones as she will accept—and then treat her as if she were fifty years old—and wore glasses!"

"She does wear glasses—abominable yellow horn rimmed spectacles!" I announced excitedly.—"Have you never seen them?"

The Duchesse's eyes flashed—.

"I have not said I ever met Miss Sharp, Nicholas—"

I knew the affair was now hopeless—and that I would only risk the real displeasure of my dear old friend if I continued in this way. So I subsided.—I had some instinct too that I would not receive sympathy even if I owned that my intentions were strictly honourable.

"I will say no more—except that should you know these people *cherè Duchesse*—and you ever discover that I could help them in any way—that you will call upon me to any extent."

She looked at me very searchingly and said laconically.

"*Bien.*"

Then we talked of other things, and I tried to reingratiate myself—The war was going better—Foch would wish to push his advantage. Things must have some end—in the near future.—When was I going to England?—All these subjects we discussed.

"When I am out of the hands of these doctors and have my new leg and eye—I will return, and then, I want to go into Parliament."

The Duchesse warmed up at once.—That was just the thing for me to do—that and to marry some nice girl of my own world, of which there must be an embarrassment of choice—with all the men killed in my country!

"I would want such an exceptional woman, Duchesse!"

"Do not look for the moon, my son—Be thankful if she has been sufficiently well brought up to have a decent conduct—the manners of the young girls now revolt me.—I try to go with the times——but these new fashions are disgusting."

"Do you think a woman ought to be perfectly innocent and ignorant of life to make the marriage happy—" I asked.

"The insides of the minds of young girls one is never sure of, but the *tenue* should be correct at all costs, so that they may have something to uphold them as well as religion—which is no longer so surrounding as it used to be."

"Duchesse, I want someone who would love me passionately, and whom I could passionately love."

"For that, my poor boy—" and she sighed—"it is not found among young girls—these things come after one knows, and can discriminate—put them aside from your thoughts—they are temptations which one resists if one can, and at all events makes no scandals about.—Love! *Mon Dieu*, it is the song of the poets, it cannot happen in the world—with satisfaction—It must be a pain always—Do your duty to your race, and your class—and try not to mix up sentiment with it!"

"There is no hope of my finding someone I could really love, then?"

"I do not know—in your own country it may be—here it is the wife of someone else who holds the charm—and if it were not for *tenue* society could not exist.

"All that one must ask of the young is that they act with discretion, so that they can reach the autumn of life without scandals against their names—If the *Bon Dieu* adds love—then they have been indeed fortunate."

"But Duchesse—with your great heart—have you never loved—?"

Her eyes seemed to grow beautiful and young again—they diffused a fire—.

"Loved—Nicholas—! All women love once in their lives—happy for them if it has not burnt their souls in its passage—Happy if the *Bon Dieu* has let it merge into love for humanity—" And soft tears dimmed the dark blue brilliancy.

I leaned forward and kissed her hand with deep devotion—then the ancient servitor came in and she was called to a ward—but I left feeling that if there is really some barrier of family between Alathea and me—there would be no use in my appealing to the Duchesse—Sorrows she understands—and war and suffering—and self-sacrifice—Love she understands and passion—and all that appertains thereto—but all these things go to the wall before the conception of the meaning of *noblesse oblige* which ruled when Adelaide de Mont Orgeuil—wedded the Duc de Courville-Hautevine, in the eighties! The only thing left now was to telephone to Maurice—.

He came in for a few minutes just before dinner—.

He has questioned Alwood Chester of the American Red Cross, who had told him that Miss Sharp had been Miss Sharp always while she worked for them, and that no one knew anything further about her.

Well!—if her father is a convict, and her mother—in a mad house, and her sister consumptive—I still want her for herself—.

Is that true—Could I face disease and insanity coming into my family—?

I don't know—All I know is that I do not believe whatever curse hangs over the rest it has touched her—She is the picture of health and balance and truth—Her every action is noble—and I love her—I love her—there!

Next day she came in at ten as usual—She brought all the chapters annotated—. As her attitude towards me had been as cold as it was possible for an attitude to be, I cannot say that there was any added shade of contempt since her interview with Suzette—What had passed between them perhaps Burton will be able gradually to discover—.

I controlled myself, and behaved with a businesslike reserve—She had nothing to snub me for, or to disturb her—She took the papers at twelve o'clock—and I sighed as she left the room—I had watched her furtively for nearly two hours—Her face was a mask—And she might indeed really have been concentrating upon the work in hand. Her hands are whitening considerably—. I believe their redness had something to do with her little brother, perhaps she put very hot things on his chest.—I have never seen such a white skin—it shows like mother of pearl against the cheap black frock—The line of the throat is like my fascinating Nymph with the shell—indeed the mouth is not unlike her's also. I wonder if she has dimp—but I had better not think of those things—!

I am now determined to ask her to marry me on the first occasion I can screw up my courage sufficiently. I have decided what I am going to say. I am going to be quite matter of fact—I shan't tell her that I love her even—I feel if I can secure her first I shall have a better chance afterwards. If she thought I loved her, her nature is of that honest kind that she might think it was dishonorable to make so uneven a bargain with me—but if she just thinks I want her for my secretary and to play to me—and even perhaps that there is some brute part which she despises mixed up in my feeling for her—and which I would promise to keep in check—she may feel that it is fair for her to take my name, and my money, and give me nothing in return.

After lunch, which we did not have together, George Harcourt came in, and diverted me until four o'clock.

After we had discussed the war news for a long time he began as usual about Violetta—.

She was perfection!—She had fulfilled all he had ever asked of a woman—but—or rather in consequence of this—she had begun to bore him, while a new vixen with no heart and the brain of a rabbit—now drew him strangely!

"And what are you going to do about it, my dear George?"

"Deceive her of course, Nicholas. It is a painful necessity that my kind heart forces me to perpetrate."

He was smoking contemplatively.

I laughed—.

"You see, dear boy—one can't be brutal with the little darlings, so that is the only course open to one, for their limited reasoning power does not enable them to grasp that it is not one's fault at all when one ceases to care—the trouble lies with their own weakening attraction.—So one has to go on bluffing until they themselves weary, or find out inadvertently that one's affection has been transferred!"

"Don't you think there are some to whom you could tell the truth?"

"I have not met any—if they do exist."

"If I were a woman it would insult me far more for a man to think I was so stupid that he could deceive me, than if he said frankly he no longer cared."

"Probably—but then women don't reason in that way—you might prove by every law of logic that it was because they themselves had disillusioned you, and that you had no control over the coming or going of your emotion—but at the end of your peroration they would still reproach you for being a fickle brute, and believe themselves blameless, and sinned against!"

"It is all very difficult!"—I sighed unconsciously—.

—"Are you in some mess, my son?" George asked concernedly.—"In your case with Suzette, money can always smooth things—she has perhaps been annoying?"

"I have entirely finished with Suzette—George, how a man pays for all his follies—Have you, with all your affairs, ever got off scot free?"

George leaned back in his chair—his well cut face which expresses as a rule a rather kindly whimsical cynicism grew stern—and his very voice altered.

"Nicholas—one has to pay one's shot every time—A man pays in money, or in jewels or in disgrace, or in regret and remorse—and he has to calculate beforehand to what extent that which he desires is worth the price which will become due—It is a brainless idiot who does not calculate, or who laments when he has to stump up. I admit women are of supreme interest to me, and their companionship and affection—bought or otherwise—are necessary to my existence—So I resignedly discharged my debt every time."

"How will you pay it then about Violetta whom you say is an angel, and blameless?"

"I shall have some disgusting moments of discomfort and remorse—and feel a moral Bluebeard—I shan't go scot free—."

"And she—? That won't help her."

"She will pay in tears for having been weak enough to love me—she will feel the consolation of martyrdom—and soon forget me."

"And you don't think one incurs some kind of hoodoo—in indulging in these things—I am thinking of Suzette—her shadow—almost one would say projected by fate, is what is causing me trouble now, not any deliberate action she is committing against me."

"Part of the price, my boy! You can't steal anything, or do anything against the law, be it of man or of morals or of the spirit—that you don't have to pay for it—and there is no use in haggling beforehand or in squealing after. The thing is to learn early enough in life what is worth while and what you really want, before you lay up for yourself limitations."

"That is true—."

"Now let us analyse what gains and losses you have had in the Suzette business. Let us take the gains first—You had a jolly little companion during some months of pain and weariness—She helped you over a difficult moment—You were not leading her astray. To be the friend of war-heroes was her *métier*—you paid her highly in solid cash—You are under no obligation to her—. But the law has decreed that man must have no illicit relations, so the force of that current, or belief, or whatever it is, makes you pay some price for having broken the law—Accept it and get through with it—And if the price has been too heavy decide not to incur such debts again. The whole bother occurs because you don't look ahead, my boy! There was a case when I was a youngster and just joined my Battalion of Guards which will illustrate what I mean, of Bobby Bulteel, Hartelford's brother.—He cheated at cards—He was a kind of cousin of my mother's so the family felt the scandal awfully—He was kicked out of course, and utterly broke, and Lady Hilda Marchant ran off with him, and left her husband. She adored the fellow who had every charm—Well that was not worth while—The odds are too heavy for anyone ever to have the ghost of a chance to pull cheating off. He was simply a fool, you see. Take chances, but never when the scales have gone beyond the angle of forty-five degrees!"—Then having finished his cigar George rose in the best of tempers—.

"You may take it from me Nicholas—it sounds old fashioned—but to behave like a gentleman and always be ready to discharge your obligations, are the best rules for life.——Ta ta, dear boy—Shall look in on you soon again—" and he went!

Of course his logic is unanswerable—So I had better accept the shadow of Suzette falling upon my relation with Alathea, and try to gain my end in spite of it—And what is my very end?

Not of course that I shall spend the rest of my life as Alathea's husband-in-name-only, hungry and longing and miserable—but that after securing her certain companionship I shall overcome her prejudices, conquer her aversion, and make her love me.—But to have the chance to do all this it is absolutely necessary that I shall be near her always—So my idea of marriage is not so far-fetched after all!

And if she will accept me, someday, upon *any terms*—provided they do not mean separation—I shall believe that half the battle is won—I feel more cheerful already!—How sound reasoning does one good, even if it is as baldly brutal as George's!

XVII

Burton gave forth some information this evening, as he was dressing me for dinner. He had now discovered from Pierre how Suzette had behaved when she intruded upon Alathea. She had entered the room—"Passing Pierre without so much as asking his leave, and he with his wooden leg not so nimble as might be!" She had gone to the writing table and demanded my address. "An affair of business which must be attended to at once," she had announced. Pierre standing at the door had heard all this. Burton added "He said that Mam'zelle was that scented and that got up, of course Miss Sharp must have known what she was."

Alathea apparently had answered with dignity, that she had received no orders to give any address, but that letters would be forwarded.

"She took no more notice of Mam'zelle than if she was a chair," Pierre had told him—who, having his own troubles with women, was prepared to see a conflict! Suzette became nonplussed, and losing her temper a little told Alathea that she hoped she would get as much out of the situation as she herself had done! Alathea continued writing as though she had not heard, and then told her quite politely in French, that if she would kindly leave whatever letters were to be sent on, she would see that they went that night, and had added:

"Now, I need not detain you longer." Suzette became furious, and stamping, said she was "Mademoiselle la Blonde," and had more right there than Alathea!

Pierre had here interfered, and catching hold of Suzette's arm, had dragged her from the room.

I tingled with shame and wrath. That the person I respect most in the world should have been exposed to such a scene—! Burton too was horrified—.

I had the most awful sensation of discomfort—the very fact of having to hear of all this through servants was sufficiently disgusting, without the events themselves being so degrading.

What must Alathea think of me! And I cannot even allude to the subject. How wonderful her dignity has been that she has allowed no extra contempt to come into her manner.

How shall I have the pluck to ask her to marry me? I mean to do so to-morrow when she comes.

Saturday:

I am going to write the events of these last days down without any comment.

I came in to the sitting-room after Alathea had arrived. She was writing at her desk in the little salon. I looked in and asked her if she would come in and speak to me. Then I got to my chair. She entered obediently with the block in her hand, ready to begin work.

"Will you sit down, please," I said, indicating a chair, where she would face me and the light, so that no shade of her expression should be lost upon me. (I shall become quite an expert in reading mouths. I am obliged to study hers so closely!)

I felt less nervous than I have ever felt when with her. I thought there was the faintest shade of alertness in her manner.

"I am going to say something which will surprise you very much, Miss Sharp," I began.

She raised her head a little.

"I will put the case to you quite baldly—I am very rich as you know—I am still horrid to look at—I am lonely and I want a companion who would play the piano to me, and who would help me to write books, and who would travel with me. I cannot have any of these simple things because of the scandal people would make—so there is only one course open to me—that is to go through the marriage ceremony—Miss Sharp—under those terms will you marry me?"

Her attitude had become tense—her face did not flush, it became very pale. She remained perfectly silent for a moment. I felt just the same as I used to do before going over the top—a queer kind of excitement—a wonder if I'd come through or not.

As she did not answer I went on. "I would not expect anything from you except a certain amount of your company. There would not be any question of living with me as a wife—I would promise even to keep in check that side which you once saw and which I was so sorry about. I would settle lots of money on you, and give anything to your family you might wish. I would not bother you, you would be quite free—only I would like you to take interest in my work in a way—and to play to me—even if you would not talk to me."

My voice broke a little at the end of this; I was conscious of it, and of how weak it was of me. Her hands clasped together suddenly—and she appeared as though she was going to speak, then remained silent.

"Won't you answer me at all?" I pleaded.

"It is such a strange proposal—I would wish to refuse it at once——"

"It is quite bald, I know," I interrupted quickly. "I want to buy you—that is all—you can name the price. I know if you consented it would merely be for the same reason which makes you work. I presume it is for your family, not for yourself; therefore, I am counting upon that to influence you. Whatever you would want for your family I should be delighted to give you."

She twisted her locked hands—the first sign of real emotion I have seen in her.

"You would marry me—without knowing anything about me? It is very strange—."

"Yes. I think you are extremely intelligent—if you would consent to talk to me sometimes. I want to go into Parliament—when I am patched up and more decent looking, and I believe you would be of the greatest help to me."

"You mean the whole thing simply as a business arrangement?"

"I have already stated that."

She started to her feet.

"The bargain," I went on, "would be quite a fair one. I am offering to buy a thing which is not for sale—therefore, I am willing to pay whatever would tempt the owner to part with it. I am not mixing up any sentiment in the affair. I want the brain of you for my scheme of life, and the laws of the quaintly civilized society to which we belong, do not permit me to hire it—I must buy it outright. I put it to you net—is there any way we can effect this deal?"

Her lips were quivering—.

"You would say this, no matter what you might hear of my family?"

"I am quite unconcerned as to their history. I have observed you, and you possess all the qualities which I want in the partner who can help me to live my new life. For me you are just a personality—" (thus I lied valiantly!) "not a woman."

"Can I believe you?" she asked a little breathlessly.

"You are thinking of that day when I kissed you—" her lips told me by their sudden drawing in, that she was agitated.

"Well—I expect really that you know men well enough, Miss Sharp, to know that they have sudden temptations—but that a strong will can overcome them. I was very much moved about your grief that afternoon, and the suppressed emotion, and the exasperation you had caused me, unbalanced me—I am quite unlikely ever to feel again—if you will marry me, I will give you my word I will never touch you, or expect anything, of you except what you agree to give in the bargain. You can lead your own life—and I can lead mine."

I felt suddenly that these last words were not very wise—for they aroused in her mind the thought that I should go on having friends like Suzette. I hastened to add—

"You will have my deepest respect, and as my wife shall be treated with every courtesy and honour."

She sat down again and raised her hands to her eyes as though to remove her glasses, and then remembered and dropped them.

"I see that you would rather not answer to-day, Miss Sharp—you might prefer to go now and think about it?"

"Thank you." She turned and walked back into the little salon without a word more, and when she went I closed my eye exhausted with the great strain.

But I did not feel altogether hopeless until Burton came in to tell me lunch was ready and said that Alathea had gone.

"The young lady said as how she would not be back she expected, and she took her own pens and things in her bag. She was as white as a lily, give you my word, Sir Nicholas."

I am ashamed to say that I felt a little faint then. Had I overstepped the mark, and should I never see her again?

A whole party of the fluffies were coming to dinner, and we were to have a very gay evening. I ordered my one horse Victoria and went for a drive in the *Bois*, to calm myself, and the trees with their early autumn tints seemed to mock at me. I could see too much beauty in them, and it hurt. Everything hurt! This was certainly the worst afternoon I have had to bear since I came to on No-Man's Land near Langemarke. But I suppose at dinner I played the game, for Coralie and the rest congratulated me.

"Getting quite well, Nicholas! And of a *chic*! *Va!*"

We played poker afterwards and the stakes were high, and I was the winner the whole time, until I could see anxiety creep into more than one eye (pair of eyes! I have got so accustomed to writing of eyes in the singular that I forget!) We had quantities of champagne and some exotic musicians Maurice had procured for me, and a nude Hindoo dancer.

Everyone went more or less mad.

They left about four in the morning, all rather drunk, if one must write it. But the more I had drunk the more hideously sober and filled with anguish I seemed to become, until when I had called the last cheery good-night and was at last alone in my bed, I felt as if the end had come, and that death would be the next and only good thing which could happen to me.

I have never before had this strange detached sense in such measure as this night. As of a hungry agonized spirit standing outside its wretched body, and watching its feeble movements, conscious of their futility, conscious of being chained to the miserable thing, and only knowing rebellion and agony.

Burton gave me a sleeping draught, and I slept far into the next day to awake more unhappy than ever, obsessed with self-contempt and degradation.

In the afternoon, I received a note from Maurice, telling me that he had inadvertently heard that a fellow in the American Red Cross had seen Miss Sharp's passport, when she had been sent down to Brest for them, and the name on it was Alathea Bulteel Sharp, and judging that the second name sounded as if it might be a well-known English one, he hastened to tell me, in case it should be a clue. I could not think where I had heard it before, or with what memory it was connecting in my brain. I had a feeling it was something to do with George Harcourt. I puzzled for a while, and then I looked back over the pages of my journal, and there found what I had written of his conversation—Bobby Bulteel—Hartelford's brother—cheating at cards—and married to Lady Hilda Marchant——

Of course!—The whole thing became plain to me! This would account for everything. I hobbled up and got down the peerage. I turned to the Hartelford title, and noted the brothers—the Hon'bles—John Sinclair, Charles Henry, and Robert Edgar. This last must be "Bobby" Then I read the usual things—"Educated at Eton and Christchurch, etc., etc." "Left the Guards in ." "Married in —Lady Hilda Farwell, only daughter of the Marquess of Braxted (title extinct) and divorced wife of William Marchant, Esquire." "Issue—"

"Alathea—born , John Robert born , and Hilda born ."

So the whole tragic story seemed to unfold itself before me.

Alathea is the child of that great love and sacrifice of her Mother—I read again the words George had used: "She adored the fellow who had every charm." All the world might cast him out, but that one faithful woman gave up home and name and honour, to follow him in his disgrace. That was love indeed, however misplaced! I looked again at the dates and made a calculation of the time divorces took then, and I saw that my little darling girl could only have escaped illegitimacy by perhaps a few hours!

What had her life been? I pictured it. They must have hidden diminished heads in hole and corner places during the dreary years. Such a man as Bobby Bulteel must have been, as George said, a weakling. The Hartlefords were poor as church mice, and were not likely to assist a scapegrace, who had dishonoured them. I remembered hearing that on the old Lord Braxted's death years ago, Braxted was sold to the Merrion-Walters, Ironfounders from Leeds. No doubt the old man had cut his daughter off without the traditional shilling, but even so, some hundreds a year must have been theirs. What then did the poverty of Alathea suggest? That some constant drain must be going on all the time. Could the scapegrace still be a gambler, and that could account for it? This seemed the most probable explanation.

Then all over me there rushed a mad worship for my little love. Her splendid unselfishness, her noble self-sacrifice, her dignity, her serenity. I could have kissed the ground under her feet.

I made Burton spend untold time telephoning to the Embassy, and then to Versailles to Colonel Harcourt—would he not dine with me? He was sorry he was engaged but he would lunch the next day. Then when the long evening was in front of me alone—I could hardly bear it. And, driven to desperation at last, when Burton was undressing me, I said to him:

"Did you ever know anything of the Hartlefords, Burton—Bulteel is the family name?"

"Can't say as I did personally, Sir Nicholas," he answered, "but of course, when I was a young boy taking my first fourth-footman's place, before I came to your father, Sir Guy, at Her Grace of Wiltshire's, I could not help hearing of the scandal about the cheating at cards. The whole nobility and gentry was put to about it, and nothing else was talked of at dinner."

"Try and tell me what you remember of the story."

So Burton held forth in his own way for a quarter of an hour. There had been no possible doubt of the crime, it was the week after the Derby, and Bulteel had lost heavily it was said. He was caught red-handed and got off abroad that night, and the matter would have been hushed up probably but for the added sensation of Lady Hilda's elopement with him. That set society by the ears, and the thing was the thrill of the season. Mr. Marchant had been "all broken-up" by it, and delayed the divorce so that as far as Burton could remember, Captain Bulteel could not marry Lady Hilda for more than a year afterwards. All this coincided with what I already knew. Lord Braxted too, "took on fearful," and died of a broken heart it was said, leaving every cent to charity. The entail had been cut in the generation before and the title became extinct at his death.

I did not tell Burton then of my discovery, and lay long hours in the dark, thinking and thinking.

What did the Duchesse's attitude mean? In the eyes of the Duchesse de Courville-Hautevine, *neé* Adelaide de Mont Orgeuil—to cheat at cards would be the worst of all the cardinal sins. Such a man as Bobby Bulteel must be separated from his kind. She knew Lady Hilda probably (the Duchesse often stayed in England with my mother) and she probably felt a disapproving pity for the poor lady. The great charity of her mind would be touched by suffering, if the suffering was apparent, and perhaps she had some affection for the girl Alathea. But no affection could bridge the gulf which separated the child of an outcast from her world. The sins of the father would inevitably be visited upon the children by an unwritten law, and although she might love Alathea herself, she could not countenance her union with me. The daughter of a man who had cheated at cards should go into a convent. I instinctively felt somehow that this would be her viewpoint.

Does Alathea know this tragedy about her father? Has she had to live always under this curse? Oh! The pity of it all.

Morning found me more restless and miserable than I have ever been, and it brought no sign of my love!

XVIII

George Harcourt was called suddenly to Rome that morning and so even hearing him talk further about the Bulteels was denied me for the time. I passed some days of the cruelest unrest. There was no sign of Alathea. I allowed Maurice to drag me out into the world and spent my evenings among my kind.

A number of my old pals have been killed lately, such an irony when the war seems to be drawing to a close! There is still an atmosphere of tension and unrestfulness in the air, though.

After an awful week George Harcourt came back and dropped in to see me. I opened fire at once, and asked him to tell me all that he knew of the Bulteels, especially his old brother officer Bobby.

"I have a particular reason for asking, George," I said.

"Very curious your speaking of them, Nicholas, because there has just been the devil of a fuss in the French Foreign Legion about that infernal blackguard; it came to my knowledge in my work."

"Has he been cheating at cards again?"

George nodded.

"Tell me from the beginning."

So he started—many of the bits I already knew. Lady Hilda had been a great friend of his and he dwelt upon the life of suffering she had had.

"There were a few years of frantic love and some sort of happiness, I expect, and then funds began to give out, and Bobbie's insane desire to gamble led him into the shadiest society, at Baden-Baden and Nice, and other warm spots. Poor Hilda used to go about with him then in a shamed, defiant way, running from any old friend, or staring over his head. I happened upon them once or twice in my wanderings; then I lost sight of them for some years, and the next thing was someone told me the poor woman had broken down and was a nervous wreck, and two children had been born in quick succession, when the first one was about eleven years old, and the whole family were in miserable straits. I think relations paid up that time—with the understanding that never again were they to be applied to. And since then I have heard nothing until the other day it came to my ears that the eldest girl—she must be over twenty now, was supporting the entire family. One of the children died lately, and now Bobby has put the cap on it. I am sorry for them, but Bobby is impossible."

Oh! My poor little girl, what a life! How I longed to take her out of it!

He went on.

"Strange how certain instincts show themselves under every condition. Bobby was no physical coward, and to talk to and mix with casually, the most perfect gentleman you ever met. Awfully well read and a topper at classics and history, and sang like a bird. Hehad the grand manner, and could attract any woman, though to give the devil his due—I believe for some years he was faithful to Lady Hilda."

"I should think so!" I said indignantly. "After accepting her great sacrifice!"

"Nothing lasts, my dear boy, that is not fundamental. Bobby was a rotter through and through, and so he couldn't even behave decently to the woman who had given up everything for him, once her charm went. But—that something in human beings which is unaccountable, when they are well bred, made him join the French Foreign Legion immediately war broke out, and behave with great gallantry."

"What brought on the last episode?"
"He was probably bored in the dull post where he was, with not much fighting to do lately, and resorted to his old game to cover up losses, which he could not pay, and had the bad luck to be caught for the second time. I told you he was a fool and did not know how to calculate the price of his follies."
"When did you hear of this?"
"Only last night on my return, and there will be a disgusting scandal, and the old story will be raked up and it is pretty beastly for Englishmen."
"Can money keep it quiet, George?"
"I expect so, but who would be fool enough to pay for such a fellow?"
"I would, and will, if you can manage it without letting my name appear."
"My dear boy, how does it interest you? Why should you do such a quixotic thing? It is twenty-five thousand francs."
"Only twenty-five thousand francs! I'll give you the cheque this minute George, if you can, in your own way, free the poor devil."
"But Nicholas—you must be mad my dear boy!—Or you have some strong motive I do not know of."
"Yes, I have—I want this chap freed from disaster, not for his sake, but for the sake of the family. What must that poor lady have gone through, and that poor girl!"
George looked at me with his whimsical cynical eye.
"It's awfully decent of you, Nicholas," was all he said though, and I reached for my cheque-book, and wrote a cheque for thirty thousand francs with my stylo.
"You may need the extra five thousand, George—to make sure of the thing, and I count on you to patch it up as soon as you can."
He left after that, promising to see into the affair at once, and telephone me the result—and when he had gone I tried to think over what it all means?
Alathea did not know of this when I asked her to marry me last week. She must never know that I am paying, even if that makes matters easy enough for her to refuse me. The reason of her long silence is because this fresh trouble has fallen upon them, I am sure. I feel so awfully, not being able to comfort her. The whole burden upon those young shoulders.—
Just as I wrote that yesterday, Burton came in to say that Miss Sharp was in the little salon, and wished to see me, and I sent him to pray her to come in. I rose from my chair to bow to her when she entered, she never shakes hands. I was awfully pained to see the change in her. Her poor little white face was thin and woebegone and even her lips pale, and her air was not so proud as usual.
"Won't you sit down," I said with whatever of homage I could put into my voice.
She was so humbled and miserable, that I knew she would even have taken off her glasses if I had asked her to, but of course I would not do that.
She seemed to find it hard to begin. I felt troubled for her and started.
"I am awfully glad that you have come back."
She locked her hands together, in the shabby, black suede gloves.
"I have come to tell you that if you will give me twenty-five thousand francs this afternoon, I will accept your offer, and will marry you."
I held out my hand in my infinite joy, but I tried to control all other exhibition of emotion.
"That is awfully good of you—I can't say how I thank you," I said in a voice which sounded quite stern. "Of course I will give you anything in the world you want." And again I reached for my cheque-book and wrote a cheque for fifty thousand and handed it to her.
She looked at it, and went crimson.
"I do not want all that, twenty-five thousand is enough. That is the price of the bargain."
I would not let this hurt me.
"Since you have consented to marry me, I have the right to give you what I please—you may need more than you have suggested, and I want everything to be smooth and as you would wish."
She trembled all over.
"I—I cannot argue now, I must go at once; but I will think over what I must say about it."
"If you are going to be my wife, you must know that all that is mine will be yours; so how can a few thousand francs more or less now make any difference, though if you have any feeling concerning it, you can pay me back out of your first month's dress allowance!" and I tried to smile.
She started to her feet.
"When shall I see you again?" I pleaded.
"In two days."
"When will you marry me?"
"Whenever you arrange."
"Must you go now?"
"Yes—I must—I am grateful for your generosity, I will fulfill my side of the bargain."
"And I mine."
I tried to rise, and she handed me my crutch, and then went towards the door, there she turned.
"I will come on Friday at ten o'clock as usual, Good-bye," and she bowed and left me.
What a remarkable way to become an engaged man!! But only joy filled me at that moment. I wanted to shout and sing—and thank God!
Alathea will be mine, and surely it will only be a question of time before I can make her love me, my little girl!
I rang for Burton. I must have rung vigorously for he came in hurriedly.

"Burton," I said, "Congratulate me, my old friend—Miss Sharp has promised to marry me."
For once Burton's imperturbability deserted him, he almost staggered and put his hand to his head.
"God bless my soul, Sir Nicholas," he gasped, and then went on, "Beg pardon, Sir, but that is the best piece of news I ever did hear in my life."
And his dear old eyes were full of tears while he blew his nose vigorously.
"It will be a very quiet wedding, Burton. We shall have it at the Consulate, and I suppose at the church in the *Rue d'Agesseau*, if Miss Sharp is a Protestant—I have never asked her."
"The wedding don't so much matter, Sir Nicholas. It is having the young lady always here to look after you."
"Without her glasses, Burton!"
"As you say Sir, without them horn things." And there was a world of understanding in his faithful eyes.
He left the room presently with the walk of a boy, so elated was he, and I was left alone, thrilling in every nerve with triumph. How I long for Friday I cannot possibly say.
In the afternoon Maurice and Alwood Chester, and Madame de Clerté came to see me, and all exclaimed at my improved appearance.
"Why you look like a million dollars, Nicholas," Alwood said, "What is up, old bird?"
"I am getting well, that is all."
"We are going to have a party on Sunday to introduce you to the loveliest young girl in Paris," Solonge announced. "The daughter of a friend of mine without a great dot, but that does not matter for you, Nicholas. We think that you should marry and marry a *jeune fille francaise*!"
"That is sweet of you. I have shown how I appreciate young girls, have not I?"
"For that—no!" she laughed, "But the time has come—."
I felt amused, what will Alathea think of these, my friends? Solonge is the best of them.
Maurice had an air of anxiety underneath his watchful friendliness. He's fine enough to *feel* atmospheres, or whatever it is that comes from people, not in words. He felt that some great change had taken place in me, and he was not sure what aspect it would have in regard to himself. He came back after he had seen Madame de Clerté to her coupé!—She has essence also now,—and his rather ridiculous, kindly, effeminate, little dark face was appealing.
"*Eh bien, mon ami?*" he said.
"*Eh bien?*"
"There is something, Nicholas, what? Was the clue of any use to you?"
"Yes, thank you a thousand times, Maurice, I could trace the whole thing. Miss Sharp comes of a very distinguished family, which I know all about. Her uncle is a miserable Earl! That is respectable enough, especially a tenth Earl! And her maternal grandfather was a 'Marquess.'"
"*Vrai, mon vieux?*"
"Quite true!"
Maurice was duly interested.
"You were right then about the breeding, it always does show."
I had difficulty in not telling him my news, but I thought it wiser to remain silent until after Friday! Friday! Day of days!
Maurice suspected that there was something beyond in all this, and was not sure which course would be the best to pursue; one of sympathy or unconsciousness. He decided upon the latter and presently left me.
Then I telephoned to Cartier to have some rings sent up to look at. I have a feeling that I must be very discreet about giving Alathea presents, or she will be resentful and even suspect that my bargain is not entirely a business one. I am afraid I seemed a little too pleased at our interview; I must be indifferently aloof on Friday.
I suppose I had better not give her my mother's pearls until after the ceremony. I wonder if there will be a fuss when I suggest her going to the *Rue de la Paix* for clothes? I apprehend that there will be a stubborn resistance to almost everything I would wish to do.
How will the Duchesse take it! Probably philosophically, once it is an accomplished fact.
At that moment Burton brought me in a note from that very lady! I opened it eagerly, and its contents made me smile.
The Duchesse wrote to remind me of a request I once made her, that if a certain family were in trouble that I would assist them to any amount. Twenty-five thousand francs were now absolutely necessary on the moment, if I could send them to her by bearer, I would know that I was doing a good deed!
For the third time that day I reached for my cheque-book and wrote a cheque, but for only the sum asked on this occasion, and then when Burton had brought me note paper, I sent a little word with it, to the Duchesse, and when I was alone again I laughed aloud.
Three people determined upon it must surely save the scapegrace!—I wonder which of the three will get there first!
I would not go out anywhere to dinner, I wanted to be alone to think over the whole strange turn of fate. Do strong desires influence events? Or are all these things settled beforehand? Or is there something in reincarnation, which Alathea believes in, and the actions of one life cause that which looks like fate in the next? We shall have many talks on this subject, I hope.
I wonder, how long it will take for my little love to come voluntarily into my arms?——?

XIX

Saturday.

I wonder how long I shall go on writing in this Journal? I suppose once I should be happy it would not be necessary; well the moment has not yet come, in spite of my being the *fiancé* of the woman I desire.

At ten o'clock I was waiting for her in the sitting-room, and I was thinking of that other time when I waited in anxiety, in case she did not return at all. I was very excited, but it was more the exhilaration I used to feel when we were going to have some stunning marauding expeditions over No-Man's Land. The old zest was in my veins.

I heard Alathea's ring, and after she had taken off her hat she came into the room. I believed that her anxieties must be assuaged because George Harcourt had telephoned late on Thursday night to say that he had been successful, and that he had four thousand francs to hand back to me, the affair having been concluded for twenty-six thousand. So what was my surprise to see Alathea's face below her glasses more woebegone than ever! At first it gave me a stab of pain. Does she really hate me so? She did not mention the money, so I wonder if it is that she does not yet know her father is cleared? I bowed as coldly as I used always to do, and she asked me if I had a chapter ready for her to type? I answered that I had not, because I had been too busy with other things to have composed anything.

"I think we had better discuss the necessary arrangements for our marriage before we can settle down to our old work," I said.

"Very well."

"I shall have to have your full name and your father's and mother's and all that, you know, to make it legal. My lawyer will attend to all the formalities—they are quite considerable, I believe. He arrives from London on Monday. I got him a passport by pulling a lot of strings."

She actually trembled. It seemed as if the idea of all this had not come to her, some of the value of her sacrifice would be diminished if the family skeleton should be laid bare, I could see she felt, so I reassured her.

"Believe me, I do not wish you to tell me anything about your family. As long as you can give just sufficient facts to satisfy the law, I have no curiosity to see them unless I can be of use."

"Thank you."

"I think a fortnight is the quickest that everything can be settled in.—Will you marry me on the seventh of November, Miss Sharp?"

"Yes."

"Do you care for the church ceremony, or will the one at the Consulate do?"

"I should think that would be quite enough for us."

The ring cases were all lying upon the table by me—I pointed to them.

"I wonder if you would choose an engagement ring?" and I began opening the lids. "It is customary, you know," I went on as she started reluctantly. I intended to be firm with her in all the points where I had rights.

"Don't you think it is a little ridiculous?" she asked. "A ring for a mere business arrangement?"

I would not allow myself to be hurt, but I was conscious that I felt a little angry.

"You would prefer not to choose a ring then? Very well, I will decide for you," and I took up one really magnificent single stone diamond, set as only Cartier can set stones.

"This is the last thing in modernity," and I handed it to her. "A hard white diamond of egregious size, it cannot fail to be a reminder of our hard business bargain, and I shall ask you to be good enough to wear it."

I suppose she saw that I was not pleased, for she drew in her lips a little, but she took the ring.

Her hands seemed very restless as she held it, they were certainly not nearly so red as they formerly were.

"Am I to put it on now?"

"Please."

She did so, only she put it on her right third finger, her cheeks growing pink.

"Why do you do that?" I asked.

"What?"

"Put the ring on the wrong hand."

She changed it reluctantly, then she burst out:

"I suppose I ought to thank you for such a very splendid gift, but I can't, because I would much rather not have it, please do let us keep to business in every way, and please don't give me any more presents. I am going to be just your secretary, with my wages commuted into some lump sum, I suppose."

I felt more angry, and I think she saw it. I remained silent, which forced her to speak.

"Do you intend that I shall live here, in the flat?"

"Of course. Will you please choose which of the two guest rooms you would prefer, they both have bathrooms, and you will have the decoration re-done as you wish."

Silence.

My exasperation augmented.

"Will you also please engage a maid, and go and order every sort of clothes which you ought to have. I know by the way you were dressed when I saw you in the *Bois* that Sunday, that your taste is perfect."

She stiffened as I spoke. It was quite plain to be seen that she loathed taking anything from me, but I had no intention of ceding a single point where I had the right to impose my will.

"You see you will be known as my wife, therefore you must dress according to the position, and have everything my mother used to have. Otherwise, people would not respect you, and only think that you were invidiously placed."

Her cheeks flamed again at the last words.

"It is difficult to picture it all," she said; "Tell me exactly what you expect of me daily."

"I expect that when you have breakfasted, in your room if you wish, that you will come and talk to me, perhaps do a little writing, or go out to drive, or what you wish, and that we shall lunch, and in the afternoon do whatever turns up. You will want to go out and see your friends and do what you please. And perhaps you will play to me as often as you feel inclined, and after dinner we can go to the theatre, or read, or do whatever you like. And as soon as my treatments with these doctors are concluded, and I have my new leg and eye, and we shall hope war is finished, we can travel, or go back to England, and then I shall begin taking up a political career, and I shall hope you will take a real interest in that and help me as though I were your brother."

"Very well."

"You will order the clothes to-day?"

"Yes."

She was subdued now, the programme was not very formidable, except that it contained daily companionship with me.

"Have you told the Duchesse de Courville-Hautevine yet that we are engaged?" I asked after a moment's pause.

Discomfort grew in her manner.

"No."

"Do you think that she will not approve of the marriage?"

"She may not."

"Perhaps you would rather that I told her?"

"As you please."

"I want you to understand something quite clearly, Alathea." She started when I said her name, "and that is that I expect you to treat me with confidence, and tell me anything which you think that I ought to know, so that we neither of us can be put in a false position, beyond that, believe me, I have no curiosity. I desire a companionship of brain, and a sort of permanent secretary who does not feel hostile all the time, that is all."

I could see that she was controlling herself with all her will, and that she was overwrought and intensely troubled. I knew that some barrier was between us which I could not at present surmount. All she said after a minute was:

"How did you know that my name was 'Alathea'?"

"I heard your little sister call you that the day I saw you in the *Bois*. I think it a very beautiful name."

Silence.

Her discomfort seemed to come to a climax, for after a little she spoke.

"The twenty-five thousand francs beyond the twenty-five I asked you for, I cannot return to you. I feel very much about it, and that you should pay for my clothes, and give me presents. It is the hardest thing I ever had to do in my life,—to take all this."

"Do not let it bother you, I am quite content with the bargain. Perhaps you would rather go now after we have selected which room you will have."

"Thank you."

She gave me my crutch, and I led the way and she followed. I knew instinctively that she would choose the room which was furthest from mine. She did!

"This will do," she said immediately we entered it.

"The look-out is not so nice, it only gets the early morning sun," I ventured to remark.

"It is quieter."

"Very well."

"It was rather arranged for a man, and is perhaps severe. Do you wish anything changed?"

She did not appear to take any more interest in it than if it had been a hotel room. She had given it the merest glance, although it is quite a little masterpiece in its way, of William and Mary—even the panelling being English, and of the time, and the old rose silk window and bed curtains.

"I don't want anything altered, thank you."

It seemed a strange moment, to be talking thus calmly to the woman who, in a fortnight, will be my wife. I feel that a volcano is really working under our feet, and that adds to the excitement!

When we got back to the sitting-room I offered to send the carriage for her to go and do her shopping, but she refused, and I thought it was wiser to let her go. We shall have years to talk in presently, and there is always the danger of our coming to an open rupture, and the bargain being off, if we see much of one another now.

"Good-bye," she said a little nervously, and I bowed and said "Good-bye," and she went from the room.

And when she had gone I laughed aloud, and began to analyse the situation.

George Harcourt has paid the gambling debt, therefore the fifty thousand I gave Alathea cannot have been used for that. Some fresh worry is perhaps upon the wretched family. The obvious thing for me to do is to go and see the Duchesse, and yet I have some strange sort of wish that it should be Alathea herself who tells me everything, and not that she becomes aware, by inference, that I must know. I feel that our future happiness depends upon her giving up all this stubborn pride. What is at the back of her mind? I do not know. That resentment and dislike of me has only become crystallized since the Suzette affair. I am sure she thinks that Suzette is my mistress still, and this insults her, but she reasons that with the bargain as it is, she has not the smallest right to object. She is furious with herself to think that it should matter to her. That is a thought! Why indeed should it matter if she is utterly indifferent to me? Is it possible? Can it be that? No—I dare not think of it, but, in any case it will be the most thrilling situation, once she is my wife.

I believe it would be wisest for me not to go to the Duchesse's but simply to write her a note telling her of my news, then anything she may tell me will be gratuitous.

I had just finished doing this when once again a letter was brought in from that lady, and this time it was to thank me for my cheque, and to tell me that it had been the means of preventing a most disagreeable scandal and bringing peace to a family!

Sardonic mirth overcame me. So three separate people seem to be under the impression that they have paid this gambler's debts! Each apparently unaware that there was anyone else in the running! It looks as if "Bobby" had wolfed the lot! Does Alathea know, and is this the extra cause of her worry?

I sent my note back by the Duchesse's messenger, who still waited, and went to my luncheon.

In about an hour the telephone rang—a request from the Hotel de Courville that I should repair there immediately without fail.

"Her Grace spoke herself," Burton said, "and said it was most important, Sir Nicholas."

"Very well, order the carriage. By the way. Burton, did you congratulate Miss Sharp?"

Burton coughed.

"I did make so bold, Sir Nicholas, as to tell the young lady how very glad I was, but she took it queer like, she stiffened up and said it was only a business arrangement, to be able to write your letters and do your work without people talking about it. That seemed funny to me, so I said nothing more."

"Burton it is funny for the moment, Miss Sharp is only marrying me for some reason for her family, the same one which forces her to work, but I hope I can make her think differently about it some day."

"Pardon the liberty I am taking, Sir Nicholas, but perhaps she don't like the idea of Mam'zelle, and don't know she's gone for good."

"That is probably the case."

Burton's wise old face expressed complete understanding, as he left the room, and presently I was on my way to the Hotel de Courville, a sense of exhilaration and of excitement and joy in my heart!

XX

The Duchesse was playing impatiently with her glasses when I was announced by the servant of ninety! Her face expressed some strong feeling. I was not sure if it was tinged with displeasure or no. She helped me to sit down, and then she began at once.

"Nicholas, explain yourself. You tell me you are engaged to your secretary! So this has been going on all the time, and you have not told me. I, who was your mother's oldest friend!"

"Dear Duchesse, you are mistaken, it has only just been settled. No one was more surprised at my offer than Miss Sharp herself."

"You know her real name, Nicholas? And her family history? You have guessed, of course, from my asking you for the twenty-five thousand francs, that they were in some difficulty?"

"Yes, I know Alathea is the daughter of the Honorable Robert and Lady Hilda Bulteel."

"She has told you all of the story, perhaps?—but you cannot know what the money was for, because the poor child does not know it herself. It is more just that I should inform you, since you are going to marry into the family."

"Thank you, Duchesse."

She then began, and gave me a picture of her old friendship with Lady Hilda, and of the dreadful calamity which had befallen in her going off with Bobby Bulteel.

"It was one of those cases of mad love, Nicholas, which fortunately seem to have died out of the modern world, though for the truth I must say that one more *séduisant* than *ce joli Bulteel*, I have never met! One could not, of course, acknowledge them for a crime like that, but I have ever been fond of poor Hilda and that sweet little child. She was born here, in this hotel. Poor Hilda came to me in her great trouble, and I was in deep mourning myself then for my husband,—the house is large, and it could all pass quietly."

I reached forward and took the Duchesse's hand and kissed it, and she went on:

"Alatheé is my godchild, one of my names is Alatheé. The poor little one, she adored her father, in all those first years. They wandered much and only came to Paris at intervals, and each time they came, a little poorer, a little more troubled, and then after a lapse I heard those two were born at Nice—wretched little decadents, when my poor Hilda was a mass of nerves and disillusion. Alatheé was eleven then. It was, *par hazard*, when she was about fourteen that she heard of her father's crime. She was the gayest, most sweet child before that, through all their poverty, but from that moment her character was changed. It destroyed something in her spirit, one must believe. She set firmly to education, decided she would be a secretary, cultivated herself, worked, worked, worked! She worshipped her mother, and resented immensely her father's treatment of her."

"She must always have had a wonderful character."

"For that, yes," and the Duchesse paused a moment, then went on:

"Quite a tremendous character, and as Bobby sank and poor Hilda became more ill, and wretched, that child has risen in strength, and supported them all. Since the war came they have almost lived upon her earnings. The father is without conscience, and of a selfishness unspeakable! His money all went to him for his use, and Alatheé was left to supplement the mother's wretched two or three thousand francs a year. And now that brute has again cheated at cards, and poor Hilda came to me in her great distress, and remembering your words, Nicholas, I called upon you. It would have been too cruel for the poor woman to have had to suffer again. Hilda took the money and gave it to this infamous husband, and the affair was settled that night. Alatheé knows nothing about it."

Light was dawning upon me. The admirable Bobby has evidently played upon the feelings of both wife and daughter!

"Duchesse, why did you not wish me to know the real name, and would not help me at all about 'Miss Sharp,'—won't you now tell me your reason?"

The Duchesse shaded her eyes from the fire with a hand-screen, and it came between us, and I could not see her face, but her voice changed.

"I was greatly surprised to find the girl in your flat one day. I had not understood with whom she was working. I was not pleased about it, frankly, Nicholas, because one cannot help knowing of your existence and your friends, and I feared your interest for a secretary might be as for them, and I disliked that my godchild should run such a risk. When *jeunes filles* of the world have to take up menial positions they are of course open to such situations, and have to expect difficulties. I wished to protect her as well as I could."

Suddenly I saw myself, and the utterly rotten life I had led, that this, my old friend, even, could not be sure of my chivalry. I loathed the lax, cheap honor of the world and its hypocrisy. I could not even be indignant with the Duchesse, judging me from that standpoint. She was right, but I did tell her that men had a slightly different angle in looking upon such things in England, where women worked, and were respected in all classes, and that the idea of making love to any secretary would never have entered my head. It was the intelligence and the dignity of Alathea herself which had made me desire her for a companion.

"It is well that you are English, Nicholas. No Frenchman of family could have married the daughter of a man who had cheated at cards."

"Even if the girl was good and splendid like Alathea, Duchesse?"

"For that, no, my son, we have little left but our traditions, and our names, and those things matter to us. No, frankly, I could not have permitted the union had you been my son."

So I had been right in my analysis of what would be the bent of my old friend's mind.

"You are pleased now, though, dear Duchesse?" I pleaded.

"It seems impossible, from my point, and I would not have encouraged it, but since it is done, I can but wish my dear Alatheé and you, my dear boy true happiness."

Again I took and kissed her kind hand.

"In England, especially in this war time, questions are not asked, *n'est ce pas*? She can be 'Sharp' simply and not Bulteel, then it may pass. For the girl, herself, you have a rare jewel, Nicholas—unselfish, devoted, true, but the will of the devil! You shall not be able to turn her as you wish, if her ideas go the other way!"

"Duchesse, the situation is peculiar, there is no question of love in it. Alathea is marrying me merely that she may give money to her family. I am marrying that I may have a secretary without scandal. We are not going to be really husband and wife."

The Duchesse dropped her fire-screen, her clever-eyes were whimsical and sparkling.

"*Tiens*!" she said, and never has the delicious word conveyed so much meaning! "You believe that truly Nicholas? Alatheé is a very pretty girl when properly dressed—"

"And without glasses!"

"As you say, without glasses, which I hear cover her fine eyes when in your society!"

"I asked her to marry me under those terms, and it was only upon those terms she accepted me."

The Duchesse laughed.

"A nice romance! Well, my son, I wish you joy!"

"Duchesse," and I leaned forward, "do you really think I can make her love me? Am I too awful? Is there a chance?"

The Duchesse patted my arm and her face shone with kindliness.

"Of course, foolish boy!" And she broke into French, using the "thee" and "thou" again affectionately. 'I was very handsome!—that which remained,—and all would look the same as ever when the repairing should be complete!'

"So very tall and fine, Nicholas, and hair of a thickness, and what is best of all, that air of a great gentleman. Yes, yes, women will always love thee, *sans* eye, *sans* leg, do not disturb thyself!"

"Don't tell her I love her, Duchesse," I pleaded. "We have much to learn of each other. If she did not believe it was a bargain equal on both sides, she would not marry me at all!"

The Duchesse agreed about this.

"Whatever she has promised she will perform, but why she does not love thee already I cannot tell."

"She dislikes me, she thinks I am a rotter, and I expect she was right, but I shall not be in the future, and then perhaps she will change."

When I left the Hotel de Courville it had been arranged that the Duchesse would receive my wife with honour, her world only knowing that I had married an English "Miss Sharp."

I heard no more of my *fiancée* until next morning, when she telephoned. Did I wish her to come that day?

Burton answered that I hoped she would, about eleven o'clock.

I intended to tell her that I thought that it might be wiser now if she did not come again until the wedding, as once we were engaged I would not allow her to run the risk of meeting anyone and giving a false impression. I think the strain would be too great in any case.

I did not come in to the salon until she was there, and she rose as I entered. She was whiter than ever, and very stern.

"I have been thinking," she said, before I could speak, "that if I promise to fulfill the bargain, and live here in the flat with you, going through the ceremony at the Consulate is quite unnecessary. Your caprice of having me for your wife merely in name in England, may pass, and it seems ridiculous to be tied. I am quite indifferent to what anyone thinks of me. I would prefer it like that."

"Why?" I asked, and wondered for a moment what had occurred.

"There are so many stupid law things, if there is a marriage, and if you have the same from me without, surely you see that it is better."

I first thought that it was this fear of my knowing her family history which was at the root of this suggestion, but then I remembered that she would know that I would hear it in any case from the Duchesse. What then could it be?

I felt cruel, I was not going to make things too easy for her. If she has the will of the devil, she has also the pride!

"If you are indifferent to such an invidious position as your new idea would place us in, I am not, I do not wish my friends to think that I am such a cad as presumably to have taken advantage of your being my secretary."

"You wish to go on with the marriage then?"

"Of course."

She clasped her hands together suddenly, as if she could control herself no longer, and I thought of what she had said to Burton about feeling that she could not fight any more. I would not allow myself to sympathize with her. I was longing in every nerve of my being to take her into my arms, and tell her that I loved her, and knew everything, but I would not do this. I cannot let her master me, or we shall never have any peace. I will not tell her that I love her until her pride is broken, and I have made her love me and come to me voluntarily.

She was silent.

"I have informed the Duchesse de Courville that we are engaged. I saw her yesterday."

She started perceptibly.

"She has told you my real name?"

"I have known that for some time. I thought I had made it plain to you that I am not interested about the subject, we need not mention it again, you have only to talk to old Robert Nelson, my lawyer, when he comes on Monday. He will tell you the settlements I propose to make, and you can discuss with him as to whether or not you think them satisfactory. Perhaps you on your side will tell me what reason you have strong enough to make a girl of your natural self-respect, willing to take the position of my apparent mistress?"

She burst out for a second, throwing out her hands, then controlling herself.

"No, I won't tell you.—I will tell you nothing, I will just stick to the bargain if I must. You have no right to my thoughts, only my actions!"

I bowed; disagreeable as she was, there was a distinctly pleasant zest in fighting!

"Perhaps of your courtesy, you will take off those glasses now, since I am aware that you only wear them to conceal your eyes, and not that they are necessary for your sight."

She flushed with annoyance.

"And if I refuse?"

I shrugged my shoulders.

"I shall think it very childish of you."

With a petulance which I had never seen in her she tossed her head.

"I don't care, at present I will not."

I frowned but did not speak. This will be discussed between us later. My fighting spirit is up, she *shall* obey me!

"Did you order the clothes yesterday?"

"Yes."

"Enough, I hope."

"Yes."

"Well, now, I have a suggestion to make which I am sure will please you, and that is that you will appoint some meeting place with Mr. Nelson for Tuesday morning, since you do not trust my good taste far enough even to let me know your home address. Perhaps at the Hotel de Courville, if the Duchesse will permit, and that then we do not meet until the seventh of November at the ceremony. Mr. Nelson will arrange with you all the law of the thing and what witnesses you must have, and everything, and this will save these useless discussions, and give you a little breathing space."

This seemed to subdue her, and she agreed less defiantly.

"And now I will not detain you longer," I said stiffly. "*Au revoir* until the seventh of November at whatever hour is arranged, or if we must meet before at the signing of the contract," and I bowed.

She bowed also, and walked haughtily to the door, and left.

And greatly exhilarated, I decided to go and lunch with Maurice at the Ritz.

As I came from the lift, Madame Bizot's daughter came out of the concierge's lodge with her baby, and it was making its same little cooing, gurgling noises that caused me so to feel that time when Alathea first began to interest me. I stopped and spoke to the mother, a comely young woman, and the little creature put out its tiny hand and clasped one of my fingers, and over me there came a weird thrill. Shall I ever hear noises like that, and have a son of Alathea's and mine to take my hand. Well the game of her subjection is interesting enough anyway, and rather ashamed of my emotion, I went on into the Victoria and was crawled to the Ritz.

Here I ran into a fellow in the Flying Corps, who told me that Nina's boy, Johnnie, had been killed the night before, in his first fight with a Boche plane. I do not know that any of the tragedies of the war have affected me more. My poor Nina! She really loved her son. I telegraphed to her at once my fondest sympathies, and the thought of her grief would not leave me all the way, war-hardened as I am.

I did not tell Maurice of my approaching wedding. I have a plan that he shall only know when I ask him to come to the Hotel de Courville to be presented to my wife.

The Fluffies have returned from Deauville, and Coralie and Alice joined us at luncheon. They have the most exquisite new garments, and were full of sparkle and gaiety. Alice's wedding, to the rich neutral, seems really to be coming off. Her air was one of subdued modesty and gentleness, and when I congratulated her she made the tenderest acceptance of it, which would havedone justice to a young virgin of the *ancien regime*! Coralie met my eye with her shrewd small ones, and we looked away! After lunch we sat in the hall for a little, Maurice taking Alice to try on her clothes, so Coralie and I were left alone.

"You are looking quite well now Nicholas," she whispered, "Why don't you ask me to come and dine with you, at your adorable flat,—alone?"
"You would be bored with me before the evening was over."
"Arrange it, and try! Always there are the others, except that night at Versailles. There is an air with you Nicholas,—one has forgotten all about your eye. I have thought and thought of you.—You have interfered with all my pleasures in life!"
"I am going back to England quite soon, Coralie, won't you come now to the *rue de la Paix* and let me buy you a little souvenir of all the lovely times we have had together in the last year?"
So she came, and selected a gem of an opera glass. An opera glass is discreet, it can be accepted by anyone; even a woman determined to impress my mind with her dignity and charm, as Coralie was attempting to do, upon our expedition. She had made up her mind that I should no longer be just a benefit to the three of them, but her own especial property, and she is clever enough to see that I am in a mood to admire dignity and discretion! I spent a most amusing hour with her, enjoying myself in the spirit of watching a good play at the *Comedie Français*. At about four o'clock, when we returned to the Ritz, Coralie was baffled. I could see that she was keener than ever, and beginning to be a little worried and unsure of herself!
As I drove back to my flat, taking a roundabout way through the Bois, I mused and analysed things. And what is the psychological reason for some presents being quite correct to give and some not? It all goes back to the re-creative instinct and through what this manifests itself. Gifts which have any relation to the body, to give it pleasure, or to decorate it, are the expressions of the sex relationship, and so presumably the subconscious mind, which only sees the truth in everything, only feels harmonious when these gifts are given by either parents or relations, as a dower, so to speak, or the husband or prospective husband. Hence through the ages, the unconscious relegation of certain presents as acceptable only from certain people. Any present which gives pleasure to the mind alone is the tribute of friendship, but those to touch the body are presumably not. I could give Coralie an opera glass as a mark of my esteem, but a bracelet which she would wear on her arm would have another meaning!
Alathea resents every present, those for the body because they suggest my possession of her, those for the mind because she feels no friendship for me at all!
Well, well!
What will she do I wonder during the fortnight of our engagement? I feel that I can afford to wait with patience and certainty. But the thought that I do not even know my *fiancée's* address, and that she is resentful and defiant, and rebellious at everything, and yet intends to marry me, on the seventh of November, is really almost humorous!
And now it behooves me to put my house in order, and map out exactly what I mean to do!

XXI

The days go slowly on, my preparations are complete. My good friend Nelson arrived on Monday and took charge of the affair. He was entirely aware of the Bulteel story, it was the great scandal of twenty-five years ago. He expressed no opinion as to my marrying into such a family, but went about the business end with diligence. I made a very nice settlement upon Alathea, more than he thought was necessary. Then he spoke of arrangements for possible children, and fixed that, too. I wonder what she will say when she reads that part! I have settled with the Duchesse, who is entering into the spirit of the thing with her usual delicious whimsical understanding, that some time soon after the wedding she shall ask about ten of our principal mutual friends to come in the afternoon, and she will present Alathea to them, and if anyone makes comments upon the matter, she will say that she is the daughter of an old English friend, and even if Coralie recognizes her as the girl who was with me at Versailles, she will not dare to say a word about any protegée of the Duchesse's. She is much too afraid of offending her, being received at the Hotel de Courville herself on sufferance only because of her birth and family. As for Maurice, I can manage him! Now I am beginning to wonder what Alathea would prefer to do? I don't want to see her until the ceremony, but I suppose I must.
The Duchesse has arranged that I should meet my *fiancée* in her sitting-room and sign the contract there on the day before the wedding, five days from now. Alathea, she tells me is like a frozen image, but faithful to her promise to me, my dear old friend has not made any comment or tried to aid matters. I think she rejoices that I shall have such an interesting time in the breaking down of the barrier.
Nina writes heartbrokenly; Johnnie was very dear to her; sorrow seems to have brought out all that is best in her. She says she feels that she just drifted along, taking all good and happiness for granted, and not doing enough for other people, and that now she is going to devote her life to making Jim happy and contented, and hopes some day, not too far off, to have another child to care for. Darling old Nina! She always was the best sort in the world.
Of Suzette I have heard nothing, although Burton says he caught sight of her on the stairs just whisking into the flat above mine, which has been taken by a lovely actress, a cousin of hers, who has married a rich retired Jew *antiquaire*!
There are still possibilities of complications here!
But I feel quite serene, Alathea will be mine. She cannot get away from me. I can insidiously, from day to day, carry out my plan of winning her, and the tougher the fight is, the more it will be worth while afterwards!
November th.
To-day was really wonderful! Mr. Nelson has presumably seen Alathea and her family several times. I have refused to hear anything about it, and he arrived with her alone at the Hotel de Courville. I had understood that her mother was coming with her, but she was ill and did not turn up.
The Duchesse and I were talking when the two were announced. Alathea was in a nice little grey frock and had her glasses on. I think she knew the Duchesse would not approve of that camouflage, because there was an air of

defiance about her, her rebellious Cupid's bow of a mouth was shut sternly, she was even quite repellant,—she has never attracted me more!

The Duchesse was sweet to her and made no remark about the glasses, but was called back to the ward almost immediately for a little, and while she was gone Mr. Nelson read over the settlement.

"I think you are giving me a great deal too much," Alathea said annoyedly. "I shall feel uncomfortable,—and chained."

"I intend my wife to have this." I answered quietly. "So I am afraid you will have to agree."

She pulled in her lips but said no more until the part about the children came, when she started to her feet, her cheeks crimson.

"What is this ridiculous clause?" she asked angrily.

Old Mr. Nelson looked unspeakably shocked. "It is customary in all marriage settlements, my dear young lady," he said reprovingly, and Alathea looked at me with suspicion, but she said nothing, and the Duchesse, returning then to the room, all was soon signed, sealed and delivered! Mr. Nelson withdrew, saying he would call for Miss Bulteel next day for the wedding.

When we were alone the Duchesse kissed us both.

"I hope for your happiness, my children," she said. "I know you both, and your droll characters, the time will come when you may know each other, and in any case, I feel that you will both remember that *tenue*, a recognition of correct behaviour, helps all situations in life, and the rest is in the hands of the *Bon Dieu*."

Then she left us again, and Alathea sat stiffly down upon an uncompromising little Louis XV *canapé* out of my reach. I did not move or speak, indeed I lit a cigarette casually.

Alathea's face was a study! I watched her lazily. How had I ever thought her plain? Even in those first days, disguised with the horn spectacles, and the tornback hair, the contour of her little face is so perfectly oval, and her neck so round and long, but not too long. There is not the least look of scragginess about her, just extreme slenderness, a small-boned creature of perhaps five foot four or five, with childish outline. To-day in the becoming little grey frock, and even with the glasses on she is lovely, perhaps she seems so to me because I now know that the glasses are not necessary. The expression of her mouth said, "Am I being tricked? Does the man mean to seize me when he gets me alone? Shall I run away and have done with it?"

She was restless, her old serenity seems to have deserted her.

"I wanted to ask you," I began calmly, "What you would like to do immediately after the wedding. I mean would you prefer that we went to Versailles? The passport business makes everything so difficult, or would you rather go down to the Riviera? Or just stay at the flat?"

"I don't care in the least," she replied ungraciously.

"Then if you don't care, we will stay at the flat, because if I do not interrupt my treatment I shall be the sooner well to go to England. Have you engaged a maid?"

"Yes."

"You will give orders that your trunks are sent in in the morning, then, and that she has everything ready for you."

"Very well."

All this time her face was turned away from me as much as possible. For one second a fear came to me that after all perhaps it is real hate she has for me, which will be unsurmountable, and I was impelled to ask her:

"Alathea, do you detest the idea of marrying me so much that you would rather break the whole thing?"

She turned and faced me now, and I feel sure blue fire was coming from those beautiful eyes, could I have seen them!

"It is not a question of what I would wish or not, nor of my feelings in any way. I am going through with the ceremony, and shall be your permanent secretary, because I am under great monetary obligations to you, and wish for security for my family in the future. You put it to me that you wanted to buy me, and I could name the price—you have overpaid it. I shall not go back upon my promise, only I want to feel perfectly sure that you will expect nothing more of me than what we have arranged."

"I shall expect nothing more; your sense of the fitness of things will suggest to you not to make either of us look ridiculous in public by your being over disagreeable to me, we shall carry on with a semblance of mutual respect, I hope."

She bowed.

The temptation to burst out and tell her of my feelings was extraordinary. I absolutely trembled with the control it required not to rise from my chair and go and take her hands; but I restrained every sign and appeared as indifferent as she is. The Duchesse came back in a few moments and I said I would go.

I did not even then shake hands with Alathea, and the Duchesse came out into the passage with me, to see me safe into the lift, she is always so kind to anything crippled.

"Nicholas," she whispered, "Her manner to you is very cruel, but do not be discouraged!—I feel that it is more promising than if she were kind. She has also had a dreadful time with the father, who has now been transferred to the *poste* in the desert in Africa. One must hope for good, and her poor mother is going off to Hyères with little Hilda and their faithful old maid, the only servant they had, so after the wedding you will have your bride all to yourself!"

"Perhaps the thought of that is what is making her so reluctant and icy to-day!"

The Duchesse laughed as she handed me my crutch and closed the lift door. "Time will tell, my son!" and she waved her hand as I disappeared below.

And now I am alone before the crackling fire in my sitting-room,—and I wonder how many men have spent the eve of their marriages in so quiet a manner? I feel no excitement even. I have re-read this journal, it is a pretty poor literary effort, but it does chronicle my emotions, and the gradual growing influence Alathea has been exercising upon me. By putting down what happens between us each day like this, I can then review progress once a week, and can take stock of little shades which would not be remembered otherwise.

At that moment the telephone rang, and George Harcourt asked if he might come round and smoke a cigar.

"Your pre-war ones are so good, Nicholas," he said. He was in at the Ritz, from Versailles, for the night.

I answered "Yes." I like to talk to old George, I don't know why I call him old always, he is forty-eight perhaps, and absolutely well preserved, and women love him passionately, more perhaps than when he was young.

When we were settled in two comfortable arm chairs before the fire, he held forth as usual. He had arranged the affairs of Bobby Bulteel only in the nick of time. "I have all the receipts, Nicholas, to hand to you," he said.

"The wretched creature was overcome with gratitude. We had a long chat, and he plans to clear out and start life afresh in the Argentine as soon as War is over and he can be released from his commission. He is bound to end in hell with his temperament, but it won't matter so long as poor Lady Hilda is not dragged down too. He agreed to leave the family here unmolested now, and not return for years to them, when he does retire from the army."

Then I told my old friend that I intended to marry the daughter on the morrow. He was very surprised.

"I could not imagine what your interest could be, Nicholas, unless it had something to do with a woman, but where did you ever meet the girl, my dear boy?"

I explained.

"You might come to the wedding, George," I said.

He promised he would, then he smoked for a minute or two in silence. "Pretty terrible thing, marriage," and he puffed blue rings with perfect precision. "I have never been able to face it. What has made you slip into the mesh?"

"Because I think I have found someone who will be a good companion and not bore me."

"You are not in love then? It is a sensible arrangement, and in that way you have a chance of happiness; also the girl has had a hard life, and may be grateful for comfort and kindness."

"What do you suppose men really want, George?"

"The continuous stimulation of the hunting instinct, of course. It is satiety which kills everything, but what a small percentage of women know how to keep it alive, on the mental side!"

I waited for him to go on.

"You see, dear boy, love which is only the camouflaged aspect of the creative instinct, cannot really hold, but a clever woman acts as a spur to the mind, keeps it hunting in the abstract, as well as gratifying, not too generously, the physical desires. Unfortunately it has never been my good fortune to encounter such a being, so I have never been able to remain faithful. You are very much in luck if Bobby's girl shows intelligence. She ought to be a remarkable creature because she was born at the white heat of passion on both parents' side, and self-sacrifice and devotion added on the mother's."

"She is, George."

"My best wishes, Nicholas. I think you are wise, probably wounded as you are, it will be nice for you to have an agreeable companion," and he sighed.

"You have quite finished with Violetta?"

"Now that is the odd part," and he actually removed his cigar from his lips. "I thought I had, but when I went to see her with the certain intention of deceiving her and backing out gracefully,—that vixen Carmencita was drawing me so strongly!—I found Violetta quite tranquil. She said she had realized that I was cooling off, and her rule was to hold nothing which did not wish to stay, so she was quite prepared to part from me. She was very tender, she looked beautiful, and you know when it came to saying farewell, I found myself quite unable to do so! I had prepared a lot of lies about my not being justified in giving the time from my work, but before I could tell them Violetta had forestalled me by assuring me that she knew I must really stick closer to my office, and she would no longer expect much of my company. You know, Nicholas, I suddenly found her charm renewed tenfold, and I could only congratulate myself upon the fact that the affair with Carmencita had not gone far enough to amount to anything, and now I am in pursuit of Violetta again, and 'pon my soul, Nicholas, if she only keeps me wondering, I believe I shall be really in love!"

"Shall you marry, George?"

He looked almost bashful.

"It is just possible,—Violetta is a widow."

Then our eyes met and we both laughed aloud.

"You can contemplate happiness, George with your widow, because you feel that she now knows how to handle you, and I contemplate happiness with my little girl, because I respect her character and adore every inch of her, and by Jove! old man, I believe we shall both get what we are looking for!"

Then our talk drifted to politics and the war, and it was just about midnight before old George left, and when he had gone I opened the window wide, and looked out on the night, there was a half moon almost set, and the air was still, and very warm for the beginning of November. There are nights like that, mysterious and electric when all sorts of strange forces seem to be abroad. And something of romance in me exalted my spirit, and I found myself saying a prayer that I might be true to my trust, and have strength enough of will to wait patiently until my Alathea comes voluntarily into my arms.

And how I wonder what she is thinking about, there at Auteuil?

I went along into the room which is to be hers to-morrow, and I saw that it was all arranged, except the flowers, which would come in fresh in the morning. And then I hobbled back to my own room and rang for Burton. The faithful creature waits for me no matter how late I am.

When I was safely in bed, he came over to me, and his dear old face showed emotion.

"I do indeed wish you happiness, Sir Nicholas, to-morrow will be the best day of my life."

We shook hands silently, and he left me, still writing in this journal!

I feel no excitement, rather as if another act in the drama of life was ended, that is all, and that to-morrow I am starting upon a new one which will decide whether the end of the play shall be tragedy or content?

XXII

I am not going to describe the wedding in this Journal. A civil ceremony is not interesting in its baldness. I had literally no emotions, and Alathea looked as pale as her white frock. She wore a little sable toque and a big sable cloak I had sent her the night before, by Nelson. The ring was the new diamond hoop set in platinum. No more gold fetters for modern girls!

Old George and Mr. Nelson were our witnesses, and the whole thing was over in a few minutes, and we were being congratulated. Burton was by far the happiest face there, as he helped me into the automobile, lent by the Embassy. Alathea had just shaken hands with Mr. Nelson and been wished joy by George. I wonder what he thought of the glasses, which even for the wedding she had not taken off!

"May you know every happiness, Lady Thormonde," he said. "Take care of Nicholas and make him quite well, he is the best fellow on earth."

Alathea thanked him coldly. He is such a citizen of the world that he showed no surprise, and finally we were off on our way to the flat.

Here Madame Bizot and her daughter, and the baby, awaited us! And in the creature's tiny hand was a bunch of violets. This was the first time Alathea smiled. She bent and kissed the wee face. These people know and love her. I stayed behind a few moments to express my substantial appreciation of their friendly interest. Burton had been beside the chauffeur to help me in and out, and while we had been driving Alathea had not spoken a word. She had turned from me, and her little body was drawn back as far in the corner as possible.

My own emotions were queer. I did not feel actually excited. I felt just as I used when we were going to take up a new position on the line where great watchfulness would be necessary to succeed.

The maid Alathea had engaged arrived in the morning, and I had had the loveliest flowers put in all the rooms. Pierre intended to outdo himself for the wedding *déjeuner*, I knew, and Burton had been able to find somewhere a really respectable looking footman, not too obviously wounded.

Alathea handed me my crutch as we got out of the lift. Perhaps she thinks this is going to be one of her new duties!

We went straight into the sitting-room and I sat down in my chair. Her maid, named Henriette, had taken her cloak and hat in the hall, and I suppose from sheer nervousness, and to cover the first awkward moments, Alathea buried her face in the big bowl of roses on a table near another arm chair, before she sat down in it.

"What lovely flowers!" she said. They were the first words she had spoken to me directly.

"I wondered what would be your favorites. You must tell me for the future. I just had roses because they happen to be mine."

"I like roses best too."

I was silent for quite two minutes. She tried to keep still, then I spoke, and I could hear a tone of authority in my voice.

"Alathea, again I ask you please to remove your glasses, as I told you before, I know that you wear them only so that I may not see your eyes, not for sight or light or anything. To keep them on is a little undignified and ridiculous now, and irritates me very much."

She colored and straightened herself.

"To remove my glasses was not part of the bargain. You should have made it a condition if you had wanted to impose it. I do not admit that you have the least right to ask me to take them off, and I prefer to wear them."

"For what possible reason?"

"I will not tell you."

I felt my temper rising. If I had not been a cripple I could not have resisted the temptation to rise and seize her in my arms, tear the d—— d things off! and punish her with a thousand kisses. As it was, I felt an inward rage. What a fool I had been not to have actually made the removal of them a *sine qua non* before I signed the contract!

"It is very ungenerous of you, and shows a spirit of hostility which I think we agreed that you would drop."

Silence.

The desire to punish her physically, beat her, make her obey me, was the only thing I felt. A nice emotion for a wedding day!

"Do you mean to wear them all the time, even when we go out in the world?" I asked when I could control my voice.

"Probably."

"Very well then, I consider you are breaking the bargain in spirit, if not in the letter. You, yourself, said you were going to be my permanent secretary—no secretary in the world would insist upon doing something she knew to be a great irritation to her employer."

Silence.

"You are only lowering yourself in my estimation by showing this obstinacy. Since we have now to live together, I would rather not have to grow to despise you for childishness."

She started to her feet, and with violence threw the glasses on to the table. Her beautiful eyes flashed at me; the lashes are that peculiar curly kind, not black, but soft and dusky, a little lighter near the skin. It is the first time I have ever seen such eyelashes on a woman's lids. One sees them quite often on little boys, especially little vagabonds in the street. The eyes themselves are intensely blue, and with everything of passion and magnetism, and attraction, in them. It is no wonder she wore glasses while having to face the world by herself! A woman with eyes like that would not be safe alone in any avocation where men could observe her. I have never seen such expressive, fascinating eyes in my life. I thrilled in every fibre of my being, and with triumph also to think that our first battle should be won!

"Thank you," I said, making my voice very calm. "I had grown so to respect your balance and serenity, I should have been sorry to have to change my opinion."

I could see that she was palpitating with fury at having been made to obey. I felt it wise to turn the conversation.

"I suppose lunch will be ready soon."

She went towards the door then, and left me. I wondered what she would say when she got to her room and found the three sapphire bangles waiting for her on the dressing table!

I had written on a card inside the lid of the box:

"To Alathea with her husband's best wishes."

Burton announced lunch before she returned to the sitting-room. I sent him to say that it was ready, and a moment after she came in. She had the case in her hand which she put down on the table, and her cheeks were very pink, her eyes she kept lowered.

"I wish you would not give me presents," she gasped a little breathlessly, coming close up to my chair. "I do not care to receive them, you have loaded me with things—the sables, the diamond ring, the clothes, everything, and now these."

I took the case and opened it, removing the bangles.

"Give me your wrist," I said sternly.

She looked at me too surprised at my tone to speak.

I put out my hand and took her bare arm, her sleeves were to the elbows, and I deliberately put the three bracelets on while she stood petrified.

"I have had enough of your disagreeable temper," I said in the same voice. "You will wear these, and anything else I choose to give you, though your rudeness will soon remove my desire to give you anything."

She was absolutely flabbergasted, but I had touched her pride.

"I apologize if I have seemed rude," she said at last. "I—suppose you have the right really—only—" And her whole slender body quivered with a wave of rebellion.

"Let us say no more about the matter, but go into lunch, only you will find that I am not such a weakling, as you no doubt supposed you would have to deal with." I hobbled up from my chair, Burton discreetly not having entered the room. Alathea gave me my crutch, and we went in to the dining-room.

While the servants were in there I led the conversation upon the war news, and ordinary subjects, and she played the game, but when we were alone with the coffee, I filled her glass with Benedictine, which she had refused when Burton handed the liqueurs. She had taken no wine at all.

"Now drink whatever toast you like," I told her. "I am going to drink one to the time when you don't hate me so much and we can have a little quiet friendship and peace."

She sipped her glass, and her eyes became inscrutable. What she was thinking of I do not know.

I find myself watching those eyes all the time. Every reflection passes through them, they are as expressive of all shades of emotion as the eyes of a cat, though the beautiful Madonna tenderness I have never seen again since the day when she held the child in her arms, and I was rude to her.

When we went back into the salon I knew that I was passionately in love with her. Her restiveness is absolutely alluring, and excites all my hunting instinct. She looks quite lovely, and the subtle magnetism which drew me the first days, even when she appeared poor and shabby, and red of hand, is stronger than ever—I felt that I wanted to crush her in my arms and devour her, the blood thumped in my temples, I had to use every atom of my will with myself, and lay back in my chair and closed my eye.

She went straight to the piano and began to play. It seemed as though she were talking, telling me of the passion in her soul. She played weird Russian dances and crashed agonizing chords, then she played laments, and finally a soft and soothing thing of McDowell's, and every note had found an echo in me, and I had followed, it almost seemed, all her pain.

"You play divinely, child," I said, when she had finished. "I am going to rest now, will you give me some tea later on?"

"Yes," and her voice was quite meek, while she helped me with my crutch, and I went to the door of my room.

"I would like you to wear nice soft teagowns. My eye gets so wearied with everything bright after a while. I hope—you have got all you want, and that your room is comfortable?"

"Yes, thanks."

I bowed and went on into my room and shut the door. Burton was waiting to help me to lie down.

"It has been a very tiring day for you, Sir Nicholas," he said, "and for her Ladyship also."

"Go and have a rest yourself, Burton, you have been up since cock crow, the new man Antoine can call me at five." And soon I was in a land of blissful dreams.

Of course it was the very irony of fate that Suzette should have selected this very afternoon to come in and thank me for the Villa which she was just now going down to see—!

Antoine opened the door to her while Burton was out. I heard afterwards that she told him she had an appointment with me when he had hesitated about letting her in. She was quite quietly dressed and had no great look of the *demi-monde*, and a new footman, blunted with war service, was probably impervious even to the very strong scent which she was saturated with—that perfume which I had never been able entirely to cure her liking for, and which she reverted to using always when she went away from me, and had to be corrected of again and again when she returned.

Antoine came to my room by the passage, and said "a lady was in the salon to see me by appointment."

For a moment I was not suspicious. I thought it might be Coralie, and fearing Alathea might be somewhere about, and it might be awkward for her, I hastened to rise and go in to see and get rid of the inopportune guest. I told Antoine he must never let anyone in again without permission.

It was just growing dim in the salon, about half-past four o'clock, and a figure rose from the sofa by the fire as I entered.

"*Mon chou—mon petit cheri*!" I heard, simultaneously with a softly closing sound of the door behind the screen, which masks the entrance to the room from the hall—Antoine leaving I supposed at the time, probably it was Alathea I surmised afterwards!

"Suzette!" I exclaimed angrily. "Why do you come here?"

She flew to me and held out her arms, expressing affection and grateful thanks. She had come for no other reason only just to express her friendly appreciation! To get rid of her was all I desired. I never was more angry, but to show it would have been the poorest game. I did not tell her it was my wedding day. I just said I was expecting some relatives, and that I knew she would understand and would go at once.

"Of course," she said, and shook me by the hand. I was still standing with my crutch. She was passing to see her cousin Madame Angier, in the flat above, and could not resist the temptation to come in.

"It must be the very last time, Suzette," I said. "I have given you all that you wanted, and I would rather not see you again."

She pouted, but agreed, and I drew her to the door and saw her into the corridor, and even followed her to the front door. She was chatting all the time. I did not answer. I was speechless with rage, and could have sworn aloud, when at last I heard the door shut between us, then I strode back into my room, praying that Alathea *had* been unaware of my visitor.

Nemesis, on one's wedding day!

I waited until five and then went back into the sitting-room to my chair, and Antoine brought in the tea, and turned on the lights, and a moment or two afterwards Alathea came in. Her eyes were stony, and as she advanced up the room she sniffed the air disgustedly, her fine nostrils quivering. Suzette's pungent perfume was no doubt still present to one coming from outside!

Hauteur, contempt and disgust, expressed themselves in my little darling's blue eyes. There was nothing to be said—*qui s'excuse s'accuse—!*

She wore a soft lavender frock, and was utterly delectable, and when I reflected that but for this impassable barrier, which my own action in the past had been the means of erecting between us, I might now have made her love me, and that on this, our wedding day, she might have been coming into my arms. I could have groaned aloud.

"May I open the window," she said with the air of an offended Empress.

"Yes, do, open it wide," and then I laughed aloud cynically. I could as easily have cried.

Alathea would not of course have spoken about her suspicions, to do so would have inferred that she took an interest in me beyond that of a secretary; every impression she always has given me is that nothing in my life can matter to her one jot. But I know that this affair of Suzette does matter to her, that she resents it bitterly, that it is the cause of her smouldering anger with me. She resents it because she is a woman, and, how I wish I might believe that it is because she is not as indifferent towards me as she pretends.

She poured out the tea. I expect my face looked like the devil, I did not speak, I knew I was frowning angrily. A rising wind blew the curtain out and banged the window. She got up and shut it, then she threw some cedar dust on the fire from the box which it is kept in on a table near. She had seen Burton do this no doubt. I love the smell of cedar burning.

Then she came back and poured out the tea and we both drank it silently.

The room looked so comfortable and home like, with its panelling of old pitch pine, cleaned of its paint and mellowed and waxed, so that it seems like deep amber, showing up the greyish pear-wood carvings. One might have been in some room in old England of about . Everything looked the setting for a love scene. The glowing lamps, apricot shaded, and the firelight, and the yellow roses everywhere, and two human beings who belonged to one another and were young, and not cold of nature, sitting there with faces of stone, and in each one's heart bitterness. Again I laughed aloud.

The mocking sound seemed to disturb my bride. She allowed her tea cup to rattle as she put it down nervously.

"Would you like me to read to you," she asked icily.

And I said "Yes."

And presently her beautiful cultivated voice was flowing along. It was an article in the *Saturday Review* she had picked up, and I did not take in what it was about. I was gazing into the glowing logs, and trying to see visions, and gain any inspiration of how to find a way out of this tangle of false impression. I must wait and see, and endeavor when we get more accustomed to one another—somehow to let Alathea know the truth.

When she finished the pages she stopped.

"I think he is quite right," she said, but I had not heard what the argument was, so I could only say "Yes!"

"Will it interest you going to England?" I then asked.

"I dare say."

"I have a place there you know. Shall you care to live in it after the war is over?"

"I believe it is the duty of people to live in their homes if they have inherited them as a trust."

"And I can always count upon you to do your duty."

"I hope so."

Then I exerted myself and talked to her about politics and what were my views and aims. She entered into this stiffly, and so an hour passed, but all the time I could feel that her inner self was disturbed, and more resentful and rebellious than ever. We had been two puppets making conversation all the time, neither had said anything naturally.

At last the pretense ended, and we went to our separate rooms to dress for dinner.

Burton had returned by now, and I told him of the detestable thing which had happened, at which he was much concerned.

"Best of her sort was Mam'zelle, Sir Nicholas, but I've always said they bring trouble, every one of them,—if I may make so bold!"

And as I hobbled back into the salon to meet my wife for our first dinner alone, once more I heartily agreed with him!

XXIII

Alathea looked perfectly lovely when she came into the salon dressed for dinner. It is the first time I have seen her in anything pertaining to the evening. She had a gauzy tea-gown on, of a shade of blue like her eyes. Her nut brown hair was beautifully done, with the last "look" like Coralie's, showing her tiny head. Whether she likes it or no, I must give her some pearl earrings, and my mother's pearls. That will be a moment! But I had better wait a little while. Her eyes were shining with excitement or resentment, or a mixture of both. She was purely feminine. She intended to attract me I am certain, her subconscious mind did at all events, even though she would not have admitted it to herself. She was smarting still about Suzette. The situation fills her with distrust and uneasiness, but I know now, after analysing every point, when I could not sleep last night, that she is not really indifferent to me. And it is because she is not, that she is angry.

I registered a vow that I would *make* her love me without explaining about Suzette, fate can let her find out for herself.

I had not come to the comforting conclusion that she is not indifferent at the beginning of the evening though, so the sense of self-confidence and triumph did not uplift me then. I was still worried at the events of the afternoon.

I had troubled to put on a tail coat and white waistcoat, not a dinner jacket as usual, and had even a buttonhole of a gardenia, found by Burton for this great occasion!

I looked into her eyes with my one blue one, which is I suppose, as blue as her own. She instantly averted her glance.

"I cannot offer you my arm, milady," I said rather sarcastically, "So we will have to go in after each other."

She bowed and led the way.

The table was too beautifully decorated, and the dinner a masterpiece! while the champagne was iced to perfection, and the Burgundy a poem! The pupils of Alathea's eyes before the partridge came, were black as night. Burton discreetly marshalled Antoine out of the room each time after the dishes were handed.

"When will you get your new eye?" my wife—I like to write that!—asked in the first interval when we were alone, "and your new leg?"

"I suppose they will both be restored to me in a day or two. It will be so wonderful to walk again."

"I should think so."

Then something seemed to strike her suddenly, of how hateful it must all have been for me. Her hard expression changed and she almost whispered:

"It—will seem like a new life."

"I mean to make a new life, if you will help me. I want to get away from all the old useless days. I want to do things which are worth while."

"Shall you soon go into Parliament?"

"I suppose it will take a year or two, but we shall begin to pave the way directly we go back to England, and I hope that will be for Christmas."

She avoided looking at me. I could never catch her eye, but her adorable little profile was good enough to contemplate, the crisp curl by her ear delighted me, and another in the nape of her neck filled me with wild longings to kiss it, and the pearly skin beneath it!

I think I deserve great praise for the way I acted, for the whole thing was acting. I was cold, and as haughty and aloof as she was herself, but I used every art I knew of to draw her out and make her talk.

She is such a lady that she fell into the stride and spoke politely as if to some stranger who had taken her into dinner at a party.

At last we talked of the Duchesse, and we discussed her interesting character, such a marvel of the *ancien régime*!

"She is so very good and charitable," Alathea said, "and has always a twinkle in her eye which carries her through things."

"You laugh sometimes, too?" I asked with assumed surprise. "That is delightful! I adore the 'twinkle in the eye,' but I was afraid you would never unbend far enough so that we could laugh together!"

I think this offended her.

"Life would be impossible without a sense of humor, even if it is a grim one."

"Well, nothing need be grim any more, and we can both smile at the rather absurd situation between us, which, however, suits us both admirably. You will never interfere with me, or I with you."

"No—" There was a tone in this which let me feel that her thoughts had harked back to Suzette.

"The Duchesse is going to have a little tea party for us on Saturday, you know, so that you may be introduced as my wife."

Alathea became embarrassed at once.

"Will people know my real name?"

"No—we shall tell no stories, but we shall not be communicative. You will be introduced as an old English friend of the Duchesse's."

She looked at me for an instant and there was gratitude in her expression.

"Alathea, I want you to forget all about the troubles which must have clouded your life. They are all over now, and some day, perhaps you will introduce me to your mother and little sister."

"I will, of course when they come back from the South. My mother has often been so ill."

"I want you to feel that I would do anything for them. Are you sure they have all they want?"

She protested.

"Indeed—yes, far more. You have given too much already."

She raised her head with that indescribable little gesture of hauteur, which becomes her so beautifully. I could read her mind. It said, "I loathe receiving anything from him, with that woman in the background!"

When we went into the salon I wondered what she would do. I did not speak. She took my crutch and shook up my cushion, taking great care not to touch me. I could not look up. I knew that a powerful electric current would pass from my eye to hers, if I did, and that she would see that I was only longing to take her to my heart.

I remained silent and gazed into the fire. She sat down quietly on the sofa at the side, so that I would have to turn my head to look at her. Thus we remained for quite five minutes, speechless. The air throbbed with emotion. I dared not move.

At last she said, "Would you care that I should read to you again, or play?"

"Play for a little." My voice was chilly. I was quite determined the iciness should come from me first, not her, for a few days.

She went to the piano, and she began the Debussy she had played that afternoon when I had first asked her to play—I never can remember its name—and when she had finished she stopped.

"What made you play that now?" I asked.

"I felt like it."

"It wrenches my nerves. What makes you feel all unrestful and rebellious and defiant, Alathea, am I not keeping the bargain?"

"Yes, of course."

"You are bored to death then?"

"No, I am wondering."

"Wondering what?"

She did not answer. I could not see her without getting up out of my chair.

"Please come here," I asked in an indifferent cold voice. "You know it is so difficult for me to move."

She came back and sat down upon the sofa again. The light of the apricot lamp fell softly on her hair.

"Now tell me about what you were wondering."

Her mouth grew stubborn and she did not speak.

"It is so unlike you to do these very female things, beginning sentences and not going on. I never saw anyone so changed; once I looked upon you as the model for all that was balanced, and unlike your sex. It was I who used to feel nervous and ineffectual, now, ever since we have been engaged, you seem to be disturbed, and to have lost your serenity. Don't you think as it is the first evening that we are alone together that it would be a wise thing to try and get at each other's point of view? Tell me the truth Alathea, what has caused the alteration in you?"

Now she looked straight at me, and there was defiance in her expressive eyes.

"That is just what I was wondering about. It is true, I seem to have lost my serenity, I am self-conscious—I am conscious of you."

A delicious sensation of joy flowed through me, and the feeling of triumph began which is with me still. If she is conscious of me—!

"Do you mind if I smoke?" I asked with complete casualness to hide my emotions. She shook her head, and I lit a cigarette.

"You were uneasy because you did not trust me, you thought underneath there might be some trap, and that I would seize you once you belonged to me. There was a moment when I might have felt inclined to do so, though I would never have broken my word, but you have cured me of all that, and there is nothing to prevent our being quite good acquaintances,—even if your prejudice does not ever allow you to be friends."

For a second a blank look came into her expression. I was banking on my knowledge of the psychology of a human mind, the predatory instinct must inevitably be aroused in her by my attitude of indifference, if I can only act well enough and keep it up! I should certainly win in a fairly short space of time. But she is so attractive, I do not yet know if I shall have the strength of mind to do so.

"Are you not going to give me some regular work to do each day?" she asked with a tone of mock respect in her voice. "None of the letters have been answered lately, or the bills paid."

"Yes. I scrambled through them all myself while I was waiting, but if you will look over the book again, we might finally send it to a publisher."

"Very well."

"I don't want you to feel that you have ever to stay in or do any work you don't feel inclined for. We shall have lots of time, for the rest of our lives. No doubt to-morrow you would wish to spend with your mother, if she is going away."

"I said good-bye to her this morning. There is no need for me to go back. I came prepared to stay. Unless of course you would rather be alone, then I can go out for a walk." This last with a peculiar tone in the words.

"Naturally you will want to go for walks, and drives, and shopping. You don't imagine that I shall expect you to be a prisoner, just waiting on my beck and call!"

"Yes, that is how I took the bargain. It is quite unfair otherwise. I am here as a paid dependant and receiving really too high wages for any possible work I can give in return. I would not have entered into it otherwise or on any other terms. I loathe to receive favors."

"Madame Lucifer!"

She flashed blue sparks at me!

"I am not forced to command you to work you know," I went on "that is not part of the bargain, the bargain is entirely concerned with my not asking *you* to give me any favors, personal favors, like affection, or caresses, etcetera, or that I shall ever expect you to be really my wife."

She frowned.

"Well, you may put your mind entirely at rest, you have been so awfully disagreeable to me for so long, ever since we were at Versailles in the summer, that you don't attract me at all now, except your intellect and your playing. So if you will talk sometimes and play sometimes, that will be all right. I don't desire anything else. Now, assured about this, can't you be at ease and restful again?"

I know why she wore glasses. She cannot control the expression of her eyes! The pupils dilate and contract and tell one wonderful things! I know that this attitude of mine is having a powerful effect upon her, the feminine in her hates to feel that she has lost power over me—even over my senses. I could have laughed aloud, I was so pleased with my success, but I did not dare to look at her much, or I could never have kept the game up. She was more delectable than I can ever describe.

"It would interest me so much to know why your hands used to be so red," I asked after a little pause. "They are getting so much whiter now."

"I had work to do, dishes to wash, our old nurse was too ill, as well as my mother, and my little brother then—" there was a break in her soft voice. "I do not like red hands any more than you do. They distressed my father always. I will try to take care of them now."

"Yes—do."

The evening post had come in, and been put by Burton discreetly on a side table. He naturally thought such mundane things could not interest me on my wedding night. I caught sight of the little pile and asked Alathea to bring them to me.

She did. One from Coralie was lying on top and one immediately under it from Solonge de Clerté! Alathea saw that they were both in female writing. The rest were bills and business.

"Do you permit me to open them?" I asked punctiliously.

"Of course," and she reddened. "Are you not master here? How absurd to ask me!"

"It is not; you are Lady Thormonde, even if you are not my wife, and have a right to courtesy."

She shrugged her shoulders.

"Why did you put—'To Alathea from her husband' on the bracelets? You are 'Sir Nicholas' and not my husband."

"It was a *bêtise*, a slip of the pen; I admit you are right," and indifferently I opened Coralie's effusion, smiling over it. I put up my hand as if to shade my eye, and looked at Alathea through the fingers. She was watching me with an expression of slightly anxious interest. I could almost have believed that she was *jealous*!

My triumph increased.

I removed my hand and appeared only to be intent upon Coralie's letter.

"Perhaps we each have friends which might bore the other, so when you want to have parties tell me, and I will arrange to go out, and when I want to, I will tell you. In that way we can never have any jars."

"Thank you, but I have no friends except the Duchesse, or very humble people who don't want to come to parties."

"But you will be making plenty of new friends now. I have some which you will meet out in the world which I daresay you won't care about, and some who come and dine with me sometimes, who probably you would dislike."

"Yes,—I know."

"How do you know?" I asked innocently, affecting surprise.

"I used to hear them when I was typing."

I smiled. I did not defend them.

"If you should chance to meet, would you be civil to them?"

"Of course, 'Coralie,' 'Odette,' and 'Alice,' the Duchesse has often described them all! It was 'Coralie' who came to talk to you at Versailles in the park, was it not?"

Her voice was contemptuously amused and indifferent, but her little nostrils quivered. Underneath she was disturbed I knew.

"Yes, Coralie is charming, she knows more about how to put clothes on becomingly than any other woman."

"Do they dine often? Because I could perhaps arrange to go and have my music lesson with Monsieur Trani on those evenings, twice a week or oftener?"

"You would refuse to meet them?" I pretended to be annoyed.

"Certainly not, one does not do ridiculous things like that. I will meet whoever you wish. I only thought it might spoil your pleasure if I were there, unless of course you have told them that I am only a permanent secretary masquerading under the name of your wife—so that they need not restrain themselves."

Her face had become inscrutable. She was quite calm now. I grew uncertain again for a moment. Had I carried the bluff far enough?

"They have all quite charming manners, but as you infer they might not be so amused to come to the dinner of a married man. I think the last part of your speech was rather a reflection upon my sense of being a gentleman though. I of course have not informed anyone of our quaint relations.—But remember you told me once you did not think I was a gentleman, so I must not be offended now."

She did not speak, she was looking down and her eyelashes made a shadow on her cheeks. Her mouth was sad.

Suddenly something pathetic about her touched me. She is such a gallant little fighter. She has had such an ugly cruel life, and Oh! God she is growing to love me, and soon shall I be able to tell her that I worship the ground she walks on, and appreciate her proud spirit and great self-respect? But I cannot chance anything. I must go on and follow what I know to be sound psychological reasoning.

I felt my will weakening then, she looked so perfectly exquisite there in the corner of the sofa. We were alone.—It was nearly ten o'clock at night, the flowers were scenting the air, the lights were soft, the dinner had been perfection. After all I am a man, and she legally belongs to me. I felt the blood rushing wildly in my veins. I had to clench my hands and shut my eye.

"I expect you are tired now," I said a little breathlessly. "So I will say good-night—Milady, and hope that you will sleep well the first night in your new home."

I got up and she came forward quickly to hand me my crutch.

"Good-night," she whispered quite low, but she never looked at me, then she turned and went slowly from the room, never glancing back. And when she had gone instead of going to bed I once more sank into my chair. I felt queerly faint, my nerves are not sound yet I expect.

Well, what a strange wedding night!

Burton's face was a mask when he came to undress me. Among the many strange scenes he has witnessed and assisted at, after forty years spent in ministering to the caprices of the aristocracy, I believe he thinks this is the strangest!

When I was in bed and he was about to go, I suddenly went into a peal of bitter laughter. He stopped near the door.

"Beg pardon, Sir Nicholas?" he said as though I had called to him.

"Aren't women the weirdest things in the world, Burton!"

"They are indeed, Sir Nicholas," and he smiled. "One and all, from Mam'zelle to ladies like her Ladyship, they do like to feel that a man belongs to themselves."

"You think that is it, Burton?"

"Not a doubt of it, Sir Nicholas."

"How do you know them so well, never having married, you old scallywag!"

"Perhaps that's why, Sir. A married man looses his spirit like—and his being able to see!"

"I seem lonely, don't I Burton," and I laughed again.

"You do, Sir Nicholas, but if I may make so bold as to say so, I don't think you will be so very long. Her Ladyship sent out for a cup of tea directly she got to her room."

And with an indescribable look of blank innocence in his dear old eyes, this philosopher, and profound student of women, respectfully left the room!

XXIV

The day after my marriage I did not come into the salon until just before luncheon, at half-past twelve o'clock. My bride was not there.

"Her Ladyship has gone out walking, Sir Nicholas," Burton informed me as he settled me in my chair.

I took up a book which was lying upon the table. It was a volume of Laurence Hope's "Last Poems." It may have come in a batch of new publications sent in a day or two ago, but I had not remarked it. It was not cut all through, but someone had cut it up to the th page and had evidently paused to read a poem called "Listen Beloved," the paper knife lay between the leaves. Whoever it was must have read it over and over, for the book opened easily there, and one verse struck me forcibly:

"Sometimes I think my longing soul remembers
A previous love to which it aims and strives,
As if this fire of ours were but the embers
Of some wild flame burnt out in former lives.
Perchance in earlier days I *did* attain
That which I seek for now, so all in vain.
Maybe my soul and thine were fused and wed
In some great night, long since dissolved and dead."

And then my eye travelled on to the bottom of the page.

"Or has my spirit a divine prevision
Of vast vague passions stored in days to be
When some strong souls shall conquer their division
And two shall be as one eternally."

We are both strong souls, shall we have the strength to conquer outside things and be really "one eternally"?

Alathea must have been looking at this not an hour or more ago, what did it make her think of, I wonder?

I determined to ask her to read the whole poem presently, when we should be sitting together in the afternoon.

It had come on to rain and was a wretched dismal day, I wondered why Alathea had gone out. Probably she is as restless as I am, and being free to move, she can express her mood in rapid walking!

I began to plan my course of action.

To go on disturbing her as much as possible—

To give her the impression that I once thought her perfection, but that she herself has disillusioned me, and that I am indifferent to her now.

That I am cynical, but am amused to discuss love in the abstract.

That I have friends who divert me, and that I really only want her to be a secretary and companion, and that any interest I may show in her is merely for my own vanity, because she is, to the world, my wife!

If I can only keep this up, and not soften should I see her distressed, and not weaken or give the show away, I must inevitably win the game, perhaps sooner than I dare hope!

I felt glad she had not been there, so that I could pull myself together, and put my armour on, so to speak, before we met.

I heard her come in just before luncheon and go to her room, and then she came on to the sitting-room without her hat.

Her taste is as good as Coralie's, probably her new clothes come from the same place, she appeared adorable, and now that I can observe her at leisure, she seems extremely young,—the childish outline, and the perfect curve of the little cheek! She does not look over eighteen years old, in spite of the firm mouth and serene manner.

I had the poems in my hand.

"I see you have been reading these," I remarked after we had given each other a cold good-morning.

The pupils of her eyes contracted for a second, she was annoyed with herself that she had left the paper cutter in the book.

"Yes."

"After lunch will you read to me?"

"Of course."

"You like poetry?"

"Yes, some."

"This kind?"

Her cheeks became softly pink.

"Yes, I do. I daresay I should have more classical tastes, but these seem real, these poems, as if the author had meant and felt what she was writing about. I am no judge of poetry in the abstract, I only like it if it expresses some truth, and some thought—which appeals to me."

This was quite a long speech for her!

"Then poems about love appeal to you?" I asked surprised.

"Why not?"

"Why not indeed, only you always have seemed so austere and aloof, I hardly thought such a subject would have interested you!"

She gave a little shrug of her shoulders.

"Perhaps even the working bees have dreams."

"Have you ever been in love?"

She laughed softly, the first time I have ever heard her laugh. It gave me a thrill.

"I don't think so! I have never talked to any men. I mean men of our class."

This relieved me.

"But you dream?"

"Not seriously."

Burton announced luncheon at that moment, and we went in.

We spoke of the rain, and she said she liked being out in the wet. She had walked all down the *Avenue Henri Martin* to the *Bois*. We spoke of the war news, and the political situation, and at last we were alone again in the salon.

"Now read, will you please."

I lay back in my chair and shaded my eye with my hand.

"Do you want any special poem?"

"Read several, and then get to 'Listen Beloved,' there is a point in it I want to discuss with you."

She took the book and settled herself with her back to the window, a little behind me.

"Come forward, please. It is more comfortable to listen when one can see the reader."

She rose reluctantly, and pulled her chair nearer me and the fire, then she began. She chose those poems the least sensuous, and the more abstract. I watched her all the time. She read "Rutland Gate," and her voice showed how she sympathized with the man. Then she read "Atavism," and her little highly bred face looked savage! I realized with a quiver of delight that she is the most passionate creature,—of course she is, with that father and mother! Wait until I have awakened her enough, and she will break through all the barriers of convention and reserve, and pride.

Ah! That will be a moment!

"Now read 'Listen Beloved.'"

She turned the pages, found it, and began, and when she reached the two verses which had so interested me, she looked up for a second, and her lovely eyes were misty and far away. Then she went on and finished, letting the book drop in her lap.

"That accords with your theory of reincarnation, that souls meet again and again?"

"Yes."

"In one of the books I got upon the subject it said all marriages were karmic debts or rewards. I wonder what our marriage is, don't you? Perhaps we were two enemies who injured each other, and now have to make up by being of use, each to each."

"Probably," she was looking down.

"Do you ever have that strange feeling that you are searching for something all the time, something of the soul, that you are unsatisfied?"

"Yes, often."

"Read those last verses again."

Her voice is the most beautiful I have ever heard, modulated, expressive, filled with vibrant vitality and feeling, but this is the first time she has read anything appertaining to love. I could hear that she was restraining all emphasis, and trying to give the sensuous passionate words a commonplace cold interpretation. Never before has she read so monotonously. I knew, ("sensed" is the modern word), that this was because she probably felt and understood every line and did not want to let me see it. Suddenly I found myself becoming suffused with emotion.

Why all the delay, the fencing, the fighting, to obtain this desired thing! This woman—my mate!

That she is my mate I know. My mate because my love is not based upon the senses alone, but is founded upon reverence and respect. I hope—believe—I *am certain* that we shall one day realize the truth of the words:

"When some strong-souls shall conquer their division,
And two shall be as one eternally!
Finding at last upon each others breasts
Unutterable calm and infinite rest."

For me, that means love, not the mere gratifying of the hunting instinct, not the mere primitive passion for the longed for body, but a union of the souls, which can be satisfied, having soared beyond the laws of change.

What is it which causes unrest? Obviously because something is wanting upon one of the planes on which we love, and so that part which is unsatisfied, unconsciously struggles to have its hunger assuaged elsewhere.

There is no aspect of mind, body and soul in me, which I feel would find no counterpart in Alathea. If I reached out to any height spiritually, she could go as high, or higher. The cleverest working of the brain I could hope to manifest would find a complete comprehension in her. And as for the body! Any student of physiognomy can see that those delicate little nostrils show passion, and that cupid's bow of a mouth will delight in kisses!

Oh! My loved one, do not make we wait too long!

Ye Gods! What a state of exaltation I was in when I wrote those lines last night! But they are the truth, even if I now laugh at my expansion!

I wonder how many men are romantic underneath like I am and ashamed to show it?

When Alathea had finished the verses for the second time, she again dropped the book in her lap.

"What is your conception of love?" I asked casually.

"As I shall always have to crush it out of my life from now onward I would rather not contemplate what my conception of it might have been."

"Why must you crush it out?" I asked blandly. "Your fidelity to me was not part of the bargain, fidelity has to do with the sex relationships, which do not concern us. One would not ask a secretary to become a nun, on account of one. One would only ask her to behave decently, so as not to shock the world's idea of the situation she was supposed to be filling."

Her face grew subtle, a look came into the eyes which might have come into George's or mine. I suddenly realized how well she really knows the world from the hard school the circumstances of her life have caused her to learn in.

"Then I may take a lover, some day, should I desire to?" she asked a little cynically.

"Certainly, if you tell me about it and don't deceive me, or make me look ridiculous. The bargain would be too unfair to you at your age otherwise."

She looked straight into my eye now and hers were a little fierce.

"And you—shall you take a mistress?"

I watched the smoke of my cigarette curling.

"Possibly," I answered lazily, as though the matter were too much a foregone conclusion to discuss. "Should you mind?"

A faint movement showed in her throat as if she had stopped herself swallowing. She looked down. I know she finds it very difficult to lie, and could not possibly do so if we were gazing at each other.

"Why should I mind?"

"No of course, why should you?"

She looked up then, but not at me. Her eyes flashed and her lip curled in contempt.

"Two seems vulgar though," she snapped.

"I agree with you, the idea wounds my aesthetic senses."

"Then we need not expect another—in the flat just yet?"

At last it was out!

I appeared not to understand, and smoked on calmly, and before I could answer the telephone rang. She handed me the instrument, and I said "Hello." It was Coralie! She spoke very distinctly, and Alathea, who was near, must have been able to hear most of the words in the silence.

"Nicholas, I am going to be by myself this evening, you will have a dinner for me? Just us alone, *hein?*"

I permitted my face to express pleasure and amusement. *My wife* watched me agitatedly.

"*Non, chère Amie*—Alas! To-night I am engaged. But I shall see you soon."

"*Est il vrai—ce mensonge-la?*"

Coralie said this loud!

I put up my hand so as to be able to continue observing Alathea's face. It was the picture of disgust and resentment.

"Yes, it is perfectly true, Coralie—*Bon soir.*"

In a temper, one could gather, Coralie put the receiver down! And I laughed aloud.
"You see I prefer your intellectual conversation to any of my friends!" I told Alathea.
Alathea's cheeks were a bright pink.
"It is not that," her tone was sarcastic, "so much as that you probably have a sense of *tenue*, as the Duchesse says. After a little while you will not have to observe it so strictly," and she rose from her chair and went to the window. "If you are going to rest now, I would wish to go out," her voice was a little hoarse.
"Yes, do go, and if you will be near the *rue de la Paix* go into Roberts' and ask if the new menthol preparation has come, and if so bring it back to me, it takes ages for things to be sent now."
"I was not going to the *rue de la Paix*. I was going to a hospital."
"Never mind then, and don't hurry back, Burton will give me my tea. So *au revoir* until dinner Miladi."
I had to say all this because I was at breaking point, and could not any longer have kept up the game, but would have made an ignominious surrender, and have told her I loved her, and loathed the idea of a mistress, and would certainly murder any lover she should ever glance at!
She went from the room without a word more. And left alone I tried to sleep, but it was no good. I was too excited. I don't think I am such a fool as to flatter myself. I am trying to look at the situation abstractedly. And it seems to me that Alathea is certainly interested in me, certainly jealous of Suzette, of Coralie, furious with herself for being so, really convinced now that she has lost her hold upon me,—and is uneasy, rebellious, disturbed and unhappy!
All this is perfectly splendid,—my darling little girl!
After a while I went to sleep in my chair, and was awakened by Burton coming in to turn on the lamps.
"Her Ladyship has ordered tea in her room, Sir Nicholas," he told me, "Shall I bring yours here?"
"Her Ladyship has come in then?" I said.
"Her Ladyship did not go out, Sir," Burton answered surprised.
What did this mean I wondered? But I saw no sign of Alathea until she came in ready for dinner as the clock struck eight.
She was pale but perfectly composed, she had evidently been having some battle with herself and had won.
All through dinner she talked more politely and indifferently than she has for a long time. She was brilliantly intelligent, and I had a most delightful repast. We both came up to the scratch, I think.
She longs to visit Italy, she told me; she has not been there since she was a child. I said I would take her directly the war would be over, and things in the way of travel had become possible again. How strong her will must be to have so mastered herself. No slightest sign of emotion, one way or another, showed now. She was the serene, aloof companion of the day at Versailles, before Suzette's shadow fell upon us. I grew puzzled, as the evening wore on, and just a little unsure of myself. Had I gone too far? Had I over disgusted her? Had all interest died out, and so is she enabled to fulfill the bargain without any more disturbance of mind?
I asked her to play to me at last, I was growing so apprehensive, and she went from one divine thing to another for quite an hour, and then at ten o'clock stopped and said a dignified and casual "good-night" leaving me sitting in my chair.
I heard twelve and one strike after I too went to bed, no sleep would come, I was reviewing things, and strengthening my courage. Then I got up and hobbled into the salon to get the "Last Poems," the door was open, why I don't know, nor do I know what impelled me to go out into the passage and towards Alathea's room, some powerful magnet seemed to draw me. The carpets are very deep and soft, no noise of footfalls can be heard. I crept near the door and stopped. What was that faint sound? I listened, yes it was a sob. I crept nearer.
Alathea was crying.
A soft continued moaning as of one in resigned distress. I could hardly bear it. I could hardly prevent myself from opening the door and going to her to comfort her.
My darling, darling little girl!
Flight was my only resource. So I left her to her tears, and returned to my bed, and when I was safely there and could think, a wild sense of triumph and power and satisfaction filled me! The weight, which all the evening her marvelous self-control had been able to make me feel, lifted from my heart, and I rejoiced!
Is it possible that the primitive instinct of the joy of conquest could make of me such a brute!
It gave me pleasure to know that my little love suffered!
The sooner would she belong to me—quite!

XXV

Marriage is the most turbulent state I could have imagined! Whether or not Alathea and I will ever get the tangle straightened out I am not certain. Now as I write—Saturday afternoon, the ninth of November, —it looks as if we were parted forever, and I am so irritated and angry that as yet I feel no grief.
The quarrel all arose from my fault, I suppose. When Alathea came into the sitting-room at about ten o'clock she had blue circles round her eyes, and knowing what caused them I determined to ask her about them and disturb her as much as possible! This was mean of me.
"You poor child! You look as if you had been crying all night. I do hope nothing is troubling you?"
Her cheeks flushed.
"Nothing, thank you."
"Your room cannot be properly aired then, or something. I have never seen you looking so wretchedly. I do wish you would be frank with me. Something must have worried you. People don't look like that for nothing."
She clasped her hands together.
"I hate this talk about me. What does it matter how I look, or am, so long as I do the things I am engaged for?"

I shrugged my shoulders. "I suppose it ought not to, but one has a feeling that one hates anyone under one's roof to be unhappy."

"I am not unhappy. I mean not more unhappy than I have always had to be."

"But the causes which made you sad before have been removed surely, only things which are occurring now from day to day between you and me, can bring fresh trouble. Is it something I have done?"

Silence.

"Alathea, if you knew how you exasperate me by your silences! I was always taught that it was very rude not to answer when one was spoken to."

"It depends upon who speaks, and what about, and whether they have a right to an answer."

"Then the inference is that I have no right to an answer, when you are silent?"

"Probably."

I grew irritated.

"Well, I think I have a right, I ask you a plain question—have I done anything which has caused you distress—distress which is so evident that you must have been crying!"

She threw up her arms.

"Why on earth cannot you keep to business, it is quite unfair. If I were really your secretary and nothing more you would never persecute me for answers like this!"

"Yes I would. I have a perfect right to know why anyone in my service is unhappy. Your fencing tells me that it *is* something which I have done which has hurt you, and I insist upon knowing what it is."

"I shall not tell you," defiantly.

"I am very angry with you, Alathea," my voice was stern.

"I don't care!" hers was passionate.

"I think you are very rude."

"You have told me that before—well I am rude then! I will tell you nothing. I will do nothing but just be your servant to obey orders which relate to the work I have been engaged for."

I felt so furious I had to lie back in my chair and shut my eye.

"You have a very poor sense of a bargain, if you only keep it in the letter. Your underneath constant hostility makes everything so difficult, the inference of your whole attitude toward me, and of everything you say and do, is that you feel injured, that you have some grudge against me."

I tried to speak levelly.

"What on earth have I ever done to you except treat you with every courtesy? Except that one day when you had the baby in your arms and I was rude, but apologized, and that one other time when I kissed you, and God knows I was sorry enough afterwards and have regretted it ever since. What *is* the reason of your attitude; it is absolutely unfair?"

This seemed to upset her considerably. She hated the idea that she was thought unfair. It may have made her realize too that she *had* a definite sense of injury. She lost her temper, she stamped her scrap of a foot.

"I hate you!" she burst out. "You and your bargain! I wish I was dead!" and then she sank into the sofa and covered her face with her hands, and by the shaking of her shoulders, I saw that she was crying!

If I had been cool enough to think then, I suppose I could have reasoned that all this was probably most flattering to me, and an extra proof of her state of mind, but the agitation it had plunged me into made me unable to balance things, and I too allowed my temper to get the better of me, and I got up as best I could and seizing my crutch, I walked towards my bedroom door.

"I shall expect an apology," was all I said, and went in and left her alone.

If we are to go on fighting like this, life won't be worth living!

I tried to calm myself and went in the window, but the servants came into the room to make the bed, so I was forced to go back again to the sitting-room. Alathea had gone into the little salon, I suppose, because for the same reason, she could not have returned to her room. I sat down in my chair quite exhausted. I did not feel like reading or doing anything.

It was to-day that we were to go to the Duchesse's in the afternoon for Alathea to be presented to our friends as my wife! I wondered if she had forgotten this!

After an hour Burton came in with the second post.

"You do look badly, Sir Nicholas!" he said. His face was perplexed and troubled. "Can I get you anything?"

"Where is Her Ladyship, Burton?"

Then he told me that she had gone out. I could see he wanted to say something. His remarks are generally valuable.

"Out with it, Burton."

"I do think it is Mam'zelle that's causing all the trouble. As bad luck would have it, as I opened the door to let Her Ladyship out, who should come up the stairs a moment after but Mam'zelle! They must have passed on the floor below. Neither had taken the lift, which as you know, Sir Nicholas, is out of order again, since last night."

"Then she thinks Suzette has come in here to see me Burton. By Jove what a devilish complication! I think we had better move from the flat as quickly as we can."

"It seems as if it would be advisable, Sir Nicholas."

"Can you suggest anything, Burton? I really am quite knocked over to-day."

"Her Ladyship don't chat to servants like some ladies, or I could easily let her maid know that Mam'zelle don't visit here, so that won't do," he mused. "You could not tell her yourself straight out. Sir Nicholas, could you?"

"It would be difficult, because it presupposes I think she minds about it, and for me to let her know that would insult her more than anything."

"Beg pardon, Sir Nicholas, but there was a young woman some twenty years ago, who had a temper like, and I always found it was best just to make a fuss of her, and not do no reasoning. That is what they wants, Sir Nicholas, indeed it is. I've watched them in all classes for a matter of many years. You can get what you want of them if you only make a fuss of them."

"What does 'to make a fuss of' exactly mean Burton?"

"Well, it is not for me to tell you Sir, knowing ladies as you do, but it is just kissing and fondling them, and them things, makin' them feel that they're just everything,—even reasonable, Sir Nicholas."

Burton's dryly humorous face delighted me. His advice was first class, too!

"I'll think it over," I told him, and he left me alone.

That would be one way of winning or losing everything certainly! But it would also be breaking my word, and I don't believe I could do that.

Alathea came in in time for luncheon. Her face was set in a mutinous obstinate mould. We went into the dining-room immediately, and so there was no chance of conversation. I noticed that she wore no bracelets or rings, nothing of mine, not even the wedding ring.

We were icy to each other during the meal, and made conversation, and when we were alone with the coffee I just said:

"I hope that you have not forgotten that at four o'clock we are to go to the Duchesse's to meet the friends that she thinks it is suitable for you to know."

Alathea started. I could see she had not registered this fact for this date.

"I would rather not go," she said resentfully.

"I daresay you would. So would I, but we owe the Duchesse gratitude for all her kindness to us, and I fear we must."

We did not speak further. I could not talk until she apologized, and I rose to go out of the room. She gave me my crutch. Her not apologizing made me burn with resentment.

I had not been in the salon a minute, however, before she came in, her face crimson. She stood in front of me.

"I apologize for showing my temper this morning. Would it not do after to-day if I just lived out somewhere, and came in and worked as before? It is a perfect farce that I live here, and wear a wedding ring, even the servants must be laughing at me."

"I notice you do not wear a wedding ring. Your whole attitude is perfectly impossible, and I demand an explanation. What is the reason of it? We made a bargain, and you are not keeping it."

"If you will give me time to work, I will pay you back the fifty thousand francs, and the clothes and jewels I can leave behind me—I want to go."

She spoke with a break in her voice now.

"Why do you want to go suddenly, there is nothing different to-day to yesterday or any other day? I refuse to be the puppet of your caprices."

She stood clasping and unclasping her hands, never looking at me.

"Alathea," I said sternly, "look me straight in the face and tell me the truth. *What* is your reason."

"I can't" still her eyes were down.

"Is there someone else?" My voice sounded fierce to my own ears. I had a sudden fear.

"But you said it would not matter if there was someone else—if I told you," she answered defiantly.

"There is someone else then?" I tried to be casual. "Look at me."

Slowly she raised her eyes until they met my one.

"No, there is no one.—I just don't want to live here, in this flat any longer."

"Unless you can give me some definite reason for this extraordinary behaviour on your part, I am afraid I must refuse to discuss the situation, and meanwhile will you please go to your room and fetch the rings and bracelets."

She turned and left without a word—I daresay she wondered what I was going to do with them.

She brought them back.

"Come here close."

She came rebelliously.

"Give me your hand."

"I won't."

"Alathea, I will seize it, crippled as I am, and make you obey me by force if you will not for asking."

Her whole face expressed furious resentment, but she is too sensible and level headed to make a scene, so she gave me her hand. I put the wedding ring back, and the big diamond one.

"Now you will wear them until you convince me of your reason so thoroughly that I myself take them off, the bracelets you can do as you like about—throw them away, or give them to your maid. And this afternoon I hope I can count upon your instincts of being a lady to make you behave so that no one can chatter about us."

She drew away her hand, as though my touch burnt her. Her expression was contemptuously haughty.

"Of course you can count upon me for this afternoon," and she turned and went out of the room again.

And now I am waiting for her to come back dressed for the Duchesse's reception, it is ten minutes to four o'clock. The volcano upon which we are living cannot go on simmering much longer, there is bound to be an explosion soon!

Later:

Things are developing! My bride and I never spoke a word on the way to the Hotel de Courville. She was looking the most desirable morsel a man could wish to present to his friends. The sable cloak and the most perfect frock and hat. Her maid is evidently a splendid hairdresser. She was "of a *chic*," as Maurice afterwards told me.

I had telephoned and broken the news to him while I was waiting for Alathea to come. He was not surprised, he pretended, and now that the marriage is an accomplished fact, he is too well bred not to fall into the attitude of delight about it. Maurice has no intention of dropping me—married or single!

Thus when we arrived, and went up in the lift to the sitting-room, we found him among the first to greet us.

The Duchesse kissed us both fondly, and said many pleasant things, and having placed me in a suitable chair, brought everyone to me, and presented Alathea to them all.

They were the very *crême de la crême* of the Faubourg who could be collected in Paris—many are still in the country. Coralie was there, with two resentful pinpoints in her clever little eyes, but the most gracious words on her lips.

They none of them could find fault with the appearance of my wife—nor her manner. She has the ways of the *ancien régime* like the Duchesse. I could see that she was having a huge success.

While everything seemed to be going beautifully and all the company had gone on into another small anti-room where the "*goûter*" was, my dear old friend came to me.

"It is not progressing Nicholas—*Hein*?"

"There is some screw very loose, Duchesse. She absolutely hates me and wants to go and live out of the flat!"

"*Tiens*!—She is jealous of some one. Nicholas, it is not possible that you have still—?"

I did not grow angry.

"No indeed, that is over long ago, but I do believe she thinks it is not. You see the person in question comes to see a relative who has married an *antiquaire* on the floor above me, and Alathea has seen her on the stairs and imagines she comes to see me!"

"And you cannot tell her?"

"I am not supposed to know it would matter to her!"

"*Bon*. Do you really love the child, Nicholas?"

"*Chère Amie*, with my whole heart. I only want her in all the world."

"And she is being impossible for you surely! I know her character—if she thinks you have a mistress—her pride is of *le diable*!"

"It is indeed."

The Duchesse laughed.

"We must see what can be done, dear boy. Imagine though what I have discovered! That infamous father took that money that you gave, when the affair had already been settled by *le Colonel* Harcourt with your money! A relation of mine attested at the investigation and had to know the facts. Nicholas, you *preux chevalier*! You paid twice, and never said a word! You are of a devotion! It was splendid of you, but my poor Hilda is heartbroken that you have been so pillaged."

At that moment the crowd returned from the other room and the Duchesse rose and left me.

Coralie now sat with me.

"*Mes compliments*, Nicholas! She is lovely! But what a fox,—thou!"

"Am I not? It is so delicious to find things out for oneself!"

Coralie laughed; she has a philosophic spirit, as I have found always those much love-battered ones possess. She accepts my defection and again looks to the main chance to see how she can benefit by it.

At last the whole thing was over, and Maurice and I had a cigarette together in the tea room.

People would be crazy, "simply crazy, my dear chap," about Alathea, he told me. She was "*séduisante*," how right I had been! How fortunate I was! When was I going to England?

He said farewells after this, and once more *my wife* and I were alone in the brougham.

Alathea wore her mask. Having been received now as my wife, and by the Duchesse whom she loves and respects, she knows she cannot go on suggesting she will not live in the flat with me. She cannot bring herself to speak about Suzette, because the inference would be that she objects. I wondered if the Duchesse had been able to say anything to her.

She did not speak at all and went straight to her room when we arrived.

It was five minutes past eight when she came in to the sitting-room.

"I am sorry if I have kept you waiting," were her first words.

At dinner we spoke ceremoniously of the party. And when we went back to the salon she went straight to the piano and played divinely for an hour.

The music soothed me. I felt less angry and disturbed.

"Won't you come over and speak now?" I called in a pause, and she came over and sat down.

"Don't let us talk to-night," she said. "I am trying to adjust things in my mind. I want to go to my mother to-morrow, if you will agree. She is ill again, and has not been able to start. From there I will tell you if I can force myself to keep on with it, or no."

"I cannot understand why it should be so difficult, the idea did not affright you when we first talked of it. You voluntarily accepted the proposal, made your bargain, promised to stick to it, and here after three days you are trying to break out, and are insinuating that the circumstances are too horrible for you to continue bearing it. Surely your reason and common sense must tell you that your behaviour is grotesque."

The same agitation which always shows when we talk thus overcame her again. She did not speak.

"I could understand it better if you were a hysterical character. You did not seem to be so, but now no ridiculous school miss of romance could be more given to the vapours. You will absolutely destroy the remaining respect I have for you, unless you tell me the truth, and what is underneath in your mind influencing you to behave so childishly."

This stung her to the quick, as I had meant that it should. She bounded up.

"Well,—I will then. I hate being in the house—with your mistress!"

She was trembling all over, and as white as marble.

I leaned back and laughed softly. My joy was so immense I could not help it.

"To begin with, I have no mistress, but if I had how can it possibly matter to you, since you hate me, and yourself arranged to be only my secretary."

"You have no mistress!" I could see she thought I was lying ignobly.

"I had one, as of course you know, but the moment I began to think that you might be an agreeable companion, I parted from her, at the time when you saw the counterfoils in the cheque-book, and changed to me from that moment."

"Then—?" she still looked incredulous.

"She has a cousin living in the flat above, married to an *anticaire*. She comes to see her. You have no doubt met on the stairs. And on our wedding day she came in here, not knowing, to thank me for a villa I had given her at Monte Carlo as a good-bye present. I am very angry that she intruded, and it shall never happen again."

"Is this true?" She was breathless.

That made me angry.

"I am not in the habit of lying," I said haughtily.

"*Mademoiselle la Blonde*," and her lips curled. "She came in while you were at St. Malo. She inferred you had not parted then!"

"That was because she was jealous, and is very temperamental. I had thought that quality was confined to her class."

I too can hit hard when I am insulted!

Alathea flashed at me. She was beginning to realize that she was at a disadvantage.

"You are not unutterably shocked that I should have had a—friend, are you?"

Her face grew contemptuous.

"No, my father had one. Men are all beasts."

"They may be in the abstract, but are not when they can find a woman worth love and respect."

She shrugged her shoulders.

"My mother is an angel."

"Now that your mind is at rest as to this question, have you any other cause of complaint against me? Though why it should matter to you what I do or don't do in this respect, as long as I am courteous to you, and fulfill my side of the bargain, I cannot think. One could imagine you were jealous!"

"Jealous!" she flared furiously. "Jealous, I! How ridiculous.—One has to care to be jealous!" and then she flounced out of the room.

Yes,—even when they appear all that is balanced, there is nothing so amazing as a woman!

XXVI

Sunday:

I slept last night soundly for some strange reason, and woke quite late on Sunday morning.

One frequently has some sense of depression or some sense of exhaltation before one is quite conscious, and quite often cannot account for either state. Presumably Alathea had left me full of contemptuous indifference, but I awoke with a feeling of joy and satisfaction, which gradually changed to flatness, when I became fully aware of things.

For indeed what reason had I for great rejoicing? None, except that the menace of the Suzette bogie may be lifted.

I rang for Burton. It was nine o'clock.

"Has Her Ladyship breakfasted yet, Burton?"

"Her Ladyship breakfasted at eight, and left the house at half-past, Sir Nicholas."

My heart sank. So I was going to have a lonely morning. She had said she wanted to go to her mother, I remembered now. I did not hurry to get up. The doctors were coming with the wonderful artist who is making my new foot, at twelve o'clock, and I am to have it on to-day for the first time. This would be a surprise for Alathea when she returned to lunch. I read my journal in bed, and thought over the whole of our acquaintance. Yes, certainly she has greatly changed in the last six weeks. And possibly I am nearer my goal than I could have dared to hope.

Now my method must be to be sweet to her, and not tease her any more.

How wonderful it will be when she does love me. I have not thought much about my own feelings lately. She has kept me so often irritated and angry, but I know that there is a steady advance, and that I love her more than ever.

To see her little mutinous rebellious face softening—?—it will be worth all the waiting. But meanwhile she is out, and I had better get up!

I wonder if all the hundreds of other fellows who lost a leg below the knee and were cripples for eighteen months felt the same as I did when the new limb was fixed, and they stood upon two feet again for the first time.

A strange, almost mad sense of exaltation filled me. I could walk! I was no longer a prisoner, dependent upon the devotion of attendants!

I should no longer have to have things placed within reach, and be made to realize impotency!

It hurt and was awkward for a while.—But Oh! the joy, joy, joy!!

After the doctors and the specialist had gone with hearty congratulations, my dear old faithful servant had tears in his eyes as he dressed me.

"You must excuse me, Sir Nicholas, but I am so glad."
Excuse him! I could have hugged him in my own joy.
He arrayed me in one of Mr. Davies's pre-war masterpieces, and we both stood in front of the long glass in my bedroom, and then we solemnly shook hands!
It was too glorious!
I wanted to run about! I wanted to shout and sing. I played idiotic tricks, walking backwards and forwards, like one of Shackleton's penguins. Then I went back to the glass again, actually whistling a tune! Except for the black patch over my eye, I appeared very much the same as I used to do before the war. My shoulder is practically straight now. I am a little thinner, and perhaps my face bears traces of suffering, but in general I don't look much altered.
I wonder what Alathea will say when she sees me! I wonder if it will make any difference to her?
To-morrow morning they are going to put in my eye.
I have not written all this in my journal, it seemed too good to be true, and I had a kind of superstitious feeling that I must not even think of it, much less write, in case it did not come off. But now the moment has come! I am a man again on two feet. Hurrah!
I looked out of the window and kissed my hand to a young girl in the street. I wanted to call to her, "I could walk with you now, perhaps soon I could run!" She looked at me with the corner of her eye!
Then I planned how I would surprise Alathea! I would be in my bedroom when I knew she was in the salon before lunch, and then I would walk in!
I became excited, there was about a quarter of an hour to wait. I tried to sit down and settle to a book, but it was useless, the words conveyed no sense. I could not even read the papers!
I began listening to every sound, there were not many things passing at this time on a Sunday morning, but of course she was walking, not driving. One o'clock struck. She had not returned. Burton came in to ask if I would postpone lunch.
"Her Ladyship did not say when she would be back," he said.
"We had better not wait then. I believe now she told me she would not be in."
Burton had opened a pint of champagne. On this tremendous occasion he felt I should drink my own health!
I had begun to lose some of my joy.——I wished she had been here to share it with me.——

I have walked up and down—up and down. It is four o'clock now, and she has not returned. No doubt her mother is ill, perhaps,—perhaps—
Midnight:
I have spent a beastly day. My exhilaration has all evaporated now. I have had no one to share it with me. Maurice and everyone is leaving me discreetly alone, knowing I am supposed to be on my honeymoon—Honeymoon!
I spent the afternoon waiting, waiting. And after tea when Alathea had not arrived I began taking longer turns, walking up and down the broad corridor, and at last I paused outside her room, and a desire came over me to look in on it, and see how she had arranged it.
There was silence. I listened a moment, then I opened the door.
The fire was not lit, it all seemed cold and cheerless. I turned on the light.
Except for the tortoise-shell and gold brushes and boxes I had had put on the dressing table for her, there was not an indication that anyone stayed there, none of the usual things women have about in their rooms. One could see she looked upon it just as an hotel, and not a permanent abode. There were no photographs of her family, no books of her own, nothing.
Only the bracelets were on the table still in their case, and on looking nearer, I saw there was a bottle of scent. It had no label, and when I opened it I smelled the exquisite perfume of fresh roses that she uses. Where does she get it? It is the purest I have ever smelt in my life.
I looked at the quaint little fourpost bed that I had found in that shop at Bath, a perfect specimen of its date, about , with the old deep rose silk pressed over the shell carving.
I had an insane desire to open the drawers in the chest and touch her stockings and gloves. I had a wild feeling altogether I wanted my love, rebellious, unrelenting, anyhow! I just longed for her.
I resisted my stupidities and made myself leave the room, and then tried to feel joy again in my leg.
Burton was turning on the lamps when I got back to the salon.
"There are rumours that something is going to happen, Sir Nicholas,—talk of an Armistice I heard when I was out. Do you think Foch will do it?"
But I know all these rumours and talks, we have heard them before, so this did not affect me. I could feel nothing, as time went on, but a passionate ache. Why, why must she be so cruel to me? Why does she leave me all alone?
Alathea, I would never be so unkind to you. And yet I don't know, if I were jealous and angry, as I suppose she is, I could of course be much crueler.
Her Ladyship's maid had been given the day out by her mistress, Burton informed me, so that we could gain no information from her. We waited until half-past eight for dinner, but still my little girl did not come, and in solemn state in a white tie and tail coat, I dined—alone!
In spite of the champagne, which Burton again handed, apprehension set in. What can have happened to her? Has she had an accident? Does she mean never to return? Are all my calculations of no sense, and has she left me forever?
In despair, at ten o'clock I telephoned the Hotel de Courville.

Lady Thormonde had been there in the morning, I was told, but the Duchesse had left for Hautevine at two o'clock.—No one was in the house now.—No, they did not know Lady Hilda Bulteel's telephone number. She had no telephone they supposed.—No, they did not know the address.

Auteuil, and the name Bulteel, that is all! Perhaps something could be done on a week-day, but on a Sunday night, in war time, all was impossible. And at last in an agony of doubt and apprehension, I consented to retire to bed.

Had I made some mistake? I tried to remember. She had said she meant to decide if she could bear the situation or no, and that she was going to her mother. She wanted to be with her. She had been ill and could not start. Yes, of course that is it. The mother is ill, and they have no telephone. I must wait until the morning. She cannot really mean not to come back. In any case she would have let me know.

But what an agony of suspense!

Burton came and gave me my medicine, when I was in bed, and although I knew it was a camouflaged sleeping draught, I drank it. I just could not bear it any longer.

But I only slept until four, and now I am sitting up writing this, and I feel as if every queer force was abroad, and that all sorts of momentous things are happening.—Oh, when will daylight come—

I was awakened by cannon!

I leaped from my bed. Yes, leaped! I had been dreaming that a surprise party of Germans were attacking the trench, and I was just rallying the men for a final dash when heavy guns began a bombardment which was unexpected.—Oh God! let me get up and over the top in time!

Wild with excitement, I was now wide awake!

Yes, there were cannons booming!

Had Bertha begun again?

What was happening?

Then I heard murmurs in the street. I rang the bell violently. I had slept very late. Burton rushed in.

"An Armistice, Sir Nicholas," he cried joyously.

"It's true after all!"

An Armistice! Oh, God!

So at last, at last we have won, and it has not been all in vain!

I shook with emotion. How utterly absorbed in my own affairs I had been not to have taken in that this was coming. George Harcourt had telephoned that he had news for me, I remember now, while we were at the Hotel de Courville on Saturday, and I had paid no attention.

I was too excited all through breakfast to feel renewed anxiety about Alathea. I was accepting the fact that she had stayed with her mother. Surely, surely she would be in soon now!

The oculist, and his artist-craftsman, would be arriving soon, at eleven o'clock, if the excitement of an Armistice does not prevent them! I hope all that won't be going on when Alathea does come in!

Burton has questioned her maid. She knows nothing of Miladi's movements only that she herself had been given permission to go out for the day.

All the servants have gone more or less crazy! Pierre hopped in just now, jolly old chap! and in his excitement embraced me on both cheeks!

(He has a wooden stump, not a smart footed thing like mine, but I shall change all that now!).

Antoine could not contain himself, and heaven knows what the underservants did!

I told them all to run out and see what was happening, but Pierre said no, the *déjeuner* of Monsieur must not be neglected. Time enough in the afternoon!

Eleven came, and with it the oculist, and by luncheon time I had a second blue eye! But Oh! the shouting in the streets and the passionate joy in the air!

The two men preened themselves upon keeping this appointment upon so great a day, and indeed my gratitude was deep. But the same gladness did not hold me as when my leg was given back to me. Everything was now swallowed up in an overwhelming suspense.

What could have kept Alathea?

I walked to the glass soberly when the doctors had gone, eager to get away and join the rejoicers. And what I saw startled me. How astonishing the art of these things is now! Unless I turn my glance in some impossible way I have apparently two bright blue eyes, with the same lids and lashes, the scrap of shrapnel only injured the orb itself, and did not touch the lid, fortunately, and the socket had healed up miraculously in the last month. I am not now a disgusting object. Perhaps, possibly—Yes, can I induce her to love me soon?

But what is the good of it all? She has not returned, and now something must be done.

But on this day of days no one could be found to attend to anything! Shops were shut, post offices did not work. The city was mad with rejoicing.

At luncheon I ate,—gulped down my food. Burton's calm reassured me.

"You don't think anything has happened, do you Burton?"

"No, Sir Nicholas. Her Ladyship is no doubt with her family. I don't feel that anything is amiss. Her Grace returns to-morrow anyway, and we can hear for sure then. Would you not care to drive out and see the people, Sir? It is a day!"

But I told him no. He must go, they all could go. I would wait in and could now attend to myself! But I knew somehow that the dear old boy would not leave me.

The hours went by, the shouting grew louder, as bands passed on their way to the *Champs Elysées* to see the cannon, which I heard were now dragged there. Burton came in from time to time to tell me the news, gathered from the *concierge* below.

I telephoned to Maurice, he was wild with delight! They were going to have a great dinner at the Ritz and then go and *farandole*in the streets with the people, would not we (*we!*) join them!

Everyone was going. Odette telephoned too, and Daisy Ryven. All were rejoicing and happy.

The agony grew and grew. What if she means to leave me and has just disappeared, not telling me on purpose to punish me? At this thought I went frantically into her room again, and looked on the dressing-table. The ring cases were there in a drawer in the William and Mary looking-glass, but no rings. No, if she had not meant to return she would have left them behind her. This gave me hope.

I had the fire lit. Burton lit it, everyone else was out.

Of course the crowd has prevented her returning. There would be great difficulty in getting back from Auteuil.

Some of the fellows of the Supreme War Council rang up. They were less exhilarated by the news. A pity, they thought. Foch could have entered Berlin in a week!

At last, when I had been pacing like a restless tiger, and twilight was coming, I sank into my chair overcome with the strain.

I did not mean to feel the drivel of self pity, but it is a ghastly thing to be all alone and anxious, when everyone else is shouting for joy.

I was staring into the fire. I had not had the lights lit on purpose. I wanted the soft shadows to soothe me. Burton had gone down again to the *concierge*.

A bitterness and a melancholy I cannot describe was holding me. Of what good my leg and my eye if I am to suffer torment once more? A sense of forsakenness held me. Perhaps I dozed, because I was worn out, when suddenly I was conscious of a closing door, and opening my eye, I saw that Alathea stood before me.

A log fell and blazed brightly, and I could see that her face was greatly moved.

"I am so sorry if you have been anxious.—Burton says you have. I would have been back earlier but I was caught in the crowd."

I reached out and turned on the lamp near me, and when she saw my eye and leg, she fell upon her knees at my side.

"Oh! Nicholas," she cried brokenly, and I put out my hand and took her hand.

What a thing is joy!

My heart beat madly, the blood rushed in my veins. What was that noise I heard in my ear beyond the shouting in the street?

Was it the cooing which used to haunt my dreams?

Yes it was. And Alathea's voice was murmuring in French:

"*Pardon, pardon, j' etais si bien ingrate—Pardonnez moi—Hein?*"

I wanted to whisper:

"Darling you have returned,—nothing matters any more," but I controlled myself. She must finally surrender first!

Then she sprang to her feet and stood back to look at me. I rose too and there towered above her.

"Oh, I am so glad, so glad," she said tremulously. "How wonderful,—how miraculous!—It is for this great day!"

"I thought that you had left me altogether." I was a little breathless, "I was so very sad."

Now she looked down.

"Nicholas," (how I loved to hear her pronounce my name) "Nicholas, I have heard from my mother of your great generosity. You had helped us without ever telling me, and then paid again to stop my mother's anxiety, and again to stop mine. Oh! I am ashamed,—humbled, that I have been as I have been to you, forgive me, forgive me, I ask you to from my heart."

"I have nothing to forgive child. Come let us sit down and talk everything over," and I sank into the sofa and she came beside me.

She would not look at me, however, but her little face was gentle and shy. "I cannot understand though why you did all that. I cannot understand anything about it all.—You do not love me.—You only wanted me for your secretary, and yet you paid over a hundred thousand francs! The generosity is great."

I gazed and gazed at her.

"And you hate me," I said as coolly as I could "and let me buy you, so that you could save your family.—Your sacrifice was immense."

Suddenly she looked straight up at me, her eyes filled with passion, so that wild fire kindled in my blood.

"Nicholas,—I do not hate you."

I took both her hands and drew her to me, while outside in the street they were singing the *Marseillaise* and yelling for joy.

"Alathea, tell me the truth, what then do you feel?"

"I don't know. I wanted to murder Suzette. I could have drowned Coralie.—Perhaps you can tell me,—here in your arms—!"

And with wild abandon she fell forward into my fond embrace.

Ah! God! The bliss of the next few moments with her soft lips pressed to mine! Then I could not repeat often enough that I loved her, nor make her tell me how she loved me in return!

Afterwards, I grew masterful and ordered her to recount to me everything from the very beginning.

Yes, she had been attracted by me from the first day, but she hated the friends I had round me, and she did not like the aimlessness of my life.

"Whenever I used to be growing too contemptuous though, Nicholas, I used to remember the V.C., and then the feeling went off, but I was growing angrier and angrier with myself, because in spite of believing you only thought of me as one of them, I could not prevent myself from loving you. There is something about you that made one forget all about your leg and your eye!"

"Those cheques disgusted you!" and I kissed the little curl by her ear—she was clasped close to me now.—"That was the beginning of my determination to conquer you and have you for my own!"

She caressed my hair.

"I adore thick hair, Nicholas," she whispered, "but now you have had enough flattery! I am off to dress!"

She struggled and pretended she wanted to leave me, but I would not let her go.

"Only when I please and at a price! I want to show you that you have a husband who in spite of a wooden leg and a glass eye, is a powerful brute!"

"I love you,—strong like that," she cooed, her eyes soft with passion again. "I am not good really,—or austere,—or cold."

And I knew it was true as she paid the toll!

Presently I made her let me come and choose which frock she was to put on for dinner, and I insisted that I should stay and see her hair being brushed, and the maid, Henriette, with her French eye, beamed upon us understandingly!

While Burton almost blubbered with happiness when I told him His Ladyship and I were friends again.

"I knew it, Sir Nicholas, if you'd just made a fuss of her."

How right he was!

What a dinner we had, gay as two children, fond and foolish as sweethearts always are,—and then the afterwards!

"Let us go and see the streets," my little love implored, "I feel that we should shout our divine happiness with the crowd!"

But when we went out on the balcony to investigate, we saw that would be impossible, I am not yet steady enough on my feet to have faced that throng. So we stood there and sang and cheered with them, as they swept on towards the *Arc de Triomphe*, and gradually a delirious intoxication held us both, and I drew her back into the softly lighted room.

"Lover!" she whispered as she melted into my arms, and all I answered was, "Soul of Mine."

And now I know what the whole of those verses mean!

And so this Journal is done!

Three Weeks

CHAPTER I

Now this is an episode in a young man's life, and has no real beginning or ending. And you who are old and have forgotten the passions of youth may condemn it. But there are others who are neither old nor young who, perhaps, will understand and find some interest in the study of a strange woman who made the illumination of a brief space.

Paul Verdayne was young and fresh and foolish when his episode began. He believed in himself—he believed in his mother, and in a number of other worthy things. Life was full of certainties for him. He was certain he liked hunting better than anything else in the world—for instance. He was certain he knew his own mind, and therefore perfectly certain his passion for Isabella Waring would last for ever! Ready to swear eternal devotion with that delightful inconsequence of youth in its unreason, thinking to control an emotion as Canute's flatterers would have had him do the waves.

And the Creator of waves—and emotions—no doubt smiled to Himself—if He is not tired by now of smiling at the follies of the moles called human beings, who for the most part inhabit His earth!

Paul was young, as I said, and fair and strong. He had been in the eleven at Eton and left Oxford with a record for all that should turn a beautiful Englishman into a perfect athlete. Books had not worried him much! The fit of a hunting-coat, the pace of a horse, were things of more importance, but he scraped through his "Smalls" and his "Mods," and was considered by his friends to be anything but a fool. As for his mother—the Lady Henrietta Verdayne—she thought him a god among men!

Paul went to London like others of his time, and attended the theatres, where perfectly virtuous young ladies display nightly their innocent charms in hilarious choruses, arrayed in the latest *modes*. He supped, too, with these houris—and felt himself a man of the world.

He had stayed about in country houses for perhaps a year, and had danced through the whole of a season with all the prettiest *débutantes*. And one or two of the young married women of forty had already marked him out for their prey.

By all this you can see just the kind of creature Paul was. There are hundreds of others like him, and perhaps they, too, have the latent qualities which he developed during his episode—only they remain as he was in the beginning—sound asleep.

That fall out hunting in March, and being laid up with a sprained ankle and a broken collar-bone, proved the commencement of the Isabella Waring affair.

She was the parson's daughter—and is still for the matter of that!—and often in those days between her games of golf and hockey, or a good run on her feet with the hounds, she came up to Verdayne Place to write Lady Henrietta's letters for her. Isabella was most amiable and delighted to make herself useful.

And if her hands were big and red, she wrote clearly and well. The Lady Henrietta, who herself was of the delicate Later Victorian Dresden China type, could not imagine a state of things which contained the fact that her god-like son might stoop to this daughter of the earthy earth!

Yet so it fell about. Isabella read aloud the sporting papers to him—Isabella played piquet with him in the dull late afternoons of his convalescence—Isabella herself washed his dog Pike—that king of rough terriers! And one terrible day Paul unfortunately kissed the large pink lips of Isabella as his mother entered the room.

I will draw a veil over this part of his life.

The Lady Henrietta, being a great lady, chanced to behave as such on the occasion referred to—but she was also a woman, and not a particularly clever one. Thus Paul was soon irritated by opposition into thinking himself seriously in love with this daughter of the middle classes, so far beneath his noble station.

"Let the boy have his fling," said Sir Charles Verdayne, who was a coarse person. "Damn it all! a man is not obliged to marry every woman he kisses!"

"A gentlemen does not deliberately kiss an unmarried girl unless he intends to make her his wife!" retorted Lady Henrietta. "I fear the worst!"

Sir Charles snorted and chuckled, two unpleasant and annoying habits his lady wife had never been able to break him of. So the affair grew and grew! Until towards the middle of April Paul was advised to travel for his health.

"Your father and I can sanction no engagement, Paul, before you return," said Lady Henrietta. "If, in July, on your twenty-third birthday, you still wish to break your mother's heart—I suppose you must do so. But I ask of you the unfettered reflection of three months first."

This seemed reasonable enough, and Paul consented to start upon a tour round Europe—not having spoken the final fatal and binding words to Isabella Waring. They made their adieux in the pouring rain under a dripping oak in the lane by the Vicarage gate.

Paul was six foot two, and Isabella quite six foot, and broad in proportion. They were dressed almost alike, and at a little distance, but for the lady's scanty petticoat, it would have been difficult to distinguish her sex.

"Good-bye, old chap," she said, "We have been real pals, and I'll not forget you!"

But Paul, who was feeling sentimental, put it differently.

"Good-bye, darling," he whispered with a suspicion of tremble in his charming voice. "I shall never love any woman but you—never, never in my life."

Cuckoo! screamed the bird in the tree.

And now we are getting nearer the episode. Paris bored Paul—he did not know its joys and was in no mood to learn them. He mooned about and went to the races. His French was too indifferent to make theatres a pleasure, and the attractive ladies who smiled at his blue eyes were for him *défendues*. A man so recently parted from the only woman he could ever love had no right to look at such things, he thought. How young and chivalrous and honest he was—poor Paul!

So he took to visiting Versailles and Fontainebleau and Compiègne with a guide-book, and came to the conclusion it was all "beastly rot."

So he turned his back upon France and fled to Switzerland.

Do you know Switzerland?—you who read. Do you know it at the beginning of May? A feast of blue lakes, and snow-peaks, and the divinest green of young beeches, and the sombre shadow of dark firs, and the exhilaration of the air.

If you do, I need not tell you about it. Only in any case now, you must see it through the eyes of Paul. That is if you intend to read another page of this bad book.

It was pouring with rain when he drove from the station to the hotel. His temper was at its worst. Pilatus hid his head in mist, the Bürgenstock was invisible—it was chilly, too, and the fire smoked in the sitting-room when Paul had it lighted.

His heart yearned for his own snug room at Verdayne Place, and the jolly voice of Isabella Waring counting point, quint and quatorze. What nonsense to send him abroad. As if such treatment could be effectual as a cure for a love like his. He almost laughed at his mother's folly. How he longed to sit down and write to his darling. Write and tell how he hated it all, and was only getting through the time until he saw her six feet of buxom charms again—only Paul did not put it like that—indeed, he never thought about her charms at all—or want of them. He analysed nothing. He was sound asleep, you see, to *nuances* as yet; he was just a splendid English young animal of the best class.

He had promised not to write to Isabella—or, if he *must*, at least not to write a love-letter.

"Dear boy," the Lady Henrietta had said when giving him her fond parting kiss, "if you are very unhappy and feel you greatly wish to write to Miss Waring, I suppose you must do so, but let your letter be about the scenery and the impressions of travel, in no way to be interpreted into a declaration of affection or a promise of future union—I have your word, Paul, for that?"

And Paul had given his word.

"All right, mother—I promise—for three months."

And now on this wet evening the "must" had come, so he pulled out some hotel paper and began.

"MY DEAR ISABELLA:

"I say—you know—I hate beginning like this—I have arrived at this beastly place, and I am awfully unhappy. I think it would have been better if I had brought Pike with me, only those rotten laws about getting the little chap back to England would have been hard. How is Moonlighter? And have they really looked after that strain, do you gather? Make Tremlett come down and report progress to you daily—I told him to. My rooms look out on a beastly lake, and there are mountains, I suppose, but I can't see them. There is hardly any one in the hotel, because the Easter visitors have all gone back and the summer ones haven't come, so I doubt even if I can have a game of billiards. I am sick of guide-books, and I should like to take the next train home again. I must dress for dinner now, and I'll finish this to-night."

Paul dressed for dinner; his temper was vile, and his valet trembled. Then he went down into the restaurant scowling, and was ungracious to the polite and conciliating waiters, ordering his food and a bottle of claret as if they had done him an injury. "*Anglais*," they said to one another behind the serving-screen, pointing their thumbs at him—"he pay but he damn."

Then Paul sent for the *New York Herald* and propped it up in front of him, prodding at some olives with his fork, one occasionally reaching his mouth, while he read, and awaited his soup.

The table next to him in this quiet corner was laid for one, and had a bunch of roses in the centre, just two or three exquisite blooms that he was familiar with the appearance of in the Paris shops. Nearly all the other tables were empty or emptying; he had dined very late. Who could want roses eating alone? The *menu*, too, was written out and ready, and an expression of expectancy lightened the face of the head waiter—who himself brought a bottle of most carefully decanted red wine, feeling the temperature through the fine glass with the air of a great connoisseur.

"One of those over-fed foreign brutes of no sex, I suppose," Paul said to himself, and turned to the sporting notes in front of him.

He did not look up again until he heard the rustle of a dress.

The woman had to pass him—even so close that the heavy silk touched his foot. He fancied he smelt tuberoses, but it was not until she sat down, and he again looked at her, that he perceived a knot of them tucked into the front of her bodice.

A woman to order dinner for herself beforehand, and have special wine and special roses—special attention, too! It was simply disgusting!

Paul frowned. He brought his brown eyebrows close together, and glared at the creature with his blue young eyes.

An elderly, dignified servant in black livery stood behind her chair. She herself was all in black, and her hat—an expensive, distinguished-looking hat—cast a shadow over her eyes. He could just see they were cast down on her plate. Her face was white, he saw that plainly enough, startlingly white, like a magnolia bloom, and contained no marked features. No features at all! he said to himself. Yes—he was wrong, she had certainly a mouth worth looking at again. It was so red. Not large and pink and laughingly open like Isabella's, but straight and chiselled, and red, red, red.

Paul was young, but he knew paint when he saw it, and this red was real, and vivid, and disconcerted him.

He began his soup—hers came at the same time; she had only toyed with some caviare by way of *hors d'oeuvre*, and it angered him to notice the obsequiousness of the waiters, who passed each thing to the dignified servant to be placed before the lady by his hand. Who was she to be served with this respect and rapidity?

Only her red wine the *maître d'hôtel* poured into her glass himself. She lifted it up to the light to see the clear ruby, then she sipped it and scented its bouquet, the *maître d'hôtel* anxiously awaiting her verdict the while. "*Bon*," was all she said, and the weight of the world seemed to fall from the man's sloping shoulders as he bowed and moved aside.

Paul's irritation grew. "She's well over thirty," he said to himself. "I suppose she has nothing else to live for! I wonder what the devil she'll eat next!"

She ate a delicate *truite bleu*, but she did not touch her wine again the while. She had almost finished the fish before Paul's *sole au vin blanc* arrived upon the scene, and this angered him the more. Why should he wait for his dinner while this woman feasted? Why, indeed. What would her next course be? He found himself unpleasantly interested to know. The tenderest *selle d'agneau au lait* and the youngest green peas made their appearance, and again the *maître d'hôtel* returned, having mixed the salad.

Paul noticed with all these things the lady ate but a small portion of each. And it was not until a fat quail arrived later, while he himself was trying to get through two mutton chops *à l'anglaise*, that she again tasted her claret. Yes, it was claret, he felt sure, and probably wonderful claret at that. Confound her! Paul turned to the wine list. What could it be? Château Latour at fifteen francs? Château Margaux, or Château Lafite at twenty?—or possibly it was not here at all, and was special, too—like the roses and the attention. He called his waiter and ordered some port—he felt he could not drink another drop of his modest St. Estèphe!

All this time the lady had never once looked at him; indeed, except that one occasion when she had lifted her head to examine the wine with the light through it, he had not seen her raise her eyes, and then the glass had been between himself and her. The white lids with their heavy lashes began to irritate him. What colour could they be? those eyes underneath. They were not very large, that was certain—probably black, too, like her hair. Little black eyes! That was ugly enough, surely! And he hated heavy black hair growing in those unusual great waves. Women's hair should be light and fluffy and fuzzy, and kept tidy in a net—like Isabella's. This looked so thick—enough to strangle one, if she twisted it round one's throat. What strange ideas were those coming into his head? Why should she think of twisting her hair round a man's throat? It must be the port mounting to his brain, he decided—he was not given to speculating in this way about women.

What would she eat next? And why did it interest him what she ate or did not eat? The *maître d'hôtel* again appeared with a dish of marvellous-looking nectarines. The waiter now handed the dignified servant the finger-bowl, into which he poured rose-water. Paul could just distinguish the scent of it, and then he noticed the lady's hands. Yes, they at least were faultless; he could not cavil at *them*; slender and white, with that transparent whiteness like mother-of-pearl. And what pink nails! And how polished! Isabella's hands—but he refused to think of them.

By this time he was conscious of an absorbing interest thrilling his whole being—disapproving irritated interest.

The *maître d'hôtel* now removed the claret, out of which the lady had only drunk one glass.

(What waste! thought Paul.)

And then he returned with a strange-looking bottle, and this time the dignified servant poured the brilliant golden fluid into a tiny liqueur-glass. What could it be? Paul was familiar with most liqueurs. Had he not dined at every restaurant in London, and supped with houris who adored *crême de menthe*? But this was none he knew. He had heard of Tokay—Imperial Tokay—could it be that? And where did she get it? And who the devil was the woman, anyway?

She peeled the nectarine leisurely—she seemed to enjoy it more than all the rest of her dinner. And what could that expression mean on her face? Inscrutable—cynical was it? No—absorbed. As absolutely unconscious of self and others as if she had been alone in the room. What could she be thinking of never to worry to look about her?

He began now to notice her throat, it was rounded and intensely white, through the transparent black stuff. She had no strings of pearls or jewels on—unless—yes, that was a great sapphire gleaming from the folds of gauze on her neck. Not surrounded by diamonds like ordinary brooches, but just a big single stone so dark and splendid it seemed almost black. There was another on her hand, and yet others in her ears.

Her ears were not anything so very wonderful! Not so *very!* Isabella's were quite as good—and this thought comforted him a little. As far as he could see beyond the roses and the table she was a slender woman, and he had not noticed on her entrance if she were tall or short. He could not say why he felt she must be well over thirty—there was not a line or wrinkle on her face—not even the slight nip in under the chin, or the tell-tale strain beside the ears.

She was certainly not pretty, *certainly* not. Well shaped—yes—and graceful as far as he could judge; but pretty—a thousand times No!

Then the speculation as to her nationality began. French? assuredly not. English? ridiculous! Equally so German. Italian? perhaps. Russian? possibly. Hungarian? probably.

Paul had drunk his third glass of port and was beginning his fourth. This was far more than his usual limit. Paul was, as a rule, an abstemious young man. Why he should have deliberately sat and drank that night he never knew. His dinner had been moderate—distinctly moderate—and he had watched a refined feast of Lucullus partaken of by a woman who only *tasted* each *plat!*

"I wonder what she will have to pay for it all?" he thought to himself. "She will probably sign the bill, though, and I shan't see."

But when the lady had finished her nectarine and dipped her slender fingers in the rose-water she got up—she had not smoked, she could not be Russian then. Got up and walked towards the door, signing no bill, and paying no gold.

Paul stared as she passed him—rudely stared—he knew it afterwards and felt ashamed. However, the lady never so much as noticed him, nor did she raise her eyes, so that when she had finally disappeared he was still unaware of their colour or expression.

But what a figure she had! Sinuous, supple, rounded, and yet very slight.

"She must have the smallest possible bones," Paul said to himself, "because it looks all curvy and soft, and yet she is as slender as a gazelle."

She was tall, too, though not six feet—like Isabella!

The waiters and *maître d'hôtel* all bowed and stood aside as she left, followed by her elderly, stately, silver-haired servant.

Of course it would have been an easy matter to Paul to find out her name, and all about her. He would only have had to summon Monsieur Jacques, and ask any question he pleased. But for some unexplained reason he would not do this. Instead of which he scowled in front of him, and finished his fourth glass of port. Then his head swam a little, and he went outside into the night. The rain had stopped and the sky was full of stars scattered in its intense blue. It was warm, too, there, under the clipped trees, Paul hoped he wasn't drunk—such a beastly thing to do! And not even good port either.

He sat on a bench and smoked a cigar. A strange sense of loneliness came over him. It seemed as if he were far, far away from any one in the world he had ever known. A vague feeling of oppression and coming calamity passed through him, only he was really as yet too material and thoroughly, solidly English to entertain it, or any other subtle mental emotion for more than a minute. But he undoubtedly felt strange to-night; different from what he had ever done before. He would have said "weird" if he could have thought of the word. The woman and her sinuous, sensuous black shape filled the space of his mental vision. Black hair, black hat, black dress—and of course black eyes. Ah! if he could only know their colour really!

The damp bench where he sat was just under the ivy hanging from the balustrade of the small terrace belonging to the ground-floor suite at the end.

There was a silence, very few people passed, frightened no doubt by the recent rain. He seemed alone in the world.

The wine now began to fire his senses. Why should he remain alone? He was young and rich and—surely even in Lucerne there must be—. And then he felt a beast, and looked out on to the lake.

Suddenly his heart seemed to swell with some emotion, a faint scent of tuberoses filled the air—and from exactly above his head there came a gentle, tender sigh.

He started violently, and brusquely turned and looked up. Almost indistinguishable in the deep shadow he saw the woman's face. It seemed to emerge from a mist of black gauze. And looking down into his were a pair of eyes—a pair of eyes. For a moment Paul's heart felt as if it had stopped beating, so wonderful was their effect upon him. They seemed to draw him—draw something out of him—intoxicate him—paralyse him. And as he gazed up motionless the woman moved noiselessly back on to the terrace, and he saw nothing but the night sky studded with stars.

Had he been dreaming? Had she really bent over the ivy? Was he mad? Yes—or drunk, because now he had seen the eyes, and yet he did not know their colour! Were they black, or blue, or grey, or green? He did not know, he could not think—only they were eyes—eyes—eyes.

The letter to Isabella Waring remained unfinished that night.

CHAPTER II

Paul's head ached a good deal next morning and he was disinclined to rise. However, the sun blazed in at his windows, and a bird sang in a tree.

His temper was the temper of next day—sodden, and sullen, and ashamed. He even resented the sunshine.

But what a beautiful creature he looked, as later he stepped into a boat for a row on the lake! His mother, the Lady Henrietta, had truly reason to be proud of him. So tall and straight, and fair and strong. And at the risk of causing a second fit among some of the critics, I must add, he probably wore silk socks, and was "beautifully groomed," too, as all young Englishmen are of his class and age. And how supple his lithe body seemed as he bent over the oars, while the boat shot out into the blue water.

The mountains were really very jolly, he thought, and it was not too hot, and he was glad he had come out, even though he had eaten no breakfast and was feeling rather cheap still. Yes, very glad.

After he had advanced a few hundred yards he rested on his oars, and looked up at the hotel. Then wonder came back to him, where was she to-day—the lady with the eyes? Or had he dreamed it—and was there no lady at all?

It should not worry him anyway—so he rowed ahead, and ceased to speculate.

The first thing he did when he came in for lunch was to finish his letter to Isabella.

"P. S.—Monday," he added. "It is finer to-day, and I have had some exercise. The view isn't bad now the mist has gone. I shall do some climbing, I think. Take care of yourself, dear girl. Good-bye.

"Love from

"PAUL."

It was with a feeling of excitement that he entered the restaurant for *déjeuner*. Would she be there? How would she seem in daylight?

But the little table where she had sat the night before was unoccupied. There were the usual cloth and glass and silver, but no preparations for any specially expected guest upon it. Paul felt annoyed with himself because his heart sank. Had she gone? Or did she only dine in public? Perhaps she lunched in the sitting-room beyond the terrace, where he had seen her eyes the night before.

The food was really very good, and the sun shone, and Paul was young and hungry, so presently he forgot about the lady and enjoyed his meal.

The appearance of the Bürgenstock across the lake attracted him, as afterwards he smoked another cigar under the trees. He would hire an electric launch and go there and explore the paths. If only Pike were with him—or—Isabella!

This idea he put into execution.

What a thing was a funicular railway. How steep and unpleasant, but how quaint the tree-tops looked when one was up among them. Yes—Lucerne was a good deal jollier than Paris. And he roamed about among the trees, never noticing their beautiful colours. Presently he paused to rest. He was soothed—even peaceful. If he had Pike he could really be quite happy, he thought.

What was that rustle among the leaves above him? He looked up, and started then as violently almost as he had done the night before. Because there, peeping at him from the tender green of the young beeches, was the lady in black. She looked down upon him through the parted boughs, her black hat and long black veil making a sharp silhouette against the vivid verdure, her whole face in tender shadow and framed in the misty gauze.

Paul's heart beat violently. He felt a pulse in his throat—for a few seconds.

He knew he was gazing into her eyes, and he thought he knew they were green. They looked larger than he had imagined them to be. They were set so beautifully, too, just a suspicion of rise at the corners. And their expression was mocking and compelling—and—But she let go the branches and disappeared from view.

Paul stood still. He was thrilling all over. Should he bound in among the trees and follow her? Should he call out and ask her to come back? Should he—? But when he had decided and gained the spot where she must have stood, he saw it was a junction of three paths, and he was in perfect ignorance which one she had taken. He rushed down the first of them, but it twisted and turned, and when he had gone far enough to see ahead—there was no one in sight. So he retraced his steps and tried the second. This, too, ended in disappointment. And the third led to an opening where he could see the descending *funiculaire*, and just as it sank out of view he caught sight of a black dress, almost hidden by a standing man's figure, whom he recognised as the elderly silver-haired servant.

Paul had learnt a number of swear-words at Eton and Oxford. And he let the trees hear most of them then.

He could not get down himself until the train returned, and by that time where would she be? To go by the paths would take an eternity. This time circumstance had fairly done him.

Presently he sauntered back to the little hotel whose terrace commands the lake far below, and eagerly watching the craft upon it, he thought he caught sight of a black figure reclining in an electric launch which sped over the blue water.

Then he began to reason with himself. Why should the sight of this woman have caused him such violent emotion? Why? Women were jolly things that did not matter much—except Isabella. She mattered, of course, but somehow her mental picture came less readily to his mind than usual. The things he seemed to see most distinctly were her hands—her big red hands. And then he unconsciously drifted from all thought of her.

"She certainly looks younger in daylight," he said to himself. "Not more than thirty perhaps. And what strange hats with that shadow over her eyes. What is she doing here all alone? She must be somebody from the people in the hotel making such a fuss—and that servant—Then why alone?" He mused and mused.

She was not a *demi-mondaine*. The English ones he knew were very ordinary people, but he had heard of some of the French ladies as being quite *grande dame*, and travelling *en prince*. Yet he was convinced this was not one of them. Who *could* she be? He must know.

To go back to the hotel would be the shortest way to find out, and so by the next descending train he left the Bürgenstock.

He walked up and down under the lime-trees outside the terrace of her rooms for half an hour, but was not rewarded in any way for his pains. And at last he went in. He, too, would have a dinner worth eating, he thought. So he consulted the *maître d'hôtel* on his way up to dress, and together they evolved a banquet. Paul longed to question the man about the unknown, but as yet he was no actor, and he found he felt too much about it to do it naturally.

He dressed with the greatest care, and descended at exactly half-past eight. Yes, the table was laid for her evidently—but there were giant carnations, not roses, in the silver vase to-night. How quickly the waiters seemed to bring things! And what a frightful lot there was to eat! And dawdle as he would, by nine o'clock he had almost finished. Perhaps it would be as well to send for a newspaper again. Anything to delay his having to rise and go out. An anxious, uncomfortable gnawing sense of expectancy dominated him. How ridiculous for a woman to be so late! What cook could do justice to his dishes if they were thus to be kept waiting? She couldn't possibly have *ordered* it for half past nine, surely! Gradually, as that hour passed and his second cup of coffee had been sipped to its finish, Paul felt a sickening sense of anger and disappointment. He got up abruptly and went out. In the hall, coming from the corridor of her rooms, he met the lady face to face.

Then rage with himself seized him. Why had he not waited? For no possible reason could he go back now. And what a chance to look at her missed—and all thrown away.

He sat sullenly down in the hall, resisting the temptation to go into the beautiful night. At least he would see her on her way back. But he waited until nearly eleven, and she never appeared, and then the maddening thought came to him—she had probably passed to her rooms along the terrace outside, under the lime-tree.

He bounded up, and stalked into the starlight. He could see through the windows of the restaurant, and no one was there. Then he sat on the bench again, under the ivy—but all was darkness and silence; and thoroughly depressed, Paul at last went to bed.

Next day was so gloriously fine that youth and health sang within him. He was up and away quite early. Not a thought of this strange lady should cross his mind for the entire day, he determined as he ate his breakfast. And soon he started for the Rigi in a launch, taking the English papers with him. Intense joy, too! A letter from Isabella!

Such a nice letter. All about Pike and Moonlighter, and the other horses—and Isabella was going to stay with a friend at Blackheath, where she hoped to get better golf than at home—and Lady Henrietta had been gracious to her, and given her Paul's address, and there had been a "jolly big party" at Verdayne Place for Sunday, but none of his "pals." At least if there were, they were not in church, she added naïvely.

All this Paul read in his launch on the way to the Rigi, and for some unexplained reason the information seemed about things a long way off, and less thrilling than usual. He had a splendid climb, and when he got back to Lucerne in the evening he was thoroughly tired, and so hungry he flew down to his dinner.

It was nearly nine o'clock; at least if she came to-night he would be there to see her. But of course it did not matter if she came or not, he had conquered that ridiculous interest. He would hardly look until he reached his table. Yes, there she was, but dipping her white fingers in the rosewater at the very end of her repast.

And again, in spite of himself, a strange wild thrill ran through Paul, and he knew it was what he had been subconsciously hoping for all day—and oh, alas! it mattered exceedingly.

The lady never glanced at him. She swept from the room, her stately graceful movements delighting his eye. He could understand and appreciate movement—was he not accustomed to thoroughbreds, and able to judge of their action and line?

How blank the space seemed when she had gone—dull and unspeakably uninteresting. He became impatient with the slowness of the waiters, who had seemed to hurry unnecessarily the night before. But at last his meal ended, and he went out under the trees. The sky was so full of stars it hardly seemed dark. The air was soft, and in the distance a band played a plaintive valse tune.

There were numbers of people walking about, and the lights from the hotel windows lit up the scene. Only the ivy terrace was in shadow as he again sat down on the bench.

How had she got in last night? That he must find out—he rose, and peered about him. Yes, there was a little gate, a flight of steps, a private entrance into this suite, just round the corner.

And as he looked at it, the lady, wrapped in a scarf of black gauze, passed him, and standing aside while the silver-haired servant opened the little door with a key, she then entered and disappeared from view.

It seemed as if the stars danced to Paul. His whole being was quivering with excitement, and now he sat on the bench again almost trembling.

He did not move for at least half an hour; then the clocks chimed in the town. No, there was no hope; he would see her no more that night. He rose listlessly to go back to bed, tired out with his day's climb. And as he stood up, there, above the ivy again, he saw her face looking down upon him.

How had she crossed the terrace without his hearing her? How long had she been there? But what matter? At least she was there. And those eyes looking into his out of the shadow, what did they say? Surely they smiled at him. Paul jumped on to the bench. Now he was almost level with her face—almost—and his was raised eagerly in expectation. Was he dreaming, or did she whisper something? The sound was so soft he was not quite sure. He stretched out his arms to her in the darkness, pulling himself by the ivy nearer still. And this time there was no mistake.

"Come, Paul," she said. "I have some words to say to you."

And round to the little gate Paul flew.

CHAPTER III

Paul was never quite sure of what happened that evening—everything was so wonderful, so unusual, so unlike his ordinary life. The gate was unlocked he found when he got there, but no one appeared to be inside, and he bounded up the steps and on to the terrace. Silence and darkness—was she fooling him then? No, there she was by one of the windows; he could dimly see her outline as she passed into the room beyond, through some heavy curtains. That was why no light came through to the terrace. He followed, dropping them after him also, and then he found himself in a room as unlike a hotel as he could imagine. It may have had the usual brocade walls and gilt chairs of the "best suite," but its aspect was so transformed by her subtle taste and presence, it seemed to him unique, and there were masses of flowers—roses, big white ones—tuberoses—lilies of the valley, gardenias, late violets. The light were low and shaded, and a great couch filled one side of the room beyond the fireplace. Such a couch! covered with a tiger-skin and piled with pillows, all shades of rich purple velvet and silk, embroidered with silver and gold—unlike any pillows he had ever seen before, even to their shapes. The whole thing was different and strange—and intoxicating.

The lady had reached the couch, and sank into it. She was in black still, but gauzy, clinging black, which seemed to give some gleam of purple underneath. And if he had not been sure that in daylight he had thought they were green, he would have sworn the eyes which now looked into his were deepest violet, too.

"Come," she said. "You may sit here beside me and tell me what you think."

And her voice was like rich music—but she had hardly any accent. She might have been an Englishwoman almost, for that matter, and yet he somehow knew that she was not. Perhaps it was she pronounced each word; nothing was slurred over. Without her hat she looked even more attractive, and certainly younger. But what was age or youth? And what was beauty itself, when a woman whose face was neither young nor beautiful could make him feel he was looking at a divine goddess, and thrilling as he had never dreamt of doing in his short life?

If any one had told Paul this was going to happen to him, this experience, he would have laughed them to scorn. To begin with, he was rather shy with ladies as a rule, and had not learnt a trick of *entreprenance*. It took him quite a while to know one well enough to even talk at ease. And yet here he was, embarked upon an adventure which savoured of the Arabian Nights.

He came forward and sat down, and he could feel the pulse beating in his throat. It all seemed perfectly natural at the time, but afterwards he wondered how she had known his name was Paul—and how it had all come to pass.

"For three days you have thought of me, Paul—is it not so?" she said, half closing her lids.

But he could only blurt out "Yes!" while he devoured her with his eyes.

"We are both—how shall I say—drifting—holiday-making—trying to forget. And we must talk a little together, *n'est-ce pas*? Tell me?"

"Oh, yes!" said Paul.

"You are beautiful, you know, Paul," she went on. "So tall and straight like you English, with curly hair of gold. Your mother must have loved you as a baby."

"I suppose she did," said Paul.

"She is well? Your mother, the stately lady?"

"Very well—do you know her?" he asked, surprised.

"Long ago I have seen her, and I knew you at once, so like you are—and to your uncles, especially the Lord Hubert."

"Uncle Hubert is a rotter!"

"A—rotter?" inquired the lady. "And what is that?" And she smiled a divine smile.

Paul felt ashamed. "Oh! well, it *is* a rotter, you know—that *is*—like Uncle Hubert, I mean."

She laughed again. "You do not explain well, but I understand you. And so you only resemble the Uncle Hubert on the outside—that is good."

Paul felt jealous. Lord Hubert Aldringham's reputation—for some things—was European. "I hope so," he said with emphasis. "And you knew him well then, too?"

"I never said so," replied the lady. "I saw him once—twice perhaps—years ago—at the marriage of a princess. There, it has made you frown, we will speak no more of the Uncle Hubert!" and she leant back and laughed.

Paul felt very young. He wanted to show her he was grown up, and he wanted a number of things which had never even formed themselves in his imagination before. But she went on talking.

"And your *cotelettes* were tough, Paul, and you were so cross that first evening, and hated me! And oh! Paul, you had far too much wine for a boy like you!"

He reddened to the roots of his fair wavy hair, and then he hung his head.

"I know I did—it was beastly of me—but I was so—upset—I—"

"Look at me," she said, and she bent forward over him—a gliding feline movement infinitely sinuous and attractive.

Then he looked, his big blue eyes still cloudy with a mist of shame.

"You must tell me why you were upset, baby—Paul!"

How often she said his name! lingering over it as if it were music. It thrilled him every time.

Then he gained courage.

"But how did you know anything about it—or what I had—or what I drank? You never once raised your eyelids all the time!"

"Perhaps I can see through them when I want to—who knows!" and she laughed.

"And you wanted to—wanted to see through them?"

He was gazing at her now, and she suddenly looked down, while the most beautiful transparent pink flushed her soft white cheeks, turning her into a tender girl almost. The change was so sudden, it startled Paul, and emboldened him.

"You wanted to!" he repeated in a glad voice. "You wanted to see me?"

"Yes," she whispered, and she looked up at him, but this time there was mischief in her eyes.

"Is that why you sighed then among the ivy? What made you sigh?"

She paused a moment, and then she said slowly: "A number of things. You seemed so young, and so beautiful, and so—asleep."

"Indeed I wasn't asleep!" Paul exclaimed. "It would take a great deal more port than that to make me go to sleep. I was thinking of—" And then he saw she had not meant that kind of sleep, and felt a fool—and wondered.

She helped him out.

"All this time you have not told me why you were upset—upset enough to drink bad port. That was naughty of you, Paul."

"I was upset—over you. I was angry because I was so interested—" and he reddened again.

She leant back among the purple cushions, her figure so supple in its lines, it made him think of a snake. She half closed her eyes again—and she spoke low in a dreamy voice:

"It was fate, Paul. I knew it when I entered the room. I felt it again among the green trees, and so I ran from you—but to-night it is *plus fort que moi*—so I called you to come in."

"I am so glad—so *glad*," said Paul.

She remained silent. Her eyes in their narrowed lids gleamed at him, seeming to penetrate into his very soul. And now he noticed her mouth again. It neither drooped nor smiled, it was straight, and chiselled and strong, and small rather, and the lower lip was rounded and slightly cleft in the centre. A most appetising red flower of a mouth.

By this time Paul was more or less intoxicated with excitement, he had lost all sense of time and place. It seemed as if he had known her always—that there never had been a moment when she had not filled the whole of his horizon.

They were both silent for a couple of minutes. As far as he could gather from her inscrutable face, she was weighing things—what things?

Suddenly she sprang up, one of those fine movements of hers full of cat-like grace.

"Paul," she said, "listen," and she spoke rather fast. "You are so young, so young—and I shall hurt you—probably. Won't you go now—while there is yet time? Away from Lucerne, back to Paris—even back to England. Anywhere away from me."

She put her hand on his arm, and looked up into his eyes. And there were tears in hers. And now he saw that they were grey.

He was moved as never yet in all his life.

"I will not!" he said. "I may be young, but to-night I know—I want to live! And I will chance the hurt, because I know that only you can teach me—just how—'"

Then his voice broke, and he bent down and covered her hand with kisses.

She quivered a little and drew away. She picked up a great bunch of tuberoses, and broke off all their tops. "There, take them!" she said, pressing them into his hands, and those against his heart. "Take them and go—and dream of me. You have chosen. Dream of me to-night and remember—there is to-morrow."

Then she glided back from him, and before he realised it she had gone noiselessly away through another door.

Paul stood still. The room swam; his head swam. Then he stumbled out on to the terrace, under the night sky, the white blossoms still pressed against his heart.

He must have walked about for hours. The grey dawn was creeping over the silent world when at last he went back to the hotel and to his bed.

There he slept and dreamt—never a dream! For youth and health are glorious things. And he was tired out.

The great sun was high in the heavens when next he awoke. And the room was full of the scent of tuberoses, scattered on the pillow beside him. Presently, when his blue eyes began to take in the meaning of things, he remembered and bounded up. For was not this the commencement of his first real day?

CHAPTER IV

The problem which faced Paul, when he had finished a very late breakfast, was how he should see her soon—the lady in black.

He could not go and call like an ordinary visitor, because he did not know her name! That was wonderful—did not even know her name, or anything about her, only that his whole being was thrilling with anxiety to see her again.

The simplest thing to do seemed to descend into the hall and look at the Visitors' List, which he promptly did.

There were only a few people in the hotel; it was not hard, therefore, guessing at the numbers of the rooms, to arrive at the conviction that "Mme. Zalenska and suite" might be what he was searching for. Zalenska—she was possibly Russian after all. And what was her christian name? That he longed to know.

As he stood staring, his fair forehead puckered into a frown of thought, the silver-haired servant came up behind him and said, with his respectful, dignified bearing:

"*De la part de Madame*," handing Paul a letter the while.

What could it contain?

But this was not the moment for speculation—he would read and see.

He turned his back on the servant, and walked towards the light, while he tore open the envelope. It had the most minute sphinx in the corner, and the paper was un-English, and rather thin.

This was what he read:

"*Morning.*

"Paul, I am young to-day, and we must see the blue lake and the green trees. Come to the landing towards the station, and I will call for you in my launch. And you shall be young, too, Paul—and teach me! Give Dmitry the answer."

"The answer is, 'Yes, immediately'—tell Madame," Paul said.

And then he trod on air until he arrived at the landing she had indicated. Soon the launch glided up, he saw her there reclining under an awning of striped green.

It was a well-arranged launch, the comfortable deck-chairs were in the bows, and the steering took place from a raised perch behind the cabin, so the two were practically alone. The lady was in grey to-day, and it suited her strangely. Her eyes gleamed at him, full of mischief, under her large grey hat.

Paul drew his chair a little forward, turning it so that he could look at her without restraint.

"How good of you to send for me," he said delightedly.

She smiled a radiant smile. "Was it? I am capricious, I did not think of the good for you, only I wanted you—to please myself. I wish to be foolish to-day, Paul, and see your eyes dance, and watch the light on your curls."

Paul frowned; it was as if she thought him a baby.

Then the lady leant back and laughed, the sound was of golden bells.

"Yes, you are a baby!" she said, answering his thoughts. "A great, big, beautiful baby, Paul."

If Paul had been a girl he would have pouted.

She turned from him and gazed over the lake; it was looking indescribably beautiful, with the colours of the springtime.

"Do you see the green of those beeches by the water, Paul? Look at their tenderness, next the dark firs—and then the blue beyond—and see, there is a copper beech, he is king of them all! I would like to build a châlet up in some part like that, and come there each year in May—to read fairy-tales."

For the first time in his life Paul saw with different eyes—just the beauty of things—and forgot to gauge their sporting possibilities. An infinite joy was flooding his being, some sensation he had not dreamed about even, of happiness and fulfilment.

She appeared to him more alluring than ever, and young and gay—as young as Isabella! And then his thoughts caused him to take in his breath with a hiss—Isabella—how far away she seemed. Of course he could never love any one else—but—

"Don't think of it, then," the lady whispered. "Be young like me, and live under the blue sky."

How was it she knew his thoughts always? He blushed while he stammered: "No—I won't think of it—or anything but you—Princess."

"Daring one!" she said, "who told you to call me that? The hotel people have been talking, I suppose."

"No," said Paul, surprised, "I called you Princess just because you seem like one to me—but now I guess from what you say, you are not plain Madame Zalenska."

Her eyes clouded for a second. "Madame Zalenska does to travel with—but you shall call me what you like."

He grew emboldened.

"I suddenly feel I want so much—I want to know why your eyes were so mocking through the trees on the Bürgenstock? They drove me nearly mad, you know, and I raced about after you like a dog after a hare!"

"I thought you would—you did not control the expression when you gazed up at me! And so I was the true hare—and ran away!"

She looked down suddenly and was silent for some moments, then she turned the conversation from these personal things. She led his thoughts into new channels—made him observe the trees and sky, and the wonderful beauty of it all, and with lightning flashes took him into unknown speculations on emotions and the meaning of things.

A new existence seemed to open to Paul's view. And all the while she lay back in her chair almost motionless, only her wonderful eyes lit up the strange whiteness of her face. There was not a touch of *mauvaise honte*, or explanation of the unusualness of this situation in her manner. It had a perfect, quiet dignity, as if to look into the eyes of an unknown young man at night over an ivy terrace, and then spend a day with him alone, were the most natural things in the world to do.

Paul felt she was a queen whose actions must be left unquestioned.

Presently they came to a small village, and here she would land and lunch. And from somewhere behind the cabin Dmitry appeared, and was sent on ahead, so that when they walked into the little hotel a simple repast was waiting for them.

By this time Paul was absolutely enthralled. Never in his whole life had he spent such a morning. His imagination was expanded. He saw new vistas. His brain almost whirled. Was it he—Paul Verdayne—who was seated opposite this divine woman, drinking in her voice, and listening to her subtle curious thoughts?

And what were the commonplace, ordinary things which had hitherto occupied his mind? How had he ever wasted a moment on them?

It was his first awakening.

When it came to the end—this delightful repast—he called the waiter, and wanted to pay the bill; small enough in all conscience. But a new look appeared round the lady's mouth—imperious, with an instantaneous flash in her eyes—a pure, steel-grey they were to-day.

"Leave it to Dmitry," she said quickly. "I never occupy myself with money. They displease me, these details—and why spoil my day?"

But Paul was an Englishman, and resented any woman's paying for his food. His mouth changed, too, and looked obstinate.

"I say, you know—" he began.
Then she turned upon him.
"Understand at once," she said haughtily. "Either you leave me unjarred by your English conventionalities, or you pay these miserable francs and go back to Lucerne alone!"
Paul shrugged his shoulders. He was angry, but could not insist further.
When they got outside, her voice grew caressing again as she led the way to a path up among the young beeches.
"Paul—foolish one!" she said. "Do you not think I understand and know you—and your quaint English ways? But imagine how silly it is. I am quite aware that you have ample money to provide me with a feast of Midas—all of gold—if necessary, and you shall some day, if you really wish. But to stop over paltry sums of francs, to destroy the thread of our conversation and thoughts—to make it all banal and everyday! That is what I won't have. Dmitry is there for nothing else but to *éviter* for me these details. It is my holiday, my pleasure-day, my time of joy. I felt young, Paul. You would not make one little shadow for me—would you, *ami?*"
No voice that he had ever dreamt of possessed so many tones in it as hers—even one of pathos, as she lingered over the word "shadow," All his annoyance melted. He only felt he would change the very mainspring of his life if necessary to give her pleasure and joy.
"Of course I would not make a shadow,—surely you know that," he said, moved. "Only you see a man generally pays for a woman's food."
"When she belongs to him—but I don't belong to you, baby Paul. You, for the day, belong to me—and are my guest!"
"Very well, then, we won't talk about it," he said, resigned by the caress in her words. To belong to her! That was something, if but for one day.
"Only it must never come up again, this question", she insisted. "Should we spend more hours on this lake, or other lakes—or mountains, or rivers, or towns—let us speak never of money, or paying. If you only knew of how I hate it! the cruel yellow gold! I have heaps of it—heaps of it! and for it human beings have always paid so great a price. Just this once in life let it bring happiness and peace."
He wondered at the concentrated feeling she expressed. What could the price be? And what was her history?"
"So it is over, our little breeze," she said gently, after a pause. "And you will tease me no more, Paul?"
"I would never tease you!" he exclaimed tenderly. And, if he had dared, he would have taken her hand.
"You English are so wonderful! Full of your prejudices," she said in a contemplative way. "Bulldog tenacity of purpose, whether you are right or wrong. Things are a custom, and they must be done, or it is not 'playing the game,'" and she imitated a set English voice, her beautiful mouth pursed up, until Paul had to use violent restraint with himself to keep from kissing it. "A wonderful people—mostly gentlemen and generally honest, but of a common sense that is disastrous to sentiment or romance. If you were not so polished, and lazy and strong—and beautiful to look at, one would not consider you much beyond the German."
"Not consider us beyond a beastly German!" exclaimed Paul indignantly.
And the lady laughed like a child.
"Oh! you darling Paul!" she said. "You dear, insular, arrogant Englishman! You have no equal in the world!"
Paul was offended.
"If you had said an Austrian now—but a German—" he growled sulkily.
"The Austrians are charming," allowed the lady, "but they err the other way; they have not enough common sense, they are only great gentlemen. Also, they are naturally awake, whereas you English are naturally asleep, and you yourself are the Sleeping Beauty, Paul."
They had climbed up the path now some two hundred feet, and all around them were stripling beeches of an unnaturally exquisite green, as fresh and pure and light almost as leaves of the forced lily of the valley.
The whole world throbbed with youth and freshness, and here and there, wide of the path, by a mossy stone, a gentian raised its azure head, "small essences of sky;" the lady called them.
"Let us sit down on this piece of rock," Paul said. "I want to hear why I am the Sleeping Beauty. It is so long since I read the story. But wasn't it about a girl, not a man—and didn't she get wakened up by a—kiss?"
"She did!" said the lady, leaning back against a tree behind her; "but then it was just her faculties which were asleep, not her soul. Could a kiss wake a soul?"
"I think so," Paul whispered. He was seated on a part of the rock which jutted out a little lower than her resting-place, and he was so close as to be almost touching her. He could look up under the brim of that tantalising hat, which so often hid her from his view as they walked. He was quivering with excitement at this moment, the result of the thought of a kiss—and his blue eyes blazed with desire as they devoured her face.
"Yes—it is so," said the lady, a low note in her voice. "Because Huldebrand gave Undine a soul with a kiss."
"Tell me about it," implored Paul. "I am so ignorant. Who was Huldebrand, and what did he do?"
So she began in a dreamy voice, and you who have read De la Motte Fouqué's dry version of this exquisite legend would hardly have recognised the poetry and pathos and tender sentiment she wove round those two, and the varied moods of Undine, and the passion of her knight. And when she came to the evening of their wedding, when the young priest had placed their hands together, and listened to their vows—when Undine had found her soul at last, in Huldebrand's arms—her voice faltered, and she stopped and looked down.
"And then?" said Paul, and his breath came rather fast. "And then?"
"He was a man, you see, Paul; so when he had won her love, he did not value it—he threw it away."
"Oh, no! I don't believe it!" Paul exclaimed vehemently. "It was just this brute Huldebrand. But you don't know men—to think they do not value what they win—you don't know them, indeed!"

She looked down straight into his face, as he gazed up at her, and to his intense surprise he could have sworn her eyes were green now! as green as emeralds. And they held him and fascinated him and paralysed him, like those of a snake.

"I do not know men?" she said softly. "You think not, Paul?"

But Paul could hardly speak, he buried his face in her lap, like a child, and kept it there, kissing her gloved hands. His straw hat, with its Zingari ribbon, lay on the grass beside him, and a tiny shaft of sunlight glanced through the trees, gilding the crisp waves of his brushed-back hair into dark burnished gold.

The lady moved one hand from his impassioned caress, and touched the curl with her finger-tips. She smiled with the tenderness a mother might have done.

"There—there!" she said. "Not yet." Then she drew her hand away from him and leant back, half closing her eyes.

Paul sat up and stared around. Each moment of the day was providing new emotions for him. Surely this was what Columbus must have felt, nearing the new world. He pulled himself together. She was not angry then at his outburst, and his caress—though something in her face warned him not to err again.

"Tell me the rest," he said pleadingly. "Why did he not value Undine's love, and what made the fool throw it away?"

"Because he possessed it, you see," said the lady. "That was reason enough, surely."

Then she told him of the ceasing of Undine's wayward moods after she had received her soul—of her docility—of her tenderness—of Huldebrand's certainty of her love. Then of his inevitable weariness. And at last of the Court, and the meeting again with Hildegarde, and of all the sorrow that followed, until the end, when the fountains burst their stoppings and rushed upwards, wreathing themselves into the figure of Undine, to take her Love to death with her kiss.

"Oh! he was wise!" Paul said. "He chose to die with her kiss. He knew at last then—what he had thrown away."

"That one learns often, Paul, when it has grown—too late! Come, let us live in the sunshine. Live while we may."

And the lady rose, and giving him her hand, she almost ran into the bright light of day, where even no tender shadows fell.

CHAPTER V

Their return journey was one of quiet. The lady talked little, she leant back and looked away across the blue lake, often apparently unconscious of his presence. This troubled Paul. Had he wearied her? What should he do? He was growing aware of the fact that she was not a bit like his mother, or Isabella, or any of the other women whom he knew—people whose moods he had never even speculated about—if they had any—which he doubted.

Why wouldn't she speak? Had she forgotten him? He felt chilled and saddened.

At last, as they neared a small bay where another tempting little chalet-hotel mirrored itself in the clear water, he spoke. A note in his voice—his charming young voice—as of a child in distress.

"Are—are you cross with me?"

Then she came back from her other world. "Cross with you? Foolish one! No, I am dreaming. And I forgot that you could not know yet, or understand. English Paul! who would have me make conversation and chatter commonplaces or he feels a *gêne!* See, I will take you where I have been into this infinite sky and air"—she let her hand fall on his arm and thrilled him—"look up at Pilatus. Do you see his head so snowy, and all the delicate shadows upon him, and his look of mystery? And those dark pines—and the great chasms, and the wild anger the giants were in when they hurled these huge rocks about? I have been with them, and you and I seem such little people, Paul. We cannot throw great rocks about—we are only two small ants in this grand world."

Paul's face was puzzled, he did not believe in giants. His mind was not accustomed yet to these flights of speech, he felt stupid and irritated with himself, and in some way humiliated. The lady leant over him, her face playfully tender.

"Great blue eyes!" she said. "So pretty, so pretty! What matter whether they can see or no?" And she touched his lids with her slender fingers.

Paul quivered in his chair.

"You know!" he gasped. "You make me mad—I——But won't you teach me to see? No one wants to be blind! Teach me to see with your eyes, lady—my lady."

"Yes, I will teach you!" she said. "Teach you a number of things. Together we will put on the hat of darkness and go down into Hades. We shall taste the apples of the Hesperides—we will rob Mercure of his sandals—and Gyges of his ring. And one day, Paul—when together we have fathomed the meaning of it all—what will happen then, *enfant?*"

Her last word, "*enfant,*" was a caress, and Paul was too bewildered with joy to answer her for a moment.

"What will happen?" he said at last. "I shall just love you—that's all!"

Then he remembered Isabella Waring, and suddenly covered his face with his hands.

They stopped for tea at the quaint châlet-hotel, and after it they wandered to pick gentians. The lady was sweet and sympathetic and gay; she ceased startling him with wild fancies; indeed, she spoke of simple everyday things, and got him to tell her of his home and Oxford, and his horses and his dogs. And when they arrived at the subject of Pike, her sympathy drew Paul nearer to her than ever. Of course she would love Pike if she only knew him! Who could help loving a dog like Pike? And his master waxed eloquent. Then, when he looked away, the lady's weird chameleon eyes melted upon him in that strange tenderness which might have been a mother's watching the gambols of her babe.

The shadows were quite deep when at last they decided to return to Lucerne—a small bunch of heaven's own blue flower the only trophy of the day.

Paul had never enjoyed himself so much in his twenty-three years of life. And what would the evening bring? Surely more joy. This parting at the landing could not be good-night!

But as the launch glided nearer and nearer his heart fell, and at last he could bear the uncertainty no longer.

"And for dinner?" he said. "Won't you dine me, my Princess? Let me be your host, as you have been mine all to-day."

But a stiffness seemed to fall upon her suddenly—she appeared to have become a stranger again almost.

"Thank you, no. I cannot dine," she said. "I must write letters—and go to sleep."

Paul felt an ice-hand clutching his heart. His face became so blank as to almost pale before her eyes.

She leant forward, and smiled. "Will you be lonely, Paul? Then at ten o'clock you must come under the ivy and wish me good-night."

And this was all he could gain from her. She landed him to walk back to the hotel at the same place from which they had embarked, and the launch struck out again into the lake.

He walked fast, just to be near enough to see her step ashore on to the hotel wharf, but he could not arrive in time, and her grey figure disappearing up the terrace steps was all his hungry eyes were vouchsafed.

The weariness of dinner! What did it matter what the food was? What did it matter that a new family of quite nice English people had arrived, and sat near? A fresh young girl and a youth, and a father and mother. People who would certainly play billiards and probably bridge. What did anything matter in the world? Time must be got through, simply got through until ten o'clock—that was all.

At half-past nine he strode out and sat upon the bench. His thoughts went back in a constant review of the day. How she had looked, where they had sat, what she had said. Why her eyes seemed green in the wood and blue on the water. Why her voice had all those tones in it. Why she had been old and young, and wise and childish. Then he thought of the story of Undine and the lady's strange, snake's look when she had said: "I do not know men?—You think not, Paul?"

His heart gave a great bound at the remembrance. He permitted himself no speculation as to where he was drifting. He just sat there thrilling in every limb and every sense and every quality of his brain.

As the clocks chimed the hour something told him she was there above him, although he heard no sound.

Not a soul was in sight in this quiet corner. He bounded on to the bench to be nearer—if she should come. If she were there hiding in the shadows. This was maddening—unbearable. He would climb the balustrade to see. Then out of the blackest gloom came a laugh of silver. A soft laugh that was almost a caress. And suddenly she crept close and leant down over the ivy.

"Paul," she whispered. "I have come, you see, to wish you—good-night!"

Paul stood up to his full height. He put out his arms to draw her to him, but she eluded him and darted aside.

He gave a great sigh of pain.

Slowly she came back and bent over and over of her own accord—so low that at last she was level with his face. And slowly her red lips melted into his young lips in a long, strange kiss.

Then, before Paul could grasp her, or murmur one pleading word, she was gone.

And again he found himself alone, intoxicated with emotion under the night sky studded with stars.

CHAPTER VI

Rain, rain, rain! That was not an agreeable sound to wake to when one had not had more than a few hours' sleep, and one's only hope of the day was to see one's lady again.

So Paul thought despairingly. What would happen? No lake, or mountain climb, was possible—but see her he must. After that kiss—that divine, enthralling, undreamed-of kiss. What did it mean? Did she love him? He loved her, that was certain. The poor feeble emotion he had experienced for Isabella was completely washed out and gone now.

He felt horribly ashamed of himself when he thought about it. His parents were perfectly right, of course; they had known best, and fortunately Isabella had not perhaps believed him, and was not a person of deep feeling anyway.

But the extreme discomfort of the thought of her made him toss in his bed. What ought he to do? Rush away from Lucerne? To what good? The die was cast, and in any case he was not bound to Isabella in any way. But at least he ought to write to her and tell her he had made a mistake. That was the only honest thing to do. A terrible duty, and he must brace himself up to accomplish it.

He breakfasted in his sitting-room, his thoughts scourging him the while, and afterwards, with a bulldog determination, he faced the writing-table and began.

He tore up at least three sheets to start with—no Greek lines of punishment in his boyhood had ever appeared such a task as this. He found himself scribbling profiles on the paper, chiselled profiles with inky hair—but no words would come.

"Dear Isabella," he wrote at last. No—"My dear Isabella," then he paused and bit the pen. "I feel I ought to tell you something has happened to me. I see my parents were right when—" "Oh! dash it all," he said to himself, "it's a beastly sneaking thing to do to put it like that," and he scratched the paragraph out and began again. "I have made a mistake in my feelings for you; I know now that they were those of a brother—" "O Lord, what am I to say next, it does sound bald, this!" The poor boy groaned and ran his hands through his curly hair, then seized the pen again, and continued—"as such I shall love you always, dear Isabella. Please forgive me if I have caused you any pain. It was all my fault, and I feel a beastly cad.—Your very unhappy PAUL."

This was not a masterpiece! but it would have to do. So he copied it out on a fresh piece of paper. Then, when it was all finished and addressed he ran down and posted it himself in the hall, with some of the emotions Alexander may have experienced when he burnt his ships.

The clock struck eleven. At what time would he see the lady—*his* lady he called her now. Some instinct told him she did not wish the hotel people to be aware of their acquaintance. He felt it wiser not to send a note. He must wait and hope.

Rain or not, he was too English to stay indoors all day. So out he went and into the town. The quaint bridge pleased him; he tried to think how she would have told him to use his eyes. He must not be stupid, he said to himself, and already he began to perceive new meanings in things. Coming back, he chanced to stop and look in at the fur shop under the hotel. There were some nice skins there, and what caught his attention most was a really splendid tiger. A magnificent creature the beast must have been. The deepest, most perfectly marked, largest one he had ever seen. He stood for some time admiring it. An infinitely better specimen than his lady had over her couch. Should he buy it for her? Would she take it? Would it please her to think he had remembered it might be what she would like?

He went into the shop. It was not even dear as tigers go, and his parents had given him ample money for any follies.

"Confound it, Henrietta! The boy must have his head!" Sir Charles Verdayne had said. "He's my son, you know, and you can't expect to cure him of one wench unless you provide him with shekels to buy another." Which crudely expressed wisdom had been followed, and Paul had no worries where his banking account was concerned.

He bought the tiger, and ordered it to be sent to his rooms immediately.

Then there was lunch to be thought of. She would not be there probably, but still he had a faint hope.

She was not there, nor were any preparations made for her; but when one is twenty-three and hungry, even if deeply in love, one must eat. The English people had the next table beyond the sacred one of the lady. The girl was pretty and young, and laughing. But what a doll! thought Paul. What a meaningless wax doll! Not worth—not worth a moment's glancing at.

And the pink and white fluffy girl was saying to herself: "There is Paul Verdayne again. I wish he remembered he had met me at the De Courcys', though we weren't introduced. I must get Percy to scrape up a conversation with him. I wish mamma had not made me wear this green alpaca to-day." But Paul's blue eyes gazed through and beyond her, and saw her not. So all this prettiness was wasted.

And directly after lunch he returned to his sitting room. The tiger would probably have arrived, and he wanted to further examine it. Yes, it was there. He pulled it out and spread it over the floor. What a splendid creature—it reminded him in some way of her—his lady.

Then he went into his bedroom and fetched a pair of scissors, and proceeded to kneel on the floor and pare away the pinked-out black cloth which came beyond the skin. It looked banal, and he knew she would not like that.

Oh! he was awaking! this beautiful young Paul.

He had scarcely finished when there was a tap at the door, and Dmitry appeared with a note. The thin, remembered paper thrilled him, and he took it from the servant's hand.

"Paul—I am in the devil's mood to-day. About 5 o'clock come to me by the terrace steps."

That was all—there was no date or signature. But Paul's heart beat in his throat with joy.

"I want the skin to go to Madame," he said. "Have you any means of conveying it to her without the whole world seeing it go?"

The stately servant bowed. "If the Excellency would help him to fold it up," he said, "he would take it now to his own room, and from thence to the *appartement numero 3*."

It is not a very easy thing to fold up a huge tiger-skin into a brown paper parcel tied with string. But it was accomplished somehow and Dmitry disappeared noiselessly with it and an answer to the note:

"I will be there, sweet lady.

"Your own PAUL."

And he was.

A bright fire burnt in the grate, and some palest orchid-mauve silk curtains were drawn in the lady's room when Paul entered from the terrace. And loveliest sight of all, in front of the fire, stretched at full length, was his tiger—and on him—also at full length—reclined the lady, garbed in some strange clinging garment of heavy purple crepe, its hem embroidered with gold, one white arm resting on the beast's head, her back supported by a pile of the velvet cushions, and a heap of rarely bound books at her side, while between her red lips was a rose not redder than they—an almost scarlet rose. Paul had never seen one as red before.

The whole picture was barbaric. It might have been some painter's dream of the Favourite in a harem. It was not what one would expect to find in a sedate Swiss hotel.

She did not stir as he stepped in, dropping the heavy curtains after him. She merely raised her eyes, and looked Paul through and through. Her whole expression was changed; it was wicked and dangerous and *provocante*. It seemed quite true, as she had said—she was evidently in the devil's mood.

Paul bounded forward, but she raised one hand to stop him.

"No! you must not come near me, Paul. I am not safe to-day. Not yet. See, you must sit there and we will talk."

And she pointed to a great chair of Venetian workmanship and wonderful old velvet which was new to his view.

"I bought that chair in the town this morning at the curiosity shop on the top of Weggisstrasse, which long ago was the home of the Venetian envoy here—and you bought me the tiger, Paul. Ah! that was good. My beautiful tiger!" And she gave a movement like a snake, of joy to feel its fur under her, while she stretched out her hands and caressed the creature where the hair turned white and black at the side, and was deep and soft.

"Beautiful one! beautiful one!" she purred. "And I know all your feelings and your passions, and now I have got your skin—for the joy of my skin!" And she quivered again with the movements of a snake.

It is not difficult to imagine that Paul felt far from calm during this scene—indeed he was obliged to hold on to his great chair to prevent himself from seizing her in his arms.

"I'm—I'm so glad you like him," he said in a choked voice. "I thought probably you would. And your own was not worthy of you. I found this by chance. And oh! good God! if you knew how you are making me feel—lying there wasting your caresses upon it!"

She tossed the scarlet rose over to him; it hit his mouth.

"I am not wasting them," she said, the innocence of a kitten in her strange eyes—their colour impossible to define to-day. "Indeed not, Paul! He was my lover in another life—perhaps—who knows?"

"But I," said Paul, who was now quite mad, "want to be your lover in this!"

Then he gasped at his own boldness.

With a lightning movement she lay on her face, raised her elbows on the tiger's head, and supported her chin in her hands. Perfectly straight out her body was, the twisted purple drapery outlining her perfect shape, and flowing in graceful lines beyond—like a serpent's tail. The velvet pillows fell scattered at one side.

"Paul—what do you know of lovers—or love?" she said. "My baby Paul!"

"I know enough to know I know nothing yet which is worth knowing," he said confusedly. "But—but—don't you understand, I want you to teach me—"

"You are so sweet, Paul! when you plead like that I am taking in every bit of you. In your way as perfect as this tiger. But we must talk—oh! such a great, great deal—first."

A rage of passion was racing through Paul, his incoherent thoughts were that he did not want to talk—only to kiss her—to devour her—to strangle her with love if necessary.

He bit the rose.

"You see, Paul, love is a purely physical emotion," she continued. "We could speak an immense amount about souls, and sympathy, and understanding, and devotion. All beautiful things in their way, and possible to be enjoyed at a distance from one another. All the things which make passion noble—but without love—which *is* passion—these things dwindle and become duties presently, when the hysterical exaltation cools. Love is *tangible*—it means to be close—close—to be clasped—to be touching—to be One!"

Her voice was low—so concentrated as to be startling in contrast to the drip of the rain outside, and her eyes—half closed and gleaming—burnt into his brain. It seemed as if strange flames of green darted from their pupils.

"But that is what I want!" Paul said, unsteadily.

"Without counting the cost? Tears and—cold steel—and blood!" she whispered. "Wait a while, beautiful Paul!"

He started back chilled for a second, and in that second she changed her position, pulling the cushions around her, nestling into them and drawing herself cosily up like a child playing on a mat in front of the fire, while with a face of perfect innocence she looked up as she drew one of her great books nearer, and said in a dreamy voice:

"Now we will read fairy-tales, Paul."

But Paul was too moved to speak. These rapid changes were too much for him, greatly advanced though he had become in these short days since he had known her. He leant back in his chair, every nerve in his body quivering, his young fresh face almost pale.

"Paul," she cooed plaintively, "to-morrow I shall be reasonable again, perhaps, and human, but to-day I am capricious and wayward, and mustn't be teased. I want to read about Cupid and Psyche from this wonderful 'Golden Ass' of Apuleius—just a simple tale for a wet day—and you and—me!"

"Read then!" said Paul, resigned.

And she commenced in Latin, in a chanting, tender voice. Paul had forgotten most of the Latin he knew, but he remembered enough to be aware that this must be as easy as English to her as it flowed along in a rich rhythmic sound.

It soothed him. He seemed to be dreaming of flowery lands and running streams. After a while she looked up again, and then with one of her sudden movements like a graceful cat, she was beside him leaning from the back of his chair.

"Paul!" she whispered right in his ear, "am I being wicked for you to-day? I cannot help it. The devil is in me—and now I must sing."

"Sing then!" said Paul, maddened with again arising emotion.

She seized a guitar that lay near, and began in a soft voice in some language he knew not—a cadence of melody he had never heard, but one whose notes made strange quivers all up his spine. An exquisite pleasure of sound that was almost pain. And when he felt he could bear no more, she flung the instrument aside, and leant over his chair again—caressing his curls with her dainty fingers, and purring unknown strange words in his ear.

Paul was young and unlearned in many things. He was completely enthralled and under her dominion—but he was naturally no weakling of body or mind. And this was more than he could stand.

"*You* mustn't be teased. My God! it is you who are maddening me!" he cried, his voice hoarse with emotion. "Do you think I am a statue, or a table, or chair—or inanimate like that tiger there? I am not, I tell you!" and he seized her in his arms, raining kisses upon her which, whatever they lacked in subtlety, made up for in their passion and strength. "Some day some man will kill you, I suppose, but I shall be your lover—first!"

The lady gasped. She looked up at him in bewildered surprise, as a child might do who sets a light to a whole box of matches in play. What a naughty, naughty toy to burn so quickly for such a little strike!

But Paul's young, strong arms held her close, she could not struggle or move. Then she laughed a laugh of pure glad joy.

"Beautiful, savage Paul," she whispered. "Do you love me? Tell me that?"

"Love you!" he said. "Good God! Love you! Madly, and you know it, darling Queen."

"Then," said the lady in a voice in which all the caresses of the world seemed melted, "then, sweet Paul, I shall teach you many things, and among them I shall teach you how—to—LIVE."

And outside the black storm made the darkness fall early. And inside the half-burnt logs tumbled together, causing a cloud of golden sparks, and then the flames leapt up again and crackled in the grate.

CHAPTER VII

At dinner that night the lady came in after Paul was seated. She was all in black velvet, stately and dignified and fine. She passed his chair and took her seat, not the faintest sign of recognition on her face. And although he was prepared for this, for some reason his heart sank for a moment. Her demeanour was the same as on the first night he had seen her, hardly raising her eyes, eating little of the most exquisite food, and appearing totally unconscious of her neighbours or their ways.

She caused a flutter of excitement at the English table, the only other party, except two old men in a corner, who had dined so late, and they were half-way through their repast before she began hers. Paul was annoyed to see how they stared—stared at *his* lady. But what joy it was to sit there and realise that she was his—his very own! And only four nights ago he had been a rude stranger, too, criticising her every movement, and drinking too much port with annoyance over it all. And now his whole life was changed. He saw with new eyes, and heard with new ears, even his casual observation was altered and sharpened, so that he noticed the texture of the cloth and the quality of the glass, and the shape of the room and its decoration.

And how insupportably commonplace the good English family seemed! That bread-and-butter miss with her pink cheeks and fluffy hair, without a hat! Women's hair should be black and grow in heavy waves. He was certain of that now. How like them to come into a foreign restaurant hatless, just because they were English and must impose their customs! He sat and mused on it all, as he looked at his velvet-clad Queen. A sense of complete joy and satisfaction stealing over him, his wild excitement and emotion calmed for the time.

The delightful sensation of sharing a secret with her—a love-secret known only to themselves. Think, if these Philistines guessed at it even! their faces. And at this thought Paul almost laughed aloud.

With passionate interest he absorbed every little detail about his lady. How exactly she knew what suited her. How refined and *grande dame* and quiet it all was, and what an air of breeding and command she had in the poise of her little Greek head.

What did it matter what age she was, or of what nation? What did anything matter since she was his? And at that thought his heart began to beat again and cause him to speculate as to his evening.

Would she let him come back to the terrace room after dinner, or must he get through the time as best he could? When he had left her, half dazed with joy and languor, no arrangements had been made—no definite plans settled. But of course she could not mean him not to wish her good-night—not *now*. For one second before she left the room their eyes met, she raised a red rose, which she had taken from the silver vase, casually to her lips, and then passed out, but Paul knew she had meant the kiss for him, and his whole being was uplifted.

It was still pouring with rain. No possible excuse to smoke on the terrace. It might be wiser to stay in the hall. Surely Dmitry would come with some message before very long, if he was patient and waited her pleasure. But ten o'clock struck and there was no sign. Only the English youth, Percy Trevellian, had got into conversation with him, and was proposing billiards to pass the time.

Paul loved billiards—but not to-night. Heavens! what an idea! Go off to the billiard-room—now—to-night!

He said he had a headache, and answered rather shortly in fact, and then, to escape further importunity, went up to his sitting-room, there to await the turn of events, leaving poor little Mabel Trevellian gazing after him with longing eyes.

"Did you see at dinner how he stared at that foreign person, mamma?" she said. "Men are such fools! Clarkson told me, as she fastened my dress to-night, she'd heard she was some Grand Duchess, or Queen, travelling incognito for her health. Very plain and odd-looking, didn't you think so, mamma? And quite old!"

"No, dear. Most distinguished. Not a girl, of course, but quite the appearance of a Princess," said Mabel's mother, who had seen the world.

Paul meanwhile paced his room—an anxious excitement was now his portion. Surely, surely she could not mean him not to see her—not to say one little good-night. What should he do? What possible plan invent? As eleven chimed he could bear it no longer. Rain or no, he must go out on the terrace!

"Those mad English!" the porter said to himself, as he watched Paul's tall figure disappear in the dripping night.

And there till after twelve he paced the path under the trees. But no light showed; the terrace gate was locked. It was chilly and wet and miserable, and at last he crept back utterly depressed, to bed. But not to sleep. Even his youth and health were not proof against the mad emotions of the day. He tossed and turned, a thousand questions singing in his brain. Was it really he who had been chosen by this divine woman for her lover? And if so, why was he alone now instead of holding her in his arms? What did it all mean? Who was she? Where would it end? But here he refused to think further. He was living at all events—living as he had never dreamed was possible.

And yet, poor Paul, he was only on the rim of all that he was soon to know of life.

At last he fell asleep, one sentence ringing in his ears—"Tears and—cold steel—and blood!" But if he was young, he was a gallant gentleman, and Fear had no place in his dreams.

CHAPTER VIII

Next day they went to the Bürgenstock to stay. It was all arranged with consummate simplicity. Paul was to start for a climb, he told his valet, and for a week they would leave Lucerne. Mme. Zalenska was not very well, it appeared, and consented to try, at the suggestion of the amiable manager—inspired by Dmitry—a few days in higher air. There would not be a soul in their hotel on top of the Bürgenstock probably, and she could have complete rest.

They did not arrive together, Paul was the first. He had not seen her. Dmitry had given him his final instructions, and he awaited her coming with passionate impatience.

He had written to her, on awaking, a coherent torrent of love, marvellously unlike the letter which had gone to poor Isabella only a few days before. In this to his lady he had said he could not bear it *now*, the uncertainty of seeing her, and had suggested the Bürgenstock crudely, without any of the clever details which afterwards made it possible.

He—Paul Verdayne, not quite twenty-three years old, and English—to suggest without a backward thought or a qualm that a lady whom he had known five days should come and live with him and be his love! None of his friends accustomed to his bashful habits would have believed it. Only his father perhaps might have smiled.

As for the Lady Henrietta, she would have fainted on the spot. But fortune favoured him—they did not know.

No excitement of the wildest day's hunting had ever made his pulses bound like this! Dmitry had arranged everything. Paul was a young English secretary to Madame, who had much writing to do. And in any case it is not the affair of respectable foreign hotels to pry into their clients' relationship when a large suite has been engaged.

Paul's valet, the son of an old retainer of the family, was an honest fellow, and devoted to his master—but Sir Charles Verdayne had decided to make things doubly sure.

"Tompson," he had said, the morning before they left, "however Mr. Verdayne may amuse himself while you are abroad, your eyes and mouth are shut, remember. No d——d gossip back to the servants here, or in hotels, or houses—and, above all, no details must ever reach her Ladyship. If he gets into any thundering mess let me know—but mum's the word, d'y understand, Tompson?"

"I do, Sir Charles," said Tompson, stolidly.

And he did, as events proved.

The rooms on the Bürgenstock looked so simple, so unlike the sitting-room at Lucerne! Just fresh and clean and primitive. Paul wandered through them, and in the one allotted to himself he came upon Anna—Madame's maid, whom Dmitry had pointed out to him—putting sheets as fine as gossamer on his bed; with the softest down pillows. How dear of his lady to think thus of him!—her secretary.

The tiger—his tiger—had arrived in the sitting-room, and some simple cushions of silk; sweet-peas and spring flowers decorated the vases—there were no tuberoses, or anything hot-house, or forced.

The sun blazed in at the windows, the green trees all washed and fresh from the rain gladdened his eye, and down below, a sapphire lake reflected the snow-capped mountains. What a setting for a love-dream. No wonder Paul trod on air!

The only possible crumpled rose-leaves were some sentences in the lady's reply to his impassioned letter of the morning:

"Yes, I will come, Paul—but only on one condition, that you never ask me questions as to who I am, or where I am going. You must promise me to take life as a summer holiday—an episode—and if fate gives us this great joy, you must not try to fetter me, now or at any future time, or control my movements. You must give me your word of honour for this—you will never seek to discover who or what was your loved one—you must never try to follow me. Yes, I will come for now—when I have your assurance—but I will go when I will go—in silence."

And Paul had given his word. He felt he could not look ahead. He must just live in this gorgeous joy, and trust to chance. So he awaited her, thrilling in all his being.

About tea time she drove up in a carriage—she and Dmitry having come the long way round.

And was it not right that her secretary should meet and assist her out, and conduct her to her apartments?

How beautiful she looked, all in palest grey, and somehow the things had a younger shape. Her skirt was short, and he could see her small and slender feet, while a straw hat and veil adorned her black hair. Everything was simple, and as it should be for a mountain top and unsophisticated surroundings.

Tea was laid out on the balcony, fragrant Russian tea, and when Dmitry had lit the silver kettle lamp he retired and left them alone in peace.

"Darling!" said Paul, as he folded her in his arms—"darling!—darling!"

And when she could speak the lady cooed back to him:

"So sweet a word is that, my Paul. Sweeter in English than in any other language. And you are glad I have come, and we shall live a little and be quite happy here in our pretty nest, all fresh and not a bit too grand—is it not so? Oh! what joys there are in life; and oh! how foolish just to miss them."

"Indeed, *yes*," said Paul.

Then they played with the tea, and she showed him how he was to drink it with lemon. She was sweet as a girl, and said no vague, startling things; it was as if she were a young bride, and Paul were complete master and lord! Wild happiness rushed through him. How had he ever endured the time before he had met her?

When they had finished they went out. She must walk, she said, and Paul, being English, must want exercise! Oh! she knew the English and their exercise! And of course she must think of everything that would be for the pleasure of her lover Paul.

And he? You old worn people of the world, who perhaps are reading, think what all this was to Paul—his young strong life vibrating to passionate joys, his imagination kindled, his very being uplifted and thrilled with happiness! His charming soul expanded, he found himself saying gracious tender phrases to her. Every moment he was growing more passionately in love, and in each new mood she seemed the more divine. Not one trace of her waywardness of the day before remained. Her eyes, as they glanced at him from under her hat, were bashful and sweet, no look of the devil to provoke a saint. She talked gently.

He must take her to the place where she had peeped at him through the trees. And—

"Oh! Paul!" she said. "If you had known that day, how you tempted me, looking up at me, your whole soul in your eyes! I had to run, run, run!"

"And now I have caught you, darling mine," said Paul. "But you were wrong. I had no soul—it is you who are giving me one now."

They sat on the bench where he had sat. She was getting joy out of the colour of the moss, the tints of the beeches, every little shade and shape of nature, and letting Paul see with her eyes.

And all the while she was nestling near him like a tender ring-dove to her mate. Paul's heart swelled with exultation. He felt good, as if he could be kind to every one, as if his temper were a thing to be ashamed of, and all his faults, as if for ever he must be her own true knight and defender, and show her he was worthy of this great gift and joy. And ah! how could he put into words his tender worshipping love?

So the afternoon faded into evening, and the young crescent moon began to show in the sky—a slender moon of silver, only born the night before.

"See, this is our moon," said the lady, "and as she waxes, so will our love wax—but now she is young and fresh and fair, like it. Come, my Paul. Let us go to our house; soon we shall dine, and I want to be beautiful for you."

So they went in to their little hotel.

She was all in white when Paul found her in their inner salon, where they were to dine alone, waited on only by Dmitry. Her splendid hair was bound with a fillet of gold, and fell in two long strands, twisted with gold, nearly to her knees. Her garment was soft and clinging, and unlike any garment he had ever seen. They sat on a sofa together, the table in front of them, and they ate slowly and whispered much—and before Paul could taste his wine, she kissed his glass and sipped from it and made him do the same with hers. The food was of the simplest, and the only things exotic were the great red strawberries at the end.

Dmitry had left them, placing the coffee on the table as he went, and a bottle of the rare golden wine.

Then this strange lady grew more tender still. She must lie in Paul's arms, and he must feed her with strawberries. And the thought came to him that her mouth looked as red as they.

To say he was intoxicated with pleasure and love is to put it as it was. It seemed as if he had arrived at a zenith, and yet he knew there would be more to come. At last she raised herself and poured out the yellow wine—into one glass.

"My Paul," she said, "this is our wedding might, and this is our wedding wine. Taste from this our glass and say if it is good."

And to the day of his death, if ever Paul should taste that wine again, a mad current of passionate remembrance will come to him—and still more passionate regret.

Oh! the divine joy of that night! They sat upon the balcony presently, and Elaine in her worshipping thoughts of Lancelot—Marguerite wooed by Faust—the youngest girl bride—could not have been more sweet or tender or submissive than this wayward Tiger Queen.

"Paul," she said, "out of the whole world tonight there are only you and I who matter, sweetheart. Is it not so? And is not that your English word for lover and loved—'sweetheart'?"

And Paul, who had never even heard it used except in a kind of joke, now knew it was what he had always admired. Yes, indeed, it was "sweetheart"—and she was his!

"Remember, Paul," she whispered when, passion maddening him, he clasped her violently in his arms—"remember—whatever happens—whatever comes—for now, to-night, there is no other reason in all of this but just—I love you—I love you, Paul!"

"My Queen, my Queen!" said Paul, his voice hoarse in his throat.

And the wind played in softest zephyrs, and the stars blazed in the sky, mirroring themselves in the blue lake below.

Such was their wedding night.
Oh! glorious youth! and still more glorious love!

CHAPTER IX

Who can tell the joy of their awakening? The transcendent pleasure to Paul to be allowed to play with his lady's hair, all unbound for him to do with as he willed? The glory to realise she was his—his own—in his arms? And then to be tenderly masterful and give himself lordly airs of possession. She was almost silent, only the history of the whole world of passion seemed written in her eyes—slumbrous, inscrutable, their heavy lashes making shadows on her soft, smooth cheeks.

The ring-dove was gone, a thing of mystery lay there instead—unresisting, motionless, white. Now and then Paul looked at her half in fear. Was she real? Was it some dream, and would he wake in his room at Verdayne Place among the sporting prints and solid Chippendale furniture to hear Tompson saying, "Eight o'clock, sir, and a fine day"?

Oh, no, no, she was real! He raised himself, and bent down to touch her tenderly with his forefinger. Yes, all this fascination was indeed his, living and breathing and warm, and he was her lover and lord. Ah!

The same coloured orchid-mauve silk curtains as at Lucerne were drawn over the open windows, so the sun in high heaven seemed only as dawn in the room, filtering though the *jalousies* outside. But what was time? Time counts as one lives, and Paul was living now.

It was twelve o'clock before they were ready for their dainty breakfast, laid out under the balcony awning.

And the lady talked tenderly and occupied herself with the fancies of her lord, as a new bride should.

But all the time the mystery stayed in her eyes. And the thought came to Paul that were he to live with her for a hundred years, he would never be sure of their real meaning.

"What shall we do with our day, my Paul?" she said presently. "See, you shall choose. Shall we climb to the highest point on this mountain and look at our kingdom of trees and lake below? Or shall we rest in the launch and glide over the blue water, and dream sweet dreams? Or shall we drive in the carriage far inland to a quaint farmhouse I know, where we shall see people living in simple happiness with their cows and their sheep? Decide, sweetheart—decide!"

"Whatever you would wish, my Queen," said Paul.

Then the lady frowned, and summer lightnings flashed from her eyes.

"Of course, what I shall wish! But I have told you to choose, feeble Paul! There is nothing so irritates me as these English answers. Should I have asked you to select our day had I decided myself? I would have commanded Dmitry to make the arrangements, that is all. But no! to-day I am thy obedient one. I ask my Love to choose for me. To-morrow I may want my own will; to-day I desire only thine, beloved," and she leant forward and looked into his eyes.

"The mountain top, then!" said Paul, "because there we can sit, and I can gaze at you, and learn more of life, close to your lips. I might not touch you in the launch, and you might look at others at the farm—and it seems as if I could not bear one glance or word turned from myself today!"

"You have chosen well. *Mylyi moi.*"

The strange words pleased him; he must know their meaning, and learn to pronounce them himself. And all this between their dainty dishes took time, so it was an hour later before they started for their walk.

Up, up those winding paths among the firs and larches—up and up to the top. They dawdled slowly until they reached their goal. There, aloof from the beaten track, safe from the prying eyes of some chance stranger, they sat down, their backs against a giant rock, and all the glory of their lake and tree-tops to gaze at down below.

Paul had carried her cloak, and now they spread it out, covering their couch of moss and lichen. A soft languor was over them both. Passion was asleep for the while. But what exquisite bliss to sit thus, undisturbed in their eyrie—he and she alone in all the world.

Her words came back to him: "Love means to be clasped, to be close, to be touching, to be One!" Yes, they were One.

Then she began to talk softly, to open yet more windows in his soul to joy and sunshine. Her mind seemed so vast, each hour gave him fresh surprises in the perception of her infinite knowledge, while she charmed his fancy by her delicate modes of expression and un-English perfect pronunciation, no single word slurred over.

"Paul," she said presently, "how small seem the puny conventions of the world, do they not, beloved? Small as those little boats floating like scattered flower-leaves on the great lake down there. They were invented first to fill the place of the zest which fighting and holding one's own by the strength of one's arm originally gave to man. Now, he has only laws to combat, instead of a fiercer fellow creature—a dull exchange forsooth! Here are you and I—mated and wedded and perfectly happy—and yet by these foolish laws we are sinning, and you would be more nobly employed yawning with some bony English miss for your wife—and I by the side of a mad, drunken husband. All because the law made us swear a vow to keep for ever stationary an emotion! Emotion which we can no more control than the trees can which way the wind will blow their branches! To love! Oh! yes, they call it that at the altar—'joined together by God!' As likely as not two human creatures who hate each other, and are standing there swearing those impossibilities for some political purpose and advantage of their family. They desecrate the word love. Love is for us, Paul, who came together because our beings cried, 'This is my mate!' I should say nothing of it—oh no! if it had no pretence—marriage. If it were frankly a contract—'Yes, I give you my body and my dowry.' 'Yes, you give me your name and your state.' It is of the coarse, horrible things one must pass through in life—but to call the Great Spirit's blessing upon it, as an exaltation! To stand there and talk of love! Ah—that is what must make God angry, and I feel for Him."

Paul noticed that she spoke as if she had no realisation of the lives of lesser persons who might possibly wed because they were "mated" as well—not for political reasons or ambition of family. Her keen senses divined his thought.

"Yes, beloved, you would say—?"

"Only that supposing you were not married to any one else, we should be swearing the truth if we swore before God that we loved. I would make any vows to you from my soul, in perfect honesty, for ever and ever, my darling Queen."

His blue eyes, brimming with devotion and conviction of the truth of his thought, gazed up at her. And into her strange orbs there came that same look of tenderness that once before had made them as a mother's watching the gambols of her babe.

"There, there," she said. "You would swear them and hug your chains of roses—but because they were chains they would turn heavy as lead. Make no vows, sweetheart! Fate will force you to break them if you do, and then the gods are angry and misfortune follows. Swear none, and that fickle one will keep you passionate, in hopes always to lure you into her pitfalls—to vow and to break—pain and regret. Live, live, Paul, and love, and swear nothing at all."

Paul was troubled. "But, but," he said, "don't you believe I shall love you for ever?"

The lady leant back against the rock and narrowed her eyes.

"That will depend upon me, my Paul," she said. "The duration of love in a being always depends upon the loved one. I create an emotion in you, as you create one in me. You do not create it in yourself. It is because something in my personality causes an answering glow in yours that you love me. Were you to cease to do so, it would be because I was no longer able to call forth that answer in you. It would not be your fault any more than when you cease to please me it will be mine. That is where people are unjust."

"But surely," said Paul, "it is only the fickle who can change?"

"It is according to one's nature; if one is born a steadfast gentleman, one is more likely to continue than if one is a *farceur*—prince or no—but it depends upon the object of one's love—whether he or she can hold one or not. One would not blame a needle if it fell from a magnet, the attraction of the magnet being in some way removed, either by a stronger at the needle's side, or by some deadening of the drawing quality in the magnet itself—and so it is in love. Do you follow me, Paul?"

"Yes." said Paul gloomily. "I must try to please you, or you will throw me away."

"You see," she continued, "the ignorant make vows, and being weaklings—for the most part—vanity and fate easily remove their inclination from the loved one; it may not be his fault any more than a broken leg keeping him from walking would be his fault, beyond the fact that it was *his* leg; but we have to suffer for our own things—so there it is. We will say the weakling's inclination wants to make him break his vows; so he does, either in the letter or spirit—or both! And then he feels degraded and cheap and low, as all must do who break their sacred word given of their own free will when inclination prompted them to. So how much better to make no vow; then at least when the cord of attraction snaps, we can go free, still defying the lightning in our untarnished pride."

"Oh! darling, do not speak of it," cried Paul, "the cord of attraction between us can never snap. I worship, I adore you—you are just my life, my darling one, my Queen!"

"Sweet Paul!" she whispered, "oh! so good, so good is love, keep me loving you, my beautiful one—keep my desire long to be your Queen."

And after this they melted into one another's arms, and cooed and kissed, and were foolish and incoherent, as lovers always are and have been from the beginning of old time. More concentrated—more absorbed—than the sternest Eastern sage—absorbed in each other.

The spirit of two natures vibrating as One.

CHAPTER X

That evening it was so warm and peaceful they dined at the wide-open balcony windows. They could see far away over the terrace and down to the lake, with the distant lights towards Lucerne. The moon, still slender and fine, was drawing to her setting, and a few cloudlets floated over the sky, obscuring the stars here and there.

The lady was quiet and tender, her eyes melting upon Paul, and something of her ring-dove mood was upon her again. Not once, since they had been on the Bürgenstock, had she shown any of the tigerish waywardness that he had had glimpses of at first. It seemed as if her moods, like her chameleon eyes, took colour from her surroundings, and there all was primitive simplicity and nature and peace.

Paul himself was in a state of ecstasy. He hardly knew whether he trod on air or no. No siren of old Greek fable had ever lured mortal more under her spell than this strange foreign woman thing—Queen or Princess or what you will. Nothing else in the world was of any consequence to him—and it was all the more remarkable because subjection was in no way part of his nature. Paul was a masterful youth, and ruled things to his will in his own home.

The lady talked of him—of his tastes—of his pleasures. There was not an incident in his life, or of his family, that she had not fathomed by now. All about Isabella even—poor Isabella! And she told him how she sympathised with the girl, and how badly he had behaved.

"Another proof, my Paul, of what I said today—no one must make vows about love."

But Paul, in his heart, believed her not. He would worship her for ever, he knew.

"Yes," she said, answering his thoughts. "You think so, beloved, and it may be so because you do not know from moment to moment how I shall be—if I shall stay here in your arms, or fly far away beyond your reach. You love me because I give you the stimulus of uncertainty, and so keep bright your passion, but once you were sure, I should become a duty, as all women become, and then my Paul would yawn and grow to see I was no longer young, and that the expected is always an *ennui* when it comes!"

"Never, never!" said Paul, with fervour.

Presently their conversation drifted to other things, and Paul told her how he longed to see the world and its people and its ways. She had been almost everywhere, it seemed, and with her talent of word-painting, she took him with her on the magic carpet of her vivid description to east and west and north and south.

Oh! their *entr'actes* between the incoherence of just lovers' love were not banal or dull. And never she forgot her tender ways of insinuated caresses—small exquisite touches of sentiment and grace. The note ever of One—that they were fused and melted together into one body and soul.

Through all her talk that night Paul caught glimpses of the life of a great lady, surrounded with state and cares, and now and then there was a savage echo which made him think of things barbaric, and wonder more than ever from whence she had come.

It was quite late before the chill of night airs drove them into their salon, and here she made him some Russian tea, and then lay in his arms, and purred love-words to him, and nestled close like a child who wants petting to cure it of some imaginary hurt. Only, in her tenderest caresses he seemed at last to feel something of danger. A slumbering look of passion far under the calm exterior, but ready to break forth at any moment from its studied control.

It thrilled and maddened him.

"Beloved, beloved!" he cried, "let us waste no more precious moments. I want you—I want you—my sweet!"

* * * * *

At the first glow of dawn, he awoke, a strange sensation, almost of strangling and suffocation, upon him. There, bending over, framed in a mist of blue-black waves, he saw his lady's face. Its milky whiteness lit by her strange eyes—green as cats' they seemed, and blazing with the fiercest passion of love—while twisted round his throat he felt a great strand of her splendid hair. The wildest thrill as yet his life had known then came to Paul; he clasped her in his arms with a frenzy of mad, passionate joy.

CHAPTER XI

The next day was Sunday, and even through the silk blinds they could hear the rain drip in monotonous fashion. Of what use to wake? Sleep is blissful and calm when the loved one is near.

Thus it was late when Paul at last opened his eyes. He found himself alone, and heard his lady's voice singing softly from the sitting-room beyond, and through the open door he could perceive her stretched on the tiger, already dressed, reclining among the silk pillows, her guitar held in her hands.

"Hasten, hasten, lazy one. Thy breakfast awaits thee," she called, and Paul bounded up without further delay.

This day was to be a day of books, she said, and she read poetry to him, and made him read to her—but she would not permit him to sit too near her, or caress her—and often she was restless and moved about with the undulating grace of a cat. She would peep from the windows, and frown at the scene. The lake was hidden by mist, the skies cried, all nature was weeping and gloomy.

And at last she flung the books aside, and crept up to Paul, who was huddled on the sofa, feeling rather morose from her decree that he must not touch or kiss her.

"Weeping skies, I hate you!" she said. Then she called Dmitry in a sharp voice, and when he appeared from the passage where he always awaited her pleasure, she spoke to him in Russian, or some language Paul knew not, a fierce gleam in her eyes. Dmitry abased himself almost to the floor, and departing quickly, returned with sticks and lit a blazing pine-log fire in the open grate. Then he threw some powder into it, and with stealthy haste drew all the orchid-silk curtains, and departed from the room. A strange divine scent presently rose in the air, and over Paul seemed to steal a spell. The lady crept still nearer, and then with infinite sweetness, all her docility of the first hours of their union returned, she melted in his arms.

"Paul—I am so wayward to-day, forgive me," she said in a childish, lisping voice. "See, I will make you forget the rain and damp. Fly with me to Egypt where the sun always shines."

And Paul, like a sulky, hungry baby, who had been debarred, and now received its expected sweetmeat, clasped her and kissed her for a few minutes before he would let her speak.

"See, we are getting near Cairo," she said, her eyes half closed, while she settled herself among the cushions, and drew Paul down to her until his head rested on her breast, and her arms held him like a mother with a child.

Her voice was a dream-voice as she whispered on. "Do you not love those minarets and towers against the opal sky, and the rose-pink granite hills beyond? And look, Paul, at this peep of the Nile—those are the water-buffaloes—those strange beasts—you see they are pulling that ridiculous water-drawer—just the same as in Pharaoh's time. Ah! I smell the scent of the East. Look at the straight blue figures, the lines so pleasing and long. The dignity, the peace, the forever in it all.... Now we are there. See the brilliant crowd all moving with little haste, and listen to the strange noise. Look at the faces of the camels, disdainful and calm, and that of an old devil-man with tangled hair....

"Come—come from this; I want the desert and the Sphinx!

"Ah! it is bright day again, and we have all the green world between us and the great vast brown tract of sand. And those are the Pyramids clear-cut against the turquoise sky, and soon we shall be there, only you must observe this green around us first, my Paul—the green of no other country in all the world—pure emerald—nature's supreme concentrated effort of green for miles and miles. No, I do not want to live in that small village in a brown mud hut, shared with another wife to that gaunt blue linen-clad man; I would kill them all and be free. I want to go on, beloved—on to the desert for you and me alone, with its wonderful passion, and wonderful peace...."

Her voice became still more dreamy; there was a cadence in it now as if some soul within were forcing her to chant it all, with almost the lilt of blank verse.

"Oh! the strange drug of the glorious East, flooding your senses with beauty and life. 'Tis the spell of the Sphinx, and now we are there, close in her presence. Look, the sun has set....

"Hush! hush! beloved! we are alone, the camels and guides afar off—we are alone, sweetheart, and we go on together, you and I and the moon. See, she is rising all silver and pure, and blue is the sky, and scented the night. Look, there is the Sphinx! Do you see the strange mystery of her smile and the glamour of her eyes? She is a goddess, and she knows men's souls, and their foolish unavailing passion and pain—never content with the *Is* which they have, always regretting the *Was* which has passed, and building false hopes on the phantom *May be.* But you and I, my lover, my sweet, have fathomed the riddle which is hid in the smile of our goddess, our Sphinx—we have guessed it, and now are as high gods too. For we know it means to live in the present, and quaff life in its full. Sweetheart, beloved—joy and life in its full——"....

Her voice grew faint and far away, like the echo of some exquisite song, and the lids closed over Paul's blue eyes, and he slept.

The light of all the love in the world seemed to flood the lady's face. She bent over and kissed him, and smoothed his cheek with her velvet cheek, she moved so that his curly lashes might touch her bare neck, and at last she slipped from under him, and laid his head gently down upon the pillows.

Then a madness of tender caressing seized her. She purred as a tiger might have done, while she undulated like a snake. She touched him with her finger-tips, she kissed his throat, his wrists, the palms of his hands, his eyelids, his hair. Strange, subtle kisses, unlike the kisses of women. And often, between her purrings, she murmured love-words in some strange fierce language of her own, brushing his ears and his eyes with her lips the while.

And through it all Paul slept on, the Eastern perfume in the air still drugging his sense.

It was quite dark when he awoke again, and beside him—seated on the floor, all propped with pillows, his lady reclined her head against his shoulder. And as he looked down at her in the firelight's flickering gleam, he saw that her wonderful eyes were wet with great glittering tears.

"My soul, my soul!" he said tenderly, his heart wrung with emotion. "What is it, sweetheart—why have you these tears? Oh! what have I done—darling, my own?"

"I am weary," she said, and fell to weeping softly, and refused to be comforted.

Paul's distress was intense—what could have happened? What terrible thing had he done? What sorrow had fallen upon his beloved while he selfishly slept? But all she would say was that she was weary, while she clung to him in a storm of passion, as if some one threatened to take her out of his arms. Then she left him abruptly and went off to dress.

But later, at dinner, it seemed as if a new and more radiant light than ever glowed on her face. She was gay and caressing, telling him merry tales of Paris and its plays. It was as if she meant to efface all suggestion of sorrow or pain—and gradually the impression wore off in Paul's mind, and ere it came to their sipping the golden wine, all was brightness and peace.

"See," she said, looking from the window just before they retired to rest, "the sky has stopped crying, and there are our stars, sweetheart, come out to wish us good-night. Ah! for us tomorrow once more will be a glorious day."

"My Queen," said Paul; "rain or fine, all days are glorious to me, so long as I have you to clasp in my arms. You are my sun, moon and stars—always, for ever."

She laughed a laugh, the silver echo of satisfaction and joy.

"Sweet Paul," she lisped mischievously, "so good you have been, so gentle with my moods. You must have some reward. Listen, beloved while I tell it to you."

But what she said is written in his heart!

CHAPTER XII

His lady was so intensely *soignée*—that is what pleased Paul. He had never thought about such things, or noticed them much in other women, but she was a revelation.

No Roman Empress with her bath of asses' milk could have had a more wonderful toilet than she. And ever she was illusive, and he never quite got to the end of her mystery. Always there was a veil, when he least expected it, and so these hours for the most part were passed at the boiling-point of excitement and bliss. The experiences of another man's whole lifetime Paul was going through in the space of days.

It was the Monday following the wet Sunday when an incident happened which soon came back to him, and gave him food for reflection.

They would spend the day in the launch, she decided, going whither they wished, stopping here to pick gentians, going there under the shadow of trees—landing where and when they desired—even sleeping at Flüclen if the fancy took them to. Anna was sent on with their things in case this contingency occurred. And earth, water and sky seemed smiling them a welcome.

Just before they started, Dmitry, after the gentlest tap, noiselessly entered Paul's room. Paul was selecting some cigars from a box, and looked up in surprise as the stately servant cautiously closed the door.

"Yes, Dmitry, what is it?" he said half impatiently.

Dmitry advanced, and now Paul saw that he carried something in his hand. He bowed low with his usual courtly respect. Then he stammered a little as he began to speak.

The substance of his sentence, Paul gathered, was that the Excellency would not be inconveniencing himself too much, he hoped, if he would consent to carry this pistol. A very good pistol, he assured him, which would take but little room.

Paul's surprise deepened. Carry a pistol in peaceful Switzerland! It seemed too absurd.

"What on earth for, my friend?" he said.

But Dmitry would give no decided answer, only that it was wiser, when away from one's home and out with a lady, never to go unarmed. Real anxiety peeped from his cautious grey eyes.

Did Paul know how to shoot? And would he be pardoned for asking the Excellency such a question?—but in England, he heard, they dealt little with revolvers—and this was a point to be assured of.

Yes, Paul knew how to shoot! The idea made him laugh. But now he came to think of it, he had not had great practice with a revolver, and might not do so well as with a gun or rifle. But the whole thing seemed so absurd, he did not think it of much consequence.

"Of course I'll take it to please you, Dmitry," he said, "though I wish you would tell me why."

However, Dmitry escaped from the room without further words, his finger upon his lips.

The lady was looking more exquisitely white than usual; she wore soft pale mauve, and appeared in Paul's eyes a thing of joy.

When they were seated on the launch in their chairs, she let him hold her hand, but she did not talk much at first; only now he understood her silences, and did not worry over them—so great a teacher is love to quicken the perception of man.

He sat there, and gazed at her, and tried to realise that it was really he who was experiencing all this happiness. This wonderful, wonderful woman—and he was her lover.

At last something in her expression of sadness caught his watchful eye, and an ache came into his mind to know where hers had gone.

"Darling," he said tenderly, "mayn't I come there, too?"

She turned towards him—a shadow was in her eyes.

"No, Paul," she said. "Not there. It is a land of rocks and precipices—not for lovers."

"But if you can go—where is the danger for me, my Queen? Or, if there is danger, then it is my place to stand by your side."

"Paul, my sweet Paul," she whispered, while her eyes filled with mist, "I was thinking how fair the world could be, perhaps, if fate allowed one to meet one's mate while there was yet time. Surely two souls together, like you and I, might climb to Paradise doing deeds of greatness by the way. But so much of life is like a rushing torrent tearing along making a course for itself, without power to choose through what country it will pass, until it meets the ocean and is swallowed up and lost. If one could only see—only know in time—could he change the course? Alas! who can tell?"

Her voice was sad, and as ever it wrung Paul's heart.

"My darling one," he said, "don't think of those odd things. Only remember that I am here beside you, and that I love you, love you so—"

"My Paul!" she murmured, and she smiled a strange, sweet smile, "do you know, I find you like a rare violin which hitherto has been used by ordinary musicians to play their popular airs upon, but which is now highly strung and being touched by the bow of an artist who loves it. And oh! the exquisite sounds which are coming, and will yet come forth to enchant the ear, and satisfy the sense. All the capacity is there, Paul, in you, beautiful one—only I must bring it out with my bow of love! And what a progress you have made already—a great, great progress. Think, only a few days ago you had never noticed the colours of this lake, or even these great mountains, they said nothing to you at all except as places to take your exercise upon. Life, for you, was just eating and sleeping and strengthening your muscles." And she laughed softly.

"I know I was a Goth," said Paul. "I can hardly realise it myself, the change that has happened to me. Everything now seems full of joy."

"Your very phrases are altered, Paul, and will alter more yet, while our moon waxes and our love grows."

"Can it grow? Can I possibly love you more intensely than I do now—surely no!" he exclaimed passionately. "And yet—"

"And yet?"

"Ah! yes, I know it. Yes, it can grow until it is my life—my very life."

"Yes, Paul," she said, "your life"—and her strange eyes narrowed again, the Sphinx's inscrutable look of mystery in their chameleon depths.

Then her mood altered, she became gay and laughing, and her wit sparkled like dry champagne, while the white launch glided through the blue waters with never a swirl of foam.

"Paul," she said presently, "to-morrow we will go up the Rigi to the Kaltbad, and look from the little kiosk over the world, and over the Bernese Oberland. It gives me an emotion to stand so high and see so vast a view—but to-day we will play on the water and among the trees."

He had no desires except to do what she would do, so they landed for lunch at one of the many little inviting hotels which border the lake in sheltered bays. All through the meal she entertained him with subtle flattery, drawing him out, and making him shine until he made flint for her steel. And when they came to the end she said with sudden, tender sweetness:

"Paul—it is my caprice—you may pay the bill to-day—just for to-day—because—Ah! you must guess, my Paul! the reason why!"

And she ran out into the sunlight, her cheeks bright pink.

But Paul knew it was because now she *belonged* to him. His heart swelled with joy—and who so proud as he?

She had gone alone up a mountain path when he came out to join her, and stood there laughing at him provokingly from above. He bounded up and caught her, and would walk hand in hand, and made her feel that he was master and lord through the strength of his splendid, vigorous youth. He pretended to scold her if she stirred from him, and made her stand or walk and obey him, and gave himself the airs of a husband and prince.

And the lady laughed in pure ecstatic joy. "Oh! I love you, my Paul—like this, like this! Beautiful one! Just a splendid primitive savage beneath the grace, as a man should be. When I feel how strong you are my heart melts with bliss!"

And Paul, to show her it was true, seized her in his arms, and ran with her, placing her on a high rock, where he made her pay him with kisses and tell him she loved him before he would lift her down.

And it was his lady's caprice, as she said, that this state of things should last all day. But by night time, when they got to Flüelen, the infinite mastery of her mind, and the uncertainty of his hold over her, made her his Queen again, and Paul once more her worshipping slave.

* * * * *

Now, although his master was quite oblivious of posts, Tompson was not, and that Monday he took occasion to go into Lucerne, whence he returned with a pile of letters, which Paul found on again reaching the Bürgenstock, after staying the night at Flüelen in a little hotel.

That had been an experience! His lady quite childish in her glee at the smallness and simplicity of everything.

"Our picnic," she called it to Paul—only it was a wonderfully *recherché* picnic, as Anna of course had brought everything which was required by heart of sybarite for the passing of a night.

Ah! they had been happy. The Queen had been exquisitely gracious to her slave, and entranced him more deeply than ever. And here at the Bürgenstock, when he got into his room, his letters stared him in the face.

"Damned officiousness!" he said to himself, thinking of Tompson.

He did not want to be reminded of any existence other than the dream of heaven he was now enjoying.

Oh! they were all very real and material, these epistles—quite of earth! One was from his mother. He was enjoying Lucerne, she hoped, and she was longing for his return. She expected he also was craving for his home and horses and dogs. All were well. They—she and his father—were moving up to the town house in Berkeley Square the following week until the end of June, and great preparations were already in contemplation for his twenty-third birthday in July at Verdayne Place. There was no mention of Isabella except a paragraph at the end. Miss Waring was visiting friends at Blackheath, he was informed. Ah, so far away it all seemed! But it brought him back from heaven. The next was his father's writing. Laconic, but to the point. This parent hoped he was not wasting his time—d—d short in life! and that he was cured of his folly for the parson's girl, and found other eyes shone bright. If he wanted more money he was to say so.

Several were from his friends, banal and everyday. And one was from Tremlett, his own groom, and this was full of Moonlighter and—Pike! That gave him just a moment's feeling—Pike! Tremlett had "made so bold" as to have some snapshots done by a friend, and he ventured to send one to his master. The "very pictur'" of the dog, he said, and it was true. Ah! this touched him, this little photograph of Pike.

"Dear little chap," he said to himself as he looked. "My dear little chap."

And then an instantaneous desire to show it to his lady came over him, and he went back to the sitting-room in haste.

There she was—the post had come for her too, it seemed, and she looked up with an expression of concentrated fierceness from a missive she was reading as he entered the room. Her marvellous self-control banished all but love from her eyes after they had rested on him for an instant, but his senses—so fine now—had remarked the first glance, just as his eye had seen the heavy royal crown on the paper as she hastily folded it and threw it carelessly aside.

"Darling!" he said "Oh! look! here is a picture of Pike!"

And if it had been the most important document concerning the fate of nations the lady could not have examined it with more enthralled interest and attention than she did this snapshot photograph of a rough terrier dog.

"What a sweet fellow!" she said. "Look at his eye! so intelligent; look at that *patte*! See, even he is asking one to love him—and I do—I do—"

"Darling!" said Paul in ecstasy, "oh, if we only had him here, wouldn't that be good!"

And he never knew why his lady suddenly threw her arms round his neck, and kissed him with passionate tenderness and love, her eyes soft as a dove's.

"Oh, my Paul," she said, a break in her wonderful voice, whose tones said many things, "my young, darling, English Paul!"

Presently they would drive to see that quaint farm she wanted to show him. The day was very warm, and to rest in the comfortable carriage would be nice. Paul thought so, too. So after a late lunch they started. And once or twice on the drive through the most peaceful and beautiful scenery, a flash of the same fierceness came into the lady's eyes, gazing away over distance as when she had read her letter, and it made Paul wonder and long to ask her why. He never allowed himself to speculate in coherent thought words even as to who she was, or her abode in life. He had given his word, and was an Englishman and would keep it, that was all. But in his subconsciousness there dwelt the conviction that she must be some Queen or Princess of a country south in Europe—half barbaric, half advanced. That she was unhappy and hated it all, he more than divined. It was a proof of the strength of his character that he did not let the terrible thought of inevitable parting mar the bliss of the tangible now. He had promised her to live while the sun of their union shone, and he had the force to keep his word.

But oh! he wished he could drive all care from her path, and that this glorious life should go on for ever.

When they got to the farm in the soft late afternoon light, the most gracious mood came over his lady. It was just a Swiss farmhouse of many storeys, the lower one for the cows and other animals, and the rest for the family and industries. All was clean and in order, with that wonderful outside neatness which makes Swiss châlets look like painted toy houses popped down on the greensward without yard or byre. And these people were well-to-do, and it was the best of its kind.

The *Bäuerin*, a buxom mother of many little ones, was nursing another not four weeks old, a fat, prosperous infant in its quaint Swiss clothes. Her broad face beamed with pride as she welcomed the gracious lady. Old acquaintances they appeared, and they exchanged greetings. Foreign languages were not Paul's strong point, and he caught not a word of meaning in the German *patois* the good woman talked. But his lady was voluble, and seemed to know each flaxen-haired child by name, though it was the infant which longest arrested her attention. She held it in her arms. And Paul had never seen her look so young or so beautiful.

The good woman left them alone while she prepared some coffee for them in the adjoining kitchen, followed by her troop of *kinder*. Only the little one still lay in the lady's arms. She spoke not a word—she sang to it a cradle-song, and the thought came to Paul that she seemed as an angel, and this must be an echo of his own early heaven before his life had descended to earth.

A strange peace came over him as he sat there watching her, his thoughts vague and dreamy of some beautiful sweet tenderness—he knew not what.

Ere the woman returned with the coffee the lady looked up from her crooning and met his eyes—all her soul was aglow in hers—while she whispered as he bent over to meet her lips:

"Yes, some day, my sweetheart—yes."

And that magic current of sympathy which was between them made Paul know what she meant. And the gladness of the gods fell upon him and exalted him, and his blue eyes swam with tears.

Ah! that was a thought, if that could ever be!

All the way back in the carriage he could only kiss her. Their emotion seemed too deep for words.

And this night was the most divine of any they had spent on the Bürgenstock. But there was in it an essence about which only the angels could write.

CHAPTER XIII

Do you know the Belvedere at the Rigi Kaltbad, looking over the corner to a vast world below, on a fair day in May, when the air is clear as crystal and the lake ultra-marine? When the Bernese Oberland undulates away in unbroken snow, its pure whiteness like cold marble, the shadows grey-blue?

Have you seen the tints of the beeches, of the pines, of the firs, clinging like some cloak of life to the hoary-headed mountains, a reminder that spring is eternal, and youth must have its day, however grey beards and white heads may frown?

Ah—it is good!

And so is the air up there. Hungry and strong and—young.

Paul and his lady stood and looked down in rapt silence. It was giving her, as she said, an emotion, but of what sort he was not sure. They were all alone. No living soul was anywhere in view.

She had been in a mood, all day when she seldom raised her eyes. It reminded him of the first time he had seen her, and wonder grew again in his mind. All the last night her soul had seemed melted into his in a fusion of tenderness and trust, exalted with the exquisite thought of the wish which was between them. And he had felt at last he had fathomed its inmost recess.

But to-day, as he gazed down at her white-rose paleness, the heavy lashes making their violet shadow on her cheek—her red mouth mutinous and full—the conviction came back to him that there were breadths and depths and heights about which he had no conception even. And an ice hand clutched his heart. Of what strange thing was she thinking? leaning over the parapet there, her delicate nostrils quivering now and then.

"Paul," she said at last, "did you ever want to kill any one? Did you ever long to have them there at your mercy, to choke their life out and throw them to hell?"

"Good God, no!" said Paul aghast.

Then at last she looked up at him, and her eyes were black with hate. "Well, I do, Paul. I would like to kill one man on earth—a useless, vicious weakling, too feeble to deserve a fine death—a rotting carrion spoiling God's world and encumbering my path! I would kill him if I could—and more than ever today."

"Oh, my Queen, my Queen!" said Paul, distressed. "Don't say such things—you, my own tender woman and love—"

"Yes, that is one side of me, and the best—but there is another, which he draws forth, and that is the worst. You of calm England do not know what it means—the true passion of hate."

"Can I do nothing for you, beloved?" Paul asked. Here was a phase which he had not yet seen.

"Ah!" she said, bitterly, and threw up her head. "No! his high place protects him. But for his life I would conquer all fate."

"Darling, darling—" said Paul, who knew not what to say.

"But, Paul, if a hair of your head should be hurt, I would kill him myself with these my own hands."

Once Paul had seen two tigers fight in a travelling circus-van which came to Oxford, and now the memory of the scene returned to him when he looked at his lady's face. He had not known a human countenance could express such fierce, terrible rage. A quiver ran through him. Yes, this was no idle boast of an angry woman—he felt those slender hands would indeed be capable of dealing death to any one who robbed her of her mate.

But what passion was here! What force! He had somehow never even dreamt such feelings dwelt in women—or, indeed, in any human creatures out of sensational books. Yet, gazing there at her, he dimly understood that in himself, too, they could rise, were another to take her from him. Yes, he could kill in suchlike case.

They were silent for some moments, each vibrating with passionate thoughts; and then the lady leant over and laid her cheek against the sleeve of his coat.

"Heart of my heart," she said, "I frighten and ruffle you. The women of your country are sweet and soft, but they know not the passion I know, my Paul—the fierceness and madness of love—"

Paul clasped her in his arms.

"It makes me worship you more, my Queen," he said. "Englishwomen would seem like wax dolls now beside you and your exquisite face—they will never again be anything but shadows in my life. It can only hold you, the one goddess and Queen."

Her eyes were suffused with a mist of tenderness, the passion was gone; her head was thrown back against his breast, when suddenly her hand inadvertently touched against the pocket where Dmitry's pistol lay. She started violently, and before he could divine her purpose she snatched the weapon out, and held it up to the light.

Her face went like death, and for a second she leant against the parapet as if she were going to faint.

"Paul," she gasped with white lips, "this is Dmitry's pistol. I know it well. How did you come by it?—tell me, beloved. If he gave it to you, then it means danger, Paul—danger—"

"My darling," said Paul, in his strong young pride "fear nothing, I shall never leave you. I will protect you from any danger in the world, only depend upon me, sweetheart. Nothing can hurt you while I am here."

"Do you think I care a *sou* for my life?" she said, while she stood straight up again with the majesty of a queen. "Do you think I feared for me—for myself? Oh! no, my own lover, never that! They can kill me when they choose, but they won't; it is you for whom I fear. Only your danger could make me cower, no other in the whole world."

Paul laughed with joy at her speech. "There is nothing to fear at all then, darling," he said. "I can take care of myself, you know. I am an Englishman."

And even in the tumult of her thoughts the lady found time to smile with tender amusement at the young insular arrogance of his last words. An Englishman, forsooth! Of course that meant a kind of god untouched by the failings of other nations. A great rush of pride in him came over her and gladdened her. He was indeed a splendid picture of youth and strength, as he stood there, the sunlight gilding his fair hair, and all the magnificent proportions of his figure thrown into relief against the background of grey stone and sky, an *insouciante* smile on his lips, and all the light of love and self-confidence in his fine blue eyes.

She responded to the fire in them, and appeared to grow comforted and at peace. But all the way back through the wood to the Kalibad Hotel she glanced furtively into the shadows, while she talked gaily as she held Paul's arm.

And he never asked her a question as to where she expected the danger to come from. No anxiety for his own safety troubled him one jot—indeed, an unwonted extra excitement flooded his veins, making him enjoy himself with an added zest.

Dmitry as usual awaited them at the hotel; his face was serene, but when Paul's back was turned for a moment while he lit a cigarette, the lady questioned her servant with whispered fierceness in the Russian tongue. Apparently his answer was satisfactory, for she looked relieved, and presently, seated on the terrace, they had a merry tea—the last they would have on mountain tops, for she broke it gently to Paul that on the morrow she must return to Lucerne. Paul felt as if his heart had stopped beating. Return to Lucerne! O God! not to part—surely not to part—so soon!

"No, no," she said, the thought making her whiten too. "Oh no! my Paul, not that—yet!"

Ah—he could bear anything if it did not mean parting, and he used no arguments to dissuade her. She was his Queen and must surely know best. Only he listened eagerly for details of how matters could be arranged there. Alas! they could never be the same as this glorious time they had had.

"You must wait two days, sweetheart," she said, "before you follow me. Stay still in our nest if you will, but do not come on to Lucerne."

"I could not stand it," said Paul. "Oh! darling, don't kill me with aching for your presence two whole days! It is a lifetime! not to be endured—"

"Impatient one!" she laughed softly. "No—neither could I bear not to see you, sweetheart, but we must not be foolish. You must stay on in our rooms and each morning I will meet you somewhere in the launch. Dmitry knows every inch of the lake, and we can pass most of days thus, happy at last—"

"But the nights!" said Paul, deep distress in his voice. "What on earth do you think I can do with the nights?"

"Spend them in sleep, my beloved one," the lady said, while she smiled a soft fine smile.

But to Paul this idea presented the poorest compensation—and in spite of his will to the contrary his thoughts flew ahead for an instant to the inevitable days and nights when—Ah! no, he could not face the picture. Life would be finished for him when that time came.

The thought of only a temporary parting on the morrow made them cling together for this, their last evening, with almost greater closeness and tenderness than usual. Paul could hardly bear his lady out of his sight, even while she dressed for dinner, when they got back to the Bürgenstock, and twice he came to the door and asked plaintively how long she would be, until Anna took pity on him, and implored to be allowed to ask him to come in while she finished her mistress's hair. And that was a joy to Paul! He sat there by the dressing-table, and played with the things, opening the lids of gold boxes, and sniffing bottles of scent with an air of right and possession which made his lady smile like a purring cat. Then he tried on her rings, but they would only go on to the second joint of his little finger, as he laughingly showed her—and finally he pushed Anna aside, and insisted upon putting the last touches himself to the glorious waves of black hair.

And all the while he teased the maid, and chaffed her in infamous French, to her great delight, while his lady looked at him, whole wells of tenderness deep in her eyes. Paul had adorable ways when he chose. No wonder both mistress and maid should worship him.

The moon was growing larger, her slender contours more developed, and the stars seemed fainter and farther off. Nothing more exquisite could be dreamed of, thought Paul, than the view from their balcony windows, the light on the silver snows. And he would let no thought that it was the last night they would see it together mar the passionate joy of the hours still to be. His lady had never been more sweet; it was as if this wayward Undine had at last found her soul, and lay conquered and unresisting in her lover's strong arms.

Thus in perfect peace and happiness they; passed their last night on the Bürgenstock.

CHAPTER XIV

The desolation which came over Paul when next day before lunch time he found himself alone on the terrace, looking down vainly trying to distinguish his lady's launch as it glided over the blue waters, seemed unendurable. An intense depression filled his being. It was as if a limb had been torn from him; he felt helpless and incomplete, and his whole soul drawn to Lucerne.

The green trees and the exquisite day seemed to mock him. Alone, alone—with no prospect of seeing his Queen until the morrow, when at eleven he was to meet her at the landing-steps at the foot of the *funiculaire*.

But that was to-morrow, and how could he get through to-day?

After an early lunch he climbed to their rock at the summit, and sat there where they had sat together—alone with his thoughts.

And what thoughts!

What was this marvellous thing which had happened to him? A fortnight ago he was in Paris, disgusted with everything around him, and fancying himself in love with Isabella Waring. Poor Isabella! How had such things ever been possible? Why, he was a schoolboy then—a child—an infant! and now he was a man, and knew what life meant in its greatest and best. That was part of the wonder of this lady, with all her intense sensuousness and absence of what European nations call morality; there was yet nothing low or degrading in her influence, its tendency was to exalt and elevate into broad views and logical reasonings. Nothing small would ever again appeal to Paul. His whole outlook was vaster and more full of wide thoughts.

And then among the other emotions in his breast came one of deep gratitude to her. For, apart from her love, had she not given him the royalest gift which mankind could receive—an awakened soul? Like her story of Undine it had truly been born with that first long kiss.

Then his mind flew to their after-kisses, the immense divine bliss of these whole six days.

Was it only six days since they had come there? Six days of Paradise. And surely fate would not part them now. Surely more hours of joy lay in store for them yet. The moon was seven days old—and his lady had said, "While she waxes our love will wax." Thus, even by that calculation, there was still time to live a little longer.

Paul's will was strong. He sternly banished all speculations as to the future. He remembered her counsel of the riddle which lay hidden in the eyes of the Sphinx—to live in the present and quaff life in its full.

He was in a mood of such worship that he could have kissed the grey rock because she had leant against it. And to himself he made vows that, come what might, he would ever try to be worthy of her great spirit and teaching. Dmitry's pistol still lay in his pocket; he took it out and examined it—all six chambers were loaded. A deadly small thing, with a finely engraved stock made in Paris. There was a date scratched. It was about a year old.

What danger could they possibly have dreaded for him?—he almost laughed. He stayed up on the highest point until after the sun had set; somehow he dreaded going back to the rooms where they had been so happy—going back alone! But this was weakness, and he must get over the feeling. After dinner he would spend the evening writing his letters home. But when this solitary meal was over, the moon tempted him out on to the terrace, and there he stayed obsessed with passionate thoughts until he crept in to his lonely couch.

He could not sleep. It had no memories there to comfort him. He got up, and went across the sitting-room to the room his lady had left so lately. Alas! it was all dismantled of her beautiful things. The bed unmade and piled with uncovered hotel pillows, and a large German eiderdown, on top of folded blankets, it all looked ghastly and sad and cold. And more depressed than ever he crept back to his own bed.

Next morning was grey—not raining, but dull grey clouds all over the sky. Not a tempting prospect to spend it in a launch on the lake. A wind, too, swept the water into small rough wavelets. Would she come? The uncertainty was almost agony. He was waiting long before the time appointed, and walked up and down anxiously scanning the direction towards Lucerne.

Yes, that was the launch making its way along, not a moment late. Oh! what joy thrilled his being! He glowed all over—in ten minutes or less he could clasp her hands.

But when the launch came in full view, he perceived no lady was there—only Dmitry's black form stood alone by the chairs.

Paul's heart sank like lead. He could hardly contain his anxiety until the servant stepped ashore and handed him a letter, and this was its contents:

"My beloved one—I am not well to-day—a foolish chill. Nothing of consequence, only the cold wind of the lake I could not face. At one o'clock, when Lucerne is at lunch, come to me by the terrace gate. Come to me, I cannot live without you, Paul."

"What is it, Dmitry?" he said anxiously. "Madame is not ill, is she? Tell me—"

"Not ill—oh no!" the servant said, only Paul must know Madame was of a delicacy at times in the cold weather, and had to be careful of herself. He added, too, that it would be wiser if Paul would lunch early before they started, because, as he explained, it was not for the people of the hotel to know he was there, and how else could he eat?

All of which advice was followed, and at one o'clock they landed at Lucerne, and Paul walked quickly towards his goal, Dmitry in front to see that the way was clear. Yes—there was no one about for the moment, and like ghosts they glided through the little terrace door, and Paul went into the room by the window, while Dmitry held the heavy curtains, and then disappeared.

It was empty—the fact struck a chill note, in spite of the great bowls of flowers and the exquisite scent. His tiger was there, and the velvet pillows of old. All was warm and luxurious, as befitting the shrine of his goddess and Queen. Only he was alone—alone with his thoughts.

An incredible excitement swept through him, his heart beat to suffocation in the longing for her to come. Was it possible—was it true that soon she would be in his arms? A whole world of privation and empty hours to make up for in their first kiss.

Then from behind the screen of the door to her room she came at last—a stately figure in long black draperies, her face startlingly white, and her head wrapped in a mist of black veil. But who can tell of the note of gladness and welcome she put into the two words, "My Paul!"?

And who can tell of the passionate joy of their long, tender embrace, or of their talk of each one's impossible night? His lady, too, had not slept, it appeared. She had cried, she said, and fought with her pillow, and been so wicked to Anna that the good creature had wept. She had torn her fine night raiment, and bitten a handkerchief through! But now he had come, and her soul was at rest. What wonder, when all this was said in his ear with soft, broken sighs and kisses divine, that Paul should feel like a god in his pride!

Then he held her at arms'-length and looked at her face. Yes, it was very pale indeed, and the violet shadows lay under her black lashes. Had she suffered, his darling—was she ill? But no, the fire in her strange eyes gave no look of ill-health.

"I was frightened, my own," he said, "in case you were really not well. I must pet and take care of you all the day. See, you must lie on the sofa among the cushions, and I will sit beside you and soothe you to rest." And he lifted her in his strong arms and carried her to the couch as if she had been a baby, and settled her there, every touch a caress.

His lady delighted in these exhibitions of his strength. He had grown to understand that he could always affect her when he pretended to dominate her by sheer brute force. She had explained it to him thus one day:

"You see, Paul, a man can always keep a woman loving him if he kiss her enough, and make her feel that there is no use struggling because he is too strong to resist. A woman will stand almost anything from a passionate lover. He may beat her and pain her soft flesh; he may shut her up and deprive her of all other friends—while the motive is raging love and interest in herself on his part, it only makes her love him the more. The reason why women become unfaithful is because the man grows casual, and having awakened a taste for passionate joys, he no longer gratifies them—so she yawns and turns elsewhere."

Well, there was no fear of her doing so if he could help it! He was more than willing to follow this receipt. Indeed, there was something about her so agitating and alluring that he knew in his heart all men would feel the same towards her in a more or less degree, and wild jealousy coursed through his veins at the thought.

"My Paul," she said, "do you know I have a plan in my head that we shall go to Venice?"

"To Venice!" said Paul in delight. "To Venice!"

"Yes—I cannot endure any more of Lucerne, parted from you, with only the prospect of snatched meetings. It is not to be borne. We shall go to that home of strange joy, my lover, and there for a space at least we can live in peace."

Paul asked no better gift of fate. Venice he had always longed to see, and now to see it with her! Ah! the very thought was ecstasy to him, and made the blood bound in his veins.

"When, when, my darling?" he asked. "Tomorrow? When?"

"To-day is Friday," she said. "One must give Dmitry time to make the arrangements and take a palace for us. Shall we say Sunday, Paul? I shall go on Sunday, and you can follow the next day—so by Tuesday evening we shall be together again, not to part until—the end."

"The end?" said Paul, with sinking heart.

"Sweetheart," she whispered, while she drew his face down to hers, "think nothing evil. I said the end—but fate alone knows when that must be. Do not let us force her hand by speculating about it. Remember always to live while we may."

And Paul was more or less comforted, but in moments of silence all through the day he seemed to hear the echo of the words—The End.

CHAPTER XV

It was a beautiful apartment that Dmitry had found for them on the Grand Canal in Venice, in an old palace looking southwest. A convenient door in a side canal cloaked the exit and entry of its inhabitants from curious eyes—had there been any to indulge in curiosity; but in Venice there is a good deal of the feeling of live and let live, and the *dolce far niente* of the life is not conducive to an over-anxious interest in the doings of one's neighbours.

Money and intelligence can achieve a number of things in a short space of time, and Dmitry had had both at his command, so everything, including a *chef* from Paris and a retinue of Italian servants, was ready when on the Tuesday evening Paul arrived at the station.

What a wonderland it seemed to him, Venice! A wonderland where was awaiting him his heart's delight—more passionately desired than ever after three days of total abstinence.

As after the Friday afternoon he had spent more or less in hiding in the terrace-room, his lady had judged it wiser for him not to come at all to Lucerne, and on the Saturday had met him at a quiet part of the shore of the lake, beyond the landing-steps of the *funiculaire*, and for a few short hours they had cruised about on the blue waters—but her sweetest tenderness and ready wit had not been able entirely to eliminate the feeling of unrest which troubled them. And then there were the nights, the miserable evenings and nights of separation. On the Sunday she had departed to Venice, and after she had gone, Paul had returned for one day to Lucerne, leaving again on the Monday, apparently as unacquainted with Madame Zalenska as he had been the first night of his arrival.

He had not seen her since Saturday. Three whole days of anguishing longing. And now in half an hour at least she would be in his arms. The journey through the beautiful scenery from Lucerne had been got through at night—all day from Milan a feverish excitement had dominated him, and prevented his taking any interest in outward surroundings. A magnetic attraction seemed drawing him on—on—to the centre of light and joy—his lady's presence.

Dmitry and an Italian servant awaited his arrival; not an instant's delay for luggage called a halt. Tompson and the Italian were left for that, and Paul departed with his trusty guide.

It was about seven o'clock, the opalescent lights were beginning to show in the sky, and their reflection in the water, as he stooped his tall head to enter the covered gondola. It was all too beautiful and wonderful to take in at once, and then he only wanted wings the sooner to arrive, not eyes to see the passing objects. Afterwards the strange soft cry of the gondoliers and the sights appealed to him; but on this first evening every throb of his being was centred upon the one moment when he should hold his beloved one to his heart.

He could hardly contain his impatience, and walk sedately beside Dmitry when they ascended the great stone staircase—he felt like bounding up three steps at a time. Dmitry had been respectfully silent. Madame was well—that was all he would say. He opened the great double door with a latch-key, and Paul found himself in vast hall almost unfurnished but for some tapestry on the walls, and a huge gilt marriage-chest, and a couple of chairs. It was ill lit, and there was something of decay and gloom in its aspect.

On they went, through other doors to a salon, vast and gloomy too, and then the glory and joy of heaven seemed to spring upon Paul's view when the shrine of the goddess was reached—a smaller room, whose windows faced the Grand Canal, now illuminated by the setting sun in all its splendour, coming in shafts from the balcony blinds. And among the quaintest and most old-world surroundings, mixed with her own wonderful personal notes of luxury, his lady rose from the tiger couch to meet him.

His lady! His Queen!

And, indeed, she seemed a queen when at last he held her at arms'-length to look at her. She was garbed all ready for dinner in a marvellous garment of shimmering purple, while round her shoulders a scarf of brilliant pale emerald gauze, all fringed with gold, fell in two long ends, and on her neck and in her ears great emeralds gleamed—a pear-shaped one of unusual brilliancy fell at the parting of her waves of hair on to her white smooth forehead. But the colour of her eyes he could not be sure of—only they were two wells of love and passion gazing into his own.

All the simplicity of the Bürgenstock surroundings was gone. The flowers were in the greatest profusion, rare and heavy-scented; the pillows of the couch were more splendid than ever; cloths of gold and silver and wonderful shades of orange and green velvet were among the purple ones he already knew. Priceless pieces of brocade interwoven with gold covered the screens and other couches; and, near enough to pick up when she wanted them, stood jewelled boxes of cigarettes and bonbons, and stands of perfume.

Her expression, too, was altered. A new mood shone there; and later, when Paul learnt the history of the wonderful women of *cinquecento* Venice, it seemed as if something of their exotic voluptuous spirit now lived in her.

This was a new queen to worship—and die for, if necessary. He dimly felt, even in these first moments, that here he would drink still deeper of the mysteries of life and passionate love.

"Beztzenny-moi," she said, "my priceless one. At last I have you again to make me *live*. Ah! I must know it is really you, my Paul!"

They were sitting on the tiger by now, and she undulated round and all over him, feeling his coat, and his face, and his hair, as a blind person might, till at last it seemed as if she were twined about him like a serpent. And every now and then a narrow shaft of the glorious dying sunlight would strike the great emerald on her forehead, and give forth sparks of vivid green which appeared reflected again in her eyes. Paul's head swam, he felt intoxicated with bliss.

"This Venice is for you and me, my Paul," she said. "The air is full of love and dreams; we have left the slender moon behind us in Switzerland; here she is nearing her full, and the summer is upon us with all her richness and completeness—the spring of our love has passed." Her voice fell into its rhythmical cadence, as if she were whispering a prophecy inspired by some presence beyond.

"We will drink deep of the cup of delight, my lover, and bathe in the wine of the gods. We shall feast on the tongues of nightingales, and rest on couches of flowers. And thou shalt cede me thy soul, beloved, and I will give thee mine—"

But the rest was lost in the meeting of their lips.

* * * * *

They dined on the open loggia, its curtains drawn, hiding them from the view of the palaces opposite, but not preventing the soft sounds of the singers in the gondolas moored to the poles beneath from reaching their ears. And above the music now and then would come the faint splash of water, and the "Stahi"—"Premé" of some moving gondolier.

The food was of the richest, beginning with strange fishes and quantities of *hors d'oeuvres* that Paul knew not, accompanied by *vodka* in several forms. And some of the *plats* she would just taste, and some send instantly away.

And all the while a little fountain of her own perfume played from a group of sportive cupids in silver, while the table in the centre was piled with red roses. Dmitry and two Italian footmen waited, and everything was done with the greatest state. A regal magnificence was in the lady's air and mien. She spoke of the splendours of Venice's past, and let Paul feel the atmosphere of that subtle time of passion and life. Of here a love-scene, and there a murder. Of wisdom and vice, and intoxicating emotion, all blended in a kaleidoscope of gorgeousness and colour.

And once again her vast knowledge came as a fresh wonder to Paul—no smallest detail of history seemed wanting in her talk, so that he lived again in that old world and felt himself a Doge.

When they were alone at last, tasting the golden wine, she rose and drew him to the loggia balustrade. Dmitry had drawn back the curtains and extinguished the lights, and only the brilliant moon lit the scene; a splendid moon, two nights from the full. There she shone straight down upon them to welcome them to this City of Romance.

What loveliness met Paul's view! A loveliness in which art and nature blended in one satisfying whole.

"Darling," he said, "this is better than the Bürgenstock. Let us go out on the water and float about, too."

It was exceedingly warm these last days of May, and that night not a zephyr stirred a ripple. A cloak and scarf of black gauze soon hid the lady's splendour, and they descended the staircase hand in hand to the waiting open gondola.

It was a new experience of joy for Paul to recline there, and drift away down the stream, amidst the music and the coloured lanterns, and the wonderful, wonderful spell of the place.

The lady was silent for a while, and then she began to whisper passionate words of love. She had never before been thus carried away—and he must say them to her—as he held her hand—burning words, inflaming the imagination and exciting the sense. It seemed as if all the other nights of love were concentrated into this one in its perfect joy.

Who can tell of the wild exaltation which filled Paul? He was no longer just Paul Verdayne, the ordinary young Englishman; he was a god—and this was Olympus.

"Look, Paul!" she said at last. "Can you not see Desdemona peeping from the balcony of her house there? And to think she will have no happiness before her Moor will strangle her to-night! Death without joys. Ah! that is cruel. Some joys are well worth death, are they not, my lover, as you and I should know?"

"Worth death and eternity," said Paul. "For one such night as this with you a man would sell his soul."

It was not until they turned at the opening of the Guidecca to return to their palazzo that they both became aware of another gondola following them, always at the same distance behind—a gondola with two solitary figures in it huddled on the seats.

The lady gave a whispered order in Italian to her gondolier, who came to a sudden stop, thus forcing the other boat to come much nearer before it, too, arrested its course. There a moonbeam caught the faces of the men as they leant forward to see what had occurred. One of them was Dmitry, and the other a younger man of the pure Kalmuck type whom Paul had never seen.

"Vasili!" exclaimed the lady, in passionate surprise. "Vasili! and they have not told me!"

She trembled all over, while her eyes blazed green flames of anger and excitement. "If it is unnecessary they shall feel the whip for this."

Her cloak had fallen aside a little, disclosing a shimmer of purple garment and flashing emeralds. She looked barbaric, her raven brows knit. It might have been Cleopatra commanding the instant death of an offending slave.

It made Paul's pulses bound, it seemed so of the picture and the night. All was a mad dream of exotic emotion, and this was just an extra note.

But who was Vasili? And what did his presence portend? Something fateful at all events.

The lady did not speak further, only by the quiver of her nostrils and the gleam in her eyes he knew how deeply she was stirred.

Yes, one or the other would feel the whip, if they had been over-zealous in their duties!

It seemed out of sheer defiance of some fate that she decided to go on into the lagoon when they passed San Georgio. It was growing late, and Paul's thoughts had turned to greater joys. He longed to clasp her in his arms, to hold her, and prove her his own. But she sat there, her small head held high, and her eyes fearless and proud—thus he did not dare to plead with her.

But presently, when she perceived the servants were no longer following, her mood changed, the sweetness of the serpent of old Nile fell upon her, and all of love that can be expressed in whispered words and tender hand-clasps, she lavished upon Paul, after ordering the gondolier to hasten back to the palazzo. It seemed as if she, too, could not contain her impatience to be again in her lover's arms.

"I will not question them to-night," she said when they arrived, and she saw Dmitry awaiting her on the steps. "To-night we will live and love at least, my Paul. Live and love in passionate bliss!"

But she could not repress the flash of her eyes which appeared to annihilate the old servant. He fell on his knees with the murmured words of supplication:

"O Imperatorskoye!" And Paul guessed it meant Imperial Highness, and a great wonder grew in his mind.

Their supper was laid in the loggia again, and under the windows the musicians still played and sang a gentle accompaniment to their sighs of love.

But later still Paul learnt what fiercest passion meant, making other memories as moonlight unto sunlight—as water unto wine.

CHAPTER XVI

To some natures security hath no charm—the sword of Damocles suspended over their heads adds to their enjoyment of anything. Of such seemed Paul and his lady. It was as if they were snatching astonishing pleasures from the very brink of some danger, none the less in magnitude because unknown.

They did not breakfast until after one o'clock the next day, and then she bade him sleep—sleep on this other loggia where they sat, which gave upon the side canal obliquely, while looking into a small garden of roses and oleanders below. Here were shade and a cool small breeze.

"We are so weary, my beloved one," the lady said. "Let us sleep on these couches of smooth silk, sleep the heavy hours of the afternoon away, and go to the Piazza when the heat of the sun has lessened in measure."

An immense languor was over Paul—he asked nothing better than to rest there in the perfumed shade, near enough to his loved one to be able to stretch out his arm and touch her hair. And soon a sweet sleep claimed him, and all was oblivion and peace.

The lady lay still on her couch for a while, her eyes gleaming between their half-closed lids. But at last, when she saw that Paul indeed slept deeply, she rose stealthily and crept from the place back to the room, the gloomy vast room within, where she summoned Dmitry, and ordered the man she had called Vasili the night before into her presence. He came with cringing diffidence, prostrating himself to the ground before her, and kissing the hem of her dress, mute adoration in his dark eyes, like those of a faithful dog—a great scar showing blue on his bronzed cheek and forehead.

She questioned him imperiously, while he answered humbly in fear. Dmitry stood by, an anxious, strained look on his face, and now and then he put in a word.

Of what danger did they warn her, these two faithful servants? One came from afar for no other purpose, it seemed. Whatever it was she received the news in haughty defiance. She spoke fiercely at first, and they humbled themselves the more. Then Anna appeared, and joined her supplications to theirs, till at last the lady, like a pettish child chasing a brood of tiresome chickens, shooed them all from the room, 'twixt laughter and tears. Then she threw up her arms in rage for a moment, and ran back to the loggia where Paul still slept. Here she sat and looked at him with burning eyes of love.

He was certainly changed in the eighteen days since she had first seen him. His face was thinner, the beautiful lines of youth were drawn with a finer hand. He was paler, too, and a shadow lay under his curly lashes. But even in his sleep it seemed as if his awakened soul had set its seal upon his expression—he had tasted of the knowledge of good and evil now.

The lady crept near him and kissed his hair. Then she flung herself on her own couch, and soon she also slept.

It was six o'clock before they awoke, Paul first—and what was his joy to be able to kneel beside her and watch her for a few seconds before her white lids lifted themselves! An attitude of utter weariness and *abandon* was hers. She was as a child tired out with passionate weeping, who had fallen to sleep as she had flung herself down. There was something even pathetic about that proud head laid low upon her clasped arms.

Paul gazed and gazed. How he worshipped her! Wayward, tigerish, beautiful Queen. But never selfish or small. And what great thing had she not done for him—she who must have been able to choose from all the world a lover—and she had chosen him. How poor and narrow were all the thoughts of his former life, everywhere hedged in with foolish prejudice and ignorant certainty. Now all the world should be his lesson-book, and some day he would show her he was worthy of her splendid teaching and belief in him, and her gift of an awakened soul. He bent still lower on his knees, and kissed her feet with deepest reverence. She stirred not. She was so very pale—fear came to him for an instant—and then he kissed her mouth.

Her wonderful eyes unclosed themselves with none of the bewildered stare people often wake with when aroused suddenly. It seemed that even in her sleep she had been conscious of her loved one's presence. Her lips parted in a smile, while her heavy lashes again swept her cheeks.

"Sweetheart," she said, "you could awake me from the dead, I think. But we are living still, my Paul—waste we no more time, in dreams."

They made haste, and were soon in the gondola on their way to the Piazza.

"Paul," she said, with a wave of her hand which included all the beauty around, "I am so glad you only see Venice now, when your eyes can take it in, sweetheart. At first it would have said almost nothing to you," and she smiled playfully. "In fact, my Paul would have spent most of his time in wondering how he could get exercise enough, there being so few places to walk in! He would have bought a nigger boy with a dish for his father, and some Venetian mirrors for his aunts, and perhaps—yes—a piece of Mr. Jesurum's lace for his mother, and some blown glass for his friends. He would have walked through St. Mark's, and thought it was a tumble-down place, with uneven pavements, and he would have noticed there were a 'jolly lot of pigeons' in the square! Then he would have been captious with the food at his hotel, grumbled at the waiters, scolded poor Tompson—and left for Rome!"

"Oh! darling!" said Paul, laughing too, in spite of his protest. "Surely, surely, I never was so bad as that—and yet I expect it is probably true. How can I ever thank you enough for giving me eyes and an understanding?"

"There—there, beloved," she said.

They walked through the Piazza; the pigeons amused Paul, and they stopped and bought corn for them, and fed the greedy creatures, ever ready for the unending largess of strangers. One or two, bolder than the rest, alighted on the lady's hat and shoulder, taking the corn from between her red lips, and Paul felt jealous even of the birds, and drew her on to see the Campanile, still standing then. They looked at it all, they looked at the lion, and finally they entered St. Mark's.

And here Paul held her arm, and gazed with bated breath. It was all so beautiful and wonderful, and new to his eyes. He had scarcely ever been in a Roman Catholic church before, and had not guessed at the gorgeous beauty of this half-Byzantine shrine. They hardly spoke. She did not weary him with details like a guide-book—that would be for his after-life visits—but now he must see it just as a glorious whole.

"They worshipped here, and endowed their temple with gold and jewels," she whispered, "and then they went into the Doge's Palace, and placed a word in the lion's mouth which meant death or destruction to their best friends! A wonderful people, those old Venetians! Sly and fierce—cruel and passionate—but with ever a shrewd smile in their eye, even in their love-affairs. I often ask myself, Paul, if we are not too civilised, we of our time. We think too much of human suffering, and so we cultivate the nerves to suffer more, instead of hardening them. Picture to yourself, in my grandfather's boyhood we had still the serfs! I am of his day, though it is over—I have beaten Dmitry—"

Then she stopped speaking abruptly, as though aware she had localised her nation too much. A strange imperious expression came into her eyes as they met Paul's—almost of defiance.

Paul was moved. He began as if to speak, then he remembered his promise never to question her, and remained silent.

"Yes, my Paul—you have promised, you know," she said. "I am for you, your love—your love—but living or dead you must never seek to know more!"

"Ah!" he cried, "you torture me when you speak like that. 'Living or dead.' My God! that means us both—we stand or fall together."

"Dear one"—her voice fell softly into a note of intense earnestness—"while fate lets us be together—yes—living or dead—but if we must part, then either would be the cause of the death of the other by further seeking—never forget that, my beloved one. Listen"—her eyes took a sudden fierceness—"once I read your English book, 'The Lady and the Tiger.' You remember it, Paul? She must choose which she would give her lover to—death and the tiger, or to another and more beautiful woman. One was left, you understand, to decide the end one's self. It caused question at the moment; some were for one choice, some for the other—but for me there was never any hesitation. I would give you to a thousand tigers sooner than to another woman—just as I would give my life a thousand times for your life, my lover."

"Darling," said Paul, "and I for yours, my fierce, adorable Queen. But why should we speak of terrible things? Are we not happy today, and now, and have you not told me to live while we may?"

"Come!" she said, and they walked on down to the gondola again, and floated away out to the lagoon. But when they were there, far away from the world, she talked in a new strain of earnestness to Paul. He must promise to do something with his life—something useful and great in future years.

"You must not just drift, my Paul, like so many of your countrymen do. You must help to stem the tide of your nation's decadence, and be a strong man. For me, when I read now of England, it seems as if all the hereditary legislators—it is what you call your nobles, eh?—these men have for their motto, like Louis XV.,*Après moi le déluge*—It will last my time. Paul, wherever I am, it will give me joy for you to be strong and great, sweetheart. I shall know then I have not loved just a beautiful shell, whose mind I was able to light for a time. That is a sadness, Paul, perhaps the greatest of all, to see a soul one has illuminated and awakened to the highest point gradually slipping back to a browsing sheep, to live for *la chasse* alone, and horses, and dogs, with each day no higher aim than its own mean pleasure. Ah, Paul!" she continued with sudden passion, "I would rather you were dead—dead and cold with me, than I should have to feel you were growing a *rien du tout*—a thing who will go down into nothingness, and be forgotten by men!"

Her face was aflame with the *feu sacré*. The noble brow and line of her throat will ever remain in Paul's memory as a thing apart in womankind. Who could have small or unworthy thoughts who had known her—this splendid lady?

And his worship grew and grew.

CHAPTER XVII

That night, as they looked from the loggia on the Grand Canal after dinner, the moonlight making things almost light as day, Dmitry begged admittance from the doorway of the great salon. The lady turned imperiously, and flashed upon him. How dared he interrupt their happy hour with things of earth? Then she saw he was loth to speak before Paul, and that his face was grey with fear.

Paul realised the situation, and moved aside, pretending to lean from the wide windows and watch the passing gondolas, his wandering attention, however, fixing itself upon one which was moored not far from the palazzo, and occupied by a solitary figure reclining motionless in the seats. It had no coloured lights, this gondola, or merry musicians; it was just a black object of silence, tenanted by one man.

Dmitry whispered, and the lady listened, a quiver of rage going through her lithe body. Then she turned and surveyed the moored gondola, the same storm of passion and hate in her eyes as once before had come there, at the Rigi Kaltbad Belvedere.

"Shall I kill the miserable spy? Vasili would do it this night," she hissed between her clenched teeth. "But to what end? A day's respite, perhaps, and then another, and another to face."

Dmitry raised an imploring hand to draw her from the wide arched opening, where she must be in full view of those watching below. She motioned him furiously aside, and took Paul's hand. "Come, my lover," she said, "we will look no more on this treacherous stream! It is full of the ghosts of past murders and fears. Let us return to our shrine and shut out all jars; we will sit on our tiger and forget even the moon. Beloved one—come!"

And she led him to the open doorway, but the hand which held his was cold as ice.

A tumult of emotion was dominating Paul. He understood now that danger was near—he guessed they were being watched—but by whom? By the orders of—her husband? Ah! that thought drove him mad with rage—her husband! She—his own—the mate of his soul—of his body and soul—was the legal belonging of somebody else! Some vile man whom she hated and loathed, a "rotting carrion spoiling God's earth." And he—Paul—was powerless to change this fact—was powerless altogether except to love her and die for her if that would be for her good.

"Queen," he said, his voice hoarse with passion and pain, "let us leave Venice—leave Europe altogether—let me take you away to some far land of peace, and live there in safety and joy for the rest of our lives. You would always be the empress of my being and soul."

She flung herself on the tiger couch, and writhed there for some moments, burying her clenched fists in the creature's deep fur. Then she opened wide her arms, and drew Paul to her in a close, passionate embrace.

"*Moi-Lioubimyi*—My beloved—my darling one!" she whispered in anguish. "If we were lesser persons—yes, we could hide and live for a time in a tent under the stars—but we are not They would track me, and trap us, and sooner or later there would be the end, the ignominious, ordinary end of disgrace—" Then she clasped him closer, and whispered right in his ear in her wonderful voice, now trembling with love.

"Sweetheart—listen! Beyond all of this there is that thought, that hope, ever in my heart that one day a son of ours shall worthily fill a throne, so we must not think of ourselves, my Paul, of the Thou, and the I, and the Now, beloved. A throne which is filled most ignobly at present, and only filled at all through my birth and my family's influence. Think not I want to plant a cheat. No! I have a right to find an heir as I will, a splendid heir who shall redeem the land—the spirit of our two selves given being by love, and endowed by the gods. Ah! think of it, Paul. Dream of this joy and pride, it will help to still the unrest we are both suffering now. It must quiet this wild, useless rage against fate. Is it not so, my lover?"

Her voice touched his very heartstrings, but he was too deeply moved to answer her for a moment. The renewal of this thought exalted his very soul. All that was noble and great in his nature seemed rising up in one glad triumph-song.

A son of his and hers to fill a throne! Ah! God, if that were so!

"I love the English," she whispered. "I have known the men of all nations—but I love the English best. They are straight and just—the fine ones at least. They are brave and fair—and fearless. And our baby Paul shall be the most splendid of any. Beloved one, you must not think me a visionary—a woman dreaming of what might never be—I see it—I know it. This will come to pass as I say, and then we shall both find consolation and rest."

Thus she whispered on until Paul was intoxicated with joy and glory, and forgot time and place and danger and possible parting. A host of triumphant angels seemed singing in his ears.

Then she read him poetry, and let him caress her, and smiled in his arms.

But towards morning, if he had awakened, he would have found his lady prostrate with silent weeping. The intense concentrated grief of a strong nature taking its farewell.

CHAPTER XVIII

Now this Thursday was the night of the full moon. A cloudless morning sky promised a glorious evening.

The lovers woke early, and had their breakfast on the loggia overlooking the oleander garden. The lady was in an enchanting mood of sunshine, and no one could have guessed of the sorrow of her dawn vigil thoughts. She was wayward and playful—one moment petting Paul with exquisite sweetness, the next teasing his curls and biting the lobes of his ears. She never left him for one second—it seemed she must teach him still more subtle caresses, and call forth even new shades of emotion and bliss. All fear was banished, only a brilliant glory remained. She laughed and half-closed her eyes with provoking smiles. She undulated about, creeping as a serpent over her lover, and kissing his eyelids and hair. They were so infinitely happy it was growing to afternoon before they thought of leaving their loggia, and then they started in the open gondola, and glided away through quaint, narrow canals until they came to the lagoon.

"We shall not stay in the gondola long, my Paul," she said. "I cannot bear to be out of your arms, and our palace is fair. And oh! my beloved, to-night I shall feast you as never before. The night of our full moon! Paul, I have ordered a bower of roses and music and song. I want you to remember it the whole of your life."

"As though I could forget a moment of our time, my sweet," said Paul. "It needs no feasts or roses—only whatever delights you to do, delights me too."

"Paul," she cooed after a while, during which her hand had lain in his and there had been a soft silence, "is not this a life of joy, so smooth and gliding, this way of Venice? It seems far from ruffles and storms. I shall love it always, shall not you? and you must come back in other years and study its buildings and its history, Paul—with your new, fine eyes."

"We shall come together, my darling," he answered. "I should never want anything alone."

"Sweetheart!" she cooed again in his ears; and then presently, "Paul," she said, "some day you must read 'Salammbo,' that masterpiece of Flaubert's. There is a spirit of love in that which now you would understand—the love which looked out of Matho's eyes when his body was beaten to jelly. It is the love I have for you, my own—a love 'beyond all words or sense'—as one of your English poets says. Do you know, with the strange irony of things, when a woman's love for a man rises to the highest point there is in it always an element of *the wife*? However wayward and tigerish and undomestic she may be, she then desires to be the acknowledged possession and belonging of the man, even to her own dishonour. She desires to reproduce his likeness, she wants to compass his material good. She will think of his food, and his raiment, and his well-being, and never of her own—only, if she is wise she will hide all these things in her heart, for the average man cannot stand this great light of her sweetness, and when her love becomes selfless, his love will wane."

"The average man's—yes, perhaps so," agreed Paul. "But then, what does the average person of either sex know of love at all?"

"They think they know," she said. "Really think it, but love like ours happens perhaps once in a century, and generally makes history of some sort—bad or good."

"Let it!" said Paul. "I am like Antony in that poem you read me last night. I must have you for my own, 'Though death, dishonour, anything you will, stand in the way.' He knew what he was talking about, Antony! so did the man who wrote the poem!"

"He was a great sculptor as well as a poet," the lady said. "And yes, he knew all about those wonderful lovers better far than your Shakespeare did, who leaves me quite cold when I read his view of them. Cleopatra was to me so subtle, so splendid a queen."

"Of course she was just you, my heart," said Paul. "You are her soul living over again, and that poem you must give me to keep some day, because it says just what I shall want to say if ever I must be away from you for a time. See, have I remembered it right?

"'Tell her, till I see Those eyes, I do not live—that Rome to me Is hateful,—tell her—oh!—I know not what—That every thought and feeling, space and spot, Is like an ugly dream where she is not; All persons plagues; all living wearisome; All talking empty…'.

"Yes, that is what I should say—I say it to myself now even in the short while I am absent from you dressing!"

The lady's eyes brimmed with tenderness. "Paul!—you do love me, my own!" she said.

"Oh, why can't we go on and travel together, darling?" Paul continued. "I want you to show me the world—at least the best of Europe. In every country you would make me feel the spirit of the place. Let us go to Greece, and see the temples and worship those old gods. They knew about love, did they not?"

The lady leant back and smiled, as if she liked to hear him talk.

"I often ask myself did they really know," she said. "They knew the whole material part of it at any rate. They were perhaps too practical to have indulged in the mental emotions we weave into it now—but they were wise, they did not educate the wives and daughters, they realised that to perform well domestic duties a woman's mind should not be over-trained in learning. Learning and charm and grace of mind were for the others, the *hetaerae* of whom they asked no tiresome ties. And in all ages it is unfortunately not the simple good women who have ruled the hearts of men. Think of Pericles and Aspasia—Antony and Cleopatra—Justinian and Theodora—Belisarius and Antonina—and later, all the mistresses of the French kings—even, too, your English Nelson and Lady Hamilton! Not one of these was a man's ideal of what a wife and mother ought to be. So no doubt the Greeks were right in that principle, as they were right in all basic principles of art and balance. And now we mix the whole thing up, my Paul—domesticity and learning—nerves and art, and feverish cravings for the impossible new—so we get a conglomeration of false proportions, and a ceaseless unrest."

"Yes," said Paul, and thought of his mother. She was a perfectly domestic and beautiful woman, but somehow he felt sure she had never made his father's heart beat. Then his mind went back to the argument in what the lady had said—he wanted to hear more.

"If this is so, that would prove that all the very clever women of history were immoral—do you mean that?" he asked.

The lady laughed.

"Immoral! It is so quaint a word, my Paul! Each one sees it how they will. For me it is immoral to be false, to be mean, to steal, to cheat, to stoop to low actions and small ends. Yet one can be and do all those things, and if one remains as well the faithful beast of burden to one man, one is counted in the world a moral woman! But that shining light of hypocrisy and virtue—to judge by her sentiments in her writings—your George Eliot, must be classed as immoral because, having chosen her mate without the law's blessing, she yet wrote the highest sentiments of British respectability! To me she was being immoral *only* because she was deliberately doing what—, again I say, judging by her writings—she felt must be a grievous wrong. That is immoral—deliberately to still one's conscience and indulge in a pleasure against it. But to live a life with one's love, if it engenders the most lofty aspirations, to me is highly moral and good. I feel myself ennobled, exalted, because you are my lover, and our child, when it comes to us, will have a noble mind."

The thought of this, as ever, made Paul thrill; he forgot all other arguments, and a quiver ran through him of intense emotion; his eyes swam and he clasped more tightly her hand. The lady, too, leant back and closed her eyes.

"Oh! the beautiful dream!" she said, "the beautiful, beautiful—certainly!

Sweetheart, let us have done with all this philosophising and go back to our palace, where we are happy in the temple of the greatest of all Gods—the God of Love!"

Then she gave the order for home.

But on the way they stopped at Jesurum's, and she supervised Paul's purchases for his mother, and allowed him to buy herself some small gifts. And between them they spent a good deal of money, and laughed over it like happy children. So when they got back to the palazzo there was joy in their hearts like the sunlight of the late afternoon.

She would not let Paul go on to the loggia overlooking the Grand Canal. He had noticed as they passed that some high screens of lilac-bushes had been placed in front of the wide arched openings. No fear of prying eyes from opposite houses now! And yet they were not too high to prevent those in the loggia from seeing the moon and the sky. Their feast was preparing evidently, and he knew it would be a night of the gods.

But from then until it was time to dress for dinner his lady decreed that they should rest in their rooms.

"Thou must sleep, my Paul," she said, "so that thy spirit may be fresh for new joys."

And it was only after hard pleading she would allow him to have it that they rested on the other loggia couches, so that his closing eyes might know her near.

CHAPTER XIX

No Englishwoman would have thought of the details which made the Feast of the Full Moon so wonderful in Paul's eyes. It savoured rather of other centuries and the days of Imperial Rome, and indeed, had his lady been one of Britain's daughters, he too might have found it a little *bizarre*. As it was, it was all in the note—the exotic note of Venice and her spells.

The lady had gone to her room when he woke on the loggia, and he had only time to dress before the appointed moment when he was to meet her in the little salon.

She was seated on the old Venetian chair she had bought in Lucerne when Paul entered—the most radiant vision he had yet seen. Her garment was pale-green gauze. It seemed to cling in misty folds round her exquisite shape; it was clasped with pearls; the most magnificent ones hung in a row round her throat and fell from her ears. A diadem confined her glorious hair, which descended in the two long strands twisted with chains of emeralds and diamonds. Her whole personality seemed breathing magnificence and panther-like grace. And her eyes glowed with passion, and mystery, and force.

Paul knelt like a courtier, and kissed her hand. Then he led her to their feast.

Dmitry raised the curtain of the loggia door as they approached, and what a sight met Paul's view!

The whole place had been converted into a bower of roses. The walls were entirely covered with them. A great couch of deepest red ones was at one side, fixed in such masses as to be quite resisting and firm. From the roof chains of roses hung, concealing small lights—while from above the screen of lilac-bushes in full bloom the moon in all her glory mingled with the rose-shaded lamps and cast a glamour and unreality over the whole.

The dinner was laid on a table in the centre, and the table was covered with tuberoses and stephanotis, surrounding the cupid fountain of perfume. The scent of all these flowers! And the warm summer night! No wonder Paul's senses quivered with exaltation. No wonder his head swam.

They had scarcely been seated when from the great salon, whose open doors were hidden by falling trellises of roses, there came the exquisite sounds of violins, and a boy's plaintive voice. A concert of all sweet airs played softly to further excite the sense. Paul had not thought such musicians could be obtained in Venice, and guessed, and rightly, that, like the cook and the artist who had designed it, they hailed from Paris, to beautify this night.

Throughout the repast his lady bewildered him with her wild fascination. Never before had she seemed to collect all her moods into one subtle whole, cemented together by passionate love. It truly was a night of the gods, and the exaltation of Paul's spirit had reached its zenith.

"My Paul," she said, when at last only the rare fruits and the golden wine remained, and they were quite alone—even the musicians had retired, and their airs floated up from a gondola below. "My Paul, I want you never to forget this night—never to think of me but as gloriously happy, clasped in your arms amid the roses. And see, we must drink once more together of our wedding wine, and complete our souls' delight."

An eloquence seemed to come to Paul and loosen his tongue, so that he whispered back paeans of worship in language as fine as her own. And the moon flooded the loggia with her light, and the roses gave forth their scent. It was the supreme effort of art and nature to cover them with glorious joy.

"My darling one," the lady whispered in his ear, as she lay in his arms on the couch of roses, crushed deep and half buried in their velvet leaves, "this is our souls' wedding. In life and in death they can never part more."

* * * * *

Dawn was creeping through the orchid blinds of their sleeping chamber when this strange Queen disengaged herself from her lover's embrace, and bent over him, kissing his young curved lips. He stirred not—the languor of utter prostration was upon him, and held him in its grasp. In the uncertain light his sleep looked pale as death.

The lady gazed at him, an anguish too deep for tears in her eyes. For was not this the end—the very end? Fierce, dry sobs shook her. There was something terrible and tigerish in her grief. And yet her will made her not linger—there was still one thing to do.

She rose and turned to the writing-table by the window, then drawing the blind aside a little she began rapidly to write. When she had finished, without reading the missive over, she went and placed it with a flat leather jewel-case on her pillow beside Paul. And soon she commenced a madness of farewells—all restrained and gentle for fear he should awake.

"My love, my love," she wailed between her kisses, "God keep you safe—though He may never bring you back to me."

Then with a wild, strangled sob, she fled from the room.

CHAPTER XX

A hush was over everything when Paul first awoke—the hush of a hot, drowsy noontide.

He stretched out his arm to touch his loved one, as was his custom, to draw her near and envelop her with caresses and greeting—an instinct which came to him while yet half asleep.

But his arm met empty space. What was this? He opened his eyes wide and sat up in bed. He was alone—where had she gone? He had slept so late, that was it. She was playing one of her sweet tricks upon him. Perhaps she was even hiding behind the curtain which covered the entrance to the side loggia where they were accustomed to breakfast. He would look and see. He rose quickly and lifted the heavy drapery. No—the loggia was untenanted, and breakfast was laid for one! That was the first chill—for one! Was she angry at his drowsiness? Good God! what could it mean? He staggered a little, and sat on the bed, clutching the fine sheet. And as he did so it disclosed the letter and the flat leather case, which had fallen from the pillow and become hidden in the clothes.

A deadly faintness came over Paul. For a few seconds he trembled so his shaking fingers refused to hold the paper. Then with a mighty effort he mastered himself, and tearing the envelope open began to read.

It was a wonderful letter. The last passionate cry of her great loving heart. It passed in review their glorious days in burning words—from the first moment of their meeting. And then, towards the end, "My Paul," she wrote, "that first night you were my caprice, and afterwards my love, but now you are my life, and for this I must leave you, to save that life, sweet lover. Seek me not, heart of my heart. Believe me, I would not go if there were any other way. Fate is too strong for us, and I must bow my head. Were I to remain even another hour, all Dmitry's watching could not keep you safe. Darling, while I thought they menaced me alone, it only angered me, but now I know that you would pay the penalty, I can but go. If you follow me, it will mean death for us both. Oh! Paul, I implore you, by our great love, go into safety as soon as you can. You must leave Venice, and return straight to England, and your home. Darling—beloved—lover—if we never meet again in this sad world let this thought stay with you always, that I love you—heart and mind—body and soul—I am utterly and forever YOURS."

As he read the last words the room became dark for Paul, and he fell back like a log on the bed, the paper fluttering to the floor from his nerveless fingers.

She was gone—and life seemed over for him.

Here, perhaps an hour later, Tompson found him still unconscious, and in terrified haste sent off for a doctor, and telegraphed to Sir Charles Verdayne:

"Come at once, TOMPSON."
But ere his father could arrive on Sunday, Paul was lying 'twixt life and death, madly raving with brain fever.
And thus ended the three weeks of his episode.

CHAPTER XXI

Have any of you who read crept back to life from nearly beyond the grave? Crept back to find it shorn of all that made it fair? After hours of delirium to awaken in great weakness to a sense of hideous anguish and loss—to the prospect of days of aching void and hopeless longing, to the hourly, momentary sting of remembrance of things vaster than death, more dear than life itself? If you have come through this valley of the shadow, then you can know what the first days of returning consciousness meant to Paul.

He never really questioned the finality of her decree, he *sensed* it meant parting for ever. And yet, with that spring of eternal hope which animates all living souls, unbidden arguings and possibilities rose in his enfeebled brain, and deepened his unrest. Thus his progress towards convalescence was long and slow.

And all this time his father and Tompson had nursed him in the old Venetian palazzo with tenderest devotion.

The Italian servants had been left, paid up for a month, but the lady and her Russian retinue had vanished, leaving no trace.

Both Tompson and Sir Charles knew almost the whole story now from Paul's ravings, and neither spoke of it—except that Tompson supplied some links to complete Sir Charles' picture.

"She was the most splendid lady you could wish to see, Sir Charles," the stolid creature finished with. "Her servants worshipped her—and if Mr. Verdayne is ill now, he is ill for no less than a Queen."

This fact comforted Tompson greatly, but Paul's father found in it no consolation.

The difficulty had been to prevent his mother from descending upon them. She must ever be kept in ignorance of this episode in her son's life. She belonged to the class of intellect which could never have understood. It would have been an undying shock and horrified grief to the end of her life—excellent, loving, conventional lady!

So after the first terrible danger was over, Sir Charles made light of their son's illness. Paul and he were enjoying Venice, he said, and would soon be home. "D—d hard luck the boy getting fever like this!" he wrote in his laconic style, "but one never could trust foreign countries' drains!"

And the Lady Henrietta waited in unsuspecting, well-bred patience.

Those were weary days for every one concerned. It wrung his father's heart to see Paul prostrate there, as weak as an infant. All his splendid youth and strength conquered by this raging blast. It was sad to have to listen to his ever-constant moan:

"Darling, come back to me—darling, my Queen."

And even after he regained consciousness, it was equally pitiful to watch him lying nerveless and white, blue shadows on his once fresh skin. And most pitiful of all were his hands, now veined and transparent, falling idly upon the sheet.

But at least the father realised it could have been no ordinary woman whose going caused the shock which—even after a life of three weeks' continual emotion—could prostrate his young Hercules. She must have been worth something—this tiger Queen.

And one day, contrary to his usual custom, he addressed Tompson:

"What sort of a looking woman, Tompson?"

And Tompson, although an English valet, did not reply, "Who, Sir Charles?"—he just rounded his eyes stolidly and said in his monotonous voice:

"She was that forcible-looking, a man couldn't say when he got close, she kind of dazzled him. She had black hair, and a white face, and—and—witch's eyes, but she was very kind and overpowering, haughty and generous. Any one would have known she was a Queen."

"Young?" asked Sir Charles.

Tompson smoothed his chin: "I could not say, Sir Charles. Some days about twenty-five, and other days past thirty. About thirty-three to thirty-five, I expect she was, if the truth were known."

"Pretty?"

The eyes rounded more and more. "Well, she was so fascinatin', I can't say, Sir Charles—the most lovely lady I ever did see at times, Sir Charles."

"Humph," said Paul's father, and then relapsed into silence.

"She'd a beast of a husband; he might have been a King, but he was no gentleman," Tompson ventured to add presently, fearing the "Humph" perhaps meant disapprobation of this splendid Queen. "Her servants were close, and did not speak good English, so I could not get much out of them, but the man Vasili, who came the last days, did say in a funny lingo, which I had to guess at, as how he expected he should have to kill him some time. Vasili had a scar on his face as long as your finger that he'd got defending the Queen from her husband's brutality, when he was the worse for drink, only last year. And Mr. Verdayne is so handsome. It is no wonder, Sir Charles—"

"That will do, Tompson," said Sir Charles, and he frowned.

The fatal letter, carefully sealed up in a new envelope, and the leather case were in his despatch-box. Tompson had handed them to him on his arrival. And one day when Paul appeared well enough to be lifted into a long chair on the side loggia, his father thought fit to give them to him.

Paul's apathy seemed paralysing. The days had passed, since the little Italian doctor had pronounced him out of danger, in one unending languid quietude. He expressed interest in no single thing. He was polite, and indifferent, and numb.

"He must be roused now," Sir Charles said to the doctor. "It is too hot for Venice, he must be moved to higher air," and the little man had nodded his head.

So this warm late afternoon, as he lay under the mosquito curtains—which the coming of June had made necessary in this paradise—his father said to him:

"I have a letter and a parcel of yours, Paul: you had better look at them—we hope to start north in a day or two—you must get to a more bracing place."

Then he had pushed them under the net-folds, and turned his back on the scene.

The blood rushed to Paul's face, but left him deathly pale after a few moments. And presently he broke the seal. The minute Sphinx in the corner of the paper seemed to mock at him. Indeed, life was a riddle of anguish and pain. He read the letter all over—and read it again. The passionate words of love warmed him now that he had passed the agony of the farewell. One sentence he had hardly grasped before, in particular held balm. "Sweetheart," it said, "you must not grieve—think always of the future and of our hope. Our love is not dead with our parting, and one day there will be the living sign—" Yes, that thought was comfort—but how should he know?

Then he turned to the leather case. His fingers were still so feeble that with difficulty he pressed the spring to open it.

He glanced up at his father's distinguished-looking back outlined against the loggia's opening arches. It appeared uncompromising. A fixed determination to stare at the oleanders below seemed the only spirit animating this parent.

Yes—he must open the box. It gave suddenly with a jerk, and there lay a dog's collar, made of small flexible plates of pure beaten gold, mounted on Russian leather, all of the finest workmanship. And on a slip of paper in his darling's own writing he read:

"This is for Pike, my beloved one; let him wear it always—a gift from me."

On the collar itself, finely engraved, were the words, "Pike, belonging to Paul Verdayne."

Then the floodgates of Paul's numbed soul were opened, a great sob rose in his breast. He covered his face with his hands, and cried like a child.

Oh! her dear thought! her dear, tender thought—for Pike! His little friend!

And Sir Charles made believe he saw nothing, as he stole from the place, his rugged face twitching a little, and his keen eyes dim.

CHAPTER XXII

They did not go north, as Sir Charles intended, an unaccountable reluctance on Paul's part to return through Switzerland changed their plans. Instead, by a fortunate chance, the large schooner yacht of a rather eccentric old friend came in to Venice, and the father eagerly accepted the invitation to go on board and bring his invalid.

The owner, one Captain Grigsby, had been quite alone, so the three men would be in peace, and nothing could be better for Paul than this warm sea air.

"Typhoid fever?" Mark Grigsby had asked.

"No," Sir Charles had replied, "considerable mental tribulation over a woman."

"D—d kittle cattle!" was Captain Grigsby's polite comment. "A fine boy, too, and promising—"

"Appears to have been almost worth while," Sir Charles added, "from what I gather—and, confound it, Grig, we'd have done the same in our day."

But Captain Grigsby only repeated: "D—d kittle cattle!"

And so they weighed anchor, and sailed along the Italian shores of the sun-lit Adriatic.

These were better days for Paul. Each hour brought him back some health and vigour. Youth and strength were asserting their own again, and the absence of familiar objects, and the glory of the air and the blue sea helped sometimes to deaden the poignant agony of his aching heart. But there it was underneath, an ever-present, dull anguish. And only when he became sufficiently strong to help the sailors with the ropes, and exert physical force, did he get one moment's respite. The two elder men watched him with kind, furtive eyes, but they never questioned him, or made the slightest allusion to his travels.

And the first day they heard him laugh Sir Charles looked down at the white foam because a mist was in his eyes.

They had coasted round Italy and Sicily, and not among the Ionian Isles, as had been Captain Grigsby's intention.

"I fancy the lady came from some of those Balkan countries," Sir Charles had said. "Don't let us get in touch with even the outside of one of them."

And Mark Grigsby had grunted an assent.

"The boy is a fine fellow," he said one morning as they looked at Paul hauling ropes. "He'll probably never get quite over this, but he is fighting like a man, Charles—tell me as much as you feel inclined to of the story."

So Sir Charles began in his short, broken sentences:

"Parson's girl to start with—sympathy over a broken collar-bone. The wife behaved unwisely about it, so the boy thought he was in love. We sent him to travel to get rid of that idea. It appears he met this lady in Lucerne—seems to have been an exceptional person—a Russian, Tompson says—a Queen or Princess *incog.*,the fellow tells me—but I can't spot her as yet. Hubert will know who she was, though—but it does not matter—the woman herself was the thing. Gather she was quite a remarkable woman—ten years older than Paul."

"Always the case," growled Captain Grigsby.

Sir Charles puffed at his pipe—and then: "They were only together three weeks," he said. "And during that time she managed to cram more knowledge of everything into the boy's head than you and I have got in a lifetime. Give you my word, Grig, when he was off his chump in the fever, he raved like a poet, and an orator, and he was only an ordinary sportsman when he left home in the spring! Cleopatra, he called her one day, and I fancy that was the keynote—she must have been one of those exceptional women we read of in the sixth form."

"And fortunately never met!" said Captain Grigsby.

"I don't know," mused Sir Charles. "It might have been good to live as wildly even at the price. We've both been about the world, Grig, since the days we fastened on our cuirasses together for the first time, and each thought himself the devil of a fine fellow—but I rather doubt if we now know as much of what is really worth having as my boy there—just twenty-three years old."

"Nonsense!" snapped Captain Grigsby—but there was a tone of regret in his protest.

"Lucky to have got off without a knife or a bullet through him—dangerous nations to grapple with," he said.

"Yes—I gather some pretty heavy menace was over their heads, and that is what made the lady decamp, so we've much to be thankful for," agreed Sir Charles.

"Had she any children?" the other asked.

"Tompson says no. Rotten fellow the husband, it appears, and no heir to the throne, or principality, or whatever it is—so when I have had a talk with Hubert—Henrietta's brother, you know—the one in the Diplomatic Service, it will be easy to locate her—gathered Paul doesn't know himself."

"Pretty romance, anyway. And what will you do with the boy now, Charles?"

Paul's father puffed quite a long while at his meerschaum before he answered, and then his voice was gruffer than ever with tenderness suppressed.

"Give him his head, Grig," he said. "He's true blue underneath, and he'll come up to the collar in time, old friend—only I shall have to keep his mother's love from harrying him. Best and greatest lady in the world, my wife, but she's rather apt to jog the bridle now and then."

At this moment Paul joined them. His paleness showed less than usual beneath the sunburn, and his eyes seemed almost bright. A wave of thankful gladness filled his father's heart.

"Thank God," he said, below his breath. "Thank God."

The weather had been perfection, hardly a drop of rain, and just the gentlest breezes to waft them slowly along. A suitable soothing idle life for one who had but lately been near death. And each day Paul's strength returned, until his father began to hope they might still be home for his birthday the last day of July. They had crept up the coast of Italy now, when an absolute calm fell upon them, and just opposite the temple of Paestum they decided to anchor for the night.

For the last evenings, as the moon had grown larger, Paul had been strangely restless. It seemed as if he preferred to tire himself out with unnecessary rope-pulling, and then retire to his berth the moment that dinner was over, rather than go on deck. His face, too, which had been controlled as a mask until now, wore a look of haunting anguish which was grievous to see. He ate his dinner—or rather, pretended to play with the food—in absolute silence.

Uneasiness overcame Sir Charles, and he glanced at his old friend. But Paul, after lighting a cigar, and letting it out once or twice, rose, and murmuring something about the heat, went up on deck.

It was the night of the full moon—eight weeks exactly since the joy of life had finished for him.

He felt he could not bear even the two kindly gentlemen whose unspoken sympathy he knew was his. He could not bear anything human. To-night, at least, he must be alone with his grief.

All nature was in a mood divine. They were close enough inshore to see the splendid temples clearly with the naked eye. The sky and the sea were of the colour only the Mediterranean knows.

It was hot and still, and the moon in her pure magnificence cast her never-ending spell.

Not a sound of the faintest ripple met his ear. The sailors supped below. All was silence. On one side the vast sea, on the other the shore, with this masterpiece of man's genius, the temple of the great god Poseidon, in this vanished settlement of the old Greeks. How marvellously beautiful it all was, and how his Queen would have loved it! How she would have told him its history and woven round it the spirit of the past, until his living eyes could almost have seen the priests and the people, and heard their worshipping prayers!

His darling had spoken of it once, he remembered, and had told him it was a place they must see. He recollected her very words:

"We must look at it first in the winter from the shore, my Paul, and see those splendid proportions outlined against the sky—so noble and so perfectly balanced—and then we must see it from the sea, with the background of the olive hills. It is ever silent and deserted and calm, and death lurks there after the month of March. A cruel malaria, which we must not face, dear love. But if we could, we ought to see it from a yacht in safety in the summer time, and then the spell would fall upon us, and we would know it was true that rose-trees really grew there which gave the world their blossoms twice a year. That was the legend of the Greeks."

Well, he was seeing it from a yacht, but ah, God! seeing it alone—alone. And where was she?

So intense and vivid was his remembrance of her that he could feel her presence near. If he turned his head, he felt he should see her standing beside him, her strange eyes full of love. The very perfume of her seemed to fill the air—her golden voice to whisper in his ear—her soul to mingle with his soul. Ah yes, in spirit, as she had said, they could never be parted more.

A suppressed moan of anguish escaped his lips, and his father, who had come silently behind him, put his hand on his arm.

"My poor boy," he said, his gruff voice hoarse in his throat, "if only to God I could do something for you!"

"Oh, father!" said Paul.

And the two men looked in each other's eyes, and knew each other as never before.

CHAPTER XXIII

Next day there was a fresh breeze, and they scudded before it on to Naples. Here Paul seemed well enough to take train, and so arrive in England in time for his birthday. He owed this to his mother, he and his father both felt. She had been looking forward to it for so long, as at the time of his coming of age the festivities had been interrupted by the sudden death of his maternal grandfather, and the people had all been promised a continuance of them on this, his twenty-third birthday. So, taking the journey by sufficiently easy stages, sleeping three nights on the way, they calculated to arrive on the eve of the event.

The Lady Henrietta would have everything in readiness for them, and her darling Paul was not to be over-hurried. Only guests of the most congenial kind had been invited, and such a number of nice girls!

The prospect was perfectly delightful, and ought to cause any young man pure joy.

It was with a heart as heavy as lead Paul mounted the broad steps of his ancestral home that summer evening, and was folded in his mother's arms. (The guests were all fortunately dressing for dinner.)

Captain Grigsby had been persuaded to abandon his yacht and accompany them too.

"Yes, I'll come, Charles," he said. "Getting too confoundedly hot in these seas; besides, the boy will want more than one to see him through among those cackling women."

So the three had travelled together through Italy and France—Switzerland had been strictly avoided.

"Paul! darling!" his mother exclaimed, in a voice of pained surprise as she stood back and looked at him. "But surely you have been very ill. My darling, darling son—"

"I told you he had had a sharp attack of fever, Henrietta," interrupted Sir Charles quickly, "and no one looks their best after travelling in this grilling weather. Let the boy get to his bath, and you will see a different person."

But his mother's loving eyes were not to be deceived. So with infinite fuss, and terms of endearment, she insisted upon accompanying her offspring to his room, where the dignified housekeeper was summoned, and his every imaginable and unimaginable want arranged to be supplied.

Once all this would have irritated Paul to the verge of bearish rudeness, but now he only kissed his mother's white jewelled hand. He remembered his lady's tender counsel to him, given in one of their many talks: "You must always reverence your mother, Paul, and accept her worship with love." So now he said:

"Dear mother, it is so good of you, but I'm all right—fever does knock one over a bit, you know. You'll see, though, being at home again will make me perfectly well in no time—and I'll be as good as you like, and eat and drink all Mrs. Elwyn's beef-teas and jellies, and other beastly stuff, if you will just let me dress now, like a darling."

However, his mother was obliged to examine and assure herself that his beautiful hair was still thick and waving—and she had to pause and sigh over every sharpened line of his face and figure—though the thought of being permitted to lavish continuous care for long days to come held a certain consolation for her.

At last Paul was left alone, and there came a moment he had been longing for. He had sent written orders that Tremlett should bring Pike, and leave him in his dressing-room beyond—and all the while his mother had talked he had heard suppressed whines and scratchings. Somehow he had not wanted to see his dog before any of the people; the greeting between himself and his little friend must be in solitude, for was there not a secret link between them in that golden collar given by his Queen?

And Pike would understand—he certainly would understand!

If short, passionate barks, and a madness of wagging tail-stump, accompanied by jumps of crazy joy, could comfort any one—then Paul had his full measure when the door was opened, and this rough white terrier bounded in upon him, and, frantic with welcome and ecstasy, was with difficulty quieted at last in his master's fond arms.

"Oh! Pike, Pike!" Paul said, while tears of weakness flowed down his cheeks. "I can talk to you—and when you wear her collar you will know my Queen—our Queen."

And Pike said everything of sympathy a dog could say. But it was not until late at night, when the interminable evening had been got through, that his master had the pleasure of trying his darling's present on.

That first evening of his homecoming was an ordeal for Paul. He was still feeble, and dead tired from travelling, to begin with—and to have to listen and reply to the endless banalities of his mother's guests was almost more than he could bear.

They were a nice cheery company of mostly young friends. Pretty girls and his own boon companions abounded, and they chaffed and played silly games after dinner—until Paul could have groaned.

Captain Grigsby had eventually caught Sir Charles' eye:

"You will have the boy fainting if you don't get him off alone soon," he said. "These girls would tire a man in strong health!"

And at last Paul had escaped to his own room.

He leant out of his window, and looked at the gibbous moon. Pike was there on the broad sill beside him, under his arm, and he could feel the golden collar on the soft fur neck—a wave of perhaps the most hopeless anguish he had yet felt was upon his spirit now. The unutterable blankness—the impossible vista of the endless days to come, with no prospect of meeting—no aim—no hope. Yes, she had said there was one hope—one hope which could bring peace to their crud unrest. But how and when should he ever know? And if it were so—then more than ever he should be by her side. The number of beautiful things he would want to say to her about it all—the oceans of love he would desire to pour upon her—the tender care which should be his hourly joy. To honour and worship her, and chase all pain away. And he did not even know her name, or the country where one day this hope should reign. That was incredible—and it would be so easy to find out. But he had promised her never to make inquiries, and he would keep his word. He saw her reason now; it had arisen in an instinct of tender protection for himself. She had known if he knew her place of abode no fear of death would keep him from trying to see her. Ah! he had had the tears—and why not the cold steel and blood? It was no price to pay could he but hear once more her golden voice, and feel her loving, twining arms.

He was only held back by the fear of the danger for her. And instead of being with her, and waiting on her footsteps, he should have to spend his next hours with those ridiculous Englishwomen! Those foolish, flippant girls! One had quoted poetry to him at dinner, the very scrap his lady had spoken a line of—this new poet's, who was taking the world of London by storm that year: "Loved with a love beyond all words or sense!" And it had sounded like bathos or sacrilege. What did these dolls know of love, or life? Chattering parrots to weary a man's brain! Yes, the Greeks were right, it would be better to keep them spinning flax, and uneducated.

And so in his young intolerance, maddened by pain, he saw all things gibbous like the mocking moon. Pike stirred under his arm and licked his hand, a faint whine of love making itself heard in the night.

"O God!" said Paul, as he buried his face in his hands, "let me get through this time as she would have me do; let me not show the anguish in my heart, but be at least a man and gentleman."

CHAPTER XXIV

The neighbours and his parents were astonished at the eloquence of Paul's speech at the great dinner given to the tenants next day. No one had guessed at his powers before, and the county papers, and indeed some London reporters, had predicted a splendid political future for this young orator. It had been quite a long speech, and contained sound arguments and common sense, and was expressed in language so lofty and refined that it sent ecstatic admiration through his mother's fond breast.

And all the time Paul spoke he saw no sea of faces below him—only his soul's eyes were looking into those strange chameleon orbs of his lady. He said every word as if she had been there, and at the end it almost seemed she must have heard him, so soft a peace fell on his spirit. Yes, she would have been pleased with her lover, he knew, and that held large grains of consolation. And so these days passed in well-accomplished duty; and at last all the festivities were over, and he could rest.

Captain Grigsby and his father had helped him whenever they could, and an eternal bond of friendship was cemented between the three.

"By Jove, Charles! You ought to be thundering proud of that boy!" Captain Grigsby said the morning of his departure for Scotland on August 10. "He's come up to the scratch like a hero, and whatever the damage, the lady must have been well worth while to turn him out polished like that. Gad! Charles, I'd take a month's journey to see her myself."

And Paul's father grunted with satisfaction as he said: "I told you so."

Thus the summer days went by in the strengthening of Paul's character—trying always to live up to an ideal—trying ever to dominate his grief—but never trying to forget.

By the autumn shooting time his health was quite restored, and except that he looked a year or so older there were no outward traces of the passing through that valley of the shadow, from whence he had escaped with just his life.

But the three weeks of his lady's influence had changed the inner man beyond all recognition. His spirit was stamped with her nameless distinction, and all the vistas she had opened for him to the tree of knowledge he now followed up. No smallest incident of his day seemed unconnected with some thought or wish of hers—so that in truth she still guided and moulded him by the power of her great soul.

But in spite of all these things, the weeks and months held hours of aching longing and increasing anxiety to know how she fared. If she should be ill. If their hope was coming true, then now she must be suffering, and suffering all alone. Sometimes the agony of the thought was more than Paul could bear, and took him off with Pike alone into the leafless woods which crowned a hill at the top of the park. And then he would pause, and look out at the view, and the dull November sky, a madness of agonising unrest torturing his heart.

The one thing he felt glad of was the absence of his Uncle Hubert, who had been made Minister in a South American Republic, and would not return to England for more than a year. So there would be no temptation to question him, or perchance to hear one of his clever, evil jests which might contain some allusion to his lady. Lord Hubert Aldringham was fond of boasting of his royal acquaintances, and was of a mind that found "not even Lancelot brave, nor Galahad clean." Now all Paul could do was to wait and hope. At least his Queen had his address. She could write to him, even though he could not write to her—and surely, surely, some news of her must come.

Thus the winter arrived, and the hunting—hunting that he had been sure was what he liked best in all the world.

And now it just served to pass the time and distract some hours from the anguishing ache by its physical pleasure. But in that, as in everything he did at this time, Paul tried to outshine his fellows, and gain one more laurel to lay at the feet of his Queen. Socially he was having an immense success. He began to be known as some one worth listening to by men, and women hung on his words. It was peculiarly delightful to find so young and beautiful a creature with all the knowledge and fascinating *cachet* of a man of the world. And then his complete indifference to them piqued and allured them still more. Always polite and chivalrous, but as aloof as a mountain top. Paul had no small vanity to be soothed by their worship into forgetting for one moment his Queen. So his shooting-visits passed, and his experience of life grew.

Isabella had returned at Christmas, engaged to a High Church curate, and beaming with satisfaction and health. And it gave Paul, and indeed them both, pleasure to meet and talk for an hour. She was a good sort always, and if he marvelled to himself how he had even been even mildly attracted by her, he did not let it appear in his manner.

But one thing jarred.

"My goodness, Paul, how smart Pike's collar is!" Isabella had said. "Did you ever! You extravagant boy! It is good enough for a lady's bracelet. You had better give it to me! It will make the finest wedding gift I'll have!"

But Paul had snatched Pike up, the blood burning in his cheeks, and had laughed awkwardly and turned the conversation.

No one's fingers but his own were ever allowed to touch the sacred gold.

About this time his mother began to have the idea he ought really to marry. His father had been thirty at the time of his wedding with herself, and she had always thought that was starting too late. Twenty-three was a good age, and a sweet, gentle wife of Paul's would be the joy of her declining years—to say nothing of several grandchildren. But when this matter was broached to him first, Paul laughed, and when it became a daily subject of conversation, he almost lost that quick temper of his, which was not quite yet under perfect control.

"I tell you what it is, mother," he said, "if you tease me like this I shall go away on a voyage round the world!"

So the Lady Henrietta subsided into pained silence, and sulked with her adored son for more than a day.

"Paul is so unaccountably changed since his visit abroad," she said to her husband plaintively. "I sometimes wonder, Charles, if we really know all the people he met."

And Sir Charles had replied, "Nonsense! Henrietta—the lad is a man now, and immensely improved; do leave him in peace."

But when he was alone the father had smiled to himself—rather sadly—for he saw a good deal with his shrewd eyes, though he said no words of sympathy to his son. He knew that Paul was suffering still, perhaps as keenly as ever, and he honoured his determination to keep it all from view.

So the old year died, and the new one came—and soon February would be here. Ah! with what passionate anxiety the end of that month was awaited by Paul, only his own heart knew.

CHAPTER XXV

The days passed on, March had almost come, and Paul heard nothing. His father noticed the daily look of strain, and his mother anxiously inquired if he were dull, and if he would not like her to have some people to stay, and thus divert him in some fashion. And Paul had answered with what grace he could.

An intense temptation came over him to read all the Court news. He longed to pick up the ladies' papers he saw in his mother's sitting-room; such journals, he knew, delighted to publish the doings of royal lives. But the stern self-control which now he practised in all the ruling of his life prevented him. No, he had promised never to investigate—and neither in the letter, nor the spirit, would he break his word, whatever the suffering. The news, when it came, must be from his beloved one direct.

But oh! the unrest of these hours. Had their hope come true?—and how was she? The days passed in a gnawing anxiety. He was so restless he could hardly fix his attention on anything. It required the whole of his will to keep him taking in the sense of the Parliamentary books which were now his study. The constant query would raise its head between each page—"What news of my Queen?—what news of my Queen?"

Each mail as it came in made his heart beat, and often his hand trembled as he lifted his pile of letters. But no sight of her writing gladdened his eyes, until he began to be like the sea and its tides, rising twice a day in a rushing hope with the posts, and sinking again in disappointment.

He grew to look haggard, and his father's heart ached for him in silence. At length one morning, when he had almost trained himself not to glance at his correspondence, which came as he was dawdling over an early breakfast, his eye caught a foreign-looking letter lying on the top. It was no hand he knew—but something told him it contained a message—from his Queen.

He dominated himself; he would not even look at the postmark until he was away up in his own room. No eye but Pike's must see his joy—or sorrow and disappointment. And so the letter burnt in his pocket until his sanctum was reached, and then with agonised impatience he opened the envelope.

Within was another of the familiar paper he knew, and ah! thank God, addressed in pencil in his lady's own hand. Inside it contained an enclosure, but the sheet was blank. With wildly beating heart and trembling fingers Paul undid the smaller packet's folded ends. And there the morning sunbeams fell on a tiny curl of hair, of that peculiar nondescript shade of infant fairness which later would turn to gold. It was less than an inch long, and of the fineness of down, while in tender care it had been tied with a thread of blue silk.

Written on the paper underneath were the words:

"Beloved, he is so strong and fair, thy son, born the 19th of February."

For a moment Paul closed his eyes, and as once before a choir of seraphims were singing in his ears.

Then he looked at this minute lock again, and touched it with his forefinger. The strangest emotion he had ever known quivered through his being—the concentrated sensation of what he used to feel when his lady had spoken of their hope—a weird, tremulous, physical thrill. The dear small curl of hair! The actual, tangible proof of his own living son. He lifted it with the greatest reverence to his lips, and a mist of joy swam in his blue eyes. Ah! it was all too wonderful—too divine the thought! The essence of their great love—this child of his and hers. His and hers! Yes, their hope had not deceived them. It was true! It was true!

Then his mind rose in passionate worship of his lady. His goddess and Queen—the mainspring of his watch of life—the supreme and absolute mistress of his heart and soul. Never had he more madly desired and loved her than this day. He kissed and kissed her words in deep devotion.

But how and where was she?—was she well?—was she ill? Had she been suffering? Oh! that he could fly to her. More than ever the terrible gall of their separation came to him. It was his right, by every law of nature, to now be by her side.

But she was well—she must be well, or she would have said, and surely he soon would see her.

It was like a voice from heaven, her little written words, bridging the impossible—drawing him back to the knowledge and certainty that she was there, for him to love, and one day to go to. Fate could never be so unjust as to part him from—the mother of his child.

And then a state of mad ecstasy came over Paul with that vision; he could not stay in the house; he must go out under God's sky, and let his soul-thoughts fly into space. Dazzling pictures came to him; surely the spring was in his heart breaking through the frozen ground like a single golden crocus he saw at his feet—surely, surely the sun of life would shine again, and living he should see her.

He strode away, Pike gambolling beside him, and racing ahead and back again, seeming to understand and participate in his master's inward joy.

Paul hardly noticed where he went, his thoughts exalting him so that he did not even heed to choose his favourite haunt, the wood against the sky-line. It was as if great blocks of icy fear and anguish were melting in the warmth. Hope and glory shone on his path, almost blinding him.

He left the park far behind, and struck away across the moor. As he passed some gipsy vans a swarthy young woman looked out, an infant in her arms, and gave him a smiling greeting. But Paul stopped and said good-day, tossing her a sovereign with laughing, cheery words—for her little child—and so passed on, his glad face radiant as the morn.

But the woman called after him in gratitude:

"Blessings on your honour. Your own will grace a throne."

And the strange coincidence of her prophecy set fresh thrills of delight bounding in Paul's veins.

He walked and walked, stopping to lunch at an inn miles away. He could not bear even to see his parents—or the familiar scenes at home; and as once before he had felt in his grief—he and his joy must be alone to-day.

When he turned to come back in the late afternoon, the torrent of his wild happiness had crystallised itself into coherent thought and question. Surely she would send him some more words and make some plan to see him. But at least he was in touch with her again and knew she was his own—his own. The silence had broken, and human ingenuity would find some way of meeting.

The postmark was Vienna—though that meant nothing at all; she could have sent Dmitry there to post the letter. But at best, even if it were Russia, a few days' journey only separated him from his darling and—his son! Then the realisation of that proud fact of parenthood came over him again. He said the words aloud, "My son!"

And with a cry of wild exaltation he vaulted a gate like a schoolboy and ran along the path, Pike bounding in the air in frantic sympathy. Thus Paul returned to his home again, hope singing in his heart.

* * * * *

But even his father did not guess why that night at dinner he raised his champagne glass and drank a silent toast—his eyes gazing into distance as if he there saw heaven.

CHAPTER XXVI

Of course as the days went by the sparkle of Paul's joy subsided. An infinite unrest took its place—a continual mad desire for further news. Supposing she were ill, his darling one? Many times a day he read her words; the pencil writing was certainly feeble and shaky—supposing—But he refused to face any terrible picture. The letter had come on the 2d of March; his son had been eleven days old then—two days and a half to Vienna—that brought it to eight when the letter was posted—and from whence had it come there? If he allowed two days more, say—she must have written it only five or six days after the baby's birth.

Paul knew very little about such things, though he understood vaguely that a woman might possibly be very ill even after then. But surely, if so, Anna or Dmitry would have told him on their own initiative. This thought comforted him a little, but still anxiety—like a sleuth-hound—pursued his every moment. He would not leave home—London saw him not even for a day. Some word might come in his absence, some message or summons to go to her, and he would not chance being out of its reach. More than ever all their three weeks of happiness was lived over again—every word she had said had sunk for ever in his memory. And away in his solitary walks, or his rides home from hunting in the dusk of the afternoon, he let them echo in his heart.

But the desire to be near her was growing an obsession.

Some days when a wild gallop had made his blood run, triumphant thoughts of his son would come to him. How he should love to teach him to sit a horse in days to come, to ride to hounds, and shoot, and be an English gentleman. Oh! why was she a Queen, his loved one, and far away—why not here, and his wife, whom he could cover with devotion and honour? Surely that would be enough for them both—a life of trust and love and sweetness; but even if it were not—there was the world to choose from, if only they were together.

The two—Paul and his father—were a silent pair for the most part, as they jogged along the lanes on their way back from hunting.

One afternoon, when this sense of parenthood was strong upon Paul, he went in to tea in his mother's sitting-room. And as he leant upon the mantelpiece, his tall, splendid figure in its scarlet coat outlined against the bright blaze, his eye took in—perhaps for the first time—the immense number of portraits of himself which decorated this apartment—himself in every stage, from infantile days upward, through the toy rocking-horse period to the real dog companion—in Eton collars and Fourth of June hats—in cricketing flannels and Oxford Bullingdon groups—and then not so many, until one taken last year. How young it looked and smiling! There was one particular miniature of him in the holy of holiest positions in the centre of the writing-table—a real work of art, well painted on ivory. It was mounted in a frame of fine pearls, and engraved with the name and date at the back:

"Paul Verdayne—aged five years and three months."

It was a full-length picture of him standing next a great chair, in a blue velvet suit and a lace turn-over collar, while curls of brightest gold fell rippling to his neck—rather short bunchy curls which evidently would not be repressed.

"Was I ever like that, mother?" he said.

And the Lady Henrietta, only too enchanted to expand upon this enthralling subject, launched forth on a full description.

Like it! Of course! Only much more beautiful. No child had ever had such golden curls, or such eyes or eye-lashes! No child had ever, in fact, been able to compare with him in any way, or ever would! The Lady Henrietta's delicate shell-tinted cheeks flushed rose with joy at the recollection.

"Darling mother," said Paul, as he kissed her, "how you loved me. And how cold I have often been. Forgive me—"

Then he was silent while she fondled him in peace, his thoughts turning as ever to his lady. She, too, probably, would be foolish, and tender, and sweet over her son—and how his mother would love her grandchild. Oh! how cruel, how cruel was fate!

Then he asked: "Mother, does it take women a long time to get well when they have children? Ladies, I mean, who are finely nurtured? They generally get well, though, don't they—and it is quite simple—"

And the Lady Henrietta blushed as she answered:

"Oh! yes, quite simple—unless some complications occur. Of course there is always a faint danger, but then it is so well worth it. What a strange thing to ask, though, dear boy! Were you thinking of Cousin Agatha?"

"Cousin Agatha!" said Paul vaguely, and then recollected himself. "Oh, yes, of course—how is she?"

But when he went off to his room to change, his mother's words stayed with him—"unless some complications occur"—and the thought opened a fresh field of anxious wonderment.

At last it all seemed unbearable. A wild idea of rushing off to Vienna came to him—to rush there on the clue of a postmark—but common sense put this aside. It might be the means of just missing some message. No, he must bear things and wait. This silence, perhaps, meant good news—and if by the end of April nothing came, then he should have to break his promise and investigate.

About this time Captain Grigsby again came to stay with them. And the next day, as he and his host smoked their pipes while they walked up and down the sunny terrace, he took occasion to give forth this information:

"I say, Charles—I have located her—have you?"

"No! By Jove!" said Paul's father. "Hubert is away, you know, and I have just let the thing slide—"

"About the end of February did you notice the boy looking at all worried?"

Sir Charles thought a moment.

"Yes—I recollect—d—d worried and restless—and he is again now."

"Ah! I thought so!" said Mark Grigsby, as though he could say a good deal more.

"Well, then—out with it, Grig," Sir Charles said impatiently.

And Captain Grigsby proceeded in his own style to weave together a chain of coincidences which had struck him, until this final certainty. They were a clear set of arguments, and Paul's father was convinced, too.

"You see, Tompson told you in the beginning she was Russian," Captain Grigsby said after talking for some time, "and the rest was easy to find out. We're not here to judge the morals of the affair, Charles; you and I can only be thundering glad your grandson will sit on that throne all right."

He had read in one paper—he proceeded to say—that a most difficult political situation had been avoided by the birth of this child, as there was no possible heir at all, and immense complications would ensue upon the death of the present ruler—the scurrilous rag even gave a *résumé* of this ruler's dissolute life, and a broad hint that the child could in no case be his; but, as they pithily remarked, this added to the little prince's welcome in Ministerial circles, where the lady was greatly beloved and revered, and the King had only been put upon his tottering throne, and kept there, by the fact of being her husband. The paper added, the King had taken the chief part in the rejoicings over the heir, so there was nothing to be said. There were hints also of his mad fits of debauchery and drunkenness, and a suppressed tale of how in one of them he had strangled a keeper, and had often threatened the Queen's life. Her brother, however, was with her now, and would see Russian supremacy was not upset.

"Husband seems a likely character to hobnob with, don't he, Charles? No wonder she turned her eye on Paul, eh?" Mark Grigsby ended with.

But Sir Charles answered not, his thoughts were full of his son.

All the forces of nature and emotion seemed to be drawing him away from peaceful England towards a hornets' nest, and he—his father—would be powerless to prevent it.

CHAPTER XXVII

April's days were lengthening out in showers and sunshine and cold east wind. Easter and a huge party had come and gone at Verdayne Place, and the Lady Henrietta had had her hopes once more blighted by noticing Paul's indomitable indifference to all the pretty girls.

He was going to stand for Parliament in the autumn, when their very old member should retire, and he made that an excuse for his isolation; he was working too hard for social functions, he said. But in reality life was growing more than he could bear.

Captain Grigsby had sold the old *Blue Heather* and bought a new steam yacht of seven hundred tons—large enough to take him round the world, he said—and he had had her put in commission for the Mediterranean, and she was waiting for him now at Marseilles. Would Paul join him for a trip? he asked, and Paul hesitated for a moment.

If no news came by Friday—this was a Monday—then he should go to London and deliberately find out his lady's name and kingdom. In that case to cruise in those waters might suit his book passing well.

So he asked for a few days' grace, and Captain Grigsby gave a friendly growl in reply, and thus it was settled. By Saturday he was to give his answer.

Tuesday passed, and Wednesday, and on Thursday a telegram came for Paul which drove him mad with joy. It was short and to the point: "Meet Dmitry in Paris," Then followed an address. By rushing things he could just catch the night boat.

He went to his father's room, where Sir Charles was discussing affairs with his land steward. The man retired.

"Father," said Paul, "I am going immediately to Paris. I have not even time to wait and see my mother—she is out driving, I hear. Will you understand, father, and make it all right with her?"

And Sir Charles said, as he wrung his son's hand:

"Take care of yourself, Paul—I understand, my boy—and remember, Grig and I are with you to the bone. Wire if you want us—and let me have your news."

So they had parted without fuss, deep feeling in their hearts.

Paul had telegraphed to the address given, for Dmitry, that he would be in Paris, and at what hotel, by the following morning. He chose a large caravanserai as being more suitable to unremarked comings and goings, should Dmitry's visit be anything of a secret one. And with intense impatience he awaited the faithful servant's visit.

He was eating his early breakfast in his sitting-room when the old man appeared. In all the journey Paul had not allowed himself any speculation—he would see and know soon, that was enough. But he felt inclined to grind this silver-haired retainer's hand with joy as he made his respectful obeisance.

"The Excellency was well?"

"Yes." And now for his news.

Madame had bid him come and see the Excellency here in Paris, as not being so inaccessible as England—and first, Yes, Madame was well—There was something in his voice as he said this which made Paul exclaim and question him closely, but he would only repeat that—Yes, his lady was well—a little delicate still, but well—and the never-sufficiently-to-be-beloved son was well, too, his lady had told him to assure the Excellency—and was the portrait of his most illustrious father. And the old man lowered his eyes, while Paul looked out of the window, and thrilled all over. Circumstances made things very difficult for Madame to leave the southern country where she was at present, but she had a very strong desire to see the Excellency again—if such meeting could be managed.

He paused, and Paul exclaimed that of course it could be managed, and he could start that night.

But Dmitry shook his head. That would be impossible, he said. Much planning would be needed first. A yacht must be taken, and not until the end of May would it be safe for the Excellency to journey south. At that time Madame would be in a château on the seacoast, and if the Excellency in his cruise could be within sight, he might possibly land at a suitable moment and see her for a few hours.

Paul thought of Captain Grigsby.

"I will come in a yacht, whenever I may," he said to Dmitry.

So they began to settle details. Paul imagined from Dmitry continuing to call his Queen plain "Madame" that she still wished to preserve her incognito, so, madly as he desired to know, he would wait until he saw her face to face, and then ask to be released from his promise. The time had come when he could bear the mystery no longer, but he would not question Dmitry. All his force was turned to extracting every detail of his darling's health and well-being from the old servant, and in his guarded, respectful manner he answered all he could.

His lady had indeed been very ill, Paul gathered—at death's door. Ah! this was terrible to hear—but lately she was mending rapidly, only she had been too ill to plan or make any arrangements to see him. How all this made his heart ache! Something had told him his passionate anxiety had not been without cause. Dmitry continued: Madame's life was not a happy one, the Excellency must know, and the difficulties surrounding her had become formidable once or twice. However, the brother of Madame was with her now, and had been made guardian of her son—so things were peaceful and the cause of all her trouble would not dare to menace further.

For once Dmitry had let himself go, as he spoke, and a passionate hate appeared in his quiet eyes. The "Trouble" was of so impossible a viciousness that only the nobility and goodness of Madame had prevented his assassination numbers of times. He was hated, he said, hated and loathed; his life—spent in continual drunkenness, and worse, unspeakable wickedness—was not worth a day's purchase, but for her. The son of Madame would be loved forever, for her sake, so the Excellency need not fear for that, and Madame's brother was there, and would see all was well.

Then Paul asked Dmitry if his lady had been aware that he had been ill in Venice. And he heard that, Yes, indeed, she had kept herself informed of all his movements, and had even sent Vasili back on learning of his danger, and was on the point of throwing all prudence to the winds and returning herself. Oh! Madame had greatly suffered in the past year—the old man said, but she was more beautiful than ever, and of the gentleness of an angel, taking continuous pleasure in her little son—indeed, Anna had said this was her only joy, to caress the illustrious infant and call him Paul—such name he had been christened—after a great-uncle. And again Dmitry lowered his eyes, and again Paul looked out of the window and thrilled.

Paul! She had called him Paul, their son. It touched him to the heart. Oh! the mad longing to see her! Must he wait a whole month? Yes—Dmitry said there was no use his coming before the 28th of May, for reasons which he could not explain connected with the to-be-hated Troublesome one.

Every detail was then arranged, and Dmitry was to send Paul maps, and a chart, and the exact description and name of the place where the yacht was to lie. The whole thing would take some time, even if they were to depart to-morrow.

"The yacht is at Marseilles now," Paul said, "and we shall start on the cruise next week. Let me have every last instruction *poste restante*, at Constantinople—and for God's sake send me news to Naples on the way."

Dmitry promised everything, and then as he made his obeisance to go, he slipped a letter into Paul's hand. Madame had bidden him give the Excellency this when they had talked and all was settled. He would leave again that night, and his present address would find him till six o'clock if the Excellency had aught to send in return.

And then he backed out with deep bows, and Paul stood there, clasping his letter, a sudden spring of wild joy in his heart.

And what a letter it was! The very soul of his loved one expressed in her own quaint words.

First she told him that now she expected he knew who she was, and as they were to meet again—which in the beginning she feared might never be—all reason for her incognito was over. Then she told him—to make sure he knew—her name and kingdom. "But, sweetheart," she added, "remember this—my proudest titles ever are to be thy Loved one, and the Mother of thy son." Here Paul kissed the words, madly thrilling with pride and worship. She spoke of her still undying love, and of her anguishing sorrow all the winter at their separation, and at length the joy of their little one's arrival.

"Thy image, my Paul! English and beautiful, as I said he would be—not black and white like me. And oh! beloved, thou must always increase thy knowledge of statesmancraft to help me to train him well."

Then she made a glorious picture of their child's future, and Paul lay back in his chair and closed his eyes—the brightness of it all dazzled him—while his heart flew to her in passionate adoration. She went on to speak of their possible meeting. Her villa was but two hundred yards from the sea, only he must follow exactly all Dmitry's instructions, or there might be danger for them both; but at all costs she *could not live* much longer without seeing her lover.

"Thou art more than a lover *now*, my Paul—and I am more than ever THINE."

Thus it ended. And Paul spent most of the rest of his day reading and re-reading it, and writing his worshipping answer.

By night both he and Dmitry had started on their homeward journeys.

CHAPTER XXVIII

The Lady Henrietta was desolated when Paul and his father announced their intention of taking a month or six weeks' cruise with Captain Grigsby. So unnecessary, she said, at this time of the year, almost the beginning of May, when England was really getting most enjoyable. And they were obliged to pacify her as best they could.

The Mediterranean! Such miles off—and so eccentric, too, starting when other people would be leaving! Really, she had never ceased regretting ever having tolerated her son's travels the year before. Since then there had been no certainty in any of his movements.

"Darling mother," said Paul, "I must see the world."

And Sir Charles had snorted and chuckled, as was his habit.

So they sailed away from Marseilles, this party of three, like a gunboat under sealed orders. A cruise to the Greek Isles, and beyond, was what they said attracted them. "Especially the beyond!" Captain Grigsby had added, with a grunt to Sir Charles. And if the ardour of love and impatience boiled in Paul's veins, the spirit of interested adventure animated his old friend and his parent.

They had not spoken much on the subject to the young man. He had briefly asked Mark Grigsby to do him this service to take him to a far sea in the new *Blue Heather*, and there to land him when he should give the word.

May was a fair month, and an adventure is an adventure all the world over, so Mark Grigsby had given a joyful assent.

Then Sir Charles had suggested accompanying them, and was welcomed by the other two as a third for their party with extra pleasure.

"I shall grow a young man again before I have done, Grig!" he had said happily. But down in his heart lurked some undefined fear for Paul, and that was the real reason for his journey.

They had a pleasant voyage, and picked up letters at Naples, which only added to Paul's impatience to be there. But they were not to arrive before the end of May, so the Grecian Archipelago could be investigated.

Life in these sunny seas was a joy to all concerned, and Paul's eyes—illuminated by his lady's ever-present spirit—saw beauties and felt shades and balances of which his companions never dreamed. So they came at last to the Bosphorus and Constantinople.

Here full instructions awaited them. That night Paul took his father and his friend some way into his confidence, as he showed them the chart and read aloud the directions. On the 29th of May, should the weather prove favourable, they were to anchor towards night at a certain spot—latitude and longitude given—and when they heard a sea-bird cry sharply three times, Paul was to come ashore to where he would see a green light. Vasili would be waiting for him, and from there it was but a few steps to the garden gate of the villa by the sea, in which his lady was passing the summer. It all seemed perfectly simple—only, the directions added, he must leave again before dawn, and the yacht be out of sight before daylight, as complications had occurred since the letter to Naples, and the To-be-hated one had not left the capital, so things were not so easy to manage, or safe.

Paul's impatience knew no bounds. The concentrated pent-up longing of all these months was animating him. To see his lady again! To clasp her! To kiss her—to kneel to her—and give her homage and worship. And to behold his little son. Always he carried the minute flaxen curl in a locket, and often he had looked at it, and tried to picture the wee head from which it had been cut. But she—his love—would bring his son to him—and perhaps let him hold him in his arms. Ah! he shut his eyes and imagined the tender scene. Would she be changed? Should he see the traces of suffering? But he would caress all memory of pain away, and surely this meeting would only be the forerunner of others to come. Fate could never intend such deep, true love as theirs to be apart. An exaltation uplifted him. And if his lady were a Queen, and wore a crown, he felt himself the greatest king on earth, for was not he the absolute ruler of her heart? And who could wish for a more glorious kingdom?

The hours from Constantinople seemed longer than the whole voyage. He could hardly keep his attention to talk coherently about ordinary things at meals, and his father and Mark Grigsby left him practically alone.

At last, at last, the 29th of May dawned, boiling hot and cloudlessly fair.

For obvious reasons they stayed beyond sight of the coast until darkness fell, and then came close inshore. It was a starlit night, with not a breath of air, and no moon would illuminate their whereabouts.

Paul dressed with the greatest care; never had he been more particular over his toilet. Tompson found him *exigeant!*

He had broadened and filled out in the past year, and his fair face was tanned, and blooming with health and excitement.

"The best-looking young devil a woman's eye could light on!" Mark Grigsby said, as he and Sir Charles watched him descend the gangway to the boat, when the impatiently awaited signal had been given.

"God keep him safe, Grig," was all Sir Charles could mutter, with a grunt in his throat.

The maddest excitement was racing through Paul, as he held the tiller-ropes and made straight for the light. And once he felt in his pocket to assure himself he had not forgotten Dmitry's pistol, which he had cleaned and loaded himself that afternoon.

He knew this adventure might be a dangerous one, simple as it looked superficially, and now he was an expert revolver shot, thanks to constant practice.

The light proved to be in a little sheltered cove, with a small landing-stage. And—yes—the man who held it was the Kalmuck, Vasili.

"Welcome, welcome to the *Siyatelstvo*," he whispered, as he kissed Paul's hand. And then in perfect silence they began to ascend a path. Presently it stopped abruptly. They had come up perhaps not fifty feet, when their way was barred by a great nail-studded door.

"Hist!" said Vasili softly, and instantly it was opened from within, and Dmitry peered anxiously at them.

"Ah, the saints be blessed, the Excellency is safe," he said. But they must not delay a minute, he added. The Excellency must return to the waiting boat! A slight but unexpected ill-fortune had befallen them, connected with the to-be-execrated Troublesome one, and it would not be safe for the Imperial Highness if the Excellency should land tonight. She had sent him to say that the Excellency was to keep out at sea for two days, and return steaming past, and if he saw a white flag flying from the villa roof, then at night he was to anchor and come ashore at this same time. If not, for the moment he must go on back to Constantinople, where news and further instructions would be sent him.

As he spoke Dmitry indicated the return path, and bid the Excellency follow him, and hasten, hasten. This was a terrible blow to Paul, but the thought that he might bring danger to his beloved one made him not hesitate a moment.

They descended the path in silence, and as he stepped into the boat the old servant whispered, the Imperial Highness had bid him assure the Excellency that all was well, the meeting was only deferred, when they should have several days together in safety. "The saints protect the Excellency," the faithful creature added. Then, when Paul was safely in the boat, he stood back to make sharply three times the sea-bird's cry.

The weird minor notes floating out on the night seemed a wailing echo of the agonised disappointment in Paul's heart—more than once a mad impulse to go back convulsed his being before he reached the yacht—but it was not till afterwards that he remembered as a strange circumstance the fact that with Dmitry's first words at the nail-studded door Vasili had vanished into darkness.

CHAPTER XXIX

The two days out at sea were a raging impatience to Paul, in which he learnt to understand all the torments of Tantalus. To know and feel her near, and yet not to be allowed to get to her! It was an impossible cruelty.

The two grey-headed men's hearts ached for him, and Captain Grigsby delivered himself of this aphorism:

"Say what you will, Charles, but youth pays the devil of a long price for its pleasures. Here you and I snored like a couple of porpoises all last night, while the boy paced the deck and cursed everything."

And Sir Charles had only grunted, for he was feeling very deeply for his son.

There was a fresh breeze blowing when the time was up and they sighted land again, and long before any possible shore could be examined, Paul stood—his strongest glasses in his hand—on the look-out.

At length they came in full view, and alas! there could be no mistake, the flagstaff upon the villa roof was empty.

To the day of his death Paul will keep a vivid picture of the pure white-columned house. No semi-Oriental architecture met his view, but a beautiful marble structure in the graceful Ionic style, seeming a suitable habitation for his Queen.

It was approached by groves of ilex, from a wall at the edge of the sea. And now Paul could discern the landing-stage, and the great studded door.

A sensation of foreboding—a wild, mad anxiety, filled his being. What had happened? Why might he not land? Then for the first time that fact of Vasili's vanishment came into his mind. Was there something sinister in it? Had he scented any danger to his Queen, and gone to see? A whirlwind of questions and frenzied speculation shook Paul's brain. But there was nothing to be done now but to cram on all steam and make for Constantinople.

He looked again. The green *jalousies* were lowered over the windows, all seemed peaceful, silent and deserted. No living being wandered in the gardens. It might have been a mausoleum for the dead. And as this thought came to him Paul almost cried aloud.

Then he dominated himself. How weak and intolerably foolish to imagine evil where perhaps none was! Why should his thoughts fly to terrible reasons for the postponement of his joy, when in truth they could as well be of the simplest? A sudden call to the city—a descent of some undesirable spying eye—a hundred and one possible things, all much more likely than any ones of fear.

He would not permit another moment of wonder. He would regain his calm and wait like a man for certainty. Thus his face wore an iron mask and his thoughts an iron band. And presently they came to Constantinople.

But of what followed afterwards it is difficult to write. For fate struck Paul on that warm June morning, and blasted his life, so that for many days he only saw red, and lived in hell.

Every one knows the story which at the time convulsed Europe. How a certain evil-living King, after a wild orgie of mad drunkenness, rode out with two boon companions to the villa of his Queen, and there, forcing an entrance, ran a dagger through her heart before her faithful servants could protect her. And most people were glad, too, that this brute paid the penalty of his crime by his own death—his worthless life choked out of him by the Queen's devoted Kalmuck groom.

But only Paul and his father, and Mark Grigsby, know the details, which were told in Dmitry's heart-broken letter. How that night, the 29th of May, at the hour the Excellency was expected, he—Dmitry—was waiting in the garden to meet him and conduct him through the gloom, when, while he stood there under the stars, the Imperial Highness had called him softly, telling him to take the message down to the Excellency, which he did. How he had never dreamed that immediate danger threatened her, or that the King was there, or he would not have left her for any peril to the Excellency, who was after all a man and could fight. And How Vasili, being younger and more quick of wit, had suspected, hearing his message as he gave it to the Excellency, that all was not well, and had hastened to the house—too late to save his Queen.

And then the faithful servant took up Anna's tale. How this good girl had been watching on the side of the villa towards the town, and had heard the King come battering at the gate. How she had flown to warn her mistress, but that the *Imperatorskoye* had sent her back to watch, saying she herself would call Dmitry to protect them. Of course—as they now guessed—on purpose that Anna should not hear her message to him—as the Queen knew full well if he—Dmitry—heard from Anna the King was there, and she—the Queen—in danger, he would not leave her, even to do her bidding. Then of how the King had thrust the frightened servants aside, and strode with threats and oaths into the hall, accompanied by his two vile men. And how Anna had implored the Queen to hide while there was yet time. But how that shining one had stood only listening intently for the sea-bird's cry, and then when she heard it, had turned in triumph to the entering King, saying to Anna that nothing mattered now the Excellency was safe!

On her face, as she looked at this monster, was no dread of death, or aught but scorn and fearless pride. How Anna, seeing the dagger, had screamed, and tried to get between, but had been seized by one of the execrated men, and there been forced to watch the murder of her worshipped Queen. Ah! that had been a moment the saints could never efface! The splendid lady had stood quite still, her head thrown back, while this hound of hell had lurched towards her—hissing through his evil teeth this dreadful sentence: "Since thou hast at last obeyed me and found me an heir, making the people love me, I have no more use for thee. It will be a joy to kill thee!"

And with that he had plunged the dagger in her heart.

Of all that followed the Excellency would know. How Vasili had entered, scattering the minions like a mad bull, and springing upon the villainous King, had torn his life out on the marble floor.

Thus ended the letter.

Ah, God! For Paul had come the tears. But for her—cold steel and blood.

And so, as ever, the woman paid the price.

CHAPTER XXX

Now some of you who read will think her death was just, because she was not a moral woman. But others will hold with Paul she was the noblest lady who ever wore a crown. And in all cases she is beyond our puny reasonings.

But her work in Paul's heart still lives, and will live to the end of his life. Although for long months after the agony of that June day, nothing but hate and passion and misery had the ruling of him.

He could not bear his kind. His father and Captain Grigsby had left the yacht to him and let him cruise alone. But who can know of the hideous, ghastly hours that Paul spent then, ever obsessed with this one bitter thought? Why had he not gone back? Why had he not gone back when that impulse had seized him? Why had Vasili, and not he, had the satisfaction of killing this vile slayer of his Queen?

Even the remembrance of his child did not rouse him. It was safe with the Grand Duke Peter—a king at four months old! But what of sons, or kings or countries—nothing could make up for the loss of his Queen! And to think that she had died to save him! Save him from what? A brush with three besotted drunkards, whom it would have been great joy to kill!

There were moments when Paul went mad with passion, and lay and writhed in his berth. So long months passed, and at last he dominated himself enough to come back to his home.

And if the Lady Henrietta had exclaimed that he appeared ill before on his return, she was dumb now with sorrow at the change. For Paul had looked upon Medusa's head of horror, and, as well as his heart, his face seemed turned to stone. He was gentle with his mother, and let her caress him as much as she would, but nothing any one could say could move him—even Pike's joyous greeting.

The whole of God's world was his enemy—for was he not alone there, robbed of his mate? Presently the reaction from this violence came, and an intense apathy set in. A saltless, tasteless existence. What was Parliament to him? What was his country or his nation? or even his home? Only the hunting when it came gave him some relief, and then if the run were fast enough, or the jumps prodigiously high, or his horses sufficiently fresh to be difficult, his blood ran again for a brief space. But beyond this life was hell, and often he was tempted to use that little pistol of Dmitry's, and end it, and sleep. Only the inherent manly English spirit in him, deep down somewhere, prevented him.

All this time his father grieved and grieved, and the Lady Henrietta spent hours in tears and prayer. Sir Charles had told her their son had met with a great sorrow, and they must bow their heads and leave him in peace, so there were no more gay young parties at Verdayne Place, and gone for ever were the visions of the grandchildren. Only Mark Grigsby was a constant visitor, but then—he knew.

Thus a year passed away, and Paul left on a voyage round the world. An Englishman's stern duty to be a man at all costs was calling him at last—bidding him in change of scene to try and overcome the paralysing dominion of his grief. But as far as that went the experiment proved futile. If moments came when circumstances did divert him, such as one or two great storms he happened to come across, and one or two exciting situations—still, when things were fair and peaceful, back would rush the ever-living ache. That passionate void and loss for which there seems no remedy.

Gentle, pleasant women longed to lavish worship upon him, and Paul talked and was polite, but all their sweetness touched him no more than summer ripples stir the bottom of a lake. He seemed impervious to any human influence, though when the look of a mountain or the colour of beech-trees would remind him of the Bürgenstock anguish as fresh as ever stabbed his heart. Yet all this while, unknown to himself, his faculties were developing. He read deeply. He had unconsciously grown to apply his darling's lucid reasoning to every detail of his judgment of life. It was as if it had before been written in cypher for him, and she had now given him the key. His mind was untiring in its efforts to master subjects, as his splendid physique seemed tireless in all manner of sport.

Thus he saw the world and its peoples, and was an honoured guest among the great ones of the earth. But the hardness of adamant was in him. He had no beliefs—no ambitions. He dissected everything with all the pitiless certainty of a surgeon's cold knife. And if his life contained an aim at all, it was to get through with it and find oblivion in eternal sleep.

Thoughts of his little son would sometimes come to him, but when they did he thrust them back, and shut his heart up in a casing of ice.

To feel—was to suffer! That perhaps was his only creed; that and a blind, sullen rage against fate. This was the lesson his suffering had taught him, and they were weary years before he knew another side.

The first time he saw a tiger in India was one of the landmarks in the history of his inner emotions. He had gone to shoot the beasts with a well-known Rajah, and it had chanced he came upon a magnificent creature at very close quarters and had shot it on sight. But when it lay dead, its wonderful body gracefully moving no more, a sickening regret came over Paul. Of all things in creation none reminded him so forcibly of his lost worshipped Queen. In a flash came back to him the first day she had lain on the skin which had been his gift. Out of the jungle her eyes seemed to gleam. In his ears rang her words, "I know all your feelings and your passions. And now I have your skin—for the joy of my skin." Yes, she had loved tigers, and been in sympathy with them always, and here was one whose joy of life he had ended!

No, he could never kill one more. After this expedition for weeks he was restless—the incident seemed to have pierced through his carefully cultivated calm. For days and days, fresh as in the first hours of his grief, came an infinite sensation of pain—just hideous personal pain.

So time, and his journeys, went on. But no country and no change of scene could dull Paul's sense of loss, and the great vast terrible finality of all hope.

The hackneyed phrase would continually ring in his brain of—Never again—never again! Ah! God! it was true he would hold his beloved one—never again. And often unavailing rebellion against destiny would rise up in him, and he would almost go mad and see red once more. Then he would rush away from civilisation out into the wild.

But these violent emotions were always followed by a heavy, numb lethargy until some echo or resemblance roused him to suffering again. The scent of tuberoses caused him anguish unspeakable. One night in New York he was obliged to leave the opera because a woman he was with wore some in her dress.

Thus, with all his strong will, there were times when he could not control himself or his grief.

He had been absent from England for over two years, when the news came to him far out in America of his Uncle Hubert's death. So he had gone to join the world of spirits in the vast beyond! Paul did not care! His only feeling was one of relief. No more fear of hearing, perhaps, some chance idle word. But he remembered his mother had loved her handsome brother, and he wrote a tender letter home.

Then something in the Lady Henrietta's answer touched him vaguely and decided him to return. After all—because life was a black barren waste to him—what right had he to dim all joy in the two who had given him being? Yes, he would go back, and try to pick up the threads anew.

There were great quiet rejoicings in his parents' hearts at their son's third homecoming. And like a wild beast tamed for a time to perform tricks in a circus, Paul conformed to the ordinary routine. The question of his entering Parliament was mooted again, but this he put aside. As yet he could face no ties. He would do his best by staying at home most of the year—but when that call of anguish was upon him, he must be free once more to roam.

Then hope began to bloom in the Lady Henrietta's heart as flowers after rain. Surely this great unknown grief was passing—surely her adored one would settle down again.

CHAPTER XXXI

But the months went by without healing Paul's grief. Time only coated it with a dull, callous crust. He had got into a hard way of taking everything as it came. He did not fly from society, or ape the manners of the misanthrope; he went to London, and stayed about and played the game. But all with a stony, bald indifference which made people wonder.

No faintest inkling of his story had ever leaked out. And it seemed an incomprehensible attitude towards life for a young and fortunate man. Those who had looked for great things from his birthday speech shook their heads sadly at the unfulfilment.

So time passed on, until one day at the beginning of February, nearly five years after the light had gone out of his life, a circumstance happened which proved a turning-point of great magnitude.

It was quite a small thing—just the brutalised hardness in a gipsy woman's face!

The sun was setting that late afternoon when he strode home across the moor with Pike, and they came upon some gipsy vans. Paul looked up—it was no unaccustomed sight, only they happened to be in exactly the same spot where the like had stood that morning long ago, when in his exuberant happiness at the news of his little son's birth he had tossed the young woman the sovereign.

The door of the last van was open, and there, sitting on the steps in an attitude of dull sullen idleness, was the same swarthy lass, only now she was altered sadly! No more the proud young mother met his view, but a hard, gaunt, evil-looking woman.

She knew him instantly, and her black eyes fiercened; as he came up close to her she said without any greeting: "I lost him, your honour—him and my Bill in the same blasted year, and I ain't never had no other."

Paul stopped and peered into her brown face in the fading light.

"So we have been both through hell since then, my poor girl?" he said.

The gipsy woman laughed with bitter harshness as she echoed back the one word "Hell!"—and afterwards she added with a wail: "Yes, they're dead! and there won't be never no meeting."

And Paul went on—but her face haunted him.

Was there the same hard change in himself, he wondered? Was he, too, brutalised and branded with the five years of hell? Surely if so he had gone on a lower road than his darling would have had him travel.

Then out of the mist of the dying day came the memory of her noble face as it had been in that happy hour when they had floated out to the lagoon, and she had told him—her eyes alight with the *feu sacré*—her wishes for his future.

But what had he done to carry them out—those lofty wishes? Surely nothing. For, obsessed with his own selfish anguish, he had lived on with no single worthy aim, with no aim at all except to forget and deaden his suffering.

Forget! Ah God! that could never be. For had she not said there was an eternal marriage of their souls—in life or in death they could never be parted?

And he had tried to break this sacred tender bond, when he should have cherished every memory to comfort his deep pain with its sweetness. What had he done? Let sorrow sink him to the level of the poor gipsy girl, instead of trying to do some fine thing as a tribute to his lady's noble teaching.

He strode on in the dusk towards his home, his thoughts lashing him with shame and remorse.

And that night, when he and Pike were alone in his own panelled room, he broke the seal of those beautiful letters which, with directions for them to be buried with his body at his death, had lain in a packet hidden away from sight all these years, freighted with agonised memory.

He read them over carefully, from the first brief note to the last long cry of love which Dmitry had brought him to Paris. Then he lay back in his chair, while his strong frame shook with sobs, and his eyes were blinded by scorching, bitter tears.

But suddenly it seemed as if his lady's spirit stood beside him in the firelight's flickering gleam, whispering words of hope, pleading to come back from the cold grave to his heart, there to abide and comfort him.

He heard her golden voice once more, and it fell like soft, healing rain, so that he stretched out his arms, and cried aloud:

"My darling, beloved one, forgive me for these five wasted years—sweetheart, come back to me never to part again. Come back to my heart, and dwell there, Angel Queen!"

* * * * *

Then, as the days went on, all the world altered for him. Instead of the terrible bitterness against fate which had ruled his heart, a new tenderness grew there. It seemed now as though he were never alone, but lived in her ever-present memory. And with this golden change came thoughts of his child—that little life neglected for so long. What had he done? What cruel, terrible thing had he done in his selfish pain?

Each year Dmitry had sent him a letter of news, and each year that day had held ghastly hours for him in the reopening of old anguish—the missive to be read and quickly thrust out of sight, the thought of it to be strangled and forgotten.

And now the little one would soon be five years old, and his father's living eyes had never seen him! But this should no more be so, and he wrote at once to Dmitry.

By return of post came the answer. The Excellency indeed would be welcome. The Regent—the Grand Duke Peter—had bidden him say that if the Excellency should be travelling for pleasure, as the nobility of his country often did, he would gladly be received by the Regent, who was himself a great *chasseur* and *voyageur*. The Excellency would then see the never-to-be-sufficiently-beloved baby King. Of this glorious child he—Dmitry—found it difficult to write. It was as if the *Imperatorskoye* breathed again in his spirit, while he was the portrait of his illustrious father, proving how deeply and well the *Imperatorskoye* must have loved that father. If the Excellency could arrive in time for the Majesty's fifth birthday, on the 19th of February, there was to be a special ceremony in the great church which the Regent thought might be of interest to the Excellency.

Paul wired back he would travel night and day to be in time, and he instructed Dmitry to have the necessary arrangements made that he might go straight to the church, in case unforeseen delay should not permit him to arrive until that morning.

It was in a shaft of sunlight from the great altar window that Paul first saw his son. The tiny upright figure in its blue velvet suit, heavily trimmed with sable, standing there proudly. A fair, rosy-cheeked, golden-haired English child—the living reality of that miniature painted on ivory and framed in fine pearls, which made the holy of holies on Lady Henrietta's writing-table.

And as he gazed at his little son, while the organ pealed out a Te Deum and the sweet choir sang, a great rush of tenderness filled Paul's heart, and melted forever the icebergs of grief and pain.

And as he knelt there, watching their child, it seemed as if his darling stood beside him, telling him that he must look up and thank God, too—for in her spirit's constant love, and this glory of their son, he would one day find rest and consolation.

THE END.

Beyond The Rocks, A Love Story

I

The hours were composed mostly of dull or rebellious moments during the period of Theodora's engagement to Mr. Brown. From the very first she had thought it hard that she should have had to take this situation, instead of Sarah or Clementine, her elder step-sisters, so much nearer his age than herself. To do them justice, either of these ladies would have been glad to relieve her of the obligation to become Mrs. Brown, but Mr. Brown thought otherwise.

A young and beautiful wife was what he bargained for.

To enter a family composed of three girls—two of the first family, one almost thirty and a second very plain—a father with a habit of accumulating debts and obliged to live at Bruges and inexpensive foreign sea-side towns, required a strong motive; and this Josiah Brown found in the deliciously rounded, white velvet cheek of Theodora, the third daughter, to say nothing of her slender grace, the grace of a young fawn, and a pair of gentian-blue eyes that said things to people in the first glance.

Poor, foolish, handsome Dominic Fitzgerald, light-hearted, débonair Irish gentleman, gay and gallant on his miserable pension of a broken and retired Guardsman, had had just sufficient sense to insist upon magnificent settlements, certainly prompted thereto by Clementine, who inherited the hard-headedness of the early defunct Scotch mother, as well as her high cheek-bones. That affair had been a youthful *mésalliance*.

"You had better see we all gain something by it, papa," she had said. "Make the old bore give Theodora a huge allowance, and have it all fixed and settled by law beforehand. She is such a fool about money—just like you—she will shower it upon us; and you make him pay you a sum down as well."

Captain Fitzgerald fortunately consulted an honest solicitor, and so things were arranged to the satisfaction of all parties concerned except Theodora herself, who found the whole affair far from her taste.

That one must marry a rich man if one got the chance, to help poor, darling papa, had always been part of her creed, more or less inspired by papa himself. But when it came to the scratch, and Josiah Brown was offered as a husband, Theodora had had to use every bit of her nerve and self-control to prevent herself from refusing.

She had not seen many men in her nineteen years of out-at-elbows life, but she had imagination, and the one or two peeps at smart old friends of papa's, landed from stray yachts now and then, at out-of-the-way French watering-places, had given her an ideal far, far removed from the personality of Josiah Brown.

But, as Sarah explained to her, such men could never be husbands. They might be lovers, if one was fortunate enough to move in their sphere, but husbands—never! and there was no use Theodora protesting this violent devotion to darling papa, if she could not do a small thing like marrying Josiah Brown for him!

Theodora's beautiful mother, dead in the first year of her runaway marriage, had been the daughter of a stiff-necked, unforgiving old earl; she had bequeathed her child, besides these gentian eyes and wonderful, silvery blond hair, a warm, generous heart and a more or less romantic temperament.

The heart was touched by darling papa's needs, and the romantic temperament revolted by Josiah Brown's personality.

However, there it was! The marriage took place at the Consulate at Dieppe, and a perfectly miserable little bride got into the train for Paris, accompanied by a fat, short, prosperous, middle-class English husband, who had accumulated a large fortune in Australia, quite by accident, in a comparatively few years.

Josiah Brown was only fifty-two, though his head was bald and his figure far from slight. He had a liver, a chest, and a temper, and he adored Theodora.

Captain Fitzgerald had felt a few qualms when he had wished his little daughter good-bye on the platform and had seen the blue stars swimming with tears. The two daughters left to him were so plain, and he hated plain people about him; but, on the other hand, women must marry, and what chance had he, poor, unlucky devil, of establishing his Theodora better in life?

Josiah Brown was a good fellow, and he, Dominic Fitzgerald, had for the first time for many years a comfortable balance at his bankers, and could run up to Paris himself in a few days, and who knows, the American widow, fabulously rich—Jane Anastasia McBride—might take him seriously!

Captain Dominic Fitzgerald was irresistible, and had that fortunate knack of looking like a gentleman in the oldest clothes. If married for the third time—but this time prosperously, to a fabulously rich American—his well-born relations would once more welcome him with open arms, he felt sure, and visions of the best pheasant shoots at old Beechleigh, and partridge drives at Rothering Castle floated before his eyes, quite obscuring the fading smoke of the Paris train.

"A pretty tough, dull affair marriage," he said to himself, reminded once more of Theodora by treading on a white rose in the station. "Hope to Heavens Sarah prepared her for it a bit." Then he got into a *fiacre* and drove to the hotel, where he and the two remaining Misses Fitzgerald were living in the style of their forefathers.

Josiah Brown's valet, Mr. Toplington, who knew the world, had engaged rooms for the happy couple at the Grand Hotel. "We'll go to the Ritz on our way back," he decided, "but at first, in case there's scenes and tears, it's better to be a number than a name." Mademoiselle Henriette, the freshly engaged French maid, quite agreed with him. The Grand, she said, was "*plus convenable pour une lune de Miel*—" Lune de Miel!

II

It was a year later before Theodora saw her family again. A very severe attack of bronchitis, complicated by internal catarrh, prostrated Josiah Brown in the first days of their marriage, and had turned her into a superintendent nurse for the next three months; by that time a winter at Hyères was recommended by the best physicians, and off they started.

Hyères, with a semi-invalid, a hospital nurse, and quantities of medicine bottles and draught-protectors, is not the ideal place one reads of in guide-books. Theodora grew to hate the sky and the blue Mediterranean. She used to sit on her balcony at Costebelle and gaze at the olive-trees, and the deep-green velvet patch of firs beyond, towards the sea, and wonder at life.

She longed to go to the islands—anywhere beyond—and one day she read *Jean d'Agrève*; and after that she wondered what Love was. It took a mighty hold upon her imagination. It seemed to her it must mean Life.

It was the beginning of May before Josiah Brown thought of leaving for Paris. England would be their destination, but the doctors assured him a month of Paris would break the change of climate with more safety than if they crossed the Channel at once.

Costebelle was a fairyland of roses as they drove to the station, and peace had descended upon Theodora. She had fallen into her place, a place occupied by many wives before her with irritable, hypochondriacal husbands.

She had often been to Paris in her maiden days; she knew it from the point of view of a cheap boarding-house and snatched meals. But the unchecked gayety of the air and the *façon* had not been tarnished by that. She had played in the Tuilleries Gardens and watched Ponchinello at the Rond Point, and later been taken once or twice to dine at a cheap café in the Bois by papa. And once she had gone to Robinson on a coach with him and some aristocratic acquaintances of his, and eaten luncheon up the tree, and that was a day of the gods and to be remembered.

But now they were going to an expensive, well-managed private hotel in the Avenue du Bois, suitable to invalids, and it poured with rain as they drove from the Gare de Lyon.

All this time something in Theodora was developing. Her beautiful face had an air of dignity. The set of her little Greek head would have driven a sculptor wild—and Josiah Brown was very generous in money matters, and she had always known how to wear her clothes, so it was no wonder people stopped and turned their heads when she passed.

Josiah Brown possessed certainly not less than forty thousand a year, and so felt he could afford a carriage in Paris, and any other fancy he pleased. His nerves had been too shaken by his illness to appreciate the joys of an automobile.

Thus, daily might be seen in the Avenue des Acacias this ill-assorted pair, seated in a smart victoria with stepping horses, driving slowly up and down. And a number of people took an interest in them.

Towards the middle of May Captain Fitzgerald arrived at the Continental, and Theodora felt her heart beat with joy when she saw his handsome, well-groomed head.

Oh yes, it had been indeed worth while to make papa look so prosperous as that—so prosperous and happy—dear, gay papa!

He was about the same age as her husband, but no one would think of taking him for more than forty. And what a figure he had! and what manners! And when he patted her cheek Theodora felt at once that thrill of pride and gratification she had always experienced when he was pleased with her, from her youngest days.

She was almost glad Sarah and Clementine should have remained at Dieppe. Thus she could have papa all to herself, and oh, what presents she would send them back by him when he returned!

Josiah Brown despised Dominic Fitzgerald, and yet stood in awe of him as well. A man who could spend a fortune and be content to live on odds and ends for the rest of his life must be a poor creature. But, on the other hand, there was that uncomfortable sense of breeding about him which once, when Captain Fitzgerald had risen to a situation of dignity during their preliminary conversations about Theodora's hand, had made Josiah Brown unconsciously say "Sir" to him.

He had blushed and bitten his tongue for doing it, and had blustered and patronized immoderately afterwards, but he never forgot the incident. They were not birds of a feather, and never would be, though the exquisite manners of Dominic Fitzgerald could carry any situation.

Josiah was not altogether pleased to see his father-in-law. He even experienced a little jealousy. Theodora's face, which generally wore a mask of gentle, solicitous meekness for him, suddenly sparkled and rippled with laughter, as she pinched her papa's ears, and pulled his mustache, and purred into his neck, with joy at their meeting.

It was that purring sound and those caressing tricks that Josiah Brown objected to. He had never received any of them himself, and so why should Dominic Fitzgerald?

Captain Fitzgerald, for his part, was enchanted to clasp his beautiful daughter once more in his arms; he had always loved Theodora, and when he saw her so quite too desirable-looking in her exquisite clothes, he felt a very fine fellow himself, thinking what he had done for her.

It was not an unnatural circumstance that he should look upon the idea of a dinner at the respectable private hotel, with his son-in-law and daughter, as a trifle dull for Paris, or that he should have suggested a meal at the Ritz would do them both good.

"Come and dine with me instead, my dear child," he said, with his grand air. "Josiah, you must begin to go out a little and shake off your illness, my dear fellow."

But Josiah was peevish.

Not to-night—certainly not to-night. It was the evening he was to take the two doses of his new medicine, one half an hour after the other, and he could not leave the hotel. Then he saw how poor Theodora's face fell, and one of his sparks of consideration for the feelings of others came to him, and he announced gruffly that his wife might go with her father, if she pleased, provided she crept into her room, which was next door to his own, without the least noise on her return.

"I must not be disturbed in my first sleep," he said; and Theodora thanked him rapturously.

It was so good of him to let her go—she would, indeed, make not the least noise, and she danced out of the room to get ready in a way Josiah Brown had never seen her do before. And after she had gone—Captain Fitzgerald came back to fetch her—this fact rankled with him and prevented his sleep for more than twenty minutes.

"My sweet child," said Captain Fitzgerald, when he was seated beside his daughter in her brougham, rolling down the Champs-Elysées, "you must not be so grateful; he won't let you out again if you are."

"Oh, papa!" said Theodora.

They arrived at the Ritz just at the right moment. It was a lovely night, but rather cold, so there were no diners in the garden, and the crowd from the restaurant extended even into the hall.

It was an immense satisfaction to Dominic Fitzgerald to walk through them all with this singularly beautiful young woman, and to remark the effect she produced, and his cup of happiness was full when they came upon a party at the lower end by the door; prominent, as hostess, being Jane Anastasia McBride—the fabulously rich American widow.

In a second of time he reviewed the situation; a faint coldness in his manner would be the thing to draw—and it was; for when he had greeted Mrs. McBride without gush, and presented his daughter with the air of just passing on, the widow implored them with great cordiality to leave their solitary meal and join her party. Nor would she hear of any refusal.

The whole scene was so novel and delightful to Theodora she cared not at all whether her father accepted or no, so long as she might sit quietly and observe the world.

Mrs. McBride had perceived immediately that the string of pearls round Mrs. Josiah Brown's neck could not have cost less than nine thousand pounds, and that her frock, although so simple, was the last and most expensive creation of Callot Sœurs. She had always been horribly attracted by Captain Fitzgerald, ever since that race week at Trouville two summers ago, and fate had sent them here to-night, and she meant to enjoy herself.

Captain Fitzgerald acceded to her request with his usual polished ease, and the radiant widow presented the rest of her guests to the two new-comers.

The tall man with the fierce beard was Prince Worrzoff, married to her niece, Saidie Butcher. Saidie Butcher was short, and had a voice you could hear across the room. The sleek, fair youth with the twinkling gray eyes was an Englishman from the Embassy. The disagreeable-looking woman in the badly made mauve silk was his sister, Lady Hildon. The stout, hook-nosed bird of prey with the heavy gold chain was a Western millionaire, and the smiling girl was his daughter. Then, last of all, came Lord Bracondale—and it was when he was presented that Theodora first began to take an interest in the party.

Hector, fourteenth Lord Bracondale of Bracondale (as she later that night read in the *Peerage*) was aged thirty-one years. He had been educated at Eton and Oxford, served for some time in the Fourth Lifeguards, been unpaid attaché at St. Petersburg, was patron of five livings, and sat in the House of Lords as Baron Bracondale; creation, 1505; seat, Bracondale Chase. Brothers, none. Sister living, Anne Charlotte, married to the fourth Earl of Anningford.

Theodora read all this over twice, and also even the predecessors and collateral branches—but that was while she burned the midnight oil and listened to the snorts and coughs of Josiah Brown, slumbering next door.

For the time being she raised her eyes and looked into Lord Bracondale's, and something told her they were the nicest eyes she had ever seen in this world.

Then when a voluble French count had rushed up, with garrulous apologies for being late, the party was complete, and they swept into the restaurant.

Theodora sat between the Western millionaire and the Russian Prince, but beyond—it was a round table, only just big enough to hold them—came her hostess and Lord Bracondale, and two or three times at dinner they spoke, and very often she felt his eyes fixed upon her.

Mrs. McBride, like all American widows, was an admirable hostess; the conversation never flagged, or the gayety for one moment.

The Western millionaire was shrewd, and announced some quaint truths while he picked his teeth with an audible sound.

"This is his first visit to Europe," Princess Worrzoff said afterwards to Theodora by way of explanation. "He is so colossally rich he don't need to worry about such things at his time of life; but it does make me turn to hear him."

Captain Fitzgerald was in his element. No guest shone so brilliantly as he. His wit was delicate, his sallies were daring, his looks were insinuating, and his appearance was perfection.

Theodora had every reason to tingle with pride in him, and the widow felt her heart beat.

"Isn't he just too bright—your father, Mrs. Brown?" she said as they left the restaurant to have their coffee in the hall. "You must let me see quantities of you while we are all in Paris together. It is a lovely city; don't you agree with me?"

And Theodora did.

Lord Bracondale was of the same breed as Captain Fitzgerald—that is, they neither of them permitted themselves to be superseded by any other man with the object of their wishes. When they wanted to talk to a woman they did, if twenty French counts or Russian princes stood in the way! Thus it was that for the rest of the evening Theodora found herself seated upon a sofa in close proximity to the man who had interested her at dinner, and Mrs. McBride and Captain Fitzgerald occupied two arm-chairs equally well placed, while the rest of the party made general conversation.

Hector Bracondale, among other attractions, had a charming voice; it was deep and arresting, and he had a way of looking straight into the eyes of the person he was talking to.

Theodora knew at once he belonged to the tribe whom Sarah had told her could never be husbands.

She wondered vaguely why, all the time she was talking to him. Why had husbands always to be bores and unattractive, and sometimes even simply revolting, like hers? Was it because these beautiful creatures could not be bound to any one woman? It seemed to her unsophisticated mind that it could be very nice to be married to one of them; but there was no use fighting against fate, and she personally was wedded to Josiah Brown.

Lord Bracondale's conversation pleased her. He seemed to understand exactly what she wanted to talk about; he saw all the things she saw and—he had read *Jean d'Agrève*!—they got to that at the end of the first half-hour, and then she froze up a little; some instinct told her it was dangerous ground, so she spoke suddenly of the weather, in a banal voice.

Meanwhile, from the beginning of dinner, Lord Bracondale had been saying to himself she was the loveliest white flower he had yet struck in a path of varied experiences. Her eyes so innocent and true, with the tender expression of a fawn; the perfect turn of her head and slender pillar of a throat; her grace and gentleness, all appealed to him in a maddening way.

"She is asleep to the whole of life's possibilities," he thought. "What can her husband be about, and *what* an intoxicatingly agreeable task to wake her up!"

He had lived among the world where the awaking of young wives, or old wives, or any woman who could please man, was the natural course of the day. It never even struck him then it might be a cruel thing to do. A woman once married was always fair game; if the husband could not retain her affections that was his lookout.

Hector Bracondale was not a brute, just an ordinary Englishman of the world, who had lived and loved and seen many lands.

He read Theodora like an open book: he knew exactly why she had talked about the weather after *Jean d'Agrève*. It thrilled him to see her soft eyes dreamy and luminous when they first spoke of the book, and it flattered him when she changed the conversation.

As for Theodora, she analyzed nothing, she only felt that perhaps she ought not to speak about love to one of those people who could never be husbands.

Captain Fitzgerald, meanwhile, was making tremendous headway with the widow. He flattered her vanity, he entertained her intelligence, and he even ended by letting her see she was causing him, personally, great emotion.

At last this promising evening came to an end. The Russian Prince, with his American Princess, got up to say good-night, and gradually the party broke up, but not before Captain Fitzgerald had arranged to meet Mrs. McBride at Doucet's in the morning, and give her the benefit of his taste and experience in a further shopping expedition to buy old bronzes.

"We can all breakfast together at Henry's," he said, with his grand manner, which included the whole party; and for one instant force of habit made Theodora's heart sink with fear at the prospect of the bill, as it had often had to do in olden days when her father gave these royal invitations. Then she remembered she had not been sacrificed to Josiah Brown for nothing, and that even if dear, generous papa should happen to be a little hard up again, a few hundred francs would be nothing to her to slip into his hand before starting.

The rest of the party, however, declined. They were all busy elsewhere, except Lord Bracondale and the French Count—they would come, with pleasure, they said.

Theodora wondered what Josiah would say. Would he go? and if not, would he let her go? This was more important.

"Then we shall meet at breakfast to-morrow," Lord Bracondale said, as he helped her on with her cloak. "That will give me something to look forward to."

"Will it?" she said, and there was trouble in the two blue stars which looked up at him. "Perhaps I shall not be able to come; my husband is rather an invalid, and—"

But he interrupted her.

"Something tells me you will come; it is fate," he said, and his voice was grave and tender.

And Theodora, who had never before had the opportunity of talking about destiny, and other agreeable subjects, with beautiful Englishmen who could only be—lovers—felt the red blood rush to her cheeks and a thrill flutter her heart. So she quickened her steps and kept close to her father, who could have dispensed with this mark of affection.

"Dearest child," he said, when they were seated in the brougham, "you are married now and should be able to look after yourself, without staying glued to my side so much—it is rather bourgeois."

Poor Theodora was crushed and did not try to excuse herself.

"I am afraid Josiah won't go, papa dear," she said, timidly; "and in case he does not allow me to either, I want you to have these few louis, just for the breakfast. I know how generous you are, and how difficult things have been made for you, darling." And she nestled to his side and slipped about eight gold pieces, which she had fortunately found in her purse, into his hand.

Captain Fitzgerald was still a gentleman, although a good many edges of his sensitive perceptions had been rubbed off.

He kissed his daughter fondly while he murmured: "Merely a loan, my pet, merely a loan. You were always a jewel to your old father!"

Whenever her parent accused himself of being "old," Theodora knew he was deeply touched, and her tender heart overflowed with gladness that she was able to smooth the path of such a darling papa.

"I will come and see you in the morning, my child," he said, as they stopped at the door of her hotel, "and I will manage Josiah."

So Theodora crept up to her apartment, comforted; and in the salon it was she caught sight of the *Peerage*.

Josiah Brown bought one every year and travelled with it, although until he met the Fitzgerald family he had not known a single person connected with it; but it pleased him to be able to look up his wife's name, and to read that her mother was the daughter of a real live earl and her father the brother of a baronet.

"Hector! I like the name of Hector," were the last coherent thoughts which floated through the brain of Theodora before sleep closed her broad, white lids.

Meanwhile, Lord Bracondale had gone on to sup at the Café de Paris, with Marion de Beauvoison and Esclarmonde de Chartres; and among the diamonds and pearls and scents and feathers he suddenly felt a burning disgust, and a longing to be out again in the moonlight—alone with his thoughts.

"Mais qu'as tu, mon vieux chou?" they said. "Ce bel Hector chéri—il a un béguin pour quelqu'un—mais ce n'est pas pour nous autres!"

III

Josiah Brown cut the top off his *œuf à la coque* with a knife at his *premier déjeuner* next day. The knife grated on the shell in a determined way, and Theodora felt her heart sink at the prospect of broaching the subject of the breakfast at the Café Henry.

"I am so glad the rain has stopped," she said, nervously. "It was raining when I woke this morning."

"Indeed," replied Josiah. "And what kind of an evening did you pass with that father of yours?"

"A very pleasant one," said Theodora, crumbling her roll. "Papa met some old friends, and we all dined together at the Ritz. I wish you had been able to come, it might have done you good, it was so gay!"

"I am not fit for gayety," said her husband, peevishly, scooping out spoonfuls of yolk. "And who were the party, pray?"

Theodora obediently enumerated them all, and the high-sounding title of the Russian Prince, to say nothing of the English lord and lady, had a mollifying effect on Josiah Brown. He even remembered the name of Bracondale—had he not been a grocer's assistant in the small town of Bracondale for a whole year in his apprenticeship days?

"Papa wants us to breakfast to-day with him at Henry's for you to meet some of them," Theodora said, with more confidence.

Josiah had taken a second egg and his frown was gone.

"We'll see about it, we'll see about it," he grunted; but his wife felt more hopeful, and was even unusually solicitous of his wants in the way of coffee and marmalade and cream. Josiah was shrewd if he did happen to be deeply self-absorbed in his health, and he noticed that Theodora's eyes were brighter and her step more elastic than usual.

He knew he had bought "one of them there aristocrats," as his old aunt, who had kept a public-house at New Norton, would have said. Bought her with solid gold—he had no illusions on this subject, and he quite realized if the solid gold had not been amassed out of England, so that to her family he could be represented as "something from the colonies—rather rough, but such a good fellow"—even Captain Fitzgerald's impecuniosity and rapacity would not have risen to his bait.

He was also grateful to Theodora—she had been so meek always, and such a kind and unselfish nurse. With his impaired constitution and delicate chest he had given up all hopes of looking on her as a wife again, just yet; but, as a nurse and an ornament—a peg to hang the evidences of his wealth upon—she was little short of perfection. He could have been frantically in love with her if she had only been the girl from the station bar in Melbourne. Josiah Brown was not a bad fellow.

By the time Mr. Toplington advanced in his dignified way with the accurately measured tonic on a silver tray and the single acid drop to remove the taste, Josiah Brown had decided to go and partake food with his father-in-law at Henry's. If he had been good enough to entertain the Governor of Australia, he was quite good enough for Russian princes or English lords, he told himself. Thus it was that Captain Fitzgerald, who came in person in a few minutes to indorse his invitation, found an unusually cordial reception awaiting him.

"I am too delighted, my dear Josiah," he said, "that you have decided to come out of your shell. Moping would kill a cat; and I shall order you the plainest chicken and soufflé aux fraises."

"Josiah can eat almost anything, papa. I don't think you need worry about that," said Theodora, who hoped to make her husband enjoy himself. And then Captain Fitzgerald left to meet his widow.

All the morning, while she walked up and down under the trees in the Avenue du Bois beside her husband, who leaned upon her arm, Theodora's thoughts were miles away. She felt stimulated, excited, intensely interested in the hour, afraid they would be late. Twice she answered at random, and Josiah got quite cross.

"I asked you which you considered would do me most good when we return to England, to continue seeing Sir Baldwin once a week or to have Dr. Wilton permanently in the house with us, and you answer that you quite agree with me! Agree with what? Agree with which? You are talking nonsense, girl!"

Theodora apologized gently, and her white velvet cheeks became tinged with wild roses. It seemed as if the victoria, with its high-steppers, would never come and pick them up; and it must be at least quarter of an hour's drive to Henry's. She did not understand where it was exactly, but papa had said the coachman would know.

If some one had told her, as Clementine certainly would have done had she been there, that she was simply thus interested and excited because she wished to see again Lord Bracondale, she would have been horrified. She never had analyzed sensations herself, and the day had not yet arrived when she would begin to do so.

At last they were rolling down the Champs-Elysées. The mass of chestnut blooms in full glory, the tender green still fresh and springlike, the sky as blue as blue, and every creature in the street with an air of gayety—that Paris alone seems to inspire in the human race. It entered into her blood, this rush of spring and hope and laughter and life, and a radiant creature got out of the carriage at Henry's door.

The two men were waiting for them—Lord Bracondale and the French Count—her father and Mrs. McBride had not yet appeared.

Theodora introduced them to her husband, and Lord Bracondale said:

"Mrs. McBride is always late. I have found out which is your father's table; don't you think we might go and sit down?"

And they did. Theodora got well into the corner of the velvet sofa, the Count on one side and Lord Bracondale on the other, with Josiah beyond the Count.

They made conversation. The Frenchman was voluble and agreeable, and the next ten minutes passed without incident.

Josiah, not quite at ease, perhaps, but on the whole not ill-pleased with his situation. The Count took all ups and downs as of the day's work, sure of a good breakfast, sooner or later, unpaid for by himself. And Lord Bracondale's thoughts ran somewhat thus:

"She is even more beautiful in daylight than at night. She can't be more than twenty—what a skin! like a white gardenia petal—and, good Lord, what a husband! How revolting, how infamous! I suppose that old schemer, her father, sold her to him. Her eyes remind one of forgotten fairy tales of angels. Can anything be so sweet as that little nose and those baby-red lips. She has a soul, too, peeping out of the blue when she looks up at one. She reminds me of Praxiteles' Psyche when she looks down. Why did I not meet her long ago? I believe I ought not to stay now—something tells me I shall fall deeply into this. And what a voice!—as gentle and caressing as a tender dove. A man would give his soul for such a woman. As guileless as an infant saint, too—and sensitive and human and understanding. I wish to God I had the strength of mind to get up and go this minute—but I haven't—it is fate."

"Oh, how naughty of papa," said Theodora, "to be so late! Are you very hungry, Josiah? Shall we begin without them?"

But at that moment, with rustling silks and delicate perfume, the widow and Captain Fitzgerald came in at the door and joined the party.

"I am just too sorry," the lady said, gayly. "It is all Captain Fitzgerald's fault—he would try to restrain me from buying what I wanted, and so it made me obstinate and I had to stay right there and order half the shop."

"How I understand you!" sympathized Lord Bracondale. "I know just that feeling of wanting forbidden fruit. It makes the zest of life."

He had foreseen the disposition of the party, and by sitting in the outside corner seat at the end knew he would have Theodora almost *en tête-à-tête*, once they were all seated along the velvet sofa beyond Josiah Brown.

"What do you do with yourself all the time here?" he asked, lowering his voice to that deep note which only carries to the ear it is intended for. "May one ever see you again except at a chance meal like this?"

"I don't know," said Theodora. "I walk up and down in the side allées of the Bois in the morning with my husband, and when he has had his sleep, after déjeuner, we drive nearly all the afternoon, and we have tea, at the Pré Catalan and drive again until about seven, and then we come in and dine, and I go to bed very early. Josiah is not strong enough yet for late hours or theatres."

"It sounds supernaturally gay for Paris!" said Lord Bracondale; and then he felt a brute when he saw the cloud in the blue eyes.

"No, it is not gay," she said, simply. "But the flowers are beautiful, and the green trees and the chestnut blossoms and the fine air here, and there is a little stream among the trees which laughs to itself as it runs, and all these things say something to me."

He felt rebuked—rebuked and interested.

"I would like to see them all with you," he said.

That was one of his charms—directness. He did not insinuate often; he stated facts.

"You would find it all much too monotonous," she answered. "You would tire of them after the first time. And you could if you liked, too, because I suppose you are free, being a man, and can choose your own life," and she sighed unconsciously.

And there came to Hector Bracondale the picture of her life—sacrificed, no doubt, to others' needs. He seemed to see the long years tied to Josiah Brown, the cramping of her soul, the dreary desolation of it. Then a tenderness came over him, a chivalrous tenderness unfelt by him towards women now for many a long day.

"I wonder if I can choose my life," he said, and he looked into her eyes.

"Why can you not?" She hesitated. "And may I ask you, too, what you do with yourself here?"

He evaded the question; he suddenly realized that his days were not more amusing than hers, although they were filled up with racing and varied employments—while the thought of his nights sickened him.

"I think I am going to make an immense change and learn to take pleasure in the running brooks," he said. "Will you help me?"

"I know so little, and you know so much," and her sweet eyes became soft and dreamy. "I could not help you in any way, I fear."

"Yes, you could—you could teach me to see all things with fresh eyes. You could open the door into a new world."

"Do you know," she said, irrelevantly, "Sarah—my eldest sister—Sarah told me it was unwise ever to talk to strangers except in the abstract—and here are you and I conversing about our own interests and feelings—are not we foolish!" She laughed a little nervously.

"No, we are not foolish because we are not strangers—we never were—and we never will be."

"Are not strangers—?"

"No—do you not feel that sometimes in life one's friendships begin by antipathy—sometimes by indifference—and sometimes by that sudden magnetism of sympathy as if in some former life we had been very near and dear, and were only picking up the threads again, and to such two souls there is no feeling that they are strangers."

Theodora was too entirely unsophisticated to remain unmoved by this reasoning. She felt a little thrill—she longed to continue the subject, and yet dared not. She turned hesitatingly to the Count, and for the next ten minutes Lord Bracondale only saw the soft outline of her cheek.

He wondered if he had been too sudden. She was quite the youngest person he had ever met—he realized that, and perhaps he had acted with too much precipitation. He would change his tactics.

The Count was only too pleased to engage the attention of Theodora. He was voluble; she had very little to reply. Things went smoothly. Josiah was appreciating an exceedingly good breakfast, and the playful sallies of the fair widow. All, in fact, was *couleur de rose.*

"Won't you talk to me any more?" Lord Bracondale said, after about a quarter of an hour. He felt that was ample time for her to have become calm, and, beautiful as the outline of her cheek was, he preferred her full face.

"But of course," said Theodora. She had not heard more than half what the Count had been saying; she wished vaguely that she might continue the subject of friendship, but she dared not.

"Do you ever go to Versailles?" he asked. This, at least, was a safe subject.

"I have been there—but not since—not this time," she answered. "I loved it: so full of memories and sentiment, and Old-World charm."

"It would give me much pleasure to take you to see it again," he said, with grave politeness. "I must devise some plan—that is, if you wish to go."

She smiled.

"It is a favorite spot of mine, and there are some alleés in the park more full of the story of spring than your Bois even."

"I do not see how we can go," said Theodora. "Josiah would find it too long a day."

"I must discuss it with your father; one can generally arrange what one wishes," said Lord Bracondale.

At this moment Mrs. McBride leaned over and spoke to Theodora. She had, she said, quite converted Mr. Brown. He only wanted a little cheering up to be perfectly well, and she had got him to promise to dine that evening at Armenonville and listen to the Tziganes. It was going to be a glorious night, but if they felt cold they could have their table inside out of the draught. What did Theodora think about it?

Theodora thought it would be a delicious plan. What else could she think?

"I have a large party coming," Mrs. McBride said, "and among them a compatriot of mine who saw you last night and is dying to meet you."

"Really," said Theodora, unmoved.

Lord Bracondale experienced a sensation of annoyance.

"I shall not ask you, Bracondale," the widow continued, playfully. "Just to assert British superiority, you would try to monopolize Mrs. Brown, and my poor Herryman Hoggenwater would have to come in a long, long second!"

Josiah felt a rush of pride. This brilliant woman was making much of his meek little wife.

Lord Bracondale smiled the most genial smile, with rage in his heart.

"I could not have accepted in any case, dear lady," he said, "as I have some people dining with me, and, oddly enough, they rather suggested they wanted Armenonville too, so perhaps I shall have the pleasure of looking at you from the distance."

The conversation then became general, and soon after this coffee arrived, and eventually the adieux were said.

Mrs. McBride insisted upon Theodora accompanying her in her smart automobile.

"You leave your wife to me for an hour," she said, imperiously, to Josiah, "and go and see the world with Captain Fitzgerald. He knows Paris."

"My dear, you are just the sweetest thing I have come across this side of the Atlantic," she said, when they were whizzing along in her car. "But you look as if you wanted cheering too. I expect your husband's illness has worried you a good deal."

Theodora froze a little. Then she glanced at the widow's face and its honest kindliness melted her.

"Yes, I have been anxious about him," she said, simply, "but he is nearly well now, and we shall soon be going to England."

Mrs. McBride had not taken a companion on this drive for nothing, and she obtained all the information she wanted during their tour in the Bois. How Josiah Brown had bought a colossal place in the eastern counties, and intended to have parties and shoot there in the autumn. How Theodora hoped to see more of her sisters than she had done since her marriage. The question of these sisters interested Mrs. McBride a good deal.

For a man to have two unmarried daughters was rather an undertaking.

What were their ages—their habits—their ambitions? Theodora told her simply. She guessed why she was being interrogated. She wished to assist her father, and to say the truth seemed to her the best way. Sarah was kind and humorous, while Clementine had the brains.

"And they are both dears," she said, lovingly, "and have always been so good to me."

Mrs. McBride was a shrewd woman, full of American quickness, lightning deduction, and a phenomenal insight into character. Theodora seemed to her to be too tender a flower for this world of east wind. She felt sure she only thought good of every one, and how could one get on in life if one took that view habitually! The appallingly hard knocks fate would give one if one was so trusting! But as the drive went on that gentle something that seemed to emanate from Theodora, the something of pure sweetness and light, affected her, too, as it affected other people. She felt she was looking into a deep pool of crystal water, so deep that she could see no bottom or fathom the distance of it, but which reflected in brilliant blue God's sky and the sun.

"And she is by no means stupid," the widow summed up to herself. "Her mind is as bright as an American's! And she is just too pretty and sweet to be eaten up by these wolves of men she will meet in England, with that unromantic, unattractive husband along. I must do what I can for her."

By the time she had dropped Theodora at her hotel the situation was quite clear. Of course the girl had been sacrificed to Josiah Brown; she was sound asleep in the great forces of life; she was bound to be hideously unhappy, and it was all an abominable shame, and ought to have been prevented.

But Mrs. McBride never cried over spilled milk.

"If I decide to marry her father," she thought, as she drove off, "I shall keep my eye on her, and meanwhile I can make her life smile a little perhaps!"

IV

Theodora did not wonder why she felt in no exalted state of spirits as she dressed for dinner. She seldom thought of herself at all, or what her emotions were, but the fact remained there was none of the excitement there had been over the prospect of breakfast. Her husband, on the contrary, seemed quite fussy.

"A devilish fine woman," he had described Mrs. McBride. "Acts like a tonic upon me; does me more good than a pint of champagne!"

"Is she not delightful?" agreed Theodora; "so very kind and gay. I am sure the dinner will do you good, Josiah, and perhaps we might give one in return. What do you say?"

Josiah said, "Certainly!" He could give a meal with the best of them! They would consult that father of hers, who knew Paris so well, and ask him to help them to arrange a regular "slap-up treat."

And so they arrived at Armenonville. It was a divine night, quite warm, and a soft three-quarter moon.

Mrs. McBride had everything arranged to perfection. Their table was just where it should be, the menu was all that heart of gourmet could desire, and the company sparkling.

Theodora found herself seated beside Mr. Harryman Hoggenwater and an elderly Austrian, and before the *hors d'œuvres* were cleared away both gentlemen had decided to make love to her.

It was when the *bisque d'écrevisses* was being handed she became conscious that, not two tables off, there was an empty one simply arranged with flowers, and almost at the same instant Lord Bracondale and his party arrived upon the scene.

All Theodora's perceptions seemed to be sharpened. She knew without turning her head the table was for them, and that they were advancing towards it. She had felt their arrival almost before their automobile stopped; and now she would not look up.

A strange sensation, as of excitement, tingled through her. She longed to ascertain if the woman was good-looking who made the third in this party of three. She peeped eventually—with the corner of her eye. Lord Bracondale had so placed his guests that he himself faced Theodora, and the lady had her back turned to her.

Thus Theodora's curiosity could not be gratified.

"She is English," she decided; "that round shaped back always is—and very well-bred looking, and not much taste in dress. I wonder if she is old or young—and if that is the husband. Yes, he is unattractive—it must be the husband—and oh, I wonder what they are talking about! Lord Bracondale seems so interested!"

And if she had known it was—

"Really, Monica, how fortunate to have secured you at short notice like this," Lord Bracondale was saying. "I only found I had a free evening at breakfast, and I met Jack on my way to the polo-ground just in the nick of time."

"We love coming," Mrs. Ellerwood replied. "For unsophisticated English people it is a great treat. We go back on Saturday—every one will be asking what is keeping you here so long."

"My plans are vague," Lord Bracondale said, casually. "I might come back any day, or I may stay until well into June—it quite depends upon how amused I am. I rather love Paris."

And to himself he was thinking—

"How I wish that atrocious woman over there with the paradise plume would keep her hat out of the way. Ah, that is better! How lovely she looks to-night! What an exquisite pose of head! And what are those two damned foreigners saying to her, I wonder. Underbred brute, the American, Herryman Hoggenwater! What a name! She is laughing—she evidently finds him amusing. Abominably cattish of the widow not to ask me. I wonder if she has seen me yet. I want to make her bow to me. Ah!" For just then magnetism was too strong for Theodora, and, in spite of her determination, their eyes met.

A thrill, little short of passion, ran through Lord Bracondale as he saw the wild roses flushing her white cheeks—the exquisite flattery to his vanity. Yes, she had seen him, and it already meant something to her.

He raised his champagne glass and sipped a sip, while his eyes, more ardent than they had ever been, sought her face.

And Theodora, for her part, felt a flutter too. She was angry with herself for blushing, such a school-girlish thing to do, Sarah had always told her. She hoped he had not noticed it at that distance—probably not. And what did he mean by drinking her health like that? He—oh, he was—

"Now, truly, Mrs. Brown, you are cruel," Mr. Herryman Hoggenwater said, pathetically, interrupting her thoughts. "I tell you I am simply longing to know if you will come for a drive in my automobile, and you do not answer, but stare into space."

Theodora turned, and then the young American understood that for all her gentle looks it would be wiser not to take this tone with her.

He admired her frantically, he was just "crazy" about her, he told Mrs. McBride later. And so now he exerted himself to please and amuse her with all the vivacity of his brilliant nation.

Theodora was enjoying herself. Environment and atmosphere affected her strongly. The bright pink lights, the sense of night and the soft moon beyond the wide open balcony windows, the scents of flowers, the gayety, and, above all, the knowledge that Lord Bracondale was there, gazing at her whenever opportunity offered, with eyes in which she, unlearned as she was in such things, could read plainly admiration and unrest.

It all went to her head a little, and she became quite animated and full of repartee and sparkle, so that Josiah Brown could hardly believe his eyes and ears when he glanced across at her. This his meek and quiet mouse!

His heart swelled with pride when Mrs. McBride leaned over and said to him:

"You know, Mr. Brown, you have got the most beautiful wife in the world, and I hope you value her properly."

It was this daring quality in his hostess Josiah appreciated so much. "She's not afraid to say anything, 'pon my soul," he said to himself. "I rather think I know my own possession's value!" he answered aloud, with a pompous puffing out of chest, and a cough to clear the throat.

The Austrian Prince on Theodora's right hand pleased her. He had a quiet manner, and the freemasonry of breeding in two people, even of different nations, drew her to talk naturally to him in a friendly way.

He was a fatalist, he told her; what would be would be, and mortals like himself and herself were just scattered leaves, like barks floating down a current where were mostly rocks ahead.

"Then must we strike the rocks whether we wish it or no?" asked Theodora. "Cannot we help ourselves?"

"Ah, madame, for that," he said, "we can strive a little and avoid this one and that, but if it is our fate we will crash against them in the end."

"What a sad philosophy!" said Theodora. "I would rather believe that if one does one's best some kind angel will guide one's bark past the rocks and safely into the smooth waters of the pool beyond."

"You are young," he said, "and I hope you will find it so, but I fear you will have to try very hard, and circumstances may even then be too strong for you."

"In that case I must go under altogether," said Theodora; but her eyes smiled, and that night at least such a possibility seemed far enough away from her.

The Austrian looked across at her husband. Such marriages were rare in his country, and he had thought so too in England. He wondered what their story could be. He wondered how soon she would take a lover—and he realized how infinitely worth while that lover would find his situation.

He wished he were not so old. If she must break up her bark on the rocks, he could take the place of steersman with pleasure. But he was a courteous gentleman and he said none of these things aloud.

Meanwhile, Lord Bracondale was not enjoying his dinner. For the first time for several years he found himself jealous! He, unlike Theodora, knew the meaning of every one of his sensations.

"She is certainly interested in Prince Carolstein," he thought, as he watched her; "he has a European reputation for fascination. She has not looked this way once since the entrées. I wish I could hear what they are talking about. As for that young puppy Hoggenwater, I would like to kick him round the room! Lord, look how he is leaning over her! It sickens me! The young fool!"

Mrs. Ellerwood turned round in her seat and surveyed the room. They had almost come to the end of dinner, and could move their chairs a little. She had the true Englishwoman's feeling when among foreigners—that they were all there as puppets for her entertainment.

"Look, Hector," she said—they were cousins—"did you ever see such a lovely woman as that one over there among the large party, in the black chiffon dress?"

Then Hector committed a *bêtise*.

"Where?" said he, his eyes persistently fixed in another direction.

"There; you can't mistake her, she looks so pure white, and fair, among all these Frenchwomen The one with the blue eyes and the lovely hat with those sweeping feathers. She is exquisitely dressed, and both those men look fearfully devoted to her. Can't you see? Oh, you are stupid!"

"My dear Monica," said Jack Ellerwood, who joined rarely in the conversation, "Hector has been sitting facing this way all through dinner. He is a man who can appreciate what he sees, and I do not fancy has missed much—have you, Hector?" and he smiled a quiet smile.

Mrs. Ellerwood looked at Lord Bracondale and laughed.

"It is I who am stupid," she said. "Naturally you have seen her all the time, and know her probably. Are they cocottes, or Americans, or Russian princesses, or what?—the whole collection?"

"If you mean that large party in the corner, they are most of them friends and acquaintances of mine," he said, rather icily—she had annoyed him—"and they belong to the aristocracies of various nations. Does that satisfy you? I am afraid they are none of them demimondaines, so you will be disappointed this time!"

Mrs. Ellerwood looked at him; she understood now.

"He is in love with the white woman," she thought; "that is why he was so anxious to dine here to-night, when Jack suggested Madrid; that is why he stays in Paris. It is not Esclarmonde de Chartres after all! How excited Aunt Milly will be! I must find out her name."

"She is a beautiful creature," said Jack Ellerwood, as if to himself, while he carefully surveyed Theodora from his position at the side of the table.

Hector Bracondale's irritation rose. Relations were tactless, and he felt sorry he had asked them.

"You must tell me her name, Hector," pleaded Mrs. Ellerwood; "the very white, pretty one I mean."

"Now just to punish your curiosity I shall do no such thing."

"Hector, you are a pig."

"Probably."

"And so selfish."

"Possibly."

"Why mayn't I know? You set a light to all sorts of suspicions."

"Doubly interesting for you, then."

"Provoking wretch!"

"Don't you think you would like some coffee? The waiter is trying to hand you a cup."

Mrs. Ellerwood laughed. She knew there was no use teasing him further; but there were other means, and she must employ them. Theodora had become the pivot upon which some of her world might turn.

The object of this solicitude was quite unconscious of the interest she had created. She did not naturally think she could be of importance to any one. Had she not been the youngest and snubbed always?

The same thought came to her that was conjuring the brain of Lord Bracondale: would there be a chance to speak to-night, or must they each go their way in silence? He meant to assist fate if he could, but having Monica Ellerwood there was a considerable drawback.

Mrs. McBride's party were to take their coffee in one of the *bosquets* outside, and all got up from their table in a few minutes to go out. They would have to pass the *partie à trois*, who were nearer the door. Monica would take her most searching look at them, Lord Bracondale thought; now was the time for action. So as Mrs. McBride came past with Captain Fitzgerald, he rose from his seat and greeted her.

"You have been exceedingly mean," he whispered. "What are you going to do for me to make up for it?"

The widow had a very soft spot in her heart for "Ce beau Bracondale," as she called him, and when he pleaded like that she found him hard to resist.

"Come and see me to-morrow at twelve, and we will talk about it," she said.

"To-morrow!" exclaimed Lord Bracondale; "but I want to talk to her to-night!"

"Get rid of your party, then, and join us for coffee," and the widow smiled archly as she passed on.

Theodora bowed with grave sweetness as she also went by, and most of the others greeted Hector, while one woman stopped and told him she was going to have an automobile party in a day or two, and she hoped he would come.

When they had all gone on Mrs. Ellerwood said:

"I wonder why Americans are so much smarter than we poor English? I can't bear them as a nation though, can you?"

"Yes," said Lord Bracondale. "I think the best friends I have in the world are American. The women particularly are perfectly charming. You feel all the time you are playing a game with really experienced adversaries, and it makes it interesting. They are full of resource, and you know underneath you could never break their hearts. I am not sure if they have any in their own country, but if so they turn into the most wonderful and exquisite bits of mechanism when they come to Europe."

"And you admire that."

"Certainly—hearts are a great bore."

"You were always a cynic, Hector; that is perhaps what makes you so attractive."

"Am I attractive?"

"I can't judge," said Mrs. Ellerwood, nettled for a moment. "I have known you too long, but I hear other women saying so."

"That is comforting, at all events," said Lord Bracondale. "I always have adored women."

"No, you never have, that is just it. You have let them adore you, and utterly spoil you; so now sometimes, Hector, you are insupportable."

"You just said I was attractive."

"I shall not argue further with you," said Mrs. Ellerwood, pettishly.

"And I think we ought to be saying good-night, Hector," interrupted the silent Jack. "We are making an early start for Fontainebleau to-morrow, and Monica likes any amount of sleep."

This did not suit Mrs. Ellerwood at all; but if Jack spoke seldom he spoke to some purpose when he did, and she knew there was no use arguing.

So with a heart full of ungratified curiosity, she at last allowed herself to be packed into Hector's automobile and driven away.

"Of course he'll go and join that other party now, Jack! What *did* you make me come away for, you tiresome thing!" she said to her husband.

"He has done me many a turn in the past," said Jack, laconically.

"Then you think—?"

But Jack refused to think.

V

Theodora was sitting rather on the outskirts of the party in the *bosquet*, her two devoted admirers still on either side of her. All the chairs were arranged informally, and hers was against the opening, so that it proved easy for Lord Bracondale to come up behind her unperceived.

She believed he had gone. She could not see distinctly from where she was, but she had thought she saw the automobile whizzing by. She recognized Mrs. Ellerwood's hat. An unconscious feeling of blankness came over her. She grew more silent.

A lady beyond the Prince spoke to him, and at that moment Mr. Hoggenwater rose to put down her coffee-cup, and in this second of loneliness a deep voice said in her ear:

"I could not go—I wanted to say good-night to you!"

Then Theodora experienced a new emotion; she could not have told herself what it was, but suddenly a gladness spread through her spirit; the moon looked more softly bright, and her sweet eyes dilated and glowed, while that voice, gentle as a dove's, trembled a little as she said:

"Lord Bracondale! Oh, you startled me!"

He drew a chair and sat down behind her.

"How shall we get rid of your Hogginheimer millionaire?" he whispered. "I feel as if I wanted to kill every one who speaks to you to-night."

The half light, the moon, Paris, and the spring-time! Theodora spent the next hour in a dream—a dream of bliss.

Mrs. McBride, with her all-seeing eye, perceived the turn events had taken. She was full of enjoyment herself; she had quite—almost quite—decided to listen to the addresses of Captain Fitzgerald, therefore her heart, not her common-sense, was uppermost this night.

It could not hurt Theodora to have one evening of agreeable conversation, and it would do Herryman Hoggenwater a great deal of good to be obstacled; thus she expressed it to herself. That last success with Princess Waldersheim had turned his empty head. So she called him and planted him in a safe place by an American girl, who would know how to keep him, and then turned to her own affairs again.

The Prince was a man of the world, and understood life. So Theodora and Lord Bracondale were left in peace.

The latter soon moved his chair to a position where he could see her face, rather behind her still, which entailed a slightly leaning over attitude. They were beyond the radius of the lights in the *bosquet.*

Lord Bracondale was perfectly conversant with all moves in the game; he knew how to talk to a woman so that she alone could feel the strength of his devotion, while his demeanor to the world seemed the least compromising.

Theodora had not spoken for a moment after his first speech. It made her heart beat too fast.

"I have been watching you all through dinner," he continued, with only a little pause. "You look immensely beautiful to-night, and those two told you so, I suppose."

"Perhaps they did!" she said. This was her first gentle essay at fencing. She would try to be as the rest were, gay and full of badinage.

"And you liked it?" with resentment.

"Of course I did; you see, I never have heard any of these nice things much. Josiah has always been too ill to go out, and when I was a girl I never saw any people who knew how to say them."

She had turned to look at him as she said this, and his eyes spoke a number of things to her. They were passionate, and resentful, and jealous, and full of something disturbing. Thrills ran through poor Theodora.

His eyes had been capable of looking most of these things before to other women, when he had not meant any of them, but she did not know that.

"Well," he said, "they had better not return or recommence their compliments, because I am not in the mood to be polite to them to-night."

"What is your mood?" asked Theodora, and then felt a little frightened at her own daring.

"My mood is one of unrest—I would like to be away alone with you, where we could talk in peace," and he leaned over her so that his lips were fairly close to her ear. "These people jar upon me. I would like to be sitting in the garden at Amalfi, or in a gondola in Venice, and I want to talk about all your beautiful thoughts. You are a new white flower for me, as different as an angel from the other women in the world."

"Am I?" said she, in her tender tones. "I would wish that you should always keep that good thought of me. We shall soon go our different ways. Josiah has decided to leave next week, and we are not likely to meet in England."

"Yes, we are likely to meet—I will arrange it," he said.

There was nothing hesitating about Hector Bracondale—his way with women had always been masterful—and this quality, when mixed with a sudden bending to their desires, was peculiarly attractive. To-night he was drifting—drifting into a current which might carry him beyond his control.

It was now several years since he had been in love even slightly. His position, his appearance, his personal charm, had all combined to spoil a nature capable of great things. Life had always been too smooth. His mother adored him. He had an ample fortune. Every marriageable girl in his world almost had been flung at his head. Women of all classes with one consent had done their best to turn him into a coxcomb and a beast. But he continued to be a man for all that, and went his own way; only as no one can remain stationary, the crust of selfishness and cynicism was perhaps thickening with years, and his soul was growing hidden still deeper beneath it all. From the beginning something in Theodora had spoken to the best in him. He was conscious of feelings of dissatisfaction with himself when he left her, of disgust with the days of unmeaning aims.

He had begun out of idle admiration; he had continued from inclination; but to-night it was *plus fort que lui*, and he knew he was in love.

The habit of indulging any emotion which gave him pleasure was still strong upon him; it was not yet he would begin to analyze where this passion might lead him—might lead them both.

It was too deliciously sweet to sit there and whisper to her sophistries and reasonings, to take her sensitive fancy into new worlds, to play upon her feelings—those feelings which he realized were as fine and as full of tone as the sounds which could be drawn from a Stradivarius violin.

It was a night of new worlds for them both, for if Theodora had never looked into any world at all, he also had never even imagined one which could be so quite divine as this—this shared with her in the moonlight, with the magic of the Tzigane music and the soft spring night.

He had just sufficient mastery over himself left not to overstep the bounds of respectful and deep interest in her. He did not speak a word of love. There was no actual sentence which Theodora felt obliged to resent—and yet through it all was the subtle insinuation that they were more than friends—or would be more than friends.

And when it was all over, and Theodora's pulses were calmer as she lay alone on her pillow, she had a sudden thrill of fear. But she put it aside—it was not her nature to think herself the object of passions. "I would be a very silly woman to flatter myself so," she said to herself, and then she went to sleep.

Lord Bracondale stayed awake for hours, but he did not sup with Esclarmonde de Chartres or Marion de Beauvoison. And the Café de Paris—and Maxims—and the afterwards—saw him no more.

Once again these houris asked each other, "Mais qu'est-ce qu'il a! Ce bel Hector? Oú se cache-t-il?"

VI

Before she went to bed in her hotel in the Rue de Rivoli, Monica Ellerwood wrote to her aunt.

PARIS, *May 15th.*

"MY DEAR AUNT MILLY,—We have had a delicious little week, Jack and I, quite like an old honeymoon pair—and to-day we ran across Hector, who has remained hidden until now. He is looking splendid, just as handsome and full of life as ever, so it does not tell upon his constitution, that is one mercy! Not like poor Ernest Bretherton, who, if you remember, was quite broken up by her last year. And I have one good piece of news for you, dear Aunt Milly. I do not believe he is so frantically wrapped up in this Esclarmonde de Chartres woman after all—in spite of that diamond chain at Monte Carlo. For to-night he took us to dine at Armenonville—although Jack particularly wanted to go to the Madrid—and when we got there we saw at once why! There was a most beautiful woman dining there with a party, and Hector never took his eyes off her the whole of dinner, Jack says—I had my back that way—and he got rid of us as soon as he could and went and joined them. Very young she looked, but I suppose married, from her pearls and clothes—American probably, as she was perhaps too well dressed for one of us; but quite a lady and awfully pretty. Hector was so snappish about it, and would not tell her name, that it makes me sure he is very much in love with her, and Jack thinks so too. So, dear Aunt Milly, you need have no more anxieties about him, as she can't have been married long, she looks so young, and so must be quite safe. Jack says Hector is thoroughly able to take care of himself, anyway, but I know how all these things worry you. If I can find out her name before I go I will, though perhaps you think it is out of the frying-pan into the fire, as it makes him no more in the mood to marry Morella Winmarleigh than before. Unless, of course, this new one is unkind to him. We shall be home on Saturday, dear Aunt Milly, and I will come round to lunch on Sunday and give you all my news.

"Your affectionate niece,

"MONICA ELLERWOOD".

Which epistle jarred upon Hector's mother when she read it over coffee at her solitary dinner on the following night.

"Poor dear Monica!" she said to herself. "I wonder where she got this strain from—her father's family, I suppose—I wish she would not be so—bald."

Then she sat down and wrote to her son—she was not even going to the opera that night. And if she had looked up in the tall mirror opposite, she would have seen a beautiful, stately lady with a puckered, plaintive frown on her face.

If a woman absolutely worships a man, even if she is only his mother, she is bound to spend many moments of unhappiness, and Lady Bracondale was no exception to the general rule. Hector had always gone his own way, and there were several aspects of his life she disapproved of. These visits to Paris—his antipathy to matrimony—his boredom with girls—such nice girls she knew, too, and had often thrown him with!—his delight in big-game shooting in alarming and impossible countries—and, above all, his absolute indifference to Morella Winmarleigh, the only woman who really and truly in her heart of hearts Lady Bracondale thought worthy of him, although she would have accepted several other girls as choosing the lesser evil to bachelorhood. But Morella Winmarleigh was perfection! She owned the enormous property adjoining Bracondale; she was twenty-six years old, of unblemished reputation, nice looking, and not—not one of those modern women who are bound to cause anxieties. Under any circumstances one could count upon Morella Winmarleigh behaving with absolute propriety. A girl born to be a mother-in-law's joy.

But Hector persistently remained at large. It was not that he openly defied his mother—he simply made love to her whenever they were together, twisted her round his finger, and was off again.

"To see mother with Hector," Lady Annigford said, "is a wonderful sight. Although I adore him myself, I am not at the stage she is! She sits there beaming on him exactly like an exceedingly proud and fond cat with new kittens. He treats her as if she were a young and beautiful woman, caresses her, pets her, pays not the least attention to anything she says, and does absolutely what he pleases!"

Hector and Lady Bracondale together had often made the women who were in love with him jealous.

When she had finished her letter the stately lady read it over carefully—she had a certain tact, and Hector must be cajoled to return, not irritated. Monica's epistle, in spite of that touch of vulgarity which she had deplored, had held out some grains of comfort. She had been getting really anxious over this affair with the—French person. Even to herself Lady Bracondale would not use any of the terms which usually designate ladies of the type of Esclarmonde de Chartres.

Since her brother-in-law Evermond had returned from Monte Carlo bringing that disturbing story of the diamond chain, she had been on thorns—of such a light mind and always so full of worldly gossip, Evermond!

Hector had gone from Monte Carlo to Venice, and then to Paris, where he had been for more than a month, and she had heard that men could become quite infatuated and absolutely ruined by these creatures. So for him to have taken a fancy to a married American was considerably better than that. She had met several members of this nation herself in England, and were they not always very discreet, with well-balanced heads! So altogether the puckered frown soon left her smooth brow, and she was able to resume the knitting of a tie she was doing for her son, with a spirit more or less at rest, though she sighed now and then as she remembered Morella Winmarleigh could not be expected to wait forever—and her cherished vision of perfectly behaved, vigorously healthy grandchildren was still a long way from being realized. For with such a mother what perfect children they would be! This was always her final reflection.

VII

At twelve o'clock punctually Lord Bracondale was ushered into Mrs. McBride's sitting-room at the Ritz, the day after her dinner-party at Armenonville. He expected she would not be ready to receive him for at least half an hour; having said twelve he might have known she meant half-past, but he was in a mood of impatience, and felt obliged to be punctual.

He was suffering more or less from a reaction. He had begun towards morning to realize the manner in which he had spent the evening was not altogether wise. Not that he had the least intention of not repeating his folly—indeed, he was where he was at this hour for no other purpose than to enlist the widow's sympathy, and her co-operation in arranging as many opportunities for similar evenings as together they could devise.

After all, she only kept him waiting twenty minutes, and he had been rather amused looking at the piles of bric-à-brac obsequious art dealers had left for this rich lady's inspection.

A number of spurious bronzes warranted pure antique, clocks, brocades, what not, lying about on all the available space.

"And I wonder what it will look like in her marble palace halls," he thought, as he passed from one article to another.

"I am just too sorry to keep you, mon cher Bracondale," Mrs. McBride said, presently, suddenly opening the adjoining door a few inches, "but it is a quite exasperating hat which has delayed me. I can't get the thing on at the angle I want. I—"

"Mayn't I come and help, dear lady?" interrupted Hector. "I know all about the subject. I had to buy forty-seven at Monte Carlo, and see them all tried on, too—and only lately! Do ask Marie to open that door a little wider; I will decide in a minute how it should be."

"Insolent!" said the widow, who spoke French with perfect fluency and a quite marvellously pure American accent. But she permitted the giggling and beaming Marie to open the door wide, and let Hector advance and kiss her hand.

He then took a chair by the dressing-table and inspected the situation.

Seven or eight dainty bandboxes strewed the floor, some of their contents peeping from them—feathers, aigrettes, flowers, impossible birds—all had their place, and on the sofa were three *chef d'œuvres* ruthlessly tossed aside. While in the widow's fair hands was a gem of gray tulle and the most expensive feather heart of woman could desire.

"You see," she said, plaintively, "it is meant to go just so," and she placed it once more upon her head, a handsome head of forty-five, fresh and well preserved and comely. "But the vile-tempered thing refuses to stay there once I let go, and no pin will correct it."

"Base ingratitude," said Lord Bracondale, with feeling; "but couldn't you stuff these in the hiatus," and he tenderly lifted a bunch of nut-brown curls from the dressing-table. "They would fill up the gap and keep the fractious thing steady."

"Of course they would," said Mrs. McBride; "but I have a rooted objection to auxiliary nature trimmings. That bunch was sent with the hat, and Marie has been trying to persuade me to wear it ever since we began this struggle. But I won't! My hair's my own, and I don't mean to have any one else's alongside of it. There is my trouble."

"If milor were to hold madame's 'at one side, while I de other, madame might force her emerald parrot pin through him," suggested Marie, which advice was followed, and the widow beamed with satisfaction at the gratifying result.

"There!" she exclaimed, with a sigh of relief, "that will do; and I am just ready. Gloves, handkerchief—oh! and my purse, Marie." And in five minutes more she was leading the way back into her sitting-room.

"I have not ordered lunch until one o'clock," she said, "so we have oceans of time to talk and tell each other secrets. Sit down, jeune homme, and confess to me." She pointed to a *bergère*, but it was filled with Italian embroideries. "Marie, take this rubbish away!" she called, and presently some chairs were made clear.

"And what must I confess?" asked Hector, when they were seated. "That I am frantically in love with you, and your coldness is driving me wild?"

"Certainly not!" said the widow, while she rose again and began to arrange some giant roses in a wonderful basket which looked as if it had just arrived—her shrewd eye had seen the card, "From Captain Fitzgerald, with his best bonjour." "Certainly not! We are going to talk truth, or, to punish you, I shall not ask you to meet her again, and I shall warn her father of your strictly dishonorable intentions."

"You would not be so cruel!"

"Yes I would. And it is what I ought to do, anyway. She is as innocent as a woolly lamb, and unsophisticated and guileless, and will probably be falling in love with you. You take the wind out of the sails of that husband of hers, you see!"

"Do I?" said Hector, with overdone incredulity.

She looked at him. His long, lithe limbs stretched out, every line indicative of breeding and strength. She noted the shape of his head, the perfect grooming, his lazy, insolent grace, his whimsical smile. Englishmen of this class were certainly the most provokingly beautiful creatures in the world.

"It is because they have done nothing but order men, kill beasts, and subjugate women for generations," she said to herself. "Lazy, naughty darlings! If they came to our country and worked their brains a little, they would soon lose that look. But it would be a pity," she added—"yes, a pity."

"What are you thinking of?" asked Lord Bracondale, while she gazed at him.

"I was thinking you are a beautiful, useless creature. Just like all your nation. You think the world is made for you; in any case, all the women and animals to kill are."

"What an abominable libel! But I am fond of both things—women and animals to kill."

"And you class them equally—or perhaps the animals are ahead."

"Indeed not always," said Hector, reassuringly. "Some women have quite the first place."

"You are too flattering!" retorted the widow. "Those sentiments are all very well for your own poor-spirited, down-trodden women, but they won't do for Americans! A man has to learn a number of lessons before he is fitted to cope with them."

"Oh, tell me," said Hector.

"He has got to learn to wait, for one thing, to wait about for hours if necessary, and not to lose his temper, because the woman can't make up her mind to be in time for things, or to change it often as to where she will dine. Then he has to learn to give up any pleasure of his own for hers—and travel when she wants to travel, or stay home when she wants to go alone. If he is an Englishman he don't have brains enough to make the money, but he must let her spend what he has got how she likes, and not interfere with her own."

"And in return he gets?"

"The woman he happens to want, I suppose." And the widow laughed, showing her wonderfully preserved brilliant white teeth.

"You enunciate great truths, belle dame!" said Hector, "and your last sentence is the greatest of all—'*The woman he happens to want.*'"

"Which brings us back to our muttons—in this case only a defenceless baby lamb. Now tell me what you are here for, trying to cajole me with your good looks and mock humility."

"I am here to ask you to help me to see her again, then," said Hector, who knew when to be direct. "I have only met her three times, as you know, but I have fallen in love, and she is going away next week, and there is only one Paris in the world."

"You can do a great deal of mischief in a week," Mrs. McBride said, looking at him again critically. "I ought not to help you, but I can't resist you—there! What can we devise?"

It is possible the probability of Theodora's father making a fourth may have had something thing to do with her complaisance. Anyway, it was decided that if feasible the four should spend a day at Versailles.

They should go in their two automobiles in time for breakfast at the Réservoirs. They would start, Theodora in Mrs. McBride's with her, and Captain Fitzgerald with Lord Bracondale, and each couple could spend the afternoon as they pleased, dining again at the Réservoirs and whirling back to Paris in the moonlight. A truly rural and refreshing programme, good for the soul of man.

"And I can rely upon you to get rid of the husband?" said Lord Bracondale, finally. "I do not see the poetry of the affair with his bald head and mutton-chop whiskers as an accessory."

"Leave that to Captain Fitzgerald and myself," Mrs. McBride said, proudly. "I have a scheme that Mr. Brown shall spend the day with Clutterbuck R. Tubbs, examining some new machinery they are both interested in. Leave it to me!" The part of *Deus ex machina* was always a rôle the widow loved.

Then they descended to an agreeable lunch in the restaurant, with a numerous party of her friends as usual, and Lord Bracondale felt afterwards full of joy and hope, to continue his sinful path unrepenting.

The days that intervened before Theodora saw him again were uneventful and full of blankness. The walks in the Bois appeared more tedious than ever in the morning, the drives in the Acacias more exasperating. It was a continual alertness to see if she caught sight of a familiar face, but she never did. Fate was against them, as she sometimes is when she means to compensate soon after by some glorious day of the gods. And although Lord Bracondale called at her hotel and walked where he thought he should see her, and even drove in the Acacias, they had no meeting.

Josiah did not feel himself sufficiently strong to stand the air of theatres, and they went nowhere in the evenings. He was keeping himself for his own dinner-party, which was to take place at the Madrid on the Monday.

Captain Fitzgerald had arranged it, and besides Mrs. McBride several of his friends were coming, and a special band of wonderfully talented Tziganes, who were delighting Paris that year, had been engaged to play to them. If only the weather should remain fine all would be well.

A surprise awaited Theodora on Saturday morning. A friendly note from Mrs. McBride arrived, asking her if she would spend the day with her at Versailles, as she had asked her husband to do her a favor and lunch with Mr. Clutterbuck R. Tubbs.

Theodora awaited Josiah's presence at the *premier déjeuner*, which they took in their salon, with absolute excitement. He came in, a pompous smile on his face.

"Good-day, my love," he said, blandly. "That charming widow writes me this morning, asking if I will do her a favor, and take her friend, Mr. Clutterbuck Tubbs, to examine that machinery for the separation of fats we both have an interest in, and he suggests I should lunch with him, as he is very anxious to have my opinion upon the merits of it."

"Yes," said Theodora.

"She also says," referring to the letter in his hand, "she will take charge of you for the day, and take you to Versailles, which I know you wish to go to. She wants an answer at once, as she will call for you at twelve o'clock if we accept."

"I have heard from her, too," said Theodora. "What shall you answer, Josiah?" and she looked out of the window.

"Oh, I may as well go, I think. There is money in the invention, or that old gimlet-eye would not be so keen about it; I talked the matter over with him at Armenonville the other night."

"Then shall you write or shall I?" said Theodora, as evenly as she could. "Her servant is waiting."

VIII

Theodora hummed to herself a glad little *chansonnette* as she changed her breakfast negligee for the freshest and loveliest of her spring frocks. She did not know why she was so happy. There had been no word of any one else being of the party, only she and Mrs. McBride, but Versailles would be exquisite on such a day, and something whispered to her that she might not yawn.

The most radiant vision awaited the widow, when, with unusual punctuality, her automobile stopped at the hotel door. She came in. She was voluble, she flattered Josiah. So good of him to take Mr. Tubbs—and she hoped it would not tire him. Theodora should be well looked after. They might be late and even dine at Versailles, she said, and Mr. Brown was not to be anxious—*she* would be responsible for the safe return of his beautiful little wife. (Theodora was five foot seven at least, but her small head and extreme slenderness gave people the feeling she was little—something to be protected and guarded always.)

Josiah was affable. Mrs. McBride's words were so smooth and so many, he had no time to feel Theodora was going to dine out without him, or that anything had been arranged for ultimate ends.

The automobile had almost reached Suresnes before the widow said to her guest:

"Your father and Lord Bracondale have promised to meet us at the Réservoirs. Captain Fitzgerald told me how you wanted to go to Versailles, and how your husband is not strong enough to take these excursions, so I thought we might have this little day out there, while he is engaged with Mr. Clutterbuck Tubbs."

"How sweet of you!" said Theodora.

As they rushed through the smiling country, both women's spirits rose, and Mrs. McBride's were the spirits of experience and did not mount without due cause. Since she had been a girl in Dakota and passionately in love with her first husband—the defunct McBride was a second venture—she had not met a man who could quicken her pulse like Captain Fitzgerald. It was a curious coincidence that they both had already two partners to regret. It was an extra link between them, and Jane McBride, who was superstitious, read the omen to mean that this time each had met his true mate.

"If he is irresistible to-day, I think I shall clinch matters," she was saying to herself.

While Theodora's musings ran:

"How beautiful Versailles will look, and I dare say he will know all about its history, and be able to tell me interesting things; and oh! I am so glad I put on this frock, and oh! I am so happy."

And aloud they spoke of paradise plumes and the new gray, and the merits and demerits of Callot and Doucet and Jeanne Valez. And the widow said some bright American things about husbands and the world in general that conveyed crisp truths.

The drive seemed all too short, and there were their two cavaliers in the court-yard awaiting them at the Réservoirs, having arrived just before them.

To the end of her life Theodora will remember that glorious May day. Its even minutest detail, the color of the chestnut-trees, the tint of the sky, the scent in the air, every line of his figure and turn of his head, every look in his eyes—and they were many and varied—and also and alas! every growing emotion in her own heart. But at the moment all was gladness, and exquisite, young, irresponsible joy. *Sans arrière-pensée* or disquieting reflection.

She wondered which of the two men was the handsomer as she got out of the automobile—dear, darling papa or Lord Bracondale; both were quite show creatures of their age, and both were of the same class and knowledge of *savoir-vivre.* Every one said such polite and gracious things, it was all so smooth and gay, and it seemed so natural that they should take a turn up towards the château while breakfast was being prepared.

Half-past one o'clock was time enough to eat, the widow said.

"I want to show you a number of spots I love," Hector announced, choosing a different path to the other pair. "And it is a day we can be happy in, can't we?"

"I want to be happy," said Theodora.

"Then we shall go no farther now; we shall sit on this seat and admire the view. See, we are quite alone and undisturbed; all the world has gone home to breakfast."

Then he looked at her, and though he really did try at this stage to be reasonable, something of the intense attraction he felt for her blazed in his eyes.

She was sufficiently delectable a picture to turn the sagest head. There was something so absolutely pure white about that skin, it seemed good to eat, flawless, unlined, unblemished, under this brilliant light.

The way her silvery blond hair grew was just the right way a woman's hair ought to grow, he thought; low on a high, broad brow, rippling and soft, and quantities of it. What could it be like to caress it, to run one's fingers through it, to bury one's face in it? Ah! and then there were her tender eyes, dewy and shadowed with dark lashes, and so intensely blue. His glance wandered farther afield. Such a figure! slender and graceful and fine. There was something almost childish about it all; the innocent look of a very young girl, with the polish of the woman, garbed by an artist. It seemed the great pearls in her ears were not more milkily white than her throat, and he was sure were also her little slender hands, that did not fidget, but lay idly in her lap, holding her blue parasol. He would like to have taken off her gloves to see.

Passionate devotion was surging up in his breast.

And he was an Englishman, and it was still the morning. There was no moon now and he had not even breakfasted! This shows sufficiently to what state he had come.

"I want you to tell me all about Versailles," she said, looking to the left and the gray wing beyond the chapel. "Its histories and its meanings. I used to read about it all after Sarah brought me here once for our treat, but you probably are learned upon the subject, and I want to know."

"I would much rather hear what you did when Sarah brought you here for your treat," he said.

"Oh! it was a very simple day," and she leaned back and laughed softly at the recollection. "Papa was very hard up at that time, you know, and we were rather poor, so we came as cheaply as we could, Sarah, Clementine, and I, and I remember there were some very snuffy men in the train—we could not go first-class, you see—and one of them rather frightened me."

"The brute!" said Hector.

"I think I was about fourteen."

"And even then perfectly beautiful, I expect," he commented to himself.

"We walked up from the station, and oh! we saw all the galleries and we ran all over the park, but we missed the way to Trianon somehow and never saw that, and when we got back here we were too tired to start again. We had only had sandwiches, you see, that we brought with us, and some funny little drinks at a café down there," and she pointed vaguely towards the lake, "because we found we had only one franc fifty between us all. But we were so happy, and Clementine knows a great deal, and told us many things which were quite different from what was in the guide-books—but it seems so long, long ago. Do you know it must be six years." And she looked at him seriously.

"Half a lifetime!" agreed Hector, with a whimsical smile.

"Oh! you are laughing at me!" she said, and there was a cloud in the blue stars which looked up at him.

He made a movement nearer her—while his deep voice took every tone of tenderness.

"Indeed, indeed I am not—you dear little girl! I love to hear of your day. I was only smiling to think that six years ago you were a baby child, and I was then an old man in feeling—let me see, I was twenty-five, and I was in Russia."

He stopped suddenly; there were some circumstances which, sitting there beside her, he would rather not remember connected with Russia.

This was one of the peculiarities of Theodora. There was something about her which seemed to wither up all low or vicious things. It was not that she filled people with ascetic thoughts of saints and angels and their mother in heaven, only she seemed suddenly to enhance simple joys with beauty and charm.

They talked on for half an hour, and with every moment he discovered fresh qualities of sweetness and light in her gentle heart.

She was not ill educated either, but she had never speculated upon things, she took them for granted just as they were, and *Jean d'Agrève* was probably the only awakening book she had ever read.

Hector all at once seemed to realize his mother's vision, and to understand for the first time what marriage might mean. That to possess this exquisite bit of God's finished work for his very own, to live with her in the country, at old Bracondale, to see her honored and adored, surrounded by little children—his children—would be a dream of bliss far, far beyond any dream he had ever known. A domestic, tender dream of sweetness that he had always laughed at before as a final thing when life's other joys should be over, and now it seemed suddenly to be the only heaven and completion of his soul's desire.

Then he remembered Josiah Brown with a hideous pang of pain and bitterness—and they went in to lunch.

Theodora was so gay! Captain Fitzgerald and Mrs. McBride were already seated when they joined them in the restaurant. Most of the other visitors had finished—it was almost two o'clock.

There was a good deal of black middle in the widow's eyes, Theodora noticed, and wondered to herself if she had had a happy and exciting hour too. Papa looked complacent and handsomer than ever, she thought. She did hope it was going well. And she wondered how they were to dispose of their afternoon.

The widow soon settled this. She had, she said, a wild desire to rush through the air for a little—she *must* have her chauffeur go at full speed—somewhere—anywhere—her nerves needed calming! And Captain Fitzgerald had agreed to accompany her. Their destination was unknown, and they might not be back for tea, so Lord Bracondale must take the greatest care of Theodora and give her some if they did not turn up. They certainly would for dinner, but eight o'clock would be time enough for that.

When your destination is unknown you can never say how many hours it will take to get there and back, she pointed out. And no one felt inclined to argue with her about this obvious truth!

Now if Theodora had been a free unmarried girl, or a freer widow, it is highly probable fate would not have arranged this long afternoon in blissful surroundings undisturbed by any one. As it was, who knows if the goddess settled it with a smile on her lip or a tear in her eye? It was settled, at all events, and looked as if it were going to contain some moments worth remembering.

IX

"And what is your pleasure, fair queen?" Hector said, as they listened to the diminishing noise of the widow's Mercédès. "We are alone, and we have the world before us. Issue your commands."

"No," said Theodora, and she pouted her red lips. "I want you to settle that. I want you to arrange for whatever you think would give me the greatest pleasure. Then I shall know if you understand me and guess what I would like."

This was the most daring speech she had ever made, and she was surprised at her own temerity.

"Very well," he said. "That means you belong to me until they return," and a thrill ran through him. "Has not your father, has not your hostess, given you into my charge? And, now you yourself have sealed the compact, we shall see if I can make you happy."

As he said the words "you belong to me," Theodora thrilled too—a sensation as of an electric shock almost quivered through her. Belonged to him—ah!—what would that mean?

He called his chauffeur, who started the automobile and drove under the covered *porte cochère* where they stood.

Lord Bracondale had not spoken all the time he was helping her in and arranging rugs with the tenderest solicitude, but when they were settled and started—it was a coupé with a great deal of glass about it, so that they got plenty of air—he turned to her.

"Now, do you know what I am going to do with you, madame? I shall only unfold my plans bit by bit, and watch your face to see if I have chosen well. I am going to take you first to the Petit Trianon, and we are going to walk leisurely through the rooms. I am not going to worry you with much sight-seeing and tourists and lessons of history, but I want you to glance at this setting of the life picture of poor Marie Antoinette, because it is full of sentiment and it will make you appreciate more the *hameau* and her playground afterwards. Something tells me you would rather see these things than all the fine pictures and salons of the stiff château."

"Oh yes," said Theodora; "you have guessed well this time."

"Then here we are, almost arrived," he said, presently.

They had been going very fast, and could see the square, white house in front of them, and when they alighted at the gates she found the guardian was an old friend of Lord Bracondale's, and they were left free to wander alone in the rooms between the batches of tourists.

But every one knows the Petit Trianon, and can surmise how its beauties appealed to Theodora.

"Oh, the poor, poor queen!" she said, with a sad ring in her expressive voice, when they came to the large salon; "and she sat here and played on her harpsichord—and I wonder if she and Fersen were ever alone—and I wonder if she really loved him—"

Then she stopped suddenly; she had told herself she must never talk about love to any one. It was a subject that she must have nothing to do with. It could never come her way, now she was married to Josiah Brown, and it would be unwise to discuss it, even in the abstract.

The same beautiful, wild-rose tint tinged the white velvet as once before when she had spoken of *Jean d'Agrève*, and again Lord Bracondale experienced a sensation of satisfaction.

But this time he would not let her talk about the weather. The subject of love interested him, too.

"Yes, I am sure she did," he said, "and I always shall believe Fersen was her lover; no life, even a queen's, can escape one love."

"I suppose not," said Theodora, very low, and she looked out of the window.

"Love is not a passion which asks our leave if he may come or no, you see," Hector continued, trying to control his voice to sounddispassionate and discursive—he knew he must not frighten her. "Love comes in a thousand unknown, undreamed-of ways. And then he gilds the world and makes it into heaven."

"Does he?" almost whispered Theodora.

"And think what it must have been to a queen, married to a tiresome, unattractive Bourbon—and Fersen was young and gallant and thoughtful for her slightest good, and, from what one hears and has read, he must have understood her, and been her friend as well—and sometimes she must have forgotten about being a queen for a few moments—in his arms—"

Theodora drew a long, long breath, but she did not speak.

"And perhaps, if we knew, the remembrance of those moments may have been her glory and consolation in the last dark hours."

"Oh! I hope so!" said Theodora.

Then she walked on quickly into the quaint, little, low-ceilinged bedroom. Oh, she must get out into the air—or she must talk of furniture, or curtain stuffs, or where the bath had been!

Love, love, love! And did it mean life after all?—since even this far-off love of this poor dead queen had such power to move her. And perhaps Fersen was like—but this last thought caused her heart to beat too wildly.

There were no roses now, she was very pale as she said: "It saddens me, this. Let us go out into the sun."

They descended the staircase again almost in silence, and on through the little door in the court-yard wall into the beautiful garden beyond.

"Show me where she was happy, where you know she was happy before any troubles came. I want to be gay again," said Theodora.

So they walked down the path towards the *hameau.*

"What have I done?" Lord Bracondale wondered. "Her adorable face went quite white. Her soul is no longer the open book I have found it. There are depths and depths, but I must fathom them all."

"Oh, how I love the spring-time!" exclaimed Theodora, and her voice was full of relief. "Look at those greens, so tender and young, and that peep of the sky! Oh, and those dear, pretty little dolls' houses! Let us hasten; I want to go and play there, and make butter, too! Don't you?"

"Ah, this is good," he said; "and I want just what you want."

Her face was all sweet and joyous as she turned it to him.

"Let's pretend we lived then," she said, "and I am the miller's daughter of this dear little mill, and you are the bailiff's son who lives opposite, and you have come with your corn to be ground. Oh, and I shall make a bargain, and charge you dear!" and she laughed and swung her parasol back, while the sun glorified her hair into burnished silver.

"What bargain could you make that I would not agree to willingly?" he asked.

"Perhaps some day I shall make one with you—or want to—that you will not like," she said, "and then I shall remind you of this day and your gallant speech."

"And I shall say then as I say now. I will make any bargain with you, so long as it is a bargain which benefits us both."

"Ah, you are a Normand, you hedge!" she laughed, but he was serious.

They walked all around the *laiterie*, and all the time she was gay and whimsical, and to herself she was saying, "I am unutterably happy, but we must not talk of love."

"Now you have had enough of this," Lord Bracondale said, when they were again in view of the house, "and I am going to take you into a forest like the babes in the woods, and we shall go and lose ourselves and forget the world altogether. The very sight of these harmless tourists in the distance jars upon me to-day. I want you alone and no one else. Come."

And she went.

"I have never been here before," said Theodora, as they turned into the Forest of Marly. "And you have been wise in your choice so far. I love trees."

"You see how I study and care for the things which belong to me," said Hector. It gave him ridiculous pleasure to announce that sentence again—ridiculous, unwarrantable pleasure.

Theodora turned her head away a little. She would like to have continued the subject, but she did not dare.

Presently they came to a side *allée*, and after going up it about a mile the automobile stopped, and they got out and walked down a green glade to the right.

Oh, and I wonder if any of you who read know the Forest of Marly, and this one green glade that leads down to the centre of a star where five avenues meet? It is all soft grass and splendid trees, and may have been a *rendezvous de chasse* in the good old days, when life—for the great—was fair in France.

It is very lonely now, and if you want to spend some hours in peace you can almost count upon solitude there.

"Now, is not this beautiful?" he asked her, as they neared the centre, "and soon you will see why I carry this rug over my arm. I am going to take you right to the middle of the star until you see five paths for you to choose from, all green and full of glancing sunlight, and when you have selected one we will penetrate down it and sit under a tree. Is it good—my idea?"

"Very good," said Theodora. Then she was silent until they reached the *rond-point.*

There was that wonderful sense of aloofness and silence—hardly even the noise of a bird. Only the green, green trees, and here and there a shaft of sunlight turning them into the shade of a lizard's back.

An ideal spot for—poets and dreamers—and lovers—Theodora thought.

"Now we are here! Look this way and that! Five paths for us to choose from!"

Then something made Theodora say, "Oh, let us stay in the centre, in this one round place, where we can see them all and their possibilities."

"And do you think uncertain possibilities are more agreeable perhaps than certain ends?" he asked.

"I never speculate," said Theodora.

"As you will, then," he said, while he looked into her eyes, and he placed the rug up against a giant tree between two avenues, so that their view really only extended down three others now.

"We have turned our backs on the road we came," he said, "and on another road that leads in a roundabout way to the Grande Avenue again. So now we must look into the unknown and the future."

"It seems all very green and fair," said Theodora, and she leaned back against the tree and half closed her eyes.

He lay on the grass at her feet, his hat thrown off beside him, and in a desert island they could not have been more alone and undisturbed.

The greatest temptation that Hector Bracondale had ever yet had in his life came to him then. To make love to her, to tell her of all the new thoughts she had planted in his soul, of the windows she had opened wide to the sunlight. To tell her that he loved her, that he longed to touch even the tips of her fingers, that the thought of caressing her lips and her eyes and her hair drove the blood coursing madly through his veins. That to dream of what life could be like, if she were really his own, was a dream of intoxicating bliss.

And something of all this gleamed in his eyes as he gazed up at her—and Theodora, all unused to the turbulence of emotion, was troubled and moved and yet wildly happy. She looked away down the centre avenue, and she began to speak fast with a little catch in her breath, and Hector clinched his hands together and gazed at a beetle in the grass, or otherwise he would have taken her in his arms.

"Tell me the story of all these avenues," she said; "tell me a fairy story suitable to the day."

And he fell in with her mood. So he began:

"Once upon a time there was a fairy prince and princess, and a witch had enchanted them and put them in a green forest, but had set a watch-dog over Love—so that the poor Cupid with his bow and arrows might not shoot at them, and they were told they might live and enjoy the green wood and find what they could of sport and joy. But Cupid laughed. 'As if,' he said, 'there is anything in a green wood of good without me—and my shafts!' So while the watch-dog slept—it was a warm, warm day in May, just such as this—he shot an arrow at the prince and it entered his heart. Then he ran off laughing. 'That is enough for one day,' he said. And the poor prince suffered and suffered because he was wounded and the princess had not received a dart, too—and could not feel for him."

"Was she not even sympathetic?" asked Theodora, and again there was that catch in her breath.

"Yes, she was sympathetic," he continued, "but this was not enough for the prince; he wanted her to be wounded, too."

"How very, very cruel of him," said Theodora.

"But men are cruel, and the prince was only a man, you know, although he was in a green forest with a lovely princess."

"And what happened?" asked Theodora.

"Well, the watch-dog slept on, so that a friendly zephyr could come, and it whispered to the prince: 'At the end of all these allées, which lead into the future, there is only one thing, and that is Love; he bars their gates. As soon as you start down one, no matter which, you will find him, and when he sees your princess he will shoot an arrow at her, too.'"

"Oh, then the princess of course never went down an allée," said Theodora—and she smiled radiantly to hide how her heart was beating—"did she?"

"The end of the story I do not know," said Lord Bracondale; "the fairy who told it to me would not say what happened to them, only that the prince was wounded, deeply wounded, with Love's arrow. Aren't you sorry for the prince, beautiful princess?"

Theodora opened her blue parasol, although no ray of sunshine fell upon her there. She was going through the first moment of this sort in her life. She was quite unaccustomed to fencing, or to any intercourse with men—especially men of his world. She understood this story had himself and herself for hero and heroine; she felt she must continue the badinage—anything to keep the tone as light as it could be, with all these new emotions flooding her being and making her heart beat. It was almost pain she experienced, the sensation was so intense, and Hector read of these things in her eyes and was content. So he let his voice grow softer still, and almost whispered again:

"And aren't you sorry for the prince—beautiful princess?"

"I am sorry for any one who suffers," said Theodora, gently, "even in a fairy story."

And as he looked at her he thought to himself, here was a rare thing, a beautiful woman with a tender heart. He knew she would be gentle and kind to the meanest of God's creatures. And again the vision of her at Bracondale came to him—his mother would grow to love her perhaps even more than Morella Winmarleigh! How she would glorify everything commonplace with those tender ways of hers! To look at her was like looking up into the vast, pure sky, with the light of heaven beyond. And yet he lay on the grass at her feet with his mind full of thoughts and plans and desires to drag this angel down from her high heaven—into his arms!

Because he was a man, you see, and the time of his awakening was not yet.

X

Man is a hunter—a hunter always. He may be a poor thing and hunt only a few puny aims, or he may be a strong man and choose big game. But he is hunting, hunting—something—always.

And primitive life seems like the spectrum of light—composed of three primary colors, and white and black at the beginning and ending of it. And the three colors of blue, red, and yellow have their counterparts in the three great passions in man—to hunt his food, to continue his species, and to kill his enemy.

And white and black seem like birth and death—and there is the sun, which is the soul and makes the colors, and allows of all combinations and graduations of beautiful other shades from them for parallels to all other qualities and instincts, only the original are those great primary forces—to hunt his food, to continue his species, and to kill his enemy.

And if this is so to the end of time, man will be the same, I suppose, until civilization has emasculated the whole of nature and so ends the world! Or until this wonderful new scientist has perfected his researches to the point of creating human life by chemical process, as well as his present discovery of animating jellyfish!

Who knows? But by that time it will not matter to any of us!

Meanwhile, man is at the stage that when he loves a woman he wishes to possess her, and, in a modified form, he wishes to steal her, if necessary, from another, or kill the enemy who steals her from him.

But the Sun of the Soul is there, too, so the poor old world is not in such a very bad case after all.

And how the *bon Dieu* must smile sadly to Himself when He looks down on priests and nuns and hermits and fanatics, and sees how they have distorted His beautiful scheme of things with their narrow ideas. Trying to eliminate the red out of His spectrum, instead of ennobling and glorifying it all with the Sun of the Soul.

And all of you who are great reasoners and arguers will laugh at this ridiculous little simile of life drawn by a woman; but I do not care. I have had my outburst, and said what I wanted to. So now we can get back to the two—who were not yet lovers—under their green tree in the Forest of Marly.

"But you must be able to guess the end," Theodora was saying; "and oh, I want to know, if all the roads were barred by love—how did they get out of the wood?"

"They took him with them," said Lord Bracondale, and he touched the edge of her dress gently with a wild flower he had picked in the grass, while into his eyes crept all the passion he felt and into his voice all the tenderness.

Now if Theodora had ever read *La Faute de L'Abbé Mouret* she would have known just what proximity and the spring-time was doing for them both.

But she had not read, and did not know. All she was conscious of was a wild thrilling of her pulses, an extraordinary magnetic force that seemed to draw her—draw her nearer—nearer to what? Even that she did not know or ask herself. Beyond that it was danger, and she must fly from it.

"I do not want to talk of any of those things to-day," she said, suddenly dropping her parasol between them. "I only want to laugh and be amused, and as you were to devise schemes for my happiness, you must amuse me."

He looked up at her again and he noticed, for all this brave speech, that her hands were trembling as she clutched the handle of her blue parasol.

Triumph and joy ran through him. He could afford to wait a little longer now, since he knew that he must mean something, even perhaps a great deal, to her.

And so for the next half-hour he played with her, he skimmed over the surface of danger, he enthralled her fancy, and with every sentence he threw the glamour of his love around her, and fascinated her soul. All his powers of attraction—and they were many—were employed for her undoing.

And Theodora sat as one in a dream.

At last she felt she *must* wake—must realize that she was not a happy princess, but Theodora, who must live her dull life—and this—and this—where was it leading her to?

So she clasped her hands together suddenly, and she said:

"But do you know we have grown serious, and I asked you to amuse me, Lord Bracondale!"

"I cannot amuse you," he said, lazily, "but shall I tell you about my home, which I should like to show you some day?" And again he began to caress the farthest edge of her dress with his wild flower. Just the smallest movement of smoothing it up and down that no one could resent, but which was disturbing to Theodora. She did not wish him to stop, on the contrary—and yet—

"Yes, I would like to hear of that," she said. "Is it an old, old house?"

"Oh, moderately so, and it has nooks and corners and views that might appeal to you. I believe I should find them all endowed with fresh charm myself, if I could see them with you"—and he made the turning-point of his flower a few inches nearer her hand.

Theodora said nothing; but she took courage and peeped at him again. And she thought how powerful he looked, and how beautifully shaped; and she liked the fineness of the silk of his socks and his shirt, and the cut of his clothes, and the wave of his hair—and last of all, his brown, strong, well-shaped hands.

And then she fell to wondering what the general scheme of things could be that made husbands possess none of these charms; when, if they did, it could all be so good and so delicious, instead of a terribly irksome duty to live with them and be their wives.

"You are not listening to a word I am saying!" said Hector. "Where were your thoughts, cruel lady?"

She was confused a little, and laughed gently. "They were away in a land where you can never come," she said.

He raised himself on his elbow, and supported his head on his hand, while he answered, eagerly:

"But I must come! I want to know them, all your thoughts. Do you know that since we met on Monday you have never been for one instant out of my consciousness. And you would not listen then to what I told you of friendship when it is born of instantaneous sympathy—it is because in some other life two souls have been very near and dear. And that is our case, and I want to make you feel it so, as I do. Tell me that you do—?"

"I do not know what I do feel," said Theodora. "But perhaps—could it be true that we met when we lived before; and when was that? and who were we?"

"It matters not a jot," said he. "So long as you feel it too—that we are not only of yesterday, you and I. There is some stronger link between us."

For one second they looked into each other's eyes, and each read the other's thoughts mirrored there; and if his said, in conscious, passionate words, "I love you," hers were troubled and misty with possibilities. Then she jumped up from her seat suddenly, and her voice trembled a little as she said:

"And now I want to go out of the wood."

He rose too and stood beside her, while he pointed to the glade to the left of the centre they were facing.

"We must penetrate into the future then," he said, "because I told my chauffeur to meet us on the road where I think that will lead to. We cannot go back by the way we have come."

And she did not answer; she was afraid, because she remembered all those avenues were barred by—love.

As he walked beside her, Hector Bracondale knew that now he must be very, very careful in what he said. He must lull her fears to sleep again, or she would be off like a lark towards high heaven, and he would be left upon earth.

So he exerted himself to interest and amuse her in less agitating ways. He talked of his home and his mother and his sister. He wanted Theodora to meet them. She would like Anne, he said, and his mother would love her, he knew. And again the impossible vision same to him, and he felt he hated the face of Morella Winmarleigh.

Usually when he had been greatly attracted by a married woman before, he had unconsciously thought of her as having the qualities which would make her an adorable mistress, a delicious friend, or a holiday amusement. There had never been any reverence mixed up with the affair, which usually had the zest of forbidden fruit, and was hurried along by passion. It had always only depended upon the woman how far he had got beyond these stages; but, as he thought of Theodora, unconsciously a picture always came to him of what she would be were she his wife. And it astonished him when he analyzed it; he, the scoffer at bonds, now to find this picture the fairest in the world!

And as yet he was hardly even dimly growing to realize that fate would turn the anguish of this desire into a chastisement of scorpions for him.

Things had always been so within his grasp.

"We shall go to England on Tuesday," Theodora said, as they sauntered along down the green glade. "It is so strange, you know, but I have never been there."

"Never been to England!" Hector exclaimed, incredulously.

"No!" and she smiled up at him. All was at peace now in her mind, and she dared to look as much as she pleased.

"No. Papa used to go sometimes, but it was too expensive to take the whole family; so we were left at Bruges generally, or at Dieppe, or where we chanced to be. If it was the summer, often we have spent it in a Normandy farm-house."

"Then how have you learned all the things you know?" he asked.

"That was not difficult. I do not know much," she said, gently, "and Sarah taught me in the beginning, and then I went to convents whenever we were in towns, and dear papa was so kind and generous always; no matter how hard up he was he always got the best masters available for me—and for Clementine. Sarah is much older, and even Clementine five years."

"I wonder what on earth you will think of it—England, I mean?" He was deeply interested.

"I am sure I shall love it. We have always spoken of it as home, you know. And papa has often described my grandfather's houses. Both my grandfathers had beautiful houses, it seems, and he says, now that I am rich and cannot ever be a trouble to them, the family might be pleased to see me."

She spoke quite simply. There never was room for bitterness or irony in her tender heart. And Hector looked down upon her, a sort of worship in his eyes.

"Papa's father is dead long ago; it is his brother who owns Beechleigh now," she continued—"Sir Patrick Fitzgerald. They are Irish, of course, but the place is in Cambridgeshire, because it came from his grandmother."

"Yes, I know the old boy," said Hector. "I see him at the turf—a fiery, vile-tempered, thin, old bird, about sixty."

"That sounds like him," said Theodora.

"And so you are going to make all these relations' acquaintance. What an experience it will be, won't it?" His voice was full of sympathy. "But you will stay in London. They are all there now, I suppose?"

"My Grandfather Borringdon, my mother's father, never goes there, I believe; he is very old and delicate, we have heard. But I have written to him—papa wished me to do so; for myself I do not care, because I think he was unkind to my mother, and I shall not like him. It was cruel never to speak to her again—wasn't it?—just because she married papa, whom she loved very much—papa, who is so handsome that he could never have really been a husband, could he?"

Then she blushed deeply, realizing what she had said.

And the quaintness of it caused Hector to smile while he felt its pathos.

How *could* they all have sacrificed this beautiful young life between them! And he slashed off a tall green weed with his stick when he thought of Josiah Brown—his short, stumpy, plebeian figure and bald, shiny head, his common voice, and his pompousness—Josiah Brown, who had now the ordering of her comings and goings, who paid for her clothes and gave her those great pearls—who might touch her and kiss her—might clasp and caress her—might hold her in his arms, his very own, any moment of the day—or night! Ah, God! that last thought was impossible—unbearable.

And for one second Hector's eyes looked murderous as they glared into the distance—and Theodora glanced up timidly, and asked, in a sympathetic voice: What was it? What ailed him?

"Some day I will tell you," he said. "But not yet."

Then he asked her more about her family and her plans.

They would stay in London at Claridge's for a week or so, and go down to Bessington Hall for Whitsuntide. It would be ready for them then. Josiah had had it all furnished magnificently by one of those people who had taste and ordered well for those who could afford to pay for it. She was rather longing to see it, she said—her future home—and she could have wished she might have chosen the things herself. Not that it mattered much either way.

"I am very ignorant about houses," she explained, "because we never really had one, you see, but I think, perhaps, I would know what was pretty from museums and pictures—and I love all colors and forms."

He felt sure she would know what was pretty. How delightful it would be to watch her playing with his old home! The touches of her gentle fingers would make everything sacred afterwards.

At last they came to the end of the green glade—and temptation again assailed him. He *must* ruffle the peace of her soft eyes once more.

"And here is the barrier," he said, pointing to a board with "*Terrain réservé*" upon it—*Réserveé pour la chasse de Monsieur le Président*, "The barrier which Love keeps—and I want to take him with us as the prince and princess did in the fairy tale."

"Then you must carry him all by yourself," laughed Theodora. "And he will be heavy and tire you, long before we get to Versailles."

This time she was on her guard—and besides they were walking—and he was no longer caressing the edge of her dress with his wild flower; it was almost easy to fence now.

But when they reached the automobile and he bent over to tuck the rug in—and she felt the touch of his hands and perceived the scent of him—the subtle scent, not a perfume hardly, of his coat, or his hair, a wild rush of that passionate disturbance came over her again, making her heart beat and her eyes dilate.

And Hector saw and understood, and bit his lips, and clinched his hands together under the rug, because so great was his own emotion that he feared what he should say or do. He dared not, dared not chance a dismissal from the joy of her presence forever, after this one day.

"I will wait until I know she loves me enough to certainly forgive me—and then, and then—" he said to himself.

But Fate, who was looking on, laughed while she chanted, "The hour is now at hand when these steeds of passion whose reins you have left loose so long will not ask your leave, noble friend, but will carry you whither they will."

XI

They were both a little constrained upon the journey back to Versailles—and both felt it. But when they turned into the Porte St. Antoine Theodora woke up.

"Do you know," she said, "something tells me that for a long, long time I shall not again have such a happy day. It can't be more than half-past five or six—need we go back to the Reservoirs yet? Could we not have tea at the little café by the lake?"

He gave the order to his chauffeur, and then he turned to her.

"I, too, want to prolong it all," he said, "and I want to make you happy—always."

"It is only lately that I have begun to think about things," she said, softly—"about happiness, I mean, and its possibilities and impossibilities. I think before my marriage I must have been half asleep, and very young."

And Hector thought, "You are still, but I shall awake you."

"You see," she continued, "I had never read any novels, or books about life until *Jean d'Agrève*. And now I wonder sometimes if it is possible to be really happy—really, really happy?"

"I know it is," he said; "but only in one way."

She did not dare to ask in what way. She looked down and clasped her hands.

"I once thought," she went on, hurriedly, "that I was perfectly happy the first time Josiah gave me two thousand francs, and told me to go out with my maid and buy just what I wished with it; and oh, we bought everything I could think Sarah and Clementine could want, numbers and numbers of things, and I remember I was fearfully excited when they were sent off to Dieppe. But I never knew if I chose well or if they liked them all quite, and now to do that does not give me nearly so much joy."

Soon they drew up at the little café and ordered tea, which he guessed probably would be very bad and they would not drink. But tea was English, and more novel than coffee for Theodora, and that she must have, she said.

She was so gracious and sweet in the pouring of it out, when presently it came, and the elderly waiter seemed so sympathetic, and it was all gay and bright with the late afternoon sun streaming upon them.

"The garçon takes us for a honeymoon couple," Hector said; "he sees you have beautiful new clothes, and that we have not yet begun to yawn with each other."

But Theodora had not this view of honeymoons. To her a honeymoon meant a nightmare, now happily a thing of the past, and almost forgotten.

"Do not speak of it," she said, and she put out her hands as if to ward off an ugly sight, and Hector bent over the table and touched her fingers gently as he said:

"Forgive me," and he raged within himself. How could he have been so gauche, so clumsy and unlike himself. He had punished them both, and destroyed an illusion. He meant that she should picture herself and him as married lovers, and she had only seen—Josiah Brown. They both fell into silence and so finished their repast.

"I want you to walk now," Hector said, "through some delicious allées where I will show you Encelădus after he was struck by the thunders of Zeus. You will like him, I think, and there is fine greensward around him where we can sit awhile."

"I was always sorry for him," said Theodora; "and oh, how I would like to go to Sicily and see Ætna and his fiery breath coming forth, and to know when the island quakes it is the poor giant turning his weary side!"

To go to Sicily—and with her! The picture conjured up in Hector's imagination made him thrill again.

Then he told her about it all, he charmed her fancy and excited her imagination, and by the time they came to their goal the feeling of jar had departed, and the dangerous sense of attraction—of nearness—had returned.

It was nearly seven o'clock, and here among the trees all was in a soft gloom of evening light.

"Is not this still and far away?" he said, as they sat on an old stone bench. "I often stay the whole morning here when I spend a week at Versailles."

"How peaceful and beautiful! Oh, I would like a week here, too!" and Theodora sighed.

"You must not sigh, beautiful princess," he implored, "on this our happy day."

The slender lines of her figure seemed all drooping. She reminded him more than ever of the fragment of Psyche in the Naples Museum.

"No, I must not sigh," she said. "But it seems suddenly to have grown sad—the air—what does it mean? Tell me, you who know so many things?" There was a pathos in her voice like a child in distress.

It communicated itself to him, it touched some chords in his nature hitherto silent. His whole being rushed out to her in tenderness.

"It seems to me it is because the time grows nearer when we must go back to the world. First to dinner with the others, and then—Paris. I would like to stay thus always—just alone with you."

She did not refute this solution of her sadness. She knew it was true. And when he looked into her eyes, the blue was troubled with a mist as of coming tears.

Then passion—more mighty than ever—seized him once more. He only felt a wild desire to comfort her, to kiss away the mist—to talk to her. Ah!

"Theodora!" he said, and his voice vibrated with emotion, while he bent forward and seized both her hands, which he lifted to his face—she had not put on her gloves again after the tea—her cool, little, tender hands! He kissed and kissed their palms.

"Darling—darling," he said, incoherently, "what have I done to make your dear eyes wet? Oh, I love you so, I love you so, and I have only made you sad."

She gave a little, inarticulate cry. If a wounded dove could sob, it might have been the noise of a dove, so beseeching and so pathetic. "Oh, please—you must not," she said. "Oh, what have you done!—you have killed our happy day."

And this was the beginning of his awakening. He sat for many moments with his head buried in his hands. What, indeed, had he done!—and they would be turned out of their garden of Eden—and all because he was a brute, who could not control his passion, but must let it run riot on the first opportunity.

He suffered intensely. Suffered, perhaps, for the first time in his life.

She had not said one word of anger—only that tone in her voice reached to his heart.

He did not move and did not speak, and presently she touched his hands softly with her slender fingers, it seemed like the caress of an angel's wing.

"Listen," she said, so gently. "Oh, you must not grieve—but it was too good to be true, our day. I ought to have known to where we were drifting, I am wicked to have let you say all you have said to-day, but oh, I was asleep, I think, and I only knew that I was happy. But now you have shown me—and oh, the dream is broken up. Come, let us go back to the world."

Then he raised his eyes to her face, and they were haggard and miserable.

How her simple speech, blaming herself who was all innocent, touched his heart and filled him with shame at his unworthiness.

"Oh, forgive me!" he pleaded. "Oh, please forgive me! I am mad, I think, I love you so—and I had to tell you—and yes, I will say it all now, and then you can punish me. From the first moment I looked into your angel eyes it has been growing, you are so true and so sweet, and so miles beyond all other women in the world. Each minute I have loved you more—and all the time I thought to win you. Yes, you may well turn away, and shrink from me now that you know the brute I am. I thought I would make you love me, and you would forgive me then. But I have suddenly seen your soul, my darling, and I am ashamed, and I can only ask you to forgive me and let me worship you and be your slave—I will not ask for any return—only to worship you and be your slave—that I may show you I am not all brute and may earn your pardon."

And then Theodora's blindness fell from her and she knew that she loved him—she had faced the fact at last. And all over her being there thrilled a mad, wild joy. It surged up and crushed out fear and pain—for just one moment—and then she too, in her turn, covered her face with her hands.

"Oh, hush! hush!" she said. "What have you done—what have we both done!"

It was characteristic of her that now she realized she loved him she did not fence any longer, she never thought of concealing it from him or of blaming him. They were sinners both, he and she equally guilty.

Another woman might have argued, "He is fooling me; perhaps he has said these things before—I must at least hide my own heart," but not Theodora. Her trust was complete—she loved him—therefore he was a perfect knight—and if he was wicked she was wicked too.

Her gentian eyes were full of tears as she let fall her hands and looked at him. "Oh yes, I have been asleep—I should have known from the beginning why, why I wanted to see you so much—I should never have come—and I should have understood in the wood that we could not leave it without bringing Love with us—and now we may not be happy any more."

And then it was his turn to be exalted with wild joy.

"Do you know what you have said," he whispered, breathless. "Your words mean that you love me—Theodora—darling mine." And once again passion blazed in his eyes, and he would have taken her in his arms; but she put up her hands and gently pushed him from her.

"Yes," she said, simply, "I love you, but that only makes it all the harder—and we must say good-bye at once, and go our different ways. You who are so strong and know so much—I trust you, dear—you must help me to do what is right."

She never thought of reproaching him, of telling him, as she very well could have done, that he had taken cruel advantage of her unsophistication. All her mind was full of the fact that they were both very sad and wicked and must help each other.

"I *cannot* say good-bye," he said, "now that I know you love me, darling; it is impossible. How can we part—what will the days be—how could we get through our lives?"

She looked at him, and her eyes were the eyes of a wounded thing—dumb and pitiful, and asking for help.

Then the something that was fine and noble in Hector Bracondale rose up in him—the crust of selfishness and cynicism fell from him like a mask. He suddenly saw himself as he was, and she—as she was—and a determination came over him to grow worthy of her love, obey her slightest wish, even if it must break his heart.

He dropped upon his knees beside her on the greensward, and buried his face in her lap.

"Darling—my queen," he said. "I will do whatever you command—but oh, it need not be good-bye. Don't let me sicken and die out of your presence. I swear, on my word of honor, I will never trouble you. Let me worship you and watch over you and make your life brighter. Oh, God! there can be no sin in that."

"I trust you!" she said, and she touched the waves of his hair. "And now we must not linger—we must come at once out of this place. I—I cannot bear it any more."

And so they went—into an *allée* of close, cropped trees, where the gloom was almost twilight; but if there was pain there was joy too, and almost peace in their hearts.

All the anguish was for the afterwards. Love, who is a god, was too near to his kingdom to admit of any rival.

"Hector," she whispered, and as she said his name a wild thrill ran through him again. "Hector—the Austrian Prince at Armenonville said life was a current down which our barks floated, only to be broken up on the rocks if it was our fate; and I said if we tried very hard some angel would steer us past them into smooth waters beyond; and I want you to help me to find the angel, dear—will you?"

But all he could say was that she was the angel, the only angel in heaven or earth.

And so they came at last to the Bason de Neptune, and on through the side door into the Réservoirs—and there was the widow's automobile that moment arrived.

XII

Every one behaved with immense propriety—they said just what they should have said, there was no *gêne* at all. And when they went up the stairs together to arrange their hair and their hats for dinner, the elder woman slipped her arm through Theodora's.

"I am going to marry your father, my dear," she said, "and I want you to be the first to wish me joy."

The dinner went off with great gayety. The widow especially was full of bright sayings, and Captain Fitzgerald made the most devoted lover. Not too elated by his good-fortune, and yet thoroughly happy and tender. He continually told himself that fate had been uncommonly kind to mix business and pleasure so dexterously, for if the widow had not possessed a cent, he still would have been glad to marry her.

He had been quite honest with her on their drive, explaining his financial situation and his disadvantages, which he said could only be slightly balanced by his devotion and affection—but of those he would lay the whole at her feet.

And the widow had said:

"Now look here, I am old enough just to know what my money is worth—and if you like to put it as a business speculation for me, I consider, in buying the companion for the rest of my life who happens to suit me, I am laying out the sum to my own advantage."

After that there was no more to be said, and he had spent his time making love to her like any Romeo of twenty, and both were content.

All through dinner a certain strange excitement dominated Theodora. She felt there would be more deep emotion yet to come for her before the day should close.

How were they going back to Paris?

The moon had risen pure and full, she could see it through the windows. The night was soft and warm, and when the last sips of coffee and liqueurs were finished it was still only nine o'clock.

On an occasion when no personal excitement was stirring Captain Fitzgerald he probably would have hesitated about approving of Theodora spending the entire evening alone with Lord Bracondale. She was married, it was true—but to Josiah Brown—and Dominic Fitzgerald knew his world. To-night, however, neither the widow nor he had outside thoughts beyond themselves. Indeed, Mrs. McBride was so overflowing with joy she had almost a feeling of satisfaction in the knowledge that the others would possibly be happy too—when she thought of them at all!

Again she decided the situation for every one, and again fate laughed.

There was no use staying any longer at Versailles, because the park gates were shut and they could not stroll in the moonlight, but a drive back and a few turns in the Bois with a little supper at Madrid would be a fitting ending to the day.

"You must meet us at Madrid at half-past ten," she said; "and Dominic"—the name came out as if from long habit—"telephone for a table in the bosquet—Numero 3—I like that garçon best, he knows my wants."

And so they got into their separate automobiles.

"Let us have all the windows down," said Theodora, "to get all the beautiful air—it is such a lovely night."

Her heart was beating as it had never beat before. How could she control herself! How keep calm and ordinary during the enchanting drive! Her hands were cold as ice, while flaming roses burned in the white velvet cheeks.

And Hector saw it all and understood, and passion surged madly in his veins. For a mile or two there was silence—only the moonlight and the swift rushing through the air, and the wild beating of their hearts. And so they came to the long, dark stretch of wood by St. Cloud. And the devil whispered sophistries and fate continued to laugh. Then passion was too strong for him.

"Darling," he said, and his fine resolutions fled to the winds, while his deep voice was hoarse and broken. "My darling!—God! I love you so—beyond all words or sense—Oh, let us be happy for this one night—we must part afterwards I know, and I will accept that—but just for to-night there can be no sin and no harm in being a little happy—when we are going to pay for it with all the rest of our lives. Let us have the memory of one hour of bliss—the angels themselves could not grudge us that."

One hour of bliss out of a lifetime! Would it be a terrible sin, Theodora wondered, a terrible, unforgivable sin to let him kiss her—to let him hold her just once in his arms.

There was no light in the coupé—he had seen to that—only the great lamps flaring in the road and the moonlight.

She clasped her hands in an agony of emotion. She was but a dove in the net of an experienced fowler, but she did not know or think of that, nor he either. They only knew they loved each other passionately, and this situation was more than they could bear.

"Oh, I trust you!" she said. "If you tell me it is not a terrible sin I will believe you—I do not know—I cannot think—I—"

But she could speak no more because she was in his arms.

The intense, unutterable joy—the maddening, intoxicating bliss of the next hour! To have her there, unresisting—to caress her lips and eyes and hair—to murmur love words—to call her his very own! Nothing in heaven could equal this, and no hell was a price too great to pay—so it seemed to him. It was the supremest moment of his life; and how much more of hers who knew none other, who had never received the kisses of men or thrilled to any touch but his!

After a little she drew herself away and shivered. She knew she was wicked now—very, very wicked—but it was again characteristic of her that having made her decision there was no vacillation about her. The die was cast—for that night they were to be happy, and all the rest of her life should be penitence and atonement.

But to-night there was no room for anything but joy. She had never dreamed in her most secret thoughts of moments so gloriously sweet as these—to have a lover—and such a lover! And it was true—it must be true—that they had lived before, and all this passion was not the growth of one short week.

It seemed as if it was all her life, all her being—it could mean nothing now but Hector—Hector—Hector! And over and over again he made her whisper in his ear that she loved him—nor could she ever tire of hearing him say he worshipped her.

Oh, they were foolish and tender and wonderful, as lovers always are.

He had given his orders beforehand and the chauffeur was a man of intelligence. They drove in the most beautiful *allée* when they came to the Bois—and no incident ruffled the exquisite peace and bliss of their time.

Suddenly Hector became aware of the fact it was just upon half-past ten, and they were almost in sight of Madrid, which would end it all.

And a pang of hideous pain shot through him, and he did not speak.

In the distance the lights blazed into the night, and the sight of them froze Theodora to ice.

It was finished then—their hour of joy.

"My darling," he exclaimed, passionately, "good-bye, and remember all my life is in your hands, and I will spend it in worship of you and thankfulness for this hour of yourself you have given to me. I am yours to do with as you will until death do us part."

"And I," said Theodora, "will never love another man—and if we have sinned we have sinned together—and now, oh, Hector, we must face our fates."

Her voice tore his very heartstrings in its unutterable pathos.

And in that last passionate kiss it seemed as if they exchanged their very souls.

Then they drove into the glare of the restaurant lights, having tasted of the knowledge of good and evil.

XIII

"What have I done? What have I done?" Hector groaned to himself in anguish as he paced up and down his room at the Ritz an hour after the party had broken up, and he had driven Mrs. McBride back in his automobile, leaving hers to father and daughter.

All through supper Theodora had sat limp and white as death, and every time she had looked at him her eyes had reminded him of a fawn he had wounded once at Bracondale, in the park, with his bow and arrow, when he was a little boy. He remembered how fearfully proud he had been as he saw it fall, and then how it had lain in his arms and bled and bled, and its tender eyes had gazed at him in no reproach, only sorrow and pain, and a dumb asking why he had hurt it.

All the light of the stars seemed quenched, no eyes in the world had ever looked so unutterably pathetic as Theodora's eyes, and gradually as they sat and talked platitudes and chaffed with the elderly fiancées, it had come to him how cruel he had been—he who had deliberately used every art to make her love him—and now, having gained his end, what could he do for her? What for himself? Nothing but sorrow faced them both. He had taken brutal advantage of her gentleness and innocence—when chivalry alone should have made him refrain.

He saw himself as he was—the hunter and she the hunted—and the knowledge that he would pay with all the anguish and regret of a passionate, hopeless love—perhaps for the rest of his life—did not balance things to his awakened soul. If his years should be one long, gnawing ache for her, what of hers? And she was so young. His life, at all events, was a free one; but hers tied to Josiah Brown! And this thought drove him to madness. She belonged to Josiah Brown—not to him whom she loved—but to Josiah Brown, plebeian and middle-aged and exacting. He knew now that he ought to have gone away at once, the next day after they had met. His whole course of conduct had been weak and absolutely self-indulgent and wicked.

Who was he to dare to have raised his eyes to this angel, and try to scorch even the hem of her clothing! And now he had only brought suffering upon her and dimmed the light in God's two stars, which were her eyes.

And then wild passion shook him, and he could only live again the divine moments when she had nestled unresisting in his arms. Would it have made things better or worse if he had not yielded to the temptation of that hour of night and solitude?

After all, the sin was in making her love him, not in just holding her and kissing her lips. And at least, at least, they would have that exquisite memory of moments of unutterable bliss to keep for the rest of their lives.

His windows were wide open, and he leaned upon the balcony and gazed out at the moon. What good had all his life been? What benefit had he brought to any one? Then he seemed to see a clear vision of Theodora's short existence. Every picture she had unconsciously shown him was of some gentle thought of unselfishness for others.

And now he had laid a burden upon her shoulders, when he would not hurt a hair of her head—that dear, exquisite head which had lain upon his breast only two hours ago, and could never lie there again. He knew this was the end.

Then anguish and remorse seized him, and he buried his face on his crossed arms.

And Theodora staggered up to her room like one half dead. Mercifully Josiah Brown, had gone to bed, leaving a message with Henriette, Theodora's maid, that on no account was she to make any noise or disturb him.

Henriette adored her mistress—as who did not who served her?—and she felt distressed to see madame so pale. Doubtless madame had had a most tiring day. Madame had, and was thankful when at last she was left alone with her thoughts. Then she, too, opened wide the windows and gazed at the moon.

She had no cause for remorse for evil conduct like Hector. She had made no plans for the entrapping of any soul, and yet she felt forlorn and wicked. Oh yes, she was awake now and knew where she had been drifting. And so love had come at last, and indeed, indeed it meant life. This blast had struck her, and she had been blind in not recognizing it at once.

But oh, how sweet it was!—love—and it seemed as if it could make everything good and fair. If he and she who loved each other could have belonged to each other, surely they might have shed joy and gladness and kindness on all around.

Then she lay on her bed and did not try to reason any more; she only knew she loved Hector Bracondale with all her heart and being, and that she was married to Josiah Brown.

And what would the days be when she never saw him? And he, too, he would be sad—and then there was poor Josiah—who was so generous to her. He could not help being vulgar and unsympathetic, and her duty was to make him happy. Well, she could do that, she would try her very best to do that.

But thrills ran through her with the recollection of the moments in the drive to Paris—oh, why had no one told her or warned her all her life about this good thing love? At last, worn out with all emotions, sleep gently closed her eyes.

And fate up above laughed no more. Her sport was over for a time, she had made a sorry ending to their happy day.

XIV

Josiah had been too much fatigued on his machinery hunt with Mr. Clutterbuck R. Tubbs. They had lunched too richly, he said, and stood about too long, and so all the Sunday he was peevish and fretful, and required Theodora's constant attention. She must sit by his bedside all the morning, and drive round and round all the afternoon.

He told her she was not looking well. These excursions did not suit either of them, and he would be glad to get to England.

He asked a few questions about Versailles, and Theodora vouchsafed no unnecessary information. Nor did she tell him of her father's good-fortune. The widow had expressly asked her not to. She wished it to appear in the New York *Herald* first of all, she said. And they could have a regular rejoicing at the banquet on Monday night.

"Men are all bad," she had told Theodora during their ante-dinner chat. "Selfish brutes most of them; but nature has arranged that we happen to want them, and it is not for me to go against nature. Your father is a gentleman and he keeps me from yawning, and I have enough money to be able to indulge that and whatever other caprices I may have acquired; so I think we shall be happy. But a man in the abstract—don't amount to much!" And Theodora had laughed, but now she wondered if ever she would think it was true. Would Hector ever appear in the light of a caprice she could afford, to keep her from yawning? Could she ever truly say, "He don't amount to much!" Alas! he seemed now to amount to everything in the world.

The unspeakable flatness of the day! The weariness! The sense of all being finished! She did not even allow herself to speculate as to what Hector was doing with himself. She must never let her thoughts turn that way at all if she could help it. She must devote herself to Josiah and to getting through the time. But something had gone out of her life which could never come back, and also something had come in. She was awake—she, too, had lived for one moment like in *Jean d'Agrève*—and it seemed as if the whole world were changed.

Captain Fitzgerald did not appear all day, so the Sunday was composed of unadulterated Josiah. But it was only when Theodora was alone at last late at night, and had opened wide her windows and again looked out on the moon, that a little cry of anguish escaped her, and she remembered she would see Hector to-morrow at the dinner-party. See him casually, as the rest of the guests, and this is how it would be forever—for ever and ever.

Lord Bracondale had passed what he termed a dog's day. He had gone racing, and there had met, and been bitterly reproached by, Esclarmonde de Chartres for his neglect.

Qu'est-ce qu'il a eu pour toute une semaine?

He had important business in England, he said, and was going off at once; but she would find the bracelet she had wished for waiting for her at her apartment, and so they parted friends.

He felt utterly revolted with all that part of his life.

He wanted nothing in the world but Theodora. Theodora to worship and cherish and hold for his own. And each hour that came made all else seem more empty and unmeaning.

Just before dinner he went into the widow's sitting-room. She was alone, Marie had said in the passage—resting, she thought, but madame would certainly see milord. She had given orders for him to be admitted should he come.

"Now sit down near me, beau jeune homme," Mrs. McBride commanded from the depths of her sofa, where she was reclining, arrayed in exquisite billows of chiffon and lace. "I have been expecting you. It is not because I have been indulging in a little sentiment myself that my eyes are glued shut—you have a great deal to confess—and I hope we have not done too much harm between us."

Hector wanted sympathy, and there was something in the widow's directness which he felt would soothe him. He knew her good heart. He could speak freely to her, too, without being troubled by an over-delicacy of *mauvaise honte*, as he would have been with an Englishwoman. It would not have seemed sacrilege to the widow to discuss with him—who was a friend—the finest and most tender sentiments of her own, or any one else's, heart. He drew up a *bergère* and kissed her hand.

"I have been behaving like a damned scoundrel," he said.

"My gracious!" exclaimed Mrs. McBride, with a violent jerk into a sitting position. "You don't say—"

Then, for the first time for many years, a deep scarlet blush overspread Hector's face, even up to his forehead—as he realized how she had read his speech—how most people of the world would have read it. He got up from his chair and walked to the window.

"Oh, good God!" he said, "I don't mean that."

The widow fell back into her pillows with a sigh of relief.

"I mean I have deliberately tried to make her unhappy, and I have succeeded—and myself, too."

"That is not so bad then," and she settled a cushion. "Because unhappiness is only a thing for a time. You are crazy for the moon, and you can't get it, and you grieve and curse for a little, and then a new moon arises. What else?"

"Well, I want you to sympathize with me, and tell me what I had better do. Shall I go back to England to-morrow morning, or stay for the dinner-party?"

"You got as far, then, as telling each other you loved each other madly—and are both suffering from broken hearts, after one week's acquaintance."

"Don't be so brutal!" pleaded Hector.

And she noticed that his face looked haggard and changed. So her shrewd, kind eyes beamed upon him.

"Yes, I dare say it hurts; but having broken up your cake, you can't go on eating it. Why, in Heaven's name, did you let affairs get to a climax?"

"Because I am mad," said Hector, and he stretched out his arms. "I cannot tell you how much I love her. Haven't you seen for yourself what a darling she is? Every dear word she speaks shows her beautiful soul, and it all creeps right into my heart. I worship her as I might an angel, but I want her in my arms."

Mrs. McBride knew the English. They were not emotional or *poseurs* like some other nations, and Hector Bracondale was essentially a man of the world, and rather a whimsical cynic as well. So to see him thus moved must mean great things. She was guilty, too, for helping to create the situation. She must do what she could for him, she felt.

"You should pull yourself together, mon cher Bracondale," she said; "it is not like you to be limp and undecided. You had better stay for the party, and make yourself behave like a gentleman, and how you mean to continue. We have passed the days when 'Oh no, we never mention him' is the order, and 'never meeting,' and that sort of thing. You are bound to meet unless you go into the wilds. And you must face it and try to forget her."

"I can never forget her," he said, in a deep voice; "but, as you say, I must face it and do my best."

"You see," continued the widow, "the girl has only been married a year, and her husband is the most unattractive human being you could find along a sidewalk of miles; but he is her husband, anyway, and she may have children."

Hector clinched his hands in a convulsive movement of anguish and rage.

"And you must realize all these possibilities, and settle a path for yourself and stick to it."

"Oh, I couldn't bear that!" he said. "It would be better I should take her away myself now, to-day."

"You will do no such thing!" said the widow, sternly, and she sat up again. "You forget I am going to marry her father, and I shall look upon her as my daughter and protect her from wolves—do you hear? And what is more, she is too good and true to go with you. She has a backbone if you haven't; and she'll see it her duty to stick to that lump of middle-class meat she is bound to—and she'll do her best, if she suffers to heart-break. It is she, the poor, little white dove, that you and I have wounded between us, that I pity, not you—great, strong man!"

Mrs. McBride's eyes flashed.

"Oh, you are all the same, you Englishmen. Beasts to kill and women to subjugate—the only aims in life!"

"Don't!" said Hector. "I am not the animal you think me. I worship Theodora, and I would devote my life and its best aims to secure her happiness and do her honor; but don't you see you have drawn a picture that would drive any man mad—"

"I said you had to face the worst, and I calculate the worst for you would be to see her with some little Browns along. My! How it makes you wince! Well, face it then and be a man."

He sat for a moment, his head buried in his hands—then—

"I will," he said, "I will do what I can; but oh, when you have the chance you will be good to her, won't you, dear friend?"

"There, there!" said the widow, and she patted his hand. "I had to scold you, because I see you have got the attack very badly and only strong measures are any good; but you know I am sorry for you both, and feel dreadfully, because I helped you to it without enough thought as to consequences."

There was silence for a few minutes, and she continued to stroke his hand.

"Dominic has run down to Dieppe to see those daughters of his," she said, presently, "and won't be back to-night. I meant to be all alone and meditate and go to bed early; but you can dine with me, if you wish, up here, and we will talk everything over. Our plans for the future, I mean, and what will be best to do; I kind of feel like your mother-in-law, you know." Which sentence comforted him.

This woman was his friend, and so kind of heart, if sometimes a little plain-spoken.

And late that night he wrote to Theodora.

"My darling," he began. "I must call you that even though I have no right to. *My* darling—I want to tell you these my thoughts to-night, before I see you to-morrow as an ordinary guest at your dinner-party. I want you to know how utterly I love you, and how I am going to do my best with the rest of my life to show you how I honor you and revered you as an angel, and something to live for and shape my aims to be worthy of the recollection of that hour of bliss you granted me. Dearest love, does it not give you joy—just a little—to remember those moments of heaven? I do not regret anything, though I am all to blame, for I knew from the beginning I loved you, and just where love would lead us. But it was not until I saw the peep into your soul, when you never reproached me, that I began to understand what a brute I had been—how unworthy of you or your love. Darling, I don't ask you to try and forget me—indeed, I implore you not to do so. I think and believe you are of the nature which only loves once in a lifetime, and I am world-worn and experienced enough to know I have never really loved before. How passionately I do now I cannot put into words. So let us keep our love sacred in our hearts, my darling, and the knowledge of it will comfort and soothe the anguish of separation. Beloved one, I am always thinking of you, and I want to tell you my vision of heaven would be to possess you for my wife. My happiest dream will always be that you are there—at Bracondale—queen of my home and my heart, darling. *My* darling! But however it may be, whether you decide to chase away every thought of me or not, I want you to know I will go on worshipping you, and doing my utmost to serve you with my life.—For ever and ever your devoted lover."

And then he signed it "Hector," and not "Bracondale."

The widow had promised to give it into Theodora's own hand on the morrow.

He added a postscript:

"I want you to meet my mother and my sister in London. Will you let me arrange it? I think you will like Anne. And oh, more than all I want you to come to Bracondale. Write me your answer that I may have your words to keep always."

Mrs. McBride came round in the morning to the private hotel in the Avenue du Bois, to ask the exact time of the dinner-party, she said. She wanted to see for herself how things were going. And the look in Theodora's eyes grieved her.

"I am afraid it has gone rather deeply with her," she mused. "Now what can I do?"

Theodora was unusually sweet and gentle, and talked brightly of how glad she was for her father's happiness, and of their plans about England; but all the time Jane McBride was conscious that the something which had made her eyes those stars of gracious happiness was changed—instead there was a deep pathos in them, and it made her uncomfortable.

"I wish to goodness I had let well alone, and not tried to give her a happy day," she said to herself.

Just before leaving, she slipped Hector's letter into Theodora's hand. "Lord Bracondale asked me to give you this, my child," she said, and she kissed her. "And if you will write the answer, will you post it to him to the Ritz."

All over Theodora there rushed an emotion when she took the letter. Her hands trembled, and she slipped it into the bodice of her dress. She would not be able to read it yet. She was waiting, all ready dressed, for Josiah to enter any moment, to take their usual walk in the Bois.

Then she wondered what would the widow think of her action, slipping it into her dress—but it was done now, and too late to alter. And their eyes met, and she understood that her future step-mother was wide awake and knew a good many things. But the kind woman put her arm round her and kissed her soft cheek.

"I want you to be my little daughter, Theodora," she said. "And if you have a heartache, dear, why I have had them, too—and I'd like to comfort you. There!"

XV

The dinner-party went off with great éclat. Had not all the guests read in the New York *Herald* that morning of Captain Fitzgerald's good-fortune? He with his usual *savoir-vivre* had arranged matters to perfection. The company was chosen from among the nicest of his and Mrs. McBride's friends.

The invitations had been couched in this form: "I want you to meet my daughter, Mrs. Josiah Brown, my dear lady," or "dear fellow," as the case might be. "She is having a little dinner at Madrid on Monday night, and so hopes you will let me persuade you to come."

And the French Count, and Mr. Clutterbuck R. Tubbs and his daughter, Theodora had asked herself. Also the Austrian Prince. The party consisted of about twenty people—and the menu and the Tziganes were as perfect as they could be, while the night might have been a night of July—it happened to be that year when Paris was blessed with a gloriously warm May.

Lord Bracondale was late: had not the post come in just as he was starting, and brought him a letter, whose writing, although he had never seen it before, filled him with thrills of joy.

Theodora had found time during the day to read and reread his epistle, and to kiss it more than once with a guilty blush.

And she had written this answer:

"I have received your letter, and it says many things to me—and, Hector, it will comfort me always, this dear letter, and to know you love me.

"I have led a very ordinary life, you see, and the great blast of love has never come my way, or to any one whom I knew. I did not realize, quite, it was a real thing out of books—but now I know it is; and oh, I can believe, if circumstances were different, it could be heaven. But this cannot alter the fact that for me to think of you much would be very wrong now. I do love you—I do not deny it—though I am going to try my utmost to put the thought away from me and to live my life as best I can. I do not regret anything either, dear, because, but for you, I would never have known what life's meaning is at all—I should have stayed asleep always; and you have opened my eyes and taught me to see new beauties in all nature. And oh, we must not grieve, we must thank fate for giving us this one peep into paradise—and we must try and find the angel to steer our barks for us beyond the rocks. Listen—I want you to do something for me to-night. I want you not to look at me much, or tempt me with your dear voice. It will be terribly hard in any case, but if you will be kind you will help me to get through with it, and then, and then—I hardly dare to look ahead—but I leave it all in your hands. I would like to meet your mother and sister—but when, and where? I feel inclined to say, not yet, only I know that is just cowardice, and a shrinking from possible pain in seeing you. So I leave it to you to do what is best, and I trust to your honor and your love not to tempt me beyond bearing-point—and remember, I am trying, trying hard, to do what is right—and trying not to love you.

"And so, good-bye. I must never say this again—or even think it unsaid; but to-night, oh! Yes, Hector, know that I love you! THEODORA."

And all the way to Madrid, as he flew along in his automobile, his heart rejoiced at this one sentence—"Yes, Hector, know that I love you!"

The rest of the world did not seem to matter very much. How fortunate it is that so often Providence lets us live on the pleasure of the moment!

He sat on her left hand—the Austrian Prince was on her right—and studiously all through the repast he tried to follow her wishes and the law he had laid down for himself as the pattern of his future conduct.

He was gravely polite, he never turned the conversation away from the general company, including her neighbors in it all the time, and only when he was certain she was not noticing did he feast his eyes upon her face.

She was looking supremely beautiful. If possible, whiter than usual, and there was a shadow in her eyes as of mystery, which had not been there before—and while their pathos wrung his heart, he could not help perceiving their added beauty. And he had planted this change there—he, and he alone. He admired her perfect taste in dress—she was all in pure white, muslin and laces, and he knew it was of the best, and the creation of the greatest artist.

She looked just what *his* wife ought to look, infinitely refined and slender and stately and fair.

Morella Winmarleigh would seem as a large dun cow beside her.

Then suddenly they both remembered it was only a week this night since they had met. Only seven days in which fate had altered all their lives.

The Austrian Prince wondered to himself what had happened. He had not been blind to the situation at Armenonville, and here they seemed like polite hostess and guest, nothing more.

"They are English, and they are very well bred, and they are very good actors," he thought. "But, mon Dieu! were I ce beau jeune homme!"

And so it had come to an end—the feast and the Tziganes playing, and Theodora will always be haunted by that last wild Hungarian tune. Music, which moved every fibre of her being at all times, to-night was a torture of pain and longing. And he was so near, so near and yet so far, and it seemed as if the music meant love and separation and passionate regret, and the last air most passionate of all, and before the final notes died away Hector bent over to her, and he whispered:

"I have got your letter, and I love you, and I will obey its every wish. You must trust me unto death. Darling, good-night, but never good-bye!"

And she had not answered, but her breath had come quickly, and she had looked once in his eyes and then away into the night.

And so they shook hands politely and parted. And next day Mr. and Mrs. Josiah Brown crossed over to England.

XVI

It was pouring with rain the evening Lord Bracondale arrived from Paris at the family mansion in St. James's Square. He had only wired at the last moment to his mother, too late to change her plans; she was unfortunately engaged to take Morella Winmarleigh to the opera, and was dining early at that lady's house, so she could only see him for a few moments in her dressing-room before she started.

"My darling, darling boy!" she exclaimed, as he opened the door and peeped in. "Streatfield, bring that chair for his lordship, and—oh, you can go for a few minutes."

Then she folded him in her arms, and almost sobbed with joy to see him again.

"Well, mother," he said, when she had kissed him and murmured over him as much as she wished. "Here I am, and what a sickening climate! And where are you off to?"

"I am going to dine with Morella Winmarleigh," said Lady Bracondale, "early, to go to the opera, and then I shall take her on to the Brantingham's ball. Won't you join us at either place, Hector? I feel it so dreadfully, having to rush off like this, your first evening, darling."

She stood back and looked at him. She must see for herself whether he was well, and if this riotous life she feared he had been leading lately had not too greatly told upon him. Her fond eyes detected an air of weariness: he looked haggard, and not so full of spirits as he usually was. Alas! if he would only stay in England!

"I am rather tired, mother; I may look in at the opera, but I can't face a ball. How is Anne, and what is she doing to-night?" he said.

"Anne has a bad cold. We have had such weather—nothing but rain since Sunday night! She is dining at home and going to bed early. I have just had a telephone message from her; she is longing to see you, too."

"I think I shall go round and dine with her then," said Hector, "and join you later."

They talked on for about ten minutes before he left her to dress, running against Streatfield in the passage. She had known him since his birth, and beamed with joy at his return.

He chaffed her about growing fat, and went on his way to telephone to his sister.

"His lordship looks pale, my lady," said the demure woman, as she fastened Lady Bracondale's bracelet. She, too, disapproved of Paris and bachelorhood, but she did not love Morella Winmarleigh.

"Oh, you think so, Streatfield?" Lady Bracondale exclaimed, in a worried voice. "Now that we have got him back we must take great care of him. His lordship will join me at the opera. Are you sure he likes those aigrettes in my hair?"

"Why, it's one of his lordship's favorite styles, my lady. You need have no fears," said the maid.

And thus comforted, Lady Bracondale descended the great staircase to her carriage.

She was still a beautiful woman, though well past fifty. Her splendid, dark hair had hardly a thread of gray in it, and grew luxuriantly, but she insisted upon wearing it simply parted in the middle and coiled in a mass of plaits behind, while one braid stood up coronet fashion well at the back of her head. She was addicted to rich satins and velvets, and had a general air of Victorian repose and decorum. There was no attempt to retain departed youth; no golden wigs or red and white paint disfigured her person, which had an immense natural dignity and stateliness. It made her shiver to see some of her contemporaries dressed and arranged to represent not more than twenty years of age. But so many modern ways of thought and life jarred upon her!

"Mother is still in the early seventies; she has never advanced a step since she came out," Anne always said, "and I dare say she was behind the times even then."

Meanwhile, Hector was dressing in his luxurious mahogany-panelled room. Everything in the house was solid and prosperous, as befitted a family who had had few reverses and sufficient perspicacity to marry a rich heiress now and then at right moments in their history.

This early Georgian house had been in the then Lady Bracondale's dower, and still retained its fine carvings and Old-World state.

"How shall I see her again?" was all the thought which ran in Lord Bracondale's head.

"She won't be at a ball, but she might chance to have thought of the opera. It would be a place Mr. Brown would like to exhibit her at. I shall certainly go."

Lady Anningford was tucked up on a sofa in her little sitting-room when her brother arrived at her charming house in Charles Street. Her husband had been sent off to a dinner without her, and she was expecting her brother with impatience. She loved Hector as many sisters do a handsome, popular brother, but rather more than that, and she had fine senses and understood him.

She did not cover him with caresses and endearments when she saw him; she never did.

"Poor Hector has enough of them from mother," she explained, when Monica Ellerwood asked her once why she was so cold. "And men don't care for those sort of things, except from some one else's sister or wife."

"Dear old boy!" was all she said as he came in. "I am glad to see you back."

Then in a moment or two they went down to dinner, talking of various things. And all through it, while the servants were in theroom, she prattled about Paris and their friends and the gossip of the day; and she had a shocking cold in her head, too, and might well have been forgiven for being dull.

But when they were at last alone, back in the little sitting-room, she looked at him hard, and her voice, which was rather deep like his, grew full of tenderness as she asked: "What is it, Hector? Tell me about it if I can help you."

He got up and stood with his back to the wood fire, which sparkled in the grate, comforting the eye with its brightness, while the wind and rain moaned outside.

"You can't help me, Anne; no one can," he said. "I have been rather badly burned, but there is nothing to be done. It is my own fault—so one must just bear it."

"Is it the—eh—the Frenchwoman?" his sister asked, gently.

"Good Lord, no!"

"Or the American Monica came back so full of?"

"The American? What American? Surely she did not mean my dear Mrs. McBride?"

"I don't know her name," Anne said, "and I don't want you to say a thing about it, dear, if I can't help you; only it just grieves me to see you looking so sad and distrait, so I felt I must try if there is anything I can do for you. Mother has been on thorns and dying of fuss over this Frenchwoman and the diamond chain—("How the devil did she hear about that?" thought Hector)—until Monica came back with a tale of your devotion to an American."

"One would think I was eighteen years old and in leading-strings still, upon my word," he interrupted, with an irritated laugh. "When will she realize I can take care of myself?"

"Never," said Lady Anningford, "until you have married Morella Winmarleigh; then she would feel you were in good hands."

He laughed again—bitterly this time.

"Morella Winmarleigh! I would not be faithful to her for a week!"

"I wonder if you would be faithful to any woman, Hector? I have often thought you do not know what it means to love—really to love."

"You were perfectly right once. I did not know," he said; "and perhaps I don't now, unless to feel the whole world is a sickening blank without one woman is to love—really to love."

Anne noticed the weariness of his pose and the vibration in his deep voice. She was stirred and interested as she had never been. This dear brother of hers was not wont to care very much. In the past it had always been the women who had sighed and longed and he who had been amused and pleased. She could not remember a single occasion in the last ten years when he had seemed to suffer, although she had seen him apparently devoted to numbers of women.

"And what are you going to do?" she asked, with sympathy, "She is married, of course?"

"Yes."

"Hector, don't you want me to speak about it?"

He took a chair now by his sister's sofa, and he began to turn over the papers rather fast which lay on a table near by.

"Yes, I do," he said, "because, after all, you can do something for me. I want you to be particularly kind to her, will you, Anne, dear?"

"But, of course; only you must tell me who she is and where I shall find her."

"You will find her at Claridge's, and she is only the wife of an impossible Australian millionaire called Brown—Josiah Brown."

"Poor dear Hector, how terrible!" thought Anne. "It is not the American, then?" she said, aloud.

"There never was any American," he exclaimed. "Monica is the most ridiculous gossip, and always sees wrong. If she had not Jack to keep her from talking so much she would not leave one of us with a rag of character."

"I will go to-morrow and call there, Hector," Lady Anningford said. "My cold is sure to be better; and if she is not in, shall I write a note and ask her to lunch? The husband, too, I suppose?"

"I fear so. Anne, you are a brick."

Then he said good-night, and went to the opera.

Left to herself, Lady Anningford thought: "I suppose she is some flashy, pretty creature who has caught Hector's fancy, the poor darling. One never has chanced to find an Australian quite, quite a lady. I almost wish he would marry Morella and have done with it."

Then she lay on her sofa and pondered many things.

She was a year older than her brother, and they had always been the closest friends and comrades.

Lady Anningford was more or less a happy and contented woman now, but there had been moments in her life scorched by passion and infinite pain. Long ago in the beginning when she first came out she had had the misfortune to fall in love with Cyril Lamont, married and bad and attractive. It had given him great pleasure to evade the eye of Lady Bracondale, pure dragon and strict disciplinarian. Anne was a good girl, but she was eighteen years old and had tasted no joy. She was not an easy prey, and her first year had passed in storms of emotion suppressed to the best of her powers.

The situation had been full of shades and contrasts. The outward, a strictly guarded lamb, the life of the world and aristocratic propriety; and the inward, a daily growing mad love for an impossible person, snatched and secret meetings after tea in country-houses, walks in Kensington Gardens, rides along lonely lanes out hunting, and, finally, the brink of complete ruin and catastrophe—but for Hector.

"Where should I be now but for Hector?" her thoughts ran.

Hector was just leaving Eton in those days, and had come up and discovered matters, while she sobbed in his arms, at the beginning of her second season. He had comforted her and never scolded a word, and then he had gone out armed with a heavy hunting-crop, found Cyril Lamont, and had thrashed the man within an inch of his life. It was one of Hector's pleasantest recollections, the thought of his cowering form, his green silk smoking-jacket all torn, and his eyes sightless. Cyril Lamont's talents had not run in the art of self-defence, and he had been very soon powerless in the hands of this young athlete.

The Lamonts went abroad that night, and stayed there for quite six months, during which time Anne mended her broken heart and saw the folly of her ways.

Hector and she had never alluded to the matter all these years, only they were intimate friends and understood each other.

Lady Bracondale adored Hector and was fond of Anne, but had no comprehension of either. Anne was a *frondeuse*, while her mother's mind was fashioned in carved lines and strict boundaries of thought and action.

XVII

Meanwhile, Hector reached the opera, and made his way to the omnibus box where he had his seat.

He felt he could not stand Morella Winmarleigh just yet. The second act of "Faust" was almost over, and with his glass he swept the rows of boxes in vain to find Theodora. He sat a few minutes, but restlessness seized him. He must go to the other side and ascertain if she could be discovered from there. Morella Winmarleigh's box commanded a good view for this purpose, so after all he would face her.

He looked up at her opposite. She sat there with his mother, and she seemed more thoroughly wholesomely unattractive than ever to him.

He hated that shade of turquoise blue she was so fond of, and those unmeaning bits and bows she had stuck about. She was a large young woman with a stolid English fairness.

Her hair had the flaxen ends and sandy roots one so often sees in those women whose locks have been golden as children. It was a thin, dank kind of hair, too, with no glints anywhere. Her eyes were blue and large and meaningless and rather prominent, and her lightish eyelashes seemed to give no shade to them.

Morella's orbs just looked out at you like the bow-windows of a sea-side villa—staring and commonplace. Her features were regular, and her complexion, if somewhat all too red, was fresh withal; so that, possessing an income of many thousands, she passed for a beauty of exceptional merit.

She had a good maid who used her fingers dexterously, and did what she could with a mistress devoid of all sense of form or color.

Miss Winmarleigh went to the opera regularly and sat solidly through it. The music said nothing to her, but it was the right place for her to be, and she could talk to her friends before going on to the numerous balls she attended.

If she loved anything in the world she loved Hector Bracondale, but her feelings gave her no anxieties. He would certainly marry her presently, the affair would be so suitable to all parties; meanwhile, there was plenty of time, and all was in order. The perfect method of her account-books, in which the last sixpence she spent in the day was duly entered, translated itself to her life. Method and order were its watchwords; and if the people who knew her intimately—such as her chaperon, Mrs. Herrick, and her maid, Gibson—thought her mean, she was not aware of their opinion, and went her way in solid rejoicing.

Lady Bracondale was really attached to her. Morella's decorum, her absence of all daring thought in conversation, pleased her so. She had none of that feeling when with Miss Winmarleigh she suffered in the company of her daughter Anne, who said things so often she did not quite understand, yet which she dimly felt might have two meanings, and one of them a meaning she most probably would disapprove of.

She loved Anne, of course, but oh, that she could have been more like herself or Morella Winmarleigh!

Both women saw Hector in the omnibus box, and saw him leave it, and were quite ready with their greetings when he joined them.

Miss Winmarleigh had a slight air of proprietorship about her, which every one knew when Hector was there. And most people thought as she did, that he would certainly marry her in the near future.

He was glad it was not between the acts—there was no excuse for conversation after their greeting, so he searched the house in peace with his glasses.

And although he was hoping to see Theodora, his heart gave a great bound of surprised joy when, on the pit tier, almost next the box he had just left, he discovered her. He supposed it was a box often let to strangers that season, as he could not remember whose the name was as he had passed. He got back into the shadow, that his gaze should not be too remarkable. She had not caught sight of him yet, or so it seemed.

There she sat with her husband and another woman, whom he recognized as one of those kind creatures who go everywhere in society and help strangers when suitably compensated for their trouble.

Where on earth could she have come across Mrs. Devlyn? he wondered. A poisonous woman, who would fill her ears with tales of all the world. Then he guessed, and rightly, the introduction had been effected by Captain Fitzgerald, who would probably have known her in his own day.

Theodora appeared wrapped in the music, and was an enthralling picture of loveliness; her fineness seemed to make all the women's faces who were near look coarse, and her whiteness turned them into gypsies. She wore a gown of black velvet with no relief whatever, only her dazzling skin and her great pearls. He feasted his eyes upon her—eyes hungry with a week's abstinence; for he had felt it more prudent to remain in Paris for some days after she had left.

He looked round the rest of the house, and understood all the other men could, and probably would, gaze too. And then he began to feel hot and jealous! This was different from Paris, where she was more or less a tourist; but here, how long would she be left in peace without siege being laid to her? He knew his world and the men it contained. Yes, at that moment the door at the back of the box opened and Delaval Stirling came in, Josiah Brown making way for him to sit in front. Delaval Stirling—this was too much!

And Theodora turned with her adorable smile and greeted him, so it showed they had met before—greeted him with pleasure. Good God! How much could happen in a week! Why had he stayed in Paris?

If Morella Winmarleigh had glanced round at his face, even her thick perceptions must have grasped the disturbance which was marked there, as he stood back in the shadow and gazed with angry eyes.

The moment she had seen him come into the box Mrs. Devlyn had said, "I want you to notice a man over there, Mrs. Brown, in the box exactly opposite; on the grand tier—do you see?"

"Yes," said Theodora, and she perceived him shaking hands with Miss Winmarleigh before he caught sight of her, so she was forearmed and turned to the stage.

"He is nice-looking, don't you think so?" continued Mrs. Devlyn, without a pause. "He is going to marry that girl in the box; she is one of the richest heiresses of the day—Miss Winmarleigh. I always point out Hector Bracondale to strangers or foreigners; he is quite a show Englishman."

"Bracondale? Lord Bracondale?" interrupted Josiah Brown. "We met him in Paris, did we not, my love?" turning to Theodora. "He dined with us our last evening. Where is he?"

"Oh, you know him, then!" said Mrs. Devlyn, disappointed. "I wanted to be the first to point him out to you. They will make a handsome pair, won't they—he and Miss Winmarleigh?"

"Very," said Theodora, listlessly, with an air of dragging her thoughts from the music with difficulty, while she suddenly felt sick and cold.

"And are they to be married soon?"

"I don't know exactly; but it has been going on for years, and we all look upon it as a settled thing. She is always about with his mother."

"Is that Lord Bracondale's mother—the lady with the coronet of plaits and the huge white aigrette with the diamond drops in it?" Theodora asked. Her voice was schooled, and had no special tones in it. But oh, how she was thrilling with interest and excitement underneath!

"Yes, that is Lady Bracondale. She is quite a type; always dresses in that old-fashioned way, and won't know a soul who is not of her own set. She is a cousin of one of my husband's aunts. I must introduce you to her."

"She looks pretty haughty," announced Josiah Brown. "I should not care to tread on her toes much." And then he remembered he had seen her years ago driving through the little town of Bracondale.

Theodora asked no more questions. She kept her eyes fixed on the stage, but she knew Hector had raised his glasses now and was scanning the box, and had probably seen her.

What ought it to matter to her that he should be going to marry Miss Winmarleigh? He could be nothing to her—only—only—but perhaps it was not true. This woman, Mrs. Devlyn, whom she began to feel she should dislike very much, had said it was looked upon as settled, not that it was a fact. How could a man be going to marry one woman and make desperate love to another at the same time? It was impossible—and yet—she would *not* look in any case. She would not once raise her eyes that way.

And so in these two boxes green jealousy held sway, and while Hector glared across at Theodora she smiled at Delaval Stirling, and spoke softly of the music and the voices, though her heart was torn with pain.

"Do you see Hector Bracondale is back again, Delaval?" Mrs. Devlyn said. "Do you know why he stayed in Paris so long? I heard—" And she whispered low, so that Theodora only caught the name "Esclarmonde de Chartres" and their modulated mocking laughter.

How they jarred upon her! How she felt she should hate London among all these people whose ways she did not know! She turned a little, and Josiah's vulgar familiar face seemed a relief to her, and her tender eyes melted in kindliness as she looked at him.

"You are very pale to-night, my love," he said. "Would you like to go home?"

But this she would not agree to, and pulled herself together and tried to talk gayly when the curtain went down.

And Hector blamed his own folly for having come up to this box at all. Here he must be glued certainly for a few moments; now that they could talk, politeness could not permit him to fly off at once.

"The house is very full," Miss Winmarleigh said—it was a remark she always made on big nights—"and yet hardly any new faces about."

"Yes," said Hector.

"Does it compare with the Opera-House in Paris, Hector?" Miss Winmarleigh hardly ever went abroad.

"No," said Hector.—Not only had Delaval Stirling retained his seat, but Chris Harford, Mrs. Devlyn's brother, had entered the box now and was assiduously paying his court. "Damned impertinence of the woman, forcing her relations upon them like that," he thought.—"Oh—er—no—that is, I think the Paris Opera-House is a beastly place," he said, absently, "a dull, heavy drab brown and dirty gilding, and all the women look hideous in it."

"Really," said Morella. "I thought everything in Paris was lovely."

"You should go over and see for yourself," he said, "then you could judge. I think most things there are lovely, though."

Miss Winmarleigh raised her glasses now and examined the house. Her eyes lighted at last on Theodora.

"Dear Lady Bracondale," she said, "do look at that woman in black velvet. What splendid pearls! Do you think they are real? Who is it, I wonder, with Florence Devlyn?"

But Hector felt he could not stay and hear their remarks about his darling, so he got up, and, murmuring he must have a talk to his friends in the house, left the box.

He was thankful at least Theodora was sitting on the pit tier—he could walk along the gangway and talk to her from the front.

She saw him coming and was prepared, so no wild roses tinged her cheeks, and her greeting was gravely courteous, that was all.

An icy feeling crept over him. What was the change, this subtle change in voice and eyes? He suddenly had the agonizing sensation of being a great way off from her, shut out of paradise—a stranger. What had happened? What had he done?

Every one knows the Opera-House, and where he would be standing, and the impossibility of saying anything but the most banal commonplaces, looking up like that.

Then Josiah leaned forward, proud of his acquaintanceship with a peer, and said in a distinct voice:

"Won't you come into the box, Lord Bracondale? There is plenty of room." He had not taken to either Delaval Stirling or Chris Harford, and thought a change of company would not come amiss. They had ignored him, and should pay for it.

Hector made his way joyfully to the back, and, entering, was greeted affably by his host, so the other two men got up to leave to make room for him.

He sat down behind Theodora, and Mrs. Devlyn saw it would be wiser to conciliate Josiah by her interested conversation.

She hoped to make a good thing out of this millionaire and his unknown wife, and it would not do to ruffle him at this stage of the affair.

Theodora hardly turned, thus Hector was obliged to lean quite forward to speak to her.

"I have seen my sister to-night," he said, "and she wants so much to meet you. I said perhaps she would find you to-morrow. Will you be at home in the afternoon any time?"

"I expect so," replied Theodora. She was longing to face him, to ask him if it was true he was going to marry that large, pink-faced young woman opposite, who was now staring down upon them with fixed opera-glasses; but she felt frozen, and her voice was a frozen voice.

Hector became more and more unhappy. He tried several subjects. He told her the last news of her father and Mrs. McBride. She answered them all with the same politeness, until, maddened beyond bearing, he leaned still farther forward and whispered in her ear:

"For God's sake, what is it? What have I done?"

"Nothing," said Theodora. What right had she to ask him any question, when for these seven nights and days since they had parted she had been disciplining herself not to think of him in any way? She must never let him know it could matter to her now.

"Nothing? Then why are you so changed? Ah, how it hurts!" he whispered, passionately. And she turned and looked at him, and he saw that her beautiful eyes were no longer those pure depths of blue sky in which he could read love and faith, but were full of mist, as of a curtain between them.

He put his hand up to touch the little gold case he carried always now in his waistcoat-pocket, which contained her letter. He wanted to assure himself it was there, and she had written it—and it was not all a dream.

Theodora's tender heart was wrung by the passionate distress in his eyes.

"Is that your mother over there you were with?" she asked, more gently. "How beautiful she is!"

"Yes," he said, "my mother and Morella Winmarleigh, whom the world in general and my mother in particular have decided I am going to marry."

She did not speak. She felt suddenly ashamed she could ever have doubted him; it must be the warping atmosphere of Mrs. Devlyn's society for these last days which had planted thoughts, so foreign to her nature, in her. She did not yet know it was jealousy pure and simple, which attacks the sweetest, as well, as the bitterest, soul among us all. But a thrill of gladness ran through her as well as shame.

"And aren't you going to marry her, then?" she said, at last. "She is very handsome."

Hector looked at her, and a wave of joy chased out the pain he had suffered. That was it, then! They had told her this already, and she hated it—she cared for him still.

"Surely you need not ask me," he said, deep reproach in his eyes. "You must be very changed in seven days to even have thought it possible."

The shame deepened in Theodora. She was, indeed, unlike herself to have been moved at all by Mrs. Devlyn's words, but she would never doubt again, and she must tell him that.

"Forgive me," she said, quite low, while she looked away. "I—of course I ought to be pleased at anything which made you happy, but—oh, I hated it!"

"Theodora," he said, "I ask you—do not act with me ever—to what end? We know each other's hearts, and I hope it would pain you were I to marry any other woman, as much as in like circumstances it would pain me."

"Yes, it would pain me," she said, simply. "But, oh, we must not speak thus! Please, please talk of the music, or the—the—oh, anything but ourselves."

And he tried hard for the few moments which remained before the curtain rose again. Tried hard, but it was all dust and ashes; and as he left the box and returned to his own seat next door his heart felt like lead. How would he be able to follow the rules he had laid down for himself during his week of meditations in Paris alone?

"You see, dear Lady Bracondale," Morella Winmarleigh had been saying, "Hector knows that woman with the pearls. He is sitting talking to her now."

"Hector knows every one, Morella. Lend me your glasses, mine do not seem to work to-night. Yes, I suppose by some she would be considered pretty," Lady Bracondale continued, when the lorgnette was fixed to her focus. "What do you think, dear?"

"Pretty!" exclaimed Miss Winmarleigh. "Oh no! Much too white, and, oh—er—foreign-looking. We must find out who she is."

The matter was not difficult. Half the house had been interested in the new-comer, the beautiful new-comer with the wonderful pearls, who must be worth while in some way, or she would not be under the wing of Florence Devlyn.

By the time Hector again entered their box in the last act, Miss Winmarleigh had obtained all the information she wanted from one of the many visitors who came to pay their court to the heiress. And the information reassured her. Only the wife of a colonial millionaire; no one of her world or who could trouble her.

Early next morning, while she sat in her white flannel dressing-gown, her hair screwed in curling-pins, after the Brantinghams' ball, she wrote in her journal the customary summary of her day, and ended with: "H.B. returned—same as usual, running after a new woman, nobody of importance; but I had better watch it, and clinch matters between him and me before Goodwood. Ordered the pink silk after all, from the new little dressmaker, and beat her down three pounds as to price. Begun Marvaloso hair tonic."

Then, as it was broad daylight, after carefully replacing in its drawer this locked chronicle of her maiden thoughts, she retired to bed, to sleep the sleep of those just persons whose digestions are as strong as their absence of imagination.

XVIII

Next day Lady Anningford called, as she had promised, at Claridge's, and found Mrs. Brown at home, although it was only three o'clock in the afternoon.

She had not two minutes to wait in the well-furnished first-floor sitting-room, but during that time she noticed there were one or two things about which showed the present occupant was a woman of taste, and there were such quantities of flowers. Flowers, flowers, everywhere.

Theodora entered already dressed for her afternoon drive. She came forward with that perfect grace which characterized her every movement.

If she felt very timid and nervous it did not show in her sweet face, and Lady Anningford perceived Hector had every excuse for his infatuation.

"I am so fortunate to find you at home, Mrs. Brown," she said. "My brother has told me so much about you, and I was longing to meet you. May we sit down on this sofa and talk a little, or were you just starting for your drive?"

"Of course we may sit down," said Theodora. "My drive does not matter in the least. It was so good of you to come."

And her inward thought was that she would like Hector's sister. Anne's frankness and *sans gêne* were so pleasing.

They exchanged a few agreeable sentences while each measured the other, and then Lady Anningford said:

"You come from Australia, don't you?"

"Australia!" smiled Theodora, while her eyes opened wide. "Oh no! I have never been out of France and Belgium and places like that. My husband lived in Melbourne for some years, though."

"I thought it could not be possible," quoth Anne to herself.

"Then you don't know much of England yet?" she said, aloud.

"It is my first visit; and it seems very dull and rainy. This is the only really fine day we have had since we arrived."

Anne soon dexterously elicited an outline of Theodora's plans and what she was doing. They would only remain in town until Whitsuntide, perhaps returning later for a week or two; and Mrs. Devlyn, to whom her father had sent her an introduction, had been kind enough to tell them what to do and how to see a little of London. She was going to a ball to-night. The first real ball she had ever been to in her life, she said, ingenuously.

And Lady Anningford looked at her and each moment fell more under her charm.

"The ball at Harrowfield House, I expect, to meet the King of Guatemala," she said, knowing Lady Harrowfield was Florence Devlyn's cousin.

"That is it," said Theodora.

"Then you must dance with Hector—my brother," she said.

She launched his name suddenly; she wanted to see what effect it would have on Theodora. "He is sure to be there, and he dances divinely."

She was rewarded for her thrust: just the faintest pink came into the white velvet cheeks, and the blue eyes melted softly. To dance with Hector! Ah! Then the radiance was replaced by a look of sadness, and she said, quietly:

"Oh, I do not think I shall dance at all. My husband is rather an invalid, and we shall only go in for a little while."

No, she must not dance with Hector. Those joys were not for her—she must not even think of it.

"How extraordinarily beautiful she is!" Anne thought, when presently, the visit ended, she found herself rolling along in her electric brougham towards the park. "And I feel I shall love her. I wonder what her Christian name is?"

Theodora had promised they would lunch in Charles Street with her the next day if her husband should be well enough after the ball. And Anne decided to collect as many nice people to meet them as she could in the time.

At the corner of Grosvenor Square she met an old friend, one Colonel Lowerby, commonly called the Crow, and stopped to pick him up and take him on with her.

He was the one person she wanted to talk to at this juncture. She had known him all her life, and was accustomed to prattle to him on all subjects. He was always safe, and gruff, and honest.

"I have just done something so interesting, Crow," she told him, as they went along towards Regent's Park, to which sylvan spot she had directed her chauffeur, to be more free to talk in peace to her companion. Some of her friends were capable of making scandals, even about the dear old Crow, she knew.

"And what have you done?" he asked.

"Of course you have heard the tale from Uncle Evermond, of Hector and the lady at Monte Carlo?"

He nodded.

"Well, there is not a word of truth in it; he is in love, though, with the most beautiful woman I have ever seen in my life—and I have just been to call upon her. And to-morrow you have got to come to lunch to meet her—and tell me what you think."

"Very well," said the Crow. "I was feeding elsewhere, but I always obey you. Continue your narrative."

"I want you to tell me what to do, and how I can help them."

"My dear child," said the Crow, sententiously, as was his habit, "help them to what? She is married, of course, or Hector would not be in love with her. Do you want to help them to part or to meet? or to go to heaven or to hell? or to spend what Monica Ellerwood calls 'a Saturday to Monday amid rural scenery,' which means both of those things one after the other!"

"Crow, dear, you are disagreeable," said Lady Anningford, "and I have a cold in my head and cannot compete with you in words to-day."

"Then say what you want, and I'll listen."

"Hector met them in Paris, it seems, and must have fallen wildly in love, because I have never seen him as he is now."

"How is he?—and who is 'them'?"

"Why, she and the husband, of course, and Hector is looking sad and distrait—and has really begun to feel at last."

"Serve him right!"

"Crow, you are insupportable! Can you not see I am serious and want your help?"

"Fire away, then, my good child, and explain matters. You are too vague!"

So she told him all she knew—which was little enough; but she was eloquent upon Theodora's beauty.

"She has the face of an angel," she ended her description with.

"Always mistrust 'em," interjected the Crow.

"Such a figure and the nicest manner, and she is in love with Hector, too, of course—because she could not possibly help herself—could she?—if he is being lovely to her."

"I have not your prejudiced eyes for him—though Hector certainly is a decent fellow enough to look at," allowed Colonel Lowerby. "But all this does not get to what you want to do for them."

"I want them to be happy."

"Permanently, or for the moment?"

"Both."

"An impossible combination, with these abominably inconsiderate marriage laws we suffer under in this country, my child."

"Then what ought I to do?"

"You can do nothing but accelerate or hinder matters for a little. If Hector is really in love, and the woman, too, they are bound to dree their weird, one way or the other, themselves. You will be doing the greatest kindness if you can keep them apart, and avoid a scandal if possible."

"My dear Crow, I have never heard of your being so thoroughly unsympathetic before."

"And I have never heard of Hector being really in love before, and with an angel, too—deuced dangerous folk at the best of times!"

"Then there are mother and Morella Winmarleigh to be counted with."

"Neither of them can see beyond their noses. Miss Winmarleigh is sure of him, she thinks—and your mother, too."

"No; mother has her doubts."

"They will both be anti?"

"Extremely anti."

"To get back to facts, then, your plan is to assist your brother to see this 'angel,' and smooth the path to the final catastrophe."

"You worry me, Crow. Why should there be a catastrophe?"

"Is she a young woman?"

"A mere baby. Certainly not more than twenty or so."

"Then it is inevitable, if the husband don't count. You have not described him yet."

"Because I have never seen him," said Lady Anningford. "Hector did say last night, though, that he was an impossible Australian millionaire."

"These people have a strong sense of personal rights—they are even blood-thirsty sometimes, and expect virtue in their women. If he had been just an English snob, the social bauble might have proved an immense eye-duster; but when you say Australian it gives me hope. He'll take her away, or break Hector's head, before things become too embarrassing."

"Crow, you are brutal."

"And a good thing, too. That is what we all want, a little more brutality. The whole of the blessed show here is being ruined with this sickly sentimentality. Flogging done away with; every silly nerve pandered to. By Jove! the next time we have to fight any country we shall have an anæsthetic served round with the rations to keep Tommy Atkins's delicate nerves from suffering from the consciousness of the slaughter he inflicts upon the enemy."

"Crow, you are violent."

"Yes, I am. I am sick of the whole thing. I would reintroduce prize-fighting and bear-baiting and gladiatorial shows to brace the nation up a bit. We'll get jammed full of rotten vices like those beastly foreigners soon."

"I did not bring you into Regent's Park to hear a tirade upon the nation's needs, Crow," Anne reminded him, smiling, "but to get your sympathy and advice upon this affair of Hector. You know you are the only person in the world I ever talk to about intimate things."

"Dear Queen Anne," he said, "I will always do what I can for you. But I tell you seriously, when a man like Hector loves a woman really, you might as well try to direct Niagara Falls as to turn him any way but the one he means to go."

"He wants me to be kind to her. Do you advise me just to let the thing drop, then?"

"No; be as kind as you like—only don't assist them to destruction."

"She goes into the country on Saturday for Whitsuntide, as we all do. Hector is going down to Bracondale alone."

"That looks desperate. I shall see Hector, and judge for myself."

"You must be sure to go to the ball at Harrowfield House to-night, then," Anne said. "They are both going. I say both because I know she is, and so, of course, Hector will be there too. I shall go, naturally, and then we can decide what we can do about it after we have seen them together."

And all this time Theodora was thinking how charming Anne was, and how kind, and that she felt a little happier because of her kindness. And, hard as it would be, she would not leave Josiah's side that night or dance with Hector.

And Hector was thinking—

"What is the good of anything in this wide world without her? I *must* see her. For good or ill, I cannot keep away."

He was deep in the toils of desire and passionate love for a woman belonging to someone else and out of his reach, and for whom he was hungry. Thus the primitive forces of nature were in violent activity, and his soul was having a hard fight.

It was the first time in his life that a woman had really mattered or had been impossible to obtain.

He had always looked upon them as delightful accessories: sport first, and woman, who was only another form of sport, second.

He had not neglected the obligations of his great position, but they came naturally to him as of the day's work. They were not real interests in his life. And when stripped of the veneer of civilization he was but a passionate, primitive creature, like numbers of others of his class and age.

While the elevation of Theodora's pure soul was an actual influence upon him, he had thought it would be possible—difficult, perhaps—but possible to obey her—to keep from troubling her—to regulate his passion into worship at a distance. But since then new influences had begun to work—prominent among them being jealousy.

To see her surrounded by others—who were men and would desire her, too—drove him mad.

Josiah was difficult enough to bear. The thought that he was her husband, and had the rights of this position, always turned him sick with raging disgust; but that was the law, and a law accepted since the beginning of time. These others were not of the law—they were the same as himself—and would all try to win her.

He had no fear of their succeeding, but, to watch them trying, and he himself unable to prevent them, was a thought he could not tolerate.

He had no settled plan. He did not deliberately say to himself: "I will possess her at all costs. I will be her lover, and take her by force from the bonds of this world." His whole mind was in a ferment and chaos. There was no time to think of the position in cold blood. His passion hurried him on from hour to hour.

This day after the opera, when the hideous impossibility of the situation had come upon him with full force, he felt as Lancelot—

"His mood was often like a fiend, and rose and drove him into wastes and solitudes for agony, Who was yet a living soul."

There are all sorts of loves in life, but when it is the real great passion, nor fear of hell nor hope of heaven can stem the tide—for long!

He had gone out in his automobile, and was racing ahead considerably above the speed limit. He felt he must do something. Had it been winter and hunting-time, he would have taken any fences—any risks. He returned and got to Ranelagh, and played a game of polo as hard as he could, and then he felt a little calmer. The idea came to him as it had done to Anne. Lady Harrowfield was Florence Devlyn's cousin; she would probably have squeezed an invitation for her protégées for the royal ball to-night. He would go—he must see Theodora. He must hold her in his arms, if only in the mazes of the waltz.

And the thought of that sent the blood whirling madly once more in his veins.

Everything he had looked upon so lightly up to now had taken a new significance in reference to Theodora. Florence Devlyn, for instance, was no fit companion for her—Florence Devlyn, whom he met at every decent house and had never before disapproved of, except as a bore and a sycophant.

XIX

Harrowfield House, as every one knows, is one of the finest in London; and with the worst manners, and an inordinate insolence, Lady Harrowfield ruled her section of society with a rod of iron. Indeed, all sections coveted the invitations of this disagreeable lady.

Her path was strewn with lovers, and protected by a proud and complacent husband, who had realized early he never would be master of the situation, and had preferred peace to open scandal.

She was a woman of sixty now, and, report said, still had her lapses. But every incident was carried off with a high-handed, brazen daring, and an assumption of right and might and prerogative which paralyzed criticism.

So it was that with the record of a *demimondaine*—and not one kind action to her credit—Lady Harrowfield still held her place among the spotless, and ruled as a queen.

There was not above two years' difference between her age and Lady Bracondale's; indeed, the latter had been one of her bridesmaids; but no one to look at them at a distance could have credited it for a minute.

Lady Harrowfield had golden hair and pink cheeks, and her *embonpoint* retained in the most fashionable outline. And if towards two in the morning, or when she lost at bridge, her face did remind on-lookers of a hideous colored mask of death and old age—one can't have everything in life; and Lady Harrowfield had already obtained more than the lion's share.

This night in June she stood at the top of her splendid staircase, blazing with jewels, receiving her guests, among whom more than one august personage, English and foreign, was expected to arrive; and an unusually sour frown disfigured the thick paint of her face.

It all seemed like fairy-land to Theodora as, accompanied by Josiah, and preceded by Mrs. Devlyn, she early mounted the marble steps with the rest of the throng.

She noticed the insolent stare of her hostess as she shook hands and then passed on in the crowd.

She felt a little shy and nervous and excited withal. Every one around seemed to have so many friends, and to be so gay and joyous, and only she and Josiah stood alone. For Mrs. Devlyn felt she had done enough for one night in bringing them there.

It was an immense crowd. At a smaller ball Theodora's exquisite beauty must have commanded instant attention, but this was a special occasion, and the world was too occupied with a desire to gape at the foreign king to trouble about any new-comers. Certainly for the first hour or so.

Josiah was feeling humiliated. Not a creature spoke to them, and they were hustled along like sheep into the ballroom.

A certain number of men stared—stared with deep interest, and made plans for introductions as soon as the crowd should subside a little.

Theodora was perfectly dressed, and her jewels caused envy in numbers of breasts.

She was too little occupied with herself to feel any of Josiah's humiliation. This society was hers by right of birth, and did not disconcert her; only no one could help being lonely when quite neglected, while others danced.

Presently, a thin, ill-tempered-looking old man made his way with difficulty up to their corner; he had been speaking to Mrs. Devlyn across the room.

"I must introduce myself," he said, graciously, to Theodora. "I am your uncle, Patrick Fitzgerald, and I am so delighted to meet you and make your acquaintance."

Theodora bowed without *empressement*. She had no feeling for these relations who had been so indifferent to her while she was poor and who had treated darling papa so badly.

"I only got back to town last night, or I and my wife would have called at Claridge's before this," he continued. And then he said something affable to Josiah, who looked strangely out of place among this brilliant throng.

For whatever may compose the elements of the highest London society, the atoms all acquire a certain air after a little, and if within this *fine fleur* of the aristocracy there lurked some Jews and Philistines and infidels of the middle classes, they were not quite new to the game, and had all received their gloss. So poor Josiah stood out rather by himself, and Sir Patrick Fitzgerald felt a good deal ashamed of him.

Theodora's fine senses had perceived all this long ago—the contrast her husband presented to the rest of the world—and it had made her stand closer to him and treat him with more deference than usual; her generous heart always responded to any one or anything in an unhappy position.

And through all his thick skin Josiah felt something of her tenderness, and glowed with pride in her.

Sir Patrick Fitzgerald continued to talk, and even paid his niece some bluff compliments. Her manner was so perfect, he decided! Gad! he could be proud of his new-found relation. And though the husband was nothing but a grocer still, and looked it every inch, by Jove, he was rich enough to gild his vulgarity and be tolerated among the highest.

Thus the uncle was gushing and lavish in his invitations and offers of friendship. They must come to Beechleigh for Whitsuntide. He would hear of no refusal. Going home! Oh, what nonsense! Home was a place one could go to at any time. And he would so like to show them Beechleigh at its best, where her father had lived all his young life.

Josiah was caught by his affable suggestions. Why should they not go? Only that morning he had received a letter from his agent at Bessington Hall to say the place, unfortunately, would not be completely ready for them. Why, then, should they not accept this pleasant invitation?

Theodora hesitated—but he cut her short.

"I am sure it is very good of you, Sir Patrick, and my wife and I will be delighted to come," he said.

By this time the excitement of the royal entrance and quadrille had somewhat subsided, and several people felt themselves drawn to be presented to the beautiful young woman in white with the really fine jewels, and before she knew where she was, Theodora found herself waltzing with a wonderfully groomed, ugly young marquis.

She had meant not to dance—not to leave her husband's side; but fate and Josiah had ordered otherwise.

"Not dance! What nonsense, my love! Go at once with his lordship," he had said, when Sir Patrick had presented Lord Wensleydown. And wincing at the sentence, Theodora had allowed herself to be whirled away.

Her partner was not more than nine-and-twenty; but he had all the blasé airs of a man of forty. He began to say *entreprenant* things to Theodora after three turns round the room.

She was far too unsophisticated to understand their ultimate meaning, but they made her uncomfortable.

He gazed at her loveliness with that insulting look of sensual admiration which some men think the highest compliment they can pay to a woman. And just in the middle of all this, Hector Bracondale arrived upon the scene. He had been searching for her everywhere; in that crowd one could miss any one with ease. He stood and watched her before she caught sight of him—watched her pure whiteness in the clutches of this beast of prey. Saw his burning looks; noted his attitude; imagined his whisperings—and murderous feelings leaped to his brain.

How dared Wensleydown! How dared any one! Ah, God! and he was powerless to prevent it. She was the wife of Josiah Brown over there, smiling and complacent to see *his* belonging dancing with a marquis!

"Hector, dearest, what is the matter?" exclaimed Lady Anningford, coming up at that moment to her brother's side. She was with Colonel Lowerby, and they had made a tour of the rooms on purpose to see Theodora. "You appear ready to murder some one. What has happened?"

Hector looked straight at her. She was a very tall woman, almost his height, and she saw pain and rage and passion were swimming in his eyes, while his deep voice vibrated as he answered:

"Yes, I want to murder some one—and possibly will before the evening is over."

"Hector! Crow, leave me with him, like the dear you always are," she whispered to Colonel Lowerby, "and come and find me again in a few minutes."

"Hector, what is it?" she asked, anxiously, when they stood alone.

"Look!" said Lord Bracondale. "Look at Wensleydown leaning over Theodora." He was so moved that he uttered the name without being aware of it. "Did you ever see such a damned cad as he is? Good God, I cannot bear it!"

"He—he is only dancing with her," said Anne, soothingly. What had come to her brother, her whimsical, cynical brother, who troubled not at all, as a rule, over anything in the world?

"Only dancing with her! I tell you I will not bear it. Where is the Crow? Why did you send him off? I can't stay with you; I must go and speak to her, and take her away from this."

"Hector, for Heaven's sake do not be so mad," said Lady Anningford, now really alarmed. "You can't go up and seize a woman from her partner in the middle of a waltz. You must be completely crazy! Dear boy, let us stay here by the door until the music finishes, and then I will speak to her before they can leave the room to sit out."

She put her hand on his arm to detain him, and started to feel how it trembled.

What passion was this? Surely the Crow was right, after all, and it could only lead to some inevitable catastrophe. Anne's heart sank; the lights and the splendor seemed all a gilded mockery.

At that moment Morella Winmarleigh advanced with Evermond Le Mesurier—their uncle Evermond—who, having other views for his own amusement, left her instantly at Anne's side and disappeared among the crowd.

"How impossible to find any one in this crush!" Miss Winmarleigh said. There was a cackly tone in her voice, especially when raised above the din of the music, which was peculiarly irritating to sensitive ears.

Hector felt he hated her.

Anne still kept her hand on his arm, and flight was hopeless.

Just then a Royalty passed with their hostess, and claimed Lady Anningford's attention, so Hector was left sole guardian of Morella Winmarleigh.

She cackled on about nothing, while his every sense was strained watching Theodora, to see that she did not leave the room without his knowledge.

She was whirling still in the maze of the waltz, and each time she passed fresh waves of rage surged in Hector's breast, as he perceived the way in which Lord Wensleydown held her.

"Why, there is the woman who was at the opera last night," exclaimed Morella, at last. "How in the world did an outsider like that get here, I wonder? She is quite pretty, close—don't you think so, Hector? Oh, I forgot, you know her, of course; you talked to her last night, I remember."

Hector did not answer; he was afraid to let himself speak.

Morella Winmarleigh was looking her best. A tonged, laced, flounced best; and she was perfectly conscious of it, and pleased with herself and her attractions.

She meant to keep Lord Bracondale with her for the rest of the evening if possible, even if she had to descend to tricks scarcely flattering to her own vanity.

"Do let us go for a walk," she said. "I have not yet seen the flower decorations in the yellow salon, and I hear they are particularly fine."

Hector by this time was beside himself at seeing Theodora converging with her partner towards the large doors at the other end of the ballroom.

"No," he said. "I am very sorry, but I am engaged for the next dance, and must go and hunt up my partner. Where can I take you?"

Hector engaged for a dance? An unknown thing, and of course untrue. What could this mean? Who would he dance with? That colonial creature? This must be looked into and stopped at once.

Miss Winmarleigh's thin under-lip contracted, and a deeper red suffused her blooming cheeks.

"I really don't know," she said. "I am quite lost, and I am afraid you can't leave me until I find some one to take care of me." And she giggled girlishly.

That such a large cow of a woman should want protection of any sort seemed quite ridiculous to Hector—maddeningly ridiculous at the present moment. Theodora had disappeared, having seen him standing there with Morella Winmarleigh, who she had been told he was going to marry.

He was literally white with suppressed rage. The Royalty had commandeered Anne, and among the dozens of people he knew there was not one in sight with whom he could plant Morella Winmarleigh; so he gave her his arm, and hurried along the way Theodora had disappeared.

"Are you going to Beechleigh for Whitsuntide?" Morella asked. "I am, and I think we shall have a delightful party."

Hector was not paying the least attention. Theodora was completely out of sight now, and might be lost altogether, for all they were likely to overtake her among this crowd and the numberless exits and entrances.

"Beechleigh!" he mumbled, absently. "Who lives there? I don't even know. I am going home."

"Why, Hector, of course you know! The Fitzgeralds—Sir Patrick and Lady Ada. Every one does."

Then it came to him. These were Theodora's uncle and aunt. Was it possible she could be going there, too? He recollected she had told him in Paris her father had written to this brother of his about her coming to London. She might be going. It was a chance, and he must ascertain at once.

Sir Patrick Fitzgerald he knew at the Turf, and now that he thought of it he knew Lady Ada by sight quite well, and he was aware he would be a welcome guest at any house. If Theodora was going, he expected the thing could be managed. Meanwhile, he must find her, and get rid of Morella Winmarleigh. He hurried her on through the blue salon and the yellow salon and out into the gallery beyond. Theodora had completely disappeared.

Miss Winmarleigh kept up a constant chatter of commonplaces, to which, when he replied at all, he gave random answers.

And every moment she became more annoyed and uneasy.

She had known Hector since she was a child. Their places adjoined in the country, and she saw him constantly when there. Her stolid vanity had never permitted the suggestion to come to her that he had always been completely indifferent to her. She intended to marry him. His mother shared her wishes. They were continually thrown together, and the thought of her as a probable ending to his life when all pleasures should be over had often entered his head.

Before he met Theodora, if he had ever analyzed his views about Morella, they probably would have been that she was a safe bore with a great many worldly advantages. A woman who you could be sure would not take a lover a few years after you had married her, and whom he would probably marry if she were still free when the time came.

His flittings from one pretty matron to another had not caused her grave anxieties. He could not marry them, and he never talked with girls or possible rivals. So she had always felt safe and certain that fate would ultimately make him her husband.

But this was different—he had never been like this before. And uneasiness grabbed at her well-regulated heart.

"Ah, there is my mother!" he exclaimed, at last, with such evident relief that Morella began to feel spiteful.

They made their way to where Lady Bracondale was standing. She beamed upon them like a pleased pussy-cat. It looked so suitable to see them thus together!

"Dearest," she said to Morella, "is not this a lovely ball? And I can see you are enjoying yourself."

Miss Winmarleigh replied suitably, and her stolid face betrayed none of her emotion.

"Mother," said Hector, "I wish you would introduce me to Lady Ada Fitzgerald when you get the chance. I see her over there."

This was so obvious that Morella, who never saw between the lines, preened with pleasure. After all, he wished to spend Whitsuntide with her, and this anxiety to find Lady Bracondale had been all on that account. Lady Bracondale, who was acquainted with Miss Winmarleigh's plans, made the same interruption, and joy warmed her being.

She was only too pleased to do whatever he wished. And the affair was soon accomplished.

Hector made himself especially attractive, and Lady Ada Fitzgerald decided he was charming.

The way paved for possible contingencies, he escaped from this crowd of women, and once more began his search for Theodora. She would certainly return to Josiah some time. To go straight to him would be the best plan.

Josiah was standing absolutely alone by one of the windows in the ballroom, and looked pitiably uncomfortable and ill at ease in his knee-breeches and silk stockings.

He had experienced such pleasure when he had tried them on, and had enjoyed walking through the hall at Claridge's to his carriage, knowing the people there would be aware it meant he was going to meet the most august Royalty.

But now he felt uncomfortable, and kept standing first on one leg, then on the other. Theodora had not returned to him yet: the next dance had not begun.

This great world contained discomfort as well as pleasure, he decided.

Hector walked straight over to him and was excessively polite and agreeable, and Josiah's equanimity was somewhat restored.

What could have happened to Theodora? Where had that beast Wensleydown taken her? Not to supper—surely not to supper?—were Lord Bracondale's thoughts.

And then with the first notes of the next dance she reappeared. It seemed to him she was looking superbly lovely: a faint pink suffused her cheeks, and her eyes were shining with the excitement of the scene.

A mad rush of passion surged over Hector; his turn had come, he thought.

Lord Wensleydown seemed loath to release her, and showed signs of staying to talk awhile. So Hector interposed at once.

"May I not have this dance? I have been looking for you everywhere," he said.

Theodora told him she was tired, and she stood close to her husband; tired—and also she was quite sure Josiah would be bored left all alone, so she wished to stay with him.

But Mrs. Devlyn made a reappearance just then, and as they spoke they saw Josiah give her his arm and lead her away.

Thus Theodora was left standing alone with Lord Bracondale.

Fate seemed always to nullify her good intentions.

It was an exquisite waltz, and the music mounted to both their brains.

For one moment the room appeared to reel in front of her, and then she found herself whirling in his arms. Oh, what bliss it was, after this long week of separation! What folly and maddening bliss!

Her senses were tingling; her lithe, exquisite, willowy body thrilled and quivered in his embrace. And they both realized what a waltz could be, as a medium for joy.

"We will only have two turns until the crowd gets impossible again," he whispered, "and then I will take you to supper."

Lady Anningford had been rejoined by the Crow, and now stood watching them. She and her companion were silent for a moment, and then:

"By Jove!" Colonel Lowerby said. "She is certainly worth going to hell for, to look at even—and they don't appear as if they would take long on the road."

XX

"Oh, Crow, dear, what are we to do, then?" said Lady Anningford. "Surely, surely you don't anticipate any sudden catastrophe? In these days people never run away—"

"No," said the Crow. "They stay at home until the footman, or the man's last mistress, or the woman's dearest friend, send anonymous letters to the husband."

"But—"

"Well, I tell you, Queen Anne, to me this appears serious. I know Hector pretty well, and I have never seen him as far gone as this before. The woman—she is a mere child—looks as unsophisticated as a baby, and probably is. She won't have the least idea of managing the affair. She will tumble headlong into it."

"Well, what is to be done, then?" exclaimed Anne, piteously.

"You had better talk to him quietly. He is very fond of you. Though nothing, I am afraid, will be of the least use," said the Crow.

"But if she is going into the country they won't meet," reasoned Anne. "You saw the dreadful-looking husband just now. Will he be the colonial who will object, do you think, or the English snob who won't?"

But the Crow refused to give any more opinions except in general.

It all came, he said, from the ridiculous marriage laws in this over-civilized country. Why should not people eminently suited to each other be allowed to be happy?

"It is too bad, Crow," said Anne. "You take it for granted that Hector has the most dishonorable intentions towards Mrs. Brown. He may worship her quite in the abstract."

"Fiddle-dee-dee, my child!" said Colonel Lowerby. "Look at him! You don't understand the fundamental principles of human nature if you say that. When a man is madly in love with a woman, nature says, 'This is your mate,' not a saint of alabaster on a church altar. There are numbers of animals about who find a 'mate' in every woman they come across. But Hector is not that sort. Look at his face—look at him now they are passing us, and tell me if you see any abstract about it?"

Anne was forced to admit she did not; and it was with intense uneasiness she saw her brother and his partner stop, and disappear through one of the doors towards the supper-room.

When her mother perceived the situation—or Morella—disagreeable moments would begin at once for everybody!

Meanwhile, the culprits were extremely happy.

With the finest and noblest intention in the world, Theodora was too young, and too healthy, not to have become exhilarated with the dance and the scene. Something whispered, Why should she not enjoy herself to-night? What harm could there be in dancing? Every one danced—and Josiah, himself, had left her alone.

Hector had not said a word that she must rebuke him for; they had just waltzed and thrilled, and been—happy!

And now she was going to eat some supper with him, and forget there were any to-morrows.

They found a secluded corner, and spent half an hour in perfect peace. Hector was an artist in pleasing women—and to-night, though he never once transgressed in words, she could feel through it all that he loved her—loved her madly. His voice was so tender and deep, and his thought for her slightest wish and comfort so evident; he was masterful, too, and settled what she was to do—where to sit, and now and then he made her look at him.

He was just so wildly happy he could not stop to count the cost; and while he worshipped her more deeply than when they had sat on the soft greensward at Versailles, even the whole sight of her pure soul now could not stop him—now he knew she loved him, and that there were possible others on the scene. She had trusted him—had appealed to his superior strength; he did not forget that fact quite—but here at a ball was not the place to analyze what it would mean. They were just two guests dancing and supping like the rest, and were supremely content.

He found out where she was going for Whitsuntide, but said nothing of his own intentions.

The blindness and madness of love was upon him and held him in complete bondage. The first shock, which her look of the wounded fawn had given him, was over. They had suffered, and made good resolutions, and parted, and now they had met again. And he could not, and would not, think where they might drift to.

To be near her, to look into her eyes, to be conscious of her personality was what he asked at the moment, what he must have. The rest of time was a blank, and meaningless. It is not every man who loves in this way—fortunately for the rest of the world! Many go through life with now and then a different woman merely as an episode, as far as anything but a physical emotion is concerned. Sport, or their own ambitions, fill up their real interests, and no woman could break their hearts.

But Hector was not of these. And this woman had it in her power to make his heaven or hell.

They had both passed through moments of exalted sentiment, even a little dramatic in their tragedy and renunciation, but circumstance is stronger always than any highly strung emotion of good or evil. At the end of their good-bye at Madrid their story should have closed, as the stories in books so often do, with the hero and heroine worked up to some wonderful pitch of self-sacrifice and drama. They so seldom tell of the flatness of the afterwards. The impossibility of retaining a balance on this high pinnacle of moral valor, where circumstance, which is a commonplace and often material thing, decrees that the lights shall not be turned out with the ring-down of the curtain.

Unless death finishes what is apparently the last act, there is always the to-morrow to be reckoned with—out of the story-book. So while exalted—he by his sudden worship of that pure sweetness of soul in Theodora which he had discovered, she by her innocence and desire to do right—they had been able to tune their minds to an idea of a tender good-bye, full of sentiment and vows of abstract devotion, and adherence to duty.

And if he had gone to the ends of the earth that night the exaltation, as a memory, might have continued, and time might have healed their hurts—time and the starvation of absence and separation. But fate had decreed they should meet again, and soon; and all the forces which precipitate matters should be employed for their undoing.

For all else in life Hector was no weakling. He had always been a strong man, physically and morally.

His views were the views of the world. It seemed no great sin to him to love another man's wife. All his friends did the same at one period or another.

It was only when Theodora had awakened him that he had begun even to think of controlling himself.

It was to please her, not because he was really convinced of the right and necessity of their course of action, that he had said good-bye and agreed to worship her in the abstract.

He had been highly moved and elevated by her that night in Paris. And when he wrote the letter his honest intention had been to follow its words.

He did not recognize the fact that without the zeal of blind faith as to the right, human nature must always yield to inclination.

So they sat there and ate their supper, and forgot to-morrow, and were radiantly happy.

As they had gone down the stairs Monica Ellerwood had joined Lady Bracondale in the gallery above.

"Oh! Look, Aunt Milly!" she had said. "Hector is with the American I told you about in Paris. Do you see, going down to supper. Oh, isn't she pretty! and what jewels—look!"

And Lady Bracondale had moved forward in a manner quite foreign to her usual dignity to catch sight of them.

"It is the same woman he talked to at the opera last night," she said. "She is not an American, but a Mrs. Brown, an Australian millionaire's wife, we were told. She is certainly pretty. Oh—eh—you said Hector was devoted to her in Paris?"

"Why, of course! You can ask Jack."

"I do not think we need worry, though, dear, because I am happy to say Hector shows great signs of wishing to be with Morella."

And with this pleasing thought she had turned the conversation.

"I think we must go back now," said Theodora, after she had finished the last monster strawberry on her plate. "Josiah may be waiting for me."

Oh, she had been so happy! There was that sense vibrating through everything that he loved her, and they were together—but now it must end.

So they made their way up the stairs and back to the ballroom.

Mrs. Devlyn had abandoned Josiah, and he stood once more alone and supremely uncomfortable. A pang of remorse seized Theodora; she wished she had not stayed so long; she would not leave him again for a moment.

He had supped, it appeared, been hurried over it because Mrs. Devlyn wished to return, and was now feeling cross and tired. He was quite ready to leave when Theodora suggested it, and they said good-night to Hector and descended to find their carriage. But in that crowd it was not such an easy matter.

There was a long wait in the hall, where they were joined by the assiduous Marquis and Delaval Stirling. And Hector, from a place on the stairs, had all his feelings of jealous rage aroused again in watching them while he was detained where he was by his hostess.

Meanwhile, Sir Patrick Fitzgerald had gone about telling every one of the beauty of his new-found niece, and had brought his wife to be introduced to her just after Theodora had left.

Since his scapegrace brother was going to make such an advantageous marriage, and this niece had proved a lovely woman, and rich withal, he quite admitted the ties of blood were thicker than water.

Lady Ada was not of like opinion; she had enough relations of her own, and resented his having asked the Browns to Beechleigh for Whitsuntide.

"My party was all made up but for one extra man," she said, "whom I think I have found; and we did not need these people."

XXI

Lord Bracondale arrived at his sister's house in Charles Street about a quarter of an hour before her luncheon guests were due.

Anne rushed down to see him, meeting her husband on the stairs.

"Oh, don't come in yet, Billy, like a darling," she said, "I want to talk to Hector alone."

And the meek and fond Lord Anningford had obediently retired to his smoking-room.

"Well, Hector," she said, when she had greeted him, "and so you are going to the Fitzgeralds' for Whitsuntide, and not to Bracondale, mother tells me this morning. She is in the seventh heaven, taking it for a sign, as you had to manœuvre so to be asked, that things are coming to a climax between you and Morella."

"Morella? Is she going?" said Hector, absently. He had quite forgotten that fact, so perfectly indifferent was he to her movements, and so completely had his own aims engrossed him.

"Why—dear boy!" Anne gasped. The whole scene, highly colored by repetition, had been recounted to her. How Morella had told him of her plans, and how he had at once got introduced to Lady Ada, and played his cards so skilfully that the end of the evening produced the invitation.

"Oh yes, of course, I remember she is going," he said, impatiently. "Anne, you haven't asked that beast Wensleydown to-day, have you?"

"No, dear. What made you think so?"

"I saw you talking to him in the park this morning, and I feared you might have. I shall certainly quarrel with him one of these days."

"You will have an opportunity, then, at Beechleigh, as he will be there. He is always with the Fitzgeralds," Anne said, and she tried to laugh. "But don't make a scandal, Hector."

She saw his eyes blaze.
"He is going there, is he?" he said, and then he stared out of the window.
Anne knew nothing of the relationship between Theodora and Sir Patrick. She never for a moment imagined the humble Browns would be invited to this exceptionally smart party. And yet she was uneasy. Why was Hector going? What plan was in his head? Not Morella, evidently. But she had never believed that would be his attraction.
And Hector was too preoccupied to enlighten her.
"Is mother coming to lunch?" he asked.
"Yes, by her own request. I had not meant to ask her—Oh, well, you know, she is never very pleased at your having new friends, and I thought she might fix Mrs. Brown with that stony stare she has sometimes, and we would be happier without her; but she was determined to come."
"It is just as well," he said, "because she will have to get accustomed to it. I shall ask my friends the Browns down to Bracondale on every occasion, and as she is hostess there the stony stare won't answer."
"Manage her as best you may," said Anne. "But you know how she can be now and then—perfectly annihilating to unfortunate strangers."
Hector's finely chiselled lips shut like a vise.
"We shall see," he said. "And who else have you got? None of the Harrowfield-Devlyn crew, I hope—"
"Hector, how strange you are! I thought you and Lady Harrowfield were the greatest friends, so of course I asked her. No one in London can make a woman's success as she can."
"Or mar it so completely if she takes a dislike! Have you ever heard of her doing a kindness to any one? I haven't!" he said, irritably.
Then he walked to the window and back quickly.
"I tell you I am sick of it all, Anne. Last night, whoever I spoke to had something vile to impute or insinuate about every one they mentioned; and Lady Harrowfield, with a record of her own worse than the lowest, rode a high horse of virtue, and was more spiteful than all the rest put together. I loathe them, the whole crew. What do they know of anything good or pure or fine? Painted Jezebels, the lot of them!"
"Hector!" almost screamed Lady Anningford. "What has come over you, my dear boy?"
"I will tell you," he said; and his voice, which had been full of passion, now melted into a tone of deep tenderness. "I love a woman whose pure goodness has taught me there are other possibilities in life beyond the aims of these vile harpies of our world—a woman whose very presence makes one long to be better and nobler, whose dear soul has not room for anything but kind and loving thoughts of sweetness and light. Oh, Anne, if I might have her for my own, and live away down at Bracondale far from all this, I think—I think I, too, could learn what heaven would mean on earth."
"Dear Hector!" said Anne, who was greatly moved. "Oh, I am so sorry for you! But what is to be done? She is married to somebody else, and you will only injure her and yourself if you see too much of her."
"I know," he said. "I realize it sometimes—this morning, for instance—and then—and then—"
He did not add that the thought of Lord Wensleydown and the rest swarming round Theodora drove him mad, deprived him of his power of reasoning, and filled him with a wild desire to protect her, to be near her, to keep her always for himself, always in his sight.
"Anne," he said, at last, "promise me you will go out of your way to be kind to her. Don't let these other odious women put pin-points into her, because she is so innocent, and all unused to this society. She is just my queen and my darling. Will you remember that?"
And as Anne looked she saw there were two great tears in his eyes—his deep-gray eyes which always wore a smile of whimsical mockery—and she felt a lump in her throat.
This dear, dear brother! And she could do nothing to comfort him—one way or another.
"Hector, I will promise—always," she said, and her voice trembled. "I am sure she is sweet and good; and she is so lovely and fascinating—and oh, I wish—I wish—too!"
Then he bent down and kissed her, just as his mother and Lady Harrowfield came into the room.
Anne felt glad she had not informed them they were to meet the Browns, as was her first intention. She seemed suddenly to see with Hector's eyes, and to realize how narrow and spiteful Lady Harrowfield could be.
Most of the guests arrived one after the other, and were talking about the intimate things they all knew, when "Mr. and Mrs. Brown" were announced, and the whole party turned to look at them, while Lady Harrowfield tittered, and whispered almost audibly to her neighbor:
"These are the creatures Florence insisted upon my giving an invitation to last night. I did it for her sake, of course, so wretchedly poor she is, dear Florence, and she hopes to make a good thing out of them. Look at the man!" she added. "Has one ever sees such a person, except in a pork-butcher's shop!"
"I have never been in one," said Hector, agreeably, a dangerous flash in his eyes; "but I hear things are too wonderfully managed at Harrowfield House—though I had no idea you did the shopping yourself, dear Lady Harrowfield."
She looked up at him, rage in her heart. Hector had long been a hopeless passion of hers—so good-looking, so whimsical, and, above all, so indifferent! She had never been able to dominate and ride rough-shod ever him. When she was rude and spiteful he answered her back, and then neglected her for the rest of the evening.
But why should he defend these people, whom, probably, he did not even know?
She would watch and see.
Then they went in to luncheon, without waiting for two or three stray young men who were always late.
And Theodora found herself sitting between the Crow and a sleek-looking politician; while poor Josiah, extremely ill at ease, sat at the left hand of his hostess.

Anne had purposely not put Hector near Theodora; with her mother there she thought it was wiser not to run any risks.

Lady Bracondale was sufficiently soothed by her happy dream of the cause of Hector's visit to Beechleigh to be coldly polite to Theodora, whom Anne had presented to her before luncheon. She sat at the turn of the long, oval table just one off, and was consequently able to observe her very carefully.

"She is extremely pretty and looks well bred—quite too extraordinary," she said to herself, in a running commentary. "Grandfather a convict, no doubt. She reminds me of poor Minnie Borringdon, who ran off with that charming scapegrace brother of Patrick Fitzgerald. I wonder what became of them?"

Lady Bracondale deplored the ways of many of the set she was obliged to move in—Delicia Harrowfield, for instance. But what was one to do? One must know one's old friends, especially those to whom one had been a bridesmaid!

The Crow, who had begun by being determined to find Theodora as cunning as other angels he was acquainted with, before the second course had fallen completely under her spell.

No one to look into her tender eyes could form an adverse opinion about her; and her gentle voice, which only said kind things, was pleasing to the ear.

"'Pon my soul, Hector is not such a fool as I thought," Colonel Lowerby said to himself. "This seems a bit of pure gold—poor little white lady! What will be the end of her?"

And opposite, Hector, with great caution, devoured her with his eyes.

Theodora herself was quite happy, though her delicate intuition told her Lady Harrowfield was antagonistic to her, and Hector's mother exceedingly stiff, while most of the other women eyed her clothes and talked over her head. But they all seemed of very little consequence to her, somehow.

She was like the sun, who continues to shine and give warmth and light no matter how much ugly imps may look up and make faces at him.

Theodora was never ill at ease. It would grieve her sensitive heart to the core if those she loved made the faintest shade of difference in their treatment of her—but strangers! They counted not at all, she had too little vanity.

Both her neighbors, the young politician and the Crow, were completely fascinated by her. She had not the slightest accent in speaking English, but now and then her phrasing had a quaint turn which was original and attractive.

Anne was not enjoying her luncheon-party. The impression of sorrow and calamity which the conversation with her brother had left upon her deepened rather than wore off.

Josiah's commonplace and sometimes impossible remarks perhaps helped it.

She seemed to realize how it must all jar on Hector. To know his loved one belonged to this worthy grocer—to understand the hopelessness of the position!

Anne was proud of her family and her old name. It was grief, too, to think that after Hector the title would go to Evermond Le Mesurier, the unmarried and dissolute uncle, if he survived his nephew, and then would die out altogether. There would be no more Baron Bracondales of Bracondale, unless Hector chose to marry and have sons. Oh, life was a topsy-turvy affair at the best of times, she sighed to herself.

Just before the ladies left the table, Josiah had announced their intended visit to Beechleigh, and his wife's relationship to Sir Patrick Fitzgerald and the old Earl Borringdon.

It came as a thunderclap to Lady Anningford. This accounted for Hector's eagerness to obtain the invitation—accounted for Theodora's exceeding look of breeding—accounted for many things.

She only trusted her mother had not heard the news also. So much better to leave her in her fool's paradise about Morella.

If Lady Harrowfield knew, she said nothing about it. She absolutely ignored Theodora, as though she had never shaken hands with her in her own house the night before. Theodora wondered at her manners—she did not yet know Mayfair.

The conversation turned upon some of the wonderful charities they were all interested in, and Theodora thought how good and kind of them to help the poor and crippled. And she said some gentle, sympathetic things to a lady who was near her. And Anne thought to herself how sweet and beautiful her nature must be, and it made her sadder and sadder.

Presently they all began to discuss the ball at Harrowfield House. It had been too lovely, they said, and Lady Harrowfield joined in with one of her sharp thrusts.

"Of course it could not be just as one would have wished. I was obliged to ask all sorts of people I had never even heard of," she said. "The usual grabbing for invitations, you know, to see the Royalties. Really, the quaint creatures who came up the stairs! I almost laughed in their faces once or twice."

"But don't you like to feel what pleasure you gave them, the poor things?" Theodora said, quite simply, without the least sarcasm. "You see, I know you gave them pleasure, because my husband and I were some of them—and we enjoyed it, oh, so much!"

And she smiled one of her adorable smiles which melted the heart of every one else in the room. But of Lady Harrowfield she made an enemy for life. The venomous woman reddened violently—under her paint—while she looked this upstart through and through. But Theodora was quite unconscious of her anger. To her Lady Harrowfield seemed a poor, soured old woman very much painted and ridiculous, and she felt sorry for unlovely old age and ill-temper.

Meanwhile, Lady Bracondale was being favorably impressed. She was a most presentable young person, this wife of the Australian millionaire, she decided.

Anne took the greatest pains to be charming to Theodora. They were sitting together on a sofa when the men came into the room.

Hector could keep away no longer. He joined them in their corner, while his face beamed with joy to see the two people he loved best in the world apparently getting on so well together.

"What have you been talking about?" he asked.

"Nothing very learned," said Anne. "Only the children. I was telling Mrs. Brown how Fordy's pony ran away in the park this morning, and how plucky he had been about it."

"They are rather nice infants," said Hector. "I should like you to see them," and he looked at Theodora. "Mayn't we have them down, Anne?"

Lady Anningford adored her offspring, and was only too pleased to show them; but she said:

"Oh, wait a moment, Hector, until some of these people have gone. Lady Harrowfield hates children, and Fordy made some terrible remarks about her wig last time."

"I wish he would do it again," said Hector. "She took the skin off every one the whole way through lunch."

"But Colonel Lowerby told me she was one of the cleverest women in London!" exclaimed Theodora; "and surely it is not very clever just to be bitter and spiteful!"

"Yes, she is clever," said Anne, with a peculiar smile, "and we are all rather under her thumb."

"It is perfectly ridiculous how you pander to her!" Hector said, impatiently. "I should never allow my wife to have anything but a distant acquaintance with her if I were married," and he glanced at Theodora.

Lady Anningford's duties as hostess took her away from them then, and he sat down on the sofa in her place.

"Oh, how I hate all this!" he said. "How different it is to Paris! It grates and jars and brings out the worst in one. These odious women and their little, narrow ways! You will never stay much in London—will you, Theodora?"

"I have always to do what Josiah wishes, you know; he rather likes it, and means us to come back after Whitsuntide, I think."

Hector seemed to have lost the power of looking ahead. Whitsuntide, and to be with her in the country for that time, appeared to him the boundary of his outlook.

What would happen after Whitsuntide? Who could say?

He longed to tell her how his thoughts were forever going back to the day at Versailles, and the peace and beauty of those woods—how all seemed here as though something were dragging him down to the commonplace, away out of their exalted dream, to a dull earth. But he dared not—he must keep to subjects less moving. So there was silence for some moments.

Theodora, since coming to London, had begun to understand it was possible for beautiful Englishmen to be husbands now and then, and that the term is not necessarily synonymous with "bore" and "duty"—as she had always thought it from her meagre experience.

She could not help picturing what a position of exquisite happiness some nice girl might have—some day—as Hector's wife. And she looked out of the window, and her eyes were sad. While the vision which floated to him at the same moment was of her at his side at Bracondale, and the delicious joy of possessing for their own some gay and merry babies like Fordy and his little brother and sister. And each saw a wistful longing in the other's eyes, and they talked quickly of banal things.

XXII

The Crow stayed on after all the other guests had left. He knew his hostess wished to talk to him.

It had begun to pour with rain, and the dripping streets held out no inducement to them to go out.

They pulled up their two comfortable arm-chairs to the sparkling wood fire, and then Colonel Lowerby said:

"You look sad, Queen Anne. Tell me about it."

"Yes, I am sad," said Anne. "The position is so hopeless. Hector loves her—loves her really—and I do not wonder at it; and she seems just everything that one could wish for him. A thousand times above Morella in intellect and understanding. All the things Hector and I like she sees at once. No need of explaining to her, as one has to to mother and Morella always."

"Yes," said the Crow. He did not argue with her as usual.

"It seems so fearful to think of her forever bound to that dreadful old grocer, whom she treats with so much deference and gentleness. The whole thing has made me sad. Hector is perfectly miserable; and, do you know, they are going to Beechleigh for Whitsuntide. Sir Patrick Fitzgerald is her uncle—and, of course, Hector is going, too, and—"

She did not finish her sentence. Her voice died away in a pathetic note as she gazed into the fire.

The Crow fidgeted; he had been devoted to Anne since she was a child of ten, and he hated to see her troubled.

"Look here," he said. "I investigated her thoroughly at luncheon, and I don't often make a mistake, do I?"

"No," said Anne. "Well—?"

"Well, she appeared to me to have some particular quality of sweetness—you were right about her looking like an angel—and I think she has got an angel's nature more or less; and when people are really like that there is some one up above looks after them, and I don't think we need worry much—you and I."

"Dear old Crow!" said Anne; "you do comfort me. But all the same, angel or not, Hector is so attractive—and he is a man, you know, not one of these anæmic, artistic, æsthetic things we see about so often now; and thrown together like that—how on earth will they be able to help themselves?"

The Crow was silent.

"You see," she continued, "beyond Morella, who is too absolutely unalluring and respectable to come to harm anywhere, and Miss Linwood, who only cares for bridge, there will hardly be another woman in the house who has not got a lover, and the atmosphere of those things is catching—don't you think so?"

"It is nature," said Colonel Lowerby. "A woman in possession of her health and faculties requires a mate, and when her husband is attending to sport or some other man's wife, she is bound to find one somewhere. I don't blame the poor things."

"Oh, nor I!" said Anne. "I don't ever blame any one. And just one, because you love him, seems all right, perhaps. It is six different ones in a year, and a seventh to pay the bills, that I find vulgar."

"Dans les premières passions, les femmes aiment l'amant; et dans les autres, elles aiment l'amour," quoted the Crow. "It was ever the same, you see. It is the seventh to pay the bills that seems vulgar and modern."

"Billy and I stayed there for the pheasant shoot last November, and I assure you we felt quite out of it, having no little adventures at night like the rest. Lady Ada is the picture of washed-out respectability herself, and so—to give her some reflected color, I suppose—she asks always the most go-ahead, advanced section of her acquaintances."

"Well, I shall be there this time," said the Crow; "she invited me last week."

This piece of news comforted Lady Anningford greatly. She felt here would be some one to help matters if he could.

"Morella will be perfectly furious when she gets there and finds she was not the reason of Hector's empressement for the invitation. And in her stolid way she can be just as spiteful as Lady Harrowfield."

"Yes, I know."

Then they were both silent for a while—Anne's thoughts busy with the mournful idea of the end of the House of Bracondale should Hector never marry, and the Crow's of her in sympathy, his eyes watching her face.

At last she spoke.

"I believe it would be best for Hector to go right away for a year or so," she sighed. "But, however it may be, I fear, alas! it can only end in tears."

XXIII

Beechleigh was really a fine place, built by Vanbrugh in his best days.

Three tiers of fifteen tall windows looked to the north in a front and two short wings, while colonnades led down to splendid wrought-iron gates, and blocks of buildings constructed in the same stately style. Fifteen more windows faced the south; and the centre one of the first floor led, with sweeping steps, to a terrace, while seven casements adorned each of the eastern and western sides.

On the southern side the view, for that rather flat country, was superb.

It gave, from a considerable elevation—through a wide opening of giant oaks and elms—a peep of the lake a mile below, and on in a long avenue of turf to a vista of smiling country.

On the splendid terrace peacocks spread their tails, and vases of carved stone broke at intervals the gray old balustrade.

Inside the house was equally nobly planned: all the rooms of great height and perfect proportion, and filled with pictures and tapestries and bronzes and antiques of immense value.

It had come to these spendthrift Irish Fitzgeralds through their grandmother, the last of an old ducal race. And two generations of Hibernian influence had curtailed the fine fortune which went with it, until Sir Patrick often felt it no easy matter to make both ends meet in the luxurious and gilded fashion which was necessary to himself and his friends.

If he and Lady Ada pinched and scraped when alone, keeping few servants on board wages, the parties, at all events, were done with all their wonted regal splendor.

"I shall stay with you, Patrick, as long as you can afford this cook," Lady Harrowfield said once to him; "but when you begin to economize, don't trouble to ask me. I hate poor people, when it shows."

A promising son, on the true Fitzgerald lines, was at Oxford now, and gave many anxious crows'-feet full opportunity of developing round his mother's faded eyes.

A plain daughter, Barbara, was pushed into corners and left much to herself. And a brilliant, flashing, up-to-date niece of Lady Ada's took always the first place.

Mildred was so clever, and her lovers were so well chosen, and so thoroughly of the right set or of great wealth; while a puny husband was helped to something in South Africa, when the man in possession was a Jew—or as agent for tea and jam in the colonies—when he happened to be only a colossally successful Englishman. And once, during a prominent politician's reign, poor Willie Verner enjoyed a few months in his own land as secretary to a newly started Radical club.

This Whitsuntide party was perhaps the smartest of the year.

By Saturday evening over thirty people would be gathered together under the Beechleigh roof.

Josiah, though exceedingly proud and pleased at the invitation, felt nervous at the thought of the visit. Not so Mr. Toplington, who, although he knew he should probably have to blush for his master, and might get a very secondary place in the "room," still felt he would hold his own when he could let it be known what magnificent wages he received from Mr. Brown.

"A long sight more than I'd get out of any lord," he thought. "And money is money. And all classes feels it."

Theodora, on the contrary, was neither proud nor pleased. She looked forward to the visit with excitement and dread.

Hector would be there, among all these people whom she did not know. And her awakened heart had begun to tell her that she loved him wildly, and to see him could only be alternate mad joy and remorse and anguish.

It was still drizzling on the Saturday afternoon when they arrived. So tea awaited them in the great saloon which made the centre of the north side of the house. Several of the rest of the guests had come down in the same train, but they did not know them, nor did any of them trouble themselves much to speak to them on the short drive from the station. A few words, that was all, addressed to Theodora. Josiah was ignored.

Sir Patrick had always been an excellent host. His genial Irish smile, when in action, concealed the ill-tempered lines of his thin old face. He greeted his guests cordially, and made them welcome to his home.
Lady Ada had the inherited bad manners of her family, the De Baronsvilles, who had come over with the Conqueror, and when one has a *cachet* like that there is no need to trouble one's self further. Thus, while Mildred flashed brilliant witticisms about, plain Barbara saw after the guests' tea and sugar, and if they took cream or lemon, and tiresome things like that. And as every one knew every one else, and the same party met continuously all over England, things were very gay and friendly.
Only Theodora and Josiah were completely out of it all, and several of the guests, who resented the intrusion of these strangers into their charmed circle, would take care on every opportunity to make them feel it.
Hector did not get there until half an hour later, in his automobile, which was the mode of arrival with more than two-thirds of the company.
And until the dressing-gong sounded, a continuous teuf-teuf-teuf might have been heard as, one after another, the cars whizzed up to the door.
Of course, in a troop of over thirty people, naturally some had kind hearts and good manners, but the prevailing tone of this coterie of *crème de la crème* was one of pure selfishness and blunt and material brutality.
If you were rich and suited them, you were given a nickname probably, and were allowed to play cards with them, and lose your money for their benefit. If you were non-congenial you did not exist—that was all. You might be sitting in a chair, but they only saw it and an empty space—you did not even cumber their ground.
To do them justice, they preferred people of their own exalted station; outsiders seldom made their way into this holy of holies, however rich they were—unless, of course, they happened to be Mildred's lovers. That situation for a man held special prerogatives, and was greatly coveted by pretenders to this circle of grace.
Intellectual intelligence was not important. Some of the women of this select company had been described by an agricultural duke who had stayed there as having just enough sense to come in out of the rain.
Sir Patrick Fitzgerald occasionally departed from the strict limits of this set in the big parties—especially lately, when money was becoming scarcer, several financial friends who could put him on to good things had been included, the result being that Lady Harrowfield had not always shed the light of her countenance upon the festivities.
Lord Harrowfield drew most of his income from a great, populous manufacturing city in the north, so neither he nor his countess had need to smile at mere wealth.
And Lady Harrowfield had said, frankly, "Let me know if it is a utility party, Patrick, or for just ourselves, because if you are going to have these creatures I sha'n't come."
This time, however, she had not been so exigent. It happened to suit some other arrangements of hers to spend Whitsuntide at Beechleigh, so she consented to chaperon Morella Winmarleigh without asking for a list of the guests.
Hector had never conformed to any special set; he went here, there, and everywhere, and was welcomed by all. But somehow, until this occasion, Beechleigh had never seen him within its gates, although Lady Harrowfield had praised him, and Mildred had sighed for him in vain.
He saw the situation at a glance when he came into the saloon: Josiah and Theodora sitting together, neglected by every one but Barbara. They could not have been more than half an hour in the house, he knew, for he had found out when the trains got in.
Barbara was a good sort; he remembered now he had met her before somewhere. She had evidently taken to the new cousin; but Mildred had not.
Hitherto Mildred had been the undisputed and acknowledged beauty of every party, and she resented Theodora's presence because she was clever enough not to have any illusions upon the matter of their mutual looks. She saw Theodora was beautiful and young and charming, and had every advantage of perfect Paris clothes. Uncle Patrick had been a fool to ask her, and she must take measures to suppress her at once.
Sir Patrick, on the other hand, was very pleased with himself for having given the invitation. He had made inquiries, and found that Josiah was a man of great and solid wealth, with interests in several things which could be of particular use to himself, and he meant to obtain what he could out of him.
As for Theodora, no living man could do anything but admire her, and Sir Patrick was not an Irishman for nothing.
Hector behaved with tact; he did not at once fly to his darling, but presently she found him beside her. And the now habitual thrill ran over her when he came near.
He saw the sudden, convulsive clasp of her little hands together; he knew how he moved her, and it gave him joy.
The next batch of arrivals contained Lord Wensleydown, who showed no hesitation as to his desired destination in the saloon. He made a bee-line for Theodora, and took a low seat at her feet.
Hector, with more caution, was rather to one side. Rage surged up in him, although his common-sense told him as yet there was nothing he could openly object to in Wensleydown's behavior.
The little picture of these five people—Barbara engaging Josiah, and the two men vying with each other to please Theodora—was gall and wormwood to Mildred. Freddy Wensleydown had always been one of her most valued friends, and for Hector she had often felt she could experience a passion.
Lord Wensleydown had an immense *cachet*. He was exceedingly ugly and exceedingly smart, and was known to have quite specially attractive methods of his own in the art of pleasing beautiful ladies. He was always unfaithful, too, and they had to make particular efforts to retain him for even a week.
Hector knew him intimately, of course; they had been in the same house at Eton, and were comrades of many years' standing, and until Theodora's entrance upon the scene, Hector had always thought of him as a coarse, jolly

beast of extremely good company and quaintness. But now! He had no words adequate in his vocabulary to express his opinion about him!

To Theodora he appeared an ugly little man, who reminded her of the statue of a satyr she knew in the Louvre. That was all!

At this juncture Lady Harrowfield, accompanied by Morella Winmarleigh, her lord, and one of her *âmes damnées*, a certain Captain Forester, appeared upon the scene.

Their entrance was the important one of the afternoon, and Lady Ada and Sir Patrick could not do enough to greet and make them welcome.

The saloon was so large and the screens so well arranged, that for the first few seconds neither of the ladies perceived the fact of Theodora's presence. But when it burst upon them, both experienced unpleasant sensations.

Lady Harrowfield's temper was bad in any case on account of the weather, and here, on her arrival, that she should find the impertinent upstart who had made her look foolish at the Anningford luncheon, was an extra straw.

Morella felt furious. It began to dawn upon her this might be Hector's reason in coming, not herself at all; and one of those slow, internal rages which she seldom indulged in began to creep in her veins.

Thus it was that poor Theodora, all unconscious of any evil, was already surrounded by three bitter enemies—Mildred, Lady Harrowfield, and Morella Winmarleigh. It did not look as though her Whitsuntide could be going to contain much joy.

It was a good deal after six o'clock by now. Bridge-tables had already appeared, and most of the company had commenced to play. Barbara saw the look in Mildred's eye as she came across, and, ignoring Theodora quite, tried to carry off Lord Wensleydown.

"You must come, Freddy," she said. "Lady Harrowfield wants to begin her rubber."

Barbara, knowing what this move meant, and blushing for her cousin's rudeness, nervously introduced Theodora to her.

"How d' do," said Mildred, staring over her head. "Don't detain Lord Wensleydown, please, because Lady Harrowfield hates to be kept waiting."

Theodora rose and smiled, while she said to Barbara: "I am rather tired. Mayn't I go to my room for a little rest before dinner?"

"Take him, Lady Mildred, do," said Hector; "we don't want him," and he laughed gayly. His beautiful, tender angel might be a match for these people after all. At any rate, he would be at her side to protect her from their claws.

Lord Wensleydown frowned. Mildred was being a damned nuisance, he said to himself, and he insisted upon accompanying Theodora to the bottom of the great staircase, which rose to magnificent galleries in the hall adjoining the saloon.

Sir Patrick had advanced and engaged Josiah in conversation.

He knew his guests' ways and how they would boycott him, and, with a serious question like those Australian shares on the *tapis*, he was not going to have Josiah insulted and ruffled just yet.

"Don't stay up-stairs all the time," Hector had managed to whisper, while Mildred and Lord Wensleydown stood arguing; "they are sure not to dine till nine; there are two hours before you need dress, and we can certainly find some nice sitting-room to talk in."

But Theodora, with immense self-denial, had answered: "No, I want to write a long letter to papa and my sisters. I won't come down again until dinner."

And he was forced to be content with the memory of her soft smile and the evident regret in her eyes.

XXIV

Theodora was greatly interested in Beechleigh. To her the home of her fathers was full of sentiment, and the thought that her grandfather had ruled there pleased her. How she would love and cherish it were it her home now! Every one of these fine things must have some memory.

Then the pictures of as far back as she could remember came to her, and she saw again their poor lodgings in the cheap foreign towns and their often scanty fare. And with a fresh burst of love and pride in him, she remembered her father's invariable cheerfulness—cheerfulness and gayety—in such poverty! And after he had been used to—this! For all the descriptions of Captain Fitzgerald had given her no idea of the reality.

Now she knew what love meant, and could realize her mother's story. Oh, she would have acted just in the same way, too.

Dominic had been forgiven by his brother after his first wife's death, and had come back to enjoy a short spell of peace and prosperity. And who could wonder that Lady Minnie Borringdon, in her first season, and full of romance, should fall headlong in love with his wonderfully handsome face, and be only too ready to run off with him from an angry and unreasonable parent! She was a spoiled and only child who had never been crossed. Then came that fatal Derby, and the final extinction of all sympathy with the scapegrace. The Fitzgeralds had done enough for him already, and Lord Borringdon had no intention of doing anything at all, so the married lovers crept away in high disgrace, and spent a few months of bliss in a southern town, where the sun shone and the food was cheap, and there poor, pretty Minnie died, leaving Theodora a few hours old.

And now at Beechleigh Theodora looked out of her window on the north side—the southern rooms were kept for greater than she—and from there she could see a vast stretch of park, with the deer cropping the fine turf, and the lions frowning while they supported the ducal coronet over the great gates at the end of the court-yard and colonnade.

It was truly a splendid inheritance, and she glowed with pride to think she was of this house.

So she wrote a long letter to her dear ones—her sisters at Dieppe, and papa, still in Paris, and even one to Mrs. McBride. And then she read until her maid came to dress her for dinner.

Her room was a large one, and numberless modern touches of comfort brought up-to-date the early Georgian furniture and the shabby silk hangings. A room stamped with that something which the most luxurious apartments of the wealthiest millionaire can never acquire.

Josiah looked in upon her as she finished dressing. He was, he said, most pleased with everything, and if they were a little unused to such company, still nothing could be more cordial than Sir Patrick's treatment of him.

Meanwhile, on their way up to dress, Mildred had gone in to Morella's room, and the two had agreed that Mrs. Brown should be suppressed.

It was with extra displeasure Miss Winmarleigh had learned of Theodora's relationship to Sir Patrick, and that after all she could not be called a common colonial.

There was no question about the Fitzgerald and Borringdon families, unfortunately, while Morella's grandfather had been merely a coal merchant.

"I don't think she is so wonderfully pretty, do you, Mildred?" she said.

But Mildred was a clever woman, and could see with her eyes.

"Yes, I do," she answered. "Don't be such a fool as to delude yourself about that, Morella. She is perfectly lovely, and she has the most deevie Paris clothes, and Lord Bracondale is wildly in love with her."

"And apparently Freddy Wensleydown, too," snapped Morella, who was now boiling with rage.

"Well, she is not likely to enjoy herself here," said Mildred, with her vicious laugh, which showed all her splendid, sharp teeth, as she went off to dress, her head full of plans for the interloper's suppression.

First she must have a few words with Barbara. There must be none of her partisanship. Poor, timid Barbara would not dare to disobey her, she knew. That settled, she did not fear that she would be able to make Theodora suffer considerably during the five days she would be at Beechleigh.

Sir Patrick was busy with some new arrivals who had come while they were dressing, so not a soul spoke to Theodora or Josiah when they got down to the great, white drawing-room, from which immensely high mahogany doors opened into an anteroom hung with priceless tapestry and containing cabinets of rare china. From thence another set of splendid carved doors gave access to the dining-room.

Neither Lord Wensleydown or Hector was in the room at first, so there was no man even to talk to them. Lady Ada had not introduced them to any one. And there they stood: Josiah ill at ease and uncomfortable, and Theodora quite apparently unconscious of neglect, while she looked at a picture.

All the younger women were thinking to themselves: "Who are these people? We don't want any strangers here—poaching on our preserves. And what perfect clothes! and what pearls! Why on earth did Ada ask them?"

And soon the party was complete, and Theodora found herself going in to dinner with her cousin Pat, who arrived upon the scene at the very last minute, having come from Oxford by a late train.

Mildred had taken care that neither Lord Wensleydown or Hector should be anywhere near Theodora. She had secured Lord Bracondale for herself, and did her best all through the repast to fascinate him.

And while he answered gallantly and paid her the grossest compliments, she knew he was laughing in his sleeve all the time, and it made her venom rise higher and higher.

Patrick Fitzgerald, the younger, was a dissipated, vicious youth, with his mother's faded coloring and none of the Fitzgerald charm. How infinitely her father surpassed any of the family she had seen yet, Theodora thought.

She did not enjoy her dinner. The youth's conversation was not interesting. But it was not until the ladies left the dining-room that her real penance began.

It seemed as if all the women crowded to one end of the drawing-room round Lady Harrowfield, and talked and whispered to one another, not one making way for Theodora or showing any knowledge of her presence. Barbara had gone off up to her room. She was too frightened of Mildred to disobey her, and she felt she would rather not be there to see their hateful ways to the dear, little, gentle cousin whom she thought she could love so much.

Theodora subsided on a sofa, wondering to herself if these were the manners of the great world in general. She hoped not; but although no human creature could be quite happy under the circumstances, she was not greatly distressed until she distinctly caught the name of "Mr. Brown" from the woman Josiah had taken in amid a burst of laughter, and saw Mildred, with a glance at her, ostentatiously suppress the speaker, who then continued her narration in almost a whisper, amid mocking titters of mirth.

Then anger burned in Theodora's gentle soul. They were talking about Josiah, of course, and turning him into ridicule.

She wondered, what would be the best to do. She was too far away to attempt to join in the conversation, or to be even able to swear she had heard aright, although there was no doubt in her own mind about it.

So she sat perfectly still on her great sofa, her hands folded in her lap, while two bright spots of wild rose flushed her cheeks.

She did not even pick up a book. There she sat like an alabaster statue, and most of the women were conscious of the exquisitely beautiful picture she made.

They could not stand in this packed group all the time, the whole dozen or more of them, and they gradually broke up into twos and threes about the large room.

They were delightfully friendly with one another, and all seemed in the best of spirits and tempers.

Most of them had no ulterior motive in their behavior to Theodora; it was merely the feeling that they were not the hostess and responsible. It was none of their business if Ada neglected her guests, and they all knew plenty of people and did not care to enlarge their acquaintance gratuitously.

So when they came in from the dining-room more than one of the men understood the picture they saw, of the beautiful, little, strange lady seated alone, while the other women chatted together in groups.

Hector was feeling irritated and excited, and longing to get near Theodora. He guessed Lord Wensleydown would have the same desire, and had no intention of being interfered with. He felt he could not bear to spend an evening watching the little brute daring to lean over her. He should kill him, or commit some violence, he knew.

Thus prudence, which at another time would have held him—would have made him remember what was best for her among this crowd of hostile women—flew to the winds. He must go to her—must show her he loved and would protect her, and, above all, that he would permit no other man to usurp his place.

And Theodora, who had been suffering silently a miserable feeling of loneliness and neglect, felt her heart bound with joy at the sight of his loved, familiar face, and she welcomed him more warmly than she had ever done before.

"Have these demons of women been odious to you, darling?" he whispered, hardly conscious of the term of endearment he had used. "Do not mind them; it is only jealousy because you are so beautiful and young."

"They have not been anything at all," she said, softly; "they have just left me alone and kept to themselves, and—and laughed at Josiah, and that has made me very angry, because—what has he done to them?"

"I loathe them all!" said Hector. "They are hardly fit to be in the same room with you, dear queen—and if you really belonged to me I would take you away from them now—to-night."

His voice was a caress, and that sentence, "belonged to me," always made her heart beat with its pictured possibilities. Oh, how she loved him! Could anything else in the world really matter while he could sit there and she could feel his presence and hear his tender words?

And so they talked awhile, and then they looked up and surveyed the scene. Josiah had been joined by Sir Patrick, and they were earnestly conversing by the fireplace. One or two pairs sat about on the sofas; but the general company showed signs of flocking off to the bridge-tables, which were laid out in another drawing-room beyond. And the couples joined them gradually, until only Lord Wensleydown and Morella Winmarleigh remained near and watched them with mocking eyes.

Hector had never before realized that Morella could have so much expression in her face.

How could he ever have thought under any conceivable circumstances, even at the end of his life, it would be possible to marry her! How thankful he felt he had never paid her any attention, or from his behavior given color to his mother's hopes.

He remembered a fairy story he had read in his youth, where a magic power was given to the hero of discovering what beast each human being was growing into by grasping their hands. And he wondered, if the gift had been his, what he should now find was the destiny of those two in front of him!

Wensleydown, no doubt, would be a great, sensual goat and Morella a vicious mule. And the idea made him laugh as he turned to Theodora again, to feast his eyes on her pure loveliness.

The Crow, who had arrived late and been among the last to enter the drawing-room before dinner, had not yet had an opportunity of speaking to Mrs. Brown, as he had been dragged off among the first of the bridge-players.

Presently Mildred looked through the door from the room beyond and called: "Freddy and Morella, come and play; we must have two more to make up the numbers. Uncle Patrick will bring Lord Bracondale presently."

Josiah and Theodora did not count at all, it seemed!

"What intolerable insolence!" said Hector, through his teeth. "I shall not play bridge or stir from here."

And Lord Wensleydown called back: "Do give one a moment to digest one's dinner, dear Lady Mildred. Miss Winmarleigh does not want to come yet, either. We are very—interested—and happy here."

Morella tittered and played with her fan. The dull, slow rage was simmering within her. Even her vanity could not misinterpret the meaning of Hector's devotion to Mrs. Brown. He was deeply in love, of course, and she, Morella, was robbed of her hopes of being Lady Bracondale. Her usually phlegmatic nature was roused in all its narrow strength. She was like some silent, vengeful beast waiting a chance to spring.

And so the evening wore away. Sir Patrick drew Josiah into the bridge-room, and made him join one of the tables where they were waiting for a fourth—Josiah, who was a very bad player, and did not really care for cards! But luck favored him, and the woman opposite restrained the irritable things she had ready to say to him when she first perceived how he played his hand.

And all the while Hector sat by Theodora, and learned more and more of her fair, clear mind. All the thoughts she had upon every subject he found were just and quaint and in some way illuminating. It was her natural sweetness of nature which made the great charm—that quality which Mrs. McBride had remarked upon, and which every one felt sooner or later.

Nothing of the ascetic saint or goody *poseuse*. She did not walk about with a book of poems under her arm, and wear floppy clothes and talk about her own and other people's souls. She was just human and true and attractive.

Theodora had perhaps no religion at all from the orthodox point of view; but had she been a Mohommedan or a Confucian or a Buddhist, she would still have been Theodora, full of gentleness and goodness and grace.

The entire absence of vanity and self-consciousness in her prevented her from feeling hurt or ruffled even with these ill-mannered women. She thought them rude and unpleasant, but they could not really hurt her except by humiliating Josiah. Her generosity instantly fired at that.

Both she and Hector perceived that Morella and Lord Wensleydown sat there watching them for no other reason but to disconcert and tease them, and it roused a spirit of resistance in both. While this was going on they would not move.

And Hector employed the whole of his self-control to keep himself from making actual love to her, and they talked of many things, and she understood and was grateful.

Presently, apparently, Morella could stand it no longer, for she rose rather abruptly and said to Lord Wensleydown:

"Come, let us play bridge."

They went on into the other room, and Theodora and Lord Bracondale were left quite alone.

"I should like to find Josiah," said Theodora. "Shall we not go, too?"

And they also followed upon the others' heels. Lady Ada happened to be out at her table, and some tardy sense of her duties as a hostess came to her, for she crossed over to where Theodora stood by the door and made some ordinary remark about hoping it would be fine on the morrow so they could enjoy the gardens.

And while she talked and looked into the blue eyes something attracted and softened her. She was very gentle and pretty, after all, the new niece, she decided, and Mildred had been quite wrong in saying she was an upstart and must be snubbed.

Lady Ada had a nervous way of blinking her light lashes in a fashion which suggested she might suffer from headache.

To Theodora she seemed a sad woman, full of cares, and she felt a kindly pity for her and no resentment for her rudeness.

Mildred looked up, and a frown of annoyance darkened her face.

The "creature" should certainly not make a conquest of her hostess if she could help it!

It was the first time Theodora had ever been into a company of people like this, and her eyes wandered over the scene when Lady Ada had to go back to her place.

"Tell me what you are thinking of?" said Hector, in her ear.

"I was thinking," she answered, "it is so interesting to watch people's faces. It seems to me so queer a way to spend one's time, the whole of one's intelligence set upon a game of cards and a few pieces of money for hours and hours together."

"They don't look attractive, do they?" he laughed.

"No, they look haggard, and worried, and old," she said. "Even the young ones look old and watchful, and so intent and solemn."

Lady Harrowfield had been losing heavily, and a deep mauve shade glowed through all her paint. She was a bad loser, and made all at her table feel some of her chagrin and wrath. In fact, candidates for the light of her smile found it advisable to let her win when things became too unpleasant.

There was a dreary silence over the room, broken by the scoring and remarks upon the games, and those who were out wandered into the saloon beyond, where iced drinks of all sorts were awaiting the weary.

"Every one must enjoy themselves how they can, of course," said Theodora. "It is absurd to try and make any one else happy in one's own way, but oh, I hope I shall not have to pass the time like that, ever! I don't think I could bear it."

The voices became raised at the table where Josiah sat. He had made some gross mistake in the game and his partner was being fretful over it. Her complaints amounted to real rudeness when the counting began. She had lost twenty pounds on this rubber, all through his last foolish play, she let it be known.

Josiah was angry with himself and deeply humiliated. He apologized as well as he could, but to no purpose with the wrathful dame.

And Theodora slipped behind his chair, and laid her hand upon his shoulder in what was almost a caress, and said, in a sweet and playful voice:

"You are a naughty, stupid fellow, Josiah, and of course you must pay the losses of both sides to make up for being such a wicked thing," and she patted his shoulders and smiled her gentle smile at the angry lady, as though they were children playing for counters or sweets, and the twenty pounds was a nothing to her husband, as indeed it was not. Josiah would cheerfully have paid a hundred to finish the unpleasant scene.

He was intensely grateful to her—grateful for her thought for him and for her public caress.

And the lady was so surprised at the turn affairs had taken that she said no more, and, allowing him to pay without too great protest, meekly suggested another rubber. But Josiah was not to be caught again. He rose, and, saying good-night, followed his wife and Lord Bracondale into the saloon.

XXV

After the rain and gloom of the week, Sunday dawned gloriously fine. There was to be a polo match on Monday in the park, which contained an excellent ground—Patrick and his Oxford friends against a scratch team. The neighborhood would watch them with interest. But the Sunday was for rest and peace, so all the morning the company played croquet, or lay about in hammocks, and more than half of them again began bridge in the great Egyptian tent which served as an out-door lounge on the lawn. It was reached from the western side down wide steps from the terrace, and beautiful rose gardens stretched away beyond.

Theodora had spent a sleepless night. There was no more illusion left to her on the subject of her feelings. She knew that each day, each hour, she was growing more deeply to love Hector Bracondale. He absorbed her thoughts, he dominated her imagination. He seemed to mean the only thing in life. The situation was impossible, and must end in some way. How could she face the long months with Josiah down at their new home, with the feverish hopes and fears of meetings! It was too cruel, too terrible; and she could not lead such a life. She had thought in Paris it would be possible, and even afford a certain amount of quiet happiness, if they could be strong enough to remain just friends. But now she knew this was not in human nature. Sooner or later fate would land them in some situation of temptation too strong for either to resist—and then—and then—She refused to face that picture. Only she writhed as she lay there and buried her face in the fine pillows. She did not permit herself any day-dreams of what might have been. Romauld himself, as he took his vows, never fought harder to regain his soul from the keeping of Claremonde than did Theodora to suppress her love for Hector Bracondale. Towards morning, worn out with fatigue, she fell asleep, and in her dreams, released from the control of her will, she spent moments of passionate bliss in his arms, only to wake and find she must face again the terrible reality. And cruellest thought of all was the thought of Josiah.

She had so much common-sense she realized the position exactly about him. She had not married him under any false impression. There had been no question of love—she had frankly been bought, and had as frankly detested him. But his illness and suffering had appealed to her tender heart—and afterwards his generosity. He was not unselfish, but, according to his lights, he heaped her with kindness. He could not help being common and ridiculous. And he had paid with solid gold for her, gold to make papa comfortable and happy, and she must fulfil her part of the bargain and remain a faithful wife at all costs.

This visit must be the last time she should meet her love. She must tell him, implore him—he who was free and master of his life; he must go away, must promise not to follow her, must help her to do what was right and just. She had no sentimental feeling of personal wickedness now. How could it be wicked to love—to love truly and tenderly? She had not sought love; he had come upon her. It would be wicked to give way to her feelings, to take Hector for a lover; but she had no sense of being a wicked woman as things were, any more than if she had badly burned her hand and was suffering deeply from the wound; she would have considered herself wicked for having had the mischance thus to injure herself. She was intensely unhappy, and she was going to try and do what was right. That was all. And God and those kind angels who steered the barks beyond the rocks would perhaps help her.

Hector for his part, had retired to rest boiling with passion and rage, the subtle, odious insinuations of Mildred ringing in his ears. The remembrance of the menace on Morella's dull face as she had watched Theodora depart, and, above all, Wensleydown's behavior as they all said good-night: nothing for him actually to take hold of, and yet enough to convulse him with jealous fury.

Oh, if she were only his own! No man should dare to look at her like that. But Josiah had stood by and not even noticed it.

Passionate jealousy is not a good foster-parent for prudence.

The Sunday came, and with it a wild, mad longing to be near her again—never to leave her, to prevent any one else from so much as saying a word. Others besides Wensleydown had begun to experience the attraction of her beauty and charm. If considerations of wisdom should keep him from her side, he would have the anguish of seeing these others take his place, and that he could not suffer.

And as passion in a man rages higher than in the average woman, especially passion when accelerated by the knowledge of another's desire to rob it of its own, so Hector's conclusions were not so clear as Theodora's.

He dared not look ahead. All he was conscious of was the absolute determination to protect her from Wensleydown—to keep her for himself.

And fate was gathering all the threads together for an inevitable catastrophe, or so it seemed to the Crow when the long, exquisite June Sunday evening was drawing to a close and he looked back on the day.

He would have to report to Anne that the two had spent it practically together; that Morella had a sullen red look on her face which boded ill for the part she would play, when she should be asked to play some part; that Mildred had done her best to render Theodora uncomfortable and unhappy, and thus had thrown her more into Hector's protection. The other women had been indifferent or mocking or amused, and Lady Harrowfield had let it be seen she would have no mercy. Her comments had been vitriolic.

Hector and Theodora had not gone out of sight, or been any different to the others; only he had never left her, and there could be no mistaking the devotion in his face.

For the whole day Sir Patrick had more or less taken charge of Josiah. He was finding him more difficult to manipulate over money matters than he had anticipated. Josiah's vulgar, round face and snub nose gave no index to his shrewdness; with his mutton-chop whiskers and bald head, Josiah was the personification of the smug grocer.

As she went to dress for dinner it seemed to Theodora that her heart was breaking. She was only flesh and blood after all, and she, too, had felt her pulses throbbing wildly as they had walked along by the lake, when all the color and lights of the evening helped to excite her imagination and exalt her spirit. They had been almost alone, for the other pair who composed the *partie carrée* of this walk were several yards ahead of them.

Each minute she had been on the verge of imploring him to say good-bye—to leave her—to let their lives part, to try to forget, and the words froze on her lips in the passionate, unspoken cry which seemed to rise from her heart that she loved him. Oh, she loved him! And so she had not spoken.

There had been long silences, and each was growing almost to know the other's thoughts—so near had they become in spirit.

When she got to her room her knees were trembling. She fell into a chair and buried her face in her hands. She shivered as if from cold.

Josiah was almost angry with her for being so late for dinner. Theodora hardly realized with whom she went in; she was dazed and numb. She got through it somehow, and this night determined to go straight to her room rather than be treated as she had been the night before. But one of the women whom the intercourse of the day had drawn into conversation with her showed signs of friendliness as they went through the anteroom, and drew her towards a sofa to talk. She was fascinated by Theodora's beauty and grace, and wanted to know, too, just where her clothes came from, as she did not recognize absolutely the models of any of the well-known *couturières*, and they were certainly the loveliest garments worn by any one in the party.

One person draws another, and soon Theodora had three or four around her—all purring and talking frocks. And as she answered their questions with gentle frankness, she wondered what everything meant. Did any of them feel—did any of them love passionately as she did?—or were they all dolls more or less bored and getting through life? And would she, too, grow like them in time, and be able to play bridge with interest until the small hours?

Later some of the party danced in the ballroom, which was beyond the saloon the other way, and now a definite idea came to Hector as he held Theodora in his arms in the waltz. They could not possibly bear this life. Why should he not take her away—away from the smug grocer, and then they could live their life in a dream of bliss in Italy, perhaps, and later at Bracondale. He had a great position, and people soon forget nowadays.

His pulses were bounding with these wild thoughts, born of their nearness and the long hours of strain. To-morrow he would tell her of them, but to-night—they would dance.

And Theodora felt her very soul melt within her. She was worn out with conflicting emotions. She could not fight with inclination any longer. Whatever he should say she would have to listen to—and agree with. She felt almost faint. And so at the end of the first dance she managed to whisper:

"Hector, I am tired. I shall go to bed." And in truth when he looked at her she was deadly white.

She stopped by her husband.

"Josiah," she said, "will you make my excuses to Lady Ada and Uncle Patrick? I do not feel well; I am going to my room."

Hector's distress was intense. He could not carry her up in his arms as he would have wished, he could not soothe and pet and caress her, or do anything in the world but stand by and see Josiah fussing and accompanying her to the stairs and on to her room. She hardly said the word good-night to him, and her very lips were white. Wensleydown's face, as he stood with Mildred, drove him mad with its mocking leer, and if he had heard their conversation there might have been bloodshed.

Josiah returned to the saloon, and made his way to the bridge-room to Sir Patrick and his hostess; but Hector still leaned against the door.

"He'll probably go out on the terrace and walk in the night by himself," thought the Crow, who had watched the scene, "and these dear people will say he has gone to meet her, and it is a ruse her being ill. They could not let such a chance slip, if they are both absent together."

So he walked over to Hector and engaged him in conversation.

Hector would have thought of this aspect himself at another time, but to-night he was dazed with passion and pain.

"Come and smoke a cigar on the terrace, Crow," he said. "One wants a little quiet and peace sometimes."

And then the Crow looked at him with his head on one side in that wise way which had earned for him his sobriquet.

"Hector, old boy, you know these damned people here and their ways. Just keep yourself in evidence, my son," he said, as he walked away.

And Hector thanked him in his heart, and went across and asked Morella to dance.

Up in her room Theodora lay prostrate. She could reason no more—she could only sob in the dark.

Next day she did not appear until luncheon-time. But the guests at Beechleigh always rose when they pleased, and no one remarked her absence even, each pair busy with their own affairs. Only Barbara crept up to her room to see how she was, and if she wanted anything. Theodora wondered why her cousin should have been so changed from the afternoon of their arrival. And Barbara longed to tell her. She moved about, and looked out of the window, and admired Theodora's beautiful hair spread over the pillows. Then she said:

"Oh, I wish you came here often and Mildred didn't. She is a brute, and she hates you for being so beautiful. She made me keep away, you know. Do you think me a mean coward?" Her poor, plain, timid face was pitiful as she looked at Theodora, and to her came the thought of what Barbara's life was probably among them all, and she said, gently:

"No, indeed, I don't. It was much better for you not to annoy her further; she might have been nastier to me than even she has been. But why don't you stand up for yourself generally? After all, you are Uncle Patrick's daughter, and she is only your mother's niece."

"They both love her far more than they do me," said Barbara, with hanging head.

And then they talked of other things. Barbara adored her home, but her family had no sentiment for it, she told Theodora; and Pat, she believed, would like to sell the whole thing and gamble away the money.

Just before luncheon-time, when Theodora was dressed and going down, Josiah came up again to see her. He had fussed in once or twice before during the morning. This time it was to tell her a special messenger had come from his agent in London to inform him his presence was absolutely necessary there the first thing on Tuesday morning. Some turn of deep importance to his affairs had transpired during the holiday. So he would go up by an early train. He had settled it all with Sir Patrick, who, however, would not hear of Theodora's leaving.

"The party does not break up until Wednesday or Thursday, and we cannot lose our greatest ornament," he had said.

"I do not wish to stay alone," Theodora pleaded. "I will come with you, Josiah."

But Josiah was quite cross with her.

"Nothing of the kind," he said. These people were her own relations, and if he could not leave her with them it was a strange thing! He did not want her in London, and she could join him again at Claridge's on Thursday. It would give him time to run down to Bessington to see that all was ready for her reception. He was so well now he looked forward to a summer of pleasure and peace.

"A second honeymoon, my love!" he chuckled, as he kissed her, and would hear no more.

And having planted this comforting thought for her consolation he had quitted the room.

Left alone Theodora sank down on the sofa. Her trembling limbs refused to support her; she felt cold and sick and faint.

A second honeymoon. Oh, God!

XXVI

At luncheon, when Theodora descended from her room, the whole party were assembled and already seated at the several little tables. The only vacant place left was just opposite Hector.

And there they faced each other during the meal, and all the time her eyes reminded him of the wounded fawn again, only they were sadder, if possible, and her face was pinched and pale, not the exquisite natural white of its usual fresh, soft velvet.

Something clutched at his heart-strings. What extra sorrow had happened to her since last night? What could he do to comfort and protect her? There was only one way—to take her with him out of it all.

After the first nine days' wonder, people would forget. It would be an undefended suit when Josiah should divorce her, and then he would marry her and have her for his very own. And what would they care for the world's sneers?

His whole being was thrilled and exalted with these thoughts; his brain was excited as with strong wine.

To have her for his own!

Even the memory of his mother only caused him a momentary pang. No one could help loving Theodora, and she—his mother—would get over it, too, and learn her sweetness and worth.

He was wildly happy now that he had made up his mind—so surely can passionate desire block out every other feeling.

The guests at their table were all more or less civil. Theodora's unassuming manner had disarmed them, and as savage beasts had been charmed of old by Orpheus and his lute, so perhaps her gentle voice had soothed this company—the women, of course; there had been no question of the men from the beginning.

Mildred's programme to make Mrs. Brown suffer was not having the success her zeal in promoting it deserved.

The weather was still glorious, and after lunch the whole party flocked out on the terrace.

A terrible nervous fear was dominating Theodora. She could not be alone with Hector, she did not dare to trust herself. And there would be the to-morrow and the Wednesday—without Josiah—and the soft warmth of the evenings and the glamour of the nights.

Oh, everything was too cruel and impossible! And wherever she turned she seemed to see in blazing letters, "A second honeymoon!"

The first was a horrible, fearsome memory which was over long ago, but the thought of a second—now that she knew what love meant, and what life with the loved one might mean—Oh, it was unbearable—terrible—impossible! better, much better, to die and have done with it all.

She kept close to Barbara, and when Barbara moved she feverishly engaged the Crow in conversation—any one—something to save her from any chance of listening to Hector's persuasive words. And the Crow's kind heart was pained by the hunted expression in her eyes. They seemed to ask for help and sanctuary.

"Shall we walk down to the polo-field, Mrs. Brown?" he said, and she gladly acquiesced and started with him.

If she had been a practised coquette she could not have done anything more to fan the flame of Hector's passion.

Lady Harrowfield had detained him on the top of the steps, and he saw her go off with the Crow and was unable to rush after them.

And when at last he was free he felt almost drunk with passion.

He had learned of Josiah's intended departure on the morrow, and that Theodora would join him again on the Thursday, and his mind was made up. On Wednesday night he would take her away with him to Italy. She should never belong to Josiah any more. She was his in soul and mind already, he knew, and she should be his in body, too, and he would cherish and love and protect her to the end of his life.

Every detail of his plan matured itself in his brain. It only wanted her consent, and that, when opportunity should be given him to plead his cause, he did not greatly fear would be refused.

Hitherto he had ever restrained himself when alone with her, had dominated his desire to make love to her; had never once, since Paris, given way to passion or tender words during their moments together.

But he remembered that hour of bliss on the way from Versailles; he remembered how she had thrilled, too, how he had made her feel and respond to his every caress.

Yes—she was not cold, his white angel!

He was playing in the scratch team of the polo match, and the wild excitement of his thoughts, coursing through his blood, caused him to ride like a mad thing.

Never had he done so brilliantly.

And Theodora, while she was every now and then convulsed with fear for him, had moments of passionate admiration.

The Crow remained at her side in the tent. He knew Hector would not be jealous of him, and the instinct of the brink of calamity was strong upon him, from the look in Theodora's eyes.

He used great tact—he turned the conversation to Anne and the children, and then to Lady Bracondale and Hector's home, all in a casual, abstract way, and he told her of Lady Bracondale's great love for her son, and of her hopes that he would marry soon, and how that Hector would be the last of his race—for Evermond Le Mesurier did not count—and many little tales about Bracondale and its people.

It was all done so wisely and well; not in the least as a note of warning. And all he said sank deep into Theodora's heart. She had never even dreamed of the plan which was now matured in Hector's brain—of going away with him. He, as really a lover, was not for her, that was a foregone conclusion. It was the fear of she knew not what which troubled her. She was too unsophisticated and innocent to really know—only that to be with him now was a continual danger; soon she knew she would not be able to control herself, she must be clasped in his arms.

And then—and then—there was the picture in front of her of Josiah and the "second honeymoon."

Thus while she sat there gazing at the man she passionately loved playing polo, she was silently suffering all the anguish of which a woman's heart is capable.

The only possible way was to part from Hector forever—to say the last good-bye before she should go, like a sheep, to the slaughter.
When she was once more the wife of Josiah she could never look upon his face again.
And if Hector had known the prospect that awaited her at Bessington Hall, it would have driven him—already mad—to frenzy.
The day wore on, and still Theodora's fears kept her from allowing a tête-à-tête when he dismounted and joined them for tea.
But fate had determined otherwise. And as the soft evening came several of the party walked down by the river—which ran on the western side below the rose-gardens and the wood of firs—to see Barbara's many breeds of ducks and water-fowl.
Then Hector's determination to be alone with her conquered for the time. Theodora found herself strolling with him in a path of meeting willows, with a summer-house at the end, by the water's bank.
They were quite separated from the others by now. They, with affairs of their own to pursue, had spread in different directions.
And it was evening, and warm, and June.
There was a strange, weird silence between them, and both their hearts were beating to suffocation—hers with the thought of the anguish of parting forever, his with the exaltation of the picture of parting no more.
They came to the little summer-house, and there they sat down and surveyed the scene. The evening lights were all opalescent on the water, there was peace in the air and brilliant fresh green on the trees, and soft and liquid rose the nightingale's note. So at last Hector broke the silence.
"Darling," he said, "I love you—I love you so utterly this cannot go on. I must have you for my own—" and then, as she gasped, he continued in a torrent of passionate words.
He told her of his infinite love for her; of the happiness he would fill her life with; of his plan that they should go away together when she should leave Beechleigh; of the joy of their days; of the tender care he would take of her; and every and each sentenceended with a passionate avowal of his love and devotion.
Then a terrible temptation seized Theodora. She had never even dreamed of this ending to the situation; and it would mean no second honeymoon of loathsome hours, but a glorious fulfilment of all possible joy.
For one moment the whole world seemed golden with happiness; but it was only of short duration. The next instant she remembered Josiah and her given word.
No, happiness was not for her. Death and sleep were all she could hope for; but she must not even hope for them. She must do what was right, and be true to herself, *advienne que pourra*. And perhaps some angel would give her oblivion or let her drink of Lethe, though she should never reach those waters beyond the rocks.
He saw the exaltation in her beautiful face as he spoke, and wild joy seized him. Then he saw the sudden droop of her whole body and the light die out of her eyes, and in a voice of anguish he implored her:
"Darling, darling! Won't you listen to what I say to you? Won't you answer me, and come with me?"
"No, Hector," she said, and her voice was so low he had to bend closer to hear.
He clasped her to his side, he covered her face with kisses, murmuring the tenderest love-words.
She did not resist him or seek to escape from his sheltering, strong arms. This was the end of her living life, why should she rob herself of a last joy?
She laid her head on his shoulder, and there she whispered in a voice he hardly recognized, so dominated it was by sorrow and pain: "It must be good-bye, beloved; we must not meet. Ah! never any more. I have been meaning to say this to you all the day. I cannot bear it either. Oh, we must part, and it must end; but oh, not—not in that way!"
He tried to persuade her, he pleaded with her, drew pictures of their happiness that surely would be, talked of Italy and eternal summer and exquisite pleasure and bliss.
And all the time he felt her quiver in his arms and respond to each thought, as her imagination took fire at the beautiful pictures of love and joy. But nothing shook her determination.
At last she said: "Dearest, if I were different perhaps, stronger and braver, I could go away and live with you like that, and keep it all a glorious thing; but I am not—only a weak creature, and the memory of my broken word, and Josiah's sorrow, and your mother's anguish, would kill all joy. We could have blissful moments of forgetfulness, but the great ghost of remorse would chase for me all happiness away. Dearest, I love you so; but oh, I could not live, haunted like that; I should just—die."
Then he knew all hope was over, and the mad passion went out of him, and his arms dropped to his sides as if half life had fled. She looked up in his face in fear at its ghastly whiteness.
And at this moment, through the parted willows, there appeared the sullen, mocking eyes of Morella Winmarleigh.
She pushed the bushes aside, and, followed by Lord Wensleydown, she came towards the summer-house.
Her slow senses had taken in the scene. Hector was evidently very unhappy, she thought, and that hateful woman had been teasing him, no doubt.
Thus her banal mind read the tragedy of these two human lives.

XXVII

Morella Winmarleigh had been taking an evening stroll with Lord Wensleydown. They had come upon the two in the summer-house quite by accident, but now they had caught them they would stick to them, and make their walk as tiresome as possible, they both decided to themselves.
After very great emotion such as Hector and Theodora had been experiencing, to have this uncongenial and hateful pair as companions was impossible to bear.
Neither Hector or Theodora stirred or made room for them on the seat.

"Isn't this a sweet place, Lord Wensleydown?" Miss Winmarleigh said. "Why have you never brought me here before? How did you find it, Hector?" turning to him in a determined fashion. "You will have to show us the way back, as we are quite lost!" and she giggled irritatingly.

"The first turn to the right at the end of the willows," said Hector, with what politeness he could summon up, "and I am sure you will be able to get to the house quite safely. As you are in such a hurry, don't let us keep you. Mrs. Brown and I are going the other way by the river, when we do start."

"Oh, we are not in a hurry at all," said Lord Wensleydown. "Do come with us, Mrs. Brown, we are feeling so lonely."

Theodora rose. She could bear no more of this.

"Let us go," she said to Hector, and they started, leading the way. And for a while they heard the others in mocking titters behind them, but presently, when near the house, they quickened their pace, and were again alone and free from their tormentors.

They had not spoken at all in this hateful walk, and now he turned to her.

"My darling," he said, "life seems over for me."

"And for me, too, Hector," she said. "And when we come to this dark piece of wood I want you to kiss me once more and say good-bye forever, and go out of my life." There was a passionate sob in her voice. "And oh! *Bien-aimé*, please promise me you will leave to-morrow. Do not make it more impossible to bear than it already is."

But he was silent with pain. A mad, reckless revolt at fate flooded all his being.

It was past eight o'clock now, and when they came to the soothing gloom of the dark firs he crushed her in his arms, and a great sob broke from him and rent her heart.

"My darling, my darling! Good-bye," he said, brokenly. "You have taught me all that life means; all that it can hold of pleasure and pain. Henceforth, it is the gray path of shadows; and oh, God take care of you and grant us some peace."

But she was sobbing on his breast and could not speak.

"And remember," he went on, "I shall never forget you or cease to worship and adore you. Always know you have only to send me a message, a word, and I will come to you and do what you ask, to my last drop of blood. I love you! Oh, God! I love you, and you were made for me, and we could have been happy together and glorified the world."

Then he folded her again in his arms and held her so close it seemed the breath must leave her body, and then they walked on silently, and silently entered the house by the western garden door.

The evening was a blank to Theodora. She dressed in her satins and laces, and let her maid fasten her wonderful emeralds on throat and breast and hair. She descended to the drawing-room and walked in to dinner with some strange man—all as one in a dream. She answered as an automaton, and the man thought how beautiful she was, and what a pity for so beautiful a woman to be so stupid and silent and dull.

"Almost wanting," was his last comment to himself as the ladies left the dining-room.

Then Theodora forced herself to speak—to chatter to a now complacent group of women who gathered round her. Those emeralds, and the way the diamonds were set round them, proved too strong an attraction for even Lady Harrowfield to keep far away.

She was going to have her rubies remounted, and this seemed just the pattern she would like.

So the time passed, and the men came into the room. But Hector was not with them. He had found a telegram, it transpired, which had been waiting for him on his return, and it would oblige him to go to Bracondale immediately, so he was motoring up to London that night. He had acted his part to the end, and no one guessed he was leaving the best of his life behind him. When Theodora realized he was gone she suddenly felt very faint; but she, too, was not of common clay, and breeding will tell in crises of this sort, so she sat up and talked gayly. The evening passed, and at last she was alone for the night.

There are moralists who will assure us the knowledge of having done right brings its own consolation. And in good books, about good women, the heroine experiences a sense of peace and satisfaction after having resigned the forbidden joy of her life. But Theodora was only a human being, so she spent the night in wild, passionate regret.

She had done right with no stern sense of the word "Right" written up in front of her, but because she was so true and so sweet that she must keep her word and not betray Josiah. She did not analyze anything. Life was over for her, whatever came now could only find her numb. By an early train Josiah left for London.

"Take care of yourself, my love," he had said, as he looked in at her door, "and write to me this afternoon as to what train you decide to leave by on Thursday."

She promised she would, and he departed, thoroughly satisfied with his visit among the great world.

The day was spent as the other days, and after lunch Theodora escaped to her room. She must write her letter to Josiah for the afternoon's post. She had discovered the train left at eleven o'clock. It did not take her long, this little note to her husband, and then she sat and stared into space for a while.

The terrible reaction had begun. There was no more excitement, only the flatness, the blank of the days to look forward to, and that unspeakable sense of loss and void. And oh, she had let Hector go without one word of her passionate love! She had been too unnerved to answer him when he had said his last good-bye to her in the wood.

She seized the pen again which had dropped from her hand. She would write to him. She would tell him her thoughts—in a final farewell. It might comfort him, and herself, too.

So she wrote and wrote on, straight out from her heart, then she found she had only just time to take the letters to the hall.

She closed Hector's with a sigh, and picking up Josiah's, already fastened, she ran with them quickly down the stairs.

There was an immense pile of correspondence—the accumulation of Whitsuntide.

The box that usually received it was quite full, and several letters lay about on the table.

She placed her two with the rest, and turned to leave the hall. She could not face all the company on the lawn just yet, and went back to her room, meeting Morella Winmarleigh bringing some of her own to be posted as she passed through the saloon.

When Miss Winmarleigh reached the table curiosity seized her. She guessed what had been Theodora's errand. She would like to see her writing and to whom the letters were addressed.

No one was about anywhere. All the correspondence was already there, as in five minutes or less the post would go.

She had no time to lose, so she picked up the last two envelopes which lay on the top of the pile and read the first:

To Josiah Brown, Esq.,
Claridge's Hotel,
Brook Street,
London, W.

and the other:

The Lord Bracondale,
Bracondale Chase,
Bracondale.

"The husband and—the lover!" she said to herself. And a sudden temptation came over her, swift and strong and not to be resisted.

Here would be revenge—revenge she had always longed for! while her sullen rage had been gathering all these last days. She heard the groom of the chambers approaching to collect the letters; she must decide at once. So she slipped Theodora's two missives into her blouse and walked towards the door.

"There is another post which goes at seven, isn't there, Edgarson?" she asked, "and the letters are delivered in London to-morrow morning just the same?"

"Yes, ma'am, they arrive by the second post in London," said the man, politely, and she passed on to her room.

Arrived there, excitement and triumph burned all over her. Here, without a chance of detection, she could crush her rival and see her thoroughly punished, and—who knows?—Hector might yet be caught in the rebound.

She would not hesitate a second. She rang for her maid.

"Bring me my little kettle and the spirit-lamp. I want to sip some boiling water," she said. "I have indigestion. And then you need not wait—I shall read until tea."

She was innocently settled on her sofa with a book when the maid returned. She was a well-bred servant, and silently placed the kettle and glass and left the room noiselessly. Morella sprang to her feet with unusual agility. Her heavy form was slow of movement as a rule.

The door once locked, she returned to the sofa and began operations.

The kettle soon boiled, and the steam puffed out and achieved its purpose.

The thin, hand-made paper of the envelope curled up, and with no difficulty she opened the flap.

Hector's letter first and then Josiah's. All her pent-up, concentrated rage was having its outlet, and almost joy was animating her being.

Hector's was a long letter; probably very loving, but that did not concern her.

It would be most unladylike to read it, she decided—a sort of thing only the housemaids would do. What she intended was to place them in the wrong envelopes—Hector's to Josiah, and Josiah's to Hector. It was a mistake any one might make themselves when they were writing, and Theodora, when it should be discovered, could only blame her own supposed carelessness. Even if the letter was an innocent one, which was not at all likely. Oh, dear, no! She knew the world, however little girls were supposed to understand. She had kept her eyes open, thank goodness; and it would certainly not be an epistle a husband would care to read—a great thing of pages and pages like that. But even if it were innocent, it was bound to cause some trouble and annoyance; and the thought of that was honey and balm to her.

She slipped them into the covers she had destined for them and pressed down the damp gum. So all was as it had been to outward appearance, and she felt perfectly happy. Then when she descended to tea she placed them securely in the box under some more of her own for the seven-o'clock post, and went her way rejoicing.

XXVIII

Next morning, over a rather late breakfast in his sitting-room at Claridge's, Josiah's second post came in.

All had gone well with his business in the City the day before, and in the afternoon he had run down to Bessington Hall, returning late at night.

He was feeling unusually well and self-important, and his thoughts turned to pleasant things: To the delight of having Theodora once more as a wife; of his hope of founding a family—the Browns of Bessington—why not? Had not a boy at the gate called him squire?

"Good-day to 'e, squire," he had said, and that was pleasant to hear.

If only his tiresome cough would keep off in the autumn, he might himself shoot the extensive coverts he had ordered to be stocked on the estate. He had heard there were schools for would-be sportsmen to learn the art of handling a gun, and he would make inquiries.

All the prospect was fair.

He picked up his letters and turned them over. Nothing of importance. Ah, yes! there was Theodora's. The first letter she had ever written him, and such a long one! What could the girl have to say? Surely not all that about trains! He opened the envelope with a knife which lay by his plate, and this is what he read—read with whitening face and sinking heart:

"BEECHLEIGH, *June 5th.*

"HECTOR, MY BELOVED!—Oh, for this last time I must think of you as that! Dearest, we are parted now and may never meet again, and the pain of it all kept me silent yesterday, when my heart was breaking with the anguish and longing to tell you how I loved you, how you were not going away suffering alone. Oh, it has all crept upon us, this great, great love! It was fate, and it was useless to struggle against it. Only we must not let it be the reason of our doing wrong—that would be to degrade it, and love should not live in an atmosphere of degradation. I could not go away with you, could not have you for my lover without breaking a bargain—a bargain over which I have given my word. Of course I did not know what love meant when I was married. In France one does not think of that as connected with a husband. It was just a duty to be got through to help papa and my sisters. But my part of the bargain was myself, and in return for giving that I have money and a home, and papa and Sarah and Clementine are comfortable and happy. And as Josiah has kept his side of it, so I must keep mine, and be faithful to him always in word and deed. Dearest, it is too terrible to think of this material aspect to a bond which now I know should only be one of love and faith and tenderness. But it *is* a bond, and I have given my word, and no happiness could come to us if I should break it, *as Josiah has not broken his.* And oh, Hector, you do not know how good he has always been to me, and generous and indulgent! It is not his fault that he is not of our class, and I must do my utmost to make him happy, and atone for this wound which I have unwittingly given him, and which he is, and must always remain, unconscious of. Oh, if something could have warned me, after that first time we met, that I would love you—had begun to love you—even then there would have been time to draw back, to save us both, perhaps, from suffering. And yet, and yet, I do not know, we might have missed the greatest and noblest good of all our lives. Dearest, I want you to keep the memory of me as something happy. Each year, when the spring-time comes and the young fresh green, I want you to look back on our day at Versailles, and to say to yourself, 'Life cannot be all sad, because nature gave the earth the returning spring.' And some> spring must come for us, too—if only in our hearts.

"And now, O my beloved, good-bye! I cannot even tell to you the anguish which is wringing my heart. It is all summed up in this. I love you! I love you! and we must say forever a farewell!

"THEODORA.

"P.S.—I am sending this to your home."

As he read the last words the paper slipped from Josiah's nerveless hands, and for many minutes he sat as one stricken blind and dumb. Then his poor, plebeian figure seemed to crumple up, and with an inarticulate cry of rage and despair he fell forward, with his head upon his out-stretched arms across the breakfast-table.

How long he remained there he never knew. It seemed a whole lifetime later when he began to realize things—to know where he was—to remember.

"Oh, God!" he said. "Oh, God!"

He picked up the letter and read it all over again, weighing every word.

Who was this thief who had stolen his wife? Hector? Hector? Yes, it was Lord Bracondale; he remembered now he had heard him called that at Beechleigh. He would like to kill him. But was he a thief, after all? or was not—he—Josiah the thief? To have stolen her happiness, and her life. Her young life that might have been so fair, though how did he know that at the time! He had never thought of such things. She was what he desired, and he had bought her with gold. No, he was not a thief, he had bought her with gold, and because of that she was going to keep to her bargain, and make him a true and faithful wife.

"Oh, God!" he said again. "Oh, God!"

Presently the business method of his life came back to him and helped him. He must think this matter over carefully and see if there was any way out. It all looked black enough—his future, that but an hour ago had seemed so full of promise. He rang for the waiter and gave orders to have the breakfast things taken away. That accomplished, he requested that he should not be disturbed upon any pretext whatsoever. And then, drawn up to his writing-table, he began deliberately to think.

Yes, from the beginning Theodora had been good and meek and docile. He remembered a thousand gentle, unselfish things she had done for him. Her patience, her kindness, her unfailing sympathy in all his ills, the consideration and respect with which she treated him. When—when could this thing have begun? In Paris? Only these short weeks ago—was love so sudden a passion as that? Then he turned to the letter again and once more read it through. Poor Theodora, poor little girl, he thought. His anger was gone now; nothing remained but an intolerable pain. And this lord—of her own class—her own class! How that thought hurt. What of him? He was handsome and young, and just the mate for Theodora. And she had said good-bye to him, and was going to do her best to make him—Josiah—happy. He gave a wild laugh. Oh, the mockery of it all, the mockery of it all! Well, if she could renounce happiness to keep her word, what could he do for her in return? She must never know of the mistake she had made in putting the letters into the wrong envelopes. That he could save her from. But the man? He would know—for he must have got the note intended for him—Josiah. What must be done about that? He thought and thought. And at last he drew a sheet of paper forward and wrote, in his neat, clerklike hand, just a few lines.

And these were they:

"MY LORD,—You will have received, I presume, a communication addressed to you and intended for me. The enclosed speaks for itself. I send it to you because it is my duty to do so. If I were a young man, though I am not of your class, I would kill you. But I am growing old, and my day is over. All I ask of you is never, *under any circumstances*, to let my wife know of her mistake about the letters. I do not wish to grieve her, or cause her more suffering than you have already brought upon her.

"Believe me,
"Yours faithfully,
"JOSIAH BROWN."

Then he got down the *Peerage* and found the correct form of superscription he must place upon the envelope.

He folded the two letters, his own and Theodora's, and, slipping them in, sealed the packet with his great seal which was graven with a deep J.B. And lest he should change his mind, he rang the bell for the waiter, and had it despatched to the post at once—to be sent by express. If possible it must reach Lord Bracondale at the same time as the other letter—Theodora's letter to himself in the wrong envelope.

And then poor Josiah subsided into his chair again, and suffered and suffered. He was conscious of nothing else—just intense, overwhelming suffering.

When his secretary, from his office in the City, came in about luncheon-time to transact some important business, he was horrified and distressed to see the change in his patron; for Josiah looked crumpled and shrivelled and old.

"I caught a chill coming from Bessington last night," he explained, "and I will send for Toplington to give me a draught if you will kindly touch the bell."

Then he tried to concentrate his mind on his affairs and get through the day. But the gray look kept growing and growing, and the secretary decided towards evening to suggest sending for Theodora. Josiah, however, would not hear of this. He was not ill, he said, it was merely a chill; he would be quite restored by a night's rest, and Mrs. Brown would be with him, anyway, in the morning. Of what use to alarm her unnecessarily. But he had unfortunately mislaid her letter with the exact time of her train, so he had better telegraph to her before six o'clock to make sure. He wrote it out himself. Just:

"Stupidly mislaid your letter. What time did you say for the carriage to meet your train?"JOSIAH."

And about eight o'clock her reply came, and then he went to bed, wondering if he had reached the summit of human suffering or if there would be more to come.

XXIX

Late that night, in the old panelled library at Bracondale, Hector walked up and down. He, too, was suffering, suffering intensely, his only grain of comfort being that he was alone. His mother was away in the north with Anne, and he had the place to himself. In his hand was Theodora's letter. As Josiah had calculated, knowing cross-country posts, both his and hers had arrived at the same time.

Hector paced and paced up and down, his thoughts maddening him.

And so three people were unhappy now—not he and his beloved one alone. This was the greater calamity.

But how he had misjudged Josiah! The common, impossible husband had behaved with a nobility, a justice, and forbearance which he knew his own passionate nature would not have been capable of. It had touched him to the core, and he had written at once in reply, enclosing Theodora's letter about the arrival of the train.

"DEAR SIR,—I am overcome with your generosity and your justice. I thank you for your letter and for your magnanimity in forwarding the enclosure it contained. I understand and appreciate the sentiment you express when you say, had you been younger you would have killed me, and I on my side would have been happy to offer you any satisfaction you might have wished, and am ready to do so now if you desire it. At the same time, I would like you to know, in deed, I have never injured you. My deep and everlasting grief will be that I have brought pain and sorrow into the life of a lady who is very dear to us both. My own life is darkened forever as well, and I am going away out of England for a long time as soon as I can make my arrangements. I will respect your desire never to inform your wife of her mistake, and I will not trouble either of you again. Only, by a later post, I intend to answer her letter and say farewell.

"Believe me,
"Yours truly,
"BRACONDALE."

This he had despatched some hours ago, but his last good-bye to Theodora was not yet written. What could he say to her? How could he tell her of all the misery and anguish, all the pain which was racking his being; he, who knew life and most things it could hold, and so could judge of the fact that nothing, nothing, counted now but herself—and they should meet no more, and it was the end. A blank, absolute end to all joy. Nothing to exist upon but the remembrance of an hour or two's bliss and a few tender kisses.

And as Josiah had done, he could only say: "Oh, God! Oh, God!"

On top of his large escritoire there stood a minute and very perfect copy of the fragment of Psyche, which he had so intensely admired. He turned to it now as his only consolation; the likeness to Theodora was strong; the exact same form of face, and the way her hair grew; the pure line of the cheek, and the angle which the head was set on to the column of her throat—all might have been chiselled from her. How often had he seen her looking down like that. Perhaps the only difference at all was that Theodora's nose was fine, and not so heavy and Greek; otherwise he had her there in front of him—his Theodora, his gift of the gods, his Psyche, his soul. And wherever he should wander—if in wildest Africa or furthest India, in Alaska or Tibet—this little fragment of white marble should bear him company.

It calmed him to look at it—the beautiful Greek thing.

And he sat down and wrote to his loved one his good-bye.

He told her of his sorrow and his love, and how he was going away from England, he did not yet know where, and should be absent many months, and how forever his thoughts from distant lands would bridge the space between them, and surround her with tenderness and worship.

And her letter, he said, should never leave him—her two letters; they should be dearer to him than his life. He prayed her to take care of herself, and if at any time she should want him to send for him from the ends of the earth. Bracondale would always find him, sooner or later, and he was hers to order as she willed.

And as he had ended his letter before, so he ended this one now:

"For ever and ever your devoted

"LOVER."

After this he sat a long time and gazed out upon the night. It was very dark and cloudy, but in one space above his head two stars shone forth for a moment in a clear peep of sky, and they seemed to send him a message of hope. What hope? Was it, as she had said, the thought that there would be a returning spring—even for them?

XXX

And the summer wore away and the dripping autumn came, and with each week, each day almost, Josiah seemed to shrivel.

It was not very noticeable at first, after the ten days of sharp illness which had prostrated him when he received the fatal letter.

He appeared to recover almost from that, and they went down to Bessington Hall at the beginning of July. But there was no further talk of a second honeymoon.

Theodora's tenderness and devotion never flagged. If her heart was broken she could at least keep her word, and try to make her husband happy. And so each one acted a part, with much zeal for the other's welfare.

It was anguish to Josiah to see his wife's sweet face grow whiter and thinner; she was so invariably bright and cheerful with him, so considerate of his slightest wish.

His pride and affection for her had turned into a sort of adoration as the days wore on. He used to watch her silently from behind a paper, or when she thought he slept. Then the mask of smiles fell from her, and he saw the pathetic droop of her young, fair head and the mournful gloom that would creep into her great, blue eyes.

And he was the stumbling-block to her happiness. She had sent away the man she loved in order to stay and be true to him, to minister to his wants, and do her utmost to render him happy. Oh, what could he do for her in return? What possible thing?

He lavished gifts upon her; he lavished gifts upon her sisters, upon her father; their welfare, he remembered, was part of the bargain. At least she would know these—her dear ones—had gained by it, and, so far, her sacrifice had not been in vain.

This thought comforted him a little. But the constant gnawing ache at his heart, and the withdrawal of all object to live for, soon began to tell upon his always feeble constitution.

Of what use was anything at all? His house or his lands! His pride in his position—even his title of "squire," which he often heard now. All were dead-sea fruit, dust and ashes; there never would be any Browns of Bessington in the years to come. There never would be anything for him, never any more.

For a week in September Captain and Mrs. Dominic Fitzgerald had paid them a visit, and the brilliant bride had cheered them up for a little and seemed to bring new life with her. She expressed herself as completely satisfied with her purchase in the way of a husband; it was just as she had known, three was a lucky number for her, and Dominic was her soul's mate, and they were going to lead the life they both loved, of continual movement and change and gayety.

But the situation at Bessington distressed her.

"Why, my dear, they are just like a couple of sick paroquets," she said to her husband. "Mr. Brown don't look long for this world, and Theodora is a shadow! What in the Lord's name has been happening to them?"

But Dominic could not enlighten her. Before they left she determined to ascertain for herself.

The last evening she said to Theodora, who was bidding her good-night in her room:

"I had a letter from your friend Lord Bracondale last week, from Alaska. He asks for news of you. Did you see him after he came from Paris? He was only a short while in England, I understand."

"Yes, we saw him once or twice," said Theodora, "and we made the acquaintance of his sister."

"He always seemed to be very fond of her. Is she a nice sort of woman?"

"Very nice."

"I hear the mother is clean crazy with him for going off again and not marrying that heiress they are so set upon. But why should he? He don't want the money."

"No," said Theodora.

"Was he at Beechleigh when you were there?"

"Yes."

"And Miss Winmarleigh, too?"

"Yes, she was there."

"Oh!" said Mrs. Fitzgerald. "A great lump of a woman, isn't she?"

"She is rather large."

This was hopeless—a conversation of this sort—Jane Fitzgerald decided. It told her nothing.

Theodora's face had become so schooled it did not, even to her step-mother's sharp eyes, betray any emotion.

"I am glad if the folly is over," she thought to herself. "But I shouldn't wonder if it Wasn't something to do with it still, after all. If it is not that, what can it be?" Then she said aloud: "He is going through America, and we shall meet him when we get back in November, most likely. I shall persuade him to come down to Florida with us, if I can. He seems to be aimlessly wandering round, I suppose, shooting things; but Florida is the loveliest place in the world, and I wish you and Josiah would come, too, my dear."

"That would be beautiful," said Theodora, "but Josiah is not fit for a long journey. We shall go to the Riviera, most probably, when the weather gets cold."

"Have you no message for him then, Theodora, when I see him?"

And now there was some sign. Theodora clasped her hands together, and she said in a constrained voice:

"Yes. Tell him I hope he is well—and I am well—just that," and she walked ever to the dressing-table and picked up a brush, and put it down again nervously.

"I shall tell him no such thing," said her step-mother, kindly, "because I don't believe it is true. You are not well, dear child, and I am worried about you."

But Theodora assured her that she was, and all was as it should be, and nothing further could be got out of her; so they kissed and wished each other good-night. And Jane Fitzgerald, left to herself, heaved a great sigh.

Next day, after this cheery pair had gone, things seemed to take a deeper gloom.

The mention of Hector's name and whereabouts had roused Theodora's dormant sorrows into activity again; and with all her will and determination to hide her anguish, Josiah could perceive an added note of pathos in her voice at times and less and less elasticity in her step.

Once he would have noticed none of these things, but now each shade of difference in her made its impression upon him.

And so the time wore on, their hearts full of an abiding grief.

When October set in Josiah caught a bad cold, which obliged him to keep to his bed for days and days. He did not seem very ill, and assured his wife he would be all right soon; but by November, Sir Baldwin Evans, who was sent for hurriedly from London, broke it gently to Theodora that her husband could not live through the winter. He might not even live for many days. Then she wept bitter tears. Had she been remiss in anything? What could she do for him? Oh, poor Josiah!

And Josiah knew that his day was done, as he lay there in his splendid, silk-curtained bed. But life had become of such small worth to him that he was almost glad.

"Now, soon she can be happy—my little girl," he said to himself, "with the one of her class. It does not do to mix them, and I was a fool to try. But her heart is too kind ever to quite forget poor old Josiah Brown."

And this thought comforted him. And that night he died.

Then Theodora wept her heart out as she kissed his cold, thin hand.

When they got the telegram in New York at Mrs. Fitzgerald's mansion, Hector was just leaving the house, and Captain Fitzgerald ran after him down the steps.

"My son-in-law, Josiah Brown, is dead," he said. "My wife thought you would be interested to hear. Poor fellow, he was not very old either—only fifty-two."

Hector almost staggered for a moment, and leaned against the gilded balustrade. Then he took off his hat reverently, while he said, in his deep, expressive voice:

"There lived no greater gentleman."

And Captain Fitzgerald wondered if he were mad or what he could mean, as he watched him stride away down the street.

But when he told his wife, she understood, for she had just learned from Hector the whole story.

And perhaps—who knows? Far away in Shadowland Josiah heard those words, "There lived no greater gentleman." And if he did—they fell like balm on his sad soul.

XXXI

It was eighteen months after this before they met again—Hector and Theodora; and now it was May, and the flowers bloomed and the birds sang, and all the world was young and fair—only Morella Winmarleigh was growing into a bitter old maid.

At twenty-eight people might have taken her for a matron of ten years older.

She had wondered for weeks what was the result of her action with the letters. She hoped daily to hear of some catastrophe and scandal falling upon the head of Theodora. But she heard nothing. It was only after Josiah's death that details were wafted to her through the Fitzgeralds.

How poor Mr. Brown had never really recovered from a slight stroke he had had on leaving Beechleigh, and of Theodora's goodness and devotion to him, and of his worship of her. And Morella had the maddening feeling that if she had left well alone this death might never have occurred, and her hated rival might not now be a free and beautiful widow, with no impediment between herself and Hector when they should choose to meet.

She had meant to be revenged and punish them, and it seemed she had only cleared their path to happiness. There was really no justice in this world!

Theodora had gone to meet her father and step-mother in Paris.

Her sisters were married and very happy, she hoped. Prosperity had wonderfully embellished their attractions, and even Sarah had found a mate.

And Lady Bracondale remained her placid, stately self. Her grief and disappointment over Hector's departure from England had passed away by now, as so had her treasured dream of receiving Morella Winmarleigh as a daughter. But Anne whispered to her that she need not worry forever, and some day soon her brother might choose a bride whom even she would love.

Hector had continued his wanderings over the world for many months after Josiah's death. He felt, should he return to England, nothing could keep him from Theodora.

And she, too, had travelled and explored fresh scenes, and was now a supremely beautiful and experienced woman—courted and flattered, and besieged by many adorers.

But she was still Theodora, with only one love in her heart and one dream in her soul—to meet Hector again and spend the rest of her life in the shelter of his arms.

She heard of him often through her step-mother; and sometimes she saw Anne—and both Hector and she understood, and knew the time would come when they could be happy.

Jane Anastasia Fitzgerald had romantic notions. This pretty pair, whom she looked upon as of her own producing, must meet again under her auspices in like circumstances as they had done on the happy and never-to-be-forgotten day when she herself had promised her heart and hand to Dominic Fitzgerald.

"There is something lucky about Versailles," she said, "and they shall experience it, too!"

So she planned a picnic, and arranged it with Hector before he reached Paris. He was not to show himself or communicate with Theodora; he was just to be there at the Réservoirs and wait for their arrival.

And the gods smiled—and the day was fine—and the trees were green—as had been another day, two years ago.

And oh, the wild, mad joy that surged up in their hearts when their eyes met once more!

They could not speak, it seemed, even the words of politeness; so they wandered away into the spring woods, silent and glad; and it was not until they reached the shrine of old Enceladus that Hector clasped Theodora again in his arms, and gave rein to all the passionate love and delirious happiness which was flooding his being.

There one can leave them—together—for always—looking out upon the realization of that fair dream of life.

Safe in each other's arms, in those smooth waters, beyond the rocks.

THE END

His Hour

CHAPTER I

The Sphinx was smiling its eternal smile. It was two o'clock in the morning. The tourists had returned to Cairo, and only an Arab or two lingered near the boy who held Tamara's camel, and then gradually slunk away; thus, but for Hafis, she was alone—alone with her thoughts and the Sphinx.

The strange, mystical face looked straight at her from the elevation where she sat. Its sensual mocking calm penetrated her brain. The creature seemed to be laughing at all humanity—and saying—"There is no beyond—live and enjoy the things of the present—Eat, drink, and be merry, for to-morrow you die, and I—I who sit here and know, tell you there is no beyond. The things you can touch and hold to your bodies are the only ones worth grasping."

"No, no!" said Tamara, half aloud, "I will not—I will not believe it."

"Fool," said the Sphinx. "What is your soul? And if you have one, what have you done with it hitherto? Are you any light in the world?—No, you have lived upon the orders of others, you have let your individuality be crushed these twenty-four years—since the day you could speak. Just an echo it is—that fine thing, your soul! Show it then, if you have one! Do you possess an opinion? Not a bit of it. You simply announce platitudes that you have been taught were the right answers to all questions! Believe me, you have no soul. So take what you can—a body! You certainly have that, one can see it—well, snatch what it can bring you, since you have not enough will to try for higher things. Grasp what you may, poor weakling. That is the wisdom sitting here for eternity has taught me."

Tamara stirred her hands in protest—but she knew the indictment was true. Yes, her life had been one long commonplace vista of following leads—like a sheep.

But was it too late to change? Had she the courage? Dared she think for herself? If not, the mystic message of the Sphinx's smile were better followed: "Eat, drink, and be merry, for to-morrow you die."

The blue of the sky seemed to soothe her, and speak of hope. Could any other country produce a sky of so deep a sapphire as the night sky of Egypt? All around was intense sensuous warmth and stillness almost as light as day.

How wise she had been to break through the conventionality which surrounded her—and it had required some nerve—so as to be able to come here alone, on this one of her last nights in Egypt.

She half smiled when she thought of Millicent Hardcastle's face when she had first suggested it.

"My dear Tamara, what—what an extraordinary thing for a woman to do! Go to the Sphinx all alone at two o'clock in the morning. Would not people think it very strange?"

Tamara felt a qualm for a second, but was rebellious.

"Well, perhaps—but do you know, Millicent, I believe I don't care. That carven block of stone has had a curious effect upon me. It has made me think as I have never done before. I want to take the clearest picture away with me—I must go."

And even Mrs. Hardcastle's mild assertion that it could equally well be viewed and studied at a more reasonable hour did not move Tamara, and while her friend slumbered comfortably in her bed at Mena House, she had set off, a self-conscious feeling of a truant schoolboy exalting and yet frightening her.

Tamara was a widow. James Loraine had been everything that a thoroughly respectable English husband ought to be. He had treated her with kindness, he had given her a comfortable home—he had only asked her to spend ten months of the year in the country, and he had never caused her a moment's jealousy.

She could not remember her heart having beaten an atom faster—or slower—for his coming or going. She had loved him, and her sisters and brother, and father, all in the same devoted way, and when pneumonia had carried him off nearly two years before, she had grieved with the measure the loss of any one of them would have caused her—that was sincerely and tenderly.

They were such a nice family, Tamara's!

For hundreds of years they had lived on the same land, doing their duty to their neighbors and helping to form that backbone of England of which we hear so much nowadays, in its passing away.

They had been members of Parliament, of solid Whig, and later of Unionist, views. They had been staunch Generals, Chairmen of Quarter-Sessions, riders to hounds, subscribers to charities, rigid church-goers, disciplined, orthodox, worthy members of society.

Underdown was their name, and Underwood their home.

That Tamara should have been given that Russian appellation, in a group of Gladys, Mabels and Dorothys, must have surely indicated that fate meant her to follow a line not quite so mapped out as that of her sisters'. The very manner of her entry into the world was not in accordance with the Underdown plan.

Her mother, Lady Gertrude Underdown, had contracted a friendship with the wife of the First Secretary of the Russian Embassy.

Foreigners were not looked upon with favor in the home circle, and instead of staying only the two months of May and June, as she was fully entitled to, in London, she had insisted upon remaining for July as well that year—to be near her friend Vera and enjoy the gay world.

The Squire had grumbled, but acquiesced, though when afterward a fourth daughter was presented to him with a request that she might have Princess Vera for a godmother and a Russian name to be called by, he felt himself justified in carping at fate.

"Foreign fandangoes," he designated such ideas. However, Lady Gertrude was very ill, and had to be humored, so the affair took place, and Tamara the baby was christened, with due state.

There were no more Russian suggestions in the family; the son and heir who arrived a year later became plain Tom, and then Lady Gertrude Underdown made her bow to the world and retired to the family vault in Underwood Church.

They were all estimably brought up by an aunt, and hardly ever left the country until each one came up in turn to be presented at Court, and go through a fairly dull season among country neighbors on the same bent.

Two of them, including Tamara, had secured suitable husbands, and at the age of twenty-three years the latter had been left a well-dowered widow.

She had worn mourning for just the right period, had looked after her affairs—handed James' place over with a good grace to James' brother and an unliked sister-in-law, and finally, when she was wearing grays and mauves, two years almost after her loss, she had allowed herself to be persuaded into taking a trip to Egypt with her friend, Millicent Hardcastle, who was recovering from influenza.

It had caused the greatest flutter at Underwood, this journey abroad! None of them had been further than Dresden, where each girl had learned German for a year or so before her presentation.

And what had Egypt done for Tamara? Lifted just one pretty white eyelid, perhaps. Stirred something which only once or twice in her life she had been dimly conscious of. Everything had been a kind of shock to her. A shock of an agreeable description. And once driving at night in the orange groves of Ghezireh, after some open-air fête, the heavy scent and intoxicating atmosphere had made her blood tingle. She felt it was almost wrong that things should so appeal to her senses. Anything which appealed deliberately to the senses had always been considered as more than almost wrong at Underwood Chase.

The senses were improper things which Aunt Clara for her part never quite understood why the Almighty should have had the bad taste to permit in human beings.

But the Sphinx was again talking to Tamara—only this time in the voice of a young man—who without a word of warning had risen from a bank of sand where he had been stretched motionless and unperceived.

"A fine goddess, is she not, Madame," he said. And to add to the impertinence of a stranger's addressing her at all, Tamara was further incensed by the voice being that of a foreigner!

But it was an extraordinarily pleasant voice, deep and tuneful, and the "*Insolent*" stood over six feet high and was as slender as Tamara herself almost—in spite of his shoulders and air of strength.

She hardly knew what to answer, he had spoken with such ease and assurance, almost with the tone of one who hails a fellow worshiper and has a right to exchange sympathy.

Tamara had been startled, too, by the sudden rising of the man when she thought she was alone, but at last she answered slowly, "Yes."

"I often come here at night," he went on, "when those devils of tourists have gone back in their devil of a tramway. Then you get her alone—and she says things to you. You think so, too, isn't it?"

"Yes," again said Tamara, convulsed with wonder at herself for speaking at all.

"At first I was angry when I saw your camel against the sky and saw you come and dismount and sit and look, I like to have her all to myself. But afterwards when I watched you I saw you meant no harm—you aren't a tourist, and so you did not matter."

"Indeed," said Tamara, the fine in her grasping the situation, the Underdown training resenting its unconventionality.

"Yes," he continued, unconcerned. "You can't look at that face and feel we any of us matter much—can you?"

"No," said Tamara.

"How many thousand years has she been telling people that? But it drives me mad, angry, furious, to see the tourists! I want to strangle them all!"

He clenched his hand and his eyes flashed.

Tamara peeped up at him—he was not looking at her—but at the Sphinx. She saw that he was extremely attractive in spite of having un-English clothes, which were not worn with ease. Gray flannel of unspeakable cut, and boots which would have made her brother Tom shriek with laughter. The Underdown part of her whispered, could he be quite a gentleman? But when he turned his face full upon her in the moonlight, that doubt vanished completely. He might even be a very great gentleman, she thought.

"Would you like to see a bit of the Arabian Nights?" he asked her.

Tamara rose. This really ought not to go on, this conversation—and yet—

"Yes, I would," she said.

"Well, the spell is broken of the Sphinx," he continued. "She can't talk to me with you there, and she can't talk to you with me near, so let us go and see something else that is interesting together."

"What?" asked Tamara.

"The Sheikh's village down below. Half the people who come don't realize it is there, and the other half would be afraid to ride through it at night—but they know me and I will take care of you."

Without the least further hesitation he called Hafis and the camel, spoke to them in Arabic, and then stood ready to help Tamara up. She seemed hypnotized, when she was settled in the high saddle. She began to realize that she was going into the unknown with a perfect stranger, but she did not think of turning back.

"What do you ride?" she asked.

"See," he said, and he made a strange low whistle, which was instantly answered by an equally strange low whinny of a horse, and a beautiful Arab appeared from the foot of the rocks—where all things were in shadow—led by a little brown boy.

"I am taking him back with me," he said, "Isn't he a beauty. I only bought him a week ago, and he already knows me."

Then he was in the saddle with the lightest bound, and Tamara, who had always admired Tom on a horse, knew that she had never seen anyone who seemed so much a part of his mount as this quaint foreigner. "I suppose he is an Austrian," she said to herself, and then added with English insular arrogance, "Only Austrians are like us."

The young man appeared quite indifferent to anything she thought. He prepared to lead the way down beyond the Sphinx, apparently into the desert.

Now that he was in front of her, Tamara could not help admiring the lines of his figure. He was certainly a very decent shape, and certainly knew how to ride.

Then it came to her that this was a most singular adventure, and the faint pink mounted to her clear cheeks when she remembered how dreadfully shocked Millicent would be—or any of the family! But it was her night of rebellion, so things must take their course.

The young man rode in front until they were on the flat desert, then he drew rein and waited for her.

"You see," he said, "we skirt these rocks and then we shall ride through the village. One can very well imagine it has been the same always."

They entered the little town. The streets were extremely narrow and the dark houses gave an air of mystery—a speculation—what could be going on behind those closed shutters? Here and there a straight blue-clad figure slunk away round a corner. There was a deep silence and the moonlight made the shadows sharp as a knife. Then a shaft of red light would shoot from some strange low hovel as they passed, and they could see inside a circle of Arab Bedouins crouching over a fire. There seemed no hilarity, their faces were solemn as the grave.

Presently, in the narrowest and darkest street, there was a sound of tom-toms, strains of weird music and voices, and through the chinks of the half-opened shutters light streamed across the road—while a small crowd of Arabs were grouped about the gate in the wall holding donkeys and a camel.

"A wedding," said the young man. "They have escorted the bride. What pleasure to raise a veil and see a black face! But each one to his taste."

Tamara looked up at the window. She wondered what could be happening within—were the other wives there as well? She would have liked to have asked.

The young man saw her hesitation and said laconically—

"Well?"

"They are having a party," Tamara replied, with lame obviousness.

"Of course," said the young man. "Weddings and funerals—equally good occasions for company. They are so wise they leave all to fate; they do not tear their eyes out for something they cannot have—and fight after disappointment. They are philosophers, these Arabs."

The little crowd round the gate now barred the road, half good humoredly, half with menace.

"So, so," said the young man, riding in front. Then he laughed, and putting his hand in his pocket, brought out a quantity of silver and flung it among them with merry words in Arabic, while he pointed to the windows of the house.

Then he seized the bridle of Tamara's camel and started his horse forward. The crowd smiled now and began scrambling for the baksheesh, and so they got through in peace.

Neither spoke until they were in a silent lane again.

"Sometimes they can be quite disagreeable," he said, "but it is amusing to see it all. The Sheikh lives here—he fancies the pyramids belong to him, just as the Khedive fancies all Egypt is his—life is mostly imagination."

Now Tamara could see his face better as he looked up to her superior height on the camel. He had a little moustache and peculiarly chiseled lips—too chiseled for a man, she thought for a moment, until she noticed the firm jaw. His eyes were sleepy—slightly Oriental in their setting, and looked very dark, and yet something made her think that in daylight they might be blue or gray.

He did not smile at all; as he spoke his face was grave, but when something made him laugh as they turned the next corner, it transformed him. It was the rippling spontaneous gaiety of a child.

Two goats had got loose from opposite hovels and were butting at one another in the middle of the road.

He pulled up his horse and watched.

"I like any fight," he said.

But the goats fled in fear of him, so they went on.

Tamara was wondering why she felt so stupid. She wanted to ask her strange companion a number of questions. Who he was? What he was doing at the Sphinx?—and indeed in Egypt. Why he had spoken to her at all?—and yet appeared absolutely indifferent as they rode along! He had not asked her a single question or expressed the least curiosity. For some reason she felt piqued.

Presently they emerged at the end of the village where there was a small lake left by the retirement of the Nile. The moon, almost full, was mirrored in it. The scene was one of extreme beauty. The pyramids appeared an old rose pink, and everything else in tones of sapphire—not the green-blue of moonlight in other countries. All was breathlessly still and lifeless. Only they two, and the camel boys, alone in the night.

The dark line of trees which border the road faced them, and they rode slowly in that direction.

"You are going to the hotel, I suppose?" he said. "I will see you safely to it."

And they climbed the bank on to the avenue from Cairo.

"And you?" Tamara could not prevent herself from asking. "Where do you go?"

"To hell, sometimes," he answered, and his eyes were full of mist, "but tonight I shall go to bed for a change."

Tamara was nonplussed. She felt intensely commonplace. She was even a little cross with herself. Why had she asked a question?

The Arab horse now took it into his head to curvet and bound in the air for no apparent reason, but the young man did not stir an inch—he laughed.

"Go on, my beauty," he said. "I like you to be so. It shows you are alive."

As they approached the hotel, Tamara began to hope no one would see them. No one who could tell Millicent that she had a companion. She bent down and said rather primly to the young man who was again at her side:

"I am quite safe now, thank you. I need not trouble you any further. Good-bye! and I am so obliged to you for showing me a new way home."

He looked up at her, and his whole face was lit with a whimsical smile.

"Yes, at the gate," he said. "Don't be nervous. I will go at the gate."

Tamara did not speak, and presently they came to the turning into the hotel. Then he stopped.

"I suppose we shall meet again some day," he said. "They have a proverb here, 'Meet before dawn—part not till dawn.' They see into the future in a few drops of water in any hollow thing. Well, good-night"—and before she could answer he was off beyond the hotel up the road and then turning to the right on a sand-path, galloped out of sight into what must be the vast desert.

Where on earth could he be going to?—possibly the devil—if one knew.

CHAPTER II

When Tamara woke in the morning the recollection of her camel ride seemed like a dream. She sat for a long time at the window of her room looking out toward the green world and Cairo. She was trying to adjust things in her mind. This stranger had certainly produced an effect upon her.

She wondered who he was, and how he would look in daylight—and above all whither he had galloped into the desert. Then she wondered at herself. The whole thing was so out of her line—so bizarre—in a life of carefully balanced proprieties. And were the thoughts the Sphinx had awaked in her brain true? Yes, certainly she had been ruled by others always—and had never developed her own soul.

She was very sensitive—that last whimsical smile of the unknown had humiliated her. She felt he had laughed at her prim propriety in wishing to get rid of him before the gate. Indeed, she suddenly felt he might laugh at a good many of the things she did. And this ruffled her serenity. She put up her slender hands and pushed the thick hair back from her forehead with an impatient gesture. It all made her dissatisfied with herself and full of unrest.

"You don't tell me a thing about your Sphinx excursion last night, Tamara," Millicent Hardcastle said at breakfast, rather peevishly. They were sipping coffee together in the latter's room in dressing-gowns. "Was it nice, and had the tourists quite departed?"

"It was wonderful!" and Tamara leant back and looked into distance. "There were no tourists, and it made me think a number of new things—we seem such ordinary people, Millicent."

Mrs. Hardcastle glanced up surprised, not to say offended, with coffee cup poised in the air.

"Yes—you may wonder, but it is true, Milly—we do the same things every day, and think the same thoughts, and are just thoroughly commonplace and uninteresting."

"And you came to these conclusions from gazing at the Sphinx?" Mrs. Hardcastle asked.

"Yes," said Tamara, the pink deepening for a moment in her cheeks. In her whole life she hardly ever had had a secret. "I sat there, Millicent, in the sand opposite the strange image, and it seemed to smile and mock at all little things; it appeared perfectly ridiculous that we pay so much attention to what the world says or thinks. I could not help looking back to the time when you and I were at Dresden together. What dull lives we have both led since! Yours perhaps more filled than mine has been, because you have children; but really we have both been browsing like sheep."

Mrs. Hardcastle now was almost irritated.

"I cannot agree with you," she said. "Our lives have been full of good and pleasant things—and I hope, dear, we have both done our duty."

This, of course, ended the matter! It was so undoubtedly true—each had done her duty.

After breakfast they started for a last donkey-ride, as they must return to Cairo in time for the Khedive's ball that night, which, as distinguished English ladies, they were being taken to by their compatriots at the Agency. Then on the morrow they were to start for Europe. Mrs. Hardcastle could not spare more time away from her babies. Their visit had only been of four short weeks, and now it was December 27, and home and husband called her.

For Tamara's part, she could do as she pleased; indeed, for two pins she would have stayed on in Egypt.

But that was not the intention of fate!

"Do let us go up that sand-path, Millicent," she said, when they turned out of the hotel gate. "We have never been there, and I would like to see where it leads to—perhaps we shall get quite a new vista from the top——"

And so they went.

What she expected to find she did not ask herself. In any case they rode on, eventually coming out at a small enclosure where stood a sort of bungalow in those days—it is probably pulled down now, but then it stood with a wonderful view over the desert, and over the green world. Tamara had vaguely observed it in the distance before, but imagined it to be some water-tower of the hotel, it was so bare and gaunt. It had been built by some mad Italian, they heard afterward, for rest and quiet.

It was a quaint place with tiny windows high up, evidently to light a studio, and there was a veranda to look at the view towards the Nile.

When they got fairly close they could see that on this veranda a young man was stretched at full length. A long wicker chair supported him, while he read a French novel. They—at least Tamara—could see the yellow back of the book, and also, one regrets to add, she was conscious that the young man was only clothed in blue and white striped silk pyjamas!—the jacket of which was open and showed his chest—and one foot, stretched out and hanging over the back of another low chair, was—actually bare!

Mrs. Hardcastle touched her donkey and hurried past—the path went so very near this unseemly sight! And Tamara followed, but not before the young man had time to raise himself and frown with fury. She almost imagined she heard him saying "Those devils of tourists!" Then with the corner of her eye ere they got out of sight, she perceived that a blue-clad Arab brought coffee on a little tray.

She glowed with annoyance. Did he think she had come to look at him? Did he—he certainly was quite uninterested, for he must have recognized her; but perhaps not; people look so different in large straw hats to what they appear with scarves of chiffon tied over their heads. But why had she come this way at all? She wished a thousand times she had suggested going round the pyramids instead.

"Tamara," said Mrs. Hardcastle, when they were safely descending the further sand-path, with no unclothed young giant in view, "did you see there was a *man* in that chair? What a dreadful person to be lying on the balcony—undressed!"

"I never noticed," said Tamara, without a blush. "I am surprised at you having looked, Millie—when this view is so fine."

"But, my dear child, I could not possibly help seeing him. How you did not notice, I can't think; he had pyjamas on, Tamara—and *bare feet!"*

Mrs. Hardcastle almost whispered the last terrible words.

"I suppose he felt hot," said Tamara; "it is a grilling day."

"But really, dear, no nice people, in any weather, remain—er—undressed at twelve o'clock in the day for passers-by to look at—do they?"

"Well, perhaps he isn't a nice person," allowed Tamara. "He may be mad. What was he like, since you saw so much, Millicent?"

Mrs. Hardcastle glanced over her shoulder reproachfully. "You really speak as though I had looked on purpose," she said. "He seemed very long—and not fat. I suppose, as his hair was not very dark, he must be an Englishman."

"Oh, dear, no!" exclaimed Tamara. "Not an Englishman." Then seeing her friend's expression of surprise, "I mean, it isn't likely an Englishman would lie on his balcony in pyjamas—at least not the ones we see in Cairo; they—they are too busy, aren't they?"

This miserably lame explanation seemed to satisfy Millicent. It was too hot and too disagreeable, she felt, clinging to the donkey while it descended the steep path, to continue the subject further, having to turn one's head over the shoulder like that; but when they got on the broad level she began again:

"Possibly it was a madman, Tamara, sent here with a keeper—in that out-of-the-way place. How fortunate we had the donkey boys with us!"

Tamara laughed.

"You dear goose, Millie, he couldn't have eaten us up, you know; and he was not doing the least harm, poor thing. We should not have gone that way; it may have been his private path."

"Still, no one should lie about undressed," Mrs. Hardcastle protested. "It is not at all nice. Girls might have been riding with us, and how dreadful it would have been then."

"Let us forget it, pet!" Tamara laughed, "and trot on and get some real exercise."

So off they started.

Just as they were turning out of the hotel gate, late in the same afternoon, a young man on an Arab horse passed the carriage. He was in ordinary riding dress, and looked a slim, graceful sight as he trotted ahead.

He never glanced their way. But while Tamara felt a sudden emotion of sorts, Mrs. Hardcastle exclaimed:

"Look, look! I am sure that is he—the mad man who wore those pyjamas."

CHAPTER III

The Khedive's ball was a fairly fine sight, Tamara thought, but driving through the streets took such a ridiculously long time, the crowd was so great. The palace itself was, and probably is still, like all other palaces that are decorated in that nondescript style of Third Empire France—not a thing of beauty. But the levée uniforms of the officers gave an air of brilliance contrasted with the civilians of the Government of Egypt. Tamara thought their dress very ugly, it reminded her of a clergyman's at a children's party, where he has been decorated with caps and sham orders from the crackers to amuse the little guests. It seemed strange to see the English faces beneath the fez. She and Millicent Hardcastle walked about and talked to their friends. There were many smart young gallants in the regiments then quartered in Cairo, who enjoyed dancing with the slender, youthful widow with the good jewels and pretty dress, and soon Tamara found herself whirling with a gay hussar.

"Let us stop near the Royalties and look at the Russians," he said. "You know, a Grand Duke arrived to-day, and must be here to-night."

They came to a standstill close to the little group surrounding the Khedive, and amid the splendid uniforms of the Grand Duke's suite there was one of scarlet, the like of which Tamara had never seen before.

Afterward she learned it was a Cossack of the Emperor's escort, but at the moment it seemed like a gorgeous fancy dress. The high boots and long, strangely graceful coat, cut with an Eastern hang, the white under-dress, the way the loose scarlet sleeves fell at the wrist, showing the white tight ones, the gold and silver trimmings and the arms, stuck in the quaint belt, all pleased her eye extremely; and then she recognized its wearer as the young man of the Sphinx.

How dress changes a person! she thought. He looked at ease now in this gorgeous garment, and a very prince for a fairy tale. That accounted for the dreadful gray flannel—he was a soldier and unaccustomed to wearing ordinary clothes. She had heard that in foreign countries even the officers wore their uniforms habitually; not as the English do, merely as an irksome duty.

He did not appear to see her, but when she began dancing again, and paused once more for breath, she was close to him as he stood some way apart and alone.

Their eyes met. His had the same whimsical provoking smile in them which angered and yet attracted her. He made no move to bow to her, nor did he take any steps to be introduced. She burnt with annoyance.

"He might at least have been presented; it is too impertinent otherwise!" she thought.

She knew she was looking her best: a fair, distinguished woman as young and fresh as a girl. Hardly a man in the room was unconscious of her presence. Anger lent an extra brightness to her eyes and cheeks. She went on dancing wildly.

The next time she was near the stranger was some half an hour later, although not once was she able to banish the scarlet form from her view. He did not dance. He talked now and then to his Prince, and then he was presented to the official ladies, with the rest of the suite. He looked bored.

Tamara would not ask his name, which she could have done with ease, as every one was interested in the Russians and glad to talk about them. She avoided the English group of bigwigs where they were standing, and where she had her place—And when they passed the tall Cossack again she turned upon him a witheringly unconscious glance.

However, this was not to continue the whole night, for presently she was requested by one of the attachés to come and be presented to the Grand Duke, and when she had made her curtsey the suite came up in turn.

"Prince Milaslávski," and she heard one of his friends call him "Gritzko." The name fell pleasantly on her ears—"Gritzko"! Why was he such a wretch as to humiliate her so? She felt horribly small. She ought never to have let him speak to her at the Sphinx. She was being thoroughly punished for her unconventionality now!

She said a few words in French to each of the others, and then, as he still stood there with that provoking smile in his splendid eyes, she turned away almost biting her lip with shame and rage.

Before she knew it she was dancing with a fierce count in green and silver. Their conversation was interesting.

"You are here since long, Madame?"

"No, Monsieur, only a few weeks, and I go to-morrow."

"Ah! you dance beautifully!"

"Do I? I am glad——"

The Russian Count held her very tightly, and they stopped quite out of breath, where the screened windows half-hid the poor ladies of the harem, who watched the throng from their safe retreat.

The Count bowed—and Tamara bowed. A section, not the whole dance, was evidently the Russian custom.

Then a voice said close to her ear:

"May I, too, have the honor of a turn, Madame?" and she looked up into the eyes of the Prince.

For a second she hesitated. Her first impulse was to scornfully say no, but she quickly realized that would be undignified and absurd; so she said yes, coldly, and let him place his arm about her. The band was playing a particularly sensuous valse, which drove all young people mad that year, and—if the Count had danced well—this man's movements were heaven. Tamara did not speak a word. She purposely did not look at him, but drooped her proud head so that the flashing diamonds of her tiara were all he could have seen of her.

He put no special meaning into the way he held her; he just danced divinely; but there was something in the creature himself of a perfectly annoying attractiveness—or so it seemed to Tamara.

They at last paused for a moment, and then he spoke. He made not the slightest allusion to the Sphinx incident. He spoke gravely of Cairo, and the polo, and the races, and said that his Grand Duke had arrived that day. He was not on his staff, but was indeed travelling in Egypt for his own amusement and delectation, he said.

He had been there since November, it seemed, and had been up the Nile, and had fortunately been able to secure a little bungalow at Mena, where he could spend some hours of peace.

Then Tamara laughed. She remembered Millicent Hardcastle's consternation over those unfortunate pyjamas. She wondered if Millicent would realize that she—Tamara—was dancing with their wearer now! When she laughed he put his arm around her once more and began dancing. This time he held her rather closely, and suddenly as she laughed again to herself provokingly, he clasped her tight.

"If you laugh like that I will kiss you—here in the room," he said.

Tamara stopped dead short. She blazed with anger.

"How dare you be so impertinent?" she said.

They were up in a corner; everyone's back was turned to them happily, for in one second he had bent and kissed her neck. It was done with such incredible swiftness and audacity that even had they been observed it must only have looked as though he bent to pick up something she had dropped. But the kiss burned into Tamara's flesh.

She could hardly keep the tears of outraged pride from her eyes.

"How dare you! How dare you!" she hissed. "Truly you are making me ashamed of having let you speak to me last night!"

"Last night?" he said, while he forcibly drew her hand within his arm and began walking toward the group of her friends. "Last night you were afraid some should see me from the hotel, and to-night you dare me. Do it once more and I will kiss your lips!"

Tamara went dead white; she felt as if the ground were sinking beneath her feet; her knees trembled. In all her smooth, conventionally ordered life she had never experienced such a strong emotion.

The Prince glanced at her, and the fierceness went out of his eyes. He bowed gravely with the most courtly homage, and left her standing by Millicent's side.

Then Tamara remembered she was a lady, and that tenue was expected of her; so she turned to her friend gaily and said how she was enjoying the ball; but her fine nostrils quivered at intervals for the rest of the night.

"Thank God!" she said to herself, when a few hours later she got into bed—"Thank God! we are going tomorrow. I shall never see him again, and no one shall ever know."

CHAPTER IV

Next day they started, escorted to the station by a troup of gushing friends. Their compartment was a bower of flowers, and as each moment went by Tamara's equanimity was restored by the thought that she would soon be out of the land of her disgrace.

It is a tiresome journey to Alexandria—dusty and glaring and not of great interest. They hurried on board the ship when they arrived, without even glancing at their fellow passengers following in the gangway. Neither woman was a perfect sailor and both were quite overcome with fatigue. It promised to be a disagreeable night, too, so they retired at once to their cabins, and were soon asleep.

The next day, which was Sunday, the wind blew, but by the afternoon calmed down again, and Tamara decided to dress and go on deck.

"Mrs. Hardcastle went up some hours ago; she was ready for luncheon, ma'am," her maid told her.

"She left a message for you to join her when you woke."

The ship was the usual sort of ship that goes from Alexandria to Trieste, and the two English ladies had secured places for their chairs in the most protected spot. Tamara rather looked forward to being able to sit there in the moonlight and enjoy the Mediterranean.

Her maid preceded her with her rug and cushion and book, and it was not until she was quite settled that she took cognizance of an empty chair at her other side.

"You lazy child!" Millicent Hardcastle said. "To sleep all day like this! It has been quite beautiful since luncheon, and I have had a most agreeable time. That extremely polite nice young Russian Prince we met at the Khedive's ball is here, dear; indeed, that is his chair next you. He is with Stephen Strong. We have been talking for hours."

Tamara felt suddenly almost cold.

"I never saw him in the train or coming on board," she said, with almost a gasp.

"Nor did I, and yet he must have been just behind us. Our places at meals are next him, too. So fortunate he was introduced, because one could not talk to a strange man, even on a boat. I never can understand those people who pick up acquaintances promiscuously; can you, dear?"

"No," said Tamara, feebly.

She was pondering what to do. She could not decline to know the Prince without making some explanation to Millicent. She also could not flatter him so much. She must just be icily cold, and if he should be further impertinent she could remain in her cabin.

But what an annoying contretemps! And she had thought she should never see him again!—and here until Wednesday afternoon, she would be constantly reminded of the most disgraceful incident in her career. All brought upon herself, too, by her own action in having lapsed from the rigid rules in which Aunt Clara had brought her up.

If she had not answered him at the Sphinx—he could not have—but she refused to dwell upon the shame of this recollection.

She had quite half an hour to grow calm before the cause of her unrest came even into sight, and when he did, it was to walk past in the company of their old friend, Stephen Strong.

The Prince raised his cap gravely, and Tamara comforted herself by noticing again how badly his clothes fitted him! How unsuitable, and even ridiculous, they were to English eyes—That gave her pleasure! Also she must have a little fun with Millicent.

"Has it struck you, Millie, the Prince is the same young man we saw in the pyjamas on the veranda? I am surprised at your speaking to such a person, even if he has been introduced!"

Mrs. Hardcastle raised an aggrieved head.

"Really, Tamara," she said, "I had altogether forgotten that unpleasant incident. I wish you had not reminded me of it. He is a most respectful, modest, unassuming young man. I am sure he would be dreadfully uncomfortable if he were aware we had seen him so."

"I think he looked better like that than he does now," Tamara rejoined, spitefully. "Did you ever see such clothes?"

Mrs. Hardcastle whisked right round in her chair and stared at her friend. She was shocked, in the first place, that Tamara should speak so lightly of a breach of decorum; and, secondly, she was astonished at another aspect of the case.

"I thought you never saw him at all that morning!" she exclaimed.

Tamara was nettled.

"Your description was so vivid; besides, I looked back!"

"You *looked back!* Tamara! after I had told you he wasn't dressed! My dear, how could you?"

"Well, I did.—Hush! he is coming toward us," and Tamara hurriedly opened a book and looked down.

"At last Mrs. Loraine has arrived on deck," she heard Millicent say; and then, for convention's sake she was obliged to glance up and bow coldly.

The young man did not seem the least impressed; he sat down and pulled his rug round his knees and gazed out at the sea. The sun had set, and the moon would soon rise in all her full glory.

There was hardly twilight and the ship's electric lights were already being lit. The old Englishman, Stephen Strong, greeted her and took the chair at Mrs. Hardcastle's other side. That lady was in one of her chatty moods, when each nicely expressed sentence fell from her lips directly after the other—all so pleasant and easy to understand. No one ever felt with Millicent he need use an atom of brain. These are the women men like.

Tamara pretended to read her book, but she was conscious of the near proximity of the Prince. Nothing so magnetic in the way of a personality had ever crossed her path as yet.

He sat as still as a statue gazing at the sea. An uncontrollable desire to look at him shook Tamara, but she dominated it. The discomfort at last grew so great that she almost trembled.

Then he spoke:

"Have you cat's eyes?" he asked.

Now, when there was a legitimate chance to look at him, she found her orbs glued to her book.

"Of course not!" she said, icily.

"Then of what use to pretend you are reading in this gloom? The miserable lantern is not good for a gleam."

Tamara was silent. She even turned a page. She would be irritating, too!

"That ball was a sight," he continued. "Did you see the harem ladies peeping from their cage? They looked fat and ugly enough to be wisely kept there. What a lot of fools they must have thought us, cavorting for their amusement."

"Poor women!" said Tamara. Her voice was the primmest thing in voices she had ever heard.

"Why poor women?" he asked. "They have all the pleasures of the body, and no anxieties; nothing but the little excitement of trying now and then to poison their rivals! It is the poor Khedive!—Think of his having to wade through all that fat mass to find one pretty one!"

The tone of this conversation displeased Tamara. She did not wish to enter into the ethics of the harem. She wished he would be silent again, only that deep voice of his was so pleasant! His English was wonderful, too, with hardly the least accent; and when she did allow herself to look at him she could not help admiring the way his hair grew, back from a forehead purely Greek. His nose was short and rather square, while those too beautifully chiseled lips of his had an expression of extraordinary charm. His whole personality breathed attraction, every human being who approached him was conscious of it. As for his eyes, they were enormous, with broad full lids, mystical, passionate, and yet unconcerned. Always they suggested something Eastern, though on the whole he was fair. Tamara's own soft brown hair was only a shade lighter than his.

She was not sure yet, but now thought his eyes were gray.

She could have asked him a number of questions she wanted answered, but she refrained. He suddenly turned and looked at her full in the face. He had been gazing fixedly at the sea, and these movements of quickness were disconcerting, especially as Tamara found herself caught in the act of studying his features.

"What on earth made you go to the Sphinx?" he asked.

Anger rose in Tamara; the inference was not flattering, in his speech, or the tone in which he uttered it.

"To count the number of stones the creature is made of, of course," she said. "Those technical things are what one would go for at that time of night."

And now her companion rippled with laughter, infectious, joyous laughter.

"Ah, you are not so stupid as I thought!" he said, frankly. "You looked poetic and fine with that gauze scarf around your head sitting there—and then afterwards. Wheugh! It was like a pretty wax doll. I regretted having wasted the village on you. All that is full of meaning for me."

Tamara was interested in spite of her will to remain reserved, although she resented the wax-doll part.

"Yes?"—he faltered.

"You can learn all the lessons you want in life from the Sphinx," he went on. "What paltry atoms you and I are, and how little we matter to anyone but ourselves! She is cruel, too, and does not hesitate to tear one in pieces if she wishes and she could make one ready to get drunk on blood."

Tamara rounded her sweet eyes.

"Then the village there, full of men with the passions of animals, living from father to son forever the same, wailing for a death, rejoicing at a birth, taking strong physical pleasure in their marriage rights and their women, and beating them when they are tired; but you are too civilized in your country to understand any of these things."

Tamara was stirred; she felt she ought to be shocked.

Contrary to her determination, she asked a question:

"Then you are not civilized in yours?"

"Not nearly so badly," he said. "The primitive forces of life still give us emotions, when we are not wild; when we are then it is the jolliest hell."

Tamara was almost repulsed. How could one be so odd as this man? she thought. Was he a type, or was he mad, or just only most annoyingly attractive and different from any one else? She found herself thrilled. Then with a subtle change he turned and almost tenderly wrapped the rug, which had blown a little down, more securely round her.

"You have such a small white face," he said, the words a caress. "One must see that you are warm and the naughty winds do not blow you away."

Tamara shivered; she could not have told why.

After this the conversation became general.

Millicent joined in with her obvious remarks. The sea was much smoother; they would be able to eat some dinner; she had heard there was a gipsy troupe on board in the third-class, and how nice it would be to have some music!

And something angered Tamara in the way the Prince assisted in all this, out-commonplacing her friend in commonplaces with the suavest politeness, while his grave face betrayed him not even by a twinkle in the eye. Only when he caught hers; then he laughed a sudden short laugh, and he whispered:

"What a perfect woman! everything in the right place. Heaven! at the best times she would do her knitting, and hand one a child every year! I'll marry when I can find a wife like that!"

Tamara was furious. She resented his ridicule of Millicent, and she was horrified at the whole speech; so, gathering her rug together, she said she was cold, and asked Mr. Strong to pace the deck with her. Nor would she take the faintest further notice of the Prince, until they all went below to the evening meal.

At dinner he seemed to be practically a stranger again. He was Tamara's neighbor, but he risked no startling speeches; in fact, he hardly spoke to her, contenting himself with discussing seafaring matters with the captain, and an occasional remark to Stephen Strong, who sat beyond Mrs. Hardcastle. It was unnecessary for her to have decided beforehand to snub him; he did not give her the chance.

CHAPTER V

On Monday they heard they would arrive at Brindisi on the Tuesday morning, and Tamara persuaded Mrs. Hardcastle to agree to disembarking there instead of going on to Trieste.

"We shall be home all the sooner," she said. And so it was settled. But there was still all Monday to be got through.

It was a perfect day, the blue Mediterranean was not belying its name. Tamara felt in great spirits, as she came on deck at about eleven o'clock, to find Millicent taking a vigorous walk round and round with the Russian Prince. They seemed to be laughing and chattering like old friends. Again Tamara resented it.

"He is only making fun of poor Millie," she thought, "who never sees a thing," and she settled herself in her chair and let her eyes feast on the blue sea——

What should she do with her life? This taste of change and foreign skies had unsettled her. How could she return to Underwood and the humdrum everyday existence there? She seemed to see it mapped out on a plain as one who stood on a mountain. She seemed to realize that always there had been dormant in her some difference from the others. She remembered now how often she perceived things that none of them saw, and she knew it was because of this that it had grown into a habit with her from early childhood to suppress the expression of her thoughts, and keep them to herself—until outwardly, at all events, she was of the same stolid mould as her family. The dears! they could not help it.

But about one point she was determined. She would think and act for herself in future. Aunt Clara's frown should not prohibit any book or any action. The world should teach her what it could.

Tamara had received a solid education; now she would profit by it, and instead of letting all her knowledge lie like a bulb in a root-house, she would plant it and tend it, and would hope to see sweet flowers springing forth.

"Next summer I shall be twenty-five years old," she said to herself, "and the whole thing has been a waste."

Each time the energetic promenaders passed her chair she heard a few words of their conversation, on hunting often, and the dogs, and the children, Bertie's cleverness, and Muriel's chickenpox, but always the Prince seemed interested and polite.

Presently the old man, Stephen Strong, came up and took Mrs. Hardcastle's chair.

"May I disturb your meditations?" he said. "You look so wise."

"No, I am foolish," Tamara answered. "Now you who know the world must come and talk and teach me its meaning."

He was rather a wonderful old man, Stephen Strong, purely English to look at, and purely cosmopolitan in habits and life. He had been in the diplomatic service years ago, and had been in Egypt in the gorgeous Ismail time; then a fortune came his way, and he traveled the earth over. There were years spent in Vienna and Petersburg and Paris, and always the early winter back in the land of the Sphinx.

"The world," he said, as he arranged himself in the chair, "is an extremely pleasant place if one takes it as it is, and does not quarrel with it. One must not be intolerant, and one must not be hypercritical. See it all and make allowances for the weakness of the human beings who inhabit it."

"Yes," said Tamara, "I know you are right; but so many of us belong to a tribe who think their point of view the only one. I do, for instance; that is why I say I am foolish."

The walkers passed again.

"There is a type for you to study," Stephen Strong said. "Prince Milaslávski. I have known him for many years, since he was a child almost; he is about twenty-nine or thirty now, and really a rather interesting personality."

"Yes," said Tamara, honestly, "I feel that. Tell me about him?"

Stephen Strong lit a cigar and puffed for a few seconds, then he settled himself with the air of a person beginning a narrative.

"He came into his vast fortune rather too young, and lived rather fiercely. His mother was a Basmanoff; that means a kind of Croesus in Russia. He is a great favorite with the powers that be, and is in the Cossacks of the Escort. Something in their wild freedom appealed to him more than any other corps. He is a Cossack himself on the mother's side, and the blood is all rather wild, you know."

Tamara looked as she felt—interested.

"They tell the most tremendous stories about him," the old man went on, "hugely exaggerated, of course; but the fact remains, he is a fascinating, restless, dauntless character."

"What sort of stories?" asked Tamara, timidly.

"Not all fit for your ears, gentle lady," laughed Stephen Strong. "Sheer devilment, mostly. It was the amusement in the beginning to dare him to anything, the maddest feats. He ran off with a nun once, it is said, for a bet, and deposited her in the house of the man she had loved before her vows were taken. That was in Poland. Then he has orgies sometimes at his country place, when every one is mad for three days on end. It causes terrible scandal. Then he comes back like a lamb, and purrs to all the old ladies. They say he obeys neither God nor the Devil—only the Emperor on this earth."

"How dreadful!" force of habit made Tamara say, while her thoughts unconsciously ran into interested fascination.

"He is absolutely fearless, and as cool as an Englishman, and there are not any mean things told about him, though," Steven Strong continued, "and indeed sometimes he lives the simplest country life with his horses and dogs, and his own people worship him, I believe. But there is no wildest prank he is incapable of if his blood is up."

"I think he looks like it," said Tamara. "Is it because he habitually wears uniform that his ordinary clothes fit so badly? To our eyes he seems dressed like some commis voyageur."

"Of course," said Stephen Strong. "And even in Paris I don't suppose you would approve of him in that respect, but if you could see him in Petersburg, then I believe you would be like all the rest."

"All which rest?" asked Tamara.

"Women. They simply adore him. Bohemians, great ladies, actresses, dancers, and——"

He was just going to mention those of another world, when he felt Tamara would hardly understand him, so he stopped short.

Something in her rose up in arms.

"It shows how foolish they are," she said.

Stephen Strong glanced at her sideways, and if she could have read his thoughts they were:

"This sweet Englishwoman is under Gritzko's spell already, and how she is battling against it! She won't have a chance, though, if he makes up his mind to win."

But Tamara, for all her gentle features, was no weakling; only her life had been a long hibernation; and now the spring had come, and soon the time of the finding of honey and a new life.

"What can he be talking about to my friend, Mr. Strong?" she asked, as the two passed again. "Millicent is one of the last women he can have anything in common with; she would simply die of horror if she heard any of these stories—and he can't be interested in a word she says."

"He always does the unexpected," and Stephen Strong laughed as he said it. He himself was amused at this ill-matched pair.

"Mrs. Hardcastle is agreeable to look at, too," he continued.

Tamara smiled scornfully.

"That is the lowest view to take. One should be above material appearance."

"Charming lady!" said Stephen Strong. "Yes, indeed you do not know the world."

Tamara was not angry. She looked at him and smiled, showing her beautiful teeth.

"Of course you think me a goose," she said, "but I warned you I was one. Tell me, shall I ever grow out of it—tell me, you who know?"

"If the teacher is young and handsome enough to make your heart beat," said her old companion. And then Millicent and the Prince joined them.

Mrs. Hardcastle's round blue eyes were flashing brightly, and her fresh face was aglow with exercise and enjoyment.

"Tamara dear, you are too incorrigibly lazy. Why do you sit here instead of taking exercise? and you have no idea of the interesting things the Prince has been telling me. All about a Russian poet called—oh, I can't pronounce the name, but who wrote of a devil—not exactly Faust, you know, though something like it."

Tamara noticed that amused, whimsical, mocking gleam in the Cossack's great eyes, but Millicent went gaily on, unconscious of anything but herself.

"I mean those mythical, strange sort of devils who come to earth, you know, and—and—make love to ladies—a sort of Satan like in Marie Corelli's lovely book. You remember, Tamara, the one you were so funny about, laughing when you read it."

"You mean 'The Demon' of Lermontoff, probably, Millicent, don't you?" Tamara said. "A friend of my mother's translated it into English, and I have known it since I was a child. I think it must be very fine in the original," and she looked at the Prince.

In one moment his face became serious and sympathetic.

"You know our great poet's work, then?" he said, surprised. "One would not have thought it!"

Then again Tamara's anger rose. There was always the insinuation in his remarks, seemingly unconscious, and therefore the more irritating, that she was a commonplace fool.

"Her name—the heroine's—is the same as my own," she said, gravely; but there was a challenge in her eyes.

"Tamara!" he said. "Well—it could be—a devil might come your way, but you would kneel and pray, and eat bonbons, and not listen to him."

"It would depend upon the devil," she said.

"Those who live the longest will see the most," and the Prince put back his head and laughed with real enjoyment at his thoughts, just as he had done when the two goats had butted at one another in the road.

Tamara felt her cheeks blaze with rage, but she would not enter the lists, in spite of the late challenge in her eyes.

Mr. Strong had vacated Millicent's chair and taken his own. The party soon settled into their legitimate places, and Tamara again took up her book.

"No, don't read," the Prince said. "You get angry at once with me when we talk, and the red comes into your cheeks, and I like it."

Exasperation was almost uncontrollable in Tamara. She remained silent, only the little ear next the Prince burned scarlet.

"Some day you will come to Russia," he said, "and then you will learn many things."

"I have no desire to go there," said Tamara, lying frankly, as it had always been her great wish, and indeed her godmother, who never forgot her, had often begged her to visit that northern clime; but Russia!—as well have suggested the moon at Underwood.

"It would freeze you, perhaps, or burn you—who can tell?" the Prince said. "One would see when you got there. I have an old lady, a dear friend, with white hair and a mole on her cheek—someone who sees straight. She would be good for your education."

Tamara thought it would be wiser not to show any further annoyance, so she said lightly:

"Yes, I am only sixteen, and have never left the schoolroom; it would be delightful to be taught how to live."

He turned and smiled at her.

"You hardly look any more—twenty, perhaps, and—never kissed!"

A memory rose up of a scorched neck, and suddenly Tamara's long eyelashes rested on her cheek.

Then into his splendid eyes came a fierce, savage, passionate gleam, which she did not see, but dimly felt, and he said in a low voice a little thick:

"And—as—yet—never really kissed."

"Milly," said Tamara, as calmly as she could, "what time do we get into Brindisi to-morrow morning? And think of it, on Thursday night we shall be at home."

Home seemed so very safe!

The Prince did not come in to luncheon, something was the matter with his Arab horse, and he had gone to see to it just before—a concern on his face as of the news of illness to his nearest kin.

Tamara was gay and charming, and laughed with Stephen Strong and the captain in quite an unusual way for her. They both thought her an adorable woman. Poor Tamara! and so she really was.

About tea-time Prince Milaslávski turned up again.

"He is all right now," he said, sure that his listeners were in perfect sympathy with him. "It was those fools down there. I have made them suffer, I can say," and then he turned to Stephen Strong. "Among the steerage there is an Alexandrian gipsy troupe. I have ordered them up to sing to us to-night, since Madame wished it," and he turned upon Millicent an air of deep devotion.

"Common ragged creatures, but one with some ankles and one with a voice. In any case, we must celebrate these ladies' last night."

And thus the terrible present end to their acquaintance fell about!

Nothing could have been more charming than the Prince was until dinner-time, and indeed through that meal, only he made Stephen Strong change places with him, so that he might be next Mrs. Hardcastle, much to that lady's delight.

"He is really too fascinating," she said, as she came into Tamara's cabin to fetch her for the evening meal. "I hardly think Henry would like his devotion to me. What do you think, dear?"

"I am sure he would be awfully jealous, Milly darling; you really must be careful," Tamara said. And with a conscious air of complacent pleasantly tickled virtue Mrs. Hardcastle led the way to the saloon.

It was not possible, Tamara thought, that anything so terribly unpleasant as the Prince's having too much champagne at dinner, could have accounted for his simply scandalous behavior after; and yet surely that would have been the kindest thing to say. But, no, it was not that.

This was, in brief, the scene which was enacted on the upper deck:

With the permission of the captain, the gipsy troupe were brought, and began their performance, tame enough at the commencement until the Prince gave orders for them to be supplied with unlimited champagne, and then the wildest dancing began. They writhed and gesticulated and undulated in a manner which made Millicent cling on to her chair, grow crimson in the face, and finally start to her feet.

But the worst happened when the Prince rose and, taking a tambourine, began, with a weird shriek, to beat it wildly, his eyes ablaze and his lips apart.

Then, seizing the chief dancer and banging it upon her head, he held his arm about her heaving breast, as she turned to him with a serpentine movement of voluptuous delight.

In a second he had caught hold of her, and had lifted and swung her far out over the dark blue waters, then, with a swirl to the side, held her suspended in the air above the open deck below.

"Ha, ha!" yelled the troupe, in frenzied pleasure, and, nimble as a cat, one rough dark man rushed down the ladder and caught the hanging woman in his arms. Then they all clapped and cheered and shrieked with joy, while the Prince, putting his hands in his pockets, pulled out heaps of gold and flung it among them.

"Back to hell, rats!" he shouted, laughing. "See, you have frightened the ladies. You should all be killed!"

For Tamara and Millicent had risen, and with stately steps had quitted the scene.

It was all too terrible and too vulgarly melodramatic, Tamara thought, especially that touching of the woman and that flinging of the gold, the latter caused by the same barbaric instinct which made him throw the silver in the Sheikh's village by the moonlit Sphinx, only this was worse a thousandfold.

The next morning the two ladies left the ship at Brindisi before either the Prince or Stephen Strong was awake. Both were silent upon the subject of the night before, until Millicent at last said when they were in the train:

"Tamara—you won't tell Henry or your family, will you, dear? Because really, last night he was so fascinating—but that dancing! I am sure you feel, with me, we could have died of shame."

CHAPTER VI

When Tamara reached Underwood and saw a letter from her Russian godmother among the pile which awaited her, she felt it was the finger of fate, and when she read it and found it contained not only New Year's wishes, but an invitation couched in affectionate and persuasive terms that she should visit St. Petersburg, she suddenly, and without consulting her family, decided she would go.

"There is something drawing me to Russia," she said to herself. "One gets into the current of things. I felt it in the air. And why should I hesitate now I am free? Why should I not accept, just because one Russian man has horrified me. It is, I suppose, a big city, and perhaps I shall never see him there."

So she announced her decision to the dumfounded household, and in less than a week took the Nord Express.

"The Court, alas! is in mourning,"—her godmother had written,—"so you will see no splendid Court balls, but I daresay we can divert you otherwise, Tamara, and I am so anxious to make the acquaintance of my godchild."

The morning after she left them Aunt Clara expressed herself thus at breakfast:

"I see a great and most unwelcome change in dear Tamara since she returned from Egypt, I had hoped Millicent Hardcastle would be all that was steadying and well-balanced as a companion for her, but it seems this modern restlessness has got into her blood. I tremble to think what ideas she will bring from Russia. Almost savages they are there!—She may be sent to Siberia or something dreadful, and we may never see her again."

"Oh! come Aunt Clara!" Tom Underdown protested, as he buttered his toast. "I think you are a little behind the times. There is a Russian at Oxford with me and he is the decentest chap in the world. You speak as though they almost lived on raw fish!"

"My dear Tom," said Miss Underdown, severely. "I was reading only yesterday, in the 'Christian Clarion,' how one of their Emperors cut off everyone's head. Dreadful customs they have, it seems; and one of their Empresses—Catherine, I think; her name was. Well, dear, it is too shocking to speak of—and most people were sent to the mines!"

"Oh! hang it all, Aunt Clara, you can't have looked at the date! You can hunt up just those jolly kind of stories about our Henry VIII. if you want to, you know, and our Elizabeth wasn't the saint they made out. And as for Siberia, I am going there myself some day, on the Trans-Siberian Railway. Tamara will be all right. I wish to heavens she had taken me with her. We have got dry rot in this house, that is what is the matter with us!"

"Tom!" almost gasped Miss Underdown. "Your manners are extremely displeasing, and the tone of your remarks is far from what one could wish!"

Meanwhile Tamara was speeding on her way to the North, her interest and excitement in her journey deepening with each mile.

The snow and the vast forests impressed her from the train windows. Every smallest shade made its effect upon her brain. Tamara was sensitive to all form and color. She was a person who apprehended things, and from the habit of keeping all her observations to herself perhaps the faculty of perception had grown the keener.

The silence seemed to be the first thing she remarked on reaching the frontier. The porters were so grave and quiet, with their bearded kindly faces, many of them like the saints and Biblical characters in Sunday-school picture books at home.

And finally she arrived at St. Petersburg, and found her godmother waiting for her on the platform. They recognized each other immediately. Tamara had several photographs of the Princess Ardácheff.

"Welcome, *ma filleule*," that lady cried, while she shook her hand. "After all these years I can have you in my house."

They said all sorts of mutually agreeable things on their way thither, and they looked at each other shyly.

"She is not beautiful," ran the Princess' comments. "Though she has a superb air of breeding—that is from her poor mother—but her eyes are her father's eyes. She is very sweet, and what a lovely skin—yes, and eyelashes—and probably a figure when one can see beneath the furs—tall and very slender in any case. Yes, I am far from disappointed—far."

And Tamara thought:

"My godmother is a splendid looking lady! I like her bright brown eyes and that white hair; and what a queer black mole upon her left cheek, like an early eighteenth-century beauty spot. Where have I heard lately of someone with a mole———?

"You fortunately see our city with a fresh mantle of snow, Tamara," the Princess said, glancing from the automobile window as they sped along. "It is not, alas! always so white as this."

It appeared wonderful to Tamara—so quite unlike anything she had imagined. The tiny sleighs seemingly too ridiculously small for the enormously padded coachman on the boxes—the good horses with their sweeping tails—the unusual harness. And, above all, again the silence caused by the snow.

Her first remark was almost a childish one of glee and appreciation, and then she stopped short. What would her godmother think of such an outburst! She must return to the contained self-repression of the time before her visit to the Sphinx—surely in this strange land!

The Princess Ardácheff's frank face was illuminated with a smile.

"She is extremely young," she thought, "in spite of her widowhood, but I like her, and I know we shall be friends."

Just then they arrived at her house in the Serguiefskaia. It had not appeared to Tamara that they were approaching any particularly fashionable quarter. A fine habitation seemed the neighbor of quite a humble one, and here there was even a shop a few doors down, and except for the very tall windows there was nothing exceptionally imposing on the outside. But when they entered the first hall and the gaily-liveried suisse and two footmen had removed their furs, and the Princess' snow boots, then Tamara perceived she was indeed in a glorious home.

Princess Ardácheff's house was, and is, perhaps the most stately in all Petersburg.

As they ascended the enormous staircase dividing on the first landing, and reaching the surrounding galleries above in two sweeps, a grave major-domo and more footmen met them, and opened wide the doors of a lofty room. It was full of fine pictures and objets d'art, and though the furniture dated from the time of Alexander II., and even a little earlier—when a flood of frightful taste pervaded all Europe—still the stuffs and the colors were beautiful and rich, and time had softened their crudity into a harmonious whole.

Be the decorations of a house what they will, it is the mistress of it who gives the rooms their soul. If hers is vulgar, so will the rooms be, even though Monsieur Nelson himself has but just designed them in purest Louis XVI. But the worst of all are those which look as though their owner constantly attended bazaars, and brought the superfluous horrors she secured there back with her. Then there are vapid rooms, and anaemic rooms, and fiddly, and messy rooms, and there are monuments of wealth with no individuality at all.

Tamara felt all these *nuances* directly, and she knew that here dwelt a woman of natural refinement and a broad outlook.

She sank into an old-fashioned sofa, covered with silk a quarter of an inch thick, and the atmosphere seemed to breathe life and completeness.

Tea and quantities of different little *bonnes bouches* awaited them. But if there was a samovar she did not recognize it as such; in fact, she had seen nothing which many writers describe as "Russian."

The Princess talked on in a fashion of perfect simplicity and directness. She told her that her friends would all welcome her and be glad that an Englishwoman should really see their country, and find it was not at all the grotesque place which fancy painted it.

"We are so far away that you do not even imagine us," she said. "You English have read that there was an Ivan the Terrible and a Peter the Great, who crushed through your Evelyn's hedges, and was a giant of seven foot high! Many of you believe wolves prowl in the streets at night, and that among the highest society Nihilists stalk, disguised as heaven knows what! While the sudden disappearance of a member of any great or small family can be accounted for by a nocturnal visit of police, and a transportation in chains to Siberian mines! Is it not so, Tamara?"

Tamara laughed. "Yes, indeed," she said. "I am sure that is what Aunt Clara thinks now! Are we not a ridiculously insular people, Marraine?"

She said the last word timidly and put out her hand. "May I call you Marraine, Princess?" she asked. "I never knew my mother, and it sounds nice."

"Indeed, yes!" the Princess said, and she rose and kissed Tamara. "Your mother was very dear to me, long ago, before you were born, we spent a wild season together of youth and happiness. You shall take the place of my child Tamara, if she had lived."

Before they had finished drinking their tea, other guests came in—a tall old General in a beautiful uniform, and two ladies, one young and the other old. They all spoke English perfectly, and were so agreeable and *sans façon*, Tamara's first impression was distinctly good.

Presently she heard the elder lady say to her godmother:

"Have you seen Gritzko since his return, Vera? One hears he has a wild fit on and is at Milasláv with———" the rest of the words were almost whispered. Tamara found herself unpleasantly on the alert—how ridiculous, though, she thought—Gritzko!—there might be a dozen Gritzkos in Petersburg.

"No, he returns tonight," Princess Ardácheff said; "but I never listen to these tales, and as no matter what he does we all forgive him, and let him fly back into our good graces as soon as he purses up that handsome mouth of his—it is superfluous to make critiques upon his conduct—it seems to me!"

The lady appeared to agree to this, for she laughed, and they talked of other things, and soon all left.

And when they were gone—"Tonight I have one or two of my nicest friends dining," the Princess said, "whom I wish you to know, so I thought if you rested now you would not be too tired for a little society," and she carried Tamara off to her warm comfortable bedroom, an immense apartment in gorgeous Empire taste, and here was a great bunch of roses to greet her, and her maid could be seen unpacking in the anti-chamber beyond.

The company, ten or twelve of them, were all assembled when Tamara reached one of the great salons, which opened from the galleries surrounding the marble hall. She came in—a slender willowy creature, with a gentle smile of contrition—was she late?

And then the presentations took place. What struck her first was that dark or fair, fat-faced or thin, high foreheads or low, all the ladies wore *coiffées* exactly the same—the hair brushed up from the forehead and tightly *ondulés*. It gave a look of universal distinction, but in some cases was not very becoming. They were beautifully dressed in mourning, and no one seemed to have much of a complexion, from an English point of view, but before the end of the evening Tamara felt she had never met women with such charm. Surely no other country could produce the same types, perfectly simple in manner—perfectly at ease. Extremely highly educated, with a wide range of subjects, and a knowledge of European literature which must be unsurpassed. Afterwards when she knew them better she realized that here was one place left in Europe where there were no *parvenues* and no snobs—or if there were any, they were beautifully concealed. Such absolute simplicity and charm can only stay in a society where no one is trying "to arrive," all being there naturally by birth. There could be no room for the *métier*adopted by several impecunious English ladies of title—that of foisting anyone, however unsuitable, upon society and their friends for a well-gilded consideration.

In Russia, at least, it is the round peg in the round hole. No square peg would have a chance of admission. Thus there are the ease and elegance of one large and interesting family.

It seemed to Tamara that each one was endowed with natural fascination. They made no "frais" for her. There were no compliments or gushing welcomes. They were just casual and delightful and made her feel at home and happy with them all.

They took "Zacouska" in an ante-room. Such quantities of strange dishes! There seemed enough for a whole meal, and Tamara wondered how it would be possible to eat anything further! At dinner she sat between a tall old Prince and a diplomat. The uniforms pleased her and the glorious pearls of the ladies. Such pearls—worth a king's ransom!

Then she was interested to see the many different sorts of wine, and the extreme richness of the food, and finally the shortness of the meal.

The pretty custom of the men kissing the hostess' hand as they all left the dining-room together, she found delightful.

They were drinking coffee in the blue salon, and most of the party had retired to the bridge tables laid out, and Tamara, who played too badly, sat by the fire with her godmother and another lady, when suddenly the door opened and, with an air of complete insouciance and assurance, Prince Milaslávski came in.

"I want some coffee, Tantine," he said, kissing the Princess' hand, while he nodded to everyone else. "I was passing and so came in to get it."

"Gritzko—back again!" the whole company cried, and the Princess, beaming upon him fond smiles, gave him the coffee, while she murmured her glad welcome.

The society now began to chaff him as to his doings, which he took with the utmost *sang froid*.

"That old cat of a Marianne Mariuski sets about as usual one of her stories. I am having an orgie at Milasláv, and this time with a seraglio of Egyptian houris—the truth being I only brought back by the merest chance one small troupe of Alexandrian dancers, and two performing bears. They made us laugh for three days, Serge, Sasha, and the rest!"

"Gritzko, will you never learn wisdom," said one lady, the Princess Shébanoff, plaintively, while the others all laughed. "Were they pretty, and what were they like?" they asked.

"The bears?—little angels, especially Fatima,—and with the manners of Princesses," and he bowed to an old lady who was surveying him severely through her pince-nez, while she held her cards awry. "Which reminds me we are failing in ours, Tantine, you have not presented me to the English lady, who is, I perceive, a stranger."

During all this Tamara had sat cold and silent. She was angry with herself that this man's entrance should cause her such emotion—or rather commotion and sensation. Why should he make her feel nervous and stupid, unsure of herself, and uncertain what to do. Invariably he placed her at some disadvantage, and left the settling of their relations to himself. Whereas all such regulations ought to have been in her hands. Now she was without choice again, she could only bow stiffly as her godmother said his name and her name, and Prince Milaslávski took a chair by her side and began making politenesses as though he were really a stranger.

Had she just arrived? Did she find Russia very cold? Was she going to stay long? etc., etc.

To all of which Tamara answered in monosyllables, while two bright spots of rose color burned in her cheeks.

The Prince was astonishingly good looking in his Cossack's uniform, and his eyes had a laugh in them, but a shadow round as if bed had not seen him for several nights.

His whole manner to Tamara was different from any shade it had formerly worn. It was as if a courtly Russian were welcoming an honored guest in his aunt's house.

He did not mock or tease, or announce startling truths; he was pleasant and ordinary and serene.

He and the Princess Ardácheff were no real blood relations; the first wife of her late husband had been his mother's sister, but the tradition of aunt had gone on in the family and the Princess loved him almost as a son. He had always called her "Tantine" as though she had been his real aunt.

"What did you think of Gritzko Milaslávski, Tamara?" she asked, when all the guests were gone, and the two had retired to Tamara's room. "He is one of the dearest characters when you know him—but a terrible tease."

"He seemed very pleasant," Tamara said blankly, while she picked up a book. Even to speak of him caused her unease.

"He is not at all the type of an ordinary Russian," the Princess continued. "He has traveled so much, he is so *fin* there is almost a French touch in him. I am afraid you will find our young men rather dull as a rule. They are very hard worked at their military duties, and have not much time for *les dames du monde*."

"No?" said Tamara. "Well, the women seem to make up for it. I have never met so many clever delightful ones."

"It is our education," the Princess said. "You see from babyhood we learn many languages, and thus the literatures of countries are open to us before we begin to analyze anything, and English especially we know well, because in that language there are so many books for young girls."

"In England," said Tamara, "what may be given to young girls seems to rule everything, no one is allowed a thought for herself, every idea almost is brought down to that dead level—one rebels after a while—but tell me, Marraine, if I may ask, what makes them all so tired and gray looking, the people I have seen tonight I mean. Do they sit up very late at parties, or what is it?"

"In the season, yes, but it is not that, it is our climate and our hot closed-up rooms, and the impossibility of taking proper exercise. In the summer you will not know them for the same faces."

And then she kissed her goddaughter good-night, but just at the door she paused. "You were not shocked about the Alexandrian dancers, I hope, child?" she said. "If one knew the truth, they were poor people who were starving, probably, and Gritzko paid them money and helped them out of the kindness of his heart—those are the sort of things he generally does I find when I investigate, so I never pay attention to what he says."

Tamara, left to herself, gazed into the glowing embers of her wood fire.

"I wonder—I wonder," she said. But what she wondered she hardly dared admit—even to herself.

CHAPTER VII

The next day was the last of the Russian old year—the 13th of January new style—and when Tamara appeared about ten o'clock in her godmother's own sitting-room, a charming apartment full of the most interesting miniatures and bibelots collected by the great Ardácheff, friend of Catherine II., she found the Princess already busy at her writing table.

"Good-morning, my child," she said. "You behold me up and working at a time when most of my countrywomen are not yet in their baths. We keep late hours here in the winter, while it is dark and cold. You will get quite accustomed to going to bed at two and rising at ten; but to-night, if it pleases you to fall in with what is on the tapis for you, I fear it will be even four in the morning before you sleep. Prince Milaslávski has telephoned that he gives a party at his house on the Fontonka, to dine first and then go on to a café to hear the Bohemians sing. It is a peculiarity of the place these Bohemians—we shall drink in the New Year and then go. It will not bore you. No? Then it is decided," and she pressed a lovely little Faberger enamel bell which lay on the table near, and one of the innumerable servants, who seemed to be always waiting in the galleries, appeared. She spoke to him in Russian, and then took up the telephone by her side, and presently was in communication with the person she had called.

"It is thou, Gritzko? Awake? Of course she is awake, and here in the room. Yes, it is arranged—we dine—not until nine o'clock?—you cannot be in before. Bon. Now promise you will be good.—Indeed, yes.—Of course any English lady would be shocked at you—So!—I tell you she is in the room—pray be more discreet," and she smiled at Tamara, and then continued her conversation. "No, I will not talk in Russian, it is very rude.—If you are not completely *sage* at dinner we shall not go on.—I am serious! Well, good-bye,"—and with a laugh the Princess put the receiver down.

"He says nothing would shock you—he is sure you understand the world! Well, we must amuse ourselves, and try and restrain him if he grows too wild."

"He is often wild, then?" Tamara said.

The Princess rose and stood by the window looking out on the thickly falling snow.

"I am afraid—a little—yes, though never in the wrong situation; above all things Gritzko is a gentleman; but sometimes I wish he would take life less as a game. One cannot help speculating how it can end."

"Has he no family?" Tamara asked.

"No, everyone is dead. His mother worshipped him, but she died when he was scarcely eighteen, and his father before that. His mother is his adored memory. In all the mad scenes which he and his companions, I am afraid, have enacted in the Fontonka house, there is one set of rooms no one has dared to enter—her rooms—and he keeps flowers there, and an ever-burning lamp. There is a strange touch of sentiment and melancholy in Gritzko, and of religion too. Sometimes I think he is unhappy, and then he goes off to his castle in the Caucasus or to Milasláv, and no one sees him for weeks. Last year we hoped he would marry a charming Polish girl—he quite paid her attention for several nights; but he said she laughed one day when he felt sad, and answered seriously when he was gay, and made crunching noises with her teeth when she eat biscuits!—and her mother was fat and she might grow so too! And for these serious reasons he could not face her at breakfast for the rest of his life! Thus that came to an end. No one has any influence upon him. I have given up trying. One must accept him as he is, or leave him alone—he will go his own way."

Tamara had ceased fighting with herself about the interest she took in conversations relating to the Prince. She could not restrain her desire to hear of him, but she explained it now by telling herself he was a rather lurid and unusual foreign character, which must naturally be an interesting study for a stranger.

"It was an escape for the girl at least, perhaps," she said, when the Princess paused.

"Of that I am not sure; he is so tender to children and animals, and his soul is full of generosity and poetry—and justice too. Poor Gritzko," and the Princess sighed.

Then Tamara remembered their conversation during their night ride from the Sphinx, and she felt again the humiliating certainty of how commonplace he must have found her.

Presently the Princess took her to see the house. Every room filled with relics of the grand owners who had gone before. There were portraits of Peter the Great, and the splendid Catherine, in almost every room.

"An Empress so much misjudged in your country, Tamara," her godmother said. "She had the soul and the necessities of a man, but she was truly great."

Tamara gazed up at the proud *débonnaire* face, and she thought how at home they would think of the most unconventional part of her character, to the obliteration of all other aspects, and each moment she was realizing how ridiculous and narrow was the view from the standpoint from which she had been made to look at life.

For luncheon quite a number of guests arrived, the Princess, she found afterward, was hardly ever alone.

"I don't care to go out, Tamara, as a rule, to déjeuner," she said, "but I love my house to be filled with young people and mirth."

The names were very difficult for Tamara to catch, especially as they all called each other by their *petits noms*—all having been friends since babyhood, if not, as often was the case, related by ties of blood; but at last she began to know that "Olga" was the Countess Gléboff, and "Sonia," the Princess Solentzeff-Zasiekin—both young, under thirty, and both attractive and quite *sans gêne*.

"Olga" was little and plump, with an oval face and rather prominent eyes, but with a way of saying things which enchanted Tamara's ear. Her manner was casualness itself, and had a wonderful charm; and another thing struck her now that she saw them in daylight, not a single woman present—and there were six or seven at least—had even the slightest powder on her face. They were as nature made them, not the faintest aid from art in any way. "They cannot be at all coquette like the French," she thought, "or even like us in England, or they could not all do their hair like that whether it suits them or no! But what charm they have—much more than we, or the French, or any one I know."

They were all so amusing and gay at lunch and talked of teeny scandals with a whimsical humor at themselves for being so small, which was delightful, and no one said anything spiteful or mean. Quantities of pleasant things were planned, and Tamara found her days arranged for a week ahead.

That night, as they drove to Prince Milaslávski's dinner, an annoying sense of excitement possessed Tamara. She refused to ask herself why. Curiosity to see the house of this strange man—most likely—in any case, emotion enough to make her eyes bright.

It was one of the oldest houses in Petersburg, built in the time of Catherine, about 1768, and although in a highly florid rococo style of decoration, as though something gorgeous and barbaric had amalgamated with the Louis XV., still it had escaped the terrible wave of 1850 vandalism, and stood, except for a few Empire rooms, a monument of its time.

Everything about it interested Tamara. The strange Cossack servants in the hall; the splendid staircase of stone and marble, and then finally they reached the salons above.

"One can see no woman lives here," she thought, though the one they entered was comfortable enough. Huge English leather armchairs elbowed some massively gilt seats of the time of Nicholas I., and an ugly English high fender with its padded seat, surrounded the blazing log fire.

The guests were all assembled, but host, there was not!

"What an impertinence to keep them waiting like this," Tamara thought! However, no one seemed to mind but herself, and they all stood laughing or sitting on the fender in the best of spirits.

"I will bet you," said Olga Gléboff, in her attractive voice, "that Gritzko comes in with no apology, and that we shall none of us be able to drag from him where he has been!"

As she spoke he entered the room.

"Ah! you are all very early," he said, shaking their hands in frank welcome. "So good of you, dear friends. Perhaps I am a little late, you will forgive me, I know; and now for Zacouska, a wolf is tearing at my vitals, I feel, and yours too. It is nine o'clock!"

Then the dining-room doors at the side opened and they all went in *en bande*, and gathered round the high table, where they began to eat like hungry natural people, selecting the dishes they wanted. Some of the men taking immense spoonfuls of caviare, and spreading them on bread, like children with jam. All were so joyous and so perfectly without ceremony. Nothing could be more agreeable than this society, Tamara thought.

Some of the men were elderly, and a number the husbands of the various ladies; there were a few young officers and several diplomats from the Embassies, too. But young or old, all were gay and ready to enjoy life.

"You must taste some vodka, Madame," Prince Milaslávski said, pouring a small glass at Tamara's side. "You will not like it, but it is Russian, and you must learn. See I take some, too, and drink your health!"

Tamara bowed and sipped the stuff, which she found very nasty, with a whiff of ether in it. And then they all trouped to the large table in this huge dining-hall.

Tamara sat on her host's right hand, and Princess Sonia on his left.

To-night his coat was brown and the underdress black, it was quite as becoming as the others she had seen him in, with the strange belt and gold and silver trimmings and the Eastern hang of it all, and his great dark gray-blue eyes blazed at Tamara now and then with a challenge in them she could hardly withstand.

"Now tell us, Gritzko, what did you do in Egypt this year?" Princess Sonia said. "It is the first time that no histories of your ways have come to our ears—were you ill?—or bored? We feared you were dead."

"On the contrary, I was greatly alive," he answered gravely. "I was studying mummies and falling in love with the Sphinx. And just at the end I had a most interesting kind of experience; I came upon what looked like a woman, but turned out to be a mummy and later froze into a block of ice!"

"Gritzko!" they called in chorus. "Can anyone invent such impossible stories as you!"

"I assure you I am speaking the truth. Is it not so, Madame?" And he looked at Tamara and smiled with fleeting merry mockery in his eyes. "See," and he again turned to his guests, "Madame has been in Egypt she tells me, and should be able to vouch for my truth."

Tamara pulled herself together.

"I think the Sphinx must have cast a spell over you, Prince," she said, "so that you could not distinguish the real from the false. I saw no women who were mummies and then turned into ice!"

Some one distracted Princess Sonia's attention for a moment, and the Prince whispered, "One can melt ice!"

"To find a mummy?" Tamara asked with grave innocence. "That would be the inverse rotation."

"And lastly a woman—in one's arms," the Prince said.

Tamara turned to her neighbor and became engrossed in his conversation for the rest of the repast.

All the women, and nearly all the men, spoke English perfectly, and their good manners were such that even this large party talked in the strange guest's language among themselves.

"One must converse now as long as one can," her neighbor told her, "because the moment we have had coffee everyone will play bridge, and no further sense will be got out of them. We are a little behind the rest of the world always in Petersburg, and while in England and Paris this game has had its day, here we are still in its claws to a point of madness, as Madame will see."

And thus it fell about.

Prince Milaslávski gave Tamara his arm and they found coffee awaiting them in the salon when they returned there, and at once the rubbers were made up. And with faces of grave pre-occupation this lately merry company sat down to their game, leaving only the Prince and one lady and Tamara unprovided for.

"Yes, I can play," she had said, when she was asked, "but it bores me so, and I do it so badly; may I not watch you instead?"

The lady who made the third had not these ideas, and she sat down near a table ready to cut in. Thus the host and his English guest were left practically alone.

"I did not mean you to play," he said, "I knew you couldn't—I arranged it like this."

"Why did you know I couldn't?" Tamara asked. "I am too stupid perhaps you think!"

"Yes—too stupid and—too sweet."

"I am neither stupid—nor sweet!" and her eyes flashed.

"Probably not, but you seem so to me.—Now don't get angry at once, it makes our acquaintance so fatiguing, I have each time to be presented over again."

Then Tamara laughed.

"It really is all very funny," she said.

"And how is the estimable Mrs. Hardcastle?" he asked, when he had laughed too—his joyous laugh. "This is a safe subject and we can sit on the fender without your wanting to push me into the fire over it."

"I am not at all sure of that," answered Tamara. She could not resist his charm, she could not continue quarrelling with him; somehow it seemed too difficult here in his own house, so she smiled as she went on. "If you laugh at my Millicent, I shall get very angry indeed."

"Laugh at your Millicent! The idea is miles from my brain—did not I tell you when I could find a wife like that I would marry—what more can I say!" and the Prince looked at her with supreme gravity. "Did she tell 'Henry' that a devil of a Russian bear had got drunk and flung a gipsy into the sea?"

"Possibly. Why were you so—horrible that night?"

"Was I horrible?"

"Probably not, but you seemed so to me," Tamara quoted his late words.

"I seem horrible—and you seem sweet."

"Surely the stupid comes in too!"

"Undoubtedly, but Russia will cure that, you will not go away for a long time."

"In less than four weeks."

"We shall see," and the Prince got up and lit another cigarette. "You do not smoke either? What a little good prude!"

"I am not a prude!" Tamara's ire rose again. "I have tried often with my brother Tom, and it always makes me sick. I would be a fool, not a prude, to go on, would not I?"

"I am not forcing you to smoke. I like your pretty teeth best as they are!"

Rebellion shook Tamara. It was his attitude toward her—one of supreme unconcerned command—as though he had a perfect right to take his pleasure out of her conversation, and play upon her emotions, according to his mood. She could have boxed his ears.

"How long ago is it since we danced in Egypt—a fortnight, or more? You move well, but you don't know anything about dancing," he went on. "Dancing is either a ridiculous jumping about of fools, who have no more understanding of its meaning than a parcel of marionettes. Or it is an expression of some sort of emotion. The Greeks understood that in their Orchiesis, each feeling had its corresponding movement. For me it means a number of things. When a woman is slender and pliant and smooth of step, and if she pleases me otherwise, then it is not waste of time!—Tonight I shall probably get drunk again," and he flicked the ash off his cigarette with his little finger; and even though Tamara was again annoyed with him, she could not help noticing that his hands were fine and strong.

"But you were not drunk on the ship—you could not even plead that," she said, almost shocked at herself for speaking of anything so horrible.

"It is the same thing. I feel a mad supercharge of life—an intoxication of the senses, perhaps. It has only one advantage over the champagne result. I am steady on my feet, and my voice is not thick!"

Tamara did not speak.

"I wonder what this music we shall hear will say to you. Will it make the milk and water you call blood in your veins race?—it will amuse me to see."

"I am not made for your amusement, Prince. How dare you always treat me as you do?" And Tamara drew herself up haughtily. "And if my veins contain milk and water, it is at least my own."

"You dared me once before, Madame," he said, smiling provokingly. "Do you think it is quite wise of you to try it again?"

"I do not care if it is wise or no. I hate you!" almost hissed poor Tamara.

Then his eyes blazed, as she had never seen them yet. He moved nearer to her, and spoke in a low concentrated voice.

"It is a challenge. Good. Now listen to what I say. In a little short time you shall love me. That haughty little head shall lie here on my breast without a struggle, and I shall kiss your lips until you cannot breathe."

For the second time in her life Tamara went dead white—he saw her pale even to her lips. And since the moment was not yet, and since his mood was not now to make her suffer, he bent over with contrition and asked her to forgive him in a tender voice.

"Madame—I am only joking—but I am a brute," he said.

Tamara rose and walked to the bridge tables, furious with herself that he could have seen his power over her, even though it were only to cause rage.

He came up behind her and sat down and began to talk nicely again—about the sights to be seen in the capital, and the interesting museums and collections of pictures and arms. Nothing could be more correct than his manner, and the bridge players who were within earshot smiled, while Countess Olga thought.

"Either Gritzko has just been making love to the Englishwoman, or he is immensely bored—The latter from his face."

CHAPTER VIII

The company stopped their game about a quarter to twelve, and tables and champagne and glasses were brought in, and hand in hand they made a circle and drank in the New Year.

Tamara took care to stand by Princess Ardácheff, but her host looked at her as he raised his glass. Then they descended to the hall, and were wrapped in their furs again to go to the café where the Bohemians were to sing.

Tamara and the Princess were already in the latter's coupé when Prince Milaslávski called out: "Tantine—! take me too—I am slim and can sit between you, and I want to arrive soon, I have sent my motor on with Serge and Valonne."

And without waiting he got in.

They had to sit very close, and Tamara became incensed with herself, because in spite of all her late rage with the Prince, she experienced a sensation which was disturbing and unknown. The magnetic personality of the man was so strong. He bent and whispered something to the Princess, and then as though sharing a secret, he leaned the other way, and whispered to Tamara, too. The words were nothing, only some ordinary nonsense, of which she took no heed. But as he spoke his lips touched her ear. A wild thrill ran through her, she almost trembled, so violent was the emotion the little seemingly accidental caress caused. A feeling she had never realized in the whole of her life before. Why did he tease her so. Why did he always behave in this maddening manner! and choose moments when she was defenseless and could make no move. Of one thing she was certain, if she should stay on in Russia she must come to some understanding with him if possible, and prevent any more of these ways—absolutely insulting to her self-respect.

So she shrunk back in her corner and gave no reply.

"Are you angry with me?" he whispered. "It was the shaking of the automobile which caused me to come too near you. Forgive me, I will try not to sin again,"—but as he spoke he repeated his offense!

Tamara clasped her hands together, tightly, and answered in the coldest voice—

"I did not notice anything, Prince, it must be a guilty conscience which causes you to apologize."

"In that case then all is well!" and he laughed softly.

The Princess now joined in the conversation.

"Gritzko, you must tell Mrs. Loraine how these gipsies are, and what she will hear—she will think it otherwise so strange."

He turned to Tamara at once.

"They are a queer people who dwell in a clan. They sing like the fiend—one hates it or loves it, but it gets on the nerves, and if a man should fancy one of them, he must pay the chief, not the girl. Then they are faithful and money won't tempt them away. But if the man makes them jealous, they run a knife into his back."

"It sounds exciting at all events," Tamara said.

"It is an acquired taste, and if you have a particularly sensitive ear the music will make you feel inclined to scream. It drives me mad."

"Gritzko," the Princess whispered to him. "You promise to be *sage*, dear boy, do you not? Sometimes you alarm me when you go too far."

"Tantine!" and he kissed her hand. "Your words are law!"

"Alas! if that were only true," she said with a sigh.

"Tonight all shall be suited to the eleven thousand virgins!" and he laughed. "Or shall I say suited to an English *grande dame*—which is the same!"

They had crossed the Neva by now, and presently arrived at a building with a gloomy looking door, and so to a dingy hall, in which a few waiters were scurrying about. They seemed to go through endless shabby passages, like those of a lunatic asylum, and finally arrived at a large and empty room—empty so far as people were concerned—for at the end there were sofas and a long narrow table, and a few smaller ones with chairs.

The tables were already laid, with dishes of raw ham and salted almonds and various *bonnes bouches*, while brilliant candelabra shone amidst numerous bottles of champagne.

The company seemed to have forgotten the gloom that playing bridge had brought over them, and were as gay again as one could wish, while divesting themselves of their furs and snow-boots.

And soon Tamara found herself seated on the middle sofa behind the long table, Count Gléboff on her right, and the French Secretary, Count Valonne, at her left, while beyond him was Princess Sonia, and near by all the rest.

Their host stood up in front, a brimming glass in his hand.

Then there filed in about twenty-five of the most unattractive animal-looking females, dressed in ordinary hideous clothes, who all took their seats on a row of chairs at the farther end. They wore no national costume nor anything to attract the eye, but were simply garbed as concierges or shop-girls might have been; and some were old, gray-haired women, and one had even a swollen face tied up in a black scarf! How could it be possible that any of these could be the "fancy" of a man!

They were followed by about ten dark, beetle-browed males, who carried guitars.

These were the famous Bohemians! Their appearance at all events was disillusioning enough. Tamara's disappointment was immense.

But presently when they began to sing she realized that there was something—something in their music—even though it was of an intense unrest.

She found it was the custom for them to sing a weird chant song on the name of each guest, and every one must drink to this guest's health, all standing, and quaffing the glasses of champagne down at one draught.

That they all remained sober at the end of the evening seemed to do great credit to their heads, for Tamara, completely unaccustomed to the smoke and the warm room, feared even to sip at her glass.

The toasting over, every one sat down, Prince Milaslávski and a Pole being the only two in front of the table, and they with immense spirit chaffed the company, and called the tunes.

The music was of the most wild, a queer metallic sound, and the airs were full of unexpected harmonies and nerve-racking chords. It fired the sense, in spite of the hideous singers.

They all sat there with perfectly immovable faces and entirely still hands,—singing without gesticulations what were evidently passionate love-songs! Nothing could have been more incongruous or grotesque!

But the fascination of it grew and grew. Every one of their ugly faces remained printed on Tamara's brain. Long afterward she would see them in dreams.

How little we yet know of the force of sounds! How little we know of any of the great currents which affect the world and human life!

And music above any other art stirs the sense. Probably the Greek myth of Orpheus and his lute was not a myth after all; perhaps Orpheus had mastered the occult knowledge of this great power. Surely it would be worth some learned scientist's while to investigate from a psychological point of view how it is, and why it is, that certain chords cause certain emotions, and give base or elevating visions to human souls.

The music of these gipsies was of the devil, it seemed to Tamara, and she was not surprised at the wild look in Prince Milaslávski's eyes, for she herself—she, well brought up, conventionally crushed English Tamara,—felt a strange quickening of the pulse.

After an hour or so of this music, two of the younger Bohemian women began to dance, not in the least with the movements that had shocked Mrs. Hardcastle in the Alexandrian troupe on the ship, but a foolish valsing, while the shoulders rose and fell and quivered like the flapping wings of some bird. The shoulders seemed the talented part, not the body or hips.

And then about three o'clock the entire troupe filed out of the room for refreshment and rest. The atmosphere was thick with smoke, and heated to an incredible extent. Some one started to play the piano, and every one began to dance a wild round—a mazurka, perhaps—and Tamara found herself clasped tightly in the arms of her Prince.

She did not know the step, but they valsed to the tune, and all the time he was whispering mad things in Russian in her ear. She could not correct him, because she did not know what they might mean.

"Doushka," he said at last. "So you are awake; so it is not milk and water after all in those pretty blue veins! God! I will teach you to live!"

And Tamara was not angry; she felt nothing except an unreasoning pleasure and exultation.

The amateur bandsman came to a stop, and another took his place; but the spell fortunately was broken, and she could pull herself together and return to sane ways.

"I am tired," she said, when the Prince would have gone on, "and I am almost faint for want of air." So he opened a window and left her for a moment in peace.

She danced again with the first man who asked her, going quickly from one to another so as to avoid having to be too often held by the Prince. But each time she felt his arm round her, back again would steal the delicious mad thrill.

"I hope you are amusing yourself, dear child," her godmother said. "This is a Russian scene; you would not see it in any other land."

And indeed Tamara was happy, in spite of her agitation and unrest.

She sat down now with Olga Gléboff, and they watched the others while they took breath. The Prince was dancing with Princess Shébanoff, and her charming face was turned up to him with an adoring smile.

"Poor Tatiane,—" Countess Olga said low to herself.

When the gipsies returned, their music grew wilder than ever, and some of the solos seemed to touch responsive chords in Tamara's very bones.

The Prince sat next her on the sofa now, and every few moments he would bend over to take an almond, or light a cigarette, so that he touched her apparently without intention, but nevertheless with intent. And the same new and intoxicating sensation would steal through her, and she would draw her slender figure away and try to be stiff and severe, but with no effect.

It was long after five o'clock before it was all done, and they began to wrap up and say "Goodnight." And the troupe, bowing, went out to another engagement they had.

"They sing all night and sleep in the day," Count Gléboff told Tamara, as they descended the stairs. "At this time of the year they never see daylight, only sometimes the dawn."

"Tantine," said the Prince, "order your motor to go back. I sent for my troika, and it is here. We must show Madame Loraine what a sleigh feels like."

And the Princess agreed.

Oh! the pleasure Tamara found when presently they were flying over the snow, the side horses galloping with swift, sure feet. And under the furs she and her godmother felt no cold, while Gritzko, this wild Prince, sat facing them, his splendid eyes ablaze.

Presently they stopped and looked out on the Gulf of Finland and a vast view. Above were countless stars and a young, rising moon.

It was striking seven as they went to their rooms.

Such was Tamara's first outing in this land of the North.

CHAPTER IX

Six days went past before Tamara again saw the Prince. Whether he was busy or kept away because he wished to, she did not know—and would not ask—but a piqued sensation gradually began to rise as she thought of him.

"I must arrange for you to go to Tsarsköi-Sélo to see the ceremony of the Emperor blessing the waters on the 6th of our January, Tamara," her godmother said, a day or two after the Bohemian feast. "I have seen it so often, and I do not wish to stand about in the cold, but Sonia's husband is one of the aides-de-camp, and, as you know, she lives at Tsarsköi. Olga is going out there, and will take you with her, and you three can go on; it will interest you, I am sure."

And Tamara had gladly acquiesced.

Tsarsköi-Sélo, which they reached after half an hour's train, seemed such a quaint place to her. Like some summer resort made up of wooden villas, only now they were all covered with snow. She and Countess Olga had gone together to Princess Sonia's house, and from there to the palace grounds, where they followed snow-cleared paths to a sort of little temple near the lake, where they were allowed to stand just outside the line of Cossacks and watch for the coming procession.

The sky was heavy, and soon the snow began to fall intermittently in big, fluffy flakes. This background of white showed up the brilliant scarlet uniforms of the escort. Standing in long rows, they were an imposing sight. And Tamara admired their attractive faces, many so much more finely cut than the guards further on. They wore fierce beards, and they all seemed to be extremely tall and slim, with waists which would not have disgraced a girl. And, at the end of the line at the corner where they stood, she suddenly saw the Prince. He was talking to some other officers, and apparently did not see them. Tamara grew angry with herself at finding how the very sight of him moved her. The procession, soon seen advancing, was as a lesser interest, her whole real concentration being upon one scarlet form.

From the time the signal was given that the Emperor had started from the palace all the heads were bare—bare in a temperature many degrees below freezing and in falling snow! It was the Prince who gave the word of command, and while he stood at attention she watched his face. It was severe and rigid, like the face of a statue. On duty he was evidently a different creature from the wild Gritzko of gipsy suppers. But there was no use arguing with herself—he attracted her in every case.

Then the procession advanced, and she looked at it with growing amazement. This wonderful nation! so full of superstition and yet of common sense. It seemed astonishing that grown-up people should seriously assist at this ceremony of sentiment.

First came the choir-boys with thick coats covering their scarlet gowns; then a company of singing men; then the priests in their magnificent robes of gold and silver, and then the Emperor, alone and bareheaded. Afterward followed the Grand Dukes and the standard of every guard regiment and finally all the aides-de-camps.

When the Emperor passed she glanced again at the Prince. The setness of his face had given place to a look of devotion. There was evidently a great love for his master in his strange soul. When the last figure had moved beyond the little temple corner, the tension of all was relaxed, and they stood at ease again, and Gritzko appeared to perceive the party of ladies, and smiled.

"I am coming to get some hot coffee after lunch, Sonia," he called out. "I promised Marie."

"Does it not give them cold?" Tamara asked, as she looked at the Cossacks' almost shaven bare heads. "And they have no great-coats on! What can they be made of, poor things?"

"They get accustomed to it, and it is not at all cold to-day, fortunately," Countess Olga said. "They would have their furs on if it were. Don't you think they are splendid men? I love to see them in their scarlet; they only wear it on special occasions and when they are with the Emperor, or at Court balls or birthdays. I am so glad you see Gritzko in his."

Tamara did not say she had already seen the Prince in the scarlet coat; none of her new friends were aware that they had met before in Egypt.

All this time the guns were firing, and soon the ceremony of dipping the cross in the water was over, and the procession started back again.

It was the same as when it came, only the priests were wiping the cross in a napkin, and presently all passed out of sight toward the palace, and the three ladies walked quickly back to the waiting sleigh, half-frozen with cold.

About ten minutes after they had finished lunch, and were sitting at coffee in Princess Sonia's cosy salon—so fresh and charming and like an English country house—they heard a good deal of noise in the passage, and the Prince came in. He was followed by a sturdy boy of eight, and carried in his arms a tiny girl, whose poor small body looked wizened, while in her little arms she held a crutch.

"We met in the hall—my friend Marie and I," he said, as he bent to kiss Princess Sonia's hand, and then the other two ladies', "and we have a great deal to say to one another."

"These are my children, Mrs. Loraine," Princess Sonia said. "They were coming down to see you; but now Gritzko has appeared we shall receive no attention, I fear," and she laughed happily, while the little boy came forward, and with beautiful manners kissed Tamara's hand.

"You are an English lady," he said, without the slightest accent. "Have you a little boy, too?"

Tamara was obliged to own she had no children, which he seemed to think very unfortunate.

"Marie always has to have her own way, but while she is with Gritzko she is generally good," he announced.

"How splendidly you speak English!" Tamara said. "And only eight years old! I suppose you can talk French, too, as well as Russian?"

"Naturally, of course," he replied, with fine contempt. "But I'll tell you something—German I do very badly. We have a German governess, and I hate her. Her mouth is too full of teeth."

"That certainly is a disadvantage," Tamara agreed.

"When Gritzko gets up with us he makes her in a fine rage! She spluttered so at him last week the bottom row fell out. We were glad!"

Princess Sonia now interrupted: "What are you saying, Peter?" she said. "Poor Fräulein! You know I shall have to forbid Gritzko from going to tea with you. You are all so naughty when you get together!"

There was at once a fierce scream from the other side of the room.

"Maman! we will have Gritzko to tea! I love him!—Je l'aime!" and the poor crippled tiny Marie nearly strangled her friend with a frantic embrace.

"You see, Maman, we defy you!" the Prince said, when he could speak.

The little boy now joined his sister, and both soon shrieked with laughter over some impossible tale which was being poured into their ears; and Princess Sonia said softly to Tamara:

"He is too wonderful with children—Gritzko—when he happens to like them—isn't he, Olga? All of ours simply adore him, and I can never tell you of his goodness and gentleness to Marie last year when she had her dreadful accident. The poor little one will be well some day, we hope, and so I do not allow myself to be sad about it; but it was a terrible grief."

Tamara looked her sympathy, while she murmured a few words. Princess Sonia was such a sweet and charming lady.

More visitors now came in, and they all drank their coffee and tea, but the Prince paid no attention to any one beyond casual greetings; he continued his absorbing conversation with his small friends.

Tamara was surprised at this new side of him. It touched her. And he was such a gloriously good-looking picture as he sat there in his scarlet coat, while Marie played with the silver cartridges across his breast, and Peter with his dagger.

When she and Countess Olga left to catch an early afternoon train he came too. He had to be back in Petersburg, he said. Nothing could look more desolate than the tracts of country seen from the train windows, so near the capital and yet wild, uncultivated spaces, part almost like a marsh. There seemed to be nothing living but the lonely soldiers who guarded the Royal line a hundred yards or so off. It depressed Tamara as she gazed out, and she unconsciously sighed, while a sad look came into her eyes.

The Prince and Countess Olga and another officer, who had joined them, were all chaffing gaily while they smoked their cigarettes, but Gritzko appeared to be aware of everything that was passing, for he suddenly bent over and whispered to Tamara:

"Madame, when you have been here long enough you will learn never to see what you do not wish." Then he turned back to the others, and laughed again.

What did he mean? she wondered. Were there many things then to which one must shut one's eyes?

She now caught part of the conversation that was going on.

"But why won't you come, Gritzko?" Countess Olga was saying. "It will be most amusing—and the prizes are lovely, Tatiane, who has seen them, says."

"I?—to be glued to a bridge table for three solid evenings. Mon Dieu!" the Prince cried. "Having to take what partner falls to one's lot! No choice! My heavens! nothing would drag me. Whatever game I play in life, I will select my lady myself."

"You *are* tiresome!" Countess Olga said. When they got to the station the Princess's coupé was waiting, as well as the Gléboff sleigh.

"Good-bye, and a thousand thanks for taking me," Tamara said, and they waved as Countess Olga drove off. And then the Prince handed her into the coupé and asked her if she would drop him on the way.

For some time after they were settled under the furs and rushing along, he seemed very silent, and when Tamara ventured a few remarks he answered mechanically. At last after a while:

"You are going to this bridge tournament at the Varishkine's, I suppose?" he suddenly said. "It ought to be just your affair."

"Why my affair?" Tamara asked, annoyed. "I hate bridge."

"So you do. I forgot. But Tantine will take you, all the same. Perhaps, if nothing more amusing turns up, I will drop in one night and see; but—wheugh!" and he stretched himself and spread out his hands—"I have been impossibly *sage* for over a fortnight. I believe I must soon break out."

"What does that mean, Prince—to 'break out'?"

"It means to throw off civilized things and be as mad as one is inclined," and he smiled mockingly while some queer, restless spirit dwelt in his eyes. "I always break out when things make me think, and just now—in the train—when you looked at the sad country——"

"That made you think?" said Tamara, surprised.

"Well—never mind, good little angel. And now good-bye," and he kissed her hand lightly and jumped out; they had arrived at his house.

Tamara drove on to the Serguiefskaia with a great desire to see him again in her heart.

* * * * *

And so the days passed and the hours flew. Tamara had been in Russia almost three weeks; and since the blessing of the waters the time had been taken up with a continual round of small entertainments. The Court mourning prevented as yet any great balls; but there were receptions, and "bridges" and dinners, and night after night they saw the same people, and Tamara got to know them fairly well. But after the excursion to Tsarsköi-Sélo for several days she did not see the Prince. His military duties took up his whole time, her godmother said. And when at last he did come it was among a crowd, and there was no possible chance of speech.

"This bores me," he announced when he found the room full of people, and he left in ten minutes, and they did not see him again for a week, when they met him at a dinner at the English Embassy.

Then he seemed cool and respectful and almost commonplace, and Tamara felt none of the satisfaction she should have done from this changed order of things.

At the bridge tournament he made no appearance whatever.

"Why do we see Prince Milaslávski so seldom when we go out, Marraine?" she asked her godmother one day. "I thought all these people were his intimate friends!"

"So they are, dear; but Gritzko is an odd creature," the Princess said. "He asked me once if I thought he was an *imbécile* or a performing monkey, when I reproached him for not being at the balls. He only goes out when he is so disposed. If some one person amuses him, or if he suddenly wants to see us all. It is merely by fits and starts—always from the point of view of if he feels inclined, never from the observance of any social law, or from obligation."

"Why on earth do you put up with such manners?" Tamara exclaimed with irritation.

"I do not know. We might not in any one else, but Gritzko is a privileged person," the Princess said. "You can't imagine, of course, dear, because you do not know him well enough, but he has ways and *façons* of coaxing. He will do the most outrageous things, and make me very angry, and then he will come and put his head in my lap like a child, and kiss my hands, and call me 'Tantine,' and, old woman as I am, I cannot resist him. And if one is unhappy or ill, no one can be more tender and devoted." Then she added dreamily:—"While as a lover I should think he must be quite divine."

Tamara took another cup of tea and looked into the fire. She was ashamed to show how this conversation interested her.

"Tatiane Shébanoff is madly in love with him, poor thing, and I do not believe he has ever given her any real encouragement," the Princess continued. "I have seen him come to a ball, and when all the young women are longing for him to ask them to dance, he will go off with me, or old Countess Nivenska, and sit talking half the night, apparently unaware of any one else's presence."

"It seems he must be the most exasperating, tiresome person one has ever heard of, Marraine," Tamara exclaimed. "He rides over you all, and you cannot even be angry, and continually forgive him."

"But then he has his serious side," the Princess went on, eager to defend her favorite. "He is now probably studying some deep military problem all this time, and that is why we have not seen him,"—and then noticing the scornful pose of Tamara's head she laughed. "Don't be so contemptuous, dear child," she—said. "Perhaps you too will understand some day."

"That is not very likely," Tamara said.

But alas! for the Princess' optimistic surmises as to the Prince's occupations, a rumor spread toward the end of the week of the maddest orgie which had taken place at the Fontonka house. It sounded like a phantasmagoria in which unclothed dancers, and wild beasts, and unheard-of feats seemed to float about. And the Princess sighed as she refuted the gossip it caused.

"Oh, my poor Gritzko! if he might only even for a while remain in a state of grace," she said.

And Tamara's interest in him, in spite of her shocked contempt, did not decrease.

And so the time went on.

She was gradually growing to know the society better, and to get a peep at the national point of view. They were a wonderfully uncomplex people, with the perfect ease which only those at the bottom of the social ladder who have not started to climb at all, and those who have reached the top, like these, can have. They were casually friendly when the strangers pleased them, and completely unimpressed with their intrinsic worth if they did not. They seemed to see in a moment the shades in people, and only to select the best. And when Tamara came to talk seriously with even the most apparently frivolous, she found they all had the same trace of vague melancholy and mystery, as though they were grasping in the dark for something spiritual they wished to seize. Their views and boundaries of principles in action seemed to be limitless, just as their vast country seems to have no landmarks for miles. One could imagine the unexpected happening in any of their lives. And the charm and fascination of them continued to increase.

It was late one afternoon when Prince Milaslávski again came prominently into view on Tamara's horizon.

She was sitting alone reading in the blue salon when he walked unceremoniously in.

"Give me some tea, Madame," he said. "The Princess met me in the hall, and told me I should find you here; so now let us begin by this."

Tamara poured it out and leaned back in the sofa below the beautiful Falconet group, which made—and makes—the glory of the blue salon in the Ardácheff House. She felt serene. These two weeks of unawakened emotions and just pleasant entertainments since the day at Tsarsköi had given her fresh poise.

"And what do you think of us by now, Madame?" he asked.

"I think you are a strange band," she said. "You are extremely intellectual, you are brilliant, and yet in five minutes all intelligence can fade out of your faces, and all interest from your talks, and you fly to bridge."

"It is because we are primitive and unspoilt; this is our new toy, and we must play with it; the excitement will wane, and a fresh one come——" he paused and then went on in another tone—

"You in England have many outlets for your supervitality—you cannot judge of other nations who have not. You had a magnificent system of government. It took you about eight hundred years to build up, and it was the admiration of the world—and now you are allowing your Socialists and ignorant plebeian place hunters to pull it all to pieces and throw it away. That is more foolish surely, than even to go crazy over bridge!"

Tamara sighed.

"Have you ever been in England, Prince?" she asked.

He sat down on the sofa beside her.

"No—but one day I shall go, Paris is as far as I have got on the road as yet."

"You would think us all very dull, I expect, and calculating and restrained," Tamara said softly. "You might like the hunting, but somehow I do not see you in the picture there—"

He got up and moved restlessly to the mantlepiece, where he leaned, while he stirred his tea absently. There was almost an air of bravado in the insouciant tone of his next remark—

"Do you know, I did a dreadful thing," he said. "And it has grieved me terribly, and I must have your sympathy. I hurt my Arab horse. You remember him, Suliman, at the Sphinx?"

"Yes," said Tamara.

"I had a little party to some of my friends, and we were rather gay—not a party you would have approved of, but one which pleased us all the same—and they dared me to ride Suliman from the stables to the big saloon."

"And I suppose you did?" Tamara's voice was full of contempt.

He noticed the tone, and went on defiantly:

"Of course; that was easy; only the devil of a carpet made him trip at the bottom again, and he has strained two of his beautiful feet. But you should have seen him!" he went on proudly. "As dainty as the finest gentleman in and out the chairs, and his great success was putting his forelegs on the fender seat!"

"How you have missed your metiér!" Tamara said, and she leant back in her sofa and surveyed him as he stood, a graceful tall figure in his blue long coat. "Think of the triumph you would have in a Hippodrome!"

He straightened himself suddenly, his great eyes flashed, and over his face came a fierceness she had not guessed.

"I thought you had melted a little—here in our snow, but I see it is the mummy there all the same," he said.

Tamara laughed. For the first time it was she who held the reins.

"Even to the wrappings,"—and she gently kicked out the soft gray folds of her skirt.

He took a step nearer her, and then he stood still, and while the fierceness remained in his face, his eyes were full of pain.

She glanced up at him, and over her came almost a sense of indignation that he should so unworthily pass his time.

"How you waste your life!" she said. "Oh! think to be a man, and free, and a great landowner. To have thousands of peasants dependent upon one's frown. To have the opportunity of lifting them into something useful and good. And to spend one's hours and find one's pleasure in such things as this! Riding one's favorite horse at the risk of its and one's own neck, up and down the stairs. Ah! I congratulate you, Prince!"

He drew himself up again, as if she had hit him, and the pain in his eyes turned to flame.

"I allow no one to criticize my conduct," he said. "If it amused me to ride a bear into this room and let it eat you up, I would not hesitate."

"I do not doubt it," and Tamara laughed scornfully. "It would be in a piece with all the rest."

He raised his head with an angry toss, and then they looked at each other like two fighting cats, when fortunately the door opened, and the Princess came in.

In a moment he had laughed, and resumed his habitually insouciant mien.

"Madame has been reading me a lecture," he said. "She thinks I am wasted in the Emperor's escort, and a circus is my place."

Tamara did not speak.

"Why do you seem always to quarrel so, Gritzko?" the Princess said, plaintively. "It really quite upsets me, dear boy."

"You must not worry, Tantine," and he kissed the Princess' hand. "We don't quarrel; we are the best of friends; only we tell one another home truths. I came this afternoon to ask you if you will come to Milasláv next week. I think Madame ought to see Moscow, and we might make an excursion from there just for a night," and he looked at Tamara with a lifting of the brows.

"Then, Tantine, she could see how I cow my peasants with a knout, and grind them to starvation. It would be an interesting picture for her to take back to England."

"I should enjoy all that immensely, of course," Tamara said, pleasantly. "Many thanks, Prince."

"I shall be so honored," and he bowed politely; then, turning to the Princess: "You will settle it, won't you, Tantine?"

"I will look at our engagements, dear boy. We will try to arrange it. I can tell you at the ballet," and the Princess smiled encouragingly up at him. "My godchild has not seen our national dancing yet, so we go to-night with Prince Miklefski and Valonne."

"Then it is au revoir," he said, and kissing their hands he left them.

When the door was shut and they were alone.

"Tamara, what had you said to Gritzko to move him so?" the Princess asked. "I, who know every line of his face, tell you I have not seen him so moved since his mother's death."

So Tamara told her, describing the scene.

"My dear, you touched him in a tender spot," her godmother said. "His mother was a saint almost to those people at Milasláv; they worshipped her. She was very beautiful and very sweet, and after her husband's death she spent nearly all her life there. She started schools to teach the peasants useful things, and she encouraged them and cared for their health; and her great wish was that Gritzko should carry out her schemes. She was no advanced Liberal, the late Princess, but she had such a tender heart, she longed to bring happiness to those in her keeping, and teach them to find happiness themselves."

"And he has let it all slide, I suppose," Tamara said.

"Well, not exactly that," and the Princess sighed deeply; "but I dare say these over gay companions of his do not leave him much time for the arrangement such things require. Ah! if you knew, Tamara," she went on, "how fond I am of that boy, and how I feel the great and noble parts of his character are running to waste, you would understand my grief."

"You are so kind, dear Marraine," Tamara said. "But surely he must be very weak."

"No, he is not weak; it is a dare-devil wild strain in him that seems as if it must out. He has a will of iron, and never breaks his word; only to get him to be serious, or give his word, is as yet an unaccomplished task. I sometimes think if a great love could come into his life it would save him—his whole soul could wake to that."

Tamara looked down and clasped her hands.

"But it does not seem likely to happen, does it, Marraine?"

The Princess sighed again.

"I would like him to love you, dear child," she said; and then as Tamara did not answer she went on softly almost to herself: "My brother Alexis was just such another as Gritzko. That season he spent with me in London, when your mother and I were young, he played all sorts of wild pranks. We three were always together. He was killed in a duel after, you know. It was all very sad."

Tamara stroked her godmother's hand.

"Dear, dear Marraine," she said.

Then they checked sentiment and went to dress for dinner, arm in arm. They had grown real friends in these three short weeks.

CHAPTER X

The scene at the ballet was most brilliant, as it is always on a Sunday night. The great auditorium, with its blue silk-curtained boxes, the mass of glittering uniforms, and the ladies in evening-dress, although they were all in black, made a gay spectacle almost like a gala night. Then it is so delightful to have one's eyes pleased with what is on the stage and yet be able to talk.

But Tamara, as she sat and looked at it, was not enjoying herself. She was overcome with a vague feeling of unrest. She hated having to admit that the Prince was the cause of it. She could not look ahead; she was full of fear. She knew now that when he was near her she experienced certain emotion, that he absorbed far too much of her thoughts. He did not really care for her probably, and if he did, how could one hope to be happy with such a wild, fierce man? No, she must control herself; she must conquer his influence over her, and if she could not she could at least go away. England seemed very uninteresting and calm—and safe!

Filled with these sage resolutions she tried to fix her eyes on the stage, but unconsciously they continually strayed to a tall blue figure which was seated in the front row of the stalls with a number of officers of the Chevaliers Gardes. And when the curtain went down,—and instead of the Prince joining them in the box, as she fully expected he would do, he calmly leaned against the orchestra division and surveyed the house with his glasses—she felt a sudden pang, and talked as best she might to the many friends who thronged to pay the Princess court.

Gritzko did not even glance their way! he stood laughing with his comrades, and it would have been impossible to imagine anything more insouciant and attractive and provoking than the creature looked.

"No wonder Tatiane Shébanoff is in love with him—or that actress—or—the rest!" Tamara thought.

And then a wave of rage swept over her. She at least would not give in and join this throng! To be his plaything. *She would* be mistress of herself and her thoughts!

But alas! all these emotions not unmixed with pique, spoilt the ballet's second act!

For the interval after it, the two ladies got up and went into the little ante-chamber beyond the box. Tamara was glad. There she could not see what this annoying Prince would do.

What he did do was to open the door in a few minutes and saunter in. He greeted Tamara with polite indifference, and having calmly displaced Count Valonne, sat down by the Princess' side.

Valonne was a charming person, and he and Tamara were great friends. He chatted on now, and she smiled at him, but with ears preternaturally sharpened she heard the conversation of the other pair.

It was this.

"Tantine, I am feeling the absolute devil tonight. Will you come and have supper with me after this infernal ballet is over?"

"Gritzko—what is it? Something has disturbed you!"

He leant forward and rested his chin on his hands. "Well, your haughty guest touched me with too sharp a spur, perhaps," he said, "but she was right. I do waste my life. I have been thinking of my mother. I believe she might not be pleased with me sometimes. And then I felt mad, and now I must do something to forget. So if you won't sup—"

"Oh! Gritzko!" the Princess said.

"I telephoned home and ordered things to be ready. I know you don't like a restaurant. Say you will come," and he kissed her hand. "I have asked all the rest." And the Princess had to consent!

"You must promise not to quarrel any more with my godchild if we do. I am sure you frighten and upset her, Gritzko—promise me," she said. He laughed.

"I upset her! She is too cold and good to be upset!"

Tamara still continued to talk to Valonne, and presently they all moved into the box, and the Prince sat down beside her, and again as he leaned over in the shaded light that nameless physical thrill crept over her. Was she really cold, she asked herself. If so, why should she shiver as she was shivering now?

"I wonder if you have any heart at all, Madame?" he said. "If under the mummy's wrappings there is some flesh and blood?"

Then she turned and answered him with passion. "Of course there is," she said.

He bent over still nearer. "Just for to-night, shall we not quarrel or spar?" he whispered. "See, I will treat you as a sister and friend. I want to be petted and spoilt—I am sad."

Tamara, of course, melted at once! His extraordinarily attractive voice was very deep and had a note in it which touched her heart.

"Please don't be sad," she said softly. "Perhaps you think I was unkind to-day, but indeed it was only because—Oh! because it seemed to me such waste that you—you should be like that."

"It hurt like the fiend, you know," he said, "the thought of the damned circus. I think we are particularly sensitive as a race to those sort of things. If you had been a man I would have killed you."

"I hated to hear what you told me," and Tamara looked down. "It seemed so dreadful—so barbaric—and so childish for a man who really has a brain. If you were just an animal person like some of the others are, it would not have mattered; but you—please I would like you never to do any of these mad things again—"

Then she stopped suddenly and grew tenderly pink. She realized the inference he must read in her words.

He did not speak for a moment, only devoured her with his great blue-gray eyes. Of what he was thinking she did not know. It made her uncomfortable and a little ashamed. Why had she melted, it was never any use. So she drew herself up stiffly and leaned back in her seat.

Then down at the side by the folds of her dress he caught her hand while he said quite low:

"Madame, I must know—do you mean that?"

"Yes," she said, and tried to take away her hand. "Yes, I mean that I think it dreadful for any human being to throw things away—and Oh! I would like you to be very great."

He did not let go her hand, indeed he held it the more tightly.

"You are a dear after all, and I will try," he said. "And when I have pleased you you must give me a reward."

"Alas! What reward could I give you, Prince," she sighed.

"That I will tell you when the time comes."

Thus peace seemed to be restored, and soon the curtain fell for the interval before the last act, and the Prince got up and went out of the box.

He did not reappear again, but was waiting for them to start for his house.

"I met Stephen Strong, Tantine," he said. "He left me at Trieste, you know, and only arrived in Petersburg to-day. He has got a cousin with him, Lord something, so I have asked them both to come along. They will be a little late they said."

"It is not Jack Courtray by chance—is it?" Tamara asked, in an interested voice, as they went. "Mr. Strong has a cousin who lives near us in the country and he is always traveling about."

"Yes, I think that is the name—Courtray. So you know him then!" and the Prince leant forward from the seat which faced them. "An ami d'enfance?"

"We used to play cricket and fish and bird's-nest," she said. "Tom—my brother Tom—was his fag at Eton—he is one of my oldest friends—dear old Jack."

"How fortunate I met him to-night!"

"Indeed, yes."

Then her attention was diverted, as it always was each time she saw the blazing braziers and heaped up flaming piles of wood at the corners of the streets, since she had been in Russia. "How glad I am there is something to make the poor people warm," she said.

"When it gets below twelve degrees it is difficult to enjoy life, certainly," the Prince agreed. "And, indeed, it is hard sometimes not to freeze."

It was a strange lurid picture, the Isvostchiks drawn round, while the patient horses with their sleighs stood quiet some little distance off.

How hard must existence be to these poor things.

Supper could not be ready for half an hour, the Prince told them when they got to the Fontonka House, and as they all arrived more or less together, they soon paired off for bridge.

"I am going to show Mrs. Loraine my pictures," the host said. "She admires our Catherine and Peter the Great."

And in the salon where they all sat, he began pointing out this one and that, making comments in a distrait voice. But when they came to the double doors at the end he opened them wide, and led Tamara into another great room.

"This is the ballroom," he said. "It is like all ballrooms, so we shall not linger over that. I have two Rembrandts in my own apartment beyond which it may interest you to see, and a few other relics of the past."

He was perfectly matter of fact, his manner had not a shade of gallantry in it, and Tamara accepted this new situation and followed him without a backward thought.

They seemed to go through several sheet-shrouded salons and came out into a thoroughly comfortable room. Its general aspect of decoration had a Byzantine look, and on the floor were several magnificent bear skins, while around the walls low bookcases with quantities of books stood. And above them many arms were crossed. Over the mantlepiece a famous Rembrandt frowned, and another from the opposite wall. But it was strange there were no photographs of dancers or actresses about as Tamara would have thought.

The Prince talked intelligently. He seemed to know of such things as pictures, and understood their technique. And if he had been an elderly art critic he could not have been more aloof.

Presently Tamara noticed underneath the first picture there was hung a quaint sword. Something in its shape and workmanship attracted her attention, and she asked its history.

The Prince took it down and placed it in her hand.

"That sword belonged to a famous person," he said—"a Cossack—Stenko Razin was his name—a robber and a brigand and a great chief. He loved a lady, a Persian Princess whom he had captured, and one day when out on his yacht on the Volga, being drunk from a present of brandy some Dutch travellers had brought him, he clasped her in his arms. She was very beautiful and gentle and full of exquisite caresses, and he loved her more than all his wealth. But mad thoughts mounted to his brain, and after making an oration to the Volga for all the riches and plunder she had brought him, he reproached himself that he had never given this river anything really valuable in return, and then exclaiming he would repair his fault, unclasped the clinging arms of his mistress and flung her overboard."

"What a horrible brute!" exclaimed Tamara, and she put down the sword.

The Prince took it up and drew it from its sheath.

"The Cossacks had a wild strain in them even in those days," he said. "You must not be too hard on me for merely riding my horse!"

"Would you be cruel like that, too, Prince?" Tamara asked; and she sat down for a second on the arm of a carved chair. And when he had put the sword back in its place, he bent forward and leaned on the back of it.

"Yes, I could be cruel, I expect," he said. "I could be even brutal if I were jealous, or the woman I loved played me false, but I would not be cruel to her while it hurt myself. Razin lost his pleasure for days through one mad personal act. It would have been more sensible to have kept her until he was tired of her, or she had grown cold to him. Don't you agree with me about that?"

"It is a horrible history and I hate it," Tamara said. "Such ways I do not understand. For me love means something tender and true which could never want to injure the thing it loved."

He looked at her gravely.

"Lately I have wondered what love could mean for me. Tell me what you think, Madame," he said.

She resolved not to allow any emotion to master her, though she was conscious of a sudden beating of her heart.

"You would torture sometimes, and then you would caress."

"I would certainly caress."

He moved from his position and walked across the room, while he talked as though the words burst from him.

"Yes, I should demand unquestioning surrender, and if it were refused me, then I might be cruel. And if my love were cold or capricious, *then* I would leave her. But if she loved me truly—my God, it would be bliss."

"Think how it would hurt her when you did those foolish things though," Tamara said.

He stopped short in his restless walk.

"No one does foolish things when he is happy, Madame. All such outbursts are the froth of a soul in its seething. But if one were satisfied—" he paused, and then he went on again. "Oh! If you knew!—In the desert in Egypt I used to think I had found rest, sometimes. I am sated with this life here. A quoi bon, Madame!—the same thing year after year!—and then since I have known you. I have wondered if perhaps you in your country could teach me peace."

"So many of you are so déséquilibrés," Tamara said. "You seem to be so polished and sensible and even great, and then in a moment you are off at a tangent, displaying that want of discipline that we at home would not permit in a child."

"Yes it is true."

"It seems that you love, and must have, or you hate and must kill. There are storms and passions, and the gaiety of children and their irresponsibility, and all on the top is good manners and smiles, but underneath—I have a feeling I know not what volcano may burst."

"Tonight I feel one could flame with me." He came up close now and looked into her eyes, as if he were going to say something, and then he restrained himself.

Tamara did not move, she looked at him gravely.

"You all seem as if you had no aim," she said. "You are not interested in the politics of your country. You don't seem to do anything but kill time—Why?"

"Our country!" he said, and he flung himself into a seat near. "It would be difficult to make you understand about that. In the old days of the serfs, it was all very well. One could be a good landlord and father to them all, but now——" Then he got up restlessly and paced the room. "Now there are so many questions. If one would think it would drive one mad, but I am a soldier, Madame, so I do not permit myself to speculate at all."

"Things are not then as you would wish?" she asked.

"As I would wish—no, not as I would wish—but as I told you, I do not mix myself up with them. I only obey the Emperor and shall to the end of my life."

Tamara saw she had stirred too deep waters. His face wore a look of profound melancholy. She had never felt so drawn toward him. She let her eyes take in the picture he made. There was something very noble about his brow and the set of his head. Who could tell what thoughts were working in his brain. Presently he got up again and knelt by her side—his movements had the grace and agility of a cat. He took her hand and kissed it.

"Madame, please don't make me think," he said. "The question is too great for one man to help. I do not go with the Liberals or any of the revolt. Indeed I am far on the other side. Good to this country should all have come in a different, finer way, and now it must work out its own salvation as best it may. For me, my only duty is to my master. Nothing else could count." His eyes which looked into hers seemed great sombre pools of unrest and pain.

She did not take away her hand and he kissed it again.

Then the clock on the mantlepiece chimed one, and she started to her feet.

"Oh! Prince, should we not be thinking of supper," she said. "Come, let us forget we have been serious and go back and eat!"

He rose.

"They have probably gone in without us, they know me so well," he said; "but as you say, we will no more be serious, we will laugh."

Then he took her hand, and merrily, like two children, they ran through all the big empty rooms to find exactly what he had predicted had occurred. The party were at supper quite unconcerned!

It was such a gay scene. Princess Sonia and Serge Grekoff were busily cutting raw ham, by their places; while others drank tea or vodka or champagne, or helped themselves from various dishes the servants had brought up. There was no ceremony or stiffness, each one did as he pleased.

And there sitting by Olga Gléboff, already perfectly at home, was Lord Courtray; and further down the Princess Ardácheff sat by Stephen Strong.

"Gritzko—we could not wait!" Countess Olga said.

Then both the Englishmen got up and greeted Tamara.

"Fancy seeing you here, Tamara! What a bit of luck!" Jack Courtray said.

CHAPTER XI

Jack Courtray was a thoroughly good all-around sportsman, and had an immense success with women as a rule. His methods were primitive and direct. When not hunting or shooting, he went straight to the point with a beautiful simplicity unhampered by sentiment, and then when wearied with one woman, moved on to the next.

He was a tremendously good fellow every man said. Just a natural animal creature, whom grooming and polishing in the family for some hundred or so of years had made into a gentleman.

He was as ignorant as he could well be. To him the geography of the world meant different places for sport. India represented tigers and elephants. It had no towns or histories that mattered, it had jungles and forests. Africa said lions. Austria, chamois—and Russia, bears!

Women were either sisters, or old friends and jolly comrades—like Tamara. Or they came under the category of sport. A lesser sport, to be indulged in when the rarer beasts were not obtainable for his gun—but still sport!

He found himself in a delightful milieu. The prospect of certain bears in the near future—a dear old friend to frolic with in the immediate present, and the problematic joys of a possible affair to be indulged in meanwhile. No wonder he was in the best of spirits, and when Tamara, without *arrière pensée*, took the empty place at his side, he bent over her and filled her plate with the thinnest ham he had been able to cut, with all the apparent air of a devoted lover. And if she had looked up she would have seen that the Prince suddenly had begun to watch her with a fierceness in his eyes.

"This is a jolly place," Jack Courtray said. He had just the faintest lisp, which sounded rather attractive, and Tamara, after the storms and emotions of the past few days, found a distinct pleasure and rest in his obviousness.

It is an ill wind which blows no one any good, for presently the Prince turned and devoted himself to Tatiane Shébanoff.

She was quite the prettiest of all this little clique, petite and fair and sweet. Divorced from a brute of a husband a year or so ago, and now married to an elderly Prince.

And she loved Gritzko with passion, and while she was silent about it, her many friends told him so.

For his part he remained unconcerned, and sometimes troubled himself about her, and sometimes not.
And so the evening wore on, and apparently it had no distinct sign that it was to be one of the finger-posts of fate.
When all had finished supper, they moved back into another great room.
"You must notice this, Tamara, it is very Russian," her godmother said.
It was an immense apartment with a great porcelain stove at one corner, and panelled with wood, and it suggested to Tamara, for no sane reason, something of an orthodox church! One end was bare, and the other carpeted with great Persian rugs, had huge divans spread about; there was an electric piano and an organ, and there were also crossed foils, and masks, and everything for a fencing bout.
The Prince went to the piano and started a valse. Then he came up to Tamara and asked her to dance.
There was no trace left of his respectful friendliness! His sleepy eyes were blazing, he had never looked more oriental, or more savage, or more intense.
It was almost with a thrill of fear that Tamara yielded herself to his request. He clasped her so tightly she could hardly breathe, all she knew was she seemed to be floating in the air, and to be crushed against his breast.
"Prince, please, I am suffocating!" she cried at last.
Then he swung her off her feet, and stopped by an armchair, and Tamara subsided into it, panting, not able to speak. And all across her milk-white chest there were a row of red marks from the heavy silver cartridges, which cross in two rows in the Cossack dress.
"I would like those brands of me to last forever," the Prince said.
Tamara lay back in the chair a prey to tumultuous emotions. She ought to be disgusted she supposed, and of course she was—such an uncivilized horrible thought! but at the same time every nerve was tingling and her pulse was beating with the strange thrills she had only lately begun to dream of.
"Tamara! By jove! What have you done to your neck?" Jack Courtray said, as he came up.
And Tamara was glad she had a gauze scarf over her arm, which she wrapped around carelessly as she said:
"Nothing, Jack—let's dance!"
"What an awfully decent chap our host is, isn't he!" Lord Courtray said, as they ambled along in their valse. "And jolly good-looking too—for a foreigner. These Russians are men after my own heart!"
"Yes, he is good-looking," admitted Tamara. "If he weren't so wild; but don't you think he has a frightfully savage expression, Jack?"
"If you are intending to play with him, old girl, take my advice, you had better look out," and he laughed his merry laugh as they stopped because the piano stopped.
Meanwhile the Prince had left the room.
"Gritzko has gone to telephone for a Tzigane band," Princess Sonia said. "And to the club and to the reception at Madame Sueboffs, and soon we shall have enough people for a contre-danse—and some real fun."
That it was almost three o'clock in the morning never seemed to have struck anyone!
"Now, tell me everything, Tamara," Lord Courtray said, as they sat down on one of the big divans. "Give me a few wrinkles. I can see one wants to comprehend these tent ropes."
"Well, first they are the nicest people you could possibly meet, Jack," Tamara said. "And don't imagine because they skylark like this, and sit up all night, that they aren't most dignified when they have to be. That is their charm, this sense of the fitness of things. They have not got to have any pretence like some of us have. Not one of them has a scrap of pose. They are nice to you because they like you, or they leave you entirely alone if they do not. And some days when they are all together they will whisper and titter and have jokes among themselves, leaving you completely out in the cold—what would really be fearful ill-manners with us, but it is not in the least, it is just they have forgotten you are there, and as likely as not you will be the center of the whispering in the next minute. They are all like volcanoes with the most beautiful Faberger enamel on the top."
"And the men? I suppose they make awful love?"
"I don't think so," went on Tamara, while she stupidly blushed. "They all seem to be just merry friends, and the young ones don't go out very much. I don't mean the quite, quite young who dance with girls, but the young men. My godmother says they are very hard worked, and in their leisure they like to have dinners in their regiments—or at restaurants—with, with other sort of ladies, where they can do what they please. It seems a little elementary—don't you think so?"
"Jolly common-sense!" said Jack Courtray.
"And then, you see, if by chance, when they are in the world, if they do fall in love, it is possible for the lady to get a divorce here without any scandal and fuss, and the whole clan stick to their own member, no matter how much in the wrong she may be, and so all is arranged, and life seems much simpler and apparently happier than it is with us. If it is really so I cannot say, I have not been here long enough to judge."
"It sounds a kind of Utopia," and Lord Courtray laughed. And just then the Prince came into the room again, and over to them and they got up and the two men went off together to examine the foils.
Presently the band arrived and more guests, and soon the contre-danse was begun. That grown-up people could seriously take pleasure in this amazing romp was a new and delightful idea to Tamara.
It was a sort of enormous quadrille with numerous figures and farandole, while one sat on a chair between the figures, as at a cotillon. And toward the end the company stamped and cried, and the band sang, and nothing could have been more gay and exciting and wild.
Before they began, the Prince came up to Tamara and said:
"I want you to dance this with me. I have had it on purpose to show you a real Russian sight."
They had moved into the ballroom by then, which was now a blaze of light, while as if by magic the sheet coverings had been removed from the chairs.

And the Prince exerted himself to amuse and please his partner, and did not again clasp her too tight, only whenever she had turns with her countryman, his eyes would flame, and he would immediately interrupt them and carry her off.

Tamara felt perfectly happy, she was no longer analyzing and questioning, and she was no longer fighting against her inclination. She abandoned herself to the rushing stream of life.

It was about five o'clock when some one suggested supper at the Islands was now the proper thing. This was the delightful part about them—on no occasion was there ever a halt for the consideration of ways and means. They wanted some particular amusement and—had it! Convention, from an English point of view, remained an unknown quantity.—Now those who decided to continue the feasting all got into their waiting conveyances.

With the thermometer at fifteen degrees Reaumur, a coachman's life is not one altogether to be envied in Russia, but apparently custom will make anything endurable.

"I know you like the troika, Tamara," Princess Ardácheff said. "So you go with Olga and Gritzko and your friend—only be sure you wrap up your head."

And when they were all getting in, the Countess Gléboff said:

"It is so terribly cold tonight, Gritzko. I am going to sit with my back to the horses, so as not to get the wind in my face."

When they were tucked in under the furs this arrangement seemed to Jack Courtray one of real worth, for he instantly proceeded to take Countess Olga's hand, while he whispered that he was cold and she could not be so inhuman as to let a poor stranger freeze!

It seemed amusing to look from the windows of a private room, down upon a gay supping throng, in the general salle at the restaurant on the Islands, while Tziganes played and their supper was being prepared.

"Who could think it was five o'clock in the morning! What a lesson for our rotten old County Council in London," Jack Courtray said. "By Jove! this is the place for me!" and he proceeded to make violent love to Olga Gléboff, to who's side he remained persistently glued.

And then the gayest repast began; nothing could have been more entertaining or full of wild *entrain*, and yet no one over-did it, or was vulgar or coarse.

At the last moment, when they were all starting for home about seven o'clock, Countess Olga decided she could not face the cold of the open sleigh, and Lord Courtray and she got into her motor instead.

It was done so quickly, Tamara was already packed into the troika, and the outside steeds were prancing in their desire to be off.

"The horses won't stand," the Prince said, and he jumped in beside her and gave the order to go. Thus Tamara found herself alone with him flying over the snow under the stars.

There was a delicious feeling of excitement in her veins. They neither of them spoke for a while, but the Prince drew nearer and yet nearer, and presently his arm slipped round her, and he folded her close.

"Doushka," he whispered. "I hate the Englishman—and life is so short. Let us taste it while we may," and then he bent and kissed her lips!

Tamara struggled against the intense intoxicating emotion she was experiencing. What frightful tide was this which had swept into her well-ordered life! She vainly put up her arms and tried to push him away, but with each sign of revolt he held her the tighter.

"Darling," he said softly in her ear. "My little white soul. Do not fight, it is perfectly useless, because I *will* do what I wish. See, I will be gentle and just caress you, if you do not madden me by trying to resist!"

Then he gathered her right into his arms, and again bent and most tenderly kissed her. All power of movement seemed to desert Tamara. She only knew that she was wildly happy, that this was heaven, and she would wish it never to end.

She ceased struggling and closed her eyes, then he whispered all sorts of cooing love words in Russian and French, and rubbed his velvet eyelids against her cheek, and every few seconds his lips would come to meet her lips.

At last, when they had crossed the Troitzka bridge, he permitted her to release herself, and only held her hands under the furs, because dawn was breaking and they could be observed.

But when they turned into the wide Serguiefskaia, which seemed deserted, he bent once more and this time with wildest passion he seemed to draw her very soul through her lips.

Then ere she could speak, they drew up at the door, and he lifted her out, and before the Suisse and the waiting footmen.

"Good-night, Madame—sleep well," he calmly said.

But Tamara, trembling with mad emotion, rushed quickly to her room.

CHAPTER XII

In life there comes sometimes a tidal wave in the ebb of which all old landmarks are washed out. And so it was with Tamara. She had fallen into bed half dead with fatigue and emotion, but when she woke the sickly gray light of a Russian winter mid-day pouring into her room, and saw her maid's stolid face, back rushed the events of the night, and she drew in her breath with almost a hiss. Yes, nothing could ever be the same again. "Leave me, Johnson," she said, "I am too tired, I cannot get up yet."

And the respectful maid crept from the room.

Then she lay back in her pillows and forced herself to face the position, and review what she had done, and what she must now do.

First of all, she loved Gritzko, that she could no longer argue with herself about. Secondly, she was an English lady, and could not let herself be kissed by a man whose habit it was to play with whom he chose, and then pass on. She was free, and he was free, it followed his caressing then—divine as it had been—was an absolute insult. If he wanted her so much he should have asked her to marry him. He had not done so, therefore the only thing which remained for her to do, was to go away. The sooner the better.

Then she thought of all the past.

From the moment of the good-bye at the Sphinx it had been a humiliation for her. Always, always, he had been victor of the situation. Had she been ridiculously weak? What was this fate which had fallen upon her? What had she done to draw such circumstances? Then even as she lay there, communing sternly with herself, a thrill swept over her, as her thoughts went back to that last passionate kiss. And her slender hands clenched under the clothes.

"If he really loved me," she sighed, "I would face the uncertain happiness with him. I know now he causes me emotions of which I never dreamed and for which I would pay that price. But I have no single proof that he does really love me. He may be playing in the same way with Tatiane Shébanoff—and the rest." And at this picture her pride rose in wild revolt.

Never, never! should he play with her again at least!

Then she thought of all her stupid ways, perhaps if she had been different, not so hampered by prejudice, but natural like all these women here, perhaps she could have made him really love her.—Ah!—if so.

This possibility, however, brought no comfort, only increased regret.

The first thing now to be done was to restrain herself in an iron control. To meet him casually. To announce to her godmother that she must go home, and as soon as the visit to Moscow should be over, she would return to England. She must not be too sudden, he would think she was afraid. She would be just stiff and polite and serene, and show him he was a matter of indifference to her, and that she had no intention to be trifled with again!

At last, aching in mind and body, she lay still. Meanwhile, below in the blue salon, the Princess Ardácheff was conversing with Stephen Strong.

"Yes, mon ami," she was saying. "You must come—we go in a week—the day after my ball, to show Tamara Moscow, and from there to spend a night at Milasláv. Olga and Sonia and her husband and the Englishman, and Serge Grekoff and Valonne are coming, and it will be quite amusing."

"Think of the travelling and my old bones!" And Stephen Strong smiled. "But since it is your wish, dear Princess, of course I must come."

They were old and very intimate friends these two, and with him thePrincess was accustomed to talk over most of her plans.

He got up and lit a cigarette, then he walked across the room and came back again, while his hostess surveyed him with surprise. At last he sat down.

"Vera, tell me the truth," he said. "How are things going? I confess last night gave me qualms."

The Princess gazed at him inquiringly.

"Why qualms?"

"You see, Gritzko is quite an exceptional person, he is no type of a Russian or any other nation that one can reckon with, he is himself, and he has the most attractive magnetic personality a man could have."

"Well, then?"

"And if you knew the simple unsophisticated atmosphere in which your godchild has been brought up——."

"Stephen, really,"—and the Princess tapped her foot impatiently. "Please speak out. Say what you mean."

"She is no more fitted to cope with him than a baby, that is what I mean."

"But why should she cope with him? Are not men tiresome!" and the Princess sighed. "Can't you see I want them to love one another. It is just that—if she would not snub and resist him—all would be well."

"It did not look much like resistance last night," said Stephen Strong. "And if Gritzko is only playing the fool, and means nothing serious, then I think it is a shame."

"You don't suggest, surely, that I should interfere with fate?"

"Only to the extent of not giving him unlimited opportunities. You remember that season in London—and your brother Alexis—and her mother, and what came of that!"

The Princess put her hands up with a sudden gesture and covered her eyes.

"Oh! Stephen! how cruel of you to bring it back to me," she said; "but this is quite different—they are free—and it is my dearest wish that Tamara and Gritzko should be united." Then she continued in another tone. "I think you are quite wrong in any case. My plan is to throw them together as much as possible—he will see her real worth and delicate sweetness—and they will get over their quarrelling. It is her reserve and resistance which drives him mad. Sometimes I do not know how he will act."

"No, one can never count upon how he will act!" and Stephen Strong smiled. "But since you are satisfied I will say no more, only between you don't break my gentle little countrywoman's heart."

"You hurt me very much, Stephen!" the Princess said. "You—you—of all people, who know the tie there is between Tamara and me. You to suggest even that I would aid in breaking her heart."

"Dear Vera, forgive me," and he kissed her plump white hand. "I will suggest nothing, and will leave it all to you, but do not forget a man's passions, and Gritzko, as we know, is not made of snow!"

"You all misjudge him, my poor Gritzko," the Princess said, hardly mollified. "He has the noblest nature underneath, but some day you will know."

It was late in the afternoon when Tamara appeared, to find a room full of guests having tea. Her mind was made up, and she had regained her calm.

She would use the whole of her intelligence and play the game. She would be completely at ease and indifferent to Gritzko and would be incidentally as nice as possible to Jack. And so get through the short time before she must go home. "For," she had reasoned with herself sadly, "If he had loved me really he would never have behaved as he has done."

So when the Prince and Lord Courtray came in together presently, her greeting to both was naturalness itself, and she took Jack off to a distant sofa with friendly familiarity, and conversed with him upon their home affairs.

"By Jove! you know, Tamara, you are awfully improved, my child," Lord Courtray said, presently. "You've acquired some kind of a look in your eye! If I wasn't so taken with that darling little Countess Olga I should feel inclined to make love to you myself."

"You dear silly old Jack!" Tamara said.

It was Lord Courtray's fashion, when talking to any woman, even his own mother, to lean over her with rather a devoted look. And Tamara glancing up caught sight of Prince Milaslávski's face. It wore an expression which almost filled her with fear. Of all things she must provoke no quarrel between him and dear old Jack, who was quite blameless in the affair.

At the same time there was a consolation in the knowledge that she could make him feel.

She thought it wiser soon to rise and return to the general group, while Jack, on his own amusement bent, now took his leave.

She sat down by Stephen Strong, she was in a most gracious mood it seemed.

"You have heard of our excursion to Moscow, Mr. Strong," she said. "The Princess says you must come too, I am looking forward to it immensely."

"We ought to have a most promising time in front of us," that old cynic replied, while he puffed rings of smoke. "It all should be as full of adventure as an egg is full of meat!"

"I have been reading up the guide books, so as to be thoroughly learned and teach Jack—he is so terribly ignorant always, worse than Tom!" and she laughed.

"We must try and see the whole show, and if the snow lasts, as it promises to do, we should have a delightful time."

"Gritzko," Princess Ardácheff said. "How many versts is it from Moscow to Milasláv?"

The Prince had been leaning on the mantlepiece without speaking for some moments, listening to Tamara's conversation, but now he joined in, and sinking into a chair beside her, answered from there.

"Thirty versts, Tantine—we shall go in troikas—but you must send your servants on the night before."

Then he turned to Tamara, who seemed wonderfully absorbed, almost whispering to Stephen Strong. "Did you sleep well, Madame?" he said. There was an expression of mocking defiance in his glance, which angered Tamara. However, faithful to her resolutions, she kept herself calm.

"Never better, thank you, Prince. It was a most interesting evening, and I am learning the customs of the country," she said. "The thing which strikes me most is your wonderful chivalry to women—especially strange women."

They looked into one another's eyes and measured swords, and if she had known it she had never so deeply attracted him before.

She had broached the subject of her return to England to her godmother, who had laughed the idea to scorn, but now she spoke to Gritzko as if it were an established fact.

"I go home from Moscow, you know," she said.

"You find our country too cold?" he asked.

"It is too full of contrasts, freezing one moment and thawing the next, and while outside one is turned to ice, indoors one is consumed with heat; it is upsetting to the equilibrium."

"All the same, you will not go," and he leaned back in the chair with his provoking lazy smile.

"Indeed, I shall."

"We shall see. There are a number of things for you to learn yet."

"What things?"

The Prince lit a cigarette. "The possibilities of the unknown fires you have lit," he said. "You remember the night at the Sphinx, when we said good-bye. I told you a proverb they have there about meeting before dawn, and not parting until dawn. Well, that dawn has not arrived yet. And I have no intention—for the moment—that it shall arrive."

Tamara felt excited, and as ever his tone of complete omnipotence annoyed her. At the same time to see him sitting there, his eyes fixed with deep interest on her face, thrilled and exalted her. Oh! she certainly loved him! Alas! and it would be dreadfully difficult to say good-bye. But those three words in his sentence stung her pride—"for the moment." Yes, there was always this hint of caprice. Always he gave her the sensation of instability, there was no way to hold him. She must ever guard her emotions and ever be ready to fence.

And now that she had taken a resolve to go home, to linger no more, she was free to tease him as much as she could. To feel that she could, gave her a fillip, and added a fresh charm to her face.

"You think you can rule the whole world to your will, Prince," she said.

"I can rule the part of it I want, as you will find," he retorted fiercely. She made a pouting moue and tapped her little foot, then she laughed.

"How amusing it would be if you happened to be mistaken this time," she cooed. Then she rapidly turned to the Princess Sonia, who had just come in, and they all talked of the great ball which was to take place in the house in a week. The first after the period of the deep mourning.

"We cannot yet wear colors, but whites and grays and mauves—and won't it be a relief from all this black," Princess Sonia said.

When they had all gone and Tamara was dressing for dinner, she felt decidedly less depressed. She had succeeded better than she had hoped. She had contrived to outwit the Prince, when he had plainly shown his intention was to continue talking to her, she had turned from one to another, and finally sat down by a handsome Chevalier Garde. In companies she had a chance, but when they were alone!—however, that was simple, because she must arrange that they should never be alone.

CHAPTER XIII

It was perhaps a fortunate thing that for three days after this the Prince was kept at his military duties at Tsarsköi-Sélo, and could not come to Petersburg, for he was in a mood that could easily mean mischief. Tamara also was inclined to take things in no docile spirit.

She felt very unhappy, underneath her gay exterior. It was not agreeable to her self-respect to realize she was fleeing from a place because she loved a man whose actions showed he did not entertain the same degree of feeling for her. No amount of attention from any other quite salved that ever-constant inward hurt.

She went often through strange moments. In the middle of a casual conversation suddenly back would come a wave of remembrance of the dawn drive in the troika, and she would actually quiver with physical emotion as the vivid recollection of the bliss of it would sweep over her.

Then she would clench her hands and determine more fiercely than ever to banish such memories. But with all her will, hardly for ten minutes at a time could she keep Gritzko from her thoughts. His influence over her was growing into an obsession.

She wondered why he did not come. She would not ask her godmother. The three days passed in a feverish, gnawing unrest; and on the third evening they went to the ballet again.

Opposite them, in a box, a very dark young woman was seated. She had a hard, determined face, and she was well dressed, and not too covered with jewels.

"That is a celebrated lady," Count Valonne said. "You must look at her, Madame Loraine; she was one of the best dancers at the ballet, and last year she tried to commit suicide in a charmingly dramatic way at one of Gritzko's parties. She was at the time perhaps his *chère amie*—one never knows, but in all cases violently in love with him—and is still, for the matter of that—or so it is said—and in the middle of rather a wild feast he was giving for her, she suddenly drank off some poison, after making the terrifying announcement of her intention! We were all petrified with horror, but he remained quite calm, and, seizing her, he poured a whole bottle of salad oil down her throat, and then sent for a doctor!—Of course the poor lady recovered, and the romantic end was quite *raté!*—She was perfectly furious, one heard—and married a rich slate merchant the week after. Wasn't it like Gritzko? He said the affair was vulgar, and he sent her a large diamond bracelet, and never spoke to her again!"

Tamara felt her cheeks burn—and her pride galled her more than ever. So she and the ex-dancer were in the same boat?—but she at least would not try to commit suicide and be restored by—salad oil!

"How perfectly ridiculous!" she said, with rather a bitter little laugh. "What complete bathos!"

"It was unfortunate, was it not?" Valonne went on, and he glanced at Tamara sideways.

He guessed that she was interested in the Prince; but Valonne was a charming creature with an understanding eye, and in their set was in great request. He knew exactly the right thing to talk about to each different person, as a perfect diplomat should, and he was too tactful and sympathetic to tease poor Tamara. On the contrary, he told her casually that Gritzko had been on some duty these three days, in case she did not know it.

From the beginning Tamara always had liked Valonne.

Then into the box came the same good-looking Chevalier Garde, Count Varishkine, whom she had talked to on the last occasion of Gritzko's visit, and the spirit of hurt pride caused her to be most gracious with him. Meanwhile the Princess Ardácheff watched her with a faint sensation of uneasiness, and at last whispered to Stephen Strong:

"Does not my godchild seem to be developing new characteristics, Stephen? She is so very stately and quiet; and yet to-night it would almost seem she is being flirtatious with Boris Varishkine.—I trust we shall have no complications. What do you think?"

Mr. Strong laughed.

"It will depend upon how much it angers Gritzko. It could come to mean anything—bloodshed, a scandal, or merely bringing things to a crisis between them.—Let us hope, for the latter."

"Indeed, yes."

"You must remember, for an Englishwoman it would be very difficult to grasp all the possibilities in the character of Gritzko. We are not accustomed to these tempestuous headlong natures in our calm country."

"Fortunately Boris and Gritzko are very great friends."

"I never heard that the warmest friendship prevented jealousy between men," Stephen Strong said, a little cynically—he had suffered a good deal in his youth.

"I am delighted we are going to Moscow. There will be no Boris, and I shall arrange for my two children to be together as much as possible. I feel that is the surest way," the Princess answered; and they talked of other things.

After the ballet was over the party went on to supper at Cubat's in a private room, contrary to the Princess' custom. But it was Stephen Strong's entertainment, and he had no house to invite them to.

As they passed down the passage to their salon the door of another opened as a waiter came out, and loud laughter and clatter of glass burst forth, and above the din one shrill girl's treble screamed:

"Gritzko! Oh, Gritzko!"

The food nearly choked Tamara when they reached their room, and supper began. It was not, of course, a heinous crime for the Prince to be entertaining ladies of another world. But on the top of everything else it raised a wild revolt in her heart, and a raging disgust with herself. Never, never should she unbend to him again. She *would not* love him.

Alas! for the impotency of human wills! Only the demonstrations of love can be controlled, the emotion itself comes from heaven—or hell, and is omnipotent. Poor Tamara might as well have determined to keep the sun from rising as to keep herself from loving Gritzko.

She was quite aware that men—even the nicest men—like Jack and her brother Tom, sometimes went out with people she would not care to know; but to have the fact brought under her very observation disgusted her fine senses. To realize that the man she loved was at the moment perhaps kissing some ordinary woman, revolted and galled her immeasurably. But if she had known it this night, at least, the Prince was innocent. He had strolled into that room with some brother officers, and was not the giver of the feast. And a few minutes after Mr. Strong's party had begun their repast he opened the door.

"May I come in, Stephen?" he asked. "I heard you were all here, Serge saw you. I have just arrived from Tsarsköi, and must eat."

And of course he was warmly welcomed and pressed to take a seat, while Valonne chaffed him in an undertone about the joys he had precipitately left.

Tamara's face was the picture of disdain. But the Prince sat beside her godmother, apparently unconcerned. He did not trouble to address her specially, and before the end of supper, in spite of rage and disgust and anger—and shame, she was longing for him to talk to her.

The only consolation she had was once when they went out, as she looked up sweetly at Count Varishkine she caught a fierce expression stealing over Gritzko's face.

So even though he did not love her really he could still feel jealous; that was something, at all events!

Thus in these paltry rages and irritations, these two human beings passed the next three days—when their real souls were capable of something great.

Prince Milaslávski, to every one's surprise, appeared continuously in the world.

Tamara and the Princess met him everywhere, and while the Princess did her best to throw them together, Tamara maneuvered so that not once could he speak to her alone, while she was assiduously charming to every one else. Now it was old Prince Miklefski or Stephen Strong, now one of the husbands, or Jack, and just often enough to give things a zest she was bewitching to the handsome Chevalier Garde.

And the strange, fierce light in Gritzko's eyes did not decrease.

The night before the Ardácheff ball they were going to a reception at one of the Embassies for a foreign King and Queen, who were paying a visit to the Court, and Tamara dressed with unusual care, and fastened her high tiara in her soft brown hair.

The Prince should see her especially attractive, she thought.

But when they arrived at the great house and walked among the brilliant throng no Prince was to be seen!—It might be he had no intention to come.

Presently Tamara went off to the refreshment room with her friend Valonne.

The conversation turned to Gritzko with an easy swing.

He seemed on the brink of one of his maddest fits. Valonne had seen him in the club just before dinner.

"If you really go to England I think he will follow you, Madame," he said.

"How ridiculous!" and Tamara laughed. "How can it make a difference to him whether I go or no? We do not exist for one another," and she fanned herself rather rapidly, while Valonne smiled a fine smile.

"I should not be quite sure of that," he said. "If I might predict, I should say you will be lucky if you get away from here without being the cause of a duel of some sort."

"A duel!" Tamara was startled. "How dreadful, and how silly! But why? I thought dueling had quite gone out in all civilized countries; and in any case, why fight about me? And who should fight? Surely you are only teasing me, Count Valonne."

"Duels are real facts here, I am afraid," he said. "Gritzko has already engaged in two of them. He is not quarrelsome, but just never permits any one to cross his wishes or interfere with his game."

"But what *is* his game? You speak as though it were some kind of cards or plot. What do you mean?" and Tamara, with heightened color, lifted her head.

"The game of Gritzko?" and Count Valonne laughed. "Frankly, I think he is very much in love with you, Madame," he said. "So by that you can guess what would be any man's game."

"You have a vivid imagination, and are talking perfect nonsense." Tamara laughed nervously. "I refuse to be the least upset by such ideas!"

At the moment up came Count Boris Varishkine, and after a while she went off with him to a sofa by the window, and there was seated in deep converse when the Prince came in.

He looked at them for a second and then made straight for the Princess Ardácheff, who was just about to arrange her rubber of bridge.

"Tantine, I want to talk to you," he said.

And the Princess at once left the cardroom and returned with him. They found a quiet corner opposite Tamara and her Garde, and there sat down.

"Tantine, I brought you here to look over there.—What does that mean?"

The Princess put up her glasses to gain time.

"Nothing, dear boy. Tamara is merely amusing herself like all the rest of us at a party. Are you jealous, Gritzko?" she asked.

He looked at her sharply, and for a moment unconsciously fingered the dagger in his belt.

"Yes, I believe I am jealous. I am not at all sure that I do not love your charming friend," he said.

"Well, why don't you marry her then?" suggested the Princess.

"Perhaps I shall—if she does not drive me to doing something mad first. I don't know what I intend. It may be to go off to the Caucasus, or to stay and make her love me so deeply that she will forgive me—no matter what I do."

He paused a moment, and his great eyes filled with mist, and then the wild light grew.

"If ever she becomes my Princess, she shall be entirely for me. I will not let her have a look or thought for any other man. All must be mine—unshared, and then she shall be my queen."

Princess Ardácheff leant back and looked at him. He was in his blue uniform with the scarlet underdress; and even she—old woman and fond friend—could not help picturing the gorgeous joy such a fate would give—to have him for a lover! to see his fierce, proud head bent in devotion, to feel his tender caress. Tamara must be an unutterable fool if she should hesitate.

But what he had said was not reassuring in its prospect of calm. She felt she must put in some small word of admonition.

"You will be careful won't you, Gritzko?" she ventured to suggest. "Remember, Tamara is an Englishwoman, and not accustomed to your ways."

"It will depend upon herself," he said. "If she goes on teasing me I do not know what I shall do. If she does not—"

"You will be good?"

"Possibly. But one thing, Tantine, I will not be interfered with either by her friend the Englishman or Boris Varishkine."

At this moment Tamara looked up and caught the two pairs of eyes fixed upon her. And into her spirit flowed a devilment.—Duels! They were all nonsense. She should certainly play a little with her new friend.

In her whole life before she came to Russia she had never been really flirtatious. She was in no way a coquette, rather a simple creature who recked little of men. But the simplest woman develops feline qualities under certain provocation; and her pride was deeply hurt.

Count Boris Varishkine asked nothing better than to fall in with her views. He was, however, like most of his countrymen, sincere, and not merely passing the time.

Jack Courtray came up, too, and joined them, his Countess Olga had sent him temporarily from her side. And Tamara scintillated and sparkled as she talked to them both in a way which surprised herself.

This society was very diplomatic, and it amused her to watch the representatives of the different nations—the English and the Russians standing out as so much the finest men.

Presently the little group was joined by Stephen Strong.

"Isn't this an amusing party, Mrs. Loraine?" he said.

"Yes," said Tamara. "And I am beginning to be able to place the members of the different countries. Don't you think the Russians look much the most like us, Mr. Strong?"

"The Russians, dear lady? When you have traveled a little more you will see that term covers half the types of the earth—but I agree. What we see here in Petersburg are very much like us—a trifling difference in the way the eyes are set, and the way the hair is brushed; and, given the same uniforms, half these smart young men might be our English Guards."

"We do not resemble you in character, though," said Count Varishkine. "You can feel just what you like, or not at all, whereas we are storm-tossed, and have not yet learnt the arts of pretence."

"We're a deuced cold-blooded race, aren't we, Tamara?" Jack Courtray said, and he grinned his happy grin.

The little party looked so merry and content Princess Ardácheff hardly liked to disturb them, but was impelled to by a look in Gritzko's face.

"Tamara, dear," she said, as she joined them, "I am so very tired after last night, for once shall we go home reasonably early?"

And Tamara rose gladly to her feet.

"Of course, Marraine, I too am dropping with fatigue," she said.

The Prince spoke a few words to Stephen Strong, and Jack joined in; so that the three were a pace or so to one side when the two ladies wished them goodnight.

"Come and see me early tomorrow, Jack," Tamara said. "I want to show you Tom's letter from home," and she looked up with an alluring smile, feeling the Prince was watching her; then, turning to Count Boris, "I am sure you will regret your bargain in having asked me to dance the Mazurka tomorrow night," she said. "I do not know a single figure or a step—but I hope we shall have some fun. I am looking forward to it."

"More than fun!" the young man said, with devotion, as he kissed her hand.

Then they walked to say goodnight to the hostess, and Gritzko seemed to disappear. But when they got down into the hall they saw him already in his furs.

The Princess' footman began to hand Tamara her snowboots and cloak, but Gritzko almost snatched them from the man's hand. She made no protest, but let him help her to put them on and wrap her up, while her godmother thought it advisable to walk toward the door.

"Tonight was your moment, Madame," he said, in a low voice. "But the gods are often kind to me, and my hour will come!"

Tamara summoned everything she knew of provokingness into her face as she looked up and answered:

"Tant pis! et bon soir! Monsieur le démon de Lermontoff!"

Then she felt it prudent to run quickly after the Princess and get into the automobile!

CHAPTER XIV

It was twenty-four hours later. The night of the Ardácheff ball had come. The glorious house made the background of a festive scene. The company waited all round the galleries for the arrival of the Grand Dukes and the foreign King and Queen.

And Tamara stood by her godmother's side at the top of the stairs, a strange excitement flooding her veins.

Since the night before they had heard nothing of the Prince. And as each guest came in view, past the splendid footmen grouped like statues on every six steps, both women watched with quickening pulses for one insouciant Cossack face.

The Royalties arrived in a gorgeous train, and yet neither Gritzko nor Count Varishkine.

It might mean nothing, but it was curious all the same. The opening *contre-danse* was in full swing, and still they never came, and by the time of the second valse after it Tamara was a prey to a vague fear. While the Princess' uneasiness grew more than vague.

Tamara could not enjoy herself. She talked at random, she made her partners continually promenade through the salons, and her eyes constantly scanned the doors.

The immense ballroom, quite two stories high, presented a brilliant sight with its stately decorations of the time of Alexander I. And all the magnificent jewels and uniforms, and the flowers. Somehow a riot of roses takes an extra charm when outside the thermometer measures zero. And no one would have believed, looking at this dignified throng, that they could be the same people who could frolic wildly at a Bohemian supper.

There is a great deal in breeding, after all, and the knowledge of the fitness of things which follows in its train.

Tamara was valsing with Jack Courtray, and they stopped to look at the world.

"Are they not a wonderful people, Jack? Could anything be more decorous and dignified than they are tonight? And yet if you watch, in the *contre-danse* their eyes have the same excited look as when we wildly capered after supper in Prince Milaslávski's house."

"Which reminds me—why is he not here?" asked Jack.

"I wish I knew," Tamara said. "Jack, be a dear and go and forage about and get hold of Serge Grekoff, if you can see him, or Mr. Strong, or Sasha Basmanoff, or some one who might know—but it seems as if none of them are here."

"As interested as that?" and Lord Courtray laughed. "Well, my child, I'll do my best," so he relinquished her for the next turn and left her with Valonne, who had just arrived.

"Apparently I shall have to go partnerless for the Mazurka," Tamara carelessly said while she watched the Frenchman's face with the corner of her eye. "I was engaged for it to Count Varishkine, and he has never turned up. I do wonder what has happened to him. Do you know?"

"I told you you would be lucky if you got away from here without some row of sorts, Madame," and Valonne smiled enigmatically.

"What do you mean? Please tell me?" and Tamara turned pale.

"I mean nothing; only I fancy you will only see one of them tonight; which it will be is still on the cards."

A cold, sick feeling came over Tamara.

"You are not insinuating that they have been fighting?" she asked, with a tremble in her voice which she could not control.

But Valonne reassured her.

"I am insinuating nothing," he said, with a calm smile. "Let us have one more turn before this charming valse stops."

And, limp and nerveless, Tamara allowed herself to be whirled around the room; nor could she get anything further out of Valonne.

When it was over she sought in vain for her godmother or Jack or Stephen Strong. The Princess was engaged with the Royalties and could not be approached, and neither of the men were to be seen.

The next half-hour was agony, in which, with a white face and fixed smile, Tamara played her part, and then just before the Mazurka was going to begin Gritzko came in.

It seemed as if her knees gave way under her for a moment, and she sat down in a seat. The relief was so great. Whatever had happened he at least was safe.

She watched him securing two chairs in the best place, and then he crossed over to where she sat by the door to the refreshment room.

"Bon soir, Madame," he said. "Will you take me as a substitute for your partner, Count Varishkine?" and he bowed with a courtly grace which seemed suited to the scene. "He is, I regret to say, slightly indisposed, and has asked me to crave your indulgence for him, and let me fill his place."

For a moment Tamara hesitated; she seemed to have lost the power of speech; she felt she must control her anxiety and curiosity, so at last she answered gravely:

"I am so very sorry! I hope it is nothing serious. He is so charming, Count Varishkine."

"Nothing serious. Shall we take our places? I have two chairs there not far from Olga and your friend," and the Prince prepared to lead the way. Tamara, now that the tension was over, almost thought she would refuse, but the great relief and joy she felt in his presence overcame her pride, and she meekly followed him across the room.

They passed the Princess on the way, and as she apparently gave some laughing reply to the Ambassador she was with, she hurriedly whispered in Tamara's ear:

"Pour l'amour de Dieu! Be careful with Gritzko tonight, my child."

When they were seated waiting for the dance to begin Tamara noticed that the Prince was very pale, and that his eyes, circled with blue shadows, seemed to flame.

The certainty grew upon her that some mysterious tragic thing had taken place; but, frightened by the Princess' words, she did not question him.

She hardly spoke, and he was silent, too. It seemed as though now he had gained his end and secured her as a partner it was all he meant to do.

Presently he turned to her and asked lazily:

"Have you been amused since the Moravian reception? How have you passed the time? I have been at Tsarsköi again, and could not come to see Tantine."

"We have been quite happy, thanks, Prince," Tamara said. "Jack Courtray and I have spent the day studying the lovely things in the Hermitage. We must see what we can before we both go home."

Gritzko looked at her.

"I like him—he is a good fellow—your friend," and then he added reflectively: "But if he spends too much time with you I hope the bears will eat him!"

This charitable wish was delivered in a grave, quiet voice, as though it had been a blessing.

"How horrible you are!" Tamara flashed. "Jack to be eaten by bears! Poor dear old Jack! What has he done?"
"Nothing, I hope,—as yet; but time will tell. Now we must begin to dance."
And they rose, called to the center by the Master of the Ceremonies to assist in a figure.
While the Prince was doing his part she noticed his movements seemed languid and not full of his usual wild *entrain*, and her feeling of unease and dread of she knew not what increased.
Tamara was very popular, and was hardly left for a moment on her chair when the flower figures began, so their conversations were disjointed, and at last almost ceased, and unconsciously a stiff silence grew up between them, caused, if she had known it, on his side, by severe physical pain.
She was surprised that he handed all his flowers to her but did not ask her to dance, nor did he rise to seek any other woman. He just sat still, though presently, when magnificent red roses were brought in in a huge trophy, and Serge Grekoff was seen advancing with a sheaf of them to claim Tamara, he suddenly asked her to have a turn, and got up to begin.
She placed her hand on his arm, and she noticed he drew in his breath sharply and winced in the slightest degree. But when she asked him if something hurt him, and what it was, he only laughed and said he was well, and they must dance; so away they whirled.
A feverish anxiety and excitement convulsed Tamara. What in heaven's name had occurred?
When they had finished and were seated again she plucked up courage to ask him:
"Prince, I feel sure Count Varishkine is not really ill. Something has happened. Tell me what it is."
"I never intended you to dance the Mazurka with him," was all Gritzko said.
"And how have you prevented it?" Tamara asked, and grew pale to her lips.
"What does it matter to you?" he said. "Are you nervous about Boris?"
And now he turned and fully looked at her, and she was deeply moved by the expression in his face.
He was suffering extremely, she could distinguish that, but underneath the pain there was a wild triumph, too. Her whole being was wrung. Love and fear and solicitude, and, yes, rebellion also had its place. And at last she said:
"I am nervous, not for Count Varishkine, but for what you may have done."
He leaned back and laughed with almost his old irresponsible mirth.
"I can take care of my own deeds, thanks, Madame," he said.
And then anger rose in Tamara beyond sympathy for pain.
She sat silent, staring in front of her, the strain of the evening was beginning to tell. She hardly knew what he said, or she said, until the Mazurka was at an end, all the impression it left with her was one of tension and fear. Then the polonaise formed, and they went in to supper.
Here they were soon seated next their own special friends, and Gritzko seemed to throw off all restraint. He drank a great deal, and then poured out a glass of brandy and mixed it with the champagne.
He had never been more brilliant, and kept the table in a roar, while much of his conversation was addressed to Tatiane Shébanoff, who sat on his left hand.
Tamara appeared as though she were turned into stone.
And so the night wore on. It was now four o'clock in the morning. The company all went to the galleries again to watch the departure of the King and Queen. And, leaning on the marble balustrade next the Prince, Tamara suddenly noticed a thin crimson stream trickle from under his sleeve to his glove.
He saw it, too, and with an impatient exclamation of annoyance he moved back and disappeared in the crowd. The rest of the ball for Tamara was a ghastly blank, although they kept it up with immense spirit until very late.
She seemed unable to get near the Princess, she was always surrounded, and when at last she did come upon her in deep converse with Valonne.
"Tamara, dear," she said, "you must be so dreadfully tired. Slip off to bed. They will go on until daylight," and there was something in her face which prevented any questions.
So, cold and sick with apprehension, poor Tamara crept to her room, and, dismissing her weary maid, sat and rocked herself over her fire.
What horrible thing had occurred?
What was the meaning of that thin stream of blood?

CHAPTER XV

Tamara and her godmother did not meet until nearly lunchtime next day. A little before that meal the Princess came into her room. Tamara was still in bed, perfectly exhausted with the strain of the night. The Princess wore an anxious look of care, as she walked from the window to the dressing table and then back again. Finally she sat down and took up a glove which was lying on a cushion near.
"Tamara, you saw I talked last night with Valonne, and this morning I sent for Serge Grekoff, but he would not come, so I got Valonne again." She paused an instant. "I was extremely worried last night about Gritzko. I dare say you were not to blame, dear, but—"
"Please tell me, Marraine," and poor Tamara sat up and pushed her hair back.
"It appears, as far at I can gather, they all dined at the Fontonka house—Boris Varishkine and Gritzko have always been great friends—and at the end of dinner—Valonne imagines, because no one is sure what took place between them at this stage—Gritzko, it is supposed, said to Boris in quite an amiable way that he did not wish him to dance the Mazurka with you, but to relinquish his right in his—Gritzko's—favor."
She paused again, and Tamara's eyes fixed themselves in fascinated fear on her face. The Princess, after smoothing out the glove in her hand with a nervous energy, went on:
"They had all had quite enough champagne, of course, and apparently Boris refused, and suggested that they should toss up, and whoever won the toss should have first shot in the dark."
"Yes," said Tamara faintly.

"You know, dear, our boys are often very wild, and they have a game they play when they are at the end of their tether for something to do when quartered in some hopeless outpost—a kind of blind-man's-buff—only it is all in the dark, and the blind man stands in the middle of the room and the rest clap hands and then dodge, and he fires his revolver at the point the sound seems to come from, and the object is not to get shot. You may have noticed Sasha Basmanoff has no left thumb? He lost it last year on just such a night."

"Oh! Marraine, how dreadful!" Tamara said.

"It is perhaps not a very civilized game," the Princess continued, "but we are not discussing that, I am telling you what occurred. Well, from this point Valonne and the rest were eyewitnesses. Gritzko and Boris, still laughing in rather a strained way, said they had some slight difference of opinion to settle, and had decided to do it in the ballroom, in the dark. I won't go into details of how many steps to the right or left, the impromptu seconds arranged, only it was settled when Sasha at one end and Serge at the other should shut the doors they should both fire, and if in three times neither was shot, both should give up their claim."

"It is too horrible! and for such a trifle," Tamara said, clutching the bedclothes, and the Princess went on.

"Valonne said they were both hit in the first round, and all the company burst into the room. Nothing seemed very serious, and they laughed and shook hands. So Valonne left to be in time for the ball, but this morning, he told me, he found Boris Varishkine had had a shoulder wound which bled very badly and quite prevented his coming, while Gritzko was shot through the flesh of the right arm, and as soon as they could bind it up decently, as you know, he came on."

Tamara's face was as white as her pillow. She clasped her hands with a movement of anguish.

"Oh! Marraine, I am too unhappy," she wailed. "Indeed, indeed, I did nothing to cause this. You heard me, I only said to Count Varishkine I was looking forward to the dance. He is impossible, Gritzko. Oh! let me go home!"

"Alas! my child, what would be the good of that? If you went off tonight instead of coming to Moscow, it might create a talk; what we want is to prevent a scandal, to hush everything up. None of these men will tell, and your name will not be dragged into it. And if we go on our trip amicably as was arranged it will discountenance rumor. Gritzko and Boris are quite friends again. And if anything about the shooting does leak out, if no one has further cause for connecting you with it, they will generally think it merely one of Gritzko's mad parties. For heaven's sake let it all blow over, and after Moscow and a reasonable time, not to appear too hurried, you shall go home."

"But meanwhile, how can I know that he won't shoot at Jack? or do some other awful thing! He does not love me really a bit, Marraine. It is all out of pride and devilment because he wants to win and conquer me and add me to his scalps, and I won't be conquered. I tell you I won't!" and Tamara clenched her hands.

The Princess did not know what to say, she was not perfectly sure in her own mind as to Gritzko's feelings, and she was too thoroughly acquainted with his ways to hazard any theory as to his possible acts. She felt it might not be fair to assure her godchild that he truly loved her. She could only think of tiding over matters for the time being.

"Tamara, dearest, could you at least try to keep the peace on our trip?" she asked. "Be gentle with him, and do not excite him in any way."

Tamara buried her face in her pillows, she was too English to be dramatic and sob; but when she spoke her soft voice trembled a little and her eyes glistened with tears.

"He is horribly cruel, Marraine," she said.

"Why should he treat me as he does. I won't—I won't bear it."

The Princess sighed.

"Tamara, forgive me for asking you, but I must, I feel I must. Do you—love him, child?"

Then passion flamed up in Tamara's white face, her secret was her own, and she would defend it even from this kind friend—so—"I believe I hate him!" she said.

After a while the Princess left her, they having come to the agreement that Tamara should do all that she could to keep the peace; but when she was alone she decided to speak to Gritzko as little as possible herself, and to ignore him completely. There would be no Boris and no one to make him jealous. She would occupy herself with Stephen Strong, and the sight-seeing, and even Sonia's husband, who was a bore and old, too; but the prospect held out no charms for her. She knew that she loved him deeply—this wild, fierce Gritzko—more deeply than ever today, and the tears, one after another, trickled down her pale cheeks.

If there was not a chance of any happiness, at least she must go home keeping some rag of self-respect. She firmly determined that he should not see the slightest feeling on her side, it should be restrained or perhaps capricious even, as his own.

Their train for Moscow started at nine o'clock, and the whole party had arranged to dine at the Ardácheff house at seven and then go to the station.

Nothing of the scandal of the night seemed to have transpired, for no one even hinted at anything about it.

Gritzko was still very pale, but appeared none the worse, and the atmosphere seemed to have resumed a peaceful note.

The five sleeping compartments reserved for this party of ten were all in a row in one carriage, and Tamara and the Princess, on the plea of fatigue, immediately retired to their berths for the night, Tamara not having addressed a single direct word to Gritzko. So far, so well. But when she was comfortably tucked into the top berth, and an hour or so later was just falling off to sleep, he knocked at the door, and the Princess believing it to be the ticket-collector opened it, and he put his head in. The shade was drawn over the lamp and the compartment was in a blue gloom. Tamara was startled by hearing her godmother say:

"Gritzko! Thou! What do you want, dear boy, disturbing us like this?"

"I came to ask you to tie up my arm," he said. "I was practising with a pistol yesterday, and it went off and the bullet grazed the skin, and the damned thing has begun bleeding again. I know you are a trained nurse, Tantine. Serge, who is with me, has tried and made a ridiculous mess of it, so I brought the bandage to you."

He now pulled back the shade and they saw he was standing there quite *sans gêne* in the same kind of blue silk pyjamas Tamara remembered to have seen once before, and his eyes, far from being tragic or serious, had the naughtiest, most mischievous twinkle in them, while he whispered to the Princess and enlisted her sympathy for his pain.

"Gritzko, dearest child, but you are suffering! But let me see! only wait in the passage until I have my dressing-gown, and then come in again."

Tamara now thought it prudent to crouch down in the clothes and pretend to be asleep, while the kind Princess got up and arranged herself.

Then with a gentle tap this poor wounded one came in.

Tamara was conscious that her godmother was murmuring horrified and affectionate solicitations, as she busily set to work. She was also conscious that Gritzko was standing with his shoulder leant against her berth. He was so tall he could look at her, in spite of her retirement to the farthest side, and she was horribly conscious of the magnetic power exercised by his eyes. She longed quite to open hers, she longed really to look. She felt so nervous she almost gave a silly little laugh, but her will won, and her long eyelashes remained resting on her cheek.

"You darling. You are doing it beautifully!" he presently said, and then more softly, "I had no idea how pretty your friend is! and how soundly she sleeps! Do you think I might kiss her, Tantino? I have always wanted to, only she is of such a severity I have been too frightened. May I, Tantine?" And his voice sounded coaxing and sweet, and Tamara felt sure he was caressing the Princess' hair with his free hand, for that lady kept murmuring.

"Tais toi!—Gritzko—have done! How can I bind your arm if you conduct yourself so! Not a moment of stillness! Truly what a naughty child—keep still!" Then she spoke more severely to him in Russian, and he laughed while he answered, and then presently the bandage was done, and standing on tip-toe he looked full at Tamara.

"And you think I must not kiss her? Oh! you are a most cruel Tantine! She is sound asleep and would never know, and it would be just one of the things which could cool my fever and help my arm."

But the Princess interposed, sternly, and getting really annoyed with him, he was forced to go. But first he kissed her hand and thanked her and purred affection and gratitude with his astonishing charm, and the Princess' voice grew more and more mollified as she said: "There—there—what a boy! Gritzko, dear child, begone!"

And all this while, with her long eyelashes resting upon her cheek, Tamara apparently slept peacefully on.

But when the door was safely shut and bolted, the Princess addressed her.

"You are not really asleep, Tamara, I suppose," she said. "You have heard? Is he not difficult. What is one to do with him? I can never remain angry long. Those caresses! Mon Dieu! I wish you would love each other and marry and go and live at Milasláv, and then we others might have a little peace and calm!"

"Marry him," and Tamara raised herself in bed. "One might as well marry a panther in a jungle, it would be quite as safe!" she said.

But the Princess shook her head. "There you are altogether wrong," she replied. "Once there were no continuous obstacles to his will, he would be gentle and adoring, he would be as tender and thoughtful as he is to me when I am ill."

Then into Tamara's brain there rushed visions of the unutterable pleasure this tenderness would mean, and she said:

"Don't let us talk;—I want to sleep, Marraine."

And in the morning they arrived at Moscow.

CHAPTER XVI

The whole day of the sight-seeing passed with comparative smoothness, Tamara persistently remained with Sonia's husband or Stephen Strong, when any moment came that she should be alone with any man.

She was apparently indifferent to Gritzko,—considering that she was throbbing with interest in his every movement and inwardly longing to talk to him—she kept up the *rôle* she had set herself to play very well. It was not an agreeable one, and but for the inward feverish excitement she would have suffered much pain.

Gritzko for his part seemed whimsically indifferent for most of the time, but once now and then the Princess, who watched things as the god in the car, experienced a sense of uneasiness. And yet she could not suggest any other line of conduct for Tamara to pursue. But on the whole the day was a success.

The two young English guests had both been extremely interested in what they saw. Stephen Strong was an old hand and knew it intimately, and the whole party was so merry and gay. The snow fortunately had held, and they rushed about in little sleighs seeing the quaint buildings and picturesque streets and the churches with their bright gilt domes. Moscow was really Russian, Prince Solentzeff-Zasiekin told them, unlike Petersburg, which at a first glance might be Berlin or Vienna, or anywhere else; but Moscow is like no other city in the world.

"How extremely good you Russians must be," Tamara said. "The quantities of churches you have, and everywhere the people seem so devout. Look at them kissing that Ikon in the street! Such faith is beautiful to see."

"Our faith is our safeguard," her companion said. "When the people become sufficiently educated to have doubts then, indeed, a sad day will come."

"They have such grave patient faces, don't you think?" said Stephen Strong. "It is not exactly a hopeless expression, it is more one of resignation. Whenever I come here I feel of what use is strife, and yet after a while they make one melancholy."

They were waiting by the house of the Romanoffs, for their guide to open the door, and just then a batch of beggars passed, their wild hair and terribly ragged sheepskins making them a queer gruesome sight. They craved alms with the same patient smile with which they thanked when money was given. Misery seemed to stalk about a good deal.

"How could a great family have lived in this tiny house?" Tamara asked. "Really, people in olden times seem to have been able to double up anywhere. Pray look at this bedroom and this ridiculous bed!"

"It will prepare you for what you are coming to at Milasláv," Gritzko said. "A row of tent stretchers for everyone together in the hall!"

Tamara made no answer, she contrived to move on directly he spoke, and her reply now was to the general company, as it had been all day.

If she had looked back then she would have seen a gleam in his eyes which boded no peace. She thought she was doing everything for the best, but each rebuff was adding fuel to that wild fire in his blood.

By the end of the day, after walks through the Treasury and museums, and what not, and never having been able to speak to Tamara, his temper was at boiling point. But he controlled it, and his face wore a mask, which disarmed even the Princess' fears.

Their dinner was very gay, and the Russians asked Lord Courtray what had impressed him most.

"I like the story of Ivan the Terrible putting his jolly old alpenstock through the fellow's foot on the stairs when he came with the letter," Jack said. "Sensible sort of thing to do. Kept the messenger in place."

Meanwhile Tamara was conversing in a lower voice with Stephen Strong.

"The more you stay in this country, the more it fascinates you," he said. "And you feel you have got back to some of the fierce primitive passions of nature. Here, in Moscow, the whole earth must be stained with wild orgies and blood, and yet they are full of poetry and romance. Even Ivan the Terrible had his religious side, and every creature of them believes in the saints and the priests. It is said the impostor who posed as Ivan's son might have succeeded had he not been too kind, he showed clemency to Shuisky and his enemies and did not have them torn to pieces, so the people would not believe he could be the Terrible's son! And they chased him to that window you remember we saw in the old palace of the Kremlin and there he had to throw himself out."

"It makes one wonder what can arise from a history of such horrible crimes," Tamara said.

"You must not forget that the country is practically three hundred years behind the times, though," Stephen Strong went on. "No doubt quite as great horrors marked others if we look at them at an equivalent stage of development. It is missing this point which makes most strangers, and many foreign historians, so unjust to Russia and her people. The national qualities are immeasurably great, but as a civilized nation they are so very young."

"I believe one could grow to love them," Tamara said. "I have never had the feeling that I am among strangers since I have been here."

Then she wondered vaguely why Stephen Strong smiled softly to himself.

By the end of dinner, Gritzko's eyes were blazing, and he suggested every sort of astonishing way to spend the night. But Princess Ardácheff, as the doyenne of the party, prudently put her foot down, and insisted upon bed. For had they not a whole morning of sight-seeing still to do on the morrow, and then their thirty versts in troikas to arrive at Milasláv. So the ladies all trouped off to rest.

"Leave your door open into my room, Tamara dear, if you do not mind," her godmother said. "I am always nervous in hotels—"

"I trust everything is going quietly," she added to herself, "but one never can tell."

Next day the whole sky was leaden with unfallen snow. Nothing more strange and gloomy and barbaric than Moscow looked could have been imagined, Tamara thought. It brought out the gilt domes and the unusual colors of things in a lurid way.

Their first visit was to the Church of the Assumption, where the emperors are crowned. Its great beauty and rich colors pleased the eye. The totally different arrangement of things from any other sort of church—the shape and the absence of chairs or seats—the hidden altar behind the doors of the sanctuary—the numerous pictures and frescoed walls—all gave it a mysterious, wonderful charm, and here again the two English were struck by the people's simple faith.

"We would catch every sort of disease kissing those Ikons after filthy ulcerated beggars," Stephen Strong said to Tamara. "But the belief that only good can come to them brings only good. The study of these people makes one less materialistic and full of common sense. One puts more credence in things occult."

A service was just beginning, it was some high saint's day, and the beautiful singing, the boys' angel voices and the deep bass of the priests, unaccompanied by any instruments or organ, impressed Tamara far more in this old temple than the services had done in any of the St. Petersburg churches.

A peace fell on her soul, and just as the gipsies' music had been of the devil, so this seemed to come from heaven itself. She felt calmed and happier when they came out.

After an early lunch they saw from the hotel windows three troikas drawn up. Two of them Gritzko's, and one belonging to Prince Solentzeff Zasiekin, who had also a country place in the neighbourhood.

The two, which had come a day or so before from Milasláv, were indeed wonderful turn-outs. The Prince prided himself upon his horses, which were renowned throughout Europe.

The graceful shaped sleighs, with the drivers in their quaint liveries standing up to drive, always unconsciously suggest that their origin must have been some chariot from Rome.

Gritzko's colors were a rich greenish-blue, while the reins and velvet caps and belts of the drivers were a dull cerise; the caps were braided with silver, while they and the coats and the blue velvet rugs were lined and bordered with sable. One set of horses was coal black, and the others a dark gray. Everything seemed in keeping with the buildings, and the semi-Byzantine scene with its Oriental note of picturesque grace.

"Which will you choose to go in, Madame?" Gritzko asked. "Shall you be drawn by the blacks or the grays?"

"I would prefer the blacks," Tamara replied. "I always love black horses, and these are such beautiful ones." And so it was arranged.

"If you will come with Stephen and me, Tantino," the Prince said, "we shall be the lighter load and get there first. Madame Loraine and Olga can go with Serge and Lord Courtray, they will take the blacks; that leaves Valonne for Sonia and her husband. Will this please everyone?"

Apparently it did, for thus they started. It was an enchanting drive over the snow. They seemed to fly along, once they had left the town, and the weird bleak country, unmarked by any boundaries, impressed both Tamara and Jack. And while Tamara was speculating upon its mystical side, Lord Courtray was gauging its possibilities for sport.

They at last skirted a dark forest, which seemed to stretch for miles, and then after nearly three hours' drive arrived at the entrance to Milasláv.

They went through a wild, rough sort of park, and then came in view of the house—a great place with tall Ionic pillars supporting the front, and wings on each side—while beyond, stretching in an irregular mass, was a wooden structure of a much earlier date.

It all appeared delightfully incongruous and a trifle makeshift to Tamara and Jack when they got out of their sleigh and were welcomed by their host.

A bare hall, at one side showing discolored marks of mould on the wall, decorated in what was the Russian Empire style, a beautiful conception retaining the classic lines of the French and yet with an added richness of its own. Then on up to a first floor above a low *rez de chaussée* by wide stairs. These connecting portions of the house seemed unfurnished and barren,—walls of stone or plaster with here and there a dilapidated decoration. It almost would appear as if they were meant to be shut off from the living rooms, like the hall of a block of flats. The whole thing struck a strange note. There were quantities of servants in their quaint liveries about, and when finally they arrived in a great saloon it was bright and warm, though there was no open fireplace, only the huge porcelain stove.

Here the really beautiful, though rather florid Alexander I. style struggled from the walls with an appalling set of furniture of the period of Alexander II. But the whole thing had an odd unfinished look, and a fine portrait of the Prince's grandfather in one panel was entirely riddled with shot!

Some splendid skins of bears and wolves were on the floor, and there was a general air of the room being lived in—though magnificence and dilapidation mingled everywhere. The very rich brocade on one of the sofas had the traces of great rents. And while one table held cigarette cases and cigar boxes in the most exquisitely fine enamel set with jewels, on another would be things of the roughest wood. And a cabinet at the side filled with a priceless collection of snuff boxes and *bon-bonnières* of Catherine's time had the glass of one door cracked into a star of splinters.

Tamara had a sudden sensation of being a million miles away from England and her family: it all came as a breath of some other life. She felt strangely nervous, she had not the least notion why. There was a reckless look about things which caused a weird thrill.

"If it were only arranged, what capabilities it all has," she thought; "but as it is, it seems to speak of Gritzko and fierce strife."

Tea and the usual quantities of *bonnes bouches* and vodka waited them and a bowl of hot punch.

And all three English people, Stephen Strong, Tamara and Jack, admired their host's gracious welcome, and his courtly manners. Not a trace of the wild Gritzko seemed left.

Tamara wondered secretly what their sleeping accommodation would be like.

"Tantine, you must act hostess for me. Will you show these ladies their rooms," the Prince said. "Dinner is at eight o'clock, but you have lots of time before for a little bridge if you want."

He took them through the usual amount of reception-rooms—a billiard-room and library, and small boudoir—and then they came out on another staircase which led to the floor above. Here he left them and returned to the men.

"This was done up by the late Princess, Tamara," her godmother said. "Even twenty years ago the taste was perfectly awful, as you can see. The whole house could be made beautiful if only there was someone who cared—though I expect we shall be comfortable enough."

The top passage proved to be wide, but only distempered in two colors, like the walls of a station waiting-room. Not the slightest attempt to beautify or furnish with carved chairs, and cabinets of china, and portraits and tapestry on the walls, as in an English house. In the passage all was as plain as a barrack.

Tamara's room and the Princess' joined. They were both gorgeously upholstered in crude blue satin brocade, and full of gilt heavy furniture, but in each there was a modern brass bed.

They were immense apartments, and warm and bright, monuments of the taste of 1878.

"Is it not incredible, Marraine, that with the beautiful models of the eighteenth century in front of them, people could have perpetrated this? Waves of awful taste seem to come, and artists lose their sense of beauty and produce the grotesque."

"This is a paradise compared to some," the Princess laughed. "You should see my sister-in-law's place!"

One bridge table was made up already when they got back to the saloon, and Sonia, Serge Grekoff and Valonne, only waited the Princess' advent to begin their game.

It seemed to be an understood thing that Gritzko and his English guest should be left out, and so practically alone.

"I feel it is my duty to learn to play better," Tamara said, "so I am going to watch."

He put down his hand and seized her wrist. "You shall certainly not," he said. "You cannot be so rude as deliberately to controvert your host. It is my pleasure that you shall sit here and talk."

His eyes were flashing, and Tamara's spirit rose.

"What a savage you are, Prince," she laughed. "Everything must be only as you wish! That I want to watch the bridge does not enter into your consideration."

"Not a bit."

"Well, then, since I must stay here I shall be disagreeable and not say a word."

And she sat down primly and folded her hands.

He lit a cigarette, and she noticed his hand trembled a little, but his voice was quite steady, and in fact low as he said:

"I tell you frankly, if you go on treating me as you have done today, whatever happens is on your head."

"Do you mean to strangle me then?—or have me torn up by dogs?" and Tamara smiled provokingly. With all the others in the room, and almost within earshot, she felt perfectly safe.

She had suffered so much, it seemed good to oppose him a little, when it could not entail a duel with some unoffending man!

"I do not know yet what I shall be impelled to do, only I warn you, if you tease me, you will pay the price." And he puffed a cloud of smoke.

"He can do nothing tonight," Tamara thought, "and tomorrow we are going back to Moscow, and then I am returning home." A spirit of devilment was in her. Nearly always it had been he who regulated things, and now it was her turn. She had been so very unhappy, and had only the outlook of dullness and regret. Tonight she would retaliate, she would do as she felt inclined.

So she leaned back in her chair and smiled, making a tantalizing moue at him, while she said, mockingly:

"Aren't you a barbarian, Prince! Only the days of Ivan the Terrible are over, thank goodness!"

He took a chair and sat down quietly, but the tone of his voice should have warned her as he said:

"You are counting upon the unknown."

She peeped at him now through half-closed alluring lids, and she noticed he was very pale.

In her quiet, well-ordered life she had never come in contact with real passion. She had not the faintest idea of the vast depths she was stirring. All she knew was she loved him very much, and the whole thing galled her pride horribly. It seemed a satisfaction, a salve to her wounded vanity, to be able to make him feel, to punish him a little for all her pain.

"Think! This time next week. I shall be safe in peaceful England, where we have not to combat the unknown."

"No?"

"No. Marraine and I have settled everything. I take the Wednesday's Nord Express after we get back to Petersburg."

"And tomorrow is Friday, and there are yet five days. Well, we must contrive to show you some more scenes of our uncivilized country, and perhaps after all you won't go."

Tamara laughed with gay scorn. She put out her little foot and tapped the edge of the great stove.

"For once I shall do as I please, Prince. I shall not ask your leave!"

His eyes seemed to gleam, and he lay perfectly still in his chair like some panther watching its prey. Tamara's blood was up. She would not be dominated! She continued mocking and defying him until she drove him gradually mad.

But on one thing she had counted rightly, he could do nothing with them all in the room.

First one and then another left their game, and joined them for a few minutes, and then went back.

And so in this fashion the late afternoon passed and they went up to dress.

No one was down in the great saloon when Tamara and the Princess descended for dinner, but as they entered, Stephen Strong and Valonne came in from the opposite door and joined them near the stove, and Tamara and Valonne talked, while the other two wandered to a distant couch.

"Have you ever been to any of these wonderful parties one hears have taken place, Count Valonne?" she asked.

Valonne smiled his enigmatic smile. "Yes," he said. "I have once or twice—perhaps you think this room shows traces of some rather violent amusements, and really on looking round, I believe it does!"

Tamara shivered slightly. She had the feeling known as a goose walking over her grave.

"It is as if wild animals played here—hardly human beings," she said. "Look at that cabinet, and the sofa, and—and—that picture! One cannot help reflecting upon what caused those holes. One's imagination can conjure up extraordinary things."

"Not more extraordinary than the probable facts," and Valonne laughed as if at some astonishing recollection. "You have not yet seen our host's own rooms though, I expect?"

"Why?" asked Tamara. "But can they possibly be worse than this?"

"No, that is just it. He had them done up by one of your English firms, and they are beautifully comfortable and correct. His sitting-room is full of books, and a few good pictures, and leads into his bedroom and dressing-room; and as for the bathroom it is as perfect as any the best American plumber could invent!"

Valonne had spent years at Washington, and in England too, and spoke English almost as a native.

"He is the most remarkable contrast of wildness and civilization I have ever met."

"It always seems to me as though he were trying to crush something—to banish something in himself," said Tamara. "As though he did these wild things to forget."

"It is the limitless nature warring against an impossible bar. If he were an Englishman he would soar to be one of the greatest of your country, Madame," Valonne said. "You have not perhaps talked to him seriously; he is extraordinarily well read; and then on some point that we of the Occident have known as children, he will be completely ignorant, but he never bores one! Nothing he does makes one feel heavy like lead!"

Tamara looked so interested, Valonne went on.

"These servants down here absolutely idolize him; they have all been in the house since he or they were born. For them he can do no wrong. He has a gymnasium, and he keeps two or three of them to exercise him, and wrestle with him, and last year Basil, the second one, put his master's shoulder out of joint, and then tried to commit suicide with remorse. You can't, until you have been here a long time, understand their strange natures. So easily moved to passion, so fierce and barbaric, and yet so full of sentiment and fidelity. I firmly believe if he were to order them to set fire to us all in our beds tonight, they would do it without a word! He is their personal 'Little Father.' For them there is a trinity to worship and respect—the Emperor, God, and their Master."

Tamara felt extremely moved. A passionate wild regret swept over her. Oh! why might not fate let him love her really, so that they could be happy. How she would adore to soothe him, and be tender and gentle and obedient, and bring him peace!

But just at that moment, with an air of exasperating insouciant insolence, he came into the room and began chaffing with Valonne, and turning to her said something which set her wounded pride again all aflame, and burning with impotence and indignation she, as the strange guest, put her hand on his arm to go in to dinner.

Zacouska was partaken of, and then the serious repast began. Every one was in the highest spirits. Countess Olga and Lord Courtray looked as though they were getting on with giant strides. Jack had got to the whispering stage, which Tamara knew to be a serious one with him. The whole party became worked up to a point of extra gaiety. On her other hand sat Sonia's husband, Prince Solentzeff-Zasiekin. But Gritzko sparkled with brilliancy and seemed to lead the entire table.

There was something so extremely attractive about him in his character of host that Tamara felt she dared hardly look at him or she could not possibly keep up this cold reserve if she did!

So she turned and talked, and apparently listened, with scarcely a pause to her right-hand neighbor's endless dissertations upon Moscow, and while she answered interestedly, her thoughts grew more and more full of rebellion and unrest.

It was as if a needle had an independent will, and yet was being drawn by a magnet against itself. She had to use every bit of her force to keep her head turned to Prince Solentzeff-Zasiekin, and when Gritzko did address her, only to answer him in monosyllables, stiffly, but politely, as a stranger guest should.

By the end of dinner he was again wild with rage and exasperation.

When they got back to the great saloon, they found the end of it had been cleared and a semicircle of chairs arranged for them to sit in and watch some performance. It proved to be a troupe of Russian dancers and some Cossacks who made a remarkable display with swords, while musicians, in their national dress, accompanied the performance.

Tamara and Lord Courtray had seen this same sort of dancing in London when Russian troupes gave their "turns," but never executed with such wonderful fire and passion as this they witnessed now. The feats were quite extraordinary, and one or two of the women were attractive-looking creatures.

Gritzko's attitude toward them was that of the benevolent master to highly trained valued hounds. Indeed this feeling seemed to be mutual, the hounds adoring their master with blind devotion, as all his belongings did.

During most of the time he sat behind the Princess, and whispered whatever conversation he had in her ear; but every now and then he would move to Princess Sonia or Countess Olga, and lastly subsided close to Tamara, and bending over leaned on the back of her chair.

He did not speak, but his close proximity caused her to experience the exquisite physical thrill she feared and dreaded. When her heart beat like that, and her body tingled with sensation, it was almost impossible to keep her head.

His fierceness frightened her, but when he was gentle, she knew she melted at once, and only longed to be in his arms. So she drew herself up and shrank forward away from him, and began an excited conversation with Stephen Strong.

Gritzko got up abruptly and strode back to the Princess. And soon tables and supper were brought in, and there was a general move.

Tamara contrived to outwit him once more when he came up to speak. It was the only way, she felt. No half-measures would do now. She loved him too much to be able to unbend an inch with safety. Otherwise it would be all over with her, and she could not resist.

They had been standing alone for an instant, and he said, looking passionately into her eyes:

"Tamara, do you know you are driving me crazy—do you think it wise?"

"I really don't care whether my conduct is wise or not, Prince," she replied. "As I told you, tonight, and from now onward, I shall do as I please." And she gathered all her forces together to put an indifferent look on her face.

"So be it then," he said, and turned instantly away, and for the rest of the time never addressed her again.

The long drive in the cold had made every one sleepy, and contrary to their usual custom, they were all ready for bed soon after one o'clock, and to their great surprise Gritzko made no protest, but let the ladies quietly go.

Tamara's last thoughts before she closed her weary eyes were, what a failure it all had been! She had succeeded in nothing. She loved him madly, and she was going back home. And if she had made him suffer, it was no consolation! She would much rather have been happy in his arms!

Meanwhile, Gritzko had summoned Ivan, his major domo, and the substance of his orders to that humble slave was this. That early on the morrow the stove was to be lit in the hut by the lake, where at the time when the woodcock came in quantities he sometimes spent the night waiting for the dawn.

"And see that there is fodder for the horses," he added. "And that Stépan drives my troika with the blacks, and let the brown team be ready, too, but neither of these to come round until the grays have gone. And in the hut put food—cold food—and some brandy and champagne."

The servant bowed in obedience and was preparing to leave the room.

"Oil the locks and put the key in my overcoat pocket," his master called again. And then he lit another cigarette and drawing back the heavy curtains looked out on the night.

It was inky black, the snow had not yet begun to fall.

All promised well.

CHAPTER XVII

Tamara had just begun to dress when her godmother came into her room next day.

"There is going to be a terrible snow storm, dear," she said. "I think we should get down fairly early and suggest to Gritzko that we start back to Moscow before lunch. It is no joke to be caught in this wild country. I will send you in Katia."

Tamara's maid had been left in Petersburg, and indeed her godmother's, an elderly Russian accustomed to these excursions, had been the only one brought.

"I won't be more than half an hour dressing," she said. "Don't go down without me, Marraine."

And the Princess promised and returned to her room.

"It has been a real success, our little outing, has it not?" she said, when later they were descending the stairs. "Gritzko has been so quiet and nice. I am so happy, dear child, that you can go away now without that uncomfortable feeling of quarreling. There was one moment when he got up from behind your chair last night I feared you had angered him about something, but afterward he was so gentle and charming when we talked I felt quite reassured."

"Yes, indeed," feebly responded Tamara. "The party has been positively tame!"

They found their host had gone with Jack and the rest of the men to the stables to inspect his famous teams. But Princess Sonia and Countess Olga were already down. They were smoking lazily, and had almost suggested a double dummy of their favorite game.

They hailed the two with delight, and soon the four began a rubber, and Tamara, who hated it, had to keep the whole of her attention to try and avoid making some mistake.

Thus an hour past, and first Stephen Strong and then the other men came in.

Jack Courtray was enthusiastic about the horses, and indeed the whole thing. He and Gritzko had arranged to go on a bear-hunt the following week, and everything looked *couleur de rose*—except the sky, that continued covered with an inky pall.

The Princess beckoned to Gritzko and took him aside. She explained her fears about the storm, and the necessity of an earlier start, to which he agreed.

"I am going to ask you to let us take Katia with us, we have only the one maid, and must have her in Moscow when we arrive," she said.

So thus it was arranged. The Princess and Stephen Strong and Katia were to start first, and Sonia and her husband would take both Serge and Valonne, leaving Gritzko to bring Tamara, Olga and Lord Courtray last.

All through the early lunch, which was now brought in, nothing could have been more lamblike than their host. He exerted himself to be sweetly agreeable to every one, and the Princess, generally so alert, felt tranquil and content, while Tamara almost experienced a sense of regret.

Only Count Valonne, if he had been asked, would have suggested—but he was not officious and kept his ideas to himself.

The snow now began to fall, just a few thin flakes, but it made them hurry their departure.

In the general chatter and chaff no one noticed that Gritzko had never once spoken directly to Tamara, but she was conscious of it, and instead of its relieving her, she felt a sudden depression.

"You will be quite safe with Olga and your friend, dearest," the Princess whispered to her as she got into the first troika which came round. "And we shall be only just in front of you."

So they waved adieu.

Then Princess Sonia's party started. The cold was intense, and as the team of blacks had not yet appeared, the host suggested the two ladies should go back and wait in the saloon.

"Don't you think our way of herding in parties here is quite ridiculous," he said to Jack, when Olga and Tamara were gone. "After the rest get some way on, I'll have round the brown team too. It is going to be a frightful storm, and we shall go much better with only two in each sleigh."

Jack was entirely of his opinion, from his English point of view, a party of four made two of them superfluous. Countess Olga and himself were quite enough. So he expressed his hearty approval of this arrangement, and presently as they smoked on the steps, the three brown horses trotted up.

"I'll go and fetch Olga," Gritzko said, and as luck would have it he met her at the saloon door.

"I had forgotten my muff," she said, "and had just run up to fetch it."

Then he explained to her about the storm and the load, and since it was a question of duty to the poor horses, Countess Olga was delighted to let pleasure go with it hand in hand. And she allowed herself to be settled under the furs, with Jack, without going back to speak to Tamara. Indeed, Gritzko was so matter of fact she started without a qualm.

"We shall overtake you in ten minutes," he said. "The blacks are much the faster team." And they gaily waved as they disappeared beyond the bend of the trees. Then he spoke to his faithful Ivan. "In a quarter of an hour let the blacks come round." And there was again the gleam of a panther in his eyes as he glanced at the snow.

All this while Tamara, seated by the saloon stove, was almost growing uneasy at being left so long alone. What could Olga be doing to stay such a time?

Then the door opened, and the Prince came in.

"We must start now," he said, in a coldly polite tone. "The storm is coming, and four persons made too heavy a load; so Lord Courtray and Olga have gone on."

Tamara's heart gave a great bound, but his face expressed nothing, and her sudden fear calmed.

He was ceremoniously polite as he helped her in. Nor did he sit too near her or change his manner one atom as they went along. He hardly spoke; indeed they both had to crouch down in the furs to shelter from the blinding snow. And if Tamara had not been so preoccupied with keeping her woollen scarf tight over her head she would have noticed that when they left the park gate they turned to the right, in the full storm, not to the left, where it was clearer and which was the way they had come.

At last the Prince said something to the coachman in Russian, and the man shook his head—the going was terribly heavy. They seemed to be making tracks for themselves through untrodden snow.

"Stépan says we cannot possibly go much further, and we must shelter in the shooting hut," Gritzko announced, gravely; and again Tamara felt a twinge of fear.

"But what has become of the others?" she asked. "Why do we not see their tracks?"

"They are obliterated in five minutes. You do not understand the Russian storm," he said.

Tamara's heart now began to beat again rather wildly, but she reasoned with herself; she was no coward, and indeed why had she any cause for alarm? No one could be more aloof than her companion seemed. She was already numb with cold too, and her common sense told her shelter of any sort would be acceptable.

They had turned into the forest by now, and the road—if road it could be called—was rather more distinct.

It was a weird scene. The great giant pine trees, and the fine falling flakes penetrating through, the quickly vanishing daylight, and the mist rising from the steaming horses as they galloped along; while Stépan stood there urging them on like some northern pirate at a ship's prow.

At last the view showed the white frozen lake, and by it a rough log hut. They came upon it suddenly, so that Tamara could only realize it was not large and rather low, when they drew up at the porch.

At the time she was too frozen and miserable to notice that the Prince unlocked the door, but afterward she remembered she should have been struck by the strangeness of his having a key.

He helped her out, and she almost fell she was so stiff with cold, and then she found herself, after passing through a little passage, in a warm, large room. It had a stove at one end, and the walls, distempered green, had antlers hung round. There was one plain oak table and a bench behind it, a couple of wooden armchairs, a corner cupboard, and an immense couch with leather cushions, which evidently did for a bed, and on the floor were several wolf skins.

The Prince made no explanation as to why there was a fire, he just helped her off with her furs without a word; he hung them up on a peg and then divested himself of his own.

He wore the brown coat to-day, and was handsome as a god. Then, after he had examined the stove and looked from the window, he quietly left the room.

The contrast of the heat after the intense cold without made a tingling and singing in Tamara's ears. She was not sure, but thought she heard the key turn in the lock. She started to her feet from the chair where she sat and rushed to try the door, and this time her heart again gave a terrible bound, and she stood sick with apprehension.

The door was fastened from without.

For a few awful moments which seemed an eternity, she was conscious of nothing but an agonized terror. She could not reason or decide how to act. And then her fine courage came back, and she grew more calm.

She turned to the window, but that was double, and tightly shut and fastened up. There was no other exit, only this one door. Finding escape hopeless, she sat down and waited the turn of events. Perhaps he only meant to frighten her, perhaps there was some reason why the door must be barred; perhaps there were bears in this terribly lonely place.

She sat there reasoning with herself and controlling her nerves for moments which appeared like hours, and then she heard footsteps in the passage, breaking the awful silence, and the door opened, and Gritzko strode into the room.

He locked it after him, and pocketed the key; then he faced her. What she saw in his passionate eyes turned her lips gray with fear.

And now everything of that subtle thing in womankind which resists capture, came uppermost in Tamara's spirit. She loved him—but even so she would not be taken.

She stood holding on to the rough oak table like a deer at bay, her face deadly white, and her eyes wide and staring.

Then stealthily the Prince drew nearer, and with a spring seized her and clasped her in his arms.

"Now, now, you shall belong to me," he cried. "You are mine at last, and you shall pay for the hours of pain you have made me suffer!" and he rained mad kisses on her trembling lips.

A ghastly terror shook Tamara. This man whom she loved, to whom in happier circumstances she might have ceded all that he asked, now only filled her with frantic fear. But she would not give in, she would rather die than be conquered.

"Gritzko—oh, Gritzko! please—please don't!" she cried, almost suffocated.

But she knew as she looked at him that he was beyond all hearing.

His splendid eyes blazed with the passion of a wild beast. She knew if she resisted him he would kill her. Well, better death than this hideous disgrace.

He held her from him for a second, and then lifted her in his arms.

But with the strength of terrified madness she grasped his wounded arm, and in the second in which he made a sudden wince, she gave an eel-like twist and slipped from his grasp, and as she did so she seized the pistol in his belt and stood erect while she placed the muzzle to her own white forehead.

"Touch me again, and I will shoot!" she gasped, and sank down on the bench almost exhausted behind the rough wooden table.

He made a step forward, but she lifted the pistol again to her head and leant her arm on the board to steady herself. And thus they glared at one another, the hunter and the hunted.

"This is very clever of you, Madame," he said; "but do you think it will avail you anything? You can sit like that all night, if you wish, but before dawn I will take you."

Tamara did not answer.

Then he flung himself on the couch and lit a cigarette, and all that was savage and cruel in him flamed from his eyes.

"My God! what do you think it has been like since the beginning?" he said. "Your silly prudish fears and airs. And still I loved you—madly loved you. And since the night when I kissed your sweet lips you have made me go through hell—cold and provoking and disdainful, and last night when you defied me, then I determined you should belong to me by force; and now it is only a question of time. No power in heaven or earth can save you—Ah! if you had been different, how happy we might have been! But it is too late; the devil has won, and soon I will do what I please."

Tamara never stirred, and the strain of keeping the pistol to her head made her wrist ache.

For a long time there was silence, and the great heat caused a mist to swim before her eyes, and an overpowering drowsiness—Oh, heaven!—if unconsciousness should come upon her!

Then the daylight faded quite, and the Prince got up and lit a small oil lamp and set it on the shelf. He opened the stove and let the glow from the door flood through the room.

Then he sat down again.

A benumbing agony crept over Tamara; her brain grew confused in the hot, airless room. It seemed as if everything swam round her. All she saw clearly were Gritzko's eyes.

There was a deathly silence, but for an occasional moan of the wind in the pine trees. The drift of snow without showed white as it gradually blocked the window.

Were they buried here—under the snow? Ah! she must fight against this horrible lethargy.

It was a strange picture. The rough hut room with its skins and antlers; the fair, civilized woman, delicate and dainty in her soft silk blouse, sitting there with the grim Cossack pistol at her head—and opposite her, still as marble, the conquering savage man, handsome and splendid in his picturesque uniform; and just the dull glow of the stove and the one oil lamp, and outside the moaning wind and the snow.

Presently Tamara's elbow slipped and the pistol jerked forward. In a second the Prince had sprung into an alert position, but she straightened herself, and put it back in its place, and he relaxed the tension, and once more reclined on the couch.

And now there floated through Tamara's confused brain the thought that perhaps it would be better to shoot in any case—shoot and have done with it. But the instinct of her youth stopped her—suicide was a sin, and while she did not reason, the habit of this belief kept its hold upon her.

So an hour passed in silence, then the agonizing certainty came upon her that there must be an end. Her arm had grown numb.

Strange lights seemed to flash before her eyes—Yes,—surely—that was Gritzko coming toward her—!

She gave a gasping cry and tried to pull the trigger, but it was stiff, her fingers had gone to sleep and refused to obey her. The pistol dropped from her nerveless grasp.

So this was the end! He would win.

She gave one moan—and fell forward unconscious upon the table.

With a bound Gritzko leaped up, and seizing her in his arms carried her into the middle of the room. Then he paused a moment to exult in his triumph.

Her little head, with its soft brown hair from which the fur cap had fallen, lay helpless on his breast. The pathetic white face, with its childish curves and long eyelashes, resting on her cheek, made no movement. The faint, sweet scent of a great bunch of violets crushed in her belt came up to him.

And as he fiercely bent to kiss her white, unconscious lips, suddenly he drew back and all the savage exultation went out of him.

He gazed at her for a moment, and then carried her tenderly to the couch and laid her down. She never stirred. Was she dead? Oh, God!

In frightful anguish he put his ear to her heart; it did not seem to beat.

In wild fear he tore open her blouse and wrenched apart her fine underclothing, the better to listen. Yes, now through only the bare soft skin he heard a faint sound. Ah! saints in heaven! she was not dead.

Then he took off her boots and rubbed her cold little silk-stockinged feet, and her cold damp hands, and presently as he watched, it seemed as if some color came back to her cheeks, and at last she gave a sigh and moved her head without opening her eyes—and then he saw that she was not unconscious now, but sleeping.

Then the bounds of all his mad passion burst, and as he knelt beside the couch, great tears suffused his eyes and trickled down his cheeks.

"My Doushka! my love!" he whispered, brokenly. "Oh, God! and I would have hurt you!"

He rose quickly, and going to the window opened the ventilator at the top, picked up the pistol from the table and replaced it in his belt, and then he knelt once more beside Tamara, and with deepest reverence bent down and kissed her feet.

"Sleep, sleep, my sweet Princess," he said softly, and then crept stealthily from the room.

CHAPTER XVIII

The light was gray when Tamara awoke, though the lamp still burned—more than three parts of the window was darkened by snow—only a peep of daylight flickered in at the top.

Where was she! What had happened? Something ghastly—but what?

Then she perceived her torn blouse, and with a terrible pang remembrance came back to her.

She started up, and as she did so realized she was only in her stockinged feet.

For a moment she staggered a little and then fell back on the couch.

The awful certainty—or so it seemed to her—of what had occurred came upon her, Gritzko had won—she was utterly disgraced.

The whole training of her youth thundered at her. Of all sins, none had been thought so great as this which had happened to her.

She was an outcast. She was no better than poor Mary Gibson whom Aunt Clara had with harshness turned from her house.

She—a lady!—a proud English lady! She covered her face with her hands. What had her anguish of mind been before, when compared with this! She had suffered hurt to her pride the day after he had kissed her, but now that seemed as nothing balanced with such hideous disgrace.

She moaned and rocked herself to and fro. Wild thoughts came—where was the pistol? She would end her life.

She looked everywhere, but it was gone.

Presently she crouched down in a corner like a cowed dog, too utterly overcome with shame and despair to move.

And there she still was when Gritzko entered the room.

She looked up at him piteously, and with unconscious instinct tried to pull together her torn blouse.

In a flash he saw what she thought, and one of those strange shades in his character made him come to a resolve. Not until she should lie willingly in his arms—herself given by love—should he tell her her belief was false.

He advanced up the room with a grave quiet face. His expression was inscrutable. She could read nothing from his look. Her sick imagination told her he was thus serene because he had won, and she covered her face with her hands, while her cheeks flamed, and she sobbed.

Her weeping hurt him—he nearly relented—but as he came near she looked up.

No! Not in this mood would he win her! and his resolve held.

She did not make him any reproaches; she just sat there, a crumpled, pitiful figure in a corner on the floor.

"The snowstorm is over," he said in a restrained voice; "we can get on now. Some of my Moujiks got here this morning, and I have been able to send word to the Princess that she should not be alarmed."

Then, as Tamara did not move, he put out his hand and helped her up. She shuddered when he touched her, and her tears burst out afresh. Where was all her pride gone—it lay trampled in the dust.

"You are tired and hungry, Madame," he said, "and here is a looking-glass and a comb and brush," and he opened a door of the tall cupboard which filled the corner opposite the stove, and took the things out for her. "Perhaps you might like to arrange yourself while I bring you some food."

"How can I face the others,—with this blouse!" she exclaimed miserably, and then her cheeks crimsoned again, and she looked down.

He did not make any explanation of how it had got torn—the moment was a wonderful one between them.

Over Tamara crept some strange emotion, and he walked to the door quickly to prevent himself from clasping her in his arms, and kissing away her fears.

When she was alone the cunning of all Eve's daughters filled her. Above all things she must now use her ingenuity to efface these startling proofs. She darted to the cupboard and searched among the things there, and eventually found a rough housewife, and chose out a needle and coarse thread. It was better than nothing, so she hurriedly drew off the blouse, then she saw her torn underthings—and another convulsive pang went through her—but she set to work. She knew that however she might make even the blouse look to the casual eyes of her godmother, she could never deceive her maid. Then the thought came that fortunately Johnson was in Petersburg, and all these things could be left behind at Moscow. Yes, no one need ever know.

With feverish haste she cobbled up the holes, glancing nervously every few moments to the door in case Gritzko should come in. Then she put the garment on again—refastened her brooch and brushed and recoiled her hair. What she saw in the small looking-glass helped to restore her nerve. Except that her eyes were red, and she was very pale, she was tidy and properly clothed.

She sat down by the table and tried to think. These outside things could still look right, but nothing could restore her untarnished pride.

How could she ever take her blameless place in the world again.

Once more it hurt Gritzko terribly to see the woebegone, humbled, hopeless look on her face as he came in and put some food on the table. He cut up some tempting bits and put them on her plate, while he told her she must eat—and she obeyed mechanically. Then he poured out a tumbler of champagne and made her drink it down. It revived her, and she said she was ready to start. But as she stood he noticed that all her proud carriage of head was gone.

"My God! what should I feel like now?" he said to himself, "if it were really true!"

He wrapped her in her furs with cold politeness, his manner had resumed the stiffness of their yesterday's drive.

Suddenly she felt it was not possible there could be this frightful secret between them. It must surely be all a dreadful dream.

She began to speak, and he waited gravely for what she would say; but the words froze on her lips when she saw the pistol in his belt—that brought back the reality. She shuddered convulsively and clenched her hands. He put on his furs quietly and then opened the door.

He lifted her into the troika which was waiting outside. Stépan's face, as he stood holding the reins, was as stolid as though nothing unusual had occurred.

So they started.

"I told the messenger to tell Tantine that we were caught in the snow," he said, "and had to take shelter at the farm.—There is a farm a verst to the right after one passes the forest. It contains a comfortable farmer's wife and large family, and though you found it too confoundedly warm in their kitchen you passed a possible night.

"Very well," said Tamara with grim meekness.

Then there was silence.

Her thoughts became a little confused with the intense cold and the effect of the champagne, and once or twice she dozed off; and when he saw this he drew her close to him and let her sleep with her head against his arm, while he wrapped the furs round her so that she felt no cold. Then he kept watch over her tenderly, fondest love in his eyes. She would wake sometimes with a start and draw herself away, but soon fell off again, and in this fashion, neither speaking, the hours passed and they gradually drew near Moscow.

Then she woke completely with a shudder and sat up straight, and so they came to the hotel and found the Princess and the others anxiously waiting for them.

"What an unfortunate contretemps, Tamara, dear child," her godmother said, "that wicked storm! We only just arrived safely, and poor Olga and your friend fared no better than you! Imagine! they, too, had to take shelter in that second village in a most horrible hovel, which they shared with the cows. It has been too miserable for you all four I am afraid."

But Gritzko was obliged to turn quickly away to hide the irrepressible smile in his eyes—really, sometimes, fate seemed very kind.

So there was no scandal, only commiseration, and both Countess Olga and Tamara were petted and spoilt—while, if there was a roguish note in Valonne's sympathetic condolences, none of them appeared to notice it.

However, no petting seemed to revive Tamara.

"You have caught a thorough chill, I fear, dearest," the Princess said; and as they had missed their sleeping berths engaged for the night before, and were unable to get accommodation on the train again for the night, they were forced to remain in Moscow until the next day, so the Princess insisted upon her godchild going immediately to bed, while the rest of the party settled down to bridge.

"It is a jolly thing, a snowstorm!" Lord Courtray said to Gritzko. "Isn't it? 'Pon my soul I have never enjoyed the smell of cows and hay so much in my life!"

But upstairs in the stiff hotel bedroom Tamara sobbed herself to sleep.

CHAPTER XIX

The journey back to Petersburg passed in a numb, hopeless dream for Tamara. She did her best to be natural and gay, but her white face, pinched and drawn, caused her godmother to feel anxious about her.

Gritzko had bidden them goodbye at the train—he was going back to Milasláv to arrange for his and Jack's bear-hunt—and would not be in the capital for two more days. That would be the Tuesday, and Tamara was to leave on Wednesday evening by the Nord Express.

He had kissed her hand with respectful reverence as he said farewell, and the last she saw of him was standing there in his gray overcoat and high fur collar, a light in his eyes as they peered from beneath his Astrakhan cap.

The Princess sent for the doctor next day—they arrived late at night at the Ardácheff house.

"Your friend has got a chill, and seems to have had a severe shock," he said when he came from Tamara's room. "Make her rest in bed today, and then distract her with cheerful society."

And the Princess pondered as she sat in the blue salon alone. A shock—what had happened? Could fear of the storm have caused a shock? She felt very worried.

And poor Tamara lay limp in her bed; but every now and then she would clench her hands in anguish as some fresh aspect of things struck her. The most ghastly moment of all came when she remembered the eventual fate of Mary Gibson.

What if she also should have—

"No! Oh, no!" she unconsciously screamed aloud; and her godmother, coming into the room, was really alarmed.

From this moment onward the horror of this thought took root in her brain, and she knew no peace. But her will and her breeding came to her rescue. She would not lie there like an invalid; she would get up and dress and go down to tea. She would chaff with the others who would all swarm to see her. No one should pity or speculate about her. And she made Johnson garb her in her loveliest teagown, and then she went to the blue salon.

And amidst the laughter and fun they had talking of their adventure, no one but Stephen Strong remarked the feverish unrest in her eyes, or the bright, hectic flush in her cheeks.

When night came and she was alone again, her thoughts made a hell; she could not sleep; she paced her room. If Gritzko should not return on Tuesday. If she should never see him again. What—what would happen—if—she—too—like poor Mary Gibson—

Next day—the Tuesday—at about eleven o'clock, a servant in the Milaslávski livery arrived with a letter, a stiff-looking, large, sealed letter. She had never seen Gritzko's writing before and she looked at it critically as she tremblingly broke it open.

It was written from Milasláv the day they had left Moscow. It was short and to the point, and her eyes dilated as she read.

It began thus:

"To Madame Loraine,

"Madame,—I write to ask you graciously to accord me the honor of your hand. If you will grant me this favor I will endeavor to make you happy.

"I have the honor, Madame, to remain,

"Your humble and devoted serviteur,

"Gregoir Footnote 1: "Gritzko" is the diminutive of "Gregoir." Milaslávski."

And as once before in her life Tamara's knees gave way under her, and she sat down hurriedly on the bed—all power of thought had left her.

"The messenger waits, ma'am," her maid said, stolidly, from the door.

Then she pulled herself together and went to the writing-table. Her hand trembled, but she steadied it, and wrote her answer.

"To Prince Milaslávski,—

"Monsieur,—I have no choice. I consent

"Yours truly,

"Tamara Loraine."

And she folded it, and placing it in the envelope, she sealed it with her own little monogram seal, in tender blue wax, and handed it to her maid, who left the room.

Then she stared in front of her—her arms crossed on the table—but she could not have analyzed the emotions which were flooding her being.

Her godmother found her there still as an image when presently she came to ask after her health.

"Tamara! dearest child. You worry me dreadfully. Confide in me, little one. Tell me what has happened?" and she placed her kind arms around her goddaughter's shoulders and caressed and comforted her.

Tamara shivered, and then stood up. "I am going to marry Gritzko, Marraine," she said. "I have just sent him my answer."

And the Princess had too much tact to do more than embrace her, and express her joy, and give her her blessing. All as if the news contained no flaw, and had come in the most delightful manner.

Then she left her alone in her room.

Yes, this was the only thing to be done, and the sooner the ceremony should be over the better. Lent would come on in a few short weeks; that would be the excuse to hasten matters, and this idea was all Tamara was conscious of as she finished dressing.

At twelve o'clock, with formal ceremony, Prince Milaslávski sent to ask if the Princess Ardácheff could receive him—and soon after he was shown up into the first salon, where the hostess awaited him.

He was dressed in his blue and scarlet uniform, and was groomed with even extra care, she noticed, as he advanced with none of his habitual easy familiarity to greet her.

"I come to ask your consent to my marriage with your goddaughter, Tantine," he said, with grave courtesy, as he kissed her hand. "She has graciously promised to become my wife, and I have only to secure your consent to complete my felicity."

"Gritzko! my dear boy!" was all the Princess could murmur. "If—if—you are sure it is for the happiness of you both nothing of course could give me greater joy; but—"

"It will be for our happiness," he answered, letting the hinted doubt pass.

Then his ceremonious manner melted a little, and he again kissed his old friend's hand. "Dear Tantine, have no fears. I promise you it shall be for our happiness."

The Princess was deeply moved. She knew there must be something underneath all this, but she was accustomed to believe Gritzko blindly, and she felt that if he gave his word, things must be right. She would ask no questions.

"Will you go and fetch my fiancée like the darling you are," he said presently, "I want you to give her to me."

And the Princess, quite overcome with emotion, left the room.

It was not like a triumphant prospective Princess and bride that Tamara followed her godmother, when they returned together. She looked a slender drooping girl, in a clinging dove-colored gown, and she hardly raised her eyes from the carpet. Her trembling hand was cold as death when the Princess took it and placed it in Gritzko's, and as they stood receiving her blessing she kissed them both, and then hurriedly made her exit.

When they were alone Tamara remained limp and still, her eyes fixed on the ground. It was he who broke the silence—as he took her left hand, and touched it with his lips.

He drew from her finger her wedding ring and carelessly put it on a table—while he still held her hand—then he placed his gift in the wedding ring's place, a glittering thing of an immense diamond and ruby.

Tamara shivered. She looked down at her hand, it seemed as if all safe and solid things were slipping from her with the removal of that plain gold band. She made no remark as to the beauty of the token of her engagement, she did not thank him, she remained inert and nerveless.

"I thank you, Madame, for your consent," he said stiffly, "I will try to make you not regret it." He used no word of love, nor did he attempt any caresses, although if she had looked up she would have seen the passionate tenderness brimming in his eyes, which he could not conceal. But she did not raise her head, and it all seemed to her part of the same thing—he knew he had sinned against her, and was making the only reparation a gentleman could offer.

And even now with her hand in his, and the knowledge that soon she would be his Princess, there was no triumph or joy, only the sick sense of humiliation she felt. Passion, and its result—necessity—not love, had brought about this situation.

So she stood there in silence. It required the whole force of Gritzko's will to prevent him from folding her shrinking pitiful figure in his strong arms, and raining down kisses and love words upon her. But the stubborn twist in his nature retained its hold. No, that glorious moment should come with a blaze of sunlight when all was won, when he had made her love him in spite of everything.

Meanwhile nothing but reserved homage, and a settling of details.

"You will let the marriage take place before Lent, won't you?" he said, dropping her hand.

And Tamara answered dully.

"I will marry you as soon as you wish," and she turned and sat down.

He leant on the mantlepiece and looked at her. He understood perfectly the reason which made her consent to any date—and he smiled with some strange powerful emotion—and yet his eye had a whimsical gleam.

"You are afraid that something can happen—isn't it?" he said. "Well, I shall be most pleased when that day comes."

But poor Tamara could not bear this—the crystalizing of her fears! With a stifled cry, she buried her face in the cushions. He did not attempt to comfort her—though he could hardly control his longing to do so. Instead of which he said gravely, "I suppose you must communicate with your family? They will come here perhaps for the wedding? You have not to ask any one's consent by the laws of your country, have you?—being a widow."

Tamara with a shamed crimson face half raised her head.

"I am free to do as I choose," she said, and she looked down in crushed wretchedness. "Yes, I suppose they will come to the wedding."

"Lent is such an excellent excuse," he went on. "And all this society is accustomed to my doing as I please, so there will be no great wonder over the haste—only I am sorry if it inconveniences you—such hurried preparation."

"How long is it before Lent?" Tamara asked without interest.

"Just under a month—almost four weeks—shall the wedding take place in about a fortnight? Then we can go south to the sun to spend our honeymoon."

"Just as you will;" Tamara agreed in a deadly resigned voice. "I am always confused with the dates—the difference between the English and Russian—will you write down what it will be that I may send it to my father?"

He picked up a calendar which lay upon the table, and made the calculations, then he jotted it all down on a card and handed it to her.

She took it and never looking at him rose and made a step toward the door, and as she passed the table where he had put her wedding ring she surreptitiously secured it.

"I suppose you are staying for lunch?" she said in the same monotonous voice. "Can I go now?—do you want to say any more?"

"Tamara!" he exclaimed, with entreaty in his tone, and then with quick repression he bowed gravely and once more touched her hand with his lips—ere he held open the door for her.

"I will be here when you return—I will await your pleasure."

So she left the room quietly. And when she was gone he walked wildly up and down for a moment—then he bent and passionately kissed the cushion she had leant on.

Tamara would learn what his love meant—when the day should come.

CHAPTER XX

The lunch passed off with quiet reserve—there was no one present but Stephen Strong. Tamara endeavored to behave naturally and answered Gritzko whenever he spoke to her. He, too, played his part, but the tone of things did not impose upon Stephen Strong.

As they were leaving the diningroom, on the plea of finding something, Tamara went to her room, and Gritzko took his leave.

"I will fetch you for the French plays tonight, Tantine," he said, "and probably will come back to tea—tell Tamara," and so he left, and the two old friends were alone.

They stirred their coffee and then lit cigarettes—there was an awkward silence for a moment, and then the Princess said:

"Stephen, I count upon you to help us all over this. I do not, and will not, even guess what has happened, but of course something has. Only tell me, do you think he loves her? I cannot bear the idea of Tamara's being unhappy."

The old Englishman puffed rings of smoke.

"If she is prepared never to cross his will, but let him be absolute master of her body and soul, while he makes continuous love to her, I should think she will be the happiest woman in the world. She is madly infatuated with him. She has been ever since we came from Egypt—I saw the beginning on the boat—and I warned you, as you know, when I thought he was only fooling."

"In Egypt!—they had met before then!" the Princess exclaimed, surprised; "how like Gritzko to pretend he did not know her,—and be introduced all over again! They had already quarreled, I suppose, and that accounts for the cat and dog like tone there has always been between them."

"Probably," said Stephen Strong; "but now I think we can leave it to chance. You may be certain that to marry her is what he wishes most to do,—or he would not have asked her."

"Not even if—he thought he ought to?"

"No—dear friend. No! I believe I know Gritzko even better than you do. If there was a sense of obligation, and no desire in the case, he would simply shoot her and himself, rather than submit to a fate against his inclination. You may rest in peace about that. Whatever strain there is between them, it is not of that sort. I believe he adores her in his odd sort of way, just let them alone now and all will be well."

And greatly comforted the Princess was able to go out calling.

The news was received with every sort of emotion,—surprise, chagrin, joy, excitement, speculation, and there were even those among them who averred they had predicted this marriage all along.

"Fortunately we like her," Countess Olga said. "She is a good sort, and perhaps she will keep Gritzko quiet, and he may be faithful to her."

But this idea was laughed to scorn, until Valonne joined in with his understanding smile.

"I will make you a bet," he said; "in five years' time they will still be love-birds. She will be the only one among this party who won't have been divorced and have moved on to another husband."

"You horribly spiteful cat!" Princess Sonia laughed. "But I am sure we all hope they will be happy."

Meanwhile Jack Courtray had come in at once to see Tamara.

"Well, upon my word! fancy you marrying a foreigner, old girl!" he said; "but you have got just about the best chap I have ever met, and I believe you'll be jolly happy."

And Tamara bent down so that he should not see the tears which gathered in her eyes, while she answered softly, "Thank you very much, Jack; but no one is ever sure of being happy."

And even though Lord Courtray's perceptions were rather thick he wondered at her speech—it upset him.

"Look here, Tamara," he said, "don't you do it then if it is a chancy sort of thing. Don't go and tie yourself up if you aren't sure you love him."

Love him!—good God!—

Pent-up feeling overcame Tamara. She answered in a voice her old playmate had never dreamed she possessed—so concentrated and full of passion. In their English lives they were so accustomed to controlling every feeling into a level commonplace that if they had had time to think, both would have considered this outburst melodramatic.

"Jack," Tamara said, "you don't know what love is. I tell you I know now—I love Gritzko so that I would rather be unhappy with him than happy with any one else on earth. And if they ask you at home, say I would not care if he were a Greek, or a Turk, or an African nigger, I would follow him to perdition.—There!"—and she suddenly burst into tears and buried her face in her hands.

Yes, it was true. In spite of shame and disgrace, and fear, she loved him—passionately loved him.

Of course Jack, who was the kindest-hearted creature, at once put his arm around her and took out his handkerchief and wiped her eyes, while he said soothingly:

"I say, my child—there! there!—this will never do," and he continued to pet and try to comfort her, but all she could reply was to ask him to go, and to promise her not to say anything about her outburst of tears to any one.

And, horribly distressed, Jack did what she wished, running against Gritzko in the passage as he went out; but they had met before that day, so he did not stop, but, nodding in his friendly way, passed down the stairs.

Tamara sat where he had left her, the tears still trickling over her cheeks, while she stared into the fire. The vision she saw there of her future did not console her.

To be married to a man whom she knew she would daily grow to love more—every moment of her time conscious that the tie was one of sufferance, her pride and self respect in the dust—it was a miserable picture.

Gritzko came in so quietly through the anteroom that, lost in her troubled thoughts, she did not hear him until he was quite close. She gave a little startled exclamation and then looked at him defiantly—she was angry that he saw her tears.

His face went white and his voice grew hoarse with overmastering emotion.

"What has happened between you and your friend, Madame? Tell me the truth. No man should see you cry! Tell me everything, or I will kill him."

And he stood there his eyes blazing.

Then Tamara rose and drew herself to her full height, while a flash of her vanished pride returned to her mien, and with great haughtiness she answered in a cold voice:

"I beg you to understand one thing, Prince, I will not be insulted by suspicions and threats against my friends. Lord Courtray and I have been brought up as brother and sister. We spoke of my home, which I may never see again, and I told him what he was to say to them there when they asked about me. If I have cried I am ashamed of my tears, and when you speak and act as you have just done, it makes me ashamed of the feeling which caused them."

He took a step nearer, he admired her courage.

"What was the feeling which caused them? Tell me, I must know,—" he said; but as he spoke he chanced to notice she had replaced her wedding ring, it shone below his glittering ruby.

"That I will not bear!" he exclaimed, and with almost violence he seized her wrist and forcibly drew both rings from her finger, and then replaced his own.

"There shall be no token of another! No gold band there but mine, and until then, no jewel but this ruby!"

Then he dropped her hand and turning, threw the wedding ring with passion in the fire!

Tamara made a step forward in protest, and then she stood petrified while her eyes flashed with anger.

"Indeed, yes, I am ashamed I cried!" she said at last between her teeth.

He made some restless paces, he was very much moved.

"I must know—" he began. But at that moment the servants came in with the tea, and Tamara seized the opportunity while they were settling the tray to get nearer the door, and then fled from the room, leaving Gritzko extremely disturbed.

What could she mean? He knew in his calmer moments he had not the least cause to be jealous of Jack. What was the inference in her words? Two weeks seemed a long time to wait before he could have all clouds dispersed, all things explained—as she lay in his arms. And this thought—to hold her in his arms—drove him wild. He felt inclined to rush after her, to ask her to forgive him for his anger, to kiss and caress her, to tell her he loved her madly and was jealous of even the air she breathed until he should hear her say she loved him.

He went as far as to write a note.

"Madame," he began—He determined to keep to the severest formality or he knew he would never be able to play his part until the end.—"I regret my passion just now. The situation seemed peculiar as I came in. I understand there was nothing for me to have been angry about,—please forgive me. Rest now. I will come and fetch you at quarter to eight.

"Gritzko."

And as he went away he had it sent to her room.

And when Tamara read it the first gleam of comfort she had known since the night at the hut illumined her thoughts. If he should love her—after all!—But no, this could not be so; his behavior was not the behavior of love. But in spite of the abiding undercurrent of humiliation and shame, the situation was intensely exciting. She feverishly looked forward to the evening. Her tears seemed to have unlocked her heart—she was no longer numb. She was perfectly aware that no matter what he had done she wildly loved him. He had taken everything from her, dragged her down from her pedestal, but that last remnant of self-respect she would keep. He should not know of this crowning humiliation—that she still loved him. So her manner was like ice when he came into the room, and the chill of it communicated itself to him. They hardly spoke on the way to the Théâtre Michel, and when they entered the box she pretended great interest in the stage, while, between the acts, all their friends came in to give their congratulations.

Tamara asked to be excused from going on to supper and the ball which was taking place. And she kept close to her godmother while going out, and so contrived that she did not say a word alone with Gritzko. It was because he acquiesced fully in this line of conduct that she was able to carry it through, otherwise he would not have permitted it for a moment.

He realized from this night that the situation could only be made possible if he saw her rarely and before people—alone with her, human nature would be too strong. So with the most frigid courtesy and ceremony between them the days wore on, and toward the beginning of the following week Gritzko went off with Jack Courtray on the bear-hunt. He could stand no more.

But after he was gone Tamara loathed the moments. She was overwrought and overstrung. Harassed by the wailing and expostulations of her family for what they termed her "rash act," worried by dressmakers and dozens of letters to write, troubled always with the one dominating fear, at last she collapsed and for two days lay really ill in a darkened room.

Then Gritzko returned, and there were only five days before the wedding. He had sent her flowers each morning as a lover should, and he had loaded her with presents,—all of which she received in the same crushed spirit. With the fixed idea in her brain that he was only marrying her because as a gentleman he must, none of his gifts gave her any pleasure. And he, with immense control of passion had played his part, only his time of probation was illumined by the knowledge of coming joy. Whereas poor Tamara, as the time wore on, lost all hope, and grew daily paler and more fragile-looking.

Her father had a bad attack of the gout, and could not possibly move; but her brother Tom and her sister, Lady Newbridge, and Millicent Hardcastle were to arrive three days before the wedding.

CHAPTER XXI

The night of the bear-hunter's return there was to be a small dinner at the Ardácheff house. The Princess had arranged that there should be a party of six; so that while the four played bridge the fiancés might talk to one another. She was growing almost nervous, and indeed it had required all Stephen Strong's assurance that things eventually would come right to prevent her from being actually unhappy.

"Let 'em alone!" the old man said. "Take no notice! you won't regret it."

Tamara had only got up from her bed that afternoon and was very pale and feeble. She wore a white clinging dress and seemed a mere slip of a girl. The great string of beautiful pearls, Gritzko's latest gift, which had arrived that morning, was round her neck, and her sweet eyes glanced up sadly from the blue shadows which encircled them.

Gritzko was already there when the Princess and Tamara reached the first salon, and his eyes swam with passionate concern when he saw how Tamara had been suffering. He could not restrain the feeling in his voice as he exclaimed:

"You have been ill!—my sweet lady! Oh! Tantine, why did you not send for me? How could you let her suffer?"

And a sudden wave of happiness came over Tamara when he kissed her hand. She was so weak the least thing could have made her cry.

But her happiness was short-lived, for Gritzko—afraid yet of showing what was in his heart—seemed now colder than ever; though he was exulting within himself at the thought that the moment would come soon when all this pretence should end.

Tamara, knowing nothing of these things, felt a new sinking depression. In five days she would be his wife, and then when he had paid the honorable price—how would he treat her?—

He was looking wildly attractive tonight, his voice had a thousand tones in it when he addressed the others, he was merry and witty and gay—and almost made love to the Princess—only to his fiancée did he seem reserved.

The food appeared impossible to swallow. She almost felt at last as though she were going to faint. The hopeless anguish of the situation weighed upon her more than ever; for alas! she felt she loved him now beyond any pride, every barrier was broken down. She had no more anger or resentment for the night at the hut. All his many sins were forgiven.

Dinner was an impossible penance, and with a feverish excitement she waited for the time when they should be alone.

It seemed an eternity before coffee was finished and the four retired to their bridge. Then the two passed out of the room and on into the blue salon.

It was extremely difficult for both of them. The Prince could scarcely control his mad longing to caress her. Only that strange turn in his character held him. Also the knowledge that once he were to grant himself an inch he could never restrain the whole of his wild passion, and there were yet five days before she should be really his—.

Tamara looked a white, frozen shape as she almost fell into the sofa below the Falconet group. Cupid with his laughing eyes peeped down and mocked her. Gritzko did not sit beside her. He took a chair and leant on a table near.

"We had good sport," he said dryly. "Your friend can hit things. We got two bears."

"Jack must have been pleased," Tamara answered dully.

"And your family—they arrive on Monday, isn't it?" he asked. "Your brother and sister and the estimable Mrs. Hardcastle?" and he laughed as he always did at the mention of Millicent. "They will wonder, won't they, why you are marrying this savage! but they will not know."

"No!" said Tamara. "They must never know." Gritzko's face became whimsical, a disconcerting, mischievous provoking smile stole into his eyes.

"Do you know yourself?" he asked.

She looked up at him startled. It was her habit now never to meet his eyes. Indeed, the sense of humiliation under which she lived had changed all her fearless carriage of head.

"Why do you ask such questions? I might as well ask you why are you marrying me. We both know that we cannot help it," and there was a break in her voice which touched him profoundly.

"Answer for yourself please, I may have several other reasons," he said coldly, and got up and walked across the room picking up a bibelot here and there, and replacing it restlessly.

Tamara longed to ask him what these reasons were. She was stirred with a faint hope, but she had not the courage, the intensity of her feeling made her dumb.

"They—Tantine—or Sonia—have explained to you all the service, I suppose," he said at last. "It is different to yours in your country. It means much more—"

"And is more easily broken."

"That is so, but we shall not break ours, except by death," and he raised his head proudly. "From Wednesday onward the rest of your life belongs to me."

Tamara shivered. If she could only overcome this numbness which had returned—if she could only let her frozen heart speak; this was surely the moment, but she could not, she remained silent and white and lifeless.

He came over to the sofa.

"Tamara," he said, and his voice vibrated with suppressed passion. "Will you tell me the truth? Do you hate me,—or what do you feel for me?"

She thought he meant only to torture her further; she would not answer the question.

"Is it not enough that you have conquered me by force? Why should you care to know what my feelings are? As you say, after Wednesday I shall belong to you—You can strangle me at Milasláv if you wish. My body will be yours, but my soul you shall never soil or touch, you have no part or lot in that matter, Prince."

His eyes filled with pain.

"I will even have your soul," he said. Then, as though restraining further emotion, he went on coldly. "I have arranged that after the wedding we go to my house, and do not start for the South until Saturday. There are some things I wish to show you there. Will that be as you wish?"

"I have no wishes, it is as you please," Tamara answered monotonously.

He gave an impatient shrug, and walked up and down the room, his will kept its mastery, but it was a tremendous strain. Her words had stung him, her intense quiet and absence of emotion had produced a faint doubt. What if after all he should never be able to make her love him. For the first time in his life a hand of ice clutched his heart. He knew in those moments of agony that she meant the whole world to him.

He glanced at her slender graceful figure so listlessly leaning against the blue cushions, at her pale ethereal face, and then he turned abruptly away toward the door to the other salon.

"Come," he said, "it is of no avail to talk further, we will say goodnight." Tamara rose. The way to her room led from the opposite side.

"Goodnight then," she said, "make my adieu to Sonia and the rest. I shall go to bed," and she walked that way. The whole floor was between them, as she looked back. He stood rigid by the other door.

Then with great strides he was beside her, and had taken her in his arms.

"Ah! God!" he said, as he fiercely kissed her, and then almost flung her from him, and strode from the room.

And Tamara went on to her own, trembling with excitement.

This was passion truly, but what if some love lurked underneath?—and when she reached her great white bed she fell upon her knees, and burying her face in her hands she prayed to God.

* * * * *

Now of what use to write of the days that followed—the stiff restrained days—or of the arrival of Tom Underdown and his sister, and Millicent Hardcastle—or of the splendid Russian ceremonies in the church or the quieter ones at the Embassy. All that it concerns us to know is that Gritzko and Tamara were at last alone on this their wedding night. Alone with all their future before them. Both their faces had been grave and solemn through all the vows and prayers, but afterward his had shone with a wild triumph. And as they had driven to his house on the Fontonka he had held Tamara's hand but had not spoken.

It was a strange eventful moment when he led her up the great stairs between the rows of bowing servants—up into the salons all decorated with flowers. Then, still never speaking, he opened the ballroom doors, and when they had walked its great length and came to the rooms beyond, he merely said:

"These you must have done by that man in Paris—or how you please," as though the matter were aloof, and did not interest him. And then instead of turning into his own sitting-room, he opened a door on the right, which Tamara did not know, and they entered what had been his mother's bedroom. It was warmed and lit, but it wore that strange air of gloom and melancholy which untenanted rooms, consecrated to the memory of the dead, always have, in spite of blue satin and bright gilding.

"Tamara," he said, and he took her hand, "these were my mother's rooms. I loved her very much, and I always thought I would never let any woman—even my wife—enter them. I have left them just as she used them last. But now I know that is not what she would have wished."

His deep voice trembled a little with a note of feeling in it which was new, and which touched Tamara's innermost being.

"I want you to see them now with me, and then while we are in the South all these things shall be taken away, and they shall be left bare and white for you to arrange them when we come back, just as you would like. I want my mother's blessing to rest on us—which it will do—"

Then he paused, and there was a wonderful silence, and when he went on, his tones were full of a great tenderness.

"Little one, in these rooms, some day I will make you happy."

Tamara trembled so she could hardly stand, the reaction from her misery was so immense. She swayed a little and put out her hand to steady herself by the back of a chair. He thought she was going to fall, seeing her so white, and he put his arm round her as he led her through the room and into the sitting-room, and then beyond again to a little sanctuary. Here a lamp swung before the Ikon, and the colors were subdued and rich, while the virgin's soft eyes looked down upon them. There were fresh lilies, too, in a vase below, and their scent perfumed the air. He knelt for a second and whispered a prayer, then he rose, and they looked into each other's eyes—and their souls met—and all shadows rolled away.

"Tamara!" he said, and he held out his arms—and with a little inarticulate cry almost of pain Tamara fell into them—and he folded her to his heart—while he bent and kissed her hair.

Then he held her from him and looked deep into her eyes.

"Sweetheart—am I forgiven?" he asked, and when she could speak she answered:

"Yes—you are forgiven."

Then he questioned again.

"Tamara, do you love me?"

But he saw the answer in her sweet face, and did not wait for her to speak, but kissed her mouth.

Then he lifted her in his arms like a baby and carried her back through the ghostly rooms to his warm human sitting-room, and there he laid her tenderly down upon the couch and knelt beside her.

"Oh, my heart," he said. "What this time has been—since you promised to marry me!—but I would not change it—I wanted you to love me beyond everything—beyond anger with me, beyond—fear—beyond your pride. Now tell me you do. My sweet one. Moia Doushka. I must know. I *must* know. You mean my life—tell me?"

And passion overcame Tamara, and she answered him in a low voice of vibrating emotion.

"Gritzko! do you think I care for what you have done or will do! You know very well I have always loved you!" And she put up her mouth for him to kiss her. Then he went quite mad for a few moments with joy—he caressed her as even on the dawn-drive she had never dreamed, and presently he said with deep earnestness.

"Darling, we must live for one another—in the world of course for duty; but our real life shall be alone at Milasláv for only you and me. You must teach me to be calm and to banish impossible thoughts. You must make yourself my center—Tamara, you must forget all your former life, and give yourself to me, sweetheart. My country must be your country, my body your body, and my soul your soul. I love you better than heaven or earth—and you are mine now till death do us part."

Then the glory of paradise seemed to descend upon Tamara, as he bent and kissed her lips.

Oh! what did anything else matter in the world since after all he loved her! This beautiful fierce lover!

Visions of enchantment presented themselves—a complete intoxication of joy.

He held her in his arms, and all the strange passion and mystic depths which had fascinated her always, now dwelt in his eyes, only intensified by delirious love.

"Do you remember, Sweetheart, how you defied and resisted me? Darling! Heart of mine! but I have conquered you and taken you, in spite of all! You cannot struggle any more, you are my own. Only you must tell me that you give me, too, your soul. Ah! you said once I should have no part or lot in that matter. Tamara, tell me that I have it?"

And Tamara thrilled with ecstasy as she whispered, "Yes, you have it."

She cared not at all about pride—she did not wish to struggle, she adored being conquered. Her entire being was merged in his.

He held her from him for a second and the old whimsical smile full of tender mischief stole into his eyes.

"That night at the hut—when you dropped the pistol when—well, don't you want to know what really did happen?" he said.

She buried her face in his scarlet coat.

"Oh, no, no, no!" she cried. "It is all forgotten and forgiven."

Then with wild passion he clasped her to his breast.

"Oh! Love!" he said. "My sweet Princess; the gods are very kind to us, for all happiness is yet to come—! I did but kiss your little feet."

Red Hair

Branches Park,
November 3.

I wonder so much if it is amusing to be an adventuress, because that is evidently what I shall become now. I read in a book all about it; it is being nice looking and having nothing to live on, and getting a pleasant time out of life—and I intend to do that! I have certainly nothing to live on, for one cannot count £300 a year; and I am extremely pretty, and I know it quite well, and how to do my hair, and put on my hats, and those things—so, of course, I am an adventuress! I was not intended for this rôle—in fact, Mrs. Carruthers adopted me on purpose to leave me her fortune, as at that time she had quarrelled with her heir, who was bound to get the place. Then she was so inconsequent as not to make a proper will—thus it is that this creature gets everything, and I nothing!

I am twenty, and up to the week before last, when Mrs. Carruthers got ill and died in one day, I had had a fairly decent time at odd moments when she was in a good temper.

There is no use pretending even when people are dead, if one is writing down one's real thoughts. I detested Mrs. Carruthers most of the time. A person whom it was impossible to please. She had no idea of justice, or of anything but her own comfort, and what amount of pleasure other people could contribute to her day.

How she came to do anything for me at all was because she had been in love with papa, and when he married poor mamma—a person of no family—and then died, she offered to take me, and bring me up, just to spite mamma, she has often told me. As I was only four I had no say in the matter, and if mamma liked to give me up that was her affair. Mamma's father was a lord, and her mother I don't know who, and they had not worried to get married, so that is how it is poor mamma came to have no relations. After papa was dead, she married an Indian officer and went off to India, and died, too, and I never saw her any more—so there it is; there is not a soul in the world who matters to me, or I to them, so I can't help being an adventuress, and thinking only of myself, can I?

Mrs. Carruthers periodically quarrelled with all the neighbors, so beyond frigid calls now and then in a friendly interval, we never saw them much. Several old, worldly ladies used to come and stay, but I liked none of them, and I have no young friends. When it is getting dark, and I am up here alone, I often wonder what it would be like if I had—but I believe I am the kind of cat that would not have got on with them too nicely—so perhaps it is just as well. Only, to have had a pretty—aunt, say—to love one—that might have been nice.

Mrs. Carruthers had no feelings like this; "stuff and nonsense," "sentimental rubbish," she would have called them. To get a suitable husband is what she brought me up for, she said, and for the last years had arranged that I should marry her detested heir, Christopher Carruthers, as I should have the money and he the place.

He is a diplomat, and lives in Paris, and Russia, and amusing places like that, so he does not often come to England. I have never seen him. He is quite old—over thirty—and has hair turning gray.

Now he is master here, and I must leave—unless he proposes to marry me at our meeting this afternoon, which he probably won't do.

However, there can be no harm in my making myself look as attractive as possible under the circumstances. As I am to be an adventuress, I must do the best I can for myself. Nice feelings are for people who have money to live as they please. If I had ten thousand a year, or even five, I would snap my fingers at all men, and say, "No, I make my life as I choose, and shall cultivate knowledge and books, and indulge in beautiful ideas of honor and exalted sentiments, and perhaps one day succumb to a noble passion." (What grand words the thought, even, is making me write!) But as it is, if Mr. Carruthers asks me to marry him, as he has been told to do by his aunt, I shall certainly say yes, and so stay on here, and have a comfortable home. Until I have had this interview it is hardly worth while packing anything.

What a mercy black suits me! My skin is ridiculously white. I shall stick a bunch of violets in my frock—that could not look heartless, I suppose. But if he asks me if I am sad about Mrs. Carruthers's death, I shall not be able to tell a lie.

I am sad, of course, because death is a terrible thing, and to die like that, saying spiteful things to every one, must be horrid—but I can't, I can't regret her. Not a day ever passed that she did not sting some part of me; when I was little, it was not only with her tongue—she used to pinch me, and box my ears until Dr. Garrison said it might make me deaf, and then she stopped, because she said deaf people were a bore, and she could not put up with them.

I shall not go on looking back. There are numbers of things that even now make me raging to remember.

I have only been out for a year. Mrs. Carruthers got an attack of bronchitis when I was eighteen, just as we were going up to town for the season, and said she did not feel well enough for the fatigues, and off we went to Switzerland. And in the autumn we travelled all over the place, and in the winter she coughed and groaned, and the next season would not go up until the last court, so I have only had a month of London. The bronchitis got perfectly well—it was heart-failure that killed her, brought on by an attack of temper because Thomas broke the Carruthers vase. I shall not write of her death, or the finding of the will, or the surprise that I was left nothing but a thousand pounds and a diamond ring.

Now that I am an adventuress, instead of an heiress, of what good to chronicle all that! Sufficient to say if Mr. Carruthers does not obey his orders and offer me his hand this afternoon, I shall have to pack my trunks and depart by Saturday, but where to is yet in the lap of the gods.

He is coming by the 3.20 train, and will be in the house before four, an ugly, dull time; one can't offer him tea, and it will be altogether trying and exciting.

He is coming ostensibly to take over his place, I suppose, but in reality it is to look at me, and see if in any way he will be able to persuade himself to carry out his aunt's wishes. I wonder what it will be like to be married to some one you don't know and don't like? I am not greatly acquainted yet with the ways of men. We have not had any that you could call that here, much—only a lot of old wicked sort of things, in the autumn, to shoot the pheasants, and play bridge with Mrs. Carruthers. The marvel to me was how they ever killed anything, such antiques they were! Some politicians and ambassadors, and creatures of that sort; and mostly as wicked as could be. They used to come trotting down the passage to the school-room, and have tea with mademoiselle and me on the slightest provocation, and say such things! I am sure lots of what they said meant something else, mademoiselle used to giggle so. She was rather a good-looking one I had the last four years, but I hated her. There was never any one young and human who counted.

I did look forward to coming out in London, but being so late, every one was preoccupied when we got there, and no one got in love with me much. Indeed, we went out very little; a part of the time I had a swollen nose from a tennis-ball at Ranelagh, and people don't look at girls with swollen noses.

I wonder where I shall go and live! Perhaps in Paris—unless, of course, I marry Mr. Carruthers. I don't suppose it is dull being married. In London all the married ones seemed to have a lovely time, and had not to bother with their husbands much.

Mrs. Carruthers always assured me love was a thing of absolutely no consequence in marriage. You were bound to love some one some time, but the very fact of being chained to him would dispel the feeling. It was a thing to be looked upon like measles, or any other disease, and was better to get it over and then turn to the solid affairs of life. But how she expected me to get it over when she never arranged for me to see any one, I don't know.

I asked her one day what I should do if I got to like some one after I am married to Mr. Carruthers, and she laughed one of her horrid laughs, and said I should probably do as the rest of the world. And what do they do, I wonder? Well, I suppose I shall find out some day.

Of course there is the possibility that Christopher (do I like the name of Christopher, I wonder?)—well, that Christopher may not want to follow her will.

He has known about it for years, I suppose, just as I have, but I believe men are queer creatures, and he may take a dislike to me. I am not a type that would please every one. My hair is too red—brilliant, dark, fiery red, like a chestnut when it tumbles out of its shell, only burnished like metal. If I had the usual white eyelashes I should be downright ugly, but, thank goodness! by some freak of nature mine are black and thick, and stick out when you look at me sideways, and I often think when I catch sight of myself in the glass that I am really very pretty—all put together—but, as I said before, not a type to please every one.

A combination I am that Mrs. Carruthers assured me would cause anxieties. "With that mixture, Evangeline," she often said, "you would do well to settle yourself in life as soon as possible. Good girls don't have your coloring." So you see, as I am branded as bad from the beginning, it does not much matter what I do. My eyes are as green as pale emeralds, and long, and not going down at the corners with the Madonna expression of Cicely Parker, the vicar's daughter. I do not know yet what is being good, or being bad; perhaps I shall find out when I am an adventuress, or married to Mr. Carruthers.

All I know is that I want to *live*, and feel the blood rushing through my veins. I want to do as I please, and not have to be polite when I am burning with rage. I want to be late in the morning if I happen to fancy sleeping, and I want to sit up at night if I don't want to go to bed! So, as you can do what you like when you are married, I really hope Mr. Carruthers will take a fancy to me, and then all will be well! I shall stay up-stairs until I hear the carriage wheels, and leave Mr. Barton—the lawyer—to receive him. Then I shall saunter down nonchalantly while they are in the hall. It will be an effective entrance. My trailing black garments, and the great broad stairs—this is a splendid house—and if he has an eye in his head he must see my foot on each step! Even Mrs. Carruthers said I have the best foot she had ever seen. I am getting quite excited—I shall ring for Véronique and begin to dress!... I shall write more presently.

Thursday evening.

It is evening, and the fire is burning brightly in my sitting-room, where I am writing. *My* sitting-room!—did I say? Mr. Carruthers's sitting-room, I meant—for it is mine no longer, and on Saturday, the day after to-morrow, I shall have to bid good-bye to it forever.

For—yes, I may as well say it at once—the affair did not walk; Mr. Carruthers quietly, but firmly, refused to obey his aunt's will, and thus I am left an old maid!

I must go back to this afternoon to make it clear, and I must say my ears tingle as I think of it.

I rang for Véronique, and put on my new black afternoon frock, which had just been unpacked. I tucked in the violets in a careless way, saw that my hair was curling as vigorously as usual, and not too rebelliously for a demure appearance, and so, at exactly the right moment, began to descend the stairs.

There was Mr. Carruthers in the hall. A horribly nice-looking, tall man, with a clean-shaven face and features cut out of stone, a square chin, and a nasty twinkle in the corner of his eye. He has a very distinguished look, and that air of never having had to worry for his things to fit; they appear as if they had grown on him. He has a cold, reserved manner, and something commanding and arrogant in it that makes one want to contradict him at once; but his voice is charming—one of that cultivated, refined kind, which sounds as if he spoke a number of languages, and so does not slur his words. I believe this is diplomatic, for some of the old ambassador people had this sort of voice.

He was standing with his back to the fire, and the light of the big window with the sun getting low was full on his face, so I had a good look at him. I said in the beginning that there was no use pretending when one is writing one's own thoughts for one's own self to read when one is old, and keeping them in a locked-up journal, so I shall always tell the truth here—quite different things to what I should say if I were talking to some one and describing to them this scene. Then I should say I found him utterly unattractive, and, in fact, I hardly noticed him! As it was, I noticed him very much, and I have a tiresome inward conviction that he could be very attractive indeed, if he liked.

He looked up, and I came forward with my best demure air as Mr. Barton nervously introduced us, and we shook hands. I left him to speak first.

"Abominably cold day," he said, carelessly. That was English and promising!

"Yes, indeed," I said. "You have just arrived?"

And so we continued in this *banal* way, with Mr. Barton twirling his thumbs, and hoping, one could see, that we should soon come to the business of the day; interposing a remark here and there which added to the *gêne* of the situation.

At last Mr. Carruthers said to Mr. Barton that he would go round and see the house, and I said tea would be ready when they got back. And so they started.

My cheeks would burn, and my hands were so cold, it was awkward and annoying—not half the simple affair I had thought it would be up-stairs.

When it was quite dark and the lamps were brought, they came back to the hall, and Mr. Barton, saying he did not want any tea, left us to find papers in the library.

I gave Mr. Carruthers some tea, and asked the usual things about sugar and cream. His eye had almost a look of contempt as he glanced at me, and I felt an angry throb in my throat. When he had finished he got up and stood before the fire again. Then, deliberately, as a man who has determined to do his duty at any cost, he began to speak.

"You know the wish, or, rather, I should say, the command, my aunt left me," he said. "In fact, she states that she had always brought you up to the idea. It is rather a tiresome thing to discuss with a stranger, but perhaps we had better get it over as soon as possible, as that is what I came down here to-day for. The command was I should marry you." He paused a moment. I remained perfectly still, with my hands idly clasped in my lap, and made myself keep my eyes on his face.

He continued, finding I did not answer, just a faint tone of resentment creeping into his voice—because I would not help him out, I suppose. I should think not! I loved annoying him!

"It is a preposterous idea in these days for any one to dispose of people's destinies in this way, and I am sure you will agree with me that such a marriage would be impossible."

"Of course I agree," I replied, lying with a tone of careless sincerity. I had to control all my real feelings of either anger or pleasure for so long in Mrs. Carruthers's presence that I am now an adept.

"I am so glad you put it so plainly," I went on, sweetly. "I was wondering how I should write it to you, but now you are here it is quite easy for us to finish the matter at once. Whatever Mrs. Carruthers may have intended me to do, I had no intention of obeying her; but it would have been useless for me to say so to her, and so I waited until the time for speech should come. Won't you have some more tea?"

He looked at me very straightly, almost angrily, for an instant; presently, with a sigh of relief, he said, half laughing:

"Then we are agreed; we need say no more about it!"

"No more," I answered; and I smiled, too, although a rage of anger was clutching my throat. I do not know who I was angry with—Mrs. Carruthers for procuring this situation, Christopher for being insensible to my charms, or myself for ever having contemplated for a second the possibility of his doing otherwise. Why, when one thinks of it calmly, should he want to marry me, a penniless adventuress with green eyes and red hair that he had never seen before in his life? I hoped he thought I was a person of naturally high color, because my cheeks from the moment I began to dress had been burning and burning. It might have given him the idea the scene was causing me some emotion, and that he should never know!

He took some more tea, but he did not drink it, and by this I guessed that he also was not as calm as he looked!

"There is something else," he said—and now there was almost an awkwardness in his voice—"something else which I want to say, though perhaps Mr. Barton could say it for me, but which I would rather say straight to you, and that is, you must let me settle such a sum of money on you as you had every right to expect from my aunt, after the promises I understand she always made to you——"

This time I did not wait for him to finish. I bounded up from my seat, some uncontrollable sensation of wounded pride throbbing and thrilling through me.

"Money! Money from you!" I exclaimed. "Not if I were starving." Then I sat down again, ashamed of this vehemence. How would he interpret it! But it galled me so—and yet I had been ready an hour ago to have accepted him as my husband! Why, then, this revolt at the idea of receiving a fair substitute in gold? Really, one is a goose, and I had time to realize, even in this tumult of emotion, that there can be nothing so inconsistent as the feelings of a girl.

"You must not be foolish!" he said, coldly. "I intend to settle the money whether you will or no, so do not make any further trouble about it!"

There was something in his voice so commanding and arrogant, just as I noticed at first, that every obstinate quality in my nature rose to answer him.

"I do not know anything about the law in the matter; you may settle what you choose, but I shall never touch any of it," I said, as calmly as I could. "So it seems ridiculous to waste the money, does it not? You may not, perhaps, be aware I have enough of my own, and do not in any way require yours."

He became colder and more exasperated.

"As you please, then," he said, snappishly, and Mr. Barton fortunately entering at that moment, the conversation was cut short, and I left them.

They are not going back to London until to-morrow morning, and dinner has yet to be got through. Oh, I do feel in a temper! and I can never tell of the emotions that were throbbing through me as I came up the great stairs just now. A sudden awakening to the humiliation of the situation! How had I ever been able to contemplate marrying a man I did not know, just to secure myself a comfortable home! It seems preposterous now. I suppose it was because I have always been brought up to the idea, and, until I came face to face with the man, it did not strike me as odd. Fortunately he can never guess that I had been willing to accept him; my dissimulation has stood me in good stead. Now I am animated by only one idea—to appear as agreeable and charming to Mr. Carruthers as possible. The aim and object of my life shall be to make him regret his decision. When I hear him imploring me to marry him, I shall regain a little of my self-respect! And as for marriage, I shall have nothing to do with the horrid affair! Oh, dear, no! I shall go away free and be a happy adventuress. I have read the *Trois Mousquetaires* and *Vingt Ans Après*—mademoiselle had them—and I remember milady had only three days to get round her jailer, starting with his hating her; whereas Mr. Carruthers does not hate me, so that counts against my only having one evening. I shall do my best!

Thursday night.

I was down in the library, innocently reading a book, when Mr. Carruthers came in. He looked even better in evening dress, but he appeared ill-tempered, and no doubt found the situation unpleasant.

"Is not this a beautiful house?" I said, in a velvet voice, to break the awkward silence, and show him I did not share his unease. "You had not seen it before, for ages, had you?"

"Not since I was a boy," he answered, trying to be polite. "My aunt quarrelled with my father—she was the direct heiress of all this—and married her cousin, my father's younger brother—but you know the family history, of course——"

"Yes."

"They hated each other, she and my father."

"Mrs. Carruthers hated all her relations," I said, demurely.

"Myself among them?"

"Yes," I said, slowly, and bent forward so that the lamplight should fall upon my hair. "She said you were too much like herself in character for you ever to be friends."

"Is that a compliment?" he asked, and there was a twinkle in his eye.

"We must speak no ill of the dead," I said, evasively.

He looked slightly annoyed—as much as these diplomats ever let themselves look anything.

"You are right," he said. "Let her rest in peace."

There was silence for a moment.

"What are you going to do with your life now?" he asked, presently. It was a bald question.

"I shall become an adventuress," I answered, deliberately.

"A *what?*" he exclaimed, his black eyebrows contracting.

"An adventuress. Is not that what it is called? A person who sees life, and has to do the best she can for herself."

He laughed. "You strange little lady!" he said, his irritation with me melting. And when he laughs you can see how even his teeth are; but the two side ones are sharp and pointed, like a wolf's.

"Perhaps, after all, you had better have married me!"

"No, that would clip my wings," I said, frankly, looking at him straight in the face.

"Mr. Barton tells me you propose leaving here on Saturday. I beg you will not do so. Please consider it your home for so long as you wish—until you can make some arrangements for yourself. You look so very young to be going about the world alone!"

He bent down and gazed at me closer—there was an odd tone in his voice.

"I am twenty, and I have been often snubbed," I said, calmly. "That prepares one for a good deal. I shall enjoy doing what I please."

"And what are you going to please?"

"I shall go to Claridge's until I can look about me."

He moved uneasily.

"But have you no relations—no one who will take care of you?"

"I believe none. My mother was nobody particular, you know—a Miss Tonkins by name."

"But your father?" He sat down now on the sofa beside me; there was a puzzled, amused look in his face; perhaps I was amazing him.

"Papa? Oh, papa was the last of his family. They were decent people, but there are no more of them."

He pushed one of the cushions aside.

"It is an impossible position for a girl—completely alone. I cannot allow it. I feel responsible for you. After all, it would do very well if you married me. I am not particularly domestic by nature, and should be very little at home, so you could live here and have a certain position, and I would come back now and then and see you were getting on all right."

One could not say if he was mocking or no.

"It is too good of you," I said, without any irony. "But I like freedom, and when you were at home it might be such a bore——"

He leaned back and laughed merrily.

"You are candid, at any rate!" he said.

Mr. Barton came into the room at that moment, full of apologies at being late. Immediately after, with the usual ceremony, the butler entered and pompously announced, "Dinner is served, sir." How quickly they recognize the new master!

Mr. Carruthers gave me his arm, and we walked slowly down the picture-gallery to the banqueting-hall, and there sat down at the small, round table in the middle, that always looks like an island in a lake.

I talked nicely at dinner. I was dignified and grave, and quite frank. Mr. Carruthers was not bored. The chef had outdone himself, hoping to be kept on. I never felt so excited in my life.

I was apparently asleep under a big lamp, after dinner, in the library, a book of silly poetry in my lap, when the door opened and he—Mr. Carruthers—came in alone, and walked up the room. I did not open my eyes. He looked for just a minute—how accurate I am! Then he said, "You are very pretty when asleep!"

His voice was not caressing or complimentary—merely as if the fact had forced this utterance.

I allowed myself to wake without a start.

"Was the '47 port as good as you hoped?" I asked, sympathetically.

He sat down. I had arranged my chair so that there was none other in its immediate neighborhood. Thus he was some way off, and could realize my whole silhouette.

"The '47 port? Oh yes; but I am not going to talk of port. I want you to tell me a lot more about yourself, and your plans——"

"I have no plans—except to see the world."

He picked up a book and put it down again; he was not perfectly calm.

"I don't think I shall let you. I am more than ever convinced you ought to have some one to take care of you—you are not of the type that makes it altogether safe to roam about alone."

"Oh! as for my type," I said, languidly, "I know all about that. Mrs. Carruthers said no one with this combination of color could be good, so I am not going to try. It will be quite simple."

He rose quickly from his chair and stood in front of the great log fire, such a comical expression on his face.

"You are the quaintest child I have ever met," he said.

"I am not a child, and I mean to know everything I can."

He went over towards the sofa again and arranged the cushions—great, splendid, fat pillows of old Italian brocade, stiff with gold and silver.

"Come!" he pleaded. "Sit here beside me, and let us talk; you are miles away there, and I want to—make you see reason."

I rose at once and came slowly to where he pointed. I settled myself deliberately. There was one cushion of purple and silver right under the light, and there I rested my head.

"Now talk!" I said, and half closed my eyes.

Oh, I was enjoying myself! The first time I have ever been alone with a real man! They—the old ambassadors and politicians and generals—used always to tell me I should grow into an attractive woman—now I meant to try what I could do.

Mr. Carruthers remained silent, but he sat down beside me, and looked and looked right into my eyes.

"Now talk, then," I said again.

"Do you know, you are a very disturbing person," he said, at last, by way of a beginning.

"What is that?" I asked.

"It is a woman who confuses one's thoughts when one looks at her. I do not now seem to have anything to say, or too much——"

"You called me a child."

"I should have called you an enigma."

I assured him I was not the least complex, and that I only wanted everything simple, and to be left in peace, without having to get married or worry to obey people.

We had a nice talk.

"You won't leave here on Saturday," he said, presently, apropos of nothing. "I do not think I shall go myself to-morrow. I want you to show me all over the gardens, and your favorite haunts."

"To-morrow I shall be busy packing," I said, gravely, "and I do not think I want to show you the gardens; there are some corners I rather loved; I believe it will hurt a little to say good-bye."

Just then Mr. Barton came into the room, fussy and ill at ease. Mr. Carruthers's face hardened again, and I rose to say good-night.

As he opened the door for me—"Promise you will come down to give me my coffee in the morning," he said.

"Qui vivra verra," I answered, and sauntered out into the hall. He followed me, and watched as I went up the staircase.

"Good-night!" I called, softly, as I got to the top, and laughed a little—I don't know why.

He bounded up the stairs, three steps at a time, and before I could turn the handle of my door he stood beside me.

"I do not know what there is about you," he said, "but you drive me mad. I shall insist upon carrying out my aunt's wish, after all! I shall marry you, and never let you out of my sight—do you hear?"

Oh, such a strange sense of exaltation crept over me—it is with me still! Of course, he probably will not mean all that to-morrow, but to have made such a stiff block of stone rush up-stairs and say this much now is perfectly delightful!

I looked at him up from under my eyelashes. "No, you will not marry me," I said, calmly, "or do anything else I don't like; and now, really, good-night," and I slipped into my room and closed the door. I could hear he did not stir for some seconds. Then he went off down the stairs again, and I am alone with my thoughts!

My thoughts! I wonder what they mean! What did I do that had this effect upon him? I intended to do something, and I did it, but I am not quite sure what it was. However, that is of no consequence. Sufficient for me to know that my self-respect is restored and I can now go out and see the world with a clear conscience.

He has asked me to marry him—and *I* have said I won't!

BRANCHES PARK,
Thursday night, *November 3.*

DEAR BOB,—

A quaint thing has happened to me! Came down here to take over the place, and to say decidedly I would not marry Miss Travers, and I find her with red hair and a skin like milk, and a pair of green eyes that look at you from a forest of black eyelashes with a thousand unsaid challenges. I should not wonder if I commit some folly. One has read of women like this in the *cinque-cento* time in Italy, but up to now I had never met one. She is not in the room ten minutes before one feels a sense of unrest, and desire for one hardly knows what—principally to touch her, I fancy. Good Lord! what a skin! pure milk and rare roses—and the reddest Cupid's bow of a mouth! You had better come down at once (these things are probably in your line) to save me from some sheer idiocy. The situation is exceptional—she and I practically alone in the house, for old Barton does not count. She had nowhere to go, and as far as I can make out has not a friend in the world. I suppose I ought to leave. I will try to on Monday; but come down to-morrow by the 4.00 train.

Yours,
CHRISTOPHER.

P. S.—'47 port A1, and two or three brands of the old aunt's champagne exceptional, Barton says—we can sample them. Shall send this up by express; you will get it in time for the 4.00 train.

A letter from Mr. Carruthers which came into Evangeline's possession later, and which she put into her journal at this place.—EDITOR'S NOTE.

BRANCHES,
Friday night, *November 4th.*

This morning Mr. Carruthers had his coffee alone. Mr. Barton and I breakfasted quite early, before nine o'clock, and just as I was calling the dogs in the hall for a run, with my out-door things already on, Mr. Carruthers came down the great stairs with a frown on his face.

"Up so early!" he said. "Are you not going to pour out my tea for me, then?"

"I thought you said coffee! No, I am going out," and I went on down the corridor, the wolf-hounds following me.

"You are not a kind hostess!" he called after me.

"I am not a hostess at all," I answered back—"only a guest."

He followed me. "Then you are a very casual guest, not consulting the pleasure of your host."

I said nothing. I only looked at him over my shoulder as I went down the marble steps—looked at him and laughed, as on the night before.

He turned back into the house without a word, and I did not see him again until just before luncheon.

There is something unpleasant about saying good-bye to a place, and I found I had all sorts of sensations rising in my throat at various points in my walk. However, all that is ridiculous and must be forgotten. As I was coming round the corner of the terrace, a great gust of wind nearly blew me into Mr. Carruthers's arms. Odious weather we are having this autumn!

"Where have you been all the morning?" he said, when we had recovered ourselves a little. "I have searched for you all over the place."

"You do not know it all yet, or you would have found me," I said, pretending to walk on.

"No, you shall not go now!" he exclaimed, pacing beside me. "Why won't you be amiable, and make me feel at home?"

"I do apologize if I have been unamiable," I said, with great frankness. "Mrs. Carruthers always brought me up to have such good manners."

After that he talked to me for half an hour about the place.

He seemed to have forgotten his vehemence of the night before. He asked all sorts of questions, and showed a sentiment and a delicacy I should not have expected from his hard face. I was quite sorry when the gong sounded for luncheon and we went in.

I have no settled plan in my head. I seem to be drifting—tasting for the first time some power over another human being. It gave me delicious thrills to see his eagerness when contrasted with the dry refusal of my hand only the day before.

At lunch I addressed myself to Mr. Barton; he was too flattered at my attention, and continued to chatter garrulously.

The rain came on and poured and beat against the window-panes with a sudden, angry thud. No chance of further walks abroad. I escaped up-stairs while the butler was speaking to Mr. Carruthers, and began helping Véronique to pack. Chaos and desolation it all seemed in my cosey rooms.

While I was on my knees in front of a great wooden box, hopelessly trying to stow away books, a crisp tap came to the door, and without more ado my host—yes, he is that now—entered the room.

"Good Lord! what is all this?" he exclaimed. "What are you doing?"

"Packing," I said, not getting up.

He made an impatient gesture.

"Nonsense!" he said. "There is no need to pack. I tell you I will not let you go. I am going to marry you and keep you here always."

I sat down on the floor and began to laugh.

"You think so, do you?"

"Yes."

"You can't force me to marry you, you know—can you? I want to see the world. I don't want any tiresome man bothering after me. If I ever do marry, it will be because—oh, because—" and I stopped and began fiddling with the cover of a book.

"What?"

"Mrs. Carruthers said it was so foolish—but I believe I should prefer to marry some one I liked. Oh, I know you think that silly—" and I stopped him as he was about to speak—"but of course, as it does not last, anyway, it might be good for a little to begin like that—don't you think so?"

He looked round the room, and on through the wide-open double doors into my dainty bedroom, where Véronique was still packing.

"You are very cosey here; it is absurd of you to leave it," he said.

I got up off the floor and went to the window and back. I don't know why I felt moved—a sudden sense of the cosiness came over me. The world looked wet and bleak outside.

"Why do you say you want me to marry you, Mr. Carruthers?" I said. "You are joking, of course."

"I am not joking. I am perfectly serious. I am ready to carry out my aunt's wishes. It can be no new idea to you, and you must have worldly sense enough to realize it would be the best possible solution of your future. I can show you the world, you know."

He appeared to be extraordinarily good-looking as he stood there, his face to the dying light. Supposing I took him at his word, after all!

"But what has suddenly changed your ideas since yesterday? You told me you had come down to make it clear to me that you could not possibly obey her orders."

"That was yesterday," he said. "I had not really seen you—to-day I think differently."

"It is just because you are sorry for me; I suppose I seem so lonely," I whispered, demurely.

"It is perfectly impossible, what you propose to do—to go and live by yourself at a London hotel—the idea drives me mad."

"It will be delightful—no one to order me about from day to night!"

"Listen," he said, and he flung himself into an arm-chair. "You can marry me, and I will take you to Paris, or where you want, and I won't order you about—only I shall keep the other beasts of men from looking at you."

But I told him at once that I thought that would be very dull. "I have never had the chance of any one looking at me," I said, "and I want to feel what it is like. Mrs. Carruthers always assured me I was very pretty, you know, only she said that I was certain to come to a bad end, because of my type, unless I got married at once, and then if my head was screwed on it would not matter; but I don't agree with her."

He walked up and down the room impatiently.

"That is just it," he said. "I would rather be the first—I would rather you began by me. I am strong enough to ward off the rest."

"What does 'beginning by you' mean?" I asked, with great candor. "Old Lord Bentworth said I should begin with him, when he was here to shoot pheasants last autumn; he said it could not matter, he was so old; but I didn't——"

Mr. Carruthers bounded up from his chair.

"You didn't what! Good Lord! what did he want you to do?" he asked, aghast.

"Well," I said, and I looked down for a moment; I felt stupidly shy. "He wanted me to kiss him."

Mr. Carruthers looked almost relieved. It was strange.

"The old wretch! Nice company my aunt seems to have kept!" he exclaimed. "Could she not take better care of you than that—to let you be insulted by her guests?"

"I don't think Lord Bentworth meant to insult me. He only said he had never seen such a red, curly mouth as mine; and as I was bound to go to the devil some day with that, and such hair, I might begin by kissing him—he explained it all."

"And were you not very angry?" his voice wrathful.

"No, not very; I could not be, I was shaking so with laughter. If you could have seen the silly old thing, like a wizened monkey, with dyed hair and an eye-glass—it was too comic! I only told you because you said the sentence 'begin with you,' and I wanted to know if it was the same thing——"

Mr. Carruthers's eyes had such a strange expression—puzzle and amusement, and something else. He came over close to me.

"Because," I went on, "if so—I believe if that is always the beginning, I don't want any beginnings. I haven't the slightest desire to kiss any one. I should simply hate it."

Mr. Carruthers laughed. "Oh, you are only a baby child, after all!" he said.

This annoyed me. I got up with great dignity. "Tea will be ready in the white drawing-room," I said, stiffly, and walked towards my bedroom door.

He came after me.

"Send your maid away, and let us have it up here," he said. "I like this room."

But I was not to be appeased thus easily, and deliberately called Véronique and gave her fresh directions.

"Poor old Mr. Barton will be feeling so lonely," I said, as I went out into the passage. "I am going to see that he has a nice tea," and I looked back at Mr. Carruthers over my shoulder. Of course, he followed me, and we went together down the stairs.

In the hall a footman with a telegram met us. He tore it open impatiently. Then he looked quite annoyed.

"I hope you won't mind," he said, "but a friend of mine, Lord Robert Vavasour, is arriving this afternoon. He is a—er—great judge of pictures. I forgot I asked him to come down and look at them; it clean went out of my head."

I told him he was host, and why should I object to what guests he had.

"Besides, I am going myself to-morrow," I said, "if Véronique can get the packing done."

"Nonsense! How can I make you understand that I do not mean to let you go at all?"

I did not answer—only looked at him defiantly.

Mr. Barton was waiting patiently for us in the white drawing-room, and we had not been munching muffins for five minutes when the sound of wheels crunching the gravel of the great sweep—the windows of this room look out that way—interrupted our made conversation.

"This must be Bob arriving," Mr. Carruthers said, and went reluctantly into the hall to meet his guest.

They came back together presently, and he introduced Lord Robert to me.

I felt at once he was rather a pet. Such a shape! Just like the Apollo Belvedere! I do love that look, with a tiny waist and nice shoulders, and looking as if he were as lithe as a snake, and yet could break pokers in half like Mr. Rochester in *Jane Eyre*.

He has great, big, sleepy eyes of blue, and rather a plaintive expression, and a little fairish mustache turned up at the corners, and the nicest mouth one ever saw; and when you see him moving, and the back of his head, it makes you think all the time of a beautifully groomed thorough-bred horse. I don't know why. At once—in a minute—when we looked at each other, I felt I should like "Bob." He has none of Mr. Carruthers's cynical, hard expression, and I am sure he can't be nearly as old—not more than twenty-seven or so.

He seemed perfectly at home—sat down and had tea, and talked in the most casual, friendly way. Mr. Carruthers appeared to freeze up, Mr. Barton got more *banal*, and the whole thing entertained me immensely.

I often used to long for adventures in the old days with Mrs. Carruthers, and here I am really having them!

Such a situation! I am sure people would think it most improper! I alone in the house with these three men! I felt I really would have to go—but where?

Meanwhile I have every intention of amusing myself.

Lord Robert and I seemed to have a hundred things to say to each other. I do like his voice—and he is so perfectly *sans gêne* it makes no difficulties. By the end of tea we were as old friends. Mr. Carruthers got more and more polite and stiff, and finally jumped up and hurried his guest off to the smoking-room.

I put on such a duck of a frock for dinner—one of the sweetest, chastened simplicity, in black, showing peeps of skin through the thin part at the top. Nothing could be more demure or becoming, and my hair would not behave, and stuck out in rebellious waves and curls everywhere.

I thought it would be advisable not to be in too good time, so sauntered down after I knew dinner was announced.

They were both standing on the hearth-rug. I always forget to count Mr. Barton; he was in some chair, I suppose, but I did not notice him.

Mr. Carruthers is the taller—about one inch. He must be a good deal over six feet, because the other one is very tall, too; but now that one saw them together, Mr. Carruthers's figure appeared stiff and set besides Lord Robert's, and he hasn't got nearly such a little waist. But they really are lovely creatures, both of them, and I don't yet know which I like best.

We had such an engaging time at dinner! I was as provoking as I could be in the time, sympathetically, absorbingly interested in Mr. Barton's long stories, and only looking at the other two now and then from under my eyelashes; while I talked in the best demure fashion that I am sure even Lady Katherine Montgomerie—a neighbor of ours—would have approved of.

They should not be able to say I could not chaperone myself in any situation.

"Dam good port this, Christopher," Lord Robert said, when the '47 was handed round. "Is this what you asked me down to sample?"

"I thought it was to give your opinion about the pictures?" I exclaimed, surprised. "Mr. Carruthers said you were a great judge."

They looked at each other.

"Oh—ah—yes," said Lord Robert, lying transparently. "Pictures are awfully interesting. Will you show me them after dinner?"

"The light is too dim for a connoisseur to investigate them properly," I said.

"I shall have it all lit by electricity as soon as possible; I wrote about it to-day," Mr. Carruthers announced, sententiously. "But I will show you the pictures myself, to-morrow, Bob."

This at once decided me to take Lord Robert round to-night, and I told him so in a velvet voice while Mr. Barton was engaging Christopher's attention.

They stayed such a long time in the dining-room after I left that I was on my way to bed when they came out into the hall, and could with difficulty be persuaded to remain—for a few moments.

"I am too awfully sorry," Lord Robert said. "I could not get away. I do not know what possessed Christopher; he would sample ports, and talked the hind-leg off a donkey, till at last I said to him straight out I wanted to come to you. So here I am. Now you won't go to bed, will you?—please, please."

He has such pleading blue eyes, imploring pathetically, like a baby in distress, it is quite impossible to resist him—and we started down the gallery.

Of course, he did not know the difference between a Canaletto and a Turner, and hardly made a pretence of being interested; in fact, when we got to the end where the early Italians hang, and I was explaining the wonderful texture of a Madonna, he said:

"They all look sea-sick and out of shape. Don't you think we might sit in that comfy window-seat and talk of something else?" Then he told me he loved pictures, but not this sort.

"I like people to look human, you know, even on canvas," he said. "All these ladies appear as if they were getting enteric, like people used in Africa; and I don't like their halos and things; and all the men are old and bald. But you must not think me a Goth. You will teach me their points, won't you?—and then I shall love them."

I said I did not care a great deal for them myself, except the color.

"Oh, I am so glad!" he said. "I should like to find we admired the same things; but no picture could interest me as much as your hair. It is the loveliest thing I have ever seen, and you do it so beautifully."

That did please me. He has the most engaging ways—Lord Robert—and he is very well informed, not stupid a bit, or thick, only absolutely simple and direct. We talked softly together, quite happy for a while.

Then Mr. Carruthers got rid of Mr. Barton and came towards us. I settled myself more comfortably on the velvet cushions. Purple velvet cushions and curtains in this gallery, good old relics of early Victorian taste. Lots of the house is awful, but these curtains always please me.

Mr. Carruthers's face was as stern as a stone bust of Augustus Cæsar. I am sure the monks in the Inquisition looked like that. I do wonder what he was going to say, but Lord Robert did not give him time.

"Do go away, Christopher," he said. "Miss Travers is going to teach me things about Italian Madonnas, and I can't keep my attention if there is a third person about."

I suppose if Mr. Carruthers had not been a diplomat he would have sworn, but I believe that kind of education makes you able to put your face how you like, so he smiled sweetly and took a chair near.

"I shall not leave you, Bob," he said. "I do not consider you are a good companion for Miss Evangeline. I am responsible for her, and I am going to take care of her."

"Then you should not have asked him here if he is not a respectable person," I said, innocently. "But Italian Madonnas ought to chasten and elevate his thoughts. Anyway, your responsibility towards me is self-constituted. I am the only person whom I mean to obey," and I settled myself deliberately in the velvet pillows.

"Not a good companion!" exclaimed Lord Robert. "What dam cheek, Christopher! I have not my equal in the whole Household Cavalry, as you know."

They both laughed, and we continued to talk in a sparring way—Mr. Carruthers sharp and subtle, and fine as a sword-blade; Lord Robert downright and simple, with an air of a puzzled baby.

When I thought they were both wanting me very much to stay, I got up and said good-night.

They both came down the gallery with me, and insisted upon each lighting a candle from the row of burnished silver candlesticks in the hall, which they presented to me with great mock-homage. It annoyed me—I don't know why—and I suddenly froze up and declined them both, while I said good-night again stiffly, and walked in my most stately manner up the stairs.

I could see Lord Robert's eyebrows puckered into a more plaintive expression than ever while he let the beautiful silver candlestick hang, dropping the grease onto the polished oak floor.

Mr. Carruthers stood quite still, and put his light back on the table. His face was cynical and rather amused. I can't say what irritation I felt, and immediately decided to leave on the morrow—but where to, fate or the devil could only know.

When I got to my room a lump came in my throat. Véronique had gone to bed, tired out with her day's packing.

I suddenly felt utterly alone—all the exaltation gone. For the moment I hated the two down-stairs. I felt the situation equivocal and untenable, and it had amused me so much an hour ago.

It is stupid and silly, and makes one's nose red, but I felt like crying a little before I got into bed.

BRANCHES,
Saturday afternoon, *November 5th.*

This morning I woke with a headache, to see the rain beating against my windows, and mist and fog—a fitting day for the 5th of November. I would not go down to breakfast. Véronique brought me mine to my sitting-room fire, and, with Spartan determination, I packed steadily all the morning.

About twelve a note came up from Lord Robert. I put it in.

DEAR MISS TRAVERS,—

Why are you hiding? Was I a bore last night? Do forgive me and come down. Has Christopher locked you in your room? I will murder the brute if he has!

Yours very sincerely,
ROBERT VAVASOUR.

"Can't; I am packing," I scribbled in pencil on the envelope, and gave it back to Charles, who was waiting in the hall for the answer. Two minutes after, Lord Robert walked into the room, the door of which the footman had left open.

"I have come to help you," he said, in that voice of his that sounds so sure of a welcome you can't snub him. "But where are you going?"

"I don't know," I said, a little forlornly, and then bent down and vigorously collected photographs.

"Oh, but you can't go to London by yourself!" he said, aghast. "Look here, I will come up with you, and take you to my aunt, Lady Merrenden. She is such a dear, and I am sure when I have told her all about you she will be delighted to take care of you for some days until you can hunt round."

He looked such a boy, and his face was so kind, I was touched.

"Oh no, Lord Robert! I cannot do that, but I thank you. I don't want to be under an obligation to any one," I said, firmly. "Mr. Carruthers suggests a way out of the difficulty—that I should marry him, and stay here. I don't think he means it, really, but he pretends he does."

He sat down on the edge of a table already laden with books, most of which overbalanced and fell crash on the floor.

"So Christopher wants you to marry him—the old fox?" he said, apparently oblivious of the wreck of literature he had caused. "But you won't do that, will you? And yet I have no business to say that. He is a dam good friend, Christopher."

"I am sure you ought not to swear so often, Lord Robert; it shocks me, brought up as I have been," I said, with the air of a little angel.

"Do I swear?" he asked, surprised. "Oh no, I don't think so—at least, there is no 'n' to the end of the 'dams,' so they are only an innocent ornament to conversation. But I won't do it, if you don't wish me to."

After that he helped me with the books, and was so merry and kind I soon felt cheered up, and by lunchtime all were finished and in the boxes ready to be tied up and taken away. Véronique, too, had made great progress in the adjoining room, and was standing stiff and *maussade* by my dressing-table when I came in. She spoke respectfully in French, and asked me if I had made my plans yet, for, as she explained to me, her own position seemed precarious, and yet, having been with me for five years, she did not feel she could leave me at a juncture like this. At the same time she hoped mademoiselle would make some suitable decision, as she feared, respectfully, it was "une si drôle de position pour une demoiselle du monde," alone with "ces messieurs."

I could not be angry; it was quite true what she said.

"I shall go up this evening to Claridge's, Véronique," I assured her—"by about the 5.15 train. We will wire to them after luncheon."

She seemed comforted, but she added—in the abstract—that a rich marriage was what was obviously mademoiselle's fate, and she felt sure great happiness and many jewels would await mademoiselle if mademoiselle could be persuaded to make up her mind. Nothing is sacred from one's maid. She knew all about Mr. Carruthers, of course. Poor old Véronique! I have a big, warm corner for her in my heart. Sometimes she treats me with the frigid respect one would pay to a queen, and at others I am almost her *enfant*, so tender and motherly she is to me. And she puts up with all my tempers and moods, and pets me like a baby just when I am the worst of all.

Lord Robert had left me reluctantly when the luncheon gong sounded.

"Haven't we been happy?" he said, taking it for granted I felt the same as he did. This is a very engaging quality of his, and makes one feel sympathetic, especially when he looks into one's eyes with his sleepy blue ones. He has lashes as long and curly as a gypsy's baby.

Mr. Carruthers was alone in the dining-room when I got in; he was looking out of the window, and turned round sharply as I came up the room. I am sure he would like to have been killing flies on the panes if he had been a boy. His eyes were steel.

"Where have you been all the time?" he asked, when he had shaken hands and said good-morning.

"Up in my room, packing," I said, simply. "Lord Robert was so kind he helped me. We have got everything done; and may I order the carriage for the 5.15 train, please?"

"Certainly not. Confound Lord Robert!" Mr. Carruthers said. "What business is it of his? You are not to go. I won't let you. Dear, silly little child!—" his voice was quite moved. "You can't possibly go out into the world all alone. Evangeline, why won't you marry me? I—do you know, I believe—I shall love you——"

"I should have to be *perfectly sure* that the person I married loved me, Mr. Carruthers," I said, demurely, "before I consented to finish up my life like that."

He had no time to answer, for Mr. Barton and Lord Robert came into the room.

There seemed a gloom over luncheon. There were pauses, and Lord Robert had a more pathetic expression than ever. His hands are a nice shape—but so are Mr. Carruthers's; they both look very much like gentlemen.

Before we had finished, a note was brought in to me. It was from Lady Katherine Montgomerie. She was too sorry, she said, to hear of my lonely position, and she was writing to ask if I would not come over and spend a fortnight with them at Tryland Court.

It was not well worded, and I had never cared much for Lady Katherine, but it was fairly kind, and fitted in perfectly with my plans.

She had probably heard of Mr. Carruthers's arrival, and was scandalized at my being alone in the house with him.

Both men had their eyes fixed on my face when I looked up, as I finished reading the note.

"Lady Katherine Montgomerie writes to ask me to Tryland," I said. "So if you will excuse me I will answer it, and say I will come this afternoon," and I got up.

Mr. Carruthers rose, too, and followed me into the library. He deliberately shut the door and came over to the writing-table where I sat down.

"Well, if I let you go, will you tell her then that you are engaged to me, and I am going to marry you as soon as possible?"

"No, indeed I won't," I said, decidedly. "I am not going to marry you, or any one, Mr. Carruthers. What do you think of me? Fancy my consenting to come back here forever, and live with you, when I don't know you a bit! And having to put up with your—perhaps—kissing me, and—and—things of that sort. It is perfectly dreadful to think of!"

He laughed as if in spite of himself. "But supposing I promised not to kiss you?"

"Even so," I said, and I couldn't help biting the end of my pen. "It could happen that I might get a feeling I wanted to kiss some one else—and there it is! Once you're married, everything nice is wrong!"

"Evangeline! I won't let you go—out of my life—you strange little witch! You have upset me, disturbed me—I can settle to nothing. I seem to want you so very much."

"Pouf!" I said, and I pouted at him.

"You have everything in your life to fill it—position, riches, friends. You don't want a green-eyed adventuress."

I bent down and wrote steadily to Lady Katherine. I would be there about six o'clock, I said, and thanked her in my best style.

"If I let you go, it is only for the time," Mr. Carruthers said as I signed my name. "I *intend* you to marry me—do you hear?"

"Again I say, 'Qui vivre verra!'" I laughed and rose with the note in my hand.

Lord Robert looked almost ready to cry when I told him I was off in the afternoon.

"I shall see you again," he said. "Lady Katherine is a relation of my aunt's husband, Lord Merrenden. I don't know her myself, though."

I do not believe him. How can he see me again? Young men do talk a lot of nonsense!

"I shall come over on Wednesday to see how you are getting on," Mr. Carruthers said. "Please do be in."

I promised I would, and then I came up-stairs.

And so it has come to an end, my life at Branches. I am going to start a new phase of existence, my first beginning as an adventuress!

How completely all one's ideas can change in a few days! This day three weeks ago Mrs. Carruthers was alive. This day two weeks ago I found myself no longer a prospective heiress, and only three days ago I was contemplating calmly the possibility of marrying Mr. Carruthers; and now, for heaven, I would not marry any one! And so, for fresh woods and pastures new! Oh, I want to see the world, and lots of different human beings; I want to know what it is makes the clock go round—that great big clock of life. I want to dance and to sing and to laugh, and to *live*—and—and—yes, perhaps some day to kiss some one I love!

TRYLAND COURT HEADINGTON,
Wednesday, *November 9th.*

Goodness gracious! I have been here four whole days, and I continually ask myself how I shall be able to stand it for the rest of the fortnight. Before I left Branches, I began to have a sinking at the heart. There were horribly touching farewells with housekeepers and people I have known since a child, and one hates to have that choky feeling, especially as just at the end of it, while tears were still in my eyes, Mr. Carruthers came out into the hall and saw them; so did Lord Robert!

I blinked and blinked, but one would trickle down my nose. It was a horribly awkward moment.

Mr. Carruthers made profuse inquiries as to my comforts for the drive, in a tone colder than ever, and insisted upon my drinking some cherry brandy. Such fussing is quite unlike his usual manner, so I suppose he, too, felt it was a tiresome *quart d'heure.* Lord Robert did not hide his concern; he came up to me and took my hand while Christopher was speaking to the footman who was going with me.

"You are a dear," he said, "and a brick, and don't you forget I shall come and stay with Lady Katherine before you leave, so you won't feel you are all among strangers."

I thanked him, and he squeezed my hand so kindly. I do like Lord Robert.

Very soon I was gay again and *insouciante*, and the last they saw of me was smiling out of the brougham window as I drove off in the dusk. They both stood upon the steps and waved to me.

Tea was over at Tryland when I arrived—such a long, damp drive! And I explained to Lady Katherine how sorry I was to have had to come so late, and that I could not think of troubling her to have up fresh for me; but she insisted, and after a while a whole new lot came, made in a hurry with the water not boiling, and I had to gulp down a nasty cup—Ceylon tea, too! I hate Ceylon tea! Mr. Montgomerie warmed himself before the fire, quite shielding it from us, who shivered on a row of high-backed chairs beyond the radius of the hearth-rug.

He has a way of puffing out his cheeks and making a noise like "Burrrr," which sounds very bluff and hearty until you find he has said a mean thing about some one directly after. And while red hair looks very well on me, I do think a man with it is the ugliest thing in creation. His face is red, and his nose and cheeks almost purple, and fiery whiskers, fierce enough to frighten a cat in a dark lane.

He was a rich Scotch manufacturer, and poor Lady Katherine had to marry him, I suppose; though, as she is Scotch herself, I dare say she does not notice that he is rather coarse.

There are two sons and six daughters—one married, four grown-up, and one at school in Brussels—and all with red hair! But straight and coarse, and with freckles and white eyelashes. So, really, it is very kind of Lady Katherine to have asked me here.

They are all as good as gold on top, and one does poker-work, and another binds books, and a third embroiders altar-cloths, and the fourth knits ties—all for charities, and they ask every one to subscribe to them directly they come to the house. The tie and the altar-cloth ones were sitting working hard in the drawing-room—Kirstie and Jean are their names; Jessie and Maggie, the poker-worker and the bookbinder, have a sitting-room to themselves—their work-shop they call it. They were there still, I suppose, for I did not see them until dinner. We used to meet once a year at Mrs. Carruthers's Christmas parties ever since ages and ages, and I remember I hated their tartan sashes, and they generally had colds in their heads, and one year they gave every one mumps, so they were not asked the next. The altar-cloth one, Jean, is my age, the other three are older.

It was really very difficult to find something to say, and I can quite understand common people fidgeting when they feel worried like this. I have never fidgeted since eight years ago, the last time Mrs. Carruthers boxed my ears for it. Just before going up to dress for dinner Mr. Montgomerie asked blank out if it was true that Mr. Carruthers had arrived. Lady Katherine had been skirting round this subject for a quarter of an hour.

I only said yes, but that was not enough, and, once started, he asked a string of questions, with "Burrrr" several times in between. Was Mr. Carruthers going to shoot the pheasants in November? Had he decided to keep on the chef? Had he given up diplomacy? I said I really did not know any of these things, I had seen so little of him.

Lady Katherine nodded her head, while she measured a comforter she was knitting, to see if it was long enough.

"I am sure it must have been most awkward for you, his arriving at all; it was not very good taste on his part, I am afraid, but I suppose he wished to see his inheritance as soon as possible," she said.

I nearly laughed, thinking what she would say if she knew which part of his inheritance he had really come to see. I do wonder if she has ever heard that Mrs. Carruthers left me to him, more or less, in her will!

"I hope you had your old governess with you, at least," she continued, as we went up the stairs, "so that you could feel less uncomfortable—really a most shocking situation for a girl alone in the house with an unmarried man!"

I told her Mr. Barton was there, too, but I had not the courage to say anything about Lord Robert; only that Mr. Carruthers had a friend of his down who was a great judge of pictures, to see them.

"Oh, a valuer, I suppose. I hope he is not going to sell the Correggios," she exclaimed.

"No, I don't think so," I said, leaving the part about the valuer unanswered.

Mr. Carruthers's being unmarried seemed to worry her most; she went on about it again before we got to my bedroom door.

"I happened to hear a rumor at Miss Sheriton's" (the wool-shop in Headington, our town) "this morning," she said, "and so I wrote at once to you. I felt how terrible it would be for one of my own dear girls to be left alone with a bachelor like that. I almost wonder you did not stay up in your own rooms."

I thanked her for her kind thought, and she left me at last.

If she only knew! The unmarried ones who came down the passage to talk to mademoiselle were not half so saucy as the old fellows with wives somewhere. Lord Bentworth was married, and he wanted me to kiss him, whereas Colonel Grimston had no wife, and he never said Bo! to a goose. And I do wonder what she thought Mr. Carruthers was going to do to me, that it would have been wise for me to stay up in my rooms. Perhaps she thinks diplomats, having lived in foreign places, are sort of wild beasts.

My room is frightful after my pretty rosy chintzes at Branches. Nasty yellowish wood furniture, and nothing much matching; however, there are plenty of wardrobes, so Véronique is content.

They were all in the drawing-room when I got down, and Malcolm, the eldest son, who is in a Highland militia regiment, had arrived by a seven-o'clock train.

I had that dreadful feeling of being very late and Mr. Montgomerie wanting to swear at me, though it was only a minute past a quarter to eight.

He said "Burrrr" several times, and flew off to the dining-room with me tucked under his arm, murmuring it gave no cook a chance to keep the dinner waiting. So I expected something wonderful in the way of food, but it is not half so good as our chef sent up at Branches. And the footmen are not all the same height, and their liveries don't fit like Mrs. Carruthers always insisted that ours should do.

Malcolm *is* a titsy pootsy man. Not as tall as I am, and thin as a rail, with a look of his knees being too near together. He must be awful in a kilt, and I am sure he shivers when the wind blows—he has that air. I don't like kilts—unless men are big, strong, bronzed creatures that don't seem ashamed of their bare bits. I saw some splendid specimens marching, once, in Edinburgh, and they swung their skirts just like the beautiful ladies in the Bois, when mademoiselle and I went out of the Allée Mrs. Carruthers told us to try always to walk in.

Lady Catherine talked a great deal at dinner about politics and her different charities, and the four girls were so respectful and interested, but Mr. Montgomerie contradicted her whenever he could. I was glad when we went into the drawing-room.

That first evening was the worst of all, because we were all so strange; one seems to get acclimatized to whatever it is after a while.

Lady Katherine asked me if I had not some fancy-work to do. Kirstie had begun her ties, and Jean the altar-cloth, again.

"Do let Maggie run to your room and fetch it for you," she said.

I was obliged to tell her I never did any. "But I—I can trim hats," I said; it really seemed awful not to be able to do anything like them, I felt I must say this as a kind of defence for myself.

However, she seemed to think that hardly a lady's employment.

"How clever of you!" Kirstie exclaimed. "I wish I could, but don't you find that intermittent? You can't trim them all the time. Don't you feel the want of a constant employment?"

I was obliged to say I had not felt like that yet, but I could not tell them I particularly loved sitting perfectly still, doing nothing.

Jessie and Maggie played Patience at two tables which folded up, and which they brought out and sat down to with a deliberate accustomed look which made me know at once they did this every night, and that I should see those tables planted exactly on those two spots of carpet every evening during my whole stay. I suppose it is because they cannot bring the poker-work and the bookbinding into the drawing-room.

"Won't you play us something?" Lady Katherine asked, plaintively. Evidently it was not permitted to do nothing, so I got up and went to the piano.

Fortunately I know heaps of things by heart, and I love them, and would have gone on and on, so as to fill up the time, but they all said "Thank you" in a chorus after each bit, and it rather put me off.

Mr. Montgomerie and Malcolm did not come in for ages, and I could see Lady Katherine getting uneasy. One or two things at dinner suggested to me that these two were not on the best terms, perhaps she feared they had come to blows in the dining-room. The Scotch, Mrs. Carruthers said, have all kinds of rough customs that other nations do not keep up any longer.

They did turn up at last, and Mr. Montgomerie was purple all over his face, and Malcolm a pale green, but there were no bruises on him; only one could see they had had a terrible quarrel.

There is something in breeding, after all, even if one is of a barbarous country. Lady Katherine behaved so well, and talked charities and politics faster than ever, and did not give them time for any further outburst, though I fancy I heard a few "damns" mixed with the "burrrrs," and not without the "n" on just for ornament, like Lord Robert's.

It was a frightful evening.

Wednesday, *November 9th.*
(Continued.)

Malcolm walked beside me going to church the next day. He looked a little less depressed, and I tried to cheer him up.

He did not tell me what his worries were, but Jean had said something about it when she came into my room as I was getting ready. It appears he has got into trouble over a horse called Angela Grey—Jean gathered this from Lady Katherine; she said her father was very angry about it, as he had spent so much money on it.

To me it does not sound like a horse's name, and I told Jean so, but she was perfectly horrified, and said it must be a horse, because they were not acquainted with any Angela Grey, and did not even know any Greys at all. So it must be a horse!

I think that a ridiculous reason, as Mrs. Carruthers said all young men knew people one wouldn't want to; and it was silly to make a fuss about it, and that they couldn't help it, and they would be very dull if they were as good as gold, like girls.

But I expect Lady Katherine thinks differently about things to Mrs. Carruthers, and the daughters the same.

I shall ask Lord Robert when I see him again if it is a horse or not.

Malcolm is not attractive, and I was glad the church was not far off.

No carriages are allowed out on Sunday, so we had to walk; and coming back it began to rain, and we could not go round the stables, which I understand is the custom here every Sunday.

Everything is done because it is the custom, not because you want to amuse yourself.

"When it rains and we can't go round the stables," Kirstie said, "we look at the old *Illustrated London News*, and go on our way from afternoon church."

I did not particularly want to do that, so stayed in my room as long as I could. The four girls were seated at a large table in the hall, each with a volume in front of her when I got down at last. They must know every picture by heart, if they do it every Sunday it rains—they stay in England all the winter.

Jean made room for me beside her.

"I am at the 'Sixties,'" she said. "I finished the 'Fifties' last Easter." So they evidently do even this with a method.

I asked her if there were not any new books they wanted to read, but she said Lady Katherine did not care for their looking at magazines or novels unless she had been through them first, and she had not time for many, so they kept the few they had to read between tea and dinner on Sunday.

By this time I felt I should do something wicked; and if the luncheon gong had not sounded, I do not know what would have happened.

Mr. Montgomerie said rather gallant things to me when the cheese and port came along, while the girls looked shocked, and Lady Katherine had a stony stare. I suppose he is like this because he is married. I wonder, though, if young married men are the same. I have never met any yet.

By Monday night I was beginning to feel the end of the world would come soon. It is ten times worse than ever having had to conceal all my feelings and abjectly obey Mrs. Carruthers. Because she did say cynical, entertaining things sometimes to me, and to her friends, that made one laugh. And one felt it was only she who made the people who were dependent upon her do her way, because she herself was so selfish, and that the rest of the world were free if once one got outside.

But Lady Katherine and the whole Montgomerie *milieu* give you the impression that everything and everybody must be ruled by rules; and no one could have a right to an individual opinion in any sphere of society.

You simply can't laugh—they asphyxiate you. I am looking forward to this afternoon and Mr. Carruthers coming over. I often think of the days at Branches, and how exciting it was, with those two, and I wish I were back again.

I have tried to be polite and nice to them all here, and yet they don't seem absolutely pleased.

Malcolm gazes at me with sheep's eyes. They are a washy blue, with the family white eyelashes (how different to Lord Robert's!). He has the most precise, regulated manner, and never says a word of slang; he ought to have been a young curate, and I can't imagine his spending money on any Angela Greys, even if she is a horse or not.

He speaks to me when he can, and asks me to go for walks round the golf course. The four girls play for an hour and three-quarters every morning. They never seem to enjoy anything—the whole of life is a solid duty. I am sitting up in my room, and Véronique has had the sense to have my fire lighted early. I suppose Mr. Carruthers won't come until about four—an hour more to be got through. I have said I must write letters, and so have escaped from them and not had to go for the usual drive.

I suppose he will have the sense to ask for me, even if Lady Katherine is not back when he comes.

This morning it was so fine and frosty a kind of devil seemed to creep into me. I have been *so* good since Saturday, so when Malcolm said, in his usual prim, priggish voice, "Miss Travers, may I have the pleasure of taking you for a little exercise," I jumped up without consulting Lady Katherine, and went and put my things on, and we started.

I had a feeling that they were all thinking I was doing something wrong, and so, of course, it made me worse. I said every kind of simple thing I could to Malcolm to make him jump, and looked at him now and then from under my eyelashes. So when we got to a stile, he did want to help me, and his eyes were quite wobblish. He has a giggle right up in the treble, and it comes out at such unexpected moments, when there is nothing to laugh at. I suppose it is being Scotch—he has just caught the meaning of some former joke. There would never be any use in saying things to him like to Lord Robert and Mr. Carruthers, because one would have left the place before he understood, if even then.

There was an old Sir Thomas Farquharson who came to Branches, and he grasped the deepest jokes of Mrs. Carruthers—so deep that even I did not understand them—and he was Scotch. It may be they are like that only when they have red hair.

When I was seated on top of a stile, Malcolm suddenly announced:

"I hear you are going to London when you go. I hope you will let me come and see you; but I wish you lived here always."

"I don't," I said, and then I remembered that sounded rather rude, and they had been kind to me. "At least, you know, I think the country is dull; don't you—for always?"

"Yes," he replied, primly, "for men, but it is where I should always wish to see the woman I respected."

"Are towns so wicked?" I asked, in my little-angel voice. "Tell me of their pitfalls, so that I may avoid them."

"You must not believe everything people say to you, to begin with," he said, seriously. "For one so young as you, I am afraid you will find your path beset with temptations."

"Oh, do tell me what!" I implored. "I have always wanted to know what temptations were. Please tell me. If you come to see me—would you be a temptation, or is temptation a thing and not a person?" I looked at him so beseechingly he never for a second saw the twinkle in my eye.

He coughed pompously. "I expect I should be," he said modestly. "Temptations are—er—er—Oh, I say, you know, I say—I don't know what to say."

"Oh, what a pity!" I said, regretfully. "I was hoping to hear all about it from you, especially if you are one yourself; you must know."

He looked gratified, but still confused.

"You see, when you are quite alone in London, some man may make love to you."

"Oh, do you think so, *really*?" I asked, aghast. "That, I suppose, would be frightful, if I were by myself in the room. Would it do, do you think, if I left the sitting-room door open and kept Véronique on the other side?"

He looked at me hard, but he only saw the face of an unprotected angel, and, becoming reassured, he said, gravely:

"Yes, it might be just as well."

"You do surprise me about love," I said. "I had no idea it was a violent kind of thing like that. I thought it began with grave reverence and respect, and after years of offering flowers and humble compliments, and bread-and-butter at tea-parties, the gentleman went down upon one knee and made a declaration—'Clara Maria, I adore you; be mine'—and then one put out a lily-white hand and, blushing, told him to rise; but that can't be your sort, and you have not yet explained what temptation means."

"It means more or less wanting to do what you ought not to."

"Oh, then," I said, "I am having temptation all the time; aren't you? For instance, I want to tear up Jean's altar-cloth, and rip Kirstie's ties, and tool bad words on Jessie's bindings, and burn Maggie's wood-boxes."

He looked horribly shocked and hurt, so I added at once:

"Of course, it must be lovely to be able to do these things; they are perfect girls, and so clever, only it makes me feel like that because I suppose I am—different."

He looked at me critically. "Yes, you are different; I wish you would try and be more like my sisters, then I should not feel so nervous about your going to London."

"It is too good of you to worry," I said, demurely. "But I don't think you need, you know. I have rather a strong suspicion I am acquainted with the way to take care of myself," and I bent down and laughed right in his face, and jumped off the stile onto the other side.

He did look such a teeny shrimp climbing after me! But it does not matter what is their size, the vanity of men is just the same. I am sure he thought he had only to begin making love to me himself and I would drop like a ripe peach into his mouth.

I teased him all the way back, until when we got in to lunch he did not know whether he was on his head or his heels. Just as we came up to the door he said:

"I thought your name was Evangeline; why did you say it was Clara Maria?"

"Because it is not!" I laughed over my shoulder, and ran into the house.

He stood on the steps, and if he had been one of the stable-boys he would have scratched his head.

Now I must stop and dress. I shall put on a black tea-frock I have. Mr. Carruthers shall see I have not caught frumpdom from my hosts.

Night.

I do think men are the most horrid creatures—you can't believe what they say or rely upon them for five minutes! Mrs. Carruthers was right; she said, "Evangeline, remember, it is quite difficult enough to trust one's self without trusting a man."

Such an afternoon I have had! That annoying feeling of waiting for something all the time and nothing happening. For Mr. Carruthers did not turn up, after all. How I wish I had not dressed and expected him!

He is probably saying to himself he is well out of the business, now I have gone. I don't suppose he meant a word of his protestations to me. Well, he need not worry. I had no intention of jumping down his throat; only I would have been glad to see him, because he is human, and not like any one here.

Of course, Lord Robert will be the same, and I shall probably never see either of them again. How can Lord Robert get here when he does not know Lady Katherine? No; it was just said to say something nice when I was leaving, and he will be as horrid as Mr. Carruthers.

I am thankful, at least, that I did not tell Lady Katherine; I should have felt such a goose. Oh! I do wonder what I shall do next. I don't know at all how much things cost; perhaps three hundred a year is very poor. I am sure my best frocks always were five or six hundred francs each, and I dare say hotels run away with money. But for the moment I am rich, as Mr. Barton kindly advanced some of my legacy to me; and, oh, I am going to see life! and it is absurd to be sad! I shall go to bed, and forget how cross I feel.

They are going to have a shoot here next week—pheasants. I wonder if they will have a lot of old men. I have not heard all who are coming.

Lady Katherine said to me after dinner this evening that she was sorry, as she was afraid it would be most awkward for me their having a party, on account of my deep mourning, and I, if I felt it dreadfully, I need not consider they would find me the least rude if I preferred to have dinner in my room.

I don't want to have dinner in my room. Think of the stuffiness of it! And perhaps hearing laughter going on down-stairs.

I can always amuse myself watching faces, however dull they are. I thanked her, and said it would not be at all necessary, as I must get accustomed to seeing people. I could not count upon always meeting hostesses with such kind thoughts as hers, and I might as well get used to it.

She said "Yes," but not cordially.

To-morrow Mrs. Mackintosh, the eldest daughter, is arriving with her four children. I remember her wedding five years ago. I have never seen her since.

She was very tall and thin, and stooped dreadfully, and Mrs. Carruthers said Providence had been very kind in giving her a husband at all. But when Mr. Mackintosh tittuped down the aisle with her, I did not think so.

A wee, sandy fellow about up to her shoulder!

Oh, I would hate to be tied to that! I think to be tied to anything could not be very nice. I wonder how I ever thought of marrying Mr. Carruthers offhand!

I feel now I shall never marry, for years. Of course one can't be an old maid, but for a long time I mean to see life first.

TRYLAND,
Thursday, ***November 10th.***

BRANCHES,
Wednesday.

DEAR MISS TRAVERS,—

I regret exceedingly I was unable to come over to Tryland to-day, but hope to do so before you leave. I trust you are well, and did not catch cold on the drive.

Yours, very truly,
CHRISTOPHER CARRUTHERS.

This is what I get this morning! Pig!

Well, I sha'n't be in if he does come. I can just see him pulling himself together once temptation (it makes me think of Malcolm!) is out of his way; he no doubt feels he has had an escape, as I am nobody very grand.

The letters come early here, as everywhere, but in a bag which only Mr. Montgomerie can open, and one has to wait until every one is seated at breakfast before he produces the key and deals them all out.

Mr. Carruthers's was the only one for me, and it had "Branches" on the envelope, which attracted Mr. Montgomerie's attention, and he began to "burrrr," and hardly gave me time to read it before he commenced to ask questions apropos of the place, to get me to say what the letter was about. He is a curious man.

"Carruthers is a capital fellow, they tell me—er. You had better ask him over quietly, Katherine, if he is all alone at Branches"—this with one eye on me in a questioning way.

I remained silent.

"Perhaps he is off to London, though?"

I pretended to be busy with my coffee.

"Best pheasant-shoot in the county, and a close borough under the old régime. Hope he will be more neighborly—Er—suppose he must shoot 'em before November?"

I buttered my toast.

Then the "burrrrs" began. I wonder he does not have a noise that ends with d—n simply. It would save him time.

"Couldn't help seeing your letter was from Branches. Hope Carruthers gives you some news?"

As he addressed me deliberately, I was obliged to answer:

"I have no information. It is only a business letter," and I ate toast again.

He "burrred" more than ever, and opened some of his own correspondence.

"What am I to do, Katherine," he said, presently—"that confounded fellow Campion has thrown me over for next week, and he is my best gun? At short notice like this, it's impossible to replace him with the same class of shot."

"Yes, dear," said Lady Katherine, in that kind of voice that has not heard the question. She was deep in her own letters.

"Katherine!" roared Mr. Montgomerie. "Will you listen when I speak—burrrr!" and he thumped his fist on the table.

Poor Lady Katherine almost jumped, and the china rattled.

"Forgive me, Anderson," she said, humbly; "you were saying——?"

"Campion has thrown me over," glared Mr. Montgomerie.

"Then I have perhaps the very thing for you," Lady Katherine said, in a relieved way, returning to her letters. "Sophia Merrenden writes this morning, and among other things tells me of her nephew, Lord Robert Vavasour—you know, Torquilstone's half-brother. She says he is the most charming young man and a wonderful shot—she even suggests" (looking back a page), "that he might be useful to us, if we are short of a gun."

"Damned kind of her!" growled Mr. Montgomerie.

I hope they did not notice, but I had suddenly such a thrill of pleasure that I am sure my cheeks got red. I felt frightfully excited to hear what was going to happen.

"Merrenden, as you know, is the best judge of shooting in England," Lady Katherine went on, in an injured voice. "Sophia is hardly likely to recommend his nephew so highly if he were not pretty good."

"But you don't know the puppy, Katherine."

My heart fell.

"That is not the least consequence; we are almost related. Merrenden is my first cousin, you forget that, I suppose!"

Fortunately I could detect that Lady Katherine was becoming obstinate and offended. I drank some more coffee. Oh, how lovely if Lord Robert comes!

Mr. Montgomerie "burrred" a lot first, but Lady Katherine got him round, and before breakfast was over it was decided she should write to Lord Robert and ask him to come to the shoot. As we were all standing looking out of the window at the dripping rain, I heard her say, in a low voice:

"Really, Anderson, we must think of the girls sometimes. Torquilstone is a confirmed bachelor and a cripple—Lord Robert will certainly one day be duke."

"Well, catch him if you can," said Mr. Montgomerie. He is coarse sometimes.

I am not going to let myself think much about Lord Robert. Mr. Carruthers has been a lesson to me. But if he does come, I wonder if Lady Katherine will think it funny of me not saying I knew him when she first spoke of him. It is too late now, so it can't be helped.

The Mackintosh party arrived this afternoon. Marriage must have quite different effects on some people. Numbers of the married women we saw in London were lovely—prettier, I always heard, than they had been before—but Mary Mackintosh is perfectly awful. She can't be more than twenty-seven, but she looks forty, at least; and stout, and sticking out all in the wrong places, and flat where the stick-outs ought to be. And the four children. The two eldest look much the same age, the next a little smaller, and there is a baby, and they all squall, and although they seem to have heaps of nurses, poor Mr. Mackintosh has to be a kind of under one. He fetches and carries for them, and gives his handkerchief when they slobber, but perhaps it is he feels proud that a person of his size had these four enormous babies almost all at once like that.

The whole thing is simply dreadful.

Tea was a pandemonium! The four aunts gushing over the infants, and feeding them with cake, and gurgling with "tootsie-wootsie popsy-wopsy" kind of noises. They will get to do "burrrrs," I am sure, when they get older. I wonder if the infants will come down every afternoon when the shoot happens. The guests will enjoy it.

I said to Jean as we came up-stairs that I thought it seemed terrible to get married; did not she? But she was shocked, and said no, marriage and motherhood were sacred duties, and she envied her sister.

This kind of thing is not my idea of bliss. Two really well-behaved children would be delicious, I think; but four squalling imps all about the same age is *bourgeois*, and not the affair of a lady.

I suppose Lord Robert's answer cannot get here till about Saturday. I wonder how he arranged it? It is clever of him. Lady Katherine said this Mr. Campion who was coming is in the same regiment, the 3d Life Guards. Perhaps when—— But there is no use my thinking about it, only somehow I am feeling so much better to-night—gay, and as if I did not mind being very poor—that I was obliged to tease Malcolm a little after dinner. I *would* play Patience, and never lifted my eyes from the cards.

He kept trying to say things to me to get me to go to the piano, but I pretended I did not notice. A palm stands at the corner of a high Chippendale writing-bureau, and Jessie happened to have put the Patience-table behind that rather, so the rest of them could not see everything that was happening. Malcolm at last sat very near beside me, and wanted to help with the aces—but I can't bear people being close to me, so I upset the board, and he had to pick up all the cards on the floor. Kirstie, for a wonder, played the piano then—a cake-walk—and there was something in it that made me feel I wanted to move—to dance, to undulate—I don't know what—and my shoulders swayed a little in time to the music. Malcolm breathed quite as if he had a cold, and said, right in my ear, in a fat voice:

"You know you are a devil—and I——"

I stopped him at once, and looked up for the first time, absolutely shocked and surprised.

"Really, Mr. Montgomerie, I do not know what you mean," I said.

He began to fidget.

"Er—I mean—I mean—I awfully wish to kiss you."

"But I do not a bit wish to kiss you," I said, and I opened my eyes wide at him.

He looked like a spiteful bantam, and fortunately at that moment Jessie returned to the Patience, and he could not say any more.

Lady Katherine and Mrs. Mackintosh came into my room on the way up to bed. She—Lady Katherine—wanted to show Mary how beautifully they had had it done up; it used to be hers before she married. They looked all round at the dead-daffodil-colored cretonne and things, and at last I could see their eyes often straying to my night-gown, and dressing-gown, laid out on a chair beside the fire.

"Oh, Lady Katherine, I am afraid you are wondering at my having pink silk," I said, apologetically, "as I am in mourning; but I have not had time to get a white dressing-gown yet."

"It is not that, dear," said Lady Katherine, in a grave duty voice. "I—I—do not think such a night-gown is suitable for a girl."

"Oh, but I am very strong," I said. "I never catch cold."

Mary Mackintosh held it up, with a face of stern disapproval. Of course it has short sleeves ruffled with Valenciennes, and is fine linen cambric nicely embroidered. Mrs. Carruthers was always very particular about them, and chose them herself at Doucet's. She said one never could know when places might catch on fire.

"Evangeline, dear, you are very young, so you probably cannot understand," Mary said. "But I consider this garment not in any way fit for a girl, or for any good woman for that matter. Mother, I hope my sisters have not seen it."

I looked so puzzled.

She examined the stuff, one could see the chair through it, beyond.

"What *would* Alexander say if I were to wear such a thing!"

This thought seemed to almost suffocate them both; they looked genuinely pained and shocked.

"Of course it would be too tight for you," I said, humbly; "but it is otherwise a very good pattern, and does not tear when one puts up one's arms. Mrs. Carruthers made a fuss at Doucet's because my last set tore so soon, and they altered these."

At the mention of my late adopted mother, both of them pulled themselves up.

"Mrs. Carruthers, we know, had very odd notions," Lady Katherine said, stiffly. "But I hope, Evangeline, you have sufficient sense to understand now for yourself that such a—a—garment is not at all seemly."

"Oh, why not, dear Lady Katherine?" I said, "You don't know how becoming it is."

"Becoming!" almost screamed Mary Mackintosh, "But no nice-minded woman wants things to look becoming in bed!"

The whole matter appeared so painful to them I covered up the offending "nighty" with my dressing-gown, and coughed. It made a break, and they went away, saying good-night frigidly.

And now I am alone. But I do wonder why it is wrong to look pretty in bed, considering nobody sees one, too!

TRYLAND COURT,
Monday, *November 14th.*

I have not felt like writing; these last days have been so stodgy—sticky, I was going to say. Endless infant talk. The methods of head nurses, teething, the knavish tricks of nursemaids, patent foods, bottles, bibs—everything. Enough to put one off forever from wishing to get married. And Mary Mackintosh sitting there all out of shape, expounding theories that can have no results in practice, as there could not be worse-behaved children than hers.

They even try Lady Katherine, I can see, when the two eldest, who come in while we are at breakfast each day, take the jam-spoon, or something equally horrid, and dab it all over the cloth. Yesterday they put their hands in the honey-dish which Mr. Montgomerie was helping himself to, and then after smearing him (the "burrrs" were awful), they went round the table to escape being caught, and fingered the backs of every one's chair and the door-handle, so that one could not touch a thing without getting sticky.

"Alexander, dearie," Mary said. "Alec must have his mouth wiped."

Poor Mr. Mackintosh had to get up and leave his breakfast, catch these imps, and employ his table-napkin in vain.

"Take 'em up-stairs, do—burrrr," roared their fond grandfather.

"Oh, father, the poor darlings are not really naughty," Mary said, offended. "I like them to be with us all as much as possible. I thought they would be such a pleasure to you."

Upon which, hearing the altercation, both infants set up a yell of fear and rage, and Alec, the cherub of four and a half, lay on the floor and kicked and screamed until he was black in the face.

Mr. Mackintosh is too small to manage two, so one of the footmen had to come and help him to carry them up to their nursery. Oh, I would not be in his place for the world!

Malcolm is becoming so funny. I suppose he is attracted by me. He makes kind of love in a priggish way whenever he gets the chance, which is not often, as Lady Katherine contrives to send one of the girls with us on all our walks; or if we are in the drawing-room, she comes and sits down beside us herself. I am glad, as it would be a great bore to listen to a quantity of it.

How silly of her, though! She can't know as much about men as even I do; of course, it only makes him all the more eager.

It is quite an object-lesson for me. I shall be impossibly difficult myself if I meet Mr. Carruthers again, as he has no mother to play these tricks for him.

Lord Robert's answer came on Saturday afternoon. It was all done through Lady Merrenden.

He will be delighted to come and shoot on Tuesday, to-morrow. Oh, I am so glad, but I do wonder if I shall be able to make him understand not to say anything about having been at Branches while I was there. Such a simple thing, but Lady Katherine is so odd and particular.

The party is to be a large one—nine guns. I hope some will be amusing, though I rather fear.

Tuesday night.

It is quite late, nearly twelve o'clock, but I feel so wide awake I must write.

I shall begin from the beginning, when every one arrived.

They came by two trains early in the afternoon, and just at tea-time, and Lord Robert was among the last lot.

They are mostly the same sort as Lady Katherine, looking as good as gold; but one woman, Lady Verningham, Lady Katherine's niece, is different, and I liked her at once.

She has lovely clothes, and an exquisite figure, and her hat on the right way. She has charming manners, too, but one can see she is on a duty visit.

Even all this company did not altogether stop Mary Mackintosh laying down the law upon domestic—infant domestic—affairs. We all sat in the big drawing-room, and I caught Lady Verningham's eye, and we laughed together. The first eye with a meaning in it I have seen since I left Branches.

Everybody talked so agreeably, with pauses, not enjoying themselves at all, when Jean and Kirstie began about their work, and explained it, and tried to get orders, and Jessie and Maggie too, and specimens of it all had to be shown, and prices fixed. I should hate to have to beg, even for a charity.

I felt quite uncomfortable for them, but they did not mind a bit, and their victims were noble over it.

Our parson at Branches always got so red and nervous when he had to ask for anything, one could see he was quite a gentleman; but women are different, I suppose.

I longed for tea.

While they are all very kind here, there is that asphyxiating atmosphere of stiffness and decorum which affects every one who comes to Tryland. A sort of "the gold must be tried by fire and the heart must be wrung by pain" kind of suggestion about everything.

They are extraordinarily cheerful, because it is a Christian virtue, cheerfulness; not because they are brimming over with joy, or that lovely feeling of being alive and not minding much what happens, you feel so splendid, like I get on fine days.

Everything they do has a reason, or a moral, in it. This party is because pheasants have to be killed in November, and certain people have to be entertained, and their charities can be assisted through them. Oh, if I had a big house, and were rich, I would have lovely parties, with all sorts of nice people, because I wanted to give them a good time and laugh myself. Lady Verningham was talking to me just before tea, when the second train-load arrived.

I tried to be quite indifferent, but I did feel dreadfully excited when Lord Robert walked in. Oh, he looked such a beautiful creature, so smart, and straight, and lithe!

Lady Katherine was frightfully stiff with him; it would have discouraged most people, but that is the lovely part about Lord Robert, he is always absolutely *sans gêne*!

He saw me at once, of course, and came over as straight as a die the moment he could.

"How do, Robert?" said Lady Verningham, giving him her fingers in such an attractive way. "Why are you here, and why is our Campie not? Thereby hangs some tale, I feel sure."

"Why, yes," said Lord Robert, and he held her hand. Then he looked at me with his eyebrow up. "But won't you introduce me to Miss Travers? To my great surprise she seems to have forgotten me."

I laughed, and Lady Verningham introduced us, and he sat down beside us, and every one began tea.

Lady Verningham had such a look in her eye!

"Robert, tell me about it," she said.

"I hear they have five thousand pheasants to slay," Lord Robert said, looking at her with his innocent smile.

"Robert, you are lying," she said, and she laughed. She is so pretty when she laughs; not very young, over thirty I should think, but such a charm—as different as different can be from the whole Montgomerie family.

I hardly spoke; they continued to tease one another, and Lord Robert ate most of a plate of bread-and-butter that was near.

"I am damed hungry, Lady Ver!" he said. She smiled at him; she evidently likes him very much.

"Robert! You must not use such language here!" she said.

"Oh, doesn't he say them often?—those dams!" I burst out, not thinking for a moment; then I stopped, remembering. She did seem surprised.

"So you have heard them before. I thought you had only just met casually," she said, with such a comic look of understanding, but not absolutely pleased. I stupidly got crimson. It did annoy me, because it shows so dreadfully on my skin. She leaned back in her chair and laughed.

"It is delightful to shoot five thousand pheasants, Robert," she said.

"Now, isn't it?" replied Lord Robert. He had finished the bread-and-butter.

Then he told her she was a dear, and he was glad something had suggested to Mr. Campion that he would have other views of living for this week.

"You are a joy, Robert," she said. "But you will have to behave here. None of the tricks you played at Fotherington in October, my child. Aunt Katherine would put you in a corner. Miss Travers has been here a week, and can tell you I am truthful about it."

"Indeed, *yes*," I said.

"But I *must* know how you got here!" she commanded.

Just then, fortunately, Malcolm, who had been hovering near, came up and joined us, and would talk too; but if he had been a table or a chair he could not have mattered less to Lord Robert. He is quite wonderful. He is not the least rude, only perfectly simple and direct, always getting just what he wants, with rather an appealing expression in his blue eyes. In a minute or two he and I were talking together, and Malcolm and Lady Verningham a few yards off. I felt so happy. He makes one like that, I don't know for what reason.

"Why did you look so stonily indifferent when I came up?" he asked. "I was afraid you were annoyed with me for coming."

Then I told him about Lady Katherine, and my stupidly not having mentioned meeting him at Branches.

"Oh, then I stayed with Christopher after you left, I see," he said. "Had I met you in London?"

"We won't tell any stories about it. They can think what they please."

"Very well," he laughed. "I can see I shall have to manœuvre a good deal to talk quietly to you here, but you will stand with me, won't you, out shooting to-morrow?"

I told him I did not suppose we should be allowed to go out, except perhaps for lunch, but he said he refused to believe in such cruelty.

Then he asked me a lot of things about how I had been getting on, and what I intended to do next. He has the most charming way of making one feel that one knows him very well, he looks at one every now and then straight in the eyes, with astonishing frankness. I have never seen any person so quite without airs. I don't suppose he is ever thinking a bit the effect he is producing. Nothing has two meanings with him, like with Mr. Carruthers. If he had said I was to stay and marry him, I am sure he would have meant it, and I really believe I should have stayed.

"Do you remember our morning packing?" he said, presently, in such a caressing voice. "I was so happy; weren't you?"

I said I was.

"And Christopher was mad with us. He was like a bear with a sore head after you left, and insisted upon going up to town on Monday, just for the day. He came over here on Tuesday, didn't he?"

"No, he did not," I was obliged to say, and I felt cross about it still, I don't know why.

"He is a queer creature," said Lord Robert, "and I am glad you have not seen him. I don't want him in the way. I am a selfish brute, you know."

I said Mrs. Carruthers had always brought me up to know men were that, so such a thing would not prejudice me against him.

He laughed. "You must help me to come and sit and talk again after dinner," he said. "I can see the red-haired son means you for himself, but of course I shall not allow that."

I became uppish.

"Malcolm and I are great friends," I said, demurely. "He walks me round the golf-course in the park, and gives me advice."

"Confounded impertinence!" said Lord Robert.

"He thinks I ought not to go to Claridge's alone when I leave here, in case some one made love to me. He feels if I looked more like his sisters it would be safer. I have promised that Véronique shall stay at the other side of the door if I have visitors."

"Oh, he is afraid of that, is he? Well, I think it is very probable his fears will be realized, as I shall be in London," said Lord Robert.

"But how do you know," I began, with a questioning, serious air—"how do you know I should listen? You can't go on to deaf people, can you?"

"Are you deaf?" he asked. "I don't think so; anyway, I would try to cure your deafness." He bent close over to me, pretending to pick up a book.

Oh, I was having such a nice time!

All of a sudden I felt I was really living, the blood was jumping in my veins, and a number of provoking, agreeable things came to the tip of my tongue to say, and I said them. We were so happy.

Lord Robert is such a beautiful shape, that pleased me too; the perfect lines of things always give me a nice emotion. The other men look thick and clumsy beside him, and he does have such lovely clothes and ties.

We talked on and on. He began to show me he was deeply interested in me. His eyes, so blue and expressive, said even more than his words. I like to see him looking down; his eyelashes are absurdly long and curly, not jet black like mine and Mr. Carruthers's, but dark brown and soft and shaded, and, oh! I don't know how to say quite why they are so attractive. When one sees them half resting on his cheek it makes one feel it would be nice to put out the tip of one's finger and touch them. I never spent such a delightful afternoon. Only, alas! it was all too short.

"We will arrange to sit together after dinner," he whispered, as even before the dressing-gong had rung, Lady Katherine came and fussed about, and collected every one, and more or less drove them off to dress, saying, on the way up-stairs, to me, that I need not come down if I had rather not.

I thanked her again, but remained firm in my intention of accustoming myself to company.

Stay in my room, indeed, with Lord Robert at dinner—never!

However, when I did come down he was surrounded by Montgomeries, and pranced into the dining-room with Lady Verningham.

I had such a bore! A young Mackintosh, cousin of Mary's husband, and on the other side the parson. The one talked about botany in a hoarse whisper, with a Scotch accent, and the other gobbled his food, and made kind of pious jokes in between the mouthfuls.

I said, when I had borne it bravely up to the ices, I hated knowing what flowers were composed of, I only liked to pick them. The youth stared, and did not speak much more. For the parson, "Yes" now and then did, and like that we got through dinner.

Malcolm was opposite me, and he gaped most of the time. Even he might have been better than the botanist, but I suppose Lady Katherine felt these two would be a kind of half mourning for me. No one could have felt gay with them.

After dinner Lady Verningham took me over to a sofa with her, in a corner. The sofas here don't have pillows, as at Branches, but fortunately this one is a little apart, though not comfortable, and we could talk.

"You poor child!" she said; "you had a dull time. I was watching you. What did that Mactavish creature find to say to you?"

I told her, and that his name was Mackintosh, not Mactavish.

"Yes, I know," she said. "But I call the whole clan Mactavish; it is near enough, and it does worry Mary so, she corrects me every time. Now don't you want to get married, and be just like Mary?" There was a twinkle in her eye.

I said I had not felt wild about it yet. I wanted to go and see life first.

But she told me one couldn't see life unless one were married.

"Not even if one is an adventuress, like me?" I asked.

"A *what*?"

"An adventuress," I said. "People do seem so astonished when I say that. I have got to be one, you know, because Mrs. Carruthers never left me the money after all, and in the book I read about it, it said you were that if you had nice clothes, and—and—red hair—and things—and no home."

She rippled all over with laughter.

"You duck!" she said. "Now you and I will be friends. Only you must not play with Robert Vavasour. He belongs to me. He is one of my special and particular own pets. Is it a bargain?"

I do wish now I had the pluck then to say straight out that I rather liked Lord Robert, and would not make any bargain, but one is foolish sometimes when taken suddenly. It is then when I suppose it shows if one's head is screwed on, and mine wasn't to-night. But she looked so charming, and I felt a little proud, and perhaps ashamed to show that I am very much interested in Lord Robert, especially if he belongs to her, whatever that means; and so I said it was a bargain, and of course I had never thought of playing with him; but when I came to reflect afterwards, that is a promise, I suppose, and I sha'n't be able to look at him any more under my eyelashes. And I don't know why I feel very wide awake and tired, and rather silly, and as if I wanted to cry to-night.

However, she was awfully kind to me, and lovely, and has asked me to go and stay with her, and lots of nice things, so it is all for the best, no doubt. But when Lord Robert came in, and came over to us, it did feel hard having to get up at once and go and pretend I wanted to talk to Malcolm.

I did not dare to look up often, but sometimes, and I found Lord Robert's eyes were fixed on me with an air of reproach and entreaty, and the last time there was wrath as well.

Lady Verningham kept him with her until every one started to go to bed.

There had been music and bridge, and other boring diversions happening, but I sat still. And I don't know what Malcolm had been talking about; I had not been listening, though I kept murmuring "Yes" and "No."

He got more and more *empressé*, until suddenly I realized he was saying, as we rose:

"You have promised! Now remember, and I shall ask you to keep it—to-morrow."

And there was such a loving, mawkish, wobbly look in his eyes, it made me feel quite sick. The horrible part is I don't know what I have promised any more than the man in the moon. It may be something perfectly dreadful, for all I know. Well, if it is a fearful thing, like kissing him, I shall have to break my word, which I never do for any consideration whatever.

Oh, dear, oh, dear! It is not always so easy to laugh at life as I once thought. I almost wish I were settled down, and had not to be an adventuress. Some situations are so difficult. I think now I shall go to bed.

I wonder if Lord Robert—— No, what is the good of wondering; he is no longer my affair.

I shall blow out the light.

---

300 Park Street,
Saturday night, *November 19th.*

I do not much care to look back to the rest of my stay at Tryland. It is an unpleasant memory.

That next day after I last wrote, it poured with rain, and every one came down cross to breakfast. The whole party appeared, except Lady Verningham, and breakfast was just as stiff and boring as dinner. I happened to be seated when Lord Robert came in, and Malcolm was in the place beside me. Lord Robert hardly spoke, and looked at me once or twice with his eyebrows right up.

I did long to say it was because I had promised Lady Ver I would not play with him that I was not talking to him now like the afternoon before. I wonder if he ever guessed it. Oh, I wished then, and I have wished a hundred times since, that I had never promised at all. It seemed as if it would be wisest to avoid him, as how could I explain the change in myself? I hated the food, and Malcolm had such an air of proprietorship it annoyed me as much as I could see it annoyed Lady Katherine. I sniffed at him, and was as disagreeable as could be.

The breakfasts there don't shine, and porridge is pressed upon people by Mr. Montgomerie. "Capital stuff to begin the day—burrrr," he says.

Lord Robert could not find anything he wanted, it seemed. Every one was peevish. Lady Katherine has a way of marshalling people on every occasion; she reminds me of a hen with chickens, putting her wings down and clucking and chasing till they are all in a corner. And she is rather that shape, too, very much rounded in front. The female brood soon found themselves in the morning-room, with the door shut, and no doubt the male things fared the same with their host—anyway, we saw no more of them till we caught sight of them passing the windows in scutums and mackintoshes, a depressed company of sportsmen.

The only fortunate part was that Malcolm had found no opportunity to remind me of my promise, whatever it was, and I felt safer.

Oh, that terrible morning! Much worse than when we were alone; nearly all of them, about seven women beyond the family, began fancy-work.

One, a Lady Letitia Smith, was doing a crewel silk blotting-book that made me quite bilious to look at, and she was very short-sighted, and had such an irritating habit of asking every one to match her threads for her. They knitted ties and stockings, and crocheted waistcoats and comforters and hoods for the North Sea fishermen, and one even tatted. Just like housemaids do in their spare hours to trim Heaven knows what garment of unbleached calico.

I asked her what it was for, and she said for the children's pinafores in her "guild" work. If one doesn't call that waste of time, I wonder what is.

Mrs. Carruthers said it was much more useful to learn to sit still and not fidget than to fill the world with rubbish like this.

Mary Mackintosh dominated the conversation. She and Lady Letitia Smith, who have both small babies, revelled in nursery details, and then whispered bits for us, the young girls not to hear. We caught scraps though, and it sounded grewsome, whatever it was about. Oh, I do wonder when I get married if I shall grow like them!

I hope not.

It is no wonder married men are obliged to say gallant things to other people, if, when they get home, their wives are like that.

I tried to be agreeable to a lady who was next me. She was a Christian Scientist, and wore glasses. She endeavored to convert me, but I was abnormally thick-headed that day, and had to have things explained over and over, so she gave it up at last.

Finally, when I felt I should do something desperate, a footman came to say Lady Verningham wished to see me in her room, and I bounded up, but as I got to the door I saw them beginning to shake their heads over her.

"Sad that dear Ianthe has such irregular habits of breakfasting in her room; so bad for her," etc., etc. But, thank Heaven, I was soon outside in the hall, where her maid was waiting for me.

One would hardly have recognized that it was a Montgomerie apartment, the big room overlooking the porch, where she was located, so changed did its aspect seem. She had numbers of photographs about, and the loveliest gold toilet things, and lots of frilled garments, and flowers, and scent-bottles; and her own pillows propping her up, all blue silk, and lovely muslin embroideries; and she did look such a sweet, cosey thing among it all, her dark hair in fluffs round her face, and an angelic lace cap over it. She was smoking a cigarette, and writing numbers of letters with a gold stylograph pen. The blue silk quilt was strewn with correspondence, and newspapers, and telegraph forms. And her garment was low-necked, of course, and thin like mine. I wondered what Alexander would have thought if he could have seen her in contrast to Mary. I know which I would choose if I were a man.

"Oh, there you are!" she exclaimed, looking up, and puffing smoke clouds. "Sit on the bye-bye, snake-girl. I felt I must rescue you from the hoard of holies below, and I wanted to look at you in the daylight. Yes, you have extraordinary hair, and real eyelashes and complexion, too. You are a witch thing, I can see, and we shall all have to beware of you."

I smiled. She did not say it rudely, or I should have been uppish at once. She has a wonderful charm.

"You don't speak much, either," she continued. "I feel you are dangerous. That is why I am being so civil to you; I think it wisest. I can't stand girls as a rule." And she went into one of her ripples of laughter. "Now say you will not hurt me."

"I should not hurt any one," I said. "Unless they hurt me first, and I like you, you are so pretty."

"That is all right," she said. "Then we are comrades. I was frightened about Robert last evening, because I am so attached to him; but you were a darling after dinner, and it will be all right now. I told him you would probably marry Malcolm Montgomerie, and he was not to interfere."

"I shall do nothing of the kind!" I exclaimed, moving off the bed. "I would as soon die as spend the rest of my life here at Tryland."

"He will be fabulously rich one day, you know, and you could get round père Montgomerie in a trice, and revolutionize the whole place. You had better think of it."

"I won't," I said, and I felt my eyes sparkle. She put up her hands as if to ward off an evil spirit, and she laughed again. "Well, you sha'n't then. Only don't flash those emeralds at me; they give me quivers all over."

"Would *you* like to marry Malcolm?" I asked and I sat down again. "Fancy being owned by that! Fancy seeing it every day! Fancy living with a person who never sees a joke from week's end to week's end! Oh!"

"As for that—" and she puffed smoke. "Husbands are a race apart—there are men, women, and husbands; and if they pay bills, and shoot big game in Africa, it is all one ought to ask of them; to be able to see jokes is superfluous. Mine is most inconvenient, because he generally adores me, and at best only leaves me for a three weeks' cure at Homburg, and now and then a week at Paris; but Malcolm could be sent to the Rocky Mountains, and places like that, continuously; he is quite a sportsman."

"That is not my idea of a husband," I said.

"Well, what is your idea, snake-girl?"

"Why do you call me 'snake-girl'?" I asked. "I hate snakes."

She took her cigarette out of her mouth, and looked at me for some seconds.

"Because you are so sinuous; there is not a stiff line about your movements, you are utterly wicked-looking and attractive, too, and un-English, and what in the world Aunt Katherine asked you here for with those hideous girls I can't imagine. I would not have, if my three angels were grown up, and like them—" Then she showed me the photographs of her three angels—they are pets.

But my looks seemed to bother her, for she went back to them.

"Where do you get them from? Was your mother some other nation?"

I told her how poor mamma had been rather an accident, and was nobody much. "One could not tell, you see; she might have had any quaint creature beyond the grand-parents—perhaps I am mixed with Red Indian or nigger."

She looked at me searchingly.

"No, you are not; you are Venetian. That is it—some wicked, beautiful friend of a Doge, come to life again."

"I know I am wicked," I said. "I am always told it; but I have not done anything yet, or had any fun out of it, and I do want to."

She laughed again.

"Well, you must come to London with me when I leave here on Saturday, and we will see what we can do."

This sounded so nice, and yet I had a feeling that I wanted to refuse; if there had been a tone of patronage in her voice, I would have in a minute. We sat and talked a long time, and she did tell me some interesting things.

The world, she assured me, was a delightful place if one could escape bores, and had a good cook and a few friends. After a while I left her, as she suddenly thought she would come down to luncheon.

"I don't think it would be safe, at the present stage, to leave you alone with Robert," she said.

I was angry.

"I have promised not to play with him; is that not enough?" I exclaimed.

"Do you know, I believe it is, snake-girl," she said, and there was something wistful in her eyes; "but you are twenty, and I am past thirty, and—he is a man. So one can't be too careful." Then she laughed, and I left her putting a toe into a blue satin slipper and ringing for her maid.

I don't think age can matter much; she is far more attractive than any girl, and she need not pretend she is afraid of me. But the thing that struck me then, and has always struck me since, is that to have to *hold* a man by one's own manœuvres could not be agreeable to one's self-respect. I would *never* do that under any circumstances; if he would not stay because it was the thing he wanted to do most in the world, he might go. I should say, "Je m'en fiche!"

At luncheon, for which the guns came in—no nice picnic in a lodge as at Branches—I purposely sat between two old gentlemen, and did my best to be respectful and intelligent. One was quite a nice old thing, and at the end began paying me compliments. He laughed and laughed at everything I said. Opposite me were Malcolm and Lord Robert, with Lady Ver between them. They both looked sulky. It was quite a while before she could get them gay and pleasant. I did not enjoy myself.

After it was over, Lord Robert deliberately walked up to me.

"Why are you so capricious?" he asked. "I won't be treated like this. You know very well I have only come here to see you. We are such friends—or were. Why?"

Oh, I did want to say I was friends still, and would love to talk to him. He seemed so adorably good-looking, and such a shape! And his blue eyes had the nicest flash of anger in them.

I could have kept my promise to the letter, and yet broken it in the spirit, easily enough, by letting him understand by inference; but of course one could not be so mean as that when one was going to eat her salt, so I looked out of the window and answered coldly that I was quite friendly and did not understand him, and I immediately turned to my old gentleman and walked with him into the library. In fact, I was as cool as I could be without being actually rude, but all the time there was a flat, heavy feeling round my heart. He looked so cross and reproachful, and I did not like him to think me capricious.

We did not see them again until tea—the sportsmen, I mean. But tea at Tryland is not a friendly time; it is just as stiff as other meals. Lady Ver never let Lord Robert leave her side, and immediately after tea everybody who stayed in the drawing-room played bridge, where they were planted until the dressing-bell rang.

One would have thought Lady Katherine would have disapproved of cards, but I suppose every one must have one contradiction about them, for she loves bridge, and played for the lowest stakes with the air of a "needy adventurer" as the books say.

I can't write the whole details of the rest of the visit. I was miserable, and that is the truth. Fate seemed to be against Lord Robert speaking to me, even when he tried, and I felt I must be extra cool and nasty because I—oh, well, I may as well say it—he attracts me very much. I never once looked at him from under my eyelashes, and after the next day he did not even try to have an explanation.

He glanced with wrath sometimes, especially when Malcolm hung over me, and Lady Ver said his temper was dreadful.

She was so sweet to me, it almost seemed as if she wanted to make up to me for not letting me play with Lord Robert.

(Of course, I would not allow her to see I minded that.)

And finally Friday came, and the last night.

I sat in my room from tea until dinner. I could not stand Malcolm any longer. I had fenced with him rather well up to then, but that promise of mine hung over me. I nipped him every time he attempted to explain what it was, and to this moment I don't know, but it did not prevent him from saying tiresome, loving things, mixed with priggish advice. I don't know what would have happened, only when he got really horribly affectionate, just after tea, I was so exasperated I launched this bomb.

"I don't believe a word you are saying—your real interest is Angela Grey."

He nearly had a fit, and shut up at once. So, of course, it is not a horse. I felt sure of it. Probably one of those people Mrs. Carruthers said all young men knew—their adolescent measles and chicken-pox, she called them.

All the old men talked a great deal to me, and even the other two young ones; but these last days I did not seem to have any of my usual spirits. Just as we were going to bed on Friday night Lord Robert came up to Lady Ver; she had her hand through my arm.

"I can come to the play with you on Saturday night, after all," he said. "I have wired to Campion to make a fourth, and you will get some other woman, won't you?"

"I will try," said Lady Ver, and she looked right into his eyes; then she turned to me. "I shall feel so cruel leaving you alone, Evangeline" (at once, almost, she called me Evangeline; I should never do that with strangers), "but I suppose you ought not to be seen at a play just yet."

"I like being alone," I said. "I shall go to sleep early."

Then they settled to dine all together at her house, and go on; so, knowing I should see him again, I did not even say good-bye to Lord Robert, and he left by the early train.

A number of the guests came up to London with us.

My leave-taking with Lady Katherine had been coldly cordial. I thanked her deeply for her kindness in asking me there. She did not renew the invitation; I expect she felt a person like me, who would have to look after themselves, was not a suitable companion to her altar-cloth and poker workers.

Up to now, she told Lady Ver, of course I had been most carefully brought up and taken care of by Mrs. Carruthers, although she had not approved of her views. And having done her best for me at this juncture, saving me from staying alone with Mr. Carruthers, she felt it was all she was called upon to do. She thought my position would become too unconventional for their circle in future! Lady Ver told me all this with great glee. She was sure it would amuse me, it so amused her, but it made me a teeny bit remember the story of the boys and the frogs!

Lady Ver now and then puts out a claw which scratches, while she ripples with laughter. Perhaps she does not mean it.

This house is nice, and full of pretty things, as far as I have seen. We arrived just in time to fly into our clothes for dinner. I am in a wee room four stories up, by the three angels. I was down first, and Lord Robert and Mr. Campion were in the drawing-room. Sir Charles Verningham is in Paris, by-the-way, so I have not seen him yet.

Lord Robert was stroking the hair of the eldest angel, who had not gone to bed. The loveliest thing she is, and so polite, and different to Mary Mackintosh's infants.

He introduced Mr. Campion stiffly, and returned to Mildred—the angel.

Suddenly mischief came into me, the reaction from the last dull days; so I looked straight at Mr. Campion from under my eyelashes, and it had the effect it always has on people—he became interested at once. I don't know why this does something funny to them. I remember I first noticed it in the school-room at Branches. I was doing a horrible exercise upon the *participe passé*, and feeling very *égarée*, when one of the old ambassadors came in to see mademoiselle. I looked up quickly, with my head a little down, and he said to mademoiselle, in a low voice, in German, that I had the strangest eyes he had ever seen, and that uplook under the eyelashes was the affair of the devil!

Now I knew even then the affair of the devil is something attractive, so I have never forgotten it, although I was only about fifteen at the time. I always determined I would try it when I grew up and wanted to create emotions. Except Mr. Carruthers and Lord Robert, I have never had much chance, though.

Mr. Campion sat down beside me on a sofa, and began to say at once that I ought to be going to the play with them. I spoke in my velvet voice, and said I was in too deep mourning, and he apologized so nicely, rather confused.

He is quite a decent-looking person, smart and well groomed, like Lord Robert, but not that lovely shape. We talked on for about ten minutes. I said very little, but he never took his eyes off my face. All the time I was conscious that Lord Robert was fidgeting and playing with a china cow that was on a table near, and just before the butler announced Mrs. Fairfax he dropped it on the floor and broke its tail off.

Mrs. Fairfax is not pretty; she has reddish-gold hair, with brown roots, and a very dark skin, but it is nicely done—the hair, I mean, and perhaps the skin too, as sideways you can see the pink sticking up on it. It must be rather a nuisance to have to do all that, but it is certainly better than looking like Mary Mackintosh. She doesn't balance nicely—bits of her are too long or too short. I do like to see everything in the right place—like Lord Robert's figure. Lady Ver came in just then, and we all went down to dinner. Mrs. Fairfax gushed at her a good deal. Lady Ver does not like her much—she told me in the train—but she was obliged to wire to her to come, as she could not get any one else Mr. Campion liked on so short a notice.

"The kind of woman every one knows, and who has no sort of pride," she said.

Well, even when I am really an adventuress I sha'n't be like that.

Dinner was very gay.

Lady Ver, away from her decorous relations, is most amusing. She says anything that comes into her head. Mrs. Fairfax got cross because Mr. Campion would speak to me; but as I did not particularly take to her, I did not mind, and just amused myself. As the party was so small, Lord Robert and I were obliged to talk a little, and once or twice I forgot and let myself be natural and smile at him. His eyebrows went up in that questioning, pathetic way he has, and he looked so attractive—that made me remember again, and instantly turn away. When we were coming into the hall, while Lady Ver and Mrs. Fairfax were up putting on their cloaks, Lord Robert came up close to me and whispered:

"I *can't* understand you. There is some reason for your treating me like this, and I will find it out. Why are you so cruel, little, wicked tiger cat?" and he pinched one of my fingers until I could have cried out.

That made me so angry.

"How dare you touch me!" I said. "It is because you know I have no one to take care of me that you presume like this."

I felt my eyes blaze at him, but there was a lump in my throat. I would not have been hurt if it had been any one else, only angry; but he had been so respectful and gentle with me at Branches, and I had liked him so much. It seemed more cruel for him to be impertinent now.

His face fell; indeed, all the fierceness went out of it, and he looked intensely miserable.

"Oh, don't say that!" he said, in a choked voice. "I—oh, that is the one thing you know is not true."

Mr. Campion, with his fur coat fastened, came up at that moment, saying gallant things, and insinuating that we must meet again, but I said good-night quietly, and came up the stairs without a word more to Lord Robert.

"Good-night, Evangeline, pet," Lady Ver said, when I met her on the drawing-room landing, coming down. "I do feel a wretch, leaving you, but to-morrow I will really try and amuse you. You look very pale, child; the journey has tried you, probably."

"Yes, I am tired," I tried to say in a natural voice, but the end word shook a little, and Lord Robert was just behind, having run up the stairs after me, so I fear he must have heard.

"Miss Travers—please—" he implored, but I walked on up the next flight, and Lady Ver put her hand on his arm and drew him down with her, and as I got up to the fourth floor I heard the front door shut.

And now they are gone and I am alone. My tiny room is comfortable, and the fire is burning brightly. I have a big arm-chair and books, and this, my journal, and all is cosey—only I feel so miserable.

I won't cry and be a silly coward.

Why, of course it is amusing to be free. And I am *not* grieving over Mrs. Carruthers's death—only perhaps I am lonely, and I wish I were at the theatre. No, I don't—I—Oh, the thing I do wish is that—that—*no*, I won't write it even.

Good-night, journal!

---

300 Park Street,
Wednesday, *November 23d.*

Oh, how silly to want the moon! But that is evidently what is the matter with me. Here I am in a comfortable house with a kind hostess, and no immediate want of money, and yet I am restless, and sometimes unhappy.

For the four days since I arrived Lady Ver has been so kind to me, taken the greatest pains to try and amuse me and cheer me up. We have driven about in her electric brougham and shopped, and agreeable people have been to lunch each day, and I have had what I suppose is a *succès*. At least she says so.

I am beginning to understand things better, and it seems one must have no real feelings, just as Mrs. Carruthers always told me, if one wants to enjoy life.

On two evenings Lady Ver has been out, with numbers of regrets at leaving me behind, and I have gathered that she has seen Lord Robert, but he has not been here, I am glad to say.

I am real friends with the angels, who are delightful people, and very well brought up. Lady Ver evidently knows much better about it than Mary Mackintosh, although she does not talk in that way.

I can't think what I am going to do next. I suppose soon this kind of drifting will seem quite natural, but at present the position galls me for some reason. I *hate* to think people are being kind out of charity. How very foolish of me, though!

Lady Merrenden is coming to lunch to-morrow. I am interested to see her, because Lord Robert said she was such a dear. I wonder what has become of him. He has not been here—I wonder—No, I am *too* silly.

Lady Ver does not get up to breakfast, and I go into her room and have mine on another little tray, and we talk, and she reads me bits out of her letters.

She seems to have a number of people in love with her—that must be nice.

"It keeps Charlie always devoted," she said, "because he realizes he owns what the other men want."

She says, too, that all male creatures are fighters by nature; they don't value things they obtain easily, and which are no trouble to keep. You must always make them realize you will be off like a snipe if they relax their efforts to please you for one moment.

Of course there are heaps of humdrum ways of living, where the husband is quite fond, but it does not make his heart beat, and Lady Ver says she couldn't stay on with a man whose heart she couldn't make beat when she wanted to.

I am curious to see Sir Charles.

They play bridge a good deal in the afternoon, and it amuses me a little to talk nicely to the man who is out for the moment, and make him not want to go back to the game.

I am learning a number of things.

Night.

Mr. Carruthers came to call this afternoon. He was the last person I expected to see when I went into the drawing-room after luncheon, to wait for Lady Ver. I had my out-door things on, and a big black hat, which is rather becoming, I am glad to say.

"You here!" he exclaimed, as we shook hands.

"Yes, why not me?" I said.

He looked very self-contained and reserved, I thought, as if he had not the least intention of letting himself go to display any interest. It instantly aroused in me an intention to change all that.

"Lady Verningham kindly asked me to spend a few days with her when we left Tryland," I said, demurely.

"Oh, you are staying here! Well, I was over at Tryland the day before yesterday—an elaborate invitation from Lady Katherine to 'dine and sleep quietly,' which I only accepted as I thought I should see you."

"How good of you," I said, sweetly. "And did they not tell you I had gone with Lady Verningham?"

"Nothing of the kind. They merely announced that you had departed for London, so I supposed it was your original design of Claridge's, and I intended going round there some time to find you."

Again I said it was so good of him, and I looked down.

He did not speak for a second or two, and I remained perfectly still.

"What are your plans?" he asked, abruptly.

"I have no plans."

"But you must have—that is ridiculous—you must have made some decision as to where you are going to live!"

"No, I assure you," I said, calmly, "when I leave here on Saturday I shall just get into a cab and think of some place for it to take me to, I suppose, as we turn down Park Lane."

He moved uneasily, and I glanced at him up from under my hat. I don't know why he does not attract me now as much as he did at first. There is something so cold and cynical about his face.

"Listen, Evangeline," he said, at last. "Something must be settled for you. I cannot allow you to drift about like this. I am more or less your guardian, you know—you must feel that."

"I don't a bit," I said.

"You impossible little—witch." He came closer.

"Yes, Lady Verningham says I am a witch, and a snake, and all sorts of bad, attractive things, and I want to go somewhere where I shall be able to show these qualities. England is dull. What do you think of Paris?"

Oh, it did amuse me launching forth these remarks; they would never come into my head for any one else!

He walked across the room and back. His face was disturbed.

"You shall not go to Paris—alone. How can you even suggest such a thing?" he said.

I did not speak. He grew exasperated.

"Your father's people are all dead, you tell me, and you know nothing of your mother's relations. But who was she? What was her name? Perhaps we could discover some kith and kin for you."

"My mother was called Miss Tonkins," I said.

"*Called* Miss Tonkins?"

"Yes."

"Then it was not her name. What do you mean?"

I hated these questions.

"I suppose it was her name. I never heard she had another."

"Tonkins," he said—"Tonkins," and he looked searchingly at me with his monk-of-the-Inquisition air.

I can be so irritating, not telling people things, when I like, and it was quite a while before he elicited the facts from me, which Mrs. Carruthers had often hurled at my head in moments of anger, that poor mamma's father had been Lord de Brandreth and her mother, Heaven knows who!

"So you see," I ended with, "I haven't any relations, after all, have I?"

He sat down upon the sofa.

"Evangeline, there is nothing for it; you must marry me," he said.

I sat down opposite him.

"Oh, you are funny!" I said. "You, a clever diplomat, to know so little of women! Who in the world would accept such an offer?" and I laughed and laughed.

"What am I to do with you?" he exclaimed, angrily.

"Nothing." I laughed still, and I looked at him with my "affair-of-the-devil" look. He came over and forcibly took my hand.

"Yes, you are a witch," he said—"a witch who casts spells and destroys resolutions and judgments. I determined to forget you, and put you out of my life—you are most unsuitable to me, you know—but as soon as I see you I am filled with only one desire. I *must* have you for myself. I want to kiss you—to touch you. I want to prevent any other man from looking at you—do you hear me, Evangeline?"

"Yes, I hear," I said; "but it does not have any effect on me. You would be awful as a husband. Oh, I know all about them!" and I looked up. "I saw several sorts at Tryland, and Lady Verningham has told me of the rest, and I know you would be no earthly good in that rôle!"

He laughed, in spite of himself, but he still held my hand.

"Describe their types to me, that I may see which I should be," he said, with great seriousness.

"There is the Mackintosh kind—humble and 'titsy pootsy,' and a sort of under-nurse," I said.

"That is not my size, I fear."

"Then there is the Montgomerie—selfish and bullying, and near about money."

"But I am not Scotch."

"No—well, Lord Kestervin was English, and he fussed and worried, and looked out trains all the time."

"I will have a groom of the chambers."

"And they were all casual and indifferent to their poor wives—and boresome—and bored! And one told long stories, and one was stodgy, and one opened his wife's letters before she was down!"

"Tell me the attributes of a perfect husband, then, that I may learn them," he said.

"They have to pay all the bills——"

"Well, I could do that."

"And they have not to interfere with one's movements. And one must be able to make their hearts beat."

"Well, you could do *that*!" and he bent nearer to me. I drew back.

"And they have to take long journeys to the Rocky Mountains for months together, with men friends."

"Certainly not!" he exclaimed.

"There, you see!" I said; "the most important part you don't agree to. There is no use talking further."

"Yes, there is! You have not said half enough. Have they to make your heart beat, too?"

"You are hurting my hand."

He dropped it.

"Have they?"

"Lady Ver said no husband could do that. The fact of their being one kept your heart quite quiet, and often made you yawn; but she said it was not necessary, as long as you could make theirs so that they would do all you asked."

"Then do women's hearts never beat—did she tell you?"

"Of course they beat. How simple you are for thirty years old! They beat constantly for—oh—for people who are not husbands."

"That is the result of your observations, is it? You are probably right and I am a fool."

"Some one said at lunch yesterday that a beautiful lady in Paris had her heart beating for you," I said, looking at him again.

He changed—so very little. It was not a start, or a wince even—just enough for me to know he felt what I said.

"People are too kind," he said. "But we have got no nearer the point. When will you marry me?"

"I shall marry you—never! Mr. Carruthers," I said, "unless I get into an old maid soon and no one else asks me! Then if you go on your knees I may put out the tip of my fingers, perhaps!" and I moved towards the door, making him a sweeping and polite courtesy.

He rushed after me.

"Evangeline!" he exclaimed. "I am not a violent man as a rule; indeed, I am rather cool, but you would drive any one perfectly mad. Some day some one will strangle you—witch!"

"Then I had better run away to save my neck," I said, laughing over my shoulder as I opened the door and ran up the stairs, and I peeped at him from the landing above. He had come out into the hall. "Good-bye," I called, and, without waiting to see Lady Ver, he tramped down the stairs and away.

"Evangeline, what *have* you been doing?" she asked, when I got into her room, where her maid was settling her veil before the glass, and trembling over it. Lady Ver is sometimes fractious with her—worse than I am with Véronique, far.

"Evangeline, you look naughtier than ever—confess at once."

"I have been as good as gold," I said.

"Then why are those two emeralds sparkling so, may one ask?"

"They are sparkling with conscious virtue," I said, demurely.

"You have quarrelled with Mr. Carruthers—go away, Welby! Stupid woman, can't you see it catches my nose!"

Welby retired meekly. (After she is cross, Lady Ver sends Welby to the theatre. Welby adores her.)

"Evangeline, how dare you! I see it all. I gathered bits from Robert. You have quarrelled with the very man you must marry!"

"What does Lord Robert know about me?" I said. That made me angry.

"Nothing; he only said Mr. Carruthers admired you at Branches."

"Oh!"

"He is too attractive—Christopher! He is one of the 'married women's pets,' as Ada Fairfax says, and has never spoken to a girl before. You ought to be grateful we have let him look at you—minx!—instead of quarrelling, as I can see you have." She rippled with laughter, while she pretended to scold me.

"Surely I may be allowed that chastened diversion!" I said. "I can't go to theatres!"

"Tell me about it," she commanded, tapping her foot.

But early in Mrs. Carruthers's days I learned that one is wiser when one keeps one's own affairs to one's self, so I fenced a little, and laughed, and we went out to drive finally, without her being any the wiser. Going into the park, we came upon a troop of the 3d Life Guards, who had been escorting the king to open something, and there rode Lord Robert in his beautiful clothes and a floating plume. He did look so lovely, and *my* heart suddenly began to beat—I could feel it, and was ashamed, and it did not console me greatly to reflect that the emotion caused by a uniform is not confined to nursemaids.

Of course it must have been the uniform and the black horse—Lord Robert is nothing to me. But I hate to think that, mamma's mother having been nobody, I should have inherited these common instincts!

---

300 Park Street,
Thursday evening, *November 24th.*

Lady Merrenden is so nice—one of those kind faces that even a tight fringe in a net does not spoil. She is tall and graceful, past fifty perhaps, and has an expression of Lord Robert about the eyes. At luncheon she was sweet to me at once, and did not look as if she thought I must be bad just because I have red hair, like elderly ladies do generally.

I felt I wanted to be good and nice directly. She did not allude to my desolate position or say anything without tact, but she asked me to lunch as if I had been a queen and would honor her by accepting. For some reason I could see Lady Ver did not wish me to go—she made all sorts of excuses about wanting me herself—but also, for some reason, Lady Merrenden was determined I should, and finally settled it should be on Saturday, when Lady Ver is going down to Northumberland to her father's, and I am going—where? Alas! as yet I know not.

When she had gone Lady Ver said old people without dyed hair or bridge proclivities were tiresome, and she smoked three cigarettes, one after the other as fast as she could. (Welby is going to the theatre again to-night!)

I said I thought Lady Merrenden was charming. She snapped my head off for the first time, and then there was silence, but presently she began to talk, and fix herself in a most becoming way on the sofa—we were in her own sitting-room, a lovely place, all blue silk and French furniture and attractive things. She said she had a cold and must stay in-doors. She had changed immediately into a tea-gown, but I could not hear any cough.

"Charlie has just wired he comes back to-night," she announced, at length.

"How nice for you!" I sympathized; "you will be able to make his heart beat!"

"As a matter of fact, it is extremely inconvenient, and I want you to be nice to him, and amuse him, and take his attention off me, like a pet, Evangeline," she cooed; and then: "What a lovely afternoon for November! I wish I could go for a walk in the park," she said.

I felt it would be cruel to tease her further, and so announced my intention of taking exercise in that way with the angels.

"Yes, it will do you good, dear child," she said, brightly, "and I will rest here and take care of my cold."

"They have asked me to tea in the nursery," I said, "and I have accepted."

"Jewel of a snake-girl!" she laughed—she is not thick.

"Do you know the Torquilstone history?" she said, just as I was going out of the door.

I came back—why, I can't imagine, but it interested me.

"Robert's brother—half-brother, I mean—the duke, is a cripple, you know, and he is *toqué* on one point too—their blue blood. He will never marry, but he can cut Robert off with almost the bare title if he displeases him."

"Yes," I said.

"Torquilstone's mother was one of the housemaids. The old duke married her before he was twenty-one, and she, fortunately, joined her beery ancestors a year or so afterwards; and then much later he married Robert's mother, Lady Etheldrida Fitz Walter. There is sixteen years between them—Robert and Torquilstone, I mean."

"Then what is he *toqué* about blue blood for, with a *tache* like that?" I asked.

"That is just it. He thinks it is such a disgrace that even if he were not a humpback he says he would never marry to transmit this stain to the future Torquilstones—and if Robert ever marries any one without a pedigree enough to satisfy an Austrian prince, he will disown him and leave every sou to charity."

"Poor Lord Robert!" I said, but I felt my cheeks burn.

"Yes, is it not tiresome for him? So, of course, he cannot marry until his brother's death, there is almost no one in England suitable."

"It is not so bad, after all," I said; "there is always the delicious rôle of the 'married woman's pet,' open to him, isn't there?" and I laughed.

"Little cat!" but she wasn't angry.

"I told you I only scratched when I was scratched first," I said, as I went out of the room.

The angels had started for their walk, and Véronique had to come with me at first to find them. We were walking fast down the path beyond Stanhope Gate, seeing their blue velvet pelisses in the distance, when we met Mr. Carruthers.

He stopped and turned with me.

"Evangeline, I was so angry with you yesterday," he said. "I very nearly left London and abandoned you to your fate, but now that I have seen you again—" He paused.

"You think Paris is a long way off!" I said, innocently.

"What have they been telling you?" he said, sternly, but he was not quite comfortable.

"They have been saying it is a fine November, and the Stock Exchange is no place to play in, and if it weren't for bridge they would all commit suicide. That is what we talk of at Park Street."

"You know very well what I mean. What have they been telling you about me?"

"Nothing, except that there is a charming French lady who adores you, and whom you are devoted to—and I am so sympathetic. I like Frenchwomen, they put on their hats so nicely."

"What ridiculous gossip! I don't think Park Street is the place for you to stay. I thought you had more mind than to chatter like this."

"I suit myself to my company." I laughed, and waited for Véronique, who had stopped respectfully behind. She came up reluctantly. She disapproves of all English unconventionality, but she feels it her duty to encourage Mr. Carruthers.

"Should she run on and stop the young ladies," she suggested, pointing to the angels in front.

"Yes, do," said Mr. Carruthers, and before I could prevent her she was off.

Traitress! She was thinking of her own comfortable quarters at Branches, I know.

The sharp, fresh air got into my head. I felt gay, and without care. I said heaps of things to Mr. Carruthers, just as I had once before to Malcolm, only this was much more fun, because Mr. Carruthers isn't a red-haired Scotchman and can see things.

It seemed a day of meetings, for when we got down to the end we encountered Lord Robert walking leisurely in our direction. He looked as black as night when he caught sight of us.

"Hello, Bob!" said Mr. Carruthers, cheerfully. "Ages since I saw you. Will you come and dine to-night? I have a box for this winter opera that is on, and I am trying to persuade Miss Travers to come. She says Lady Verningham is not engaged to-night, she knows, and we might dine quietly and all go; don't you think so?"

Lord Robert said he would, but he added, "Miss Travers would never come out before—she said she was in too deep mourning." He seemed aggrieved.

"I am going to sit in the back of the box and no one will see me," I said. "And I do love music so."

"We had better let Lady Verningham know at once then," said Mr. Carruthers.

Lord Robert announced he was going there now, and would tell her.

I knew that. The blue tea-gown with the pink roses, and the lace cap, and the bad cold were not for nothing. (I wish I had not written this; it is spiteful of me, and I am not spiteful, as a rule. It must be the east wind.)

Thursday night, *November 24th.*

"Now that you have embarked upon this—" Lady Ver said, when I ventured into her sitting-room, hearing no voices, about six o'clock. (Mr. Carruthers had left me at the door at the end of our walk, and I had been with the angels at tea ever since.) "Now that you have embarked upon this opera, I say, you will have to dine at Willis's with us. I won't be in when Charlie arrives from Paris. A blowy day like to-day his temper is sure to be impossible."

"Very well," I said.

Of what use, after all, for an adventuress like me to have sensitive feelings.

"And I am leaving this house at a quarter to seven, I wish you to know, Evangeline, pet," she called after me, as I flew off to dress. As a rule Lady Ver takes a good hour to make herself into the attractive darling she is in the evening. She has not to do much, because she is lovely by nature, but she potters and squabbles with Welby, to divert herself, I suppose.

However, to-night, with the terror upon her of a husband fresh from a rough Channel passage going to arrive at seven o'clock, she was actually dressed and down in the hall when I got there punctually at 6.45, and in the twinkle of an eye we were rolling in the electric to Willis's. I have only been there once before, and that to lunch in Mrs. Carruthers's days with some of the ambassadors; and it does feel gay going to a restaurant at night. I felt more excited than ever in my life, and such a situation, too!

Lord Robert—*fruit défendu!*—and Mr. Carruthers—*empressé*—and to be kept in bounds!

More than enough to fill the hands of a maiden of sixteen fresh from a convent, as old Count Someroff used to say when he wanted to express a really difficult piece of work.

They were waiting for us just inside the door, and again I noticed that they were both lovely creatures, and both exceptionally distinguished looking.

Lady Ver nodded to a lot of people before we took our seats in a nice little corner. She must have an agreeable time with so many friends. She said something which sounds so true in one of our talks, and I thought of it then.

"It is wiser to marry the life you like, because after a little the man doesn't matter." She has evidently done that, but I wish it could be possible to have both—the man and the life. Well! Well!

One has to sit rather close on those sofas, and as Lord Robert was not the host, he was put by me. The other two at a right-angle to us.

I felt exquisitely gay—in spite of having an almost high black dress on and not even any violets.

It was dreadfully difficult not to speak nicely to my neighbor, his directness and simplicity are so engaging, but I did try hard to concentrate myself on Christopher and leave him alone, only—I don't know why—the sense of his being so near me made me feel, I don't quite know what. However, I hardly spoke to him—Lady Ver shall never say I did not play fair—though, insensibly, even she herself drew me into a friendly conversation, and then Lord Robert looked like a happy school-boy.

We had a delightful time.

Mr. Carruthers is a perfect host. He has all the smooth and exquisite manners of the old diplomats, without their false teeth and things. I wish I were in love with him, or even I wish something inside me would only let me feel it was my duty to marry him; but it jumps up at me every time I want to talk to myself about it, and says, "Absolutely impossible."

When it came to starting for the opera, "Mr. Carruthers will take you in his brougham, Evangeline," Lady Ver said, "and I will be protected by Robert. Come along, Robert," as he hesitated.

"Oh, I say, Lady Ver!" he said, "I would love to come with you, but won't it look rather odd for Miss Evangeline to arrive alone with Christopher? Consider his character!"

Lady Ver darted a glance of flame at him and got into the electric, while Christopher, without hesitation, handed me into his brougham. Lord Robert and I were two puppets, a part I do not like playing.

I was angry altogether. She would not have dared to have left me go like this if I had been any one who mattered. Mr. Carruthers got in, and tucked his sable rug round me. I never spoke a word for a long time, and Covent Garden is not far off, I told myself. I can't say why I had a sense of *malaise.*

There was a strange look in his face as a great lamp threw a light on it. "Evangeline," he said, in a voice I have not yet heard, "when are you going to finish playing with me? I am growing to love you, you know."

"I am very sorry to hear it," I said, gently. "I don't want you to. Oh, please *don't*!" as he took my hand. "I—I—if you only knew how I *hate* being touched!"

He leaned back and looked at me. There is something which goes to the head a little about being in a brougham with nice fur rugs alone with some one at night. The lights flashing in at the windows, and that faint scent of a very good cigar. I felt fearfully excited. If it had been Lord Robert, I believe—well——

He leaned over very close to me. It seemed in another moment he would kiss me, and what could I do then? I couldn't scream, or jump out in Leicester Square, could I?

"Why do you call me Evangeline?" I said, by way of putting him off. "I never said you might."

"Foolish child!—I shall call you what I please. You drive me mad. I don't know what you were born for. Do you always have this effect on people?"

"What effect?" I said, to gain time; we had got nearly into Long Acre.

"An effect that causes one to lose all discretion. I feel I would give my soul to hold you in my arms."

I told him I did not think it was at all nice or respectful of him to talk so—that I found such love revolting.

"You tell me in your sane moments I am most unsuitable to you—you try to keep away from me—and then when you get close you begin to talk this stuff! I think it is an insult!" I said, angry and disdainful. "When I arouse devotion and tenderness in some one, then I shall listen, but to you and to this—never!"

"Go on," he said. "Even in the dim light you look beautiful when cross."

"I am not cross," I answered. "Only absolutely disgusted."

By that time, thank goodness, we had got into the stream of carriages close to the opera-house. Mr. Carruthers, however, seemed hardly to notice this.

"Darling," he said, "I will try not to annoy you; but you are so fearfully provoking. I—tell you truly, no man would find it easy to keep cool with you."

"Oh, I don't know what it is, being cool, or not cool," I said, wearily. "I am tired of every one. Even as tiny a thing as Malcolm Montgomerie gets odd like this!"

He leaned back and laughed, and then said, angrily: "Impertinence! I will wring his neck!"

"Thank Heaven we have arrived!" I exclaimed, as we drove under the portico. I gave a great sigh of relief.

Really, men are very trying and tiresome, and if I shall always have to put up with these scenes through having red hair, I almost wish it were mouse-colored, like Cicely Parker's. Mrs. Carruthers often said, "You need not suppose, Evangeline, that you are going to have a quiet life with your coloring; the only thing one can hope for is that you will screw on your head."

Lady Ver and Lord Robert were already in the hall waiting for us, but the second I saw them I knew she had been saying something to Lord Robert. His face, so gay and *debonnaire* all through dinner, now looked set and stern, and he took not the slightest notice of me as we walked to the box—the big one next the stage on the pit tier.

Lady Ver appeared triumphant—her eyes were shining with big blacks in the middle, and such bright spots of pink in her cheeks—she looked lovely; and I can't think why, but I suddenly felt I hated her. It was horrid of me, for she was so kind, and settled me in the corner behind the curtain where I could see and not be seen, rather far back, while she and Lord Robert were quite in the front. It was "Carmen"—the opera. I had never seen it before.

Music has such an effect—every note seems to touch some emotion in me. I feel wicked, or good, or exalted, or—or—oh, some queer feeling that I don't know what it is—a kind of electric current down my back, and as if—as if I would like to love some one and have them to kiss me. Oh, it sounds perfectly dreadful what I have written, but I can't help it—that is what some music does to me, and I said always I should tell the truth here.

From the very beginning note to the end I was feeling—feeling—Oh, how I understand her—Carmen!—*fruit défendu* attracted her so—the beautiful, wicked, fascinating snake. I also wanted to dance, and to move like that, and I unconsciously quivered perhaps. I was cold as ice, and fearfully excited. The back of Lord Robert's beautifully set head impeded my view at times. How exquisitely groomed he is! And one could see at a glance *his* mother had not been a housemaid! I never have seen anything look so well bred as he does.

Lady Ver was talking to him in a cooing, low voice after the first act, and the second act, and indeed even when the third act had begun. He seemed much more *empressé* with her than he generally does. It—it hurt me, that and the music and the dancing, and Mr. Carruthers whispering passionate little words at intervals, even though I paid no attention to them; but altogether I, too, felt a kind of madness.

Suddenly Lord Robert turned round, and for five seconds looked at me, his lovely, expressive blue eyes swimming with wrath and reproach and—oh, how it hurt me!—contempt. Christopher was leaning over the back of my chair, quite close, in a devoted attitude.

Lord Robert did not speak, but if a look could wither I must have turned into a dead oak-leaf. It awoke some devil in me. What had *I* done to be annihilated so! *I* was playing perfectly fair—keeping my word to Lady Ver, and—oh, I felt as if it were breaking my heart.

But that look of Lord Robert's! It drove me to distraction, and every instinct to be wicked and attractive that I possess came up in me. I leaned over to Lady Ver, so that I must be close to him, and I said little things to her, never one word to him; but I moved my seat, making it certain the corner of his eye must catch sight of me, and I allowed my shoulders to undulate the faintest bit to that Spanish music. Oh, I can dance as Carmen, too! Mrs. Carruthers had me taught every time we went to Paris. She loved to see it herself.

I could hear Christopher breathing very quickly. "My God!" he whispered, "a man would go to hell for you."

Lord Robert got up abruptly and went out of the box.

Then it was as if Don José's dagger plunged into my heart, not Carmen's. That sounds high-flown, but I mean it—a sudden, sick, cold sensation, as if everything was numb. Lady Ver turned round pettishly to Christopher. "What on earth is the matter with Robert?" she said.

"There is a Persian proverb which asserts a devil slips in between two winds," said Christopher. "Perhaps that is what has happened in this box to-night."

Lady Ver laughed harshly, and I sat there still as death. And all the time the music and the movement on the stage went on. I am glad she is murdered in the end—glad! Only I would like to have seen the blood gush out. I am fierce—fierce—sometimes.

---

300 Park Street,
Friday morning, *November 25th.*

I know just the meaning of dust and ashes, for that is what I felt I had had for breakfast this morning, the day after "Carmen."

Lady Ver had given orders she was not to be disturbed, so I did not go near her, and crept down to the dining-room, quite forgetting the master of the house had arrived. There he was, a strange, tall, lean man with fair hair, and sad, cross, brown eyes, and a nose inclined to pink at the tip—a look of indigestion about him, I feel sure. He was sitting in front of a *Daily Telegraph* propped up on the teapot, and some cold, untasted sole on his plate.

I came forward. He looked very surprised.

"I—I'm Evangeline Travers," I announced.

He said "How d'you do?" awkwardly. One could see without a notion what that meant.

"I'm staying here," I continued. "Did you not know?"

"Then won't you have some breakfast? Beastly cold, I fear," politeness forced him to utter. "No, Ianthe never writes to me. I had not heard any news for a fortnight, and I have not seen her yet."

Manners have been drummed into me from early youth, so I said, politely, "You only arrived from Paris late last night, did you not?"

"I got in about seven o'clock, I think," he replied.

"We had to leave so early—we were going to the opera," I said.

"A Wagner that begins at unearthly hours, I suppose?" he murmured, absently.

"No, it was 'Carmen,' but we dined first with my—my—guardian, Mr. Carruthers."

"Oh!"

We both ate for a little. The tea was greenish black—and lukewarm. No wonder he has dyspepsia.

"Are the children in, I wonder?" he hazarded, presently.

"Yes," I said. "I went to the nursery and saw them as I came down."

At that moment the three angels burst into the room, but came forward decorously and embraced their parent. They do not seem to adore him as they do Lady Ver.

"Good-morning, papa," said the eldest, and the other two repeated it in chorus. "We hope you have slept well and had a nice passage across the sea."

They evidently had been drilled outside.

Then, nature getting uppermost, they patted him patronizingly.

"Daddie, darling, have you brought us any new dolls from Paris?"

"And I want one with red hair, like Evangeline," said Yseult, the youngest.

Sir Charles seemed bored and uncomfortable; he kissed his three exquisite bits of Dresden china, so like and yet unlike himself—they have Lady Ver's complexion, but brown eyes and golden hair like his.

"Yes; ask Harbottle for the packages," he said. "I have no time to talk to you. Tell your mother I will be in for lunch," and making excuses to me for leaving so abruptly—an appointment in the City—he shuffled out of the room.

I wonder how Lady Ver makes his heart beat! I *don't* wonder she prefers—Lord Robert.

"Why is papa's nose so red?" said Yseult.

"Hush!" implored Mildred. "Poor papa has come off the sea."

"I don't love papa," said Corisande, the middle one. "He's cross, and sometimes he makes darling mummie cry."

"We must always love papa," chanted Mildred, in a lesson voice. "We must always love our parents, and grandmamma, and grandpapa, and aunts and cousins—amen." The "amen" slipped out unawares, and she looked confused, and corrected herself when she had said it.

"Let's find Harbottle. Harbottle is papa's valet," Corisande said, "and he is much thoughtfuller than papa. Last time he brought me a Highland boy doll, though papa had forgotten I asked for it."

They all three went out of the room, first kissing me, and courtesying sweetly when they got to the door. They are never rude or boisterous, the three angels—I love them.

Left alone, I did feel like a dead fish. The column "London Day by Day" caught my eye in the *Daily Telegraph*, and I idly glanced down it, not taking in the sense of the words, until "The Duke of Torquilstone has arrived at Vavasour House, St. James's, from abroad," I read.

Well, what did it matter to me—what did anything matter to me?—Lord Robert had met us in the hall again, as we were coming out of the opera; he looked very pale, and he apologized to Lady Ver for his abrupt departure. He had got a chill, he said, and had gone to have a glass of brandy, and was all right now, and would we not come to supper, and various other *empressé* things, looking at her with the greatest devotion. I might not have existed.

She was capricious, as she sometimes is. "No, Robert, I am going home to bed. I have got a chill, too," she said.

And the footman announcing the electric at that moment, we flew off and left them, Christopher having fastened my sable collar with an air of possession which would have irritated me beyond words at another time, but I felt cold and dead, and utterly numb.

Lady Ver did not speak a word on the way back, and kissed me frigidly as she went into her room; then she called out:

"I am tired, snake-girl; don't think I am cross. Good-night." And so I crept up to bed.

To-morrow is Saturday and my visit ends. After my lunch with Lady Merrenden, I am a wanderer on the face of the earth.

Where shall I wander to? I feel I want to go away by myself, away where I shall not see a human being who is English. I want to forget what they look like; I want to shut out of my sight their well-groomed heads; I want—oh, I do not know what I do want.

Shall I marry Mr. Carruthers? He would eat me up, and then go back to Paris to the lady he loves. But I should have the life I like—and the Carruthers's emeralds are beautiful—and I love Branches—and—and——

"Her ladyship would like to see you, miss," said a footman.

So I went up the stairs.

Lady Ver was in a darkened room, soft pink blinds right down beyond the half-drawn blue silk curtains.

"I have a fearful head, Evangeline," she said.

"Then I will smooth your hair," and I climbed up behind her and began to run over her forehead with the tips of my fingers.

"You are really a pet, snake-girl," she said, "and you can't help it."

"I can't help what?"

"Being a witch. I knew you would hurt me when I first saw you, and I tried to protect myself by being kind to you."

"Oh, dear Lady Ver!" I said, deeply moved. "I would not hurt you for the world, and indeed you misjudge me. I have kept the bargain to the very letter—and spirit."

"Yes, I know you have to the letter, at least, but why did Robert go out of the box last night?" she demanded, wearily.

"He said he had got a chill, did not he?" I replied, lamely. She clasped her hands passionately.

"A chill! You don't know Robert. He never had a chill in his life," she said. "Oh, he is the dearest, dearest being in the world. He makes me believe in good and all things honest. He isn't vicious, and isn't a prig, and he knows the world, and he lives in its ways like the rest of us, and yet he doesn't begin by thinking every woman is fair game and undermining what little self-respect she may have left to her."

"Yes," I said. I found nothing else to say.

"If I had had a husband like that I would never have yawned," she went on; "and besides, Robert is too masterful and would be too jealous to let one divert one's self with another."

"Yes," I said again, and continued to smooth her forehead.

"He has sentiment, too—he is not matter-of-fact and brutal—and oh, you should see him on a horse!—he is too, too beautiful." She stretched out her arms in a movement of weariness that was pathetic and touched me.

"You have known him a long, long time?" I said, gently.

"Perhaps five years, but only casually until this season. I was busy with some one else before. I have played with so many." Then she roused herself up. "But Robert is the only one who has never made love to me. Always dear and sweet, and treating me like a queen, as if I were too high for that, and having his own way, and not caring a pin for any one's opinion. And I have wanted him to make love to me often. But now I realize it is no use. Only, you sha'n't have him, snake-girl! I told him as we were going to the opera you were as cold as ice, and were playing with Christopher, and I am going to take him down to Northumberland with me to-morrow out of your way. He shall be my devoted friend, at any rate. You would break his heart, and I shall still hold you to your promise."

I said nothing.

"Do you hear? I say: *You* would break his heart. He would be only capable of loving straight to the end. The kind of love any other woman would die for—but—you—You are Carmen."

At all events, not *she*, nor any other woman, shall ever see what I am or am not. My heart is not for them to peck at. So I said, calmly:

"Carmen was stabbed!"

"And serve her right! Fascinating, fiendish demon!" Then she laughed, her mood changing.

"Did you see Charlie?" she said.

"We breakfasted together."

"Cheerful person, isn't he?"

"No," I said. "He looked cross and ill."

"Ill!" she said, with a shade of anxiety. "Oh, you only mean dyspeptic."

"Perhaps."

"Well, he always does when he comes from Paris. If you could go into his room and see the row of photographs on his mantelpiece, you might guess why."

"Pictures of 'Sole Dieppoise' and 'Poulet à la Victoria aux Truffes,' no doubt," I hazarded.

She doubled up with laughter. "Yes, just that," she said. "Well, he adores me in his way, and will bring me a new Cartier ring to make up for it—you will see at luncheon."

"He is a perfect husband, then."

"About the same as you will find Christopher. Only Christopher will start by being an exquisite lover. There is nothing he does not know, and Charlie has not an idea of that part. Heavens!—the dulness of my honeymoon!"

"Mrs. Carruthers said all honeymoons were only another parallel to going to the dentist or being photographed. Necessary evils to be got through for the sake of the results."

"The results!"

"Yes, the nice house and the jewels and the other things."

"Oh! Yes, I suppose she was right, but if one had married Robert one would have had both." She did not say both what—but oh, I knew!

"You think Mr. Carruthers will make a fair husband, then?" I asked.

"You will never really know Christopher. I have been acquainted with him for years. You will never feel he would tell you the whole truth about anything. He is an epicure, and an analyst of sensations. I don't know if he has any gods—he does not believe in them if he has; he believes in no one, and nothing, but perhaps himself. He is violently in love with you for the moment, and he wants to marry you, because he cannot obtain you on any other terms."

"You are flattering," I said, rather hurt.

"I am truthful. You will probably have a delightful time with him, and keep him devoted to you for years, because you are not in love with him; and he will take good care you do not look at any one else. I can imagine if one were in love with Christopher he would break one's heart, as he has broken poor Alicia Verney's."

"Oh, but how silly! People don't have broken hearts now; you are talking like out of a book, dear Lady Ver."

"There are a few cases of broken hearts, but they are not for book reasons—of death and tragedy, etc.—they are because we cannot have what we want, or keep what we have—" and she sighed.

We did not speak for a few minutes, then she said, quite gayly:

"You have made my head better; your touch is extraordinary; in spite of all, I like you, snake-girl. You are not found on every gooseberry-bush."

We kissed lightly, and I left her and went to my room.

Yes, the best thing I can do is to marry Christopher. I care for him so little that the lady in Paris won't matter to me, even if she is like Sir Charles's "Poulet à la Victoria aux Truffes." He is such a gentleman, he will at least be kind to me and refined and considerate—and the Carruthers emeralds are divine, and just my stones. I shall have them reset by Cartier. The lace, too, will suit me, and the sables, and I shall have the suite that Mrs. Carruthers used at Branches done up with pale, pale green, and burn all the early Victorians! And no doubt existence will be full of triumphs and pleasure.

But oh—I wish—I wish it were possible to obtain—"both!"

---

300 Park Street,
Friday night.

Luncheon passed off very well. Sir Charles returned from the City improved in temper, and, as Lady Ver had predicted, presented her with a Cartier jewel. It was a brooch, not a ring, but she was delighted, and purred to him.

He was a little late, and we were seated, a party of eight, when he came in. They all chaffed him about Paris, and he took it quite good-humoredly—he even seemed pleased. He has no wit, but he looks like a gentleman, and I dare say as husbands go he is suitable.

I am getting quite at home in the world, and can speak to any one. I listen, and I do not talk much, only when I want to say something that makes them think.

A very nice man sat next me to-day; he reminded me of the old generals at Branches. We had quite a war of wits, and it stimulated me.

He told me, among other things, when he discovered who I was, that he had known papa—papa was in the same Guards with him—and that he was the best-looking man of his day. Numbers of women were in love with him, he said, but he was a faithless being, and rode away.

"He probably enjoyed himself—don't you think so?—and he had the good luck to die in his zenith," I said.

"He was once engaged to Lady Merrenden, you know. She was Lady Sophia Vavasour then, and absolutely devoted to him, but Mrs. Carruthers came between them and carried him off—she was years older than he was, too, and as clever as paint."

"Poor papa seems to have been a weak creature, I fear."

"All men are weak," he said.

"And then he married and left Mrs. Carruthers, I suppose?" I asked. I wanted to hear as much as I could.

"Ye-e-s," said my old colonel. "I was best man at the wedding."

"And what was she like, my mamma?"

"She was the loveliest creature I ever saw," he said—"as lovely as you, only you are the image of your father, all but the hair—his was fair."

"No one has ever said I was lovely before. Oh, I am so glad if you think so," I said. It did please me. I have often been told I am attractive and extraordinary, and wonderful and divine, but never just lovely. He would not say any more about my parents, except that they hadn't a sou to live on, and were not very happy—Mrs. Carruthers took care of that.

Then, as every one was going, he said: "I am awfully glad to have met you. We must be pals, for the sake of old times," and he gave me his card for me to keep his address, and told me if ever I wanted a friend to send him a line—Colonel Tom Carden, The Albany.

I promised I would.

"You might give me away at my wedding," I said, gayly. "I am thinking of getting married, some day!"

"That I will," he promised; "and, by Jove! the man will be a fortunate fellow."

Lady Ver and I drove after luncheon—me paid some calls, and went in to tea with the Montgomeries, who had just arrived at Brown's Hotel for a week's shopping.

"Aunt Katherine brings those poor girls up always at this time, and takes them to some impossible old dressmaker of her own in the daytime, and to Shakespeare or a concert at night, and returns with them equipped in more hideous garments each year. It is positively cruel," said Lady Ver, as we went up the stairs to their *appartement.*

There they were, sitting round the tea-table just as at Tryland—Kirstie and Jean embroidering and knitting, and the other two reading new catalogues of books for their work.

Lady Ver began to tease them. She asked them all sorts of questions about their new frocks, and suggested they had better go to Paris once in a way. Lady Katherine was like ice. She strongly disapproved of my being with her niece, one could see.

The connection with the family she hoped would be ended with my visit to Tryland. Malcolm was arriving in town, too, we gathered, and Lady Ver left a message to ask him to dine to-night.

Then we got away.

"If one of those lumps of suet had a spark of spirit they would go straight to the devil," Lady Ver said as we went down the stairs. "Think of it—ties and altar-cloths in London! Mercifully they could not dine to-night. I had to ask them, and they generally come once while they are up—the four girls and Aunt Katherine—and it is with the greatest difficulty I can collect four young men for them if they get the least hint whom they are to meet. I generally secure a couple of socially budding Jews, because I feel the subscriptions for their charities which they will pester whoever they do sit next for are better filched from the Hebrew than from some pretty, needy Guardsman. Oh, what a life!"

She was so kind to me on the way back; she said she hated leaving me alone on the morrow, and that I must settle now what I was going to do or she would not go. I said I would go to Claridge's, where Mrs. Carruthers and I had always stayed, and remain quietly alone with Véronique. I could afford it for a week. So we drove there and made the arrangement.

"It is absolutely impossible for you to go on like this, dear child," she said. "You must have a chaperone; you are far too pretty to stay alone in a hotel. What *can* I do for you?"

I felt so horribly uncomfortable I was really at my wits' end. Oh, it is no fun being an adventuress, after all, if you want to keep your friends of the world as well.

"Perhaps it won't matter if I don't see any one for a few days," I said. "I will write to Paris. My old mademoiselle is married there to a flourishing poet, I believe—perhaps she would take me as a paying guest for a little."

"That is very visionary—a French poet! Horrible, long-haired, frowsy creature! Impossible! Surely you see how necessary it is for you to marry Christopher as soon as you can, Evangeline, don't you?" she said, and I was obliged to admit there were reasons.

"The truth is, you can't be the least eccentric or unconventional if you are good-looking and unmarried," she continued. "You may snap your fingers at society, but if you do you won't have a good time, and all the men will either foolishly champion you or be impertinent to you."

"Oh, I realize it," I said, and there was a lump in my throat.

"I shall write to Christopher to-morrow," she went on, "and thank him for our outing last night, and I shall say something nice about you and your loneliness, and that he, as a kind of relation, may go and see you on Sunday, as long as he doesn't make love to you, and he can take you to the Zoo—don't see him in your sitting-room. That will give him just the extra fillip, and he will go, and you will be demure, and then by those stimulating lions' and tigers' cages you can plight your troth. It will be quite respectable. Wire to me at once on Monday to Sedgwick, and you must come back to Park Street directly I return on Thursday, if it is all settled."

I thanked her as well as I could. She was quite ingenuous and quite sincere. I should be a welcome guest as Christopher's fiancée, and there was no use my feeling bitter about it—she was quite right.

As I put my hand on Malcolm's skinny arm going down to the dining-room, the only consolation was my fate had not got to be him. I would rather be anything in the world than married to that!

I tried to be agreeable to Sir Charles. We were only a party of six. An old Miss Harpenden, who goes everywhere to play bridge, and Malcolm, and one of Lady Ver's young men, and I. Sir Charles is absent, and brings himself back. He fiddles with the knives and forks, and sprawls on the table rather, too. He looks at Lady Ver with admiration in his eyes. It is true, then, in the intervals of Paris, I suppose, she can make his heart beat.

Malcolm made love to me after dinner. We were left to talk when the others sat down to bridge in the little drawing-room.

"I missed you so terribly, Miss Travers," he said, priggishly, "when you left us that I realized I was extremely attracted by you."

"No, you don't say so!" I said, innocently. "Could one believe a thing like that?"

"Yes," he said, earnestly. "You may, indeed, believe it."

"Do not say it so suddenly, then," I said, turning my head away so that he could not see how I was laughing. "You see, to a red-haired person like me these compliments go to my head."

"Oh, I do not want to flurry you," he said, affably. "I know I have been a good deal sought after—perhaps on account of my possessions"—this with arrogant modesty—"but I am willing to lay everything at your feet if you will marry me."

"Everything?" I asked.

"Yes, everything."

"You are too good, Mr. Montgomerie—but what would your mother say?"

He looked uneasy and slightly unnerved.

"My mother, I fear, has old-fashioned notions, but I am sure if you went to her dressmaker—you—you would look different."

"Should you like me to look different, then? You wouldn't recognize me, you know, if I went to her dressmaker."

"I like you just as you are," he said, with an air of great condescension.

"I am overcome," I said, humbly. "But—but—what is this story I hear about Miss Angela Grey? A lady, I see in the papers, who dances at the Gaiety, is it not? Are you sure she will permit you to make this declaration without her knowledge?"

He became petrified.
"Who has told you about her?" he asked.
"No one," I said. "Jean said your father was angry with you on account of a horse of that name, but I chanced to see it in the list of attractions at the Gaiety, so I conclude it is not a horse; and if you are engaged to her, I don't think it is quite right of you to try and break my heart."
"Oh, Evangeline—Miss Travers!" he spluttered. "I am greatly attached to you—the other was only a pastime—a—a—Oh, we men, you know—young and—and—run after—have our temptations, you know. You must think nothing about it. I will never see her again, except just to finally say good-bye. I promise you."
"Oh, I could not do a mean thing like that, Mr. Montgomerie," I said. "You must not think of behaving so on my account. I am not altogether heartbroken, you know; in fact, I rather think of getting married, myself."
He bounded up.
"Oh, you have deceived me, then!" he said, in self-righteous wrath. "After all I said to you that evening at Tryland, and what you promised then! Yes, you have grossly deceived me."
I could not say I had not listened to a word he had said that night and was utterly unconscious of what I had promised. Even his self-appreciation did not deserve such a blow as that, so I softened my voice and natural anger at his words, and said, quite gently:
"Do not be angry. If I have unconsciously given you a wrong impression I am sorry, but if one came to talking of deceiving, you have deceived me about Miss Grey, so do not let us speak further upon the matter. We are quits. Now, won't you be friends as you have always been?" and I put out my hand and smiled frankly in his face. The mean little lines in it relaxed, he pulled himself together, and took my hand and pressed it warmly. From which I knew there was more in the affair of Angela Grey than met the eye.
"Evangeline," he said. "I shall always love you; but Miss Grey is an estimable young woman—there is not a word to be said against her moral character—and I have promised her my hand in marriage, so perhaps we had better say good-bye."
"Good-bye," I said; "but I consider I have every reason to feel insulted by your offer, which was not, judging from your subsequent remarks, worth a moment's thought."
"Oh, but I love you!" he said, and by his face, for the time, this was probably true. So I did not say any more, and we rose and joined the bridge players. And I contrived that he should not speak to me again alone before he said good-night.
"Did Malcolm propose to you?" Lady Ver asked as we came up to bed. "I thought I saw a look in his eye at dinner."
I told her he had done it in a kind of a way, with a reservation in favor of Miss Angela Grey.
"That is too dreadful!" she said. "There is a regular epidemic in some of the Guards regiments just now to marry these poor, common things with high moral characters and indifferent feet. But I should have thought the cuteness of the Scot would have protected Malcolm from their designs. Poor Aunt Katherine!"

CLARIDGE'S,
Saturday, *November 26th.*

Lady Ver went off early to the station to catch her train to Northumberland this morning, and I hardly saw her to say good-bye. She seemed out of temper, too, on getting a note—she did not tell me who it was from or what it was about, only she said immediately after that I was not to be stupid. "Do not play with Christopher further," she said, "or you will lose him. He will certainly come and see you to-morrow. He wrote to me this morning in answer to mine of last night, but he says he won't go to the Zoo, so you will have to see him in your sitting-room, after all. He will come about four."
I did not speak.
"Evangeline," she said, "promise me you won't be a fool."
"I—won't be a fool," I said.
Then she kissed me and was off, and a few moments after I also started for Claridge's.
I have a very nice little suite right up at the top, and if only it were respectable for me, and I could afford it, I could live here very comfortably by myself for a long time.
At a quarter to two I was ringing the bell at 200 Carlton House Terrace—Lady Merrenden's house—with a strange feeling of excitement and interest. Of course, it must have been because once she had been engaged to papa. In the second thoughts take to flash, I remembered Lord Robert's words when I talked of coming to London alone at Branches—how he would bring me here, and how she would be kind to me until I could "hunt round."
Oh, it came to me with a sudden stab. He was leaning over Lady Ver in the northern train by now.
Such a stately, beautiful hall it is when the doors open, with a fine staircase going each way, and full of splendid pictures, and the whole atmosphere pervaded with an air of refinement and calm.
The footmen are tall, and not too young, and even at this time of the year have powdered hair.
Lady Merrenden was up-stairs in the small drawing-room, and she rose to meet me, a book in her hand, when I was announced.
Her manners are so beautiful in her own home—gracious, and not the least patronizing.

"I am so glad to see you," she said. "I hope you won't be bored, but I have not asked any one to meet you, only my nephew Torquilstone is coming. He is a great sufferer, poor fellow, and numbers of faces worry him at times——"

I said I was delighted to see her alone. No look more kind could be expressed in a human countenance than is expressed in hers. She has the same exceptional appearance of breeding that Lord Robert has—tiny ears and wrists and head; even dressed as a char-woman Lady Merrenden would look like a great lady.

Very soon we were talking without the least restraint. She did not speak of people or of very deep things, but it gave one the impression of an elevated mind and a knowledge of books, and wide thoughts. Oh, I could love her so easily.

We had been talking for nearly a quarter of an hour. She had incidentally asked me where I was staying now, and had not seemed surprised or shocked when I said Claridge's, and by myself.

All she said was: "What a lonely little girl! But I dare say it is very restful sometimes to be by one's self, only you must let your friends come and see you, won't you?"

"I don't think I have any friends," I said. "You see, I have been out so little, but if you would come and see me—oh, I should be so grateful."

"Then you must count me as one of your rare friends!" she said.

Nothing could be so rare or so sweet as her smile. Fancy papa throwing over this angel for Mrs. Carruthers! Men are certainly unaccountable creatures.

I said I would be too honored to have her for a friend, and she took my hand.

"You bring back the long ago," she said. "My name is Evangeline, too—Sophia Evangeline—and I sometimes think you may have been called so in remembrance of me."

What a strange, powerful factor love must be! Here were these two women, Mrs. Carruthers and Lady Merrenden—the very opposites of each other—and they had evidently both adored papa, and both, according to their natures, had taken an interest in me in consequence, the child of a third woman who had superseded them both! Papa must have been extraordinarily fascinating, for to the day of her death Mrs. Carruthers had his miniature on her table, with a fresh rose beside it—his memory the only soft spot, it seemed, in her hard heart.

And this sweet lady's eyes melted in tenderness when she spoke of the long ago, although she does not know me well enough yet to say anything further. To me papa's picture is nothing so very wonderful—just a good-looking young Guardsman, with eyes shaped like mine, only gray, and light, curly hair. He must have had "a way with him," as the servants say.

At that moment the Duke of Torquilstone came in. Oh, such a sad sight!

A poor, humpbacked man, with a strong face and head and a soured, suspicious, cynical expression. He would evidently have been very tall but for his deformity—a hump stands out on his back almost like Mr. Punch. He can't be much over forty, but he looks far older; his hair is quite gray.

Not a line or an expression in him reminded me of Lord Robert, I am glad to say.

Lady Merrenden introduced us, and Lord Merrenden came in then, too, and we all went down to luncheon.

It was a rather small table, so we were all near one another and could talk.

The dining-room is immense.

"I always have this little table when we are such a small party," Lady Merrenden said. "It is more cosey, and one does not feel so isolated."

How I agreed with her!

The duke looked at me searchingly, often, with his shrewd little eyes. One could not say if it was with approval or disapproval.

Lord Merrenden talked about politics and the questions of the day. He has a courteous manner, and all their voices are soft and refined. And nothing could have been more smooth and silent than the service.

The luncheon was very simple and very good, but not half the number of rich dishes like at Branches, or Lady Ver's. There was only one bowl of violets on the table, but the bowl was gold, and a beautiful shape, and the violets nearly as big as pansies. My eyes wandered to the pictures—Gainsborough's and Reynolds's and Romney's—of stately men and women.

"You met my other nephew, Lord Robert, did you not?" Lady Merrenden said, presently. "He told me he had gone to Branches, where I believe you lived."

"Yes," I said, and—oh, it is too humiliating to write!—I felt my cheeks get crimson at the mention of Lord Robert's name. What could she have thought? Can anything be so young-ladylike and ridiculous!

"He came to the opera with us the night before last," I continued. "Mr. Carruthers had a box, and Lady Verningham and I went with them." Then, recollecting how odd this must sound in my deep mourning, I added, "I am so fond of music."

"So is Robert," she said. "I am sure he must have been pleased to meet a kindred spirit there."

Sweet, charming, kind lady! If she only knew what emotions were really agitating us in that box that night! I fear the actual love of music was the least of them.

The duke, during this conversation and from the beginning mention of Lord Robert's name, never took his eyes off my face—it was very disconcerting; his look was clearer now, and it was certainly disapproving.

We had coffee up-stairs, out of such exquisite Dresden cups, and then Lord Merrenden showed me some miniatures. Finally it happened that the duke and I were left alone for a minute looking out of a window onto the Mall.

His eyes pierced me through and through. Well, at all events, my nose and my ears and my wrists are as fine as Lady Merrenden's—poor mamma's odd mother does not show in me on the outside, thank goodness! He did not say much, only commonplaces about the view. I felt afraid of him, and rather depressed. I am sure he dislikes me.

"May I not drive you somewhere?" my kind hostess said. "Or, if you have nowhere in particular to go, will you come with me?"

I said I should be delighted. An ache of loneliness was creeping over me. I wanted to put off as long as possible getting back to the hotel. I wanted to distract my thoughts from dwelling upon to-morrow and what I was going to say to Christopher. To-morrow—that seems the end of the world!

She has beautiful horses, Lady Merrenden, and the whole turn-out, except she herself, is as smart as can be. She really looks a little frumpish out-of-doors, and perhaps that is why papa went on to Mrs. Carruthers. Goodness and dearness like this do not suit male creatures as well as caprice, it seems.

She was so good to me, and talked in the nicest way. I quite forgot I was a homeless wanderer, and arrived at Claridge's about half-past four in almost good spirits.

"You won't forget I am to be one of your friends," Lady Merrenden said, as I bid her good-bye.

"Indeed I won't," I replied, and she drove off, smiling at me.

I do wonder what she will think of my marriage with Christopher.

Now it is night. I have had a miserable, lonely dinner in my sitting-room. Véronique has been most gracious and coddling—she feels Mr. Carruthers in the air, I suppose—and so I must go to bed.

Oh, why am I not happy, and why don't I think this is a delightful and unusual situation, as I once would have done? I only feel depressed and miserable, and as if I wished Christopher at the bottom of the sea. I have told myself how good-looking he is, and how he attracted me at Branches, but that was before—Yes, I may as well write what I was going to—before Lord Robert arrived. Well, he and Lady Ver are talking together on a nice sofa by now, I suppose, in a big, well-lit drawing-room, and—Oh, I *wish*, I *wish* I had never made any bargain with her—perhaps, now, in that case—Ah, well——

Sunday afternoon.

No, I can't bear it. All the morning I have been in a fever, first hot and then cold. What will it be like? Oh, I shall faint when he kisses me. And I know he will be dreadful like that; I have seen it in his eye. He will eat me up. Oh, I am sure I shall hate it. No man has ever kissed me in my life, and I can't judge, but I am sure it is frightful—unless—I feel as if I shall go crazy if I stay here any longer. I can't—I can't stop and wait and face it. I must have some air first. There is a misty fog. I would like to go out and get lost in it, and I *will*, too! Not get lost, perhaps, but go out in it, and alone. I won't have even Véronique. I shall go by myself into the park. It is growing nearly dark, though only three o'clock. I have got an hour. It looks mysterious, and will soothe me, and suit my mood, and then, when I come in again, I shall perhaps be able to bear it bravely, kisses and all.

CLARIDGE'S,
Sunday evening, *November 27th.*

I have a great deal to write, and yet it is only a few hours since I shut up this book and replaced the key on my bracelet.

By a quarter-past three I was making my way through Grosvenor Square. Everything was misty and blurred, but not actually a thick fog—or any chance of being lost. By the time I got into the park it had lifted a little. It seemed close and warm, and as I went on I got more depressed. I have never been out alone before—that in itself seemed strange, and ought to have amused me.

The image of Christopher kept floating in front of me; his face seemed to have the expression of a satyr. Well, at all events, he would never be able to break my heart like "Alicia Verney's"—nothing could ever make me care for him. I tried to think of all the good I was going to get out of the affair, and how really fond I was of Branches.

I walked very fast; people loomed at me, and then disappeared in the mist. It was getting almost dusk, and suddenly I felt tired and sat down on a bench.

I had wandered into a side path where there were no chairs. On the bench before mine I saw, as I passed, a tramp huddled up. I wondered what his thoughts were, and if he felt any more miserable than I did. I dare say I was crouching in a depressed position, too.

Not many people went by, and every moment it grew darker. In all my life, even on the days when Mrs. Carruthers taunted me about mamma being nobody, I have never felt so wretched. Tears kept rising in my eyes, and I did not even worry to blink them away. Who would see me, and who in the world would care if they did see?

Suddenly I was conscious that a very perfect figure was coming out of the mist towards me, but not until he was close to me, and stopping, with a start, peered into my face, did I recognize it was Lord Robert.

"Evangeline!" he exclaimed, in a voice of consternation. "I—what, oh! what is the matter?"

No wonder he was surprised. Why he had not taken me for some tramp, too, and passed on, I don't know.

"Nothing," I said, as well as I could, and tried to tilt my hat over my eyes. I had no veil on, unfortunately. "I have just been for a walk. Why do you call me Evangeline and why are you not in Northumberland?"

He looked so tall and beautiful, and his face had no expression of contempt or anger now, only distress and sympathy.

"I was suddenly put on guard yesterday, and could not get leave. I am going to-morrow," he said, not answering the first part, "but, oh, I can't bear to see you sitting here alone and looking so, so miserable. Mayn't I take you home? You will catch cold in the damp."

"Oh no, not yet. I won't go back yet," I said, hardly realizing what I was saying. He sat down beside me and slipped his hand into my muff, pressing my clasped fingers, the gentlest, friendliest caress a child might have made in sympathy. It touched some foolish chord in my nature, some want of self-control inherited from mamma's ordinary mother, I suppose; anyway the tears poured down my face. I could not help it. Oh, the shame of it! To sit crying in the park, in front of Lord Robert, of all people in the world, too!

"Dear, dear little girl," he said, "tell me about it," and he held my hand in my muff with his strong, warm hand.

"I—I have nothing to tell," I said, choking down a sob. "I am ashamed for you to see me like this, only—I am feeling so very miserable."

"Dear child!" he said. "Well, you are not to be—I won't have it. Has some one been unkind to you? Tell me, tell me." His voice was trembling with distress.

"It's—it's nothing," I mumbled.

I dared not look at him, I knew his eyebrows would be up in that way that attracts me so dreadfully.

"Listen," he whispered almost, and bent over me. "I want you to be friends with me so that I can help you. I want you to go back to the time we packed your books together. God knows what has come between us since—it is not of my doing. But I want to take care of you, dear little girl, to-day. It—oh, it hurts me so to see you crying here!"

"I—would like to be friends," I said. "I never wanted to be anything else, but I could not help it, and I can't now."

"Won't you tell me the reason?" he pleaded. "You have made me so dreadfully unhappy about it. I thought all sorts of things. You know I am a jealous beast."

There can't in the world be another voice as engaging as Lord Robert's, and he has a trick of pronouncing words that is too attractive; and the way his mouth goes when he is speaking, showing his perfectly chiselled lips under the little mustache! There is no use pretending. I was sitting there on the bench going through thrills of emotion and longing for him to take me in his arms. It is too frightful to think of. I must be bad, after all.

"Now you are going to tell me everything about it," he commanded. "To begin with: what made you suddenly change at Trylands after the first afternoon—and then, what is it that makes you so unhappy now?"

"I can't tell you either," I said, very low. I hoped the common grandmother would not take me as far as doing mean tricks to Lady Ver.

"Oh, you have made me wild!" he exclaimed, letting go my hand and leaning both elbows on his knees, while he pushed his hat to the back of his head—"perfectly mad with fury and jealousy! That brute Malcolm! And then looking at Campion at dinner, and, worst of all, Christopher in the box at 'Carmen'! Wicked, naughty little thing! And yet underneath I have a feeling it is for some absurd reason, and not for sheer devilment. If I thought that, I would soon get not to care. I did think it at 'Carmen.'"

"Yes, I know," I said.

"You know what?" he looked up, startled; then he took my hand again and sat close to me.

"Oh, please, please don't, Lord Robert!" I said.

It really made me quiver so with the loveliest feeling I have ever known, that I knew I should never be able to keep my head if he went on.

"Please, please don't hold my hand," I said. "It—it makes me not able to behave nicely."

"Darling," he whispered, "then it shows that you like me, and I sha'n't let go until you tell me every little bit."

"Oh, I can't, I can't!" I felt too tortured, and yet, waves of joy were rushing over me. That *is* a word, "darling," for giving feelings down the back.

"Evangeline," he said, quite sternly, "will you answer this question, then: Do you like me, or do you hate me? Because, as you must know very well, I love you."

Oh, the wild joy of hearing him say that! What in the world did anything else matter? For a moment there was a singing in my ears, and I forgot everything but our two selves. Then the picture of Christopher waiting for me, with his cold cynic's face and eyes blazing with passion, rushed into my vision, and the duke's critical, suspicious, disapproving scrutiny, and I felt as if a cry of pain, like a wounded animal, escaped me.

"Darling, darling, what is it? Did I hurt your dear little hand?" Lord Robert exclaimed, tenderly.

"No," I whispered, brokenly; "but I cannot listen to you. I am going back to Claridge's now, and I am going to marry Mr. Carruthers."

He dropped my hand as if it stung him.

"Good God! Then it is true," was all he said.

In fear I glanced at him, his face looked gray in the quickly gathering mist.

"Oh, Robert!" I said, in anguish, unable to help myself. "It isn't because I want to. I—I—oh, probably I love you, but I must; there is nothing else to be done."

"Isn't there?" he said, all the life and joy coming back to his face. "Do you think I will let Christopher, or any other man in the world have you, now that you have confessed that?" and, fortunately, there was no one in sight, because he put his arms round my neck and drew me close and kissed my lips.

Oh, what nonsense people talk of heaven! Sitting on clouds and singing psalms and things like that! There can't be any heaven half so lovely as being kissed by Robert. I felt quite giddy with happiness for several exquisite seconds, then I woke up. It was all absolutely impossible, I knew, and I must keep my head.

"Now you belong to me," he said, letting his arm slip down to my waist, "so you must begin at the beginning, and tell me everything."

"No, no," I said, struggling feebly to free myself, and feeling so glad he held me tight. "It is impossible, all the same, and that only makes it harder. Christopher is coming to see me at four, and I promised Lady Ver I would not be a fool, and would marry him."

"A fig for Lady Ver," he said, calmly. "If that is all, you leave her to me—she never argues with me."

"It is not only that; I—I promised I would never play with you."

"And you certainly never shall," he said, and I could see a look in his eye as he purposely misconstrued my words, and then he deliberately kissed me again. Oh, I like it better than anything else in the world! How could any one keep their head with Robert quite close, making love like that?

"You certainly never—never—shall," he said again, with a kiss between each word. "I will take care of that. Your time of playing with people is over, mademoiselle. When you are married to me, I shall fight with any one who dares to look at you."

"But I shall never be married to you, Robert," I said, though as I could only be happy for such a few moments I did not think it necessary to move away out of his arms. How thankful I was to the fog! and no one passing! I shall always adore fogs.

"Yes, you will," he announced, with perfect certainty, "in about a fortnight, I should think. I can't and won't have you staying at Claridge's by yourself. I shall take you back this afternoon to Aunt Sophia. Only all that we can settle presently; now for the moment I want you to tell me you love me, and that you are sorry for being such a little brute all this time."

"I did not know it until just now, but I think—I probably do love you—Robert," I said.

He was holding my hand in my muff again, the other arm round my waist. Absolutely disgraceful behavior in the park. We might have been Susan Jane and Thomas Augustus, and yet I was perfectly happy, and felt it was the only natural way to sit.

A figure appeared in the distance—we started apart.

"Oh, really, really—" I gasped—"we—— you—must be different."

He leaned back and laughed.

"You sweet darling! Well, come, we will go for a drive in a hansom; we will choose one without a light inside. Albert Gate is quite close—come!" and he rose, and taking my arm, not offering his to me, like in books, he drew me on down the path.

I am sure any one would be terribly shocked to read what I have written, but not so much if they knew Robert, and how utterly adorable he is, and how masterful, and simple, and direct. He does not split straws or bandy words. I had made the admission that I loved him, and that was enough to go upon.

As we walked along I tried to tell him it was impossible, that I must go back to Christopher, that Lady Ver would think I had broken my word about it. I did not, of course, tell him of her bargain with me over him, but he probably guessed that, because before we got into the hansom even, he had begun to put me through a searching cross-examination as to the reasons for my behavior at Tryland, and Park Street, and the opera. I felt like a child with a strong man, and every moment more idiotically happy and in love with him.

He told the cabman to drive to Hammersmith, and then put his arm round my waist again, and held my hand, pulling my glove off backward first. It is a great, big, granny muff of sable I have, Mrs. Carruthers's present on my last birthday. I never thought then to what charming use it would be put.

"Now I think we have demolished all your silly little reasons for making me miserable," he said. "What others have you to bring forward as to why you can't marry me in a fortnight?"

I was silent—I did not know how to say it—the principal reason of all.

"Evangeline, darling," he pleaded. "Oh, why will you make us both unhappy? Tell me, at least."

"Your brother, the duke," I said, very low. "He will never consent to your marrying a person like me, with no relations."

He was silent for a second, then: "My brother is an awfully good fellow," he said; "but his mind is warped by his infirmity. You must not think hardly of him; he will love you directly he sees you, like every one else."

"I saw him yesterday," I said.

Robert was so astonished.

"Where did you see him?" he asked.

Then I told him about meeting Lady Merrenden, and her asking me to luncheon, and about her having been in love with papa, and about the duke having looked me through and through with an expression of dislike.

"Oh, I see it all," said Robert, holding me closer. "Aunt Sophia and I are great friends, you know; she has always been like my mother, who died when I was a baby. I told her all about you when I came from Branches, and how I had fallen deeply in love with you at first sight, and that she must help me to see you at Tryland; and she did, and then I thought you had grown to dislike me, so when I came back she guessed I was unhappy about something, and this is her first step to find out how she can do me a good turn. Oh, she is a dear!"

"Yes, indeed, she is," I said.

"Of course she is extra interested in you if she was in love with your father. So that is all right, darling; she must know all about your family, and can tell Torquilstone. Why, we have nothing to fear!"

"Oh yes, we have," I said. "I know all the story of what your brother is *toqué* about. Lady Ver told me. You see, the awkward part is mamma was really nobody; her father and mother forgot to get married, and although mamma was lovely and had been beautifully brought up by two old ladies at Brighton, it was a disgrace for papa marrying her. Mrs. Carruthers has often taunted me with this."

"Darling!" he interrupted, and began to kiss me again, and that gave me such feeling I could not collect my thoughts to go on with what I was saying for a few minutes. We both were rather silly, if it is silly to be madly, wildly happy, and oblivious of everything else.

"I will go straight to Aunt Sophia now, when I take you back to Claridge's," he said, presently, when we had got a little calmer.

I wonder what kisses do that it makes one have that perfectly lovely sensation down the back, just like certain music does, only much, much more so. I thought they would be dreadful things when it was a question of Christopher, but Robert! Oh, well, as I said before, I can't think of any other heaven.

"What time is it?" I had sense enough to ask presently.

He lit a match and looked at his watch.

"Ten minutes past five," he exclaimed.

"And Christopher was coming about four," I said; "and if you had not chanced to meet me in the park by now I should have been engaged to him, and probably trying to bear his kissing me."

"My God!" said Robert, fiercely; "it makes me rave to think of it," and he held me so tight for a moment I could hardly breathe.

"You won't have any one else's kisses ever again in this world, and that I tell you," he said, through his teeth.

"I—I don't want them," I whispered creeping closer to him. "And I never have had any, never any one but you, Robert."

"Darling," he said, "how that pleases me!"

Of course, if I wanted to I could go on writing pages and pages of all the lovely things we said to each other, but it would sound, even to read to myself, such nonsense that I can't, and I couldn't make the tone of Robert's voice, or the exquisite fascination of his ways—tender, and adoring, and masterful. It must all stay in my heart, but oh! it is as if a fairy with a wand had passed and said "bloom" to a winter tree. Numbers of emotions that I had never dreamed about were surging through me—the floodgates of everything in my soul seemed opening in one rush of love and joy. While we were together nothing appeared to matter, all barriers melted away.

Fate would be sure to be kind to lovers like us.

We got back to Claridge's about six, and Robert would not let me go up to my sitting-room until he had found out if Christopher had gone.

Yes, he had come at four, we discovered, and had waited twenty minutes, and then left, saying he would come again at half-past six.

"Then you will write him a note, and give it to the porter for him, saying you are engaged to me and can't see him," Robert said.

"No, I won't do that. I am not engaged to you, and cannot be until your family consent and are nice to me," I said.

"Darling!" he faltered, and his voice trembled with emotion. "Darling, love is between you and me—it is our lives. However, that can go. The ways of my family—nothing shall ever separate you from me or me from you, I swear it! Write to Christopher."

I sat down at a table in the hall and wrote:

"DEAR MR. CARRUTHERS,—

"I am sorry I was out."

then I bit the end of my pen.

"Don't come and see me this evening. I will tell you why in a day or two.

"Yours sincerely,
"EVANGELINE TRAVERS."

"Will that do?" I said, and I handed it to Robert, while I addressed the envelope.

"Yes," he said, and waited while I sealed it up and gave it to the porter. Then, with a surreptitious squeeze of the hand, he left me to go to Lady Merrenden.

I have come up to my little sitting-room a changed being. The whole world revolves for me upon another axis, and all within the space of three short hours.

CLARIDGE'S,
Sunday night, *November 27th.*

Late this evening, about eight o'clock, when I had relocked my journal, I got a note from Robert. I was just going to begin my dinner.

I tore it open, inside was another; I did not wait to look who from, I was too eager to read his. I paste it in:

"CARLTON HOUSE TERRACE.

"MY DARLING,—

"I have had a long talk with Aunt Sophia, and she is everything that is sweet and kind, but she fears Torquilstone will be a little difficult (*I don't care, nothing* shall separate us now). She asks me not to go and see you again to-night as she thinks it would be better for you that I should not go to the hotel so late. Darling, read her note, and you will see how nice she is. I shall come round to-morrow, the moment the beastly stables are finished, about twelve o'clock. Oh, take care of yourself! What a difference to-night and last night! I was feeling horribly miserable and reckless, and to-night! Well, you can guess. I am not half good enough for you, darling beautiful queen, but I think I shall know how to make you happy. I love you.

"Good-night my own.
"ROBERT."

"Do please send me a tiny line by my servant. I have told him to wait."

I have never had a love-letter before. What lovely things they are. I felt thrills of delight over bits of it. Of course I see now that I must have been dreadfully in love with Robert all along, only I did not know it quite. I fell into a kind of blissful dream, and then I roused myself up to read Lady Merrenden's. I sha'n't put hers in, too; it fills up too much, and I can't shut the clasp of my journal. It is a perfectly sweet little letter, just saying Robert had told her the news, and that she was prepared to welcome me as her dearest niece, and to do all she could for us. She hoped I would not think her very tiresome and old-fashioned suggesting Robert had better not see me again to-night, and, if it would not inconvenience me, she would herself come round to-morrow morning and discuss what was best to be done.

Véronique said Lord Robert's valet was waiting outside the door, so I flew to my table and began to write. My hand trembled so I made a blot, and had to tear that sheet up; then I wrote another. Just a little word. I was frightened; I couldn't say loving things in a letter; I had not even spoken many to him—yet.

"I loved your note," I began; "and I think Lady Merrenden is quite right. I will be here at twelve, and very pleased to see you." I wanted to say I loved him, and thought twelve o'clock a long way off, but of course one could not write such things as that, so I ended with just,

"Love from"
"EVANGELINE."

Then I read it over, and it did sound "missish" and silly. However, with the man waiting there in the passage, and Véronique fussing in and out of my bedroom, besides the waiters bringing up my dinner, I could not go tearing up sheets and writing others, it looked so flurried, so it was put into an envelope. Then, in one of the seconds I was alone, I nipped off a violet from a bunch on the table and pushed it in, too. I wonder if he will think it sentimental of me! When I had written the name, I had not an idea where to address it. His was written from Carlton House Terrace, but he was evidently not there now, as his servant had brought it. I felt so nervous and excited, it was too ridiculous—I am very calm as a rule. I called the man, and asked him where was his lordship now? I did not like to say I was ignorant of where he lived.

"His Lordship is at Vavasour House, madam," he said, respectfully, but with the faintest shade of surprise that I should not know. "His lordship dines at home this evening with his grace."

I scribbled a note to Lady Merrenden. I would be delighted to see her in the morning at whatever time suited her. I would not go out at all, and I thanked her. It was much easier to write sweet things to her than to Robert.

When I was alone I could not eat. Véronique came in to try and persuade me. I looked so very pale, she said, she feared I had taken cold. She was in one of her "old-mother" moods, when she drops the third person sometimes, and calls me "*mon enfant.*"

"Oh, Véronique, I have not got a cold; I am only wildly happy," I said.

"Mademoiselle is doubtless fiancée to Mr. Carruthers. *Oh, mon enfant adorée*," she cried, "*que je suis contente!*"

"Gracious, no!" I exclaimed. This brought me back to Christopher with a start. What would he say when he heard?

"No, Véronique, to some one much nicer—Lord Robert Vavasour."

Véronique was frightfully interested. Mr. Carruthers she would have preferred, to me, she admitted, as being more solid, more "*rangé*," "*plus à la fin de ses bêtises*," but, no doubt, "milor" was charming too, and for certain one day mademoiselle would be duchess. In the meanwhile what kind of coronet would mademoiselle have on her trousseau?

I was obliged to explain that I should not have any, or any trousseau, for an indefinite time, as nothing was settled yet. This damped her a little.

"*Un frère de duc, et pas de couronne!*" After seven years in England she was yet unable to understand these strange habitudes, she said.

She insisted upon putting me to bed directly after dinner, "to be prettier for *milor demain*!" and then when she had tucked me up, and was turning out the light in the centre of the room, she looked back. "Mademoiselle is too beautiful like that," she said, as if it slipped from her. "*Mon Dieu! il ne s'embêterai pas, le monsieur!*"

CLARIDGE'S,
Monday morning.

I wonder how I lived before I met Robert. I wonder what use were the days. Oh, and I wonder, I wonder, if the duke continues to be obdurate about me, if I shall ever have the strength of mind to part from him so as not to spoil his future.

Such a short time ago—not yet four weeks—since I was still at Branches, and wondering what made the clock go round, the great, big clock of life.

Oh, now I know. It is being in love—frightfully in love, as we are. I must try and keep my head, though, and remember all the remarks of Lady Ver about things and men. Fighters all of them, and they must never feel quite sure. It will be dreadfully difficult to tease Robert, because he is so direct and simple, but I must try, I suppose. Perhaps being so very pretty as I am, and having all the male creatures looking at me with interest, will do, and be enough to keep him worried, and I won't have to be tiresome myself. I hope so, because I really do love him so extremely, I would like to let myself go, and be as sweet as I want to.

I am doing all the things I thought perfectly silly to hear of before. I kissed his letter, and slept with it on the pillow beside me, and this morning woke at six, and turned on the electric light to read it again. The part where the "darlings" come is quite blurry, I see, in daylight—that is where I kissed most, I know.

I seem to be numb to everything else. Whether Lady Ver is angry or not does not bother me. I did play fair. She could not expect me to go on pretending when Robert had said straight out he loved me. But I am sure she will be angry, though, and probably rather spiteful about it.

I will write her the simple truth in a day or two, when we see how things go. She will guess by Robert not going to Sedgwick.

CLARIDGE'S,
Monday afternoon.

At half-past eleven this morning Lady Merrenden came, and the room was all full of flowers that Robert had sent, bunches and bunches of violets and gardenias. She kissed me, and held me tight for a moment, and we did not speak. Then she said, in a voice that trembled a little:

"Robert is so very dear to me—almost my own child—that I want him to be happy; and you, too, Evangeline—I may call you that, may not I?"

I squeezed her hand.

"You are the echo of my youth, when I, too, knew the wild spring-time of love. So, dear, I need not tell you that you may count upon my doing what I can for you both."

Then we talked and talked.

"I must admit," she said at last, "that I was prejudiced in your favor for your dear father's sake, but in any case my opinion of Robert's judgment is so high, I would have been prepared to find you charming, even without that. He has the rarest qualities, he is the truest, most untarnished soul in this world.

"I don't say," she went on, "that he is not just as the other young men of his age and class; he is no Galahad, as no one can be with truth who is human and lives in the world. And I dare say kind friends will tell you stories of actresses and other diversions, but I who know him tell you, you have won the best and greatest darling in London."

"Oh, I am sure of it," I said. "I don't know why he loves me so much, he has seen me so little; but it began from the very first minute, I think, with both of us. He is such a nice shape."

She laughed. Then she asked me if she was right in supposing all these *contretemps* we had had were the doing of Lady Ver. "You need not answer, dear," she said. "I know Ianthe. She is in love with Robert herself; she can't help it; she means no harm, but she often gets these attacks, and they pass off. I think she is devoted to Sir Charles, really."

"Yes," I said.

"It is a queer world we live in, child," she continued, "and true love and suitability of character are such a rare combination, but from what I can judge, you and Robert possess them."

"Oh, how dear of you to say so!" I exclaimed.

"You don't think I *must* be bad, then, because of my coloring?"

"What a ridiculous idea, you sweet child!" she laughed. "Who has told you that!"

"Oh, Mrs. Carruthers always said so—and—and the old gentlemen, and—even Mr. Carruthers hinted I probably had some odd qualities. But you do think I shall be able to be fairly good—don't you?"

She was amused, I could see, but I was serious.

"I think you probably might have been a little wicked if you had married a man like Mr. Carruthers," she said, smiling, "but with Robert I am sure you will be good. He will never leave you a moment, and he will love you so much you won't have time for anything else."

"Oh, that is what I shall like—being loved," I said.

"I think all women like that," she sighed. "We could all of us be good if the person we love went on being demonstrative. It is the cold, matter-of-fact devotion that kills love, and makes one want to look elsewhere to find it again."

Then we talked of possibilities about the duke. I told her I knew his *toquade*, and she, of course, was fully acquainted with mamma's history.

"I must tell you, dear, I fear he will be difficult," she said. "He is a strangely prejudiced person, and obstinate to a degree, and he worships Robert, as we all do."

I would not ask her if the duke had taken a dislike to me, because I *knew* he had.

"I asked you to meet him on Saturday on purpose," she continued. "I felt sure your charm would impress him, as it had done me, and as it did my husband, but I wonder now if it would have been better to wait. He said after you were gone that you were much too beautiful for the peace of any family, and he pitied Mr. Carruthers if he married you. I don't mean to hurt you, child; I am only telling you everything, so that we may consult how best to act."

"Yes, I know," I said, and I squeezed her hand again; she does not put out claws like Lady Ver.

"How did he know anything about Mr. Carruthers"—I asked—"or me, or anything?" She looked ashamed.

"One can never tell how he hears things. He was intensely interested to meet you, and seemed to be acquainted with more of the affair than I am. I almost fear he must obtain his information from the servants."

"Oh, does not that show the housemaid in him? Poor fellow!" I said. "He can't help it, then, any more than I could help crying yesterday before Robert in the park. Of course we would neither of us have done these things if it were not for the *tache* in our backgrounds, only, fortunately for me, mine wasn't a housemaid, and was one generation farther back, so I would not be likely to have any of those tricks."

She leaned back in her chair and laughed. "You quaint, quaint child, Evangeline," she said.

Just then it was twelve o'clock, and Robert came in.

Oh, talk of hearts beating! If mine is going to go on jumping like this every time Robert enters a room, I shall get a disease in it in less than a year.

He looked too intensely attractive. He was not in London clothes; just serge things, and a guard's tie, and his face was beaming, and his eyes shining like blue stars.

We behaved nicely—he only kissed my hand, and Lady Merrenden looked away at the clock even for that. She has tact.

"Isn't my Evangeline a darling, Aunt Sophia?" he said. "And don't you love her red hair?"

"It is beautiful," said Lady Merrenden.

"When you leave us alone I am going to pull it all down"; and he whispered, "Darling, I love you," so close that his lips touched my ear, while he pretended he was not doing anything. I say, again, Robert has ways that would charm a stone image.

"How was Torquilstone last night?" Lady Merrenden asked, "and did you tell him anything?"

"Not a word," said Robert. "I wanted to wait and consult you both which would be best. Shall I go to him at once, or shall he be made to meet my Evangeline again, and let her fascinate him, as she is bound to do, and then tell him?"

"Oh, tell him straight!" I exclaimed, remembering his proclivities about the servants and that Véronique knows. "Then he cannot ever say we have deceived him."

"That is how I feel," said Robert.

"You take Evangeline to lunch, Aunt Sophia, and I will go back and feed with him, and tell him, and then come to you after."

"Yes, that will be best," she said, and it was settled that she should come in again and fetch me in an hour, when Robert should leave to go to Vavasour House. He went with her to the lift, and then he came back.

No—even in this locked book I am not going to write of that hour—it was too divine. If I had thought just sitting in the park was heaven, I now know there are degrees of heaven, and that Robert is teaching me up towards the seventh.

Monday afternoon.
(Continued.)

I forgot to say a note came from Christopher by this morning's post—it made me laugh when I read it, then it went out of my head; but when Lady Merrenden returned for me, and we were more or less sane again—Robert and I—I thought of it; so apparently did he. "Did you by chance hear from Christopher, whether he got your note last night or no?" he said.

I went and fetched it from my bedroom when I put on my hat. Robert read it aloud:

"TRAVELLERS' CLUB,
"Sunday night.

"'*Souvent femme varie—fol qui se fie!*' Hope you found your variation worth while!

C. C."

"What dam cheek!" he said, in his old way. He hasn't used any "ornaments to conversation" since we have been—oh, I want to say it—engaged!

Then his eyes flashed. "Christopher had better be careful of himself! He will have to be answerable to me now."

"Do be prudent, Evangeline dear," Lady Merrenden said, gayly, "or you will have Robert breaking the head of every man in the street who even glances at you. He is frantically jealous."

"Yes, I know I am," said Robert, rearranging the tie on my blouse with that air of *sans gêne* and possession that pleases me so.

I belong to him now, and if my tie isn't as he likes he has a perfect right to retie it, no matter who is there. That is his attitude—not the *least* ceremony or stuff, everything perfectly simple and natural.

It does make things agreeable. When I was, "Miss Travers" and he "Lord Robert," he was always respectful and unfamiliar—except that one night when rage made him pinch my finger. But now that I am *his* Evangeline and he is *my* Robert (thus he explained it to me in our paradise hour), I am his queen and his darling, but at the same time his possession and belonging, just the same as his watch or his coat—I adore it—and it does not make me the least "uppish," as one might have thought.

"Come, come, children," Lady Merrenden said at last, "we shall all be late."

So we started, dropping Robert at Vavasour House on our way. It is a splendid place, down one of those side streets looking on the Green Park, and has a small garden that side. I had never been down to the little square where it is before, but, of course, every one can see its splendid frontage from St. James's Park, though I had never realized it was Vavasour House.

"Good luck!" whispered Lady Merrenden as Robert got out, and then we drove on.

Several people were lunching at Carlton House Terrace: cabinet ministers, and a clever novelist, and the great portrait painter, besides two or three charming women—one as pretty and smart as Lady Ver, but the others more ordinary looking, only so well mannered. No real frumps like the Montgomeries. We had a delightful lunch, and I tried to talk nicely and do my best to please my dear hostess. When they had all left I think we both began to feel excited, and long apprehensively for the arrival of Robert. So we talked of the late guests.

"It amuses my husband to see a number of different kinds of people," she said; "but we had nothing very exciting to-day, I must confess, though sometimes the authors and authoresses bore me, and they are often very disappointing—one does not any longer care to read their books after seeing them."

I said I could quite believe that.

"I do not go in for budding geniuses," she continued. "I prefer to wait until they have arrived, no matter their origin; then they have acquired a certain outside behavior on the way up, and it does not *froissé* one so. Merrenden is a great judge of human nature, and variety entertains him. Left to myself, I fear I should be quite contented with less gifted people who were simply of one's own world."

In all her talk one can see her thought and consideration for Lord Merrenden and his wishes and tastes.

"I always feel it is so cruel for him, our having no children," she said. "The earldom becomes extinct, so I must make him as happy as I can."

What a dear and just woman!

At last we spoke of Robert, and she told me stories of his boyhood, amusing Eton scrapes, and later feats. And how brave and splendid he had been in the war; and how the people all adored him at Torquilstone; and of his popularity and influence with them. "You must make him go into Parliament," she said.

Then Robert came into the room. Oh, his darling face spoke, there was no need for words. The duke, one could see, had been obdurate.

"Well," said Lady Merrenden.

Robert came straight over to me and took my face in his two hands. "Darling," he said, "before everything I want you to know I love you better than anything else in the world, and nothing will make any difference," and he kissed me deliberately before his aunt. His voice was so moved, and we all felt a slight lump in our throats I know; then he stood in front of us, but he held my hand.

"Torquilstone was horrid, I can see," said Lady Merrenden. "What did he say, Robert? Tell us everything. Evangeline would wish it too, I am sure, as well as I."

Robert looked very pale and stern; one can see how firm his jaw is in reality, and how steady his dear, blue eyes.

"I told him I loved Evangeline, whom I understood he had met yesterday, and that I intended to marry her."

"And he said?" asked Lady Merrenden, breathless.

I only held tighter Robert's hand.

"He swore like a trooper, he thumped his glass down on the table and smashed it—a disgusting exhibition of temper—I was ashamed of him. Then he said never, as long as he lived and could prevent it; that he had heard something of my infatuation, so as I am not given that way he had made inquiries, and found the family was most unsatisfactory. Then he had come here yesterday on purpose to see you—darling," turning to me, "and that he had judged for himself. The girl was a 'devilish beauty' (his words, not mine), with the naughtiest, provoking eyes, and a mouth—No, I can't say the rest, it makes me too mad," and Robert's eyes flashed.

Lady Merrenden rose from her seat and came and took my other hand. I felt as if I could not stand too tall and straight.

"The long and short of it is, he has absolutely refused to have anything to do with the matter, says I need expect nothing further from him, and we have parted for good and all."

"Oh, Robert!" It was almost a cry from Lady Merrenden.

Robert put his arms round me, and his face changed to radiance.

"Well, I don't care; what does it matter? A few places and thousands in the dim future—the loss of them is nothing to me if I only have my Evangeline now."

"But, Robert dearest," Lady Merrenden said, "you can't possibly live without what he allows you—what have you of your own? About eighteen hundred a year, I suppose, and you know, darling boy, you are often in debt. Why, he paid five thousand for you as lately as last Easter. Oh, what is to be done?" and she clasped her hands.

I felt as if turned to stone. Was all this divine happiness going to slip from my grasp? Yes, it looked like it, for I could never drag Robert into poverty and spoil his great future.

"He can't leave away Torquilstone, and those thousands of profitless acres," Lady Merrenden went on; "but, unfortunately, all the London property is at his disposition. Oh, I must go and talk to him!"

"No," said Robert. "It would not be the least use, and would look as if we were pleading." His face had fallen to intense sadness as Lady Merrenden spoke of his money.

"Darling," he said, in a broken voice. "No, it is true it would not be fair to make you a beggar. I should be a cad to ask you. We must think of some way of softening my brother after all."

Then I spoke.

"Robert," I said, "if you were only John Smith I would say I would willingly go and live with you in a cottage, or even in a slum; but you are not, and I would not for *anything in the world* drag you down out of what is your position in life. That would be a poor sort of love. Oh, my dear," and I clasped tight his hand, "if everything fails, then we must part and you must forget me."

He folded me in his arms, and we heard the door shut. Lady Merrenden had left us alone. Oh, it was anguish and divine bliss at the same time the next half-hour.

"I will never forget you, and never in this world will I take another woman, I swear to God!" he said, at the end of it. "If we must part, then life is finished for me of all joy."

"And for me, too, Robert!"

We said the most passionate vows of love to each other, but I will not write them here; there is another locked book where I keep them—the book of my soul.

"Would it be any good if Colonel Tom Carden went and spoke to him?" I asked, presently. "He was best man at papa's wedding, and knows all there is to be known of poor mamma; and do you think that as mamma's father was Lord de Brandreth—a very old barony I believe it is—oh, can it make any difference to the children's actual breeding, their parents not having been through the marriage ceremony? I—I—don't know much of that sort of things."

"My sweet," said Robert, and through all our sorrow he smiled and kissed me—"my sweet, sweet Evangeline."

"But does the duke know all the details of the history?" I asked, when I could speak; one can't when one is being kissed.

"Every little bit, it seems. He says he will not discuss the matter of that—I must know it is quite enough, as I have always known his views; but if it was not sufficient, your wild, wicked beauty is. You would not be faithful to me for a year, he said. I could hardly keep from killing him when he hurled that at my head."

I felt my temper rising. How frightfully unjust—how cruel! I went over and looked in the glass—a big mirror between the windows—drawing Robert with me.

"Oh, tell me, tell me, what is it? Am I so very bad looking? It is a curse, surely, that is upon me."

"Of course you are not bad looking, my darling!" exclaimed Robert. "You are perfectly beautiful—a slender, stately, exquisite tiger-lily—only—only—you don't look cold—and it is just your red hair, and those fascinating green eyes, and your white, lovely skin and black eyelashes that, that—Oh, you know, you sweetheart! You don't look like bread-and-butter, you are utterly desirable, and you would make any one's heart beat."

I thought of the night at "Carmen."

"Yes, I am wicked," I said; "but I never will be again—only just enough to make you always love me, because Lady Ver says security makes yawns. But even wicked people can love with a great, great love, and that can keep them good. Oh, if he only knew how utterly I love you, Robert, I am sure, sure, he would be kind to us!"

"Well, how shall we tell him?"

Then a thought came to me, and I felt all over a desperate thrill of excitement.

"Will you do nothing until to-morrow?" I said. "I have an idea which I will tell to no one. Let us go back to Claridge's now, and do not come and see me again until to-morrow at twelve. Then, if this has failed we will say good-bye. It is a desperate chance."

"And you won't tell me what it is?"

"No. Please trust me; it is my life as well as yours, remember."

"My queen!" he said. "Yes, I will do that, or anything else you wish, only *never, never* good-bye. I am a man, after all, and have numbers of influential relations. I can do something else in life just be a Guardsman, and we shall get enough money to live quite happily on, though we might not be very grand people. I will never say good-bye—do you hear? Promise me you will never say it, either."

I was silent.

"Evangeline, darling!" he cried in anguish, his eyebrows right up in the old way, while two big tears welled up in his beautiful eyes. "My God! won't you answer me?"

"Yes, I will," I said, and I threw all my reserve to the winds, and flung my arms round his neck, passionately.

"I love you with my heart and soul, and pray to God we shall never say good-bye."

When I got back to Claridge's, for the first time in my life I felt a little faint. Lady Merrenden had driven me back herself, and left me with every assurance of her devotion and affection for us. I had said good-bye to Robert for the day at Carlton House Terrace.

They do not yet know me, either of them, quite; or what I can and will do.

I felt to carry out my plan I must steady my mind a little, so I wrote my journal, and that calmed me.

Of all the things I was sure of in the world, I was most sure that I loved Robert far too well to injure his prospects. On the other hand, to throw him away without a struggle was too cruel to both of us. If mamma's mother was nobody, all the rest of my family were fine old fighters and gentlemen, and I really prayed to their shades to help me now.

Then I rang and ordered some iced water, and when I had thought deeply for a few minutes while I sipped it, I sat down to my writing-table. My hand did not shake, though I felt at a deadly tension. I addressed the envelope first, to steady myself:

"To
"His Grace
"The Duke of Torquilstone,
"Vavasour House,
"St. James's, S.W.

Then I put that aside.

"I am Evangeline Travers who writes,"

I began, without any preface;

"and I ask if you will see me—either here in my sitting-room this evening, or I will come to you at Vavasour House. I understand your brother, Lord Robert, has told you that he loves me and wishes to marry me, and that you have refused your consent, partly because of the history of my family, but chiefly because my type displeases you. I believe, in days gone by, the prerogative of a great noble like you was to dispense justice. In my case it is still your prerogative by courtesy, and I ask it of you. When we have talked for a little, if you then hold to your opinion of me, and *convince me* that it is for your brother's happiness, I swear to you on my word of honor I will never see him again.

"Believe me,
"Yours faithfully,
"EVANGELINE TRAVERS."

I put it hastily in the envelope and fastened it up. Then I rang the bell, and had it sent by a messenger in a cab, who was to wait for an answer. Oh, I wonder if in life I shall ever have to go through another twenty-five minutes like those that passed before the waiter brought a note up to me in reply.

Even if the journal won't shut I must put it in:

"VAVASOUR HOUSE, ST. JAMES'S,
"*November 28th.*

"DEAR MADAM,—

"I have received your letter, and request you to excuse my calling upon you at your hotel this evening, as I am unwell; but if you will do me the honor to come to Vavasour House on receipt of this, I will discuss the matter in question with you, and trust you will believe that you may rely upon my *justice.*

"I remain, madam,
"Yours truly,
"TORQUILSTONE."

"His grace's brougham is waiting below for you, madam," the waiter said, and I flew to Véronique.

I got her to dress me quickly. I wore the same things, exactly, as he had seen me in before—deep mourning they are, and extremely becoming.

In about ten minutes Véronique and I were seated in the brougham and rolling on our way. I did not speak.

I was evidently expected, for as the carriage stopped the great doors flew open and I could see into the dim and splendid hall.

A silver-haired, stately old servant led me along through a row of powdered footmen, down a passage all dimly lit with heavily shaded lights. (Véronique was left to their mercies.) Then the old man opened a door, and without announcing my name, merely, "The lady, your grace," he held the door, and then went out and closed it softly.

It was a huge room splendidly panelled with dark, carved *boiserie* Louis XV., the most beautiful of its kind I had ever seen—only it was so dimly lit with the same shaded lamps one could hardly see into the corners.

The duke was crouching in a chair and looked fearfully pale and ill, and had an inscrutable expression on his face. Fancy a man so old-looking, and crippled, being even Robert's half-brother.

I came forward—he rose with difficulty, and this is the conversation we had.

"Please don't get up," I said. "If I may sit down opposite you."

"Excuse my want of politeness," he said, pointing to a chair; "but my back is causing me great pain to-day."

He looked such a poor, miserable, soured, unhappy creature, I could not help being touched.

"Oh, I am so sorry!" I said. "If I had known you were ill I would not have troubled you now."

"Justice had better not wait," he replied, with a whimsical, cynical, sour smile. "State your case."

Then he suddenly turned on an electric lamp near me, which made a blaze of light in my face. I did not jump, I am glad to say; I have pretty good nerves.

"My case is this: To begin with, I love your brother better than anything else in the world."

"Possibly—a number of women have done so," he interrupted. "Well?"

"And he loves me," I continued, not noticing the interruption.

"Agreed. It is a situation that happens every day among young fools. You have known each other about a month, I believe."

"Under four weeks," I corrected.

He laughed—bitterly.

"It cannot be of such vital importance to you, then, in that short time."

"It is of vital importance to me, and you know your brother's character; you will be able to judge as well as I if, or not, it is a matter of vital importance to him."

He frowned. "Well, your case?"

"First, to demand on what grounds you condemned me as a 'devilish beauty'? And why you assume that I should not be faithful to Robert for a year?"

"I am a rather good judge of character," he said.

"You cannot be, or you would see that whatever accident makes me have this objectionable outside, the me that lives within is an honest person who never breaks her word."

"I can only see red hair, and green eyes, and a general look of the devil."

"Would you wish people always to judge by appearances, then?" I said; "because, if so, I see before me a prejudiced, narrow-minded, cruel-tempered, cynical man—jealous of youth's joys. But *I* would not be so unjust as to stamp you with these qualities because of that!"

He looked straight at me, startled. "I may be all these things," he said. "You are probably right."

"Then, oh, please don't be!" I went on quickly. "I want you to be kind to us. We—oh, we do, do so wish to be happy, and we are both so young, and life will be so utterly blank and worthless for all those years to the end if you part us now."

"I did not say I would part you," he said, coldly. "I merely said I refused to give Robert any allowance, and I shall leave everything in my power away from the title. If you like to get married on those terms you are welcome to."

Then I told him that I loved Robert far too much to like the thought of spoiling his future.

"We came into each other's lives," I said. "We did not ask it of fate, she pushed us there, and I tried not to speak to him because I had promised a friend of mine I would not, as she said she liked him herself, and it made us both dreadfully unhappy; and every day we mattered more to each other until yesterday, when I thought he had gone away for good and I was too miserable for words, we met in the park, and it was no use pretending any longer. Oh, you *can't* want to crush out all joy and life for us, just because I have red hair! It is so horribly unjust."

"You beautiful siren!" he said. "You are coaxing me. How you know how to use your charms and your powers, and what *man* could resist your tempting face!"

I rose in passionate scorn.

"How dare you say such things to me!" I said. "I would not stoop to coax you. I will not again ask you for any boon. I only wanted you to do me the justice of realizing you had made a mistake in my character—to do your brother the justice of conceding the point that he has some right to love whom he chooses. But keep your low thoughts to yourself—evil, cruel man! Robert and I have got something that is better than all your lands and money—a dear, great love, and I am glad—glad he will not in the future receive anything that is in your gift. I shall give him the gift of myself, and we shall do very well without you;" and I walked to the door, leaving him huddled in the chair.

Thus ended our talk on justice.

Never has my head been so up in the air. I am sure had Cleopatra been dragged to Rome in Augustus's triumph she would not have walked with more pride and contempt than I through the hall of Vavasour House.

The old servant was waiting for me, and Véronique, and the brougham.

"Call a hansom, if you please," I said, and stood there like a statue while one of the footmen had to run into St. James's Street for it.

Then we drove away, and I felt my teeth chatter while my cheeks burned. Oh, what an end to my scheme and my dreams of, perhaps, success!

But what a beast of a man! What a cruel, warped, miserable creature. I will not let him separate me from Robert—never, never! He is not worth it. I will wait for him—my darling—and if he really loves me, some day we can be happy, and if he does not—but, oh, I need not fear.

I am still shaking with passion, and shall go to bed. I do not want any dinner.

Tuesday morning, *November 29th.*

Véronique would not let me go to bed, she insisted upon my eating, and then after dinner I sat in an old but lovely wrap of whitecrêpe, and she brushed out my hair for more than an hour—there is such a tremendous lot of it, it takes time.

I sat in front of the sitting-room fire and tried not to think. One does feel a wretch after a scene like that. At about half-past nine I heard noises in the passage of people, and with only a preliminary tap Robert and Lady Merrenden came into the room. I started up, and Véronique dropped the brush in her astonishment, and then left us alone.

Both their eyes were shining and excited, and Robert looked crazy with joy; he seized me in his arms, and kissed me, and kissed me, while Lady Merrenden said, "You darling Evangeline! you plucky, clever girl! Tell us all about it!"

"About what?" I said, as soon as I could speak.

"How you managed it."

"Oh, I must kiss her first, Aunt Sophia!" said Robert. "Did you ever see anything so divinely lovely as she looks with her hair all floating like this, and it is all mine, every bit of it!"

"Yes, it is," I said, sadly, "and that is about all of value you will get."

"Come and sit down," said Robert, "Evangeline, you darling—and look at this."

Upon which he drew from his pocket a note. I saw at once it was the duke's writing, and I shivered with excitement. He held it before my eyes.

"Dear Robert," it began. "I have seen her. I am conquered. She will make a magnificent duchess. Bring her to lunch to-morrow. Yours, TORQUILSTONE."

I really felt so intensely moved I could not speak.

"Oh, tell us, dear child, how did it happen, and what did you do, and where did you meet!" said Lady Merrenden.

Robert held my hand.

Then I tried to tell them as well as I could, and they listened breathlessly. "I was very rude, I fear," I ended with, "but I was so angry."

"It is glorious," said Robert. "But the best part is that you intended to give me yourself with no prospect of riches. Oh, darling, that is the best gift of all!"

"Was it disgustingly selfish of me?" I said. "But when I saw your poor brother so unhappy-looking, and soured, and unkind, with all his grandeur, I felt that to us, who know what love means, to be together was the thing that matters most in all the world."

Lady Merrenden then said she knew some people staying here who had an apartment on the first floor, and she would go down and see if they were visible. She would wait for Robert in the hall, she said, and she kissed us good-night and gave us her blessing.

What a dear she is! What a nice pet, to leave us alone!

Robert and I passed another hour of bliss, and I think we must have got to the sixth heaven by now—Robert says the seventh is for the end, when we are married. Well, that will be soon. Oh, I am too happy to write coherently!

I did not wake till late this morning, and Véronique came and said my sitting-room was again full of flowers. The darling Robert is!

I wrote to Christopher and Lady Ver in bed, as I sipped my chocolate. I just told Lady Ver the truth, that Robert and I had met by chance and discovered we loved each other, so I knew she would understand, and I promised I would not break his heart. Then I thanked her for all her kindness to me, but I felt sad when I read it over; poor, dear Lady Ver—how I hope it won't really hurt her, and that she will forgive me!

To Christopher I said I had found my "variation" worth while, and I hoped he would come to my wedding some day soon.

Then I sent Véronique to post them both.

To-day I am moving to Carlton House Terrace. What a delight that will be! and in a fortnight—or at best three weeks—Robert says we shall quietly go and get married, and Colonel Tom Carden can give me away after all.

Oh, the joy of the dear, beautiful world, and this sweet, dirty, entrancing, fog-bound London! I love it all—even the smuts!

CARLTON HOUSE TERRACE,
Thursday night.

Robert came to see me at twelve, and he brought me the loveliest, splendid diamond and emerald ring, and I danced about like a child with delight over it. He has the most exquisite sentiment, Robert—every little trifle has some delicate meaning, and he makes me *feel* and *feel*.

Each hour we spend together we seem to discover some new bit of us which is just what the other wants. And he is so deliciously jealous and masterful and—oh, I love him—so there it is!

I am learning a lot of things, and I am sure there are lots to learn still.

At half-past one Lady Merrenden came and fetched us in the barouche, and off we went to Vavasour House, with what different feelings to last evening!

The pompous servants received us in state, and we all three walked on to the duke's room.

There he was, still huddled in his chair, but he got up—he is better to-day.

Lady Merrenden went over and kissed him.

"Dear Torquilstone," she said.

"Morning, Robert," he mumbled, after he had greeted his aunt. "Introduce me to your fiancée."
And Robert did, with great ceremony.
"Now, I won't call you names any more," I said, and I laughed in his face. He bent down and kissed my forehead.
"You are a beautiful tiger-cat," he said; "but even a year of you would be well worth while."
Upon which Robert glared, and I laughed again, and we all went in to lunch.
He is not so bad, the duke, after all.

CARLTON HOUSE TERRACE,
December 21st.

Oh, it is three weeks since I wrote, but I have been too busy and too happy for journals. I have been here ever since, getting my trousseau, and Véronique is becoming used to the fact that I can have no coronet on my lingerie.
It is the loveliest thing in the world being engaged to Robert.
He has ways! Well, even if I really were as bad as I suppose I look, I could never want any one else. He worships me, and lets me order him about, and then he orders me about, and that makes me have the loveliest thrills. And if any one even looks at me in the street—which of course they always do—he flashes blue fire at them, and I feel—oh, I feel, all the time!
Lady Merrenden continues her sweet kindness to us, and her tact is beyond words, and now I often do what I used to wish to—that is, touch Robert's eyelashes with the tips of my fingers.
It is perfectly lovely.
Oh, what in the world is the good of anything else in life but being frantically in love as we are!
It all seems, to look back upon, as if it were like having porridge for breakfast, and nothing else every day, before I met Robert.
Perhaps it is because he is going to be very grand in the future, but every one has discovered I am a beauty, and intelligent. It is much nicer to be thought that than just to be a red-haired adventuress.
Lady Katherine, even, has sent me a cairngorm brooch and a cordial letter. (I should now adorn her circle!)
But oh, what do they all matter—what does anything matter but Robert! All day long I know I am learning the meaning of "to dance and to sing and to laugh and *to live.*"
The duke and I are great friends. He has ferreted out about mamma's mother, and it appears she was a Venetian music-mistress of the name of Tonquini, or something like that, who taught Lord de Brandreth's sisters—so perhaps Lady Ver was right after all, and far, far back in some other life I was the friend of a Doge.
Poor, dear Lady Ver! She has taken it very well after the first spiteful letter, and now I don't think there is even a tear at the corner of her eye.
Lady Merrenden says it is just the time of the year when she usually gets a new one, so perhaps she has now, and so that is all right.
The diamond serpent she has given me has emerald eyes—and such a pointed tongue.
"It is like you, snake-girl," she said; "so wear it at your wedding."
The three angels are to be my only bridesmaids.
Robert loads me with gifts, and the duke is going to let me wear all the Torquilstone jewels when I am married, besides the emeralds he has given me himself. I really love him.
Christopher sent me this characteristic note with the earrings which are his gift, great big emeralds set with diamonds:
"So sorry I shall not see you on the happy day, but Paris, I am fortunate enough to discover, still has joys for me.

"C. C.

"Wear them; they will match your eyes."
And to-morrow is my wedding-day, and I am going away on a honeymoon with Robert—away into the seventh heaven. And oh, and oh, I am certain, *sure*, neither of us will yawn!

THE END

The Reason Why

CHAPTER I

People often wondered what nation the great financier, Francis Markrute, originally sprang from. He was now a naturalized Englishman and he looked English enough. He was slight and fair, and had an immaculately groomed appearance generally—which even the best of valets cannot always produce. He wore his clothes with that quiet, unconscious air which is particularly English. He had no perceptible accent—only a deliberate way of speaking. But Markrute!—such a name might have come from anywhere. No one knew anything about him, except that he was fabulously rich and had descended upon London some ten years previously from Paris, or Berlin, or Vienna, and had immediately become a power in the city, and within a year or so, had grown to be omnipotent in certain circles.

He had a wonderfully appointed house in Park Lane, one of those smaller ones just at the turn out of Grosvenor Street, and there he entertained in a reserved fashion.

It had been remarked by people who had time to think—rare cases in these days—that he had never made a disadvantageous friend, from his very first arrival. If he had to use undesirables for business purposes he used them only for that, in a crisp, hard way, and never went to their houses. Every acquaintance even was selected with care for a definite end. One of his favorite phrases was that "it is only the fool who coins for himself limitations."

At this time, as he sat smoking a fine cigar in his library which looked out on the park, he was perhaps forty-six years old or thereabouts, and but for his eyes—wise as serpents'—he might have been ten years younger.

Opposite to him facing the light a young man lounged in a great leather chair. The visitors in Francis Markrute's library nearly always faced the light, while he himself had his back to it.

There was no doubt about this visitor's nation! He was flamboyantly English. If you had wished to send a prize specimen of the race to a World's Fair you could not have selected anything finer. He was perhaps more Norman than Saxon, for his hair was dark though his eyes were blue, and the marks of breeding in the creature showed as plainly as in a Derby winner. Francis Markrute always smoked his cigars to the end, if he were at leisure and the weed happened to be a good one, but Lord Tancred (Tristram Lorrimer Guiscard Guiscard, 24th Baron Tancred, of Wrayth in the County of Suffolk) flung his into the grate after a few whiffs, and he laughed with a slightly whimsical bitterness as he went on with the conversation.

"Yes, Francis, my friend, the game here is played out; I am thirty, and there is nothing interesting left for me to do but emigrate to Canada, for a while at least, and take up a ranch."

"Wrayth mortgaged heavily, I suppose?" said Mr. Markrute, quietly.

"Pretty well, and the Northern property, too. When my mother's jointure is paid there is not a great deal left this year, it seems. I don't mind much; I had a pretty fair time before these beastly Radicals made things so difficult."

The financier nodded, and the young man went on: "My forbears got rid of what they could; there was not much ready money to come into and one had to live!"

Francis Markrute smoked for a minute thoughtfully.

"Naturally," he said at last. "Only the question is—for how long? I understand a plunge, if you settle its duration; it is the drifting and trusting to chance, and a gradual sinking which seem to me a poor game. Did you ever read de Musset's 'Rolla'?"

"The fellow who had arrived at his last night, and to whom the little girl was so kind? Yes: well?"

"You reminded me of Jacques Rolla, that is all."

"Oh, come! It is not as bad as that!" Lord Tancred exclaimed—and he laughed. "I can collect a few thousands still, even here, and I can go to Canada. I believe there is any quantity of money to be made there with a little capital, and it is a nice, open-air life. I just looked in this afternoon on my way back from Scotland to tell you I should be going out to prospect, about the end of November and could not join you for the pheasants on the 20th, as you were good enough to ask me to do."

The financier half closed his eyes. When he did this there was always something of importance working in his brain.

"You have not any glaring vices, Tancred," he said. "You are no gambler either on the turf or at cards. You are not over addicted to expensive ladies. You are cultivated, for a sportsman, and you have made one or two decent speeches in the House of Lords. You are, in fact, rather a fine specimen of your class. It seems a pity you should have to shut down and go to the Colonies."

"Oh, I don't know! And I have not altogether got to shut down," the young man said, "only the show is growing rather rotten over here. We have let the rabble—the most unfit and ignorant—have the casting vote, and the machine now will crush any man. I have kept out of politics as much as I can and I am glad."

Francis Markrute got up and lowered the blind a few inches—a miserable September sun was trying to shine into the room. If Lord Tancred had not been so preoccupied with his own thoughts he would have remarked this restlessness on the part of his host. He was no fool; but his mind was far away. It almost startled him when the cold, deliberate voice continued:

"I have a proposition to make to you should you care to accept it. I have a niece—a widow—she is rather an attractive lady. If you will marry her I will pay off all your mortgages and settle on her quite a princely dower."

"Good God!" said Lord Tancred.

The financier reddened a little about the temples, and his eyes for an instant gave forth a flash of steel. There had been an infinite variety of meanings hidden in the exclamation, but he demanded suavely:

"What point of the question causes you to exclaim 'Good God'?"

The sang-froid of Lord Tancred never deserted him.

"The whole thing," he said—"to marry at all, to begin with, and to marry an unknown woman, to have one's debts paid, for the rest! It is a tall order."

"A most common occurrence. Think of the number of your peers who have gone to America for their wives, for no other reason."

"And think of the rotters they are—most of them! I mayn't be much catch, financially; but I have one of the oldest names and titles in England—and up to now we have not had any cads nor cowards in the family, and I think a man who marries a woman for money is both. By Jove! Francis, what are you driving at? Confound it, man! I am not starving and can work, if it should ever come to that."

Mr. Markrute smoothed his hands. He was a peculiarly still person generally.

"Yes, it was a blunder, I admit, to put it this way. So I will be frank with you. My family is also, my friend, as old as yours. My niece is all I have left in the world. I would like to see her married to an Englishman. I would like to see her married to you of all Englishmen because I like you and you have qualities about you which count in life. Oh, believe me!"—and he raised a protesting finger to quell an interruption—"I have studied you these years; there is nothing you can say of yourself or your affairs that I do not know."

Lord Tancred laughed.

"My dear old boy," he said, "we have been friends for a long time; and, now we are coming to hometruths, I must say I like your deuced cold-blooded point of view on every subject. I like your knowledge of wines and cigars and pictures, and you are a most entertaining companion. But, 'pon my soul I would not like to have your niece for a wife if she took after you!"

"You think she would be cold-blooded, too?"

"Undoubtedly; but it is all perfectly preposterous. I don't believe you mean a word you are saying—it is some kind of a joke."

"Have you ever known me to make such jokes, Tancred?" Mr. Markrute asked calmly.

"No, I haven't, and that is the odd part of it. What the devil do you mean, really, Francis?"

"I mean what I say: I will pay every debt you have, and give you a charming wife with a fortune."

Lord Tancred got up and walked about the room. He was a perfectly natural creature, stolid and calm as those of his race, disciplined and deliberate in moments of danger or difficulty; yet he never lived under self-conscious control as the financier did. He was rather moved now, and so he walked about. He was with a friend, and it was not the moment to have to bother over disguising his feelings.

"Oh, it is nonsense, Francis; I could not do it. I have knocked about the world as you know, and, since you are aware of everything about me, you say, you have probably heard some of my likings—and dislikings. I never go after a woman unless she attracts me, and I would never marry one of them unless I were madly in love with her, whether she had money or no; though I believe I would hate a wife with money, in any case—she'd be saying like the American lady of poor Darrowood: 'It's my motor and you can't have it to-day.'"

"You would marry a woman then—if you were in love, in spite of everything?" Francis Markrute asked.

"Probably, but I have never been really in love; have you? It is all story-book stuff—that almighty passion, I expect. They none of them matter very much after a while, do they, old boy?"

"I have understood it is possible for a woman to matter," the financier said and he drew in his lips.

"Well, up to now I have not," Lord Tancred announced, "and may the day be far off when one does. I feel pretty safe!"

A strange, mysterious smile crept over Mr. Markrute's face.

"By the way, also, how do you know the lady would be willing to marry me, Francis? You spoke as if I only had to be consulted in the affair."

"So you have. I can answer for my niece; she will do as I wish, and, as I said before, you are rather a perfect picture of an English nobleman, Tancred. You have not found women recalcitrant, as a rule—no?"

Lord Tancred was not inordinately vain, though a man, and he had a sense of humor—so he laughed.

"'Pon my word it is amusing, your turning into a sort of matrimonial agent. Can't you see the fun of the thing yourself?"

"It seems quite natural to me. You have every social advantage to offer a woman, and a presentable person; and my niece has youth, and some looks, and a large fortune. But we will say no more about it. I shall be glad to be of any service I can to you, anyway, in regard to your Canadian scheme. Come and dine to-night; I happen to have asked a couple of railway magnates with interests out there, and you can get some information from them."

And so it was arranged, and Lord Tancred got up to go; but just at the door he paused and said with a laugh:

"And shall I see the niece?"

The financier had his back turned, and so he permitted the flicker of a smile to come over his mouth as he answered:

"It might be; but we have dismissed the subject of the niece."

And so they parted.

At the sound of the closing of the door Mr. Markrute pressed the button of a wonderful trifle of Russian enamel and emeralds, which lay on his writing table, and a quiet servant entered the room.

"Tell the Countess Shulski I wish to speak to her here immediately, please," he said. "Ask her to descend at once."

But he had to walk up and down several times, and was growing impatient, before the door opened and a woman came slowly into the room.

CHAPTER II

The financier paused in his restless pacing as he heard the door open and stood perfectly still, with his back to the light. The woman advanced and also stood still, and they looked at one another with no great love in their eyes, though she who had entered was well worth looking at, from a number of points of view. Firstly, she had that arresting, compelling personality which does not depend upon features, or coloring, or form, or beauty. A subtle force of character—a radiating magnetism—breathed from her whole being. When Zara Shulski came into any assemblage of people conversation stopped and speculation began.

She was rather tall and very slender; and yet every voluptuous curve of her lithe body refuted the idea of thinness. Her head was small and her face small, and short, and oval, with no wonderfully chiseled features, only the skin was quite exceptional in its white purity—not the purity of milk, but the purity of rich, white velvet, or a gardenia petal. Her mouth was particularly curved and red and her teeth were very even, and when she smiled, which was rarely, they suggested something of great strength, though they were small and white. And now I am coming to her two wonders, her eyes and her hair. At first you could have sworn the eyes were black; just great pools of ink, or disks of black velvet, set in their broad lids and shaded with jet lashes, but if they chanced to glance up in the full light then you knew they were slate color, not a tinge of brown or green—the whole iris was a uniform shade: strange, slumberous, resentful eyes, under straight, thick, black brows, the expression full of all sorts of meanings, though none of them peaceful or calm. And from some far back Spanish-Jewess ancestress she probably got that glorious head of red hair, the color of a ripe chestnut when it falls from its shell, or a beautifully groomed bright bay horse. The heavy plaits which were wound tightly round her head must have fallen below her knees when they were undone. Her coiffure gave you the impression that she never thought of fashion, nor changed its form of dressing, from year to year. And the exquisite planting of the hair on her forehead, as it waved back in broad waves, added to the perfection of the Greek simplicity of the whole thing. Nothing about her had been aided by conscious art. Her dress, of some black clinging stuff, was rather poor, though she wore it with the air of a traditional empress. Indeed, she looked an empress, from the tips of her perfect fingers to her small arched feet.

And it was with imperial hauteur that she asked in a low, cultivated voice with no accent:

"Well, what is it? Why have you sent for me thus peremptorily?"

The financier surveyed her for a moment; he seemed to be taking in all her points with a fresh eye. It was almost as though he were counting them over to himself—and his thoughts ran: "You astonishingly attractive devil. You have all the pride of my father, the Emperor. How he would have gloried in you! You are enough to drive any man mad: you shall be a pawn in my game for the winning of my lady and gain happiness for yourself, so in the end, Elinka, if she is able to see from where she has gone, will not say I have been cruel to you."

"I asked you to come down—to discuss a matter of great importance: Will you be good enough to be seated, my niece," he said aloud with ceremonious politeness as he drew forward a chair—into which she sank without more ado and there waited, with folded hands, for him to continue. Her stillness was always as intense as his own, but whereas his had a nervous tension of conscious repression, hers had an unconscious, quiet force. Her father had been an Englishman, but both uncle and niece at moments made you feel they were silent panthers, ready to spring.

"So—" was all she said.

And Francis Markrute went on:

"You have a miserable position—hardly enough to eat at times, one understands. You do not suppose I took the trouble to send for you from Paris last week, for nothing, do you? You guessed I had some plan in my head, naturally."

"Naturally," she said, with fine contempt. "I did not mistake it for philanthropy."

"Then it is well, and we can come to the point," he went on. "I am sorry I have had to be away, since your arrival, until yesterday. I trust my servants have made you comfortable?"

"Quite comfortable," she answered coldly.

"Good: now for what I want to know. You have no doubt in your mind that your husband, Count Ladislaus Shulski, is dead? There is no possible mistake in his identity? I believe the face was practically shot away, was it not? I have taken the precaution to inform myself upon every point, from the authorities at Monte Carlo, but I wish for your final testimony."

"Ladislaus Shulski is dead," she said quietly, in a tone as though it gave her pleasure to say it. "The woman Féto caused the fray, Ivan Larski shot him in her arms; he was her lover who paid, and Ladislaus the *amant du coeur* for the moment. She wailed over the body like a squealing rabbit. She was there lamenting his fine eyes when they sent for me! They were gone for ever, but no one could mistake his curly hair, nor his cruel, white hands. Ah! it was a scene of disgust! I have witnessed many ugly things but that was of the worst. I do not wish to talk of it; it is passed a year ago. Féto heaped his grave with flowers, and joined the hero, Larski, who was allowed to escape, so all was well."

"And since then you have lived from hand to mouth, with those others." And here Francis Markrute's voice took on a new shade: there was a cold hate in it.

"I have lived with my little brother, Mirko, and Mimo. How could I desert them? And sometimes we have found it hard at the end of the quarter—but it was not always as bad as that, especially when Mimo sold a picture—"

"I will not hear his name!" Francis Markrute said with some excitement. "In the beginning, if I could have found him I would have killed him, as you know, but now the carrion can live, since my sister is dead. He is not worth powder and shot."

The Countess Shulski gave the faintest shrug of her shoulders, while her eyes grew blacker with resentment. She did not speak. Francis Markrute stood by the mantelpiece, and lit a cigar before he continued; he knew he must choose his words as he was dealing with no helpless thing.

"You are twenty-three years old, Zara, and you were married at sixteen," he said at last. "And up to thirteen at least I know you were very highly educated—You understand something of life, I expect."

"Life!" she said—and now there was a concentrated essence of bitterness in her voice. "*Mon Dieu!* Life—and men!"

"Yes, you probably think you know men."

She lifted her upper lip a little, and showed her even teeth—it was like an animal snarling.

"I know that they are either selfish weaklings, or cruel, hateful brutes like Ladislaus, or clever, successful financiers like you, my uncle. That is enough! Something we women must be always sacrificed to."

"Well, you don't know Englishmen—"

"Yes, I remember my father very well; cold and hard to my darling mother"—and here her voice trembled a little—"he only thought of himself, and to rush to England for sport—and leave her alone for months and months: selfish and vile—all of them!"

"In spite of that I have found you an English husband whom you will be good enough to take, madame," Francis Markrute announced authoritatively.

She gave a little laugh—if anything so mirthless could be called a laugh.

"You have no power over me; I shall do no such thing."

"I think you will," the financier said with quiet assurance, "if I know you. There are terms, of course—"

She glanced at him sharply: the expression in those somber eyes was often alert like a wild animal's, about to be attacked; only she had trained herself generally to keep the lids lowered.

"What are the terms?" she asked.

And as she spoke Francis Markrute thought of the black panther in the Zoo, which he was so fond of going to watch on Sunday mornings, she reminded him so of the beast at the moment.

He had been constrained up to this, but now, the question being one of business, all his natural ease of manner returned, and he sat down opposite her and blew rings of smoke from his cigar.

"The terms are that the boy Mirko, your half-brother, shall be provided for for life. He shall live with decent people, and have his talent properly cultivated—"

He stopped abruptly and remained silent.

Countess Shulski clasped her hands convulsively in her lap, and with all the pride and control of her voice there was a note of anguish, too, which would have touched any heart but one so firmly guarded as Francis Markrute's.

"Ah, God!" she said so low that he could only just hear her, "I have paid the price of my body and soul once for them. It is too much to ask it of me a second time—"

"That is as you please," said the financier.

He seldom made a mistake in his methods with people. He left nothing to chance; he led up the conversation to the right point, fired his bomb, and then showed absolute indifference. To display interest in a move, when one was really interested, was always a point to the adversary. He maintained interest could be simulated when necessary, but must never be shown when real. So he left his niece in silence, while she pondered over his bargain, knowing full well what would be the result. She got up from her chair and leaned upon the back of it, while her face looked white as death in the dying afternoon's light.

"Can you realize what my life was like with Ladislaus?" she hissed. "A plaything for his brutal pleasures, to begin with; a decoy duck to trap the other men, I found afterwards; tortured and insulted from morning to night. I hated him always, but he seemed so kind beforehand—kind to my darling mother, whom you were leaving to die."—Here Francis Markrute winced and a look of pain came into his hard face while he raised a hand in protest and then dropped it again, as his niece went on—"And she was beginning to be ill even at that time and we were so poor—so I married him."

Then she swept toward the door with her empress air, the rather shabby, dark dress making a swirl behind her; and as she got there she turned and spoke again, with her hand on the bronze tracery of the fingerplate, making, unconsciously, a highly dramatic picture, as a sudden last ray of the sinking sun shot out and struck the glory of her hair, turning it to flame above her brow.

"I tell you it is too much," she said, with almost a sob in her voice. "I will not do it." And then she went out and closed the door.

Francis Markrute, left alone, leant back in his chair and puffed his cigar calmly while he mused.

What strange things were women! Any man could manage them if only he reckoned with their temperaments when dealing with them, and paid no heed to their actual words. Francis Markrute was a philosopher. A number of the shelves of this, his library, were filled with works on the subject of philosophy, and a well-thumbed volume of the fragments of Epicurus lay on a table by his side. He picked it up now and read: "He who wastes his youth on high feeding, on wine, on women, forgets that he is like a man who wears out his overcoat in the summer." He had not wasted his youth either on wine or women, only he had studied both, and their effects upon the thing which, until lately, had interested him most in the world—himself. They could both be used to the greatest advantage and pleasure by a man who apprehended things he knew.

Then he turned to the *Morning Post* which was on a low stand near, and he read again a paragraph which had pleased him at breakfast:

"The Duke of Glastonbury and Lady Ethelrida Montfitchet entertained at dinner last night a small party at Glastonbury House, among the guests being—" and here he skipped some high-sounding titles and let his eye feast upon his own name, "Mr. Francis Markrute."

Then he smiled and gazed into the fire, and no one would have recognized his hard, blue eyes, as he said softly: "Ethelrida! *belle et blonde!*"

CHAPTER III

While the financier was contentedly musing in his chair beside the fire, his niece was hurrying into the park, wrapped in a dark cloak and thick veil. She had slipped out noiselessly, a few minutes after she left the library. The sun had completely set now and it was damp and cold, with the dead leaves, and the sodden autumn feeling in the air. Zara Shulski shivered, in spite of the big cloak, as she peered into the gloom of the trees, when she got nearly to the Achilles statue. The rendezvous had been for six o'clock; it was now twenty minutes past, and it was so bad for Mirko to wait in the cold. Perhaps they would have gone on. But no; she caught sight of two shabby figures, close up under the statue, when she got sufficiently near.

They came forward eagerly to meet her. And even in the half light it could be seen that the boy was an undersized little cripple of perhaps nine or ten years old but looking much younger; as it could also be seen that even in his worn overcoat and old stained felt hat the man was a gloriously handsome creature.

"What joy to see you, Chérisette!" exclaimed the child. "Papa and I have been longing and longing all the day. It seemed that six would never come. But now that you are here let me eat you—eat you up!" And the thin, little arms, too long for the wizened body, clasped fondly round her neck as she lifted him, and carried him toward a seat where the three sat down to discuss their affairs.

"I know nothing, you see, Mimo," the Countess Shulski said, "beyond that you arrived yesterday. I think it was foolish of you to risk it. At least in Paris Madame Dubois would have let you stay and owe a week's rent. But here—among these strangers—"

"Now do not scold us, Mentor," the man answered, with a charming smile. "Mirko and I felt the sun had fled when you went last Thursday. It rained and rained two—three—days, and the Dubois canary got completely on our nerves; and, heavens above! the Grisoldi insisted upon cooking garlic in his food at every meal!—we had thought to have broken him of the habit, you remember?—and up, up it came from his stove. Body of Bacchus! It killed inspiration. I could not paint, my Chérisette, and Mirko could not play. And so we said: 'At least—at least the sun of the hair of our Chérisette must shine in the dark England; we, too, will go there, away from the garlic and the canary, and the fogs will give us new ideas, and we shall create wonderful things.' Is it not so, Mirko mio?"

"But, of course, Papa," the boy echoed; and then his voice trembled with a pitiful note. "You are not angry with us, darling Chérisette? Say it is not so?"

"My little one! How can you! I could never be angry with my Mirko, no matter what he did!" And the two pools of ink softened from the expression of the black panther into the divine tenderness of the Sistine Madonna, as she pressed the frail, little body to her side and pulled her cloak around it.

"Only I fear it cannot be well for you here in London, and if my uncle should know, all hope of getting anything from him may be over. He expressly said if I would come quite alone, to stay with him for these few weeks, it would be to my advantage; and my advantage means yours, as you know. Otherwise do you think I would have eaten of his hateful bread?"

"You are so good to us, Chérisette," the man Mimo said. "You have, indeed, a sister of the angels, Mirko mio; but soon we shall be all rich and famous. I had a dream last night, and already I have begun a new picture of grays and mists—of these strange fogs!"

Count Mimo Sykypri was a confirmed optimist.

"Meanwhile you are in the one room, in Neville Street, Tottenham Court Road. It is, I fear, a poor neighborhood."

"No worse than Madame Dubois'," Mimo hastened to reassure her, "and London is giving me new ideas."

Mirko coughed harshly with a dry sound. Countess Shulski drew him closer to her and held him tight.

"You got the address from the Grisoldi? He was a kind little old man, in spite of the garlic," she said.

"Yes, he told us of it, as an inexpensive resting place, until our affairs prospered, and we came straight there and wrote to you at once."

"I was greatly surprised to receive the letter. Have you any money at all now, Mimo?"

"Indeed, yes!" And Count Sykypri proudly drew forth eight bits of French gold from his pocket. "We had two hundred francs when we arrived. Our little necessities and a few paints took up two of the twenty-franc pieces, and we have eight of them left! Oh, quite a fortune! It will keep us until I can sell the 'Apache.' I shall take it to a picture dealer's to-morrow."

Countess Shulski's heart sank. She knew so well of old how long eight twenty-franc pieces would be likely to last! In spite of Mirko's care and watching of his father that gentleman was capable of giving one of them to a beggar if the beggar's face and story touched him, and any of the others could go in a present to Mirko or herself—to be pawned later, when necessity called. The case was hopeless as far as money was concerned with Count Sykypri.

Her own meager income, derived from the dead Shulski, was always forestalled for the wants of the family—the little brother whom she had promised her dead and adored mother never to desert.

For when the beautiful wife of Maurice Grey, the misanthropic and eccentric Englishman who lived in a castle near Prague, ran off with Count Mimo Sykypri, her daughter, then aged thirteen, had run with her, and the pair had been wiped off the list of the family. And Maurice Grey, after cursing them both and making a will depriving them of everything, shut himself up in his castle, and steadily drank himself to death in less than a year. And the brother of the beautiful Mrs. Grey, Francis Markrute, never forgave her either. He refused to receive her or hear news of her, even after poor little Mirko was born and she married Count Sykypri.

For on the father's side, the Markrute brother and sister were of very noble lineage; even with his bar sinister the financier could not brook the disgrace of Elinka. He had loved her so—the one soft side of his adamantine character. Her disgrace, it seemed, had frozen all the tenderness in his nature.

Countess Shulski was silent for a few moments, while both Mimo and Mirko watched her face anxiously. She had thrown back her veil.

"And supposing you do not sell the 'Apache,' Mimo? Your own money does not come in until Christmas; mine is all gone until January, and it is the cold winter approaching—and cold is not good for Mirko. What then?"

Count Sykypri moved uneasily. A tragic look grew in his handsome face; his face that was a mirror of all passing emotions; his face that had been able to express love and romance, devotion and tenderness, to wile a bird from off a tree or love from the heart of any woman. And even though Zara Shulski knew of just how little value was anything he said or did yet his astonishing charm always softened her irritation toward his fecklessness. So she repeated more gently:

"What then?"

Mimo got up and flung out his arms in a dramatic way.

"It cannot be!" he said. "I must sell the 'Apache!' Besides, if I don't: I tell you these strange, gray fogs are giving me new, wonderful thoughts—dark, mysterious—two figures meeting in the mist! Oh! but a wonderful combination that will be successful in all cases."

Mirko pressed his arm round his sister's neck and kissed her cheek, while he cooed love words in a soft Slavonic language. Two big tears gathered in Zara Shulski's deep eyes and made them tender as a dove's.

She drew out her purse and counted from it two sovereigns and some shillings which she slipped into Mirko's small hand.

"Keep these, pet, for an emergency," she said. "They are all I have, but I will—I must—find some other way for you soon: and now I shall have to go. If my uncle should suspect I am seeing you I might be powerless to help further."

They walked with her to the Grosvenor Gate, and reluctantly let her leave them; and then they watched her, as she sped across the road between the passing taxi-cabs. When they saw the light from the opening door and her figure disappearing between the tall servants who had come to open it, the two poor, shabby figures walked on with a sigh, to try to find an omnibus which would put them down somewhere near their dingy bedroom in Neville Street, Tottenham Court Road. And as they reached the Marble Arch there came on a sharp shower of icy rain.

Countess Shulski, however poorly dressed, was a person to whom servants were never impertinent; there was something in her bearing which precluded all idea of familiarity. It did not even strike Turner, or James, that her clothes were what none of the housemaids would have considered fit to wear when they went out. The remark the lordly Turner made, as he arranged some letters on the hall table, was:

"A very haughty lady, James—quite a bit of the Master about her, eh?"

But she went on to the lift, slowly, and to her luxurious bedroom, her heart full of pain and rage against fate. Here she sat down before the fire, and, resting her chin on her two hands, gazed steadily into the glowing coals.

What pictures did she see of past miseries there in the flames? Her thoughts wandered right back to the beginning. The stern, peculiar father, and the gloomy castle. The severe governesses—English and German—and her adorable, beautiful mother, descending upon the schoolroom like a fairy of light, always gay and sweet and loving. And then of that journey to a far country, where she saw an old, old, dying gentleman in a royal palace, who kissed her, and told her she would grow as beautiful as her grandmother with the red, red hair. And there in the palace was Mimo, so handsome and kind in his glittering aide-de-camp's uniform, who after that often came to the gloomy castle, and, with the fairy mother, to the schoolroom. Ah! those days were happy days! How they three had shrieked with laughter and played hide-and-seek in the long galleries!

And then the blank, hideous moment when the angel fairy had gone, and the stern father cursed and swore, and Uncle Francis' face looked like a vengeful fiend's. And then a day when she got word to meet her mother in the park of the castle. How she clung to her and cried and sobbed to be taken, too! And they—Mimo and the mother—always so kind and loving and irresponsible, consented. And then the flight; and weeks of happiness in luxurious hotels, until the mother's face grew pinched and white, and no letters but her own—returned—came from Uncle Francis. And ever the fear grew that if Mimo were absent from her for a moment Uncle Francis would kill him. The poor, adored mother! And then of the coming of Mirko and all their joy over it; and then, gradually, the skeleton of poverty, when all the jewels had been sold and all Mimo's uniform and swords; and nothing but his slender income, which could not be taken from him, remained. How he had worked to be a real artist, there in Paris! Oh! poor Mimo. He had tried, but everything was so against a gentleman; and Mirko such a delicate baby, and the mother's lovely face so often sad. And then the time of the mother's first bad illness—how they had watched and prayed, and Mimo had cried tears like a child, and the doctor had said the South was the only thing to help their angel's recovery. So to marry Ladislaus Shulski seemed the only way. He had a villa in the sun at Nice and offered it to them; he was crazy about her—Zara—at that time, though her skirts were not quite long, nor her splendid hair done up.

When her thoughts reached this far, the black panther in the Zoo never looked fiercer when Francis Markrute poked his stick between its bars to stir it up on Sunday mornings.

The hateful, hateful memories! When she came to know what marriage meant, and—a man! But it had saved the sweet mother's life for that winter. And though it was a strain to extract anything from Ladislaus, still, in the years that followed, often she had been able to help until his money, too, was all gone—on gambling and women.

And then the dear mother died—died in cold and poverty, in a poor little studio in Paris—in spite of her daughter's and Mimo's frantic letters to Uncle Francis for help. She knew now that he had been far away, in South

Africa, at the time, and had never received them, until too late; but then, it seemed as if God Himself had forsaken them. And now came the memory of her solemn promise. Mirko should never be deserted—the adored mother could die in peace about that. Her last words came back now—out of the glowing coals:

"I have been happy with Mimo, after all, my Chérisette, with you and Mimo and Mirko. It was worth while—" And so she had gasped—and died.

And here the tears gathered and blurred the flaming coals. But Zara's decision had come. There was no other way. To her uncle's bargain she must consent.

She got up abruptly and flung her hat on the bed—her cloak had already fallen from her—and without further hesitation she descended the stairs.

Francis Markrute was still seated in his library; he had taken out his watch and was calculating the time. It was twenty-five minutes to eight; his guests would be coming to dine at eight o'clock and he had not begun to dress. Would his niece have made up her mind by then?

That there could be any doubt about the fact that she would make up her mind as he wished never entered his head. It was only a question of time but it would be better, for every reason, if she arrived at the conclusion at once.

He rose from his chair with a quiet smile as she entered the room. So she had come! He had not relied upon his knowledge of a woman's temperament in vain.

She was very pale. The extra whiteness showed even on her gardenia skin, and her great eyes gleamed sullenly from beneath her lowering brows of ink.

"If the terms are for the certain happiness of Mirko I consent," she said.

CHAPTER IV

The four men—the two railway magnates, Francis Markrute, and Lord Tancred—had all been waiting a quarter of an hour before the drawing-room fire when the Countess Shulski sailed into the room. She wore an evening gown of some thin, black, transparent, woolen stuff, which clung around her with the peculiar grace her poorest clothes acquired. Another woman would have looked pitifully shabby in such a dress, but her distinction made it appear to at least three of the men as the robe of a goddess. Francis Markrute was too annoyed at the delay of her coming to admire anything; but even he, as he presented his guests to her, could not help remarking that he had never seen her look more wonderful, nor more contemptuously regal.

They had had rather a stormy scene in the library, half an hour before. Her words had been few, but their displeasure had been unconcealed. She would agree to the bare bargain, if so be this strange man were willing, but she demanded to know the reason of his willingness.

And when she was told it was a business matter between the two men, and that she would be given a large fortune, she expressed no more surprise than a disdainful curl of the lips.

For her, all men were either brutes—or fools like poor Mimo.

If she had known that Lord Tancred had already refused her hand and that her uncle was merely counting upon his own unerring knowledge of human nature—and Lord Tancred's nature in particular—she might have felt humiliated, instead of full of impotent rage.

The young man, for his part, had arrived exactly on the stroke of eight, a rare effort of punctuality for him. Some underneath excitement to see his friend Markrute's niece had tingled in his veins from the moment he had left the house.

What sort of a woman could it be who would be willing to marry a perfect stranger for the sake of his title and position? The quarter-of-an-hour's wait had not added to his calm. So when the door had eventually opened for her entry he had glanced up with intense interest, and had then drawn in his breath as she advanced up the room. The physical part of the lady at all events was extremely delectable.

But when he was presented and his eyes met hers he was startled by the look of smoldering, somber hate he saw in them.

What could it all mean? Francis must have been romancing. Why should she look at him like that, if she were willing to marry him? He was piqued and interested.

She spoke not a word as they went down to dinner, but he was no raw youth to be snubbed thus into silence. His easy, polished manner soon started a conversation upon the usual everyday things. He received "Yes" and "No" for answers. The railway magnate on her other side was hardly more fortunate, until the entrées were in full swing, then she unfroze a little; the elderly gentleman had said something which interested her.

The part which particularly irritated Lord Tancred was that he felt sure she was not really stupid—who could be stupid with such a face? And he was quite unaccustomed to being ignored by women. A like experience had not occurred to him in the whole of his life.

He watched her narrowly. He had never seen so white a skin; the admirably formed bones of her short, small face caused, even in a side light, no disfiguring shadows to fall beside the mouth and nose, nor on the cheeks; all was velvety smooth and rounded. The remote Jewish touch was invisible—save in the splendor of the eyes and lashes. She filled him with the desire to touch her, to clasp her tightly in his arms, to pull down that glorious hair and bury his face in it. And Lord Tancred was no sensualist, given to instantly appraising the outward charm of women.

When the grouse was being handed, he did get a whole sentence from her; it was in answer to his question whether she liked England.

"How can one say—when one does not know?" she said. "I have only been here once before, when I was quite a child. It seems cold and dark."

"We must persuade you to like it better," he answered, trying to look into her eyes which she had instantly averted. The expression of resentment still smoldered there, he had noticed, during their brief glance.

"Of what consequence whether I like it or no," she said, looking across the table, and this was difficult to answer! It seemed to set him upon his beam-ends. He could not very well say because he had suddenly begun to admire her very much! At this stage he had not decided what he meant to do.

An unusual excitement was permeating his being; he could not account for how or why. He had felt no sensation like it, except on one of his lion hunts in Africa when the news had come into camp that an exceptionally fine beast had been discovered near and might be stalked on the morrow. His sporting instincts seemed to be thoroughly awakened.

Meanwhile Countess Shulski had turned once more to Sir Philip Armstrong, the railway magnate. He was telling her about Canada and she listened with awakening interest: how there were openings for every one and great fortunes could be made there by the industrious and persevering.

"It has not come to a point, then, when artists could have a chance, I suppose?" she asked. Lord Tancred wondered at the keenness in her voice.

"Modern artists?" Sir Philip queried. "Perhaps not, though the rich men are beginning to buy pictures and beautiful things, too; but in a new country it is the man of sinew and determination, not the dreamer, who succeeds."

Her head then drooped a little; her interest now seemed only mechanical, as she answered again, "Yes" and "No."

Lord Tancred wondered and wondered; he saw that her thoughts were far away.

Francis Markrute had been watching things minutely while he kept up his suave small talk with Colonel Macnamara on his right hand. He was well pleased with the turn of events. After all, nothing could have been better than Zara's being late. Circumstance often played into the hand of an experienced manipulator like himself. Now if she only kept up this attitude of indifference, which, indeed, she seemed likely to do—she was no actress, he knew—things might be settled this very night.

Lord Tancred could not get her to have a single continued conversation for the remainder of dinner; he was perfectly raging with annoyance, his fighting blood was up. And when at the first possible moment after the dessert arrived she swept from the room, her eyes met his as he held the door and they were again full of contemptuous hate.

He returned to his seat with his heart actually thumping in his side.

And all through the laborious conversation upon Canada and how best to invest capital, which Francis Markrute with great skill and apparently hearty friendship prolonged to its utmost limits, he felt the attraction and irritation of the woman grow and grow. He no longer took the slightest interest in the pros and cons of his future in the Colony, and when, at last, he heard the distant tones of Tschaikovsky's *Chanson Triste* as they ascended the stairs he came suddenly to a determination. She was sitting at the grand piano in the back part of the room. A huge, softly shaded lamp shed its veiled light upon her white face and rounded throat; her hands and arms, which showed to the elbow, seemed not less pale than the ivory keys, and those disks of black velvet gazed in front of them, a whole world of anguish in their depths.

For this was the tune that her mother had loved, and she was playing it to remind herself of her promise and to keep herself firm in her determination to accept the bargain, for her little brother Mirko's sake.

She glanced at Lord Tancred as he entered. Count Ladislaus Shulski had been a very handsome man, too. She did not know enough of the English type to judge of Lord Tancred morally. She only saw that he was a splendid, physical creature who would be strong—and horrible probably—like the rest.

The whole expression of her face changed as he came and leaned upon the piano. The sorrow died out of her eyes and was replaced by a fierce defiance; and her fingers broke into a tarantella of wild sounds.

"The whole expression of her face changed as he came and leaned upon the piano."

"You strange woman!" Lord Tancred said.

"Am I strange?" she answered through her teeth. "It is said by those who know that we are all mad—at some time and at some point. I have, I think, reason to be mad to-night." And with that she crashed a final chord, rose from her seat, and crossed the room.

"I hope, Uncle Francis, your guests will excuse me," she said, with an imperial, aloof politeness, "but I am very tired. I will wish you all a good-night." She bowed to them as they expressed their regrets, and then slowly left the room.

"Goodnight, madame," Lord Tancred said, at the door. "Some day you and I will cross swords."

But he was rewarded by no word, only an annihilating glance from her sullen eyes, and he stood there and gazed at her as she passed up the stairs.

"An extraordinary and beautiful woman—your niece—eh, my dear Markrute?" he heard one of the pompous gentlemen say, as he returned to the group by the fire, and it angered him—he could not have told why.

Francis Markrute, who knew his moments, began now to talk about her, casually; how she was an interesting, mysterious character; beautiful? well, no, not exactly that—a superlative skin, fine eyes and hair, but no special features.

"I will not admit that she is beautiful, my friend," he said. "Beauty suggests gentleness and tenderness. My niece reminds me of the black panther in the Zoo, but one could not say—if she were tamed."

Such remarks were not calculated to allay the growing interest and attraction Lord Tancred was feeling. Francis Markrute knew his audience; he never wasted his words. He abruptly turned the conversation back to Canada again, until even the two magnates on their own ground were bored and said goodnight. The four men came downstairs together. As the two others were being assisted into their coats by Turner and his satellites the host said to Lord Tancred:

"Will you have a cigar with me, Tancred, before you go on to your supper party?" And presently they were both seated in mammoth armchairs in the cozy library.

"I hope, my dear boy, you have all the information you want about Canada," Mr. Markrute said. "You could not find two more influential people than Sir Philip and the Colonel. I asked—" but Lord Tancred interrupted him.

"I don't care a farthing more about Canada!" he flashed out. "I have made up my mind. If you really meant what you said to-day, I will marry your niece, and I don't care whether she has a penny or no."

The financier's plans had indeed culminated with a rush!

But he expressed no surprise, merely raised his eyebrows mildly and puffed some blue rings of smoke, as he answered:

"I always mean what I say, only I do not care for people to do things blindly. Now that you have seen my niece are you sure she would suit you? I thought, after all, perhaps not, to-night: she is certainly a difficult person. It would be no easy task for any man to control her—as a wife."

"I don't care for tame women," Lord Tancred said. "It is that very quality of difficulty which has inspired me. By George! did you ever see such a haughty bearing? It will take a man's whole intelligence to know which bit to use."

"She may close her teeth on whatever bit you use, and bolt with it. Do not say afterwards that I let you take her blindly."

"Why does she look at me with such hate?" Lord Tancred was just going to ask—and then he stopped himself. It was characteristic of him that now he had made up his mind he would not descend to questions or details—he would find all out later for himself—but one thing he must know: had she really consented to marry him? If so, she had her own reasons, of course, and desire for himself was not among them; but, somehow, he felt sure they were not sordid or paltry ones. He had always liked dangerous games—the most unbroken polo ponies to train in the country, the freshest horses, the fiercest beasts to stalk and kill—and why not a difficult wife? It would add an adorable spice to the affair. But as he was very honest with himself he knew, underneath, that it was not wholly even this instinct, but that she had cast some spell over him and that he must have her for his own.

"You might very well ask her history," Francis Markrute said. He could be so gracious when he liked, and he really admired the wholehearted dash with which Lord Tancred had surrendered; there was something big and royal about it—he himself never gambled in small sums either. "So as I expect you won't," he continued, "I will tell you. She is the daughter of Maurice Grey, a brother of old Colonel Grey of Hentingdon, whom everybody knew, and she has been the widow of an unspeakable brute for over a year. She was an immaculate wife, and devoted daughter before that. The possibilities of her temperament are all to come."

Lord Tancred sprang from his chair, the very thought of her and her temperament made him thrill. Was it possible he was already in love, after one evening?

"Now we must really discuss affairs, my dear boy," the financier went on. "Her dower, as I told you, will be princely."

"That I absolutely refuse to do, Francis," Lord Tancred answered. "I tell you I want the woman for my wife. You can settle the other things with my lawyer if you care to, and tie it all up on her. I am not interested in that matter. The only thing I really wish to know is if you are sure she will marry me?"

"I am perfectly sure." The financier narrowed his eyes. "I would not have suggested the affair to-day if I had had any doubt about that."

"Then it is settled, and I shall not ask why. I shall not ask any thing. Only when may I see her again and how soon can we be married?"

"Come and lunch with me in the city to-morrow, and we will talk over everything. I shall have seen her, and can then tell you when to present yourself. And I suppose you can have the ceremony at the beginning of November?"

"Six whole weeks hence!" Lord Tancred said, protestingly. "Must she get such heaps of clothes? Can't it be sooner? I wanted to be here for my Uncle Glastonbury's first shoot on the 2nd of November, and if we are only married then, we shall be off on a honeymoon. You must come to that shoot, by-the-way, old boy, it is the pleasantest of the whole lot he has; one day at the partridges, and a dash at the pheasants; but he only asks the jolliest parties to this early one, for Ethelrida's birthday, and none of the bores."

"It would give me great pleasure to do so," Francis Markrute said. And he looked down so that Lord Tancred should not see the joy in his eyes.

Then they shook hands most heartily, and the newly made fiancé said good-night, with the happy assurance in his ears that he might claim his bride in time to be back from a week's honeymoon for the Glastonbury shoot.

When he had gone Francis Markrute's first act was to sit down and write a four-figure check for the Cripple Children's Hospital: he believed in thankofferings. Then he rubbed his hands softly together as he went up to his bed.

CHAPTER V

Then Lord Tancred left the house in Park Lane he did not go on to the supper party at the Savoy he had promised to attend. That sort of affair had bored him, now for several years. Instead, he drove straight back to his rooms in St. James' Street, and, getting comfortably into his pet chair, he steadily set himself to think. He had acted upon a mad impulse; he knew that and did not argue with himself about it, or regret it. Some force stronger than anything he had hitherto known had compelled him to come to the decision. And what would his future life be like with this strange woman? That could not be exactly guessed. That it would contain scenes of the greatest excitement he did not doubt. She would in all cases look the part. His mother herself—the Lady Tancred, daughter of the late and sister of the present Duke of Glastonbury—could not move with more dignity: a thought which reminded him that he had better write to his parent and inform her of his intended step. He thought of all the women he had loved—or imagined he had loved—since he left Eton. The two affairs which had convulsed him during his second year at Oxford were perhaps the most serious; the Laura Highford, his last episode, was fortunately over and had always been rather tiresome. In any case none of those ladies of the world—or other world—had any reasons to reproach him, and he was free and happy. And if he wished to put down a large stake on the card of marriage he was answerable to no one.

During the last eight hundred years, ever since Amaury Guiscard of that house of Hauteville whose daring deeds gave sovereigns to half Europe, had come over with his Duke William, and had been rewarded by the gift of the Wrayth lands—seized from the Saxons—his descendants had periodically done madly adventurous things. Perhaps the quality was coming out in him!

Then he thought of his lady, personally, and not of the extraordinariness of his action. She was exasperatingly attractive. How delicious it would be when he had persuaded her to talk to him, taught her to love him, because she certainly must love him—some day! It was rather cold-blooded of her to be willing to marry him, a stranger; but he was not going to permit himself to dwell upon that. She could not be really cold-blooded with that face: its every line bespoke capability of exquisite passion. It was not the least cunning, or calculating, either. It was simply adorable. And to kiss! But here he pulled himself together and wrote to his mother a note, short and to the point, which she received by the first post next morning at her small, house in Queen Street, Mayfair; and then he went to bed. The note ran:

"My Dear Mother:

"I am going to be married at last. The lady is a daughter of Maurice Grey (a brother of old Colonel Grey of Hentingdon who died last year), and the widow of a Pole named Shulski, Countess Shulski she is called."

(He had paused here because he had suddenly remembered he did not know her Christian name!)

"She is also the niece of Francis Markrute whom you have such an objection to—or had, last season. She is most beautiful and I hope you will like her. Please go and call to-morrow. I will come and breakfast with you about ten.

"Your affectionate son, Tancred."

And this proud English mother knew here was a serious letter, because he signed it "Tancred." He usually finished his rare communications with just, "love from Tristram."

She leaned back on her pillows and closed her eyes. She adored her son but she was, above all things, a woman of the world and given to making reasonable judgments. Tristram was past the age of a foolish entanglement; there must be some strong motive in this action. He could hardly be in love. She knew him so well, when he was in love! He had shown no signs of it lately—not, really, for several years—for that well conducted—friendship—with Laura Highford could not be called being in love. Then she thought of Francis Markrute. He was so immensely rich, she could not help a relieved sigh. There would be money at all events. But she knew that could not be the reason. She was aware of her son's views about rich wives. She was aware, too, that with all his sporting tastes and modern irreverence of tradition, underneath he was of a proud, reserved nature, intensely proud of the honor of his ancient name. What then could be the reason for this engagement? Well, she would soon know. It was half-past eight in the morning, and Tristram's "about ten" would not mean later than, half-past, or a quarter to eleven. She rang the bell for her maid, and told her to ask the young ladies to put on dressing-gowns and come to her.

Soon Lord Tancred's two sisters entered the room.

They were nice, fresh English girls, and stood a good deal in awe of their mother. They kissed her and sat down on the bed. They felt it was a momentous moment, because Lady Tancred never saw any one until her hair was arranged—not even her own daughters.

"Your brother Tristram is going to be married," she said and referred to the letter lying on the coverlet, "to a Countess Shulski, a niece of that Mr. Markrute whom one meets about."

"Oh! Mother!" and "Really!" gasped Emily and Mary.

"Have we seen her?"

"Do we know her?"

"No, I think we can none of us have seen her. She certainly was not with Mr. Markrute at Cowes, and no one has been in town, except this last week for Flora's wedding. I suppose Tristram must have met her in Scotland, or possibly abroad. He went to Paris, you remember, at Easter, and again in July."

"I wonder what she is like," said Emily.

"Is she young?" asked Mary.

"Tristram does not say," replied Lady Tancred, "only that she is beautiful."

"We are so surprised," both girls gasped together.

"Yes, it is unexpected, certainly," agreed their mother, "but Tristram has judgment; he is not likely to have chosen any one of whom I should disapprove. You must be ready to call with me, directly after lunch. Tristram is coming to breakfast, so you can have yours now—in your room. I must talk to him."

And the girls, who were dying to ask a hundred thousand questions, felt that they were dismissed, and, kissing their dignified parent, they retired to their own large, back room, which they shared, in common with all their pleasures and little griefs, together.

"Isn't it too wonderful, Em?" Mary said, when they were back there, both curled up in the former's bed waiting for their breakfast. "One can see Mother is very much moved; she was so stern. I thought Tristram was devoted to Laura Highford, did not you?"

"Oh! he has been sick of that for ages and ages. She nags at him—she is a cat anyway and I never could understand it, could you, Mary?"

"Men have to be like that," said Mary, wisely, "they must have some one, I mean, to play with, and they are afraid of girls."

"How I hope she will like us, don't you?" Emily said. "Mr. Markrute is very rich and perhaps she is, too. How lovely it will be if they are able to live at Wrayth. How lovely to have it opened again—to go and stay there!"

"Yes, indeed," said Mary.

Lady Tancred awaited her son in the small front morning-room. She was quite as much a specimen of an English aristocrat as he was, with her brushed-back, gray hair, and her beautiful, hard, fine-featured face. She was supremely dignified, and dressed well and with care. She had been brought up in the school which taught the repression of all emotion—now, alas! rapidly passing away—so that she did not even tap her foot from the impatience which was devouring her, and it was nearly eleven o'clock before Tristram made his appearance!

He apologized charmingly, and kissed her cheek. His horse, Satan, had been particularly fresh, and he had been obliged to give him an extra canter twice round the Row, before coming in, and was breakfast ready?—as he was extremely hungry! Yes, breakfast was ready, and they went into the dining-room where the old butler awaited them.

"Give me everything, Michelham," said his lordship, "I am ravenous. Then you can go. Her ladyship will pour out the coffee."

The old servant beamed upon him, with a "glad to see your lordship's well!" and, surrounding his plate with hot, covered, silver dishes, quietly made his exit, and so they were alone.

Lady Tancred beamed upon her son, too. She could not help it. He looked so completely what he ought to look, she thought—magnificently healthy and handsome, and perfectly groomed. No mother could help being proud of him.

"Tristram, dear boy, now tell me all about it," she said.

"There is hardly anything to tell you, Mother, except that I am going to be married about the 25th of October—and—you will be awfully nice to her—to Zara—won't you?" He had taken the precaution to send round a note, early in the morning, to Francis Markrute, asking for his lady's full name, as he wished to tell his family; so the "Zara" came out quite naturally! "She is rather a peculiar person, and—er—has very stiff manners. You may not like her at first."

"No, dear?" said Lady Tancred hesitatingly, "Stiff manners you say? That at least is on the right side. I always deplore the modern free-and-easy-ness."

"Oh, there is nothing free-and-easy about her!" said Tristram, helping himself to a cutlet, while he smiled almost grimly. His sense of humor was highly aroused oven the whole thing; only that overmastering something which drew him was even stronger than this.

Then he felt that there was no use in allowing his mother to drag information from him; he had better tell her what he meant her to know.

"You see, Mother, the whole thing has been arranged rather suddenly. I only settled upon it last night myself, and so told you at once. She will be awfully rich, which is rather a pity in a sense—though I suppose we shall live at Wrayth again, and all that—- but I need not tell you I am not marrying her for such a reason."

"No, I know you," Lady Tancred said, "but I cannot agree with you about its being a pity that she is rich. We live in an age when the oldest and most honored name is useless without money to keep up its traditions, and any woman would find your title and your position well worth all her gold. There are things you will give her in return which only hundreds of years can produce. You must have no feeling that you are accepting anything from her which you do not equalize. Remember, it is a false sentiment."

"Oh, I expect so—and she is well bred, you know, so she won't throw it in my teeth." And Lord Tancred smiled.

"I remember old Colonel Grey," his mother continued; "years ago he drove a coach; but I don't recollect his brother. Did he live abroad, perhaps?"

This was an awkward question. The young fiancé was quite ignorant about his prospective bride's late father!

"Yes," he said hurriedly. "Zara married very young, she is quite young now—only about twenty-three. Her husband was a brute, and now she has come to live with Francis Markrute. He is an awfully good fellow, Mother, though you don't like him; extremely cultivated, and so quaintly amusing, with his cynical views on life. You will like him when you know him better. He is a jolly good sportsman, too—for a foreigner."

"And of what nation is Mr. Markrute, Tristram, do you know?" Lady Tancred asked.

Really, all women—even mothers—were tiresome at times with their questions!

"'Pon my word, I don't." And he laughed awkwardly. "Austrian, perhaps, or Russian. I have never thought about it; he speaks English so well, and he is a naturalized Englishman, in any case."

"But as you are marrying into the family, don't you think it would be more prudent, dear, to gather some information on the subject?" Lady Tancred hazarded.

And then she saw the true Tancred spirit come out, which she had often vainly tried to combat in her husband during her first years of married life, and had desisted in the end. Tristram's strong, level eyebrows joined themselves in a frown, and his mouth, clean-shaven and chiseled, shut like a vice.

"I am going to do what I am going to do, Mother," he said. "I am satisfied with my bargain, and I beg of you to accept the situation. I do not demand any information, and I ask you not to trouble yourself either. Nothing any one could say would change me—Give me some more coffee, will you, please."

Lady Tancred's hand trembled a little as she poured it out, but she did not say anything, and there was silence for a minute, while his lordship went on with his breakfast, with appetite unimpaired.

"I will take the girls and call there immediately after lunch," she said presently, "and I am to ask for the Countess Shulski. You pronounce it like that, do you not?"

"Yes. She may not be in, and in any case, perhaps, for to-day only leave cards. To-morrow or next day I'll go with you, Mother. You see, until the announcement comes out in the *Morning Post*, everything is not quite settled—I expect Zara would like it better if you did not meet until after then."

That was probably true, he reflected, since he had not even exchanged personal pledges with her yet himself!

Then, as his mother looked stiffly repulsed, his sense of humor got the better of him, and he burst into a peal of laughter, while he jumped up and kissed her with the delightful, caressing boyishness which made her love him with a love so far beyond what she gave to her other children.

"Darling," she murmured, "if you are so happy as to laugh like that I am happy, too, and will do just what you wish." Her proud eyes filled with mist and she pressed his hand.

"Mum, you are a trump!" he said, and he kissed her again and, holding her arm, he led her back into the morning-room.

"Now I must go and change these things," he announced, as he looked down at his riding clothes. "I am going to lunch with Markrute in the City to discuss all the points. So good-bye for the present. I will probably see you to-night. Call a taxi," he said to Michelham who at that moment came into the room with a note. He had kissed his mother and was preparing to leave, when just as he got to the door he turned and said:

"Don't say a word to any one, to-day, of the news—let it come out in the *Morning Post*, to-morrow. I ask it—please?"

"Not even to Cyril? You have forgotten that he is coming up from Uncle Charles' to go back to Eton," his mother said, "and the girls already know."

"Oh! Cyril. By Jove! I had forgotten! Yes, tell him; he is a first class chap, he'll understand, and, I say"—and he pulled some sovereigns from his pocket—"do give him these from me for this term."

Then with a smile he went.

And a few minutes afterwards a small, slender boy of fourteen, with only Eton's own inimitable self-confidence and delicious swagger printed upon his every line, drove up to the door, and, paying for the taxi in a lordly way, came into his mother's morning-room. There had been a gap in the family after Tristram's appearance, caused by the death, from diphtheria, of two other boys; then came the two girls of twenty and nineteen respectively and, lastly, Cyril.

His big, blue eyes rounded with astonishment and interest when he heard the important news. All he said was:

"Well, she must be a corker, if Tristram thinks her good enough. But what a beastly nuisance! He won't go to Canada now, I suppose, and we shan't have that ranch."

CHAPTER VI

Francis Markrute also saw his niece at breakfast—or rather—just after it. She was finishing hers in the little upstairs sitting-room which he had allotted to her for her personal use, when he tapped at the door and asked if he might come in.

She said "yes," and then rose, with the ceremonious politeness she always used in her dealings with him—contemptuous, resentful politeness for the most part.

"I have come to settle the details of your marriage," he said, while he waved her to be seated again and took a chair himself. At the word "marriage" her nostrils quivered, but she said nothing. She was always extremely difficult to deal with, on account of these silences of hers. She helped no one out. Francis Markrute knew the method himself and admired it; it always made the other person state his case.

"You saw Lord Tancred last night. You can have no objection to him on the ground of his person, and he is a very great gentleman, my niece, as you will find."

Still silence.

"I have arranged with him for you to be married in October—about the 25th, I suppose. So now comes the question of your trousseau. You must have clothes to fit you for so great a position. You had better get them in Paris." Then he paused, struck by the fact which he had only just noticed, that the garments she had been wearing and those she now wore were shabby enough. He realized the reason he had not before remarked this—her splendid carriage and air of breeding—and it gave him a thrill of pride in her. After all, she was his own niece.

"It will be a very great joy to dress you splendidly," he said. "I would have done so always, if I had not known where the money would go; but we are going to settle all that now, and every one can be happy."

It was not in her nature to beg and try to secure favors for her brother and Mimo without paying for them. She had agreed upon the price—herself. Now all she had to do was to obtain as much as possible for this.

"Mirko's cough has come back again," she said quietly. "Since I have consented I want him to be able to go into the warmth without delay. They are here in London now—he and his father—in a very poor place."

"I have thought it all out," Francis Markrute answered while he frowned, as he always did, at the mention of Mimo. "There is a wonderfully clever doctor at Bournemouth where the air is perfect for those delicate in the lungs. I have communicated with him; and he will take the child into his own house, where he will be beautifully cared for. There he can have a tutor, and when he is stronger he can return to Paris, or to Vienna, and have his talent for the violin cultivated. I want you to understand," he continued, "that if you agree to my terms your brother will not be stinted in any way."

And her thoughts said, "And Mimo?" but she felt it wiser not to ask anything about him just then. To have Mirko cared for by a really clever doctor, in good air, with some discipline as to bedtime, and not those unwholesome meals, snatched at odd hours at some restaurant, seemed a wonderfully good thing. If the little fellow would only be happy separated from his father; that was the question!

"Are there children in the house?" she asked. Mirko was peculiar, and did not like other little boys.

"The doctor has an only little girl of about your brother's age. He is nine and a half, is it not so? And she is delicate, too, so they could play together."

This sounded more promising.

"I would wish to go down and see the doctor first—and the home," she said.

"You shall do so, of course, when you like. I will set aside a certain sum every year, to be invested for him, so that when he grows up he will have a competence—even a small fortune. I will have a deed drawn out for you to sign; it shall be all *en règle*."

"That is well," she said. "And now give me some money, please, that I may relieve their present necessities until my brother can go to this place. I do not consent to give myself, unless I am certain that I free those I love from anxieties. I should like, immediately, a thousand francs. Forty pounds of your money, isn't it?"

"I will send the notes up in a few minutes," Francis Markrute said. He was in the best of tempers to-day. "Meanwhile, that part of the arrangement being settled, I must ask you to pay some attention to the thought of seeing your fiancé."

"I do not wish to see him," she announced.

Her uncle smiled.

"Possibly not, but it is part of the bargain. You can't marry the man without seeing him. He will come and call upon you this afternoon, and, no doubt, will bring you a ring. I trust to your honor not to show so plainly your dislike that no man could carry through his side. Please remember your brother's welfare depends upon your actual marriage. If you cause Lord Tancred to break off the match the bargain between you and me is void."

The black panther's look again appeared in her eyes, and an icy stillness settled upon her. But she began to speak rather fast, with a catch in the breath between the sentences.

"Then, since you wish this so much for your own ends, which I cannot guess, I tell you, arrange for me to go to Paris, alone, away from him, until the wedding day. He must hate the thought as much as I do. We are probably both only marionettes in your hands. Explain to the man that I will not go through the degradation of the pretence of an engagement, especially here in this England, where, *Maman* said, they parade affections, and fiancés are lovers. *Mon Dieu!* I will play my part—for the visits of ceremony to his family, which I suppose must take place even here—but beyond that, after to-day, I will not see him alone nor have any communication with him. Is it understood?"

Francis Markrute looked at her with growing admiration. She was gorgeously attractive in this mood. He obtained endless pleasure out of life by his habit of abstract observation. He was able to watch people in the throes of emotion, like a master seeing his hunters being put through their paces.

"It shall be understood," he said. He knew it was wiser to insist upon no more; her temper would never brook it. He knew he could count upon her honor and her pride to fulfill her part of the bargain if she were not exasperated beyond bearing.

"I will explain everything to Lord Tancred at luncheon," he said, "that you will receive him this afternoon, and that then you are going to Paris, and will not return until the wedding. You will concede the family interviews that are absolutely necessary, I suppose?"

"I have already said so; only let them be few and short."

"Then I will not detain you longer now. You are a beautiful woman, Zara," Francis Markrute said, as he rose and kissed her hand. "None of the royal ladies, your ancestresses, ever looked more like a queen." And he bowed himself out of the room, leaving her in her silence.

When she was alone she clenched her hands and walked up and down for a few moments, and her whole serpentine body writhed with passionate anger and pain.

Yes, she was a beautiful woman, and had a right to her life and joys like another—and now she was to be tied, and bound again to a husband!

"Les Infâmes!" she hissed aloud. "But for that part, I will not bear it! Until the wedding I will dissemble as best I can—but afterwards—!"

And if Lord Tancred could have seen her then he would have known that all the courage he had used when he faced the big lion would be needed soon again.

But before a servant brought up the envelope with the notes she had calmed herself and was preparing to go out. The good part of the news must be told to the two poor ones in their Tottenham Court Road retreat.

As she sped along in the taxi—her uncle had placed one of his several motors at her disposal, but it was not for such localities—she argued with herself that it would be wiser not to give Mimo all the money at once. She knew that that would mean not only the necessary, instantaneous move to a better lodging, but an expensive dinner at the nearest restaurant as well, and certainly bonbons and small presents for Mirko, and new clothes; twice as much would be spent, if credit could be obtained; and then there would be the worry of the bills and the anxiety. If only Mirko would consent to be parted from his fond and irresponsible parent for a time it would be so much better for his health, and his chance of becoming of some use in the world. Mimo always meant so kindly and behaved so foolishly! With the money she personally would get for her bargain Mimo should, somehow, be made comfortable in some studio in Paris where he could paint those pictures which would not sell, and might see his friends—he had still a few who, when his clothes were in a sufficiently good state, welcomed him and his charming, debonair smile. Mimo could be a delightfully agreeable guest, even though he was changed by years and poverty.

And Mirko would be in healthy surroundings; surely it was worth it, after all!

The taxi drew up in the mean street and she got out, paid the man, and then knocked at the dingy door.

A slatternly, miserable, little general servant opened it. No, the foreign gentleman and the little boy were not in, they said they would be back in a few minutes—would the lady step up and wait? She followed the lumpy, untidy figure upstairs to a large attic at the top. It was always let as a studio, apparently. It had a fine northern light from a big window, and was quite clean, though the wretched furniture spoke of better days.

Cleanliness was one of Count Sykypri's peculiarities; he always kept whatever room he was in tidy and clean. This orderly instinct seemed at variance with all the rest of his easy-going character. It was the fastidiousness of a gentleman, which never deserted him. Now Zara recognized the old traveling rug hung on two easels, to hide the little iron beds where he and Mirko slept. The new wonder, which would be bound to sell, was begun there on a third easel. It did not look extremely promising at its present stage. Mirko's violin and his father's, in their cases, were on a chair beside a small pile of music; the water-jug had in it a bunch of yellow chrysanthemums probably bought off a barrow.

The Countess Shulski had been through many vicissitudes with these two since her husband's death, but seldom—only once perhaps—had they gone down to such poverty-stricken surroundings. Generally it was some small apartment in Paris, or Florence, that they occupied, with rather scanty meals when the end of the quarter came. During Count Shulski's life she had always either lived in some smart villa at Nice, or led a wandering existence in hotels; and for months at a time, in later years, when he disappeared, upon his own pleasures bent, he would leave her in some old Normandy farmhouse, only too thankful to be free from his hateful presence. Here Mimo and Mirko would join her, and while they painted and played, she would read. Her whole inner life was spent with books. Among the shady society her husband had frequented she had been known as "The Stone." She never unbent, and while her beauty and extraordinary type attracted all the men she came across they soon gave up their pursuit. She was quite hopeless, they said—and half-witted, some added! No woman could sit silent like that for hours, otherwise. Zara thought of all these things, as she sat on the rickety chair in the Neville Street lodging. How she had loathed that whole atmosphere! How she loathed bohemians and adventurers, no words could tell.

While her mother had lived there had been none of them about. For all her personal downfall, Elinka, Markrute's sister, and an emperor's daughter, remained an absolute *grande dame*—never mixing or mingling with any people but her own belongings.

But now that she was dead, poor Mimo had sometimes gone for company into a class other than his own.

As yet Zara's thoughts had not turned upon her new existence which was to be. She had drawn a curtain over it in her mind. She knew but vaguely about life in England, she had never had any English friends. One or two gamblers had often come to the Nice villa, but except that they were better looking types and wore well made clothes, she had classed them with the rest of her husband's acquaintances. She had read numbers of English classics but practically no novels, so she could not very well picture a state of things she was ignorant about. Sufficient for the day was the evil thereof.

She was getting slightly impatient when at last the two came in.

They had been told of her arrival; she knew that by their glad, hurried mounting of the stairs and the quick opening of the door.

"Chérisette, Angel! But what joy!" And Mirko hurled himself into her arms, while Mimo kissed her hand. He never forgot his early palace manners.

"I have brought you good news," she said, as she drew out two ten-pound notes. "I have made my uncle see reason. Here is something for the present. He has such a kind and happy scheme for Mirko's health. Listen, and I will tell you about it."

They clustered around her while she explained in the most attractive manner she could the picture of the boy's future, but in spite of all that, his beautiful little face fell as he grasped that he was to leave his father.

"It will only be for a time, darling," Zara said, "just until you get quite well and strong, and learn some lessons. All little boys go to school, and come home for the holidays. You know *Maman* would have wished you to be educated like a gentleman."

"But I hate other boys, and you have taught me so well. Oh! Chérisette, what shall I do? And to whom play my violin, who will understand?"

"Oh, but Mirko mio, it is a splendid offer! Think, dear child, a comfortable home and no anxieties," Mimo said. "Truly your sister is an angel, and you must not be so ungrateful. Your cough will get quite well; perhaps I can come and lodge in the town, and we could walk together."

But Mirko pouted. Zara sighed and clasped her hands.

"If you only knew how hard it has been to obtain this much," she said, with despair in her voice. "Oh, Mirko, if you love me you will accept it! Can't you trust me that I would not ask you to go where they are hard or cruel? I am going down to the place to-morrow, to see it and judge for myself. Won't you be good and try to please me?"

Then the little cripple fell to sobbing and kissing her, nestling in her arms with his curly head against her neck.

But in the end she comforted him, the never varying gentleness toward him which she showed would have soothed the most peevish invalid.

So at last she was able to feel that her sacrifice, of which they must always remain ignorant, would not be all in vain; Mirko appeared reconciled to his fate, and would certainly benefit by more healthy surroundings. Instinct told her there would be no use even suggesting to her uncle that the child should stay with Mimo, the situation would have become an *impasse* if the boy had held out, and between them they would have had only this forty pounds until Christmas—and then very little more—and the life of hand-to-mouth poverty would have gone on and on, while here were comfort and probable health, with a certainty of welfare, and education, and a competence in the future. And who knows but Mirko might grow into a great artist one day!

This possible picture she painted in glowing colors until the child's pathetic, dark eyes glistened with pleasure.

Then she became practical; they must change their lodging and find a better one. But here Mimo interfered. They were really very comfortable where they were, he urged, humble though it looked, and changing was unpleasant. If they were able to buy some linen sheets and a new suit of clothes for each it would be much better to stay for the present, until Mirko's going to Bournemouth should be completely settled. "And even then," Count Sykypri said, "it will do for me. No one cooks garlic here, and there is no canary!"

CHAPTER VII

Neither Lord Tancred nor Francis Markrute was late at the appointment in the city restaurant where they were to lunch, and they were soon seated at a table in a corner where they could talk without being interrupted. They spoke of ordinary things for a moment. Then Lord Tancred's impatience to get at the matter which interested him became too great to wait longer, so he said laconically:

"Well?"

"I saw her this morning and had a talk"—the financier said, as he placed some caviare on his toast. "You must not overlook the fact, which I have already stated to you, that she is a most difficult problem. You will have an interesting time taming her. For a man of nerve, I cannot imagine a more thrilling task. She is a woman who has restricted all her emotion for men, and could lavish it all upon *the* man, I imagine. In any case that is 'up to you,' as our friends, the Americans, say—"

Lord Tancred thrilled as he answered:

"Yes, it shall be 'up to me.' But I want to find out all about her for myself. I just want to know when I may see her, and what is the programme?"

"The programme is that she will receive you this afternoon, about tea-time, I should say; that you must explain to her you realize you are engaged. You need not ask her to marry you; she will not care for details like that—she knows it is already settled. Be as businesslike as you can—and come away. She has made it a condition that she sees you as little as possible until the wedding. The English idea of engaged couples shocks her, for, remember, it is, on her side, not a love-match. If you wish to have the slightest success with her afterwards be careful *now*. She is going to Paris, immediately, for her trousseau. She will return about a week before the wedding, when you can present her to your family."

Tristram smiled grimly and then the two men's eyes met and they both laughed.

"Jove! Francis!" Lord Tancred exclaimed, "isn't it a wonderful affair! A real dramatic romance, here in the twentieth century. Would not every one think I was mad, if they knew!"

"It is that sort of madmen who are often the sanest," Francis Markrute answered. "The world is full of apparently sane fools." Then he passed on to a further subject. "You will re-open Wrayth, of course," he said. "I wish my niece to be a Queen of Society, and to have her whole life arranged with due state. I wish your family to understand that I appreciate the honor of the connection with them, and consider it a privilege, and a perfectly natural thing—since we are foreigners of whom you know nothing—that we should provide the necessary money for what we wish."

Lord Tancred listened; he thought of his mother's similar argument at breakfast.

"You see," the financier went on reflectively, "in life, the wise man always pays willingly for what he really wants, as you are doing, for instance, in your blind taking of my niece. Your old nobility in England is the only one of any consequence left in the world. The other countries' system of the titles descending to all the younger sons, *ad infinitum*, makes the whole thing a farce after a while. A Prince in the Caucasus is as common as a Colonel in Kentucky, and in Austria and Germany there are poor Barons in the streets. There was a time in my life when I could have had a foreign title, but I found it ridiculous, and so refused it. But in England, in spite of your amusing radicalism the real thing still counts. It is a valid asset—a tangible security for one's money—from a business point of view. And Americans or foreigners like myself and my niece, for instance, are securing substantial property and equal return, when we bring large fortunes in our marriage settlements to this country. What satisfaction comparable to the glory of her English position as Marchioness of Darrowood could Miss Clara D. Woggenheimer have got out of her millions, if she had married one of her own countrymen, or an Italian count? Yet she gives herself the airs of a benefactress to poor Darrowood and throws her money in his teeth, whereas Darrowood is the benefactor, if there is a case of it either way. But to me, a sensible business man, the bargain is equal. You don't go to an art dealer's and buy a very valuable Rembrandt for its marketable value, and then, afterwards, jibe at the picture and reproach the art dealer. Money is no good without position, and here in England you have had such hundreds of years of freedom from invasion, that you have had time, which no other country has had, to perfect your social system. Let the Radicals and the uninformed of other lands rail as they will, your English aristocracy is the finest body of thinkers and livers in the world. One hears ever of the black sheep, the few luridly glaring failures, but never of the hundreds of great and noble lives which are England's strength."

"By Jove!" said Lord Tancred, "you ought to be in the House of Lords, Francis! You'd wake them up!"

The financier looked down at his plate; he always lowered his eyes when he felt things. No one must ever read what was really passing in his soul, and when he felt, it was the more difficult to conceal, he reasoned.

"I am not a snob, my friend," he said, after a mouthful of salad. "I have no worship for aristocracy in the abstract; I am a student, a rather careful student of systems and their results, and, incidentally, a breeder of thoroughbred live stock, too, which helps one's conclusions: and above all I am an interested watcher of the progress of evolution."

"You are abominably clever," said Lord Tancred.

"Think of your uncle, the Duke of Glastonbury," the financier went on. "He fulfills his duties in every way, a munificent landlord, and a sound, level-headed politician: what other country or class could produce such as he?"

"Oh, the Duke's all right," his nephew agreed. "He is a bit hard up like a number of us at times, but he keeps the thing going splendidly, and my cousin Ethelrida helps him. She is a brick. But you know her, of course, don't you think so?"

"The Lady Ethelrida seems to me a very perfect young woman," Francis Markrute said, examining his claret through the light. "I wish I knew her better. We have few occasions of meeting; she does not go out very much into general society, as you know."

"Oh, I'll arrange that, if it would interest you. I thought you were perfectly cynical about and even rather bored with women," Lord Tancred said.

"I think I told you—was it only yesterday?—that I understood it might be possible for a woman to count—I have not time for the ordinary parrot-chatterers one meets. There are three classes of the species female: those for the body, those for the brain, and those for both. The last are dangerous. The other two merely occupy certain moods in man. Fortunately for us the double combination is rare."

Lord Tancred longed to ask under which head Francis Markrute placed his niece, but, of course, he restrained himself. He, personally, felt sure she would be of the combination; that was her charm. Yes, as he thought over things, that was the only really dangerous kind, and he had so seldom met it! Then his imagination suddenly pictured Laura Highford with her tiny mouth and pointed teeth. She had a showy little brain, absolutely no heart, and the senses of a cat or a ferret. What part of him had she appealed to? Well, thank God, that was over and done with, and he was perfectly free to make his discoveries in regard to Zara, his future wife!

"I tell you what, Francis," he said presently, after the conversation had drifted from these topics and cigars and liqueurs had come, "I would like my cousin Ethelrida to meet Countess Shulski pretty soon. I don't know why, but I believe the two would get on."

"There is no use suggesting any meetings until my niece returns from Paris," the financier said. "She will be in a different mood by then. She had not, when she came to England, quite put off her mourning; she will then have beautiful clothes, and be more acquiescent in every way. Now she would be antagonistic. See her this afternoon and be sensible; make up your mind to postpone things, until her return. And even then be careful until she is your wife!"

Lord Tancred looked disappointed. "It is a long time," he said.

"Let me arrange to give a dinner at my house, at which perhaps the Duke and Lady Ethelrida would honor me by being present, and your mother and sisters and any other member of your family you wish, let us say, on the night of my niece's return" (he drew a small calendar notebook from his pocket). "That will be Wednesday, the 18th, and we will fix the wedding for Wednesday the 25th, a week later. That gets you back from your honeymoon on the 1st of November; you can stay with me that night, and if your uncle is good enough to include me in the invitation to his shoot we can all three go down to Montfitchet on the following day. Is all this well? If so I will write it down."

"Perfectly well," agreed the prospective bridegroom—and having no notebook or calendar, he scribbled the reminder for himself on his cuff. Higgins, his superb valet, knew a good deal of his lordship's history from his lordship's cuffs!

"I don't think I shall wait for tea-time, Francis," he said, when they got out of the restaurant, into the hall. "I think I'll go now, and get it over, if she will be in. Could I telephone and ask?"

He did so and received the reply from Turner that Countess Shulski was at home, but could not receive his lordship until half-past four o'clock.

"Damn!" said that gentleman as he put the receiver down, and Francis Markrute turned away to hide his smile.

"You had better go and buy an engagement ring, hadn't you?" he said. "It won't do to forget that."

"Good Lord, I had forgotten!" gasped Tristram.

"Well, I have lots of time to do it now, so I'll go to the family jewelers, they are called old-fashioned, but the stones are so good."

So they said good-bye, the young man speeding westwards in a taxi, the lion hunter's excitement thrilling in his veins.

The financier returned to his stately office and passed through his obsequious rows of clerks to his inner sanctum. Then he lit another cigar and gave orders that he was not to be disturbed for a quarter of an hour. He reposed in a comfortable chair and allowed himself to dream. All his plans were working; there must be no rush. Great emergencies required rush, but to build to the summit of one's ambitions, one must use calm and watchful care.

CHAPTER VIII

Countess Shulski was seated in her uncle's drawing-room when Lord Tancred was announced.

It was rather a severe room, purely French, with very little furniture, each piece a priceless work of art. There were no touches of feminine influence, no comfortable sofas as in the morning-room or library, all was stiff, and dignified, and in pure style.

She had chosen to receive him there, on purpose. She wished the meeting to be short and cold. He came forward, a look of determination upon his handsome face.

Zara rose as he advanced, and bowed to him. She did not offer to shake hands, and he let his, which he had half outstretched, drop. She did not help him at all; she remained perfectly silent, as usual. She did not even look at him, but straight out of the window into the pouring rain, and it was then he saw that her eyes were not black but slate.

"You understand why I have come, of course?" he said by way of a beginning.

"Yes," she replied and said nothing more.

"I want to marry you, you know," he went on.

"Really!" she said.

"Yes, I do." And he set his teeth—certainly she was difficult!

"That is fortunate for you, since you are going to do so."

This was not encouraging; it was also unexpected.

"Yes, I am," he answered, "on the 25th of October, with your permission."

"I have already consented." And she clasped her hands.

"May I sit down beside you and talk?" he asked.

She pointed to a Louis XVI. *bergère* which stood opposite, and herself took a small armchair at the other side of the fire.

So they sat down, she gazing into the blazing coals and he gazing at her. She was facing the gloomy afternoon light, though she did not think out these things like her uncle, so he had a clear and wonderful picture of her. "How could so voluptuous looking a creature be so icily cold?" he wondered. Her wonderful hair seemed burnished like dark copper, in the double light of fire and day, and that gardenia skin looked fit to eat. He was thrilled with a mad desire to kiss her; he had never felt so strong an emotion towards a woman in his life.

"Your uncle tells me you are going away to-morrow, and that you will be away until a week before our wedding. I wish you were not going to be, but I suppose you must—for clothes and things."

"Yes, I must."

He got up; he could not sit still, he was too wildly excited; he stood leaning on the mantelpiece, quite close to her, for a moment, his eyes devouring her with the passionate admiration he felt. She glanced up, and when she saw their expression her jet brows met, while a look of infinite disgust crept over her face.

So it had come—so soon! He was just like all men—a hateful, sensual beast. She knew he desired to kiss her—to kiss a person he did not know! Her experience of life had not encouraged her to make the least allowance for the instinct of man. For her, that whole side of human beings was simply revolting. In the far back recesses of her mind she knew and felt that caresses and such things might be good if one loved—passionately loved—but in the abstract, just because of the attraction of sex, they were hideous. No man had ever had the conceded tip of her little finger, although she had been forced to submit to unspeakable exhibitions of passion from Ladislaus, her husband.

For her, Tristram appeared a satyr, but she was no timid nymph, but a fierce panther ready to defend herself!

He saw her look and drew back—cooled.

The thing was going to be much more difficult than he had even thought; he must keep himself under complete control, he knew now. So he turned away to the window and glanced out on the wet park.

"My mother called upon you to-day, I believe," he said. "I asked her not to expect you to be at home. It was only to show you that my family will welcome you with affection."

"It is very good of them."

"The announcement of the engagement will be in the *Morning Post* to-morrow. Do you mind?"

"Why should I mind?" (her voice evinced surprise). "Since it is true, the formalities must take place."

"It seems as if it could not be true. You are so frightfully frigid," he said with faint resentment.

"I cannot help how I am," she said in a tone of extreme hauteur. "I have consented to marry you. I will go through with all the necessary ceremonies, the presentations to your family, and such affairs; but I have nothing to say to you: why should we talk when once these things are settled? You must accept me as I am, or leave me alone—that is all"—and then her temper made her add, in spite of her uncle's warning, "for I do not care!"

He turned now; he was a little angry and nearly flared up, but the sight of her standing there, magnificently attractive, stopped him. This was merely one of the phases of the game; he should not allow himself to be worsted by such speeches.

"I expect you don't, but I do," he said. "I am quite willing to take you as you are, or will be."

"Then that is all that need be said," she answered coldly. "Arrange with my uncle when you wish me to see your family on my return; I will carry out what he settles. And now I need not detain you, and will say good-bye." And bowing to him she walked towards the door.

"I am sorry you feel you want to go so soon," he said, as he sprang forward to open it for her, "but good-bye." And he let her pass without shaking hands.

When he was alone in the room he realized that he had not given her the engagement ring, which still reposed in his pocket!

He looked round for a writing table, and finding one, sat down and wrote her a few words.

"I meant to give you this ring. If you don't like sapphires it can be changed. Please wear it,

and believe me to be

"Yours,

"Tancred."

He put the note with the little ring-case, inclosed both in a large envelope, and then he rang the bell.

"Send this up to the Countess Shulski," he said to the footman who presently came. "And is my motor at the door?"

It was, so he descended the stairs.

"To Glastonbury House," he ordered his chauffeur. Then he leaned back against the cushions, no look of satisfaction upon his face.

Ethelrida might be having tea, and she was always so soothing and sympathetic.

Yes, her ladyship was at home, and he was shown up into his cousin's own sitting-room.

Lady Ethelrida Montfitchet had kept house for her father, the Duke of Glastonbury, ever since she was sixteen when her mother had died, and she acted as hostess at the ducal parties, with the greatest success. She was about twenty-five now, and one of the sweetest of young women.

She was very tall, rather plain, and very distinguished.

Francis Markrute thought her beautiful. He was fond of analyzing types and breeds, and he said there were those who looked as if they had been poured into more or less fine or clumsy mould, and there were others who were sharply carved as with a knife. He loved a woman's face to look *ciselée*, he said. That is why he did not entirely admire his niece, for although the mould was of the finest in her case, her small nose was not chiseled. Numbers of English and some Austrians were chiseled, he affirmed—showing their race—but very few of other nations.

Now some people would have said the Lady Ethelrida was too chiseled—she might grow peaky, with old age. But no one could deny the extreme refinement of the young woman.

She was strikingly fair, with silvery light hair that had no yellow in it; and kind, wise, gray eyes. Her figure in its slenderness was a thing which dressmakers adored; there was so little of it that any frock could be made to look well on it.

Lady Ethelrida did everything with moderation. She was not mad about any sport or any fad. She loved her father, her aunt, her cousins of the Tancred family, and her friend, Lady Anningford. She was, in short, a fine character and a great lady.

"I have come to tell you such a piece of news, Ethelrida," Tristram said as he sat down beside her on the chintz-covered sofa. Ethelrida's tastes in furniture and decorations were of the simplest in her own room. "Guess what it is!"

"How can I, Tristram? Mary is really going to marry Lord Henry?"

"Not that I know of as yet, but I daresay she will, some day. No, guess again; it is about a marriage."

She poured him out some tea and indicated the bread and butter. Tristram, she knew, loved her stillroom maid's brown bread and butter.

"A man, or a woman?" she asked, meditatively.

"A man—ME!" he said, with reckless grammar.

"You, Tristram!" Ethelrida exclaimed, with as much excitement as she ever permitted herself. "You going to be married! But to whom?"

The thing seemed too preposterous; and her mind had instantly flown to the name, Laura Highford, before her reason said, "How ridiculous—she is married already!"—so she repeated again: "But to whom?"

"I am going to be married to a widow, a niece of Francis Markrute's; you know him." Lady Ethelrida nodded. "She is the most wonderfully attractive creature you ever saw, Ethelrida, a type not like any one else. You'll understand in a minute, when you see her. She has stormy black eyes—no, they are not really black; they are slate color—and red hair, and a white face, and, by Jove! a figure! And do you know, my dear child, I believe I am awfully in love with her!"

"You only 'believe,' Tristram! That sounds odd to be going to be married upon!" Lady Ethelrida could not help smiling.

He sipped his tea and then jumped up. He was singularly restless to-day.

"She is the kind of woman a man would go perfectly mad about when he knew her well. I shall, I know." Then, as he saw his cousin's humorous expression, he laughed boyishly. "It does sound odd, I admit," he said, "the inference is that I don't know her well—and that is just it, Ethelrida, but only to you would I say it. Look here, my dear girl, I have got to be comforted this afternoon. She has just flattened me out. We are going to be married on the 25th of October, and I want you to be awfully nice to her. I am sure she has had a rottenly unhappy life."

"Of course I will, Tristram dear," said Lady Ethelrida, "but remember, I am completely in the dark. When did you meet her? Can't you tell me something more? Then I will be as sympathetic as you please."

So Lord Tancred sat down on the sofa beside her again, and told her the bare facts: that it was rather sudden, but he was convinced it was what he wanted most to do in life; that she was young and beautiful, rich, and very reserved, and rather cold; that she was going away, until a week before the wedding; that he knew it sounded all mad, but his dear Ethelrida was to be a darling, and to understand and not reason with him!

And she did not. She had gathered enough from this rather incoherent recital to make her see that some very deep and unusual current must have touched her cousin's life. She knew the Tancred character, so she said all sorts of nice things to him, asked interested but not indiscreet questions. And soon that irritated and baffled sense left him, and he became calm.

"I want Uncle Glastonbury to ask Francis Markrute to the shoot on the 2nd of November, Ethelrida," he said, "and you will let me bring Zara—she will be my wife by then—although I was asked only as a bachelor?"

"It is my party, not Papa's, you dear old goose, you know that," Lady Ethelrida said. "Of course you shall bring your Zara and I myself will write and ask Mr. Markrute. In spite of Aunt Jane's saying that he is a cynical foreigner I like him!"

CHAPTER IX

Society was absolutely flabbergasted when it read in the *Morning Post* the announcement of Lord Tancred's engagement! No one had heard a word about it. There had been talk of his going to Canada, and much chaff upon that subject—so ridiculous, Tancred emigrating! But of a prospective bride the most gossip-loving busybody at White's had never heard! It fell like a bombshell. And Lady Highford, as she read the news, clenched her pointed teeth, and gave a little squeal like a stoat.

So he had drifted beyond her, after all! He had often warned her he would, at the finish of one of those scenes she was so fond of creating. It was true then, when he had told her before Cowes that everything must be over. She had thought his silence since had only been sulking! But who was the creature? "Countess Shulski." Was it a Polish or Hungarian name? "Daughter of the late Maurice Grey." Which Grey was that? "Niece of Francis Markrute, Esquire, of Park Lane." Here was the reason—money! How disgusting men were! They would sell their souls for money. But the woman should suffer for this, and Tristram, too, if she could manage it!

Then she wept some tears of rage. He was so adorably good looking and had been such a feather in her cap, although she had never been really sure of him. It was a mercy her conduct had always been of such an immaculate character—in public—no one could say a word. And now she must act the dear, generous, congratulating friend.

So she had a dose of sal volatile and dressed, with extra care, to lunch at Glastonbury House. There she might hear all the details; only Ethelrida was so superior, and uninterested in news or gossip.

There was a party of only five assembled, when she arrived—she was always a little late. The Duke and Lady Ethelrida, Constance Radcliffe, and two men: an elderly politician, and another cousin of the family. She could certainly chatter about Tristram, and hear all she could.

They were no sooner seated than she began:

"Is not this wonderful news about your nephew, Duke? No one expected it of him just now, though I as one of his best friends have been urging him to marry, for the last two years. Dear Lady Tancred must be so enchanted."

"I am sure you gave him good counsel," said the Duke, screwing his eyeglass which he wore on a long black ribbon into his whimsical old blue eye. "But Tristram's a tender mouth, and a bit of a bolter—got to ride him on the snaffle, not the curb."

Lady Highford looked down at her plate, while she gave an answer quite at variance with her own methods.

"Snaffle or curb, no one would ever try to guide Lord Tancred! And what is the charming lady like? You all know her, of course?"

"Why, no," said His Grace. "The uncle, Mr. Markrute, dined here the other night. He's been very useful to the Party, in a quiet way and seems a capital fellow—but Ethelrida and I have never met the niece. Of course, no one has been in town since the season, and she was not here then. We only came up, like you, for Flora's wedding, and go down to-morrow."

"This is thrilling!" said Lady Highford. "An unknown bride! Have you not even heard what she is like—young or old? A widow always sounds so attractive!"

"I am told that she is perfectly beautiful," said Lady Ethelrida from the other side of the table—there had been a pause—"and Tristram seems so happy. She is quite young, and very rich."

She had always been amiably friendly and indifferent to Laura Highford. It was Ethelrida's way to have no likes and dislikes for the general circle of her friends; her warm attachment was given to so very few, and the rest were just all of a band. Perhaps if she felt anything definite it was a tinge on the side of dislike for Laura. Thinking to please Tristram at the time she had asked her to this, her birthday party, when they had met at Cowes in August, and now she was faced with the problem how to put her off, since Tristram and his bride would be coming. She saw the glint in the light hazel eyes as she described the fiancé and her kind heart at once made her determine to turn the conversation. After all, it was perfectly natural for poor Laura to have been in love with Tristram—no one could be more attractive—and, of course, it must hurt her—this marriage. She would reserve the "putting off," until they left the dining-room and she could speak to her alone. So with her perfect tact and easy grace she diverted the current of conversation to the political situation, and luncheon went on.

But this was not what Lady Highford had come for. She wanted to hear everything she could about her rival, in order to lay her plans; and the moment Ethelrida was engaged with the politician and the Duke had turned to Mrs. Radcliffe, she tackled the cousin, in a lower voice.

He, Jimmy Danvers, had only read what she had, that morning. He had seen Tristram at the Turf on Tuesday after lunch—the day before yesterday—and he had only talked of Canada—and not a word of a lady then. It was a bolt from the blue. "And when I telephoned to the old boy this morning," he said, "and asked him to take me to call upon his damsel to-day, he told me she had gone to Paris and would not be back until a week before the wedding!"

"How very mysterious!" piped Laura. "Tristram is off to Paris, too, then, I suppose?"

"He did not say; he seemed in the deuce of a hurry and put the receiver down."

"He is probably only doing it for money, poor darling boy!" she said sympathetically. "It was quite necessary for him."

"Oh, that's not Tristram's measure," Sir James Danvers interrupted. "He'd never do anything for money. I thought you knew him awfully well," he added, surprised. Apprehension of situations was not one of his strong qualities.

"Of course I do!" Laura snapped out and then laughed. "But you men! Money would tempt any of you!"

"You may bet your last farthing, Lady Highford, Tristram is in love—crazy, if you ask me—he'd not have been so silent about it all otherwise. The Canada affair was probably because she was playing the poor old chap,—and now she's given in; and that, of course, is chucked."

Money, as the motive, Lady Highford could have borne, but, to hear about love drove her wild! Her little pink and white face with its carefully arranged childish setting suddenly looked old and strained, while her eyes grew yellow in the light.

"They won't be happy long, then!" she said. "Tristram could not be faithful to any one."

"I don't think he's ever been in love before, so we can't judge," the blundering cousin continued, now with malice prepense. "He's had lots of little affairs, but they have only been 'come and go.'"

Lady Highford crumbled her bread and then turned to the Duke—there was nothing further to be got out of this quarter. Finally luncheon came to an end, and the three ladies went up to Ethelrida's sitting-room. Mrs. Radcliffe presently took her leave to catch a train, so the two were left alone.

"I am so looking forward to your party, dear Ethelrida," Lady Highford cooed. "I am going back to Hampshire to-morrow, but at the end of the month I come up again and will be with you in Norfolk on the 2nd."

"I was just wondering," said Lady Ethelrida, "if, after all, you would not be bored, Laura? Your particular friends, the Sedgeworths, have had to throw us over—his father being dead. It will be rather a family sort of collection, and not so amusing this year, I am afraid. Em and Mary, Tristram and his new bride,—and Mr. Markrute, the uncle—and the rest as I told you."

"Why, my dear child, it sounds delightful! I shall long to meet the new Lady Tancred! Tristram and I are such dear friends, poor darling boy! I must write and tell him how delighted I am with the news. Do you know where he is at the moment?"

"He is in London, I believe. Then you really will stick to us and not be bored? How sweet of you!" Lady Ethelrida said without a change in her level voice while her thoughts ran: "It is very plucky of Laura; or, she has some plan! In any case I can't prevent her coming now, and perhaps it is best to get it over. But I had better warn Tristram, surprises are so unpleasant."

Then, after a good deal of gush about "dear Lady Tancred's" prospective happiness in having a daughter-in-law, and "dear Tristram," Lady Highford's motor was announced, and she went.

And when she had gone Lady Ethelrida sat down and wrote her cousin a note. Just to tell him in case she did not see him before she went back to the country to-morrow that her list, which she enclosed, was made up for her November party, but if he would like any one else for his bride to meet, he was to say so. She added that some friends had been to luncheon, and among them Laura Highford, who had said the nicest things and wished him every happiness.

Lady Ethelrida was not deceived about these wishes, but she could do no more.

The Duke came into her room, just as she was finishing, and warmed himself by her wood fire.

"The woman is a cat, Ethelrida," he said without any preamble. These two understood each other so well, they often seemed to begin in the middle of a sentence, of which no outsider could grasp the meaning.

"I am afraid she is, Papa. I have just been writing to Tristram, to let him know she still insists upon coming to the shoot. She can't do anything there, and they may as well get it over. She will have to be civil to the new Lady Tancred in our house."

"Whew!" whistled the Duke, "you may have an exciting party. You had better go and leave our cards to-day on the Countess Shulski, and another of mine, as well, for the uncle. We'll have to swallow the whole lot, I suppose."

"I rather like Mr. Markrute, Papa," Ethelrida said. "I talked to him the other night for the first time; he is extremely intelligent. We ought not to be so prejudiced, perhaps, just because he is a foreigner, and in the City. I've asked him on the 2nd, too—you don't mind? I will leave the note to-day; Tristram particularly wished it."

"Then we'll have to make the best of it, pet. I daresay you are right, and one ought not to be prejudiced about anything, in these days."

And then he patted his daughter's smoothly brushed head, and went out again.

Lady Ethelrida drove in the ducal carriage (the Duke insisted upon a carriage, in London), to Park Lane, and was handing her cards to her footman to leave, when Francis Markrute himself came out of the door.

His whole face changed; it seemed to grow younger. He was a fairly tall man, and distinguished looking. He came forward and said: "How do you do," through the brougham window.

Alas! his niece had left that morning *en route* for Paris—*trousseaux* and feminine business, but he was so delighted to have had this chance of a few words with her—Lady Ethelrida.

"I was leaving a note to ask you to come and shoot with my father at Montfitchet, Mr. Markrute," she said, "on the 2nd of November. Tristram says he hopes they will be back from the honeymoon in time to join us, too."

"I shall be delighted, and my niece will be delighted at your kindness in calling so soon."

Then they said a few more polite things and the financier finished by:—"I am taking the great liberty of having the book, which I told you about, rebound—it was in such a tattered condition, I was ashamed to send it to you—do not think I had forgotten. I hope you will accept it?"

"I thought you only meant to lend it to me because it is out of print and I cannot buy it. I am so sorry you have had this trouble," Lady Ethelrida said, a little stiffly. "Bring it to the shoot. It will interest me to see it but you must not give it to me." And then she smiled graciously; and he allowed her to say good-bye, and drive on. And as he turned into Grosvenor Street he mused,

"I like her exquisite pride; but she shall take the book—and many other things—presently."

Meanwhile Zara Shulski had arrived at Bournemouth. She had started early in the morning, and she was making a careful investigation of the house. The doctor appeared all that was kind and clever, and his wife gentle and sweet. Mirko could not have a nicer home, it seemed. Their little girl was away at her grandmother's for the next six weeks, they said, but would be enchanted to have a little boy companion. Everything was arranged satisfactorily. Zara stayed the night, and next day, having wired to Mimo to meet her at the station, she returned to London.

They talked in the Waterloo waiting-room; poor Mimo seemed so glad and happy. He saw her and her small bag into a taxi. She was going back to her uncle's, and was to take Mirko down next day, and, on the following one, start for Paris.

"But I can't go back to Park Lane without seeing Mirko, now," she said. "I did not tell my uncle what train I was returning by. There is plenty of time so I will go and have tea with you at Neville Street. It will be like old times, we will get some cakes and other things on the way, and boil the kettle on the fire."

So Mimo gladly got in with her and they started. He had a new suit of clothes and a new felt hat, and looked a wonderfully handsome foreign gentleman; his manner to women was always courteous and gallant. Zara smiled and looked almost happy, as they arranged the details of their surprise tea party for Mirko.

At that moment there passed them in Whitehall a motorcar going very fast, the occupant of which, a handsome young man, caught the most fleeting glimpse of them—hardly enough to be certain he recognized Zara. But it gave him a great start and a thrill.

"It cannot be she," he said to himself, "she went to Paris yesterday; but if it is—who is the man?"

He altered his plans, went back to his rooms, and sat moodily down in his favorite chair—an unpleasant, gnawing uncertainty in his heart.

CHAPTER X

Mirko, crouched up by the smoldering fire, was playing the *Chanson Triste* on his violin when the two reached the studio. He had a wonderful talent—of that there was no doubt—but his health had always been too delicate to stand any continuous study. Nor had the means of the family ever been in a sufficiently prosperous condition, in later years, to procure a really good master. But the touch and soul of the strange little fellow sounded in every wailing note. He always played the *Chanson Triste* when he was sad and lonely. He had been nearly seven when his mother died, and he remembered her vividly. She had so loved Tschaikovsky's music, and this piece especially. He had played it to her—from ear then—the afternoon she lay dying, and for him, as for them all, it was indissolubly connected with her memory. The tears were slowly trickling down Mirko's cheeks. He was going to be taken away from his father, his much loved Chérisette would not be near him, and he feared and hated strangers.

He felt he was talking to his mother with his bow. His mother who was in heaven, with all the saints and angels. What could it be like up there? It was perhaps a forest, such as Fontainebleau, only there were sure to be numbers of birds which sang like the nightingales in the Borghese Gardens—there would be no canaries! The sun always shone and *Maman* would wear a beautiful dress of blue gauze with wings, and her lovely hair, which was fair, not red like Chérisette's, would be all hanging down. It surely was a very desirable place, and quite different from the Neville Street lodging. Why could he not get there, out of the cold and darkness? Chérisette had always taught him that God was so good and kind to little boys who had crippled backs. He would ask God with all the force of his music, to take him there to *Maman*.

The sound of the familiar air struck a chill note upon Mimo and Zara, as they came up the stairs; it made them hasten their steps—they knew very well what mood it meant with the child.

He was so far away, in his passionate dream-prayer, that he did not hear them coming until they opened the door; and then he looked up, his beautiful dark eyes all wet with tears which suddenly turned to joy when he saw his sister.

"*Chérisette adorée*!" he cried, and was soon in her arms, soothed and comforted and caressed. Oh, if he could always be with her, he really, after all, would wish for no other heaven!

"We are going to have such a picnic!" Zara told him. "Papa and I have brought a new tablecloth, and some pretty cups and saucers, and spoons, and knives, and forks—and see! such buns! English buns for you to toast, Mirko mio! You must be the little cook, while I lay the table."

And the child clapped his hands with glee and helped to take the papers off; he stroked the pretty roses on the china with his delicate, little forefinger—he had Mimo's caressing ways with everything he admired and loved. He had never broken his toys, as other children do; accidental catastrophes to them had always caused him pain and weeping. And these bright, new flowery cups should be his special care, to wash, and dry, and guard.

He grew merry as a cricket, and his laughter pealed over the paper cap Mimo made for him and the towel his sister had for an apron. They were to be the servants, and Mimo a lordly guest.

And soon the table was laid, and the buns toasted and buttered; Zara had even bought a vase of the same china, in which she placed a bunch of autumn red roses, to match those painted on it and this was a particular joy.

"The Apache," which had not yet found a purchaser, stood on one easel, and from it the traveling rug hung to the other, concealing all unsightly things, and yesterday Mimo had bought from the Tottenham Court Road a cheap basket armchair with bright cretonne cushions. And really, with the flowers and the blazing fire when they sat down to tea it all looked very cozy and home-like.

What would her uncle or Lord Tancred have thought, could they have seen those tempestuous eyes of Zara's glistening and tender—and soft as a dove's!

After tea she sat in the basket chair, and took Mirko in her arms, and told him all about the delightful, new home he was going to, the kind lady, and the beautiful view of the sea he would get from his bedroom windows; how pretty and fresh it all looked, how there were pine woods to walk in, and how she would—presently—come down to see him. And as she said this her thoughts flew to her own fate—what would her "presently" be? And she gave a little, unconscious shiver almost of fear.

"What hast thou, Chérisette?" said Mirko. "Where were thy thoughts then?—not here?"

"No, not here, little one. Thy Chérisette is going also to a new home; some day thou must visit her there."

But when he questioned and implored her to tell him about it she answered vaguely, and tried to divert his thoughts, until he said:

"It is not to *Maman* in heaven, is it, dear Chérisette? Because there, there would be enough place for us both—and surely thou couldst take me too?"

When she got back to Park Lane, and entered her uncle's library he was sitting at the writing table, the telephone in his hand. He welcomed her with his eyes and went on speaking, while she took a chair.

"Yes, do come and dine.—May you see her if by chance she did not go to Paris?" He looked up at Zara, who frowned. "No—she is very tired and has gone to her room for the evening.—She has been in the country to-day, seeing some friends.—No—not to-morrow—she goes to the country again, and to Paris the following night—To the station? I will ask her, but perhaps she is like me, and dislikes being seen off," then a laugh,—and then, "All right—well, come and dine at eight—good-bye." The financier put the receiver down and looked at his niece, a whimsical smile in his eyes.

"Well," he said, "your fiancé is very anxious to see you, it seems. What do you say?"

"Certainly not!" she flashed. "I thought it was understood; he shall not come to the train. I will go by another if he insists."

"He won't insist; tell me of your day?"

She calmed herself—her face had grown stormy.

"I am quite satisfied with the home you have chosen for Mirko and will take him there to-morrow. All the clothes have come that you said I might order for him, and I hope and think he will be comfortable and happy. He has a very beautiful, tender nature, and a great talent. If he could only grow strong, and more balanced! Perhaps he will, in this calm, English air."

Francis Markrute's face changed, as it always did with the mention and discussion of Mirko—whose presence in the world was an ever-rankling proof of his loved sister's disgrace. All his sense of justice—and he was in general a just man—could never reconcile him to the idea of ever seeing or recognizing the child. "The sins of the fathers"—was his creed and he never forgot the dying Emperor's words. He had lost sight of his niece for nearly two years after his sister's death. She had wished for no communication with him, believing then that he had left her mother to die without forgiveness, and it was not until he happened to read in a foreign paper the casual mention of Count Shulski's murder, and so guessed at Zara's whereabouts, that a correspondence had been opened again, and he was able to explain that he had been absent in Africa and had not received any letters.

He then offered her his protection and a home, if she would sever all connection with the two, Mimo and Mirko, and she had indignantly refused. And it was only when they were in dire poverty, and he had again written asking his niece to come and stay with him for a few weeks, this time with no conditions attached, that she had consented, thinking that perhaps she would be able in some way to benefit them.

But now that she looked at him she felt keenly how he had trapped her, all the same.

"We will not discuss your brother's nature," he said, coldly. "I will keep my side of the bargain scrupulously, for all material things; that is all you can expect of me. Now let us talk of yourself. I have ventured to send some sables for your inspection up to your sitting room; it will be cold traveling. I hope you will select what you wish. And remember, I desire you to order the most complete trousseau in Paris, everything that a great lady could possibly want for visits and entertainments; and you must secure a good maid there, and return with all the *apanages* of your position."

She bowed, as at the reception of an order. She did not thank him.

"I will not give you any advice what to get," he went on. "Your own admirable taste will direct you. I understand that in the days of your late husband you were a beautifully dressed woman, so you will know all the best places to go to. But please to remember, while I give you unlimited resources for you to do what I wish, I trust to your honor that you will bestow none of them upon the—man Sykypri. The bargain is about the child; the father is barred from it in every way."

Zara did not answer, she had guessed this, but Mirko's welfare was of first importance. With strict economy Mimo could live upon what he possessed, if alone and if he chose to curtail his irresponsible generosities.

"Do I understand I have your word of honor about this?" her uncle demanded.

Her empress' air showed plainly now. She arose from the chair and stood haughtily drawn up:

"You know me and whether my spoken word 'is required or no," she said, "but if it will be any satisfaction to you to have it I give it!"

"Good—Then things are settled, and, I hope, to the happiness of all parties."

"Happiness!" she answered bitterly. "Who is ever happy?" Then she turned to go, but he arrested her.

"In two or three years' time you will admit to me that you know of four human beings who are ideally happy." And with this enigmatic announcement ringing in her ears, she went on up the stairs to her sitting-room.

Who were the *four* people? Herself and himself and Mimo and Mirko? Was it possible that after all his hardness towards them he meant to be eventually kind? Or was the fourth person not Mimo, but her future husband? Then she smiled grimly. It was not very likely *he* would be happy—a beast, like the rest of men, who, marrying her only for her uncle's money, having been ready to marry her for that when he had never even seen her—was yet full enough of the revolting quality of his sex to be desirous now to kiss her and clasp her in his arms!

As far as she was concerned he would have no happiness!

And she herself—what would the new life mean? It appeared a blank—an abyss. A dark curtain seemed to overhang and cover it. All she could feel was that Mirko was being cared for, that she was keeping her word to her adored mother. She would fulfill to the letter her uncle's wishes as to her suitable equipments, but beyond that she refused to think.

All the evening, when she had finished her short, solitary dinner, she played the piano in her sitting-room, her white fingers passing from one divine air to another, until at last she unconsciously drifted to the *Chanson Triste*, and Mirko's words came back to her:

"There, there would be enough place for us both"—Who knows—that might be the end of it!

And the two men heard the distant wail of the last notes as they came out of the dining-room, and, while it made the financier uncomfortable, it caused Tristram a sharp stab of pain.

CHAPTER XI

The next three weeks passed for Lord Tancred in continuously growing excitement. He had much business to see to for the reopening of Wrayth which had been closed for the past two years. He had decided to let Zara choose her own rooms, and decorate them as she pleased, when she should get there. But the big state apartments, with their tapestry and pictures, would remain untouched.

It gave him infinite pleasure—the thought of living at his old house once again—and it touched him to see the joy of the village and all the old keepers and gardeners who had been pensioned off! He found himself wondering all sorts of things—if he would have a son some day soon, to inherit it all. Each wood and broad meadow seemed to take on new interest and significance from this thought.

His home was so very dear to him though he had drilled himself into a seeming indifference. The great, round tower of the original Norman keep was still there, connected with the walls of the later house, a large, wandering edifice built at all periods from that epoch upwards, and culminating in a shocking early-Victorian Gothic wing and porch.

"I think we shall pull that wretched bit down some time," he said to himself. "Zara must have good taste—she could not look so well in her clothes, if she had not."

His thoughts were continually for her, and what she would be likely to wish; and, in the evening, when he sat alone in his own sanctum after a hard day with electricians and work-people, he would gaze into the blazing logs and dream.

The new electric light was not installed yet, and only the big, old lamps lit the shadowy oak panelling. There in a niche beside the fireplace was the suit of armor which another Tristram Guiscard had worn at Agincourt. What little chaps they had been in those days in comparison with himself and his six feet two inches! But they had been great lords, his ancestors, and he, too, would be worthy of the race. There were no wars just now to go to and fight for his country—but he would fight for his order, with his uncle, the Duke, that splendid, old specimen of the hereditary legislator. Francis Markrute who was a good judge had said that he had made some decent speeches in the House of Lords already, and he would go on and do his best, and Zara would help him. He wondered if she liked reading and poetry. He was such a magnificently healthy sportsman he had always been a little shy of letting people know his inner and gentler tastes. He hoped so much she would care for the books he did. There was a deep strain of romance in his nature, undreamed of by such women as Laura Highford, and these evenings—alone, musing and growing in love with a phantom—drew it forth.

His plan was to go to Paris—to the Ritz—for the honeymoon. Zara who did not know England would probably hate the solemn servants staring at her in those early days if he took her to Orton, one of the Duke's places which he had offered him for the blissful week. Paris was much better—they could go to the theater there—because he knew it would not all be plain sailing by any means! And every time he thought of that aspect, his keen, blue eyes sparkled with the instinct of the chase and he looked the image of the Baron Tancred who, carved in stone, with his Crusader's crossed feet, reposed in state in the church of Wrayth.

A lissom, wiry, splendid English aristocrat, in perfect condition and health, was Tristram Guiscard, twenty-fourth Baron Tancred, as he lounged in his chair before the fire and dreamed of his lady and his fate.

And when they were used to one another—at the end of the week—there would be the party at Montfitchet where he would have the joy and pride of showing his beautiful wife—and Laura would be there;—he suddenly thought of her. Poor old Laura! she had been awfully nice about it and had written him the sweetest letter. He would not have believed her capable of it—and he felt so kindly disposed towards her—little as she deserved it if he had only known!

Then when these gayeties were over, he and Zara would come here to Wrayth! And he could not help picturing how he would make love to her in this romantic setting; and perhaps soon she, too, would love him. When he got thus far in his picturings he would shut his eyes, stretch out his long limbs, and call to Jake, his solemn bulldog, and pat his wrinkled head.

And Zara, in Paris, was more tranquil in mind than was her wont. Mirko had not made much difficulty about going to Bournemouth. Everything was so pretty, the day she took him there, the sun shining gayly and the sea almost as blue as the Mediterranean, and Mrs. Morley, the doctor's wife, had been so gentle and sweet, and had drawn him to her heart at once, and petted him, and talked of his violin. The doctor had examined his lungs and said they certainly might improve with plenty of the fine air if he were very carefully fed and tended, and not allowed to catch cold.

The parting with poor Mimo had been very moving. They had said good-bye to him in the Neville Street lodging, as Zara thought it was wiser not to risk a scene at the station. The father and son had kissed and clasped one another and both wept, and Mimo had promised to come to see him soon, soon!

Then there had been another painful wrench when she herself left Bournemouth. She had put off her departure until the afternoon of the following day. Mirko had tried to be as brave as he could; but the memory of the pathetic little figure, as she saw it waving a hand to her from the window, made those rare tears brim up and splash on her glove, as she sat in the train.

In her short life with its many moments of deep anguish she had seldom been able to cry; there were always others to be thought of first, and an iron self-control was one of her inheritances from her grandfather, the Emperor, just as that voluptuous, undulating grace, and the red, lustrous hair, came from the beautiful opera dancer and great artiste, her grandmother.

She had cautioned Mrs. Morley, if she should often hear Mirko playing the *Chanson Triste*, to let her know, and she would come to him. It was a sure indication of his state of mind. And Mrs. Morley, who had read in the *Morning Post* the announcement of her approaching marriage, asked her where she could be found, and Zara had stiffened suddenly and said—at her uncle's house in Park Lane, the letters to be marked "To be forwarded immediately."

And when she had gone, Mrs. Morley had told her sister who had come in to tea how beautiful Countess Shulski was and how very regal looking, "but she had on such plain, almost shabby, black clothes, Minnie dear, and a small black toque, and then the most splendid sable wrap—those very grand people do have funny tastes, don't they? I should have liked a pretty autumn costume of green velveteen, and a hat with a wing or a bird."

The financier had insisted upon his niece wearing the sable wrap—and somehow, in spite of all things, the beautiful, dark, soft fur had given her pleasure.

And now, three weeks later, she was just returning from Paris, her beauty enriched by all that money and taste could procure. It was the eighteenth of October, exactly a week before her wedding.

She had written to Mimo from Paris, and told him she was going to be married; that she was doing so because she thought it was best for them all; and he had written back enchanted exclamations of surprise and joy, and had told her she should have his new picture, the London fog—so dramatic with its two meeting figures—for his wedding gift. Poor Mimo, so generous, always, with all he had!

Mirko was not to be told until she was actually married.

She had written to her uncle and asked him as a great favor that she might only arrive the very day of the family dinner party, he could plead for her excess of trousseau business, or what he liked. She would come by the nine o'clock morning train, so as to be in ample time for dinner; and it would be so much easier for every one, if they could get the meeting over, the whole family together, rather than have the ordeal of private presentations.

And Francis Markrute had agreed, while Lord Tancred had chafed.

"I *shall* meet her at the station, whatever you say, Francis!" he had exclaimed. "I am longing to see her."

And as the train drew up at Victoria, Zara caught sight of him there on the platform, and in spite of her dislike and resentment she could not help seeing that her fiancé was a wonderfully good-looking man.

She herself appeared to him as the loveliest thing he had ever seen in his life, with her perfect Paris clothes, and air of distinction. If he had thought her attractive before he felt ecstatic in his admiration now.

Francis Markrute hurried up the platform and Tristram frowned, but the financier knew it might not be safe to leave them to a tête-à-tête drive to the house! Zara's temper might not brook it, and he had rushed back from the city, though he hated rushing, in order to be on the spot to make a third.

"Welcome, my niece!" he said, before Lord Tancred could speak. "You see, we have both come to greet you."

She thanked them politely, and turned to give an order to her new French maid—and some of the expectant, boyish joy died out of Tristram's face, as he walked beside her to the waiting motor.

They said the usual things about the crossing—it had been smooth and pleasant—so fortunate for that time of the year—and she had stayed on deck and enjoyed it. Yes, Paris had been charming; it was always a delightful spot to find oneself in.

Then Tristram said he was glad she thought that, because, if she would consent, he would arrange to go there for the honeymoon directly after the wedding. She inclined her head in acquiescence but did not speak. The matter appeared one of complete indifference to her.

In spite of his knowledge that this would be her attitude and he need not expect anything different Tristram's heart began to sink down into his boots, by the time they reached the house, and Francis Markrute whispered to his niece as they came up the steps:

"I beg of you to be a little more gracious—the man has some spirit, you know!"

So when they got into the library, and she began to pour out the tea for them, she made conversation. But Tristram's teeth were set, and a steely light began to grow in his blue eyes.

She looked so astonishingly alluring there in her well-fitting, blue serge, traveling dress, yet he might not even kiss her white, slender hand! And there was a whole week before the wedding! And after it?—would she keep up this icy barrier between them? If so—but he refused to think of it!

He noticed that she wore his engagement ring only, on her left hand, and that the right one was ringless, nor had she a brooch or any other jewel. He felt glad—he would be able to give her everything. His mother had been so splendid about the family jewels, insisting upon handing them over, and even in the short time one or two pieces had been reset, the better to please the presumably modern taste of the new bride of the Tancreds. These, and the wonderful pearls, her uncle's gift, were waiting for her, up in her sitting-room.

"I think I will go and rest now until dinner," she said, and forced a smile as she moved towards the door.

It was the first time Tristram had ever seen her smile, and it thrilled him. He had the most frantic longing to take her in his arms and kiss her, and tell her he was madly in love with her, and wanted her never to be out of his sight.

But he let her pass out, and, turning round, he found Francis Markrute pouring out some liqueur brandy from a wonderful, old, gold-chased bottle, which stood on a side-table with its glasses. He filled two, and handed one to Tristram, while he quoted Doctor Johnson with an understanding smile:

"'Claret for boys, port for men, but brandy for heroes!' By Jove! my dear boy," he said, "you are a hero!"

CHAPTER XII

Lady Tancred unfortunately had one of her very bad headaches, and an hour before dinner, in fact before her son had left the Park Lane house, a telephone message came to say she was dreadfully sorry, it would be impossible for her to come. It was Emily who spoke to Francis Markrute, himself.

"Mother is so disappointed," she said, "but she really suffers so dreadfully. I am sure Countess Shulski will forgive her, and you, too. She wants to know if Countess Shulski will let Tristram bring her to-morrow morning, without any more ceremony, to see her and stay to luncheon."

Thus it was settled and this necessitated a change in the table arrangements.

Lady Ethelrida would now sit on the host's right hand, and Lady Coltshurst, an aunt on the Tancred side, at his left, while Zara would be between the Duke and her fiancé, as originally arranged. Emily Guiscard would have Sir James Danvers and Lord Coltshurst as neighbors, and Mary her uncle, the Duke's brother, a widower, Lord Charles Montfitchet, and his son, "Young Billy," the Glastonbury heir—Lady Ethelrida was the Duke's only child.

At a quarter before eight Francis Markrute went up to his niece's sitting-room. She was already dressed in a sapphire-blue velvet masterpiece of simplicity. The Tancred presents of sapphires and diamonds lay in their open cases on the table with the splendid Markrute yards of pearls. She was standing looking down at them, the strangest expression of cynical resignation upon her face.

"Your gift is magnificent, Uncle Francis," she said, without thanking him. "Which do you wish me to wear? Yours—or his?"

"Lord Tancred's, he has specially asked that you put his on to-night," the financier replied. "These are only his first small ones; the other jewels are being reset for you. Nothing can be kinder or more generous than the whole family has been. You see this brooch, with the large drop sapphire and diamond, is from the Duke."

She inclined her head without enthusiasm, and took her own small pearls from her ears, and replaced them by the big sapphire and diamond earrings; a rivière of alternate solitaire sapphires and diamonds she clasped round her snowy throat.

"You look absolutely beautiful," her uncle exclaimed with admiration. "I knew I could perfectly trust to your taste—the dress is perfection."

"Then I suppose we shall have to go down," she said quietly.

She was perfectly calm, her face expressionless; if there was a tempestuous suggestion in her somber eyes she generally kept the lids lowered. Inwardly, she felt a raging rebellion. This was the first ceremony of the sacrifice, and although in the abstract her fine senses appreciated the jewels and all her new and beautiful clothes and *apanages*, they in no way counterbalanced the hateful degradation.

To her it was a hideous mockery—the whole thing; she was just a chattel, a part of a business bargain. She could not guess her uncle's motive for the transaction (he had a deep one, of course), but Lord Tancred's was plain and purely contemptible. Money! For had not the whole degrading thing been settled before he had ever seen her? He was worse than Ladislaus who, at all events, had been passionately in love, in his revolting, animal way.

She knew nothing of the English customs, nor how such a thing as the arrangement of this marriage, as she thought it was, was a perfectly unknown impossibility, as an idea. She supposed that the entire family were aware of the circumstances, and were willing to accept her only for her uncle's wealth—she already hated and despised them all. Her idea was, "*noblesse oblige*," and that a great and ancient house should never stoop to such depths.

Francis Markrute looked at her when she said, "I suppose we shall have to go down," with that icy calm. He felt faintly uneasy.

"Zara, it is understood you will be gracious? and *brusquer* no one?"

But all the reply he received was a glance of scorn. She had given her word and refused to discuss that matter.

And so they descended the stairs just in time to be standing ready to receive Lord and Lady Coltshurst who were the first to be announced. He was a spare, unintelligent, henpecked, elderly man, and she, a stout, forbidding-looking lady. She had prominent, shortsighted eyes, and she used longhandled glasses; she had also three chins, and did not resemble the Guiscards in any way, except for her mouth and her haughty bearing.

Zara's manner was that of an empress graciously receiving foreigners in a private audience!

The guests now arrived in quick succession. Lord Charles and his son, "Young Billy," then Tristram and his sisters, and Jimmy Danvers, and, lastly, the Duke and Lady Ethelrida.

They were all such citizens of the world there was no awkwardness, and the old Duke had kissed his fair, prospective niece's hand when he had been presented, and had said that some day he should claim the privilege of an old man and kiss her cheek. And Zara had smiled for an instant, overcome by his charm, and so she had put her fingers on his arm, and they had gone down to dinner; and now they were talking suavely.

Francis Markrute had a theory that certain human beings are born with moral antennae—a sort of extra combination beyond the natural of the senses of sight, smell, hearing and understanding—which made them apprehend situations and people even when these chanced to be of a hitherto unknown race or habit. Zara was among those whose antennae were highly developed. She had apprehended almost instantaneously that whatever their motives were underneath, her future husband's family were going to act the part of receiving her for herself. It was a little ridiculous, but very well bred, and she must fall in with it when with them collectively like this.

Before they had finished the soup the Duke was saying to himself that she was the most attractive creature he had ever met in his life, and no wonder Tristram was mad about her; for Tristram's passionate admiration to-night could not have been mistaken by a child!

And yet Zara had never smiled, but that once—in the drawing-room.

Lady Ethelrida from where she sat could see her face through a gap in the flowers. The financier had ordered a tall arrangement on purpose: if Zara by chance should look haughtily indifferent it were better that her expression should escape the observation of all but her nearest neighbors. However, Lady Ethelrida just caught the picture of her through an oblique angle, against a background of French panelling.

And with her quiet, calm judgment of people she was wondering what was the cause of that strange look in her eyes? Was it of a stag at bay? Was it temper, or resentment, or only just pain? And Tristram had said their color was slate gray; for her part she saw nothing but pools of jet ink!

"There is some tragic story hidden here," she thought, "and Tristram is too much in love to see it." But she felt rather drawn to her new prospective cousin, all the same.

Francis Markrute seemed perfectly happy—his manner as a host left nothing to be desired; he did not neglect the uninteresting aunt, who formed golden opinions of him; but he contrived to make Lady Ethelrida feel that he wished only to talk to her; not because she was an attractive, young woman, but because he was impressed with her intelligence, in the abstract. It made things very easy.

The Duke asked Zara if she knew anything about English politics.

"You will have to keep Tristram up to the mark," he said, "he has done very well now and then, but he is a rather lazy fellow." And he smiled.

"'Tristram,'" she thought. "So his name is 'Tristram'!" She had actually never heard it before, nor troubled herself to inquire about it. It seemed incredible, it aroused in her a grim sense of humor, and she looked into the old Duke's face for a second and wondered what he would say if she announced this fact, and he caught the smile, cynical though it was, and continued:

"I see you have noticed his laziness! Now it will really be your duty to make him a first-rate fighter for our cause. The Radicals will begin to attack our very existence presently, and we must all come up to the scratch."

"I know nothing as yet of your politics," Zara said. "I do not understand which party is which, though my uncle says one consists of gentlemen, and the other of the common people. I suppose it is like in other countries, every one wanting to secure what some one above him has got, without being fitted for the administration of what he desires to snatch."

"That is about it," smiled the Duke.

"It would be reasonable, if they were all oppressed here, as in France before the great revolution, but are they?"

"Oh! dear, no!" interrupted Tristram. "All the laws are made for the lower classes. They have compensations for everything, and they have openings to rise to the top of the tree if they wish to. It is wretched landlords like my uncle and myself who are oppressed!" and he smiled delightedly, he was so happy to hear her talk.

"When I shall know I shall perhaps find it all interesting," she continued to the Duke.

"Between us we shall have to instruct you thoroughly, eh, Tristram, my boy? And then you must be a great leader, and have a salon, as the ladies of the eighteenth century did: we want a beautiful young woman to draw us all together."

"Well, don't you think I have found you a perfect specimen, Uncle!" Tristram exclaimed; and he raised his glass and kissed the brim, while he whispered:

"Darling, my sweet lady—I drink to your health."

But this was too much for Zara—he was overdoing the part—and she turned and flashed upon him a glance of resentment and contempt.

Beyond the Duke sat Jimmy Danvers, and then Emily Guiscard and Lord Coltshurst, and the two young people exchanged confidences in a low voice.

"I say, Emily, isn't she a corker?" Sir James said. "She don't look a bit English, though, she reminds me of a—oh, well, I'm not good at history or dates, but some one in the old Florentine time. She looks as if she could put a dagger into one or give a fellow a cup of poison, without turning a hair."

"Oh, Jimmy! how horrid," exclaimed Emily. "She does not seem to me to have a cruel face, she only looks peculiar and mysterious, and—and—unsmiling. Do you think she loves Tristram? Perhaps that is the foreign way—to appear so cold."

At that moment Sir James Danvers caught the glance which Zara gave her fiancé for his toast.

"Je-hoshaphat!" he exclaimed! But he realized that Emily had not seen, so he stopped abruptly.

"Yes—one can never be sure of things with foreigners," he said, and he looked down at his plate. That poor devil of a Tristram was going to have a thorny time in the future, he thought, and he was to be best man at the wedding; it would be like giving the old chap over to a tigress! But, by Jove!—such a beautiful one would be worth being eaten by—he added to himself.

And during one of Francis Markrute's turnings to his left-hand neighbor Lord Coltshurst said to Lady Ethelrida:

"I think Tristram's choice peculiarly felicitous, Ethelrida, do not you? But I fear her ladyship"—and he glanced timidly at his wife—"will not take this view. She has a most unreasonable dislike for young women with red hair. 'Ungovernable temperaments,' she affirms. I trust she won't prejudice your Aunt Jane."

"Aunt Jane always thinks for herself," said Lady Ethelrida. She announced no personal opinion about Tristram's fiancé, nor could Lord Coltshurst extort one from her.

As the dinner went on she felt a growing sense that they were all on the edge of a volcano.

Lady Ethelrida never meddled in other people's affairs, but she loved Tristram as a brother and she felt a little afraid. She could not see his face, from where she sat—the table was a long one with oval ends—but she, too, had seen the flash from Zara which had caused Jimmy Danvers to exclaim: "Jehoshaphat!"

The host soon turned back from duty to pleasure, leaving Lady Coltshurst to Lord Charles Montfitchet. The conversation turned upon types.

Types were not things of chance, Francis Markrute affirmed; if one could look back far enough there was always a reason for them.

"People are so extremely unthinking about such a number of interesting things, Lady Ethelrida," he said, "their speculative faculties seem only to be able to roam into cut and dried channels. We have had great scientists like Darwin investigating our origin, and among the Germans there are several who study the atavism of races, but in general even educated people are perfectly ignorant upon the subject, and they expect little Tommy Jones and Katie Robinson, or Jacques Dubois and Marie Blanc, to have the same instincts as your cousin, Lord Tancred, and you, for instance. Whatever individual you are dealing with, you should endeavor to understand his original group. In moments of great excitement when all acquired control is in abeyance the individual always returns to the natural action of his group."

"How interesting!" said Lady Ethelrida. "Let us look round the table and decide to what particular group each one of us belongs."

"Most of you are from the same group," he said meditatively. "Eliminating myself and my niece, Sir James Danvers has perhaps had the most intermixtures."

"Yes," said Lady Ethelrida, and she laughed. "Jimmy's grandmother was the daughter of a very rich Manchester cotton spinner; that is what gives him his sound common sense. I am afraid Tristram and the rest of us except Lord Coltshurst have not had anything sensible like that in us for hundreds of years, so what would be your speculation as to the action of our group?"

"That you would have high courage and fine senses, and highly-strung, nervous force, and chivalry and good taste, and broad and noble aims in the higher half and that in the lower portion you would run to the decadence of all those things—the fine turned to vices—yet even so I would not look for vulgarity, or bad taste, or cowardice in any of you."

"No," said Lady Ethelrida—"I hope not. Then, according to your reasoning it is very unjust of us when we say, as perhaps you have heard it said, that Lady Darrowood is to blame when she is noisy and assertive and treats Lord Darrowood with bad taste?"

"Certainly—she only does those things when she is excited and has gone back to her group. When she is under her proper control she plays the part of an English marchioness very well. It is the prerogative of a new race to be able to play a part; the result of the cunning and strength which have been required of the immediate forbears in order to live at all under unfavorable conditions. Now, had her father been a Deptford ox-slaughterer instead of a Chicago pig-sticker she could never have risen to the role of a marchioness at all. This is no new country; it does not need nor comprehend bluff, and so produces no such type as Lady Darrowood."

At this moment Lady Ethelrida again caught sight of Zara. She was silent at the instant, and a look of superb pride and disdain was on her face. Almost before she was aware of it Ethelrida had exclaimed:

"Your niece looks like an empress, a wonderful, Byzantine, Roman empress!"

Francis Markrute glanced at her, sideways, with his clever eyes; had she ever heard anything of Zara's parentage, he wondered for a second, and then he smiled at himself for the thought. Lady Ethelrida was not likely to have spoken so in that case—she would not be acting up to her group.

"There are certain reasons why she should," he said. "I cannot answer for the part of her which comes from her father, Maurice Grey, a very old English family, I believe, but on her mother's side she could have the passions of an artist and the pride of a Caesar: she is a very interesting case."

"May I know something of her?" Ethelrida said, "I do so want them to be happy. Tristram is one of the simplest and finest characters I have ever met. He will love her very much, I fear."

"Why do you say you *fear?*"

Lady Ethelrida reddened a little; a soft, warm flush came into her delicate face and made it look beautiful: she never spoke of love—to men.

"Because a great love is a very powerful and sometimes a terrible thing, if it is not returned in like measure. And, oh, forgive me for saying so, but the Countess Shulski does not look as if—she loved Tristram—much."

Francis Markrute did not speak for an instant, then he turned and gazed straight into her eyes gravely, as he said:

"Believe me, I would not allow your cousin to marry my niece if I were not truly convinced that it will be for the eventual great happiness of them both. Will you promise me something, Lady Ethelrida? Will you help me not to permit any one to interfere between them for some time, no matter how things may appear? Give them the chance of settling everything themselves."

Ethelrida looked back at him, with a seriousness equal to his own as she answered, "I promise." And inwardly the sense of some unknown undercurrent that might grow into a rushing torrent made itself felt, stronger than before.

Meanwhile Lady Coltshurst, who could just see Zara's profile all the time when she put up those irritating, longhandled glasses of hers, now gave her opinion of the bride-elect to Lord Charles Montfitchet, her neighbor on the left hand.

"I strongly disapprove of her, Charles. Either her hair is dyed or her eyes are blackened; that mixture is not natural, and if, indeed, it should be in this case then I consider it uncanny and not what one would wish for in the family."

"Oh, I say, my lady!" objected Lord Charles, "I think she is the most stunning-looking young woman I've seen in a month of Sundays!"

Lady Coltshurst put up her glasses again and glared:

"I cannot bear your modern slang, Charles, but 'stunning,' used literally, is quite appropriate. She does stun one; that is exactly it. I fear poor Tristram with such a type can look forward to very little happiness, or poor Jane to any likelihood that the Tancred name will remain free from scandal."

Lord Charles grew exasperated and retaliated.

"By George! A demure mouse can cause scandal to a name, with probably more certainty than this beauty!"

There was a member of Lady Coltshurst's husband's family whom she herself, having no children, had brought out, and who had been perilously near the Divorce Court this very season: and she was a dull, colorless little thing.

Her ladyship turned the conversation abruptly, with an annihilating glance. And fortunately, just then Zara rose, and the ladies filed out of the room: and so this trying dinner was over.

CHAPTER XIII

Nothing could exceed Zara's dignity, when they reached the drawing-room above. They at first stood in a group by the fire in the larger room, and Emily and Mary tried to get a word in and say something nice in their frank girlish way. They admired their future sister-in-law so immensely, and if Zara had not thought they were all acting a part, as she herself was, she would have been touched at their sweetness. As it was she inwardly froze more and more, while she answered with politeness; and Lady Ethelrida, watching quietly for a while, grew further puzzled.

It was certainly a mask this extraordinary and beautiful young woman was wearing, she felt, and presently, when Lady Coltshurst who had remained rather silently aloof, only fixing them all in turn with her long eyeglasses, drew the girls aside to talk to her by asking for news of their mother's headache, Ethelrida indicated she and Zara might sit down upon the nearest, stiff, French sofa; and as she clasped her thin, fine hands together, holding her pale gray gloves which she did not attempt to put on again, she said gently:

"I hope we shall all make you feel you are so welcome, Zara—may I call you Zara? It is such a beautiful name I think."

The Countess Shulski's strange eyes seemed to become blacker than ever—a startled, suspicious look grew in them, just such as had come into the black panther's on a day when Francis Markrute whistled a softly caressing note outside its bars: what did this mean?

"I shall be very pleased if you will," she said coldly.

Lady Ethelrida determined not to be snubbed. She must overcome this barrier if she could, for Tristram's sake.

"England and our customs must seem so strange to you," she went on. "But we are not at all disagreeable people when you know us!" And she smiled encouragingly.

"It is easy to be agreeable when one is happy," Zara said. "And you all seem very happy here—*sans souci*. It is good."

And Ethelrida wondered. "What can make you so unhappy, you beautiful thing, with Tristram to love you, and youth and health and riches?"

And Zara thought, "This appears a sweet and most frank lady, but how can I tell? I know not the English. It is perhaps because she is so well bred that she is enabled to act so nicely."

"You have not yet seen Wrayth, have you?" Ethelrida went on. "I am sure you will be interested in it, it is so old."

"Wr—ayth—?" Zara faltered. She had never heard of it! What was Wrayth?

"Perhaps I do not pronounce it as you are accustomed to think of it," Ethelrida said kindly. She was absolutely startled at the other's ignorance. "Tristram's place, I mean. The Guiscards have owned it ever since the Conqueror gave it to them after the Battle of Hastings, you know. It is the rarest case of a thing being so long in one family, even here in England, and the title has only gone in the male line, too, as yet. But Tristram and Cyril are the very last. If anything happened to them it would be the end. Oh! we are all so glad Tristram is going to be married!"

Zara's eyes now suddenly blazed at the unconscious insinuation in this speech. Any one who has ever watched a caged creature of the cat tribe and seen how the whole gamut of emotions—sullen endurance, suspicion, resentment, hate and rage, as well as contentment and happiness—can appear in its orbs without the slightest aid from lids or eyebrows, without the smallest alteration in mouth or chin, will understand how Zara's pools of ink spoke while their owner remained icily still.

She understood perfectly the meaning of Ethelrida's speech. The line of the Tancreds should go on through her! But never, never! That should never be! If they were counting upon that they were counting in vain. The marriage was never intended to be anything but an empty ceremony, for mercenary reasons. There must be no mistake about this. What if Lord Tancred had such ideas, too? And she quivered suddenly and caught in her breath with the horror of this thought.

And who was Cyril? Zara had no knowledge of Cyril, any more than of Wrayth! But she did not ask.

If Francis Markrute had heard this conversation he would have been very much annoyed with himself, and would have blamed himself for stupidity. He, of course, should have seen that his niece was sufficiently well coached, in all the details that she should know, not to be led into these pitfalls.

Ethelrida felt a sensation of a sort of petrified astonishment. There is a French word, *ahuri*, which expresses her emotion exactly, but there is no English equivalent. Tristram's fiancé was evidently quite ignorant of the simplest facts about him, or his family, or his home! Her eyes had blazed at Ethelrida's last speech, with a look of self-defence and defiance. And yet Tristram was evidently passionately in love with her. How could such things be? It was a great mystery. Ethelrida was thrilled and interested.

Francis Markrute guessed the ladies' lonely moments would be most difficult to pass, so he had curtailed the enjoyment of the port and old brandy and cigars to the shortest possible dimensions, Tristram aiding him. His one desire was to be near his fiancé.

The overmastering magnetic current which seemed to have drawn him from the very first moment he had seen her now had augmented into almost pain. She had been cruelly cold and disdainful at dinner whenever she had spoken to him, her contempt showing plainly in her eyes, and it had maddened and excited him; and when the other men had all drunk the fiancés' health and wished them happiness he had gulped down the old brandy, and vowed to himself, "Before a year is out I will make her love me as I love her, so help me God!"

And then they all had trooped up into the drawing-room just as Ethelrida was saying,

"The northern property, Morndale, is not half so pretty as Wrayth—"

But when she saw them enter she rose and ceded her place to Tristram who gladly sank into the sofa beside his lady.

He was to have no tête-à-tête, however, for Jimmy Danvers who felt it was his turn to say something to the coming bride came now, and leant upon the mantelpiece beside them.

"I am going to be the most severe 'best man' next Wednesday, Countess," he said. "I shall see that Tristram is at St. George's a good half-hour before the time, and that he does not drop the ring; you trust to me!" And he laughed nervously, Zara's face was so unresponsive.

"Countess Shulski does not know the English ceremony, Jimmy," Tristram interrupted quickly, "nor what is a 'best man.' Now, if we were only across the water we would have a rehearsal of the whole show as we did for Darrowood's wedding."

"That must have been a joke," said Jimmy.

"It was very sensible there; there was such a lot of fuss, and bridesmaids, and things; but we are going to be quite quiet, aren't we, Zara? I hate shows; don't you?"

"Immensely," was all she answered.

Then Sir James, who felt thoroughly crushed, after one or two more fatuous remarks moved away, and Zara arose in her character of hostess, and spoke to Lady Coltshurst.

Tristram crossed over to the Duke and rapidly began a political discussion, but while his uncle appeared to notice nothing unusual, and entered into it with interest, his kind, old heart was wrung with the pain he saw his favorite nephew was suffering.

"Mr. Markrute, I am troubled," Lady Ethelrida said, as she walked with the host to look at an exquisite Vigée le Brun across the room. "Your niece is the most interesting personality I have ever met; but, underneath, something is making her unhappy, I am sure. Please, what does it mean? Oh, I know I have promised what I did at dinner, but are you certain it is all right? And can they ever be really at peace together?"

Francis Markrute bent over, apparently to point to a *bibelot* which lay on a table under the picture, and he said in a low, vibrating tone.

"I give you my word there is some one, who is dead—whom I loved—who would come back and curse me now, if I should let this thing be, with a doubt in my heart as to their eventual happiness."

And Lady Ethelrida looked full at him and saw that the man's cold face was deeply moved and softened.

"If that is so then I will speculate no more," she said. "Listen! I will trust you!"

"You dear, noble English lady," the financier replied, "how truly I thank you!" And he let some of the emotion which he felt, gleam from his eyes, while he changed the conversation.

A few minutes after this, Lady Coltshurst announced it was time to go, and she would take the girls home. And the Duke's carriage was also waiting, and good nights were said, and the host whispered to Jimmy Danvers,

"Take Tancred along with you, too, please. My niece is overtired with the strain of this evening and I want her to go to bed at once." And to Tristram he said,

"Do not even say good night, like a dear fellow. Don't you see she is almost ready to faint? Just go quietly with the rest, and come for her to-morrow morning to take her to your mother."

So they all left as he wished, and he himself went back upstairs to the big drawing-room and there saw Zara standing like a marble statue, exactly as they had left her, and he went forward, and, bending, kissed her hand.

"Most beautifully endured, my queenly niece!" he said; and then he led her to the door and up to her room. She was perfectly mute.

But a little while afterwards, as he came to bed himself, he was startled and chilled by hearing the *Chanson Triste* being played in her sitting-room, with a wailing, passionate pathos, as of a soul in anguish.

And if he could have seen her face he would have seen her great eyes streaming with tears, while she prayed:

"*Maman*, ask God to give me courage to get through all of this, since it is for your Mirko."

CHAPTER XIV

Satan was particularly fresh next morning when Tristram took him for a canter round the Park. He was glad of it: he required something to work off steam upon. He was in a mood of restless excitement. During the three weeks of Zara's absence he had allowed himself to dream into a state of romantic love for her. He had glossed over in his mind her distant coldness, her frigid adherence to the bare proposition, so that to return to that state of things had come to him as a shock.

But, this morning, he knew he was a fool to have expected anything else. He was probably a great fool altogether, but he never changed his mind, and was prepared to pay the price of his folly. After all, there would be plenty of time afterwards to melt her dislike, so he could afford to wait now. He would not permit himself to suffer again as he had done last night. Then he came in and had his bath, and made himself into a very perfect-looking lover, to present himself to his lady at about half-past twelve o'clock, to take her to his mother.

Zara was, if anything, whiter than usual when she came into the library where he was waiting for her alone. The financier had gone to the City. She had heavy, bluish shadows under her eyes, and he saw quite plainly that, the night before, she must have been weeping bitterly.

A great tenderness came over him. What was this sorrow of hers? Why might he not comfort her? He put out both hands and then, as she remained stonily unresponsive, he dropped them, and only said quietly that he hoped she was well, and his motor was waiting outside, and that his mother, Lady Tancred, would be expecting them.

"I am ready," said Zara. And they went.

He told her as they flew along, that he had been riding in the Park that morning, and had looked up at the house and wondered which was her window; and then he asked her if she liked riding, and she said she had never tried for ten years—the opportunity to ride had not been in her life—but she used to like it when she was a child.

"I must get you a really well-mannered hack," he said joyously. Here was a subject she had not snubbed him over! "And you will let me teach you again when we go down to Wrayth, won't you?"

But before she could answer they had arrived at the house in Queen Street.

Michelham, with a subdued beam on his old face, stood inside the door with his footmen, and Tristram said gayly,

"Michelham, this is to be her new ladyship; Countess Shulski"—and he turned to Zara. "Michelham is a very old friend of mine, Zara. We used to do a bit of poaching together, when I was a boy and came home from Eton."

Michelham was only a servant and could not know of her degradation, so Zara allowed herself to smile and looked wonderfully lovely, as the old man said,

"I am sure I wish your ladyship every happiness, and his lordship, too; and, if I may say so, with such a gentleman your ladyship is sure to have it."

And Tristram chaffed him, and they went upstairs.

Lady Tancred had rigidly refrained from questioning her daughters, on their return from the dinnerparty; she had not even seen them until the morning, and when they had both burst out with descriptions of their future sister-in-law's beauty and strangeness their mother had stopped them.

"Do not tell me anything about her, dear children," she had said. "I wish to judge for myself without prejudice."

But Lady Coltshurst could not be so easily repressed. She had called early, on purpose to give her views, with the ostensible excuse of an inquiry about her sister-in-law's health.

"I am afraid you will be rather unfavorably impressed with Tristram's choice, when you have seen her, Jane," she announced. "I confess I was. She treated us all as though *she* were conferring the honor, not receiving it, and she is by no means a type that promises domestic tranquillity for Tristram."

"Really, Julia!" Lady Tancred protested. "I must beg of you to say no more. I have perfect confidence in my son, and wish to receive his future wife with every mark of affection."

"Your efforts will be quite wasted, then, Jane," her sister-in-law snapped. "She is most forbidding, and never once unbent nor became genial, the whole evening. And besides, for a lady, she is much too striking looking."

"She cannot help being beautiful," Lady Tancred said. "I am sure I shall admire her very much, from what the girls tell me. But we will not discuss her. It was so kind of you to come, and my head is much better."

"Then I will be off!" Lady Coltshurst sniffed in a slightly offended tone. Really, relations were so tiresome! They never would accept a word of advice or warning in the spirit it was given, and Jane in particular was unpleasantly difficult.

So she got into her electric brougham, and was rolled away, happily before Tristram and his lady appeared upon the scene; but the jar of her words still lingered with Lady Tancred, in spite of all her efforts to forget it.

Zara's heart beat when they got to the door, and she felt extremely antagonistic. Francis Markrute had left her in entire ignorance of the English customs, for a reason of his own. He calculated if he informed her that on Tristram's side it was purely a love match, she, with her strange temperament, and sense of honor, would never have accepted it. He knew she would have turned upon him and said she could be no party to such a cheat. He with his calm, calculating brain had weighed the pros and cons of the whole matter: to get her to consent, for her brother's sake in the beginning, under the impression that it was a dry business arrangement, equally distasteful personally to both parties—to leave her with this impression and keep the pair as much as possible apart, until the actual wedding; and then to leave her awakening to Tristram—was his plan. A woman would be impossibly difficult to please, if, in the end, she failed to respond to such a lover as Tristram! He counted upon what he had called her moral antennae to make no mistakes. It would not eventually prejudice matters if the family did find her a little stiff, as long as she did not actually show her contempt for their apparent willingness to support the bargain. But her look of scorn, the night before, when he had shown some uneasiness on this score, had reassured him. He would leave things alone and let her make her own discoveries.

So now she entered her future mother-in-law's room, with a haughty mien and no friendly feelings in her heart. She was well acquainted with the foreign examples of mother-in-law. They interfered with everything and had their sons under their thumbs. They seemed always mercenary, and were the chief agents in promoting a match, if it were for their own family's advantage. No doubt Uncle Francis had arranged the whole affair with this Lady Tancred in the first instance, and she, Zara, would not be required to keep up the comedy, as with the uncle and cousins. She decided she would be quite frank with her if the occasion required, and if she should, by chance, make the same insinuation of the continuance of the Tancred race as Lady Ethelrida had innocently done, she would have plainly to say that was not in the transaction. For her own ends she must be Lord Tancred's wife and let her uncle have what glory he pleased from the position; if that were his reason, and as for Lord Trancred's ends, he was to receive money. That was all: it was quite simple.

The two women were mutually surprised when they looked at one another. Lady Tancred's first impression was, "It is true she is a very disturbing type, but how well bred and how beautiful!" And Zara thought, "It is possible that, after all, I may be wrong. She looks too proud to have stooped to plan this thing. It may be only Lord Tancred's doing—men are more horrible than women."

"This is Zara, Mother," Tristram said.

And Lady Tancred held out her hands, and then drew her new daughter—that was to be—nearer and kissed her.

And over Zara there crept a thrill. She saw that the elder lady was greatly moved, and no woman had kissed her since her mother's death. Why, if it were all a bargain, should she tenderly kiss her?

"I am so glad to welcome you, dear," Lady Tancred said, determining to be very gracious. "I am almost pleased not to have been able to go last night. Now I can have you all to myself for this, our first little meeting."

And they sat down on a sofa, and Zara asked about her head; and Lady Tancred told her the pain was almost gone, and this broke the ice and started a conversation.

"I want you to tell me of yourself," Lady Tancred said. "Do you think you will like this old England of ours, with its damp and its gloom in the autumn, and its beautiful fresh spring? I want you to—and to love your future home."

"Everything is very strange to me, but I will try," Zara answered.

"Tristram has been making great arrangements to please you at Wrayth," Lady Tancred went on. "But, of course, he has told you all about it."

"I have had to be away all the time," Zara felt she had better say—and Tristram interrupted.

"They are all to be surprises, Mother; everything is to be new to Zara, from beginning to end. You must not tell her anything of it."

Then Lady Tancred spoke of gardens. She hoped Zara liked gardens; she herself was a great gardener, and had taken much pride in her herbaceous borders and her roses at Wrayth.

And when they had got to this stage of the conversation Tristram felt he could safely leave them to one another, so, saying he wanted to talk to his sisters, he went out of the room.

"It will be such happiness to think of your living in the old home," the proud lady said. "It was a great grief to us all when we had to shut it up, two years ago; but you will, indeed, adorn it for its reopening."

Zara did not know what to reply. She vaguely understood that one might love a home, though she had never had one but the gloomy castle near Prague; and that made her sigh when she thought of it.

But a garden she knew she should love. And Mirko was so fond of flowers. Oh! if they would let her have a beautiful country home in peace, and Mirko to come sometimes, and play there, and chase butterflies, with his excited, poor little face, she would indeed be grateful to them. Her thoughts went on in a dream of this, while Lady Tancred talked of many things, and she answered, "Yes," and "No," with gentle respect. Her future mother-in-law's great dignity pleased her sense of the fitness of things; she so disliked gush of any sort herself, and she felt now that she knew where she was and there need be no explanations. The family, one and all, evidently intended to play the same part, and she would, too. When the awakening came it would be between herself and Tristram. Yes, she must think of him now as "Tristram!"

Her thoughts had wandered again when she heard Lady Tancred's voice, saying,

"I wanted to give you this myself," and she drew a small case from a table near and opened it, and there lay a very beautiful diamond ring. "It is my own little personal present to you, my new, dear daughter. Will you wear it sometimes, Zara, in remembrance of this day and in remembrance that I give into your hands the happiness of my son, who is dearer to me than any one on earth?"

And the two proud pairs of eyes met, and Zara could not answer, and there was a strange silence between them for a second. And then Tristram came back into the room, which created a diversion, and she was enabled to say some ordinary conventional things about the beauty of the stones, and express her thanks for the gift. Only, in her heart, she determined never to wear it. It would burn her hand, she thought, and she could never be a hypocrite.

Luncheon was then announced, and they went into the dining-room.

Here she saw Tristram in a new light, with only "Young Billy" and Jimmy Danvers who had dropped in, and his mother and sisters.

He was gay as a schoolboy, telling Billy who had not spoken a word to Zara the night before that now he should sit beside her, and that he was at liberty to make love to his new cousin! And Billy, aged nineteen—a perfectly stolid and amiable youth—proceeded to start a laborious conversation, while the rest of the table chaffed about things which were Greek to Zara, but she was grateful not to have to talk, and so passed off the difficulties of the situation.

And the moment the meal was over Tristram took her back to Park Lane. He, too, was thankful the affair had been got through; he hardly spoke as they went along, and in silence followed her into the house and into the library, and there waited for her commands.

Whenever they were alone the disguises of the part fell from Zara, and she resumed the icy mien.

"Good-bye," she said coldly. "I am going into the country to-morrow for two or three days. I shall not see you until Monday. Have you anything more it is necessary to say?"

"You are going into the country!" Tristram exclaimed, aghast. "But I will not—" and then he paused, for her eyes had flashed ominously. "I mean," he went on, "must you go? So soon before our wedding?"

She drew herself up and spoke in a scathing voice.

"Why must I repeat again what I said when you gave me your ring?—I do not wish to see or speak with you. You will have all you bargained for. Can you not leave my company out of the question?"

The Tancred stern, obstinate spirit was thoroughly roused. He walked up and down the room rapidly for a moment, fuming with hurt rage. Then reason told him to wait. He had no intention of breaking off the match now, no matter what she should do; and this was Thursday; there were only five more days to get through, and when once she should be his wife—and then he looked at her, as she stood in her dark, perfect dress, with the great, sable wrap slipping from her shoulders and making a regal background, and her beauty fired his senses and made his eyes swim; and he bent forward and took her hand.

"Very well, you beautiful, unkind thing," he said. "But if you do not want to marry me you had better say so at once, and I will release you from your promise. Because when the moment comes afterwards for our crossing of swords there will be no question as to who is to be master—I tell you that now."

And Zara dragged her hand from him, and, with the black panther's glance in her eyes, she turned to the window and stood looking out.

Then after a second she said in a strangled voice,

"I wish that the marriage shall take place.—And now, please go."

And without further words he went.

CHAPTER XV

On her way to Bournemouth next day, to see Mirko, Zara met Mimo in the British Museum. They walked along the galleries on the ground floor until they found a bench near the mausoleum of Halicarnassus. To look at it gave them both infinite pleasure; they knew so well the masterpieces of all the old Greeks. Mimo, it seemed, had been down to see his son ten days before. They had met secretly. Mirko had stolen out, and with the cunning of his little brain fully on the alert he had dodged Mrs. Morley in the garden, and had fled to the near pine woods with his violin; and there had met his father and had a blissful time. He was certainly better, Mimo said, a little fatter and with much less cough, and he seemed fairly happy and quite resigned. The Morleys were so kind and good, but, poor souls! it was not their fault if they could not understand! It was not given to every one to have the understanding of his Chérisette and his own papa, Mirko had said, but so soon he would be well; then he would be able to come back to them, and in the meantime he was going to learn lessons, learn the tiresome things that his Chérisette alone knew how to teach him with comprehension. The new tutor who came each day from the town was of a reasonableness, but no wit! "Body of Bacchus!" the father said, "the poor child had not been able to make the tutor laugh once—in a week—when we met."

And then after a while it seemed that there was some slight care upon Mimo's mind. It had rained, it appeared, before the end of their stolen meeting. It had rained all the morning and then had cleared up gloriously fine, and they had sat down on a bank under the trees, and Mirko had played divinely all sorts of gay airs. But when he got up he had shivered a little, and Mimo could see that his clothes were wet, and then the rain had come on immediately again, and he had made him run back. He feared he must have got thoroughly soaked, and he had had nothing since but one postcard, which said that Mirko had been in bed, though he was now much better and longing—longing to see his Chérisette!

"Oh, Mimo! how could you let him sit on the grass!" Zara exclaimed reproachfully, when he got thus far. "And why was I not told? It may have made him seriously ill. Oh, the poor angel! And I must stay so short a while—and then this wedding—" She stopped abruptly and her eyes became black. For she knew there was no asking for respite. To obtain her brother's possible life she must be ready and resigned, at the altar at St. George's, Hanover Square, on Wednesday the 25th of October, at 2 o'clock, and, once made a wife, she must go with Lord Tancred to the Lord Warren Hotel at Dover, to spend the night.

She rose with a convulsive quiver, and looked with blank, sightless eyes at an Amazon in the frieze hard by. The Amazon—she saw, when vision came back to her—was hurling a spear at a splendid young Greek. That is how she felt she would like to behave to her future husband. Men and their greed of money, and their revolting passions!—and her poor little Mirko ill, perhaps, from his father's carelessness—How could she leave him? And if she did not his welfare would be at an end and life an abyss.

There was no use scolding Mimo; she knew of old no one was sorrier than he for his mistakes, for which those he loved best always had to suffer. It had taken the heart out of him, the anxious thought, he said, but, knowing that Chérisette must be so busy arranging to get married, he had not troubled her, since she could do nothing until her return to England, and then he knew she would arrange to go to Mirko at once, in any case.

He, Mimo, had been too depressed to work, and the picture of the London fog was not much further advanced, and he feared it would not be ready for her wedding gift.

"Oh, never mind!" said Zara. "I know you will think of me kindly, and I shall like that as well as any present."

And then she drove to the Waterloo station alone, a gnawing anxiety in her heart. And all the journey to Bournemouth her spirits sank lower and lower until, when she got there, it seemed as if the old cab-horse were a cow in its slowness, to get to the doctor's trim house.

"Yes," Mrs. Morley said as soon as she arrived, "your little brother has had a very sharp attack."

He escaped from the garden about ten days before, she explained, and was gone at least two hours, and then returned wet through, and was a little light-headed that night, and had talked of "Maman and the angels," and "Papa and Chérisette," but they could obtain no information from him as to why he went, nor whom he had seen. He had so rapidly recovered that the doctor had not thought it necessary to let any one know, and she, Mrs. Morley—guessing how busy one must be ordering a trousseau—when there was no danger had refrained from sending a letter, to be forwarded from the given address.

Here Zara's eyes had flashed, and she had said sternly,

"The trousseau was not of the slightest consequence in comparison to my brother's health."

Mirko was upstairs in his pretty bedroom, playing with a puzzle and the nurse; he had not been told of his sister's proposed coming, but some sixth sense seemed to inform him it was she, when her footfall sounded on the lower stairs, for they heard an excited voice shouting:

"I tell you I will go—I will go to her, my Chérisette!" And Zara hastened the last part, to avoid his rushing, as she feared he would do, out of his warm room into the cold passage.

The passionate joy he showed at the sight of her made a tightness round her heart. He did not look ill, only, in some unaccountable way, he seemed to have grown smaller. There was, too, even an extra pink flush in his cheeks.

He must sit on her lap and touch all her pretty things. She had put on her uncle's big pearl earrings and one string of big pearls, on purpose to show him; he so loved what was beautiful and refined.

"Thou art like a queen, Chérisette," he told her. "Much more beautiful than when we had our tea party, and I wore Papa's paper cap. And everything new! The uncle, then, is very rich," he went on, while he stroked the velvet on her dress.

And she kissed and soothed him to sleep in her arms, when he was ready for his bed. It was getting quite late, and she sang a soft, Slavonic cradle song, in a low cooing voice, and, every now and then, before the poor little fellow sank entirely to rest, he would open his beautiful, pathetic eyes, and they would swim with love and happiness, while he murmured, "Adored Chérisette!"

The next day—Saturday—she never left him. They played games together, and puzzles. The nurse was kind, but of a thickness of understanding, like all the rest, he said, and, with his sister there, he could dispense with her services for the moment. He wished, when it grew dusk and they were to have their tea, to play his violin to only her, in the firelight; and there he drew forth divine sounds for more than an hour, tearing at Zara's heart-strings with the exquisite notes until her eyes grew wet. And at last he began something that she did not know, and the weird, little figure moved as in a dance in the firelight, while he played this new air as one inspired, and then stopped suddenly with a crash of joyous chords.

"It is *Maman* who has taught me that!" he whispered. "When I was ill she came often and sang it to me, and when they would give me back my violin I found it at once, and now I am so happy. It talks of the butterflies in the woods, which are where she lives, and there is a little white one which flies up beside her with her radiant blue wings. And she has promised me that the music will take me to her, quite soon. Oh, Chérisette!"

"No, no," said Zara faintly. "I cannot spare you, darling. I shall have a beautiful garden of my own next summer, and you must come and stay with me, Mirko mio, and chase real butterflies with a golden net."

And this thought enchanted the child. He must hear all about his sister's garden. By chance there was an old number of *Country Life* lying on the table, and, the nurse bringing in the tea at the moment, they turned on the electric light and looked at the pictures; and by the strangest coincidence, when they came to the weekly series of those beautiful houses she read at the beginning of the article, "Wrayth—the property of Lord Tancred of Wrayth."

"See, Mirko," she said in a half voice; "our garden will look exactly like this."

And the child examined every picture with intense interest. One of a statue of Pan and his pipe, making the center of a star in the Italian parterre, pleased him most.

"For see, Chérisette, he, too, is not shaped as other people are," he whispered with delight. "Look! And he plays music, also! When you walk there, and I am with *Maman*, you must remember that this is me!"

It was with deep grief and foreboding that Zara left him, on Monday morning, in spite of the doctor's assurance that he was indeed on the turn to get quite well—well of this sharp attack—whether he would ever grow to be a man was always a doubt but there was no present anxiety—she could be happy on that score. And with this she was obliged to rest content.

But all the way back in the train she saw the picture of the Italian parterre at Wrayth with the statue of Pan, in the center of the star, playing his pipes.

CHAPTER XVI

The second wedding day of Zara Shulski dawned with a glorious sun. One of those autumn mornings that seem like a return to the spring—so fresh and pure the air. She had not seen her bridegroom since she got back from Bournemouth, nor any of the family; she had said to her uncle that she could not bear it.

"I am at the end of my forces, Uncle Francis. You are so clever—you can invent some good excuse. If I must see Lord Tancred I cannot answer for what I may do."

And the financier had realized that this was the truth. The strings of her soul were strained to breaking point, and he let her pass the whole day of Tuesday in peace.

She signed numbers of legal documents concerning her marriage settlements, without the slightest interest; and then her uncle handed her one which he said she was to read with care. It set forth in the wearisome language of the law the provision for Mirko's life, "in consideration of a certain agreement" come to between her uncle and herself. But should the boy Mirko return at any time to the man Sykypri, his father, or should she, Zara, from the moneys settled upon herself give sums to this man Sykypri the transaction between herself and her uncle regarding the boy's fortune would be null and void. This was the document's sense.

Zara read it over but the legal terms were difficult for her. "If it means exactly what we agreed upon, Uncle Francis, I will sign it," she said, "that is—that Mirko shall be cared for and have plenty of money for life."

And Francis Markrute replied,

"That is what is meant."

And then she had gone to her room, and spent the night before her wedding alone. She had steadily read one of her favorite books: she could not permit herself for a moment to think.
There was a man going to be hanged on the morrow, she had seen in the papers; and she wondered if, this last night in his cell, the condemned wretch was numb, or was he feeling at bay, like herself?
Then, at last she opened the window and glanced out on the moon. It was there above her, over the Park, so she turned out the lights, and, putting her furs around her, she sat for a while and gazed above the treetops, while she repeated her prayers.
And Mimo saw her, as he stood in the shadow on the pavement at the other side of Park Lane. He had come there in his sentimental way, to give her his blessing, and had been standing looking up for some time. It seemed to him a good omen for dear Chérisette's happiness, that she should have opened the window and looked out on the night.
It was quite early—only about half-past ten—and Tristram, after a banquet with his bachelor friends on the Monday night, had devoted this, his last evening, to his mother, and had dined quietly with her alone.
He felt extremely moved, and excited, too, when he left. She had talked to him so tenderly—the proud mother who so seldom unbent. How marriage was a beautiful but serious thing, and he must love and try to understand his wife—and then she spoke of her own great love for him, and her pride in their noble name and descent.
"And I will pray to God that you have strong, beautiful children, Tristram, so that there may in years to come be no lack of the Tancreds of Wrayth."
When he got outside in the street the moonlight flooded the road, so he sent his motor away and decided to walk. He wanted breathing space, he wanted to think, and he turned down into Curzon Street and from, thence across Great Stanhope Street and into the Park.
And to-morrow night, at this time, the beautiful Zara would be his! and they would be dining alone together at Dover, and surely she would not be so icily cold; surely—surely he could get her to melt.
And then further visions came to him, and he walked very fast; and presently he found himself opposite his lady's house.
An impulse just to see her window overcame him, and he crossed the road and went out of the gate. And there on the pavement he saw Mimo, also with face turned, gazing up.
And in a flash he thought he recognized that this was the man he had seen that day in Whitehall, when he was in his motor car, going very fast.
A mad rage of jealousy and suspicion rushed through him. Every devil whispered, "Here is a plot. You know nothing of the woman whom to-morrow you are blindly going to make your wife. Who is this man? What is his connection with her? A lover's—of course. No one but a lover would gaze up at a window on a moonlight night."
And it was at this moment that Zara opened the window and, for a second, both men saw her slender, rounded figure standing out sharply against the ground of the room. Then she turned, and put out the light.
A murderous passion of rage filled Lord Tancred's heart.
He looked at Mimo and saw that the man's lips were muttering a prayer, and that he had drawn a little silver crucifix from his coat pocket, and, also, that he was unconscious of any surroundings, for his face was rapt; and he stepped close to him and heard him murmur, in his well-pronounced English,
"Mary, Mother of God, pray for her, and bring her happiness!"
And his common sense reassured him somewhat. If the man were a lover, he could not pray so, on this, the night before her wedding to another. It was not in human, male nature, he felt, to do such an unselfish thing as that.
Then Mimo raised his soft felt hat in his rather dramatic way to the window, and walked up the street.
And Tristram, a prey to all sorts of conflicting emotions, went back into the Park.

It seemed to Francis Markrute that more than half the nobility of England had assembled in St. George's, Hanover Square, next day, as, with the beautiful bride on his arm, he walked up the church.
She wore a gown of dead white velvet, and her face looked the same shade, under the shadow of a wonderful picture creation, of black velvet and feathers, in the way of a hat.
The only jewels she had on were the magnificent pearls which were her uncle's gift. There was no color about her except in her red burnished hair and her red, curved mouth.
And the whole company thrilled as she came up the aisle. She looked like the Princess in a fairy tale—but just come to life.
The organ stopped playing, and now, as in a dream she knew that she was kneeling beside Tristram and that the Bishop had joined their hands.
She repeated the vows mechanically, in a low, quiet voice. All the sense of it that came to her brain was Tristram's firm utterance, "I, Tristram Lorrimer Guiscard, take thee, Zara Elinka, to be my wedded wife."
And so, at last, the ceremony was over, and Lord and Lady Tancred walked into the vestry to sign their names. And as Zara slipped her hand from the arm of her newly-made husband he bent down his tall head and kissed her lips; and, fortunately, the train of coming relations and friends were behind them, as yet, and the Bishops were looking elsewhere, or they would have been startled to observe the bride shiver, and to have seen the expression of passionate resentment which crept into her face. But the bridegroom saw it, and it stabbed his heart.
Then it seemed that a number of people kissed her: his mother and sisters, and Lady Ethelrida, and, lastly, the Duke.
"I am claiming my privilege as an old man," this latter said gayly, "and I welcome you to all our hearts, my beautiful niece."
And Zara had answered, but had hardly been able to give even a mechanical smile.

And when they got into the smart, new motor, after passing through the admiring crowds, she had shrunk into her corner, and half closed her eyes. And Tristram, intensely moved and strained with the excitement of it all, had not known what to think.

But pride made his bride play her part when they reached her uncle's house.

She stood with her bridegroom, and bowed graciously to the countless, congratulatory friends of his, who passed and shook hands. And, when soon after they had entered Lady Tancred arrived with Cyril and the girls, she had even smiled sweetly for one moment, when that gallant youth had stood on tiptoe and given her a hearty kiss! He was very small for his age, and full of superb self-possession.

"I think you are a stunner, Zara," he said. "Two of our fellows, cousins of mine, who were in church with me, congratulated me awfully. And now I hope you're soon going to cut the cake?"

And Tristram wondered why her mutinous mouth had quivered and her eyes become full of mist. She was thinking of her own little brother, far away, who did not even know that there would be any cake.

And so, eventually, they had passed through the shower of rice and slippers and were at last alone in the motorcar again; and once more she shrank into her corner and did not speak, and he waited patiently until they should be in the train.

But once there, in the reserved saloon, when the obsequious guard had finally shut the door from waving friends and last hand shakes, and they slowly steamed out of the station, he came over and sat down beside her and tenderly took her little gray-gloved hand.

But she drew it away from him, and moved further off, before he could even speak.

"Zara!" he said pleadingly.

Then she looked intensely fierce.

"Can you not let me be quiet for a moment?" she hissed. "I am tired out."

And he saw that she was trembling, and, though he was very much in love and maddeningly exasperated with everything, he let her rest, and even settled her cushion for her, silently, and took a paper and sat in an armchair near, and pretended to read.

And Zara stared out of the window, her heart beating in her throat. For she knew this was only a delay because, as her uncle had once said, the English nobility as a race were great gentlemen—and this one in particular—and because of that he would not be likely to make a scene in the train; but they would arrive at the hotel presently, and there was dinner to be got through, alone with him, and then—the afterwards. And as she thought of this her very lips grew white.

The hideous, hideous hatefulness of men! Visions of moments of her first wedding journey with Ladislaus came back to her. He had not shown her any consideration for five minutes in his life.

Everything in her nature was up in arms. She could not be just; with her belief in his baseness it seemed to her that here was this man—her husband—whom she had seen but four times in her life, and he was not content with the honest bargain which he perfectly understood; not content with her fortune and her willingness to adorn his house, but he must perforce allow his revolting senses to be aroused, he must desire to caress her, just because she was a woman—and fair—and the law would give him the right because she was his wife.

But she would not submit to it! She would find some way out.

As yet she had not even noticed Tristram's charm, that something which drew all other women to him but had not yet appealed to her. She saw on the rare occasions in which she had looked at him that he was very handsome—but so had been Ladislaus, and so was Mimo; and all men were selfish or brutes.

She was half English herself, of course, and that part of her—the calm, common sense of the nation, would assert itself presently; but for the time, everything was too strained through her resentment at fate.

And Tristram watched her from behind his *Evening Standard*, and was unpleasantly thrilled with the passionate hate and resentment and all the varying; storms of feeling which convulsed her beautiful face.

He was extremely sensitive, in spite of his daring *insouciance* and his pride. It would be perfectly impossible to even address her again while she was in this state.

And so this splendid young bride and bridegroom, not understanding each other in the least, sat silent and constrained, when they should have been in each other's arms; and presently, still in the same moods, they came to Dover, and so to the Lord Warden Hotel.

Here the valet and maid had already arrived, and the sitting-room was full of flowers, and everything was ready for dinner and the night.

"I suppose we dine at eight?" said Zara haughtily, and, hardly waiting for an answer, she went into the room beyond and shut the door.

Here she rang for her maid and asked her to remove her hat.

"A hateful, heavy thing," she said, "and there is a whole hour fortunately, before dinner, Henriette, and I want a lovely bath; and then you can brush my hair, and it will be a rest."

The French maid, full of sympathy and excitement, wondered, while she turned on the taps, how *Miladi* should look so disdainful and calm.

"*Mon Dieu!* if *Milor* was my Raoul! I would be far otherwise," she thought to herself, as she poured in the scent.

At a quarter to the hour of dinner she was still silently brushing her mistress's long, splendid, red hair, while Zara stared into the glass in front of her, with sightless eyes and face set. She was back in Bournemouth, and listening to "*Maman's* air." It haunted her and rang in her head; and yet, underneath, a wild excitement coursed in her blood.

A knock then came to the door, and when Henrietta answered it Tristram passed her by and stepped into his lady's room.

Zara turned round like a startled fawn, and then her expression changed to one of anger and hauteur.

He was already dressed for dinner, and held a great bunch of gardenias in his hand. He stopped abruptly when he caught sight of the exquisite picture she made, and he drew in his breath. He had not known hair could be so long; he had not realized she was so beautiful. And she was his wife!

"Darling!" he gasped, oblivious of even the maid, who had the discretion to retire quickly to the bathroom beyond. "Darling, how beautiful you are! You drive me perfectly mad."

Zara held on to the dressing-table and almost crouched, like a panther ready to spring.

"How dare you come into my room like this! Go!" she said.

It was as if she had struck him. He drew back, and flung the flowers down into the grate.

"I only came to tell you dinner was nearly ready," he said haughtily, "and to bring you those. But I will await you in the sitting-room, when you are dressed."

And he turned round and left through the door by which he had come.

And Zara called her maid rather sharply, and had her hair plaited and done, and got quickly into her dress. And when she was ready she went slowly into the sitting-room.

She found Tristram leaning upon the mantelpiece, glaring moodily into the flames. He had stood thus for ten minutes, coming to a decision in his mind.

He had been very angry just now, and he thought was justified; but he knew he was passionately in love, as he had never dreamed nor imagined he could be in the whole of his life.

Should he tell her at once about it? and implore her not to be so cold and hard? But no, that would be degrading. After all, he had already shown her a proof of the most reckless devotion, in asking to marry her, after having seen her only once! And she, what had her reasons been? They were forcible enough or she would not have consented to her uncle's wishes before they had even ever met; and he recalled, when he had asked her only on Thursday last if she would wish to be released, that she had said firmly that she wished the marriage to take place. Surely she must know that no man with any spirit would put up with such treatment as this—to be spoken to as though he had been an impudent stranger bursting into her room!

Then his tempestuous thoughts went back to Mimo, that foreign man whom he had seen under her window. What if, after all, he was her lover and that accounted for the reason she resented his—Tristram's—desire to caress?

And all the proud, obstinate fighting blood of the Guiscards got up in him. He would not be made a cat's-paw. If she exasperated him further he would forget about being a gentleman, and act as a savage man, and seize her in his arms and punish her for her haughtiness!

So it was his blue eyes which were blazing with resentment this time, and not her pools of ink.

Thus they sat down to dinner in silence—much to the waiters' surprise and disgust.

Zara felt almost glad her husband looked angry. He would then of his own accord leave her in peace.

As the soup and fish came and went they exchanged no word, and then that breeding that they both had made them realize the situation was impossible, and they said some ordinary things while the waiters were in the room.

The table was a small round one with the two places set at right angles, and very close.

It was the first occasion upon which Zara had ever been so near Tristram, and every time she looked up she was obliged to see his face. She could not help owning to herself, that he was extraordinarily distinguished looking, and that there were strong, noble lines in his whole shape.

At the end of their repast, for different reasons, neither of the two felt calm. Tristram's anger had died down, likewise his suspicions; after a moment's thought the sane point of view always presented itself to his brain. No, whatever her reasons were for her disdain of him, having another lover was not the cause. And then he grew intoxicated again with her beauty and grace.

She was a terrible temptation to him; she would have been so to any normal man—and they were dining together—and she was his very own!

The waiters, with their cough of warning at the door, brought coffee and liqueurs, and then bodily removed the dinner table, and shut the doors.

And now Zara knew she was practically alone with her lord for the night.

He walked about the room—he did not drink any coffee, nor even a Chartreuse—and she stood perfectly still. Then he came back to her, and suddenly clasped her in his arms, and passionately kissed her mouth.

"Zara!" he murmured hoarsely. "Good God! do you think I am a stone! I tell you I love you—madly. Are you not going to be kind to me and really be my wife?"

Then he saw a look in her eyes that turned him to ice.

"Animal!" she hissed, and hit him across the face.

And as he let her fall from him she drew back panting, and deadly white; while he, mad with rage at the blow, stood with flaming blue eyes, and teeth clenched.

"Animal!" again she hissed, and then her words poured forth in a torrent of hate. "Is it not enough that you were willing to sell yourself for my uncle's money—that you were willing to take as a bargain—a woman whom you had never even seen, without letting your revolting passions exhibit themselves like this? And you dare to tell me you love me! What do such as you know of love? Love is a true and a pure and a beautiful thing, not to be sullied like this. It must come from devotion and knowledge. What sort of a vile passion is it which makes a man feel as you do for me? Only that I am a woman. Love! It is no love—it is a question of sense. Any other would do, provided she were as fair. Remember, my lord! I am not your mistress, and I will not stand any of this! Leave me. I hate you, animal that you are!"

He stiffened and grew rigid with every word that she said, and when she had finished he was as deadly pale as she herself.

"Say not one syllable more to me, Zara!" he commanded. "You will have no cause to reprove me for loving you again. And remember this: things shall be as you wish between us. We will each live our lives and play the game. But before I ask you to be my wife again you can go down upon your knees. Do you hear me? Good night."

And without a word further he strode from the room.

CHAPTER XVII

The moon was shining brightly and a fresh breeze had risen when Tristram left the hotel and walked rapidly towards the pier. He was mad with rage and indignation from his bride's cruel taunts. The knowledge of their injustice did not comfort him, and, though he knew he was innocent of any desire to have made a bargain, and had taken her simply for her beautiful self, still, the accusation hurt and angered his pride. How dared she! How dared her uncle have allowed her to think such things! A Tancred to stoop so low! He clenched his hands and his whole frame shook.

And then as he gazed down into the moonlit waves her last words came back with a fresh lashing sting. "Leave me, I hate you, animal that you are!" An animal, forsooth! And this is how she had looked at his love!

And then a cold feeling came over him—he was so very just—and he questioned himself. Was it true? Had it, indeed, been only that? Had he, indeed, been unbalanced and intoxicated merely from the desire of her exquisite body? Had there been nothing beyond? Were men really brutes?—And here he walked up and down very fast. What did it all mean? What did life mean? What was the truth of this thing, called love?

And so he strode for hours, reasoning things out. But he knew that for his nature there could be no love without desire—and no desire without love. And then his conversation with Francis Markrute came back to him, the day they had lunched in the city, when the financier had given his views about women.

Yes, they were right, those views. A woman, to be dangerous, must appeal to both the body and brain of a man. If his feeling for Zara were only for the body then it was true that it was only lust.

But it was *not* true; and he thought of all his dreams of her at Wrayth, of the pictures he had drawn of their future life together, of the tenderness with which he had longed for this night.

And then his anger died down and was replaced by a passionate grief.

His dream lay in ruins, and there was nothing to look forward to but a blank, soulless life. It did not seem to him then, in the cold moonlight, that things could ever come right. He could not for his pride's sake condescend to any further explanation with her. He would not stoop to defend himself; she must think what she chose, until she should of herself find out the truth.

And then his level mind turned and tried to see her point of view. He must not be unjust. And he realized that if she thought such base things of him she had been more or less right. But, even so, there was some mystery beyond all this—some cruel and oppressing dark shadow in her life.

And his thoughts went back to the night they had first met, and he remembered then that her eyes had been full of hate—resentment and hate—as though he, personally, had caused her some injury.

Francis Markrute was so very clever: what plan had he had in his head? By what scorpion whip had he perhaps forced her to consent to his wishes and become his—Tristram's—wife? And once more the disturbing remembrance of Mimo returned, so that, when at last dawn came and he went back to the hotel, tired out in body and soul, it would not let him rest in his bed. His bed—in the next room his wife!

But one clear decision he had come to. He would treat her with cold courtesy, and they would play the game. To part now, in a dramatic manner, the next day after the wedding, was not in his sense of the fitness of things, was not what was suitable or seemly for the Tancred name.

And when he had left her Zara had stood quite still. Some not understood astonishment caused all her passion to die down. For all the pitifully cruel experiences of her life she was still very young—young and ignorant of any but the vilest of men. Hitherto she had felt when they were kind that it was for some gain, and if a woman relented a second she would be sure to be trapped. For her self-respect and her soul's sake she must go armed at all points. And after her hurling at him all her scorn, instead of her husband turning round and perhaps beating her (as, certainly, Ladislaus would have done), he had answered with dignity and gone out of the room.

And she remembered her father's cold mien. Perhaps there was something else in the English—some other finer quality which she did not yet understand.

The poor, beautiful creature was like some ill-treated animal ready to bite to defend itself at the sight of a man.

It spoke highly for the strength and nobility of her character that, whereas another and weaker woman would have become degraded by the sorrows of such a life, she had remained pure as the snow, and as cold. Her strong will and her pride had kept completely in check every voluptuous instinct which must certainly have always lain dormant in her. Every emotion towards man was frozen to ice.

There are some complete natures which only respond to the highest touch; when the body and soul are evenly balanced they know all that is divine of human love. It is those warped in either of the component parts who bring sorrow—and lust.

The perfect woman gives willingly of herself, body and soul, to the *one man* she loves.

But of all these things Zara was ignorant. She only knew she was exhausted, and she crept wearily to bed.

Thus neither bride nor bridegroom, on this their wedding night, knew peace or rest.

They met next day for a late breakfast. They were to go to Paris by the one o'clock boat. They were both very quiet and pale. Zara had gone into the sitting-room first, and was standing looking out on the sea when her husband came into the room, and she did not turn round, until he said "Good morning," coldly, and she realized it was he.

Some strange quiver passed over her at the sound of his voice.

"Breakfast should be ready," he went on calmly. "I ordered it for eleven o'clock. I told your maid to tell you so. I hope that gave you time to dress."

"Yes, thank you," was all she said; and he rang the bell and opened the papers, which the waiters had piled on the table, knowing the delight of young bridal pairs to see news of themselves!

And as Zara glanced at her lord's handsome face she saw a cynical, disdainful smile creep over it, at something he read.

And she guessed it was the account of their wedding; and she, too, took up another paper and looked at the headings.

Yes, there was a flaming description of it all. And as she finished the long paragraphs she raised her head suddenly and their eyes met. And Tristram allowed himself to laugh—bitterly, it was true, but still to laugh.

The lingering fear of the ways of men was still in Zara's heart and not altogether gone; she was not yet quite free from the suspicion that he still might trap her if she unbent. So she frowned slightly and then looked down at the paper again; and the waiters brought in breakfast at that moment and nothing was said.

They did not seem to have much appetite, nor to care what they ate, but, the coffee being in front of her, politeness made Zara ask what sort her husband took, and when he answered—none at all—he wanted tea—she was relieved, and let him pour it out at the side-table himself.

"The wind has got up fiercely, and it will be quite rough," he said presently. "Do you mind the sea?"

And she answered, "No, not a bit."

Then they both continued reading the papers until all pretense of breakfast was over; and he rose, and, asking if she would be ready at about half-past twelve, to go on board, so as to avoid the crowd from the London train, he went quietly out of the room, and from the windows she afterwards saw him taking a walk on the pier.

And for some unexplained psychological reason, although she had now apparently obtained exactly the terms she had decided were the only possible ones on which to live with him, she experienced no sense of satisfaction or peace!

No pair could have looked more adorably attractive and interesting than Lord and Lady Tancred did as they went to their private cabin on the boat an admiring group of Dover young ladies thought, watching from the raised part above where the steamer starts. Every one concerned knew that this thrilling bride and bridegroom would be crossing, and the usual number of the daily spectators was greatly increased.

"What wonderful chinchilla!" "What lovely hair!" and "Oh! isn't he just too splendid!" they said. And the maid and the valet, carrying the jewel case, dressing bags, cushion and sable rug, followed, to the young ladies' extra delight.

The *apanages* of a great position, when augmented by the romance of a wedding journey, are dear to the female heart.

They had the large cabin on the upper deck of the *Queen*, and it was noticed that until the London train could be expected to arrive the bridal pair went outside and sat where they could not be observed, with a view towards Dover Castle. But it could not be seen that they never spoke a word and that each read a book.

When it seemed advisable to avoid the crowd Tristram glanced up and said,

"I suppose we shall have to stay in that beastly cabin now, or some cad will snapshot us. Will you come along?"

And so they went.

"It is going to be really quite rough," he continued, when the door was shut. "Would you like to lie down—or what?"

"I am never the least ill, but I will try and sleep," Zara answered resignedly, as she undid her chinchilla coat.

So he settled the pillows, and she lay down, and he covered her up; and as he did so, in spite of his anger with her and all his hurt pride he had the most maddeningly strong desire to kiss her and let her rest in his arms. So he turned away brusquely and sat down at the farther end, where he opened the window to let in some air, and pulled the curtain over it, and then tried to go on with his book. But every pulse in his body was throbbing, and at last he could not control the overmastering desire to look at her.

She raised herself a little, and began taking the finely-worked, small-stoned, sapphire pins out of her hat. They had been Cyril's gift.

"Can I help you?" he said.

"It is such soft fur I thought I need not take it off to lie down," she answered coldly, "but there is something hurting in the back."

He took the thing with its lace veil from her, and the ruffled waves of her glorious hair as she lay there nearly drove him mad with the longing to caress.

How, in God's name, would they ever be able to live? He must go outside and fight with himself.

And she wondered why his face grew so stern. And when she was settled comfortably again and the boat had started he left her alone.

It was, fortunately, so rough that there were very few people about, and he went far forward and leant on the rail, and let the salt air blow into his face.

What if, in the end, this wild passion for her should conquer him and he should give in, and have to confess that her cruel words did not hinder him from loving her? It would be too ignominious. He must pull himself together and firmly suppress every emotion. He determined to see her as little as possible when they got to Paris, and when the ghastly honeymoon week, that he had been contemplating with so much excitement and joy should be over, then they would go back to England, and he would take up politics in earnest, and try and absorb himself in that.

And Zara, lying in the cabin, was unconscious of any direct current of thought; she was quite unconscious that already this beautiful young husband of hers had made some impression upon her, and that, underneath, for all her absorption in her little brother and her own affairs, she was growing conscious of his presence and that his comings and goings were things to remark about.

And, strengthened in his resolve to be true to the Tancred pride, Tristram came back to her as they got into Calais harbor.

CHAPTER XVIII

The servants at the Ritz, in Paris, so exquisitely drilled, made no apparent difference, when the bride and bridegroom arrived there about half-past seven o'clock, than if they had been an elderly brother and sister; and they were taken to the beautiful Empire suite on the Vendôme side of the first floor. Everything was perfection in the way of arrangement, and the flowers were so particularly beautiful that Zara's love for them caused her to cry out,

"Oh! the dear roses! I must just bury my face in them, first."

They had got through the railway journey very well; real, overcoming fatigue had caused them both to sleep, and in the automobile, coming to the hotel, they had exchanged a few stiff words.

"To-morrow night we can dine out at a restaurant," Tristram had said, "but to-night perhaps you are tired and would rather go to bed?"

"Thank you," said Zara. "Yes, I would." For she thought she wanted to write her letters to Mirko and tell him of her new name and place. So she put on a tea-gown, and at about half-past eight joined Tristram in the sitting-room. If they had not both been so strained their sense of humor would not have permitted them to refrain from a laugh. For here they sat in state, and, when the waiters were in the room, exchanged a few remarks. But Zara did notice that her husband never once looked at her with any directness, and he seemed coldly indifferent to anything she said.

"We shall have to stay here for the whole, boring week," he announced when at last coffee was on the table and they were alone. "There are certain obligations one's position obliges one to conform to. You understand, I expect. I will try to make the time as easy to bear for you as I can. Will you tell me what theaters you have not already seen? We can go somewhere every night, and in the daytime you have perhaps shopping to do; and—I know Paris quite well. I can amuse myself."

Zara did not feel enthusiastically grateful, but she said, "Thank you," in a quiet voice, and Tristram, rang the bell and asked for the list of the places of amusement, and in the most stiff, self-contained manner he chose, with her, a different one for every night.

Then he lit a cigar deliberately, and walked towards the door.

"Good-night, Milady," he said nonchalantly, and then went out.

And Zara sat still by the table and unconsciously pulled the petals off an unoffending rose; and when she realized what she had done she was aghast!

It was not until about five o'clock the next day that he came into the sitting-room again.

Milor had gone to the races, and had left a note for *Miladi* in the morning, the maid had said.

And Zara, as she lay back on her pillows, had opened it with a strange thrill.

"You won't be troubled with me to-day," she read. "I am going out with some old friends to Maisons Liafitte. I have said you want to rest from the journey, as one has to say something. I have arranged for us to dine at the Café de Paris at 7:30, and go to the Gymnâse. Tell Higgins, my valet, if you change the plan." And the note was not even signed!

Well, it appeared she had nothing further to fear from him; she could breathe much relieved. And now for her day of quiet rest.

But when she had had her lonely lunch and her letters to her uncle and Mirko were written, she found herself drumming aimlessly on the window panes, and wondering if she would go out.

She had no friends in Paris whom she wanted to see. Her life there with her family had been entirely devoted to them alone. But it was a fine day and there is always something to do in Paris—though what then, particularly, she had not decided; perhaps she would go to the Louvre.

And then she sank down into the big sofa, opposite the blazing wood fire, and gradually fell fast asleep. She slept, with unbroken deepness, until late in the afternoon, and was, in fact, still asleep there when Tristram came in.

He did not see her at first; the lights were not on and it was almost dark in the streets. The fire, too, had burnt low. He came forward, and then went back again and switched on the lamps; and, with the blaze, Zara sat up and rubbed her eyes. One great plait of her hair had become loosened and fell at the side of her head, and she looked like a rosy, sleepy child.

"I did not see you!" Tristram gasped, and, realizing her adorable attractions, he turned to the fire and vigorously began making it up.

Then, as he felt he could not trust himself for another second, he rang the bell and ordered some tea to be brought, while he went to his room to leave his overcoat. And when he thought the excuse of the repast would be there, he went back.

Zara felt nothing in particular. Even yet she was rather on the defensive, looking out for every possible attack.

So they both sat down quietly, and for a few moments neither spoke.

She had put up her hair during his absence, and now looked wide-awake and quite neat.

"I had a most unlucky day," he said—for something to say. "I could not back a single winner. On the whole I think I am bored with racing."

"It has always seemed boring to me," she said. "If it were to try the mettle of a horse one had bred I could understand that; or to ride it oneself and get the better of an adversary: but just with sharp practices—and for money! It seems so common a thing, I never could take an interest in that."

"Does anything interest you?" he hazarded, and then he felt sorry he had shown enough interest to ask.

"Yes," she said slowly, "but perhaps not many games. My life has always been too ordered by the games of others, to take to them myself." And then she stopped abruptly. She could not suppose her life interested him much.

But, on the contrary, he was intensely interested, if she had known.

He felt inclined to tell her so, and that the whole of the present situation was ridiculous, and that he wanted to know her innermost thoughts. He was beginning to examine her all critically, and to take in every point. Beyond his passionate admiration for her beauty there was something more to analyze.

What was the subtle something of mystery and charm? Why could she not unbend and tell him the meaning in those fathomless, dark eyes?—What could they look like, if filled with love and tenderness? Ah!

And if he had done as he felt inclined at the moment the ice might have been broken, and at the end of the week they would probably have been in each other's arms. But fate ordered otherwise, and an incident that night, at dinner, caused a fresh storm.

Zara was looking so absolutely beautiful in her lovely new clothes that it was not in the nature of gallant foreigners to allow her to dine unmolested by their stares, and although the tête-à-tête dinner was quite early at the Café de Paris, there happened to be a large party of men next to them and Zara found herself seated in close proximity to a nondescript Count, whom she recognized as one of her late husband's friends. Every one who knows the Café de Paris can realize how this happened. The long velvet seats without divisions and the small tables in front make, when the place is full, the whole side look as if it were one big group. Lord Tancred was quite accustomed to it; he knew Paris well as he had told her, so he ought to have been prepared for what could happen, but he was not.

Perhaps he was not on the alert, because he had never before been there with a woman he loved.

Zara's neighbor was a great, big, fierce-looking creature from some wild quarter of the South, and was perhaps also just a little drunk. She knew a good deal of their language, but, taking for granted that this Englishman and his lovely lady would be quite ignorant of what they said, the party of men were most unreserved in their remarks.

Her neighbor looked at her devouringly, once or twice, when he saw Tristram could not observe him, and then began to murmur immensely *entreprenant* love sentences in his own tongue, as he played with his bread. She knew he had recognized her. And Tristram wondered why his lady's little nostrils should begin to quiver and her eyes to flash.

She was remembering like scenes in the days of Ladislaus, and how he used to grow wild with jealousy, in the beginning when he took her out, and once had dragged her back upstairs by her hair, and flung her into bed. It was always her fault when men looked at her, he assured her. And the horror of the recollection of it all was still vivid enough.

Then Tristram gradually became greatly worried; without being aware that the man was the cause, he yet felt something was going on. He grew jealous and uneasy, and would have liked to have taken her home.

And because of the things she was angrily listening to, and because of her fear of a row, she sat there looking defiant and resentful, and spoke never a word.

And Tristram could not understand it, and he eventually became annoyed. What had he said or done to her again? It was more than he meant to stand, for no reason—to put up with such airs!

For Zara sat frowning, her mouth mutinous and her eyes black as night.

If she had told Tristram what her neighbor was saying there would at once have been a row. She knew this, and so remained in constrained silence, unconscious that her husband was thinking her rude to him, and that he was angry with her. She was so strung up with fury at the foreigner, that she answered Tristram's few remarks at random, and then abruptly rose while he was paying the bill, as if to go out. And as she did so the Count slipped a folded paper into the sleeve of her coat.

"With his English self-control and horror of a scene, he followed his wife to the door."

Tristram thought he saw something peculiar but was still in doubt, and, with his English self-control and horror of a scene, he followed his wife to the door, as she was walking rapidly ahead, and there helped her into the waiting automobile.

But as she put up her arm, in stepping in, the folded paper fell to the brightly lighted pavement and he picked it up.

He must have some explanation. He was choking with rage. There was some mystery, he was being tricked.

"Why did you not tell me you knew that fellow who sat next to you?" he said in a low, constrained voice.

"Because it would have been a lie," she said haughtily. "I have never seen him but once before in my life."

"Then what business have you to allow him to write notes to you?" Tristram demanded, too overcome with jealousy to control the anger in his tone.

She shrank back in her corner. Here it was beginning again! After all, in spite of his apparent agreement to live on the most frigid terms with her he was now acting like Ladislaus: men were all the same!

"I am not aware the creature wrote me any note," she said. "What do you mean?"

"How can you pretend like this," Tristram exclaimed furiously, "when it fell out of your sleeve? Here it is."

"Take me back to the hotel," she said with a tone of ice. "I refuse to go to the theater to be insulted. How dare you doubt my word? If there is a note you had better read it and see what it says."

So Lord Tancred picked up the speaking-tube and told the chauffeur to go back to the Ritz.

They both sat silent, palpitating with rage, and when they got there he followed her into the lift and up to the sitting-room.

He came in and shut the door and strode over beside her, and then he almost hissed,

"You are asking too much of me. I demand an explanation. Tell me yourself about it. Here is your note."

Zara took it, with infinite disdain, and, touching it as though it were some noisome reptile, she opened it and read aloud,

"Beautiful Comtesse, when can I see you again?"

"The vile wretch!" she said contemptuously. "That is how men insult women!" And she looked up passionately at Tristram. "You are all the same."

"I have not insulted you," he flashed. "It is perfectly natural that I should be angry at such a scene, and if this brute is to be found again to-night he shall know that I will not permit him to write insolent notes to my wife."

She flung the hateful piece of paper into the fire and turned towards her room.

"I beg you to do nothing further about the matter," she said. "This loathsome man was half drunk. It is quite unnecessary to follow it up; it will only make a scandal, and do no good. But you can understand another thing. I will not have my word doubted, nor be treated as an offending domestic—as you have treated me to-night." And without further words she went into her room.

Tristram, left alone, paced up and down; he was wild with rage, furious with her, with himself, and with the man. With her because he had told her once, before the wedding, that when they came to cross swords there would be no doubt as to who would be master! and in the three encounters which already their wills had had she had each time come off the conqueror! He was furious with himself, that he had not leaned forward at dinner to see the man hand the note, and he was frenziedly furious with the stranger, that he had dared to turn his insolent eyes upon his wife.

He would go back to the Café de Paris, and, if the man was there, call him to account, and if not, perhaps he could obtain his name. So out he went.

But the waiters vowed they knew nothing of the gentleman; the whole party had been perfect strangers, and they had no idea as to where they had gone on. So this enraged young Englishman spent the third night of his honeymoon in a hunt round the haunts of Paris, but with no success; and at about six o'clock in the morning came back baffled but still raging, and thoroughly wearied out.

And all this while his bride could not sleep, and in spite of her anger was a prey to haunting fears. What if the two had met and there had been bloodshed! A completely possible case! And several times in the night she got out of her bed and went and listened at the communicating doors; but there was no sound of Tristram, and about five o'clock, worn out with the anxiety and injustice of everything, she fell into a restless doze, only to wake again at seven, with a lead weight at her heart. She could not bear it any longer! She must know for certain if he had come in! She slipped on her dressing-gown, and noiselessly stole to the door, and with the greatest caution unlocked it, and, turning the handle, peeped in.

Yes, there he was, sound asleep! His window was wide open, with the curtains pushed back, so the daylight streamed in on his face. He had been too tired to care.

Zara turned round quickly to reenter her room, but in her terror of being discovered she caught the trimming of her dressing-gown on the handle of the door and without her being aware of it a small bunch of worked ribbon roses fell off.

Then she got back into bed, relieved in mind as to him but absolutely quaking at what she had done and at the impossibly embarrassing position she would have placed herself in, if he had awakened and known that she had come!

And the first thing Tristram saw, when some hours later he was aroused by the pouring in of the sun, was the little torn bunch of silk roses lying close to her door.

CHAPTER XIX

He sprang from bed and picked them up. What could they possibly mean? They were her roses, certainly—he remembered she wore the dressing-gown that first evening at Dover, when he had gone to her to give her the gardenias. And they certainly had not been there when at six o'clock he had come in. He would in that case have seen them against the pale carpet.

For one exquisite moment he thought they were a message and then he noticed the ribbon had been wrenched off and was torn.

No, they were no conscious message, but they did mean that she had been in his room while he slept.

Why had she done this thing? He knew she hated him—it was no acting—and she had left him the night' before even unusually incensed. What possible reason could she have, then, for coming into his room? He felt wild with excitement. He would see if, as usual, the door between them was locked. He tried it gently. Yes, it was.

And Zara heard him from her side, and stiffened in her bed with all the expression of a fierce wolfhound putting its hackles up.

Yes, the danger of the ways of men was not over! If she had not unconsciously remembered to lock the door when she had returned from her terrifying adventure he would have come in!

So these two thrilled with different emotions and trembled, and there was the locked harrier between them. And then Tristram rang for his valet and ordered his bath. He would dress quickly, and ask casually if she would breakfast in the sitting-room. It was so late, almost eleven, and they could have it at twelve upstairs—not in the restaurant as he had yesterday intended. He must find out about the roses; he could not endure to pass the whole day in wonder and doubt.

And Zara, too, started dressing. It was better under the circumstances to be armed at all points, and she felt safer and calmer with Henriette in the room.

So a few minutes before twelve they met in the sitting-room.

Her whole expression was on the defensive: he saw that at once.

The waiters would be coming in with the breakfast soon. Would there be time to talk to her, or had he better postpone it until they were certain to be alone? He decided upon this latter course, and just said a cold "Good morning," and turned to the *New York Herald* and looked at the news.

Zara felt more reassured.

So they presently sat down to their breakfast, each ready to play the game.

They spoke of the theaters—the one they had arranged to go to this Saturday night was causing all Paris to laugh.

"It will be a jolly good thing to laugh," Tristram said—and Zara agreed.

He made no allusion to the events of the night before, and she hardly spoke at all. And at last the repast was over, and the waiters had left the room.

Tristram got up, after his coffee and liqueur, but he lit no cigar; he went to one of the great windows which look out on the Colonne Vendôme, and then he came back. Zara was sitting upon the heliotrope Empire sofa and had picked up the paper again.

He stood before her, with an expression upon his face which ought to have melted any woman.

"Zara," he said softly, "I want you to tell me, why did you come into my room?"

Her great eyes filled with startled horror and surprise, and her white cheeks grew bright pink with an exquisite flush.

"I?"—and she clenched her hands. How did he know? Had he seen her, then? But he evidently did know, and there was no use to lie. "I was so—frightened—that—"

Tristram took a step nearer and sat down by her side. He saw the confession was being dragged from her, and he gloried in it and would not help her out.

She moved further from him, then, with grudging reluctance, she continued,

"There can be such unpleasant quarrels with those horrible men. It—was so very late—I—I—wished to be sure that you had come safely in."

Then she looked down, and the rose died out of her face, leaving it very white.

And if Tristram's pride in the decision he had come to, on the fatal wedding night, that she must make the first advances before he would again unbend, had not held him, he would certainly have risked everything and clasped her in his arms. As it was, he resisted the intense temptation to do so, and made himself calm, while he answered,

"It mattered to you, then, in some way, that I should not come to harm?"

He was still sitting on the sofa near her, and that magnetic essence which is in propinquity appealed to her; ignorant of all such emotions as she was she only knew something had suddenly made her feel nervous, and that her heart was thumping in her side.

"Yes, of course it mattered," she faltered, and then went on coldly, as he gave a glad start; "scandals are so unpleasant—scenes and all those things are so revolting. I had to endure many of them in my former life."

Oh! so that was it! Just for fear of a scandal and because she had known disagreeable things! Not a jot of feeling for himself! And Tristram got up quickly and walked to the fireplace. He was cut to the heart.

The case was utterly hopeless, he felt. He was frozen and stung each time he even allowed himself to be human and hope for anything. But he was a strong man, and this should be the end of it. He would not be tortured again.

He took the little bunch of flowers out of his pocket and handed it to her quietly, while his face was full of pain.

"Here is the proof you left me of your kind interest," he told her. "Perhaps your maid will miss it and wish to sew it on." And then without another word he went out of the room.

Zara, left alone, sat staring into the fire. What did all this mean? She felt very unhappy, but not angry or alarmed. She did not want to hurt him. Had she been very unkind? After all, he had behaved, in comparison to Ladislaus, with wonderful self-control—and—yes, supposing he were not quite a sensual brute she had been very hard. She knew what pride meant; she had abundance herself, and she realized for the first time how she must have been stinging his.

But there were facts which could not be got over. He had married her for her uncle's money and then shown at once that her person tempted him, when it could not be anything else.

She got up and walked about the room. There was a scent of him somewhere—the scent of a fine cigar. She felt uneasy of she knew not what. Did she wish him to come back? Was she excited? Should she go out? And then, for no reason on earth, she suddenly burst into tears.

They met for dinner, and she herself had never looked or been more icy cold than Tristram was. They went down into the restaurant and there, of course, he encountered some friends dining, too, in a merry party; and he nodded gayly to them and told her casually who they were, and then went on with his dinner. His manner had lost its constraint, it was just casually indifferent. And soon they started for the theater, and it was he who drew as far away as he could, when they got into the automobile.

They had a box—and the piece had begun. It was one of those impossibly amusing Paris farces, on the borderland of all convention but so intensely comic that none could help their mirth, and Tristram shook with laughter and forgot for the time that he was a most miserable young man. And even Zara laughed. But it did not melt things between them. Tristram's feelings had been too wounded for any ordinary circumstances to cause him to relent.

"Do you care for some supper?" he said coldly when they came out. But she answered. "No," so he took her back, and as far as the lift where he left her, politely saying "Good night," and she saw him disappear towards the door, and knew he had again gone out.

And going on to the sitting-room alone, she found the English mail had come in, and there were the letters on the table, at least a dozen for Tristram, as she sorted them out—a number in women's handwriting—and but two for herself. One was from her uncle, full of agreeable congratulations subtly expressed; and the other, forwarded from Park Lane, from Mirko, as yet ignorant of her change of state, a small, funny, pathetic letter that touched her heart. He was better, and again able to go out, and in a fortnight Agatha, the little daughter of the Morleys, would be returning, and he could play with her. That might be a joy—girls were not so tiresome and did not make so much noise as boys.

Zara turned to the piano, which she had not yet opened, and sat down and comforted herself with the airs she loved; and the maid who listened, while she waited for her mistress to be undressed, turned up her eyes in wonder.

"Quel drôle de couple!" she said.

And Tristram reencountered his friends and went off with them to sup.

Her ladyship was tired, he told them, and had gone to bed. And two of the Englishwomen who knew him quite well teased him and said how beautiful his bride was and how strange-looking, and what an iceberg he must be to be able to come out to supper and leave her alone! And they wondered why he then smiled cynically.

"For," said one to the other on their way home, "the new Lady Tancred is perfectly beautiful! Fancy, Gertrude, Tristram leaving her for a minute! And did you ever see such a face? It looks anything but cold."

Zara was wide-awake when, about two, he came in. She heard him in the sitting-room and suddenly became conscious that her thoughts had been with him ever since she went to bed, and not with Mirko and his letter.

She supposed he was now reading his pile of correspondence—he had such numbers of fond friends! And then she heard him shut the door, and go round into his room; but the carpets were very thick and she heard no more.

If she could have seen what happened beyond that closed door, would it have opened her eyes, or made her happy? Who can tell?

For Higgins, with methodical tidiness, had emptied the pockets of the coat his master had worn in the day, and there on top of a letter or two and a card-case was one tiny pink rose, a wee bud that had become detached from the torn bunch.

And when Tristram saw it his heart gave a great bound. So it had stayed behind, when he had returned the others, and was there now to hurt him with remembrance of what might have been! He was unable to control the violent emotion which shook him. He went to the window and opened it wide: the moon was rather over, but still blazed in the sky. Then he bent down and passionately kissed the little bud, while a scorching mist gathered in his eyes.

CHAPTER XX

So at last the Wednesday morning came—and they could go back to England. From that Saturday night until they left Paris Tristram's manner of icy, polite indifference to his bride never changed. She had no more quaking shocks nor any fear of too much ardor! He avoided every possible moment of her society he could, and when forced to be with her seemed aloof and bored.

And the freezing manner of Zara was caused no longer by haughty self-defense but because she was unconsciously numb at heart.

Unknown, undreamed-of emotion came over her, whenever she chanced to find him close, and during his long absences her thoughts followed him—sometimes with wonderment.

Just as they were going down to start for the train on the Wednesday morning a telegram was put into her hand. It was addressed "La Baronne de Tancred," and she guessed at once this would be Mimo's idea of her name. Tristram, who was already down the steps by the concierge's desk, turned and saw her open it, with a look of intense strain. He saw that as she read her eyes widened and stared out in front of them for a moment, and that her face grew pale.

For Mimo had wired, "Mirko not quite so well." She crumpled the blue paper in her hand, and followed her husband through the bowing personnel of the hotel into the automobile. She controlled herself and was even able to give one of her rare smiles in farewell, but when they started she leaned back, and again her face went white. Tristram was moved. Whom was her telegram from? She did not tell him and he would not ask, but the feeling that there were in her life, things and interests of which he knew nothing did not please him. And this particular thing—what was it? Was it from a man? It had caused her some deep emotion—he could plainly see that. He longed to ask her but was far too proud, and their terms had grown so distant he hardly liked to express even solicitude, which, however, he did.

"I hope you have not had any bad news?"

Then she turned her eyes upon him, and he saw that she had hardly heard him; they looked blank.

"What?" she asked vaguely; and then, recollecting herself confusedly, she went on, "No—not exactly—but something about which I must think."

So he was shut out of her confidence. He felt that, and carefully avoided taking any further notice of her.

When they got to the station he suddenly perceived she was not following him as he made way for her in the crowd, but had gone over to the telegraph office by herself.

He waited and fumed. It was evidently something about which she wished no one to see what she wrote, for she could perfectly well have given the telegram to Higgins to take, who would be waiting by the saloon door.

She returned in a few moments, and she saw that Tristram's face was very stern. It did not strike her that he was jealous about the mystery of the telegram; she thought he was annoyed at her for not coming on in case they should be late, so she said hurriedly, "There is plenty of time."

"Naturally," he answered stiffly as they walked along, "but it is quite unnecessary for Lady Tancred to struggle through this rabble and take telegrams herself. Higgins could have done it when we were settled in the train."

And with unexpected meekness all she said was, "I am very sorry."

So the incident ended there—but not the uneasy impression it left.

Tristram did not even make a pretense of reading the papers when the train moved on; he sat there staring in front of him, with his handsome face shadowed by a moody frown. And any close observer who knew him would have seen that there was a change in his whole expression, since the same time the last week.

The impossible disappointment of everything! What kind of a nature could his wife have, to be so absolutely mute and unresponsive as she had been? He felt glad he had not given her the chance to snub him again. These last days he had been able to keep to his determination, and at all events did not feel himself humiliated. How long would it be before he should cease to care for her? He hoped to God—soon, because the strain of crushing his passionate desires was one which no man could stand long.

The little, mutinous face, with its alluring, velvet, white skin, her slightly full lips, all curved and red, and tempting, and anything but cold in shape, and the extraordinary magnetic attraction of her whole personality, made her a most dangerous thing; and then his thoughts turned to the vision of her hair undone that he had had on that first evening at Dover. He had said once to Francis Markrute, he remembered, that these great passions were "storybook stuff." Good God! Well, in those days he had not known.

He thought, as he returned from his honeymoon this day, that he could not be more frightfully unhappy, but he was really only beginning the anguish of the churning of his soul—if he had known.

And Zara sat in her armchair, and pretended to read; but when he glanced at her he saw that it was a farce and that her expressive eyes were again quite blank.

And finally, after the uncomfortable hours, they arrived at Calais and went to the boat.

Here Zara seemed to grow anxious again and on the alert, and, stepping forward, asked Higgins to inquire if there was a telegram for her, addressed to the ship. But there was not, and she subsided once more quietly and sat in their cabin.

Tristram did not even attempt to play the part of the returning bridegroom beyond the ordinary seeing to her comfort about which he had never failed; he left her immediately and remained for all the voyage on deck.

And when they reached Dover Zara's expectancy showed again, but it was not until they were just leaving the station that a telegram was thrust through the window and he took it from the boy, while he could not help noticing the foreign form of address. And a certainty grew in his brain that it was "that same cursed man!"

He watched her face as she read it, and noticed the look of relief as, quite unconscious of his presence, his bride absently spread the paper out. And although deliberately to try and see what was written was not what he would ever have done, his eyes caught the signature, "Mimo," before he was aware of it.

Mimo—that was the brute's name!

And what could he say or do? They were not really husband and wife, and as long as she did nothing to disgrace the Tancred honor he had no valid reason for questions or complaints.

But he burnt with suspicion, and jealousy, and pain.

Then he thought over what Francis Markrute had said the first evening, when he had agreed to the marriage. He remembered how he had not felt it would be chivalrous or honorable to ask any questions, once he had blindly gone the whole length and settled she should be his; but how Francis had gratuitously informed him that she had been an immaculate wife until a year ago, and married to an unspeakable brute.

He knew the financier very well, and knew that he was, with all his subtle cleverness, a man of spotless honor. Evidently, then, if there was anything underneath he was unaware of it. But was there anything? Even though he was angry and suspicious he realized that the bearing of his wife was not guilty or degraded. She was a magnificently proud and noble-looking creature, but perhaps even the noblest women could stoop to trick from—love! And this thought caused him to jump up suddenly—much to Zara's astonishment. And she saw the veins show on the left side of his temple as in a knot, a peculiarity, like the horseshoe of the Redgauntlets, which ran in the Tancred race.

Then he felt how foolish he was, causing himself suffering over an imaginary thing; and here this piece of white marble sat opposite him in cold silence, while his being was wrung! He suddenly understood something which he had never done before, when he read of such things in the papers—how, passionately loving, a man could yet kill the thing he loved.

And Zara, comforted by the telegram, "Much better again to-day," had leisure to return to the subject which had lately begun unconsciously to absorb her—the subject of her lord!

She wondered what made him look so stern. His nobly-cut face was as though it were carved in stone. Just from an abstract, artistic point of view, she told herself, she honestly admired him and his type. It was finer than any other race could produce and she was glad she was half English, too. The lines were so slender and yet so strong; and every bone balanced—and the look of superb health and athletic strength.

Such must have been the young Greeks who ran in the Gymnasium at Athens, she thought.

And then, suddenly, an intense quiver of unknown emotion rushed over her. And if at that moment he had clasped her and kissed her, instead of sitting there glaring into space, the rest of this story need never have been written!

But the moment passed, and she crushed whatever it was she felt of the dawning of love, and he dominated the uneasy suspicions of her fidelity; and they got out of the train at Charing Cross—after their remarkable wedding journey.

CHAPTER XXI

Francis Markrute's moral antennae upon which he prided himself informed him that all was not as it should be between this young bride and bridegroom. Zara seemed to have acquired in this short week even an extra air of regal dignity, aided by her perfect clothes; and Tristram looked stern, and less joyous and more haughty than he had done. And they were both so deadly cold, and certainly constrained! It was not one of the financier's habits ever to doubt himself or his deductions. They were based upon far too sound reasoning. No, if something had gone wrong or had not yet evolutionized it was only for the moment and need cause no philosophical *deus ex machina* any uneasiness.

For it was morally and physically impossible that such a perfectly developed pair of the genus human being could live together in the bonds of marriage, and not learn to love.

Meanwhile, it was his business as the friend and uncle of the two to be genial and make things go on greased wheels.

So he exerted himself to talk at dinner—their dinner *à trois*—. He told them all the news that had happened during the week—Was it only a week—Zara and Tristram both thought!

How there were rumors that in the coming spring there might be a general election, and that the Radicals were making fresh plots to ruin the country; but there was to be no autumn session, and, as usual, the party to which they all had the honor to belong was half asleep.

And then the two men grew deep in a political discussion, so as soon as Zara had eaten her peach she said she would leave them to their talk, and say "Good night," as she was tired out.

"Yes, my niece," said her uncle who had risen. And he did what he had not done since she was a child, he stooped and kissed her white forehead. "Yes, indeed, you must go and rest. We both want you to do us justice to-morrow, don't we, Tristram? We must have our special lady looking her best."

And she smiled a faint smile as she passed from the room.

"By George! my dear boy," the financier went on, "I don't believe I ever realized what a gorgeously beautiful creature my niece is. She is like some wonderful exotic blossom—a mass of snow and flame!"

And Tristram said with unconscious cynicism,

"Certainly snow—but where is the flame?"

Francis Markrute looked at him out of the corners of his clever eyes. She had been icy to him in Paris, then! But his was not the temperament to interfere. It was only a question of time. After all, a week was not long to grow accustomed to a perfect stranger.

Then they went back to the library, and smoked for an hour or so and continued their political chat; and at last Markrute said to his new nephew-in-law blandly,

"In a year or so, when you and Zara have a son, I will give you, my dear boy, some papers to read which will interest you as showing the mother's side of his lineage. It will be a fit balance, as far as actual blood goes, to your own."

In a year or so, when Zara should have a son!

Of all the aspects of the case, which her pride and disdain had robbed him of, this, Tristram felt, was perhaps—though it had not before presented itself to him—the most cruel. He would have no son!

He got up suddenly and threw his unfinished cigar into the grate—that old habit of his when he was moved—and he said in a voice that the financier knew was strained,

"That is awfully good of you. I shall have to have it inserted in the family tree—some day. But now I think I shall turn in. I want to have my eye rested, and be as fit as a fiddle for the shoot. I have had a tiring week."

And Francis Markrute came out with him into the passage and up to the first floor, and when they got so far they heard the notes of the *Chanson Triste* being played again from Zara's sitting-room. She had not gone to bed, then, it seemed!

"Good God!" said Tristram. "I don't know why, but I wish to heaven she would not play that tune."

And the two men looked at one another with some uneasy wonder in their eyes.

"Go on and take her to bed," the financier suggested. "Perhaps she does not like being left so long alone."

Tristram went upstairs with a bitter laugh to himself.

He did not go near the sitting-room; he went straight into the room which had been allotted to himself: and a savage sense of humiliation and impotent rage convulsed him.

The next day, the express which would stop for them at Tylling Green, the little station for Montfitchet, started at two o'clock, and the financier had given orders to have an early lunch at twelve before they left. He, himself, went off to the City for half an hour to read his letters, at ten o'clock, and was surprised when he asked Turner if Lord and Lady Tancred had break-fasted to hear that her ladyship had gone out at half-past nine o'clock and that his lordship had given orders to his valet not to disturb him, in his lordship's room—and here Turner coughed—until half-past ten.

"See that they have everything they want," his master said, and then went out. But when he was in his electric brougham, gliding eastwards, he frowned to himself.

"The proud, little minx! So she has insisted upon keeping to the business bargain up till now, has she!" he thought. "If it goes on we shall have to make her jealous. That would be an infallible remedy for her caprice."

But Zara was not concerned with such things at all for the moment. She was waiting anxiously for Mimo at their trysting-place, the mausoleum of Halicarnassus in the British Museum, and he was late. He would have the last news of Mirko. No reply had awaited her to her telegram to Mrs. Morley from Paris, and it had been too late to wire again last night. And Mrs. Morley must have got the telegram, because Mimo had got his.

Some day, she hoped—when she could grow perhaps more friendly with her husband—she would get her uncle to let her tell him about Mirko. It would make everything so much more simple as regards seeing him, and why, since the paper was all signed and nothing could be altered, should there be any mystery now? Only, her uncle had said the day before the wedding,

"I beg of you not to mention the family disgrace of your mother to your husband nor speak to him of the man Sykypri for a good long time—if you ever need."

And she had acquiesced.

"For," Francis Markrute had reasoned to himself, "if the boy dies, as Morley thinks there is every likelihood that he will, why should Tristram ever know?"

The disgrace of his adored sister always made him wince.

Mimo came at last, looking anxious and haggard, and not his debonair self. Yes, he had had a telegram that morning. He had sent one, as he was obliged to do, in her name, and hence the confusion in the answer. Mrs. Morley had replied to the Neville Street address, and Zara wondered if she knew London very well and would see how impossible such a locality would be for the Lady Tancred!

But Mirko was better—decidedly better—the attack had again been very short. So she felt reassured for the moment, and was preparing to go when she remembered that one of the things she had come for was to give Mimo some money in notes which she had prepared for him; but, knowing the poor gentleman's character, she was going to do it delicately by buying the "Apache!" For she was quite aware that just money, for him to live, now that it was not a question of the welfare of Mirko, he would never accept from her. In such unpractical, sentimental ways does breeding show itself in some weak natures!

Mimo was almost suspicious of the transaction, and she was obliged to soothe and flatter him by saying that he must surely always have understood how intensely she had admired that work; and now she was rich it would be an everlasting pleasure to her to own it for her very own. So poor Mimo *was* comforted, and they parted after a while, all arrangements having been made that the telegrams—should any more come—were to go first, addressed to her at Neville Street, so that the poor father should see them and then send them on.

And as it was now past eleven o'clock Zara returned quickly back to Park Lane and was coming in at the door just as her husband was descending the stairs.

"You are up very early, Milady," he said casually, and because of the servants in the hall she felt it would look better to follow him into the library.

Tristram was surprised at this and he longed to ask her where she had been, but she did not tell him; she just said,

"What time do we arrive at your uncle's? Is it five or six?"

"It only takes three hours. We shall be in about five. And, Zara, I want you to wear the sable coat. I think it suits you better than the chinchilla you had when we left."

A little pink came into her cheeks. This was the first time he had ever spoken of her clothes; and to hide the sudden strange emotion she felt, she said coldly.

"Yes, I intended to. I shall always hate that chinchilla coat."

And he turned away to the window, stung again by her words which she had said unconsciously. The chinchilla had been her conventional "going away" bridal finery. That was, of course, why she hated the remembrance of it.

As soon as she had said the words she felt sorry. What on earth made her so often wound him? She did not know it was part of the same instinct of self-defense which had had to make up her whole attitude towards life. Only this time it was unconsciously to hide and so defend the new emotion which was creeping into her heart.

He stayed with his back turned, looking out of the window; so, after waiting a moment, she went from the room.

At the station they found Jimmy Danvers, and a Mr. and Mrs. Harcourt with the latter's sister, Miss Opie, and several men. The rest of the party, including Emily and Mary, Jimmy told them, had gone down by the eleven o'clock train.

Both Mrs. Harcourt and her sister and, indeed, the whole company were Tristram's old and intimate friends and they were so delighted to see him, and chaffed and were gay, and Zara watched, and saw that her uncle entered into the spirit of the fun in the saloon, and only she was a stranger and out in the cold.

As for Tristram, he seemed to become a different person to the stern, constrained creature of the past week, and he sat in a corner with Mrs. Harcourt, and bent over her and chaffed and whispered in her ear, and she—Zara—was left primly in one of the armchairs, a little aloof. But such a provoking looking type of beauty as hers did not long leave the men of the party cold to her charms; and soon Jimmy Danvers joined her and a Colonel Lowerby, commonly known as "the Crow," and she held a little court. But to relax and be genial and unregal was so difficult for her, with the whole contrary training of all her miserable life.

Hitherto men and, indeed, often women were things to be kept at a distance, as in one way or another they were sure to bite!

And after a while the party adjusted itself, some for bridge and some for sleep; and Jimmy Danvers and Colonel Lowerby went into the small compartment to smoke.

"Well, Crow," said Jimmy, "what do you think of Tristram's new lady? Isn't she a wonder? But, Jehoshaphat! doesn't she freeze you to death!"

"Very curious type," growled the Crow. "Bit of Vesuvius underneath, I expect."

"Yes, that is what a fellow'd think to look at her," Jimmy said, puffing at his cigarette. "But she keeps the crust on the top all the time; the bloomin' volcano don't get a chance!"

"She doesn't look stupid," continued the Crow. "She looks stormy—expect it's pretty well worth while, though, when she melts."

"Poor old Tristram don't look as if he had had a taste of paradise with his houri, for his week, does he? Before we'd heartened him up on the platform a bit—give you my word—he looked as mum as an owl," Jimmy said. "And she looked like an iceberg, as she's done all the time. I've never seen her once warm up."

"He's awfully in love with her," grunted the Crow.

"I believe that is about the measure, though I can't see how you've guessed it. You had not got back for the wedding, Crow, and it don't show now."

The Crow laughed—one of his chuckling, cynical laughs which to his dear friend Lady Anningford meant so much that was in his mind.

"Oh, doesn't it!" he said.

"Well, tell me, what do you really think of her?" Jimmy went on. "You see, I was best man at the wedding, and I feel kind of responsible if she is going to make the poor, old boy awfully unhappy."

"She's unhappy herself," said the Crow. "It's because she is unhappy she's so cold. She reminds me of a rough terrier I bought once, when I was a lad, from a particularly brutal bargeman. It snarled at every one who came near it, before they could show if they were going to kick or not, just from force of habit."

"Well?" questioned Jimmy, who, as before has been stated, was rather thick.

"Well, after I had had it for a year it was the most faithful and the gentlest dog I ever owned. That sort of creature wants oceans of kindness. Expect Tristram's pulled the curb—doesn't understand as yet."

"Why, how could a person who must always have had heaps of cash—Markrute's niece, you know—and a fine position be like your dog, Crow? You *are* drawing it!"

"Well, you need not mind what I say, Jimmy," Colonel Lowerby went on. "Judge for yourself. You asked my opinion, and as I am an old friend of the family I've given it, and time will show."

"Lady Highford's going to be at Montfitchet," Jimmy announced after a pause. "She won't make things easy for any one, will she!"

"How did that happen?" asked the Crow in an astonished voice.

"Ethelrida had asked her in the season, when every one supposed the affair was still on, and I expect she would not let them put her off—" And then both men looked up at the door, for Tristram peeped in.

"We shall be arriving in five minutes, you fellows," he said.

And soon they drew up at the little Tylling Green station, and the saloon was switched off, while the express flew on to King's Lynn.

There were motor cars and an omnibus to meet them, and Lady Ethelrida's own comfortable coupé for the bridal pair. They might just want to say a few words together alone before arriving, she had kindly thought. And so, though neither of the two were very eager for this tête-à-tête, they got in and started off. The little coupé had very powerful engines and flew along, so they were well ahead of the rest of the party and would get to the house first, which was what the hostess had calculated upon. Then Tristram could have the pleasure of presenting his bride to the assembled company at tea, without the interruptions of the greetings of the other folk.

Zara felt excited. She was beginning to realize that these English people were all of her dead father's class, not creatures whom one must beware of until one knew whether or not they were gamblers or rogues. And it made her breathe more freely, and the black panther's look died out of her eyes. She did not feel nervous, as she well might have done—only excited and highly worked up. Tristram, for his part, wished to heaven Ethelrida had not arranged to send the coupé for them. It was such a terrible temptation for him to resist for five miles, sitting so near her all alone in the dusk of the afternoon! He clenched his hands under the rug, and drew as far away from her as he could; and she glanced at him and wondered, almost timidly, why he looked so stern.

"I hope you will tell me, if there is anything special you wish me to do, please?" she said. "Because, you see, I have never been in the English country before, and my uncle has given me to understand the customs are different to those abroad."

He felt he could not look at her; the unusual gentleness in her voice was so alluring, and he had not forgotten the hurt of the chinchilla coat. If he relented in his attitude at all she would certainly snub him again; so he continued staring in front of him, and answered ordinarily,

"I expect you will do everything perfectly right, and every one will only want to be kind to you, and make you have a good time; and my uncle will certainly make love to you but you must not mind that."

And Zara allowed herself to smile as she answered,

"No, I shall not in the least object to that!"

He knew she was smiling—out of the corner of his eye—and the temptation to clasp her to him was so overpowering that he said rather hoarsely, "Do you mind if I put the window down?"

He must have some air; he was choking. She wondered more and more what was the matter with him, and they both fell into a constrained silence which lasted until they turned into the park gates; and Zara peered out into the ghostly trees, with their autumn leaves nearly off, and tried to guess from the lodge what the house would be like.

It was very enormous and stately, she found when they reached it, and, she walking with her empress air and Tristram following her, they at last came to the picture gallery where the rest of the party, who had arrived earlier, were all assembled in the center, by one of the big fireplaces, with their host and hostess having tea.

The Duke and Lady Ethelrida came forward, down the very long, narrow room (they had quite sixty feet to walk before they met them), and then, when they did, they both kissed Zara—their beautiful new relation!—and Lady Ethelrida taking her arm drew her towards the party, while she whispered,

"You dear, lovely thing! Ever so many welcomes to the family and Montfitchet!"

And Zara suddenly felt a lump in her throat. How she had misjudged them all in her hurt ignorance! And determining to repair her injustice she advanced with a smile and was presented to the group.

CHAPTER XXII

There was a good deal of running into each other's rooms before dressing for dinner among the ladies at Montfitchet, that night. They had, they felt, to exchange views about the new bride! And the opinions were favorable, on the whole; unanimous, as to her beauty and magnetic attraction; divided, as to her character; but fiercely and venomously antagonistic in one mean, little heart.

Emily and Mary and Lady Betty Burns clustered together in the latter's room. "We think she is perfectly lovely, Betty," Emily said, "but we don't know her as yet. She is rather stiff, and frightens us just a little. Perhaps she is shy. What do you think?"

"She looks just like the heroines in some of the books that Mamma does not let me read and I am obliged to take up to bed with me. Don't you know, Mary—especially the one I lent you—deeply, mysteriously tragic. You remember the one who killed her husband and then went off with the Italian Count; and then with some one else. It was frightfully exciting."

"Good gracious! Betty," exclaimed Emily. "How dreadful! You don't think our sister-in-law looks like that?"

"I really don't know," said Lady Betty, who was nineteen and wrote lurid melodramas—to the waste of much paper and the despair of her mother. "I don't know. I made one of my heroines in my last play have just those passionate eyes—and she stabbed the villain in the second act!"

"Yes, but," said Mary, who felt she must defend Tristram's wife, "Zara isn't in a play and there is no villain, and—why, Betty, no one has tragedies in real life!"

Lady Betty tossed her flaxen head, while she announced a prophecy, with an air of deep wisdom which positively frightened the other two girls.

"You mark my words, both of you, Emily and Mary—they will have some tragedy before the year is out! And I shall put it all in my next play."

And with this fearful threat ringing in their ears Tristram's two sisters walked in a scared fashion to their room.

"Betty is wonderful, isn't she, darling?" Mary said. "But, Em, you don't think there is any truth in it, do you? Mother would be so horribly shocked if there was anything like one of Betty's plays in the family, wouldn't she? And Tristram would never allow it either!"

"Of course not, you goosie," answered Emily. "But Betty is right in one way—Zara has got a mysterious face, and—and, Mary—Tristram seemed somehow changed, I thought; rather sarcastic once or twice."

And then their maid came in and put a stop to their confidences.

"She is the most wonderful person I have ever met, Ethelrida," Lady Anningford was just then saying, as she and the hostess stopped at her door and let Lady Thornby and the young Countess of Melton go on.—"She is wickedly beautiful and attractive, and there is something odd about her, too, and it touches me; and I don't believe she is really wicked a bit. Her eyes are like storm clouds. I have heard her first husband was a brute. I can't think who told me but it came from some one at one of the Embassies."

"We don't know much about her, any of us," Lady Ethelrida said, "but Aunt Jane asked us all in the beginning to trust Tristram's judgment: he is awfully proud, you know. And besides, her uncle, Mr. Markrute, is so nice. But, Anne—" and Lady Ethelrida paused.

"Well, what, dear? Tristram is awfully in love with her, isn't he?" Lady Anningford asked.

"Yes," said Lady Ethelrida, "but, Anne, do you really think Tristram looks happy? I thought when he was not speaking his face seemed rather sad."

"The Crow came down in the train with them," Lady Anningford announced. "I'll hear the whole exact impression of them after dinner and tell you. The Crow is always right."

"She is so very attractive, I am sure, to every man who sees her, Anne. I hope Lord Elterton won't begin and make Tristram jealous. I wish I had not asked him. And then there is Laura—It was awful taste, I think, her insisting upon coming, don't you?—Anne, if she seems as if she were going to be horrid you will help me to protect Zara, won't you?—And now we really must dress."

In another room Mrs. Harcourt was chatting with her sister and Lady Highford.

"She is perfectly lovely, Laura," Miss Opie said. "Her hair must reach down to the ground and looks as if it would not come off, and her skin isn't even powdered—I examined it, on purpose, in a side light. And those eyes! Je-hoshaphat! as Jimmy Danvers says."

"Poor, darling Tristram!" Laura sighed sentimentally while she inwardly registered her intense dislike of "the Opie girl." "He looks melancholy enough—for a bridegroom; don't you think so, Kate?" and she lowered her eyes, with a glance of would-be meaning, as though she could say more, if she wished. "But no wonder, poor dear boy! He loathed the marriage; it was so fearfully sudden. I suppose the Markrute man had got him in his power."

"You don't say so!" Mrs. Harcourt gasped. She was a much simpler person than her sister. "Jimmy assured me that Lord Tancred was violently in love with her, and that was it."

"Jimmy always was a fool," Lady Highford said, and as they went on to their rooms Lily Opie whispered,

"Kate, Laura Highford is an odious cat, and I don't believe a word about Mr. Markrute and the getting Lord Tancred into his power. That is only to make a salve for herself. The Duke would never have Mr. Markrute here if there was anything fishy about him. Why, ducky, you know it is the only house left in England, almost, where they have only US!"

Tristram was ready for dinner in good time but he hesitated about knocking at his wife's door. If she did not let him know she was ready he would send Higgins to ask for her maid.

His eyes were shining with the pride he felt in her. She had indeed come up to the scratch. He had not believed it possible that she could have been so gracious, and he had not even guessed that she would condescend to speak so much. And all his old friends had been so awfully nice about her and honestly admiring; except Arthur Elterton—*he* had admired rather too much!

And then this exaltation somewhat died down. It was after all but a very poor, outside show, when, in reality, he could not even knock at her door!

He wished now he had never let his pride hurl forth that ultimatum on the wedding night, because he would have to stick to it! He could not make the slightest advance, and it did not look as if she meant to do so. Tristram in an ordinary case when his deep feelings were not concerned would have known how to display a thousand little tricks for the allurement of a woman, would have known exactly how to cajole her, to give her a flower, and hesitate when he spoke her name—and a number of useful things—but he was too terribly in earnest to be anything but a real, natural man; that is, hurt from her coldness and diffident of himself, and iron-bound with pride.

And Zara at the other side of the door felt almost happy. It was the first evening in her life she had ever dressed without some heavy burden of care. Her self-protective, watchful instincts could rest for a while; these new relations were truly, not only seemingly, so kind. The only person she immediately and instinctively disliked was Lady Highford who had gushed and said one or two bitter-sweet things which she had not clearly nor literally understood, but which, she felt, were meant to be hostile.

And her husband, Tristram! It was plain to be seen every one loved him—from the old Duke, to the old setter by the fire. And how was it possible for them all to love a man, when—and then her thoughts unconsciously turned to *if*—he were capable of so base a thing as his marriage with her had been? Was it possible there could be any mistake? On the first opportunity she would question her uncle; and although she knew that gentleman would only tell her exactly as much as he wished her to know, that much would be the truth.

Dinner was to be at half-past eight. She ought to be punctual, she knew; but it was all so wonderful, and refined, and old-world, in her charming room, she felt inclined to dawdle and look around.

It was a room as big as her mother's had been, in the gloomy castle near Prague, but it was full of cozy touches—beyond the great gilt state bed, which she admired immensely—and with which she instinctively felt only the English—and only such English—know how to endow their apartments.

Then she roused herself. She *must* dress. Fortunately her hair did not take any time to twist up.

"*Miladi* is a dream!" Henriette exclaimed when at last she was ready. "*Milor* will be proud!"

And he was.

She sent Henriette to knock at his door—his door in the passage—not the one between their rooms!—just on the stroke of half-past eight. He was at that moment going to send Higgins on a like errand! and his sense of humor at the grotesqueness of the situation made him laugh a bitter laugh.

The two servants as the messengers!—when he ought to have been in there himself, helping to fix on her jewels, and playing with her hair, and perhaps kissing exquisite bits of her shoulders when the maid was not looking, or fastening her dress!

Well, the whole thing was a ghastly farce that must be got through; he would take up politics, and be a wonderful landlord to the people at Wrayth; and somehow, he would get through with it, and no one should ever know, from him, of his awful mistake.

He hardly allowed himself to tell her she looked very beautiful as they walked along the great corridor. She was all in deep sapphire-blue gauze, with no jewels on at all but the Duke's splendid brooch.

That was exquisite of her, he appreciated that fine touch. Indeed, he appreciated everything about her—if she had known.

People were always more or less on time in this house, and after the silent hush of admiration caused by the bride's entrance they all began talking and laughing, and none but Lady Highford and another woman were late.

And as Zara walked along the white drawing-room, on the old Duke's arm, she felt that somehow she had got back to a familiar atmosphere, where she was at rest after long years of strife.

Lady Ethelrida had gone in with the bridegroom—to-night everything was done with strict etiquette—and on her left hand she had placed the bride's uncle. The new relations were to receive every honor, it seemed. And Francis Markrute, as he looked round the table, with the perfection of its taste, and saw how everything was going on beautifully, felt he had been justified in his schemes.

Lady Anningford sat beyond Tristram, and often these two talked, so Lady Ethelrida had plenty of time, without neglecting him, to converse with her other interesting guest.

"I am so glad you like our old home, Mr. Markrute," she said. "To-morrow I will show you a number of my favorite haunts. It seems sad, does it not, as so many people assert, that the times are trending to take all these dear, old things away from us, and divide them up?"

"It will be a very bad day for England when that time comes," the financier said. "If only the people could study evolution and the meaning of things there would not be any of this nonsensical class hatred. The immutable law is that no one long retains any position unless he, or she, is suitable for it. Nothing endures that is not harmonious. It is because England is now out of harmony, that this seething is going on. You and your race have been fitted for what you have held for hundreds of years; that is why you have stayed: and your influence, and such as you, have made England great."

"Then how do you account for the whole thing being now out of joint?" Lady Ethelrida asked. "As my father and I and, as far as I know, numbers of us have remained just the same, and have tried as well as we can to do our duty to every one."

"Have you ever studied the Laws of Lycurgus, Lady Ethelrida?" he asked. And she shook her sleek, fine head. "Well, they are worth glancing at, when you have time," he went on. "An immense value was placed upon discipline, and as long as it lasted in its iron simplicity the Spartans were the wonder of the then known world. But after their conquest of Athens, when luxury poured in and every general wanted something for himself and forgot the good of the state, then their discipline went to pieces, and, so—the whole thing. And that, applied in a modern way, is what is happening to England. All classes are forgetting their discipline, and, without fitting themselves for what they aspire to, they are trying to snatch from some other class. And the whole thing is rotten with mawkish sentimentality, and false prudery, and abeyance of common sense."

"Yes," said Lady Ethelrida, much interested.

"Lycurgus went to the root of things," the financier continued, "and made the people morally and physically healthy, and ruthlessly expunged the unfit—not like our modern nonsense, which encourages science to keep, among the prospective parents for the future generation, all the most diseased. Moral and physical balance and proportion were the ideas of the Spartans. They would not have even been allowed to compete in the games, if they were misshapen. And the analogy is, no one unfitted for a part ought to aspire to it, for the public good. Any one has a right to scream, if he does not obtain it when he is fitted for it."

"Yes, I see," said Lady Ethelrida. "Then what do you mean when you say every class is trying to snatch something from some other class? Do you mean from the class above it? Or what? Because unless we, for instance—technically speaking—snatched from the King from whom could we snatch?"

The financier smiled.

"I said purposely, 'some other class,' instead of 'some class above it,' for this reason: it is because a certain and ever-increasing number of your class, if I may say so, are snatching—not, indeed, from the King—but from all classes *beneath them*, manners and morals, and absence of tenue, and absence of pride—things for which their class was not fitted. They had their own vices formerly, which only hurt each individual and not the order, as a stain will spoil the look of a bit of machinery but will not upset its working powers like a piece of grit. What they put into the machine now is grit. And the middle classes are snatching what they think is gentility, and ridiculous pretenses to birth and breeding; and the lower classes are snatching everything they can get from the pitiful fall of the other two, and shouting that all men are equal, when, if you come down to the practical thing, the foreman of some ironworks, say—where the opinions were purely socialistic, in the abstract—would give the last joined stoker a sound trouncing for aspirations in his actual work above his capabilities; because he would know that if the stoker were then made foreman the machinery could not work. The stokers of life should first fit themselves to be foremen before they shout."

Then, as Lady Ethelrida looked very grave, and Francis Markrute was really a whimsical person, and seldom talked so seriously to women, he went on, smiling,

"The only really perfect governments in the world are those of the Bees, and Ants, because they are both ruled with ruthless discipline and no sentiment, and every individual knows his place!"

"I read once, somewhere, that it has been discovered," said Lady Ethelrida gently—she never laid down the law—"that the reason why the wonderful Greeks came to an end was not really because their system of government was not a good one, but because the mosquitoes came and gave them malaria, and enervated them and made them feeble, and so they could not stand against the stronger peoples of the North. Perhaps," she went on, "England has got some moral malarial mosquitoes and the scientists have not yet discovered the proper means for their annihilation."

Here Tristram who overheard this interrupted:

"And it would not be difficult to give the noisome insects their English names, would it, Francis? Some of them are in the cabinet."

And the three laughed. But Lady Ethelrida wanted to hear something more from her left-hand neighbor, so she said,

"Then the inference to be drawn from what you have said is—we should aim at making conditions so that it is possible for every individual to have the chance to make himself practically—not theoretically—fit for anything his soul aspires to. Is that it?"

"Absolutely in a nutshell, dear lady," Francis Markrute said, and for a minute he looked into her eyes with such respectful, intense admiration that Lady Ethelrida looked away.

CHAPTER XXIII

In the white drawing-room, afterwards, Lady Highford was particularly gushing to the new bride. She came with a group of other women to surround her, and was so playful and charming to all her friends! She must be allowed to sit next to Zara, because, she said, "Your husband and I are such very dear, old friends. And how lovely it is to think that now he will be able to reopen Wrayth! Dear Lady Tancred is so glad," she purred.

Zara just looked at her politely. What a done-up ferret woman! she thought. She had met many of her tribe. At the rooms at Monte Carlo, and in another class and another race, they were the kind who played in the smallest stakes themselves, and often snatched the other people's money.

"I have never heard my husband speak of you," she said presently, when she had silently borne a good deal of vitriolic gush. "You have perhaps been out of England for some time?"

And Lady Anningford whispered to Ethelrida, "We need not worry to be ready to defend her, pet! She can hold her own!" So they moved on to the group of the girls.

But at the end of their conversation, though Zara had used her method of silence in a considerable degree and made it as difficult as she could for Lady Highford, still, that artist in petty spite had been able to leave behind her some rankling stings. She was a mistress of innuendo. So that when the men came in, and Tristram, from the sense of "not funking things" which was in him, deliberately found Laura and sat down upon a distant sofa with her, Zara suddenly felt some unpleasant feeling about her heart. She found that she desired to watch them, and that, in spite of what any one said to her, her attention wandered back to the distant sofa in some unconscious speculation and unrest.

And Laura was being exceedingly clever. She scented with the cunning of her species that Tristram was really unhappy, whether he was in love with his hatefully beautiful wife or not. Now was her chance; not by reproaches, but by sympathy, and, if possible, by planting some venom towards his wife in his heart.

"Tristram, dear boy, why did you not tell me? Did you not know I would have been delighted at anything—if it pleased you?" And she looked down, and sighed. "I always made it my pleasure to understand you, and to promote whatever seemed for your good."

And in his astonishment at this attitude Tristram forgot to recall the constant scenes and reproaches, and the paltry little selfishnesses of which he had been the victim during the year their—friendship—had lasted. He felt somehow soothed. Here was some one who was devoted to him, even if his wife were not!

"You are a dear, Laura," he said.

"And now you must tell me if you are really happy—Tristram." She lingered over his name. "She is so lovely—your wife—but looks very cold. And I know, dear" (another hesitation over the word), "I know you don't like women to be cold."

"We will not discuss my wife," he said. "Tell me what you have been doing, Laura. Let me see, when did I see you last—in June?"

And the venom came to boiling-point in Laura's adder gland. He could not even remember when he had said good-by to her! It was in July, after the Eton and Harrow match!

"Yes, in June," she said sadly, turning her eyes down. "And you might have told me, Tristram. It came as such a sudden shock. It made me seriously ill. You must have known, and were probably engaged—even then."

Tristram sat mute; for how could he announce the truth?

"Oh, don't let us talk of these things, Laura. Let us forget those old times and begin again—differently. You will be a dear friend to me always, I am sure. You always were—" and then he stopped abruptly. He felt this was too much lying! and he hated doing such things.

"Of course I will, dar—Tristram," Laura said, and appeared much moved.

And from where Zara was trying to talk to the Duke she saw the woman shiver and look down provokingly and her husband stretch his long limbs out; and a sudden, unknown sensation of blinding rage came over her, and she did not hear a syllable of the Duke's speech.

Meanwhile Lady Anningford had retired to a seat in a window with the Crow.

"Is it all right, Crow?" she asked, and one of his peculiarities was to understand her—as Lady Ethelrida understood the Duke—and and not ask "What?"

"Will be—some day—I expect—unless they get drowned in the current first."

"Isn't she mysterious, Crow? I am sure she has some tragic history. Have you heard anything?"

"Husband murdered by another man in a row at Monte Carlo."

"Over her?"

"I don't know for a fact, but I gather—not. You may be certain, Queen Anne, that when a woman is as quiet and haughty as Lady Tancred looks, and her manners are as cold and perfectly sure of herself as hers are, she has not done anything she is ashamed of, or regrets."

"Then what can be the cause of the coolness between them? Look at Tristram now! I think it is horrid of him—sitting like that talking to Laura, don't you?"

"A viper, Laura," growled the Crow. "She's trying to get him again in the rebound."

"I cannot imagine why women cannot leave other women's husbands alone. They are hateful creatures, most of them."

"Natural instinct of the chase," said Colonel Lowerby.

But Lady Anningford flashed.

"You are a cynic, Crow."

"And you will really show me your favorite haunts to-morrow, Lady Ethelrida?" Francis Markrute was saying to his hostess. He had contrived insidiously to detach her conversation from a group to himself, and drew her unconsciously towards a seat where they would be uninterrupted. "One judges so of people by their tastes in haunts."

Lady Ethelrida never spoke of herself as a rule. She was not in the habit of getting into those—abstract to begin with, and personal to go on with—thrilling conversations with men, which most of the modern young women delight in, and which were the peculiar joy of Lily Opie.

It was because for some unacknowledged reason the financier personally pleased her that she now drifted where he wished.

"Mine are very simple, I fear, nothing for you to investigate," she said gently.

"So I should have thought—" and he again as he had done at dinner permitted himself to look into her eyes, and going on after an imperceptible pause he said softly, "simple, and pure, and sweet ...I always think of you,

Lady Ethelrida, as the embodiment of sane things, balanced things—perfection." And his last word was almost a caress.

"I am most ordinary," she said; and she wondered why she was not angry with him, which she quite well could have been.

"It is only perfect balance in all things, if we but know it, which appeals to the sane eye," he went on, pulling himself up. "All weariness and satiety are caused in emotion; in pleasure in persons, places, or things; by the want of proportion in them somewhere which, like all simple things, is the hardest to find."

"Do you make theories about everything, Mr. Markrute?" she asked, and there was a smile in her eye.

"It is a wise thing to do sometimes; it keeps one from losing one's head."

Lady Ethelrida did not answer. She felt deliciously moved. She had often said to her friend, Anne Anningford, when they had been talking, that she did not like elderly men; she disliked to see their hair getting thin, and their chins getting fat, and their little habits and mannerisms growing pronounced. But here she found herself tremendously interested in one who, from all accounts, must be quite forty-five if not older, though it was true his brown colorless hair was excessively thick, and he was slight of build everywhere.

Now she felt she must turn the conversation to less personal things, so:

"Zara looks very lovely to-night," she said.

"Yes," replied the financier, with an air of detaching himself unwillingly from a thrilling topic, which was, indeed, what he felt. "Yes, and I hope some day they will be exceedingly happy."

"Why do you say some day?" Lady Ethelrida asked quickly. "I hoped they were happy now."

"Not very, I am afraid," he said. "But you remember our compact at dinner? They will be ideally so if they are left alone," and he glanced casually at Tristram and Laura.

Ethelrida looked, too, following his eyes.

"Yes," she said. "I wish I had not asked her—" and then she stopped abruptly, and grew a deep pink. She realized what the inference in her speech was, and if Mr. Markrute had never heard anything about the silly affair between her cousin and Lady Highford what would he think! What might she not have done!

"That won't matter," he said, with his fine smile. "It will be good for my niece. I meant something quite different."

But what he meant, he would not say.

And so the evening passed smoothly. The girls, and all the young men and the Crow, and Young Billy, and giddy, irresponsible people like that, had gathered at one end of the room; they were arranging some especial picnic for the morrow, as only some of them were going to shoot. And into their picnic plans they drew Zara, and barred Tristram out, with chaff.

"You are only an old, married man now, Tristram," they teased him with. "But Lady Tancred is young and comes with us!"

"And I will take care of her," announced Lord Elterton, looking sentimental—much to Tristram's disgust.

Ethelrida seemed to have collected a lot of rotters, he thought to himself, although it was the same party he had so enjoyed last year!

"Lady Thornby and Lady Melton and Lily Opie and her sister are going out to the shooters' lunch," Laura said sweetly. "As you are going to be deprived of your lovely wife, Tristram, I will come, too."

And so, finally good nights were said and the ladies retired to their rooms; and Zara could not think why she no longer found the atmosphere of hers peaceful and delightful, as she had done before she went down.

For the first time in her life she felt she hated a woman.

And Tristram, her husband, when he came up an hour or so later, wondered if she were asleep. Laura had been perfectly sweet, and he felt greatly soothed. Poor old Laura! He supposed she had really cared for him rather, and perhaps he had behaved casually, even though she had been impossible, in the past. But how had he ever even for five minutes fancied himself in love with her? Why, she looked quite old to-night! and he had never remarked before how thin and fluffed out her hair was. Women ought certainly to have beautifully thick hair.

And then all the pretenses of any healing of his aches fell from him, and he went and stood by the door that separated him from his loved one, and he stretched out his arms and said aloud, "Darling, if only you could understand how happy I would make you—if you would let me! But I can't even break down this hateful door as I want to, because of my vow."

And then for most of the rest of the night he tossed restlessly in his bed.

CHAPTER XXIV

The next day did not look at all promising as regards the weather, but still the shooters, Tristram among them, started early for their sport. And after the merriest breakfast at little tables in the great dining-room the intending picnickers met in conclave to decide as to what they should do.

"It is perfectly sure to rain," Jimmy Danvers said. "There is no use attempting to go to Lynton Heights. Why don't we take the lunch to Montfitchet Tower and eat it in the big hall? There we wouldn't get wet."

"Quite right, Jimmy," agreed the Crow, who, with Lady Anningford, was to chaperon the young folk. "I'm all for not getting wet, with my rheumatic shoulder, and I hear you and Young Billy are a couple of firstclass cooks."

"Then," interrupted Lady Betty enthusiastically, "we can cook our own lunch! Oh, how delightful! We will make a fire in the big chimney. Uncle Crow, you are a pet!"

"I will go and give orders for everything at once," Lady Ethelrida agreed delightedly. "Jimmy, what a bright boy to have thought of the plan!"

And by twelve o'clock all was arranged. Now, it had been settled the night before that Mr. Markrute should shoot with the Duke and the rest of the more serious men; but early in the morning that astute financier had sent a note to His Grace's room, saying, if it were not putting out the guns dreadfully, he would crave to be excused as he was expecting a telegram of the gravest importance concerning the new Turkish loan, which he would be obliged to answer by a special letter, and he was uncertain at what time the wire would come. He was extremely sorry, but, he added whimsically, the Duke must remember he was only a poor, business-man!

At which His Grace had smiled, as he thought of his guest's vast millions, in comparison to his own.

Thus it was that just before twelve o'clock when the young party were ready to start for their picnic. Mr. Markrute, having written his letter and despatched it by express to London, chanced upon Lady Ethelrida in a place where he felt sure he should find her, and, expressing his surprise that they were not already gone, he begged to be allowed to come with them. He, too, was an excellent cook, he assured her, and would be really of use. And they all laughingly started.

And if she could have seen the important letter concerning the new Turkish loan, she would have found it contained a pressing reminder to Bumpus to send down that night certain exquisitely bound books!

Above all, the young ladies had demanded they should have no servants at their picnic—everything, even the fire, was to be made by themselves. Jimmy was to drive the donkey-cart, with Lady Betty, to take all the food. The only thing they permitted was that the pots and pans and the wood for the fire might be sent on.

And they were all so gay and looked so charming and suitably clad, in their rough, short, tweed frocks.

Zara, who walked demurely by Lord Elterton, had never seen anything of the sort. She felt like a strange, little child at its first party.

Before he had started in the morning Tristram had sent her a note (he could not stand the maid and valet as verbal messengers—it made him laugh too bitterly), it was just a few lines:

"You asked me to tell you anything special about our customs, so this is to say, just put on some thick, short, ordinary suit, and mind you have a pair of thick boots."

And it was signed "Tancred"—not "Tristram."

She gave a little quiver as she read it, and then asked and found his lordship had already gone down. She was to breakfast later with the non-shooters. She would not see him, then, for the entire day. And that odious woman with whom he was so friendly would have him all to herself!

These thoughts flashed into her mind before she was aware of it, and then she crushed them out—furious with herself. For of what possible matter could her husband's doings be to her? And yet, as she started, she found herself hoping it would rain, so that the five ladies who intended joining the guns in the farmhouse, for luncheon at two, would be unable to go. For just as she had come into the saloon where some of the party were writing letters that morning she had heard Lady Highford say to Mrs. Harcourt, in her high voice, "Yes, indeed, we mean to finish the discussion this afternoon after luncheon.—Dear Tristram! There is a long wait at the Fulton beat; we shall have plenty of time alone." And then she had turned round, and seemed confused at seeing her—Zara—and gushed more than the night before.

But she did not get the satisfaction of perceiving the bride turn a hair, though as Zara walked on to the end of the room she angrily found herself wondering who was this woman, and what had she been to Tristram? What was she *now*?

Lord Elterton had already fallen in love. He was a true *cavalier* servant; he knew, like the financier, as a fine art, how to manipulate the temperaments of most women. He prided himself upon it. Indeed, he spent the greater part of his life doing nothing else. Exquisite gentleness and sympathy was his method. There were such heaps of rough, rude brutes about that one would always have a chance by being the contrast; and husbands, he reasoned, were nearly always brutes—after a while—in the opinion of their wives! He had hardly ever known this plan to fail with the most devoted wife. So although Lady Tancred had only been married a week he hoped to render her not quite indifferent to himself in some way. He had seen at once that she and Tristram were not on terms of passionate love, and there was something so piquant about flirting with a bride! He divided women as a band into about four divisions. The quite impossible, the recalcitrant, the timid, and the bold. For the impossible he did not waste powder and shot. For the recalcitrant he used insidious methods of tickling their fancies, as he would tickle a trout. For the timid he was tender and protective; and for the bold subtly indifferent: but always gentle and nice!

He was not sure yet in which of the four divisions he should have to place his new attraction—probably the second—but he frankly admitted he had never before had any experience with one of her type. Her strange eyes thrilled him: he felt, when she turned the deep slate, melting disks upon him, his heart went "down into his bloomin' boots," as Jimmy Danvers would have described the sensation. So he began with extreme gentleness and care.

"You have not been long in this country, Lady Tancred, have you? One can see it—you are so exquisitely *chic*. And how perfectly you speak English! Not the slightest accent. It is delicious. Did you learn it when very young?"

"My father was an Englishman," said Zara, disarmed from her usual chilling reserve by the sympathy in his voice. "I always spoke it until I was thirteen, and since then, too. It is a nice, honest language, I think."

"You speak numbers of others, probably?" Lord Elterton went on, admiringly.

"Yes, about four or five. It is very easy when one is moving in the countries, and certain languages are very much alike. Russian is the most difficult."

"How clever you are!"

"No, I am not a bit. But I have had time to read a good deal—" and then Zara stopped. It was so against her habit to give personal information to any one like this.

Lord Elterton saw the little check, and went on another tack. "I have been an idle fellow and am not at all learned," he said. "Tristram and I were at Eton together in the same house, and we were both dunces; but he did rather well at Oxford, and I went straight into the Guards."

Zara longed to ask about Tristram. She had not even heard before that he had been to Oxford! And it struck her suddenly how ridiculous the whole thing was. She had sold herself for a bargain; she had asked no questions of any one; she had intended to despise the whole family and remain entirely aloof; and now she found every one of her intentions being gradually upset. But as yet she did not admit for a second to herself that she was falling in love. It would be such a perfectly impossible thing to do in any case, when now he was absolutely indifferent to her and showed it in every way. It made the whole thing all the more revolting—to have pretended he loved her on that first night! Yes, with certain modifications of classes and races men were all perfectly untrustworthy, if not brutes, and a woman, if she could relax her vigilance, as regards the defense of her person and virtue, could not afford to unbend a fraction as to her emotions!

And all the time she was thinking this out she was silent, and Lord Elterton watched her, thrilled with the attraction of the unobtainable. He saw plainly she had forgotten his very presence, and, though piqued, he grew the more eager.

"I would love to know what you were thinking of," he said softly; and then with great care he pulled a bramble aside so that it should not touch her. They had turned into a lane beyond the kitchen garden and the park.

Zara started. She had, indeed, been far away!

"I was thinking—" she said, and then she paused for a suitable lie but none came, so she grew confused, and stopped, and hesitated, and then she blurted out, "I was thinking was it possible there could ever be any one whom one could believe?"

Lord Elterton looked at her. What a strange woman!

"Yes," he said simply, "you can believe me when I tell you I have never been so attracted by any one in my life."

"Oh! for that!" she answered contemptuously. *"Mon Dieu!* how often I have heard of that!"

This was not what he had expected. There was no empty boast about the speech, as there would have been if Laura Highford had uttered it—she was fond of demonstrating her conquests and power in words. There was only a weariness as of something banal and tiring. He must be more careful.

"Yes, I quite understand," he said sympathetically. "You must be bored with the love of men."

"I have never seen any love of men. Do men know love?" she asked, not with any bitterness—only as a question of fact. What had Tristram been about? Lord Elterton thought. Here he had been married to this divine creature for a whole week, and she was plainly asking the question from her heart. And Tristram was no fool in a general way, he knew. There was some mystery here, but whatever it was there was the more chance for him! So he went on very tactfully, trying insidiously to soothe her, so that at last when they had arrived Zara had enjoyed her walk.

Montfitchet Tower was all that remained of the old castle destroyed by Cromwell's Ironsides. It was just one large, square room, a sort of great hall. It had stood roofless for many years and then been covered in by the old Duke's father, and contained a splendid stone chimney piece of colossal proportions. It had also been floored, and had the raised place still, where the family had eaten "above the salt." The rest of the old castle was a complete ruin, and at the Restoration the new one had been rebuilt about a mile further up the park.

Lady Ethelrida had collected several pieces of rough oak furniture to put into this great room which in height reached three stories up, and the supports of the mantelpieces of the upper floors could be seen on the blackened stone walls. It was here she gave her school treats and tenants' summer dances, because there was a great stretch of green, turfy lawn beyond, down to the river, where they could play their games.

And on a wet day it was an ideal picnic place.

A bright wood fire was already blazing on top of the ashes that for many years had never been cleared out, and a big jack swung in front of it—for appearance sake! What fun every one seemed to be having, Zara thought, as from an oak bench she watched them all busy as bees over their preparations for the repast. She had helped to make a salad, and now sat with the Crow, and surveyed the rest.

Jimmy Danvers had turned up his sleeves and was thoroughly in earnest over his part; and he and Young Billy had gathered some brown bracken, and put it sprouting from a ham, to represent, they said, the peacock. For, they explained, a banquet in a baronial hall had to have a peacock, as well as a boar's head, and an ox roasted whole!

And suddenly Zara thought of her last picnic, with Mimo and Mirko in the Neville Street attic, when the poor little one had worn the paper cap, and had taken such pleasure in the new rosy cups. And the Crow who was watching her closely, wondered why this gay scene should make the lovely bride look so pitifully sad. "How *Maman* would have loved all this!" she was thinking, "with her gay, tender soul, and her delight in make-believe and joyous picnics." And her father—he had known all these sorts of people; they were his own class, and yet he had come to live in the great, gloomy castle, out of his own land, and expected his exquisite, young wife to stay there alone, most of the time. The hideous cruelty of men!

And there was her Uncle Francis, in quite a new character!—helping Lady Ethelrida to lay the table, as happily as a boy. Would she herself ever be happy, she wondered, ever have a time free from some agonizing strain or care? And then, from sorrow her expression changed to one of strange slumberous resentment at fate.

"Queen Anne," said the Crow, as they sat down to luncheon, "there is some tragedy hanging over that young woman. She has been suffering like the devil for at least ten minutes, and forgot I was even beside her and pretending to talk. You and Lady Ethelrida have two not altogether unkind hearts. Can't you find out what it is, and comfort her?"

CHAPTER XXV

After luncheon, which had been carried through with all the proper ceremonies of the olden time according to Jimmy Danvers and Young Billy's interpretation of them, it came on to pour with rain; so these masters of the revels said that now the medieval dances should begin, and accordingly they turned on the gramophone that stood in the corner to amuse the children at the school treats. And Mary and her admirer, Lord Henry Burns, and Emily and a Captain Hume, and Lady Betty and Jimmy Danvers, gayly took the floor, while Young Billy offered himself to the bride, as he said he as the representative of the Lord of the Castle had a right to the loveliest lady; and, with his young, stolid self-confidence, he pushed Lord Elterton aside.

Zara had not danced for a very long time—four years at least—and she had not an idea of the two-steps and barn-dances and other sorts of whirling capers that they invented; but she did her best, and gradually something of the excitement of the gay young spirits spread to her, and she forgot her sorrows and began to enjoy herself.

"You don't ever dance, I suppose, Mr. Markrute?" Lady Ethelrida asked, as she stopped, with the gallant old Crow, flushed and smiling by the daïs, where the financier and Lady Anningford sat. "If you ever do, I, as the Lady of the Castle, ask you to 'tread a measure' with me!"

"No one could resist such, an invitation," he answered, and put his arm around her for a valse.

"I do love dancing," she said, as they went along very well. She was so surprised that this "grave and reverend signor," as she called him, should be able to valse!

"So do I," said Francis Markrute—"under certain circumstances. This is one of them." And then he suddenly held her rather tight, and laughed. "Think of it all!" he went on. "Here we are, in thick boots and country clothes capering about like savages round their fire, and, for all sorts of reasons, we all love it!"

"It is just the delicious exercise with me," said Lady Ethelrida.

"And it has nothing at all to do with that reason with me," returned her partner.

And Lady Ethelrida quivered with some sort of pleasure and did not ask him what his reason was. She thought she knew, and her eyes sparkled. They were the same height, and he saw her look; and as they went on, he whispered:

"I have brought you down the book we spoke of, you know, and you will take it from me, won't you? Just as a remembrance of this day and how you made me young for an hour!"

They stopped by one of the benches at the side and sat down, and Lady Ethelrida answered softly,

"Yes, if—you wish me to—"

Lord Elterton had now dislodged Young Billy and was waltzing with Zara himself: his whole bearing was one of intense devotion, and she was actually laughing and looking up in his face, still affected by the general hilarity, when the door of the wooden porch that had been built on as an entrance opened noiselessly, and some of the shooters peeped into the room. It had been too impossibly wet to go on, and they had sent the ladies back in the motors and had come across the park on their way home, and, hearing the sound of music, had glanced in. Tristram was in front of the intruders and just chanced to catch his bride's look at her partner, before either of them saw they were observed.

He felt frightfully jealous. He had never before seen her so smiling, to begin with, and never at all at himself. He longed to kick Arthur Elterton! Confounded impertinence!—And what tommyrot—dancing like this, in the afternoon with boots on! And when they all stopped and greeted the shooters, and crowded round the fire, he said, in a tone of rasping sarcasm—in reply to Jimmy Danvers' announcement that they were back in the real life of a castle in the Middle Ages:

"Any one can see that! You have even got My Lady's fool. Look at Arthur—with mud on his boots—jumping about!"

And Lord Elterton felt very flattered. He knew his old friend was jealous, and if he were jealous then the charming, cold lady must have been unbelievingly nice to him, and that meant he was getting on!

"You are jealous because your lovely bride prefers me, Young Lochinvar," and he laughed as he quoted:

"'For so faithful in love and so dauntless in war—
There ne'er was a gallant like Young Lochinvar!'"

And Zara saw that Tristram's eyes flashed blue steel, and that he did not like the chaff at all. So, just out of some contrariness—he had been with Lady Highford all day so why should she not amuse herself, too; indeed, why should either of them care what the other did—so just out of contrariness she smiled again at Lord Elterton and said:

"'Then tread we a measure, my Lord Lochinvar.'"

And off they went.

And Tristram, with his face more set than the Crusader ancestor's in Wrayth Church, said to his uncle, Lord Charles, "We are all wet through: let us come along."

And he turned round and went out.

And as he walked, he wondered to himself how much she must know of English poetry to have been able to answer Arthur like that. If only they could be friends and talk of the books he, too, loved! And then he realized more strongly than ever the impossibility of the situation—he, who had been willing to undertake it with the joyous self-confidence with which he had started upon a lion hunt!

He felt he was getting to the end of his tether; it could not go on. Her words that night at Dover, had closed down all the possible sources he could have used for her melting.

And a man cannot in a week break through a thousand years of inherited pride.

Before the Canada scheme had presented itself he had rather thought of joining with a friend for another trip to the Soudan: it might not be too late still, when they had got over the Wrayth ordeal, the tenants' dinners, and the speeches, and the cruel mockery of it all. He would see—perhaps—what could be done, but to go on living in this daily torture he would not submit to, for the "loving her less" had not yet begun!

And when he had left, although she would not own it to herself, Zara's joy in the day was gone.

The motors came to fetch them presently, and they all went back to the Castle to dress and have tea.

Tristram's face was still stony and he had sat down in a sofa by Laura, when a footman brought a telegram to Zara. He watched her open it, with concentrated interest. Whom were these mysterious telegrams from? He saw her face change as it had done in Paris, only not so seriously; and then she crushed up the paper into a ball and threw it in the fire. The telegram had been: "Very slightly feverish again," and signed "Mimo."

"Now I remember where I have seen your wife before," said Laura. And Tristram said absently,

"Where?"

"In the waiting-room at Waterloo station—and yet—no, it could not have been she, because she was quite ordinarily dressed, and she was talking very interestedly to a foreign man." She watched Tristram's face and saw she had hit home for some reason; so she went on, enchanted: "Of course it could not have been she, naturally; but the type is so peculiar that any other like it would remind one, would it not?"

"I expect so," he said. "It could not have been Zara, though, because she was in Paris until just before the wedding."

"I remember the occasion quite well. It was the day after the engagement was announced, because I had been up for Flora's wedding, and was going down into the country."

Then in a flash it came to him that that was the very day he himself had seen Zara in Whitehall, the day when she had not gone to Paris. And rankling, uncomfortable suspicions overcame him again.

Laura felt delighted. She did not know why he should be moved at her announcement; but he certainly was, so it was worth while rubbing it in.

"Has she a sister, perhaps? Because—now I come to think of it—the resemblance is extraordinary. I remember I was rather interested at the time because the man was so awfully handsome and as you know, dear boy, I always had a passion for handsome men!"

"My wife was an only child," Tristram answered. What was Laura driving at?

"Well, she has a double then," she laughed. "I watched them for quite ten minutes, so I am sure. I was waiting for my maid, who was to meet me, and I could not leave for fear of missing her."

"How interesting!" said Tristram coldly. He would not permit himself to demand a description of the man.

"Perhaps after all it was she, before she went to Paris, and I may be mistaken about the date," Laura went on. "It might have been her brother—he was certainly foreign—but no, it could not have been a brother." And she looked down and smiled knowingly.

Tristram felt gradually wild with the stings her words were planting, and then his anger rebounded upon herself. Little natures always miscalculate the effect of their actions, as factors in their desires, for their ultimate ends.

Laura only longed—after hurting Tristram as a punishment—to get him back again; but she was not clever enough to know that to make him mad with jealousy about his wife was not the way.

"I don't understand what you wish to insinuate, Laura," he said in a contemptuous voice; "but whatever it is, it is having no effect upon me. I absolutely adore my wife, and know everything she does or does not do."

"Oh! the poor, angry darling, there, there!" she laughed, spitefully, "and was It jealous! Well, It shan't be teased. But what a clever husband, to know all about his wife! He should be put in a glass case in a museum!" And she got up and left him alone.

Tristram would like to have killed some one—he did not know whom—this foreign man, "Mimo," most likely: he had not forgotten the name!

If his pride had permitted him he would have gone up to Zara, who had now retired to her room, and asked straight out for an explanation. He would if he had been sensible have simply said he was unhappy, and he would have asked her to reassure him. It would all have been perfectly simple and soon ended if treated with common sense. But he was too obstinate, and too hurt, and too passionately in love. The bogey of his insulted Tancred pride haunted him always, and, like all foolish things, caused him more suffering than if it had been a crime.

So once more the pair dressed to go down to the ducal dinner, with deeper estrangement in their hearts. And when Tristram was ready to-night, he went out into the corridor and pretended to look at the pictures. He would have no more servants' messages!—and there he was, with a bitter smile on his face, when Lady Anningford, coming from her room beyond, stopped to talk. She wondered at his being there—a very different state of things to her own with her dear old man, she remembered, who, after the wedding day, for weeks and weeks would hardly let her out of his sight!

Then Henriette peeped out of the door and saw that the message she was being sent upon was in vain, and went back; and immediately Zara appeared.

Her dress was pale gray to-night—with her uncle's pearls—and both Lady Anningford and Tristram noticed that her eyes were slumberous and had in them that smoldering fierceness of pain. And remembering the Crow's appeal Lady Anningford slipped her hand within her arm, and was very gentle and friendly as they went down to the saloon.

CHAPTER XXVI

Now if the evening passed with pain and unrest for the bride and bridegroom, it had quite another aspect for Francis Markrute and Lady Ethelrida! He was not placed by his hostess to-night at dinner, but when the power of manipulating circumstances with skill is in a man, and the desire to make things easy to be manipulated is in a woman, they can spend agreeable and numerous moments together.

So it fell about that without any apparent or pointed detachment from her other guests Lady Ethelrida was able to sit in one of the embrasures of the windows in, the picture gallery, whither the party had migrated to-night, and talk to her interesting new friend—for that he was growing into a friend she felt. He seemed so wonderfully understanding, and was so quiet and subtle and undemonstrative, and, underneath, you could feel his power and strength.

It had been his insidious suggestion, spread among the company, which had caused them to be in the picture gallery to-night, instead of in one of the great drawing-rooms. For in a very long narrow room it was much easier to separate people, he felt.

"Of course this was not built at the time the house was, in about 1670," Lady Ethelrida said. "It was added by the second Duke, who was Ambassador to Versailles in the time of Louis XV, and who thought he would like a 'galérie des glaces' in imitation of the one there. And then, when the walls were up, he died, and it was not decorated until thirty-five years later, in the Regent's time, and it was turned into a picture gallery then."

"People's brands of individuality in their houses are so interesting," Francis Markrute said. "I believe Wrayth is a series of human fancies, from the Norman Castle upwards, is it not? I have never been there."

"Oh! Wrayth is much more interesting than this," she answered. "Parts of it are so wonderfully old; there are stone floors in the upper rooms in one of the inner courtyards. They did not suffer, you see, from the hateful Puritans, because the then Tancred was only an infant when the civil war began; and his mother was a Frenchwoman, and they stayed in France all the time, and only came back when Charles II returned. He married a Frenchwoman, too. She was a wonderful person and improved many things. Wrayth has two long galleries and a chapel of Henry the Seventh's time, and numbers of staircases in unexpected places, and then a fine suite of state rooms, built on by Adam, and then the most awful Early-Victorian imitation Gothic wing and porch which one of those dreadful people, who spoilt such numbers of places, added in 1850."

"It sounds wonderful," said the financier.

"Lots of it is very shabby, of course, because Tristram's father was always very hard up; and nothing much had been done either in the grandfather's time—except the horrible wing. But with enough money to get it right again, I cannot imagine anything more lovely than it could be."

"It will be a great amusement to them in the coming year to do it all, then. Zara has the most beautiful taste, Lady Ethelrida. When you know her better I think you will like my niece."

"But I do now," she exclaimed. "Only I do wish she did not look so sad. May I ask it because of our bargain? "—and she paused with gentle timidity—"Will you tell me?—do you know of any special reason to-day to make her unhappy? I saw her face at dinner to-night, and all the while she talked there was an anxious, haunted look in her eyes."

Francis Markrute frowned for a moment; he had been too absorbed in his own interests to have taken in anything special about his niece. If there were something of the sort in her eyes it could only have one source—anxiety about the health of the boy Mirko. He himself had not heard anything. Then his lightning calculations decided him to tell Lady Ethelrida nothing of this. Zara's anxiety would mean the child's illness, and illness, Doctor Morley had warned him, could have only one end. He wished the poor little fellow no harm, but, on the other hand, he had no sentiment about him. If he were going to die then the disgrace would be wiped away and need never be spoken about. So he answered slowly:

"There is something which troubles her now and then. It will pass presently. Take no notice of it."

So Lady Ethelrida, as mystified as ever, turned the conversation.

"May I give you the book to-morrow morning before we go to shoot?" the financier asked after a moment. "It is your birthday, I believe, and all your guests on that occasion are privileged to lay some offering at your feet. I wanted to do so this afternoon after tea, but I was detained playing bridge with your father. I have several books coming to-morrow that I do so want you to have."

"It is very kind of you. I would like to show you my sitting-room, in the south wing. Then you could see that they would have a comfortable home!"

"When may I come?"

This was direct, and Lady Ethelrida felt a piquant sensation of interest. She had never in her life made an assignation with a man. She thought a moment.

"They will start only at eleven to-morrow, because the first covert is at a corner of the park, quite near, and if it is fine we are all coming out with you until luncheon which we have in the house; then you go to the far coverts in the motors. When, I wonder, would be best?"—It seemed so nice to leave it to him.

"You breakfast downstairs at half-past nine, like this morning?"

"Yes, I always do, and the girls will and almost every one, because it is my birthday."

"Then if I come exactly at half-past ten will you be there?"

"I will try. But how will you know the way?"

"I have a bump of locality which is rather strong, and I know the windows from the outside. You remember you showed them to me to-day as we walked to the tower."

Lady Ethelrida experienced a distinct feeling of excitement over this innocent rendezvous.

"There is a staircase—but no!"—and she laughed—"I shall tell you no more. It will be a proof of your sagacity to find the clue to the labyrinth."

"I shall be there," he said, and once again he looked into her sweet, gray eyes; and she rose with a slightly faster movement than usual and drew him to where there were more of her guests.

Meanwhile Lord Elterton was losing no time in his pursuit of Zara. He had been among the first to leave the dining-room, several paces in front of Tristram and the others, and instantly came to her and suggested a tour of the pictures. He quite agreed with the financier—these long, narrow rooms were most useful!

And Zara, thankful to divert her mind, went with him willingly, and soon found herself standing in front of an immense canvas given by the Regent, of himself, to the Duke's grandfather, one of his great friends.

"I have been watching you all through dinner," Lord Elterton said, "and you looked like a beautiful storm: your dress the gray clouds, and your eyes the thunder ones—threatening."

"One feels like a storm sometimes," said Zara.

"People are so tiresome, as a rule; you can see through them in half an hour. But no one could ever guess about what you were thinking."

"No one would want to—if they knew."

"Is it so terrible as that?" And he smiled—she must be diverted. "I wish I had met you long ago, because, of course, I cannot tell you all the things I now want to—Tristram would be so confoundedly jealous—like he was this afternoon. It is the way of husbands."

Zara did not reply. She quite agreed to this, for of the jealousy of husbands she had experience!

"Now if I were married," Lord Elterton went on, "I would try to make my wife so happy, and would love her so much she would never give me cause to be jealous."

"Love!" said Zara. "How you talk of love—and what does it mean? Gratification to oneself, or to the loved person?"

"Both," said Lord Elterton, and looked down so devotedly into her eyes that the old Duke, who was near, with Laura, thought it was quite time the young man's innings should be over!

So he joined them.

"Come with me, Zara, while I show you some of Tristram's ancestors on his mother's side."

And he placed her arm in his gallantly, and led her away to the most interesting pictures.

"Well, 'pon my soul!" he said, as they went along. "Things are vastly changed since my young days. Here, Tristram—" and he beckoned to his nephew who was with Lady Anningford—"come here and help me to show your wife some of your forbears." And then he went on with his original speech. "Yes, as I was saying, things are vastly changed since I brought Ethelrida's dear mother back here, after our honeymoon!—a month in those days! I would have punched any other young blood's head, who had even looked at her! And you philander off with that fluffy, little empty-pate, Laura, and Arthur Elterton makes love to your bride! A pretty state of things, 'pon my soul!" And he laughed reprovingly.

Tristram smiled with bitter sarcasm as he answered, "You were absurdly old-fashioned, Uncle. But perhaps Aunt Corisande was different to the modern woman."

Zara did not speak. The black panther's look, on its rare day of slumberous indifference when it condescends to come to the front of the cage, grew in her eyes, but the slightest touch could make her snarl.

"Oh! you must not ever blame the women," the Duke—this *preux chevalier*—said. "If they are different it is the fault of the men. I took care that my duchess wanted me! Why, my dear boy, I was jealous of even her maid, for at least a year!"

And Tristram thought to himself that he went further than that and was jealous of even the air Zara breathed!

"You must have been awfully happy, Uncle," he said with a sigh.

But Zara spoke never a word. And the Duke saw that there was something too deeply strained between them, for his kindly meant *persiflage* to do any good; so he turned to the pictures, and drew them into lighter things; and the moment he could, Tristram rejoined Lady Anningford by one of the great fires.

Laura Highford, left alone with Lord Elterton up at the end of the long picture gallery, felt she must throw off some steam. She could not keep from the subject which was devouring her; she knew now she had made an irreparable mistake in what she had said to Tristram in the afternoon, and how to repair it she did not know at present, but she must talk to some one.

"You will have lots of chance before a year is out, Arthur," she said with a bitter smile. "You need not be in such a hurry! That marriage won't last more than a few months—they hate each other already."

"You don't say so!" said Lord Elterton, feigning innocence. "I thought they were a most devoted couple!"—Laura would be a safe draw, and although he would not believe half he should hear, out of the bundle of chaff he possibly could collect some grains of wheat which might come in useful.

"Devoted couple!" she laughed. "Tristram is by no means the first with her. There is a very handsome foreign gentleman, looking like Romeo, or Rizzio—"

"Or any other 'O,'" put in Lord Elterton.

"Exactly—in whom she is much more interested. Poor Tristram! He has plenty to discover, I fear."

"How do you come to know about it? You are a wonder, Lady Highford—always so full of interesting information!"

"I happened to see them at Waterloo together—evidently just arrived from somewhere—and Tristram thought she was safe in Paris! Poor dear!"

"You have told him about it, of course?"—anxiously.

"I did just give him a hint."

"That was wise." And Lord Elterton smiled blandly and she did not see the twinkle in his eye. "He was naturally grateful?" he asked sympathetically.

"Not now, perhaps, but some day he will be!"

Laura's light hazel eyes flashed, and Lord Elterton laughed again as he answered lightly,

"There certainly is a poor spirit in the old boy if he doesn't feel under a lifelong obligation to you for your goodness. I should, if it were me.—Look, though, we shall have to go now; they are beginning to say good night."

And as they found the others he thought to himself, "Well, men may be poachers like I am, but I am hanged if they are such weasels as women!"

Lady Anningford joined Lady Ethelrida that night in her room, after they had seen Zara to hers, and they began at once upon the topic which was thrilling them all.

"There is something the matter, Ethelrida, darling," Lady Anningford said. "I have talked to Tristram for a long time to-night, and, although he was bravely trying to hide it, he was bitterly miserable; spoke recklessly of life one minute, and resignedly the next; and then asked me, with an air as if in an abstract discussion, whether Hector and Theodora were really happy—because she had been a widow. And when I said, 'Yes, ideally so,' and that they never want to be dragged away from Bracondale, he said, so awfully sadly, 'Oh, I dare-say; but then they have children.' It is too pitiful to hear him, after only a week! What can it be? What can have happened in the time?"

"It is not since, Anne," Ethelrida said, beginning to unfasten her dress. "It was always like that. She had just the look in her eyes the night we all first met her, at Mr. Markrute's at dinner—that strange, angry, pained, sorrowful look, as though she were a furnace of resentment against some fate. I remember an old colored picture we had on a screen—it is now in the housekeeper's room—it was one of those badly-drawn, lurid scenes of prisoners being dragged off to Siberia in the snow, and there was a woman in it who had just been separated from her husband and baby and who had exactly the same expression. It used to haunt me as a child, and Mamma had it taken out of the old nursery. And Zara's eyes haunt me now in the same way."

"She never had any children, I suppose?" asked Lady Anningford.

"Never that I heard of—and she is so young; only twenty-three now."

"Well, it is too tragic! And what is to be done? Can't you ask the uncle? He must know."

"I did, to-night, Anne—and he answered, so strangely, that 'yes, there was something which at times troubled her, but it would pass.'"

"Good gracious!" said Anne. "It can't be a hallucination. She is not crazy, is she? That would be worse than anything."

"Oh, no!" cried Ethelrida, aghast. "It is not that in the least, thank goodness!"

"Then perhaps there are some terrible scenes, connected with her first husband's murder, which she can't forget. The Crow told me Count Shulski was shot at Monte Carlo, in a fray of some sort."

"That must be it, of course!" said Ethelrida, much relieved. "Then she will get over it in time. And surely Tristram will be able to make her love him, and forget them. I do feel better about it now, Anne, and shall be able to sleep in peace."

So they said good night, and separated—comforted.

But the object of their solicitude did not attempt to get into her bed when she had dismissed her maid. She sat down in one of the big gilt William-and-Mary armchairs, and clasped her hands tightly, and tried to think.

Things were coming to a crisis with her. Destiny had given her another cross to bear, for suddenly this evening, as the Duke spoke of his wife, she had become conscious of the truth about herself: she was in love with her husband. And she herself had made it impossible that he could ever come back to her. For, indeed, the tables were turned, with one of those ironical twists of Fate.

And she questioned herself—Why did she love him? She had reproached him on her wedding night, when he had told her he loved her, because in her ignorance she felt then it could only be a question of sense. She had called him an animal! she remembered; and now she had become an animal herself! For she could prove no loftier motive for her emotion towards him than he had had for her then: they knew one another no better. It had not been possible for her passion to have arisen from the reasons she remembered having hurled at him as the only ones from which true love could spring, namely, knowledge, and tenderness, and devotion. It was all untrue; she understood it now. Love—deep and tender—could leap into being from the glance of an eye.

They were strangers to each other still, and yet this cruel, terrible thing called love had broken down all the barriers in her heart, melted the disdainful ice, and turned it to fire. She felt she wanted to caress him, and take away the stern, hard look from his face. She wanted to be gentle, and soft, and loving—to feel that she belonged to him. And she passionately longed for him to kiss her and clasp her to his heart. Whether he had consented originally to marry her for her uncle's money or not, was a matter, now, of no further importance. He had loved her after he had seen her, at all events, and she had thrown it all away. Nothing but a man's natural jealousy of his possessions remained.

"Oh, why did I not know what I was doing!" she moaned to herself, as she rocked in the chair. "I must have been very wicked in some former life, to be so tortured in this!"

But it was too late now. She had burnt her ships, and nothing remained to her but her pride. Since she had thrown away joy she could at least keep that and never let him see how she was being punished.

And to-night it was her turn to look in anguish at the closed door, and to toss in restless pain of soul, on her bed.

CHAPTER XXVII

A bombshell, in the shape of Lady Betty Burns, burst into the bedroom of Emily and Mary next morning, while the two girls were sitting up in their great bed at about eight o'clock, reading their letters and sipping their tea.

"May I come in, darlings?" a voice full of purpose said, and a flaxen head peeped in.

"Why, Betty, of course!" both girls answered and, in a blue silk dressing-gown and a long fair plait of hair hanging down, Lady Betty stalked in.

None of the Council of Three, going to deliver secret sentence, could have advanced with more dignity or consciousness of the solemnity of the occasion. Emily and Mary were thrilled.

"Be prepared!" she said dramatically, while she climbed to the foot of the bed and sat down. "It is just what I told you. She's been the heroine of a murder—if she did not do it herself!"

"Heavens! Betty, who?" almost screamed the girls.

"Your sister-in-law! I had to come at once to tell you, darlings. Last night, Aunt Muriel (the young Lady Melton was her uncle's second wife and chaperoning her to the party) would drag me into her room, and I could not get to you. You would have been asleep when I at last escaped, so I determined to come the first thing this morning and tell you my news."

Four round eyes of excited horror fixed themselves upon her, so with deep importance of voice and manner, Lady Betty went on:

"I sat with Captain Hume in the picture gallery, just before we went to bed. Believe me, I have not been able to sleep all night from it, dears! Well, we had been speaking of that fighting scene by Teniers in a beer house, you know, the one which hangs by the big Snuyders. The moon—no, it could not have been the moon. It must have been the arc light over the entrance which shines in from the angle. Anyway, it felt as if it were the moon, when I drew aside the blind; and it struck my heart with a cold foreboding, as he said such things, fights, happened now sometimes, and he was at Monte Carlo when Count Shulski was shot; and, though it was hushed up by the authorities and no one hardly heard of it much, still it made a stir. And," continued Lady Betty, now rising majestically and pointing an accusing forefinger at Emily and Mary, "Countess Shulski was your sister-in-law's name!"

"Oh, hush, Betty!" said Emily, almost angrily. "You must not say such things. There might have been a lot of Count Shulskis. Foreigners are all counts."

But Lady Betty shook her head with tragic sorrow and dignity, much at variance with her sweet little childish turned-up nose.

"Alas, darlings, far be it from me to bring the terrible conviction home to you!" Great occasions like this required a fine style, she felt. "Far be it from me! But Captain Hume went on to say, that, of course, was the reason of Lady Tancred's dreadfully mysterious and remorseful look."

"It is perfectly impossible, Betty," Mary cried excitedly. "But even if her husband were shot, it does not prove she had anything to do with it."

"Of course it does!" said Lady Betty, forgetting for a moment her style. "There's always a scene of jealousy, in which the husband stabs the other man, and then falls dead himself. Unless," and this new bright thought came to her, "she were a political spy!"

"Oh, Betty!" they both exclaimed at once. And then Emily said gravely,

"Please do tell us exactly what Captain Hume really said. Remember, it is our brother's wife you are speaking of, not one of the heroines in your plays!"

Thus admonished, Lady Betty got back on to the bed, and gradually came down to facts, which were meager enough. For Captain Hume had instantly pulled himself up, it appeared; and he had merely said that, as her first husband had been killed in a row, Lady Tancred had cause to have tragedy imprinted upon her face.

"Betty, dearest," Emily then said, "please, please don't tell anything of your exciting story to any one else, will you? Because people are so unkind."

At this, Lady Betty bounced off again offendedly.

"You are an ungrateful pair," she flashed. "Before I brave meeting Jimmy Danvers in the passage again, in my dressing-gown, to come and tell you delicious things, I'll be hanged!"

And it was with difficulty that Emily and Mary mollified her, and got her to re-seat herself on the bed and have a bit of their bread-and-butter. She had fled to announce her thrilling news before her own tea had come.

"I do think men look perfectly horrid with their hair unbrushed in the morning, don't you, Em?" she said, presently, as she munched, while Mary poured her out some tea into the emptied sugar-basin and handed it to her. "Henry's fortunate, because his is curly"—Here Mary blushed—"and I believe Jimmy Danvers gets his valet to glue his down before he goes to bed. But you should see what Aunt Muriel has to put up with, when Uncle Aubrey comes in to talk to her, while I am there. The front, anyhow, and a lock sticking up in the back! There is one thing I am determined about. Before I'm married, I shall insist upon knowing how my husband stands the morning light."

"I thought you said just now Jimmy's was quite decent and glued down," Emily retorted slyly.

"Pouff!" said Lady Betty, with superb calm. "I have not made up my mind at all about Jimmy. He is dying to ask me, I know; but there is Bobby Harland, too. However, this morning—"

"You've seen Jimmy this morning, Betty!" Mary exclaimed.

"Well, how could I help it, girls?" Lady Betty went on, feeling that she was now a heroine. "I had to come to you. It was my bounden duty; and it's miles away, for Aunt Muriel always will have me in the dressing-room next her, when she takes me to stay out, and Uncle Aubrey across the passage; and it makes him so cross. But that's not it. I mean, it is not my fault, if the Duke has only arranged three new bathrooms down the bachelors' wing, and people are obliged to be waiting about for their turn, and I had to pass the entrance to that passage, and it happened to be Jimmy's, and he was just going in, when he saw me and rushed along, and said 'Good morning,' not a bit put out! I thought it would look silly to run, so I said 'Good morning,' too; and then we both giggled, and I came on. But I am rather glad after all, because now I've seen him; and he looks better—like that—than I am sure Bobby would have done, so perhaps, after all, I'll marry him! And you will be my bridesmaids, darlings, and now I must run!"

Upon such slender threads—the brushing of his hair—how often does the fate of man hang! If he but knew!

Almost every one was punctual for breakfast. They all came in with their gifts for Lady Ethelrida; and there was much chaffing and joking, and delightful little shrieks of surprise, as the parcels were opened.

Every soul loved Lady Ethelrida, from the lordly Groom of the Chambers to the humblest pantry boy and scullery maid; and it was their delight every year to present her, from them all, with a huge trophy of flowers, while the post brought countless messages and gifts of remembrance from absent friends. No one could have been more sweet and gracious than her ladyship was; and underneath, her gentle heart was beating with an extra excitement, when she thought of her rendezvous at half-past ten o'clock. Would he—she no longer thought of him as Mr. Markrute—would he be able to find the way?

"I must go and give some orders now," she said, about a quarter past ten, to the group which surrounded her, when they had all got up and were standing beside the fire. "And we all assemble in the hall at eleven." And so she slipped away.

Francis Markrute, she noticed, had retired some moments before.

"Heinrich," he had said to his Austrian valet, the previous evening, as he was helping him on with his coat for dinner, "I may want to know the locality of the Lady Ethelrida's sitting-room early to-morrow. Make it your business to become friendly with her ladyship's maid, so that I can have a parcel of books, which will arrive in the morning, placed safely there at any moment I want to, unobserved. Unpack the books, leaving their tissue papers still upon them, and bring them in when you call me. I will give you further orders then for their disposal. You understand?"

It was as well to be prepared for anything, he thought, which was most fortunate, as it afterwards turned out. He had meant to make her ask him to her sitting-room in any case, and his happiness was augmented, as they had talked in the picture gallery, when she did it of her own accord.

Lady Ethelrida stood looking out of her window, in her fresh, white-paneled, lilac-chintzed bower. Her heart was actually thumping now. She had not noticed the books, which were carefully placed in a pile down beside her writing table. Would he ever get away from her father, who seemed to have taken to having endless political discussions with him? Would he ever be able to come in time to talk for a moment, before they must both go down? She had taken the precaution to make herself quite ready to start—short skirt, soft felt hat, thick boots and all.

Would he? But as half-past ten chimed from the Dresden clock on the mantelpiece, there was a gentle tap at the door, and Francis Markrute came in.

He knew in an instant, experienced fowler that he was, that his bird was fluttered with expectancy, and it gave him an exquisite thrill. He was perfectly cognizant of the value of investing simple circumstances with delightful mystery, at times; and he knew, to the Lady Ethelrida, this trysting with him had become a momentous thing.

"You see, I found the way," he said softly, and he allowed something of the joy and tenderness he felt to come into his voice.

And Lady Ethelrida answered a little nervously that she was glad, and then continued quickly that she must show him her bookcases, because there was so little time.

"Only one short half-hour—if you will let me stay so long," he pleaded.

In his hand he carried the original volume he had spoken about, a very old edition of Shakespeare's Sonnets, from which he had carefully had one or two removed. It was exquisitely bound and tooled, and had her monogram worked into a beautiful little medallion—a work of art. He handed it to her first.

"This I ventured to have ordered for you long ago," he said. "Six weeks it is nearly, and I so feared until yesterday that you would not let me give it to you. It does not mean for your birthday: it is our original bond of acquaintance."

"It is too beautiful," said Lady Ethelrida, looking down.

"And over there by your writing table"—he had carefully ascertained this locality from Heinrich—"you will find the books that are my birthday gift, if you will give me the delight of accepting them."

She went forward with a little cry of surprise and pleasure, while, instantaneously, the wonder of how he should know where they would be presented itself to her mind.

They were about six volumes. A Heine, a couple of de Musset's, and then three volumes of selected poems, from numbers of the English poets. Lady Ethelrida picked them up delightedly. They, too, were works of art, in their soft mauve morocco bindings, *chiffré*, with her monogram like the other, and tooled with gold.

"How enchanting!" she said. "And look! They match my room. How could you have guessed—?" And then she broke off and again looked down.

"You told me, the night I dined with you at Glastonbury House, that you loved mauve as a color and that violets were your favorite flower. How could I forget?" And he permitted himself to come a step nearer to her.

She did not move away. She turned over the leaves of the English volume rather hurriedly. The paper was superlatively fine and the print a gem of art. And then she looked up, surprised.

"I have never seen this collection before," she said wonderingly. "All the things one loves under the same cover!" And then she turned to the title-page to see which edition it was; and she found that, as far as information went, it was blank. Simply,

"To The Lady Ethelrida Montfitchet

1

was inscribed upon it in gold. A deep pink flush grew on her delicate face, and she dared not raise her eyes.

It would be too soon yet to tell her everything that was in his heart, he reasoned. All could be lost by one false step. So, with his masterly self-control, he resisted all temptation to fold her in his arms, and said gently:

"I thought it would be nice to have, as you say, 'all the bits one loves' put together; and I have a very intelligent friend at my book-binder's, who, when I had selected them, had them all arranged and printed for me, and bound as I thought you might wish. It will gratify me greatly, if it has pleased you."

"Pleased me!" she said, and now she looked up; for the sudden conviction came to her, that to have this done took time and a great deal of money; and except once or twice before, casually, she had never met him until the evening, when, among a number of her father's political friends, he had dined at their London house. When could he have given the order and what could this mean? He read her thoughts.

"Yes," he said simply. "From the very first moment I ever saw you, Lady Ethelrida, to me you seemed all that was true and beautiful, the embodiment of my ideal of womanhood. I planned these books then, two days after I dined with you at Glastonbury House; and, if you had refused them, it would have caused me pain."

Ethelrida was so moved by some new, sudden and exquisite emotion that she could not reply for a moment. He watched her with growing and passionate delight, but he said nothing. He must give her time.

"It is too, too nice of you," she said softly, and there was a little catch in her breath. "No one has ever thought of anything so exquisite for me before, although, as you saw this morning, every one is so very kind. How shall I thank you, Mr. Markrute? I do not know."

"You must not thank me at all, you gracious lady," he said. "And now I must tell you that the half-hour is nearly up, and we must go down. But—may I—will you let me come again, perhaps to-morrow afternoon? I want to tell you, if it would interest you, the history of a man."

Ethelrida had turned to look at the clock, also, and had collected herself. She was too single-minded to fence now, or to push this new, strange joy out of her life, so she said,

"When the others go out for a walk, then, after lunch, yes, you may come."

And without anything further, they left the room. At the turn in the corridor to the other part of the house, he bent suddenly; and with deep homage kissed her hand, then let her pass on, while he turned to the right and disappeared towards the wing, where was his room.

CHAPTER XXVIII

Zara had, at first, thought she would not go out with the shooters. She felt numb, as if she could not pluck up enough courage to make conversation with any one. She had received a letter from Mimo, by the second post, with all details of what he had heard of Mirko. Little Agatha, the Morleys' child, was to return home the following day; and Mirko himself had written an excited little letter to announce this event, which Mimo enclosed. He seemed perfectly well then, only at the end, as she would see, he had said he was dreaming of *Maman* every night; and Mimo knew that this must mean he was a little feverish again, so he had felt it wiser to telegraph. Mirko had written out the score of the air which *Maman* always came and taught him, and he was longing to play it to his dear Papa and his Chérisette, the letter ended with.

And the pathos of it all caused Zara a sharp pain. She did not dare to look ahead, as far as her little brother was concerned. Indeed, to look ahead, in any case, meant nothing very happy.

She was just going up the great staircase at about a quarter to eleven, with the letter in her hand, when she met Tristram coming from his room, with his shooting boots on, ready to start. He stopped and said coldly—they had not spoken a word yet that day—

"You had better be quick putting your things on. My uncle always starts punctually."

Then his eye caught the foreign writing on the letter, and he turned brusquely away, although, as he reasoned with himself a moment afterwards, it was ridiculous of him to be so moved, because she would naturally have a number of foreign correspondents. She saw him turn away, and it angered her in spite of her new mood. He need not show his dislike so plainly, she thought. So she answered haughtily,

"I had not intended to come. I am tired; and I do not know this sport, or whether it will please me. I should feel for the poor birds, I expect."

"I am sorry you are tired," he answered, contrite in an instant. "Of course, you must not come if you are. They will be awfully disappointed. But never mind. I will tell Ethelrida."

"It is nothing—my fatigue, I mean. If you think your cousin will mind, I will come." And she turned, without waiting for him to answer, and went on to her room.

And Tristram, after going back to his for something he had forgotten, presently went on down the stairs, a bitter smile on his face, and at the bottom met—Laura Highford.

She looked up into his eyes, and allowed tears to gather in hers. She had always plenty at her command.

"Tristram," she said with extreme gentleness, "you were cross with me yesterday afternoon, because you thought I was saying something about your wife. But don't you know, can't you understand, what it is to me to see you devoted to another woman? You may be changed, but I am always the same, and I—I—" And here she buried her face in her hands and went into a flood of tears.

Tristram was overcome with confusion and horror. He loathed scenes. Good heavens! If any one should come along!

"Laura, for goodness' sake! My dear girl, don't cry!" he exclaimed. He felt he would say anything to comfort her, and get over the chance of some one seeing this hateful exhibition.

But she continued to sob. She had caught sight of Zara's figure on the landing above, and her vengeful spirit desired to cause trouble, even at a cost to herself. Zara had been perfectly ready, all but her hat, and had hurried exceedingly to be in time, and thus had not been five minutes after her husband.

"Tristram!" wailed Laura, and, putting up her hands, placed them on his shoulders. "Darling, just kiss me once—quickly—to say good-bye."

And it was at this stage that Zara came full upon them, from a turn in the stairs. She heard Tristram say disgustedly, "No, I won't," and saw Lady Highford drop her arms; and in the three steps that separated them, her wonderful iron self-control, the inheritance of all her years of suffering, enabled her to stop as if she had seen nothing, and in an ordinary voice ask if they were to go to the great hall.

"The woman," as she called Laura, should not have the satisfaction of seeing a trace of emotion in her, or Tristram either. He had answered immediately, "Yes," and had walked on by her side, in an absolutely raging temper.

How dare Laura drag him into a disgraceful and ridiculous scene like this! He could have wrung her neck. What must Zara think? That he was simply a cad! He could not offer a single explanation, either; indeed, she had demanded none. He did blurt out, after a moment,

"Lady Highford was very much upset about something. She is hysterical."

"Poor thing!" said Zara indifferently, and walked on.

But when they got into the hall, where most of the company were, she suddenly felt her knees giving way under her, and hurriedly sank down on an oak chair.

She felt sick with jealous pain, even though she had plainly seen that Tristram was no willing victim. But upon what terms could they be, or have been, for Lady Highford so to lose all sense of shame?

Tristram was watching her anxiously. She must have seen the humiliating exhibition. It followed, then, she was perfectly indifferent, or she would have been annoyed. He wished that she had reproached him, or said something—anything—but to remain completely unmoved was too maddening.

Then the whole company, who were coming out, appeared, and they started. Some of the men were drawing lots to see if they should shoot in the morning or in the afternoon. The party was primarily for Lady Ethelrida's birthday, and the shoot merely an accessory.

Zara walked by the Crow, who was not shooting at all. She was wearied with Lord Elterton; wearied with every one. The Crow was sententious and amused her, and did not expect her to talk.

"You have never seen your husband shoot yet, I expect, Lady Tancred, have you?" he asked her; and when she said, "No," he went on, "Because you must watch him. He is a very fine shot."

She did not know anything about shooting, only that Tristram looked particularly attractive in his shooting clothes, and that English sportsmen were natural, unceremonious creatures, whom she was beginning to like very much. She wished she could open her heart to this quaint, kind old man, and ask him to explain things to her; but she could not, and presently they got to a safe place and watched.

Tristram happened to be fairly near them; and, yes, he was a good shot—she could see that. But, at first, the thud of the beautiful pheasants falling to the ground caused her to wince—she, who had looked upon the shattered face of Ladislaus, her husband, with only a quiver of disgust! But these creatures were in the glory of their beauty and the joy of life, and had preyed upon the souls of no one.

Her wonderful face, which interested Colonel Lowerby so, was again abstracted. Something had brought back that hateful moment to her memory; she could hear Féto, the dancer's shrieks, and see the blood; and she shivered suddenly and clasped her hands.

"Do you mind seeing the birds come down?" the Crow asked kindly.

"I do not know," she said. "I was thinking of some other shooting."

"Because," the Crow went on, "the women who rage against sport forget one thing,—the birds would not exist at all, if it were not for preserving them for this very reason. They would gradually be trapped and snared and exterminated; whereas, now they have a royal time, of food and courtship and mating, and they have no knowledge of their coming fate, and so live a life of splendor up to the last moment."

"How much better! Yes, indeed, I will never be foolish about them again. I will think of that." Then she exclaimed, "Oh, that was wonderful!" for Tristram got two rocketters at right and left, and then another with his second gun. His temper had not affected his eye, it seemed.

"Tristram is one of the best all-round sportsmen I know," the Crow announced, "and he has one of the kindest hearts. I have known him since he was a toddler. His mother was one of the beauties, when I first put on a cuirass."

Zara tried to control her interest, and merely said, "Yes?"

"Are you looking forward to the reception at Wrayth on Monday? I always wonder how a person unaccustomed to England would view all the speeches and dinners, the bonfire, and triumphal arches, and those things of a home-coming. Rather an ordeal, I expect."

Zara's eyes rounded, and she faltered,

"And shall I have to go through all that?"

The Crow was nonplussed. Had not her husband, then, told her, what every one else knew? Upon what terms could they possibly be? And before he was aware of it, he had blurted out, "Good Lord!"

Then, recollecting himself, he said,

"Why, yes. Tristram will say I have been frightening you. It is not so very bad, after all—only to smile and look gracious and shake hands. They will be all ready to think you perfect, if you do that. Even though there are a lot of beastly radicals about, Old England still bows down to a beautiful woman!"

Zara did not answer. She had heard about her beauty in most European languages, since she was sixteen. It was the last thing which mattered, she thought.

Then the Crow turned the conversation, as they walked on to the next stand.

Did she know that Lady Ethelrida had commanded that all the ladies were to get up impromptu fancy dresses for to-night, her birthday dinner, and all the men would be in hunt coats? he asked. Large parties were coming from the only two other big houses near, and they would dance afterward in the picture gallery. "A wonderful new band that came out in London this season is coming down," he ended with; and, then, as she replied she had heard, he asked her what she intended to be. "It must be something with your hair down—you must give us the treat of that."

"I have left it all to Lady Ethelrida and my sisters-in-law," she said. "We are going to contrive things the whole afternoon, after lunch."

Tristram came up behind them then, and the Crow stopped.

"I was telling your wife she must give us the pleasure of seeing her hair down, to-night, for the Tomfools' dinner, but I can't get a promise from her. We will have to appeal to you to exert your lordly authority. Can't be deprived of a treat like that!"

"I am afraid I have no influence or authority," Tristram answered shortly, for with a sudden pang he thought of the only time he had seen the glorious beauty of it, her hair, spread like a cloak around her, as she had turned and ordered him out of her room at Dover. She remembered the circumstance, too, and it hurt her equally, so that they walked along silently, staring in front of them, and each suffering pain; when, if they had had a grain of sense, they would have looked into each other's eyes, read the truth, and soon been in each other's arms. But they had not yet "dree'd their weird." And Fate, who mocks at fools, would not yet let them be.

So the clouds gathered overhead, as in their hearts, and it came on to pour with rain; and the ladies made a hurried rush to the house.

The hostess did not stand near Francis Markrute during the shooting. Some shy pleasure made her avoid him for the moment. She wanted to hug the remembrance of her great joy of the morning, and the knowledge that to-morrow, Sunday, after lunch, would bring her a like pleasure. And for the time being there was the delight of thinking over what he had said, the subtlety of his gift, and the manner of its giving.

Nothing so goes to the head of a woman of refined sensibilities as the intoxicating flattery of thought-out action in a man, when it is to lay homage at her feet, and the man is a grave and serious person, who is no worshiper of women.

Ethelrida trod on air, and looked unusually sweet and gracious.

And Francis Markrute watched her quietly, with great tenderness in his heart, and not the faintest misgiving. "Slow and sure" was his motto, and thus he drew always the current of success and contentment.

His only crumpled roseleaf was the face of his niece, which rather haunted him. There seemed no improvement in the relations of the pair, in spite of Zara having had ample cause to feel jealous about Lady Highford since their arrival. Elinka, too, had had strange and unreasonable turns in her nature, that is what had made her so attractive. What if Zara and this really fine young Englishman, with whom he had mated her, should never get on? Then he laughed, when he thought of the impossibility of his calculations finally miscarrying. It was, of course, only a question of time. However, he would tell her before she left for her "home-coming" at Wrayth on Monday, what he thought it was now safe and advisable that she should know, namely, that on her husband's side the marriage had been one of headlong desire for herself, after having refused the bargain before he had seen her. That would give her some bad moments of humiliation, he admitted, which perhaps she had not deserved, though it would certainly bring her to her knees and so, to Tristram's arms.

But for once, being really quite preoccupied with his own affairs and a little unbalanced by love as well, he miscalculated the force of a woman's pride. Zara's one idea now was to hide from Tristram the state of her feelings, believing, poor, bruised, wounded thing, that he no longer cared for her, believing that she herself had extinguished the torch of love.

CHAPTER XXIX

There was an air of restrained excitement, importance and mystery among the ladies at luncheon. They had got back to the house in time to have their conclave before that meal, and everything was satisfactorily settled. Lady Anningford, who had not accompanied them out shooting, had thought out a whole scheme, and announced it upon their return amidst acclamations.

They would represent as many characters as they could from the "Idylls of the King," because the style would be such loose, hanging kinds of garments, the maids could run up the long straight seams in no time. And it would be so much more delightful, all to carry out one idea, than the usual powdered heads and non-descript things people chose for such impromptu occasions. It only remained to finally decide the characters. She considered that Ethelrida should undoubtedly be *Guinevere*; but, above all, Zara must be *Isolt*!

"Of course, of course!" they all cried unanimously, while Zara's eyes went black. "*Tristram* and *Isolt*! How splendid!"

"And I shall be *Brangaine*, and give the love potion," Lady Anningford went on. "Although it does not come into the 'Idylls of the King,' it should do so. It is just because Tennyson was so fearfully, respectably Early Victorian! I have been looking all the real thing up in the 'Morte d' Arthur' in the library, and in the beautiful edition of 'Tristram and Yseult' in Ethelrida's room."

"How perfectly enchanting!" cried Lady Betty. "I must be the *Lady of the Lake*—it is much the most dramatic part. And let us get the big sword out of the armory for *Excalibur*! I can have it, and brandish it as I enter the room."

"Oh, nonsense, Betty darling!" Ethelrida said. "You are the very picture of *Lynette*, with your enchanting nose 'tiptilted like the tender petal of a flower,' and your shameful treatment of poor Jimmy!"

And Lady Betty, after bridling a little, consented.

Then the other parts were cast. Emily should be *Enid* and Mary, *Elaine*, while Lady Melton, Lady Thornby and Mrs. Harcourt should be the *Three Fair Queens*.

"I shall be *Ettarre*," said Lily Opie. "The others are all good and dull; and I prefer her, because I am sure she wasn't! And certainly Lady Highford must be *Vivien*! She is exactly the type, in one of her tea gowns!"

Laura rather liked the idea of *Vivien*. It had *cachet*, she thought. She was very fond of posing as a mysterious enchantress, the mystic touch pleased her vanity.

So, of the whole party, only Zara did not feel content. Tristram might think she had chosen this herself, as an advance towards him.

Then the discussion, as to the garments to be worn, began. Numbers of ornaments and bits of tea-gowns would do. But with her usual practical forethought, Lady Anningford had already taken time by the forelock, and asked that one of the motors, going in to Tilling Green on a message, should bring back all the bales of bright and light-colored merinos and nunscloths the one large general shop boasted of.

And, amidst screams of delighted excitement from the girls, the immense parcel was presently unpacked.

It contained marvels of white and creams, and one which was declared the exact thing for *Isolt*. It was a merino of that brilliant violent shade of azure, the tone which is advertised as "Rickett's Paris blue" for washing clothes. It had been in the shop for years, and was unearthed for this occasion—a perfect relic of later Victorian aniline dye.

"It will be simply too gorgeously wonderful, with just a fillet of gold round her head, and all her adorable red hair hanging down," Lady Anningford said to Ethelrida.

"We shan't have to wear a stitch underneath," Lady Betty announced decidedly, while she pirouetted before a cheval glass—they were all in Lady Anningford's room—with some stuff draped round her childish form. "The gowns must have the right look, just long, straight things, with hanging sleeves and perhaps a girdle. I shall have cream, and you, Mary, as *Elaine*, must have white; but Emily had better have that mauve for *Enid*, as she was married."

"Why must *Enid* have mauve because she is married?" asked Emily, who did not like the color.

"I don't know why," Lady Betty answered, "except that, if you are married, you can't possibly have white, like Mary and me, who aren't. People are quite different—after, and mauve is very respectable for them," she went on. Grammar never troubled her little ladyship, when giving her valuable opinion upon things and life.

"I think *Enid* was a goose," said Emily, pouting.

"Not half as much as *Elaine*," said Mary. "She had secured her *Geraint*, whereas *Elaine* made a perfect donkey of herself over *Lancelot*, who did not care for her."

"I like our parts much the best, Lily's and mine," said Lady Betty. "I do give my Jim—Gareth?—a lively time, at all events! Just what I should do, if it were in real life."

"What you do do, you mean, not what you would do, Minx!" said her aunt, laughing.

And at this stage the shooters were seen advancing across the park, and the band of ladies, full of importance, descended to luncheon.

Lady Anningford sat next the Crow and told him what they had decided, in strict confidence, of course.

"We shall have the most delightful fun, Crow. I have thought it all out. At dessert I am going to hand one of the gold cups in which we are going to put a glass of some of the Duke's original old Chartreuse, to the bridal pair, as if to drink their health; and then, when they have drunk it, I am going to be overcome at the mistake of having given them a love-potion, just as in the real story! You can't tell—it may bring them together."

"Queen Anne, you wonder!" said the Crow.

"It is such a deliciously incongruous idea, you see," Lady Anningford went on. "All of us in long pre-mediaeval garments, with floating hair, and all of you in modern hunt coats! I should like to have seen Tristram in gold chain armor."

The Crow grunted approval.

"Ethelrida is going to arrange that they go in to dinner together. She is going to say it will be their last chance before they get to *King Mark*. Won't it all be perfect?"

"Well, I suppose you know best," the Crow said, with his wise old head on one side. "But they are at a ticklish pass in their careers, I tell you. The balance might go either way. Don't make it too hard for them, out of mistaken kindness."

"You are tiresome, Crow!" retorted Lady Anningford. "I never can do a thing I think right without your warning me over it. Do leave it to me."

So, thus admonished, Colonel Lowerby went on with his luncheon.

Zara's eyes looked more stormy than ever, when her husband chanced to see them. He was sitting nearly opposite her, and he wondered what on earth she was thinking about. He was filled with a concentrated bitterness from the events of the morning. Her utter indifference over the Laura incident had galled him unbearably, although he told himself, as he had done before, the unconscionable fool he was to allow himself to go on being freshly wounded by each continued proof of her disdain of him. Why, when he knew a thing, should he not be prepared for it? He had a strong will; he *would* overcome his emotion for her. He could, at least, make himself treat her, outwardly with the same apparent insolent indifference, as she treated him.

He made a firm resolve once again, he would not speak to her at all, any more than he had done the last three days in Paris. He would accept the position until the Wrayth rejoicings were over, and then he would certainly make arrangements to go and shoot lions, or travel, or something. There should be no further "perhaps" about it. Life, with the agonizing longing for her, seeing her daily and being denied, was more than could be borne.

There was something about Zara's type, the white, exquisite beauty of her skin, her slenderly voluptuous shape, the stormy suggestion of hidden passion in her slumberous eyes, which had always aroused absolutely mad emotions in men. Tristram, who was a normal Englishman, self-contained and reserved, and too completely healthy to be highly-strung, felt undreamed-of sensations rise in him when he looked at her, which was as rarely as possible. He understood now what was meant by an obsession—all the states of love he had read of in French novels and dismissed as "tommyrot." She did not only affect him with a thrilling physical passion. It was an obsession of the mind as well. He suffered acutely; as each day passed it seemed as if he could not bear any more, and the next always brought some further pain.

They had actually only been married for ten days! and it seemed an eternity of anguish to both of them, for different reasons.

Zara's nature was trying to break through the iron bands of her life training. Once she had admitted to herself that she loved her husband, her suffering was as deep as his, only that she was more practiced in the art of suppressing all emotion. But it was no wonder that they both looked pale and stern, and quite unbridal.

The sportsmen started immediately after lunch again, and the ladies returned to their delightful work; and, when they all assembled for tea, everything was almost completed. Zara had been unable to resist the current of light-hearted gayety which was in the air, and now felt considerably better; so she allowed Lord Elterton to sit beside her after tea and pour homage at her feet, with the expression of an empress listening to an address of loyalty from some distant colony; and the Crow leant back in his chair and chuckled to himself, much to Lady Anningford's annoyance.

"What in the world is it, Crow?" she said. "When you laugh like that, I always know some diabolically cynical idea is floating in your head, and it is not good for you. Tell me at once what you mean!"

But Colonel Lowerby refused to be drawn, and presently took Tristram off into the billiard-room.

It was arranged that all the men, even the husbands, were to go down into the great white drawing-room first, so that the ladies might have the pleasure of making an entrance *en bande*, to the delight of every one. And when this group of Englishmen, so smart in their scarlet hunt coats, were assembled at the end, by the fireplace, footmen opened the big double doors, and the groom of the chambers announced,

"Her Majesty, *Queen Guinevere*, and the Ladies of her Court."

And Ethelrida advanced, her fair hair in two long plaits, with her mother's all-round diamond crown upon her head, and clothed in some white brocade garment, arranged with a blue merino cloak, trimmed with ermine and silver. She looked perfectly regal, and as nearly beautiful as she had ever done; and to the admiring eyes of Francis Markrute, she seemed to outshine all the rest.

Then, their names called as they entered, came Enid and Elaine, each fair and sweet; and Vivien and Ettarre; then Lynette walking alone, with her saucy nose in the air and her flaxen curls spread out over her cream robe, a most bewitching sight.

Several paces behind her came the *Three Fair Queens*, all in wonderfully contrived garments, and misty, floating veils; and lastly, quite ten paces in the rear, walked *Isolt*, followed by her *Brangaine*. And when the group by the fireplace caught sight of her, they one and all drew in their breath.

For Zara had surpassed all expectations. The intense and blatant blue of her long clinging robe, which would have killed the charms of nine women out of ten, seemed to enhance the beauty of her pure white skin and marvelous hair. It fell like a red shining cloak all round her, kept in only by a thin fillet of gold, while her dark eyes gleamed with a new excitement. She had relaxed her dominion of herself, and was allowing the natural triumphant woman in her to have its day. For once in her life she forgot everything of sorrow and care, and permitted herself to rejoice in her own beauty and its effect upon the world before her.

"Jee-hoshaphat!" was the first articulate word that the company heard, from the hush which had fallen upon them; and then there was a chorus of general admiration, in which all the ladies had their share. And only the Crow happened to glance at Tristram, and saw that his face was white as death.

Then the two parties, about twenty people in all, began to arrive from the other houses, and delighted exclamations of surprise at the splendor of the impromptu fancy garments were heard all over the room, and soon dinner was announced, and they went in.

"My Lord Tristram," Ethelrida had said to her cousin, "I beg of you to conduct to my festal board your own most beautiful *Lady Isolt*. Remember, on Monday you leave us for the realm of *King Mark*, so make the most of your time!" And she turned and led forward Zara, and placed her hand in his; she, and they all, were too preoccupied with excitement and joy to see the look of deep pain in his eyes.

He held his wife's hand, until the procession started, and neither of them spoke a word. Zara, still exalted with the spirit of the night, felt only a wild excitement. She was glad he could see her beauty and her hair, and she raised her head and shook it back, as they started, with a provoking air.

But Tristram never spoke; and by the time they had reached the banqueting-hall, some of her exaltation died down, and she felt a chill.

Her hair was so very long and thick that she had to push it aside, to sit down, and in doing so a mesh flew out and touched his face; and the Crow, who was watching the whole drama intently, noticed that he shivered and, if possible, grew more pale. So he turned to his own servant, behind his chair, who with some of the other valets, was helping to wait, and whispered to him, "Go and see that Lord Tancred is handed brandy, at once, before the soup."

And so the feast began.

On Zara's other hand sat the Duke, and on Tristram's, Brangaine—for so she and Ethelrida had arranged for their later plan; and after the brandy, which Tristram dimly wondered why he should have been handed, he pulled himself together, and tried to talk; and Zara busied herself with the Duke. She quite came out of her usual silence, and laughed, and looked so divinely attractive that the splendid old gentleman felt it all going to his head; and his thoughts wondered bluntly, how soon, if he were his nephew, he would take her away after dinner and make love to her all to himself! But these modern young fellows had not half the mettle that he had had!

So at last dessert-time came, with its toasts for the *Queen Guinevere*. And the bridal pair had spoken together never a word; and Lady Anningford, who was watching them, began to fear for the success of her plan. However, there was no use turning back now. So, amidst jests of all sorts in keeping with the spirit of Camelot and the Table Round, at last *Brangaine* rose and, taking the gold cup in front of her, said,

"I, *Brangaine*, commissioned by her Lady Mother, to conduct the *Lady Isolt* safely to *King Mark*, under the knightly protection of the *Lord Tristram*, do now propose to drink their health, and ye must all do likewise, Lords and Ladies of Arthur's court." And she sipped her own glass, while she handed the gold cup to the Duke, who passed it on to the pair; and Tristram, because all eyes were upon him, forced himself to continue the jest. So he rose and, taking Zara's hand, while he bowed to the company, gave her the cup to drink, and then took it himself, while he drained the measure. And every one cried, amidst great excitement, "The health and happiness of *Tristram* and *Isolt*!"

Then, when the tumult had subsided a little, *Brangaine* gave a pretended shriek.

"Mercy me! I am undone!" she cried. "They have quaffed of the wrong cup! That gold goblet contained a love-potion distilled from rare plants by the Queen, and destined for the wedding wine of *Isolt* and *King Mark*! And now the *Lord Tristram* and she have drunk it together, by misadventure, and can never be parted more! Oh, misery me! What have I done!"

And amidst shouts of delighted laughter led by the Crow—in frozen silence, Tristram held his wife's hand.

But after a second, the breeding in them both, as on their wedding evening before the waiters, again enabled them to continue the comedy; and they, too, laughed, and, with the Duke's assistance, got through the rest of dinner, until they all rose and went out, two and two, the men leading their ladies by the hand, as they had come in.

And if the cup had indeed contained a potion distilled by the Irish sorceress Queen, the two victims could not have felt more passionately in love.

But Tristram's pride won the day for him, for this one time, and not by a glance or a turn of his head did he let his bride see how wildly her superlative attraction had kindled the fire in his blood. And when the dancing began, he danced with every other lady first, and then went off into the smoking-room, and only just returned in time to be made to lead out his "*Isolt*" in a final quadrille—not a valse. No powers would have made him endure the temptation of a valse!

And even this much, the taking of her hand, her nearness, the sight of the exquisite curves of her slender figure, and her floating hair, caused him an anguish unspeakable, so that when the rest of the company had gone, and good nights were said, he went up to his room, changed his coat, and strode away alone, out into the night.

Not by a glance or a turn of the head did he let his bride see how wildly her superlative attraction had kindled the fire in his blood."

CHAPTER XXX

Every one was so sleepy and tired on Sunday morning, after their night at Arthur's Court, that only Lady Ethelrida and Laura Highford, who had a pose of extreme piety always ready at hand, started with the Duke and Young Billy for church. Francis Markrute watched them go from his window, which looked upon the entrance, and he thought how stately and noble his fair lady looked; and he admired her disciplined attitude, no carousal being allowed to interfere with her duties. She was a rare and perfect specimen of her class.

His lady fair! For he had determined, if fate plainly gave him the indication, to risk asking her to-day to be his fair lady indeed. A man must know when to strike, if the iron is hot.

He had carefully prepared all the avenues; and had made himself of great importance to the Duke, allowing his masterly brain to be seen in glimpses, and convincing His Grace of his possible great usefulness to the party to which he belonged. He did not look for continued opposition in that quarter, once he should have assured himself that Lady Ethelrida loved him. That he loved her, with all the force of his self-contained nature, was beyond any doubt. Love, as a rule, recks little of the suitability of the object, when it attacks a heart; but in some few cases—that is the peculiar charm—Francis Markrute had waited until he was forty-six years old, firmly keeping to his ideal, until he found her, in a measure of perfection, of which even he had not dared to dream. His theory, which he had proved in his whole life, was that nothing is beyond the grasp of a man who is master of himself and his emotions. But even his iron nerves felt the tension of excitement, as luncheon drew to an end, and he knew in half an hour, when most of the company were safely disposed of, he should again find his way to his lady's shrine.

Ethelrida did not look at him. She was her usual, charmingly-gracious self to her neighbors, solicitous of Tristram's headache. He had only just appeared, and looked what he felt—a wreck. She was interested in some news in the Sunday papers, which had arrived; and in short, not a soul guessed how her gentle being was uplifted, and her tender heart beating with this, the first real emotion she had ever experienced.

Even the Crow, so thrilled with his interest in the bridal pair, had not scented anything unusual in his hostess's attitude towards one of her guests.

"I think Mr. Markrute is awfully attractive, don't you, Crow?" said Lady Anningford, as they started for their walk. To go to Lynton Heights after lunch on Sunday was almost an invariable custom at Montfitchet. "I can't say what it is, but it is something subtle and extraordinary, like that in his niece—what do you think?"

Colonel Lowerby paused, struck from her words by the fact that he had been too preoccupied to have noticed this really interesting man.

"Why, 'pon my soul—I haven't thought!" he said, "but now you speak of it, I do think he is a remarkable chap."

"He is so very quiet," Lady Anningford went on, "and, whenever he speaks, it is something worth listening to; and if you get on any subject of books, he is a perfect encyclopaedia. He gives me the impression of all the forces of power and will, concentrated in a man. I wonder who he really is? Not that it matters a bit in these days. Do you think there is any Jew in him? It does not show in his type, but when foreigners are very rich there generally is."

"Sure to be, as he is so intelligent," the Crow growled. "If you notice, numbers of the English families who show brains have a touch of it in the background. So long as the touch is far enough away, I have no objection to it myself—prefer folks not to be fools."

"I believe I have no prejudices at all," said Lady Anningford. "If I like people, I don't care what is in their blood."

"It is all right till you scratch 'em. Then it comes out; but if, as I say, it is far enough back, the Jew will do the future Tancred race a power of good, to get the commercial common sense of it into them—knew Maurice Grey, her father, years ago, and he was just as indifferent to money and material things, as Tristram is himself. So the good will come from the Markrute side, we will hope."

"I rather wonder, Crow—if there ever will be any more of the Tancred race. I thought last night we had a great failure, and that nothing will make that affair prosper. I don't believe they ever see one another from one day to the next! It is extremely sad."

"I told you they had come to a ticklish point in their careers," the Crow permitted himself to remind his friend, "and, 'pon my soul, I could not bet you one way or another how it will go. 'I hae me doots,' as the Scotchman said."

Meanwhile, Ethelrida, on the plea of letters to write, had retired to her room; and there, as the clock struck a quarter past three, she awaited—what? She would not own to herself that it was her fate. She threw dust in her own eyes, and called it a pleasant talk!

She looked absurdly young for her twenty-six years, just a dainty slip of a patrician girl, as she sat there on her chintz sofa, with its fresh pattern of lilacs and tender green. Everything was in harmony, even to her soft violet cloth dress trimmed with fur.

And again as the hour for the trysting chimed, her lover that was to be, entered the room.

"This is perfectly divine," he said, as he came in, while the roguish twinkle of a schoolboy, who has outwitted his mates sparkled in his fine eyes. "All those good people tramping for miles in the cold and damp, while we two sensible ones are going to enjoy a nice fire and a friendly chat."

Thus he disarmed her nervousness, and gave her time.

"May I sit by you, my Lady Ethelrida?" he said; and as she smiled, he took his seat, but not too near her—nothing must be the least hurried or out of place.

So for about a quarter of an hour they talked of books—their favorites—hers, all so simple and chaste, his, of all kinds, so long as they showed style, and were masterpieces of taste and balance. Then, as a great piece of wood fell in the open grate and made a volley of sparks, he leaned forward a little and asked her if he might tell her that for which he had come, the history of a man.

The daylight was drawing in, and they had an hour before them.

"Yes," said Ethelrida, "only let us make up the fire first, and only turn on that one soft light," and she pointed to a big gray china owl who carried a simple shade of white painted with lilacs on his back. "Then we need not move again, because I want extremely to hear it—the history of a man."

He obeyed her commands, and also drew the silk blinds.

"Now, indeed, we are happy; at least, I am," he said.

Lady Ethelrida leant back on her muslin embroidered cushion and prepared herself to listen with a rapt face.

Francis Markrute stood by the fire for a while, and began from there:

"You must go right back with me to early days, Sweet Lady," he said, "to a palace in a gloomy city and to an artiste—a ballet-dancer—but at the same time a great *musicienne* and a good and beautiful woman, a woman with red, splendid hair, like my niece. There she lived in a palace in this city, away from the world with her two children; an Emperor was her lover and her children's father; and they all four were happy as the day was long. The children were a boy and a girl, and presently they began to grow up, and the boy began to think about life and to reason things out with himself. He had, perhaps, inherited this faculty from his grandfather, on his mother's side, who was a celebrated poet and philosopher and a Spanish Jew. So his mother, the beautiful dancer, was half Jewess, and, from her mother again, half Spanish noble; for this philosopher had eloped with the daughter of a Spanish grandee, and she was erased from the roll. I go back this far not to weary you, but that you may understand what forces in race had to do with the boy's character. The daughter again of this pair became an artist and a dancer, and being a highly educated, as well as a superbly beautiful woman—a woman with all Zara's charm and infinitely more chiseled features—she won the devoted love of the Emperor of the country in which they lived. I will not go into the moral aspect of the affair. A great love recks not of moral aspects. Sufficient to say, they were ideally happy while the beautiful dancer lived. She died when the boy was about fifteen, to his great and abiding grief. His sister, who was a year or two younger than he, was then all he had to love, because political and social reasons in that country made it very difficult, about this time, for him often to see his father, the Emperor.

"The boy was very carefully educated, and began early, as I have told you, to think for himself and to dream. He dreamed of things which might have been, had he been the heir and son of the Empress, instead of the child of her who seemed to him so much the greater lady and queen, his own mother, the dancer; and he came to see that dreams that are based upon regrets are useless and only a factor in the degradation, not the uplifting of a man. The boy grew to understand that from that sweet mother, even though the world called her an immoral woman, he had inherited something much more valuable to himself than the Imperial crown—the faculty of perception and balance, physical and moral, to which the family of the Emperor, his father, could lay no claim. From them, both he and his sister had inherited a stubborn, indomitable pride. You can see it, and have already remarked it, in Zara—that sister's child.

"So when the boy grew to be about twenty, he determined to carve out a career for himself, to create a great fortune, and so make his own little kingdom, which should not be bound by any country or race. He had an English tutor—he had always had one—and in his studies of countries and peoples and their attributes, the English seemed to him to be much the finest race. They were saner, more understanding, more full of the sense of the fitness of things, and of the knowledge of life and how to live it wisely.

"So the boy, with no country, and no ingrained patriotism for the place of his birth, determined he, being free and of no nation, should, when he had made this fortune, migrate there, and endeavor to obtain a place among those proud people, whom he so admired in his heart. That was his goal, in all his years of hard work, during which time he grew to understand the value of individual character, regardless of nation or of creed; and so, when finally he did come to this country, it was not to seek, but to command." And here Francis Markrute, master of vast wealth and the destinies of almost as many human souls as his father, the Emperor, had been, raised his head. And Lady Ethelrida, daughter of a hundred noble lords, knew her father, the Duke, was no prouder than he, the Spanish dancer's son. And something in her fine spirit went out to him; and she, there in the firelight with the soft owl lamp silvering her hair, stretched out her hand to him; and he held it and kissed it tenderly, as he took his seat by her side.

"My sweet and holy one," he said. "And so you understand!"

"Yes, yes!" said Ethelrida. "Oh, please go on"—and she leaned back against her pillow, but she did not seek to draw away her hand.

"There came a great grief, then, in the life of the boy who was now a grown man. His sister brought disgrace upon herself, and died under extremely distressful circumstances, into which I need not enter here; and for a while these things darkened and embittered his life." He paused a moment, and gazed into the fire, a look of deep sorrow and regret on his sharply-cut face, and Ethelrida unconsciously allowed her slim fingers to tighten in his grasp. And when he felt this gentle sympathy, he stroked her hand.

"The man was very hard then, sweet lady," he went on. "He regrets it now, deeply. The pure angel, who at this day rules his life, with her soft eyes of divine mercy and gentleness, has taught him many lessons; and it will be his everlasting regret that he was hard then. But it was a great deep wound to his pride, that quality which he had inherited from his father, and had not then completely checked and got in hand. Pride should be a factor for noble actions and a great spirit, but not for overbearance toward the failings of others. He knows that now. If this lady, whom he worships, should ever wish to learn the whole details of this time, he will tell her even at any cost to his pride, but for the moment let me get on to pleasanter things."

And Ethelrida whispered, "Yes, yes," so he continued:

"All his life from a boy's to a man's, this person we are speaking of had kept his ideal of the woman he should love. She must be fine and shapely, and noble and free; she must be tender and devoted, and gracious and good. But he passed all his early manhood and grew to middle age, before he even saw her shadow across his path. He looked up one night, eighteen months ago, at a court ball, and she passed him on the arm of a royal duke, and unconsciously brushed his coat with her soft dove's wing; and he knew that it was she, after all those years, so he waited and planned, and met her once or twice; but fate did not let him advance very far, and so a scheme entered his head. His niece, the daughter of his dead sister, had also had a very unhappy life; and he thought she, too, should come among these English people, and find happiness with their level ways. She was beautiful and proud and good, so he planned the marriage between his niece and the cousin of the lady he worshiped, knowing by that he should be drawn nearer his star, and also pay the debt to his dead sister, by securing the happiness of her child; but primarily it was his desire to be nearer his own worshiped star, and thus it has all come about." He paused, and looked full at her face, and saw that her sweet eyes were moist with some tender, happy tears. So he leaned forward, took her other hand, and kissed them both, placing the soft palms against his mouth for a second; then he whispered hoarsely, his voice at last trembling with the passionate emotion he felt:

"Ethelrida—darling—I love you with my soul—tell me, my sweet lady, will you be my wife?"

And the Lady Ethelrida did not answer, but allowed herself to be drawn into his arms.

And so in the firelight, with the watchful gray owl, the two rested blissfully content.

CHAPTER XXXI

When Lady Ethelrida came down to tea, her sweet face was prettily flushed, for she was quite unused to caresses and the kisses of a man. Her soft gray eyes were shining with a happiness of which she had not dreamed, and above all things, she was filled with the exquisite emotion of having a secret!—a secret of which even her dear friend Anne was ignorant—a blessed secret, just shared between her lover and herself. And Lady Anningford, who had no idea that she had spent the afternoon with the financier, but believed she had religiously written letters alone, wondered to herself what on earth made Ethelrida look so joyous and not the least fatigued, as most of the others were. She really got prettier, she thought, as she grew older, and was always the greatest dear in the whole world. But, to look as happy as that and have a face so flushed, was quite mysterious and required the opinion of the Crow!

So she dragged Colonel Lowerby off to a sofa, and began at once:

"Crow, do look at Ethelrida's face! Did you ever see one so idiotically blissful, except when she has been kissed by the person she loves?"

"Well, how do you know that is not the case with our dear Ethelrida?" grunted the Crow. "She did not come out for a walk. You had better count up, and see who else stayed at home!"

So Lady Anningford began laughingly. The idea was too impossible, but she must reason it out.

"There was Lord Melton but Lady Melton stayed behind, too, and the Thornbys—all impossible. There was no one else except Tristram, who I know was in the smoking-room, with a fearful headache, and Mr. Markrute, who was with the Duke."

"Was he with the Duke?" queried the Crow.

"Crow!" almost gasped Lady Anningford. "Do you mean to tell me that you think Ethelrida would have her face looking like that about a foreigner! My dear friend, you must have taken leave of your seven senses—" and then she paused, for several trifles came back to her recollection, connected with these two, which, now that the Crow had implanted a suspicion in her breast, began to assume considerable proportions.

Ethelrida had talked of most irrelevant matters always during their good-night chats, unless the subject happened to be Zara, and she had never once mentioned Mr. Markrute personally or given any opinion about him; and yet, as Anne had seen, they had often talked. There must be something in it, but that was not enough to account for Ethelrida's face. A pale, rather purely colorless complexion like hers did not suddenly change to bright scarlet cheeks, without some practical means! And, as Anne very well knew, kisses were a very practical means! But her friend Ethelrida would never allow any man to kiss her, unless she had promised to marry him. Now, if it had been Lily Opie, she could not have been so sure, though she hoped she could be sure of any nice girl; but about Ethelrida she could take her oath. It followed, as Ethelrida had been quite pale at lunch and was not a person who went to sleep over fires, something extraordinary must have happened—but what?

"Crow, dear, I have never been so thrilled in my life," she said, after her thoughts had come to this stage. "The lurid tragedy of the honeymoon pair cannot compare in interest to anything connected with my sweet Ethelrida, for me, so it is your duty to put that horribly wise, cynical brain of yours to work and unravel me this mystery. Look, here is Mr. Markrute coming in—let us watch his face!"

But, although they subjected the financier to the keenest good-natured scrutiny, he did not show a sign or give them any clue. He sat down quietly, and began talking casually to the group by the tea-table, while he methodically spread his bread and butter with blackberry jam. Such delicious schoolroom teas the company indulged in, at the hospitable tea-table of Montfitchet! He did not seem to be even addressing Ethelrida. What could it be?

"I believe we have made a mistake after all, Crow," Lady Anningford said disappointedly. "Look—he is quite unmoved."

The Crow gave one of his chuckles, while he answered slowly, between his sips of tea:

"A man doesn't handle millions in the year, and twist and turn about half the governments of Europe, if he can't keep his face from showing what he doesn't mean you to see! Bless your dear heart, Mr. Francis Markrute is no infant!" and the chuckle went on.

"You may think yourself very wise, Crow, and so you are," Lady Anningford retorted severely, "but you don't know anything about love. When a man is in love, even if he were Machiavelli himself, it would be bound to show in his eye—if one looked long enough."

"Then your plan, my dear Queen Anne, is to look," the Crow said, smiling. "For my part, I want to see how the other pair have got on. They are my pets; and I don't consider they have spent at all a suitable honeymoon Sunday afternoon—Tristram, with a headache in the smoking-room, and the bride, taking a walk and being made love to by Arthur Elterton, and Young Billy, alternately. The kid is as wild about her as Tristram himself, I believe!"

"Then you still think Tristram is in love with her, do you, Crow?" asked Anne, once more interested in her original thrill. "He did not show the smallest signs of it last night then, if so; and how he did not seize her in his arms and devour her there and then, with all that lovely hair down and her exquisite shape showing the outline so in that dress—I can't think! He must be as cold as a stone, and I never thought him so before, did you?"

"No, and he isn't either, I tell you what, my dear girl, there is something pretty grim keeping those two apart, I am sure. She is the kind of woman who arouses the fiercest passions; and Tristram is in the state that, if something were really to set alight his jealousy, he might kill her some day."

"Crow—how terrible!" gasped Anne, and then seeing that her friend's face was serious, and not chaffing, she, too, looked grave. "Then what on earth is to be done?" she asked.

"I don't know, I have been thinking it over ever since I came in. I found him in the smoking-room, staring in front of him, not even pretending to read, and looking pretty white about the gills; and when he saw it was only me, and I asked him if his head were worse, and whether he had not better have a brandy and soda, he simply said: 'No, thanks, the whole thing is a d—— rotten show.' I've known him since he was a blessed baby you know, so he didn't mind me for a minute. Then he recollected himself, and said, yes, he would have a drink; and when he poured it out, he only sipped it, and then forgot about it, jumped up, and blurted out he had some letters to write, so I left him. I am awfully sorry for the poor chap, I can tell you. If it is not fate, but some caprice of hers, she deserves a jolly good beating, for making him suffer like that."

"Couldn't you say something to her, Crow, dear? We are all so awfully fond of Tristram, and there does seem some tragedy hanging over them that ought to be stopped at once. Couldn't you, Crow?"

But Colonel Lowerby shook his head.

"It is too confoundedly ticklish," he grunted. "It might do some good, and it might just do the other thing. It is too dangerous to interfere."

"Well, you have made me thoroughly uncomfortable," Lady Anningford said. "I shall get hold of him to-night, and see what I can do."

"Then, mind you are careful, Queen Anne—that is all that I can say," and at that moment, the Duke joining them, the tête-à-tête broke up.

Zara had not appeared at tea. She said she was very tired, and would rest until dinner. If she had been there, her uncle had meant to take her aside into one of the smaller sitting-rooms, and tell her the piece of information he deemed it now advisable for her to know; but as she did not appear, or Tristram, either, he thought after all they might be together, and his interference would be unnecessary. But he decided, if he saw the same frigid state of things at dinner, he would certainly speak to her after it; and relieved from duty, he went once more to find his lady love in her sitting-room.

"Francis!" she whispered, as he held her next his heart for a moment. "You must not stay ten minutes, for Lady Anningford or Lady Melton is sure to come in—Anne, especially, who has been looking at me with such reproachful eyes, for having neglected her all this, our last afternoon."

"I care not for a thousand Annes, Ethelrida mine!" he said softly, as he kissed her. "If she does come, will it matter? Would you rather she did not guess anything yet, my dearest?"

"Yes—" said Ethelrida, "—I don't want any one to know, until you have told my father,—will you do so to-night—or wait until to-morrow? I—I can't—I feel so shy—and he will be so surprised." She did not add her secret fear that her parent might be very angry.

They had sat down upon the sofa now, under the light of their kindly gray owl; and Francis Markrute contented himself with caressing his lady's hair, as he answered:

"I thought of asking the Duke, if I might stay until the afternoon train, as I had something important to discuss with him, and then wait and see him quietly, when all the others have gone, if that is what you would wish, my sweet. I will do exactly as you desire about all things. I want you to understand that. You are to have your own way in everything in life."

"You know very well that I should never want it, if it differed from yours, Francis." What music he found in his name! "You are so very wise, it will be divine to let you guide me!" Which tender speech showed that the gentle Ethelrida had none of the attitude of the modern bride.

And thus it was arranged. The middle-aged, but boyishly-in-love, fiancé was to tackle his future father-in-law in the morning's light; and to-night, let the household sleep in peace!

So, after a blissful interlude, as he saw in spite of the joy they found together, his Ethelrida was still slightly nervous of Lady Anningford's entrance, he got up to say good night, as alas! this would probably be the last chance they would have alone before he left.

"And you will not make me wait too long, my darling," he implored, "will you? You see, every moment away from you, will now be wasted. I do not know how I have borne all these years alone!"

And she promised everything he wished, for Francis Markrute, at forty-six, had far more allurements than an impetuous young lover. Not a tenderness, a subtlety of flattery and homage, those things so dear to a woman's heart, were forgotten by him. He really worshiped Ethelrida and his fashion of showing his feeling was in all ways to think first of what she would wish; which proved that if her attitude were unmodern, as far as women were concerned, his was even more so, among men!

Tristram had gone out for another walk alone, after the Crow had left him. He wanted to realize the details of the coming week, and settle with himself how best to get through with them.

He and Zara were to start in their own motor at about eleven for Wrayth, which was only forty miles across the border into Suffolk. They would reach it inside of two hours easily, and arrive at the first triumphal arch of the park before one; and so go on through the shouting villagers to the house, where in the great banqueting hall, which still remained, a relic of Henry IV's time, joined on to the Norman keep, they would have to assist at a great luncheon to the principal tenants, while the lesser fry feasted in a huge tent in the outer courtyard.

Here, endless speeches would have to be made and listened to, and joy simulated, and a general air of hilarity kept up; and the old housekeeper would have prepared the large rooms in the Adam wing for their reception; and they would not be free to separate, until late at night, for there would be the servants' and employés' ball, after a tête-à-tête dinner in state, where their every action would be watched and commented upon by many curious eyes. Yes, it was a terrible ordeal to go through, under the circumstances; and no wonder he wanted the cold, frosty evening air to brace him up!

At the end of his troubled thoughts he had come to the conclusion that there was only one thing to be done—he must speak to her to-night, tell her what to expect, and ask her to play her part. "She is fortunately game, even if cold as stone," he said to himself, "and if I appeal to her pride, she will help me out." So he came back into the house, and went straight up to her room. He had been through too much suffering and anguish of heart, all night and all day, to be fearful of temptation. He felt numb, as he knocked at the door and an indifferent voice called out, "Come in!"

He opened it a few inches and said: "It is I—Tristram—I have something I must say to you—May I come in?—or would you prefer to come down to one of the sitting-rooms? I dare say we could find one empty, so as to be alone."

"Please come in," her voice said, and she was conscious that she was trembling from head to foot.

So he obeyed her, shutting the door firmly after him and advancing to the fireplace. She had been lying upon the sofa wrapped in a soft blue tea-gown, and her hair hung in the two long plaits, which she always unwound when she could to take its weight from her head. She rose from her reclining position and sat in the corner; and after glancing at her for a second, Tristram turned his eyes away, and leaning on the mantelpiece, began in a cold grave voice:

"I have to ask you to do me a favor. It is to help me through to-morrow and the few days after, as best you can, by conforming to our ways. It has been always the custom in the family, when a Tancred brought home his bride, to have all sorts of silly rejoicings. There will be triumphal arches in the park, and collections of village people, a lunch for the principal tenants, speeches, and all sorts of boring things. Then we shall have to dine alone in the state dining-room, with all the servants watching us, and go to the household and tenants' ball in the great hall. It will all be ghastly, as you can see." He paused a moment, but he did not change the set tone in his voice when he spoke again, nor did he look at her. He had now come to the hardest part of his task.

"All these people—who are my people," he went on, "think a great deal of these things, and of us—that is—myself, as their landlord, and you as my wife. We have always been friends, the country folk at Wrayth and my family, and they adored my mother. They are looking forward to our coming back and opening the house again—and—and—all that—and—" here he paused a second time, it seemed as if his throat were dry, for suddenly the remembrance of his dreams as he looked at Tristram Guiscard's armor, which he had worn at Agincourt, came back to him—his dreams in his old oak-paneled room—of their home-coming to Wrayth; and the mockery of the reality hit him in the face.

Zara clasped her hands, and if he had glanced at her again, he would have seen all the love and anguish which was convulsing her shining in her sad eyes.

He mastered the emotion which had hoarsened his voice, and went on in an even tone: "What I have to ask is that you will do your share—wear some beautiful clothes, and smile, and look as if you cared; and if I feel that it will be necessary to take your hand or even kiss you, do not frown at me, or think I am doing it from choice—I ask you, because I believe you are as proud as I am,—I ask you, please, to play the game."

And now he looked up at her, but the terrible emotion she was suffering had made her droop her head. He would not kiss her or take her hand—from choice—that was the main thing her woman's heart had grasped, the main thing, which cut her like a knife.

"You can count upon me," she said, so low he could hardly hear her; and then she raised her head proudly, and looked straight in front of her, but not at him, while she repeated more firmly: "I will do in every way what you wish—what your mother would have done. I am no weakling, you know, and as you said, I am as proud as yourself."

He dared not look at her, now the bargain was made, so he took a step towards the door, and then turned and said:

"I thank you—I shall be grateful to you. Whatever may occur, please believe that nothing that may look as if it was my wish to throw us together, as though we were really husband and wife, will be my fault; and you can count upon my making the thing as easy for you as I can—and when the mockery of the rejoicings are over—then we can discuss our future plans."

And though Zara was longing to cry aloud in passionate pain, "I love you! I love you! Come back and beat me, if you will, only do not go coldly like that!" she spoke never a word. The strange iron habit of her life held her, and he went sadly from the room.

And when he had gone, she could control herself no longer and, forgetful of coming maid and approaching dinner, she groveled on the white bearskin rug before the fire, and gave way to passionate tears—only to recollect in a moment the position of things. Then she got up and shook with passion against fate, and civilization, and custom—against the whole of life. She could not even cry in peace. No! She must play the game! So her eyes had to be bathed, the window opened, and the icy air breathed in, and at last she had quieted herself down to the look of a person with a headache, when the dressing-gong sounded, and her maid came into the room.

CHAPTER XXXII

This, the last dinner at Montfitchet, passed more quietly than the rest. The company were perhaps subdued, from their revels of the night before; and every one hates the thought of breaking up a delightful party and separating on the morrow, even when it has only been a merry gathering like this.

And two people were divinely happy, and two people supremely sad, and one mean little heart was full of bitterness and malice unassuaged. So after dinner was over, and they were all once more in the white drawing-room, the different elements assorted themselves.

Lady Anningford took Tristram aside and began, with great tact and much feeling, to see if he could be cajoled into a better mood; and finally got severely snubbed for her trouble, which hurt her more because she realized how deep must be his pain than from any offense to herself. Then Laura caught him and implanted her last sting:

"You are going away to-morrow, Tristram,—into your new life—and when you have found out all about your wife—and her handsome friend—you may remember that there was one woman who loved you truly—" and then she moved on and left him sitting there, too raging to move.

After this, his uncle had joined him, had talked politics, and just at the end, for the hearty old gentleman could not believe a man could really be cold or indifferent to as beautiful a piece of flesh and blood as his new niece, he had said:

"Tristram, my dear boy,—I don't know whether it is the modern spirit—or not—but, if I were you, I'd be hanged if I would let that divine creature, your wife, out of my sight day or night!—When you get her alone at Wrayth, just kiss her until she can't breathe—and you'll find it is all right!"

With which absolutely sensible advice, he had slapped his nephew on the back, fixed in his eyeglass, and walked off; and Tristram had stood there, his blue eyes hollow with pain, and had laughed a bitter laugh, and gone to play bridge, which he loathed, with the Meltons and Mrs. Harcourt. So for him, the evening had passed.

And Francis Markrute had taken his niece aside to give her his bit of salutary information. He wished to get it over as quickly as possible, and had drawn her to a sofa rather behind a screen, where they were not too much observed.

"We have all had a most delightful visit, I am sure, Zara," he had said, "but you and Tristram seem not to be yet as good friends as I could wish."

He paused a moment, but as usual she did not speak, so he went on:

"There is one thing you might as well know, I believe you have not realized it yet, unless Tristram has told you of it himself."

She looked up now, startled—of what was she ignorant then?

"You may remember the afternoon I made the bargain with you about the marriage," Francis Markrute went on. "Well, that afternoon Tristram, your husband, had refused my offer of you and your fortune with scorn. He would never wed a rich woman he said, or a woman he did not know or love, for any material gain; but I knew he would think differently when he had seen how beautiful and attractive you were, so I continued to make my plans. You know my methods, my dear niece."

Zara's blazing and yet pitiful eyes were all his answer.

"Well, I calculated rightly. He came to dinner that night, and fell madly in love with you, and at once asked to marry you himself, while he insisted upon your fortune being tied up entirely upon you, and any children that you might have, only allowing me to pay off the mortgages on Wrayth for himself. It would be impossible for a man to have behaved more like a gentleman. I thought now, in case you had not grasped all this, you had better know." And then he said anxiously, "Zara—my dear child—what is the matter?" for her proud head had fallen forward on her breast, with a sudden deadly faintness. This, indeed, was the filling of her cup.

His voice pulled her together, and she sat up; and to the end of his life, Francis Markrute will never like to remember the look in her eyes.

"And you let me go on and marry him, playing this cheat? You let me go on and spoil both our lives! What had I ever done to you, my uncle, that you should be so cruel to me? Or is it to be revenged upon my mother for the hurt she brought to your pride?"

If she had reproached him, stormed at him, anything, he could have borne it better; but the utter lifeless calm of her voice, the hopeless look in her beautiful white face, touched his heart—that heart but newly unwrapped and humanized from its mummifying encasements by the omnipotent God of Love. Had he, after all, been too coldly calculating about this human creature of his own flesh and blood? Was there some insurmountable barrier grown up from his action? For the first moment in his life he was filled with doubt and fear.

"Zara," he said, anxiously, "tell me, dear child, what you mean? I let you go on in the 'cheat,' as you call it, because I knew you never would consent to the bargain, unless you thought it was equal on both sides. I know your sense of honor, dear, but I calculated, and I thought rightly, that, Tristram being so in love with you, he would soon undeceive you, directly you were alone. I never believed a woman could be so cold as to resist his wonderful charm—Zara—what has happened?—'Won't you tell me, child?"

But she sat there turned to stone. She had no thought to reproach him. Her heart and her spirit seemed broken, that was all.

"Zara—would you like me to do anything? Can I explain anything to him? Can I help you to be happy? I assure you it hurts me awfully, if this will not turn out all right—Zara," for she had risen a little unsteadily from her seat beside him. "You cannot be indifferent to him for ever—he is too splendid a man. Cannot I do anything for you, my niece?"

Then she looked at him, and her eyes in their deep tragedy seemed to burn out of her deadly white face.

"No, thank you, my uncle,—there is nothing to be done—everything is now too late." Then she added in the same monotonous voice, "I am very tired, I think I will wish you a good night." And with immense dignity, she left him; and making her excuses with gentle grace to the Duke and Lady Ethelrida, she glided from the room.

And Francis Markrute, as he watched her, felt his whole being wrung with emotion and pain.

"My God!" he said to himself. "She is a glorious woman, and it will—it must—come right—even yet."

And then he set his brain to calculate how he could assist them, and finally his reasoning powers came back to him, and he comforted himself with the deductions he made.

She was going away alone with this most desirable young man into the romantic environment of Wrayth. Human physical passion, to say the least of it, was too strong to keep them apart for ever, so he could safely leave the adjusting of this puzzle to the discretion of fate.

And Zara, freed at last from eye of friend or maid, collapsed on to the white bearskin in front of the fire again, and tried to think. So she had been offered as a chattel and been refused! Here her spirit burnt with humiliation. Her uncle, she knew, always had used her merely as a pawn in some game—what game? He was not a snob; the position of uncle to Tristram would not have tempted him alone; he never did anything without a motive and a deep one. Could it be that he himself was in love with Lady Ethelrida? She had been too preoccupied with her own affairs to be struck with those of others, but now as she looked back, he had shown an interest which was not in his general attitude towards women. How her mother had loved him, this wonderful brother! It was her abiding grief always, his unforgiveness,—and perhaps, although it seemed impossible to her, Lady Ethelrida was attracted by him, too. Yes, that must be it. It was to be connected with the family, to make his position stronger in the Duke's eyes, that he had done this cruel thing. But, would it have been cruel if she herself had been human and different? He had called her from struggling and poverty, had given her this splendid young husband, and riches and place,—no, there was nothing cruel in it, as a calculated action. It should have given her her heart's desire. It was she, herself, who had brought about things as they were, because of her ignorance, that was the cruelty, to have let her go away with Tristram, in ignorance.

Then the aspect of the case that she had been offered to him and refused! scourged her again; then the remembrance that he had taken her, for love. And what motive could he imagine she had had? This struck her for the first time—how infinitely more generous he had been—for he had not allowed, what he must have thought was pure mercenariness and desire for position on her part to interfere with his desire for her personally. He had never turned upon her, as she saw now he very well could have done, and thrown this in her teeth. And then she fell to bitter sobbing, and so at last to sleep.

And when the fire had died out, towards the gray dawn, she woke again shivering and in mortal fright, for she had dreamed of Mirko, and that he was being torn from her, while he played the *Chanson Triste*. Then she grew fully awake and remembered that this was the beginning of the new day—the day she should go to her husband's home; and she had accused him of all the base things a man could do, and he had behaved like a gentleman; and it was she who was base, and had sold herself for her brother's life, sold what should never be bartered for any life, but only for love.

Well, there was nothing to be done, only to "play the game"—the hackneyed phrase came back to her; he had used it, so it was sacred. Yes, all she could do for him now was, to "play the game"—everything else was—too late.

CHAPTER XXXIII

People left by all sorts of trains and motors in the morning; but there were still one or two remaining, when the bride and bridegroom made their departure, in their beautiful new car with its smart servants, which had come to fetch them, and take them to Wrayth.

And, just as the Dover young ladies on the pier had admired their embarkation, with its *apanages* of position and its romantic look, so every one who saw them leave Montfitchet was alike elated. They were certainly an ideal pair.

Zara had taken the greatest pains to dress herself in her best. She remembered Tristram had admired her the first evening they had arrived for this visit, when she had worn sapphire blue, so now she put on the same colored velvet and the sable coat—yes, he liked that best, too, and she clasped some of his sapphire jewels in her ears and at her throat. No bride ever looked more beautiful or distinguished, with her gardenia complexion and red burnished hair, all set off by the velvet and dark fur.

But Tristram, after the first glance, when she came down, never looked at her—he dared not. So they said their farewells quietly; but there was an extra warmth and tenderness in Ethelrida's kiss, as, indeed, there was every reason that there should be. If Zara had known! But the happy secret was still locked in the lovers' breasts.

"Of course it must come all right, they look so beautiful!" Ethelrida exclaimed unconsciously, waving her last wave on the steps, as the motor glided away.

"Yes, it must indeed," whispered Francis, who was beside her, and she turned and looked into his face.

"In twenty minutes, all the rest will be gone except the Crow, and Emily, and Mary, and Lady Anningford, who are staying on; and oh, Francis, how shall I get through the morning, knowing you are with Papa!"

"I will come to your sitting-room just before luncheon time, my dearest," he whispered back reassuringly. "Do not distress yourself—it will be all right."

And so they all went back into the house, and Lady Anningford, who now began to have grave suspicions, whispered to the Crow:

"I believe you are perfectly right, Crow. I am certain Ethelrida is in love with Mr. Markrute! But surely the Duke would never permit such a thing! A foreigner whom nobody knows anything of!"

"I never heard that there was any objection raised to Tristram marrying his niece. The Duke seemed to welcome it, and some foreigners are very good chaps," the Crow answered sententiously, "especially Austrians and Russians; and he must be one of something of that sort. He has no apparent touch of the Latin race. It's Latins I don't like."

"Well, I shall probably hear all about it from Ethelrida herself, now that we are alone. I am so glad I decided to stay with the dear girl until Wednesday, and you will have to wait till then, too, Crow."

"As ever, I am at your orders," he grunted, and lighting a cigar, he subsided into a great chair to read the papers, while Lady Anningford went on to the saloon. And presently, when all the departing guests were gone, Ethelrida linked her arm in that of her dear friend, and drew her with her up to her sitting-room.

"I have heaps to tell you, Anne!" she said, while she pushed her gently into a big low chair, and herself sank into the corner of her sofa. Ethelrida was not a person who curled up among pillows, or sat on rugs, or little stools. All her movements, even in her most intimate moments of affection with her friend, were dignified and reserved.

"Darling, I am thrilled," Lady Anningford responded, "and I guess it is all about Mr. Markrute—and oh, Ethelrida, when did it begin?"

"He has been thinking of me for a long time, Anne—quite eighteen months—but I—" she looked down, while a tender light grew in her face, "I only began to be interested the night we dined with him—it is a little more than a fortnight ago—the dinner for Tristram's engagement. He said a number of things not like any one else, then, and he made me think of him afterwards—and I saw him again at the wedding—and since he has been here—and do you know, Anne, I have never loved any one before in my life!"

"Ethelrida, you darling, I know you haven't!" and Anne bounded up and gave her a hug. "And I knew you were perfectly happy, and had had a blissful afternoon when you came down to tea yesterday. Your whole face was changed, you pet!"

"Did I look so like a fool, Anne?" Ethelrida cried.

Then Lady Anningford laughed happily, as she answered with a roguish eye,

"It was not exactly that, darling, but your dear cheeks were scarlet, as though they had been exquisitely kissed!"

"Oh!" gasped Ethelrida, flaming pink, as she laughed and covered her face with her hands.

"Perhaps he knows how to make love nicely—I am no judge of such things—in any case, he makes me thrill. Anne, tell me, is that—that curious sensation as though one were rather limp and yet quivering—is that just how every one feels when they are in love?"

"Ethelrida, you sweet thing!" gurgled Anne.

Then Ethelrida told her friend about the present of books, and showed them to her, and of all the subtlety of his ways, and how they appealed to her.

"And oh, Anne, he makes me perfectly happy and sure of everything; and I feel that I need never decide anything for myself again in my life!"

Which, taking it all round, was a rather suitable and fortunate conviction for a man to have implanted in his lady love's breast, and held out the prospect of much happiness in their future existence together.

"I think he is very nice looking," said Anne, "and he has the most perfect clothes. I do like a man to have that groomed look, which I must say most Englishmen have, but Tristram has it, especially, and Mr. Markrute, too. If you knew the despair my old man is to me with his indifference about his appearance. It is my only crumpled rose leaf, with the dear old thing."

"Yes," agreed Ethelrida, "I like them to be smart—and above all, they must have thick hair. Anne, have you noticed Francis' hair? It is so nice, it grows on his forehead just as Zara's does. If he had been bald like Papa, I could not have fallen in love with him!"

So once more the fate of a man was decided by his hair!

And during this exchange of confidences, while Emily and Mary took a brisk walk with the Crow and young Billy, Francis Markrute faced his lady's ducal father in the library.

He had begun without any preamble, and with perfect calm; and the Duke, who was above all a courteous gentleman, had listened, first with silent consternation and resentment, and then with growing interest.

Francis Markrute had manipulated infinitely more difficult situations, when the balance of some of the powers of Europe depended upon his nerve; but he knew, as he talked to this gallant old Englishman, that he had never had so much at stake, and it stimulated him to do his best.

He briefly stated his history, which Ethelrida already knew; he made no apology for his bar sinister; indeed, he felt none was needed. He knew, and the Duke knew, that when a man has won out as he had done, such things fade into space. And then with wonderful taste and discretion he had but just alluded to his vast wealth, and that it would be so perfectly administered through Lady Ethelrida's hands, for the good of her order and of mankind.

And the Duke, accustomed to debate and the watching of methods in men, could not help admiring the masterly reserve and force of this man.

And, finally, when the financier had finished speaking, the Duke rose and stood before the fire, while he fixed his eyeglass in his eye.

"You have stated the case admirably, my dear Markrute," he said, in his distinguished old voice. "You leave me without argument and with merely my prejudices, which I dare say are unjust, but I confess they are strongly in favor of my own countrymen and strongly against this union—though, on the other hand, my daughter and her happiness are my first consideration in this world. Ethelrida was twenty-six yesterday, and she is a young woman of strong and steady character, unlikely to be influenced by any foolish emotion. Therefore, if you have been fortunate enough to find favor in her eyes—if the girl loves you, in short, my dear fellow, then I have nothing to say.—Let us ring and have a glass of port!"

And presently the two men, now with the warmest friendship in their hearts for one another, mounted the staircase to Lady Ethelrida's room, and there found her still talking to Anne.

Her sweet eyes widened with a question as the two appeared at the door, and then she rushed into her father's arms and buried her face in his coat; and with his eyeglass very moist, the old Duke kissed her fondly—as he muttered.

"Why, Ethelrida, my little one. This is news! If you are happy, darling, that is all I want!"

So the whole dreaded moment passed off with rejoicing, and presently Lady Anningford and the fond father made their exit, and left the lovers alone.

"Oh, Francis, isn't the world lovely!" murmured Ethelrida from the shelter of his arms. "Papa and I have always been so happy together, and now we shall be three, because you understand him, too, and you won't make me stay away from him for very long times, will you, dear?"

"Never, my sweet. I thought of asking the Duke, if you would wish it, to let me take the place from him in this county, which eventually comes to you, and I will keep on Thorpmoor, my house in Lincolnshire, merely for the shooting. Then you would feel you were always in your own home, and perhaps the Duke would spend much time with us, and we could come to him here, in an hour; but all this is merely a suggestion—everything shall be as you wish."

"Francis, you are good to me," she said.

"Darling," he whispered, as he kissed her hair, "it took me forty-six years to find my pearl of price."

Then they settled all kinds of other details: how he would give Zara, for her own, the house in Park Lane, which would not be big enough now for them; and he would purchase one of those historic mansions, looking on The Green Park, which he knew was soon to be in the market. Ethelrida, if she left the ducal roof for the sake of his love, should find a palace worthy of her acceptance waiting for her.

He had completely recovered his balance, upset a little the night before by the uncomfortable momentary fear about his niece.

She and Tristram had arranged to come up to Park Lane for two nights again at the end of the week, to say good-bye to the Dowager Lady Tancred, who was starting with her daughters for Cannes. If he should see then that things were still amiss, he would tell Tristram the whole history of what Zara had thought of him. Perhaps that might throw some light on her conduct towards him, and so things could be cleared up. But he pinned his whole faith on youth and propinquity to arrange matters before then, and dismissed it from his mind.

Meanwhile, the pair in question were speeding along to Wrayth.

Of all the ordeals of the hours which Tristram had had to endure since his wedding, these occasions, upon which he had to sit close beside her in a motor, were the worst. An ordinary young man, not in love with her, would have found something intoxicating in her atmosphere—and how much more this poor Tristram, who was passionately obsessed.

Fortunately, she liked plenty of window open and did not object to smoke; but with the new air of meekness which was on her face and the adorably attractive personal scent of the creature, nearly two hours with her, under a sable rug, was no laughing matter.

At the end of the first half hour of silence and nearness, her husband found he was obliged to concentrate his mind by counting sheep jumping over imaginary stiles to prevent himself from clasping her in his arms.

It was the same old story, which has been chronicled over and over again. Two young, human, natural, normal people fighting against iron bars. For Zara felt the same as he, and she had the extra anguish of knowing she had been unjust, and that the present impossible situation was entirely her own doing.

And how to approach the subject and confess her fault? She did not know. Her sense of honor made her feel she must, but the queer silent habit of her life was still holding her enchained. And so, until they got into his own country, the strained speechlessness continued, and then he looked out and said:

"We must have the car opened now—please smile and bow as we go through the villages when any of the old people curtsey to you; the young ones won't do it, I expect, but my mother's old friends may."

So Zara leaned forward, when the footman had opened the landaulette top, and tried to look radiant.

And the first act of this pitiful comedy began.

CHAPTER XXXIV

Every sort of emotion convulsed the new Lady Tancred's heart, as they began to get near the park, with the village nestling close to its gates on the far side. So this was the home of her love and her lord; and they ought to be holding hands, and approaching it and the thought of their fond life together there with full hearts,—well, her heart was full enough, but only of anguish and pain. For Tristram, afraid of the smallest unbending, maintained a freezing attitude of contemptuous disdain, which she could not yet pluck up enough courage to break through to tell him she knew how unjust and unkind she had been.

And presently they came through cheering yokels to the South Lodge, the furthest away from the village, and so under a triumphant arch of evergreens, with banners floating and mottoes of "God Bless the Bride and Bridegroom" and "Health and Long Life to Lord and Lady Tancred." And now Tristram did take her hand and, indeed, put his arm round her as they both stood up for a moment in the car, while raising his hat and waving it gayly he answered graciously:

"My friends, Lady Tancred and I thank you so heartily for your kind wishes and welcome home."

Then they sat down, and the car went on, and his face became rigid again, as he let go her hand.

And at the next arch by the bridge, the same thing, only more elaborately carried out, began again, for here were all the farmers of the hunt, of which Tristram was a great supporter, on horseback; and the cheering and waving knew no end. The cavalcade of mounted men followed them round outside the Norman tower and to the great gates in the smaller one, where the portcullis had been.

Here all the village children were, and the old women from the almshouse, in their scarlet frieze cloaks and charming black bonnets; and every sort of wish for their happiness was shouted out. "Bless the beautiful bride and bring her many little lords and ladies, too," one old body quavered shrilly, above the din, and this pleasantry was greeted with shouts of delight. And for that second Tristram dropped his lady's hand as though it had burnt him, and then, recollecting himself, picked it up again. They were both pale with excitement and emotion, when they finally reached the hall-door in the ugly, modern Gothic wing and were again greeted by all the household servants in rows, two of them old and gray-haired, who had stayed on to care for things when the house had been shut up. There was Michelham back at his master's old home, only promoted to be groom of the chambers, now, with a smart younger butler under him.

Tristram was a magnificent orderer, and knew exactly how things ought to be done.

And the stately housekeeper, in her black silk, stepped forward, and in the name of herself and her subordinates, bade the new mistress welcome, and hoping she was not fatigued, presented her with a bouquet of white roses. "Because his lordship told us all, when he was here making the arrangements, that your ladyship was as beautiful as a white rose!"

And tears welled up in Zara's eyes and her voice trembled, as she thanked them and tried to smile.

"She was quite overcome, the lovely young lady," they told one another afterwards, "and no wonder. Any woman would be mad after his lordship. It is quite to be understood."

How they all loved him, the poor bride thought, and he had told them she was a beautiful white rose. He felt like that about her then, and she had thrown it all away. Now he looked upon her with loathing and disdain, and no wonder either—there was nothing to be done.

Presently, he took her hand again and placed it on his arm, as they walked through the long corridor, to the splendid hall, built by the brothers Adam, with its stately staircase to the gallery above.

"I have prepared the state rooms for your ladyship, pending your ladyship's choice of your own," Mrs. Anglin said. "Here is the boudoir, the bedroom, the bathroom, and his lordship's dressing-room—all en suite—and I hope your ladyship will find them as handsome, as we old servants of the family think they are!"

And Zara came up to the scratch and made a charming little speech.

When they got to the enormous bedroom, with its windows looking out on the French garden and park, all in exquisite taste, furnished and decorated by the Adams themselves, Tristram gallantly bent and kissed her hand, as he said:

"I will wait for you in the boudoir, while you take off your coat. Mrs. Anglin will show you the toilet-service of gold, which was given by Louis XIV to a French grandmother and which the Ladies Tancred always use, when they are at Wrayth. I hope you won't find the brushes too hard," and he laughed and went out.

And Zara, overcome with the state and beauty and tradition of it all, sat down upon the sofa for a moment to try to control her pain. She was throbbing with rage and contempt at herself, at the remembrance that she, in her ignorance, her ridiculous ignorance, had insulted this man—this noble gentleman, who owned all these things—and had taunted him with taking her for her uncle's wealth.

How he must have loved her in the beginning to have been willing to give her all this, after seeing her for only one night. She writhed with anguish. There is no bitterness as great as the bitterness of loss caused by oneself.

Tristram was standing by the window of the delicious boudoir when she went in. Zara, who as yet knew very little of English things, admired the Adam style; and when Mrs. Anglin left them discreetly for a moment, she told him so, timidly, for something to say.

"Yes, it is rather nice," he said stiffly, and then went on: "We shall have to go down now to this fearful lunch, but you had better take your sable boa with you. The great hall is so enormous and all of stone, it may be cold. I will get it for you," and he went back and found it lying by her coat on the chair, and brought it, and wrapped it round her casually, as if she had been a stone, and then held the door for her to go out. And Zara's pride was stung, even though she knew he was doing exactly as she herself would have done, so that instead of the meek attitude she had unconsciously assumed, for a moment now she walked beside him with her old mien of head in the air, to the admiration of Mrs. Anglin, who watched them descend the stairs.

"She is as haughty-looking as our own ladyship," she thought to herself. "I wonder how his lordship likes that!"

The great hall was a survival of the time of Henry IV with its daïs to eat above the salt, and a magnificent stone fireplace, and an oak screen and gallery of a couple of centuries later. The tables were laid down each side, as in the olden time, and across the daïs; and here, in the carved oak "Lord" and "Lady" chairs, the bride and bridegroom sat with a principal tenant and his wife on either side of them, while the powdered footmen served them with lunch.

And all the time, when one or two comic incidents happened, she longed to look at Tristram and laugh; but he maintained his attitude of cold reserve, only making some genial stereotyped remark, when it was necessary for the public effect.

And presently the speeches began, and this was the most trying moment of all. For the land-steward, who proposed their healths, said such nice things; and Zara realized how they all loved her lord, and her anger at herself grew and grew. In each speech from different tenants there was some intimate friendly allusion about herself, too, linking her always with Tristram; and these parts hurt her particularly.

Then Tristram rose to answer them in his name and hers. He made a splendid speech, telling them that he had come back to live among them and had brought them a beautiful new Lady—and here he turned to her a moment and took and kissed her hand—and how he would always think of all their interests in every way; and that he looked upon them as his dear old friends; and that he and Lady Tancred would always endeavor to promote their welfare, as long as the radicals—here he laughed, for they were all true blue to a man—would let them! And when voices shouted, "We want none of them rats here," he was gay and chaffed them; and finally sat down amidst yells of applause.

Then an old apple-cheeked farmer got up from far down the table and made a long rambling harangue, about having been there, man and boy, and his forbears before him, for a matter of two hundred years; but he'd take his oath they had none of them ever seen such a beautiful bride brought to Wrayth as they were welcoming now; and he drank to her ladyship's health, and hoped it would not be long before they would have another and as great a feast for the rejoicings over the son and heir!

At this deplorable bit of bucolic wit and hearty taste, Tristram's face went stern as death; and he bit his lips, while his bride became the color of the red roses on the table in front of her.

Thus the luncheon passed. And amidst countless hand-shakes of affection, accelerated by port wine and champagne, the bride and bridegroom, followed by the land-steward and a chosen few, went to receive and return the same sort of speeches among the lesser people in the tent. Here the allusions to marital felicity were even more glaring, and Zara saw that each time Tristram heard them, an instantaneous gleam of bitter sarcasm would steal into his eyes. So, worn out at last with the heat in the tent and the emotions of the day, at about five, the bridegroom was allowed to conduct his bride to tea in the boudoir of the state rooms. Thus they were alone, and now was Zara's time to make her confession, if it ever should come.

Tristram's resolve had held him, nothing could have been more gallingly cold and disdainful than had been his treatment of her, so perfect, in its acting for 'the game,' and, so bitter, in the humiliation of the between times. She would tell him of her mistake. That was all. She must guard herself against showing any emotion over it.

They each sank down into chairs beside the fire with sighs of relief.

"Good Lord!" he said, as he put his hand to his forehead. "What a hideous mockery the whole thing is, and not half over yet! I am afraid you must be tired. You ought to go and rest until dinner—when, please be very magnificent and wear some of the jewels—part of them have come down from London on purpose, I think, beyond those you had at Montfitchet."

"Yes, I will," she answered, listlessly, and began to pour out the tea, while he sat quite still staring into the fire, a look of utter weariness and discouragement upon his handsome face.

Everything about the whole thing was hurting him so, all the pleasure he had taken in the improvements and the things he had done, hoping to please her; and now, as he saw them about, each one stabbed him afresh.

She gave him his cup without a word. She had remembered from Paris his tastes in cream and sugar; and then as the icy silence continued, she could bear it no longer.

"Tristram," she said, in as level a voice as she could. At the sound of his name he looked at her startled. It was the first time she had ever used it!

She lowered her head and, clasping her hands, she went on constrainedly, so overcome with emotion she dared not let herself go. "I want to tell you something, and ask you to forgive me. I have learned the truth, that you did not marry me just for my uncle's money. I know exactly what really happened now. I am ashamed, humiliated, to remember what I said to you. But I understood you had agreed to the bargain before you had ever seen me. The whole thing seemed so awful to me—so revolting—I am sorry for what I taunted you with. I know now that you are really a great gentleman."

His face, if she had looked up and seen it, had first all lightened with hope and love; but as she went on coldly, the warmth died out of it, and a greater pain than ever filled his heart. So she knew now, and yet she did not love him. There was no word of regret for the rest of her taunts, that he had been an animal, and the blow in his face! The recollection of this suddenly lashed him again, and made him rise to his feet, all the pride of his race flooding his being once more.

He put down his tea-cup on the mantelpiece untasted, and then said hoarsely:

"I married you because I loved you, and no man has ever regretted a thing more."

Then he turned round, and walked slowly from the room.

And Zara, left alone, felt that the end had come.

CHAPTER XXXV

A pale and most unhappy bride awaited her bridegroom in the boudoir at a few minutes to eight o'clock. She felt perfectly lifeless, as though she had hardly enough will left even to act her part. The white satin of her dress was not whiter than her face. The head gardener had sent up some splendid gardenias for her to wear and the sight of them pained her, for were not these the flowers that Tristram had brought her that evening of her wedding day, not a fortnight ago, and that she had then thrown into the grate. She pinned some in mechanically, and then let the maid clasp the diamonds round her throat and a band of them in her hair. They were so very beautiful, and she had not seen them before; she could not thank him for them even—all conversation except before people was now at an end. Then, for her further unhappiness, she remembered he had said: "When the mockery of the rejoicings is over then we can discuss our future plans." What did that mean? That he wished to separate from her, she supposed. How could circumstance be so cruel to her! What had she done? Then she sat down for a moment while she waited, and clenched her hands. And all the passionate resentment her deep nature was capable of surged up against fate, so that she looked more like the black panther than ever, and her mood had only dwindled into a sullen smoldering rage—while she still sat in the peculiar, concentrated attitude of an animal waiting to spring—when Tristram opened the door, and came in.

The sight of her thus, looking so unEnglish, so barbaric, suddenly filled him with the wild excitement of the lion hunt again. Could anything be more diabolically attractive? he thought, and for a second, the idea flashed across him that he would seize her to-night and treat her as if she were the panther she looked, conquer her by force, beat her if necessary, and then kiss her to death! Which plan, if he had carried it out, in this case, would have been very sensible, but the training of hundreds of years of chivalry toward women and things weaker than himself was still in his blood. For Tristram, twenty-fourth Baron Tancred, was no brute or sensualist, but a very fine specimen of his fine, old race.

So, his heart beating with some uncontrollable excitement, and her heart filled with smoldering rage, they descended the staircase, arm in arm, to the admiration of peeping housemaids and the pride of her own maid. And the female servants all rushed to the balustrade to get a better view of the delightful scene which, they had heard whispered among them, was a custom of generations in the family—that when the Lord of Wrayth first led his lady into the state dining-room for their first dinner alone he should kiss her before whoever was there, and bid her welcome to her new home. And to see his lordship, whom they all thought the handsomest young gentleman they had ever seen, kiss her ladyship, would be a thrill of the most agreeable kind!

What would their surprise have been, could they have heard him say icily to his bride as he descended the stairs:

"There is a stupid custom that I must kiss you as we go into the dining-room, and give you this little golden key—a sort of ridiculous emblem of the endowment of all the worldly goods business. The servants are, of course, looking at us, so please don't start." Then he glanced up and saw the rows of interested, excited faces; and that devil-may-care, rollicking boyishness which made him so adored came over him, and he laughed up at them, and waved his hand: and Zara's rage turned to wild excitement, too. There would be the walk across the hall of sixty paces, and then he would kiss her. What would it be like? In those sixty paces her face grew more purely white, while he came to the resolve that for this one second he would yield to temptation and not only brush her forehead with his lips, as had been his intention, but for once—just for this once—he would kiss her mouth. He was past caring about the footmen seeing. It was his only chance.

So when they came to the threshold of the big, double doors he bent down and drew her to him, and gave her the golden key. And then he pressed his warm, young, passionate lips to hers. Oh! the mad joy of it! And even if it were only from duty and to play the game, she had not resisted him as upon that other occasion. He felt suddenly, absolutely intoxicated, as he had done on the wedding night. Why, why must this ghastly barrier be between them? Was there nothing to be done? Then he looked at his bride as they advanced to the table, and he saw that she was so deadly white that he thought she was going to faint. For intoxication, affects people in different ways; for her, the kiss had seemed the sweetness of death.

"Give her ladyship some champagne immediately," he ordered the butler, and, still with shining eyes, he looked at her, and said gently, "for we must drink our own healths."

But Zara never raised her lids, only he saw that her little nostrils were quivering, and by the rise and fall of her beautiful bosom he knew that her heart must be beating as madly as was his own—and a wild triumph filled him. Whatever the emotion she was experiencing, whether it was anger, or disdain, or one he did not dare to hope for, it was a considerably strong one; she was, then, not so icily cold! How he wished there were some more ridiculous customs in his family! How he wished he might order the servants out of the room, and begin to make love to her all alone. And just out of the devilment which was now in his blood he took the greatest pleasure in "playing the game," and while the solemn footmen's watchful eyes were upon them, he let himself go and was charming to her; and then, each instant they were alone he made himself freeze again, so that she could not say he was not keeping to the bargain. Thus in wild excitement for them both the dinner passed. With her it was alternate torture and pleasure as well, but with him, for the first time since his wedding, there was not any pain. For he felt he was affecting her, even if she were only "playing the game." And gradually, as the time went on and dessert was almost come, the conviction grew in Zara's brain that he was torturing her on purpose, overdoing the part when the servants were looking; for had he not told her but three hours before that he *had* loved her—using the past tense—and no man regretted a thing more! Perhaps—was it possible—he had seen when he kissed her that she loved him! And he was just punishing her, and laughing at his dominion over her in his heart; so her pride took fire at once. Well, she would not be played with! He would see she could keep to a bargain; and be icy, too, when the play was over. So when at last the servants had left the room, before coffee was brought, she immediately stiffened and fell into silence; and the two stared in front of them, and back over him crept the chill. Yes, there was no use deceiving himself. He had had his one moment of bliss, and now his purgatory would begin again.

Thus the comedy went on. Soon they had to go and open the ball, and they both won golden opinions from their first partners—hers, the stalwart bailiff, and his, the bailiff's wife.

"Although she is a foreigner, Agnes," Mr. Burrs said to his life's partner when they got home, "you'd hardly know it, and a lovelier lady I have never seen."

"She couldn't be too lovely for his lordship," his wife retorted. "Why, William, he made me feel young again!"

The second dance the bridal pair were supposed to dance together; and then when they should see the fun in full swing they were supposed to slip away, because it was considered quite natural that they might wish to be alone.

"You will have to dance with me now, I am afraid, Zara," Tristram said, and, without waiting for her answer, he placed his arm round her and began the valse. And the mad intoxication grew again in both of them, and they went on, never stopping, in a wild whirl of delight—unreasoning, passionate delight—until the music ceased.

Then Zara who, by long years of suffering, was the more controlled, pulled herself together first, and, with that ingrained instinct to defend herself and her secret love, and to save his possible true construction of her attitude, said stiffly:

"I suppose we can go now. I trust you think that I have 'played the game.'"

"Too terribly well," he said—stung back to reality. "It shows me what we have irreparably lost." And he gave her his arm and, passed down the lane of admiring and affectionate guests to their part of the house; and at the door of the boudoir he left her without a word.

So, with the bride in lonely anguish in the great state bed, the night of the home-coming passed, and the morrow dawned.

For thus the God of Pride makes fools of his worshipers.

It poured with rain the next day, but the same kind of thing went on for the different grades of those who lived under the wing of the Tancred name, and neither bride nor bridegroom failed in their rôles, and the icy coldness between them increased. They had drawn upon themselves an atmosphere of absolute restraint and it seemed impossible to exchange even ordinary conversation; so that at this, their second dinner, they hardly even kept up a semblance before the household servants, and, being free from feasting, Zara retired almost immediately the coffee had come. One of the things Tristram had said to her before she left the room was:

"To-morrow if it is fine you had better see the gardens and really go over the house, if you wish. The housekeeper and the gardeners will think it odd if you don't! How awful it is to have to conform to convention!" he went on. "It would be good to be a savage again. Well, perhaps I shall be, some day soon."

Then as she paused in her starting for the door to hear what he had further to say, he continued:

"They let us have a day off to-morrow; they think, quite naturally, we require a rest. So if you will be ready about eleven I will show you the gardens and the parts my mother loved—it all looks pretty dreary this time of the year, but it can't be helped."

"I will be ready," Zara said.

"Then there is the Address from the townspeople at Wrayth, on Thursday," he continued, while he walked toward the door to open it for her, "and on Friday we go up to London to say good-bye to my mother. I hope you have not found it all too impossibly difficult, but it will soon be over now."

"The whole of life is difficult," she answered, "and one never knows what it is for, or why?" And then without anything further she went out of the door, and so upstairs and through all the lonely corridors to the boudoir. And here she opened the piano for the first time, and tried it; and finding it good she sat a long time playing her favorite airs—but not the *Chanson Triste*—she felt she could not bear that.

The music talked to her: what was her life going to be? What if, in the end, she could not control her love? What if it should break down her pride, and let him see that she regretted her past action and only longed to be in his arms. For her admiration and respect for him were growing each hour, as she discovered new traits in him, individually, and began to understand what he meant to all these people whose lord he was. How little she had known of England, her own father's country! How ridiculously little she had really known of men, counting them all brutes like Ladislaus and his friends, or feckless fools like poor Mimo! What an impossible attitude was this one she had worn always of arrogant ignorance! Something should have told her that these people were not like that. Something should have warned her, when she first saw him, that Tristram was a million miles above anything in the way of his sex that she had yet known. Then she stopped playing, and deliberately went over and looked in the glass. Yes, she was certainly beautiful, and quite young. She might live until she were seventy or eighty, in the natural course of events, and the whole of life would be one long, dreary waste if she might not have her Love. After all, pride was not worth so very much. Suppose she were very gentle to him, and tried to please him in just a friendly way, that would not be undignified nor seem to be throwing herself at his head. She would begin to-morrow, if she could. Then she remembered Lady Ethelrida's words at the dinner party—was it possible that was only three weeks ago this very night—the words that she had spoken so unconsciously, when she had showed so plainly the family feeling about Tristram and Cyril being the last in the male line of Tancred of Wrayth. She remembered how she had been angered and up in arms then, and now a whole education had passed over her, and she fully understood and sympathized with their point of view.

And at this stage of her meditations her eyes grew misty as they gazed into distance, and all soft; and the divine expression of the Sistine Madonna grew in them, as it grew always when she held Mirko in her arms.

Yes, there were things in life which mattered far, far more than pride. And so, comforted by her resolutions, she at last went to bed.

And Tristram sat alone by the fire in his own sitting-room, and stared at that other Tristram Guiscard's armor. And he, too, came to a resolution, but not of the same kind. He would speak to Francis Markrute when they arrived on Friday night and he could get him quietly alone. He would tell him that the whole thing was a ghastly failure, but as he had only himself to blame for entering into it he did not intend to reproach any one. Only, he would frankly ask him to use his clever brain and invent some plan that he and Zara could separate, without scandal, until such time as he should grow indifferent, and so could come back and casually live in the house with her. He was only a human man, he admitted, and the present arrangement was impossible to bear. He was past the anguish of the mockery of everything to-night—he was simply numb. Then some waiting fiend made him think of Laura and her last words. What if there were some truth in them after all? He had himself seen the man twice, under the most suspicious circumstances. What if he were her lover? How could Francis Markrute know of all her existence, when he had said she had been an immaculate wife? And gradually, on top of his other miseries, trifles light as air came and tortured him until presently he had worked up a whole chain of evidence, proving the lover theory to be correct!

Then he shook in his chair with rage, and muttered between his teeth: "If I find this is true then I will kill him, and kill her, also!"

So near to savages are all human beings, when certain passions are aroused. And neither bride nor bridegroom guessed that fate would soon take things out of their hands and make their resolutions null and void.

CHAPTER XXXVI

The gardens at Wrayth were famous. The natural beauty of their position and the endless care of generations of loving mistresses had left them a monument of what nature can be trained into by human skill. They had also in the eighteenth century by some happy chance escaped the hand of Capability Brown. And instead of pulling about and altering the taste of the predecessor the successive owners had used fresh ground for their fancies. Thus the English rose-garden and the Dutch-clipped yews of William-and-Mary's time were as intact as the Italian parterre.

But November is not the time to judge of gardens, and Tristram wished the sun would come out. He waited for his bride at the foot of the Adam staircase, and, at eleven, she came down. He watched her as she put one slender foot before the other in her descent, he had not noticed before how ridiculously inadequate they were—just little bits of baby feet, even in her thick walking-boots. She certainly knew how to dress—and adapt herself to the customs of a country. Her short, serge frock and astrakhan coat and cap were just the things for the occasion; and she looked so attractive and chic, with her hands in her monster muff, he began to have that pain again of longing for her, so he said icily:

"The sky is gray and horrid. You must not judge of things as you will see them to-day; it is all really rather nice in the summer."

"I am sure it is," she answered meekly, and then could not think of anything else to say, so they walked on in silence through the courtyard and round under a deep, arched doorway in the Norman wall to the southern side of the Adam erection, with its pillars making the centerpiece. The beautiful garden stretched in front of them. This particular part was said to have been laid out from plans of Le Notre, brought there by that French Lady Tancred who had been the friend of Louis XIV. There were traces of her all over the house—Zara found afterwards. It was a most splendid and stately scene even in the dull November gloom, with the groups of statuary, and the *tapis vert*, and the general look of Versailles. The vista was immense. She could see far beyond, down an incline, through a long clearing in the park, far away to the tower of Wrayth church.

"How beautiful it all is!" she said, with bated breath, and clasped her hands in her muff. "And how wonderful to have the knowledge that your family has been here always, and these splendid things are their creation. I understand that you must be a very proud man."

This was almost the longest speech he had ever heard her make, in ordinary conversation—the first one that contained any of her thoughts. He looked at her startled for a moment, but his resolutions of the night before and his mood of suspicion caused him to remain unmoved. He was numb with the pain of being melted one moment with hope and frozen again the next; it had come to a pass now that he would not let himself respond. She could almost have been as gracious as she pleased, out in this cold, damp air, and he would have remained aloof.

"Yes, I suppose I am a proud man," he said, "but it is not much good to me; one becomes a cynic, as one grows older."

Then with casual indifference he began to explain to her all about the gardens and their dates, as they walked along, just as though he were rather bored but acting cicerone to an ordinary guest, and Zara's heart sank lower and lower, and she could not keep up her little plan to be gentle and sympathetic; she could not do more than say just "Yes," and "No." Presently they came through a door to the hothouses, and she had to be introduced to the head gardener, a Scotchman, and express her admiration of everything, and eat some wonderful grapes; and here Tristram again "played the game," and chaffed, and was gay. And so they went out, and through a clipped, covered walk to another door in a wall, which opened on the west side—the very old part of the house—and suddenly she saw the Italian parterre. Each view as she came upon it she tried to identify with what she had seen in the pictures in *Country Life*, but things look so different in reality, with the atmospheric effects, to the cold gray of a print. Only there was no mistake about this—the Italian parterre; and a sudden tightness grew round her heart, and she thought of Mirko and the day she had last seen him. And Tristram was startled into looking at her by a sudden catching of her breath, and to his amazement he perceived that her face was full of pain, as though she had revisited some scene connected with sorrowful memories. There was even a slight drawing back in her attitude, as if she feared to go on, and meet some ghost. What could it be? Then the malevolent sprite who was near him just now whispered: "It is an Italian garden, she has seen such before in other lands; perhaps the man is an Italian—he looks dark enough." So instead of feeling solicitous and gentle with whatever caused her pain—for his manners were usually extremely courteous, however cold—he said almost roughly:

"This seems to make you think of something! Well, let us get on and get it over, and then you can go in!"

He would be no sympathetic companion for her sentimental musings—over another man!

Her lips quivered for a moment, and he saw that he had struck home, and was glad, and grew more furious as he strode along. He would like to hurt her again if he could, for jealousy can turn an angel into a cruel fiend. They walked on in silence, and a look almost of fear crept into her tragic eyes. She dreaded so to come upon Pan and his pipes. Yes, as they descended the stone steps, there he was in the far distance with his back to them, forever playing his weird music for the delight of all growing things.

She forgot Tristram, forgot she was passionately preoccupied with him and passionately in love, forgot even that she was not alone. She saw the firelight again, and the pitiful, little figure of her poor, little brother as he poured over the picture, pointing with his sensitive forefinger to Pan's shape. She could hear his high, childish voice say: "See, Chérisette, he, too, is not made as other people are! Look, and he plays music, also. When I am with *Maman* and you walk there you must remember that this is me!"

And Tristram, watching her, knew not what to think. For her face had become more purely white than usual, and her dark eyes were swimming with tears.

God! how she must have loved this man! In wild rage he stalked beside her until they came quite close to the statue in the center of the star, surrounded by its pergola of pillars, which in the summer were gay with climbing roses.

Then he stepped forward, with a sharp exclamation of annoyance, for the pipes of Pan had been broken and lay there on the ground.

Who had done this thing?

When Zara saw the mutilation she gave a piteous cry; to her, to the mystic part of her strange nature, this was an omen. Pan's music was gone, and Mirko, too, would play no more.

With a wail like a wounded animal's she slipped down on the stone bench, and, burying her face in her muff, the tension of soul of all these days broke down, and she wept bitter, anguishing tears.

Tristram was dumbfounded. He knew not what to do. Whatever was the cause, it now hurt him horribly to see her weep—weep like this—as if with broken heart.

For her suffering was caused by remembrance—remembrance that, absorbed in her own concerns and heart-burnings over her love, she had forgotten the little one lately; and he was far away and might now be ill, and even dead.

She sobbed and sobbed and clasped her hands, and Tristram could not bear it any longer.

"Zara!" he said, distractedly. "For God's sake do not cry like this! What is it? Can I not help you—Zara?" And he sat down beside her and put his arm round her, and tried to draw her to him—he must comfort her whatever caused her pain.

But she started up and ran from him; he was the cause of her forgetfulness.

"Do not!" she cried passionately, that southern dramatic part of her nature coming out, here in her abandon of self-control. "Is it not enough for me to know that it is you and thoughts of you which have caused me to forget him!—Go! I must be alone!"—and like a fawn she fled down one of the paths, and beyond a great yew hedge, and so disappeared from view.

And Tristram sat on the stone bench, too stunned to move.

This was a confession from her, then—he realized, when his power came back to him. It was no longer surmise and suspicion—there was some one else. Some one to whom she owed—love. And he had caused her to forget him! And this thought made him stop his chain of reasoning abruptly. For what did that mean? Had he then, after all, somehow made her feel—made her think of him? Was this the secret in her strange mysterious face that drew him and puzzled him always? Was there some war going on in her heart?

But the comforting idea which he had momentarily obtained from that inference of her words went from him as he pondered, for nothing proved that her thoughts of him had been of love.

So, alternately trying to reason the thing out, and growing wild with passion and suspicion and pain, he at last went back to the house expecting he would have to go through the ordeal of luncheon alone; but as the silver gong sounded she came slowly down the stairs.

And except that she was very pale and blue circles surrounded her heavy eyes, her face wore a mask, and she was perfectly calm.

She made no apology, nor allusion to her outburst; she treated the incident as though it had never been! She held a letter in her hand, which had come by the second post while they were out. It was written by her uncle from London, the night before, and contained his joyous news.

Tristram looked at her and was again dumbfounded. She was certainly a most extraordinary woman. And some of his rage died down and he decided he would not, after all, demand an explanation of her now; he would let the whole, hideous rejoicings be finished first and then, in London, he would sternly investigate the truth. And not the least part of his pain was the haunting uncertainty as to what her words could mean, as regarded himself. If by some wonderful chance it were some passion in the past and she now loved him, he feared he could forgive her—he feared even his pride would not hold out over the mad happiness it would be to feel her unresisting and loving, lying in his arms!

So with stormy eyes and forced smiles the pair sat down to luncheon, and Zara handed him the epistle she carried in her hand. It ran:

"MY DEAR NIECE:

"I have to inform you of a piece of news that is a great gratification to myself, and I trust will cause you, too, some pleasure.

"Lady Ethelrida Montfitchet has done me the honor to accept my proposal for her hand, and the Duke, her father, has kindly given his hearty consent to my marriage with his daughter, which is to take place as soon as things can be arranged with suitability. I hope you and Tristram will arrive in time to accompany me to dinner at Glastonbury House on Friday evening, when you can congratulate my beloved fiancé, who holds you in affectionate regard.

"I am, my dear niece, always your devoted uncle,

"FRANCIS MARKRUTE."

When Tristram finished reading he exclaimed:

"Good Lord!" For, quite absorbed in his own affairs, he had never even noticed the financier's peregrinations! Then as he looked at the letter again he said meditatively:

"I expect they will be awfully happy—Ethelrida is such an unselfish, sensible, darling girl—"

And it hurt Zara even in her present mood, for she felt the contrast to herself in his unconscious tone.

"My uncle never does anything without having calculated it will turn out perfectly," she said bitterly—"only sometimes it can happen that he plays with the wrong pawns."

And Tristram wondered what she meant. He and she had certainly been pawns in one of the Markrute games, and now he began to see this object, just as Zara had done. Then the thought came to him.—Why should he not now ask her straight out—why she had married him? It was not from any desire for himself, nor his position, he knew that: but for what?

So, the moment the servants went out of the room to get the coffee—after a desultory conversation about the engagement until then, he said coldly:

"You told me on Monday that you now know the reason I had married you: may I ask you why did you marry me?"

She clasped her hands convulsively. This brought it all back—her poor little brother—and she was not free yet from her promise to her uncle: she never failed to keep her word.

A look of deep, tragic earnestness grew in her pools of ink, and she said to him, with a strange sob in her voice:

"Believe me I had a strong reason, but I cannot tell it to you now."

And the servants reentered the room at the moment, so he could not ask her why: it broke the current.

But what an unexpected inference she always put into affairs! What was the mystery? He was thrilled with suspicious, terrible interest. But of one thing he felt sure—Francis Markrute did not really know.

And in spite of his chain of reasoning about this probable lover some doubt about it haunted him always; her air was so pure—her mien so proud.

And while the servants were handing the coffee and still there Zara rose, and, making the excuse that she must write to her uncle at once, left the room to avoid further questioning. Then Tristram leant his head upon his hands and tried to think.

He was in a maze—and there seemed no way out. If he went to her now and demanded to have everything explained he might have some awful confirmation of his suspicions, and then how could they go through to-morrow—and the town's address? Of all things he had no right—just because of his wild passion in marrying this foreign woman—he had no right to bring disgrace and scandal upon his untarnished name: "noblesse oblige" was the motto graven on his soul. No, he must bear it until Friday night after the Glastonbury House dinner. Then he would face her and demand the truth.

And Zara under the wing of Mrs. Anglin made a thorough tour of the beautiful, old house. She saw its ancient arras hangings, and panellings of carved oak, and heard all the traditions, and looked at the portraits—many so wonderfully like Tristram, for they were a strong, virile race—and her heart ached, and swelled with pride, alternately. And, last of all, she stood under the portrait that had been painted by Sargent, of her husband at his coming of age, and that master of art had given him, on the canvas, his very soul. There he stood, in a scarlet hunt-coat—debonair, and strong, and true—with all the promise of a noble, useful life in his dear, blue eyes. And suddenly this proud woman put her hand to her throat to check the sob that rose there; and then, again, out of the mist of her tears she saw Pan and his broken pipes.

CHAPTER XXXVII

Tristram passed the afternoon outdoors, inspecting the stables, and among his own favorite haunts, and then rushed in, too late for tea and only just in time to catch the post. He wrote a letter to Ethelrida, and his uncle-in-law that was to be. How ridiculous that sounded! He would be his uncle and Zara's cousin now, by marriage! Then, when he thought of this dear Ethelrida whom he had loved more than his own young sisters, he hurriedly wrote out, as well, a telegram of affection and congratulation which he handed to Michelham as he came in to get the letters—and the old man left the room. Then Tristram remembered that he had addressed the telegram to Montfitchet, and Ethelrida would, of course, he now recollected, be at Glastonbury House, as she was coming up that day—so he went to the door and called out:

"Michelham, bring me back the telegram."

And the grave servant, who was collecting all the other letters from the post-box in the hall, returned and placed beside his master on the table a blue envelope. There were always big blue envelopes, for the sending of telegrams, on all the writing tables at Wrayth.

Tristram hurriedly wrote out another and handed it, and the servant finally left the room. Then he absently pulled out his original one and glanced at it before tearing it up; and before he realized what he did his eye caught: "To Count Mimo Sykypri"—he did not read the address—"Immediately, to-morrow, wire me your news. Chérisette."

And ere his rage burst in a terrible oath he noticed that stamps were enclosed. Then he threw the paper with violence into the fire!

There was not any more doubt nor speculation; a woman did not sign herself "Chérisette"—"little darling"—except to a lover! Chérisette! He was so mad with rage that if she had come into the room at that moment he would have strangled her, there and then.

He forgot that it was time to dress for dinner—forgot everything but his overmastering fury. He paced up and down the room, and then after a while, as ever, his balance returned. The law could give him no redress yet: she certainly had not been unfaithful to him in their brief married life, and the law recks little of sins committed before the tie. Nothing could come now of going to her and reproaching her—only a public scandal and disgrace. No, he must play his part until he could consult with Francis Markrute, learn all the truth, and then concoct some plan. Out of all the awful ruin of his life he could at least save his name. And after some concentrated moments of agony he mastered himself at last sufficiently to go to his room and dress for dinner.

But Count Mimo Sykypri would get no telegram that night!

The idea that there could be any scandalous interpretations put upon any of her actions or words never even entered Zara's brain; so innocently unconscious was she of herself and her doings that that possible aspect of the case never struck her. She was the last type of person to make a mystery or in any way play a part. The small subtly-created situations and hidden darknesses and mysterious appearances which delighted the puny soul of Laura Highford were miles beneath her feet. If she had even faintly dreamed that some doubts were troubling Tristram she would have plainly told him the whole story and chanced her uncle's wrath. But she had not the slightest idea of it. She only knew that Tristram was stern and cold, and showed his disdain of her, and that even though she had made up her mind to be gentle and try to win him back with friendship, it was almost impossible. She looked upon his increased, icy contempt of her at dinner as a protest at her outburst of tears during the day.

So the meal was got through, and the moment the coffee was brought he gulped it down, and then rose: he could not stand being alone with her for a moment.

She was looking so beautiful, and so meek, and so tragic, he could not contain the mixed emotions he felt. He only knew if he had to bear them another minute he should go mad. So, hardly with sufficient politeness he said:

"I have some important documents to look over; I will wish you good night." And he hurried her from the room and went on to his own sitting-room in the other part of the house. And Zara, quite crushed with her anxiety and sorrow about Mirko, and passionately unhappy at Tristram's treatment of her, once more returned to her lonely room. And here she dismissed her maid, and remained looking out on the night. The mist had gone and some pure, fair stars shone out.

Was that where *Maman* was—up there? And was Mirko going to her soon, away out of this cruel world of sorrow and pain? As he had once said, surely there, there would be room for them both.

But Zara was no morbidly sentimental person, the strong blood ran in her veins, and she knew she must face her life and be true to herself, whatever else might betide. So after a while the night airs soothed her, and she said her prayers and went to bed.

But Tristram, her lord, paced the floor of his room until almost dawn.

The next day passed in the same kind of way, only, it was nearly all in public, with local festivities again; and both of the pair played their parts well, as they were now experienced actors, and only one incident marked the pain of this Thursday out from the pains of the other days. It was in the schoolhouse at Wrayth, where the buxom girl who had been assistant mistress, and had married, a year before, brought her first-born son to show the lord and lady—as he had been born on their wedding day, just a fortnight ago! She was pale and wan, but so ecstatically proud and happy looking; and Tristram at once said, they—he and Zara—must be the god-parents of her boy; and Zara held the crimson, crumpled atom for a moment, and then looked up and met her husband's eyes, and saw that they had filled with tears. And she returned the creature to its mother—but she could not speak, for a moment.

And finally they had come home again—home to Wrayth—and no more unhappy pair of young, healthy people lived on earth.

Zara could hardly contain her impatience to see if a telegram for her from Mimo had come in her absence. Tristram saw her look of anxiety and strain, and smiled grimly to himself. She would get no answering telegram from her lover that day!

And, worn out with the whole thing, Zara turned to him and asked if it would matter or look unusual if she said—what was true—that she was so fatigued she would like to go to bed and not have to come down to dinner.

"I will not do so, if it would not be in the game," she said.

And he answered, shortly:

"The game is over, to-night: do as you please."

So she went off sadly, and did not see him again until they were ready to start in the morning—the Friday morning, which Tristram called the beginning of the end!

He had arranged that they should go by train, and not motor up, as he usually did because he loved motoring; but the misery of being so close to her, even now when he hoped he loathed and despised her, was too great to chance. So, early after lunch, they started, and would be at Park Lane after five. No telegram had come for Zara—Mimo must be away—but, in any case, it indicated nothing unusual was happening, unless he had been called to Bournemouth by Mirko himself and had left hurriedly. This idea so tortured her that by the time she got to London she could not bear it, and felt she must go to Neville Street and see. But how to get away?

Francis Markrute was waiting for them in the library, and seemed so full of the exuberance of happiness that she could not rush off until she had poured out and pretended to enjoy a lengthy tea.

And the change in the reserved man struck them both. He seemed years younger, and full of the milk of human kindness. And Tristram thought of himself on the day he had gone to Victoria to meet Zara, when she had come from Paris, and he had given a beggar half a sovereign, from sheer joy of life.

For happiness and wine open men's hearts. He would not attempt to speak about his own troubles until the morning: it was only fair to leave the elderly lover without cares until after the dinner at Glastonbury House.

At last Zara was able to creep away. She watched her chance, and, with the cunning of desperation, finding the hall momentarily empty, stealthily stole out of the front door. But it was after half-past six o'clock, and they were dining at Glastonbury House, St. James's Square, at eight.

She got into a taxi quickly, finding one in Grosvenor Street because she was afraid to wait to look in Park Lane, in case, by chance, she should be observed; and at last she reached the Neville Street lodging, and rang the noisy bell.

The slatternly little servant said that the gentleman was "hout," but would the lady come in and wait? He would not be long, as he had said "as how he was only going to take a telegram."

Zara entered at once. A telegram!—perhaps for her—Yes, surely for her. Mimo had no one else, she knew, to telegraph to. She went up to the dingy attic studio. The fire was almost out, and the little maid lit one candle and placed it upon a table. It was very cold on this damp November day. The place struck her as piteously poor, after the grandeur from which she had come. Dear, foolish, generous Mimo! She must do something for him—and would plan how. The room had the air of scrupulous cleanness which his things always wore, and there was the "Apache" picture waiting for her to take, in a new gold frame; and the "London Fog" seemed to be advanced, too; he had evidently worked at it late, because his palette and brushes, still wet, were on a box beside it, and on a chair near was his violin. He was no born musician like Mirko, but played very well. The palette and brushes showed he must have put them hurriedly down. What for? Why? Had some message come for him? Had he heard news? And a chill feeling gripped her heart. She looked about to see if Mirko had written a letter, or one of his funny little postcards? No, there was nothing—nothing she had not seen except, yes, just this one on a picture of the town. Only a few words: "Thank Chérisette for her letter, Agatha is *très jolie*, but does not understand the violin, and wants to play it herself. And heavens! the noise!" How he managed to post these cards was always a mystery; they were marked with the mark of doubling up twice, so it showed he concealed them somewhere and perhaps popped them into a pillar-box, when out for a walk. This one was dated two days ago. Could anything have happened since? She burned with impatience for Mimo to come in.

A cheap, little clock struck seven. Where could he be? The minutes seemed to drag into an eternity. All sorts of possibilities struck her, and then she controlled herself and became calm.

There was a large photograph of her mother, which Mimo had colored really well. It was in a silver frame upon the mantelpiece, and she gazed and gazed at that, and whispered aloud in the gloomy room:

"*Maman, adorée!* Take care of your little one now, even if he must come to you soon."

And beside this there was another, of Mimo, taken at the same time, when Zara and her mother had gone to the Emperor's palace in that far land. How wonderfully handsome he was then, and even still!—and how the air of *insouciance* suited him, in that splendid white and gold uniform. But Mimo looked always a gentleman, even in his shabbiest coat.

And now that she knew what the passion of love meant herself, she better understood how her mother had loved. She had never judged her mother, it was not in her nature to judge any one; underneath the case of steel which her bitter life had wrought her, Zara's heart was as tender as an angel's.

Then she thought of the words in the Second Commandment: "And the sins of the fathers shall be visited upon the children." Had they sinned, then? And if so how terribly cruel such Commandments were—to make the innocent children suffer. Mirko and she were certainly paying some price. But the God that *Maman* had gone to and loved and told her children of, was not really cruel, and some day perhaps she—Zara—would come into peace on earth. And Mirko? Mirko would be up there, happy and safe with *Maman.*

The cheap clock showed nearly half-past seven. She could not wait another moment, and also she reasoned if Mimo were sending her a telegram it would be to Park Lane. He knew she was coming up; she would get it there on her return, so she scribbled a line to Count Sykypri, and told him she had been—and why—and that she must hear at once, and then she left and hurried back to her uncle's house. And when she got there it was twenty minutes to eight.

Her maid had been dreadfully worried, as she had given no orders as to what she would wear—but Henriette, being a person of intelligence, had put out what she thought best,—only she could not prevent her anxiety and impatience from causing her to go on to the landing, and hang over the stairs at every noise; and Tristram, coming out of his room already dressed, found her there—and asked her what she was doing.

"I wait for *Miladi, Milor*, she have not come in," Henriette said. "And I so fear *Miladi* will be late."

Tristram felt his heart stop beating for a second—strong man as he was. *Miladi* had not come in!—But as they spoke, he perceived her on the landing below, hurrying up—she had not waited to get the lift—and he went down to meet her, while Henriette returned to her room.

"Where have you been?" he demanded, with a pale, stern face. He was too angry and suspicious to let her pass in silence, and he noticed her cheeks were flushed with nervous excitement and that she was out of breath; and no wonder, for she had run up the stairs.

"I cannot wait to tell you now," she panted. "And what right have you to speak to me so? Let me pass, or I shall be late."

"I do not care if you are late, or no. You shall answer me!" he said furiously, barring the way. "You bear my name, at all events, and I have a right because of that to know."

"Your name?" she said, vaguely, and then for the first time she grasped that there was some insulting doubt of her in his words.

She cast upon him a look of withering scorn, and, with the air of an empress commanding an insubordinate guard, she flashed:

"Let me pass at once!"

But Tristram did not move, and for a second they glared at one another, and she took a step forward as if to force her way. Then he angrily seized her in his arms. But at that moment Francis Markrute came out of his room and Tristram let her go—panting. He could not make a scene, and she went on, with her head set haughtily, to her room.

"I see you have been quarreling again," her uncle said, rather irritably: and then he laughed as he went down.

"I expect she will be late," he continued; "well, if she is not in the hall at five minutes to eight, I shall go on."

And Tristram sat down upon the deep sofa on the broad landing outside her room, and waited: the concentrated essence of all the rage and pain he had yet suffered seemed to be now in his heart.

But what had it meant—that look of superb scorn? She had no mien of a guilty person.

At six minutes to eight she opened the door, and came out. She had simply flown into her clothes, in ten minutes! Her eyes were still black as night with resentment, and her bosom rose and fell, while in her white cheeks two scarlet spots flamed.

"I am ready," she said, haughtily, "let us go," and not waiting for her husband she swept on down the stairs, exactly as her uncle opened the library door.

"Well done, my punctual niece!" he cried genially. "You are a woman of your word."

"In all things," she answered, fiercely, and went towards the door, where the electric brougham waited.

And both men as they followed her wondered what she could mean.

CHAPTER XXXVIII

The dinner for Ethelrida's betrothal resembled in no way the one for Zara and Tristram; for, except in those two hearts there was no bitter strain, and the fiancés in this case were radiantly happy, which they could not conceal, and did not try to.

The Dowager Lady Tancred arrived a few minutes after the party of three, and Zara heard her mother-in-law gasp, as she said, "Tristram, my dear boy!" and then she controlled the astonishment in her voice, and went on more ordinarily, but still a little anxiously, "I hope you are very well?"

So he was changed then—to the eye of one who had not seen him since the wedding—and Zara glanced at him critically, and saw that—yes, he was, indeed, changed. His face was perfectly set and stern, and he looked older. It was no wonder his mother should be surprised.

Then Lady Tancred turned to Zara and kissed her. "Welcome back, my dear daughter," she said. And Zara tried to answer something pleasant: above all things, this proud lady who had so tenderly given her son's happiness into her keeping must not guess how much there was amiss.

But Lady Tancred was no simpleton—she saw immediately that her son must have gone through much suffering and strain. What was the matter? It tore her heart, but she knew him too well to say anything to him about it.

So she continued to talk agreeably to them, and Tristram made a great effort, and chaffed her, and became gay. And soon they went in to dinner. And Lady Tancred sat on Francis Markrute's other side, and tried to overcome her prejudice against him. If Ethelrida loved him so much he must be really nice. And Zara sat on one side of the old Duke, and Lady Anningford on the other, and on her other side was Young Billy who was now in an idiotic state of calf love for her—to the amusement of every one. So, with much gayety and chaff the repast came to an end, and the ladies, who were all old friends—no strangers now among them—disposed themselves in happy groups about one of the drawing-rooms, while they sipped their coffee.

Ethelrida drew Zara aside to talk to her alone.

"Zara," she said, taking her soft, white hand, "I am so awfully happy with my dear love that I want you to be so, too. Dearest Zara, won't you be friends with me, now—real friends?"

And Zara, won by her gentleness, pressed Ethelrida's hand with her other hand.

"I am so glad, nothing my uncle could have done would have given me so much pleasure," she said, with a break in her voice. "Yes, indeed, I will be friends with you, dear Ethelrida. I am so glad—and touched—that you should care to have me as your friend." Then Ethelrida bent forward and kissed her. "When one is as happy as I am," she said, "it makes one feel good, as if one wanted to do all the kind things and take away all sorrow out of the world. I have thought sometimes, Zara dear, that you did not look as happy as—as—I would like you to look."

Happy! the mockery of the word!

"Ethelrida," Zara whispered hurriedly—"don't—don't ask me anything about it, please, dear. No one can help me. I must come through with it alone—but you of Tristram's own family, and especially you whom he loves so much, I don't want you ever to misjudge me. You think perhaps I have made him unhappy. Oh, if you only knew it all!—Yes, I have. And I did not know, nor understand. I would die for him now, if I could, but it is too late; we can only play the game!"

"Zara, do not say this!" said Ethelrida, much distressed. "What can it be that should come between such beautiful people as you? And Tristram adores you, Zara dear."

"He did love me—once," Zara answered sadly, "but not now. He would like never to have to see me again. Please do not let us talk of it; please—I can't bear any more."

And Ethelrida, watching her face anxiously, saw that it wore a hopeless, hunted look, as though some agonizing trouble and anxiety brooded over her. And poor Zara could say nothing of her other anxiety, for now that Ethelrida was engaged to her uncle her lips, about her own sorrow concerning her little brother, must be more than ever sealed. Perhaps—she did not know much of the English point of view yet—perhaps if the Duke knew that there was some disgrace in the background of the family he might forbid the marriage, and then she would be spoiling this sweet Ethelrida's life.

And Ethelrida's fine senses told her there was no use pressing the matter further, whatever the trouble was this was not the moment to interfere; so she turned the conversation to lighter things, and, finally, talked about her own wedding, and so the time passed.

The Dowager Lady Tancred was too proud to ask any one any questions, although she talked alone with Lady Anningford and could easily have done so: the only person she mentioned her anxiety to was her brother, the Duke, when, later, she spoke a few words with him alone.

"Tristram looks haggard and very unhappy, Glastonbury," she said simply, "have you anything to tell me about it?"

"My dear Jane," replied the Duke, "it is the greatest puzzle in the world; no one can account for it. I gave him some sound advice at Montfitchet, when I saw things were so strained, and I don't believe he has taken it, by the look of them to-night. These young, modern people are so unnaturally cold, though I did hear they had got through the rejoicings, in fine style."

"It troubles me very much, Glastonbury—to go abroad and leave him looking like that. Is it her fault? Or what—do you think?"

"'Pon my soul, I can't say—even the Crow could not unravel the mystery. Laura Highford was at Montfitchet—confound her—would come; can she have had anything to do with it, I wonder?"

Then they were interrupted and no more could be said, and finally the party broke up, with the poor mother's feeling of anxiety unassuaged. Tristram and Zara were to lunch with her to-morrow, to say good-bye, and then she was going to Paris—by the afternoon train.

And Francis Markrute staying on to smoke a cigar with the Duke, and, presumably, to say a snatched good night to his fiancé, Tristram was left to take Zara home alone.

Now would come the moment of the explanation! But she outwitted him, for they no sooner got into the brougham and he had just begun to speak than she leaned back and interrupted him:

"You insinuated something on the stairs this evening, the vileness of which I hardly understood at first; I warn you I will hear no more upon the subject!" and then her voice broke suddenly and she said, passionately and yet with a pitiful note, "Ah! I am suffering so to-night, please—please don't speak to me—leave me alone."

And Tristram was silenced. Whatever it was that soon she must explain, he could not torture her to-night, and, in spite of his anger and suspicions and pain, it hurt him to see her, when the lights flashed in upon them, huddled up in the corner—her eyes like a wounded deer's.

"Zara!" he said at last—quite gently, "what is this, awful shadow that is hanging over you?—If you will only tell me—" But at that moment they arrived at the door, which was immediately opened, and she walked in and then to the lift without answering, and entering, closed the door. For what could she say?

She could bear things no longer. Tristram evidently saw she had some secret trouble, she would get her uncle to release her from her promise, as far as her husband was concerned at least,—she hated mysteries, and if it had annoyed him for her to be out late she would tell him the truth—and about Mirko, and everything.

Evidently he had been very much annoyed at that, but this was the first time he had even suggested he had noticed she was troubled about anything, except that day in the garden at Wrayth. Her motives were so perfectly innocent that not the faintest idea even yet dawned upon her that anything she had ever done could even look suspicious. Tristram was angry with her because she was late, and had insinuated something out of jealousy; men were always jealous, she knew, even if they were perfectly indifferent to a woman. What really troubled her terribly to-night Was the telegram she found in her room. She had told the maid to put it there when it came. It was from Mimo, saying Mirko was feverish again—really ill, he feared, this time.

So poor Zara spent a night of anguish and prayer, little knowing what the morrow was to bring.

And Tristram went out again to the Turf, and tried to divert his mind away from his troubles. There was no use in speculating any further, he must wait for an explanation which he would not consent to put off beyond the next morning.

So at last the day of a pitiful tragedy dawned.

Zara got up and dressed early. She must be ready to go out to try and see Mimo, the moment she could slip away after breakfast, so she came down with her hat on: she wanted to speak to her uncle alone, and Tristram, she thought, would not be there so early—only nine o'clock.

"This is energetic, my niece!" Francis Markrute said, but she hardly answered him, and as soon as Turner and the footman had left the room she began at once:

"Tristram was very angry with me last night because I was out late. I had gone to obtain news of Mirko, I am very anxious about him and I could give Tristram no explanation. I ask you to relieve me from my promise not to tell him—about things."

The financier frowned. This was a most unfortunate moment to revive the family skeleton, but he was a very just man and he saw, directly, that suspicion of any sort was too serious a thing to arouse in Tristram's mind.

"Very well," he said, "tell him what you think best. He looks desperately unhappy—you both do—are you keeping him at arm's length all this time, Zara? Because if so, my child, you will lose him, I warn you. You cannot treat a man of his spirit like that; he will leave you if you do."

"I do not want to keep him at arm's length; he is there of his own will. I told you at Montfitchet everything is too late—"

Then the butler entered the room: "Some one wishes to speak to your ladyship on the telephone, immediately," he said.

And Zara forgot her usual dignity as she almost rushed across the hall to the library, to talk:—it was Mimo, of course, so her presence of mind came to her and as the butler held the door for her she said, "Call a taxi at once."

She took the receiver up, and it was, indeed, Mimo's voice—and in terrible distress.

It appeared from his almost incoherent utterances that little Agatha had teased Mirko and finally broken his violin. And that this had so excited him, in his feverish state, that it had driven him almost mad, and he had waited until all the household, including the nurse, were asleep, and, with superhuman cunning, crept from his bed and dressed himself, and had taken the money which his Chérisette had given him for an emergency that day in the Park, and which he had always kept hidden in his desk; and he had then stolen out and gone to the station—all in the night, alone, the poor, poor lamb!—and there he had waited until the Weymouth night mail had come through, and had bought a ticket, and got in, and come to London to find his father—with the broken violin wrapped in its green baize cover. And all the while coughing—coughing enough to kill him! And he had arrived with just enough money to pay a cab, and had come at about five o'clock and could hardly wake the house to be let in; and he, Mimo, had heard the noise and come down, and there found the little angel, and brought him in, and warmed him in his bed. And he had waited to boil him some hot milk before he could come to the public telephone near, to call her up. Oh! but he was very ill—very, very ill—and could she come at once—but oh!—at once!

And Tristram, entering the room at that moment, saw her agonized face and heard her say, "Yes, yes, dear Mimo, I will come now!" and before he could realize what she was doing she brushed past him and rushed from the room, and across the hall and down to the waiting taxicab into which she sprang, and told the man where to go, with her head out of the window, as he turned into Grosvenor Street.

The name "Mimo" drove Tristram mad again. He stood for a moment, deciding what to do, then he seized his coat and hat and rushed out after her, to the amazement of the dignified servants. Here he hailed another taxi, but hers was just out of sight down to Park Street, when he got into his.

"Follow that taxi!" he said to the driver, "that green one in front of you—I will give you a sovereign if you never lose sight of it."

So the chase began! He must see where she would go! "Mimo!" the "Count Sykypri" she had telegraphed to—and she had the effrontery to talk to her lover, in her uncle's house! Tristram was so beside himself with rage he knew if he found them meeting at the end he would kill her. His taxi followed the green one, keeping it always in view, right on to Oxford Street, then Regent Street, then Mortimer Street. Was she going to Euston Station? Another of those meetings perhaps in a waiting-room, that Laura had already described! Unutterable disgust as well as blind fury filled him. He was too overcome with passion to reason with himself even. No, it was not Euston—they were turning into the Tottenham Court Road—and so into a side street. And here a back tire on his taxi went, with a loud report, and the driver came to a stop. And, almost foaming with rage, Tristram saw the green taxi disappear round the further corner of a mean street, and he knew it would be lost to view before he could overtake it: there was none other in sight. He flung the man some money and almost ran down the road—and, yes, when he turned the corner he could see the green taxi in the far distance; it was stopping at a door. He had caught her then, after all! He could afford to go slowly now. She had entered the house some five or ten minutes before he got there. He began making up his mind.

It was evidently a most disreputable neighborhood. A sickening, nauseating revulsion crept over him: Zara—the beautiful, refined Zara—to be willing to meet a lover here! The brute was probably ill, and that was why she had looked so distressed. He walked up and down rapidly twice, and then he crossed the road and rang the bell; the taxi was still at the door. It was opened almost immediately by the little, dirty maid—very dirty in the early morning like this.

He controlled his voice and asked politely to be taken to the lady who had just gone in. With a snivel of tears Jenny asked him to follow her, and, while she was mounting in front of him, she turned and said: "It ain't no good, doctor, I ken tell yer; my mother was took just like that, and after she'd once broke the vessel she didn't live a hour." And by this time they had reached the attic door which, without knocking Jenny opened a little, and, with another snivel, announced, "The doctor, missis."

And Tristram entered the room.

CHAPTER XXXIX

And this is what he saw.

The poor, mean room, with its scrupulous neatness slightly disturbed by the evidences of the boiling of milk and the warming of flannel, and Zara, kneeling by the low, iron bed where lay the little body of a child. For Mirko had dwindled, these last weeks of his constant fever, so that his poor, small frame, undersized for his age at any time, looked now no more than that of a boy of six years old. He was evidently dying. Zara held his tiny hand, and the divine love and sorrowful agony in her face wrung her husband's soul. A towel soaked with blood had fallen to the floor, and lay there, a ghastly evidence of the "broken vessel" Jenny had spoken of. Mimo, with his tall, military figure shaking with dry sobs, stood on the other side, and Zara murmured in a tender voice of anguish: "My little one! My Mirko!" She was oblivious in her grief of any other presence—and the dying child opened his eyes and called faintly, "Maman!"

Then Mimo saw Tristram by the door, and advanced with his finger on his quivering lips to meet him.

"Ah, sir," he said. "Alas! you have come too late. My child is going to God!"

And all the manhood in Tristram's heart rose up in pity. Here was a tragedy too deep for human judgment, too deep for thoughts of vengeance, and without a word he turned and stole from the room. And as he stumbled down the dark, narrow stairs he heard the sound of a violin as it wailed out the beginning notes of the *Chanson Triste*, and he shivered, as if with cold.

For Mirko had opened his piteous eyes again, and whispered in little gasps:

"Papa—play to me the air *Mamam* loved. I can see her blue gauze wings!" And in a moment, as his face filled with the radiance of his vision he fell back, dead, into Zara's arms.

When Tristram reached the street he looked about him for a minute like a blinded man; and then, as his senses came back to him, his first thought was what he could do for her—that poor mother upstairs, with her dying child. For that the boy was Zara's child he never doubted. Her child—and her lover's—had he not called her "*Maman.*" So this was the awful tragedy in her life. He analyzed nothing as yet; his whole being was paralyzed with the shock and the agony of things: the only clear thought he had was that he must help her in whatever way he could.

The green taxi was still there, but he would not take it, in case she should want it. He walked on down the street and found a cab for himself, and got driven to his old rooms in St. James's Street: he must be alone to think.

The hall-porter was surprised to see him. Nothing was ready for his lordship—but his wife would come up—?

But his lordship required nothing, he wished to find something alone.

He did not even notice that there was no fire in the grate, and that the room was icy cold—the agony of pain in his mind and soul made him unconscious of lesser ills. He pulled one of the holland sheets off his own big chair, and sat down in it.

Poor Zara, poor, unhappy Zara!—were his first thoughts—then he stiffened suddenly. This man must have been her lover before even her first marriage!—for Francis Markrute had told him she had married very soon. She was twenty-three years old now, and the child could not have been less than six; he must have been born when she was only seventeen. What devilish passion in a man could have made him tempt a girl so young! Of course this was her secret, and Francis Markrute knew nothing of it. For one frightful moment the thought came that her husband was not really dead and that this was he: but no, her husband's name had been Ladislaus, and this man she had called "Mimo," and if the boy were the child of her marriage there need then have been no secret about his existence. There was no other solution—this Count Sykypri had been her lover when she was a mere child, and probably the concealment had gone through all her first married life. And no doubt her reason for marrying him, which she admitted was a very strong one, had been that she might have money to give to the child—and its father.

The sickening—sickening, squalid tragedy of it all!

And she, Zara, had seemed so proud and so pure! Her look of scorn, only the night before, at his jealous accusation, came back to him. He could not remember a single movement nor action of hers that had not been that of an untarnished queen. What horrible actresses women were! His whole belief had crumbled to the dust.

And the most terrible part of it all to him was the knowledge that in spite of everything he still loved her—loved her with a consuming, almighty passion that he knew nothing now could kill. It had been put to the bitterest proof. Whatever she had done he could love no other woman.

Then he realized that his life was over. The future a blank, unutterable, hopeless gray which must go on for years and years. For he could never come back to her again, nor even live in the house with her, under the semblance of things.

Then an agonizing bitterness came to him, the hideous malevolence of fate, not to have let him meet this woman first before this other man; think of the faithfulness of her nature, with all its cruel actions to himself! She had been absolutely faithful to her lover, and had defended herself from his—Tristram's—caresses, even of her finger-tips. What a love worth having, what a strong, true character—worth dying for—in a woman!

And now, he must never see her again; or, if once more, only for a business meeting, to settle things without scandal to either of them.

He would not go back to Park Lane, yet—not for a week; he would give her time to see to the funeral, without the extra pain of his presence.

The man had taken him for the doctor, and she had not even been aware of his entrance: he would go back to Wrayth, alone, and there try to think out some plan. So he searched among the covered-up furniture for his writing table, and found some paper, and sat down and wrote two notes, one to his mother. He could not face her to-day—she must go without seeing him—but he knew his mother loved him, and, in all deep moments, never questioned his will even if she did not understand it.

The note to her was very short, merely saying something was troubling him greatly for the time, so neither he nor Zara would come to luncheon; and she was to trust him and not speak of this to any one until he himself told her more. He might come and see her in Cannes, the following week.

Then he wrote to Zara, and these were his words:

"I know everything. I understand now, and however I blame you for your deception of me you have my deep sympathy in your grief. I am going away for a week, so you will not be distressed by seeing me. Then I must ask you to meet me, here or at your uncle's house, to arrange for our future separation.

"Yours,
"Tancred."

Then he rang for a messenger boy, and gave him both notes, and, picking up the telephone, called up his valet and told him to pack and bring his things here to his old rooms, and, if her ladyship came in, to see that she immediately got the note he was sending round to her. Francis Markrute would have gone to the City by now and was going to lunch with Ethelrida, so he telephoned to one of his clerks there—finding he was out for the moment—just to say he was called away for a week and would write later.

She should have the first words with her uncle. Whether she would tell him or no she must decide, he would not do anything to make her existence more difficult than it must naturally be.

And then when all this was done the passionate jealousy of a man overcame him again, and when he thought of Mimo he once more longed to kill.

CHAPTER XL

It was late in the afternoon when Zara got back to her uncle's house. She had been too distracted with grief to know or care about time, or what they would be thinking of her absence.

Just after the poor little one was dead frantic telegrams had come from the Morleys, in consternation at his disappearance, and Mimo, quite prostrate in his sorrow, as he had been at her mother's death, had left all practical things to Zara.

No doctor turned up, either. Mimo had not coherently given the address, on the telephone. Thus they passed the day alone with their dead, in anguish; and at last thought came back to Zara. She would go to her uncle, and let him help to settle things; she could count upon him to do that.

Francis Markrute, anxious and disturbed by Tristram's message and her absence, met her as she came in and drew her into the library.

The butler had handed her her husband's note, but she held it listlessly in her hand, without opening it. She was still too numb with sorrow to take notice of ordinary things. Her uncle saw immediately that something terrible had happened.

"Zara, dear child," he said, and folded her in his arms with affectionate kindness, "tell me everything."

She was past tears now, but her voice sounded strange with the tragedy in it.

"Mirko is dead, Uncle Francis," was all she said. "He ran away from Bournemouth because Agatha, the Morleys' child, broke his violin. He loved it, you know *Maman* had given it to him. He came in the night, all alone, ill with fever, to find his father, and he broke a blood vessel this morning, and died in my arms—there, in the poor lodging."

Francis Markrute had drawn her to the sofa now, and stroked her hands. He was deeply moved.

"My poor, dear child! My poor Zara!" he said.

Then, with most pathetic entreaty she went on,

"Oh, Uncle Francis, can't you forgive poor Mimo, now? *Maman* is dead and Mirko is dead, and if you ever, some day, have a child yourself, you may know what this poor father is suffering. Won't you help us? He is foolish always—unpractical—and he is distracted with grief. You are so strong—won't you see about the funeral for my little love?"

"Of course I will, dear girl," he answered. "You must have no more distresses. Leave everything to me." And he bent and kissed her white cheek, while he tenderly began to remove the pins from her fur toque.

"Thank you," she said gently, as she took the hat from his hand, and laid it beside her. "I grieve because I loved him—my dear little brother. His soul was all music, and there was no room for him here. And oh! I loved *Maman* so! But I know that it is better as it is; he is safe there, with her now, far away from all his pain. He saw her when he was dying." Then after a pause she went on: "Uncle Francis, you love Ethelrida very much, don't you? Try to look back and think how *Maman* loved Mimo, and he loved her. Think of all the sorrow of her life, and the great, great price she paid for her love; and then, when you see him—poor Mimo—try to be merciful."

And Francis Markrute suddenly felt a lump in his throat. The whole pitiful memory of his beloved sister stabbed him, and extinguished the last remnant of rancor towards her lover, which had smoldered always in his proud heart.

There was a moisture in his clever eyes, and a tremulous note in his cold voice as he answered his niece:

"Dear child, we will forget and forgive everything. My one thought about it all now, is to do whatever will bring you comfort."

"There is one thing—yes," she said, and there was the first look of life in her face. "Mirko, when I saw him last at Bournemouth, played to me a wonderful air; he said *Maman* always came back to him in his dreams when he was ill—feverish, you know—and that she had taught it to him. It talks of the woods where she is, and beautiful butterflies; there is a blue one for her, and a little white one for him. He wrote out the score—it is so joyous—and I have it. Will you send it to Vienna or Paris, to some great artist, and get it really arranged, and then when I play it we shall always be able to see *Maman*."

And the moisture gathered again in Francis Markrute's eyes.

"Oh, my dear!" he said. "Will you forgive me some day for my hardness, for my arrogance to you both? I never knew, I never understood—until lately—what love could mean in a life. And you, Zara, yourself, dear child, can nothing be done for you and Tristram?"

At the mention of her husband's name Zara looked up, startled; and then a deeper tragedy than ever gathered in her eyes, as she rose.

"Let us speak of that no more, my uncle," she said. "Nothing can be done, because his love for me is dead. I killed it myself, in my ignorance. Nothing you or I can do is of any avail now—it is all too late."

And Francis Markrute could not speak. Her ignorance had been his fault, his only mistake in calculation, because he had played with souls as pawns in those days before love had softened him. And she made him no reproaches, when that past action of his had caused the finish of her life's happiness! Verily, his niece was a noble woman, and, with deepest homage, as he led her to the door he bent down and kissed her forehead; and no one in the world who knew him would have believed that she felt it wet with tears.

When she got to her room she remembered she still carried some note, and she at last looked at the superscription. It was in Tristram's writing. In spite of her grief and her numbness to other things it gave her a sharp emotion. She opened it quickly and read its few cold words. Then it seemed as if her knees gave way under her, as at Montfitchet that day when Laura Highford had made her jealous. She could not think clearly, nor fully understand their meaning; only one point stood out distinctly. He must see her to arrange for their separation. He had grown to hate her so much, then, that he could not any longer even live in the house with her, and all her grief of the day seemed less than this thought. Then she read it again. He knew all? Who could have told him? Her Uncle Francis? No, he did not himself know that Mirko was dead until she had told him. This was a mystery, but it was unimportant. Her numb brain could not grasp it yet. The main thing was that he was very angry with her for her deception of him: that, perhaps, was what was causing him finally to part from her. How strange it was that she was always punished for keeping her word and acting up to her principles! She did not think this bitterly, only with utter hopelessness. There was no use in her trying any longer; happiness was evidently not meant for her. She must just accept things—and life, or death, as it came. But how hard men were—she could never be so stern to any one for such a little fault, for *any* fault—stern and unforgiving as that strange God who wrote the Commandments.

And then she felt her cheeks suddenly burn, and yet she shivered; and when her maid came to her, presently, she saw that her mistress was not only deeply grieved, but ill, too. So she put her quickly to bed, and then went down to see Mr. Markrute.

"I think we must have a doctor, monsieur," she said. "*Miladi* is not at all well."

And Francis Markrute, deeply distressed, telephoned at once for his physician.

His betrothed had gone back to the country after luncheon, so he could not even have the consolation of her sympathy, and where Tristram was he did not know.

For the four following days Zara lay in her bed, seriously ill. She had caught a touch of influenza the eminent physician said, and had evidently had a most severe shock as well. But she was naturally so splendidly healthy that, in spite of grief and hopelessness, the following Thursday she was able to get up again. Francis Markrute thought her illness had been merciful in a way because the funeral had all been got over while she was confined to her room. Zara had accepted everything without protest. She had not desired even to see Mirko once more. She had no morbid fancies; it was his soul she loved and remembered, not the poor little suffering body.

It came to her as a comfort that her uncle and Mimo had met and shaken hands in forgiveness, and now poor Mimo was coming to say good-bye to her that afternoon.

He was leaving England at once, and would return to his own country and his people. In his great grief, and with no further ties, he hoped they would receive him. He had only one object now in life—to get through with it and join those he loved in some happier sphere.

This was the substance of what he said to Zara when he came; and they kissed and blessed one another, and parted, perhaps for ever. The "Apache" and the "London Fog," which would never be finished now he feared—the pain would be too great—would be sent to her to keep as a remembrance of their years of life together and the deep ties that bound them by the memory of those two graves.

And Zara in her weakness had cried for a long time after he had left.

And then she realized that all that part of her life was over now, and the outlook of what was to come held out no hope.

Francis Markrute had telegraphed to Wrayth, to try and find Tristram, but he was not there. He had not gone there at all. At the last moment he could not face it, he felt; he must go somewhere away alone—by the sea. A great storm was coming on—it suited his mood—so he had left even his servant in London and had gone off to a wild place on the Dorsetshire coast that he knew of, and there heard no news of any one. He would go back on the Friday, and see Zara the next day, as he had said he would do. Meanwhile he must fight his ghosts alone. And what ghosts they were!

Now on this Saturday morning Francis Markrute was obliged to leave his niece. His vast schemes required his attention in Berlin and he would be gone for a week, and then was going down to Montfitchet. Ethelrida had written Zara the kindest letters. Her fiancé had told her all the pitiful story, and now she understood the tragedy in Zara's eyes, and loved her the more for her silence and her honor.

But all these thoughts seemed to be things of naught to the sad recipient of her letters, since the one and only person who mattered now in her life knew, also, and held different ones. He was aware of all, and had no sympathy or pity—only blame—for her. And now that her health was better and she was able to think, this ceaseless question worried her; how could Tristram possibly have known all? Had he followed her? As soon as she would be allowed to go out she would go and see Jenny, and question her.

And Tristram, by the wild sea—the storm like his mood had lasted all the time—came eventually to some conclusions. He would return and see his wife and tell her that now they must part, that he knew of her past and he would trouble her no more. He would not make her any reproaches, for of what use? And, besides, she had suffered enough. He would go abroad at once, and see his mother for a day at Cannes, and tell her his arrangements, and that Zara and he had agreed to part—he would give her no further explanations—and then he would go on to India and Japan. And, after this, his plans were vague. It seemed as if life were too impossible to look ahead, but not until he could think of Zara with calmness would he return to England.

And if Zara's week of separation from him had been grief and suffering, his had been hell.

On the Saturday morning, after her uncle had started for Dover, a note, sent by hand, was brought to Zara. It was again only a few words, merely to say if it was convenient to her, he—Tristram—would come at two o'clock, as he was motoring down to Wrayth at three, and was leaving England on Monday night.

Her hand trembled too much to write an answer.

"Tell the messenger I will be here," she said; and she sat then for a long time, staring in front of her.

Then a thought came to her. Whether she were well enough or no she must go and question Jenny. So, to the despair of her maid, she wrapped herself in furs and started. She felt extremely faint when she got into the air, but her will pulled her through, and when she got there the little servant put her doubts at rest.

Yes, a very tall, handsome gentleman had come a few minutes after herself, and she had taken him up, thinking he was the doctor.

"Why, missus," she said, "he couldn't have stayed a minute. He come away while the Count was playin' his fiddle."

So this was how it was! Her thoughts were all in a maze: she could not reason. And when she got back to the Park Lane house she felt too feeble to go any further, even to the lift.

Her maid came and took her furs from her, and she lay on the library sofa, after Henriette had persuaded her to have a little chicken broth; and then she fell into a doze, and was awakened only by the sound of the electric bell. She knew it was her husband coming, and sat up, with a wildly beating heart. Her trembling limbs would not support her as she rose for his entrance, and she held on by the back of a chair.

And, grave and pale with the torture he had been through, Tristram came into the room.

CHAPTER XLI

He stopped dead short when he saw her so white and fragile looking. Then he exclaimed, "Zara—you have been ill!"

"Yes," she faltered.

"Why did they not tell me?" he said hurriedly, and then recollected himself. How could they? No one, not even his servant, knew where he had been.

She dropped back unsteadily on the sofa.

"Uncle Francis did telegraph to you, to Wrayth, but you were not there," she said.

He bit his lips—he was so very moved. How was he to tell her all the things he had come to say so coldly, with her looking so pitiful, so gentle? His one longing was to take her to his heart and comfort her, and make her forget all pain.

And she was so afraid of her own weakness, she felt she could not bear to hear her death-knell, yet. If she could only gain a little time! It was characteristic of her that she never dreamed of defending herself. She still had not the slightest idea that he suspected Mimo of being her lover. Tristram's anger with her was just because he was an Englishman—very straight and simple—who could brook no deception! that is what she thought.

If she had not been so lately and so seriously ill—if all her fine faculties had been in their full vigor—perhaps some idea might have come to her; but her soul was so completely pure it did not naturally grasp such things, so even that is doubtful.

"Tristram—" she said, and there was the most piteous appeal in her tones, which almost brought the tears to his eyes. "Please—I know you are angry with me for not telling you about Mirko and Mimo, but I had promised not to, and the poor, little one is dead. I will tell you everything presently, if you wish, but don't ask me to now. Oh! if you must go from me soon—you know best—I will not keep you, but—but please won't you take me with you to-day—back to Wrayth—just until I get quite well? My uncle is away, and I am so lonely, and I have not any one else on earth."

Her eyes had a pleading, frightened look, like a child's who is afraid to be left alone in the dark.

He could not resist her. And, after all, her sin was of long ago—she could have done nothing since she had been his wife—why should she not come to Wrayth? She could stay there if she wished, for a while after he had gone. Only one thing he must know.

"Where is Count Sykypri?" he asked hoarsely.

"Mimo has gone away, back to his own country," she said simply, wondering at his tone. "Alas! I shall perhaps never see him again."

A petrifying sensation of astonishment crept over Tristram. With all her meek gentleness she had still the attitude of a perfectly innocent person. It must be because she was only half English, and foreigners perhaps had different points of reasoning on all such questions.

The man had gone, then—out of her life. Yes, he would take her back to Wrayth if it would be any comfort to her.

"Will you get ready now?" he said, controlling his voice into a note of sternness which he was far from feeling. "Because I am sure you ought not to be out late in the damp air. I was going in the open car, and to drive myself, and it takes four hours. The closed one is not in London, as you know." And then he saw she was not fit for this, so he said anxiously, "But are you sure you ought to travel to-day at all? You look so awfully pale."

For there was a great difference in her present transparent, snowy whiteness, with the blue-circled eyes, to her habitual gardenia hue; even her lips were less red.

"Yes, yes, I am quite able to go," she said, rising to show him she was all right. "I will be ready in ten minutes. Henriette can come by train with my things." And she walked towards the door, which he held open for her. And here she paused, and then went on to the lift. He followed her quickly.

"Are you sure you can go up alone?" he asked anxiously. "Or may I come?"

"Indeed, I am quite well," she answered, with a little pathetic smile. "I will not trouble you. Wait, I shall not be long." And so she went up.

And when she came down again, all wrapped in her furs, she found Tristram had port wine ready for her, poured out.

"You must drink this—a big glass of it," he said; and she took it without a word.

Then when they got to the door she found instead of his own open motor he had ordered one of her uncle's closed ones, which with footwarmer and cushions was waiting, so that she should be comfortable and not catch further cold.

"Thank you—that is kind of you," she said.

He helped her in, and the butler tucked the fur rug over them, while Tristram settled the cushions. Then she leaned back for a second and closed her eyes—everything was going round.

He was very troubled about her. She must have been very ill, even in the short time—and then her grief,—for, even though she had been so much separated from it, a mother always loves her child. Then this thought hurt him again. He hated to remember about the child.

She lay there back against the pillows until they had got quite out of London, without speaking a word. The wine in her weak state made her sleepy, and she gradually fell into a doze, and her head slipped sideways and rested against Tristram's shoulder, and it gave him a tremendous thrill—her beautiful, proud head with its thick waves of hair showing under her cap.

He was going to leave her so soon, and she would not know it—she was asleep—he must just hold her to him a little; she would be more comfortable like that. So, with cautious care not to wake her, he slipped his arm under the cushion, and very gently and gradually drew her into his embrace, so that her unconscious head rested upon his breast.

And thus more than two hours of the journey were accomplished.

And what thoughts coursed through his brain as they went!

He loved her so madly. What did it matter how she had sinned? She was ill and lonely, and must stay in his arms—just for to-day. But he could never really take her to his heart—the past was too terrible for that. And, besides, she did not love him; this gentleness was only because she was weak and crushed, for the time. But how terribly, bitterly sweet it was, all the same! He had the most overpowering temptation to kiss her, but he resisted it; and presently, when they came to a level crossing and a train gave a wild whistle, she woke with a start. It was quite dark now, and she said, in a frightened voice, "Where am I? Where have I been?"

Tristram slipped his arm from round her instantly, and turned on the light.

"You are in the motor, going to Wrayth," he said. "And I am glad to say you have been asleep. It will do you good."

She rubbed her eyes.

"Ah! I was dreaming. And Mirko was there, too, with *Maman*, and we were so happy!" she said, as if to herself.

Tristram winced.

"Are we near home—I mean, Wrayth?" she asked.

"Not quite yet," he answered. "There will be another hour and a half."

"Need we have the light on?" she questioned. "It hurts my eyes."

He put it out, and there they sat in the growing darkness, and did not speak any more for some time; and, bending over her, he saw that she had dozed off again. How very weak she must have been!

He longed to take her into his arms once more, but did not like to disturb her—she seemed to have fallen into a comfortable position among the pillows—so he watched over her tenderly, and presently they came to the lodge gates of Wrayth, and the stoppage caused her to wake and sit up.

"It seems I had not slept for so long," she said, "and now I feel better. It is good of you to let me come with you. We are in the park, are we not?"

"Yes, we shall be at the door in a minute."

And then she cried suddenly,

"Oh! look at the deer!" For a bold and valiant buck, startled and indignant at the motor lights, was seen, for an instant, glaring at them as they flashed past.

"You must go to bed as soon as you have had some tea," Tristram said, "after this long drive. It is half-past six. I telegraphed to have a room prepared for you. Not that big state apartment you had before, but one in the other part of the house, where we live when we are alone; and I thought you would like your maid next you, as you have been ill."

"Thank you," she whispered quite low.

How kind and thoughtful he was being to her! She was glad she had been ill!

Then they arrived at the door, and this time they turned to the left before they got to the Adam's hall, and went down a corridor to the old paneled rooms, and into his own sitting-room where it was all warm and cozy, and the tea-things were laid out. She already looked better for her sleep; some of the bluish transparency seemed to have left her face.

She had not been into this room on her inspection of the house. She liked it best of all, with its scent of burning logs and good cigars. And Jake snorted by the fire with pleasure to see his master, and she bent and patted his head.

But everything she did was filling Tristram with fresh bitterness and pain. To be so sweet and gentle now when it was all too late!

He began opening his letters until the tea came. There were the telegrams from Francis Markrute, sent a week before to say Zara was ill, and many epistles from friends. And at the end of the pile he found a short note from Francis Markrute, as well. It was written the day before, and said that he supposed he, Tristram, would get it eventually; that Zara had had a very sad bereavement which he felt sure she would rather tell him about herself, and that he trusted, seeing how very sad and ill she had been, that Tristram would be particularly kind to her. So her uncle knew, then! This was incredible: but perhaps Zara had told him, in her first grief.

He glanced up at her; she was lying back in a great leather chair now, looking so fragile and weary, he could not say what he intended. Then Jake rose leisurely and put his two fat forepaws up on her knees and snorted as was his habit when he approved of any one. And she bent down and kissed his broad wrinkles.

It all looked so homelike and peaceful! Suddenly scorching tears came into Tristram's eyes and he rose abruptly, and walked to the window. And at that moment the servants brought the teapot and the hot scones.

She poured the tea out silently, and then she spoke a little to Jake, just a few silly, gentle words about his preference for cakes or toast. She was being perfectly adorable, Tristram thought, with her air of pensive, subdued sorrow, and her clinging black dress.

He wished she would suggest going to her room. He could not bear it much longer.

She wondered why he was so restless. And he certainly was changed; he looked haggard and unhappy, more so even than before. And then she remembered how radiantly strong and splendid he had appeared, at dinner on their wedding night, and a lump rose in her throat.

"Henriette will have arrived by now," she said in a few minutes. "If you will tell me where it is I will go to my room."

He got up, and she followed him.

"I expect you will find it is the blue, Chinese damask one just at the top of these little stairs." Then he strode on in front of her quickly, and called out from the top, "Yes, it is, and your maid is here."

And as she came up the low, short steps, they met on the turn, and stopped.

"Good night," he said. "I will have some soup and suitable things for an invalid sent up to you; and then you must sleep well, and not get up in the morning. I shall be very busy to-morrow. I have a great many things to do before I go on Monday. I am going away for a long time."

She held on to the banisters for a minute, but the shadows were so deceiving, with all the black oak, that he was not sure what her expression said. Her words were a very low "Thank you—I will try to sleep. Good night."

And she went up to her room, and Tristram went on, downstairs—a deeper ache than ever in his heart.

CHAPTER XLII

It was not until luncheon time that Zara came down, next day. She felt he did not wish to see her, and she lay there in her pretty, old, quaint room, and thought of many things, and the wreck of their lives, above all. And she thought of Mirko and her mother, and the tears came to her eyes. But that grief was past, in its bitterness; she knew it was much better so.

The thought of Tristram's going tore her very soul, and swallowed up all other grief.

"I cannot, cannot bear it!" she moaned to herself.

He was sitting gazing into the fire, when she timidly came into his sitting-room. She had been too unhappy to sleep much and was again looking very pale.

He seemed to speak to her like one in a dream. He was numb with his growing misery and the struggle in his mind: he must leave her—the situation was unendurable—he could not stay, because in her present softened mood it was possible that if he lost control of himself and caressed her she might yield to him; and, then, he knew no resolutions on earth could hold him from taking her to his heart. And she must never really be his wife. The bliss of it might be all that was divine at first, but there would be always the hideous skeleton beneath, ready to peep out and mock at them: and then if they should have children? They were both so young that would be sure to happen; and this thought, which had once, in that very room, in his happy musings, given him so much joy, now caused him to quiver with extra pain. For a woman with such a background should not be the mother of a Tancred of Wrayth.

Tristram was no Puritan, but the ingrained pride in his old name he could not eliminate from his blood. So he kept himself with an iron reserve. He never once looked at her, and spoke as coldly as ice; and they got through luncheon. And Zara said, suddenly, she would like to go to church.

It was at three o'clock, so he ordered the motor without a word. She was not well enough to walk there through the park.

He could not let her go alone, so he changed his plans and went with her. They did not speak, all the way.

She had never been into the church before, and was struck with the fine windows, and the monuments of the Guiscards, and the famous tomb of the Crusader in the wall of the chancel pew where they sat; and all through the service she gazed at his carven face, so exactly like Tristram's, with the same, stern look.

And a wild, miserable rebellion filled her heart, and then a cold fear; and she passionately prayed to God to protect him. For what if he should go on some dangerous hunting expedition, and something should happen, and she should never see him again! And then, as she stood while they sang the final hymn, she stopped and caught her breath with a sob. And Tristram glanced at her in apprehension, and he wondered if he should have to suffer anything further, or if his misery were at its height.

The whole congregation were so interested to see the young pair, and they had to do some handshakings, as they came out. What would all these good people think, Tristram wondered with bitter humor, when they heard that he had gone away on a long tour, leaving his beautiful bride alone, not a month after their marriage? But he was past caring what they thought, one way or another, now.

Zara went to her room when they got back to the house, and when she came down to tea he was not there, and she had hers alone with Jake.

She felt almost afraid to go to dinner. It was so evident he was avoiding her. And while she stood undecided her maid brought in a note:

"I ask you not to come down—I cannot bear it. I will see you to-morrow morning, before I go, if you will come to my sitting-room at twelve."

That was all.

And, more passionately wretched than she had ever been in her life, she went to bed.

She used the whole strength of her will to control herself next morning. She must not show any emotion, no matter how she should feel. It was not that she had any pride left, or would not have willingly fallen into his arms; but she felt no woman could do so, unsolicited and when a man plainly showed her he held her in disdain.

So it was, with both their hearts breaking, they met in the sitting-room.

"I have only ten minutes," he said constrainedly. "The motor is at the door. I have to go round by Bury St. Edmunds; it is an hour out of my way, and I must be in London at five o'clock, as I leave for Paris by the night mail. Will you sit down, please, and I will be as brief as I can."

She fell, rather than sank, into a chair. She felt a singing in her ears; she must not faint—she was so very weak from her recent illness.

"I have arranged that you stay here at Wrayth until you care to make fresh arrangements for yourself," he began, averting his eyes, and speaking in a cold, passionless voice. "But if I can help it, after I leave here to-day I will never see you again. There need be no public scandal; it is unnecessary that people should be told anything; they can think what they like. I will explain to my mother that the marriage was a mistake and we have agreed to part—that is all. And you can live as you please and I will do the same. I do not reproach you for the ruin you have brought upon my life. It was my own fault for marrying you so heedlessly. But I loved you so—!" And then his voice broke suddenly with a sob, and he stretched out his arms wildly.

"My God!" he cried, "I am punished! The agony of it is that I love you still, with all my soul—even though I saw them with my own eyes—your lover and—your child!"

Here Zara gave a stifled shriek, and, as he strode from the room not daring to look at her for fear of breaking his resolution, she rose unsteadily to her feet and tried to call him. But she gasped and no words would come. Then she fell back unconscious in the chair.

He did not turn round, and soon he was in the motor and gliding away as though the hounds of hell were after him, as, indeed, they were, from the mad pain in his heart.

And when Zara came to herself it was half an hour later, and he was many miles away.

She sat up and found Jake licking her hands.

Then remembrance came back. He was gone—and he loved her even though he thought her—that!

She started to her feet. The blood rushed back to her brain. She must act.

She stared around, dazed for a moment, and then she saw the time tables—the Bradshaw and the A.B.C. She turned over the leaves of the latter with feverish haste. Yes, there was a train which left at 2:30 and got to London at half-past five; it was a slow one—the express which started at 3:30, did not get in until nearly six. That might be too late—both might be too late, but she must try. Then she put her hand to her head in agony. She did not know where he had gone. Would he go to his mother's, or to his old rooms in St. James's Street? She did not know their number.

She rang the bell and asked that Michelham should come to her.

The old servant saw her ghastly face, and knew from Higgins that his master intended going to Paris that night. He guessed some tragedy had happened between them, and longed to help.

"Michelham," she said, "his lordship has gone to London. Do you know to what address? I must follow him—it is a matter of life and death that I see him before he starts for Paris. Order my motor for the 2:30 train—it is quicker than to go by car all the way."

"Yes, my lady," Michelham said. "Everything will be ready. His lordship has gone to his rooms, 460 St. James's Street. May I accompany your ladyship? His lordship would not like your ladyship to travel alone."

"Very well," she said. "There is no place anywhere, within driving distance that I could catch a train that got in before, is there?"

"No, my lady; that will be the soonest," he said. "And will your ladyship please to eat some luncheon? There is an hour before the motor will be round. I know your ladyship's own footman, James, should go with your ladyship, but if it is something serious, as an old servant, and, if I may say so, a humble and devoted friend of his lordship's, I would beg to accompany your ladyship instead."

"Yes, yes, Michelham," said Zara, and hurried from the room.

She sent a telegram when at last she reached the station—to the St. James's Street rooms.

"What you thought was not true. Do not leave until I come and explain. I am your own Zara."

Then the journey began—three hours of agony, with the constant stoppages, and the one thought going over and over in her brain. He believed she had a lover and a child, and yet he loved her! Oh, God! That was love, indeed!—and she might not be in time.

But at last they arrived—Michelham and she—and drove to Tristram's rooms.

Yes, his lordship had been expected at five, but had not arrived yet; he was late. And Michelham explained that Lady Tancred had come, and would wait, while he himself went round to Park Lane to see if Lord Tancred had been there.

He made up a splendid fire in the sitting-room, and, telling Higgins not to go in and disturb her even with tea, the kind old man started on his quest—much anxiety in his mind.

Ten minutes passed, and Zara felt she could hardly bear the suspense. The mad excitement had kept her up until now. What if he were so late that he went straight to the train? But then she remembered it went at nine—and it was only six. Yes, he would surely come.

She did not stir from her chair, but her senses began to take in the room. How comfortable it was, and what good taste, even with the evidences of coming departure about! She had seen two or three telegrams lying on the little hall table, waiting for him, as she came in—hers among the number, she supposed. A motor stopped, surely!—Ah! if it should be he! But there were hundreds of such noises in St. James's Street, and it was too dark and foggy to see. She sat still, her heart beating in her throat. Yes, there was the sound of a latch key turning in the lock! And, after stopping to pick up his telegrams, Tristram, all unexpecting to see any one, entered the room.

She rose unsteadily to meet him, as he gave an exclamation of surprise and—yes—pain.

"Tristram!" she faltered. It seemed as if her voice had gone again, and the words would make no sound. But she gathered her strength, and, with pitiful pleading, stretched out her arms.

"Tristram—I have come to tell you—I have never had a lover: Mimo was at last married to *Maman*. He was her lover, and Mirko was their child—my little brother. My uncle did not wish me to tell you this for a time, because it was the family disgrace." Then, as he made a step forward to her, with passionate joy in his face, she went on:

"Tristram! You said, that night—before you would ever ask me to be your wife again, I must go down upon my knees—See—I do!—for Oh!—I love you!" And suddenly she bent and knelt before him, and bowed her proud head.

But she did not stay in this position a second, for he clasped her in his arms, and rained mad, triumphant kisses upon her beautiful, curved lips, while he murmured,

"At last—my Love—my own!"

Then when the delirium of joy had subsided a little,—with what tenderness he took off her hat and furs, and drew her into his arms, on the sofa before the fire.—The superlative happiness to feel her resting there, unresisting, safe in his fond embrace, with those eyes, which had been so stormy and resentful, now melting upon him in softest passion.

It seemed heaven to them both. They could not speak coherent sentences for a while—just over and over again they told each other that they loved.—It seemed as if he could not hear her sweet confession often enough—or quench the thirst of his parched soul upon her lips.

Then the masterfulness in him which Zara now adored asserted itself. He must play with her hair! He must undo it, and caress its waves, to blot out all remembrance of how its forbidden beauty had tortured him.—And she just lay there in his arms, in one of her silences, only her eyes were slumberous with love.

But at last she said, nestling closer,

"Tristram, won't you listen to the story that I must tell you? I want there never to be any more mysteries between us again—"

And, to content her, he brought himself back to earth—

"Only I warn you, my darling," he said, "all such things are side issues for me now that at last we have obtained the only thing which really matters in life—we know that we love each other, and are not going to be so foolish as to part again for a single hour—if we can help it—for the rest of time."

And then his whole face lit up with radiant joy, and he suddenly buried it in her hair. "See," he inurmured, "I am to be allowed to play with this exquisite net to ensnare my heart; and you are not to be allowed to spend hours in state rooms—alone! Oh! darling! How can I listen to anything but the music of your whispers, when you tell me you love me and are my very own!"

Zara did, however, finally get him to understand the whole history from beginning to end. And when he heard of her unhappy life, and her mother's tragic story, and her sorrow and poverty, and her final reason for agreeing to the marriage, and how she thought of men, and then of him, and all her gradual awakening into this great love, there grew in him a reverent tenderness.

"Oh! my sweet—my sweet!" he said. "And I dared to be suspicious of you and doubt you, it seems incredible now!"

Then he had to tell his story—of how reasonable his suspicions looked, and, in spite of them, of his increasing love. And so an hour passed with complete clearing up of all shadows, and they could tenderly smile together over the misunderstandings which had nearly caused them to ruin both their lives.

"And to think, Tristram," said Zara, "a little common sense would have made it all smooth!"

"No, it was not that," he answered fondly, with a whimsical smile in his eyes, "the troubles would never have happened at all if I had only not paid the least attention to your haughty words in Paris, nor even at Dover, but had just continued making love to you; all would have been well!—However," he added joyously, "we will forget dark things, because to-morrow I shall take you back to Wrayth, and we shall have our real honeymoon there in perfect peace."

And, as her lips met his, Zara whispered softly once more,

"Tu sais que je t'aime!"

Oh! the glorious joy of that second home-coming for the bridal pair! To walk to all Tristram's favorite haunts, to wander in the old rooms, and plan out their improvements, and in the late afternoons to sit in the firelight in his own sitting-room, and make pictures of their future joys together. Then he would tell her of his dreams, which once had seemed as if they must turn to Dead Sea fruit, but were now all bright and glowing with glad promise of fulfillment.

His passionate delight in her seemed as if it could not find enough expression, as he grew to know the cultivation of her mind and the pure thoughts of her soul.—And her tenderness to him was all the sweeter in its exquisite submission, because her general mien was so proud.

They realized they had found the greatest happiness in this world, and with the knowledge that they had achieved their desires, after anguish and pain, they held it next their hearts as heaven's gift.

And when they went to Montfitchet again, to spend that Christmas, the old Duke was satisfied!

Now, all this happened two years ago. And on the second anniversary of the Tancred wedding Mr. Francis and Lady Ethelrida Markrute dined with their nephew and niece.

And when they came to drinking healths, bowing to Zara her uncle raised his glass and said,

"I propose a toast, that I prophesied I would, to you, my very dear niece—the toast of four supremely happy people!"

And as they drank, the four joined hands.

The Damsel and the Sage,

A Woman's Whimsies

THE DAMSEL AND THE SAGE

And the Damsel said to the Sage:
"Now, what is life? And why does the fruit taste bitter in the mouth?"
And the Sage answered, as he stepped from his cave:
"My child, there was once a man who had two ears like other people. They were naturally necessary for his enjoyment of the day. But one of these ears offended his head. It behaved with stupidity, thinking thereby toenhance its value to him—it heard too much. Oh, it conducted itself with a gross stupidity. 'Out upon you,' cried the man; 'since you have overstepped the limit of the functions of an ear, I shall cut you from my head!' And so, without hesitation, he took a sword and accomplished the deed. The poor ear then lay upon the ground bleeding, and the man went about with a mutilated head."
"And what was the good of all that?" said the Damsel.
"There was no good in it," replied the Sage. "But he was a man, and he had punished the too-fond-and-foolish ear—also he hoped a new and more suitable one would grow in its place. 'Change,' he said, 'was a thing to be welcomed.'"
"And tell me, Sage, what became of the ear?" asked the Damsel.
"The ear fared better. Another man of greater shrewdness came along, and, although he had two ears of his own, he said, 'A third will not come amiss,' and he picked up the ear and heard with three ears instead of two. So he became knowing and clever because of the information he acquired in this way. The grafted ear grew and flourished, and, in spite of its remaining abnormal, it obtained a certain enjoyment out of existence."
"But who *really* benefited by all this?" inquired the Damsel.
"No one," said the Sage; "the first man went about with only one ear; the second man made himself remarkable with three—and the cut-off ear, although alive and successful, felt itself an excrescence."
"Then what *could* be the pleasure of it all?" demanded the Damsel.
"Out upon *you*!" exclaimed the Sage, in a passion. "You asked me what was life—and why the fruit tasted bitter in the mouth? I have answered you."
And he went back into his cave and barred the door.
The Damsel sat down upon a stone outside.
"It seems to me that men are fools," she said, and she clapped her hands to her two ears. "When I am angry and offended with one of you, I will cut the ear from off the head of some one else."
And she picked up an apple and ate it. And it tasted sweet.

A man will often fling away a woman who has wronged him although in doing so he is deeply hurting himself. A woman will forgive a man who has wronged her because her own personal pleasure in him is greater than her outraged pride. Hence women are more unconscious philosophers than men.

The Damsel returned again to the cave of the Sage. There were other questions she wished to ask about life. The door was hard to push ajar, but at last she obtained entrance.
"What do you want now?" he demanded, with a voice of grumbling. "Were you not content with my last utterances?"
"Yes—and no," said the Damsel. "I came to quite other conclusions myself. I would have kept the ear on my head, since cutting one off, however it had angered me, would have upset my own comfort."
"We have finished with that matter now," said the Sage, showing signs of impatience—he was still a man. "What next?"
"I want to know," said the Damsel, "why a woman who has Diamonds and Pearls and Emeralds and Rubies in her possession should set such store upon a Topaz—a yellow Topaz—the color she dislikes—and a Topaz of uneven temper and peculiar properties. She never wears this stone that it does not bruise her, now her neck, now her arm. It is restless and slips from its chain. It will not remain in the case with the other jewels. And at last she has lost it—she fears for good and all. And so now all the other stones, which seemed very well in their way, have grown of even less value in her eyes, and she can only lament the loss of her Topaz. 'I am brilliant,' cries the Diamond. 'I set off your eyes, and I love you.' 'I am soft and caressing,' whispers the Pearl. 'I lie close to your white skin and keep it cool, and I love you.' 'I am witty,' laughs the Emerald. 'I make your thoughts flash, and I love you.' 'I am the color of blood, and I would die for you,' chants the Ruby, 'and I love you.' And all these things the stones say all the day to her, and yet the woman only listens with half an ear, and their words have no effect upon her because of the charm of this tiresome Topaz. What does it all mean, Sage?"
"It means, first of all," said the Sage, "that the woman is a fool, as what is the value of a Topaz in comparison with a Diamond or a Ruby? It means, secondly, that the Topaz is a greater fool, because it would be more agreeable surely to lie close to the woman's soft neck than to be picked up by any stranger or lie neglected in the

dust. But, above and beyond everything, it means that cherries are ripest when out of reach, and that the whole world is full of fools of either opinion, who do not know when they are well off."

Upon which the Sage, with his usual lack of manners, retired into his cave and slammed his door.

The Damsel sat down upon the rock and came again to her own conclusions. The stone that apparently was a Topaz was in reality a yellow Diamond of great rarity and worth, and that was why the woman valued it so highly. Her instincts were stronger than her reason. But if she had not made herself so cheap by adoring the stone, it would not have become restless and she would not have lost it. Even stones cannot stand too much honey. If ever the woman should find this yellow Diamond again she must be told to keep it in a cool box and not caress it or place it above the others.

The Damsel thought aloud and the Sage heard her—he strode forth in a rage.

"Why do you come here demanding my advice if you moralize yourself? Out upon you again!" he thundered. "The woman will not find her Topaz, which is now revelling in the sun of freedom and will soon go down into nothingness and be forgotten. And after lamenting until her eyes look gaunt, the woman will begin to see some beauty in a Sapphire and become consoled, and so all will be well."

"I do not care what you say," said the Damsel. "*It is better to have what one wants one's self than to try and learn to like anything else that other people think better.*"

And she refastened a bracelet with great care—which contained two cat's-eyes of no value—as she went on her way.

Seize the occasion lest it pass thee by and fall into the lap of another.

No man likes shooting tame rabbits.

Most men like the hunt more than the quarry—therefore the wise woman is elusive.

It is a good hostess who never inclines her guests unconsciously to look at the clock.

Some things cause pride, some pleasure. There is only one thing which causes infinite bliss and oblivion of time, and this one thing, unless bound with chains, is called immoral.

It is a wise man who knows when he is happy and can appreciate the divine bliss of the tangible *now*. Most of us retrospect or anticipate and so lose the present.

Seize Love at whatever age he comes to you—if you can avoid being ridiculous.

More questions?" exclaimed the Sage, as the Damsel tapped gently upon the door of his cave.

"Women are never satisfied; they are as restless as the sea, and when they have received all the best advice they invariably follow their own inclinations."

"It was not to discuss women," replied the Damsel, timidly; "this time it is of a man I wish to ask."

"Begin, then, and have done quickly," growled the Sage, averting his head. The Damsel had an outline against the sky which caused ideas not tranquillizing for Hermits.

"I wish to know why a man who possessed the most beautiful and noble Bird of Paradise—a bird of rare plumage and wonderful qualities—should suddenly see more beauty in an ordinary Cockatoo, whose only attraction was its yellow feathers—a Cockatoo that screamed monotonously as it swung backward and forward on its perch, and would eat sugar out of the hand of any stranger while it cried 'Pretty Poll.' The man could not afford to buy this creature also, so he deliberately sold his exquisite Bird of Paradise to a person called Circumstance and with the money became the possessor of the Cockatoo, who pierced the drums of his ears with its eternal 'Pretty Poll' and wearied his sight with its yellow feathers. Why did the man do this?"

The Sage laughed at so simple a question.

"Because he was a man, and even a screaming Cockatoo belonging to some one else has more charm at times than the most divine Bird of Paradise belonging to himself."

"But was it worth while to sell this rare thing for a very ordinary one?" demanded the Damsel.

"Certainly not," said the Sage, impatiently. "What childish questions you ask! The thing was a folly on the face of it; but, as I said before, he was a man—and the Cockatoo belonged to some one else!"

"Then what will happen now?" asked the Damsel, placing herself in the direction in which the Sage had turned his head.

"The Bird of Paradise will still be the most beautiful and glorious and desirable bird in the world; and when the man realizes he has lost it forever he will begin to value its every feather, and will spend his days in comparing all its remembered perfections and advantages with the screams and the yellow feathers of the Cockatoo."

"And what will the Cockatoo do?" inquired the Damsel.

"It will probably continue to shriek 'Pretty Poll,' and eat sugar out of the hand of any stranger," replied the Sage, plucking his heard.

"And the man?"

"The man will go on telling every one he has bought the most divine bird in the world, in the hope that some one will offer him a large sum of money for it. The only person who gains in the affair is the Bird of Paradise, who, instead of being caged as when in the possession of the man, is absolutely free to fly with its new master, Circumstance, who only seeks to please and soothe this glorious bird and make life fair for it."

"But what will be the very end?" persisted the Damsel.

The Sage turned and looked full at her. He was angry with her importunity and would have answered sternly.

Then he saw that the ripples of her hair were golden and his voice softened.

"That will depend—upon Circumstance," he replied, and he closed his door softly in her face.

A man wishes and a woman wishes, but Circumstance frequently wins the game.

Life is short—avoid causing yawns.

It is possible for a woman to retain the amorous affection of a man for many years—if he only sees her for the two best hours out of each twenty-four.

Please open the door, Sage," entreated the Damsel, "and I will tell you a story."
The Sage pushed it ajar with his foot, but he did not come out.
"There was once upon a time a man," she said, "who unexpectedly and for no apparent reason became the possessor of a Tiger. It had been coveted by numbers of people and was of a certain value and beauty. It had an infinite variety of tricks. It was learned in caresses. It was fierce, and gentle, and it could love passionately. Altogether a large price would have been offered the man for it by many others if he had wished to sell it. In the beginning he had greatly valued the possession of this strange beast, and had fed it with his own hand. The little anxiety as to whether it would eat him or not, or rush away, had kept him interested. But gradually, as he became certain the Tiger adored him, and would show none but velvet claws and make only purring sounds, his keenness waned. He still loved it, but certainty is monotonous, and his eyes wandered to other objects. 'The Tiger is nothing but a domestic cat,' he said; 'I will pet and caress it when the mood takes me, and for the rest of the time it can purr to itself by the fire.' At last one day, after the Tiger was especially gracious and had purred with all essence of love, the man yawned. 'It is really a charming beast,' he said, 'but it is always the same; and then he went away and forgot even to feed it. The Tiger felt hungry and restless. Its quietness and gentleness became less apparent. The man on his travels chanced to think of it and sent it a biscuit. So the Tiger waited, and when the man returned and expected the usual docile caresses, it bit his hand. 'Vile beast!' said the man. 'Have I not fed and kept you for weeks, and now you bite my hand!' Now tell me, Sage, which was right—the man or the Tiger?"
"Both, and neither," said the Sage, decidedly. "The man was only obeying the eternal law in finding what he was sure of monotonous; but he mistook the nature of the beast he had to deal with. Tigers are not of the species that can ever be really monotonous, if he had known. The Tiger was foolish to allow its true nature to be so disguised by its love for the man that he was deceived into looking upon it as a domestic cat. It thought to please him thereby and so lost its hold."
"And what will be the end?" asked the Damsel.
"The man's hand will smart to the end of his life, and he will never secure another Tiger. And the Tiger will go elsewhere and console itself by letting its natural instincts have full play. It will not be foolish a second time."
But the Damsel's conclusion was different.
"No," she said. "The man's hand will heal up, and the Tiger will caress him and make him forget the bite, and they will love each other to eternity because they have both realized their own stupidity."
And without speaking further she allowed the Sage to close the door.

It is wiser to know the species one is playing with: do not offer Tigers hay—or Antelopes joints of meat.

Next day, in a pouring shower of rain, the Damsel knocked at the Sage's door. It was for shelter, she said, this time, until the storm should pass.
The Sage was fairly gracious, and to while away the time the Damsel began a story.
"A man once owned a brown Sparrow. It had no attractions, and it made a continuous and wearying noise as it chattered under the eaves. It did the same thing every day, and had monotonous domestic habits that often greatly irritated the man, but—he was accustomed to it, and did not complain. After several years a travelling Showman came along; he had a large aviary of birds of all sorts, some for sale, some not. Among them was a glorious Humming Bird of wonderful brilliancy and plumage, a creature full of beauty and grace and charm and elegance. The man became passionately attached to it; he was ready to perpetrate any folly for the sake of obtaining possession of it, and indeed he did commit numbers of regrettable actions, and at last stole the bird from the Showman and carried it away. Then, in a foreign palace, for a short while he revelled in its beauty and the joy of owning it. The Humming Bird did its best to be continually charming, but it felt its false position. And the worry and annoyance of concealing the theft from the Showman, and the different food the Humming Bird required, and the care that had to be taken of it, at last began to weary the man. He chafed and was often disagreeable to it, although he realized its glory and beauty and the feather it was in his cap. Finally, one day, in a fit of desperation, the man let the Humming Bird fly, and crept back home to the homely brown Sparrow, with its irritating noises and utter want of beauty. Why was this, Sage?"
The Sage had not to think long.
"Custom, my child," he said. "Custom forges stronger chains than the finest plumage of a Humming Bird. The man had to put himself out and exert himself to retain the Humming Bird in a way that was not agreeable to his self-love, whereas the brown Sparrow lived on always the same, causing him no trouble, and custom had deadened the sense of its want of charm."
"Then it seems to me it was rather hard upon the poor Humming Bird!" said the Damsel.
"It is always hard upon the Humming Birds," replied the Sage, and his voice was quite sad.

The rain did not cease for a long time. It was more than an hour before the Damsel left the cave

If you are a Humming Bird it is wiser for you to remain in the possession of the Travelling Showman.

LONG period elapsed after this before the Damsel again tapped at the Sage's door. He looked out morning and evening, and attributed his lack of enthusiasm for his devotions to an attack of rheumatism from the damp of his cave. At last, one morning he spied her sauntering slowly up the hill, and he retired into the back of his cell, and the Damsel had to knock twice before he opened the window shutter. She was in a gay mood, and demanded a story, so the Sage began:

"There was once upon a time a Fish with glittering scales who swam about in a deep river. It had been tempted by the flies of many Fishermen, but had laughed at them all and swam away, just under the surface of the water, so that the sun might shine on its glittering scales to please the eyes of the Fishermen and to excite their desire to secure it. It was a Fish who laughed a good deal at life. But one fine day a new Angler came along; he was young and beautiful, and seemed lazy and happy, and not particularly anxious to throw the line. The Fish peeped at him from the sheltering shadow of a rock. 'This is the most perfect specimen of a Fisherman I have ever seen,' it said to itself. 'I could almost believe it would be agreeable to swallow the fly and let him land me and put me in his basket.' The young Fisherman threw the line, and the sun caught the glittering scales of the Fish at that moment. The laziness vanished from the Fisherman, and he began to have a strong desire to secure the Fish.

"He fished for some time, and the Fish swam backward and forward, making up its mind. It saw the hook under the fly, but the attraction of the Angler growing stronger and stronger, at last it deliberately decided to come up and bite. 'I know all the emotions of swimming on the surface and letting my scales shine in the sun,' it mused, 'but I know nothing about the bank and the basket, and perhaps the tales that are drilled into the heads of us Fish from infancy about suffocation and exhaustion are not true.' And it mused again: 'He is a perfectly beautiful Fisherman and looks kind, and I want to be closer to him and let him touch my glittering scales. After all, one ought to know everything before one dies.'

"So, its heart beating and its eyes melting, the Fish deliberately rose to the surface and swallowed the fly. The hook caught in a gristly place and did not hurt much, and the novel experience of being pulled onto the green meadow delighted the Fish. It saw the Fisherman close, and felt his hands as he tenderly disengaged the hook. He was full of joy and pride at securing the difficult Fish and admired its scales. He talked aloud and told it how bright he found it, and he was altogether charming and delightful, and the Fish adored him and was glad it had been caught.

"Then after some time of this admiration and dalliance, the Fisherman put it in the basket among the cool rushes. The Fish lay quiet, still content. It had not yet begun to pant. For an hour almost the Fisherman gloried in his catch. He opened the lid frequently and smiled at the Fish.

"Then he lay down on the bank beside the basket and let his rod float idly in the stream. The sun was warm and pleasant.

"'I wish,' he said to himself, 'after all, I had not secured the Fish yet; the throwing of the fly and the excitement of trying to catch the creature are better fun than having it safely landed and lying in the basket,' and he yawned, and his eyes gradually closed and he slept.

"Now the Fish heard very plainly what he had said. Tell me, Damsel—you who ask questions and answer them finally yourself—tell me, What did the Fish do?"

The Damsel mused a moment. She stirred with her white fingers the water in the basin of the fountain that sprang from the rock close by. Then she looked at the Sage from under the shadow of her brows and answered, thoughtfully:

"The Fish was stunned at first by this truth being uttered so near it. It suddenly realized what it had done and what it had lost. 'I, who swam about freely and showed my glittering scales in the sun, am now caught and in a basket, with no prospect but suffocation and death in front of me,' it said to itself. 'I could have even supported that, and the knowledge that my scales will become dull and unattractive in the near future, if the Fisherman had only continued to lift the lid and admire me a little longer.' And it sighed and began to feel the sense of suffocation. But it was a Fish of great determination and resources. 'I have learned my lesson,' it gasped; 'the Fisherman has taught it to me himself. Now I will make a great jump and try to get out of the basket.'

"So it jumped and opened the lid. The Fisherman stirred in his sleep and put out his hand vaguely to close it again, but he was too sleepy to fasten the catch, and with less noise the Fish bounced up again and succeeded in floundering upon the grass. It lay panting and in great distress, but it looked at the beautiful Angler with regret. He was so beautiful and so desirable. 'I could almost staynow,' the Fish sighed. Then it braced itself up and gave one more bound, and this time reached the rock at the edge of the stream.

"Again the Fisherman awoke, and now casually, with his eyes still closed, fastened up the basket before he slept again; but the Fish with its third bound reached the river, and darted out into the middle of the stream.

"'Good-bye, Beautiful Angler!' it said, sadly. 'You were sweet, but you have taught me a lesson, and freedom is sweeter.'

"The splash of its reaching the water fully awakened the Fisherman, but he saw the basket with the lid shut, and had no anxieties until his eye caught the pink of the water where the Fish sheltered under the rock. Its gill was still bleeding from the hook wound, and colored a circle round it. Then he opened the lid and found the basket empty.

"'Good-bye,' said the Fish. 'Your wish has been granted, and your pleasure can begin all over again!'

"But the Fisherman suddenly realized that his rod, while he slept, had fallen into the river, and was floating away down the stream.

"'Good-bye again,' said the Fish; 'I have suffered, but I have now experience, and I am grateful to you, and my gill will heal up, and I will smile at you sometimes from just under the surface of the water, and so all is well!' And it flashed its glittering scales in the sun before it darted away out of sight in the strong current."

And the Damsel folded her hands and looked into distance.

"Thank you, Damsel," said the Sage, gently for him; "but the Fisherman could procure another rod—rods are not rarities. What then?"

"That would be for another day," said the Damsel; "and—for another Fish!" And she tripped away down the hill, and was deaf to the Sage, who gruffly called after her.

When you have caught your Fish, it may be wiser to cook it and eat it.

The sun was setting when the Damsel next came to the Cave. She had a pet falcon with her, and kept caressing it as she propounded her question.

"There lived a woman in a Castle who had three Knights devoted to her. She loved one, and her vanity was pleased with the other two. While she continued to play with them all, they all loved her to distraction; but presently her preference for the one Knight became evident, and the two others, after doing their utmost to supplant the third without success, at last left the Castle and rode away. They were no sooner gone, and things had become quiet, and no combats occurred to interrupt the lovers' intercourse, when the chosen Knight began to weary, and he, too, at last rode away, although before he had been the most ardent of all. Why was this, Sage? And what should the woman do?"

"It was because the Knight had won the prize and the woman gave him no trouble to keep it," replied the Sage. "He was bound to weary. When a man's profession is fighting and he has fought hard and succeeded, after sufficient rest he wishes to fight again. So if the woman wants her lover back, she had better first summon the other two."

For once the Damsel had nothing to say, and had no excuse to remain longer in the cave.

The Sage, however, was not in the mind to let her go so soon, so he began a question:

"Why do you caress that bird so much? It appears completely indifferent to you. Surely that is waste of time?"

"It is agreeable to waste time," replied the Damsel.

"Upon an insensible object?"

"Yes."

"More so than if it returned your caresses?"

"Probably—there is the speculation. It might one day respond, while certainly if it repaid warmly my love now, one day it would not. Nothing lasts in this world. You have told me so yourself."

The Sage was nettled.

"Yes, there is one thing that lasts, that is friendship," he said.

"Friendship!" exclaimed the Damsel; "but that is not made up of caresses. It does not make the heart beat."

"We were not talking of beating hearts," said the Sage, sententiously.

"Very well. Good-bye, then, Sage." laughed the Damsel. "You must think of more stories for me before I come again."

And, continuing to caress the falcon, she walked away, stately and fair, into the setting sun.

When she had gone the Sage wondered why there was no twilight that evening, and why it had suddenly become night.

Most men prefer to possess something that the other men want.

It would be a peaceful world if we could only realize that the fever of love is like other fevers. It comes to a crisis, and the patient either dies or is cured. It cannot last at the same point forever.

The Damsel came back again next day. She had remarked, the day she spent with him in the rain, that the Sage was not so old or so uncomely as she had at first supposed. "If he were to shave off his beard and wear a velvet doublet, he would look as well as many a cavalier of the Court," she mused. And she called out before she reached the door:

"Sage, I have come back because I want to ask you just another question. Will you not come out and sit in the sun while you answer?"

So the Sage advanced in a recalcitrant manner, but he would not sit down beside her.

Then the Damsel began:

"A woman once possessed a ball of silk. It was of so fine and rare a kind that, although of many thousand yards, it took up no space, and she unwound it daily for her pleasure without any appreciable difference in the size of the ball. At last she suddenly fancied she perceived some alteration. It came upon her as a shock, but still she continued to use the silk with the casual idea that a thing she had employed so long *must* go on forever. Then again, in about a week, there came another shock. The ball was certainly smaller, and felt cold and hard and firm. The thought came to her, 'What if it should not be silk all through and I have come to the end ofmatters? What shall I do?' Now tell me, Sage, should the woman go on to the end and find perhaps a stone? Or should she try to rewind the silk? Which is the best course?"

The Damsel took up the Sage's staff, which he had dropped for the moment, and with its point she drew geometrical figures in the sand. But the sun made shadows with her eyelashes, and the Sage felt his voice tremble, so he answered, tartly:

"That would depend upon the nature of the woman. If she continues to unwind the silk she will certainly find a piece of adamant, which has been cunningly covered with this rare, soft substance. If she tries to rewind, she will discover the thread has become tangled, and the ball can never again look smooth and even as before. She must choose which she would prefer, a clean piece of adamant or an uneven ball of silk."

"But that is no answer to my question," said the Damsel, pouting. "I asked which must she do for the best."

"Neither is better nor worse!" replied the Sage with asperity. "And there is no best."

"You are quite wrong, Sage," returned the Damsel. "There is a third course. She can cut the thread and leave the ball as it is, a coating of smooth silk still—and an undiscovered possibility inside."

"You are too much for me!" exclaimed the Sage in a fury. "Answer your own questions, to begin with, in future! I will have no more of you!" and he went into his cave and ostentatiously fastened the door.

The Damsel smiled to herself and continued to draw geometrical figures with the point of the Sage's staff in the sand.

There are always three courses in life: the good, the bad, and the—indifferent. The good gives you calm, and makes you sleep; the bad gives you emotions, and makes you weep; and the indifferent gives you no satisfaction, and makes you yawn, so—choose wisely.

One can swear to be faithful eternally, but how can one swear to love eternally? The one is a question of will, the other a sentiment beyond all human control. One might as sensibly swear to keep the wind in the south, or the sun from setting!

And yet we swear both vows—and break both vows.

A woman is always hardest upon her own sins, committed by others.
A man is sometimes lenient to them.

A fool can win the love of a man, but it requires a woman of resources to keep it.

---

he Damsel did not go away from the cave, as was her custom. She continued to draw geometrical figures in the sand. Presently she called to the Sage once more.

"Come out again, dear Sage! Listen, I have something more to say."

He unfastened the window and stood leaning on the sill.

"Well?" he said, sternly. "Well?"

"A Ring Dove once was owned by a man. It was the sweetest and most gentle of birds, besides being extremely beautiful. It adored the man and lived contentedly in its cage. The perches, which the man had had prepared especially for it, were endeared to it from association with the happy hours when it had been caressed by the man. Altogether to it the cage appeared a palace, and it lived content.

"The man was a brutal creature, more or less, and at last he cruelly ill-treated the Ring Dove, and exalted a Cuckoo in its place. This conduct greatly saddened the sweet Dove, but it over and over again forgave its tormentor, so great was its love, and even saw the Cuckoo advanced to the highest honors without anger, only a bleeding heart. How long things would have continued in this way no one knows; but the man suddenly gave the Cuckoo the Ring Dove's cage, and let the Cuckoo sleep on the perches which the Dove was accustomed to consider its very own. This overcame the gentle Dove. Its broken heart mended, and it flew away. Tell me, Sage, why did this action cure the Dove of its great love for the man, when it had borne all the blows and cruelty without resentment?"

"That is an easy question to answer," replied the Sage. "The Dove was really growing tired and seized this as a good opportunity to be off."

"Oh, how little you know of the female sex, even of Doves!" laughed the Damsel. "I can give you the true reason myself. It was the bad taste of the man in giving the Cuckoo the cage and perches of the Ring Dove, which he had consecrated to her. That cured her, and enabled her to fly away."

And the Damsel curtsied to the Sage and sauntered off, laughing and looking back over her shoulder.

An action committed in bad taste is more curing and disillusionizing to Love than the cruelest blows of rage and hate.

---

man would often be the lover of his wife—if he were married to some one else.

There come moments in life when we regret the old gods.

Time and place—temperature and temperament—and after the sunset the night—and then to-morrow.

---

ll the winter passed and the Damsel remained at the Court and the Sage in his cave. Both found the days long and their occupation insufficient.

At last, when spring came, the Damsel again mounted the hill one morning before dawn and tapped at the Sage's door.

His heart gave a bound, and he flew to open it without more ado.

"So you have come back?" he said; and his voice was eager, though it was a gray light and he could not see her plainly.

"Yes," said she; "I want you to tell me one more story of life before I go on a long voyage."

So the Sage began:

"There was once upon a time a man of half-measures, whose brain was filled with dreams for his own glory, and he possessed a woman of flesh and blood, who loved him, and would have turned the dreams into realities. But *because* he was happy with her, and because her hair was black and her eyes were green, and her flesh like alabaster, he said to himself, 'This is a fiend and a vampire. Nothing human can be so delectable.' So he ran a stake through her body, and buried her at the cross-roads. Then he found life an emptiness, and went down into nothingness and was forgotten—"

"Oh, hush, Sage!" said the Damsel, trembling; "I wish to hear no more. Come, shave off your beard, and put on a velvet doublet, and return with me to the Court. See, life is short, and I am fair."

And the Sage suddenly felt he had found the philosopher's stone, and knew the secret he had come into the wilds to find.

So he went back to his cave, and shaved his beard, and donned a velvet doublet, long since lain by in lavender. And he took the Damsel by the hand, and they gladly ran down the hill.

And the zephyrs whispered, and the day dawned, and all the world smiled young—and gay.

Remember the tangible now.

"*Sic transit gloria mundi!*"

The letter of her mother to Elizabeth

Letter I

MONK'S FOLLY, 27th July

DEAREST ELIZABETH:

I AM glad you reached Nazeby without any mishap. Your letter was quite refreshing, but, darling, do be more careful of your grammar. Remember, one never talks grammar now-a-days in Society, it isn't done; it is considered very Newnham and Girton and patronising, but one should always know how to write one's language. Because the fashion might change some day, and it would be so *parvenu* to have to pick it up.

As I told you before you started on your round of visits, you will have a capital opportunity of making a good match. You are young, very pretty, of the bluest blood in the three kingdoms, and have a fortune—to be sure this latter advantage, while it would be more than a sufficient *dot* to catch a twelfth-century French duke, would be considered by an impecunious British peer quite beneath contempt. Your trump card, Elizabeth, is your manner, and I count upon that to do more for you than all the other attributes put together. Nature and my training have made you a perfect specimen of an *ingénue*, and I beseech you, darling, do me credit. Please forgive the coarseness of what I have said, it is only a little plain speaking between us; I shan't refer to it again; I know I can trust you.

These Horrid Smiths

From what you write I gather that the Marquis of Valmond is *épris* with Mrs. Smith. Horrid woman! the Chevingtons have met her. Mrs. Chevington was here this morning to enquire after my neuralgia. She said that Mr. Smith met his wife in Johannesburg five years ago before he "arrived." He used to wear overalls, and carry a pick on his shoulder, and spent his days digging in the earth, but he stopped at sunset, as I should think he well might, and invariably went to the same inn to refresh himself, where Mrs. Smith's mother cooked his dinner and Mrs. Smith herself gave him what she called a "corpse-reviver" from behind the bar. At night, a great many men who dug in the earth with Mr. Smith would come for "corpse-revivers," and they called Mrs. Smith "Polly," and the mother "old girl." And one day Mr. Smith found a nugget as big as a roc's egg when he was digging in the earth, and after that he stopped. The funny part was that "Polly" always said he would never find anything, and he had a wager with her that if he did she should marry him. So that is the story of their courtship and marriage, and they have millions. Mrs. Chevington vouches for the truth of it all, for Algy Chevington was out in Johannesburg at the time, and he dug in the same hole with Mr. Smith and knows all about him and "Polly," only Algy never found anything, for the flowers in Mrs. Chevington's hat were in the bonnet she wore all last spring. But let us leave these horrid Smiths; I am sure they are horrid. I can't understand how Lady Cecilia puts up with them. Mrs. Chevington says she hears Sir Trevor is one of the directors in the Yerburg Mine. Algy called him a guinea-pig, and said he wished he was one.

An Eligible Parti

Lord Valmond has fifty thousand a year and six places besides the house in Grosvenor Square. You will hardly meet a more eligible *parti*; I hear he is very fast; they say he gave Betty Milbanke, the snake-dancer at the Palace, all the diamonds she wears. If he is anything like his father was, he must be both good-looking and fascinating. The late Marquis was the handsomest man save one that I have ever seen, and could have married any of the Duchess of Rougemont's daughters if he had been a valet instead of a marquis, and the Duchess was the proudest woman in England. The girl who gets this Valmond will not only be lucky but clever; the way to attract him is to snub him; the fools that have hitherto angled for him have always put cake on their hooks; but, if I were fishing in the water in which My Lord Valmond disported himself, I should bait my hook with a common worm. It is something he has never yet seen.

The African Millionaire

Tell me more about Mr. Wertz, the African millionaire; is he the man who is building the Venetian *palazzo* in Belgrave Square? If so, it was rumoured last season that he was to be made a baron. They blackballed him at the Jockey Club in Paris, and even the Empire nobility who live in *appartements* in the Champs Élysées refused to know him; that is why he came to England. He is a gentleman, if he is a Jew; the family belong to the tribe of Levi. Algy Chevington, who knows everything about everybody, says his Holbeins are priceless, and that the Pope offered to make him a Papal Count if he would part with a "Flight into Egypt" known as the Wertz Raphael. But of course even a knighthood is better than a Papal Count, and if Mr. Wertz gives his Holbeins to the National Gallery he is sure to be created something.

You cannot be too careful of the unmarried girls you know; Miss La Touche is certainly not the sort of person for you to be intimate with. The Rooses, of course, are quite correct, they will make capital foils for you; beside Jane Roose is amiable, and has been out so many seasons that her advice will be useful. Be sure, however, to do the very opposite to what she tells you.

Lady Beatrice Carterville

If the weather is fine to-morrow, I am going to drive over in the afternoon to call on Lady Beatrice Carterville. She has a house-party, and the people who come to her are sure to be odd and amusing. My neuralgia has been better these last few days. The things I ordered from Paquin have come at last; the mauve crêpe de chine with the valenciennes lace flounces is lovely; the hat and parasol are creations, as the Society papers say. Love to Lady Cecilia and the tips of my fingers to Sir Trevor.—Your dearest Mamma.

Letter II

MONK'S FOLLY, 29th July

DARLING ELIZABETH:

Lady Beatrice's Tea

I FELT so well yesterday that I drove over in the afternoon to Lady Beatrice's to tea. I felt I must show myself as Paquin made me to someone. It was so warm that tea was served on the terrace; the view of the Quantocks steaming in the distance over the tops of the oaks in the park was charming. There were a great many people present, and when I arrived, Lady Beatrice exclaimed at the courage I showed in coming when the sun was so hot and the road so dusty. She presided at the tea-table in white piqué and a sailor hat which rested on the bridge of her nose. She is as fat as Lady Theodosia Doran and plays tennis; the rouge on her neck had stained her collar, quite a four-inch collar too, and there were finger marks of rouge on her bodice. She introduces everybody, which, while it is not the thing, certainly makes one more comfortable than the fashion at present in vogue. I always like to know the names of the people I am talking to. Everybody talked about the weather and the dust, and it was deadly dull till Lady Beatrice said she wanted to play tennis. She went off to play singles with Mr. Frame, the Low Church curate, and looked so funny, bounding about the lawn like a big rubber ball, that I nearly screamed. Most of the people strolled up and down the terrace, or leaned over the balustrade above the lake. I sat under my parasol in a Madeira chair, and was talked to by such a curious woman, a Mrs. Beverley Fruit. *A Live Authoress* It was interesting to meet a real live authoress after having read her works. I remember when Mrs. Fruit's first novel came out ten years ago it created a great sensation, but I must confess the sensation was confined to middle-class people and the Universities. Of course, everybody in Society bought it. It was all about Radicals and a silly Low Church curate who threw up his living because he didn't believe in God, and went to London and lived in the slums. Mr. Gladstone wrote a review of it, and they dramatised it in America. Mrs. Fruit has since written several other books, and each one is more bitter against Society than the last, so you may fancy how nervous I felt at being left with such a woman. But, darling, she isn't at all like her books. I was quite charmed with her; she was dressed so well, and looked quite like a lady; she lives in Berkeley Square and has a place in Essex. In the last election she canvassed the county for the Conservatives, and the Duchess of Rougemont is very, very fond of her. Lady Beatrice tells me that Mrs. Beverley Fruit's son, who is private secretary to a Cabinet Minister, is actually going to marry one of the Duchess's daughters, Lady Mabel, the one with the projecting teeth and the squint. And I am sure I think it is very brave of Mr. Fruit Junior, for Lady Mabel is both ugly and stupid. However, the connection is a good one for the Fruits, who have made their fortune out of books, which I think is decidedly less vulgar than pale ale or furniture. Mrs. Fruit is staying with Lady Beatrice.

Lady Ann Fairfax

Lady Ann Fairfax, the *Daily Sensation's* War correspondent, is also stopping at Braxome Towers. She told me that she had been through three sieges, and never felt happier than when "sniping," whatever that may be. She lived three months in a bomb-proof shelter on quarter rations, was once taken prisoner, and when exchanged was sent through the lines barefoot and with only a blanket round her. She is bringing out a book to be called "What I have been through," and I shall certainly buy it. She is rather pretty and dresses beautifully, and is very amusing; you could listen to her for hours; her stories are like shilling shockers, with a bit of Henty thrown in to give them style. She was quite breezy, and I was sorry when Lady Beatrice shouted triumphantly, "Six love, Mr. Frame!" and came up puffing like a porpoise, her hair soppy on the temples and gutters on her cheeks.

Lady Beatrice was in an awfully good humour, for Mr. Frame beat the Somerset champion last week, but, poor man! he would not dare to even dream of beating Lady Beatrice. She only suffers him to eat her cucumber sandwiches and drink her Mazawattee for the pleasure of beating him.

The drive home in the twilight was very pleasant. I brought Captain Bennett of the Coldstreams and the Earl of Mortimer as far as the Club in Taunton. They are playing for Gloucester, but, as I dislike cricket as much as you do, I shan't go to see the match. I know my frock was admired at Braxome to-day; poor Mr. Frame, who sat and ate ices near me after his thrashing, would never meet my glance directly, and I overheard Lady Beatrice tell Mrs. Beverley Fruit that I spent altogether too much on dress, while Lady Beatrice always looks as if she considered the expenditure of a five-pound note on her person an extravagance. Dear, dear Paquin!

The Missing Handkerchief

I am awfully provoked with myself, the lace handkerchief I wore to-day is missing. I am sure it was in my hand when we left Braxome, for I remember sniffing "parfum d'Arabie" in the carriage. It is really quite provoking.—Your dearest Mamma.

The Handkerchief Found

P. S.—I have just received a note from Captain Bennett saying he found my handkerchief sticking to his coat when he got into the Club, and asking if he may restore it to me in person to-morrow.

Letter III

MONK'S FOLLY, 1st August

DEAREST ELIZABETH:

A Mature Young Man

L'INGÉNUE va bien. I am so glad you managed to put that odious Mrs. Smith in her place. It is really too revolutionary to be forced to accept such people, but what you tell me about her and Lord Valmond surprises me. I can quite understand a woman of her stamp liking the admiration of Valmond, for he is young and good-looking, and a marquis, but what can he see in her? He is one of those young men who mature quickly; at fifteen he could tell whether a woman put on her chemise or her petticoat first, and at one and twenty he knew the Rake's Catechism by heart. But I have always heard that he was intelligent, and his people were never afraid of his doing something foolish. He takes his *menus plaisirs* like a gentleman, but why he should be so devoted to this Mrs. Smith I cannot conceive.She is not pretty, she is not witty; Lord Valmond is rich, surely he does not want to borrow money from her. I shall be glad when you leave Nazeby Hall; it is one thing to catch a marquis, and another thing to get scratched in the effort. You must leave at once, otherwise you will be forced to play your trump card—the art of being an *ingénue*. Leave at once, Valmond will be sure to follow. The slap on the cheek was excellent; no man ever forgets a woman who has left the print of her fingers on his face, he will either hate her or love her. If the man *is* a man and was in the wrong, he will be forced to admire the woman who could protect herself against him. Leave Nazeby, Elizabeth; Valmond is a man and a gentleman, let him know that you are a lady and virtuous.

The Handkerchief Returned

This morning, just before lunch, Fifine and I were dozing on the lawn under the big Japanese umbrella, when James came to tell me that Captain Bennett was in the drawing-room. Of course he came to return my handkerchief—it was very polite of him to bring it himself, especially as he rode all the way from Taunton in a blazing sun, along a road lying under nearly a foot of dust. Naturally, I could not let him go back without lunch, and afterwards, when I thought he would go, he asked me to let him look over my songs, as he wanted something to sing at a smoker to-night, which the Yeomanry are giving for him and the Earl of Mortimer. He tried nearly all, and tea was brought in before he got one to suit his voice, which is really *Captain Bennett*a very good one. He is a very gentlemanly man, and has a shy way of looking at one, that is quite naïve in a soldier. He wouldn't believe me when I told him I had a daughter seventeen, until I showed him your photograph. He seemed so astonished that I was obliged to tax him with being extremely ungallant. I asked him if he expected a woman to be old at thirty-five because she happened to marry at seventeen, and he gave me such a look that I felt quite uncomfortable. His eyes were not at all shy, but looked like sparks of blue fire. Just then there was the sound of a carriage driving up, and Mrs. Chevington and the Blaine girls rushed into the room. Fell in would be more correct, for so few Englishwomen know how to enter a room quickly and gracefully. They didn't know Captain Bennett, and as I thought I had had enough of him for one day, I wouldn't introduce him.

He has a horrid way of shaking hands, and left the print of my opal ring on my middle finger. I told him to keep the songs as long as he wished, but he is so awfully polite he said he would return them to-morrow. When he had gone, Daisy Blaine asked me if I had heard that he said in the Taunton Club he intended to marry money, which I thought very spiteful of her.

Mrs. Chevington was greatly agitated by the report that an American family have taken Astley Court. She said that everybody is asking Lady Beatrice Carterville if she is going to call on them. I believe, if Lady Beatrice should marry Mr. Frame, Mrs. Chevington would find an excuse for her. Whenever she passes the lions at Braxome Lodge, Mrs. Chevington is pervaded with the most sacred emotions—she has admitted as much to me. There are some people to whom blue blood is more intoxicating than champagne, and who look on a pedigree as a reservoir which you can never exhaust. The odd part of it is, that Mrs. Chevington is not a snob, she is merely common or garden respectable.

The Ghost

The Blaine girls asked a great many questions about you, and if it was true that the ghost walked every night at Nazeby (Mrs. Chevington had told them about your letter which I read to her). Blanche Blaine said she wouldn't visit such a house as Nazeby for all the possible husbands it might contain, which I think was rude of her, but admitted, when I seemed cross, that once she had a similar experience at Great Ruin Castle. Her adventure was more sensational than yours, for Mrs. Maltravers, who had the room next to her, told her their corridor was haunted and that several people who on hearing noises had come out of their rooms to see what it was, had gone mad. But the ghost has yet to walk who can frighten Blanche Blaine. Immediately after Mrs. Maltravers, who had seen Blanche into her bed-room to reassure her, she said, had kissed her good-night and left, Blanche opened her door softly and peeped cautiously into the corridor, and while she looked she distinctly saw the ghost advancing towards her; and the ghost carried a candle in one hand, and wore crimson plush knee-breeches and white stockings and its hair was powdered. And while Blanche was uncertain whether to scream or faint the ghost vanished into Mrs. Maltravers' room. Blanche said she waited to hear Mrs. Maltravers scream, but as not a sound came from her room, Blanche believed her imagination had got the better of her, so she bolted her door and went to bed.

The weather has been so fine that my neuralgia has entirely gone, and I am accepting all invitations. Write me when you reach Eaton Place.—Your dearest Mamma.

Letter IV

MONK'S FOLLY, 3rd August

DARLING ELIZABETH:

The Parkers Arrive

MRS. CHEVINGTON walked over yesterday before tea expressly to tell me, she said, that Mr. Phineas T. Parker and family, of New York, had arrived at Astley Court, having travelled down from London in a special Pullman attached to the Bristol express. I saw two of them this morning in Taunton going into St. Mary's with

Baedekers, and Lady Beatrice called on them this afternoon, and by the end of the month the Parkers will be a county family. They are fabulously rich; I forget how many hundred million dollars Mr. Parker is worth, and of course nobody asks how he made his money. Algy says they are all kings in America and it doesn't matter, but as for that it doesn't matter in England either, where at the most the millionaires are only barons.

Nobody can talk of anything but their arrival, and everybody is singing Lady Beatrice's praises for having called on them so soon. Captain Bennett, who came this afternoon to bring back the songs and stupidly left two behind, says she should be canonised. Mr. Parker and his son have already been proposed and seconded at the Taunton Club; they have been asked to dine at the mess on guest-night; and both Father Ribbit and Mr. Frame, the High Church rector and Low Church curate, have offered them pews under the pulpit, and asked them to subscribe respectively to the Convent School of the Passionate Nuns and the Daily Soup Dispensary. But rumour has it that the Parkers are Baptists, and are going to the chapel in Holmes' the grocer's back-yard. I shall drive Mrs. Chevington over to Astley to-morrow and leave your card with mine.

On coming home from Taunton this morning, Perkins drove by Braxome. You know part of the road runs through the park, and I saw Lady Beatrice's equestrian cook out for an airing on a brown cob, with a couple of Gordon setters sniffing its hoofs. She really looked quite lady-like. Mrs. Chevington says her habit was made at Redfern's. Lady Beatrice found her in the Want column of the *Standard.*

"Young woman desires situation in County Family, as cook, housemaid, or companion; cook preferred. Must have use of horse daily. Highest references."

Lady Beatrice is delighted with her, and she will hunt with the West Somerset Harriers this coming season.

Captain Bennett Dislocates his Thumb

Captain Bennett dislocated his thumb at cricket to-day, and is *hors de combat* for the rest of the match. When he came back with the songs this afternoon he was suffering such pain that he asked me if I would mind putting on a fresh bandage for him. I told him that the sight of blood always made me faint, but he assured me the skin was not broken, so I took off the old bandage and put on a new one. It seemed to give him great relief, and he said I would make a splendid nurse, and looked at me with that queer blue fire look his eyes always have, when their expression is not as timid as a bashful boy's. He is awfully stupid at conversation, and one has to do all the talking. I asked him if they fed him properly at the Club, for he always looked so hungry whenever I met him. He replied that he was literally starving, but that nothing so material as food would satisfy his hunger, and that blue fire look came back into his eyes.

Captain Bennett in Delirium

I thought he was becoming delirious from the pain of his thumb, and I begged him to go home and send for the doctor. Then he did so strange a thing that I am sure it was done in delirium; he asked me to feel how fast his pulse was beating—it went tick-tock like a Waterbury watch—and he put his arm with the bad thumb round my waist, and called me an angel in the back of his throat and was hot all over. So I knew he had fever. I wasn't a bit afraid, for I have wonderful presence of mind, as you know. I have been told it is best to humour people in delirium, so I said I was sure I was an angel, for everybody told me so, and that if he would kindly stop crushing the jet spangles on my cream-coloured crepon bodice I would act like an angel to him. He instantly obeyed, and I rose and rang for James and told him that Captain Bennett was too ill to ride back to Taunton. Whereupon, before I could finish speaking, James asked if he should tell Perkins to get ready the brougham or dog-cart, and if I thought a glass of barley-water would do Captain Bennett good.

An Ideal Servant

Such a treasure, James. Really an ideal servant; knows exactly what one wants without one's having the trouble to order it. I can't understand how Lord Froom parted with him.

Monsieur Malorme

Just then Monsieur Malorme, whom the Blaines have engaged to talk French with Bertie before he joins the Embassy in Paris, came over with a note from Blanche asking me to a garden party on Saturday. I made Captain Bennett drink the barley-water, which I think must have done him good, because he sat very quiet till James came to say Perkins was ready. Monsieur Malorme is a very good-looking young man for a Frenchman, almost as good-looking as Captain Bennett; he has beautiful teeth and hands, but a horrid way of looking out of his eyes, as if he had just winked at you. He is a Provençal and quite a gentleman; Blanche said they felt obliged to have him eat with them, for he was very superior and accustomed to the best society. When he was coaching the Duke of FitzArthur he always followed the Melton Mowbray pack, and took the Dowager Duchess in to dinner when the family were alone.

I found him quite entertaining and he made Captain Bennett laugh quite naturally, so I knew the barley-water had acted, and I said so. I told Captain Bennett that I would send a groom into Taunton with his horse, and he could take that opportunity to return the rest of my songs, if he had done with them. When he went away, he gave me such a blue fire look and squeezed my hand so horridly that I thought he was going to be delirious again.

Remembering what Blanche had said of Monsieur Malorme's superiority, I took an interest in his pursuits, asked him how long he had been in England, what he thought of our customs, and if he found Bertie an apt pupil. He replied that he had been a year in England, that he found life in Grosvenor Square *plus ravissante qu'à Paris*, and that the English women were *comme les volcanes ayant leurs cimes dans la neige*, and that Bairtee was *précoce*, which I knew was a horrid French lie, for you know it is only because Mrs. Blaine's uncle is in the Cabinet that Bertie, whose chin and forehead seem to be racing to see which can get away from the other the fastest, ever got that secretaryship in the Rue St. Honoré.

The Phonograph

James brought in whiskey and soda and cigarettes, and Monsieur Malorme, who is really quite amusing, became communicative. He assured me that Daisy Blaine was something for which there seems to be no word in French, for he substituted as an equivalent a gesture made by putting the thumb and forefinger to the lips and wafting a kiss into the air. I also gathered that he was at work on a French-English grammar, which was to revolutionise all methods of teaching at present in vogue. It seems that Monsieur Malorme speaks the grammar into phonographs, and one buys the phonograph instead of the book. Lord St. Noodle is quite delighted with the idea, and haspromised to speak into the phonograph before the grammar begins; and Monsieur Malorme hopes to persuade the French Ambassador and the Chancellor of the Exchequer to recommend it in the same way. To overcome the difficulty of speaking into each phonograph separately, Monsieur Malorme proposes to hire a room and fill it with phonographs, so that all will catch the voice at the same time. He grew quite *farouche* over it, and let one of my Bohemian goblets, which contained his whiskey and soda, fall and break. And he looked at me like Captain Bennett when the delirium was coming on, so I excused myself as having to dress for dinner, and left James to show him out. I expect to hear from you at Heaviland Manor to-morrow. I feel sure Lord Valmond will follow you, for he has a place near, which makes the excuse very plausible.—Your dearest Mamma.

Letter V

MONK'S FOLLY, 5th August

DARLING ELIZABETH:

The Dinner-party

LAST night Lady Beatrice gave a dinner for the Parkers. I wore the blue brocade with the Peter Lely bodice, and that odious Mr. Rumple took me in. I am sure Lady Beatrice decided on it at the last moment to spite me, because she overheard me ask Mr. Frame how such a champion as he liked being beaten by her ladyship every day. Captain Bennett sat on the other side of me and Mr. Frame was opposite, so I devoted myself entirely to them, and left Mr. Rumple to lap up his soup like a horse in a water-trough. Society is falling off terribly now-a-days; we are no longer county but provincial families. I really don't see why because Mr. Rumple is Lady Beatrice's lawyer that she should invite him to dine when she has a party, but of course we have no really smart set down here, and one sends into Taunton for a lawyer or a doctor to fill up a vacant place at a dinner-table, just as one sends in for meat or candles. Mr. Rumple is fat and pasty, and has a beard; his only topics of conversation were the assizes and the war. I asked him why he didn't volunteer, and he looked at me with a Dover to Calais smile, and said what did I think would become of his practice. And I replied, "I believe you are a Pro-Boer, Mr. Rumple." He turned green like a gooseberry, and then purple, and Lady Beatrice cried sharply, "What is that you are, Mr. Rumple?" "Pro-Boer," he faltered, echoing my words, and everybody was upon him at once like a pack of wolves. He isn't really anything of the sort, but a Tory who believes that because Lady Beatrice was a duke's daughter she is part of the Constitution. Algy Chevington says he is a rising man, but I prefer to know such people when the process is complete, for this rising is only another term for moulting, which is decidedly unpleasant to witness in the male species of the respectable middle-class.

In the drawing-room, before the men joined us, Mrs. Parker sang "The Star-Spangled Banner" and "Marching through Georgia," and Lady Beatrice actually joined in the chorus. Mrs. Parker's dress was *not* made at Paquin's, and she only wore one decent ring. Miss Parker, however, kept up the family's reputation for wealth, and wore ropes of diamonds round her neck, which made poor Lady Beatrice in her black and yellow satin and amethysts look positively dowdy. Mr. Parker *père* is, I think, inclined to be jovial if he got the chance. He has small bright eyes, and has lost two fingers on his left hand in the course of his "rising" process. He called me madam continually, and asked me if I thought Lady Beatrice would ever marry, which struck me as so absurd that I laughed outright. "Do you want her for your son?" I said. "God forbid!" he replied, and I thought he was going to poke me in the waist with one of the stumps of his right hand.

Lady Beatrice, as you know, would have fifty fits of the most violent epileptic form if a woman attempted to smoke in her presence, and as I saw Blanche Blaine walking up and down on the terrace with a cigar in her cheek I was on the point of joining her when I remembered my neuralgia, but I sent Mr. Parker out to her as he said he found it "darned poky" to have to listen to his wife's voice.

Captain Bennett Apologises

Captain Bennett at once took the vacant place, and began to apologise most profusely for his behaviour two days ago. He looked really miserable, and there wasn't any more blue fire in his eyes. He has to go back to Windsor to-morrow, and I shan't see him again. He wanted to know if I was sorry and if I would let him come back, and then to my amazement he declared he loved me. It was a most unfair advantage, and I told him so; we were sitting in the middle of Lady Beatrice's drawing-room. Mr. Frame and Lady Beatrice were looking at us as hard as they could, and I am sure Daisy Blaine heard every word he said. I begged him to stop, but he said recklessly he didn't care if the whole room heard; that I had encouraged *Captain Bennett's Threat*him and broken his heart. He had never loved a woman before, and if I wouldn't have him he was going to hell, and it would all be at my door. I think it was villainously low down of him, and at that moment I would have preferred Mr. Rumple to be sitting next me. I got up to go away, but he had hold of my skirt and said I should hear him out, and as I didn't care to leave yards of Paquin in his hands I submitted. Captain Bennett is a perfect brute, and I am sure he had drunk too much of Lady Beatrice's champagne. And to think how deceived I had been in him! I thought him such a nice, manly young fellow, with such good manners, and such a straight back and long legs, so smart and handsome; and he was so insulting and threatening, and had hold of my skirt so that I couldn't budge. How I hate him. As if I would ever dream of marrying a *parvenu*, even if his fortune would build a line of battle ships. When he finally let me move, he said he was going back to Windsor to blow out his brains. I told him with my sweetest smile, for Lady Beatrice scented something and was glaring at me, that if I were he I would do something original, and that I was sure he hadn't a bit of originality about him, for he talked "*Family Herald*"just like the *Family*

Herald. He laughed and said he would like to choke me, and that I had not seen the last of him, and he would have me on my knees at his feet yet. A really horrid young man. I wish he would go to South Africa; I am sure nobody would miss him.—Your dearest Mamma.

Letter VI

MONK'S FOLLY, 10th August

DARLING ELIZABETH:

The Graftons

I FELT particularly virtuous this morning, and drove over to Romford to see old Admiral and Mrs. Grafton. Such a dear Darby and Joan pair, so different from the foot-in-the-grave old couples one meets now-a-days. The Admiral was pruning roses in the dearest little garden when I drove up; he hobbled up with a wheeze and muddy fingers and opened the carriage door before Alfred had time to dismount from the box. He welcomed me to Romford with an old-school bow, and gave me an elbow to shake because his hands were full of lumps of Somersetshire clay. He asked me to sit down in the dining-room (they always shut up the drawing-room in the summer, and it is as damp as a church), while he called his wife. Mrs. Grafton, who is a dear, kissed me on both cheeks, and asked after my neuralgia and you. Although it was awfully hot, she was wearing the Queen's Indian shawl; they keep the rooms so dark that I nearly sat down on the Angora cat, which was sleeping in the most comfortable chair in the room. While the Admiral was washing his hands and choking with asthma in the next room, Mrs. Grafton told me about the rheumatism in her left shoulder, and that she had thought at first that I was the chiropodist they were expecting from Taunton.

They insisted on my seeing the kitchen garden, and were very proud that their Brussels sprouts took the first prize at the Bath Vegetable Show in the Spring. I saw the pigs being fed, and the Admiral told me that one of his sows had been given him by the Dowager Marchioness of Ealing, who had brought it to him in her arms wrapped in cotton-wool when it was a week old. The Admiral amuses himself with carpentering, and has had one of the conservatories fitted up as a tool-house, but since he mistook one of his thumbs for a shaving and nearly planed it off, he hasn't been able to finish the table for the butler's pantry. Mrs. Grafton made him show me his artificial ice-machine, and he frappéed a Veuve Clicquot for me, but the vacuum or something didn't work and the neck of the bottle broke. Then we went back to the dining-room, where the Angora cat was sharpening its claws in the lace curtains. The Admiral said, "Damn that beast, Maria!" but Mrs. Grafton gave him such a look, and said, "Oh, Arthur! how can you when he has been so ill lately. Puss, puss, purr-r, purr-r."

A servant brought in some port wine and biscuits, and the Admiral asked me if I cared to see his views of places on the Pacific station. We came to a photograph of a woman in a mantilla, whom the Admiral said was the belle of Lima, and he sighed and chuckled. "Those were days to remember; we were the fastest ship in the Navy, and when we went out of commission there wasn't a pair of black eyes from Valparaiso to Vancouver that didn't shed tears." Then Mrs. Grafton told me of the voyage she made out to the station, when she was the only woman on the steamer, and how two men quarrelled over her in Colon harbour, and another threatened to throw himself in among the man-eaters at Barbados, because she hadn't spoken to him for a whole day. The Admiral looked very savage, and wheezed terribly and called her Mrs. Grafton. They were too delightfully Jo Anderson, my jo, John. I could have spent the whole morning with them, for it is so refreshing to find people natural and sincerely attached to each other. They never spoke a word of scandal during the whole visit; and when I left, Mrs. Grafton gave me a beautiful bouquet of Maréchal Niels and said if she were a man she knew she would break her heart over me, and the dear old Admiral insisted on helping me into the carriage and gave me such a charming Early Victorian salute.

I know they only said nice things of me when I was out of sight, and I wish there were more people like them in the county.

The Parkers' Dinner-party

Blanche Blaine came to tea in the afternoon; two of her fingers are iodined and she had a leather strap round her wrist; she says she sprained her hand at tennis yesterday and can't grip her racquet. Daisy biked over to Exeter this morning with Mr. Frame to represent Taunton in the mixed doubles and ladies' singles. The Duchess of Windermere is to give the prizes. Lady Beatrice is furious because the Committee decided at the last moment to scratch her name in the ladies' doubles. I think it is quite time she gave up tennis, for she can't hit a ball and disputes every point and looks such a fright. She was so mad when she heard she had been scratched, that she refused to go over to Exeter, or to let any of her house-party go. The Parkers took a party in a special Pullman; Blanche thinks they own it, for they always have it wherever they go. The Duchess of Windermere has invited them to sit under the marquee with her.

I was sorry I could not go to their dinner-party last night. Blanche says it was awfully well done. The chef from Prince's and an army of waiters came down from London. The plate was superb, china was only used with soup and fruit—Dresden and Sèvres; the handles of the knives and forks were gold, studded with rubies, those of the spoons were silver and ebony. The favours must have cost a small fortune. Lady Beatrice, who went in with Mr. Parker, got a diamond aigrette; Blanche got two volumes of Tennyson's poems in calf; there must have been some mistake in the order, for there were not enough favours to go round, and Mr. Rumple, who sat next to Blanche, found a ten-pound note under the roll in his napkin.

As usual, Mrs. Parker wore a high-necked dress and no jewels; Miss Parker was *à la Paquin* and went in to dinner with the Duke of Clandevil. There was no attempt at precedence, and Lord Froom was in a towering rage that Mrs. Parker went in with Mr. Frame. But I think it was very bad taste of him, as his favour was a gold watch, with the Froom crest and motto in diamonds, and as the Parkers are foreigners and kings in their own country every excuse should be made for them.

Clandevil is stopping at Astley Court, and rumour has it his engagement to Miss Parker will soon be made public. I pity her, for she seems a decent sort, and we all know what the duke is. He is five years younger than she, and only the ha'penny papers published his cross-examination in the Ventry divorce. But I suppose even an American king's daughter would not refuse an English duke, and Mrs. Parker was heard to tell Mr. Frame with a sigh that it would cost such a lot to stop the leaks in a seven-acre roof.

Mr. Parker Junior

Mr. Parker, Junior, is very retiring and can hardly be got to speak or do anything. Blanche thinks him stupid, but Mrs. Chevington says he has what she calls "a head for business," for he never goes to the Stock Exchange without causing a panic. Considering the food and the presents, the dinner was a huge success, but Mr. Parker would persist in telling Lady Beatrice how he had made his money, and that fifty years ago, "when you and I were young, Lady Beatrice, I was a barefoot newsboy in Broadway."

Boys Troublesome

You amuse me with your account of the Westaways. I don't pity Lady Westaway very much for having such a daughter-in-law; if she had used tact with Billy he would probably have listened to reason. I am so glad, darling, that you are a girl and not a boy; boys are such a source of anxiety in families of our station. They are always getting into trouble, and they pick up such vulgar tastes. Why is it, I wonder, that one never hears of girls marrying beneath them, but it takes all the ingenuity we possess to keep the boys out of *mésalliance*. Billy Westaway is a fool, and there are so many like him.

Between us, I would rather have a son as bad as Clandevil than one as silly as Billy Westaway; but if it came to marrying one of them I should prefer it to be the other way about.—Your dearest Mamma.

Letter VII

HOTEL NATIONAL, LUCERNE
18th August

DARLING ELIZABETH:

Lucerne

HOW surprised you will be to see the above address. Blanche Blaine and I came here on the spur of the moment, the day after you left for Croixmare.

Glacier Garden

Blanche came over in the morning, and asked me if I would go with her to Lucerne for a fortnight. The idea struck me as rather lively, and we went up to London that night in time to catch the Club train for Paris the next day. We were lucky to get rooms at the National, for they are turning people away to-day. We have apartments on the second floor, with a lovely view of the lake and Pilatus; the only blot on the landscape is the yacht belonging to the hotel. As I write in my balcony, I can see it over the tops of the chestnuts on the *quai* bobbing alongside of the jetty with a huge "Quaker Oats" on the sail. The weather is perfect, and the air makes you feel as if you were breathing champagne. This morning we went to see the Lion, to get it over as Blanche said. We saw hundreds in the shop-windows before we got there, and they all looked so sorry for themselves, as if they thought, "We can't help it they made us like this, go a little higher up and you'll see the real thing." The real thing is made of plaster, and you pay fifty centimes to see it in a *boutique*, where they sell Swiss quartz and post-cards. The gigantic thing carved out of the rock is really quite imposing, but the crowds vulgarise it so that it no longer has the atmosphere of meditation and romance Thorvaldsen meant it to have. A party of "personally conducteds" were doing it with Baedekers in their hands and edelweiss in their hats, and they made such funny comments, and asked such quaint questions about it, I am sure that they had never heard of it before, and most of them bought post-cards and wrote on them with stylographs. Then they all went into the Glacier Garden, and the water was turned on to show them glacial action on the rocks.

At Hugenin's

On the way back, Blanche and I stopped at Hugenin's, and had champagne frappé and meringues at a table on the pavement under an awning, and some people dressed as Tyrolese peasants yodelled in the garden of a café across the street. Crowds of people passed us; some were very smartly dressed, but most of the women wore bicycle skirts with buttons in the back and felt hats with a feather at the side, and carried edelweiss. Blanche said Continental life made her feel wicked, and she bought a package of Turkish cigarettes from such a good-looking Italian boy, with a performing monkey, and a basket on his arm filled with post-cards of the Lion and Pilatus cigarettes. He was so delighted that he made the monkey go through his tricks, and some horrid men in dress suits came and stood about with their hands in their pockets and no hats on their heads. I think they must have been waiters, for presently a gong sounded and they all bolted into the Lucernerhof. The Italian boy gave us such a graceful bow when we went away that Blanche felt sure he was a Count in disguise. She said she had heard that poor Italian noblemen wandered about the Continental watering-places in the summer with monkeys, just like the poor Baronets who sing Christy Minstrel songs to banjos on the sands at Brighton, and that you could always tell them by their manners. She was sure of it, because Sir Dennis O'Desmond had told her he had made quite a lot of money that way one year.

The Hungarian Band

We got back to the National just in time to change for lunch. Thérèse had our frocks and curling-irons ready for us, and was in such a temper because her meals were not to be served in her room. We had lunch in the big *salle-à-*

manger, which is also the ball-room; the food was excellent and very well served; all the people looked smart, but we didn't know any of them. The Hungarian band played, and the conductor was such a handsome man; he wore a blue jacket trimmed with astrachan and silver buttons, and black satin knee-breeches with blue stockings. He was very tall and finely proportioned, with flashing black eyes and curly hair. Blanche, who is always jumping to conclusions, believes he is the man who eloped with the Princess de Chimay.

After lunch, we had coffee and liqueur and cigarettes in the hall. The chairs were luxurious, and as all the doors and windows were open it was delightfully breezy; there was no glare, and it was great fun watching the people.

Dip in the Lake

At three o'clock Blanche went across to the baths and had a dip in the lake, and I drew a sofa in front of my balcony and had a snooze in the shade. When Blanche came back she said the bathing was perfect, but that the boards which separated the "Herren" from the "Frauen" were riddled with holes, and that as far as privacy was concerned the two sexes might as well have bathed together. She insisted on having tea on the *terrasse* of the Kursaal where she heard a band playing. When we got there the place was deserted save for some men who were drinking beer at a table with a very *démodér* woman and little child. We afterwards recognised them as the croupiers who ran the Petits Chevaux. Later on all the tables were taken. The people were mostly cheap Germans and Americans, and they encored the Boer Volkslied which the orchestra played with great spirit. It was the first time I had heard the Transvaal National Anthem. It is like a trek in the spirit of the Marseillaise; you could hear the bullock carts rumbling over the veldt.

At the Cathedral

At six o'clock we went to the Cathedral to hear the organ. Every seat was taken, and the music was superb; the prima donna from the Dresden Opera sang. The twilight gradually faded into darkness, and they didn't light the candles. The effect of the *vox humana* was very solemn, and the music seemed to be far away up in the darkness like a chorus of angels chanting. I felt very good.

The smart people were very smart, at dinner, and all seemed to know one another. They took the best seats in the verandah afterwards, and watched the flash-light and illuminations on the Stanzerhorn. We are going to spend the day on the lake to-morrow.—Your dearest Mamma.

Letter VIII

HOTEL NATIONAL, LUCERNE
20th August

DARLING ELIZABETH:

Fluëlen

YESTERDAY Blanche and I went to Fluëlen. The boat was crowded, but we got two comfortable seats in front of the wheel and had a perfect view. The scenery was indescribably lovely, and the air was so clear that we could actually see the people walking about on the top of the Rigi. Some Swiss peasants got on at Brunen, and they all had goitre; one was such a good-looking young fellow about twenty; his neck looked positively uncomfortable, but he didn't seem to mind it at all. Nearly all the hotels are du Lac or des Alpes, and have *terrasses* planted with chestnuts, and there was always excitement when the steamer *Bicyclists*stopped. Two bicycle fiends got off at Brunen; they were English, and we saw them afterwards scorching along the Axenstrasse in clouds of dust, evidently trying to get to Fluëlen before us. It seemed so ludicrous to see bicycles in such a country as Switzerland, that I told Blanche that I was sure that people only brought them there out of a sort of bravado, and that they didn't really enjoy themselves. An American who was sitting near, overheard, and said in quite an offended way that he had biked over the Brunig from Interlaken to Lucerne, and was going over the Furka in the same manner. I replied, I believed if there was a road to the top of Titlis one would find a pair of knickerbockers astride a pneumatic trying to make the ascent. He smiled contemptuously, and said it was evident I had never ridden. I told him I had tried to learn, and had bought an Elswick, but that the day it arrived a new stable-boy rode it into Taunton without my knowledge, and punctured the tire, which was a blessing in disguise if it had saved me from making an exhibition of myself on a Swiss pass. He became quite talkative after this, and pointed out a great many things of interest like a Baedeker, without the bother of having to find the places. We saw theTellsplatte and chapel, and the American told us that there were as many arrows that had killed Gessler in various parts of Switzerland as bits of the True Cross in European churches. We thought of returning in the same steamer and having lunch on board, but he told us we ought to go to Altdorf and see the new Tell monument, and that we could get lunch at an inn there. So we thought while we were about it we might as well do all there was to be done, and return by a later boat.

At Fluëlen

At Fluëlen we had great difficulty in getting seats in any of the brakes that run to Altdorf, as everybody made a rush for them at once. However, Blanche got a bit of iron bar on the box-seat, and was held on by a German with an alpenstock and edelweiss, who linked his arm in hers, while I was smothered between a Cook's guide, who looked fagged out, and a garrulous female, who told me she came from Chicago and had been hungry ever since she left. She said they didn't know how to make pie in Europe, and had never heard of it; her family seemed specially addicted to pie, and greatly missed this delicacy on their travels. She had a letter that morning from her son, a portion of which she read to me: he was doing the capitals of Europe in three weeks, and had been fortunate in finding pie in Constantinople, quite an American pie, only it was made of pumpkin instead of Howard squash.

Our brake stopped at a des Alpes, and the proprietor came out and made us welcome in the fashion they have on the Continent, as if he were playing the host in a private house. My Chicago acquaintance at once asked for the *menu*, and you should have seen her face when she found there was no pie on it.

An Omelette Soufflée

As I was very hungry, I had the *table d'hôte* lunch, which was very good, but Blanche ordered hers *à la carte*. The only French thing on the *menu* that Blanche fancied was *omelette soufflée*. It took twenty minutes to make, and when it came it looked like a mountain. I told Blanche they must have thought her capacity enormous, but when she put her spoon into it, it gave a sort of sigh and collapsed, and before Blanche could get it on her plate there was only as much as you scrape up in a table-spoon.

As the *table d'hôte* courses were all consumed and time was pressing, she had to content herself with French rolls and honey.

The Tell Monument

Before we left Altdorf the two Englishmen whom we had seen scorching over the Axenstrasse arrived. I never saw such objects, they were fairly reeking with perspiration and covered in white dust. They looked positively filthy. I heard one asking the proprietor of the hotel if he could buy a valve in Altdorf, and they both abused the Swiss roads as if they had expected to find them like the Macadam in Hyde Park. The Tell monument was quite worth coming to see, but I think its situation in the tiny *platz* of the picturesque village, which the immense mountains seem ready to crush, makes it more imposing than it really is. I am sure if it were in a city one would hardly notice it.

A Bunch of Edelweiss

Blanche was awfully "Cooky," and bought two post-cards with it on to send to Daisy and Mrs. Chevington. At Fluëlen, too, she bought a bunch of edelweiss from a Swiss doll with goitre, and stuck it into the bow on her sailor-hat. We were quite tired when we got back to Lucerne, and had dinner in our rooms, for Thérèse had gone to bed with a *migraine* and neglected to put out our frocks or have our baths ready. I expect to hear from you to-morrow, and that you are enjoying yourself at Croixmare.—Your dearest Mamma.

Letter IX

HOTEL NATIONAL, LUCERNE
22nd August

DARLING ELIZABETH:

On the Quai

THIS morning between twelve and one, Blanche and I were strolling on the *quai* when we met Sir Charles Bevon. He seemed glad to see us, and asked if we knew any of the people in society here, and when we told him we had only been in Lucerne four days and that he was the first person we had met that we knew, he invited us to dine with him at the Schweitzerhof to-night. It is from this dinner we have just come, and I must tell you about it before I go to bed.

Anglophobia

Sir Charles asked the Marquis and the Marquise de Pivart, the Vicomte de Narjac, and Mr. Vanduzen, an American naval officer *en retraite*, to meet us. I sat between the Marquis and Mr. Vanduzen. The Marquis looks like a little black monkey, with a beard *à Henri Deux*, but his manners are so elegant one never thinks of his looks. He knows the De Croixmares very well, and when I asked him what he thought of Héloise he turned so red and looked so uncomfortable that I at once felt that Jean's charming Comtesse had *brisé son cœur* at some period of their acquaintance. He dropped the subject as soon as possible, and quite rudely began to talk of the war, and said that England was the Jew among nations. I cooled his Anglophobia for him by remarking that I would much prefer to have him talk of the Comtesse de Croixmare than attack my country. He seemed positively afraid of me after that, so I am sure there must be something between him and Héloise that he doesn't want his wife to know. He got so moody and silent that I told him I thought him very rude, and devoted myself through the rest of dinner to Mr. Vanduzen, who is elderly and "natty." Mr. Vanduzen is quite amusing, but I wish he wouldn't call people by their full names as if they were a species he was labelling for a museum, such as, "Really, Miss Blanche Blaine, you amaze me." "It was very warm to-day, was it not, Madame la Marquise de Pivart?" "Have you made the ascent of Pilatus, Sir Charles Bevon?" You know the style of man, Elizabeth, you must have met one or two like him at Nazeby or Hazeldene. If they are English they are called snobs, but when they come from the Land of Canaan on the other side of the pond they are put down quite likely as "so American."

The Marquise

The Marquise is a fascinating creature, she knows the full value of her figure as one of her attractions, and she clothes it accordingly. Her bust is like alabaster, the neck and shoulders are perfect; her eyes are rather wide apart, which gives her a naïve expression; her smile is simplicity itself, and she talks with a tabloid voice. Sir Charles seemed to admire her, for he addressed nearly all his conversation to her, and he poked me so hard under the table once or twice that I was compelled to say, "The table leg is on the other side, Sir Charles," and he gave the Marquise such a reproachful glance.

Blanche had the Vicomte all to herself, and he seemed to like it. He has an automobile and talked of nothing else, and Sir Charles says he does nothing else in Paris. He is going to take Blanche and the Marquise in it to-morrow for a spin in the valley of the Reuss.

Everybody talked at once, as they always do on the Continent, and the effort to be general was quite fatiguing to me who am accustomed to the English method of monopolising one's neighbours. The foreign custom certainly gives more "go" to a dinner, but I think when I am not the hostess I prefer conversation *à deux*.

Don Carlos

After dinner we had coffee in the salon instead of outside on the verandah, for Sir Charles said we ought to see Don Carlos and suite go in to dinner. The suite were already in the salon, and they occupied the most comfortable chairs and looked rather sulky, which I suppose was from having to wait so long for their dinner. Don Carlos has thirty rooms on the first floor, but he will neither take his meals in private or at the usual hour with everybody else. He makes quite a point of dinner, and has it in the *salle-à-manger* when the general public have finished. He must be a great advertisement for the Schweitzerhof, for crowds come nightly to see him and the Duchess go in to dinner. When they entered the salon there was as much etiquette among the suite as if they were at a *levée*. They formed themselves in a line in order of precedence; the men all kissed the Duchess's hand and the ladies curtseyed, then Don Carlos gave his arm to his wife and led the way to dinner. As the door of the *salle-à-manger* was open we could see them eating; everybody talked at once, and the suite ate as if it was the only dinner they had had for a week. I am sure they were hungry.

Don Carlos is a splendid-looking Spaniard, with exile written all over him; whether natural or cultivated, the pose was perfect—the sadness and abstraction, the forced amusement, the far-away look in the eyes—but it wasn't melodramatic, and you didn't feel like laughing. The Duchess of Madrid was *reine aux bouts des ongles* and an ideal consort for a banished monarch. She must have been very beautiful at one period of her life, and is still strikingly fine-looking. She was dressed as the great ladies on the Continent know how to dress, and wore some lovely diamonds. She had the same melancholy far-away expression as Don Carlos, and they both seemed rather bored, as if they had had too much of the suite, who are really nothing but pensioners. Sir Charles says they have not a peseta to bless themselves with, and live entirely on the bounty of Don Carlos. They follow him wherever he goes and form a sort of court for him; they are nothing but a pack of conspirators and professional revolutionists who dare not go back to Spain, and as they have all been broken in the Carlist cause, and still continue to intrigue and make themselves useful, Don Carlos has to put up with them. And I must say I think he does it right royally, keeping up a fine old Bourbon custom, for these people can still say, like the needy noblesse in Louis XIV.'s time, that they "bank with the king."

The Kursaal

When we had "done" Don Carlos and his dinner-party, Sir Charles suggested that we should go to the Kursaal and try our luck at Petits Chevaux. We found the room crowded, and most of the people looked like those I saw at the Monico in London the night Algy Chevington took me there for supper, when he couldn't get a table at the Trocadero. At first we couldn't get near the tables, but the Marquise went and stood behind the croupier, and got him a place for her. Then a man, who I am sure was a High Church curate, for he had cut off his coat collar and let his hair grow long like a French abbé, offered me his seat if I would touch his money for him. But he gave me bad luck till he was cleared out, and then I began to win. It was such fun, and I raked in quantities of gold and some five-franc pieces made of lead. The Marquise and I won, but the others had no luck, and I saw the Marquis somewhere in the back drinking beer with an impossible female, and I told him so afterwards, and that I thought it was very rude to the ladies in his party, and he looked as if he would like to choke me. The Vicomte told Blanche that he believed the croupier tampered with the machinery and could make any horse win he liked, and the croupier heard. For an instant I thought there was going to be a "scene," but the Marquise said such a *cochon* as the croupier wouldn't dare to strike the Vicomte, who it seems spends the time he can spare from automobiling in Paris in duelling. "Mais, comme il est sale, ce croupier," the Marquise said to me, and then added that the croupiers at Monte Carlo were as beautiful as Lucifer, and that a friend of hers, a Comtesse Jean d'Outremer, had eloped with one. A *bêtise* she called it. I told Sir Charles after that that I thought we had better go, and they all walked with us as far as the National. The Marquis and the Vicomte kissed my hand, and Sir Charles told me to call on the Marquise to-morrow, as she expected it. My kindest regard to Madame de Croixmare and the family at the château.—Your dearest Mamma.

Letter X

HOTEL NATIONAL, LUCERNE
24th August

DARLING ELIZABETH:

Smart People

THIS morning Blanche and I were sitting in the wicker chairs under the chestnuts on the *quai* in front of the National, when Sir Charles and the Vicomte passed. They both stopped and chatted for a while, then the Vicomte saw some very smart people who were sitting near and introduced us to them. They were the Duchesse de Vaudricourt and Mrs. Wertzelmann, the wife of the American Minister. The Duchesse is Empire and the Wertzelmanns are *nouveaux riches*, but they are at the very top of all the society here. A great many other people came up to speak to them; Blanche and I were introduced, and, as Sir Charles said, before you could say "Jack Robinson" we were *rangé*. As we both had on Paquin we felt quite as well turned out as the other women, who were beautifully dressed.You should have seen the people on the *quai* stare as they passed.

Telling Fortunes

Blanche made quite a sensation by telling fortunes, and everybody wanted their hands read. She did it awfully well, and told the right things to the right people. She told the Duchesse de Vaudricourt, who is fifty if she is a day, but makes up twenty-five, that the only tragedy in her life would be her death, and to beware of a *beau sabreur* who carried her photograph in a locket on his watch chain. When pressed as to the reason she should be cautious of this unknown, Blanche told her that he was destined to perish in a duel over her. The Duchesse was delighted, for it is said that she longs for the *éclat* of men killing themselves over her, but that up to the present no one has ever even fought about her. Mrs. Wertzelmann was to have her portrait, which has been painted by Constant, hung in the Luxembourg, and to marry her daughter to a Serene Highness, both of which Sir Charles had told us were her supreme desires. The Vicomte had a very interesting personality, and was irresistible with women and greatly respected by men, and was to die in a collision of automobiles, which made him turn rather green. Mr. Wertzelmann, the American Minister, who had joined us, held out a hand like a working-man's, and asked Blanche what was going to happen to him. She said she saw great things in the lines, and something else which she thought could only be confided to his ear in private.

He was so excited, and Blanche wrinkled her eyes at him in the prettiest way, that he insisted on taking her to the verandah of the National, and hearing the rest of his fortune in private. I don't know what Blanche told him, but he ordered champagne frappé, and when they came back his face fairly beamed.

Mrs. Wertzelmann was very gracious, and said that though we hadn't called she wanted us to come out to-morrow afternoon to her villa to a garden-party; that she hated ceremony and etiquette and calling, and we might leave our cards when we came. For it seems it is the custom here for strangers to make the first call, but it is really very silly calling at all, for nobody ever seems to be at home, and one meets the same people half-a-dozen times a day at the National, which is the rendezvous of the smart set.

Comte Belladonna

It is the thing to have tea in the garden of the National, where the Hungarian band plays from four to six. It is very *recherché*, and the prices are so high that the *canaille*, as the Marquise de Pivart calls the tourists, don't come. So this afternoon we met the same set again, and also a dear little old man, over eighty, who had the most perfect manners, and was dressed faultlessly. In fact the Marquise told me that his only occupation was dressing and paying compliments. His name is Comte Belladonna, and he has a face like the carving on a cameo. He is the most *distingué* person here, and was something to Victor Emanuel, and has seen only the best society all his life. He is quite poor, and has a pension which just about pays for his gloves and handkerchiefs, but everybody adores him; he gives tone to everything, and nothing is complete without his presence. He is like the old beaux we used to see at Cannes and Biarritz, and it is a wonder how at his age he manages to keep *Advertising Custom*pace with his invitations. Sir Charles says he has a room on the top floor of the National which he gets for nothing, for his name is always put first on the list of the hotel guests in the papers as an advertisement.

There is an Austrian nobleman at the Schweitzerhof who is accommodated there in the same way for the use of his name in the visitors' list, and I think it is very convenient, for it saves all the worry of trying to make ends meet, and one is actually paid for existing, and supported in the best style. I am sure if the Irish peers knew that there was such a custom in vogue they would move it should be adopted at Scarborough and Harrogate, and the other places, only, of course, we haven't any *villes de luxe* at home as they have on the Continent.

Comte Belladonna spends his summers at the National and his winters in Rome, where the Marquise says the Government, in consideration for his past services to the State, have given him a post in a *bureau*, where all that he has to do is to occasionally sign his name to documents of which he never reads the contents. He is quite the most youthful old boy I have ever met; he doesn't rise at six and walk ten miles before breakfast like old Lord Merriman, who hunts with the West Somerset Harriers in all weathers and golfs on the Quantocks. Comte Belladonna rises at eleven like a gilded youth, clothes himself in the most faultless flannels, and descends to the wicker chairs under the chestnuts on the *quai*, where he reads the "Osservatore Romano," and chats with the *beau monde* of Lucerne who gather there; at one he lunches like an epicure, after which he is ready for any social amusement. He is a charming polished beau, a master of ceremonies, a courtier, and he at present affects an American girl of nineteen, who is quite ready to play May to his January. But Comte Belladonna belongs to the country of Machiavelli, and *la belle Américaine* has only her face for her fortune.

Dinner at a Café

To-night we dined at a café with the Vicomte de Narjac; Sir Charles and the Wertzelmanns were the only others of the party. A troupe of Swedish singers sang and danced and passed round a tambourine, and after dinner we went to the Kursaal theatre to see "Puppenfee."—Your dearest Mamma.

Letter XI

HOTEL NATIONAL, LUCERNE
26th August

DARLING ELIZABETH:

The De Pivarts' Villa

SUCH a jolly time as we had yesterday! In the morning before lunch Blanche and I clambered up the hill behind the National to call on the De Pivarts. They live in a mite of a box of a villa. It is at the end of a street so steep that you feel as if you were going to pitch head-first down it when you begin to descend. The De Pivarts were not at home, according to a man-servant who came to the door in his shirt sleeves and without a collar, and took our cards in fingers that I am sure had previously been engaged in blacking the Marquis's boots or lighting the kitchen fire. But as we came up the hill we saw a man like the Marquis *en déshabille* leaning out of the tiny balcony, and we distinctly heard a female exclaim: "Mon Dieu, je suis perdu! Il n'y a pas des Geraudels! Marie, vite, vite, descendez à la ville pour chercher une boîte."

So we knew where the Marquise got her voice from.

In spite of the villa being so high up, the air seemed quite stuffy, for the hill is full of six-francs-a-day pensions, where there are enough Baedekers to start a library, and where they ring *ranz des vaches* instead of dinner-gongs.

Lunch at the Gütsch

We intended to lunch at the National, but Sir Charles met us on the *quai* and said he had been hunting all over the town for us, as he wanted us to lunch with him at the Gütsch, and go on to the Wertzelmanns' afterwards. In front of the Schweitzerhof we found the Vicomte, who had been automobiling all the morning, and Sir Charles asked him to join us.

The Gütsch is much higher than the De Pivarts' villa, and you reach it by a funicular which creeps straight up the side of the hill like a lift. The view was lovely and so was the cooking; we had a table in front of a huge window overlooking the *terrasse*. Afterwards we strolled in the glades of the pine forest where the light was like the pictures called "Studies in Colour," which one sees in the Academy and nowhere else.

Morale of Lucerne Society

Blanche and Sir Charles were in front, while the Vicomte and I, owing to the Vicomte's laziness, were considerably in the rear. For once he talked of something else than his automobile, but his conversation was not very edifying, save as giving me a pretty vivid idea of the *morale* of Lucerne society. The Vicomte talked the most outrageous scandal, but in so witty a way that it was impossible to take offence. He knew the *histoire* of everybody, which, if true, proves that Continental society, especially at a *ville d'eaux*, is very much the same as in English country houses where the people are smart. As he spoke in French he sailed straight into the wind, where an Englishman would have tacked a half-a-dozen times before reaching port. The voyage was quite exciting, and when I expected him every moment to be wrecked on the rocks of a Moulin Rouge episode he dexterously dropped anchor in calm water. When we got back to the Gütsch I felt as if I had been listening to one of Gyp's spiciest novels in which I knew all the characters. They manage these things differently in England, and when Mrs. Smith looks purry-purry, puss-puss at Lord Valmond you may be sure that each sees the ghost of a conscience, and it has the face of Sir Francis Jeune.

Schloss Gessler

From the Gütsch we went straight to Schloss Gessler in the Vicomte's automobile. We tore through Lucerne at top speed; it was great fun, and the Vicomte said there was no danger, for the road was straight, and that nobody would dare get in the way. Going up the hill outside of the town somebody's Maltese terrier with bells round its neck came tearing after us and got under the wheels. But we didn't stop, and as we turned into the avenue leading to the Schloss one of Mr. Wertzelmann's geese committed suicide by throwing itself in front of the automobile.

Nothing could have been more hospitable than the welcome the Wertzelmanns gave us. Everybody we knew was there, and many more whom we didn't. Mr. Wertzelmann took me to see the ruins, but all that is left is a bit of stone wall, which looks as if it had begun with the intention of encircling a kitchen-garden, but had decided to visit the stables, and never got any further. Mr. Wertzelmann told me it had once sheltered Gessler, hence the name of the Schloss, but that the place had recently been restored by a Swiss engineer who had made a fortune out of funiculars. Certainly in its present state Schloss Gessler is very fine, and the view from the terrace, which Mr. Wertzelmann insisted were the old battlements, was lovely.

We saw Mrs. Wertzelmann's portrait by Constant and heard the price it cost; we also went down to the jetty, and as many as could got into the steam launch and went for a spin on the lake. Blanche was among the number, but I preferred to remain on the lawn where the Marquise was playing croquet. Her maid had evidently found the Geraudels, for her voice was more tabloid than ever. Some people who looked as if they lived in pensions, and were no doubt Americans, who had come to pay their respects to their Minister and his handsome wife, strolled about the grounds aimlessly and looked uncomfortable. One of them carried on a polite conversation with a lackey who spoke English, and whom he addressed as "Sir." But the Wertzelmanns devoted their whole attention to their personal friends, and left the representatives of their nation to amuse themselves in their own way.

Mr. Vanduzen brought the Duchesse de Vaudricourt and Comte Belladonna in the cab with him, and I overheard him squabbling with the cabman over the fare, for, from what passed between them, I judged that the Duchesse had been a second thought with Mr. Vanduzen, who had only arranged with the cabman for himself and the Comte. The cabman evidently won, and Mr. Vanduzen arrived on the lawn so perturbed that he forgot to kiss Mrs. Wertzelmann's hand, a custom he has affected since taking up his residence abroad.

An Austrian Nobleman

Behind Mr. Vanduzen's cab there drove up a very smart landau belonging to Mrs. Solomon G. Isaacs of St. Louis, who is stopping at the National with her mother and daughter. The Austrian nobleman, whose name heads the Schweitzerhof visitors' list, for which they give him his room and food when the latter article is not supplied to him by Mrs. Isaacs, with whose daughter he is *épris*, came with them. He is even *plus distingué* than Comte Belladonna, for it is whispered he was a friend of Crown Prince Rudolph's, and knows so much about his death that the Emperor has requested him to live out of Austria. Mrs. Isaacs, who is a widow, well *conservée*, would, I think, sooner than let him slip out of the family, take him herself, but he prefers the daughter, who is an extremely beautiful and innocent girl of seventeen. The disposal of the dollars, of which they appear to possess millions, rests with Mrs. Isaacs's mother, an impossible old woman, who looks as if she had acquired the etiquette of the salon after a very thorough knowledge of that of the kitchen. Her thirst for information is apparently unquenchable, and I heard her ask Count Albert if he was related to a *hofdame* at Vienna, whose name I forget. He replied that his maternal grandmother was a Hohenzollern and his great-uncle had married a Hapsburg, which information so delighted Mrs. Johnson that she smacked her lips as if she were tasting some of the sauces she used to make in the good old days. I believe, old as she is, that she would marry Count Albert herself if he asked her; and I am sure that *he* would not hesitate to do so, if he were certain the fortune was entirely hers.

Madame Colorado

Mrs. Wertzelmann has a very pretty French woman stopping at Schloss Gessler, a Madame Colorado; she is really lovely, and has the dearest little girl in the world. Madame Colorado knows all the people you have met at Croixmare. On the way back to the National the Vicomte told me she was angelic, as I can well believe; she was married to a brute of a Chilian, who happily killed himself and left her free; she at one time thought of taking the veil, and the Vicomte says her charities in Paris are enormous and that the breath of scandal has never touched her name. I feel quite drawn to her, and shall try to know her better.

The Schweitzerhof

To-night after dinner several of us went down to the Schweitzerhof to see the fireworks and hear the music. As everybody was in the salon waiting to see Don Carlos and his Duchesse pass through on their way to dinner, we got splendid seats on the balcony. The night was superb.—Your dearest Mamma.

Letter XII

HOTEL NATIONAL, LUCERNE
28th August

DARLING ELIZABETH:

New People

THE season is in full swing, and yesterday a number of new people "descended," as the French say, at the National. First in importance were the Prince and Princesse di Spezzia from Florence; the Maréchale de Vichy-Pontoise; Mademoiselle Liane de Pougy of the Folies Bergère; and Professor Chzweiczy, who has discovered the bacillus of paralysis, and whose great scientific work "The Blot on the Brain" has been translated into all the European languages. This morning there was an enormous crowd on the *quai* in front of the hotel; Blanche said she was sure a crowned head had arrived, but I thought it was more likely that someone had had a fit, for we could see a circle had been formed round something or someone, people were tiptoeing and crushing one another, and I expected a *sergent de ville* to cry every moment, "Air! air!" as they did in Regent Street that morning when we were coming out of Fuller's and found the Duchesse of Rougemont's footman foaming on the pavement. But Blanche insisted it was an emperor, and she was backed up by Thérèse, who said it was just like the crowds she had seen in Paris when the Czar came. We found everybody we knew sitting in the hall of the hotel and in very bad humour, because it was awfully hot and stuffy, and the waiters had brought all the chairs inside lest they should be broken by the crowd. I asked the Marquise what had happened, and she said, with a shrug, it was only Liane de Pougy taking the air under the chestnuts. Professor Chzweiczy sat in the same spot all the afternoon reading "The Blot on the Brain," and the letters on the cover were so big that the Vicomte said you could distinguish them across the *quai*, but nobody paid any attention to him.

Signor Stefano Crestfallen

The Princesse di Spezzia held quite a court in the hall, and stared at everybody through her lorgnettes; they say she is at the head of Florentine society and a young Italian, who has a *magasin* on the *quai* Schweitzerhof, and comes to the dances at the National because men are scarce, has begged Mr. Vanduzen to present him. But Mr. Vanduzen refused, and Signor Stefano went off crestfallen, finding it, I daresay, quite impossible to reconcile the selling of precious stones behind a counter with his social ambitions.

Blanche spent the morning yesterday automobiling with the Vicomte and the Marquise, while I remained in the verandah to rest, as we were to drive after lunch with Sir Charles to a Schloss twenty miles away to a garden party. Mrs. Johnson kept me company, and told me that Count Albert had gone to the Rigi for the day with Mrs. Isaacs and Rosalie. She said they had been presented at Berlin and Brussels, and had intended to enjoy the same experience at Dresden last winter, as they had letters to the Minister there, but he made some paltry objection and she had not pressed the matter, though she added that she had written to the Senator, to whom the Minister owed his place, and that he would make it hot for him.

Shopping and Sightseeing

I asked her if they had been to London, and she said only for a week, and had never had such a dull time, as they knew nobody, and her room at the Carlton was so cold it gave her rheumatism. They did some shopping and sight-seeing, and had gone from the Bank to Shepherd's Bush in the Tu'penny Tube, but she preferred the Elevated in New York, because of the scenery. However, Mrs. Johnson told me quite in confidence, that if Count Albert didn't propose to Rosalie, they thought of going to London next year for the season, and she asked me if I could recommend a Countess who would run them, and she wanted to know if there was any institution to which she could write and engage one, for she had heard in St. Louis that poor Countesses did quite a business that way. I told her we were not so progressive in England as in the States, and that I did not think there was as yet any association of distressed gentlewomen where one could hire a Countess for the London season, but that perhaps if she wrote to the editor of one of the Society papers, I daresay he could provide a suitable person who would get her access to the best houses. Mrs. Johnson at once pulled a note-book out of her pocket, and jotted down the names of two or three papers I gave her, then she looked at me rather shrewdly, and asked what I thought would be the fee. I said I didn't think she could do the London season the way she would want to much under ten thousand pounds all told.

"Well," she said, "Count Albert won't cost us as much as that, and if we secure him we shan't go to London. From what I can find out Continental society is less expensive than English and just as good."

Automobile Accident

Blanche returned just before lunch in a great state of excitement: it seems that in going up the hill to the De Pivarts, something went wrong with the automobile, and it began to descend backwards at a frightful pace; the

Marquise screamed so loud that a number of people, not knowing what was the matter, rushed into the middle of the road, and the automobile knocked down one who happened to be the croupier at the Kursaal, and he was so badly hurt he had to be taken to the hospital. Just as they expected to batter down a wall at the foot of the hill, and perish horribly, the automobile suddenly stopped; they jumped out instantly, and it was just in time, for it at once blew up with such a noise, that the porter at the Pension Thorvaldsen took it for the one o'clock gun and began sounding the dinner-gong.

Blanche says that the Vicomte took it quite coolly; he declared he always knew the automobile would end like that, and he should compel the company in Paris to give him another, as they had guaranteed it to run without accident for a year. The Marquise fainted, and when Blanche left her she was in hysterics in the Pension Thorvaldsen; it all happened so quickly, that Blanche said it was all over before she could realise the danger. She was not even shaken.

Maréchale de Vichy-Pontoise

At lunch the *maître d'hôtel* made a mistake and put some Germans at the table occupied by the Maréchale de Vichy-Pontoise, and when she hobbled in, leaning on her cane, and followed by Bijou, her pug, there was no place for her to sit. She was in a towering rage, and shook her stick at the *maître d'hôtel*, and Bijou looked as if he contemplated making his lunch off the waiter's leg. A seat was eventually found for her at our table, and another for Bijou, who finished his chop in the Maréchale's lap. She glared at us several times as if she thought it was an impertinence for us to sit at the same table with her, and she frightened the waiters out of their wits and found fault with everything. I am sure she is horribly old, for Sir Charles says she was no chicken in the last year of the Empire, when her salon was the most *suivi* in Paris. Her *coiffure* is jet black, and her eyebrows are bald and pencilled in arches. She is awfully badly made up, but, as Blanche says, it would take tons of rouge to hide the gutters on her face which is lined like a railway-map. All her clothes are made in the fashion of 1870; she is covered at all times with jewels and wears a daguerreotype brooch of the late Maréchal.

But, of course, she is *très grande dame*, and everyone tries to mollify her, and they wait on her and Bijou hand and foot, and the Duchesse de Vaudricourt, who hates her because the Maréchale asked her before the Vicomte and Mr. Vanduzen if she remembered a certain ball at the Tuileries in '68, calls her "Ma chère maréchale."

Time to Retire

Thérèse has rapped twice to ask if I am ready to retire, so unless she should pull my hair out by the roots to spite me for keeping her up so late I must say good-night.—Your dearest Mamma.

Letter XIII

HOTEL NATIONAL, LUCERNE
30th August

DARLING ELIZABETH:

The Sonnenburgs

I NEVER told you of the garden party at Schloss Sonnenburg the other day, and as it will give quite another aspect of Lucerne life from that of the National and Schloss Gessler, I will try to remember what happened. It is rather difficult, for so much transpires in the course of the day that I am apt to forget what I did the day before.

A Disagreeable Drive

In the first place Baroness Sonnenburg is an Englishwoman, and Sir Charles knows her quite well. So he offered to drive us out to the Schloss and introduce us, telling us it would be quite *comme il faut*, and that the Sonnenburgs would be only too delighted to meet us. The Vicomte occupied the vacant seat in the landau, and we started immediately after lunch, for we had over twenty miles to drive. To know what dust is you must come to Switzerland in August; the road was like driving through sand, we were powdered with it, a nasty, white, itchy powder, and the flies, having devoured the horses which flew along maddened with pain, came to add their sting and buzzing to our own sufferings from the dust. I nearly shrieked with the discomfort of it all, and longed for my balcony at the National. The Vicomte began to talk of love to me, but knowing the danger of such a subject I peevishly begged him to desist, and a huge bottle-green fly, with a most irritating buzz, having drawn blood from his cheek, the Vicomte became as peevish as I. It seemed as if the journey would never end, which made the thought of the return to Lucerne *épouvantable*, and we were none of us in a good mood when a great yellow and black building, whose walls were like a draught-board, suddenly loomed out of a forest of pine trees on the brow of a steep cliff.

Warm Welcome

When we drove up to the front door two footmen in livery helped us out of the carriage, and I could have cried from the nervousness that the drive had fretted me into. However, we found a maid with brushes and water and perfumes, and when we were at all presentable again, another carriage drove up with Mrs. Johnson, Mrs. Isaacs and Rosalie, and their Austrian Count. They were in as bad a temper as we were from the dust and the flies, and I heard Mrs. Johnson say that if "Mrs. Sonnenburg hadn't been a baroness" she would never have come. We passed down a long hall whose walls were covered with family portraits, more than enough to make up the twenty-four quarterings of the Sonnenburg arms. At the end of the hall was a room into which we were shown by a footman. A grand-looking man, who was introduced by Sir Charles as Baron Sonnenburg, gave us the warmest welcome in English, and led us across the room where we were presented to his wife and mother. Baroness Sonnenburg spoke English with an accent which was not affected, for she told us she had not been in England for over twenty years. She was one of the Trevorleys of Devonshire, and the present baronet is her first cousin. I doubt if she ever heard the name of Paquin, and I suppose her clothes are made by a seamstress in Lucerne, yet there was no disguising the gentility of her appearance and the breeding of her manners.

A Pretty Custom

Blanche and I, who, from constant observation of the people we mix with, are rapidly becoming Continental, curtseyed to the Dowager Baroness and kissed the hand she held out. I think it is such a pretty custom, and one we could adopt to advantage in England, where every trace of the manners of the *ancien régime* has disappeared. Such a number of people were in the room that we did not get the chance I should have liked to converse with our hosts, and we sauntered into an enormous octagonal apartment, which we were told jutted sheer over the precipice on which the Schloss is built. The view from the windows was very fine and extensive, and it made one quite giddy to look down into the valley which is nine hundred feet below.

There was a visitors' book here which Sir Charles was signing for us when suddenly there were shrieks of surprise and everybody rushed to the windows. Through a cleft of pine woods standing out against the bright blue sky was a glittering, dazzling mass. It was the Jungfrau, Baron Sonnenburg said, and was only seen on rare occasions, and nothing could be more fortunate than that it should unveil its peerless loveliness to-day of all days for the benefit of his guests.

An Al Fresco Repast

An *al fresco* repast was served on the old battlements which have been turned out into a *terrasse*. An awkward, blushing youth was brought up to me by Baron Sonnenburg and presented as his son, and I was told he was going to England in the autumn to learn English, of which he doesn't know a word. Two rather pretty, but shockingly badly-dressed girls, were talking to two Swiss officers, but the attitudes of all were so stilted and forced that I am sure they were not enjoying the unusual liberty permitted on this occasion.

The Duchesse de Vaudricourt whispered to me that they were Baroness Sonnenburg's daughters and were considered very English. I was on the point of asking her what she thought *I* was, but thought better of it, and merely said, that from the extreme diffidence they displayed, I should have taken them for French girls whose *dot* had not yet been settled.

The Wertzelmanns

The Wertzelmanns came late; they brought Madame Colorado, who looked perfectly angelic in a marvellous white crêpe de chine, and a hat that killed you at a glance. They brought the news of the accident to the Vicomte de Narjac's automobile, and Mrs. Wertzelmann excitedly told a circle, who had gathered to admire her clothes and her jewels, that it was the sensation of the season, she had never heard of anything so dreadful. And Baron Sonnenburg, who had never seen either Blanche or the Vicomte before, and had forgotten their names already, was told how the Vicomte's automobile had run away and exploded, terribly mangling the croupier at the Kursaal, blowing the Vicomte and Miss Blaine, such a sweet English girl, to smithereens, and that the poor Marquise de Pivart had gone mad from the shock.

An Amusing Story

Mrs. Wertzelmann dwelt on the horrible details with a tenacity there was no shaking, and at every exclamation of pity uttered by her audience she but made the story more graphic. The Vicomte and Blanche, who all the while had listened quietly, unobserved by Mrs. Wertzelmann, stuffed their mouths with handkerchiefs to keep from shrieking. But when the Vicomte heard that a boatman had found one of his arms clinging to a fragment of automobile in the lake, and that they were picking his brains off the walls of the Pension Thorvaldsen, he could contain himself no longer.

You should have seen Mrs. Wertzelmann's face when she saw Blanche and the Vicomte bursting with laughter, and she looked about the *terrasse* as if she expected to see the Marquise and the croupier eating ices in Baron Sonnenburg's beach chairs; and later when we left I am sure she wondered why we drove off in the landau with the fly-bitten horses instead of in the automobile.

"If Maria once begins to tell a story," said Mr. Wertzelmann to me, "there is no stopping her. I knew she would end by putting her foot into it."

As Mrs. Wertzelmann's confusion was so great, and she volunteered no explanation, I fancy the Sonnenburgs, who do not go into Lucerne frequently, are wondering why the *Swiss and Nice Times* have given no account of the terrible automobile disaster.

Don't ask me how we got back to Lucerne, but four more pitiable-looking objects you never would wish to see. We were utterly exhausted, and I never made any appearance the next day till lunch.

I am glad you are having such a good time at Croixmare. Give my kind regards to your Godmamma and my best love to Héloise. I am glad you have been such a success; I pride myself that whether in England or in France *l'ingénue va bien.*—Your dearest Mamma.

Letter XIV

HOTEL NATIONAL, LUCERNE
1st September

DARLING ELIZABETH:

The Ball of the Season

THE invitations are out to a *cotillon* at Schloss Gessler on the 7th. It is to be a grand affair, the favours are to come from the Maison Bail at Paris, the supper and the music from the National, and the money to pay for it all out of Mr. Wertzelmann's bank account, which it goes without saying is a big one.

Count Albert's Proposal

Everybody seems to have been invited, and Mr. Wertzelmann told me he intended that it should be remembered as the ball of the season. Old Mrs. Johnson came and sat next to me on the *quai* this morning, and broke the news that Count Albert has proposed to Rosalie and been accepted. She didn't seem to like it when I said I felt sorry for the girl, because she was too good for Count Albert, who was old enough to be her father, and I advised her to look him up and all his antecedents at Vienna before the marriage ceremony. But she was quite satisfied that he was a real, live Count, because the "Schweitzerhof knew all about him." I shouldn't be surprised, however, that she takes my advice, for she is a shrewd old woman, but just fancy anyone taking a husband on a hotel guarantee!

A very pretty woman—a blonde, with a figure that the Venus de Milo might envy, and dressed, oh! là là! shades of Paquin and Worth!—passed us several times, walking up and down the *quai*. Everybody turned round to stare at her, and everybody asked who she was, and the Princesse di Spezzia, who was talking to Comte Belladonna, put up her lorgnettes. The Duchesse de Vaudricourt leaned over the arm of her chair and whispered to me:—

"Voilà la plus belle courtisane de Florence. C'est une des bijoux de M. le Prince di Spezzia. La fameuse Vittoria Lodi!"

Monsieur le Prince

Later on the Prince di Spezzia sauntered out of the National on the arm of the Marquis de Pivart, both dressed faultlessly as usual, *à l'Anglais*, and they actually stopped and spoke to the *demi-mondaine*. The Duchesse de Vaudricourt became quite excited over it, and gave me a regular *New-York-Herald-Paris-Edition* of Monsieur le Prince. He is very English in appearance, but then Poole makes all his clothes, and he could easily pass for an Englishman, which I think would please him immensely. But why—why will these smart foreigners who affect English fashions always wear lavender or buff-coloured French kid gloves? Perhaps you will say, for the same reason that Englishwomen who are for ever talking of Paris fashions wear English corsets. So under all the artificiality of civilisation national traits come out in a pair of gloves or a pair of stays!

The Prince looks as if he would improve on acquaintance, but I think it distinctly rude and bad form of him to stop and talk to such a woman as la belle Lodi within a stone's throw of his wife. The Duchesse says he has been a *mauvais sujet* since sixteen, when he disguised himself as a priest and confessed dozens of people, and if it hadn't been that his uncle was a Cardinal, he would have got into some very hot water. He drives with the Lodi daily in the Cascine at Florence, and makes her follow him wherever he goes. She has an apartment at the Schweitzerhof. The Princesse doesn't seem to mind; I don't suppose it would make any difference if she did. She is always beautifully dressed, and spends most of her time staring at people through her lorgnettes.

Professor Chzweiczy

Poor Professor Chzweiczy (you can pronounce this name to suit yourself, for nobody knows what it should be, and Blanche calls it Squeezey) sits every day on the *quai*; he holds the "Blot on the Brain" close in front of his face as if he were near-sighted. I think he must have a cast in his eyes, for they always seem to be looking over the top of the book at the people passing. I am sure that if it were known that he is one of the greatest medical scientists of the day, he would be besieged like Liane de Pougy; but nobody ever even glances at him; they have got his name spelled wrong in the hotel visitors' list, and wedged in out of sight between some people whose names have a globe-trotting sound and who look like a party of Cook's "Specials."

Liane de Pougy

Liane de Pougy sits now in the garden of the National, for the crowds nearly suffocated her on the *quai*. She is very beautiful and dresses very quietly; you would never dream that she is as well known in Paris as a monument or a boulevard. A young Frenchman has for the last two days been doing his best to attract her attention by sitting near her, and pretending to read her "L'Insaisissable." I believe that since her arrival there are nearly as many copies of this *roman vécu*, as she calls it, as Baedekers at the National. It is hard to say which is the most interesting—herself or her book. I caught her looking at the old Maréchale de Vichy-Pontoise yesterday with the most untranslatable expression. I am not quite sure but that in spite of her triumphs she would change places with the Maréchale if she could, and wear the old harridan's moustache and the daguerreotype brooch of the late Maréchal and feed Bijou and all. As it is, not a woman at the National would dream of speaking to her, and the Maréchale would as soon think of strangling Bijou as of sitting down at the same table as the famous Liane.

A Comedy

Blanche has just come in to say that a Count Fosca has arrived at the National, having automobiled all the way from Paris, and that the Vicomte is completely *bouleversé*. She is laughing so over something that Thérèse is telling her that I cannot write any more.

I can only catch the words, "Mrs. Johnson," "Prince di Spezzia," "Ascenseur," "no lights." I leave it to you to make a comedy out of the missing links.—Your dearest Mamma.

Letter XV

HOTEL NATIONAL, LUCERNE
3rd September

DARLING ELIZABETH:

A Mishap

IT rained yesterday for the first time since we have been in Lucerne. As I was looking at the lake which the wind had turned into an ocean with waves mountains high, I saw Comte Belladonna soaked to the skin hurrying along the *quai* to the hotel. Poor little old beau! He had got himself up as usual in spotless flannels, patent-leather boots, straw hat, and lavender kids, and was coming from the direction of the pension where his inamorata lives—the pretty, portionless American girl—when the rain had overtaken him. His legs, unaccustomed to the unusual exercise of running, seemed inclined one moment to run into the flower-beds on the *quai* and another to contemplate a plunge into the lake. Sheets of water fell from the brim of his straw hat, his gloves and his boots were irretrievably spoilt, and his flannels had that heavy, soppy look that bathing-suits have. He was as full of water as a sponge, and I am sure he would have been the better for a squeeze.

I called Blanche to look at him, and we both agreed that he would catch a chill after such a wetting that would carry him off. But when we went down to lunch we found him dry and chirpy, and paying his *devoirs* to the Princesse di Spezzia, as if he had made his toilet for the first time that day.

A Funny Thing

A funny thing happened in the afternoon in connection with the old beau's wetting that would have covered anybody else but such a consummate old courtier with ridicule. After lunch it cleared off, and the sun came out very hot and dried up things so quickly that everybody had tea as usual in the garden of the hotel. The Hungarian band had just finished playing a valse of Waldeuffel, and the Maréchale de Vichy-Pontoise had hobbled out into the garden and settled herself comfortably in her favourite seat next to the Princesse di Spezzia when something slowly descended from the sky performing curious evolutions. Everybody speculated as to what it could be and where it came from, when it calmly lighted on the head of the Maréchale, who gave a wizened shriek, and having disengaged herself from it shied it away savagely with the end of her stick. Bijou at once seized it in his mouth, and having gambolled about the grass with it proceeded to improvise it into a broom and sweep up the gravel path with it. The difficulty of getting him to relinquish his possession of it caused a great deal of merriment, and the young man who reads "L'Insaisissable" and ogles Liane de Pougy at the same time suddenly put his foot on it with such force that Bijou, who was scampering off as hard as he could go with an end in his mouth, was brought up short, and, having turned a rather violent somersault in the air, let go and went off whimpering to the Maréchale, who looked as if she could have eaten the young Frenchman. He picked up Bijou's mysterious plaything and held it up, so that everybody could see—a white flannel jacket, or what was left of it, of the jauntiest cut in the world. No one claiming it, he handed it to a waiter who discovered on a tag the *chiffre* of Comte Belladonna! Instead of at once withdrawing with the garment he informed the Comte that it belonged to him. The Comte, who knew it all the time and had not cared to make himself the butt of the National, examined it, shook his head, examined it again, and bursting into a laugh exclaimed to the Princesse di Spezzia with the utmost self-possession:—

"My dear Princesse, alas! this rag is indeed mine. This morning, spotless and sweet-smelling, I arrayed my old bones in it, and its mate, whose legs you may see dangling out of that window up there under the roof; but, as if envious of the figure I cut in it, the elements having determined to deprive me of it, flooded me out of it. Not being an American millionaire, I hung it out of my window to dry, and the wind did the rest. Heaven grant that the trousers do not come to look after the jacket. Pity me, Princesse, I had worn it but once; it was cut at 'Old England.' Here, garçon, it is yours now."

It was not the words, which were funny enough, but the manner in which they were uttered, that made every one laugh *with* the Comte instead of *at* him.

Signor Stefano

The Princesse is a dear; she proved to-night that she is really a *grande dame*, and that it is neither her name nor her pose which makes her one. Young Signor Stefano, a shopkeeper, we would call him in England, came again to the National to-night to dance. The proprietor, who is very anxious that these dances should be a success, has given him, and two or three other young fellows like him, the entrée. Of course, according to the Continental custom, they can ask any one they like to dance, but a natural and creditable diffidence has kept them from forcing themselves upon any of the smart set, and they are generally to be seen reversing and chasséeing with the people from the pensions, who sit at one end of the ball-room and stare at the other.

Stefano Recognised

Young Stefano is very good-looking, and dances divinely, and has attracted the attention of all of us women, and everybody who has been in the *magasin*, where he is in charge of the precious stone department, has remarked his quiet gentlemanly behaviour. I think I wrote you that he asked Mr. Vanduzen to present him to the Princesse di Spezzia and was refused, and I must say when he came into the room to-night he looked so much a gentleman and so handsome that I horrified Mr. Vanduzen by telling him to bring Stefano to me.

Princesse di Spezzia

He was covered with confusion when he was introduced, and when we danced he bumped me into two or three people, for he held me as if he were afraid of me, and we took up as much room as four people. I made him sit next me and talked to him, and cleverly turned the conversation on to the Princesse di Spezzia. He said very modestly that desire had got the better of him the other night, and he had presumed to be presented to her and had been snubbed, as he deserved. His *magasin* is transferred to Florence for the winter; he is a Florentine, and has often seen the Princesse in the Cascine and admired her very much; he told me that he had no desire to meet her as an equal, that he knew he was only a *petit bourgeois*, but that he would have been proud to be presented to such a great lady. I surprised him by saying I would ask the Princesse if she had any objection, and if not it would be easy enough to gratify his small desire. His thanks were profuse, and when I got a chance I told the Princesse the story. She was furious with Mr. Vanduzen and has cut him dead since; she wondered how he dared to refuse to present any one to her without her permission, and she declared it was one of the greatest pleasures of her position to have the people of Florence presented to her and admire her. She chatted for some time with Stefano and gave him permission to address her at any time he chose without any fear of being snubbed. I watched her closely all the time; her manner was totally free from patronage, but it let Stefano know that she was what he had always thought, the Princesse di Spezzia, the greatest lady in Florence.

She has immensely flattered his pride by her recognition and preserved her own dignity, and Blanche and I have agreed that in point of manners and etiquette she could teach any of our great ladies in England how to hold themselves.

We think she is a dear, and wish we knew how to dress as she does and to stare through lorgnettes and to endure horrid bores such as the Maréchale. I wish the Prince appreciated her more; he plays the devil devilishly well. Sir Charles says there is no question of doubt but that the family was a noble one in the days of the Roman Empire. Adieu.—Your dearest Mamma.

Letter XVI

HOTEL NATIONAL, LUCERNE
5th September

DARLING ELIZABETH:

The Vicomte

MRS. ISAACS (who, by the way, is not one of the children of Israel, if her husband was) went yesterday to Berne. The Vicomte says she carried the Almanac de Gotha instead of Baedeker, and that the porter at the hotel who bought her ticket declared that her ultimate destination is Vienna. So that I suppose they are looking up Count Albert.

The Vicomte has been like a bear with a sore head ever since Count Fosca automobiled from Paris. He behaves so childishly, as if no one in the world should have an automobile but himself. He spends several hours a day fencing with an Italian; you know duelling is his other occupation in Paris, and I expect he is going to take it up seriously till he gets a new automobile. He glares at Count Fosca and mutters "So" under his breath like a German, and I am expecting to hear daily that they are going to fight, and all over an automobile!

Ball at Schloss Gessler

But people are too much excited over the ball at Schloss Gessler on the day after to-morrow to pay much attention to the Vicomte and his grievances. Mr. Wertzelmann told me to-day that if people talked so much about the ball before it came off he wondered what they would say about it after. He never did things by halves, and this was a ball which should be remembered for years to come. It is to cost thousands of francs, and if the Russian *boyar* (don't ask me his name, I know it has an itch at the end of it) who is Mrs. Wertzelmann's devoted admirer, and practically runs Schloss Gessler, does his duty properly, I have no doubt it will be, as Mr. Wertzelmann says, something to remember.

It will be the end of the season here, and, as we have stayed longer than we intended, we shall hurry home after it. We really have managed to do other things besides frivol. We have seen the Lion and we have been to Fluëlen and drove to Schloss Sonnenburg, but there was little of the country or scenery we saw on that occasion, owing to the flies and the dust. Yesterday we added to our knowledge of the Lake of the Four Cantons by spending the night on the top of the Stanzerhorn.

The Stanzerhorn

Quite late in the afternoon Sir Charles came over to the National to ask us if we would come with him then and there to see the sunset and sunrise in the Alps from the Stanzerhorn. He assured us we would find a good hotel and that it was worth the trouble, and as we had nothing better to do we went. Thérèse filled two handbags with necessaries and we caught the last boat from Lucerne. There was nobody we knew on the boat, and Blanche said she felt game for anything, and game we were before we saw our comfortable rooms at the National again and our indispensable Thérèse and dear, dear Paquin.

As Sir Charles had described it as a "rough and ready jaunt," and "a picnic in the clouds," and turned up at the National in snuff-coloured "knickers" that looked as if Bijou had been introducing them to the gravel-path, and carrying a brand-new alpenstock with "Lucerne" and "Gütsch" and "Sonnenburg" burnt into it, we decided to wear our serge walking skirts and men's shirts and straw-hats. Blanche looked very well in hers, for it is a style that suits her, but I nearly wept at my own reflection, and I was delighted there was to be no one else of the party but Sir Charles. Blanche said my skirt was positively indecent; it came just to the tops of my boots, and was really made for bicycling and not for walking. I felt like a Gordon Highlander, and Blanche declared that if the skirt was a plaid I would have looked like one. Thérèse too went into fits of laughter, and said she was sure that Sir Charles would not recognise me. I was half inclined to give up the excursion, but Blanche said it was ridiculous, and that I couldn't possibly take Paquin to the top of the Stanzerhorn, and that I looked charming from my waist up.

I tried to discover a blush somewhere in my veins when we stood in the hall of the hotel, but somehow I couldn't find one. Fortunately for my vanity we got on to the steamboat without being recognised, and I made a mental vow that I would never employ a Taunton seamstress again. The Italian boy with the monkey and the post-cards that we saw the first day we arrived, and whom Blanche declared was a nobleman in disguise, was on board. He went second-class, and was talking to a Swiss peasant with goitre just below us. The monkey travelled first all the way to Alpnacht, for the steamboat people didn't dare touch it; it ate apples at Blanche's feet when it wasn't frightening people out of their wits by bounding about the deck. The disguised nobleman, who can't be more than seventeen, recognised us, and gave such a smile and bow! Blanche put a franc into the tin cup round the monkey's neck, and when we got off at Stanz the boy brushed off the gangplank before we stepped on it, with his cap, though the plank was spotless. As Blanche said, it gave her quite a Sir-Walter-Raleigh-Queen-Elizabeth-and-the-Cloak feeling, and we declared he was the most picturesque tramp we had ever seen, but Sir Charles, who hasn't a scrap of romance in him, said he looked as if he belonged to an Anarchist Society.

Stanz is a funny little town, and people only come to it to leave it. Some Germans with ropes and pick-axes over their shoulders, and who looked as if they meant business, got off at Stanz, and as one makes the ascent of Titlis from here, we concluded that was their destination. Sir Charles made us walk to the little *platz* to see the statue to Arnold von Winkelreid, but we preferred Tell's at Altdorf. The funicular to the top of the Stanzerhorn makes one feel goose-pimply all over; it is not only steep, but when you get near the top you look out of the car window over a sheer precipice of two thousand feet. There are two cars attached to an endless cable, and while one creeps up the mountain like a horrid antediluvian bug the other crawls down. If the cable should break, one would catapult little Stanz to atoms and the other would Jules Verne itself to the top of the Stanzerhorn.

When we got to the two thousand feet place a German woman fainted, and I felt as if I were about to develop heart failure. But Blanche and Sir Charles leaned out of the windows and raved over the scenery, while an American woman read Baedeker out loud to another. As soon as we reached the top, we went to the hotel and got rooms, but discovered to our horror that we had left our bags at Stanz and that we couldn't get them that night. We both gave it to Sir Charles, I can tell you, but he only laughed and said the proprietor's wife would fit us out all right. We at once went in search of this individual, and you may imagine our consternation when I tell you that the proprietor was a bachelor, or a widower—I believe he tried to explain which it was, but we fairly shrieked with horror—and moreover the only females belonging to the hotel were some Swiss girls with symptoms of goitre.

The proprietor was bland and apologetic, and told Sir Charles that he would see we were provided with the necessary articles before we went to bed. With this we had to be content, and went out upon a sort of promenade where there was a telescope and a man to explain the views. He seemed to have learnt his "patter" by heart, for when he was interrupted he had to begin all over. Five minutes before sunset begins they ring a gong and everybody climbs up a tiny peak where you can see only snow mountains and the lake like a cloud far below. We waited for half an hour and saw nothing else; the man of the telescope said it was the only failure of the season. It got frightfully cold all of a sudden, and we went back to the hotel wishing we were at the National.

They gave us a remarkably good *table d'hôte* dinner, considering how remote we were from everything. The people were mostly Germans, and there was such a curious German-American woman who sat next me. If she had been decently dressed she would have been quite pretty; she was very confidential, as strange Americans are inclined to be, and gave us her history from the time she was five. She fairly astounded me by saying she was known as Patsy Bolivar, the champion lady swimmer of the world, and she showed me several photographs of herself which she carries about with her, and also one of the gold belt she won in New York. Quite contrary to the usual run of celebrities, she was modest, and did not appear at all offended that I had never heard of her before.

After dinner we all went to watch the flash-light at work, and saw it turned on to the Stanz and Lucerne, in red, white, and blue. As the sunrise was to be very early we went to bed at nine in time to be ready for it. Blanche and I had connecting rooms, and we found on the pillows of our beds two spotless and neatly folded *robes de nuit*, and a hair-brush and a comb on the dressing-table, and we blessed monsieur le propriétaire. But imagine our horror, when we were ready to put on our host's garments, to find that they were in reality his own! They reached just above our knees, and had "Ricardo" embroidered in red cotton on the buttons. There was nothing to do but to make the best of it, and as it was terribly cold we hastily got into bed in our proprietor's night-shirts, and slept soundly till we heard a hideous gong and knew that it was four o'clock and sunrise. We dressed quickly, and clambered on to the little peak again, where we found everybody shivering and jumping about to keep warm, and while we waited the sun rose. I won't attempt to describe it, for I am neither Walter Scott nor Baedeker, and if you want to know what it is like you must come to Switzerland yourself and spend the night on a mountain.

We had delicious coffee and rolls before leaving: Sir Charles paid the bill for us. Would you believe it, they actually took off a franc each for the failure of the sunset the previous day. I thought it exceedingly honourable, and different from the grasping way they have at hotels in England where they have only one way of making coffee and omelette, and that is *à l'Anglaise*. We didn't dare thank the proprietor for the things he had lent us, and he said, with such a nice smile to me, as we left:—

"Madame est-elle bien dormie? Les rêves étaient-ils doux? J'espère ça."

Horrid man!

Thérèse was waiting for us when we got back, and had our baths and Paquin ready.—Your dearest Mamma.

Letter XVII

HOTEL NATIONAL, LUCERNE
7th September

DARLING ELIZABETH:

The Wertzelmann Ball

THIS is our last day here, and we leave by the express for Paris to-night. Mr. Wertzelmann said he was going to give a ball that would be remembered, and he has kept his promise. I hardly know where to begin to tell you all about it. I had one offer of marriage and one of elopement, and got home at six in the morning.

First of all, Blanche and I, looking every bit as well dressed as any of the smart women here, drove out to Schloss Gessler by ourselves. Comte Belladonna and Mr. Vanduzen hinted outrageously for the two vacant seats, but we didn't intend to have our frocks crushed to save them a few francs, and wouldn't take their hints.

The Comte eventually got Mrs. Isaacs' seat in Mrs. Johnson's landau, but Mr. Vanduzen had to hire, and just as he was about to drive off the Duchesse de Vaudricourt rushed up and begged him for a seat, as she couldn't get a cab in the town. Thérèse told me this morning that the Duchesse has no maid, and that her room is above the *escalier de service* next to the Comte's, so I fancy they keep *her* at the National too as an advertisement for the sake of her name, though it's only Louis Philippe.

When we arrived at Schloss Gessler the scene was undeniably lovely; the grounds were like fairy-land, and Mr. Wertzelmann had had the electric light brought out from Lucerne, and had tried to turn a part of the lake into a Venetian canal. Mrs. Wertzelmann, in the most lovely costume I ever saw, received in the great hall. She never looked handsomer; her dress was made entirely of point lace over white silk, and made as only Worth or Paquin ever make for American millionaires. Round her neck was a serpent of diamonds holding in its open jaws an immense emerald. Both she and Mr. Wertzelmann received their guests with the most perfect sincerity and hospitality. There was not a scrap of affectation about them; it must be nice to be so rich that you can afford to be natural. Mr. Wertzelmann wore on the lapel of his dress-coat something like a button, with the American flag on it as a badge; all the foreigners wore decorations; don't ask me what they were,—if they were not Garters or Black Eagles, they looked as well. Even Sir Charles wore an Ashantee medal; he went in his uniform especially at Mr. Wertzelmann's request, who said he wanted a bit of colour in the room, only Sir Charles's tunic is not scarlet, and he looked somewhat like a commissionaire.

Madame Colorado was angelic as usual—what a lovely nun she would make! She was helping the Wertzelmanns to receive, and she looked after the Americans from the *pensions* that the Minister felt obliged to invite. It was great fun watching the guests arrive, and as we got there early we saw everybody; the Hungarian band from the National came out in a char-à-banc, but the supper was sent out in the afternoon. The ball-room was draped with the American and Swiss flags, and the national anthems of the two countries were played before the dancing began. There was no "state set" as we have in England, and nobody paid any attention to precedence. Mrs. Wertzelmann opened the ball with young Stefano. There was something higgledy-piggledy yet very splendid about the whole function; it went with far more spirit than such things go with us; people had come to enjoy themselves, and not to be martyrised by stupid formalities and etiquette. The musicians played ravishingly; they seemed to be intoxicated with their music, and sometimes they couldn't contain themselves but sang to the waltzes. There was an *élan* in the air. Mrs. Wertzelmann's portrait by Constant had electric lights all round the frame, and there was a champagne fountain in the refreshment room. The gaiety was almost barbaric in its extravagance, and was contagious. The men said the most outrageous things. The Marquis de Pivart, who had not paid much attention to me since I chaffed him about Héloise that night at the Schweitzerhof, danced with me three times running; he dances well, but held me so tight I could hardly breathe, and his breath was so hot on my neck it burnt. He asked me if I would like to go down to the lake to see the illumination; the night was splendid and very warm, there was no dew, and you could see the snow on Titlis as the moonbeams fell on it.

Without any preamble the Marquis burst into the most passionate declarations. He told me he had loved me in secret since the first time he had met me; would I flee with him then and there, catch the night train for Berne and Paris, live like Alfred de Musset and George Sand, and a lot more idiotic bosh; and he put his arms round me, and before I could release myself he bit me on the neck. I was so frightened that for the first time in my life, Elizabeth, I lost my presence of mind—I screamed. I don't know whether any one heard or saw, and I don't care. I told him he was a brute and I hated him, and I rushed as hard as I could under a huge Bengal light where I could easily be seen. I trembled so I could scarcely stand, and some of the wax from the candle dripped upon me. He came up with excuses and more protestations of love, but I said if he didn't leave me at once I should scream for help, and I must have looked as if I meant it, for he muttered something in his horrid black beard and went away. Then I went back to the ball-room and found Blanche. I told her what had happened, and asked her if she could see the marks of his teeth. She said the place only looked a tiny bit red, and we went to the dressing-room, where I powdered it.

After that I told Blanche that I shouldn't feel safe except with the dowagers. They sat in a room by themselves and had waiters bringing them champagne and ices, and they talked the most outrageous scandal. I sat down beside Mrs. Johnson; she said I looked pale and recommended some champagne frappé, and called a waiter and ordered a glass for me and one for herself. She was very talkative and fairly peppered her conversation with French words, though she wouldn't understand you if you said, "Comment vous portez-vous?"

She told me that the Wertzelmanns were *parvenus*—mushrooms, she called them—and Mr. W. had made his money out of oil, and that they had never been into Society till they came abroad. She was very communicative also on the subject of Rosalie's marriage, which she said was to take place in Paris in the autumn and would be a very grand affair. As for Count Albert she hadn't enough praise for him, and he was so devoted and attentive in coming often to see if she wanted anything that I am sure he knows where the dollars are to come from. I tried to find out what had taken Mrs. Isaacs away so suddenly, but Mrs. Johnson is cunning, she smelt a rat, and the only reason I could extract was "business."

She made one amusing break. Mrs. Wertzelmann came in to see if all was going well with the chaperones, and exclaimed when she saw me among them. Mrs. Johnson, who evidently hates her, began to put on "side," and talked about her hotel in the Faubourg St. Germain, which she rented from the Duc de Quatre Bras, and described a ball she had given there to which all the *demi monde* had come. Funny as this was, it was made still funnier by the fact that Mrs. Wertzelmann, who knows no more of French than Mrs. Johnson, didn't see the joke.

I had by this time recovered sufficiently to go back to the ball-room, where, as it was on the stroke of midnight, the *cotillon* was about to commence. Young Stefano came up and asked me to dance it with him. The Marquis had the grace not to put in an appearance; I believe he was playing baccarat in the card-room.

The favours were very pretty and appropriate, as the Wertzelmanns did not choose them, but simply gave the Maison Bail *carte blanche*. The Duchesse de Vaudricourt was disappointed; I believe she expected to get diamonds. The Vicomte de Narjac and the Russian with an unpronounceable name and a *grande passion* for Mrs. Wertzelmann, who, I hope, knows how to contain himself better than the Marquis, led the *cotillon*. They did it awfully well, as if they had never done anything else all their lives. They went somewhere and changed their clothes, and came back with Louis Quinze perukes, crimson satin coats, with lace fichus and black knee-breeches and stockings, and diamond buckles in their pumps. They really looked quite smart, while an Englishman would have felt self-conscious and foolish, and looked it.

At two o'clock the dancing ceased, and supper was served at tête-à-tête tables on the battlements, as Mr. Wertzelmann persists in calling the *terrasse*. The supper was delicious, and there was a waiter to each chair; the Hungarian band came out and played, and paper balloons, in the shape of monsters with lights inside, were sent up in the air from the lawn.

It was awfully jolly and gay, and poor Stefano took too much champagne. It made his eyes burn like coals; he began by telling me in Italian that he should never forget me for my kindness in presenting him to the Princesse di Spezzia—they left Lucerne yesterday, and so did the Lodi—and ended by declaring he adored me. He was so fearfully earnest, and his voice was so subdued and tender, and he never attempted any liberties that I almost wished he would. I am sure he ought to have been born the Marquis, and the Marquis behind a counter. He wanted me to marry him, and told me how many lira they paid him at the shop a month, and that we could keep a *ménage*very well on his salary; we were to have rooms in the Via Tornabuoni over a Bon Marché he knew of, and dine once a week in the Cascine, and look at the smart people. It was too absurd. But he meant it, and when I told him No firmly, two tears came into his eyes, and he had such a Lion of Lucerne look that I almost laughed. And he is only seventeen! Poor Stefano! if they make love like him in Italy, I wonder how the women ever refuse. But your mamma, Elizabeth, knows her world too well to do a *bêtise*. Stefano and his love-making was just the last finishing touch to a delightful revel. When he gets the champagne out of his eyes and the Hungarian band out of his brain, he will forget me. But I think it is a mistake to admit people of such very inferior rank into our society, even if they speak grammatically and read Alfieri.

Comte Belladonna wilted at midnight; he danced once with Rosalie, and would have given anything afterwards to go back to the National. He is made more for afternoon-tea and dinner parties than for balls. He hinted several times to Mrs. Johnson that they should go, but she is as hard as nails, and waited till the end. When he finally did go, the sun was rising in the Alps; he not only looked his eighty years, but had dwindled till he looked like the boy in the Struwelpter who faded away from starvation. I expect he wished he had never come, like the Maréchale. Ah well, it has been a jolly jaunt, and in spite of the dissipation I feel the better for the change. We shall both be in England together. I wonder if you have enjoyed Croixmare as much as Blanche and I have enjoyed Lucerne. I am so glad we didn't go to Scarborough. Au revoir.—Your dearest Mamma.

Letter XVIII

CLARIDGE'S HOTEL, LONDON
14th September

DARLING ELIZABETH:

In London

BLANCHE and I are stopping here for a few days before going home. After all the gaiety of Lucerne Blanche declared it would give her the blues to drop suddenly back into Somersetshire, with its biking and tennis and gossip, so we decided to break the fall in London. Of course, town is still *en villégiature* as the French say, but I like it, as one can be so much freer than in the Season.

Bond Street is *triste* in the mornings, and as for the Park, oh, là là!—the only people one sees there are the hospital nurses and the policemen. We don't get up till eleven, and then go straight to Paquin, till one. The first day we had lunch at Prince's, but there were such funny-looking people there that we have been to the Trocadero since. I am sure those who were at Prince's were there because they had heard it was fashionable. The *maître d'hôtel*, who was chef to the bishop of St. Esau, told me that there hadn't been even a baronet across the threshold for two months. I am sure the people came from Leeds and Birmingham, and they stared at one another as if they expected to read Burke or Debrett written on their faces. At the Trocadero the music is good, and though you would never dream of calling the people smart, yet they are interesting. The women look like problem-plays, and I am sure the men spend their time between Sandown Park and St. John's Wood.

At the Empire

We went once to the Empire, but it was awfully stupid, and I never want to go again. Being September, the boxes were empty, and only a few of the orchestra stalls were taken, but the gallery and the pit seemed full, and the Aubrey Beardsley women were walking about just as usual. But such a performance! Blanche and I never laughed once for the night; we were told afterwards that you are not supposed to expect anything funny at the first-class music halls now-a-days; if you want to laugh you must go to the cheap places. A fat woman in tights and a stage smile had some performing parrots and birds, and one or two people in evening-dress, who have left the chorus of the Opera to star, sang something, and there was a huge ballet whose chief features appear to be the time and cost it takes to produce—that was all. You couldn't imagine anything more deadly dull, and a man near us slept all through the ballet. Blanche and I felt utterly exhausted after it; it was so boring. They say the Palace and the Alhambra are not a bit different; only the Palace, in place of the ballet has a Biograph, which wiggles and makes you feel cross-eyed.

At Claridge's

We found it much jollier to spend the evenings in the drawing-room at Claridge's. I don't know why we came to such a place, and I certainly never will again. There are very few people stopping in the hotel, a couple of Grand Dukes, some Americans, and the Duchess of Rougemont, who is up in town for a few days. This morning Something Pasha, with a fez, arrived from Cairo, and Eleanora, Countess of Merryone and her boy husband. I am sure it is a love-match, for he won't let her out of his sight, and looks at her as if she were something good to eat.

She must be fully twenty-five years older than he and looks it, for he hasn't a hair on his face, and blushes when you speak to him. But she keeps her youth, and when the Society papers call her beautiful they speak the truth for once.

Countess of Merryone

I remember her quite well when I was your age; she was known then as the beautiful Lady Merryone, and Society was divided into two parties, one of which declared that she was the most beautiful woman in England, and the other that Mrs. Palsgrave was. Their photographs were in all the shop windows, and their portraits in every Academy, and fashions were named after them. There was the Palsgrave toque and the Merryone bolero, and everything they did was chronicled in the papers, just as if it mattered. Each tried to outdo the other, and Mrs. Palsgrave, who had the most beautiful feet you ever saw out of marble, went to an historical fancy-ball as Cleopatra, and her feet were absolutely bare. Her portrait was afterwards painted in the costume, but it was hung at the salon, as it was considered too indecent for the Academy. And what a sensation it was when Mr. Palsgrave blew his brains out in the height of a London Season, and left so many debts that Mrs. Palsgrave to get rid of them went on the stage, where a Serene Highness saw her and fell in love with her, and married her. They say you wouldn't recognise her now, she has changed so; she lives somewhere in Germany and is as grey as a badger and as red as a lobster and bloated with beer.

But Eleanora, Countess of Merryone, is still to the fore. Merryone, who was old enough to be her grandfather, died of a fit of jealousy; then she turned Roman Catholic and went into a convent, but it sounds better in books than it is in practice, and she came out again in six months and married a Bishop within a year of Merryone's death, and buried him within another year. She has been a Primrose Dame and a Temperance lecturer and a Theosophist, and kept a stud at Newmarket, and edited a daily, and started for the North Pole but turned backat Iceland, and now she has married this boy. And she isn't a lunatic at large, but a woman who ought to have borne children, and had cares and anxieties.

Disguising Age

It makes me feel quite old, when I think of her and Mrs. Palsgrave, and see all the changes of the last eighteen years. But I won't think of time and the Burial Service yet awhile. I saw Valmond in Piccadilly to-day, and I believe I could catch him myself if I tried, for I haven't got a grey hair, at least Thérèse manages to hide them; and I haven't got a moustache, and my eyes haven't got wrinkles round the corners, and my neck hasn't begun to shrink. I am only thirty-five, Elizabeth, and a Society belle's star sets late.—Your dearest Mamma.

Letter XIX

CLARIDGE'S HOTEL, LONDON
16th September

DARLING ELIZABETH:

L'Affaire Colorado

WE met Sir Charles Bevon in Regent Street this morning. He had just arrived from the continent, and looked it, for he wore a Glengarry cap and a yellow and brown check travelling suit, and carried on his arm a hideous ulster-looking thing that had stripes all over it. He said he was going to the Café Royal to lunch, and asked us if we would join him, and, as we wanted to hear what had happened at Lucerne after we left, we accepted his invitation.

The Wertzelmanns' ball ended the season; when Sir Charles left a week after us the National was almost empty. The great sensation that followed the ball was what he called "l'affaire Colorado." You remember my mentioning the angelically beautiful creature stopping at Schloss Gessler? Well, it seems Count Fosca gave a breakfast-party at the Gütsch, and said in chaff that he believed Madame Colorado was the "*dame voilée*" of the Dreyfus Affair. This was repeated, and Madame Colorado, it seems, nearly died of mortification. Her brother was telegraphed for, and he came over at once from St. Moritz and challenged Count Fosca. He was a tiny little man, with red hair and a pale face, and looked as if Fosca's pistols would blow him to atoms. He asked Sir Charles and Mr. Vanduzen to be his *témoins*, but both of course refused. Mr. Vanduzen got positively funky, and said his Government would take away his pension, if he had anything to do with duelling. So Madame Colorado's brother asked the Marquis and the Vicomte, who jumped at the chance. I don't know whom Fosca asked. The duel excited no end of talk and scandal. The most awful things were said about Madame Colorado and Mr. Wertzelmann, and poor Madame Colorado, who had had such an unhappy marriage, and had thought of entering a convent, was simply picked to pieces. Every one made the *affaire* his or her own business, and the Duchesse de Vaudricourt declared that Madame Colorado had behaved so badly with a priest that the nuns wouldn't have her at any price. The upshot of it all was that, after the greatest publicity and scurrility, Count Fosca apologised, said his words had been entirely misquoted, that he had the greatest respect for Madame Colorado, and he took her brother and the *témoins* over to Berne in his automobile, and they all signed documents before the French Minister.

Sir Charles said that after that, Madame Colorado and her brother left Lucerne with Mrs. Wertzelmann, and Mr. Wertzelmann went to Berne to transact some diplomatic business. Sir Charles left himself immediately afterwards, and spent some days in Paris, where he met the Vicomte, who told him that Mrs. Isaacs had come back and broken off the engagement between Rosalie and Count Albert. As far as the Vicomte could ascertain she had been to Vienna to make enquiries about the Count, and found out to her horror that he had a wife and several children, and that he wasn't divorced. Mrs. Johnson gave the Count his *congé* and threatened him with all sorts of condign vengeance, but Sir Charles said Count Albert probably laughed, as no doubt it was not the first time he had tried the same little game.

Society at Lucerne

It was fun for a fortnight, but I am sure the society at Lucerne would have bored me if I had stopped much longer. Of course it hasn't got the backbone of ours at home, and all sorts of people mix in it, as you see, from millionaires to clerks. All that is asked of one is to be amusing, and, if you are an American, to spend your money.

Nobody knows anything really about anybody else, and, as everybody wants to be distracted, there are no scruples as to the means employed. I should not like to see Lucerne customs adopted in England, but after all one meets the same sort of people in London, and, to give the devil his due, I believe that the Hotel National set is no worse than Lord Valmond's or Mrs. Smith's.

Domestics

Sir Charles thinks we ought to try a winter at Rome. But I shall settle down quietly at Monk's Folly for some time to come. There is one thing I would willingly exchange with our Continental friends, and that is the domestics in our smart hotels. Here, in England, they give themselves the airs of royal servants, and condescend to wait on us inferior mortals; they make me feel positively uncomfortable with their impudent solemnity. I hear Blanche warning me from the next room not to miss the train, so good-bye till I get home.—Your dearest Mamma.

Letter XX

MONK'S FOLLY, 18th September

DARLING ELIZABETH:

At Home

HOME once more! I never knew how much I had missed it till I got back. I wonder how I ever left it, everything is so comfortable and refined. I feel quite clean again—I mean morally clean, and that's a sensation that we in our station and particular set get so seldom. I believe the return to an English home is a moral douche. I feel virtuous; I went to hear Mr. Frame preach in the morning and almost went again this evening. I half made up my mind to put aside Paquin and make a guy of myself, I felt so good; but a glimpse of Lady Beatrice in church this morning with a Taunton milliner's dream on her back, put me off, and as soon as I had taken a tiny blue pill and driven the hypochondria of Lucerne dissipation away, I shall be my old self again—the self you know, Elizabeth, all Paquin and Henry Arthur Jones.

Tipping

What an awful imposition tipping is. Servants won't look at small change now-a-days, and when I gave the boy who works the lift five shillings, his "Thank you" sounded just like "Damn you." Mrs. Chevington, who came over this afternoon, told me of an experience she had the last time she was in town, but I am sure I should never have had the courage to do what she did. She was only three days in some hotel in the West End; she had tipped the chamber-maid, the man in the lift, the *maître d'hôtel*, the waiter, and sent a half-sovereign in to the cook, and was waiting for a hansom, when up rushed a man she had never seen before to help her into it. He took off his hat and was very polite; hotel-porter was written all over him, and she supposed she ought to tip him, but said her gorge rose at it, as he had never done anything for her. However, she put a half-crown in his hat, and he never said "Thank you," which made her so savage that she took it back again. The result was that at Paddington the cabman thought she was stingy, and he was so abusive that she had to call a policeman, and compel the man to take the right fare.

But then Mrs. Chevington is masterful, and doesn't mind attracting a crowd and being insulted, while I should have fainted with mortification. I am sending you a cheque expressly for tips, for I know that in country houses they are even more grasping than in hotels. I wish Royalty would stop it, for I don't think any other means will ever avail.

Uneventful Things

Blanche came over to supper, and to spend the night, for she said she wanted to talk of the National and old times, and at home it was nothing but tennis, bicycles, and church. Things have been rather uneventful while we were away; we missed some races at Bath, to which the Parkers took a Pullman-full of people. Lady Beatrice gave a dance, and there was a Sunday-school feast at Braxome, when the boys pulled up all of Lady Beatrice's geraniums, and threw stones on the roof of the stables for the fun of hearing the horses plunge in the stalls, and, to Mr. Frame's terror, when Lady Beatrice scolded them, they made faces at her.

Monsieur Malorme

The Blaines have had to send away Monsieur Malorme; he made love to Daisy, and when she told him it was impertinent, he was so cut up that one of the footmen found him trying to hang himself with his handkerchief from a nail in the wall of his room, having first taken down a snow-storm that Mrs. Elaine had painted when she was twelve. But the only damage he succeeded in doing was to put his foot through the canvas, and pull down half the wall. The Blaines have since heard that he did a similar thing when coaching the Duke of FitzArthur. Since then, Daisy has received threatening letters in a female hand from Soho, giving her the choice between being summoned as a co-respondent, and paying ten guineas. Poor Mrs. Blaine has been awfully upset about it, and has put the matter in Mr. Rumple's hands.

I don't think there is any more gossip to tell you, save that Tom Carterville, who was at Eton with Charlie Carriston, and went out with the Yeomanry to South Africa, has come back. Lady Beatrice is so glad to have him home safe and sound that she intends to return thanks to the Almighty by entertaining a good deal.

Society Papers

Mrs. Chevington told me in the afternoon that she had read in one of the Society papers that the Smiths have taken a house in Park Lane, and that Mr. Wertz, the African millionaire you met at Nazeby, is engaged to marry Cushla O'Cork, the Irish agitatress. But then, you know, the Society papers will say anything to fill up their columns, and it must be so hard to find something new and true every week. I like your habit of always practising the *ingénue*, even in your letters to me, it helps you to act it the better. I hope you will meet Lord Valmond soon again, but of course you will, as he is sure to be visiting at the same houses. Write me all that happens, just as I write to you. There is nothing so nice as a letter full of what other people are doing.—Your dearest Mamma.

Letter XXI

MONK'S FOLLY, 29th October

DARLING ELIZABETH:

The Hockey Season

THE hockey season has begun here, and the game is played somewhere every day. Of course, I only go to look on, and can't imagine myself, in a short skirt and thick boots, rushing about a damp field. Yesterday the Blaines had a party, and I have been having twinges of neuralgia all day from it, for it was awfully wet and cold. Mrs. Blaine and I sat on an iron roller, till we were chilled to the bone. There was a fog so thick that nobody knew which side they belonged to, and Lady Beatrice, who really at her age ought to stop, got a blow on her forehead just above the nose. The play only stopped a minute for people to shout, "Dear Lady Beatrice, hope you are not hurt!" and Tom Carterville took advantage of the momentary distraction to sneak a goal. Mrs. Blaine took Lady Beatrice indoors, and, as Lady Beatrice described it to me, she filled a basin with blood. She showed me her ankles, and there wasn't a bit of white skin from the knees down, but she said hockey was great fun, and kept her in health. They always put her to keep goal, for she is so fat it is only one chance in a hundred that a ball will pass her.

Father Ribbit

Father Ribbit came to look on, and walked back to the house with me when the match was over. He said tea was the best part of hockey, and I agreed with him; he tried nearly everything on the tea-table, and talked with his mouth full of chocolate cake about the price of incense. I really can't understand how the Blaines go to his church, but Blanche says it is on account of her mother, who thinks Low Church schismatic. You should have seen Father Ribbit glare at Mr. Frame when he came into the room, looking in his hockey things as if he had been mending the roads. Father Ribbit wears a silk neckcloth with I.H.S. embroidered on it, and Blanche says he puts ashes on his head in Holy Week. Mrs. Dorking, who is a Roman Catholic, told me nothing made her laugh so much as a High Church Anglican; they were always doing odd things, which the Low Church people called "Popish Practices," but in reality nothing was more erroneous, and that she had heard that no two Ritualist priests did the same things. Mrs. Blaine had induced her once to go to Father Ribbit's, and assured her she wouldn't find any difference between her own service and his. Mrs. Dorking said she stuffed her handkerchief into her mouth to keep from shrieking, for Father Ribbit seemed to be making up rites as he went along, and didn't at all look or act like a real priest. Lady Beatrice, who happened to overhear us, and looks on Rome and Ritualism as the abomination of abomination, said she wished Henry the Eighth was alive, and that she would as soon think of inviting "that Ribbit to Braxome as a play-actor."

Tom Carterville is much improved since he went to South Africa. Before he went out he was only an overgrown boy, but the experience has made him quite manly. His mother is always telling people in his hearing what dangers he ran, and how brave he was. Like everybody else, she likes to play Aunt Sally with the poor War Office, but her grievance is that Tom hasn't been recommended for the V.C. Tom declares he never ran any danger at all, for he was never sent to the front, and never saw a Boer the whole time; and he didn't even get enteric, or kicked by a horse. But Lady Beatrice fairly beams, and says it's his modesty, and she wishes he had been shut up in Ladysmith, for she knows he would have found a way to raise the siege, and Tom looks quite foolish, and says, "Damn!"

A Maid's Audacity

One of the maids at Braxome dressed up in his khaki uniform the other day, and went into the kitchen, where she frightened the servants out of their wits at her audacity. It seems Lady Beatrice went to the servants' hall that day, a thing she has never been known to do before, and arrived there in time to hear the butler say to the maid:

"What would you do if Mr. Tom should catch you in his uniform?" To which the girl replied, suiting the action to her words, "I should salute him!"

Tom, who told me the story and put a *double entendre* in it, like a horrid boy, said it would be hard to say whether the servants were more horrified to see his mother, or his mother at the unheard-of fastness of the upper housemaid, who, he added, was a pretty little wench, and brought him his tea in the mornings before he got out of bed.

Troublesome Servants

I am almost inclined to make my peace with those bores who are always talking servants. Mine have been troubling me so much lately that I feel quite martyrised. I ordered the carriage to go to Taunton the other morning, and got myself ready, when, would you believe, that Perkins sent in to say that I couldn't go, as the roads were too heavy and the horses would slip! I sent for him and implored him to relent, and he finally let Alfred drive me in the dog-cart, and Alfred drove so fast, I thought I should be pitched out. I call it quite unkind of Perkins, and he has been with us ten years too. Then, again, the other morning Tom Carterville came to ask me if I could lend him any golf balls, and Thérèse told me afterwards that she found James peeping through the keyhole, and when she remonstrated, he threatened to blackmail me; now I know why Lord Froom got rid of him, and I have given him notice. But the worst of all, Elizabeth, is the new page. You know how hard it is to get one at all. Well, finally, in despair, I followed Mrs. Chevington's advice and sent to the workhouse in Bath for a boy. They sent me such a pretty little fellow, about twelve years old. I had him measured for his livery, and he looked such a dear in it, and was picking up his duties so quickly, but I have had to send him back to Bath to his workhouse. The kitchen cat had kittens, and cook, very foolishly, gave them to the boy, and told him to get rid of them. Some little while later, I heard a horrid miaouing on the lawn, and went to the window to see what it was. I found the new page digging a hole in the geranium beds, and something sputtering about in the earth. Fancy, Elizabeth, he was burying the poor little kittens *alive*, the little monster! Of course I couldn't keep him after that, could I?

So you see, darling, even if you are a pretty and rich widow, and only live for Paquin and a good time, you still have your troubles. Lady Beatrice says the question of servants is more troublesome than Home Rule, and I agree with her.

Give my love to Lady Theodosia, but don't tell her that I am glad she doesn't live in this part of the country.—Your dearest Mamma.

Letter XXII

MONK'S FOLLY, 31st October

DARLING ELIZABETH:

Tom Carterville Calls

TOM CARTERVILLE came again this morning to ask if I would lend him Jerry to ride to Wellington, as the equestrian cook has lamed the three saddle-horses at Braxome. I sent to ask Perkins for permission, and after I got it, Tom didn't seem in a hurry to go, and stopped so long that I had to ask him to lunch, and then he waited till tea. He is an amusing boy, but I wish he didn't look so much like his mother. When he is a little older he is going to be enormous. You know he was at Eton with Charlie Carriston, and declares there wasn't a greater sneak in the school.

Daintree Affair

I told him about Cora de la Haye and the diamond necklace, and Tom says she is just the sort of woman to make trouble, and that Lady Carriston had better put on her life-preserver, for there is going to be a storm of Charlie's brewing. He told me all about the Daintree affair; he called Daintree a rotter, and says he will never marry the girl.

You know Lady Daintree went to the War Office herself, and refused to leave till they promised to order Daintree out to South Africa at once. The girl is suing for breach of promise,—ten thousand pounds damages,—Tom says that the Daintree barony will never stand it, for it hasn't recovered from the late lord's plunging on the turf. He says that Connie Metcalfe is good enough for Daintree, who is an awful mug, and that a Gaiety girl would make as good a ladyship as a *coryphée* at the Empire. It seems to me that Lady Daintree is herself to blame for it all; if she had used tact with her son and brought him up sensibly, she wouldn't have to eat her pride now.

I asked Tom if he intended to follow the fashion and marry in the theatrical world, and have Lady Beatrice begging the War Office to send him to the Front, so that he might die sooner than disgrace her. He looked at me with a queer expression and said he preferred to follow the other fashion now in vogue, and marry a beauty twice his age. I told him I believed he was thinking of Miss Tancred of Exeter, the temperance lecturer, who read "L'Assommoir" to the Braxome tenantry last week, and who wears short hair, green goggles and a bicycle skirt, and is fifty, if she is a day. Tom laughed, and said I had hit the right nail on the head. A jolly youngster, and might do for you, Elizabeth, if Valmond turns sour. He will have Braxome and twenty thousand a year when Lady Beatrice dies.

Dinner at Astley Court

To-night I dined at Astley Court; the Parkers have a large house-party. Miss Parker is to marry Clandevil in ten days, the invitations have been out some time; it is to be a very grand affair. Both she and the Duke appear bored with one another already, and Mr. Parker has been heard to say to a compatriot that his daughter had made him promise her a title, and that he had bought her an English duke; it was a bit off colour, but good at the price.

An Odious Man

I went in to dinner with an odious man, a Mr. Sweetson; he is Mr. Parker's partner in America, and was so patronising. He wore a button with the American flag on it, just like Mr. Wertzelmann the night of the ball at Schloss Gessler, and underneath it there was another one of white enamel with "Let her go, Gallagher," in black letters on it. I wonder what it could have meant; I would have asked him, but I thought it might seem rude. The people at Croixmare couldn't have eaten worse than Mr. Sweetson; he put his napkin in his collar, and it was well he did, for he spilled his soup all over it, and he sucked his teeth when he had finished. I asked him what he thought of England, and he replied that he preferred to spend his money in his own country, and couldn't see how a man like Mr. Parker, who had the brains to make the big fortune he had, could settle down in one of the effete countries of the Old World. And he added if he had his way he would put the Monroe Doctrine into force and drive Europe altogether out of America. He became quite *farouche*, and I am sure he is an Irish-American, for they say they hate us more than the other Americans. Algy Chevington told me that Mr. Sweetson is a Tammany Tiger, whatever that is; at any rate it isn't anything nice, and I am sure Mr. Parker had better put him to eat in the servants' hall hereafter. He is some relation to Mrs. Parker, for he called her Cousin Petunia; Clandevil looked as if he could have strangled him, and Algy says Mr. Parker must have put down millions in hard cash, or Clandevil would never go through with the marriage.

Mr. Sweetson stepped on Lady Beatrice's yellow brocade after dinner, and ripped out fully a yard of stitches. You should have seen the glance she gave him; it was more terrible than the one she bestowed on Mr. Frame the day he was unlucky enough to beat her at tennis. Mr. Sweetson was awfully embarrassed; if it had been anyone less objectionable, I should have felt sorry for him. He only made matters worse by asking her what it cost, for he would send her ladyship a dress the following day at double the price. Lady Beatrice put up her *pince-nez*, and stared at him without uttering a word; then she sailed across the room and sat down beside Mrs. Chevington. "Cousin Petunia" told Mr. Sweetson that if he wanted to smoke, he would find the gentlemen in the billiard-room. He took the hint.

Mrs. Dot

Tom Carterville came and sat down next to me, and made me nearly choke with the funny things he said about the Parkers, and he believes his mother will drop them. There is such a garrulous old lady stopping at Astley, Mrs. Dot; Tom took her in to supper. She came across the room and joined us. She began to talk about the nobility, and told us she considered she belonged to it, for though she was an American, she could trace her ancestry back to the Scottish Chiefs, and she asked Tom what he thought it would cost to have Burke put her in the peerage among the collateral branches. Then she told us she was descended also from Admiral Coligny. Poor dear Coligny, she called him, and she certainly would have been a Roman Catholic, if it hadn't been for Coligny. Tom asked her quite innocently if she had left Coligny in America, and when he intended to come over. "When he comes to Astley, Mrs. Dot," he said, "be sure you let me know, I'll give him a run with the West Somerset Harriers."

"He's *dead*! Mr. Carterville," she fairly shrieked.

"Oh, I beg your pardon," he said. "I thought from the way you spoke that he was in New York or Chicago, making money like all nice Americans."

"Oh, is it possible, Mr. Carterville," she went on, "that you have never heard of Coligny, poor dear Coligny, who was killed in the St. Bartholomew Massacre!"

"With all due respect to your relation," Tom said, "I never heard of the sad catastrophe; I don't read any but the sporting papers. I suppose the what-do-you-call-it massacre was in one of your little wars on the frontier. I hope they didn't get his scalp, Mrs. Dot."

Miss Parker, who was sitting quite near and heard every word, turned round and said, "Don't you see they are making fun of you, Aunt?" Mrs. Dot turned very red and simpered, and Tom and I felt as if we were looking for the North Pole.

I do call it unkind for people to make you feel uncomfortable in their houses. These Parkers are not at all like the Wertzelmanns and the other Americans I met at Lucerne. And I am sure if Lady Beatrice does call on them, that Lady Archibald Fairoaks and the Marchioness of Runymede, who are the nicest kind of Americans, wouldn't. Good-night, darling, I shall expect to hear from you to-morrow.—Your dearest Mamma.

Novel-reading Servants

P. S.—When I got back from Astley to-night, I had the greatest difficulty to get into the house. No one answered the bell, and finally Perkins, who has a key to the kitchen, let me in that way. I went into the dining-room and rang and called; still no one came. I then went upstairs and found Thérèse, the two maids, the cook, and the new page, sitting round a blazing wood fire in my bed-room, and cook was reading "The Master Christian" to them aloud!

I cried from pure vexation, for one can't send all one's servants away at the same time. I am sure I can't see why the lower classes should have novelists, but they have everything just like us now-a-days. And when I was in town last month, at Claridge's, the Duchess of Rougemont told me she didn't know what the world was coming to, for her maid belonged to a Corelli Society, and she had actually sat next her own footman at a Paderewski Recital the last time the pianist was in London.

Letter XXIII

MONK'S FOLLY, 2nd November

DARLING ELIZABETH:

Theatricals

THE Blaines had some theatricals yesterday in St. Leo's school-house, to raise money to give Father Ribbit a host. In spite of the weather being horrid I went. They acted "My Lord in Livery," and a manager came down from a West End theatre to stage it. They only cleared two guineas when all expenses were paid, which of course won't buy a host, though Mrs. Blaine suggested they might find a second-hand one cheap in an old curiosity shop. I thought the acting was atrocious, but they were all mightily pleased with themselves, and are now thinking of playing "The Second Mrs. Tanqueray," and renting the Taunton theatre. But that is always the way with amateurs.

Church and Theatricals

Lady Beatrice is getting up tableaux at Braxome in opposition, and Mr. Frame came to-day to ask me to help. Tom brought me a nice note from his mother, imploring me to say Yes, and I have consented, and there is to be a lunch at Braxome to-morrow to decide on what we shall do. Lady Beatrice says she feels it her duty to use all her influence with the Bishop to have Father Ribbit tried by the Ecclesiastical Court. There is every sign of a church war, for Mrs. Blaine declares she will write to her uncle, who is in the Cabinet, to back up Father Ribbit. And it's nothing but church and theatricals; as you know down here in the country it is always church and something else. I shall do all I can to fan the fire, and Tom has promised to help me, for we are so terribly dull, anything will serve to wake us up a bit.

The De Mantons

I have called on the Vane-Corduroys, who have leased Shotover Park from the De Mantons. Poor Lady de Manton cried when she left it, and is living in a boarding-house on the Parade at Weston-super-mare; old Lord de Manton has gone up to London, where he thinks he can get a Chairmanship of a City Company for the sake of his name. The Honourable Agatha has gone out to South Africa on a hospital ship, and her brother, the Honourable de

Montgomery de Manton, whom, you remember, we met once on the Promenade at Cannes, and I wouldn't let you bow to him because he was walking with such an impossible woman, has joined the Imperial Yeomanry as a trooper. The family seems quite broken up; it is rather a pity, as they had been at Shotover since the Conquest. Mrs. Blaine says it is all due to Kaffirs; that Lord de Manton would set up as a stockbroker, and you know what a mess he got the lunatic asylum accounts into the year he was treasurer. But, as Mrs. Blaine says, he will probably be back at Shotover within a year, for he is just the sort of man they like to get on directorates in London, and that is such a paying profession now-a-days. He told Lady Beatrice that if worse became worst with him he knew the Colonial Office would give him an island to govern. He didn't seem very depressed when he left, but Lady de Manton was completely *bouleversée*. Tom told me that she had written to his mother to say that Weston-super-mare was intolerable; they gave her Brussels sprouts and boiled beef six days running; she wanted Lady Beatrice to help her get the post of stewardess on one of the new West Indian line steamers to Jamaica; she makes a point of the fact that she was never sick when crossing the Channel. She seems willing to do anything till poor Lord de Manton "arrives."

The Vane-Corduroys

How I digress! I started to tell you of the Vane-Corduroys, and I shunted off to the De Mantons; you will think me as garrulous as an old maid.

I don't know how the Vane-Corduroys got their money, but I think it was out of "Sparklets," though Tom says he is sure he has seen "Corduroy's Lung Tonic" on the signboards at the Underground stations. Lady Beatrice, who takes up every new person out of sheer curiosity, called, and of course everybody else had to. But Lady Beatrice, who always has a reason for everything she does, said that she did it for Lady de Manton's sake, who had told her that if the Vane-Corduroys were properly *rangé*, it would help Lord de Manton in the City. Mr. Vane-Corduroy is the very type of a company-promoter; you know what I mean—they are always paunchy, and wear frock-coats, and top-hats, and have a President-of-a-Republic air. Mrs. Vane-Corduroy has dyed hair, the colour of tawny port, and she dresses like the ready-made models at Peter Robinson's. She looks exactly like a doll, and all the time I was talking to her, I felt that if I pinched her waist, she would say "Made in England." I am sure you wind her up with a key. They have completely changed the drawing-room at Shotover—you remember what a splendid air there was about it, with the old, worm-eaten Flemish tapestry, and the oak panelling—well, they have had the upholsterers down from Maple's, and it is now spick-and-span Louis Quinze; there are foot-stools in front of all the chairs, and the De Manton ancestors have all got new gilt frames. They have two children, a boy and a girl. The girl is about twelve, and has a French governess, a strange-looking woman, something like Louise Michel, with a moustache. Mrs. Vane-Corduroy told me she had the highest references, and that she had come to them from a Russian Grand-Duke's family. The boy is at Eton.

I asked them how they thought they would like Somersetshire. Mrs. Vane-Corduroy said she missed town—there was no Church Parade, no Prince's, no Bond Street, and no dear little Dog Cemetery, like the one in the Park. She thought the latter was such a peaceful spot, and she felt quite happy to think that Fido would rest there till the Resurrection, under his little Carrara marble cross. It was evidently a very depressing subject, and Mr. Vane-Corduroy hastened to change it by saying that his wife found the country a bit lonely just at first, but people had been very kind in calling on them, and that he was sure they would like it immensely, as he intended to fill the house with people from town, and that they should always spend the season at their house in Grosvenor Square, and part of the winter at Nice; and when they were not visiting, they would either be yachting, or at their shooting-box in the highlands. In fact, he gave me to understand that they would probably never be more than a couple of months in the year at Shotover.

They have taken seats at Father Ribbit's, and they have subscribed most liberally to all the local charities. I must say I think it rather an imposition, for they hadn't been in the county a week, before they were inundated with appeals for money; but, as Lady Beatrice says, that if such people will mix in our set, they must pay for it, and besides, their names and the sums they give are published in the Taunton papers, so that it is not as if they were not getting any return for their money.

A Eulogy

I suppose it does pay in the end, for the Rector of St. William's preached a regular eulogy on Mr. Parker last Sunday, who is restoring the whole church, for he found some old dilapidated tablets in it with "Parker" on them, and he is sure they are his ancestors. He had a letter of thanks from the Bishop about it, and the *Times* devoted a column to it; said it was such things that drew America and England together, and that Mr. Parker's love of architecture was only equalled by his knowledge of it, and that St. William's restored would be an everlasting monument, in Early English Gothic, to his memory. And I don't believe Mr. Parker knows a gargoyle from a reredos.

I must stop now, darling, for Mrs. Chevington has just called, and I must go down and see her. I shall expect to hear from you to-morrow.—Your dearest Mamma.

Letter XXIV

MONK'S FOLLY, 4th November

DARLING ELIZABETH:

A Frightful Thing

SUCH a frightful thing happened yesterday. The Vane-Corduroys came to return my call in their motor-car, and it blew up at the front door. One of the wheels fell into the conservatory, and the groom was picked up insensible on the lawn. He had to be brought into the house, where he has been ever since, and is likely to be for some days, for Dr. Smart says if he is moved in his present state he will die. Fortunately for the Vane-Corduroys they had just entered the house, or they might have been killed. You never heard such a noise; it sounded like a cannonade, and Perkins says it will cost me at least one hundred pounds to repair the damage. The Vane-Corduroys apologised profusely, and looked as if they wished they had been blown up along with the groom to hide their confusion. Perkins and the gardener have been picking up bits of motor-car all over the grounds to-day. I had to send the Vane-Corduroys back to Shotover in the victoria.

Rehearsal of Tableaux

We had a rehearsal of the tableaux at Braxome in the evening. Lady Beatrice looked absurd as Britannia; she posed herself after the tail of a penny; Mr. Parker as Uncle Sam, and Mr. Vane-Corduroy as John Bull, shaking hands, were quite good, but Mr. Frame, who was working the red, white, and blue light, set fire to himself, and might have been burned to death, but for his presence of mind. He put himself out by wrapping himself in Lady Beatrice's Gobelin tapestry, which she had specially made in Paris last year. You should have seen Lady Beatrice's face, and she called him "Frame," as she always does when she is angry with him, and she told him he might have waited till they brought some water to throw over him. Mrs. Vane-Corduroy, as Lady Macbeth going to murder Duncan, would have been effective, if she hadn't laughed in the middle of it. Everybody said that Tom and I in "The Black Brunswicker's Farewell" were the best, but Tom squeezed me so, I could hardly breathe, and when the curtain dropped he said we must do it over again for an encore.

We think the tableaux will be a great success, for all the tickets on sale at Mr. Dill's, the chemist, have been sold, and he wrote to ask Lady Beatrice if he could have some more printed. Mrs. Parker told Lady Beatrice it was awfully good of her to give her drawing-room over to the "peasantry," as she calls the Taunton people.

An Excellent Chef

To-day the Vane-Corduroys had a lunch-party. They have an excellent *chef.* Mr. Vane-Corduroy said he was five years with the Duchess of Rougemont, and only left because the Duchess refused to pay for the tuning of his piano. I think the Vane-Corduroys are afraid of him. Thérèse tells me that he has a room fitted up as a studio at Shotover, and that he exhibits every year at the Salon, and only cooks from the love of it. He has his meals in his own apartments. Mrs. Vane-Corduroy showed me several photographs of Fido, and one of his grave in the Dog Cemetery; he was run over by a 'bus in the Bayswater road; and Mrs. Vane-Corduroy shed tears when she told me of it, and she said she went into mourning for him for three months, and a Royal Academician is at present at work on his portrait from one of the photographs. She intends to have it hung in the Academy next year, and when I suggested that sometimes the best pictures of the best artists were rejected, she said that Mr. Vane-Corduroy had seen about it already, for he had put the Duke of Rougemont on to something good in the City, and the Duke had promised that he would see the picture was hung, and not skied either.

Two Visitors

Two women are visiting at Shotover, friends of Mrs. Vane-Corduroy. They look as if they were made at Marshall & Snelgrove; they wore pearl necklaces over their tailor-made walking suits, and long gold chains with uncut sapphires, and their fingers are covered in rings. I forget what Mrs. Vane-Corduroy called them, but she said they were old friends of hers, and such clever girls. It seems they were left rather poorly off, and to gain a living began by giving dancing lessons to some people in Maida Vale. They succeeded so well that they now have an "Academy" in Mayfair, and go about the country as well, giving private instruction; their brother had a gymnasium in Brighton, but got the war fever at Ladysmith time, and went out to the front in Paget's Horse, and the sisters are now running the gymnasium—a School for Physical Culture, Mrs. Vane-Corduroy called it. She says that is why they know so many people we do, Elizabeth, for they spoke of Lord Valmond, and Mr. Wertz, and the Smiths, and the Duke of Clandevil, as if they were on quite intimate terms with them. I have no doubt it is very creditable of them to earn their living, but it seems strange to meet them in Society. Really everything is changing now-a-days. I am thinking of telling Lady Beatrice and suggesting to her that they should do Indian clubs or cannon balls after the tableaux, and it would be quite easy to get out a man from Taunton to put up a trapeze in the drawing-room at Braxome.—With love from your dearest Mamma.

Letter XXV

MONK'S FOLLY, 6th November

DARLING ELIZABETH:

The Tableaux

THE tableaux were a great success, and Lady Beatrice gave the Taunton people sandwiches and ginger-beer afterwards in the dining-room. Only one of her Sèvres dishes was broken, and Mr. Frame dropped a Bohemian goblet that was made in 1530, and had belonged to Wallenstein. He was so frightened that he didn't dare tell Lady Beatrice, and she believes one of the footmen did it.

The Baron

We had a champagne supper when everybody had gone; it was awfully good, and the Vane-Corduroys' *chef* did the devilled oysters *à la reine de Serbie.* Mr. Sweetson has gone back to London, so fortunately I didn't have my appetite taken away. He is giving a big dinner at the Carlton to the Copper Trust Directors in honour of a *coup* he made on the Stock Exchange by wire. I don't exactly understand what it is, but I believe he bought all the copper in the world, and that the value of the common or garden penny will go up. Mrs. Dot came, and after what happened the other night at Astley, I was particularly civil to her. She was quite good-natured, and took the olive branch. She asked me if I could recommend a dentist in Taunton; it seems that when she goes to bed she always puts her false teeth in a glass of water, and one of the maids threw them away in the slops by mistake. Fortunately she keeps two sets, upper and lower, but the spare plate was made in a great hurry and bruises her gums. I told her Fellowes in Taunton advertised to make a set while you wait, but I didn't know how long he made you wait, and she is going to him to-day. She told me a story about a Baron Finck von Finckelstein whom she met in America, quite by chance, in a restaurant where he was a waiter. The Baron has a ruin on the Rhine, and the family had become so impoverished that he decided to go to America, where he landed literally in his shirt-sleeves, and on account of his elegant manners, Mrs. Dot said, he of course got a situation as waiter in a restaurant; and the proprietor made an awfully good thing out of him, for he got one of the New York Sunday papers to devote a column to the Baron and the restaurant. It was a capital advertisement; the article was illustrated, and there were cuts of Schloss Finckelstein, the ruin on the Rhine, of the Baron as he landed in New York, of the Baron waiting in the restaurant, and of the proprietor. Mrs. Dot said that there was such a rush for tables that one had to go awfully early to get one, and that the Baron must have made quite a good thing out of it, for nobody would have dared give him less than a dollar tip. As the Baron couldn't wait on everybody, the proprietor had *édition de luxe* menus printed with the Finckelstein twenty-four quarterings on them which you could take away as souvenirs. And Tom Carterville, who was sitting next to me, said he knew the De Mantons had made a mistake in not going to America. Mrs. Dot quite jumped at the idea; she knew the family would do well, and that they would very likely get an engagement all together to travel about the country with Barnum's. She was sure that a whole family of Norman Conquest aristocrats would draw just like the Baby Venus or the Missing Link. Tom looked sheepish, and I believe Mrs. Dot is not as simple as she seems, and was getting at him.

A Subscription Ball

There is a subscription ball at the Carterville Arms in Taunton to-night. The tickets are four shillings. Lady Beatrice is the patroness, and the money will be given to the Soldiers' Widows' and Orphans' Fund. Of course everybody will go, and Paquin sent me such a dream of a frock this morning. I wish you could meet me in town next week for the Clandevil-Parker wedding, but of course if Lord Valmond is in your neighbourhood it would be folly for you to leave. I have written to Octavia to bring him to the scratch. She is so clever and such a dear, and knows how to help you just as if I myself were with you. I am expecting daily to hear you have caught him. Best of luck from—Your dearest Mamma.

An Accident

P. S. 6.30 P.M.—Mrs. Chevington came to tea this afternoon and brought the news that Mr. Vane-Corduroy was rabbit shooting this morning and blew off two of his fingers. It seems his man gave him ball cartridge by mistake, and the bullet hit Lady Beatrice's horse as she was driving past the field in which Mr. Vane-Corduroy was shooting at the time of the accident. Poor Lady Beatrice was frightened out of her wits, and Mr. Vane-Corduroy, who saw her passing and heard her scream, thought he had killed her. Mrs. Chevington says she thinks the Vane-Corduroys were more worried over killing Lady Beatrice's horse than over Mr. Vane-Corduroy's missing fingers. Mrs. Vane-Corduroy at once despatched a note to Braxome, full of the profoundest apologies, and saying they had taken the liberty of wiring instantly to Tattersall's to send down a horse to replace the one Mr. Vane-Corduroy was so unfortunate as to kill. Mrs. Chevington was at Braxome when the letter arrived. She says Tom told his mother that she should accept the new horse, as it would be undoubtedly superior to the old crock that jogged her about the country, and he thought that before Cockney millionaires turned country gentlemen they ought to take lessons at a shooting gallery.

The Ball

P. S. S. 2.30 A.M.—I have just got home from the ball at the Carterville Arms, and as I find your letter has not been posted, and I am not very sleepy, I will add a postscript to it before going to sleep.

The ball was a financial success, and the Mayor told Lady Beatrice her patronage was invaluable. He took her in to supper, and in his speech he spoke of nothing but her ladyship's virtues. As Tom said, he made you feel that the ball had been given expressly for her benefit, and not at all for the Soldiers' Widows and Orphans. Of course, the Vane-Corduroys were not present, and there was an alarming rumour at one time that Mr. Vane-Corduroy was bleeding to death. Everybody came up to Lady Beatrice, and congratulated her on her narrow escape. In fact, at supper the Mayor quite drew tears to the Taunton people's eyes when he referred to it. Lady Beatrice tried to look unconcerned, as if she deprecated the Mayor's fine compliments, but when in a faltering voice he declared how the whole countryside would miss "good, honest, steady old Jock, who had for so many years drawn her ladyship about on her errands of mercy," Lady Beatrice burst into tears, and the Mayor became so affected at the havoc he had wrought, that he wished "the bullet of the London mushroom" (poor Mr. Vane-Corduroy bleeding to death at Shotover!) had lodged in his own magisterial breast. Mr. Parker whispered to me that the Veuve Clicquot was sweeter than usual.

Tom Proposes

There was a daïs at one end of the ball-room, and here Lady Beatrice received the "canïle" as Mr. Parker expressed it. She wore purple velvet and amethysts, and looked perfectly monstrous, and the room was so hot that beads of perspiration formed on her temples, and made little lanes in the rouge on her cheeks. Nevertheless, in spite of her appearance, Lady Beatrice can be quite *grande dame* when she wishes, and she did the honours of the evening in the most dignified way. And I suppose if you are a duke's daughter, and have such a place as Braxome Towers and twenty thousand a year, you can afford to look like a scarecrow. The floors were awfully good, and all my partners danced well. But, would you believe it, that silly boy, Tom Carterville, actually proposed to me, and was quite serious about it too! We were sitting in a sort of ante-room by ourselves, and Tom, who is anything but shy, suddenly became as awkward and bashful as a school-girl, and blurted out how madly he loved me, and had ever since he saw me at Braxome the day he got back from South Africa. He looked just like his mother, and I could hardly keep from laughing, and tried to turn all he said into a joke. Then he got quite hot and perspiry and breathed hard, and he begged me to accept him; he had never loved any one as he did me, and he didn't ever think of or mind the difference in our ages. He acted just like they do in Miss Braddon, and accused me of having given him every encouragement, and wondered how God could make a woman so fair and so false. He took me by the hands and looked into my eyes, then dropped them and groaned, and wished they'd sent him to the Front in South Africa. I knew he meant all he said too, because he was so earnest, and I could have half pitied him if he hadn't looked so much like Lady Beatrice. He made me feel so uncomfortable, for I thought someone would come into the room every minute, and I begged him to take me back to the ball-room and not be a silly boy. He laughed such a queer laugh; it had a sort of sob in it, and he said quite fiercely that I didn't know how I had wounded him, but that he loved me all the same, and that if he remained in Somersetshire and was near me all the time, the wound would never heal; and he intends to go out to South Africa at once, and is going up to London to-morrow, for he wanted plenty of action and excitement and danger to help him pull himself together again.

Tom Rejected

I begged him on no account, if he loved me, to tell his mother, for she would never speak to me again. He said, did I really have such a poor opinion of him, and it hurt him cruelly, for he was a gentleman and a man of honour. I told him he could kiss me just once, if he liked, for he was so very much in earnest, and that we should part friends. But he wouldn't, for he said the memory of it would haunt him.

When we got back to the ball-room people stared at us awfully hard, and I heard that odious Mrs. Fordythe tell someone, "He is too good for that frivolous little Paquin doll." I am sure she meant me. I do wish boys wouldn't fall in love with one, for they are so serious and earnest and masterful, and make one feel as if one had really done them an injury. I whispered to Tom before he left me, right in the midst of a horrid lot of frumpy chaperones, that I hoped he would come back safe from South Africa, and he said I was rubbing it in, and he hoped the first bullet would strike home. I really thought someone would hear, he spoke so loud. And there is no telling, Elizabeth, if Tom had been older and not so much like his mother, I might have taken him, for Braxome and twenty thousand a year are not to be found at one's feet every day. But, as it is, it is quite out of the question, and I charge you not to mention a word of this to anyone, for it would be sure to get back here, and people say such nasty things. Good-night.—Your dearest Mamma.

Letter XXVI

MONK'S FOLLY, 8th November

DARLING ELIZABETH:

Typhoid Fever

MRS. BLAINE and six others of Father Ribbit's flock are down with typhoid fever. Dr. Smart and the sanitary inspector have traced it to the Communion wine at St. Leo's. The London papers have got hold of the story, and yesterday's *Daily Sensation* had an article on it headed "Bacteria in the Chalice," "Typhoid in a Cup of Holy Wine." Mr. Parker says it beats anything he ever read in an American paper, and thinks we have nothing more to learn in that line from Yankee journalism. Naturally it has been a nasty knock for the Ritualists, and will frighten people away from the sacrament at St. Leo's. Father Ribbit wrote to the Taunton papers to-day about it, and said that he will henceforth advocate the "separate vessel" system, which he understands is in vogue in America, and he is soliciting subscriptions for fifty chalices.

At Mr. Frame's, Lady Beatrice, to whom the cup is always passed first, set the fashion of wiping the rim with her handkerchief, which precaution has, till the present, been efficacious. The Chevingtons, the Blaines, and the best families who go to St. Leo's, are going to provide their own communion cups, but, as Mr. Parker said, it will be interesting to note the strength of Father Ribbit's head, for he has to drink all the wine that is left over that not a drop may be wasted, as of course it is sacred. Altogether, the typhoid at St. Leo's has opened some curious speculation, and has for the moment put all other topics out of consideration.

Mr. Vane-Corduroy has been pronounced out of danger; his mangled fingers have been successfully amputated. He will not be able to go up to town to-morrow to the wedding of Miss Parker, but the doctor says he must go to the Riviera for a change as soon as possible, as the shock to his system has been a great one. So after this week Shotover will be shut up.

Tom Enlists

Tom Carterville left for London the day after the ball, as he said, and Lady Beatrice was in consternation on getting a telegram from him saying he would sail for the Cape in the new draft of Yeomanry in a week's time. As I feel that I am in a measure responsible for the grief at Braxome and Tom's exile, I wrote him a nice little note to-day, and enclosed a bunch of forget-me-nots and my photo.

I hardly see anything of Blanche now-a-days; since she and Daisy have taken up theatricals so seriously they have no time for dropping in for tea as they used. Of course, now that Mrs. Blaine is ill, they will be busier than ever, though Mrs. Chevington, who was here this morning, says that they are both still at work rehearsing the "Second Mrs. Tanqueray." Daisy's head seems quite turned by the praise she got in that non-professional drawing-room thing, "My Lord in Livery." She told Mrs. Chevington she always knew she had acting in her, and she wants to go up to London and go on the stage. But that is always the way with amateurs. They begin with one of these pieces peculiar to Church entertainments that one never sees, save in country school-rooms, and they immediately afterwards try Sheridan or Pinero. One hardly knows which is duller to watch.

A Droll Performance

And talking of plays reminds me that I was particularly asked by Lady Beatrice to go to the Taunton Orphan Asylum this afternoon and see the children do "The Merchant of Venice." It was the drollest performance I ever remember attending. When I got there I found two long files, one of boys, the other of girls, waiting in a corridor outside of the hall. A caretaker, with a nose like Job Trotter's, was keeping the "sexes separated," and the children, who were anywhere from five years of age up to ten, were jabbering like a lot of rooks. I instinctively wondered what would happen if Mr. Trotter's authority was withdrawn for a few minutes. While I waited for the door of the hall to be opened, Lady Beatrice and the matron arrived, and Lady Beatrice, who wore a sort of short bicycle skirt, and a felt hat with a pheasant's feather in it, and looked as if she ought to have carried a bunch of edelweiss and an alpenstock with a chamois-horn handle, exclaimed, in her voice which is always down in her boots:—

"Ah, my little dears! Each good little boy and girl is going to be given an apple and a bun, and each bad little boy and girl will get a slice of bread without any butter. Now I hope you will all be good little boys and girls."

"Yes, please, ladyship," they all piped in unison, and the matron let us all into the hall.

I don't know whether it was droller to watch the brats murder Shakespeare, or the marked interest taken in the performance by Lady Beatrice, the matron, and some of the patronesses. Shylock was too absurd; he was about ten and wore a funny little goatee. He nor any of the others understood a word of what they were saying; they had learnt it by heart like the alphabet, and recited it in shrill sing-song. When Master Shylock called for the scales, they brought him a pair such as you see in doll's houses, and when he sharpened his little knife, Lady Beatrice's "little dears" stood up in their seats with excitement and squeaked like a lot of guinea-pigs. But even more comical than the children mouthing Shakespeare was the fact of the stage-manager of a London theatre, that Lady Beatrice has had down once a week for the last two months to coach the little actors, coming before the curtain and making a speech, in which he told a lie that was so big I should have thought he would have been afraid he would be struck down like Ananias. He had the cheek to tell us that the Shylock with the goatee and the doll's scales was an undeveloped Roscius—and Lady Beatrice and the matron believed him.

The matron told me that Shakespeare was such a refining influence and that the children were so much improved by his plays, and she was quite horrified when I replied I thought a pantomime would do them more good. After the performance the "little dears" sat down at long tables and devoured apples and buns, and squeaked like guinea-pigs.

Lady Beatrice said it was a huge success, and that they would try, "As You Like It," next year. When Mr. Parker said that Britons as a race had no sense of humour Lady Beatrice should have told him to go with me to see her "little dears" interpret Shakespeare. I am sure he would have changed his mind.—Your dearest Mamma.

Letter XXVII

MONK'S FOLLY, 11th November

DARLING ELIZABETH:

The Doraines

AM so glad to hear Valmond has turned up at Chevenix Castle. You have it all your own way now. I hear it was the Doraines who gave the Vane-Corduroys their first start last year. It seems the Doraines were in awfully low water and at their wit's ends what to do. Mrs. Chevington says they had almost decided to go to Boulogne when Lord Doraine met Sir Dennis O'Desmond and advised them to go to Bayswater, for he said that three months there had pulled him straight. It seems you take a house in a terrace, go to the nearest church, and buy groceries and meat in the neighbourhood, and everybody calls. That's the way the Doraines found the Vane-Corduroys. Mrs. Vane-Corduroy was presented by Lady Doraine; it cost an enormous sum, and Lord Doraine told Algy Chevington he was making quite a tidy income in Bayswater terraces. I should think Lord de Manton might follow his example, but I suppose he is too old for Society. Lady de Manton has gone up to London to him. She is not going as stewardess to Jamaica: Lord de Manton has got "put on" to something, it's to do with a Government Contract; and is very secret and mysterious. They have taken a maisonette in Chelsea, and I am so glad for poor Lady de Manton, for they treated her quite like one of themselves at her boarding-house at Weston-super-mare.

Society Beauties

Your account of the ball was amusing; Octavia looked after you, as I knew she would, and managed to play Valmond very cleverly for you. She wrote me herself to say he was so firmly hooked that he would be landed now without any difficulty. I can't help smiling at your being surprised to find that the Society beauties that the papers rave about are *quite, quite old,* and not really beautiful at all. Did you think that "age could not wither them, nor custom stale their infinite variety"? Nor was I at all surprised to hear that they flirted with boys; they always do at their age; it's their chief amusement to pick out the nicest and handsomest boys and make men of the world of them. Dolly Tenderdown may only look fifteen and behave "grown-up," but, depend on it, he knows as much of life as Lord Valmond. Those pretty youngsters have a very quick intelligence, and between the mess-room and the ball-room there is not much that they have not learnt. Immaculate to look at, my experience of them is that they are anything but clean. Tom Carterville belonged to another genus. The Dolly Tenderdown kind only grows when you fertilise the soil, but your Tom Cartervilles grow wild in any soil and in all seasons.

Boys in Society

I wish boys could be kept out of Society till they are really grown-up, they are such a nuisance. They never know how to preserve their equilibrium, for they are either intense, and make martyrs of themselves like Stefano and Tom, or horrid, fast, impertinent creatures like Dolly. And there are so many boys in Society now-a-days.

The whole Parker family are at Claridge's, and the Pullman is to take the Taunton guests up to town to-morrow. I shall stop at the Carlton, and remain in London for a few nights, and it is so much gayer there than at the Buckingham Palace *dépendances*. It is an awful time of the year for a wedding, but I suppose Miss Parker thinks that if she postpones it, Clandevil may find another bride still richer than herself. Lady Beatrice is not going; she says nothing but family business would take her to town in November. I think the Parkers feel hurt about it, because Lady Beatrice would give a sort of backbone to the marriage feast that nobody else would.

Hospital Nurses

Mrs. Blaine has been pronounced out of danger, but the girls have had to give up the "Second Mrs. Tanqueray." The hospital nurse from Bath has been so much trouble that they have had to send her back, and Daisy is nursing her mother. It seems the nurse was very pretty, and Berty, who has never been known to speak to a girl, was found in the dining-room with her at midnight with champagne and biscuits. Blanche said, not between them, for they were sitting so close together there wasn't any room, but in front of them. And poor Mrs. Blaine at 105°, and no nourishment had passed her lips for hours. Blanche will go up to the wedding with me.

Talking of hospital nurses, it seems the Vane-Corduroys had trouble with theirs too. She wasn't pretty and flirtatious, but middle-aged and "bossy," really to my mind more objectionable than the Blaines'. She had not been at Shotover an hour before she took the measure of the household; the doctor said Mr. Vane-Corduroy must be kept quiet, and the nurse refused to allow even his wife to see him. He was kept as isolated as if he had had the plague, and to amuse him nurse read "Paradise Lost" aloud to him. She terrorised Mrs. Vane-Corduroy, who fairly quaked in her presence; she kept the servants constantly doing things for her, had her meals served her whenever she fancied them, had the grooms riding into Taunton at all hours of the day and night, and made her power felt thoroughly, besides being paid I don't know how many guineas a day, and if everything was not done just as she wished it and at once, she threatened that Mr. Vane-Corduroy would die as a consequence. Her credentials were so good that even the doctor was afraid of her, but on the second day she fell foul of the *chef*. His suite of rooms was next to hers, and he was composing a *menu* at the piano, which, as it was after midnight, disturbed nurse a good deal. She complained to Mrs. Vane-Corduroy the next day, and poor Mrs. Vane-Corduroy, who is terribly afraid of her *chef*, was driven nearly distracted; nurse even sought out the *chef* himself and ordered him to obey her, and his reply was a gesture more rude than effective, and even went so far as to threaten her if she interfered with his province. That night for dinner there was something with a delicious port-wine sauce, and nurse, who never touches spirits in any shape, didn't know what she was eating, it was so disguised. It upset her equilibrium completely, first, by making her very merry and then by making her horribly sick. She was so firmly convinced that the *chef* had made an attempt to poison her that she went off the first thing the next day in high dudgeon, to the inexpressible relief of everybody at Shotover.

I have a love of a frock and hat for the wedding. I will write you next from London and let you know how the wedding went off.—Your dearest Mamma.

Letter XXVIII

THE CARLTON HOTEL
Midnight, 13th November

DARLING ELIZABETH:

The Wedding

THE Clandevil-Parker *noces* took place to-day with great ostentation, as you may imagine. You will read the report of it to-morrow in the *Morning Post*, but I shall probably be able to give you a more graphic account of it. The ceremony was performed by the Bishop of St. Esau at twelve o'clock, at St. George's, Hanover Square, assisted by other prelates of more or less note in the ecclesiastical world. There was a thick yellow fog that made several people arrive at the church after everything was over, and prevented the crowd from congregating as it would otherwise have done. Blanche and I had excellent seats, as we arrived early; the bride was late owing to the fog, and Clandevil looked awfully bored. Following the American custom, there had been a full-dress rehearsal of the ceremony the day before, and the first five rows of pews had been taken out, and the altar banked with plants. The bridesmaids were all earls' daughters, and the best man was that notorious rake, the Honourable Ralph Swift; everyone was remarking at his cleverness in keeping out of jail. You will read all about the costumes in the *Post*; the bride looked well; the lace on her dress belonged to Marie Antoinette, and the dress itself was an exact duplication of that worn by the Queen of Holland at her Coronation, saving of course the royal mantle. Breakfast was served afterwards at the Dowager Duchess *Wedding Presents* of Clandevil's in Eton Place, where the wedding presents were on show! Their value, apart from Mr. Parker's settlement on the bride, of a square mile of New York with a rental of two million dollars annually, is estimated at five hundred thousand dollars, the more costly gifts coming from across the Atlantic. Mrs. Parker gave her daughter a Holbein; Clandevil gave his bride a tiara of emeralds; the Dowager Duchess gave a hot-water bottle; Royalty sent the bride a lace handkerchief, and the bridegroom a horse-shoe scarf pin set with brilliants; the Hon. Ralph Swift gave a solid silver napkin ring; Mr. Sweetson gave a necklace of diamonds as big as walnuts; Mrs. Dot gave a dessert set of Sèvres specially made with the Clandevil arms on it. The Marchioness of Tuke, Clandevil's only sister, gave a solid silver inkstand, and Lady Doreen Fitz Mortimer and the Countess of Warbeck gave a bog-oak blotting-pad, with a tortoise-shell paper knife; the tenants at Clandevil gave a gold loving-cup, and the servants an oak chest of damask sheets; the clerks in Mr. Parker's office in New York sent five pieces of twelfth-century tapestry, and from various people in America there came many magnificent things. But Mr. Parker, Junior, the brother, who is in Chicago, made a panic on the Stock Exchange, and sent his profits; the cheque was put to the new Duchess's account at Coutts'. The happy pair left for Clandevil Castle, Tipperary, where the honeymoon will be spent. The Duchess will be presented on her marriage at the first drawing-room.

Mr. Parker seemed delighted, and talked a good deal after the breakfast of "my son the Duke;" Mrs. Parker seemed depressed, and when she kissed her daughter good-bye, said, "My child, I hope you will be happy." Mr.

Sweetson talked to me for some time on triumphant democracy, and the effete monarchies of the old world, his favourite subjects. He said it was cheaper to buy dukes in America than in England, but admitted the price fluctuated, and depended entirely on supply, which not infrequently ran short of the demand. The atmosphere of wealth was overpowering; Blanche said she felt as if she were trampling on diamonds. Everybody thinks it will be a most happy match, for there is no pretence at love on either side, and each has got what each most desired. Flaxie Frizzle, the skirt-dancer, and her two children came to the church: everybody remarked how much the boy looked like his father.

The Wedding

I should have mentioned that the food and drink were beyond cavil. Mr. Parker told me he always got his "fizz" from the Russian Court, as the best brands were sent there from France. I cannot think of any more to tell you of the wedding; the crowd and the confusion were so great, I found it difficult to take in all that happened.

Blanche and I returned to the Carlton at three o'clock, and went straight to bed to sleep off the effects. When we went to dinner at eight, we saw the Vicomte de Narjac at one of the tables; we had a long chat with him afterwards. He came over to London to purchase an English automobile, and returns to Paris in a couple of days. We told him of the grand wedding we had been to, and he said he had seen a beautifully dressed woman helped out of a hansom, and carried upstairs unconscious, and when he enquired what had happened, the porter had told him in French that she was one of the *invitées aux épousailles de M. le duc de Clandevil avec une des plus grandes héritières du Nouveau Monde*. Blanche and I set Thérèse to find out who it could have been, and she says it was the Marchioness of Portcullis; we noticed at the breakfast that she and Mr. Sweetson were drinking neat brandy, and wondered at the time what would be the result. The Vicomte was stupefied; he thought she was a demi-mondaine.

The Lucerne Set

We asked the Vicomte all about the Lucerne set. He says Mr. Wertzelmann has been transferred to St. Petersburg, and that Madame Colorado has gone to spend the winter at the American Embassy; she was such a dear friend of Mrs. Wertzelmann's. The De Pivarts are in Paris; the Marquis has a *procès* running in the Courts against the Swiss Government, and hopes he will make enough out of it to start a stud in the spring. It seems the Marquise was arrested on a steamboat on Lake Geneva, being mistaken for Mrs. Phineas *Mrs. Porter*Porter, the beautiful American, whose husband shot Monsieur Dupont in the Hotel Beau Rivage. And the New York *Paris Herald* has been full of it. Mrs. Phineas Porter lives in Paris, and Mr. Phineas Porter in Chicago; he comes over every year, and, on this occasion, said good-bye to his wife and left for Havre, but returned secretly, and found Mrs. Porter had disappeared. He traced her and Dupont, who is a prominent member of the Jockey Club, to Geneva. He arrived late at night, knocked on his wife's door at the Beau Rivage, who thought he was the chamber-maid, and forced himself in. Mrs. Porter shrieked, and Dupont, who had retired for the night, jumped out of bed, and was chased by Mr. Porter with a loaded revolver through the whole suite of apartments into the last room, and Dupont, caught in a *cul de sac* as it were, hid behind an arm-chair, where Mr. Porter killed him. As you may imagine, the affair created a scandal, for the people are so well known in Society. Mr. Porter was arrested by the police, and is now on trial. In the confusion Mrs. Porter disappeared, and has up to the present baffled all attempts to find her. The Marquise de Pivart is said to be the image of her, and, as she was embarking about a week after the affair on a steamboat, to spend the day at Chillon, she was arrested by the stupid Swiss police. The Vicomte says the Swiss authorities apologised most humbly when they discovered their mistake, but both the Marquis and the Marquise would not be satisfied with anything less than heavy damages. The *procès* has added to the Porter-Dupont *esclandre*, and the reputation of the Marquise has been torn to shreds. The Vicomte says it is very amusing to read the accounts in the *Paris Herald*, and everybody says the Marquis could get a divorce as well as the Marquise, but they swore the deepest affection for one another in the courts, and will swear anything for the chance of touching the pockets of the Swiss Government. They are always seen together just like the *ouvriers* on Sundays at Nogent-sur-Marne. The Vicomte added that the sacrifices they were making of their private feelings were well worth one hundred thousand francs, the sum they claim as damages.

A Roman Prince

Old Mrs. Johnson has found a Roman Prince in the place of Count Albert for Rosalie Isaacs. The Vicomte says he is all that can be desired. He has a palazzo like a fortress at Rome, with a priceless collection of Greek marbles which he can't sell, and was so poor that he spent one winter on the Via Corniche, with a monkey and an organ that he borrowed from his former steward, who had just returned from tramping in America with enough to start himself in a small business. But the Prince is not bogus; he has the right to stand in the presence of the King of Italy, and best of all he is a Bourbon *sur la côté gauche*. The Vicomte thinks he cost infinitely less than Clandevil cost the Parkers, and Rosalie's wedding this winter in Rome will be much more magnificent, for the Pope will marry her, and the Royal Family will be present. Mrs. Johnson must be *très fière* of her success. But, as Blanche remarked, the extraordinary part of these American marriages *Elasticity of Conscience*is the elasticity of the religious conscience. The Parkers are Baptists, yet Mr. Parker has been restoring Gothic churches, and Miss Parker, who has been "dipped," was married by the Bishop of St. Esau. And Mrs. Johnson, who told me in Lucerne that she belonged to the Plymouth Brethren, after marrying her daughter to a Jew and her granddaughter to a Roman Catholic, will actually receive the Papal benediction! But of course, as I told Blanche, one must be *à la mode*, and that I asked the Bishop of St. Esau at the wedding if he would not *A Prayer for Paquin*put in a prayer for Paquin in the Litany after "and all the nobility."

Well, my darling, I must say good-night; it is frightfully late, and the champagne that came from the Russian Court that I had this morning, has given me just a wee bit of a *migraine*.—Your dearest Mamma.

Letter XXIX

THE CARLTON HOTEL
15th November

DARLING ELIZABETH:

A Rainy Day

YESTERDAY it rained as it only can rain in London in November, and when it stopped for a few minutes there was such a nasty fog. We had breakfast in bed, and didn't get up till quite twelve; it was such a miserable day we didn't know what to do with ourselves, so we went down-stairs and sat in that jolly place with the glass roof and the palms, and there was quite a good band playing. There were very few people there, as it isn't the season, but about one o'clock a great many people began to come for lunch. Most of the men looked like Jews, and they all wore gold rings with crests on their little fingers. I am sure they were company-promoters, for presently Lord de Manton arrived with poor, tottering Lord Ardath, and joined some of the Israelite people, and they all *At Lunch*went in to lunch together. Little Dolly Daydreams of the Tivoli drove up in a hansom with that young simpleton, Percy Felton, of the Scots Greys. We could see them through the glass doors as they got out of the cab; she lifted her skirt up to her knee to keep it out of the wet, and he kissed her on the ear right in front of the porter. Lady Ann Fairfax, the war-special, had lunch with six khaki men, and they made such a noise at their table we could hear them laughing where we were. Medina, Viscountess Frogmore, and Mrs. Beverley Fruit came together and sat down near us for a few minutes when they were joined by the Bishop of St. Esau and the three had lunch together. The Viscountess was in deep mourning, her crape veil trailed on the ground behind her, and she looked very melancholy; you know her son fell at Magersfontein. A smart-looking curate, evidently late, rushed up after they sat down. Blanche says she thinks he is a protégé of the Bishop's, he paid the greatest deference to both the Bishop and Lady Frogmore after lunch when they were having coffee outside in the glass place where the band is. I am sure we shall hear of him one of these days.

A Conversation

A lank man, with long hair and a flabby face, and a woman who looked the wife of the editor of a newspaper, took the seats next us vacated by Lady Frogmore and Mrs. Fruit. The man criticised Mrs. Fruit's books; Blanche whispered to me that she thought he must be an unsuccessful author, for he hadn't a good word to say for either Mrs. Fruit or her works. The conversation turned on to "An Englishwoman's Love Letters." The woman said she was dying to know who wrote them; the man became quite mysterious, with a could-if-I-would air. She playfully tapped him on the arm with the handle of her umbrella, and guessed *he* was the author. He looked very self-satisfied, and admitted he knew who the author was, but was bound by frightful oaths never to divulge the secret. But the woman wouldn't believe him; she declared if he hadn't written the book, he didn't know who did, for she was constantly hearing people say they knew the author and the reason he did not wish his identity disclosed.

Then the conversation drifted on to Exeter Hall, and Labouchere and Stead and the Society notes in the *Daily Sensation*, and the War in South Africa, and the man talked of some poems he had written, and what the critics had said of them, and the woman listened. When he had exhausted himself, the woman began. She talked of high life just like a pocket peerage; she told anecdotes of Royalty, which she said were perfectly true; she knew what peers gambled, who married actresses, who were divorced, who had a *ménage* in St. John's Wood, and she knew what peeresses dyed their hair, and where they did it, and what they said and what they thought. She even mentioned Lady Beatrice's name, and said that it was rumoured Tom Carterville had gone back to South Africa, because he was displeased that his mother intended to marry a Low Church curate. Poor Lady Beatrice! She also mentioned me, and that I was the best dressed woman in Society (dear Paquin), and that it was considered very improper of me to let you visit at the places you did. I am sure she was the wife of a journalist, for she knew so much more about Society than Society knew about itself or her.

Lunch with the Vicomte

Just as Blanche and I were about to go to lunch, the Vicomte arrived. He looked immaculate and quite good-looking for a Frenchman; he had been inspecting automobiles the whole morning, and he was as hungry as a lion. We had lunch together in a corner, where we could see everybody; after lunch, the Vicomte had an engagement at the French Embassy, but he said he would be back to dine with us, and take us to a music hall. As the weather had mended, I said I would go to Alice Hughes to have my photograph taken, as I should have to pay if I did not keep the appointment; Blanche went to Marshall & Snelgrove to spend the afternoon. While I was waiting at the "studio," old Lady Blubber came in; she showed me her proofs, and was delighted with them. They didn't look the least bit like her; all the flabby rings under her eyes were smoothed out, and her mouth was made straight and the lump taken off the bridge of her nose. She said she should order three dozen, that they were the best likeness she had ever had taken! After that I went to a tea-shop in Bond Street, and came back to the Carlton to find that Thérèse had taken the afternoon out. As I can't, as you know, do the slightest thing for myself, I was absolutely helpless, so I just got into a wrapper, and read "Gyp" in front of the fire. By and bye Thérèse came; she was spattered with mud as if she had been spending the day in Fleet Street, and she brought with her a strong odour of malt.

Thérèse Takes an Afternoon out

When I scolded her, ever so gently, for going out without leave, she flew into a rage, and wanted to know if I wished a month's notice. Then she began to weep and pity herself, and her cheeks were the colour of lobsters, and she behaved very strangely. I told her to get my bath ready, and she fell asleep while it was filling, and the water overflowed and did no end of damage. I got very angry, and accused her of being drunk, which she indignantly denied, saying she had only been to see her mother who lives in Soho. I sent her to bed after that, and Blanche laced me up and did my hair, but I felt like a fright for the rest of the night.

Goes to the Theatre

Dinner was rather tame, as there were so few people in the room, but of course one can't expect the season to last all the year round. The Vicomte had, after great difficulty, managed to get seats for "Mr. and Mrs. Daventry." Between the acts we heard people discussing who wrote it, and in fact, it is as much of an enigma as the authorship of "An Englishwoman's Love Letters." Blanche thinks the same person wrote both.

The Vicomte thought the play very "polite," and was astonished that it had created such a sensation. He said we ought to see "La Dame aux Maximes" and "Demie-Vierge," both now running in Paris. We all agreed that the play was thoroughly representative of Society, but the unnatural parts were Daventry's suicide and the elopement of his wife with Ashurst. People don't do these things in our set. The company was excellent, and Blanche and I both wished we were Mrs. Pat Campbell to have love made to us so delightfully every night by young Du Maurier. Even the Vicomte said they didn't do it better in France, and he is sure Du Maurier did it so well, because he was half French.

Supper at the Savoy

We had supper at the Savoy. The usual sight. At a table near us was an actress *très décolletée*; six of our *jeunesse frivole* were squabbling for her smiles. We left before the lights were turned out, because the people behave so badly in the corridor. The Vicomte leaves for Paris to-morrow; he is so much nicer in England than abroad.—Your dearest Mamma.

Letter XXX

THE CARLTON HOTEL
17th November

DARLING ELIZABETH:

Elizabeth's Engagement

HAIL, Marchioness of Valmond, all hail! Your letter gave me the greatest possible pleasure. You have made the match I desired for you, and I do not know who deserves the greatest credit for it—you who hooked this fine fish, Octavia who helped you to land it, or I who taught you how to fish, and then sent you to the pool where my lord trout disported himself. But apart from chaffing, Elizabeth, I am sincerely glad for you, because Valmond really seems to love you, and as men go, he will make you a good husband. As soon as your visit to Octavia is over, you must come straight to me; we will go to Paris for the trousseau and to Rome for the winter; a little delay and absence will do Valmond good, and then, darling, we will come to England and start the season with your *noces*, which shall be done as befits a Marquis and Marchioness of Valmond.

He wrote me to-day, as did Octavia; I am replying by this same post to both. Assure them both of my unfaltering affection.

I had intended going back to Monk's Folly, but, since the news in your letter, I have decided to stop in town till you come in a day or two. Blanche sends her congratulations; she has gone home, as Daisy wanted a rest. Mrs. Blaine is on the high road to recovery, and they will most likely go to Rome with us.

The Bazaar

Blanche left last night, after going with me to the Bazaar for Distressed Gentlewomen. It was held at Mauve House, lent by the Duke of Mauve, and was under the patronage of the Duke and Duchess, but organised by Mr. Albert D. Beake, editor and proprietor of "White Lies," said to be the most successful of all the Society papers. The Bazaar was opened by Royalty, and Mr. Beake must have cleared a large sum for the Distressed Gentlewomen as well as advertised his paper and juggled himself and wife into Society for once at any rate. His wife is the woman I wrote you about the other day, who came to the Carlton to lunch, and talked so much about Society. I said at the time she was an editor's wife. Mr. Beake was everywhere, but his wife had a stall with the Duchess of Mauve, who looked awfully bored.

Lady Hildegarde

One of the features of the bazaar was the Stage Stall. Mr. Beake had got most of the best known actors and actresses to take part. It was a huge success; the people were three deep round the stall, crushing to see the professionals; they sold everything. It was rather odd to observe the stall immediately next to the stage one. Lady Hildegarde Merrioneath presided, and was assisted by some young and pretty girls. The crowd did not know who they were, and they hardly sold a thing. Lady Hildegarde, who is the most refined and aristocratic woman I know, with that mixture of Vere de Vere and sweetness which so often marks our best born women, stood in the back of her stall, looking rather amused at the complete desertion of it. Here was the type of the real aristocrat, the real great lady, and the *parvenus* couldn't see it! I felt like telling the people that they were blind and fools, that if they had any taste, any appreciation, any refinement, all the other stalls would be deserted to overwhelm Lady Hildegarde's. Mr. Beake, running about with a china pig in his hands, which he was trying to raffle, noticed that Lady Hildegarde was not a success, and he actually had the impudence to patronise her. I suppose his vulgar commercial head was turned with the thought that the bazaar was his work, and that his wife was side by side with a real live duchess. Lady Hildegarde replied with some conventional remark, and her smile seemed to me more amused than ever, as if it were all very funny and not worth being angry about. For, after all, she was Lady Hildegarde Merrioneath, and Mr. Beake was only Mr. Beake, and his actors and actresses stars whose lights went out. I shall never forget the picture Lady Hildegarde made in her deserted stall, side by side with the crowded booth of the actors. It made me think of the French Revolution, and the noblesse going to the guillotine in the tumbrils, so far above her surroundings, was Lady Hildegarde.

The Existing Régime

A little more pushing and shoving and playing the "Charity trick," and Mr. and Mrs. Beake will be like the Vane-Corduroys, if, for all I know, they are not already *rangé*. But, as Blanche said, the sentiments that pervade the mind of Mr. Beake and his kidney are the mainstay of our national life and the existing régime, and it doesn't do to guard the portals to the high born too closely. As a future marchioness, I pray you shudder when you read the Sunday papers at Chevenix Castle with the detailed account of Mr. Beake's bazaar.

Blanche and I bought nothing, nor did the few of our set who were there, which as usual left the charity to the crowd.

I saw Blanche off at Paddington, and wished I had decided to go with her; you need not be surprised if you get a telegram from me to-morrow to say I have gone home. It is wretchedly dull by myself, and I can't take Thérèse with me everywhere; besides I have to come up to my room early, as it is not proper for me to sit in the public rooms by myself at night.

Talks of Marrying again

Thérèse, in brushing out my hair to-night, asked me why I didn't marry again; she said that she knew men admired me, for one of the Vane-Corduroys' footmen at Shotover had told her I was a woman to drive men mad. Thérèse of course gauges the value of men's admiration from the footman class, but I think I have not yet got to the shady side of beauty, and that perhaps it is just as well Valmond saw you before he met me. As money will never be a consideration, and I have social position, and as I am not yet forty-five, I shall not marry for love, so I shall keep my freedom, which I enjoy so much.

Once again, my darling, I congratulate you, and wish you all happiness. Good-night.—Your dearest Mamma.

Letter XXXI

MONK'S FOLLY, 19th November

DARLING ELIZABETH:

Home again

SIMPLY couldn't endure it in town in November by myself, so came home to-day. Yesterday, after Blanche left, I counted up the things I could do by myself in order to kill time. In spite of London being so big, there are so few things one can do by oneself to amuse oneself. The early post brought me the proofs from Alice Hughes; Paquin comes out splendidly, but I look silly in the one in which I am standing near a balustrade, holding a sheaf of wheat. I have ordered a dozen of myself in a garden, under a lovely old tree, with a stuffed greyhound at my side. It looks awfully natural, and you would never dream I was more than twenty. I thought the proofs had been sent me by mistake, till I recognised my frock, and then when you look at them a long time, you see how really like you they are. They are just the thing to send one's acquaintances.

Lady Sophia Dashton's Novel

The morning was so foggy that I couldn't go out, so I put on a very *chic* costume, and sat in the glass-roof place which they call a "garden," and read Lady Sophia Dashton's novel. It is all about the Roman Emperors and the catacombs, and the love of a princess and a slave. The language is so beautiful, and the descriptions are wonderful: they seem as if they would never end, and you forget all about the story. The book has been well reviewed, and Lady Sophia has taken up literature seriously. I have heard she is making a great deal of money out of it. Mr. Beake will publish anything she writes—all the illustrated papers have got her portrait this week—and there are stories of hers now running in two of the leading Society papers. She began to write for pleasure, but has received such encouragement that she decided to win the laurel. Everybody in Society has bought her book. The whole family are talented. Her father's speeches in the House of Lords on the London drains have been edited at 7s. 6d., with the family arms on the cover; the *Times* said they had the "ring of Burke in them," and Lady Sophia's brother's "Poems in odd Moments," which have appeared in the "Temple of Folly," are to be brought out in book form. I forget the name of Lady Sophia's novel; Mrs. Jack Strawe, in recommending it to me the day of Miss Parker's wedding, said she didn't know the name, and that very few people did, but when ordering it, it was only necessary to mention Lady Sophia Dashton's name, and the bookseller would know what you meant.

I sent Thérèse to Mudie's for it, and told her to ask for any other books that were being widely read, as I like to be posted on what is being talked of. She brought back somebody's work on Aristotle, with an introduction by the Duke of Mauve, and Mrs. Katurah P. Glob's "There is no Death." Mrs. Glob is a Christian Scientist, and states in her preface that she is the seventh daughter of a seventh son. I could only get as far as what she had to say on vaccination; I make out that she preferred to "render unto Cæsar the things that are Cæsar's," rather than to incur the penalty of the law.

Dry Books

After struggling the whole morning with Glob and Aristotle and Lady Sophia, and wondering how learned people were, and how they found time to acquire so much knowledge, I had lunch. Crême velours, sole princesse, noisettes Souvaroff, pommes nouvelles, etc., with Félix Boubel, carte d'or, took the dry taste of the books completely out of my mouth.

Having spent such a morning improving my mind at the Carlton, I thought I deserved some relaxation in the afternoon.

At the Aquarium

Que faire? Should I consult Salambo, the well-known Oriental lady in Bond Street, as to the future? Should I go to Exeter Hall and observe the Ranter on his native heath? Should I go to St. James Hall and revel in Alice Gome's superb voice? I did none of these things; I took Thérèse with me and drove to that popular place of amusement, the Aquarium, as I had never been there, and I wanted to see the fishes. Alas! How sadly we English take our pleasures! The only fish at the Aquarium are some monsters of *papier maché* and a lonely *piscis vulgaris* condemned to solitary confinement in a slimy tank. Thérèse thought she would like to see the sword-swallowers, so I took seats, and while we waited, such a funny man told us he would impersonate celebrities in quick change. He did a lot of men with beards and long hair, and held up bits of cardboard to let us know who they were, and he called himself Meyerbeer and Rossini, and, as Thérèse said, without the cardboard you wouldn't have known which was which. Then he did Lord Roberts and Baden-Powell and the Prince of Wales; and when I saw him put on his Lord Roberts' wig and jerk the antimacassar off an arm-chair, I knew that he would impersonate the Queen. And he did, and you can have no idea how grotesque it was, and the curtain dropped and nobody applauded.

The sword-swallower did some amazing things, and smacked his lips, as if the swords tasted nice. His wife swallowed an electric light, and then he told us of a trick he could do which no one had ever done before in England, namely, to swallow a sword and hang weights on to the hilt, but he didn't do it, as he said he had a sore throat. I wouldn't wait for the lady who dives from a trapeze into a tank, or drop pennies into slots, or have my photo taken while I waited, though I let Thérèse have six shots at a Boer behind a kopje in the shooting gallery, but she nearly killed the attendant after the third shot.

A Rustic Footman

Thérèse was so frightened, and began to scream in French, that we had a crowd round us in no time, and a policeman came up and took our names. After that I decided the Carlton was the best place for me, till I could get my things packed and go home. When I got back to the hotel, I found some letters and a ten of diamonds on the table in my room. At a loss to know what significance it could have, I asked the porter how it came into my room. He said it had been left by a footman, but I was none the wiser till this morning, when I received a note from the Honourable Mrs. Maxolme, explaining that her footman was a simple honest rustic whom she had brought up from the country with her, and who was new to his duties. She had spent the afternoon paying calls, and before starting had explained that it was merely a case of leaving cards, and she told the youth to take charge of them and bring a sufficient number. She had paid all the calls, when she suddenly remembered I was stopping at the Carlton and she drove there. The footman gave the card to the porter, and then Mrs. Maxolme drove to a house where she wished to leave two cards, and called the footman and told him. But it seems he had exhausted all he had brought, and horrified Mrs. Maxolme by saying that he had none left, as he had only brought from the ace to the king of diamonds. Poor Mrs. Maxolme has been writing to everybody since to explain, and as she simply could not write personally so many letters, she wrote one and had the rest type-written.

Threatened with Influenza

Now, darling, I want you to come home at once and tell Valmond to bring you, as I wish to see him. I don't want to frighten you, but the fogs and the dissipation of attempting the London season in November have made me ill. I arrived here with a sore throat and a backache, and sent at once for Dr. Smart. As I write, I have a mustard-plaster on my chest and my feet in hot water, and I have just swallowed a dose of ammoniated quinine. I think I am in for influenza. I feel a perfect wreck.—Your dearest Mamma.

P. S.—Dr. Smart has just left; he says if I will go to bed for forty-eight hours, he will try to let me go to Lady Beatrice's big dinner on Saturday. He is such a dear, and has such white teeth and soft hands, he drove all my fears away with such a pooh, pooh! But when he had gone, I heard Thérèse tell the maid that I was threatened with pleuro-pneumonia and had a chill on the liver. So exaggerative these French! I cannot write any more; my hand is trembling so I can hardly hold the pen, and I believe I am roasting with fever. Bring the tea-gown I ordered at Paquin's when you come. I am longing to see you and Valmond. Don't alarm yourself about me; I am really as hard as nails—and influenza is *à la mode*.

Made in the USA
Middletown, DE
03 September 2022

73054360R00241